EVIDENCE: THE OBJECTION METHOD

Third Edition

LexisNexis Law School Publishing Advisory Board

EVIDENCE: THE OBJECTION METHOD

Third Edition

Dennis D. Prater
Connell Teaching Professor
University of Kansas School of Law

Daniel J. Capra
Philip Reed Professor of Law
Fordham University School of Law

Stephen A. Saltzburg
Howrey Professor of Trial Advocacy,
Litigation and Professional Responsibility
George Washington University Law School

Christine M. Arguello
Adjunct Professor
University of Colorado
Chief Deputy Attorney General State of Colorado

LexisNexis

ISBN: 1-4224-1177-X

Library of Congress Cataloging-in-Publication Data

Evidence : the objection method / Dennis D. Prater . . . [et al.]. — 3rd ed.
p. cm.
Includes bibliographical references and index.
ISBN 1-4224-1177-X (hardbound)
1. Evidence (Law)—United States—Cases. I. Prater, Dennis D.
KF8934.E945 2007
347.73'6—dc22 2007036037

NOTE TO USERS
To ensure that you are using the latest materials available in this area, please be sure to periodically check the LexisNexis Law School web site for downloadable updates and supplements at www.lexisnexis.com/lawschool

Editorial Offices
744 Broad Street, Newark, NJ 07102 (973) 820-2000
201 Mission St., San Francisco, CA 94105-1831 (415) 908-3200
701 East Water Street, Charlottesville, VA 22902-7587 (434) 972-7600
www.lexis.com

(Pub.3052)

PREFACE TO THE THIRD EDITION

This Third Edition plays to what we feel were the strengths of the first two editions. Most importantly, the book is stocked with transcript style problems in which lawyers present evidence and argue evidentiary points, and a trial judge is called on to rule. We hope that these problems will be useful to readers both in and out of class. In this Edition, we have made a special effort to update and amplify the problems in order to provide a real challenge for students seeking to master the rules of evidence as well as the art of objection and argument over evidentiary points in a real trial.

Of course, no argument on evidence at a trial is possible without a grounding in doctrine and a working knowledge of the Federal Rules of Evidence. To that end, this Edition carries many new and challenging cases. We also pay special attention to the important amendments to the Federal Rules of Evidence that have gone into effect since 2000. One of the authors of this book, Professor Daniel Capra, serves as Reporter to the Judicial Advisory Committee on Evidence Rules and was the principal author of those amendments and the accompanying Committee Notes. Where possible, the Reporter's perspective on the amendments has been emphasized. The important topics of expert testimony and privileges have received extensive attention and have been completely revised to take account of their increasing dominance in evidentiary development.

A few words on the format of the book. Citations included in cases are usually omitted without so specifying. Footnotes that are included in the cases are numbered as they were in the original case. Footnotes that are ours in the text are numbered sequentially from the beginning of each chapter. If we have deleted material from a case, it is noted with three asterisks. If the court has deleted material — for example from a quote taken from another case — it is noted with three periods.

This Edition continues the practice of the previous edition by including extensive excerpts from the *Federal Rules of Evidence Manual*, co-authored by Professors Stephen Saltzburg, Michael Martin, and Daniel Capra. We hope that these excerpts will help students master the important concepts of evidence that do not arise in the principal cases. We thank LexisNexis for the permission to use this material.

The co-authors owe a special debt of thanks to Professors Capra and Saltzburg, who spent countless hours in preparing new problems, finding new cases, and reworking and modernizing the material for this new edition.

The authors dedicate this book to all our families and loved ones. Their patience, endurance, and endearments provide us monumental support.

D.D.P. to Burns, Vivian, Derek, and Scott

D.J.C. to Anne, Emily, and David

S.A.S. to Susan, David, Diane, Lisa, and Mark

C.M.A. to Ron, Ronnie, Tiffany, Jennifer, and Kenny

TABLE OF CONTENTS

Page

Page

Page

Chapter 1

MODE AND ORDER OF PRESENTATION OF EVIDENCE

A. CONTROL BY THE COURT

[1] Federal Rules of Evidence 102, 403, and 611(a)

Rule 102. Purpose and Construction

These rules shall be construed to secure fairness in administration, elimination of unjustifiable expense and delay, and promotion of growth and development of the law of evidence to the end that the truth may be ascertained and proceedings justly determined.

Rule 403. Exclusion of Relevant Evidence on Grounds of Prejudice, Confusion, or Waste of Time

Although relevant, evidence may be excluded if its probative value is substantially outweighed by the danger of unfair prejudice, confusion of the issues, or misleading the jury, or by considerations of undue delay, waste of time, or needless presentation of cumulative evidence.

Rule 611. Mode and Order of Interrogation and Presentation

(a) Control by Court. The court shall exercise reasonable control over the mode and order of interrogating witnesses and presenting evidence so as to (1) make the interrogation and presentation effective for the ascertainment of the truth, (2) avoid needless consumption of time, and (3) protect witnesses from harassment or undue embarrassment.

* * *

[2] An Application of Judicial Authority

UNITED STATES v. REAVES
636 F. Supp. 1575 (E.D. Ky. 1986)

BERTELSMAN, DISTRICT JUDGE:

Both the prosecution and the defendants in this criminal tax fraud case have challenged the authority of this Court to curtail the presentation of cumulative and time wasting evidence by placing time limits on various stages of the trial.

Background

The indictment charges the defendants with setting up and participating in several spurious coal mining partnerships, not with the genuine intent of doing any mining, but solely for the purpose of providing themselves and others with fraudulent tax deductions against their earned income from other sources. When the time limits were set at a pretrial conference, there were three defendants. One pled guilty prior to trial.

Initially, the United States estimated the trial would take a month. Upon further inquiry, the Court was convinced that this time was excessive. It was apparent to the Court that the prosecution intended to introduce numerous tax returns of various individuals and partnerships page by page, making little effort to organize the voluminous evidence into a meaningful pattern or streamline the presentation of the case by the use of charts or summary exhibits. *See* Fed. R. Evid. 1006.

Thus, the Court found itself confronted with a situation where it was convinced an excessive amount of its time was about to be consumed by a wasteful, duplicative, and inefficient method of introducing evidence. It was apparent that, although little of the evidence was strictly irrelevant to the issues in the case, only about half of the time estimated was necessary to present the issues. This was not a new situation.

It would seem that early in the career of every trial lawyer, he or she has lost a case by leaving something out, and thereupon resolved never again to omit even the most inconsequential item of possible evidence from any future trial. Thereafter, in an excess of caution the attorney tends to overtry his case by presenting vast quantities of cumulative or marginally relevant evidence. In civil cases, economics place some natural limits on such zeal. The fact that the attorney's fee may not be commensurate with the time required to present the case thrice over imposes some restraint. In a criminal case, however, the prosecution, at least in the federal system, seems not to be subject to such fiscal constraints, and the attorney's enthusiasm for tautology is virtually unchecked.

Thus, this court was once subjected to the calling of ten firemen in an arson prosecution to prove a house burned down. On another occasion, fifteen bank patrons were called to prove a bank was robbed by a masked marauder that no one could identify or describe, since he was heavily disguised. The only evidence against the defendant was that he was apprehended some weeks later with large quantities of bait money.

So it was that, at the early pretrial conference in this case, the court was all too familiar with the prosecutorial penchant to regard the omission of any * * * possible evidence with the same horror as Scrooge regarded the expenditure of a shilling. Having experienced in the past the stoney-hearted indifference with which the prosecutors usually received the court's tearful entreaties concerning the state of its civil docket and the plight of those litigants unfortunate enough to have cases moldering there, the court decided to take unilateral action to keep the trial of this case within reasonable bounds. Inspired by the example of Judge Leval of the Southern District of New York in the much publicized libel suit, *Westmoreland v. CBS*, the Court entered a scheduling order which set time limits for the presentation of the various phases of the case.

The scheduling order was designed to give the United States ten days to present its case-in-chief and to impose proportionate limits on the other phases of the trial. The order worked well in practice. Actually, it was more than generous, the prosecution's case still being overlong. It was refreshing to see, however, how things started to move along as the prosecution's time began to run out. Suddenly, the prosecutors quickly reached the point with each witness and stuck to the issues, thus eliminating many objections, and the case became intelligible and interesting. Unfortunately, it ended in a mistrial because of the conduct of a witness.

* * *

Analysis

A theoretical basis for using the time limit method may be found in the venerable concept of the inherent power of the court to control its docket. This inherent power has been codified in Federal Rules of Evidence 403 and 611(a).

* * *

Fed. R. Evid. 403 recognizes the power and duty of the court to exclude cumulative evidence or evidence which consumes more time than its probative value justifies. Rule 611 *commands* the court to "exercise reasonable control over the mode and order of interrogating witnesses and presenting evidence, so as to (1) make the interrogation and presentation effective for the ascertainment of the truth, [and] (2) avoid needless consumption of time."

It is fundamental that a court has the power and duty to manage its docket and the individual cases before it to "secure fairness in administration, [and] elimination of unjustifiable expense and delay." Fed. R. Evid. 102. Modern courts recognize that the court's time is a public commodity which should not be squandered. There is an unnamed party in every lawsuit — the public. Public resources are squandered if judicial proceedings are allowed to proliferate beyond reasonable bounds. The public's right to a "just, speedy, and inexpensive determination of every action" is infringed, if a court allows a case, civil or criminal, to preempt more than its reasonable share of the court's time.

A court cannot rely on the attorneys to keep expenditures of time in trying a case within reasonable bounds. The perspectives of the court and the attorneys in trying a case differ markedly. A judge wants to reach a just result in the case and to do so expeditiously and economically. An attorney's primary concern is to WIN the case. If he believes he can win that case by proliferating the evidence of the favorable, but relatively uncontested matters so that the weaker aspects of the case will be camouflaged, it is asking too much of our fallen nature to expect him voluntarily to do otherwise.

Somehow the unfortunate trend has arisen among attorneys to make almost every case a BIG CASE. There is a tendency to want to present the evidence not once, but many times over, and to adduce needlessly cumulative evidence not only on the controverted issues but also on those which are all but uncontested. Advocates tend to confuse quantity of evidence with probative quality. Nothing lulls an attorney to the passage of time like the sound of his or her own voice. Few attorneys can tell you what time it is without describing how the clock was made.

Traditionally, judges — most of whom like this writer have been practicing attorneys themselves — have felt that the court should not interfere with an attorney's right to present a case however he saw fit. Indeed, I know of no judge who would not like to let the attorneys have as much time as they think they need to present their case. But the days when courts could afford that luxury have passed.

It has become apparent that courts must recognize that it is they, rather than the attorneys, who have a more objective appreciation of the time a case requires when balancing its needs against the exigencies of the court's docket. Courts cannot rely on the attorneys to object to needless consumption of time by adversaries. Usually, an attorney is willing to suffer through the presentation of his opponent, however redundant, if only he can have equal time.

Recent trends in litigation have brought courts to the realization that their dockets do not belong to the attorneys or litigants, nor even to the courts themselves, but to the public. It is not only in the setting of time limitations that this realization is manifesting itself, but also in such developments as the imposition of sanctions on counsel who improperly pursue unsubstantiated factual and legal positions.

* * *

One method of controlling the ill effects of burgeoning litigation is the imposition of time limits, as the court has done here. * * *

Those courts which have imposed such time limits have chosen this method of implementing their duty to control their dockets, because frequently no particular item of evidence can be ruled to be irrelevant, although taken as a whole the volume of evidence is excessive. Also, although the court may be firmly convinced that the total mass of evidence preferred is unduly cumulative, it is at a disadvantage as compared to counsel in selecting the best evidence to delineate the issues.

Setting a reasonable time limit forces counsel to conform their zeal to the need of the court to conserve its time and resources. But, subject to the time limits imposed, counsel remain in control of the case. It is still counsel's case, although it must now be presented in a reasonable time. It is counsel rather than the court who decide what evidence is to be admitted and what is to be pruned. Numerous objections or *sua sponte* interruptions by the court to debate what evidence is repetitious or cumulative are avoided. Thus, the goal of preserving the court's resources is achieved while the traditional autonomy of counsel to present their own case, subject to the exigencies of that goal, is preserved. Properly streamlined, the case is more effective for the ascertainment of truth, as mandated by Fed. R. Evid. 611(a).

* * *

The experience of this court is that the method of establishing time limits by a scheduling order works well both from the point of view of the court's docket, and also from that of the case to be tried which ends up being presented more efficiently and intelligibly.

This court holds that it has the power to impose reasonable time limits on the trial of both civil and criminal cases in the exercise of its reasonable discretion. Of course, the court must analyze each case carefully to assure that the time limits set are not arbitrary.

NOTES

1. Are there limitations on judicial authority to control the presentation of evidence?

Professors Saltzburg, Capra and Martin, in the *Federal Rules of Evidence Manual* (9th ed. 2006) have this to say about the scope of the court's power to control the evidence under Rule 611(a):

> Rule 611(a) is infrequently cited. Yet, it is a Rule that is continually used during a trial. It permits the Trial Judge to allow or disallow changes in the order of proof, rebuttal evidence, surrebuttal evidence, recall of witnesses, reopening of a case once a party has rested, and many other requests that are made in the course of a trial. *See, e.g., United States v. Soto-Beniquez*, 350 F.3d 131 (1st Cir. 2003) (rebuttal evidence properly permitted where the defendant opened the door to an issue not addressed in the government's principal case); *United States v. Puckett*, 147 F.3d 765 (8th Cir. 1998) (no abuse of discretion where the Trial Court allowed the prosecution to recall law enforcement witnesses during the trial so that evidence could be presented in chronological order); *Berroyer v. Hertz*, 672 F.2d 334 (3d Cir. 1982) (no abuse of discretion under Rule 611(a) where the Trial Court permitted the plaintiff to call a "rebuttal" witness in her case-in-chief after the defendant obtained permission to call its expert out of turn); *United States v. Burgess*, 691 F.2d 1146 (4th Cir. 1982) (upholding the Trial Judge's exclusion of surrebuttal evidence that was repetitive of evidence offered in the case-in-chief for the defense); *United States v. Gaertner*, 705 F.2d 210 (7th Cir. 1983) (the Trial Judge did not err in permitting the government to offer rebuttal evidence to refute specific testimony of defense witnesses and in rejecting surrebuttal testimony, which would have been a repetition of the defense testimony that the government had rebutted).
>
> Also, Trial Courts have sometimes exercised authority under Rule 611(a) to permit a witness to testify in narrative form, when that would expedite the trial or assist the search for truth. *See, e.g., United States v. Young*, 745 F.2d 733, 761 (2d Cir. 1984) (a Trial Judge "has broad discretion in deciding whether or not to allow narrative testimony"; it was proper in the instant case to permit narrative testimony to explain videotape evidence).

2. Do limitations on the presentation of evidence always advance fair trials?

In *Fenner v. Dependable Trucking Co.*, 716 F.2d 598 (9th Cir. 1983), the court reversed a judgment for the plaintiff in a personal injury action, finding that the defendants were denied a fair trial when the trial judge refused to grant a continuance to permit the defendants' expert to testify. The court reasoned that the trial judge had lulled the defendants into thinking that the problem of their expert's unavailability would be worked out, and that the expert's testimony was material and not cumulative. The Federal Rules of Evidence continue to provide judges with discretion in granting and denying continuances for a variety of reasons. How does a judge "lull" litigants to believing that problems will be accommodated?

In *United States v. Russell*, 717 F.2d 518 (11th Cir. 1983), the court affirmed marijuana-related convictions, finding no error in the refusal of the trial judge to grant a recess late one afternoon so that a final defense witness could testify the next morning. The court concluded that the trial judge properly found the unheard witness to be unimportant. Is it unreasonable for a trial judge to deny a continuance if a witness was unexpectedly unavailable? Does it matter whether or not a party is at fault?

3. Do the Federal Rules have specific rules for the common procedural objections used at trial?

Federal Rules 403 and 611(a) permit a judge to impose restrictions on the presentation of evidence that go beyond ruling on objections and on particular offers of evidence. You should not be surprised to find that a number of "rules" that affect trials are not set forth in evidence rules, procedure rules or statutes. For example, there are almost no statutes or rules that govern opening statements; yet, there are traditions that are enforced by courts as though they were rules. And many of the standard objections made by trial lawyers do not specifically appear anywhere in the Federal Rules of Evidence. For example, no rule of evidence specifically prohibits argumentative, compound, or ambiguous questions. Likewise, the Rules do not specifically prohibit narrative responses. Rather, the following objections are derived from the broad language of Rules 403 and 611(a), which give the judge the power to exercise reasonable control over the mode and order of interrogating witnesses and presenting evidence so as to:

a. make the interrogation and presentation effective for the ascertainment of truth;

b. avoid undue delay or needless consumption of time;

c. protect witnesses from harassment or undue embarrassment; and

d. avoid unfairly prejudicing, confusing, or misleading the jury.

Some common examples follow:

Q. What happened the day of the murder?

"Objection! The question calls for a narrative response."

This objection is generally posed to a question that is indefinite in scope, thereby making it difficult for opposing counsel to anticipate whether the substance of the witness's answer will encompass inadmissible matter. The question should give some signal about what is coming, otherwise opposing counsel will not be able to interpose a timely objection to inadmissible testimony. Variations of this objection include "too general," "indefinite," or "lacks specificity."

Q. Did you see the defendant the night of the murder?

A. Yes. He had a lot to drink and was very angry and abusive.

"Objection! Nonresponsive."

This objection is useful in situations when, although the original question as asked by the examining attorney was not objectionable, the response by the witness extends beyond the specific information requested by the examining attorney's question. If the objectionable answer was prejudicial, in addition to making the objection, the attorney should move to strike the objectionable answer and should ask the court to admonish the jury to disregard the testimony. Variations of this objection include "narrative" and "volunteered."

(Assume no one has testified that the defendant was drinking the night of the murder.)

Q. Did you see the defendant at the bar the night of the murder?

A. Yes.

Q. After the defendant had a few drinks, did you see the defendant leave the bar?

"Objection! Assumes a fact not in evidence."

When a question asserts facts that have not been established at trial, the question is objectionable because it brings to the attention of the jury facts that are not in evidence.

Q. Did you see the defendant the night of the murder and did he seem upset?

"Objection! Compound question."

When a single question seeks multiple answers, the witness's testimony will usually be ambiguous and confusing or misleading to the jury.

Q. What did you or didn't you not see if not anything when the defendant entered the bar?

"Objection! Ambiguous."

A question that is not reasonably clear and specific may not be understood by the witness, thereby making the testimony confusing and misleading to the jury. Variations of this objection include "vague," "misleading," "confusing," and "unintelligible."

Q. Once again, would you tell the jury where you were the night of the murder?

"Objection! Asked and answered."

Under Rule 403, the judge has the discretion to exclude evidence it considers to be a "waste of time." Repeating information may fall into this proscription. "Repetitive" is a variation of this objection.

Q. Your Honor, the State moves to admit Exhibits 1 through 47 which are all autopsy pictures of the victim.

"Objection! Cumulative."

Calling several witnesses to testify on the same issue or introducing numerous similar exhibits may be objectionable as cumulative.

(Assume that on direct examination the witness's testimony regarding the demeanor of the defendant was limited to the fact that the defendant was swaying when he walked and that his eyes were red. Opposing counsel begins examination with the following question.)

Q. On direct examination you testified that the defendant was drunk, didn't you?

"Objection! Misstatement of the evidence."

An attorney should make an objection based on a misstatement of the evidence when the interrogator inaccurately describes evidence or when he draws inferences that are for the jury to make.

Q. Now why would you, in your right mind, agree to such a stupid idea?

"Objection! Argumentative!"

This objection is generally made in response to a rhetorical question that attempts to assert the interrogator's meaning or the implication of the testimony.

(Assume the attorney is one foot from the witness box.)

Q. (With voice raised) Now why would you, in your right mind, agree to such a stupid idea?

"Objection! Badgering the witness."

This objection is appropriate when the examiner is attempting to unfairly intimidate the witness. Variations of this objection include "harassing the witness" and "embarrassing the witness."

B. FORM OF QUESTIONS TO WITNESSES

[1] Federal Rule of Evidence 611(c)

Rule 611. Mode and Order of Interrogation and Presentation

* * *

(c) **Leading questions.** Leading questions should not be used on the direct examination of a witness except as may be necessary to develop the witness' testimony. Ordinarily leading questions should be permitted on cross-examination. When a party calls a hostile witness, an adverse party, or a witness identified with an adverse party, interrogation may be by leading questions.

[2] Direct Examination

STRAUB v. READING CO.

220 F.2d 177 (3d Cir. 1955)

MCLAUGHLIN, CIRCUIT JUDGE:

Appellant's main ground for reversal of this district court judgment in favor of appellee is that it was deprived of a fair trial by reason of the deliberate conduct of appellee's attorney throughout the trial.

The suit was under the Federal Employers' Liability Act, 45 U.S.C.A. § 51 *et seq.* Appellee was assistant chief timekeeper for appellant. While on a ladder in the storeroom in appellant's Philadelphia terminal he fell and sustained injuries. On the merits, the disputed condition of the ladder was important. On damages, the allegation that appellee's back had been seriously injured from the fall was strongly controverted.

* * *

The proof of plaintiff's claim both as to the accident and injury was put in to an unconscionably large extent by leading questions. Little seems to have been left to a spontaneous explanatory answer. At times the witnesses seemed relatively unnecessary except as sounding boards. The defense finally stated to the court:

> Mr. McConnell: — If Your Honor please, Mr. Richter has asked quite a number of leading questions up to this point and I have not objected because to do so does our cause a greater harm in the eyes of the jury; and, as a matter of fact, I won't be able to object effectively without greater loss than gain even in the future. So I want to ask Your Honor if you won't caution him not to ask leading questions.
>
> The Court: — I will be glad to.
>
> Mr. McConnell: — Thank you very much.
>
> The Court: — I don't think the leading questions have been very productive in the way of leadership.
>
> Mr. McConnell: — But they could become so.
>
> The Court: — They could become so. Will you watch it, please?

Immediately thereafter the same sort of questions continued; for example to the plaintiff regarding an acute cervical sprain in his neck. "Q. Now, then, did that clear right up after that? A. Yes, sir." Objection was made to this on the ground "That is exactly what we have just discussed." The court commented "I don't think that offends" but suggested that in the future Mr. Richter phrase such questions "did it or did it not." The leading questions continued in this manner with the plaintiff replying correctly to the statements of his lawyer. Sometime thereafter in the further course of the direct examination of plaintiff as to his duties the following happened:

> Q. Does that involve the movements of men that are actually moving trains or assisting in the movements of trains, or in the furtherance of interstate commerce throughout the Reading system?
>
> A. Yes, sir.
>
> Mr. McConnell: — I object to the question.
>
> The Court: — What was that, Mr. McConnell?
>
> Mr. McConnell: — I object to that question as suggesting the answer that it requires.
>
> The Witness: — I check all employees.
>
> The Court: — Is that satisfactory to you, Mr. McConnell?
>
> Mr. McConnell: — Well, if the question is stricken it will be. He just practically told him what to say in it.
>
> Mr. Richter: — That is not so.
>
> The Court: — He asked what work he does and he is telling it now. If you want to go with more particularity into it —
>
> And on the next page of the transcript:
>
> Q. So that these men work in all these four states that you have just mentioned; is that correct?
>
> A. Yes.
>
> Q. Right on the Reading system?
>
> A. That is right.
>
> Q. And do you personally have to go to these different states and go in interstate commerce yourself personally?
>
> A. Yes, sir.

The testimony of Dr. John was given at least partially by affirming question statements to him by Mr. Richter. This also applied to Mr. Arinsberg, the plaintiff's witness who brought the Veterans Administration records. For example:

> Q. In other words, Mr. Arinsberg, the only thing that he came out of the war with and the government was concerned with was the question of whether there was any condition of disability due to the influenza that he had during the war.
>
> A. That is correct, anything service-connected.
>
> Q. And there was no service connection in any way with the back condition of any kind?
>
> A. That is correct.

The direct examination of witnesses on behalf of plaintiff was in part a systematic detailed presentation of the Straub claim on both its aspects, negligence and damages, by his attorney through leading questions. That course of conduct was grossly improper. It was objected to in timely fashion by the other side. Beyond question the court's attention had been sharply focused on the method being employed with the realistic reminder that the defense could not be constantly objecting, especially when nothing was done about it, because of the probable prejudice to its cause in the minds of the jury.

* * *

We think that the entire pattern of this trial shows a conscious successful effort on the part of plaintiff's attorney which resulted in a confused distorted picture going to the jury to the grave prejudice of the defense. The latter had substantial grounds for contesting the contention on behalf of plaintiff that his present back injury resulted from his fall from the ladder. They were entitled to pursue that theory within legitimate bounds. They were prevented from so doing for all practical purposes by the unwarranted conduct of the plaintiff's attorney. Contrary to the assertion of appellee prejudice and harm did result to the appellant. * * *

Regarding the leading questions, appellee asserts that this problem is within the control of the trial court. This may be true in an ordinary law suit. But where that control is lost or at least palpably ignored and the conduct is a set piece running the length of the trial which produces a warped version of the issues as received by the jury, then that body never did have the opportunity to pass upon the whole case and a judgment based on that kind of a twisted trial must be set aside. * * * Knowledge, skill and experience in the presentation of the contentions of the parties are helpful to the court and jury but misused to deprive a litigant of its day in court the result can be as it is in this appeal. Winning, so called, at all cost puts the cost too high. * * *

The judgment of the district court will be reversed and the cause remanded for a new trial.

NOTES

1. What is a leading question?

A leading question is one which clearly suggests the desired response. It is a question "which instructs the witness how to answer on material points, or puts into [the mouth of the witness] words to be echoed back." 3 Wigmore Evidence § 769 (Chadbourn rev. 1970). Questions which begin with "Isn't it true that . . . ." or end with ". . . didn't you?" are clearly leading. Many questions that call for either a "yes" or "no" answer are leading. Sometimes the inflection of the interrogator's voice may make an otherwise permissible question, objectionable as leading.

2. When are leading questions permissible?

Rule 611(c) is couched in non-mandatory ("should" versus "shall") terms, thereby giving the trial court broad discretion to allow or disallow leading questions on both direct and cross-examination. As a general matter, however, courts will require a party to elicit the testimony of favorable witnesses through the use of non-leading questions, especially if the testimony being elicited relates to a controverted substantive area about which the jury will have to deliberate. This limitation is based first on the premise that the truth can best be garnered by having the witnesses state the facts in their own words. It is also based on the presumption that a witness who provides favorable testimony to a party might be overly susceptible to the suggestive nature of the lawyer's leading questions.

Ordinarily, a witness provides favorable testimony when the party calls her to give testimony on direct examination. Rule 611(c) carves out four express exceptions to the general rule that leading questions should not be used on the direct examination of a witness. Leading questions are acceptable when necessary to develop the witness's testimony; when a party calls a hostile witness; when a party calls an adverse party; or when a party calls a witness identified with an adverse party.

3. When may leading questions be necessary to develop a witness's testimony?

One possibility is that leading questions may be allowed for preliminary matters that are not of material importance to the case. The rationale for allowing leading questions on preliminary matters is that leading questions help expedite the trial and there is little prejudice to the opposing party if the questions relate to preliminary matters or to matters that are collateral to the disputed issues in the case. *McClard v. United States*, 386 F.2d 495 (8th Cir. 1967). Another situation where it may be necessary to develop the witness's testimony is in the questioning of a witness who is having difficulty in communicating. As indicated in the Committee Note to Rule 611, the child witness and the adult with communication problems are long-recognized exceptions to the rule prohibiting leading questions on direct examination. *See, e.g., United States v. Archdale*, 229 F.3d 861 (9th Cir. 2000) (no error in the prosecution's use of leading questions in the examination of a child allegedly the victim of sexual abuse; the witness was having a difficult time testifying about a very personal matter); *United States v. Rodriguez-Garcia*, 983 F.2d 1563 (10th Cir. 1993) (no abuse of discretion in permitting the prosecutor to ask leading questions of a witness testifying through an interpreter because he did not speak English). Finally, leading questions may be used to develop the testimony of a witness whose recollection has been exhausted. *See Roberson v. United States*, 249 F.2d 737 (5th Cir. 1957) (leading questions permitted for the purpose of refreshing the recollection of the witness).

4. When is a witness a hostile witness?

A witness can be found hostile by contemptuous or surly conduct, by refusal to answer questions, or by consistent hedging on answers. *See, e.g., United States v. Meza-Urtado*, 351 F.3d 301 (7th Cir. 2003) (Allegedly leading questions asked of cooperating witnesses at drug distribution defendant's trial were not improper where the witness became conveniently "forgetful" during direct examination by the government: "In this situation, had the government asked, he could have been treated as a hostile witness and asked leading questions until the cows came home.").

5. When is a witness identified with an adverse party?

In *Haney v. Mizell Memorial Hosp.*, 744 F.2d 1467 (11th Cir. 1984), the court ruled that a nurse employed by the defendant hospital was identified with an adverse party and the plaintiff's use of leading questions to examine her was appropriate. An even more expansive application of the doctrine is found in *United States v. Hicks*, 748 F.2d 854 (4th Cir. 1984), in which the court held that a criminal defendant's girlfriend who was called by the state to testify, was a witness identified with an adverse party and could be examined with leading questions. *Compare Suarez Matos v. Ashford Presbyterian Community Hosp.*, 4 F.3d 47 (1st Cir. 1993) (leading questions should not have been permitted on direct examination, where the only indication of identification with an adverse party was that the witness had been named on that party's witness list).

6. When a witness is identified with an adverse party, is the court required to allow leading questions?

In *Rodriguez v. Banco Cent. Corp.*, 990 F.2d 7 (1st Cir. 1993), a civil racketeering suit, the court affirmed a directed verdict for the defendants, holding there was no error when the plaintiffs were precluded from using leading questions to examine certain defendants. Although the court observed that the rules generally permit leading questions to be used against an adverse party, it indicated that Rule 611(a) might empower a trial judge to disallow such questions, for example, if they would tend to distort the testimony of a witness.

7. What may the trial judge do to curb abuses in the use of leading questions?

In *United States v. Clinical Leasing Serv.*, 982 F.2d 900 (5th Cir. 1992), an action to hold corporate officers personally liable for fines imposed against their corporation, the court held there was no abuse of discretion in the trial judge's terminating one officer's direct testimony. His attorney had been specifically warned not to lead the witness, after having been warned about leading questions at least seven times previously.

[3] Cross-Examination

UNITED STATES v. McKENNA
791 F. Supp. 1101 (E.D. La. 1992)

CHARLES SCHWARTZ, JR., DISTRICT JUDGE:

* * *

II. *Motion for New Trial*

[The defendant challenged the court's prohibition of leading questions on the cross-examination of Bruno, a government witness. When faced with that restriction, defense counsel chose not to cross-examine the witness. The defendant argued that his constitutional right to confront an adverse witness was violated.]

The Court's ruling in open court was to the effect that defense counsel could not employ leading questions but that he would be given latitude, until it was established that Bruno was in fact an adverse and/or difficult witness, at which point defense counsel would then be permitted to lead him all the way through the remainder of his testimony. Defense counsel opted to rest the defendant's case at that point — that is, despite the latitude which the Court would accord and despite the fact that in the event the defense established that Mr. Bruno was in fact an "adverse" or "unfriendly" witness, the Court expressed its intention to allow defense counsel to employ leading questions from that point forward.

In *United States v. Bourgeois*, 950 F.2d 980, 986 (5th Cir. 1992), the Fifth Circuit stated: "We note at the outset that the trial court has broad discretion in limiting [even] the scope of cross-examination." In *Bourgeois*, the defendants argued that the trial court erred by restricting cross-examination of the Government's witness regarding his immunity agreement. The *Bourgeois* court held that defendant's Sixth Amendment rights were not violated and neither the comments nor the rulings cited by the defendants amounted to an abuse of the district court's discretion in limiting cross-examination.

In the case at bar, as in *Bourgeois*, *supra*, the Court allowed the defense counsel the opportunity and latitude to develop any point they desired to make on cross-examination of Bruno. The Court further indicated that upon establishing or in the event that Bruno proved to be a difficult witness, the Court would permit defense counsel to use leading questions to establish whatever they had in mind. The restrictions about which defense counsel complains are "mythical hype." The Court merely sought to control the proceedings to ensure that the testimonial evidence heard by the jury was elicited from the witness stand and was not provided by defense counsel, a duty the Court takes seriously whether the matter is of civil or criminal gender.

* * *

In the case at bar, defense counsel had ample opportunity to elicit whatever information they desired from Bruno utilizing non-leading questions. That defense counsel *refused the opportunity* to cross-examine because the Court in its discretion deemed it appropriate to impose some control on the *mode* of questioning does not in the Court's opinion constitute error on its part, nor does it convert this matter involving the imposition of reasonable limits on the mode of cross-examination into a constitutional case. "Not every limitation on cross-examination can be easily converted into a constitutional case." *United States v. Pitocchelli*, 830 F.2d 401, 404 (1st Cir. 1987). * * *

Control of the proceedings which the Court invoked in this case was neither calculated to nor could it reasonably be expected to have a substantial effect on the jury's decision. No doubt, defense counsel's "throwing in the towel" did have some effect, albeit not the effect desired by defense counsel. Defense counsel's tactical decision to refrain from interrogating Bruno on the witness stand altogether, was not a prohibition handed down by the Court. There was no such prohibition imposed on the defendant in this case. As such, McKenna does not state a Sixth Amendment violation.

Federal Rule of Evidence 611 sets forth the general rule that "[o]*rdinarily* leading questions should be permitted on cross-examination." The Fifth Circuit in *Ardoin v. J. Ray McDermott & Co.*, 684 F.2d 335, 336 (5th Cir. 1982) explained:

> The rule [*i.e.*, F.R.E. Rule 611] is not intended to be an endorsement of leading questions on cross-examination, however. The advisory committee notes make it clear that "[t]he qualification 'ordinarily' is to furnish a basis for denying the use of leading questions when the cross-examination is cross-examination in form only and not in fact, as for example the 'cross-examination' of a party by his own counsel after being called by the opponent (savoring more of re-direct) * * * ." *A trial court therefore has power to require a party cross-examining a friendly witness to employ non-leading questions. The decision whether to do so, however, lies within the district court's discretion.* [Emphasis supplied].

The rule that the extent of cross-examination and the restriction of the use of leading questions rest in the sound discretion of the trial court prevails in *criminal* as well as civil proceedings.

The defendant in this case bears the burden of demonstrating that any "restriction" imposed by the Court was clearly prejudicial. Defense counsel's decision to rest effectively pretermits the Court's inquiry into the effectiveness of cross-examination in light of the Court's ruling. * * * Moreover, in making the evidentiary ruling at issue, touted as erroneous by the defense, the Court was by no means acting on a whim, but rather the very real need to impose some reasonable boundaries on the manner in which defense counsel sought to elicit evidence and thus, ensure the fairness of the proceedings.

* * *

Accordingly and for all the above and foregoing reasons,

IT IS ORDERED that the defendant's Motion For New Trial is DENIED.

NOTES

1. When may the court restrict the use of leading questions on cross-examination?

In *Ardoin v. McDermott & Co.*, 684 F.2d 335 (5th Cir. 1992), a Jones Act case in which the court affirmed a judgment for an employer, the court observed that, if a witness is friendly to the examiner, the danger of leading questions on cross-examination is similar to that on direct. Thus, the court stated that a trial judge may choose to forbid the use of leading questions on cross-examination of a friendly witness. The court left trial judges with considerable discretion.

Professors Saltzburg, Martin and Capra, in the *Federal Rules of Evidence Manual* (9th ed. 2006), provide this comment on limiting the use of leading questions on cross-examination:

> The final two sentences of Rule 611(c) leave the state of the law confused with respect to whether the party who cross-examines a witness that the Judge has identified as hostile or adverse to the adversary can ask leading questions. To the extent that the direct examination has produced favorable evidence for the party calling the witness, leading questions by the other side would appear to be warranted. If the direct examination is favorable to the cross-examiner, Courts have justifiably treated the cross-examination as delayed direct examination and have denied the cross-examiner a chance to lead an already favorable witness. *See, e.g., Woods v. Lecureux*, 110 F.3d 1215, 1221 (6th Cir. 1997) ("a district court should be hesitant to authorize the use of leading questions when it is cross-examination in form only").

2. What special relationship between parties and witnesses may justify limits on questioning?

In *United States v. Hansen*, 583 F.2d 325 (7th Cir. 1977), the court affirmed a trial judge's ruling that one codefendant (a father) could cross-examine another codefendant (a son) only with nonleading questions.

C. SCOPE OF CROSS-EXAMINATION

[1] Federal Rule of Evidence 611(b)

Rule 611. Mode and Order of Interrogation and Presentation

* * *

(b) Scope of cross-examination. Cross-examination should be limited to the subject matter of the direct examination and matters affecting the credibility of the witness. The court may, in the exercise of discretion, permit inquiry into additional matters as if on direct examination.

* * *

UNITED STATES v. WILLIAMS
461 F.3d 441 (4th Cir. 2006)

WILLIAMS, CIRCUIT JUDGE:

Frank L. Williams appeals his conviction for being a felon in possession of a firearm in violation of 18 U.S.C.A. § 922(g)(1). * * * As to his conviction, Williams contends that the district court erred by conditioning the admission of an evidentiary demonstration he wished to perform on his willingness to testify, an error that he argues improperly enabled the Government to introduce the names of his prior convictions despite the fact he had stipulated to his felon status. We agree that the district court erred, but we conclude that the error was harmless. * * *

I.

On October 18, 2003, Officers Gene Molinaro and Jack Atkins of the Baltimore City Police Department arrested Williams for selling counterfeit music compact disks (CDs) and digital video disks (DVDs). According to the officers, Officer Molinaro discovered a gun in Williams's waistband during a search of his person after the arrest. It was later determined that Williams had several prior felony convictions, and Williams was indicted under § 922(g)(1) in the United States District Court for the District of Maryland.

Williams elected to go to trial. Prior to trial, he stipulated that he was a convicted felon so that the name and nature of his recent prior convictions — a 1991 conviction for possession with intent to distribute heroin, a 1995 conviction for possession with intent to distribute heroin and cocaine, and a 1995 handgun conviction — would not be introduced to the jury. *See Old Chief v. United States*, 519 U.S. 172, 185 (1997) (holding that Fed. R. Evid. 403 prohibits the Government from introducing the "name or nature" of a prior felony conviction in a § 922(g)(1) case when such information would tend to "lure a juror into a sequence of bad character reasoning" regarding a defendant who had stipulated to his felon status).

The prosecution called Officers Molinaro and Atkins to testify at trial. These officers testified that on the day in question, they were in a marked patrol car on a routine patrol that took them past the Upton Courts apartment complex, an area fraught with crime. As they slowed for traffic, Officer Molinaro saw Williams, who was sitting on a wall in front of the apartment complex, engaged in a transaction with a man on a bicycle. A large black bag was near Williams and he was offering CDs to the man on the bicycle with one hand while reaching with the other hand for cash from the man on the bicycle. Suspecting that Williams was illegally selling CDs, the officers stopped their patrol, got out of the car, and approached Williams. As the officers approached, the man on the bicycle rode away. Officer Molinaro asked Williams if he had a vendor's license, and when Williams answered in the negative, he was placed under arrest. Officer Atkins handcuffed Williams, and Officer Molinaro directed Williams to sit on the curb. Officer Molinaro turned his attention to Williams while Officer Atkins inspected the black bag.

Officer Molinaro testified that Williams was wearing a fanny pack and that the fanny pack was zipped closed at the time of his arrest. As Williams sat on the curb, Officer Molinaro unclipped the fanny pack to remove it. At that time, Officer Molinaro observed that the fanny pack was unzipped and the compartment was open. Officer Molinaro further noticed that Williams's underwear was pulled high above the waist of his pants so that it covered a square bulge. Pulling the underwear back, Officer Molinaro found a handgun. Officer Molinaro suspected that Williams originally had the gun in his fanny pack and, after his arrest, transferred it to his underwear. Officer Atkins discovered counterfeit DVDs and CDs in the black bag.

Williams represents — and the Government does not seriously contest — that, having stipulated to his felon status, he did not intend to testify at trial.

During cross-examination of Officer Molinaro, however, Williams sought to demonstrate to the jury that he could not have been wearing the fanny pack because its belt was too short to close around his waist. The Government objected to the demonstration, arguing that "any demonstration * * * would be testimonial" and that Williams would, therefore, be subject to cross-examination if he performed it. The district court sustained the Government's objection, providing two reasons for its ruling: (1) that the demonstration was a testimonial act and, accordingly, Williams could not perform it without subjecting himself to cross-examination and (2) that the demonstration was inadmissible because Williams had gained a significant amount of weight after he was arrested and, therefore, the demonstration was irrelevant to show that Williams was not wearing the fanny pack at the time of his arrest.[1]

After the Government rested its case, Williams sought clarification of the district court's ruling with respect to the demonstration. In explaining its decision, the district court suggested that, despite the fact it found that Williams had gained weight since his arrest, Williams would be able to perform the demonstration if he would be willing to subject himself to cross-examination on the issue of his weight. The Government informed Williams that if he chose to testify, it would seek to impeach his testimony by introducing the name of the three aforementioned prior convictions. At that time, the district court expressed doubt that the prior handgun conviction would be admissible to impeach Williams.

Williams called his wife as the opening witness in his case in defense. She stated that she had driven Williams to the apartment complex and that, at the time he got out of the car, he was not wearing a fanny pack or carrying a black bag or gun. Mrs. Williams went into the apartment complex to visit her granddaughter and Williams stayed outside. Later, someone informed Mrs. Williams that her husband was being arrested in the street. She left the building to see what was going on and observed one of the officers (presumably Officer Molinaro) talking to her husband as he was handcuffed and seated on the curb and the other officer (presumably Officer Atkins) removing DVDs, CDs, and a gun from the black bag.

During a break in Mrs. Williams's testimony, Williams again sought clarification with respect to the district court's ruling on the demonstration. This time, the district court stated what it had suggested in its second explanation of its ruling: "If [Williams] wants to take the stand, he can put * * * on [the fanny pack]* * * . That's actually the only way you get the demonstration, because then the Government gets to cross-examine as to whether the circumstances of the demonstration are sufficiently similar to what [they were at the time of Williams's arrest]." The district court also ruled that, based on the testimony that had been presented to that point, the Government could not introduce the name of the handgun conviction as

---

[1] The court instructed counsel that he could not use the defense of "[i]f the belt doesn't fit, you must acquit." The district court was apparently referring to a memorable scene from the 1995 murder trial of O.J. Simpson. A bloody glove had been found at the crime scene, and the prosecutor wanted Simpson to put on the glove in front of the jury. Simpson tried to put on the glove, but it was too small. In his closing argument, Simpson's attorney, Johnnie Cochran, told the jury, "If it doesn't fit, you must acquit." Closing Argument of Johnnie Cochran, California v. Simpson, No. BA097211, 1995 WL 697930, at *50 (Cal. Super. Ct. Sept. 28, 1995).

impeachment because its probative value did not outweigh its prejudicial effect. The district court also stated, however, "I don't know what he's going to testify to on direct, and then the direct is going to determine the scope of the cross[-examination]." After Mrs. Williams testified, Williams's counsel sought clarification from the district court on whether, if Williams testified, the Government could impeach Williams's testimony with the name of the handgun conviction. The district court responded, "it depends on what [Williams] says about a gun."

Williams decided to take the stand. He tried on the fanny pack, but it was approximately six inches too short to close around his waist. Williams also testified regarding his weight change (or lack thereof) since the time of his arrest. Williams, however, did not limit his testimony to his weight change. Instead, he gave testimony regarding the events surrounding his arrest. According to Williams, he was sitting on the wall in front of the apartment complex when a man on a bicycle approached him offering to sell him DVDs and CDs. The man showed him the DVDs and CDs, and about the same time, the man on the bicycle saw Officers Molinaro and Atkins in their patrol car and rode off. According to Williams, he (Williams) was not wearing the fanny pack, he was not selling the DVDs and CDs, the black bag did not belong to him, and he did not have the gun. Williams also stated that he had a prior drug conviction.

On cross-examination, the prosecutor briefly questioned Williams regarding his weight change since the time of his arrest. Williams also admitted, in response to questioning from the prosecutor, that he had two prior drug convictions. The following exchange then ensued:

Prosecutor:	Okay. Are you telling the ladies and gentlemen of the jury you have no knowledge of this gun?
Williams:	Yep.
Prosecutor:	Are you telling the ladies and gentlemen of the jury you did not intend to possess this gun?
Williams:	Yep.

The prosecution then asked Williams about the handgun conviction. Williams admitted that he had pled guilty to a crime involving a handgun.

The case was submitted to the jury, which returned a guilty verdict. * * *

II.

Williams contends that his proposed demonstration was not testimonial evidence and, accordingly, the district court erred by excluding the demonstration unless he took the stand. * * *

Implicit in the district court's ruling that the demonstration was a testimonial act that would subject Williams to cross-examination is the view that a defendant who offers "testimony" is subject to cross-examination, while a defendant who offers only "nontestimonial evidence" is not subject to cross-examination. Federal Rule of Evidence 611(b) supports this view. *See* Fed. R. Evid. 611(b) ("Cross-examination should be limited to the subject matter of the direct examination and matters affecting the credibility of the witness.").

While Rule 611(b) primarily sets limits for the "[s]cope of cross-examination," id., the first sentence of the Advisory Committee's Notes on Rule 611(b) presupposes that cross-examination is only proper when a witness testifies. *See* Fed. R. Evid. 611(b) 1972 advisory committee's note ("The tradition in the federal courts and in numerous state courts has been to limit the scope of cross-examination to matter testified to on direct [examination], plus matters bearing on the credibility of the witness." (emphasis added)).

Without attempting to provide an exhaustive definition of the term "testimony" in this context, we think it clear that a physical demonstration such as the one Williams proposed here is not "testimony" and, accordingly, that such a demonstration does not subject its proponent to cross-examination under Rule 611(b). Among the primary purposes of cross-examination are to "test the [testifying] witness' perceptions and memory [and to] impeach, *i.e.*, discredit, the [testifying] witness." *Davis v. Alaska*, 415 U.S. 308, 316 (1974). In the case of a physical demonstration, the proponent of the evidence does not express any perceptions or memory that could be tested, nor does he make any assertions that could be discredited. Rather, he simply presents his body, often coupled with an accouterment, as evidence to the jury. In such a situation, there simply is nothing to cross-examine.

To be sure, when one party conducts a physical demonstration the other party is entitled to introduce evidence of his own that tends to show that the demonstration does not accurately portray what it purports to represent. Such evidence is a proper response to the admission of a physical demonstration, as is cross-examining a witness who offers testimony that the demonstration accurately portrays what it purports to represent. But it is illogical to say that a defendant opens himself up to cross-examination simply by virtue of performing a physical demonstration. Such a holding is tantamount to the strange conclusion that a demonstration *itself* can be cross-examined.

* * *

We therefore conclude that a physical demonstration performed before the jury is not, without more, "testimony" that subjects the demonstrator to cross-examination under Rule 611(b). In requiring Williams to subject himself to cross-examination as a condition to admitting his demonstration, the district court erred.

Our conclusion that the district court erred does not, of course, end the matter, for we must assess the effect of the district court's error on Williams's trial. * * *

Williams argues that he was prejudiced by the district court's error because it was only by virtue of the fact he took the stand that the Government was able to introduce the names of his three prior convictions. He further contends that the jury was likely to have assumed, without considering whether the Government had proved its case, that because he had three prior convictions — one of which was for a handgun offense — he possessed a gun outside the apartment complex. *See Old Chief*, 519 U.S. at 185 (noting that "the risk of unfair prejudice [is] especially obvious" when a defendant is charged with being a felon in possession of a firearm and the name or nature of a prior gun conviction is introduced into evidence).

This is a unique case. In most cases involving an erroneous evidentiary ruling, the error itself results in the admission of inadmissible evidence — the district court incorrectly interprets a Rule of Evidence and the Government is able to introduce inadmissible evidence. Here, however, the district court's error did not alone result in the introduction of the name of Williams's prior convictions into evidence. Under the district court's ruling, Williams could have declined to take the stand, in which case the name of his prior convictions would have been inadmissible. Instead, Williams decided to take the stand, a decision that created the possibility that the name of his prior convictions would be admitted into evidence.

We are unable to say, however, that Williams brought upon himself all harm that may have resulted from his decision to take the stand, because the district court presented him with a Hobson's choice: Williams could either (1) take the stand and demonstrate the fit of the fanny pack, thereby opening himself to cross-examination, or (2) not take the stand and be free from cross-examination but forgo performing the demonstration. Because, as discussed, Williams was entitled to perform the demonstration without taking the stand, we cannot fault Williams for choosing the former option.

This conclusion, however, does not mean that all of Williams's choices are irrelevant to our harmlessness evaluation. While Williams made his decision *to take the stand* in the context of the district court's improper either/or, the district court did not impose a similar either/or with respect to *the scope of Williams's testimony*. In other words, while the district court's Rule 611(b) ruling unduly influenced Williams's decision to take the stand, once Williams decided to take the stand, he was free to say as little or as much as he pleased. Indeed, while the district court incorrectly conditioned Williams's ability to perform the demonstration on his willingness to take the stand, the district court never suggested that, once on the stand, Williams would have to testify about anything other than the fit of the fanny pack.

This distinction is an important one. * * * [T]he district court explained to Williams that the name of his prior handgun conviction would be admissible only if the scope of his direct examination was broad enough that the handgun conviction would be a proper subject of cross-examination. * * * [A]s the district court twice explained to Williams, the Government was able to introduce the evidence of his handgun conviction because Williams testified that he did not possess a handgun on the day in question. *See* Fed. R. Evid. 611(b) ("Cross-examination should be limited to the subject matter of the direct examination and matters affecting the credibility of the witness.").

In assessing whether Williams was harmed by the district court's error and the consequent admission into evidence of the name of Williams's prior handgun convictions, we believe it is relevant that he evidently considered himself better off by testifying that he did not have a gun on the day in question rather than limiting his testimony to matters relating to the fit of the fanny-pack. This choice, which Williams made with full awareness of both his ability to limit his testimony and the consequences of failing to do so, reflects a calculation of the costs and benefits of his options that courts are not prohibited from taking into account. We need not blind ourselves to Williams's own assessment that it was better for him to present to the jury his side of the story — despite the risk that the Government would introduce the name of his prior handgun conviction — than it would be for him to remain silent on this issue. To hold otherwise would both ignore the fact that Williams presented his version of the events to the jury and reward him for exacerbating the very error about which he now complains.

* * *

* * * [W]e conclude that the Government has met its burden of establishing harmlessness. The jury's knowledge of the name of Williams's prior handgun conviction is, at least in part, attributable to Williams's mistake of not limiting his testimony to the fanny pack. But even if we disregard this mistake, it is difficult to see how the jury would have returned a different verdict if Williams had demonstrated the fanny pack without being subjected to cross-examination. To be sure, there was potential prejudice in the jury's knowledge of the names of Williams's prior convictions. *See Old Chief*, 519 U.S. at 185. But the prosecution did not exploit the potential for prejudice so as to cause harm to Williams, and the district court appropriately gave a limiting instruction to the jury about the use of the convictions.

* * *

[2] The American Rule: Cross-Examination within the Subject Matter of the Direct

MACAULAY v. ANAS

321 F.3d 45 (1st Cir. 2003)

SELYA, CIRCUIT JUDGE:

After undergoing an unsuccessful surgical procedure, plaintiff-appellant Katherine Macaulay sued for negligence. The case was tried to a jury, which returned a verdict in favor of her surgeon, defendant-appellee Peter P. Anas. Macaulay appeals, assigning error to the district court's actions in * * * (3) permitting cross-examination of her treating physician with respect to matters touching upon the standard of care. Concluding, as we do, that these claims of error are without merit, we affirm.

I. BACKGROUND

We start by sketching a broad picture of the case. We bring that picture into sharper focus by adding more specific facts during our discussion of particular issues.

The appellant, like many other people, suffers from back problems. In due course, she came under the care of Dr. Anas (a well-known orthopedist). The physician recommended that she undergo spinal fusion surgery, and the appellant acquiesced.

Dr. Anas performed the surgery on September 11, 1992, at New England Baptist Hospital in Boston, Massachusetts. The operation was not a success.

When the Macaulay family moved to Philadelphia, the appellant came under the care of a different orthopedist, Dr. Todd Albert. On February 14, 1994, Dr. Albert performed corrective spinal surgery.

Displeased by what had happened on Dr. Anas's watch, the appellant brought a diversity action, in the United States District Court for the District of Massachusetts. She named as defendants Dr. Anas * * * and AcroMed Corporation (the manufacturer of the hardware used in the original surgery). She alleged, inter alia, that Dr. Anas had been negligent in using investigational bone screws, in improperly positioning them during the operation, and in failing to remove them afterwards. * * * On September 24, 2001, the jury returned a defendant's verdict. This timely appeal ensued.

II. DISCUSSION

* * *

D. CROSS-EXAMINATION

The appellant asseverates that the district court abused its discretion in allowing defense counsel to elicit standard of care testimony during his cross-examination of [the plaintiff's treating physician] Dr. Albert. In this regard, the appellant posits that she did not identify Dr. Albert as an expert witness who would offer standard of care testimony; that permitting him to discuss the standard of care undermined the physician-patient relationship; and that, in all events, the testimony should have been excluded under Fed. R. Evid. 403. The phrasing of this asseverational array distorts the real issue: whether or not the disputed cross-examination went beyond the scope of the witness's direct examination.

Dr. Albert testified by means of a videotaped deposition. During direct examination by the appellant's counsel, he testified that, in the course of spinal fusion surgery, screws are supposed to be placed inside the pedicles of the patient's spine. He then noted that several of the screws that Dr. Anas had inserted in the appellant's spine were not entirely within the pedicles. In line with this observation, he characterized the screws as "malpositioned" or "misplaced."

On cross-examination, Dr. Albert elaborated upon these statements. He reiterated that the screws were not located entirely within the pedicles of the spine (and, thus, were malpositioned or misplaced), but he then acknowledged that this fact did not necessarily signify a deviation from the applicable standard of care. In much the same vein, he said that, in characterizing the screws as malpositioned or misplaced, he did not mean to suggest that Dr. Anas had transgressed the standard of care. At trial, the district court admitted these elaborations over the appellant's objections.

It is elementary that the scope of permissible cross-examination is delimited by the scope of the witness's direct examination. *See* Fed. R. Evid. 611(b); *see also United States v. Lara*, 181 F.3d 183, 189 (1st Cir. 1999) (describing as "standard fare" a cross-examiner's ability "to inquire into issues * * * related to and made relevant by [direct examination]").

It is, of course, unrealistic to expect that direct examination and cross-examination will be perfectly congruent. *See, e.g.*, *Irons v. FBI*, 880 F.2d 1446, 1462 (1st Cir. 1989) (en banc) (noting, in dictum, that by testifying on direct examination, witnesses may "expose themselves [on cross-examination] to a range of questions which may go well beyond what the witness, or the examiner on direct, chooses to present during the case in chief"). The latter need only be reasonably related to the former, and matching the two requires the district court to make a series of judgment calls. A district court's decision either to permit questioning as falling within the scope of the direct or to exclude it as falling outside that scope is evaluated for abuse of discretion. Under this standard, a decision will be overturned only when the court misapprehends the applicable law or commits a meaningful error in judgment. Even an erroneous ruling will not justify upsetting a jury verdict unless the error affects the aggrieved party's substantial rights. *See* Fed. R. Civ. P. 61; Fed. R. Evid. 103.

Seen in this light, the pivotal question here is whether the appellant's direct examination opened the door to the disputed cross-examination. Although the appellant asserts that Dr. Albert was strictly a fact witness, not an expert witness, her direct examination did not hew to that line. In response to questions on direct, Dr. Albert testified unequivocally that the screws used in spinal fusion surgery should be placed within the boundary of the pedicles. He then testified that several of the screws that Dr. Anas had inserted in the appellant's spine were not so configured; instead, they were malpositioned or misplaced. Although the appellant labors to characterize these comments as statements of fact, they bore directly on the standard of care required in the course of performing spinal fusion surgery. The statements also suggested (or, at least, supported a reasonable inference) that Dr. Anas had violated this standard in fusing the appellant's spine. The witness's use of terms such as "malpositioned" and "misplaced" implied fault. *See* Oxford Engl. Dict. 1708 (compact ed. 1971) (defining "malpositioned" as "wrongly or badly positioned"); id. at 1815 (defining "misplaced" as "put in a wrong place"). Thus, a reasonable jury easily could have construed Dr. Albert's statements to mean that Dr. Anas had committed actionable malpractice.

The defense was not required to let this potentially damaging inference hang in the air. The ground that is covered on direct examination sets the boundaries of permissible cross-examination. Consequently, the cross-examiner had every right to probe the meaning of the witness's statements in an effort to dispel any intimation of negligence. In other words, by asking questions that related both to the standard of care and to the breach of that standard, the appellant effectively opened the door for the cross-examiner to address and clarify those issues. *See, e.g.*, *United States v. Fortes*, 619 F.2d 108, 121 (1st Cir. 1980) (holding that direct examination as to specific issues "opened the door to a full and not just selective discussion of these matters" on cross-examination).

Here, the cross-examiner merely walked through the open door and had the witness explain what he meant. Cross-examiners must be given reasonable latitude to delve into areas related to a witness's direct examination, and that latitude was not exceeded in this instance. Questions that serve primarily to clarify matters raised on direct examination are, virtually by definition, within the proper scope of cross-examination.

There is one conceivable gray area. The cross-examiner asked Dr. Albert about the reported percentage of screws that do not end up entirely within the pedicles in operations performed by experienced orthopedic surgeons throughout the United States. The witness responded that the figure is "as high as 15 to 20 percent." This general question arguably went too far. But even assuming that it exceeded the scope of the direct examination — there are arguments both ways and much leeway for the trier's judgment — any error was harmless. The statistic, in and of itself, cuts both ways, and, moreover, the same percentages were vouchsafed during the trial, without objection, by expert witnesses for both sides.

The short of it, then, is that the district court's admission of the testimony gleaned through Dr. Albert's cross-examination did not constitute an abuse of discretion. That said, the appellant's remaining objections need not detain us. The argument that the cross-examination somehow infringed upon the physician-patient relationship is jejune; it was the appellant, after all, who sued for personal injuries and made Dr. Albert's testimony a centerpiece of her case. As for the argument that the questions and answers should have been excluded under Fed. R. Evid. 403, the question is one not merely of prejudice, but of unfair prejudice. The juxtaposition of the witness's direct testimony in the context of the case as a whole rendered the evidence gleaned through cross-examination both probative and fair.

III. CONCLUSION

We need go no further. After scrutinizing the record, we are fully persuaded that the district court handled the case with consummate skill and patience. Because the appellant received a fair trial, unblemished by discernible error, the jury verdict must stand.

NOTES

1. What is the difference between restricted cross-examination (The American Rule) and wide-open cross-examination (The English Rule)?

Professors Saltzburg, Martin and Capra, in the *Federal Rules of Evidence Manual* (9th ed. 2006) describe the difference, and its implications, as follows:

> Most common-law jurisdictions adhere to the view that the scope of cross-examination as of right does not extend beyond the scope of the subject matter testified to on direct examination. This is the position taken by Rule 611(b). *See, e.g., United States v. Vasquez*, 858 F.2d 1387 (9th Cir. 1988) (in a drug prosecution, the Court held that questions concerning items in the defendant's apartment — i.e., drugs and cash — were within the scope of direct examination where the defendant claimed that he had left his apartment and had left alone).

Congress rejected the Advisory Committee's proposal that would have provided for cross-examination on any relevant subject about which the witness is knowledgeable.

The rationale of the Rule is that the party who calls the witness ordinarily should be allowed its own order of proof, and that cross-examination beyond the subject matter of direct would be an unwarranted disruption. Of course, the Rule does not mean that the witness can never be asked about the unrelated subject matter. The solution is for the adverse party to call the witness during its own case-in-chief. *See, e.g.*, *United States v. Southers*, 583 F.2d 1302 (5th Cir. 1978) (Trial Judge properly prevented the defendant from offering his good character evidence under Rule 404(a) by cross-examining government witnesses; the defendant could subsequently call these witnesses to testify for the defense).

The Rule provides that the Judge has discretion to permit a broader scope of cross-examination. It appears that Judges have often exercised this discretion, especially where the witness would be substantially inconvenienced by having to testify on two separate occasions, or where expanded cross-examination might expedite the proceedings or assist in the search for truth. Of course, the scope limitation of Rule 611(b) does not apply to impeachment of the witness's credibility. A party can impeach a witness on cross-examination even if the subject matter of the witness's credibility was not addressed on direct. This is because the witness's credibility is always an underlying issue, independent of the subject matter of the direct testimony. *See, e.g.*, *United States v. Smalley*, 754 F.2d 944, 951 (11th Cir. 1985) ("Matters affecting the credibility of the witness are always relevant on cross-examination."); *United States v. Arnott*, 704 F.2d 322, 324 (6th Cir. 1983) ("The subject matter of direct examination and issues of witness credibility are always open to cross-examination.").

2. What is the scope of re-cross-examination?

United States v. Riggi, 951 F.2d 1368 (3d Cir. 1991): The court reversed Hobbs Act and RICO (Racketeer Influenced and Corrupt Organizations) convictions arising from labor union connections to the Mafia, holding that a blanket rule barring re-cross-examination violated the defendants' confrontation rights. When important new matters were brought out by the government on re-direct, the defendants were entitled to re-cross.

In *United States v. Perez-Ruiz*, 353 F.3d 1 (1st Cir. 2003), the court held that the trial court did not abuse its discretion in denying the defendant the opportunity to recross-examine a government witness, because the defense was given ample time for a thorough and complete cross-examination and no new information was elicited on direct.

PROBLEM 1-1

Boats of Britain, Inc., sold a boat to Honest Buyer on an installment sales agreement. Honest Buyer stopped making payments when he learned the boat was not new as he claims he was told by an employee of Boats of Britain. Boats of Britain filed suit to collect the account. Honest Buyer defends and counterclaims on the theory of breach of warranty and fraud. Honest Buyer seeks punitive damages in an amount of ten percent of Boats of Britain's gross revenues.

Boats of Britain, the plaintiff, calls its president to the stand.

Plaintiff: How are you employed?
President: I work at Boats of Britain.
Plaintiff: In fact you are the president of Boats of Britain, Inc., aren't you?
Defendant: Objection! (1) ________.
Plaintiff: (2) ________.
The court: (3) ________.
President: Yes, I am President of Boats of Britain.
Plaintiff: Do you recognize the defendant sitting over there?
President: Yes, I remember the day he came in and we talked about * * * (interrupted)
Defendant: Objection! (4) ________.
The court: (5) ________.
Plaintiff: What date did you enter into a contract with the defendant?
Defendant: Objection! (6) ________.
The court: (7) ________.
Plaintiff: Have you ever met the defendant?
President: Yes.
Plaintiff: What date was that?
President: I don't remember.
Plaintiff: Would the installment sales contract refresh your memory about the date you met the defendant?
Defendant: Objection! That's leading.
Plaintiff: (8) ________.
The court: (9) ________.
President: Yes, the installment sales contract would help refresh my memory.
Plaintiff: (After the witness looks at the contract) Now do you recall the date?
President: Yes.
Plaintiff: When was it?
President: June 8, 2005.
Plaintiff: Did you have a discussion with the defendant on that date?

President: Yes.
Plaintiff: Did you discuss the condition of the boat?
President: Yes.
Plaintiff: What did you or didn't you not say if not anything?
Defendant: Objection! (10) ________.
The court: (11) ________.
Plaintiff: What did you say about the condition of the boat?
President: Nothing much, but I never said it was new.
Plaintiff: I hand you what has been marked as Plaintiff's Exhibit 1. Do you recognize it?
President: Yes, its our contract.
Plaintiff: Does your signature and the signature of the defendant appear at the bottom?
Defendant: Objection! (12) ________.
The court: (13) ________.
Plaintiff: Does your signature appear at the bottom?
President: Yes.
Plaintiff: Did you watch the defendant sign this document?
President: Yes.
Plaintiff: Your Honor, I'd like to offer Plaintiff's Exhibit 1 into evidence.
Defendant: No objection.
The court: Plaintiff's Exhibit 1 is admitted.
Plaintiff: Now then, did the defendant stop making payments after the first payment of two hundred dollars?
Defendant: We'd stipulate that no payment was made after the first two hundred dollars.
Plaintiff: We'll accept the stipulation.
Plaintiff: Do you have anything else you'd like to add?
Defendant: Objection! (14) ________.
The court: (15) ________.
Plaintiff: Again, did you say anything about the boat being new?
Defendant: Objection! (16) ________.
The court: (17) ________.
Plaintiff: No further questions.

The defendant cross-examines.

Defendant: So you just testified that you told my client the boat was new?
Plaintiff: Objection! (18) ________.
The court: (19) ________.
Defendant: Well, isn't it true * * * (interrupted)
Plaintiff: Objection! That's a leading question.
Defendant: (20) ________.
The court: (21) ________.

Defendant: Isn't it true that the boat was a used boat?
Plaintiff: Objection! Outside the scope of direct.
Defendant: (22) __________.
The court: (23) __________.
Defendant: Isn't it true that you told your bartender the day after the sale that you sold some old guy an old junker that you said was new?
Plaintiff: Objection! Outside the scope.
Defendant: (24) __________.
The court: (25) __________.
President: Maybe I'd been drinking.
Defendant: So how can you say that you are telling the truth now?
Plaintiff: Objection! (26) __________.
The court: (27) __________.
Defendant: What is the gross revenue from Boats of Britain?
Plaintiff: Objection! (28) __________.
Defendant: (29) __________.
The court: (30) __________.

Later in the trial after the plaintiff has rested, the defendant calls the plaintiff's independent certified public accountant to the stand.

Defendant: Please state your name for the record.
Witness: C.P.A. You may call me Mr. C.P.A.
Defendant: Your Honor, I would like this witness declared hostile so I may use leading questions.
The court: (31) __________.
Defendant: How are you employed?
Witness: I have my own accounting firm.
Defendant: Do you keep the plaintiff's books?
Witness: Yes.
Defendant: Do you do the plaintiff's taxes?
Witness: Yes.
Defendant: Do you prepare the prospectus for the plaintiff?
Witness: Yes.
Defendant: Do you prepare the plaintiff's financial statements?
Witness: Yes.
Defendant: Isn't it true that the plaintiff had gross revenues of more than 10,000,000 pounds for the last fiscal year?
Plaintiff: Objection! (32) __________.
Defendant: (33) __________.
The court: (34) __________.
Witness: No, I don't think so.
Defendant: (Approaches the witness and shouts) YOU'RE LYING AREN'T YOU?
Plaintiff: Objection! (35) __________.
The court: (36) __________.

Defendant: Mr. C.P.A., I hand you what has been marked for identification as Defense Composite Exhibit 1. Composite Exhibit 1. Composite Exhibit 1 consists of the books of the plaintiff for the last fiscal year, doesn't it?

Witness: Yes.

Defendant: Composite Exhibit 1 shows the plaintiff's gross revenue for the last fiscal year to be 10,001,000.99 pounds, doesn't it?

Witness: Yes.

Defendant: Mr. C.P.A., I hand you what has been marked for identification as Defense Exhibit 2. Exhibit 2 is the prospectus you prepared for the plaintiff, isn't it?

Witness: Yes.

Defendant: Exhibit 2 shows that the plaintiff's gross revenue for the last fiscal year was 10,001,000.99 pounds, doesn't it?

Witness: Yes.

Defendant: Now let me hand you Defense Exhibit 3. Exhibit 3 is the financial statement you prepared for the plaintiff, isn't it?

Plaintiff: Objection! (37) ________.

The court: (38) ________.

The plaintiff cross-examines.

Plaintiff: Now isn't it true that gross revenues have been inflated by over 50% due to seasonal fluctuations allowing for income from the previous year to be included?

Defendant: Objection! (39) ________.

The court: (40) ________.

Chapter 2

OBJECTIONS AND OFFERS OF PROOF

A. INTRODUCTION

[1] Illustration

The scene:	The courtroom is hushed. Mr. Prosecutor has left the witness stand and walked back to the counsel table. He picks up the damning piece of evidence, turns dramatically and faces the witness, holding it so that everyone can see the gun.
Mr. Prosecutor:	Isn't this gun exactly like the one you saw the defendant throw in the lake one half hour after the murder?
Defense Counsel:	(Placing his hands on counsel table, he lifts his bulk to full height.) Objection! Incompetent, irrelevant, and immaterial!
The court:	Mr. Prosecutor?
Mr. Prosecutor:	Your Honor (said in a whine), the actual gun has never been retrieved from the lake despite the best efforts of the police. I am prepared to prove by this witness that the defendant had a gun similar to this exhibit and that both guns are of the same caliber. Furthermore, I am prepared to prove that the caliber of bullet that killed the victim is the same caliber as the exhibit. The evidence is competent, relevant, and material.
The court:	Defense Counsel?
Defense Counsel:	There's a lack of foundation and exposing the jury to the gun in this fashion is an obvious ploy to prejudice the jury.
The court:	I am inclined to agree with Defense Counsel. Sustained.
Mr. Prosecutor:	But, your Honor (more whining).
The court:	Enough, Mr. Prosecutor.
Mr. Prosecutor:	May I question the witness without the jury present so that I may establish a record?
The court:	That seems like an unnecessary waste of time.
Mr. Prosecutor:	Would the court accept my statement as an offer of proof?
The court:	So noted for the record.

[2] Federal Rule of Evidence 103

Rule 103. Rulings on Evidence

(a) Effect of erroneous ruling. Error may not be predicated upon a ruling which admits or excludes evidence unless a substantial right of the party is affected, and

(1) Objection. In case the ruling is one admitting evidence, a timely objection or motion to strike appears of record, stating the specific ground of objection, if the specific ground was not apparent from the context; or

(2) Offer of proof. In case the ruling is one excluding evidence, the substance of the evidence was made known to the court by offer or was apparent from the context within which questions were asked.

Once the court makes a definitive ruling on the record admitting or excluding evidence, either at or before trial, a party need not renew an objection or offer of proof to preserve a claim of error for appeal.

(b) Record of offer and ruling. The court may add any other or further statement which shows the character of the evidence, the form in which it was offered, the objection made, and the ruling thereon. It may direct the making of an offer in question and answer form.

(c) Hearing of jury. In jury cases, proceedings shall be conducted, to the extent practicable, so as to prevent inadmissible evidence from being suggested to the jury by any means, such as making statements or offers of proof or asking questions in the hearing of the jury.

(d) Plain error. Nothing in this rule precludes taking notice of plain errors affecting substantial rights although they were not brought to the attention of the court.

B. CONTEMPORANEOUS OBJECTION

UNITED STATES v. SPRIGGS
102 F.3d 1245 (D.C. Cir. 1996)

PER CURIAM:

The four appellants, all salesmen at well-known Washington-area suburban car dealerships, were caught in an elaborate sting operation in which an undercover police officer posed as a big-time District of Columbia drug dealer seeking to buy cars with the cash proceeds of cocaine sales.

* * *

II. Trial Issues

A. Expert Testimony

The Government's first witness was Special Agent Dwight Rawls of the Food and Drug Administration. The Government offered Rawls, formerly a detective with the Metropolitan Police Department, as an expert in drug distribution, money laundering, and undercover operations. On direct examination, Rawls explained drug terminology the jury would hear on undercover tapes, methods used by drug dealers to launder money, and law enforcement efforts to detect money laundering, including "sting" operations.

Appellants challenge the following testimony elicited from Rawls midway through the Government's direct examination:

Prosecutor: As of December of 1990, what was your information about where D.C. narcotics dealers purchased their vehicles?

Rawls: In December of 1990, the dealers were beginning to move further and further out of the city. We had a list of dealerships, including Rosenthal and the Virginia group, several of the Maryland groups of dealerships where the people were actually going. Most of it, and this is based on my interviews of violators and cooperating individuals, that there is sort of an inner circle of word of mouth of who to go see where, at which dealerships and which dealerships where there are less questions asked or the pertinent questions are not asked, and that's basically how it was generated.

On cross-examination, counsel for appellant deMesones elicited similar testimony from Rawls:

> My basic testimony is that I interviewed a number of people and I also review a lot of the documents or intelligence reports that come through, and that there were two or three locations in the Rosenthal group that were pointed out as places that you could go if you wanted to purchase a car and needed some assistance in purchasing it with cash.

Appellants argue that Rawls's testimony about Rosenthal dealerships was hearsay, *see* Fed. R. Evid. 801(c), and that its admission violated their constitutional right to confront witnesses against them. Contending that the testimony was irrelevant and prejudicial, that it was evidence of prior bad acts, and that it constituted improper fact testimony by an expert witness, appellants maintain that the district court violated a host of evidentiary rules by admitting the remarks. *See* Fed. R. Evid. 402, 403, 404(b).

We agree with the Government that appellants failed to preserve these arguments for appeal. Neither appellants nor any of their co-defendants lodged contemporaneous objections to Rawls's testimony about Rosenthal. Not until a bench conference later in Rawls's cross-examination, called at the behest of the Government, did defense counsel raise concerns about the testimony. At no point during that bench conference did defendants move to strike the remarks. Although defendants asked the district court to strike Rawls's entire testimony the following day, that motion was neither timely, as required by Rule 103, nor tailored to excise the objectionable evidence. Fed. R. Evid. 103(a)(1) (objection or motion to strike must be timely); *see, e.g.*, *United States v. Pettigrew*, 77 F.3d 1500, 1516 & n. 14 (5th Cir.1996) (motion to strike expert testimony made the following day not timely).

Because appellants did not make a timely objection to the Rosenthal testimony, we review its admission for plain error. Fed. R. Crim. P. 52(b). The plain error exception to the contemporaneous objection requirement should be used sparingly, only for particularly egregious errors that seriously affect the fairness, integrity or public reputation of judicial proceedings.

[The Court found that the testimony should not have been admitted, but that the mistake did not rise to the level of plain error.]

NOTES

1. What is the procedure for making an objection?

The procedure varies from jurisdiction to jurisdiction and even from judge to judge within the same jurisdiction. In general the process is as follows:

a. The opponent of the evidence stands to address the court.

b. The opponent of the evidence says "Objection" followed by a brief description of the basis for the objection, such as "hearsay" or "lack of foundation."

c. The proponent of the evidence may respond briefly to the objection.

d. If argument is required and the case is being tried to a jury, the argument should be held outside of the presence of the jury.

e. The court will rule on the objection, although often the court rules summarily after hearing only the objection.

f. If the court sustains the objection, the proponent should make an offer of proof to preserve the matter for appeal (*see* Section E of this chapter).

2. When can pretrial objections be made?

An objection may be made pretrial or during a trial before a witness is called or evidence is offered. Such an objection is called an *in limine* objection, meaning "at the threshold." Courts need not rule on an objection when it is made early, but an early motion may put a trial judge on notice of a possible problem and can cause the judge to instruct counsel not to mention certain evidence until the trial judge rules on the objection.

In *Luce v. United States*, 469 U.S. 38, 43 (1984), a unanimous Supreme Court concluded that a defendant who objects to being impeached with a prior conviction must take the stand and be impeached in order to preserve a claim of error on appeal; it is not enough to object *in limine* and then fail to testify. The Court was concerned that a contrary rule would allow the defendant a windfall — he could argue on appeal that the trial court's erroneous pretrial ruling kept him off the stand, when in fact he might never have had an intention of taking the stand. The Court was also concerned that the harmless error determination, and indeed the determination of whether the trial court was even in error, would be unduly speculative in the absence of the defendant's testimony at trial. *Luce* leaves a defendant with prior convictions in a difficult situation — in order to preserve an objection as to the convictions, he must take the stand and face a much higher probability of a guilty verdict once the jury hears about his past.

Luce has been extended by other courts to a variety of other contexts, establishing the principle that if a pretrial ruling is dependent on an event occurring at trial, there is no right to appeal the ruling if the event never occurs. For example, in *United States v. Griffin*, 818 F.2d 97 (1st Cir. 1987), the trial judge made an *in limine* ruling that the government could elicit from a witness the fact that he had been threatened, if the defense impeached the witness with evidence that he withheld information from investigators for more than a year. Because the defense never attacked the witness, the threat evidence was not offered. The defendant could not appeal from the tentative ruling, since "it is too great a handicap to bind a trial judge to a ruling on a subtle evidentiary question, requiring the most delicate balancing, outside a precise factual context." *See also Palmieri v. DeFaria,* 88 F.3d 136 (2d Cir. 1996) (where the plaintiff decided to take an adverse judgment rather than challenge an advance ruling by putting on evidence at trial, the *in limine* ruling would not be reviewed on appeal); *United States v. Ortiz,* 857 F.2d 900 (2d Cir. 1988) (where uncharged misconduct is ruled admissible if the defendant pursues a certain defense, the defendant must actually pursue that defense at trial in order to preserve a claim of error on appeal); *United States v. Bond*, 87 F.3d 695 (5th Cir. 1996) (where the trial court rules *in limine* that the defendant would waive his Fifth Amendment privilege were he to testify, the defendant must take the stand and testify in order to challenge that ruling on appeal).

If the trial judge rules that your witness can be impeached with a prior conviction if he testifies, and you decide despite this to have him testify, you may well wish to bring out the prior conviction on direct examination. This tends to "remove the sting" of the anticipated attack from your adversary. It also prevents the jury from thinking that you are trying to hide something negative about the witness — a thought they may well have if you don't refer to the conviction on direct and it is brought out on cross-examination.

But while bringing out the objectionable evidence on direct appears to be good strategy in light of the negative pretrial ruling, it comes at a cost — it constitutes a waiver of the right to appeal from the ruling admitting the evidence. The Supreme Court in *Ohler v. United States,* 529 U.S. 753 (2000), held that a party who introduced evidence of a prior conviction on direct examination forfeited her right to appeal an *in limine* ruling that the evidence would be admissible at trial. The Court, in an opinion by Chief Justice Rehnquist, refused to depart from the general rule that "a party introducing evidence cannot complain on appeal that the evidence was erroneously admitted." The Court recognized that a defendant who did not bring out an objectionable conviction on direct examination might suffer an adverse inference that he was trying to hide that conviction from the jury. But the

Chief Justice thought this risk to be simply part of the reality that the defendant "must make choices as the trial progresses." The Court reasoned that when a defendant brings out an objectionable conviction on direct, this denies the Government "its usual right to decide, after she testifies, whether or not to use her prior conviction against her." In the Court's view, the defendant in *Ohler* sought to "short-circuit that process by offering the conviction herself (and thereby removing the sting) and still preserve its admission as a claim of error on appeal." The Court saw nothing unfair "about putting petitioner to her choice in accordance with the normal rules of trial."

3. Do pretrial objections have to be renewed at trial?

Assume that a party objects to evidence in a pretrial motion and the trial judge rules that the evidence will be admissible at trial. When the evidence is proffered at trial, must the opponent renew the objection in order to preserve a claim of error for appeal? Effective December 1, 2000, Rule 103 was amended to provide that a renewed objection or offer of proof is not required if the trial judge's initial ruling was "definitive." The Advisory Committee Note to that amendment explains the reasoning behind the new rule and how it should be applied:

> The amendment provides that a claim of error with respect to a definitive ruling is preserved for review when the party has otherwise satisfied the objection or offer of proof requirements of Rule 103(a). When the ruling is definitive, a renewed objection or offer of proof at the time the evidence is to be offered is more a formalism than a necessity. *See* Fed. R. Civ. P. 46 (formal exceptions unnecessary); Fed. R. Crim. P. 51 (same); *United States v. Mejia-Alarcon*, 995 F.2d 982, 986 (10th Cir. 1993) ("Requiring a party to renew an objection when the district court has issued a definitive ruling on a matter that can be fairly decided before trial would be in the nature of a formal exception and therefore unnecessary."). On the other hand, when the trial court appears to have reserved its ruling or to have indicated that the ruling is provisional, it makes sense to require the party to bring the issue to the court's attention subsequently. *See, e.g., United States v. Vest,* 116 F.3d 1179, 1188 (7th Cir. 1997) (where the trial court ruled *in limine* that testimony from defense witnesses could not be admitted, but allowed the defendant to seek leave at trial to call the witnesses should their testimony turn out to be relevant, the defendant's failure to seek such leave at trial meant that it was "too late to reopen the issue now on appeal"); *United States v. Valenti,* 60 F.3d 941 (2d Cir. 1995) (failure to proffer evidence at trial waives any claim of error where the trial judge had stated that he would reserve judgment on the *in limine* motion until he had heard the trial evidence).
>
> The amendment imposes the obligation on counsel to clarify whether an *in limine* or other evidentiary ruling is definitive when there is doubt on that point. *See, e.g., Walden v. Georgia-Pacific Corp.,* 126 F.3d 506, 520 (3d Cir. 1997) (although "the district court told plaintiffs' counsel not to reargue every ruling, it did not countermand its clear opening statement that all of its rulings were tentative, and counsel never requested clarification, as he might have done.").

Even where the court's ruling is definitive, nothing in the amendment prohibits the court from revisiting its decision when the evidence is to be offered. If the court changes its initial ruling, or if the opposing party violates the terms of the initial ruling, objection must be made when the evidence is offered to preserve the claim of error for appeal. The error if any in such a situation occurs only when the evidence is offered and admitted. *United States Aviation Underwriters, Inc. v. Olympia Wings, Inc.*, 896 F.2d 949, 956 (5th Cir. 1990) ("objection is required to preserve error when an opponent, or the court itself, violates a motion *in limine* that was granted"); *United States v. Roenigk,* 810 F.2d 809 (8th Cir. 1987) (claim of error was not preserved where the defendant failed to object at trial to secure the benefit of a favorable advance ruling).

A definitive advance ruling is reviewed in light of the facts and circumstances before the trial court at the time of the ruling. If the relevant facts and circumstances change materially after the advance ruling has been made, those facts and circumstances cannot be relied upon on appeal unless they have been brought to the attention of the trial court by way of a renewed, and timely, objection, offer of proof, or motion to strike. *See Old Chief v. United States,* 519 U.S. 172, 182, n.6 (1997) ("It is important that a reviewing court evaluate the trial court's decision from its perspective when it had to rule and not indulge in review by hindsight."). Similarly, if the court decides in an advance ruling that proffered evidence is admissible subject to the eventual introduction by the proponent of a foundation for the evidence, and that foundation is never provided, the opponent cannot claim error based on the failure to establish the foundation unless the opponent calls that failure to the court's attention by a timely motion to strike or other suitable motion. *See Huddleston v. United States,* 485 U.S. 681, 690, n.7 (1988) ("It is, of course, not the responsibility of the judge *sua sponte* to ensure that the foundation evidence is offered; the objector must move to strike the evidence if at the close of the trial the offeror has failed to satisfy the condition.")."

4. When is an objection sufficiently contemporaneous to preserve a claim of error for appeal?

Generally speaking, an objection must be made at the earliest practicable opportunity for it to be considered timely. In *Frederick v. Kirby Tankships, Inc.*, 205 F.3d 1277 (11th Cir. 2000) a vessel owner's objection made after a videotape containing excluded evidence was played for the jury was untimely. Although the testimony had been excluded as prejudicial pursuant to the vessel owner's pretrial motion *in limine*, he waived his right to appeal by failing to raise his objection at the proper time during the trial itself. The court stated that, while a motion *in limine* may preserve an error for appeal if there is a good reason not to object at trial, "[g]enerally, a party must object to preserve error in the admission of testimony, even when a party or a court violates an *in limine* ruling."

There is some room for flexibility, however. For example, in *United States v. Evans*, 994 F.2d 317 (7th Cir. 1993), the court held that the defendant properly preserved error as to the trial judge's prejudicially interrogating the defendant in a skeptical tone. The objection was made the next day as the first order of business after completion of the defendant's testimony. The court reasoned that it would be unfair to require the defendant to interpose an objection at the very time that the judge was questioning the witness. *See also Benjamin v. Peter's Farm Condominium Owners Assoc.*, 820 F.2d 640 (3d Cir. 1987), where the court held an objection made after the close of a case was timely when there was no demonstrable prejudice because of the delay.

5. What is a motion to strike?

The court in *Mueller v. Mueller* recognized that "[w]hen a non-responsive answer is made to a question unobjectionable in itself, or improper testimony is volunteered in response to a proper question, the remedy is to promptly move to strike out the objectionable testimony. The motion to strike should state the ground of objection and designate the portion of the testimony objected to, for it is not error to overrule a motion to strike out all of an answer when part is competent." 78 N.E.2d 667, 668 (Ind. App. 1948). A motion to strike is also appropriate when evidence has been admitted provisionally subject to further proof and the later proof is not offered.

6. When testimony is stricken from the record, should the jury be instructed to ignore the stricken testimony?

In *Moore v. N.Y. Life Ins. Co.,* the court stated that "[a]lthough the proper procedure, upon allowing a motion to strike an answer not responsive to the question, is for the court immediately to instruct the jury not to consider the answer, we think that the failure to do so in this instance, in view of the court's prompt allowance of the motion to strike, is not prejudicial error. The jury could only have interpreted the ruling of the court as meaning that the answer given by the witness was not to be regarded as evidence in the case." 146 S.E.2d 492, 500 (N.C. 1966).

7. What procedures will a trial judge use in hearing objections?

In some instances the judge will rule without hearing any argument from counsel. In other instances, the judge will have a "sidebar" conference at the end of the judge's bench in which counsel can be heard. When more time is needed and the judge is concerned that the jury will be frustrated by a sidebar conference or that the lawyers cannot easily argue complex points at sidebar, the judge may excuse the jury.

In *United States v. Adames*, 56 F.3d 737 (7th Cir. 1995), the court held there was no abuse of discretion in removing the jury from the courtroom, as opposed to holding sidebar conferences, when determining evidentiary and procedural matters in this complex drug conspiracy case.

In *United States v. Hermanek*, 289 F.3d 1076 (9th Cir. 2002), a prosecution for drug-related offenses, the court found that potentially prejudicial testimony regarding the meanings of coded words and phrases in intercepted communications was properly presented outside the presence of the jury so that the judge could determine whether it was admissible.

C. REQUIREMENT OF SPECIFIC OBJECTION

UNITED STATES v. WILSON

966 F.2d 243 (7th Cir. 1992)

MANION, CIRCUIT JUDGE.

John W. Wilson appeals his conviction and 147 month sentence for conspiracy to possess with intent to distribute more than 500 grams of cocaine in violation of 21 U.S.C. §§ 841(a)(1) and 846. * * *

I. Background

* * * At trial, the government offered testimony from one of Wilson's co-defendants and others who had engaged in drug transactions with Wilson. In addition, the government offered the testimony of the Illinois State Police Officer who arrested Wilson in August 1989. It was Wilson's August 1989 arrest that led to his [previous conviction for possession of narcotics]. At the time of the arrest, the officer performed an inventory search of Wilson's Nissan and in the trunk found a nine millimeter gun loaded with 15 rounds of nine millimeter ammunition on top of a duffle bag containing cocaine, a triple beam O'Hass scale, some empty plastic baggies and another small scale.

The government admitted the duffle bag and its contents into evidence without objection. Wilson did object, however, when the government introduced the nine millimeter gun, but the court overruled the objection. Wilson offered no evidence. * * * On appeal to this court, Wilson * * * argues that the district court should have excluded the gun because its prejudicial effect outweighed its probative value. * * *

II. Discussion

A. Admission of the Gun

In his appeal, Wilson invokes Fed. R. Evid. 403 which provides that "although relevant, evidence may be excluded if its probative value is substantially outweighed by the danger of unfair prejudice . . . ." Wilson concedes on appeal that guns are relevant to show that a defendant knowingly and intentionally possessed drugs. However, Wilson points out that he had already been convicted of possession with intent to distribute in November 1989 and could not contest that issue at [the instant] conspiracy trial. Since knowledge and intent to possess were not at issue, Wilson argues that the gun had little probative value with respect to the issue of his conspiracy while it had substantial prejudicial effect. Wilson maintains that after determining that the gun was relevant, the district court should have engaged in Rule 403 balancing.

Although Wilson objected to the admission of the gun both before and at trial, he did not raise Rule 403 or even mention the prejudicial effect of the gun before the district court. When the government proffered testimony about the gun, Wilson stated that the gun had "no relevance to today's charge [conspiracy]" without mentioning the gun's prejudicial effect. Later, at a side bar conference, the district court justified its ruling on the record by explaining that this court's decisions [have] held that guns are "tools of the [drug] trade" and are relevant when found in close proximity with the drugs. Once again, Wilson did not raise the gun's prejudicial effect.

The government argues that by not raising the prejudicial effect of the gun or Rule 403 before the district court, Wilson waived the issue on appeal. We agree. An objection based on "relevance" does not preserve an error based on Rule 403. Under Fed. R. Evid. 103(a)(1) error may not be predicated upon a ruling that admits evidence unless a timely objection appears on the record "stating the specific ground of objection, if the specific ground was not apparent from the context." Providing specific grounds for an objection alerts the district judge to the asserted nature of the error and enables opposing counsel to take proper corrective action. Fed. R. Evid. 103 Advisory Committee Notes. Wilson's objection based on "relevance" alerted the court to consider two rules of evidence: Rule 401, which defines relevant evidence, and Rule 402, which provides that relevant evidence is generally admissible, but irrelevant evidence is not. Wilson implicitly asked the court to exclude the gun under Rule 402 because it did not fit the definition in Rule 401. Rule 403, on which Wilson now relies, however, constitutes one of the exceptions to Rule 402. It provides that even if the evidence is "relevant" the court may exclude it because of its extensive prejudicial effect. Wilson's objection was not specific enough to alert the district court to Wilson's concerns about the prejudicial effect of the gun, and therefore Wilson did not properly preserve for appeal any error based on Rule 403.

* * *

Since Wilson waived his Rule 403 argument below, we must review the admission of the gun under the plain error doctrine of Fed. R. Crim. P. 52(b). Fed. R. Evid. 103(d). In order to show plain error, Wilson would have to show not only that the district court should have excluded the gun under Rule 403 but also that "but for" the erroneously admitted evidence, Wilson "probably would have been acquitted." Even if it would have been improper to admit the gun over an objection based on Rule 403, we cannot say that Wilson probably would have been acquitted but for the admission of the gun. The record is replete with evidence from which the jury could convict Wilson. Two witnesses, Moore and Gunn, testified that Wilson was their source of supply and described in detail how Wilson fronted them the cocaine so they could sell it and return part of the profit to him. Both witnesses testified about meeting Wilson at the Best Inn in Carbondale, Illinois, for drug transactions, and their testimony was corroborated by the hotel manager's testimony. Both Moore and Gunn testified about calling Wilson to attempt to obtain cocaine. Taped telephone conversations corroborated Moore's testimony that he had Wilson's beeper and home telephone numbers. Telephone numbers in Gunn's wallet corroborated Gunn's testimony. * * * In light of the wealth of evidence supporting the conspiracy charges against Wilson, we cannot conclude that the jury probably would have acquitted Wilson but for the gun. Therefore, we hold that the admission of the gun did not constitute plain error in this case.

NOTE

May a different justification for an objection be raised for the first time on appeal?

As seen in *Wilson*, when an objection made on one ground has been overruled by the trial judge, an appellate court ordinarily will refuse to consider other grounds not presented to the trial judge if later raised by the objecting party. Thus, in *United States v. Fuchs*, 467 F.3d 889 (5th Cir. 2006), where the defendant did object to a portion of the jury instructions given by the district court, but not on the same grounds on which he challenged the instructions on appeal, the Court of Appeals reviewed the challenge for plain error.

In *United States v. Nnanyererugo*, 39 F.3d 1205 (D.C. Cir. 1994), the court held in a bank fraud prosecution that a hearsay objection did not preserve for appeal a claim that a witness testifying to the bank's insured status was not competent because he lacked personal knowledge.

The plaintiff in *Brookover v. Mary Hitchcock Mem. Hosp.*, 893 F.2d 411 (1st Cir. 1990), introduced evidence that after the patient's fall the nurses in the defendant hospital said that he should have been restrained. The court held that the evidence should not have been admitted as an agent's admission because there was no proof the nurses were employees of the hospital, but that the defendant had waived the objection by asserting only the declarants' lack of personal knowledge of the circumstances.

In contrast, if an objection has been overruled by the trial judge, an appellate court may affirm the judge on a ground either not considered or adopted by the judge, so long as the appellant is not prejudiced by the ruling. The rationale is that if the evidence could have been admitted anyway but under a different ground that the appellant could not have countered, the appellant suffers no harm. Thus, in *United States v. Williams*, 837 F.2d 1009 (11th Cir. 1988), the court held that "yellow sheets" were properly admitted against a defendant charged with filing a false tax return, where the defendant's initials were identified at the bottom of several sheets. The evidence was hearsay. The government had not relied on the hearsay exemption for party-admissions at trial, but the court of appeals found that the rule would have justified admission of the evidence on that ground, so that there was no unfairness in permitting the exemption to be relied upon on appeal.

D. THE RATIONALE FOR REQUIRING SPECIFIC AND TIMELY OBJECTIONS

OWEN v. PATTON

925 F.2d 1111 (8th Cir. 1991)

BRIGHT, SENIOR CIRCUIT JUDGE.

Matthew P. Owen brought this personal injury action based on diversity of citizenship against Donald Patton, the owner of Papa Don's tavern, a young adults' hangout on a highway near Farmington, Missouri. Owen claimed that an employee of the tavern, one Brian McGee, inflicted severe blows to Owen's head at approximately midnight on January 2, 1987. In his complaint, Owen alleged that the battery occurred in the scope of McGee's employment as a bouncer at Papa Don's. Patton's answer denied that McGee worked for Papa Don's or assaulted Owen.

After a three-day trial before Magistrate Judge William S. Bahn, the jury returned a verdict for Patton. The magistrate judge entered judgment and denied Owen's post-trial motion for a new trial.

* * *

* * * [W]e turn to Owen's claim that undue prejudice resulted when defendant's counsel elicited testimony that certain of Owen's companions on the evening in question, Ronnie Mullineaux and Roger Hahn, now reside in prison. We agree that this testimony of "guilt by association" did not belong in the lawsuit and could have evoked some improper prejudice against Owen. Even so, the magistrate judge committed no error.

In cross-examining Owen, defendant's counsel asked:

Q: Where is Ronnie Mullineaux at this time?

A: I think he is in jail, sir.

Q: In the penitentiary?

A: Yes.

Q: He's doing time for what?

A: I'm not really sure, sir.

Q: Well, do you know that he's doing time for burglary, ten years?

A: No. I wasn't —

At this point, Owen's counsel asked to approach the bench, but registered no formal objection. The magistrate judge nevertheless instructed defendant's counsel to end this line of inquiry. At that time, counsel for defendant agreed to do so. Yet, only two witnesses later, defendant's counsel again engaged in a similar colloquy on cross-examination:

Q: Do you know where [Roger] Hahn is right now?

A: Prison, I think.

Q: Prison?

A: I think so.

Q: Do you know where [Ronnie] Mullineaux is?

Although Owen's counsel failed to object, the magistrate judge interrupted: "We've been through that. That's enough of that. Come on." This admonishment notwithstanding, defendant's counsel continued the same line of questioning, asking whether the witness had talked to the two incarcerated men. However, Owen's counsel still did not object.

Yes, we agree that the inquiry amounted to improper cross-examination upon an irrelevant matter. *See* Fed. R. Evid. 402. Even if relevant, the probative worth of the plaintiff's association with persons who subsequently ended up in prison did not justify its inclusion in the trial. *See* Fed. R. Evid. 403. However, without an objection, a motion to strike, a request for special instructions or a motion for mistrial, the court was not called upon to make a ruling that could result in error for failure to accommodate the plaintiff's request. Thus, we are not justified in granting a new trial even though we believe that defense counsel's tactics here bordered on misconduct.

Trial counsel must recognize that objections must be made to improper questions or any improper evidence put before the jury. Without an objection and a proper request for relief, the matter is waived and will receive no consideration on appeal absent plain error. Judge Arnold's comments in *United States v. Thornberg*, 844 F.2d 573, 575 (8th Cir. 1988), are apropos:

> In general, preserving an issue is a matter of making a timely objection to the trial court and clearly stating the grounds for the objection, so that the trial court has an opportunity to prevent or correct the error in the first instance. Unless the issue was brought to the attention of the trial court in this manner, we are loath to reverse, even if there is error, for at least two reasons. First, as a practical matter, without a timely objection a reviewing court cannot know whether the appellant knew of the error at the time it was made, but decided nevertheless to accept the ruling in the hope that it would not harm his case. Thus the reviewing court cannot be sure that the appellant did not consent to the error. Second, in most cases it is simply unfair to reverse a trial court on the basis of an issue that it has not had an opportunity to consider. In our adversarial system, so long as the proceeding is conducted within the bounds of fundamental fairness, it is not the duty of the trial court to anticipate and evaluate every possible error that might be alleged. Rather, it is the role of counsel to bring such matters to the court's attention.

Further, we cannot say that the admission of this evidence constituted plain error. Having reviewed the record, we fail to perceive any resultant injustice of sufficient magnitude to require reversal.

NOTES

1. What are the harmless error and plain error doctrines?

Rule 103(a) precludes a party from obtaining a reversal because of evidentiary error unless the error affects "fundamental rights" and a party has made a proper objection or a proper offer of proof, which is discussed below. Rule 103(d) provides an escape hatch for "plain errors affecting substantial rights." Rule 103(a) effectively recognizes the doctrine that there are "harmless errors." Rule 103(d) permits some egregious and extremely costly errors to be deemed prejudicial even though a party has failed to comply with the basic requirements of offering and objecting to evidence.

The harmless error doctrine allows an appellate court to disregard technical errors in the proceedings that do not affect substantial rights of the parties.

By comparison, the plain error doctrine allows an appellate court to consider errors affecting substantial rights of a party even if that party failed to make a timely objection. The Supreme Court has noted that "[t]he plain-error exception of Rule 52(b) to the contemporaneous-objection requirement is to be used only in those circumstances in which a miscarriage of justice would otherwise result. Especially when addressing plain error, a reviewing court cannot properly evaluate a case except by viewing such a claimed error against the entire record." *United States v. Young*, 470 U.S. 1, 2 (1985).

2. How is the harmless error standard applied?

Chapman v. California, 386 U.S. 18 (1967), held, as a matter of constitutional law, that a constitutional error cannot be deemed harmless unless a reviewing court is satisfied beyond a reasonable doubt that the error did not affect the verdict. Since *Chapman* is an interpretation of the United States Constitution, it is binding on both federal and state courts.

Lower courts, state and federal, use a variety of standards in assessing nonconstitutional errors in both civil and criminal cases. *United States v. Lamberty*, 778 F.2d 59 (1st Cir. 1985), is a case in which the court of appeals reversed a postmaster's conviction for opening another's package, because the government wrongly elicited testimony that investigators suspected the postmaster of thefts. The court stated that "[w]hen faced in a criminal case with a clearly prejudicial error, unless it is certain that the error is harmless beyond a reasonable doubt, a court should not be forced to gamble with a defendant's liberty."

Other courts use a less demanding standard and are more likely to find a nonconstitutional error harmless in a criminal case. In *United States v. Urbanik*, 801 F.2d 692 (4th Cir. 1986), the court reversed a defendant's marijuana convictions because coconspirator statements were improperly admitted. It stated that a nonconstitutional error could be harmless only where it is highly probable that the error did not affect the judgment.

In *McQueeney v. Wilmington Trust Co.*, 779 F.2d 916 (3d Cir. 1985), the court reversed a judgment for a seaman in a Jones Act case, finding that the trial judge erred in excluding evidence from which it could have been inferred that the seaman had suborned perjury of a proffered witness. It determined that the error was prejudicial, and it held that the same standard should be used for assessing the harmless or prejudicial nature of errors in civil and criminal cases. In this circuit, an error in either a civil or criminal case cannot be harmless unless the appellate court concludes that it is "highly probable" that the error did not affect a party's rights.

Other courts use a lower standard for harmless error in civil cases. In *Haddad v. Lockheed Corp.*, 720 F.2d 1454 (9th Cir. 1983), the court concluded that, although it was error in an employment discrimination suit to admit testimony of the plaintiff's ex-wife that revealed marital communications, the error was harmless. Thus, the court affirmed a judgment for the defendant. The court held that "when an appellate court ponders the probable effect of an error on a civil trial, it need only find that the jury's verdict is more probably than not untainted by the error."

Whatever the test employed, the courts generally look to the same factors in determining whether an error was harmless. Some of the factors that are relevant to the harmless error inquiry include: (1) whether erroneously admitted or excluded evidence was "cumulative" on a point or, conversely, whether it was the most powerful or only evidence in support of the point;[1] (2) whether the trial court gave timely and effective curative instructions; (3) whether erroneously admitted evidence was relied upon by counsel in argument; (4) whether the error was discrete or pervasive;[2] (5) whether evidence, though improperly admitted for one purpose, was properly admitted for another;[3] and (6) whether the error was made in a lengthy or short trial.

Of course, if more than one error was made, the appellate court must assess the cumulative effect of the errors on the verdict. However, appellate courts have understandably taken the view that no trial can be error-free, and the longer the trial, the less likely it is that a few discrete errors will have had an impact on the verdict.

3. As an attorney, why not rely on the plain error doctrine to preserve important issues for appeal?

An attorney should not plan to rely upon the plain error doctrine on appeal. While the doctrine may allow the attorney to raise issues on appeal that were not preserved in the trial court record, it also serves as evidence of attorney malpractice for not making a proper objection at trial.

Moreover, lawyers cannot expect to win reversal by arguing "plain error" in many cases. In *United States v. Olano*, 507 U.S. 725 (1993), the Supreme Court interpreted the plain error provision of Federal Rule of Criminal Procedure 52(b), which is substantially identical to the plain error provision of Federal Rule of Evidence 103(d).

The *Olano* court identified three limitations on a court's power to reverse because of errors that were not properly preserved for review in the trial court. First, there must be an error. Second, the error must be plain, which means it must be clear or obvious. Thus, even more deference is given to the trial court than under the deferential abuse of discretion standard of review. Finally, the plain error must affect substantial rights, which means in most cases that it must have been prejudicial in the sense of affecting the outcome of the case.

Most importantly, the *Olano* court stated that the language of the plain error rule (unlike that of the harmless error rule) is permissive, not mandatory. The court recognized that "the Court of Appeals should correct a plain forfeited error affecting substantial rights if the error seriously affects the

---

[1] *See, e.g.*, *United States v. Williams*, 133 F.3d 1048 (7th Cir. 1998) (error in admitting hearsay evidence identifying the defendant as the perpetrator was not harmless where other evidence of identification was "paper-thin"). Compare *United States v. Cass*, 127 F.3d 1218 (10th Cir. 1997) (erroneous admission of hearsay was harmless given the wealth of properly admitted evidence put forth by the prosecution).

[2] *United States v. Noushfar*, 78 F.3d 1442 (9th Cir. 1996) (Trial Judge committed reversible error in sending to the jury room, over the defendant's objection, 14 tapes that had not been played in the courtroom, together with a tape recorder; this was a "structural error requiring automatic reversal").

[3] *See, e.g.*, *United States v. Cordoba*, 104 F.3d 225 (9th Cir. 1997) (when a conviction is properly admitted for impeachment under Rule 609, any error in admitting the conviction under Rule 404(b) is automatically harmless).

fairness, integrity or public reputation of judicial proceedings." However, a "plain error affecting substantial rights does not, without more" mandate reversal, because otherwise the discretion afforded by Rule 52 (and by Federal Rule of Evidence 103) "would be rendered illusory." The court also made it clear that the burden is on the appellant of showing plain error and its effect on the verdict.

E. OFFER OF PROOF

UNITED STATES v. WINKLE
587 F.2d 705 (5th Cir. 1979)

ALVIN B. RUBIN, CIRCUIT JUDGE:

An intricate and clever scheme to defraud the Government of money asserted to be due for Medicare services resulted in a lengthy and complicated indictment, a protracted trial, and a verdict of guilty. The defendant seeks to overturn that verdict by charging a bevy of errors in the indictment and trial. Because we find his arguments without merit, or the errors asserted harmless beyond a reasonable doubt, we affirm.

* * *

The defendant urges that the trial court erred in excluding as hearsay his renditions of conversations with his salesmen, Matthew Rackstein and Gerald Talty, with Drs. Nessan McCann, Frank Norton and Robert Moorehead, and with his wife, Leonarda Winkle; he would have contradicted their testimony regarding the same conversations, and, therefore, this was proper impeachment and should not have been excluded as hearsay. *See* F.R.Evid. Rule 801(c). The legal proposition on which the assertion is based is correct; impeachment to demonstrate the untruth of a witness' testimony is not excludable as hearsay because it is not offered primarily to prove the truth of the matter asserted, but to contradict the prior testimony. However, a crucial prerequisite to concluding that the ruling was erroneous is missing.

Rule 103(a)(2) of the Federal Rules of Evidence provides that error may not be based on a ruling excluding evidence unless "the substance of the evidence was made known to the court by offer or was apparent from the context within which questions were asked." While some circuits have apparently taken a more lenient approach, this circuit will not even consider the propriety of the decision to exclude the evidence at issue, if no offer of proof was made at trial.

We do not require a formal proffer; but the proponent of excluded evidence must show in some fashion the substance of his proposed testimony. The defendant here gave no indication concerning what he would have testified or the manner in which his contradiction or denial of what had already been adduced would have been admissible or helpful. While the defendant was given the opportunity to do so, outside the presence of the jury, his counsel merely stated that Winkle would testify as to *his version* of the conversations that he had with Rackstein, Talty, McCann, Norton, Moorehead, and Mrs. Winkle. This was not sufficient to make known to the court the *substance* of the evidence. Because an adequate offer of proof was not made, we "may not" find error under Rule 103, as interpreted in this circuit.

* * *

[T]he convictions of the defendant are AFFIRMED.

Roney, Circuit Judge, dissenting:

I respectfully dissent. Six witnesses were allowed to testify as to conversations they had with defendant Winkle. Testifying in his own defense, Winkle attempted to testify as to his version of these conversations. The trial court allowed him to testify only as to his own remarks, apparently under the impression that testimony as to what others said in the same conversation was hearsay. As Judge Rubin points out in his opinion, this ruling was wrong.

Judge Rubin, however, would affirm the trial court's ruling on the ground that the proffer was inadequate * * *. My view of the law and the record is that a sufficient proffer was made, under the circumstances permitted by the trial court. Winkle indicated that he wanted to testify as to his recollection of the conversations previously testified to by the Government witnesses. What his recollection might be is irrelevant to the question of admissibility. He had a right to testify as to these conversations, even if his recollection was essentially the same as the testimony of the Government witnesses, which it apparently was not. The error severely curtailed the ability of the defendant to present his testimony which the jury was entitled to hear.* * *

I would reverse the conviction and remand for a new trial.

NOTES

1. When a court ruling excludes evidence, is an explicit offer of proof always necessary to preserve the issue for appeal?

In *Beech Aircraft v. Rainey*, 488 U.S. 153 (1988), a product liability case involving a fatal Navy jet crash, the Court recognized that Rule 103(a)(2) requires "that to preserve an argument that evidence was wrongly excluded the proponent must make known the substance of the evidence sought to be admitted by an offer of proof unless it was apparent from the context within which questions were asked." At the trial, Rainey's counsel asked a question and the defense objected. Rainey began to articulate his argument that the question should be allowed, but was cut off by the judge and defense counsel. Furthermore, the judge's response suggested that he understood the argument that Rainey tried to articulate. The Court decided under these circumstances that "[a]lthough, as is frequently the case in the heat of a trial, counsel did not explain the evidentiary basis of his argument as thoroughly as might ideally be desired, we are satisfied that he substantially satisfied the requirement of putting the court on notice as to his concern." Rainey therefore was not barred from pursuing the issue on appeal.

A similarly flexible approach is found in *United States v. Ballis*, 28 F.3d 1399 (5th Cir. 1994), a prosecution for bank fraud and obstructing investigation of that fraud. In *Ballis* there was a dispute as to what the defendant said at two meetings with government agents. The trial court sustained a hearsay objection when defense witnesses were called to testify to the defendant's version of the meeting. On appeal, the government argued that the defendant had not sufficiently preserved his objection, because he "proffered" the entire record of the prior motion to dismiss hearing, rather than specifically listing the parts of that testimony that he wished to present. The court declared, however, that "neither the Rules nor this Circuit require a formal offer to preserve error." Rather, all that is required is a sufficient indication that the trial court "has been informed as to what counsel intends to show by the evidence and why it should be admitted." In this case, the trial judge had chided defense counsel for "spoon feeding" the court, and expressed an "intimate familiarity" with the challenged statements on the basis of having tried related cases and ruled on the motion to dismiss. The court of appeals concluded that even a general proffer of evidence was sufficient to preserve review under these circumstances; there was no need to antagonize the trial judge by trying to do any more.

2. What is the procedure for giving an offer of proof of a witness's testimony?

There are generally four methods used to make an offer of proof of a witness's testimony. The first method is for the attorney to speak for the record concerning the anticipated content of the excluded testimony. Another method is for the attorney to introduce a statement, written by the attorney making the offer of proof, that contains what the attorney believes the witness would have said had the witness been allowed to answer the question. With this method, the attorney should mark the document as an exhibit and introduce it into the record so that it may be properly identified on appeal. The third method for making an offer of proof is for the attorney to provide a written statement, signed by the witness, that contains what the witness would have testified to had the witness been allowed to answer the question. Like the previous method, this written statement should be marked as an exhibit and introduced into the record. The final method is for the court to excuse the jury and allow the attorney to examine the witness in question and answer form.

Every method may not always be available to an attorney making an offer of proof. Under Rule 103(b), the court "may direct the making of an offer in question and answer form." Furthermore, in *Fidelity Sav. and Loan Assoc. v. Aetna Life & Cas. Co.*, 647 F.2d 933, 937 (9th Cir. 1981), the court held that the form of offers of proof is left to the discretion of the trial court and that it was not an abuse of that discretion to require an offer of proof of an expert's testimony to be in the form of a written witness statement rather than in question and answer form.

In *Porter-Cooper v. Dalkon Shield Claimants Trust*, 49 F.3d 1285 (8th Cir. 1995), a personal injury action arising out of the plaintiff's use of the Dalkon Shield, the court held that the plaintiff had not made a sufficient offer of proof to justify a claim of error regarding exclusion of expert testimony, where the plaintiff's pretrial designation of expert witnesses stated only that the expert "may testify concerning the cause and effect" of the plaintiff's injuries. A sufficient offer of proof "must express precisely the substance of the excluded evidence, which counsel accomplishes by stating with specificity what he or she anticipates will be the witness' testimony or by putting the witness on the stand."

3. Must a *pro se* litigant make an offer of proof?

In *Badami v. Flood*, 214 F.3d 994 (8th Cir. 2000), the court refused to excuse a *pro se* plaintiff from the offer of proof requirement because notwithstanding the difficulties faced by *pro se* litigants, "[a]bsent a record of the proffered evidence and the trial court's reasons for excluding it, meaningful appellate review is virtually impossible."

4. Must the cross-examiner make the same kind of offer of proof?

A cross-examiner may not be able to make an offer of proof when the purpose of cross-examination is to discover what the witness knows about some relevant point, and the cross-examiner has not prepared the witness for trial. In such a case, the cross-examiner will not be held to the same offer of proof requirement as a direct examiner. The demands put on the cross-examiner will depend on the circumstances. For example, in *Wright v. Hartford Acc. & Indem. Co.*, 580 F.2d 809 (5th Cir. 1978), the defendant cross-examined the plaintiff's expert at a deposition in a worker's compensation case. The plaintiff's motion *in limine* to exclude this cross-examination was granted and the plaintiff objected both times the defendant offered the testimony at trial. The evidence was excluded after the defendant provided no authority supporting its admission in response to the trial judge's request. Affirming a judgment for the plaintiff, the court of appeals observed that the rationale for a more relaxed requirement of an offer of proof on cross-examination is inapplicable "when, as in this case, the evidence is deposition testimony, counsel is forewarned of the objection, and the trial judge specifically requests that counsel provide support for admitting the evidence."

PROBLEM 2-1

Assume Robin Hood is on trial for murder. There is no dispute the victim was shot in the chest with an arrow. The angle of the wound would suggest the killer was a tall man. Robin Hood is a tall man who defends on the theory that someone else committed the crime. The State wants to offer a picture of the cadaver with a dowel rod stuck in the wound showing the angle of entry. The rule of law in Nottingham is that gruesome pictures may be admitted as relevant evidence over an objection of undue prejudice if the pictures will assist the jury on an essential issue in the case.

The medical examiner is called to the stand by the prosecution, and after being duly qualified as an expert witness on arrow wounds, testifies as follows:

Prosecution:	Do you have an opinion whether Defendant is the same height as the person who shot the arrow into the victim?
Medical expert:	Yes, I do.
Prosecution:	What is your opinion?

Medical expert: Robin Hood is the same height as the person who shot the arrow.

Prosecution: On what do you base your opinion?

Medical expert: Well, the victim was tied to a tree and was standing up when shot and . . . (interrupted).

Defense Counsel: Excuse me, your Honor, but I object to the witness giving his opinion first without giving the basis therefore.

Prosecution: (1) __________.

The court: (2) __________.

Prosecution: You may continue with your answer.

Medical expert: Well, the point from which the arrow was shot was level with the victim. From the angle of entry I'm, therefore, able to determine the height of the person who shot the arrow.

Defense counsel: I object, your Honor. The evidence is incompetent, irrelevant and immaterial to any issue before the court.

The court: (3) __________.

Prosecution: How do you know how tall the victim was?

Medical expert: I measured him at the scene while he was still tied to the tree and then I asked the Sheriff of Nottingham how tall Robin Hood is and he said Robin Hood is six feet tall and * * * (interrupted).

Defense counsel: Objection! The portion of the answer which deals with Mr. Hood is non-responsive, hearsay and I (4) __________.

The court: (5) __________.

Prosecution: Did you take any pictures of the deceased which would help you explain your testimony?

Medical expert: Yes.

Prosecution: Your Honor, I would like to show the witness a picture which has been marked as state's exhibit 21.

Defense counsel: Your Honor, may we approach the bench?

The court: Yes.

Defense counsel: Your Honor, I assume the state intends to offer exhibit 21. I've already seen it and (6) __________.

The court: Mr. Prosecutor?

Prosecution: (7) __________.

Defense counsel: (8) __________.

The court: I'm going to sustain the objection.

Defense counsel: Thank you, your Honor. As the prosecution, what do you do now? (9) __________.

PROBLEM 2-2

Plaintiff has brought a products liability case alleging that she suffered burns when a coffee machine manufactured by Defendant exploded and caused boiling hot water to strike her face and arms. She files a pretrial motion seeking to exclude (a) evidence that five years earlier she sued Ford Motor Co. for injuries she suffered when an airbag in her car inflated suddenly while she was sitting in a parking lot waiting for her daughter to finish school, and (b) evidence that ten years earlier she sued a movie theater when she slipped on buttered popcorn and broke her ankle. The trial judge conducts a pretrial hearing in which Defendant argues that the prior events demonstrate that Plaintiff is accident prone and litigious. The trial judge indicates that she has doubts about whether the evidence should be admitted and tells Defendant not to mention the other accidents or litigation in the opening statement.

Plaintiff is the first witness in her case. She describes the purchase of the coffee machine and her use of the machine and then is examined as follows:

Plaintiff's counsel:	Please tell the ladies and gentleman of the jury what happened on July 1 of last year.
Plaintiff:	Well, I filled the machine with water as I usually did, and while I waited for the coffee it exploded.
Plaintiff's counsel:	What do you mean exploded?
Plaintiff:	Well, it just burst open throwing scalding water all over the place.
Plaintiff's counsel:	Did any of that water strike you?
Plaintiff:	Yes, boiling water hit me in the face and on my arms.
Plaintiff's counsel:	Was it painful?
Plaintiff:	Extraordinarily painful.
Plaintiff's counsel:	What was the pain like?
Plaintiff:	I've never experienced such serious pain.
Plaintiff's counsel:	Thank you. Your witness.
Defendant:	Now, isn't it true that you were in an accident with an airbag?
Plaintiff:	Yes.
Defendant:	Isn't it also true that you filed suit against Ford Motor Co. and claimed extraordinary pain?
Plaintiff's counsel:	I object, your Honor. This is the material you excluded at the pretrial hearing.
Defendant:	Your Honor did not actually rule at the hearing.
The court:	(1) __________.
Plaintiff's counsel:	Then I object again that this type of evidence should not be admitted.
Defendant:	What kind of objection is that?
The court:	(2) __________.
Plaintiff's counsel:	Then I object because this is character evidence, and also because it is irrelevant.

Defendant:	That objection comes too late. There was no objection to my first question about the accident.
The court:	(3) ________.
Defendant:	But, your Honor, plaintiff opened the door to this testimony by saying she never experienced such serious pain. We have a right to explore that.
Plaintiff's counsel:	We never opened any such door.
The court:	(4) ________.
Defendant:	So, you sued Ford Motor Co?
Plaintiff:	Yes.
Defendant:	You asked for a million dollars?
Plaintiff:	Yes.
Defendant:	The million was for punitive damages?
Plaintiffs' counsel:	Objection. This has nothing to do with pain, and that is the only subject the court has indicated that we opened up on direct. So, I object and move to strike all testimony about the lawsuit.
Defendant:	It's late in the day to be complaining about this.
The court:	(5) ________.
Plaintiff's counsel:	Can I have a continuing objection with regard to the evidence about pain associated with prior accidents so that I do not have to rise and object each time in the presence of the jury?
The court:	You may.
Defendant:	Let me turn to something else. You sued a movie theater ten years ago when you slipped on popcorn?
Plaintiff:	Yes I did.
Defendant:	You broke your ankle when you slipped?
Plaintiff:	I did.
Defendant:	You sought damages for your pain?
Plaintiff:	I did.
Defendant:	Those were punitive damages for your pain?
Plaintiff:	Yes, I did.
Plaintiff's counsel:	Your Honor, I object. We're back to damages again. This is outside the scope of what you permitted. I move to strike all questions and answers about the movie theater accident.
Defendant:	Once again, counsel is objecting with too little too late.
Plaintiff's counsel:	But, your Honor granted me a continuing objection.
The court:	(6) ________.

Return to the illustration at the beginning of this chapter. Did the defendant make a valid objection? Was it timely?

Chapter 3
COMPETENCY

A. INTRODUCTION

The word "competency" had several meanings at common law, including a very broad usage that equated to evidence being inadmissible due to any exclusionary rule. In this chapter, we focus on two more specific aspects of competency dealing with whether a witness should be allowed to testify at all.

First we will consider whether a witness should be precluded from testifying due to an interest in the litigation, prior bad moral conduct, or lack of mental capacity. At various times during the development of the law of evidence, the parties, their spouses, perjurers, convicts, the insane, and children of tender years were not allowed to testify solely due to their status.

Next we consider the foundational requirements necessary for a witness to testify. Here, the prerequisites of the common law remain basically unchanged:

(1) the witness must take an oath or an appropriate substitute;

(2) the witness must have perceived something important to the case;

(3) the witness must recollect what was perceived;

(4) the witness must be able to communicate the testimony to the finder of fact.

B. STATUS

[1] Federal Rule of Evidence 601

Rule 601. General Rule of Competency

Every person is competent to be a witness except as otherwise provided in these rules. However, in civil actions and proceedings, with respect to an element of a claim or defense as to which State law supplies the rule of decision the competency of a witness shall be determined in accordance with State law.

[2] Competency vs. Credibility

UNITED STATES v. BEDONIE
913 F.2d 782 (10th Cir. 1990)

BRORBY, CIRCUIT JUDGE:

Defendants-appellants appeal their convictions on two counts of first degree murder in violation of 18 U.S.C. §§ 1111(a), 1153 and 2, and on two counts of using and carrying a firearm in relation to a crime of violence in violation of 18 U.S.C. §§ 924(c), 1153 and 2.

On the morning of December 5, 1987, passers-by discovered two burned-out and still smoldering Navajo police vehicles ("the panels") in a remote area ("Copper Canyon") of the Navajo Indian Reservation in the southeast corner of Utah. The charred remains of two men, later identified as Navajo police officers Roy Lee Stanley and Andy Begay, were found inside one of the panels.

On April 28, 1988, four Navajo Indians — Thomas Cly, Vinton Bedonie, Ben Atene, Jr. and Marques Atene — were each indicted on two counts of first degree murder in the deaths of Stanley and Begay (counts I and II) and two counts of using a firearm in connection therewith (counts III and IV).

* * *

Trial to a jury commenced July 18, 1988. Dr. Thomas Henry, the government's expert in forensic pathology who performed the postmortem examination of the victims' remains, testified as to the results of his examinations and, based upon those results, expressed his opinion that "Mr. Stanley * * * died of smoke inhalation and thermal burns" and that "Mr. Begay died of smoke inhalation and thermal burns."

The testimony of the government's key witnesses to the events leading up to the deaths of Begay and Stanley — Marie Haycock, Martha Chee, Boyd Atene, Raymond Fatt and Julius Crank — revealed that a bonfire party had taken place the night of December 4, 1987. The witnesses saw both appellants at the bonfire. According to Haycock, Chee and Boyd Atene, Officer Stanley arrived at the scene of the bonfire, got out of his police panel, was confronted by appellant Cly, and then was ultimately subdued and handcuffed after a fight involving Cly, appellant Bedonie and Ben Atene, Jr. Haycock, Chee and Boyd Atene each testified that they heard either one or two gunshots after the fight and both Haycock and Boyd Atene saw Bedonie carrying a gun. Boyd Atene testified that, after Stanley had been overcome, Bedonie told Boyd to walk with Bedonie to Stanley's panel. Boyd complied and, after Bedonie opened the driver's side door for him, Boyd got in the panel and Bedonie closed the door.

Haycock, Chee and Boyd Atene testified that Andy Begay arrived shortly thereafter at the bonfire in his police panel. They then heard one or two more gunshots. Haycock testified that she saw Bedonie come up behind Begay, point a gun at him and walk Begay behind his vehicle before she heard the gunshot. Haycock and Chee then left the bonfire scene. Boyd Atene testified that Cly then got into his own pickup truck, and Bedonie got in on the passenger side of the panel in which Boyd was seated. Bedonie then directed Boyd to drive Stanley's panel away from the bonfire scene and to follow Ben Atene, Jr.'s truck. Boyd and Bedonie were followed in the caravan by Begay's panel.

* * *

Appellants' argument as to competency suggests that at a certain point — when a witness has produced a certain number of prior inconsistent statements, and when those prior statements are even inconsistent with each other — the task of evaluating the credibility of the witness should be removed from the province of the jury and considered by the trial court under a competency analysis. Appellants base their argument in part on our discussion of the incompetency standard in *United States v. Gomez*, 807 F.2d 1523, 1527 (10th Cir. 1986). However, as *Gomez* makes clear: "The credibility of the witness * * * [is] for the jury to determine." However, even if credibility considerations can properly be fit under a competency rubric, the district court has "broad discretion in determining the competency of a witness to testify, and [its] decision will not be reversed in the absence of an abuse of discretion."

In that vein, we cannot conclude the district court abused its discretion in refusing to conduct a further hearing on the incompetency — or more accurately, incredibility — of the government's witnesses or in determining that the jury should properly weigh issues of credibility.

Fed. R. Evid. 601 provides that "[e]very person is competent to be a witness except as otherwise provided." "A witness may not testify to a matter unless evidence is introduced sufficient to support a finding that [he] has personal knowledge of the matter." Fed. R. Evid. 602. However, "[e]vidence to prove personal knowledge may * * * consist of the witness' own testimony." *Id.* Finally, Fed. R. Evid. 603 requires every witness "to declare that [he] will testify truthfully, by oath or affirmation."

Each of the government's key witnesses took the required oath. Haycock, Chee, Julius Crank, Fatt and Boyd Atene each testified that he or she had been at the bonfire party, and Boyd Atene testified to being present at the Copper Canyon scene when the panels were set on fire. All of these witnesses were exhaustively cross-examined in the presence of the jury both as to the substance of their prior inconsistent statements and their explanations therefor.

We consider appellants' suggested fusion of competency and credibility analysis to be regressive rather than progressive in relation to the evolution of the law in this area. The advisory committee's notes to Rule 601 state:

> No mental or moral qualifications for testifying as a witness are specified. Standards of mental capacity have proved elusive in actual application.* * * Discretion is regularly exercised in favor of allowing the testimony. A witness wholly without capacity is difficult to imagine. The question is one particularly suited to the jury as one of weight and credibility, subject to judicial authority to review the sufficiency of the evidence. Standards of moral qualification in practice consist essentially of evaluating a person's truthfulness in terms of his own answers about it.

* * * Even the most traditional bases for excluding a witness as incompetent — such as insanity or immaturity — are no longer specifically preserved by a particular federal rule:

> There is no rule which excludes an insane person as such, or a child of any specified age, from testifying, but in each case the traditional test is whether the witness has intelligence enough to make it worthwhile to hear him at all and whether he feels a duty to tell the truth.* * * The major reason for disqualification of the persons mentioned in this section to take the stand is the judges' distrust of a jury's ability to assay the words of a small child or of a deranged person. Conceding the jury's deficiencies, the remedy of excluding such a witness, who may be the only person available who knows the facts, seems inept and primitive. Though the tribunal is unskilled, and the testimony difficult to weigh, it is still better to let the evidence come in for what it is worth, with cautionary instructions. Revised Uniform Rule of Evidence 601 and the first sentence of Federal Rule of Evidence 601 reflect the above and additional reasoning by providing every person is competent to be a witness unless otherwise provided in the rules. No exception is made for mental incapacity or immaturity. As already indicated, mental derangement, where it affects the ability of the witness to observe, remember, and recount, may always be proved to attack credibility.

McCormick § 62, at 156–57 (footnotes omitted).

Appellants' argument, in asserting that a witness can be so untrustworthy as to lack the fundamental capacity of a witness, is reminiscent of another era when "moral depravity" could form the basis for excluding a witness.

> There are two objections to any attempt to establish such an incapacity. The first is that in rational experience no class of persons can safely be asserted to be so thoroughly lacking in the sense of moral responsibility or so callous to the ordinary motives of veracity as not to tell the truth (as they see it) in a large or the larger proportion of instances; or, in more accurate analysis, no such defect, if it exists, can be so well ascertainable as to justify us in predicating it for the purpose of exclusion. The second reason is that, even if such a defect existed and were ascertainable, its operation would be so uncertain and elusive that any general rule of exclusion would be as likely in a given instance to exclude the truth as to exclude falsities. It is therefore not a proper foundation for a rule of exclusion.

2 Wigmore, Evidence § 515, at 721–22 (Chadbourn rev. 1979).

This court is confident that the Federal Rules of Evidence provide sufficient avenues by which a witness's credibility can be fully explored and tested in front of the jury, and we agree with the district court that the jury is still the best arbiter for such determinations. The court gave the jurors guidelines for assessing the credibility of witnesses, instructed them as to the purpose of the prior inconsistent statement testimony, and instructed that, based on the inconsistencies or discrepancies in a witness's testimony, they could "reject all the testimony of that witness or give it such credibility as you may think it deserves."

We are not inclined to resurrect judicial notions of moral capacity as a means for disqualifying a witness. The jury system has served us well. We would not serve it well by holding that jurors are incapable of making credibility determinations. Accordingly, we conclude that the district court did not abuse its discretion in allowing the government's principal witnesses to testify at trial.

* * *

NOTES

1. When may legal rules other than rules of evidence affect competence?

There are legal provisions other than Rule 601 that may affect the competency of a witness to testify. Rules of professional conduct, for example, may bar lawyers from being witnesses in cases in which they serve as counsel. *See* Model Rule of Professional Conduct 3.7 (with some exceptions, a lawyer "shall not act as advocate at a trial in which the lawyer is likely to be a necessary witness"). In *Grizzle v. Travelers Health Network, Inc.*, 14 F.3d 261 (5th Cir. 1994), the court held there was no error in precluding a paralegal employed by the plaintiff's counsel in an ADEA case from testifying as a "fact witness." Permitting testimony by an employee of an attorney who is assisting in the preparation and prosecution of a case was found tantamount to permitting testimony by the attorney. *See also United States v. Edwards,* 154 F.3d 915 (9th Cir. 1998) (conviction was reversed where the prosecutor, acting on his own, allegedly found evidence that tied the defendant to the crime: "by putting witnesses on the stand and having them testify regarding the circumstances under which *he* found the evidence, the prosecutor implicitly and improperly vouched for the accuracy of their testimony.").

2. What effect does intoxication or drug use have on competency?

In *United States v. Hyson*, 721 F.2d 856 (1st Cir. 1983), the court affirmed the convictions of two defendants charged with a narcotics conspiracy, approving the procedure followed after it appeared that a government witness might have been under the influence of narcotics. On the first day of the witness's testimony, the trial judge asked whether the witness had taken any drugs before testifying. The judge accepted the witness's "no" answer. On the second day, the witness appeared to have difficulty speaking, so the judge suggested, and the government arranged for, a medical examination of the witness. Two days later, the examining physician reported that the witness had been under the influence of phencyclidine (PCP) when testifying, causing him to be in "an acute confusional state." The doctor suggested the effects of the drug would clear in twenty-four hours; when he repeated his examination a day later, the witness was much improved. The judge recalled the jurors, explained the situation, and told them that all of the second day's testimony of the witness was stricken. He also explained the doctor's examinations and findings and then he permitted the witness to be recalled.

In *United States v. Van Meerbeke*, 548 F.2d 415 (2d Cir. 1976), the principal government witness, while testifying in a drug case, ingested some of the heroin that was offered into evidence. Although the court affirmed the appellants' convictions, it criticized the trial judge for remaining silent at the time he first noticed the witness's actions. "Several courses were available, if sought: suspension of testimony for the day, a medical examination to determine the witness's capacity to continue with his testimony, and a stern warning to the witness outside the jury's hearing * * * ." [Apparently, that admonition would be something like "Stop snorting the evidence."] Citing Rule 601 and quoting from the Advisory Committee's Note, the court concluded it was not error to leave the jury with the task of evaluating the witness's credibility, especially since defense counsel brought out that the witness had ingested drugs on the stand. However, the Court observed, "[t]o say that a witness's credibility is properly left to the jury * * * is not to imply that a judge must in all circumstances tolerate testimony by a witness under the influence of drugs."

In *United States v. Snead,* 447 F. Supp. 1321 (E.D. Pa. 1978), the district court held that a witness for the government could testify about the occurrences on the day of a bank robbery, despite the fact that he had been consuming alcohol throughout that day.

In *United States v. Callahan*, 442 F. Supp. 1213 (D. Minn. 1978), *rev'd on other grounds*, 596 F.2d 759 (8th Cir. 1979), the trial court read Rule 601 as establishing a presumption of competence, but as allowing a witness to be excluded if "drug use negated the threshold minimal level of competency required before a witness can take the stand."

3. What effect does state law have on competency?

Rule 601 is one of three federal rules that bow to state law when state law provides the rule of decision in a case, most often a diversity case. It is not always clear, however, when state laws are properly deemed competency rules. For example, in *Legg v. Chopra*, 286 F.3d 286 (6th Cir. 2002) the court affirmed summary judgment for the defendant in a diversity medical malpractice case, because the plaintiff's expert, a Texas physician, did not satisfy the Tennessee law holding only experts licensed in Tennessee or a contiguous state to be competent in medical malpractice cases. The court held that the Tennessee statute governs "competency" within the meaning of Rule 601, since the law's structure reflects an intimate relationship between the standard of care and the qualification requirements of the medical expert who will establish that standard. The court noted that Rule 601, as thus read, does not directly conflict with Rule 702, which governs the procedural issue of the reliability of an expert witness's opinions.

One type of state law that will determine competency in cases where state law provides the rule of decision is known as the "Dead Man's Statute." The purpose of these statutes is to prohibit the living from making fraudulent claims against the estate of a decedent. The statutes generally provide that in an action against an estate, a party with a financial claim against the estate cannot testify about personal transactions or communications with the decedent. The concern is that the living party is biased by their financial interest, and will have the incentive to lie without the risk of being contradicted by the deceased. The problem with Dead Man's Statutes is that they also may prohibit testimony about valid claims. Essentially the Statutes confuse competency with credibility — the fact that a witness has a financial interest and is not subject to contradiction by a dead person can be brought out to the factfinder who will have no trouble using that information to assess the witness' credibility. Because Dead Man's Statutes can prevent testimony on valid claims, and because they confuse competency with credibility, they have fallen into disfavor. The federal rules reflect this disfavor by omitting a Dead Man's provision.

[3] Jurors

[a] Federal Rule of Evidence 606

Rule 606. Competency of Juror as Witness

(a) At the trial. A member of the jury may not testify as a witness before that jury in the trial of the case in which the juror is sitting. If the juror is called so to testify, the opposing party shall be afforded an opportunity to object out of the presence of the jury.

(b) Inquiry into validity of verdict or indictment. Upon an inquiry into the validity of a verdict or indictment, a juror may not testify as to any matter or statement occurring during the course of the jury's deliberations or to the effect of anything upon that or any other juror's mind or emotions as influencing the juror to assent to or dissent from the verdict or indictment or concerning the juror's mental processes in connection therewith. But a juror may testify about (1) whether extraneous prejudicial information was improperly brought to the jury's attention, (2) whether any outside influence was improperly brought to bear upon any juror, or (3) whether there was a mistake in entering the verdict onto the verdict form. A juror's affidavit or evidence of any statement by the juror may not be received on a matter about which the juror would be precluded from testifying.

[b] Advisory Committee Note to the 2006 Amendment to Rule 606(b)

Rule 606(b) has been amended to provide that juror testimony may be used to prove that the verdict reported was the result of a mistake in entering the verdict on the verdict form. The amendment responds to a divergence between the text of the Rule and the case law that has established an exception for proof of clerical errors. *See, e.g., Plummer v. Springfield Term. Ry.*, 5 F.3d 1, 3 (1st Cir. 1993) ("A number of circuits hold, and we agree, that juror testimony regarding an alleged clerical error, such as announcing a verdict different than that agreed upon, does not challenge the validity of the verdict or the deliberation of mental processes, and therefore is not subject to Rule 606(b)." *Teevee Toons, Inc., v. MP3.Com, Inc.*, 148 F.Supp.2d 276, 278 (S.D.N.Y. 2001) (noting that Rule 606(b) has been silent regarding inquiries designed to confirm the accuracy of a verdict's).

In adopting the exception for proof of mistakes in entering the verdict on the verdict form, the amendment specifically rejects the broader exception, adopted by some courts, permitting the use of juror testimony to prove that the jurors were operating under a misunderstanding about the consequences of the result that they agreed upon. *See, e.g., Attridge v. Cencorp Div. of Dover Techs. Int'l, Inc.*, 836 F.2d 113, 116 (2d Cir. 1987); *Eastridge Development Co., v. Halpert Associates, Inc.*, 853 F.2d 772 (10th Cir. 1988). The broader exception is rejected because an inquiry into whether the jury misunderstood or misapplied an instruction goes to the jurors' mental processes underlying the verdict, rather than the verdict's accuracy in capturing what the jurors had agreed upon. *See, e.g., Karl v. Burlington Northern R.R.*, 880 F.2d 68, 74 (8th Cir. 1989) (error to receive juror testimony on whether verdict was the result of jurors' misunderstanding of instructions: "The jurors did not state that the figure written by the foreman was different from that which they agreed upon, but indicated that the figure the foreman wrote down was intended to be a net figure, not a gross figure. Receiving such statements violates Rule 606(b) because the testimony relates to how the jury interpreted the court's instructions, and concerns the jurors' 'mental processes,' which is forbidden by the rule."); *Robles v. Exxon Corp.*, 862 F.2d 1201, 1208 (5th Cir. 1989) ("the alleged error here goes to the substance of what the jury was asked to decide, necessarily implicating the jury's mental processes insofar as it questions the jury's understanding of the court's instructions and application of those instructions to the facts of the case"). Thus, the exception established by the amendment is limited to cases such as "where the jury foreperson wrote down, in response to an interrogatory, a number different from that agreed upon by the jury, or mistakenly stated that the defendant was 'guilty' when the jury had actually agreed that the defendant was not guilty." *Id.*

It should be noted that the possibility of errors in the verdict form will be reduced substantially by polling the jury. Rule 606(b) does not, of course, prevent this precaution. *See* 8 C. Wigmore, *Evidence,* § 2350 at 691 (McNaughten ed. 1961) (noting that the reasons for the rule barring juror testimony, "namely, the dangers of uncertainty and of tampering with the jurors to procure testimony, disappear in large part if such investigation as may be desired is *made by the judge* and takes place *before the jurors' discharge* and separation") (emphasis in original). Errors that come to light after polling the jury "may be corrected on the spot, or the jury may be sent out to continue deliberations, or, if necessary, a new trial may be ordered." C. Mueller & L. Kirkpatrick, *Evidence Under the Rules* at 671 (2d ed. 1999) (citing *Sincox v. United States*, 571 F.2d 876, 878–79 (5th Cir. 1978)).

[c] Illustration

The defendant has filed a motion for a new trial.

Defendant:	Your honor, I have an affidavit signed by one of the jurors. In the affidavit he states the following:

1. One juror was drunk during the entire trial.
2. Another juror said he had read the newspaper account of the trial.
3. The jury agreed on a quotient verdict.
4. The bailiff told the jury that the defendant was a liar, that not even the judge believed the defendant.
5. One juror told another juror that he would kill him if he didn't vote for the plaintiff.
6. One juror said the attorney for the plaintiff sort of offered a juror a trip to Tahiti.
7. One juror was suffering from insane delusions.

The court: ________ .

[d] Attacking the Judgment

TANNER v. UNITED STATES
483 U.S. 107 (1987)

JUSTICE O'CONNOR delivered the opinion of the Court:

Petitioners William Conover and Anthony Tanner were convicted of conspiring to defraud the United States in violation of 18 U.S.C. § 371, and of committing mail fraud in violation of 18 U.S.C. § 1341. * * * Petitioners argue that the District Court erred in refusing to admit juror testimony at a post-verdict hearing on juror intoxication during the trial * * *

I

* * *

The day before petitioners were scheduled to be sentenced, Tanner filed a motion, in which Conover subsequently joined, seeking continuance of the sentencing date, permission to interview jurors, an evidentiary hearing, and a new trial. According to an affidavit accompanying the motion, Tanner's attorney had received an unsolicited telephone call from one of the trial jurors, Vera Asbul. * * * Juror Asbul informed Tanner's attorney that several of the jurors consumed alcohol during the lunch breaks at various times throughout the trial, causing them to sleep through the afternoons.* * * The District Court continued the sentencing date, ordered the parties to file memoranda, and heard argument on the motion to interview jurors. The District Court concluded that juror testimony on intoxication was inadmissible under Federal Rule of Evidence 606(b) to impeach the jury's verdict. The District Court invited petitioners to call any nonjuror witnesses, such as courtroom personnel, in support of the motion for new trial. Tanner's counsel took the stand and testified that he had observed one of the jurors "in a sort of giggly mood" at one point during the trial but did not bring this to anyone's attention at the time.* * *

Earlier in the hearing the judge referred to a conversation between defense counsel and the judge during the trial on the possibility that jurors were sometimes falling asleep. * * * The judge also observed that in the past courtroom employees had alerted him to problems with the jury. "Nothing was brought to my attention in this case about anyone appearing to be intoxicated," the judge stated, adding, "I saw nothing that suggested they were." * * *

Following the hearing the District Court filed an order stating that "[o]n the basis of the admissible evidence offered I specifically find that the motions for leave to interview jurors or for an evidentiary hearing at which jurors would be witnesses is not required or appropriate." The District Court also denied the motion for new trial.* * *

While the appeal of this case was pending before the Eleventh Circuit, petitioners filed another new trial motion based on additional evidence of jury misconduct. In another affidavit, Tanner's attorney stated that he received an unsolicited visit at his residence from a second juror, Daniel Hardy. * * * Despite the fact that the District Court had denied petitioners' motion for leave to interview jurors, two days after Hardy's visit Tanner's attorney arranged for Hardy to be interviewed by two private investigators. * * * The interview was transcribed, sworn to by the juror, and attached to the new trial motion. In the interview Hardy stated that he "felt like * * * the jury was on one big party." * * * Hardy indicated that seven of the jurors drank alcohol during the noon recess. Four jurors, including Hardy, consumed between them "a pitcher to three pitchers" of beer during various recesses.* * * Of the three other jurors who were alleged to have consumed alcohol, Hardy stated that on several occasions he observed two jurors having one or two mixed drinks during the lunch recess, and one other juror, who was also the foreperson, having a liter of wine on each of three occasions. * * * Juror Hardy also stated that he and three other jurors smoked marijuana quite regularly during the trial. * * * Moreover, Hardy stated that during the trial he observed one juror ingest cocaine five times and another juror ingest cocaine two or three times.* * * One juror sold a quarter pound of marijuana to another juror during the trial, and took marijuana, cocaine, and drug paraphernalia into the courthouse. * * * Hardy noted that some of the jurors were falling asleep during the trial, and that one of the jurors described himself to Hardy as "flying." * * * Hardy said that he came forward "to clear my conscience" and "[b]ecause I felt * * * that the people on the jury didn't have no business being on the jury. I felt * * * that Mr. Tanner should have a better opportunity to get somebody that would review the facts right." * * *

The District Court * * * denied petitioners' motion for a new trial. * * * We granted *certiorari* to consider whether the District Court was required to hold an evidentiary hearing, including juror testimony, on juror alcohol and drug use during the trial.* * *

II

Petitioners argue that the District Court erred in not ordering an additional evidentiary hearing at which jurors would testify concerning drug and alcohol use during the trial. Petitioners assert that, contrary to the holdings of the

District Court and the Court of Appeals, juror testimony on ingestion of drugs or alcohol during the trial is not barred by Federal Rule of Evidence 606(b). Moreover, petitioners argue that whether or not authorized by Rule 606(b), an evidentiary hearing including juror testimony on drug and alcohol use is compelled by their Sixth Amendment right to trial by a competent jury.

By the beginning of this century, if not earlier, the near-universal and firmly established common-law rule in the United States flatly prohibited the admission of juror testimony to impeach a jury verdict. * * *

Exceptions to the common-law rule were recognized only in situations in which an "extraneous influence" was alleged to have affected the jury. In *Mattox v. United States,* 146 U.S. 140 (1892), this Court held admissible the testimony of jurors describing how they heard and read prejudicial information not admitted into evidence. The Court allowed juror testimony on influence by outsiders in *Parker v. Gladden*, 385 U.S. 363, 365 (1966) (bailiff's comments on defendant), and *Remmer v. United States*, 347 U.S. 227, 228–230 (1954) (bribe offered to juror).* * * In situations that did not fall into this exception for external influence, however, the Court adhered to the common-law rule against admitting juror testimony to impeach a verdict.* * *

Lower courts used this external/internal distinction to identify those instances in which juror testimony impeaching a verdict would be admissible. The distinction was not based on whether the juror was literally inside or outside the jury room when the alleged irregularity took place; rather, the distinction was based on the nature of the allegation. Clearly a rigid distinction based only on whether the event took place inside or outside the jury room would have been quite unhelpful. For example, under a distinction based on location a juror could not testify concerning a newspaper read inside the jury room. Instead, of course, this has been considered an external influence about which juror testimony is admissible. * * * Similarly, under a rigid locational distinction jurors could be regularly required to testify after the verdict as to whether they heard and comprehended the judge's instructions, since the charge to the jury takes place outside the jury room. Courts wisely have treated allegations of a juror's inability to hear or comprehend at trial as an internal matter.* * *

Most significant for the present case, however, is the fact that lower federal courts treated allegations of the physical or mental incompetence of a juror as "internal" rather than "external" matters. In *United States v. Dioguardi*, 492 F.2d 70 (CA2 1974), the defendant Dioguardi received a letter from one of the jurors soon after the trial in which the juror explained that she had "eyes and ears that * * * see things before [they] happen," but that her eyes "are only partly open" because "a curse was put upon them some years ago." Armed with this letter and the opinions of seven psychiatrists that the letter suggested that the juror was suffering from a psychological disorder, Dioguardi sought a new trial or in the alternative an evidentiary hearing on the juror's competence. The District Court denied the motion and the Court of Appeals affirmed. The Court of Appeals noted "[t]he strong policy against any post-verdict inquiry into a juror's state of mind," and observed:

> The quickness with which jury findings will be set aside when there is proof of tampering or *external* influence, * * * parallel the

reluctance of courts to inquire into jury deliberations when a verdict is valid on its face. * * * Such exceptions support rather than undermine the rationale of the rule that possible *internal* abnormalities in a jury will not be inquired into except in the gravest and most important cases.

* * *

Substantial policy considerations support the common-law rule against the admission of jury testimony to impeach a verdict. As early as 1915 this Court explained the necessity of shielding jury deliberations from public scrutiny:

> [L]et it once be established that verdicts solemnly made and publicly returned into court can be attacked and set aside on the testimony of those who took part in their publication and all verdicts could be, and many would be, followed by an inquiry in the hope of discovering something which might invalidate the finding. Jurors would be harassed and beset by the defeated party in an effort to secure from them evidence of facts which might establish misconduct sufficient to set aside a verdict. If evidence thus secured could be thus used, the result would be to make what was intended to be a private deliberation, the constant subject of public investigation — to the destruction of all frankness and freedom of discussion and conference.

McDonald v. Pless, 238 U.S., at 267–268, 35 S. Ct., at 784.

* * *

There is little doubt that postverdict investigation into juror misconduct would in some instances lead to the invalidation of verdicts reached after irresponsible or improper juror behavior. It is not at all clear, however, that the jury system could survive such efforts to perfect it. Allegations of juror misconduct, incompetency, or inattentiveness, raised for the first time days, weeks, or months after the verdict, seriously disrupt the finality of the process. * * * Moreover, full and frank discussion in the jury room, jurors' willingness to return an unpopular verdict, and the community's trust in a system that relies on the decisions of laypeople would all be undermined by a barrage of postverdict scrutiny of juror conduct.* * *

Federal Rule of Evidence 606(b) is grounded in the common-law rule against admission of jury testimony to impeach a verdict and the exception for juror testimony relating to extraneous influences. * * *

Petitioners have presented no argument that Rule 606(b) is inapplicable to the juror affidavits and the further inquiry they sought in this case, and, in fact, there appears to be virtually no support for such a proposition. Rather, petitioners argue that substance abuse constitutes an improper "outside influence" about which jurors may testify under Rule 606(b). In our view the language of the Rule cannot easily be stretched to cover this circumstance. However severe their effect and improper their use, drugs or alcohol voluntarily ingested by a juror seems no more an "outside influence" than a virus, poorly prepared food, or a lack of sleep.

In any case, whatever ambiguity might linger in the language of Rule 606(b) as applied to juror intoxication is resolved by the legislative history of the Rule. * * * [T]he legislative history demonstrates with uncommon clarity that Congress specifically understood, considered, and rejected a version of Rule 606(b) that would have allowed jurors to testify on juror conduct during deliberations, including juror intoxication. This legislative history provides strong support for the most reasonable reading of the language of Rule 606(b) — that juror intoxication is not an "outside influence" about which jurors may testify to impeach their verdict.

* * *

Petitioners also argue that the refusal to hold an additional evidentiary hearing at which jurors would testify as to their conduct "violates the Sixth Amendment's guarantee to a fair trial before an impartial and *competent* jury." * * *

As described above, long-recognized and very substantial concerns support the protection of jury deliberations from intrusive inquiry. Petitioners' Sixth Amendment interests in an unimpaired jury, on the other hand, are protected by several aspects of the trial process. The suitability of an individual for the responsibility of jury service, of course, is examined during *voir dire*. Moreover, during the trial the jury is observable by the court, by counsel, and by court personnel. * * * Moreover, jurors are observable by each other, and may report inappropriate juror behavior to the court before they render a verdict.* * * Finally, after the trial a party may seek to impeach the verdict by nonjuror evidence of misconduct.* * * Indeed, in this case the District Court held an evidentiary hearing giving petitioners ample opportunity to produce nonjuror evidence supporting their allegations.

In light of these other sources of protection of petitioners' right to a competent jury, we conclude that the District Court did not err in deciding, based on the inadmissibility of juror testimony and the clear insufficiency of the nonjuror evidence offered by petitioners, that an additional post-verdict evidentiary hearing was unnecessary.

* * *

It is so ordered.

NOTES

1. What constitutes "extraneous prejudicial information"or "outside influence"?

Tanner indicates that reading newspaper accounts of the cases, a bailiff's comments to the jury concerning the case, or a bribe offer to a juror meet the definitions. Courts have also held that unauthorized juror experiments meet the exceptions of "extraneous prejudicial information" or "outside influence." *Miller v. Harvey*, 566 F.2d 879 (4th Cir. 1977). Thus, in *United States v. Castello*, 526 F. Supp. 847 (W.D. Tex. 1981), the trial judge granted a new trial to a defendant convicted of assault with a dangerous weapon when one juror conducted a ballistics experiment during a weekend recess and reported the results to the other jurors.

A juror may also testify about jury review of documents not admitted in evidence. *United States v. Herrero*, 893 F.2d 1512 (7th Cir. 1990). Clearly, threats to a juror or the juror's family meet the exceptions. *Krause v. Rhodes*, 570 F.2d 563 (6th Cir. 1977). *Tanner* appears to leave some room for an argument that juror incompetence may meet the exceptions as well.

2. What circumstances do not meet the exceptions?

Tanner indicates juror statements may not be used to prove that jurors were inattentive or that jurors were using alcohol or other drugs. It has been held that a juror may not testify that instructions were ignored, *Woods v. Bank of New York*, 806 F.2d 368 (2d Cir. 1986), or that jurors impermissibly discussed the possibility that one of the parties was insured, *Holden v. Porter*, 405 F.2d 878 (10th Cir. 1969). In addition, it has been held that Rule 606(b) does not allow juror statements to prove that the jury reached a compromise verdict. *United States v. Campbell*, 684 F.2d 141 (D.C. Cir. 1982). Thus, in *United States v. Briggs*, 291 F.3d 958 (7th Cir. 2002), the court held that the trial judge did not err in refusing to conduct a hearing into a juror's complaints that she had been intimidated" by other jurors into finding the defendant guilty. Because this complaint involved only "intrajury influences on the verdict," and there was no allegation of any extraneous prejudicial information or outside influence, the juror's allegations were not admissible under Rule 606(b). *See also United States v. Rutherford*, 371 F.3d 634 (9th Cir. 2004) (jurors learned of defendant's failure to testify "through their personal observations during trial, not through a prohibited route or improper ex parte contact"; no error in finding that juror testimony regarding the effect on the jury of the defendant's failure to take the stand was inadmissible under Rule 606(b)).

3. What if the jurors reached a verdict on racist or sexist grounds?

Rule 606(b) would appear to preclude testimony concerning the effect of a juror's racial or other bias on deliberations. However, assuming that *voir dire* (i.e., questioning potential jurors to determine whether they should be struck) is minimally adequate, a juror who is unwavering in his bias is likely to have lied about his feelings during *voir dire;* and this lie would ordinarily be considered a material misrepresentation, because a prospective juror who truthfully answers that he is unalterably biased will be struck for cause. Rule 606(b) applies to juror deliberations, but it does not preclude an inquiry into whether a juror lied during *voir dire*.[1] Accordingly, evidence could be

[1] *See, e.g., United States v. Henley*, 238 F.3d 1111 (9th Cir. 2001) (ordering an inquiry into whether a juror used racial epithets during the trial): Where, as here, a juror has been asked direct questions about racial bias during voir dire, and has sworn that racial bias would play no part in his deliberations, evidence of that juror's racial bias is indisputably admissible for the purpose of determining whether the juror's responses were truthful. *Hard v. Burlington Northern R.R.*, 812 F.2d 482, 485 (9th Cir. 1987) ("Statements which tend to show deceit during voir dire are not barred by Rule 606(b)"). If appellants can show that a juror failed to answer honestly a material question on voir dire, and then further show that a correct response would have provided a valid basis for a challenge for cause, then they are entitled to a new trial

presented about the juror's lies on *voir dire* in an attempt to overturn a verdict.[2] The primary focus would be on what one juror did and the way he felt before the deliberations, rather than on anything done during the deliberations. However, it appears that Rule 606(b) would limit inquiry into the effect that a biased juror might have had on other jurors; such an inquiry would appear to intrude into the thought processes of the jurors during deliberations.

Yet despite the policies behind Rule 606(b), courts in criminal cases are understandably reluctant to limit their inquiry to the *voir dire* stage when there are allegations that jurors relied on racial or other prejudices during their deliberations. As the Second Circuit has stated, courts "have hesitated to apply [Rule 606(b)] dogmatically" in the face of the defendant's Sixth Amendment right to an impartial jury. *Wright v. United States*, 732 F.2d 1048 (2d Cir. 1984). While the court must remain sensitive to the policies of finality and protection of the jury's deliberations, these policies must be tempered by the criminal defendant's right to a fair trial.[3]

4. If a juror is allowed to testify under an exception, may the juror testify to the effect that the extraneous prejudicial information or outside influence had on the jury?

The testimony is limited to the event and may not include any effect it had on any jury member. The court must then determine from all the circumstances, the effect that the information or influence had on the jury. *United States v. Simpson*, 950 F.2d 1519 (10th Cir. 1991) (juror may testify as to "*whether* any extraneous prejudicial information was improperly brought to bear" on juror deliberations, but "a juror may not testify as to the *effect* the outside information had upon the juror").

5. Is it possible to correct clerical errors in verdicts?

Rule 606(b) has been amended to provide that evidence from jurors is permitted to prove that the verdict was the result of a clerical error. The clerical error exception is limited, however, to situations in which the allegation is that the verdict entered is different from that agreed to by the jury, such as an error in addition in determining damages. The clerical error exception does not apply when the allegation is that the jury misunderstood or ignored a jury instruction. See the Advisory Committee Note to the 2006 amendment to Rule 606(b), *supra*.

---

[2] *See, e.g., United States v. Colombo*, 869 F.2d 149 (2d Cir. 1989) (accepting an affidavit from an alternate juror, averring that another juror deliberately failed to reveal a matter on *voir dire* because she thought it would hurt her chances to sit on the case: "Courts cannot administer justice in circumstances in which a juror can commit a federal crime in order to serve as a juror in a criminal case and do so with no fear of sanction so long as a conviction results.").

[3] *See Shillcutt v. Gagnon*, 827 F.2d 1155 (7th Cir. 1987) (Court properly reviewed the internal deliberative process of the jury to determine whether a racial slur during deliberations had an effect on the verdict; no denial of due process was found where only one racially derogatory comment was made during five hours of deliberations, and that comment was unrelated to any discussion of the facts; the Court concluded that Rule 606(b) "cannot be applied in such an unfair manner as to deny due process" and therefore a juror's racial bias and its effect on the deliberations was a proper subject of post-verdict inquiry).

[4] Judges

[a] Federal Rule of Evidence 605

Rule 605. Competency of Judge as Witness

The judge presiding at the trial may not testify in that trial as a witness. No objection need be made in order to preserve the point.

[b] Advisory Committee's Note to Rule 605

ADVISORY COMMITTEE'S NOTE
56 F.R.D. 183, 264

In view of the mandate of 28 U.S.C. § 455 that a judge disqualify himself in "any case in which he * * * is or has been a material witness," the likelihood that the presiding judge in a federal court might be called to testify in the trial over which he is presiding is slight. Nevertheless the possibility is not totally eliminated.

The solution here presented is a broad rule of incompetency, rather than such alternatives as incompetency only as to material matters, leaving the matter to the discretion of the judge, or recognizing no incompetency. The choice is the result of inability to evolve satisfactory answers to questions which arise when the judge abandons the bench for the witness stand. Who rules on objections? Who compels him to answer? Can he rule impartially on the weight and admissibility of his own testimony? Can he be impeached or cross-examined effectively? Can he, in a jury trial, avoid conferring his seal of approval on one side in the eyes of the jury? Can he, in a bench trial, avoid an involvement destructive of impartiality? The rule of general incompetency has substantial support. *See* Report of the Special Committee on the Propriety of Judges Appearing as Witnesses, 36 A.B.A.J. 630 (1950); cases collected in Annot. 157 A.L.R.311: McCormick § 68, p. 147; Uniform Rule 42; California Evidence Code § 703; Kansas Code of Civil Procedure § 60-442; New Jersey Evidence Rule 42. *Cf.* 6 Wigmore § 1909, which advocates leaving the matter to the discretion of the judge, and statutes to that effect collected in Annot. 157 A.L.R. 311.

The rule provides an "automatic" objection. To require an actual objection would confront the opponent with a choice between not objecting, with the result of allowing the testimony, and objecting, with the probable result of excluding the testimony but at the price of continuing the trial before a judge likely to feel that his integrity had been attacked by the objector.

NOTES

1. How does the rule affect judicial employees?

In *Kennedy v. Great Atl. & Pac. Tea Co.*, 551 F.2d 593 (5th Cir. 1977), a central issue in a personal injury action was whether the injured party slipped because of a wet spot on the floor. After the first trial ended in a mistrial because of the injured party's death, the trial judge's law clerk went with a friend to the accident scene out of curiosity. It was raining at the time, and they saw a puddle approximately where the original complainant had fallen. The clerk reported to the judge what he saw, and then phoned defense counsel to inform him of his observation and remark that the information might have a bearing on a settlement. Before the retrial the judge also disclosed the information to the plaintiff's counsel, who called the clerk and the friend to testify. Reversing a judgment for the plaintiff, the court held that the testimony of the clerk, who was so closely associated with the judge, distorted the proceedings. Citing Rule 605 as persuasive authority, the court expressed its concern that the jury might have concluded that the clerk's information had special importance and that the defendant would not be able to attack the credibility of the clerk because of his identification with the trial judge.

2. May the judge take a "view" of the scene?

In *Lillie v. United States*, 953 F.2d 1188 (10th Cir. 1992), the court reversed a judgment against the plaintiff in a Federal Tort Claims Act case because the trial judge had viewed the scene where the accident allegedly happened without notice and without providing counsel for either party the opportunity to accompany him.

C. FOUNDATIONAL COMPETENCE

[1] The Oath

[a] Federal Rule of Evidence 603

Rule 603. Oath or Affirmation

Before testifying, every witness shall be required to declare that the witness will testify truthfully, by oath or affirmation administered in a form calculated to awaken the witness' conscience and impress the witness' mind with the duty to do so.

[b] Religious Convictions

[i] Illustration

Zernog, a recent immigrant to the United States with only a limited understanding of American culture, witnessed an automobile accident. Plaintiff needs Zernog's testimony to establish the defendant was at fault and calls Zernog to the stand.

Plaintiff:	I call Zernog to the stand.
The Bailiff:	Please raise your right hand. Do you swear to tell the truth, the whole truth and nothing but the truth, so help you God?
Zernog:	I will not swear to a god.
Plaintiff:	________ .

[ii] Substitutes for the Oath

FERGUSON v. COMMISSIONER OF INTERNAL REVENUE
921 F.2d 588 (5th Cir. 1991)

PER CURIAM:

Betty Ann Ferguson appeals the Tax Court's dismissal of her petition for lack of prosecution after she refused to swear or affirm at a hearing. We find the Tax Court's failure to accommodate her objections inconsistent with both Fed. R. Evid. 603 and the First Amendment and reverse.

I.

This First Amendment case ironically arose out of a hearing in Tax Court. Although the government's brief is replete with references to income, exemptions, and taxable years, the only real issue is Betty Ann Ferguson's refusal to "swear" or "affirm" before testifying at the hearing. Her objection to oaths and affirmations is rooted in two Biblical passages, Matthew 5:33-37 and James 5:12. The passages refer only to oaths and swearing, but Ms. Ferguson explains her objection to affirmations in her brief to this court:

> Appellant is forbidden to swear as evidenced by the Bible directive from her God, and since the word "oath" has become synonymous and interchangeable with the word "affirmation," and the word "swear" [has] become synonymous and interchangeable with the word "affirm," as is evidenced in 1 U.S.C. 1 and many other authorities, it is appellant's sincere belief that "affirmation" is just an "other oath" and "affirm" falls with "swear not *at all*." Also, "affirmation" is the chosen form of those who denounce the very existence of God. Because of these things, "swear" and "affirm" are very repugnant to appellant.

Ms. Ferguson, proceeding *pro se*, requested that Judge Korner consider the following statement set forth by the Supreme Court of Louisiana in *Staton v. Fought*, 486 So. 2d 745 (La. 1986), as an alternative to an oath or affirmation:

> I, [Betty Ann Ferguson], do hereby declare that the facts I am about to give are, to the best of my knowledge and belief, accurate, correct, and complete.

Judge Korner abruptly denied her request, commenting that "[a]sking you to affirm that you will give true testimony does not violate any religious conviction that I have ever heard anybody had" and that he did not think affirming "violates any recognizable religious scruple." Because Ms. Ferguson could only introduce the relevant evidence through her own testimony, Judge Korner then dismissed her petition for lack of prosecution. She now appeals to this court.

II.

The right to free exercise of religion, guaranteed by the First Amendment to the Constitution, is one of our most protected constitutional rights. The Supreme Court has stated that "only those interests of the highest order and those not otherwise served can overbalance legitimate claims to the free exercise of religion." *Wisconsin v. Yoder*, 406 U.S. 205, 215 (1972). * * * The protection of the free exercise clause extends to all sincere religious beliefs; courts may not evaluate religious truth.* * *

Fed. R. Evid. 603, applicable in Tax Court under the Internal Revenue Code, 26 U.S.C. § 7453, requires only that a witness "declare that [she] will testify truthfully, by oath or affirmation administered in a form calculated to awaken the witness' conscience and impress the witness' mind with the duty to do so." As evidenced in the advisory committee notes accompanying Rule 603, Congress clearly intended to minimize any intrusion on the free exercise of religion:

> The rule is designed to afford the flexibility required in dealing with religious adults, atheists, conscientious objectors, mental defectives, and children. Affirmation is simply a solemn undertaking to tell the truth; no special verbal formula is required. * * *

The courts that have considered oath and affirmation issues have similarly attempted to accommodate free exercise objections. In *Moore v. United States*, 348 U.S. 966 (1955), for example, the Supreme Court held that a trial judge erred in refusing the testimony of witnesses who would not use the word "solemnly" in their affirmations for religious reasons.

In *United States v. Looper*, 419 F.2d 1405, 1407 (4th Cir. 1969), the Fourth Circuit held that the trial judge erred in refusing the testimony of a defendant who would not take an oath that referred to God. Specifically, Looper had told the trial judge, "I can't [take the oath] if it has God's name in it. If you ask me if I'll tell the truth, I can say that." The Fourth Circuit concluded that any form or statement that impressed on the mind and conscience of the witness the necessity for telling the truth would suffice as an oath, citing proposed Rule 603. The opinion closed by advising trial judges faced with religious objections to an oath or affirmation "to make inquiry as to what form of oath or affirmation would not offend defendant's religious beliefs but would give rise to a duty to speak the truth." * * *

The cases cited by the government, *United States v. Fowler*, 605 F.2d 181 (5th Cir. 1979), and *Kaltenbach v. Breaux*, 690 F. Supp. 1551 (W.D. La. 1988), are not contrary. In both cases, the witnesses completely refused to cooperate. Fowler would not accept even the simple statement, "I state that I will tell the truth in my testimony." And Kaltenbach's witness refused the very alternative proposed by Ms. Ferguson * * *.

The government [claims that the alternative oath offered by Ferguson] is insufficient because it does not acknowledge that the government may prosecute false statements for perjury. The federal perjury statute, 18 U.S.C. § 1621, makes the taking of "an oath" an element of the crime of perjury. * * * However, Ms. Ferguson has expressed her willingness to add a sentence to the statement acknowledging that she is subject to penalties for perjury. The government has cited a number of cases invalidating perjury convictions where no oath was given, but none of the cases suggest that Ms. Ferguson's proposal would not suffice as "an oath" for purposes of § 1621. * * *

The parties' briefs to this court suggest that the disagreement between Ms. Ferguson and Judge Korner might have been nothing more than an unfortunate misunderstanding. The relevant portion of their dialogue was as follows:

MS. FERGUSON: I have religious objections to taking an oath.

THE COURT: All right. You may affirm. Then in lieu of taking an oath, you may affirm.

MS. FERGUSON: Sir, may I present this to you? I do not —

THE COURT: Just a minute. The Clerk will ask you.

THE CLERK: You are going to have to stand up and raise your right hand.

MS. FERGUSON: I do not affirm either. I have with me a certified copy of a case from the Louisiana Supreme Court.

THE COURT: I don't care about a case from the Louisiana Supreme Court, Ms. Ferguson. You will either swear or you will affirm under penalties of perjury that the testimony you are about to give is true and correct, to the best of your knowledge.

MS. FERGUSON: In that case, Your Honor, please let the record show that I was willing to go under what has been acceptable by the State of Louisiana Supreme Court, the State versus —

THE COURT: We are not in the state of Louisiana, Ms. Ferguson. You are in a Federal court and you will do as I have instructed, or you will not testify.

MS. FERGUSON: Then let the record show that because of my religious objections, I will not be allowed to testify.

Ms. Ferguson contends that Judge Korner insisted that she use either the word "swear" or the word "affirm"; the government suggests instead that Judge Korner only required an affirmation which the government defines as "an alternative that encompasses all remaining forms of truth assertion that would satisfy [Rule 603]." Even Ms. Ferguson's proposed alternative would be an "affirmation" under the government's definition.

If Judge Korner had attempted to accommodate Ms. Ferguson by inquiring into her objections and considering her proposed alternative, the entire matter might have been resolved without an appeal to this court. Instead, however, Judge Korner erred not only in evaluating Ms. Ferguson's religious belief, and concluding that it did not violate any "recognizable religious scruple," but also in conditioning her right to testify and present evidence on what she perceived as a violation of that belief. His error is all the more apparent in light of the fact that Ms. Ferguson was proceeding pro se at the hearing.

We therefore REVERSE the decision of the Tax Court and REMAND this case for further proceedings not inconsistent with this opinion.

NOTES

1. What language will provide an acceptable oath or affirmation?

In *United States v. Ward*, 973 F.2d 730 (9th Cir. 1992, as amended 1993), the defendant refused to testify because the trial court did not permit him to take an altered version of the standard oath. The defendant would have taken an oath that substituted the term "fully integrated honesty" for the word "truth." The court of appeals held that the trial court was in error for refusing to accede to the defendant's demand. It found the defendant's objection to the standard oath to be based on "beliefs that are protected by the First Amendment." The court noted that there is no rigid formula for an acceptable oath. Under Federal Rule 603, an oath is sufficient if it is in a form "calculated to awaken the witness' conscience and impress the witness' mind with the duty" to tell the truth. The court stated, however, that the trial court can refuse a proffered form of oath if it is nothing but "a cleverly worded oath that creates loopholes for falsehood or attempts to create a safe harbor for perjury." For example, a proffered oath that "I would not tell a lie to stay out of jail" has been properly rejected, because the witness could later say that he lied for some purpose other than to stay out of jail, such as to protect a relative. But in *Ward*, the court found that the proffered oath was not a means to evade the sanction of perjury.

2. What does the trial judge do when a witness refuses to take an acceptable oath or affirmation?

In *United States v. Fowler*, 605 F.2d 181 (5th Cir. 1979), the court affirmed the trial judge's preclusion of the defendant's testimony after he refused either to swear or affirm that he would tell the truth or submit to cross-examination. The defendant as a party to the case suffered the pain of his refusal to submit to an oath or affirmation. An ordinary witness whose testimony is needed by the court might be ordered to submit to an oath or affirmation and held in contempt for failing to do so.

3. May the oath requirement be waived?

In *United States v. Odom*, 736 F.2d 104 (4th Cir. 1984), the court noted that failure to object in a timely fashion to the testimony of a witness who was not sworn in waives the objection.

Refer to the previous illustration. Suggest to the judge an oath or other statement that might allow the witness to testify.

[c] Children

[i] Illustration

Plaintiff places five-year-old Ima Childe on the stand.

Plaintiff:	How old are you, Miss Childe?
Witness:	I'm five (holding up one hand to show five fingers).
Plaintiff:	Do you know what a lie is?
Witness:	Yes, that's when you tell a fib.
Plaintiff:	What happens when you tell a fib?
Witness:	I have to do time out.
Plaintiff:	Do you like that?
Witness:	No, it's not fair.
Plaintiff:	Do you agree to tell nothing but the truth in this case?
Witness:	Yes.

The defendant cross-examines as follows:

Defendant:	Do you know what an oath is?
Witness:	No.
Defendant:	Do you know what perjury is?
Witness:	No.
Defendant:	Do you have to go do time out a lot?
Witness:	Yes.
Defendant:	So you've lied to your mom and dad many times?
Witness:	I think you're a mean man and I don't want to talk to you anymore.
Defendant:	Your honor, the witness is incompetent. She can't properly take an oath.

[ii] A Minimal Standard

CAPPS v. COMMONWEALTH
560 S.W.2d 559 (Ky. 1977)

STERNBERG, JUSTICE:

The appellant, Leslie Capps, was indicted by the Fayette County Grand Jury for the offense of first-degree sodomy by engaging in deviate sexual intercourse with Billy Carol Cook, a female less than 12 years of age (KRS 510.070). He was tried and convicted on December 27, 1976, and his punishment fixed at 30 years' imprisonment. * * *

[T]he appellant contends that the court abused its discretion in permitting the prosecutrix, a 5 1/2-year-old child, to testify. He argues that the witness was well coached by the Commonwealth, yet, upon cross-examination, was broken down.

The standard of competency of the child witness by which the discretion of the trial judge is to be guided is stated in *Moore v. Commonwealth*, Ky., 384 S.W.2d 498 (1964), as follows:

> When the competency of an infant to testify is properly raised it is then the duty of the trial court to carefully examine the witness to ascertain whether she (or he) is sufficiently intelligent to observe, recollect and narrate the facts and has a moral sense of obligation to speak the truth.

An independent reading and evaluation of the transcript of testimony of Billy Carol Cook and Barbara Lawrence, who testified as to the competency of the prosecutrix, are necessary.

The trial judge permitted a *voir dire* of Billy Carol Cook and Barbara Lawrence out of the hearing of the jury in order to determine the competency of the prosecutrix to testify. First of all, Barbara Lawrence, who was a social worker with the Kentucky Department of Child Services, told the judge that she had known Billy Carol since September, 1976; that the family is on AFDC benefits; and that Billy Carol had no preschool educational training, but nevertheless was a very alert five-year-old child who related well with her mother, natural father and her siblings. The testimony of the prosecutrix demonstrated that she knew where her mother worked and where her father worked, and she knew the name of the Commonwealth's Attorney. She also demonstrated her ability to knowingly tell a lie and advised that when she tells a lie or is bad, or uses bad words, her mother and father whip her. She said that she lived in Winchester, Kentucky, with her mother and father. She counted to ten for the appellant's counsel and related her favorite TV programs, one of which is Bugs Bunny, who she thought was a real person who brings her candy at Eastertime. She also expressed displeasure with counsel for appellant; referred to him as a "nut"; and stated that if he didn't stop asking such silly questions she would kill him and he would be an angel after all his blood ran out. She avowed to tell the truth. The testimony of the prosecutrix clearly and unequivocally demonstrates her to be a sassy and uncontrolled child, who has been reared in an environment conducive to being feisty and precocious.

It was not the prerogative of the trial judge to weigh the effectiveness of the testimony; that was the jury's prerogative. Whether Billy Carol Cook, measured by the standard set out in *Moore v. Commonwealth*, *supra*, was competent to testify is a question which addresses itself to the sound discretion of the court. The judge having found her competent to testify, the jury was entitled to weigh her testimony as it would the testimony of any other witness. * * * The transcript of testimony fully supports the action of the trial court in permitting Billy Carol to testify.

* * *

The judgment is affirmed.

All concur.

NOTES

1. Is it necessary that a child know the precise meaning of the oath to be considered competent to testify?

In *State v. Ayers*, 470 S.W.2d 534 (Mo. 1971), an appeal of a manslaughter conviction, the court held that the trial court did not abuse its discretion when it allowed into evidence the testimony of a twelve-year-old witness who did not understand the meaning of the oath. Although the girl did not know the meaning of the oath, "when asked what happens to a person who doesn't tell the truth, [she] replied: 'They will go to jail.' " The Supreme Court of Missouri held that "[h]er statement revealed an understanding of the obligation to speak truthfully. Her inability to explain the precise obligation of her oath did not produce an abuse of the trial court's discretion in accepting her testimony."

2. At what age is a child presumed competent?

Many states have statutes that provide a rebuttable presumption of competence if a child is over a certain age. In other words, a witness is considered competent at a certain age unless the opponent of the evidence proves otherwise. At common law, the age limit was fourteen years old, but currently most states with a statute set the age at ten or twelve years. *See* Colo. Rev. Stat. Ann. § 13-90-106 (West 1994) (10 years old); N.Y. Crim. Proc. Law § 60.20 (McKinney 1994) (12 years old).

3. If a child witness is found incompetent to testify, how else might an attorney get the child's statement into evidence?

Even if a child is incompetent to testify, the child's out-of-court statements might still be admissible under an exception to the hearsay rule. In *State v. Bouchard*, 639 P.2d 761 (Wash. App. 1982), a three-year-old child was allegedly abused by her grandfather. Although the child was incompetent to testify, the court allowed the girl's mother to testify about excited utterances made by the child shortly after the incident occurred. In *Morgan v. Foretich*, 846 F.2d 941 (4th Cir. 1988), an action by a four-year-old child and her mother alleging child abuse on the part of the child's father and his parents, the court reversed a judgment for the defendants, concluding that statements made by the child within three hours of the child's being returned to the mother following visits with the defendants should have been admitted as excited utterances. The court held that a child's out-of-court excited utterances are admissible whether or not the child would be competent to be a witness.

These cases will be more meaningful when you have had a chance to examine the hearsay rule and its exceptions. They are included here because it is somewhat counterintuitive to know that witnesses who are not permitted to take the stand where they can be cross-examined may make statements that are admitted without cross-examination.

Return to the previous illustration. Argue the objection on behalf of the proponent of the child witness.

[d] The Competent Incompetent

[i] Illustration

Plaintiff slipped and fell on a banana peel at the grocery store. The only witness who can testify that the peel was on the floor for quite some time takes the stand.

Plaintiff:	I call Sole Witness to the stand.
Defendant:	Your honor, before this witness is sworn in, I'd like to advise the court that I have in my possession a certified copy of a court order of this district wherein the court appointed a guardian over the person and a conservator over the assets of this witness. In that case the court found that the witness was suffering from insane delusions, could not tell right from wrong and was incapable of managing her own health care and estate. The witness is not capable of taking an oath and is incompetent.

[ii] Prior Determinations

UNITED STATES v. PHIBBS
999 F.2d 1053 (6th Cir. 1993)

RALPH B. GUY, JR., CIRCUIT JUDGE:

[A number of defendants were charged with narcotics distribution and related offenses. One of the defendants challenged the testimony of two witnesses on the ground of incompetency.]

Competency of Jerry Parks and Tommy McKeehan

Whited claims that witnesses Jerry Parks and Tommy McKeehan were incompetent to give testimony on grounds of mental incapacity. In the case of Parks, he had previously been found incompetent to stand trial, had a history of auditory delusions, and had spent time in mental health facilities. As for McKeehan, Whited cites an affidavit filed with the district court by his treating psychiatrist that he could not assist his counsel in an upcoming trial because he suffered from "confusion, agitation, paranoia and hallucinations." This affidavit was dated four days prior to McKeehan having entered into a plea agreement with the government. Because of such information, Whited contends that, at the very least, it was error for the court not to conduct a preliminary examination of Parks' and McKeehan's competency as witnesses.

Under Rule 601 of the Federal Rules of Evidence (General Rule of Competency), "[e]very person is competent to be a witness except as otherwise provided in these rules." The Advisory Committee Notes to Rule 601 explain that "[t]his general ground-clearing eliminates all grounds of incompetency not specifically recognized in the rules of this Article." Accordingly, "[n]o mental or moral qualifications for testifying as a witness" are specified. This is because "[s]tandards of mental capacity have proved elusive in actual application."

Thus, the Federal Rules of Evidence strongly disfavor barring witnesses on competency grounds due to mental incapacity. As we wrote in *United States v. Ramirez*, 871 F.2d 582, 584 (6th Cir. 1989):

> What must be remembered, and is often confused, is that "competency" is a matter of status not ability. Thus, the only two groups of persons specifically rendered incompetent as witnesses by the Federal Rules of Evidence are judges (Rule 605) and jurors (Rule 606). The authority of the court to control the admissibility of the testimony of persons so impaired in some manner that they cannot give meaningful testimony is to be found outside of Rule 601. For example, the judge always has the authority under Rule 403 to balance the probative value of testimony against its prejudicial effect. Similarly, under Rule 603, the inability of a witness to take or comprehend an oath or affirmation will allow the judge to exclude that person's testimony. An argument can also be constructed that a person might be impaired to the point that he would not be able to satisfy the "personal knowledge" requirement of Rule 602. Again though, it is important to remember that such decisions by a trial judge to either admit or exclude testimony will only be reversed for a clear abuse of discretion.

The district court did not rule on Parks' competency before he took the stand; later, in considering a motion for judgment of acquittal, the court indicated that Parks and McKeehan "were not crazy witnesses." Likewise, it addressed the question of McKeehan's mental capacity during a bench conference held after he had begun to testify. The court stated that it had "observed Mr. McKeehan, and he appears to the Court to be sober, cogent. He appears to the Court to know exactly where he is and what he is doing. His testimony has been direct, and his testimony has not been confused. * * * [His condition is] fodder for cross-examination, and it would appear that either the psychiatrist made an inaccurate diagnosis September the 5th or the witness has made a remarkable recovery. And the Court observes that — repeats that he does not appear to be confused today."

At a hearing on defendants' post-trial motions, the district court supplemented its findings regarding Parks' and McKeehan's competency, and the need for a special examination of their mental faculties. The court noted that

> * * * even if I had such an opinion from a psychiatrist or psychologist or whoever that gave us an independent opinion that these people were — Mr. Parks and McKeehan were total screwballs, I would — I would find those opinions to have little probative value and of little weight, and I would not — I would not accept them as being — as being conclusive on the matter. And I would not let such opinions override my own judgment after having seen — personally witnessed their performance in court.

Hence, the district court did not find that Parks and McKeehan were incapable of understanding their oath and obligation to testify truthfully. Nor did the court find, based on its observations, that their mental abilities were so limited that they did not have sufficient capacity to perceive events, to remember them, and to describe them for the benefit of the trier of fact. *See* Fed. R. Evid. 602. The court was not required, as Whited would have it, to conduct a special examination into their competency. If either Parks' or McKeehan's behavior raised concerns stemming from Rule 602 or 603, it could have excluded their testimony (or portions thereof) without any examination whatsoever. Furthermore, the court had the additional authority, pursuant to Rule 403, to exclude their testimony in light of their past or present mental state. The court chose not to take any of these measures in the circumstances. Instead, it permitted defense counsel to use the psychiatric records of Parks and McKeehan, as well as other indicia of their mental capacity, to vigorously attack their credibility.

After carefully reviewing the record, we conclude that the district court did not abuse its discretion in doing so. As long as a witness appreciates his duty to tell the truth, and is minimally capable of observing, recalling, and communicating events, his testimony should come in for whatever it is worth. It is then up to the opposing party to dispute the witness' powers of apprehension, which well may be impaired by mental illness or other factors. As we are persuaded that Parks and McKeehan were at least minimally capable of offering reliable evidence, the possible weaknesses in their testimony went to its credibility, and so were to be assessed by the jury.

NOTES

1. When, if ever, must a court order a psychiatric examination of a witness?

In *United States v. Skorniak*, 59 F.3d 750 (8th Cir. 1995), the court held there was no abuse of discretion in refusing to order a mental examination of a government witness, as the bare assertion that the witness "was not competent to testify due to his mental state" was insufficient to overcome the presumption in Rule 601 that all witnesses are competent to testify. The defendant was given ample opportunity on cross-examination to explore the witness's psychological problems and his history of drug and alcohol abuse.

In *United States v. Gutman*, 725 F.2d 417 (7th Cir. 1984), the court held that there was no error in refusing to order that a key government witness undergo a psychiatric examination or to hold a pretrial hearing on his competency. The court recognized that the trial judge has the power to condition admissibility of a witness's testimony on willingness to take a psychiatric examination, but it cautioned that the power should be used sparingly. The mental history of the witness did not create a sufficient doubt as to competency to compel a pretrial hearing and the witness' testimony was not so "incoherent" that it should have been stricken.

2. What is the effect of an insanity adjudication on the witness's competency to testify?

In *United States v. Lightly*, 677 F.2d 1027 (4th Cir. 1982), the court reversed a conviction for assault with intent to commit murder because the trial judge refused to permit a defense witness to testify on the ground that he had been found criminally insane and incompetent to stand trial and was subject to hallucinations. The court said that Rule 601 applies to persons considered to be insane to the same extent as to other persons and that where, as here, a treating physician indicated that the witness had a sufficient memory, understood the oath, and could communicate what he saw, he should have been permitted to testify. The court also found that the government had no standing to claim that the witness did not understand the incriminating nature of what he might say.

Return to the previous illustration. Argue the objection on behalf of the proponent of the witness.

[2] Perception

[a] Federal Rule of Evidence 602

Rule 602. Lack of Personal Knowledge

A witness may not testify to a matter unless evidence is introduced sufficient to support a finding that the witness has personal knowledge of the matter. Evidence to prove personal knowledge may, but need not, consist of the witness' own testimony. This rule is subject to the provisions of Rule 703, relating to opinion testimony by expert witnesses.

[b] Illustration

Defendant:	Now on direct examination you said you just caught a glimpse of the accident, isn't that true?
Witness:	Yes.
Defendant:	In fact, isn't it true that you were looking the other way when the accident took place?
Witness:	Well, I heard it happen.
Defendant:	So, you didn't see it at all, did you?
Witness:	Well, I turned my head and caught a split second look and heard the crash all at the same time and I just believe the defendant ran the light.
Defendant:	Your Honor, I request this witness' testimony be stricken, she didn't actually perceive anything. She just believes that she saw what happened, she's incompetent.

[c] Witness's Own Testimony

UNITED STATES v. DAVIS
792 F.2d 1299 (5th Cir. 1986)

Garwood, Circuit Judge:

Appellant Ronald Wayne Davis appeals his conviction of possessing firearms in interstate commerce after having been convicted of a felony in violation of 18 U.S.C. App. § 1202(a)(1). * * * Davis now claims his conviction should be reversed because of diverse asserted trial errors. We affirm.

Facts and Proceedings Below

In May 1982, Agent Don Medley of the Federal Bureau of Alcohol, Tobacco and Firearms received a report of a person carrying an illegal machine gun in Panola County, Mississippi. Agent Medley, assisted by Panola County Deputy Sheriff Bill Joiner, interviewed Billy Woods (appellant's uncle) and later Mr. Woods' wife about the machine gun. After the interview with Mrs. Woods, the officers decided to question the Woods' nephew appellant Davis who, with his wife Celeste, was in town visiting his mother and stepfather. Before speaking to Davis, Agent Medley learned that Davis had a 1980 felony conviction for possession of marijuana for which Davis had received a three-year suspended sentence. Agent Medley knew that it was illegal for Davis, as a convicted felon, to possess any firearm in interstate commerce.

On May 5, 1982, Agent Medley and Deputy Joiner found Davis at the Panola County home of his mother and stepfather. After conversing briefly with the law enforcement officers, Davis reportedly asked the officers to step inside the house so that they could see his firearms. Davis thought that if he proved to Medley and Joiner that he did not possess or have knowledge of a machine gun, he would clear himself of suspicion. After Davis displayed two pistols, two shotguns and three rifles, none fully automatic, Agent Medley told him that it was illegal for him to possess firearms. * * *

Davis was subsequently indicted on May 27, 1982 for possession in interstate commerce of these seven firearms, each described by make, model, and serial number, after having been convicted of a felony, a violation of 18 U.S.C. App. § 1202(a)(1). The offense was alleged to have been committed "on or about May 5, 1982, in the Northern District of Mississippi."

* * *

The government's primary witness at trial was Agent Medley, who testified about defendant's display of the seven firearms at the house on May 5, 1982, and his statements to the officers. These firearms were put in evidence. The records of Davis' April 1980 felony conviction were also introduced. The government called Officer Anderson of the Houston Police Department (HPD), who testified that on January 7, 1982, in Houston, he had taken two of these seven firearms from Davis. On rebuttal, Anderson further testified that the two firearms were released from the HPD property room on March 29, 1982.

The defense theory of the case * * * was that although Davis, whose 1980 conviction counsel admitted, had indeed brought the firearms from Texas to Panola County, Mississippi "around late 1981, early 1982," nonetheless, on May 5, 1982, Davis did not own or possess the guns, because he "had given the guns several months earlier to his step-father," and Davis was not living with his mother and step-father in May 1982, but was simply there on a brief visit. Davis testified in his own defense, generally as outlined in his counsel's opening statement. On direct examination, he acknowledged his 1980 conviction, and testified that he had owned these guns while he was in Texas and brought them with him when he and his wife traveled from Texas to Panola County, Mississippi during the second week of February 1982, making a complete and permanent gift of them to his stepfather when he arrived. He also stated that he and his wife then left Panola County and did not return until late April 1982, when they came back for a visit. The defense also called Davis' wife, mother, and stepfather, who gave testimony generally to like effect, although being somewhat less precise about when Davis came with the guns. The stepfather's testimony in this respect was particularly vague. In sum, Davis judicially admitted possessing the particular guns in question in interstate commerce in the Northern District of Mississippi after he had been convicted of a felony, contrary to section 1202(a)(1), but asserted that the offense was committed in mid-February 1982, not "on or about May 5, 1982," as charged in the indictment.

The jury found Davis guilty, and he was sentenced to two years in prison. This appeal follows.

Discussion

Davis first contends that government witness HPD Officer Anderson was allowed to give rebuttal testimony not adequately shown to be within his own personal knowledge, as required by Fed. R. Evid. (Rule) 602. Officer Anderson had testified on the government's case in chief that he had taken two of the guns in question from Davis on January 7, 1982 in Houston; he identified the marks he had placed on the guns at that time, identified Davis and stated that he had "tag[ged]" the guns "into the police property room." On cross-examination, he testified he was then a "uniform patrolman" and "not involved with the Narcotics Bureau full time." Anderson's presently challenged testimony came when he was recalled by the government as a rebuttal witness, and the following transpired:

> Q. [Mr. Alexander for the government]. When were those guns released out of the Houston Police Department?
>
> Mr. McDUFF [defense counsel]: Objection, Your Honor, to anything outside this witness' personal knowledge and outside any business records that he is qualified to introduce into evidence, otherwise, it is going to be hearsay.
>
> THE COURT: Overruled.
>
> MR. ALEXANDER:
>
> Q. When were these guns released from the Houston Police Department back to Mr. Davis?

A. They were released on March the 29th, 1982.

Q. All right. Where was that?

A. That was in Houston, Texas at the police property room.

Q. Were they —

MR. McDUFF: I object again. This is hearsay. There is no indication that this witness is qualified to give this information or is using business records.

MR. ALEXANDER: Your Honor, no further questions.

THE COURT: Counsel should lay a proper predicate for that information.

MR. ALEXANDER:

Q. Mr. Anderson, *do you know of your own knowledge when these guns were released?*

A. Yes, sir.

Q. When?

A. March the 29th, 1982.

MR. ALEXANDER: No further questions. (Emphasis added).

Davis' counsel then cross-examined Anderson, asking him "do you have any records with you showing when those weapons were released," to which Anderson answered that he had "a copy of the release form." Anderson replied in the negative when asked if he was "the custodian of these records" and if Davis' name appeared "on this form." Nothing was elicited on defense counsel's cross-examination indicating that Anderson did not have personal knowledge of when the guns were released, or that his testimony was based even partly on the form. Defense counsel then renewed his objection that Anderson's testimony was hearsay. The court overruled the objection. The government then established by questioning of Anderson that the form contained a description and serial numbers which matched those of the pistols introduced in evidence. The form was never offered in evidence.

Rule 602 clearly places on the proponent of the testimony the initial burden of showing that it represents the witness' personal knowledge. This is the general common law rule. The question, then, is whether the government sufficiently met this initial burden. The district court, which doubtless has at least some discretion in determining such matters, ruled that it did. While the question is a close one, we do not find that error has been demonstrated. Anderson had testified that he was a police officer, that he took the guns from Davis, marked them, and tagged them into the police property room. Thus a personal relationship between Anderson and Davis, the guns, and the property room was shown. When Anderson was asked the date the guns were released from the property room, objection was made "to anything outside this witness' personal knowledge." Thereafter, the witness answered affirmatively when asked whether he knew "of your own knowledge" when the guns were released. No objection was made to the form of this question, either as being too general or for any other reason. There is nothing in the record to suggest that Anderson did not, or even likely did not, have such personal knowledge. Davis had ample opportunity to cross-examine Anderson, or to take him on *voir dire*, to establish any lack of personal knowledge or opportunity for same, and he could have requested that this be done out of the presence of the jury. But he chose not to do any of this. Had he done so, and shown, for example, that Anderson was not present when the guns were released, Anderson's testimony in this respect would doubtless have been stricken if the prosecution did not show some other particular basis for personal knowledge. If striking the testimony were arguably an inadequate remedy, a mistrial could be considered if the matter were sufficiently prejudicial.

We do not suggest that the trial court has discretion either to do away with the foundation requirement of Rule 602 or to allow testimony that is shown to be without adequate basis in personal knowledge. Nor do we suggest that the trial court must, or even should, accept a bare minimum initial showing of personal knowledge. But we believe that the trial court has some discretion in evaluating such an initial showing, and generally does not abuse that discretion by accepting a provisionally adequate witness' testimony that he has personal knowledge, when other evidence indicates that the witness had a personal connection to the subject matter, there is nothing to suggest that the witness likely did not have or could not have had such knowledge, and its probable absence could be easily shown, but opposing counsel, despite full opportunity to do so, wholly fails to make any such showing. That being the situation here, we reject Davis' claim of reversible error in this respect.

* * *

Affirmed.

NOTES

1. What is the standard by which the judge must decide whether the witness has personal knowledge?

According to Professors Saltzburg, Martin and Capra, *Federal Rules of Evidence Manual* (9th ed. 2006):

> As long as there is enough evidence to support a finding that the witness has personal knowledge, the trial judge must let the jury decide whether the witness is really knowledgeable. *See, e.g., United States v. Hickey*, 917 F.2d 901 (6th Cir. 1990) ("Testimony should not be excluded for lack of personal knowledge unless no reasonable juror could believe that the witness had the ability and opportunity to perceive the event that he testifies about"; witness's testimony was admissible despite the fact that it may have been, "in large part, unbelievable to some and in spite of the possibility that his perception was sometimes impaired"). If the jury believes that the witness has no personal knowledge, it will disregard the testimony. Thus, the personal knowledge requirement is a matter of conditional relevancy. *See*

Advisory Committee Note to Rule 602 ("It will be observed that the rule is in fact a specialized application of the provisions of Rule 104(b) on conditional relevancy."). The witness need not be absolutely certain of the event related in order to satisfy the personal knowledge requirement; nor must the Judge be convinced. It is enough that a reasonable juror could find that the witness perceived the event. *See, e.g., M.B.A.F.B. Federal Credit Union v. Cumis Ins. Soc'y*, 681 F.2d 930 (4th Cir. 1982) (Rule 602 does not require that the witness's knowledge be positive or rise to the level of absolute certainty. Evidence is inadmissible under the rule only if in the proper exercise of the trial court's discretion it finds that the witness could not have actually perceived or observed that which he testifies to.) Moreover, perfect knowledge is not required — the witness can be vague about certain details, and still have enough knowledge to testify under Rule 602. *See, e.g., United States v. Powers*, 75 F.3d 335 (7th Cir. 1996) ("[t]he fact that a witness cannot recall specific dates does not require exclusion of that testimony," since inability to recall specific dates does not demonstrate an absence of personal knowledge; the opponent's remedy is not exclusion but rather cross-examination and impeachment). A problem in the witness's perception generally goes to weight and not admissibility. *United States v. Peyro*, 786 F.2d 826 (8th Cir. 1986) (witness who admitted substantial memory and emotional problems nonetheless had sufficient personal knowledge to testify; the Court noted that the witness's "recall and emotional problems were laid bare for the jury's consideration").

In *United States v. Owens-El*, 699 F. Supp. 815 (C.D. Cal. 1988), *aff'd*, 889 F.2d 913 (9th Cir. 1989), the trial judge ruled that when a question is raised as to whether a witness has sufficient personal knowledge to satisfy Rule 602, the testimony will be excluded only when no reasonable jury could conclude that the witness has personal knowledge. In the instant case, the jury could determine that there was evidence to support the conclusion that an assault victim had sufficient personal knowledge to make an out-of-court identification, even though the victim was later unable to testify about his identification. The witness had defensive wounds, indicating that he faced his attacker.

2. When is the foundation insufficient?

In *United States v. Lanci*, 669 F.2d 391 (6th Cir. 1982), the court upheld a ruling excluding testimony of an unavailable codefendant in an earlier state court proceeding that he "imagined" that the defendant's fingerprints appeared on FBI documents because of the defendant's curiosity about them. Because the codefendant also said that he did not know whether the defendant read the documents "or glanced through them or what," the testimony was inadmissible under Rule 602.

In *Hart v. O'Brien*, 127 F.3d 424 (5th Cir. 1997), the Court found error when the trial court permitted a police officer to testify about what was in the mind of another officer who made an arrest. The witness did not participate in the investigation, surveillance, or arrest.

3. Does use of drugs negate personal knowledge?

In *United States v. Hickey*, 917 F.2d 901 (6th Cir. 1990), a cocaine distribution prosecution, the court held that a reasonable juror could believe that a principal witness perceived the events to which he testified, even though his testimony may have been in large part unbelievable to some and his perception was sometimes impaired by his admitted drug addiction.

4. Must the witness be certain?

In *Maylie v. National Railroad Passenger Corp.*, 791 F. Supp. 477 (E.D. Pa. 1992), the district judge denied a motion for a new trial in a personal injury case. The jury found for the plaintiff and the defendant complained that a doctor should not have been permitted to testify about a surgery, because there was an insufficient showing that the doctor had personal knowledge. The doctor admitted on cross-examination that hospital records did not reveal his presence during the surgery, and stated that he could not be 100 percent certain that he was present. The court ruled that it is unnecessary for the witness to be absolutely certain of facts under Rule 602, and it is sufficient if the proponent offers evidence from which a trier of fact could find personal knowledge.

[d] Extent of Personal Knowledge

GLADDEN v. STATE

54 So. 2d 607 (Ct. App. Ala. 1951)

HARWOOD, JUDGE:

This appellant's jury trial on an affidavit charging him with operating a motor vehicle on a public highway while drunk resulted in a verdict of guilty.

The evidence presented by the state consisted of the testimony of C. M. Garrett, Sheriff of Cherokee County, and C. R. Hurley, a deputy sheriff of said county.

These officers testified that as they were driving down a state highway in Cherokee County, at a speed of about forty miles per hour, they met two cars. One was driven by the appellant. This car was driven in a "wobbly" manner, and it was necessary for the Sheriff to drive his vehicle partly off the highway to avoid a collision.

The officers immediately turned their car around and pursued the two other vehicles. They stopped these cars, with their vehicle being between the two pursued automobiles.

Two boys jumped out of one of the automobiles, and the officers chased them. During this time appellant drove his car down a side road about 200 yards, got out and walked back toward the Sheriff's automobile. He was met by the officers and placed under arrest.

Both officers testified that all of the above transactions occurred within a space of from five to ten minutes.

Sheriff Garrett testified without objection that he observed the appellant as he drove the automobile and that he was drunk, and that he was drunk when he was arrested some five or ten minutes later.

Over appellant's objection * * * Deputy Hurley was permitted to testify that the appellant was drunk at the time he was arrested.

Also over appellant's objections, on the ground that the witness was not qualified by observation or knowledge, this witness testified that in his opinion the appellant was drunk when he saw him driving on the highway.

On cross examination Hurley testified that he saw the appellant as he approached the officers' automobile; that appellant's vehicle went from one side of the road to the other, and that the Sheriff had to drive partly off the road to avoid a collision; that while he did not recognize the appellant at the moment, he did see him, and formed his opinion as to appellant's condition at this time on the few seconds that he observed him driving.

Appellant thereupon moved to exclude Hurley's testimony as to appellant's condition at the time he was driving on the highway. This motion was denied by the court.

* * *

All testimony must be based on a witness' observation of the matter about which he is testifying. Where in a proper case a non-expert is permitted to give opinion evidence, and cross-examination discloses that his opportunity for observation was insufficient to afford any reasonable basis for the conclusion expressed, his opinion testimony should be excluded on motion. Where however an opportunity for observation is shown, even though slight, a witness should be considered competent to testify as to what he did observe. Certainly we know of no way to measure a witness' capacity for observation, other than as it may be determined by a jury which hears the testimony tending to show its strength or weakness on the facts developed from examination of the witness. When such facts are shown the weight of such testimony is for the jury.

The court therefore did not err in denying the motion to exclude the testimony of the witness Hurley as to appellant's condition of sobriety at the time he observed him driving on the highway.

* * *

NOTES

1. For how long must a witness perceive an event in order to be competent to testify?

Fed. R. Evid. 602 requires that evidence be introduced "sufficient to support a finding that the witness has personal knowledge of the matter." In *Adkins v. Dirickson*, 523 F. Supp. 1281, 1284 (E.D. Pa. 1981), the court observed that "[a] witness is deemed competent to testify unless it is nearly impossible that he had first-hand observation." In other words, the slightest possibility of actual perception is sufficient to satisfy the personal knowledge requirement of Rule 602.

While interpretation of Rule 602 has been fairly liberal, courts have excluded testimony based on "sheer speculation," *United States v. Sorrentino*, 726 F.2d 876, 886 (1st Cir. 1984), or when a witness "imagined" that a fact existed. *United States v. Lanci*, 669 F.2d 391, 394–395 (6th Cir. 1982).

2. Does Rule 602 preclude testimony regarding hearsay statements?

The Rule 602 requirement of personal knowledge does not preclude testimony about a hearsay statement, assuming that the witness heard the statement being made. In *State v. Bouchard*, an appeal of an indecent liberties conviction, the mother of a three-year-old child was allowed to testify about the child's excited utterance, "Grandpa did it," made after the mother found blood around her daughter's lower abdominal and vaginal areas. 639 P.2d 761, 763 (Wash. App. 1982). Although the mother did not have personal knowledge of the event the child described, she did have personal knowledge that the child made the statement. Of course, the hearsay declarant must have personal knowledge of the event related to the witness.

3. Are there limits to the inferences that a person may draw from personal knowledge?

Another objection that might have been made in *Gladden* would have been that the witnesses were offering improper opinion. Opinion testimony by lay witnesses is governed by Rule 701, which is discussed later in the book. It is important to note that Rule 701 does put limits on the type of inferences that witnesses are permitted to draw and relate at trial. In *Gladden*, the fact that the witnesses observed the defendant not only while driving but while arrested, probably established sufficient contact between the witnesses and the defendant to support opinion testimony.

PROBLEM 3-1

Plaintiff has filed a lawsuit claiming that her stockbroker illegally "churned" her account, losing her considerable amounts of money while making a tidy sum for the broker and her brokerage house. In support of her claim, plaintiff calls the administrative assistant to the defendant broker.

Direct Examination

Plaintiff: State your name.
AA: Administrative Assistant
Plaintiff: Are you employed?
AA: No longer. I used to work for the defendant as his administrative assistant from 1997 until six months ago.
Plaintiff: During the time you worked for the defendant, did you record the trades that the defendant made?
AA: Yes, I did.
Plaintiff: Who was the broker for the plaintiff?
AA: The defendant.

Plaintiff: Are you familiar with any trades that occurred in the plaintiff's account?

Defendant: Objection! Your Honor, there is no specification as to what time period we are talking about. This witness can't have personal knowledge of trades made when she was not working there.

The court: (1) ________ .

Plaintiff: Are you familiar with any trades that occurred in the plaintiff's account from 1997 until six months ago?

AA: Yes I am.

Plaintiff: Approximately how many trades were there?

Defendant: Objection! Your Honor, she is asking for a guess, mere speculation, not personal knowledge.

The court: (2) ________ .

AA: Approximately 2,000 trades.

Plaintiff: Of the 2,000, approximately how many trades did the plaintiff authorize the defendant to make.

Defendant: Objection! Your Honor, counsel is asking for mere speculation, not personal knowledge. There is no showing that the witness has a basis for answering the question.

The court: When the plaintiff authorized a trade, how did she do it?

AA: She called the defendant.

The court: Were you on the telephone with the plaintiff and the defendant when the plaintiff called?

AA: No.

The court: (3) ________ .

Plaintiff: Well, how many of the trades were not authorized then?

Defendant: Same Objection! Your Honor, once more counsel is asking for a guess, mere speculation, not personal knowledge.

The court: (4) ________ .

Plaintiff: Did the plaintiff ever make a complaint to your knowledge about the number of trades being made in her account?

Defendant: Objection! Your Honor, there is no showing yet of personal knowledge.

The court: (5) ________ .

AA: Yes she did.

Plaintiff: What knowledge do you have of the plaintiff's complaints?

AA: The plaintiff called me on three occasions and said that there were too many trades, and she asked me to tell the defendant to lighten up on the trades.

Plaintiff: What did you do after hearing the plaintiff's complaints?

AA: Each time the plaintiff called me, I wrote a memo to the defendant and put it on the defendant's desk. I also told the defendant that on three occasions the plaintiff had asked me to request the defendant to lighten up on the trades.

Plaintiff: What effect did these calls have on the number of trades made by the defendant in the plaintiff's account?

Defendant: Objection! She cannot answer what effect something had on the defendant; only the defendant can answer that question.

The court: (6) ________ .

AA: There were as many trades a month after the complaints as before.

Plaintiff: So, in your opinion did the plaintiff's calls have any effect on the defendant?

Defendant: Objection! She cannot answer what effect something had on the defendant; only the defendant can answer that question.

The court: (7) ________ .

Cross-examination

Defendant: Isn't it true that you have a cocaine dependency and that you use cocaine on a daily basis?

Plaintiff: I object. That is outside the scope of direct and has nothing to do with the case.

The court: (8) ________ .

AA: That's true.

Defendant: Have you taken any cocaine today?

Plaintiff: Objection. That question is designed to harass and embarrass the witness.

The court: (9) ________ .

AA: Yes.

Defendant: Your Honor. We move to strike all of the direct testimony of this witness as being incompetent because of the witness's drug use.

Plaintiff: The fact that the witness is an addict does not make the witness incompetent.

The court: (10) ________ .

[3] Recollection

[a] Memory Refreshed

[i] Illustration

Plaintiff calls her most important eyewitness to the stand.

Bailiff:	Do you swear to tell the truth, the whole truth and nothing but the truth so help you God?
Witness:	I do.
Bailiff:	Please be seated.
Plaintiff:	State your name for the record.
Witness:	Truly Forgetful.
Plaintiff:	Ms. Forgetful where do you live?
Witness:	2815 Tomahawk.
Plaintiff:	I'd like to direct your attention to last June 8 at 7:00 p.m.
Witness:	Yes.
Plaintiff:	Were you at the scene of the accident involving the plaintiff in this case?
Witness:	Yes, I was.
Plaintiff:	Did you see what happened?
Witness:	Yes and I have perfect vision.
Plaintiff:	What do you remember happening?
Witness:	Nothing.
Plaintiff:	Nothing happened?
Witness:	No, I don't remember anything.
Defendant:	Your honor, I object to this witness testifying any further, Ms. Forgetful is not competent to testify.
The court:	It certainly looks that way to me (looking to plaintiff's lawyer). Counselor, this witness doesn't recall anything and is therefore incompetent to testify. Unless you have some method to proceed with this witness, I'm going to excuse Ms. Forgetful.

[ii] Federal Rule of Evidence 612

Rule 612. Writing Used to Refresh Memory

Except as otherwise provided in criminal proceedings by section 3500 of title 18 United States Code, if a witness uses a writing to refresh his memory for the purpose of testifying either;

(1) while testifying, or

(2) before testifying, if the court in its discretion determines it is necessary in the interests of justice, an adverse party is entitled to have the writing produced at the hearing, to inspect it, to cross-examine the witness thereon, and to introduce in evidence those portions which relate to the testimony of

the witness. If it is claimed that the writing contains matters not related to the subject matter of the testimony the court shall examine the writing in camera, excise any portions not so related, and order delivery of the remainder to the party entitled thereto. Any portion withheld over objections shall be preserved and made available to the appellate court in the event of an appeal. If a writing is not produced or delivered pursuant to order under this rule, the court shall make any order justice requires, except that in criminal cases when the prosecution elects not to comply, the order shall be one striking the testimony or, if the court in its discretion determines that the interests of justice so require, declaring a mistrial.

NOTE

When a witness has difficulty recalling some of the facts within personal knowledge, it is standard practice to attempt to refresh the witness's recollection. This is often done by showing the witness a prior statement or other writing that stimulates memory. Rule 612 provides that if a witness is shown a writing to refresh memory while testifying, the adverse party is entitled to have the writing produced for inspection and to cross-examine the witness with respect to it. Moreover, an adverse party may introduce into evidence those portions of the writing that relate to the testimony of the witness. The right to inspect and use a writing is unqualified if the witness uses it to refresh recollection while testifying. But if the witness uses a writing to refresh recollection *before* taking the stand, inspection and use is dependent upon the court's finding that disclosure is necessary in the interests of justice.

[iii] Any Statement or Object

BAKER v. STATE
371 A.2d 699 (Md. 1977)

MOYLAN, JUDGE:

This appeal addresses the intriguing question of what latitude a judge should permit counsel when a witness takes the stand and says, "I don't remember." What are the available keys that may unlock the testimonial treasure vaults of the subconscious? What are the brush strokes that may be employed "to retouch the fading daguerreotype of memory?" The subject is that of Present Recollection Revived.

The appellant, Teretha McNeil Baker, was convicted by a Baltimore City jury of both murder in the first degree and robbery. Although she raises two appellate contentions, the only one which we find it necessary to consider is her claim that the trial judge erroneously refused her the opportunity to refresh the present recollection of a police witness by showing him a report written by a fellow officer.

The ultimate source of most of the evidence implicating the appellant was the robbery and murder victim himself, Gaither Martin, a now-dead declarant who spoke to the jury through the hearsay conduit of Officer Bolton. When Officer Bolton arrived at the crime scene, the victim told him that he had "picked these three ladies up * * * at the New Deal Bar"; that when he took them to their stated destination, a man walked up to the car and pulled him out; that "the other three got out and proceeded to kick him and beat him." It was the assertion made by the victim to the officer that established that his money, wallet and keys had been taken. The critical impasse, for present purposes, occurred when the officer was questioned, on cross-examination, about what happened en route to the hospital. The officer had received a call from Officer Hucke, of the Western District, apparently to the effect that a suspect had been picked up. Before proceeding to the hospital, Officer Bolton took the victim to the place where Officer Hucke was holding the appellant. The appellant, as part of this cross-examination, sought to elicit from the officer the fact that the crime victim confronted the appellant and stated that the appellant was not one of those persons who had attacked and robbed him. To stimulate the present memory of Officer Bolton, appellant's counsel attempted to show him the police report relating to that confrontation and prepared by Officer Hucke.

The record establishes loudly and clearly that appellant's counsel sought to use the report primarily to refresh the recollection of Officer Bolton and that he was consistently and effectively thwarted in that attempt:

BY MR. HARLAN:

Q:	Do you have the report filed by Officer Hucke and Officer Saclolo or Saclolo?
A:	Right, I have copies.
Q:	Okay.
MR. DOORY:	I would object to that, Your Honor.
THE COURT:	I will sustain the objection. This is not his report.

BY MR. HARLAN:

Q:	Can you look at this report and refresh your recollection as to whether or not you ever had the victim in a confrontation with Mrs. Baker?
MR. DOORY:	Objection, Your Honor.
MR. HARLAN:	He can refresh —
THE COURT:	Well, he can refresh his recollection as to his personal knowledge. That's all right.
A:	That is what I am saying, I don't know who it was that we confronted really.

BY MR. HARLAN:

Q:	All right. Would you consult your report and maybe it will refresh your recollection.
THE COURT:	I think the response is he doesn't know who —
MR. HARLAN:	He can refresh his recollection if he looks at the report.
THE COURT:	He can't refresh his recollection from someone else's report, Mr. Harlan.
MR. HARLAN:	I would object, Your Honor. Absolutely he can.
THE COURT:	You might object, but —

MR. HARLAN: You are not going to permit the officer to refresh his recollection from the police report?

THE COURT: No. It is not his report. * * *

MR. HARLAN: Your Honor, I think I am absolutely within my rights to have a police officer read a report which mentions his name in it to see if it refreshes his recollection. If it doesn't refresh his recollection, then fine.

THE COURT: Well, he did that.

MR. HARLAN: You have not afforded him the opportunity to do that yet, Your Honor.

THE COURT: He says he does not know who it was before. So, he can't refresh his recollection if he does not know simply because someone else put some name in there.

MR. HARLAN: He has to read it to see if it refreshes his recollection, Your Honor.

THE COURT: We are reading from a report made by two other officers which is not the personal knowledge of this officer.

MR. HARLAN: I don't want him to read from that report. I want him to read it and see if it refreshes his recollection.

On so critical an issue as possible exculpation from the very lips of the crime victim, appellant was entitled to try to refresh the memory of the key police witness. She was erroneously and prejudicially denied that opportunity. The reason for the error is transparent. Because they both arise from the common seedbed of failed memory and because of their hauntingly parallel verbal rhythms and grammatical structures, there is a beguiling temptation to overanalogize Present Recollection Revived and Past Recollection Recorded. It is a temptation, however, that must be resisted. The trial judge in this case erroneously measured the legitimacy of the effort to revive present recollection against the more rigorous standards for the admissibility of a recordation of past memory.

It is, of course, hornbook law that when a party seeks to introduce a record of past recollection, he must establish 1) that the record was made by or adopted by the witness at a time when the witness did have a recollection of the event and 2) that the witness can presently vouch for the fact that when the record was made or adopted by him, he knew that it was accurate. * * * Had the appellant herein sought to offer the police report as a record of past recollection on the part of Officer Bolton, it is elementary that she would have had to show, *inter alia*, that the report had either been prepared by Officer Bolton himself or had been read by him and that he can now say that at that time he knew it was correct. Absent such a showing, the trial judge would have been correct in declining to receive it in evidence.

When dealing with an instance of Past Recollection Recorded, the reason for the rigorous standards of admissibility is quite clear. Those standards exist to test the competence of the report or document in question. Since the piece of paper itself, in effect, speaks to the jury, the piece of paper must pass muster in terms of its evidentiary competence.

Not so with Present Recollection Revived! By marked contrast to Past Recollection Recorded, no such testimonial competence is demanded of a mere stimulus to present recollection, for the stimulus itself is never evidence. Notwithstanding the surface similarity between the two phenomena, the difference between them could not be more basic. *It is the difference between evidence and non-evidence.* Of such mere stimuli or memory-prods, McCormick says, "[T]he cardinal rule is that they are not evidence, but only aids in the giving of evidence." When we are dealing with an instance of Present Recollection Revived, the only source of evidence is the testimony of the witness himself. The stimulus may have jogged the witness's dormant memory, but the stimulus itself is not received in evidence. * * *

The catalytic agent or memory stimulator is put aside, once it has worked its psychological magic, and the witness then testifies on the basis of the now-refreshed memory. The opposing party, of course, has the right to inspect the memory aid, be it a writing or otherwise, and even to show it to the jury. This examination, however, is not for the purpose of testing the competence of the memory aid (for competence is immaterial where the thing in question is not evidence) but only to test whether the witness's memory has in truth been refreshed. * * *

When the writing in question is to be utilized simply "to awaken a slumbering recollection of an event" in the mind of the witness, the writing may be a memorandum made by the witness himself, 1) even if it was not made immediately after the event, 2) even if it was not made of firsthand knowledge and 3) even if the witness cannot now vouch for the fact that it was accurate when made. It may be a memorandum made by one other than the witness, even if never before read by the witness or vouched for by him. It may be an Associated Press account. It may be a highly selective version of the incident at the hands of a Hemingway or an Eliot. All that is required is that it ignite the flash of accurate recall — that it accomplish the revival which is sought.

* * *

Not only may the writing to be used as a memory aid fall short of the rigorous standards of competence required of a record of past recollection, the memory aid itself need not even be a writing. What may it be? It may be anything. It may be a line from Kipling or the dolorous refrain of "The Tennessee Waltz"; a whiff of hickory smoke; the running of the fingers across a swatch of corduroy; the sweet carbonation of a chocolate soda; the sight of a faded snapshot in a long-neglected album. All that is required is that it may trigger the Proustian moment. It may be anything which produces the desired testimonial prelude, "It all comes back to me now."

* * *

Although the use of a memorandum of some sort will continue quantitatively to dominate the field of refreshing recollection, we are better able to grasp the process conceptually if we appreciate that the use of a memorandum as a memory aid is not a legal phenomenon unto itself but only an instance of a far broader phenomenon. In a more conventional mode, the process might proceed, "Your Honor, I am about to show the witness a written report, ask him to read it and then inquire if he can now testify from his own memory thus refreshed."

In a far less conventional mode, the process could just as well proceed, "Your Honor, I am pleased to present to the court Miss Rosa Ponselle who will now sing 'Celeste Aida' for the witness, for that is what was playing on the night the burglar came through the window." Whether by conventional or unconventional means, precisely the same end is sought. One is looking for the effective elixir to revitalize dimming memory and make it live again in the service of the search for truth.

Even in the more conventional mode, it is quite clear that in this case the appropriate effort of the appellant to jog the arguably dormant memory of the key police witness on a vital issue was unduly and prejudicially restricted.

Reversed

NOTES

1. Is the process of refreshing recollection subject to abuse?

Professors Saltzburg, Martin, and Capra, *Federal Rules of Evidence Manual* (9th ed. 2006), note the possibility that the process of "refreshing recollection" might be used as a backdoor to get an inadmissible document before the jury:

> It is important to recognize that there is a difference between refreshing memory with a document and introducing a document as substantive proof, most commonly under the past recollection recorded exception to the hearsay rule. A document used to refresh recollection is not admitted on behalf of the proponent of the evidence, whereas a document satisfying the hearsay exception is admitted for its truth. This distinction could give rise to possible abuse when a party either fails or refuses to qualify a record as past recollection recorded and chooses instead to "refresh" the witness's recollection. There is a possibility that the witness's recollection might not actually be refreshed (and maybe does not even need to be refreshed), and the document is essentially being used as hearsay evidence of an event. Trial judges have the discretion and the obligation to prevent a witness from relying on inadmissible evidence to "refresh" recollection when this is simply a ruse for getting the otherwise inadmissible evidence before the jury. *See, e.g., Rush v. Illinois Cent. R.R. Co.*, 399 F.3d 705 (6th Cir. 2005) (it was error to allow counsel to ask whether certain transcript statements were correct rather than asking whether the transcript refreshed recollection; the court "reach[ed] the inescapable conclusion that defense counsel impermissibly utilized the 'guise of refreshing recollect,' * * * to place before the jury [the witness's] prior, out-of-court statements regarding the manner in which Rush fell from

the CN-IC train"). *Compare United States v. Rinke*, 778 F.2d 581 (10th Cir. 1985) (government witness was properly allowed to consult a memorandum while he was giving testimony, since the memorandum was not a substitute for testimony but was merely used to refresh recollection; such a practice was not abusive given the defendant's right under Rule 612 to inspect and use the memorandum for cross-examination).

2. If an attorney uses materials, otherwise protected from disclosure by privilege or the work product doctrine, to refresh a witness's memory, do the materials remain protected?

As a general rule, when a writing is used to refresh the recollection of a witness, the opposing party has a right to inspect the refreshing tool and any protections the document had are lost. An interesting dilemma faces the trial lawyer who uses a protected document to refresh a witness's memory *before* the witness testifies. In *James Julian, Inc. v. Raytheon Co.* the court recognized that "[t]hose courts which have considered the issue have generally agreed that the use of protected documents to refresh a witness' memory prior to testifying constitutes a waiver of the protection." 93 F.R.D. 138, 145 (D. Del. 1982). So the benefits of refreshing recollection in advance may well be outweighed by the risks of waiver of privilege or work product.

3. When can the adversary offer refreshing documents as evidence?

An adversary is entitled to see a refreshing document and to offer it as evidence in support of a claim that the witness really lacks a present memory. Thus, in *United States v. Smith*, 521 F.2d 957 (D.C. Cir. 1975), a prosecution for a taxicab robbery, a police officer's report containing the cab driver's complaint and a transcript of that report as broadcast to the police department were inconsistent with the driver's testimony. When the defense sought to introduce the report and transcript, the trial judge ruled that they were inadmissible as hearsay. The court of appeals held, however, that because the officer used them to refresh his recollection before testifying as a prosecution witness, the defendant, as opposing party, should have been permitted to introduce the writings.

4. Is there a difference between pretrial and trial refreshing?

Documents used to refresh recollection at trial are always subject to examination. The trial judge has discretion to permit or to restrict discovery of documents used to refresh prior to trial. In *Cosden Oil & Chem. Co. v. Karl O. Helm A.G.*, 736 F.2d 1064 (5th Cir. 1984), a contract dispute, the court of appeals found that the trial judge did not err in declining to order a witness to turn over to counsel for an opposing party, notes that he admitted using to refresh his recollection prior to trial. Although the trial judge had authority to order the notes turned over, the judge determined that such an order was not required, especially where the witness never referred to the notes while testifying.

Return to the illustration. What questions should the lawyer ask?

[b] Past Recollection Recorded

[i] Illustration

Plaintiff:	Now Ms. Forgetful did you make a written memorandum of what you saw at the scene?
Witness:	Yes I did. It's the document in your hand.
Plaintiff:	Let me hand it to you and you just go ahead and review it. (Pause) Now, after reviewing the memorandum, do you recall what happened?
Witness:	Not really.
Plaintiff:	Well then judge, I'd like to admit the written statement.
Defendant:	Objection, lack of foundation. It's also hearsay!

[ii] Federal Rule of Evidence 803(5)

Rule 803. Hearsay Exceptions; Availability of Declarant Immaterial

The following are not excluded by the hearsay rule, even though the declarant is available as a witness:

* * *

(5) Recorded recollection. A memorandum or record concerning a matter about which a witness once had knowledge but now has insufficient recollection to enable him to testify fully and accurately, shown to have been made or adopted by the witness when the matter was fresh in the witness' memory and to reflect that knowledge correctly. If admitted, the memorandum or record may be read into evidence but may not itself be received as an exhibit unless offered by an adverse party.

[iii] Adopted Statement

UNITED STATES v. WILLIAMS
571 F.2d 344 (6th Cir. 1978)

LIVELY, CIRCUIT JUDGE:

Glen Williams was indicted for cashing government checks bearing forged endorsements in violation of 18 U.S.C. § 495. * * * There was uncontradicted evidence that the endorsements on four checks introduced as exhibits were forgeries and strong evidence that the defendant had cashed all four of them at a Detroit bar referred to in the indictment. The only substantial issue for the jury, as counsel for the defendant conceded in closing argument, was whether the government had proven beyond a reasonable doubt that Williams "intentionally cashed these checks knowing that they had forged endorsements."

Gary Ball was called as a witness by the government. Ball operated a junk yard next door to the bar where the four forged checks were cashed and he cashed checks there regularly. During a portion of the time when the forged checks were negotiated at the bar the defendant Glen Williams rented part of Ball's lot and ran a similar business there. Ball testified that when the first of the forged checks was returned by the bank the proprietor of the bar presented it to him, assuming that he had cashed it. After Ball had denied cashing the check he told the proprietor to check it out further. Ball testified, "later, he told me it was Glenn Williams that had cashed it." The witness then related his conversations with Williams about this check. After stating that Williams admitted that he had cashed the check and was willing to make it good, Ball was asked if Williams had stated where he had gotten the check. The witness answered, "Not to my knowledge, I don't remember him telling me where he got it." When the government attorney asked Ball specifically if he ever had a conversation with Williams "about a deal he had going with his landlord about checks," counsel for the defendant objected. The court directed that the question be rephrased, and this question and answer followed:

Q: Mr. Ball, I am going to rephrase my question slightly. Did you have a conversation with Mr. Williams about another check besides this one payable to Mr. Quick?

A: We had a conversation — I don't remember exactly the time or the day or when — but I asked him about the checks, and he said that he had cashed them for a landlord or a caretaker. One check, he said he had found in a hotel room.

The witness was then asked to examine a written statement which he had given to a secret service agent 15 months prior to the trial. He identified the signature at the end of the statement as his and made an incomplete reference to a "discrepancy" as he read the statement to himself. Once Ball finished reading the statement, he was asked, "Can you now remember more about these conversations than you just did a moment ago?" Ball answered, "No." The jury was then excused and a "special record" was made. The direct examination of the witness by government counsel included the following:

Q: Mr. Ball, the statement that you have in front of you now, did you give that statement to Agent Lutz of the Secret Service in about July of '75?

A: I did.

Q: Were there conversations that you had had with Mr. Williams fairly fresh in your mind at the time you made the statement?

A: They were.

Q: Did you swear to Agent Lutz that that statement was a true statement?

A: I did.

Q: You were put under oath, asked to raise your hand and so forth, to tell the truth?

A: I don't remember if I was or not.

Q: Had you told Agent Lutz before basically the same version about these conversations with Williams orally but not in writing?

A: Do you mean from the first time I talked to Mr. Lutz or up until this was taken?

Q: On previous occasions when you had talked to Mr. Lutz, did you tell him basically the same version that you put in the statement there?

A: When I first met Mr. Lutz, he was accusing me of cashing the checks. And he accused me before I even talked to Tony about this check, the Willington check, or the Quick check. It was after that they told me that I wasn't the one they were looking for that Tony asked me if I could get his money back for the check, and I told him I would try, I would talk to Glenn about it.

Q: But my question is: Did you give basically the same account to Agent Lutz orally on previous occasions before you gave this statement?

A: Basically the same account, the best of my recollection.

Q: Was that statement true and accurate to the best of your knowledge?

A: Yes.

Q: And is that statement true and accurate now to the best of your knowledge?

A: It is.

On cross-examination, still out of the presence of the jury, Ball testified that the statement was in the handwriting of Secret Service Agent Lutz and that it had not been taken down word for word by the agent. Rather, "We talked and then he wrote this out, and then I signed it." While affirming his previous testimony that the statement was true and accurate at the time he gave it, Ball now said it was true and accurate "in general." On the question of what Williams had told him about where he (Williams) had gotten the checks, the testimony was as follows:

Q: All right. On this paper, here (indicating), it says, "Glenn told me that he and his/or a landlord or caretaker were getting checks before the payee could get his mail." Is that a quote from you?

A: I think the quote from me would have probably been something like wherever Glenn stayed at, he got it from his caretaker or landlord. I don't remember ever putting in there that "before coming from the mail, getting the mail."

Q: Did Glenn ever tell you — excuse me — did Mr. Williams ever tell you that these checks were stolen checks?

A: No, he didn't.

Q: Okay. Did you intimidate, did you try to lead Officer Lutz, Agent Lutz, into believing that you believed that Glenn Williams was admitting to you a crime?

A: No, I didn't.

Q: So, what were you telling Agent Lutz that you knew?

A: That he cashed the checks at Tony's bar, and that he had got them from where he was living at to cash them, to the best of my knowledge.

Q: Did you tell Mr. — excuse me — Agent Lutz that it was your understanding that someone else was stealing checks and giving them to Glenn?

A: I didn't put it in those words. I told him it was my understanding that the checks were coming from an apartment building.

Q: Did you tell him that they were stolen checks, that Mr. Williams had told you that?

A: No, I didn't.

Q: Is there anything else in this statement that is not what you told Officer Lutz, but, rather, is what he wrote in here?

A: No, there is not; not that I know of.

Q: Would you just explain to me, Mr. Ball, did you give Officer Lutz — Agent Lutz the impression that Mr. Williams had told you that he was stealing checks?

A: No, I didn't.

Q: Did you give Agent Lutz the impression, or did you try to give him the impression, that you believed that Mr. Williams was cashing stolen checks and that he knew it?

A: No, I didn't.

Q: Did you believe, when you were signing this statement, that you were in any way incriminating Mr. Williams?

A: No, I didn't.

On redirect examination Ball admitted reading the statement before he signed it, and swearing to Agent Lutz that it was true. He contended that he had not told the agent that Williams had told him that he or the landlord or caretaker were getting the checks before the addressees picked up their mail. He also gave an explanation for his comment to Williams, "I thought you told me you had stopped this b.s.," which did not imply that the checks were stolen. He testified that he and Williams remained friends.

The district court then heard arguments of counsel after which it ruled that the statement would be admitted as "recollection of a statement that had been adopted by the witness." The District Judge held that a foundation had been adequately laid for admission of the statement, finding that his (Ball's) "relationship with the defendant here, his demeanor, his selective memory with regard to matters, convinces this Court that he is withholding and that his protestations of failure of recollection are not convincing to the Court." Following the requirements of Rule 803(5), the court did not admit the statement as an exhibit, but permitted it to be read to the jury after deleting the subjective impression, "It was my understanding that someone else was stealing the checks and giving them to Glenn." When the jury returned, and before the statement was read, Ball testified again that the statement was true and accurate at the time he gave it. Ball then read the statement.

On cross-examination, after the jury had heard the statement, Ball testified that the writing and words of the statement were those of Agent Lutz. He stated that he was frightened when the agent first accused him of passing bad checks and that he wanted to cooperate. He testified that Agent Lutz told him that he, Lutz, suspected that the landlord was involved. He didn't remember telling Lutz that Williams told him that he or his landlord was getting the checks before the payees could get their mail.

Agent Lutz testified that the statement was taken from Ball after several discussions, and at the time of the statement there was no suggestion that Ball was under suspicion or was being accused. He said the statement was taken at the Secret Service Office following a review of their prior discussions and that the witness read the statement, asserted that it was correct and said he was satisfied it was accurate when asked if he had any corrections, deletions or additions to make. Lutz testified that Ball then signed and swore to the statement.

Following denial of motions for a mistrial and for a judgment of acquittal the case was submitted to the jury and Williams was found guilty on four counts of the indictment. The only issue on appeal relates to admission of the statement signed by Gary Ball as substantive evidence. We affirm.

The first contention of Williams is that the statement should not have been admitted because it was not Ball's statement. This position is based on the fact that Agent Lutz wrote the statement in his own words. This argument misconstrues the requirements of Rule 803(5). To be admissible the memorandum or record must have been made "*or adopted by the witness* when the matter was fresh in his mind and to reflect that knowledge correctly" (emphasis added). By signing and swearing to the statement Gary Ball adopted it. This occurred approximately six months after the events recited in the statement. Ball testified unequivocally that his conversations with Williams were fresh in his mind at the time he signed the statement and that it was true and accurate statement at the time.

* * *

Appellant's second argument is that it was error to admit a statement "when the witness had clear recollection of his conversations with defendant and when he testified that a statement written by a government investigator following a conversation with the witness was inaccurate." If the record supported the quoted assertion the Ball statement would not be admissible under Rule 803(5). Rule 803(5) applies only to memoranda or records of matters "about which a witness once had knowledge but now has insufficient recollection to enable him to testify *fully and accurately*." (emphasis added). There is no doubt that Ball had sufficient recollection to testify generally about his conversations with Williams. However, the critical question about those conversations was whether Williams had told him how the checks came into his possession. This was the very aspect of the conversations which Ball testified he could not recall. Referring to one of the checks which Williams had cashed at the bar, Ball testified, "I don't remember him telling me where he got it." He further testified that Williams said that the checks came from his caretaker or landlord and that he didn't remember stating that they were taken before payees could get their mail. In addition he testified that he didn't remember saying, "I told Glenn he was nuts."

The District Judge, who observed Gary Ball testify before the jury and in the special record proceedings, concluded that the witness was exercising a "selective memory." Regardless of whether it was a deliberate act born of his friendship with the defendant, it is clear that Ball was claiming no recollection of certain features of his conversations with Williams which had been included in the statement that he had previously adopted. Once it was established that Ball's in-court testimony would be incomplete because of his insufficient recollection, the statement which he had adopted when the events were fresh in his mind, and which he repeatedly testified was accurate, became admissible under Rule 803(5). * * *

Williams makes much of the fact that Ball disputed portions of the statement on cross-examination. However Ball continued to agree that the statement was accurate "in general." He appeared to question primarily any implication to be drawn from the statement that he considered Williams guilty of a crime, yet his disagreements with the language of the statement were couched in terms of insufficient recollection. We conclude that the matters brought out in cross-examination did not preclude admissibility of the statement, but went only to the weight to be given it. * * * The jury was free to believe Ball's explanation of his intentions and impressions when he adopted the statement. They were not bound to accept the statement as conclusive evidence of the defendant's guilt. However, they were entitled to hear the statement as an accurate account of Ball's conversations with Williams, given at a time when those conversations were recent events and his memory of them was unimpaired.

* * * The Advisory Committee's Note to Exception (5) makes it clear that the method of establishing the initial knowledge of the declarant and the accuracy of the material sought to be introduced must be determined from the circumstances of each case. We find no abuse of discretion in the determination of the District Judge that the statement signed by Gary Ball should be read to the jury. It contained the indicia of trustworthiness required by Rule 803(5) and was never categorically disowned or contradicted by the witness. * * *

The judgment of the district court is affirmed.

NOTES

1. How soon after the event must the record have been made to qualify for admission under Rule 803(5)? What is "fresh" in memory?

Federal Rule of Evidence 803(5) requires that the memorandum have been made or adopted while the events discussed were fresh in the mind of the witness. In *United States v. Senak*, 527 F.2d 129 (7th Cir. 1975), the court admitted a statement made three years after the events discussed in the statement took place. The court decided that "[w]hile in at least one case there is a suggestion that the statement must be recorded contemporaneously with the event, *Dickinson Supply, Inc. v. Montana-Dakota Utilities Co.*, 423 F.2d 106, 109 n. 1 (8th Cir. 1970), we believe the better view is that the discretion of the trial judge should not be rigidly bound by an inflexible rule but rather that it should be exercised on a case-by-case basis giving consideration to all pertinent aspects including the lapse of time which reasonably and properly bear upon the likelihood of the statement being an accurate recordation of the event to which the memory related. Of course, the likelihood of accuracy only justifies admission but does not preclude an effort * * * to persuade the trier of fact that matters in the statement are not factually correct."

In *Parliament Ins. Co. v. Hanson*, 676 F.2d 1069 (5th Cir. 1982), the court of appeals affirmed a judgment in a suit on a performance bond covering an apartment construction project. It found that the trial judge properly excluded notes made by a former employee of a contractor that were offered when the employee had memory problems. The notes were made in anticipation of litigation and were not made contemporaneously with the events at issue, therefore they did not qualify as past recollection recorded.

2. Under the federal rules, why must an attorney show that a witness's memory is impaired before introducing that witness's recorded recollection?

The Advisory Committee Note to Rule 803(5) has this to say about the impaired memory requirement:

> The principal controversy attending the exception has centered, not upon the propriety of the exception itself, but upon the question whether a preliminary requirement of impaired memory on the part of the witness should be imposed. The authorities are divided. If regard be had only to the accuracy of the evidence, admittedly impairment of the memory of the witness adds nothing to it and should not be required.* * * Nevertheless, the absence of the requirement, it is believed, would encourage the use of statements carefully prepared for purposes of litigation under the supervision of attorneys, investigators, or claim adjusters.

For more on the impaired memory requirement, see *Collins v. Kibort*, 143 F.3d 331 (7th Cir. 1998) (the plaintiff was erroneously permitted to introduce a diary recording his version of various episodes at issue in the case; the plaintiff did not state that he could not recall the events recorded — in fact, he gave testimony recalling those events in detail — so the proper foundation was not laid for the diary as past recollection recorded).

3. Must there be a showing that the witness made or adopted the statement?

In *United States v. Schoenborn*, 4 F.3d 1424 (7th Cir. 1993), the court held it was error (but harmless) to admit as past recollection recorded a statement by a witness to a government agent, where the witness had refused to sign the statement when the agent showed it to him, and where the witness disavowed its accuracy on the stand. The statement could not be past recollection recorded because the requisite foundation could not be laid.

The foundation need not show that the witness remembers what was said. In *United States v. Sollars*, 979 F.2d 1294 (8th Cir. 1992), the court affirmed convictions for arson, holding there was no error in permitting the government to play a tape recording in which a defendant's stepdaughter told a BATF agent two months after the fire that she saw the defendant on the building's roof that night. The stepdaughter remembered at trial talking to the agent but could not remember what she told him, and the statement was made while her memory was still fresh.

4. Can a past recollection recorded be sent to the jury room for use by the jury during its deliberations?

To prevent a jury from giving too much weight to a written statement that cannot be effectively cross-examined, the Rule provides that the memorandum or record may be read into evidence but may not itself be received as an exhibit. However, if the party against whom the testimony is offered wishes to have the document introduced, it may be introduced.

PROBLEM 3-2

An insurance investigator takes the stand to testify about evidence he gathered at the scene of an accident on behalf of the plaintiff.

Plaintiff:	State your name.
Witness:	Insurance Agent.
Plaintiff:	Did you investigate this accident?
Witness:	Yes, I did.
Plaintiff:	When did you go to the scene of the accident?
Witness:	Ah, let's see, It was * * *
Defendant:	Objection! Your Honor, he's referring to his notes. Lack of foundation.
The court:	Do you have notes with you?
Witness:	Yes I do.
The court:	(1) ________ .
Plaintiff:	Do you currently remember what time you went to the scene?
Witness:	No.
Plaintiff:	Would referring to those notes help you remember?
Witness:	Yes.
Plaintiff:	Let's mark these Plaintiff's Exhibit 1. Please look at this but don't read aloud.
Witness:	O.K. (looks at the notes).
Plaintiff:	After referring to the notes do you recall when you went to the scene?
Defendant:	Objection! Lack of foundation. We don't know whose notes those are.
Plaintiff:	It doesn't matter.
The court:	(2) ________ .

Witness:	Friday the 13th of May at 07:00 hours.
Plaintiff:	Do you remember the exact distances between the two cars after the impact?
Witness:	No.
Plaintiff:	Would referring to those notes help you remember?
Witness:	Gosh, to be real honest with you, its been so long ago, I don't think so.
Plaintiff:	Are those notes yours?
Witness:	No.
Plaintiff:	Whose are they?
Witness:	They were written by my colleague.
Plaintiff:	When?
Witness:	Oh, I saw them about a week later.
Plaintiff:	Were they correct when written?
Witness:	Yes.
Plaintiff:	Did you agree with them?
Witness:	Yes, you see my signature is on the bottom.
Plaintiff:	When you signed at the bottom, were the events fresh in your mind?
Witness:	Yes.
Plaintiff:	Your Honor, I'd like to introduce the notes.
Defendant:	Objection! Lack of foundation. He didn't make the notes, and it wasn't at the time of the event.
Plaintiff:	He adopted them.
The court:	(3) __________ .
Plaintiff:	May I provide copies for the jury, your honor?
Defendant:	Objection! Improper procedure.
The court:	(4) __________ .
Plaintiff:	What do the notes say about the distance between the cars.
Witness:	They were 15 feet apart.

[c] Hypnotically Refreshed Memory

PEOPLE v. ZAYAS

546 N.E.2d 513 (Ill. 1989)

JUSTICE RYAN delivered the opinion of the court:

Defendant, Fernando Zayas, was convicted in the circuit court of Cook County on three counts of murder. * * * We reverse, holding that a witness other than the defendant himself may not offer testimony to the extent that it is enhanced through hypnosis.

The trial court found defendant guilty of the shooting deaths of Miguel Vargas, Luis Cuaresma and Ruben Gutierrez. These three young men were brutally murdered on the front porch of a building on Chicago's northwest side in the early morning of July 2, 1983. * * *

[Detective Atkins testified for the State. Originally, he had stated that he saw a car that night with a possible license plate number XND 405. Then he was hypnotized by Dr. Braun, a psychiatrist certified in hypnosis, hypnotized Detective Atkins. The purpose of this hypnosis was to aid Detective Atkins in recalling the license plate number of the vehicle which he partially described earlier. Over defendant's objection, Detective Atkins testified that he recalled under hypnosis that the license plate number of the vehicle was NXJ 402. Detective Atkins testified to that effect. The actual license plate number of a car that would have tied the defendant to the scene was NXJ 240.]

Defendant contends on appeal that the testimony of Detective Atkins, insofar as he related to the jury that which he recalled under hypnosis, was inadmissible. * * *

Hypnosis is, to say the least, an enigma. Its therapeutic uses range from curing smoking to helping athletes deal better with stress. Its use in criminal investigations has increased dramatically in recent years, moreover, and its successes are almost legendary. It has not, however, been a stranger to failure.

The American Medical Association has defined hypnosis as the following:

> a temporary condition of altered attention in the subject which may be induced by another person and in which a variety of phenomena may appear spontaneously or in response to [verbal] or other stimuli. These phenomena include alterations in consciousness and memory, increased susceptibility to suggestion, and the production in the subject of responses and ideas unfamiliar to him in his usual state of mind.

As this rather imprecise definition indicates, the nature of hypnosis remains largely a mystery, and can be defined only by its symptoms and manifestations. * * * Because no one really understands it, hypnosis plays a rather dubious role in judicial proceedings.

There are essentially three different rules that this court could adopt regarding the admissibility of hypnotically refreshed recollections. There is certainly no consensus as to which is most appropriate. * * *

The first approach, originally espoused in *Harding v. State* (1968), 5 Md. App. 230, 246 A.2d 302, is a rule of *per se* admissibility which places the burden on the jury to determine the witness' credibility. The second approach, which the New Jersey Supreme Court adopted in *State v. Hurd* (1981), 86 N.J. 525, 432 A.2d 86, places the burden on the trial judge to determine whether law enforcement officials have complied with an elaborate list of procedural safeguards. The third rule, which has been labeled as the "emerging consensus" (*Zani v. State* (Tex. Crim. App. 1988), 758 S.W.2d 233, 240 n. 5), is a rule of *per se* inadmissibility which relieves trial judges of the burden of determining the quality of such evidence and relieves jurors of the responsibility of determining its credibility, tasks which neither are particularly well suited to perform because of the nature of this evidence.

The rule of *per se* admissibility has sparsely been followed since 1980. In fact, even in Maryland, where this rule was born, courts no longer follow it. * * * Because of its many flaws, this court has no interest in reviving it.

The basis of the rule set forth in *Harding* was that attorneys have an opportunity to cross-examine previously hypnotized witnesses and may present their own expert witnesses to rebut the testimony of the experts that the proponents of the evidence examined. This rationale is flawed in several respects. First, previously hypnotized witnesses are virtually immune from effective cross-examination. That is, having been hypnotized, the subject gains complete confidence in his "restored" memory, forgets how it was "restored," and is unable to differentiate between that which he was able to recall before hypnosis and that which the hypnosis elicited. Any information that the hypnotist suggested, or the subject fantasized or confabulated, becomes part of the subject's "restored" memory, moreover, and the subject is likewise unable to differentiate between this data and that which he was able to independently recall prior to being hypnotized. * * *

Another problem associated with merely allowing the jury to weigh the credibility of a previously hypnotized witness is that jurors are usually unable to properly do so. The public has been barraged with misinformation concerning hypnosis and has resultantly been led to incorrectly believe that it provides a panacea for lost memory. * * * While some studies show that, when properly administered, hypnosis can increase one's quantitative memory, these studies also demonstrate that subjects tend to fill in forgotten details with details they concoct and are later unable to discern between the two. * * *

The second alternative calls for the development of a strict set of procedural safeguards. The New Jersey Supreme Court set forth an elaborate set of procedural safeguards in *Hurd*. While these checks provide the trial court with an opportunity to effectively determine whether any conspicuous suggestiveness transpired during the hypnotic session, it does little to cure other problems inherent in the process.

One problem with allowing hypnotic testimony subject to procedural safeguards is that these checks do not detect whether the hypnotist unintentionally or subconsciously implanted suggestions in the mind of the subject. In fact, hypnosis by its very nature requires the hypnotist to suggest answers to the subject. The subject, moreover, will inevitably fill in missing details and fantasize about events that never in fact happened. Procedural safeguards do nothing, furthermore, to eliminate the problems associated with bolstered witness confidence and erroneous juror perception. Finally, this second alternative puts considerable strain on a trial court in that the court is forced to hear testimony from several competing experts and then make a rather sophisticated determination of whether the probative value of the testimony will outweigh its prejudicial effect.

Because of the shortcomings of these two rules, the third standard, that of *per se* inadmissibility, has gained wide-spread acceptance. * * * [H]aving been hypnotized, the subject's memory, and therefore his testimony, becomes the product of his prehypnosis memory, his memory as genuinely augmented by hypnosis, his fantasy and confabulation, and the suggestion of the hypnotist. The subject, the hypnotist, or any other objective observer cannot later decipher these various components. * * *

As such, we find that because its reliability is suspect, and it is not amenable to verification due to the fact that even the experts cannot agree upon its effectiveness as a memory-restorative device, a witness' hypnotically induced testimony, other than that of the defendant, is not admissible in Illinois courts. The fact that information elicited through hypnosis can be corroborated, moreover, does not permit a court to admit it as evidence. We are not concerned with whether evidence is plausible but, rather, whether evidence is reliable. The trial judge emphasized that he found no suggestion in the videotaped hypnotic session and that the information elicited through hypnosis would be corroborated by [the testimony of another witness]. This seems to indicate that if Detective Atkins would have recalled a license plate number that does not exist, the judge might not have admitted the evidence for the purpose of impeaching Officer Atkins' testimony. This is incongruous.

One argument that some have raised in opposition to a *per se* rule excluding hypnotically enhanced testimony is that it runs contrary to modern evidence rules which would allow the jury to hear all the evidence and draw its own conclusions, unless the trial judge determined that certain evidence was excessively prejudicial, and that this rule usurps the exclusive power of trial judges in making such decisions which they are better equipped to make. * * * While we agree this court should be cautious when intruding upon the truth-finding functions of trial courts, we think this rule will enhance rather than hinder that process. * * * [T]he probative value of any hypnotically enhanced testimony is questionable since most scientists doubt its accuracy. Furthermore, procedural safeguards do not cure these problems. Neither trial judges, nor juries, moreover, are well suited to take such evidence for what it may be worth because of erroneous public perception. Admission of such evidence at the discretion of trial judges would also result in inconsistent results and would strain the judicial process.

The State maintains that the only problem with which this court should concern itself with regard to hypnotically induced testimony is suggestiveness, and that no such suggestiveness is found in this case. First, as indicated earlier, suggestiveness is only one of a myriad of problems that hypnosis presents when offered as testimony in court. To say that suggestiveness is absent in this case, moreover, is a misstatement, for suggestion is an essential component of any hypnotic process. The fact that Dr. Braun was unaware of the license plate number is not determinative. The possibility that Dr. Braun suggested the actual license plate number is but one of many problems this court finds with the process. Some of the other problems that the trial court did not address, and could not properly address, include whether Officer Atkins received some suggestion of the actual license plate number before hypnosis, for instance from a picture or police report, the effect of the hypnosis on Officer Atkins regarding whether the State could properly cross-examine him, and the effect of the introduction of hypnotic evidence on the jury by bolstering jury confidence in Detective Atkins' testimony * * *. Because it could not properly make these determinations, this court finds that the trial court erred by allowing such testimony.

This ruling is not inconsistent with our prior holding * * * which allowed a witness to testify as to her prehypnotic recall. The proponent of prehypnotic recall evidence, however, will bear the burden of establishing that the testimony of the previously hypnotized witness is based solely upon that witness' independent, prehypnotic recall.

The ruling in this case is also consistent with the * * * Supreme Court ruling in *Rock v. Arkansas*, 483 U.S. 44 (1987). There, the Supreme Court ruled that a defendant may, by right, introduce hypnotic evidence because the defendant's right to testify on his own behalf, among other rights, outweighs the State's interest in excluding prejudicial evidence, and certain procedural safeguards will protect the integrity of the court. Our case, however, involves a witness for the State, not the defendant himself wishing to testify. As such, there are no constitutional implications and, therefore, *Rock* does not affect the decision in this case. While the Supreme Court did implicitly acknowledge that hypnotic evidence can have some probative value, its decision does not preclude this court from adopting a *per se* rule excluding the hypnotically enhanced testimony of a witness other than the defendant.

* * *

With the foregoing in mind, this court concludes that, without the hypnotically aided testimony of Officer Atkins, the jury quite possibly could have reached a different verdict. As it was, the jury deliberated over a day, was repeatedly instructed [about the importance of reaching a verdict], and reached its verdict at 6:30 p.m. on Good Friday. For these reasons, the defendant's convictions are reversed and the cause is remanded for a new trial.

NOTES

1. Is a *per se* rule against posthypnotic testimony constitutional?

While the majority of courts have held that testimony regarding recollection after hypnosis is *per se* inadmissible, the United States Supreme Court held in *Rock v. Arkansas*, 483 U.S. 44, 62 (1987), that a "*per se* rule excluding all posthypnosis testimony infringes impermissibly on the right of a (criminal) defendant to testify on his own behalf." As a constitutional decision, *Rock* is now binding on both state and federal courts.

In *Rock,* the defendant, charged with manslaughter for shooting her husband, underwent hypnosis with a trained neuropsychologist to refresh her memory. When she sought to testify that her gun had misfired, the state trial judge limited the testimony to matters remembered and stated to the psychologist before being hypnotized, even though her refreshed memory was consistent with defense expert testimony. Remanding, the Supreme Court held that the defendant's constitutional right to testify in her own behalf was violated by the ruling. Justice Blackmun's opinion for the court observed that a defendant's right to testify in her own behalf is not only guaranteed by the Due Process Clause and the Compulsory Process Clause, but also is a necessary corollary to the Fifth Amendment's guarantee against compelled testimony. Justice Blackmun recognized that "the right to present relevant testimony is not without limitation," but cautioned that "restrictions of a defendant's right to testify may not be arbitrary or disproportionate to the purposes they are designed to serve." He found that the Arkansas rule establishing a *per se* bar against posthypnosis testimony "operates to the detriment of any defendant who undergoes hypnosis, without regard to the reasons for it, the circumstances under which it took place, or any independent verification of the information it produced." Justice Blackmun noted that procedural safeguards might reduce the possibility of suggestiveness during hypnosis and concluded that Arkansas "has not justified the exclusion of all of a defendant's testimony that the defendant is unable to prove to be the product of prehypnosis memory," and that the state courts had not considered the arguments for admitting Rock's testimony in light of the corroboration of recalled details.

But as noted in *Zayas,* the *Rock* decision is grounded in the criminal defendant's constitutional rights. Thus, nothing in *Rock* prohibits a court from adopting a *per se* rule excluding hypnotically refreshed testimony when offered by the government in a criminal case.

2. If a court does not adopt a *per se* rule of exclusion, what factors should a court consider in reviewing hypnotically refreshed testimony?

In *Mersch v. City of Dallas*, 207 F.3d 732 (5th Cir. 2000), the court affirmed summary judgment against a plaintiff who alleged that police officers used excessive force in arresting her and rejected the plaintiff's claim that hypnotically-refreshed testimony about what happened during her arrest was sufficient to create a triable issue of fact. The court listed as relevant factors in deciding whether to admit hypnotically enhanced testimony whether "1) the hypnosis is done by a psychologist or psychiatrist trained in its use and independent of either party; 2) the hypnosis is done in a neutral setting with only the hypnotist and the subject present; 3) an audio or video recording is made of all interrogations before, during and after hypnosis; 4) corroborating evidence exists; and 5) the pre-hypnosis and post-hypnosis statements substantially correspond." In this case, the hypnotically-enhanced evidence was *per se* inadmissible because it involved a hypnotized subject identifying for the first time a person she had reason to know was already under suspicion. The court agreed with the approach of two cases from other Circuits (*Borawick v. Shay*, 68 F.3d 597 (2d Cir. 1995), and *Sprynczynatyk v. General Motors Corp.*, 771 F.2d 1112 (8th Cir. 1985)), which "impose on the proponent of the hypnotically-enhanced testimony the burden of proof during the proceeding and recommend that district courts conduct pretrial evidentiary hearings on the matter."

[4] Communication

[a] Illustration

A recent immigrant to the United States is called to the stand in a personal injury case.

Plaintiff:	Do you speak English?
Witness:	Um, um, do not follow much English.
Plaintiff:	Your Honor, this witness's native language is Spanish, and we have Professor Ortiz from State University here who is willing and able to interpret our questions and the witness's answers.

Court:	Any objection?
Defendant:	None.
Court:	The clerk will administer an oath to the interpreter. [Clerk administers oath.]
Plaintiff:	Can you describe the accident? [Interpreter translates in Spanish.]
Witness:	[Interpreter translates in English.] I saw the man sitting over there [pointing to defendant] drive his car through a red light.
Court:	I see a juror with a hand up. Do you wish to communicate with the Court? If so, please write down your communication using the paper and pen that the clerk will hand you.

Court at Sidebar Conference with counsel: The note from the juror indicates that she is from the same region as the witness and that the interpretation is incorrect, that the witness said that he saw the defendant but did not see whether the light was red.

Defendant: __________

[b] Interpreters

WATSON v. STATE
596 S.W.2d 867 (Tex. Crim. App. 1980)

CLINTON, JUDGE:

This is an appeal from a conviction for the offense of murder. Appellant, having been tried as an habitual offender under the ambit of V.T.C.A. Penal Code, § 12.42(d), was sentenced to confinement for life in the Texas Department of Corrections.

Though appellant presents some eleven grounds of error for our consideration, we need not reach each of these contentions. In his second ground of error, the contention is advanced that the trial court erred in permitting, over timely objection, an incompetent witness to testify. Further, as appellant contends in his third ground of error, the error was compounded by the trial court's appointment of an interpreter who was unqualified to "translate" the witness's testimony and who was something less than neutral and detached *vis a vis* the outcome of the proceedings. We agree and now reverse the judgment below.

The State's case consisted primarily of the testimony of one Jerry Lewayne Thomas, an accomplice to the offense, which was ostensibly corroborated by the testimony of George Keilmann, Sr., husband of the deceased. The elder Keilmann had been incapacitated by a stroke which left him unable to speak save for the expression "uh-huh." Keilmann was unable to write; though he retained the ability to *hear*, his capacity to *understand* questions asked of him was shown to be impaired.

Outside of the presence of the jury, Keilmann was examined by the respective parties and the trial court to determine if in fact he was competent to testify. The witness was first asked a series of routine leading questions to which he responded with the same answer, "uh-huh," to questions calling for an affirmative answer. However the witness displayed some difficulty in attempting to communicate a negative response, responding with the same "uh-huh" when asked by the trial court how he communicated such a negative response.

As the examination progressed, the witness failed to respond, either audibly or at all, to a series of questions propounded by the prosecutor. The witness was asked if he had been driving the family pickup truck on the day of the offense, to which he responded "uh-huh." However, the son of the witness, George Keilmann, Jr., definitely feeling that his father had answered the question in the affirmative, advised the court that his father had *not* been driving the vehicle on that day.

As the witness continued to have difficulty in responding to the prosecutor's leading questions, the following exchange occurred:

DEFENSE COUNSEL: I think the issue here is whether or not this gentleman can *understand* the questions as well as to *answer* [*sic*] the questions.

THE COURT: That is true. That is true.

DEFENSE COUNSEL: So far there hasn't —

THE COURT: He can obviously hear the questions and he can obviously make a response to what he hears. *The problem is do we understand the response and is our understanding adequate enough that he can testify.* That is the only problem that is involved in the case.

At this juncture, the brother-in-law of the witness volunteered the fact that the witness would be able to respond to "yes" or "no" questions with the aid of two cards labeled "yes" and "no." However this system of interrogation ran aground quickly when the witness pointed to the "yes" card while shaking his head to seemingly indicate "no," as well as indicating in the affirmative that his name was Steve Keilmann. * * *

Sometime later, Keilmann, Sr., again was examined outside the hearing of the jury, accompanied at this time by a woman who "had been taking care" of him for some six months. In attempting to explain to the trial court how in fact she was able to distinguish Keilmann's "yes" answers from his "no" answers, the witness recounted:

> Well, his yes answers [sic] he puts quite a bit of emphasis on his yes answers and he will bow to you usually. And if he is saying no he usually grabs you. That means to halt, and then he will explain whatever he is trying to tell you over.

The woman did admit, however, that the two really did not talk as such but could "communicate."

Still outside the presence of the jury, and with his "interpreter" at his side, the witness responded in the affirmative to several leading questions and then at the behest of the trial court communicated what the interpreter felt to be "correct" negative answers to several other questions.

At the conclusion of this examination, the following colloquy ensued between the trial court and defense counsel:

THE COURT: Okay. Are you going to take objection to his testifying.

DEFENSE COUNSEL: Absolutely, Your Honor. We don't feel this is competent testimony. I don't think it has been proven the gentleman understands the questions and as far as his responses are concerned they have been very unclear. And when he has answered incorrectly they [the prosecutor] ask him again and again until he gets a correct answer. I just don't feel like this is an appropriate situation for this kind of testimony.

THE COURT: Well, it appears to me, although he is disabled, he does appear to understand the questions put to him. And I don't — while I don't always understand the responses, *she appears to understand the responses* and she knows him better and [sic] I do. So over your objection I am going to admit that testimony. * * * Because the weight of it — the admissibility is for me but the weight is for the jury.

After the jury had been brought back into the courtroom, defense counsel renewed his initial objection and additionally noted:

That this lady, there has been no foundation laid for the appropriateness of her testimony, nor do we have any evidence that she is in fact able to interpret his —

The trial court overruled this objection pointing out that he would eventually charge the jury that they were the sole judges of the credibility of the witnesses and the weight to be given their testimony.

The interpreter was sworn and in the presence of the jury, the trial court permitted Keilmann, Sr. to "testify" about the events on the day of the offense. It was thereby brought out that the witness and his late wife went to the Finney ranch on July 21, 1977 in the family pickup truck. Upon arriving at the ranch, the witness was apparently pulled out of the truck by a black man with a gun. Though the witness first denied that the gun was in fact a rifle, he later indicated that his assailant pointed a rifle at him. The witness was said to have communicated that after his wife got out of the truck, he did not see where she went nor did he see anyone strike her.

When asked if he could point out his assailant in the courtroom, the interpreter noted that the witness did not seem to understand the question. The prosecution suggested that appellant stand to facilitate the identification process to which appellant objected. The trial court sustained the objection. The witness was then asked if he remembered what the man who pulled him out of the truck looked like to which he responded no. The witness then pointed at *someone* and in response to whether that someone was the man he saw at the Finney ranch, the interpreter noted the answer was yes. The record, however, is unclear as to whom he was pointing.

On cross examination, the witness was asked to point to the man he saw at the Finney ranch and the following exchange occurred:

DEFENSE COUNSEL: Let the record reflect that the witness pointed at this man standing to my right in the red jacket. Let the record reflect the man pointed again to my left at the defendant.

THE COURT: *I can't tell from my angle which way he is pointing, Counsel.*

PROSECUTOR: Your Honor, the last time he pointed he pointed at the defendant.

DEFENSE COUNSEL: The first time he pointed at the man in the red jacket, Your Honor.

THE COURT: I am going to overrule both your objections. Let's proceed.

The witness then contradicted the earlier interpretation by agreeing that he in fact saw a man strike his wife. When asked if there were two men at the Finney ranch that day, the interpreter responded that the witness did not know. Finally, the witness indicated that the man who pulled him out of the truck later moved the truck from where it had been parked.

* * *

It has * * * been said that there are three elements which must be considered in determining whether a witness is in fact competent to testify. The first is a capacity to observe intelligently at the time of the events in question. The other elements of capacity are recollection and narration, though the former is usually merged into the latter. * * * The capacity to narrate involves on the one hand, both an ability to understand the questions asked and to frame intelligent answers and, on the other hand, a moral responsibility to tell the truth. If a person afflicted with a physical or mental disability possesses sufficient intelligence to receive correct impressions of events he sees, retains clear recollection of them and is *able to communicate them through some means* there is no reason for rejecting his testimony. * * *

It is uncontradicted that Keilmann had the ability to observe the events as they occurred, though the record is something less than lucid as to his recollection and is replete with problems of narration, as that term is defined above. Of course, the issue of a witness's competency is generally a question for the trial court and its ruling in that regard will not be disturbed on appeal unless an abuse of discretion can be shown. * * * A detailed examination of the witness's testimony compels us to hold, however, that there was such an abuse of discretion by the trial court in permitting the witness to testify.

* * * Aside from the fact that there was no showing that the witness understood an obligation for the oath, the trial judge himself recognized early on the problems inherent in attempting to have the witness testify. * * * The contradictory nature of the witness's responses, his inability to distinguish or otherwise "communicate" negative as opposed to affirmative answers, notwithstanding the leading nature of the questions asked him, all militate towards a finding that the witness was incapable of "narration" as that term is defined by commentators.

* * *

Appointment of the interpreter in the case at bar compounded an already evident abuse of discretion, inasmuch as there was no showing that the individual was in fact qualified to "interpret" the witness's testimony. * * * [T]he interpreter in the case at bar was a woman who "had been taking care of" Keilmann for some six months and who felt that she and the witness could "communicate." In eventually deciding that the woman would be permitted to interpret, the trial court stated: "while I don't always understand the responses [of the witness], she appears to understand the responses and she knows him better [than] I do."

Simply put, the trial court's own remarks would seem to indicate that there would be no conceivable manner in which the interpreter's "translation" could be tested for obviously there was no one else available to act as an intermediary in that regard. * * *

Perhaps on retrial, the witness's condition, from the therapy and training that he has undergone in the interim, will be so improved as to obviate the need for an interpreter or to adapt to some other means of communication. Regardless of what may or may not be possible, the trial court abused its discretion in permitting the elder Keilmann to testify in the unusual circumstances presented. Due process, whose essence is fundamental fairness, was denied.

For the errors pointed out, the judgment is reversed and the cause remanded.

NOTES

1. What qualifications must an interpreter possess in order to aid a witness in his testimony?

Fed. R. Evid. 604 states that "[a]n interpreter is subject to the provisions of these rules relating to qualification as an expert and the administration of an oath or affirmation to make a true translation." To qualify as an expert under Fed. R. Evid. 702, the interpreter must possess sufficient "knowledge, skill, experience, training, or education."

2. What oath must a translator take?

In *United States v. Armijo*, 5 F.3d 1229 (9th Cir. 1993), a prosecution for cocaine distribution, a court translator had translated a recorded conversation; when she testified, she was asked only to swear that she translated the tape to the best of her ability, but she did not take a standard witness oath. The court held that there was no error, because her testimony related only to the accuracy and validity of the translation, which she had sworn to translate as accurately as she could. Thus, the witness testified to no statement of fact that was not covered by the oath. The dissenting judge argued as follows: the failure to inform the witness of her duty to tell the truth on the stand and of the penalty for perjury denied the defendant's right to meaningful confrontation; the examination of the witness tested her credibility as well as the accuracy of her translation; and the standing oath she had taken as an interpreter was insufficient as an oath for a witness.

Chapter 4

RELEVANCE

A. INTRODUCTION

[1] Federal Rules of Evidence 401, 402, and 403

Rule 401. Definition of "Relevant Evidence"

"Relevant evidence" means evidence having any tendency to make the existence of any fact that is of consequence to the determination of the action more probable or less probable than it would be without the evidence.

Rule 402. Relevant Evidence Generally Admissible; Irrelevant Evidence Inadmissible

All relevant evidence is admissible, except as otherwise provided by the Constitution of the United States, by Act of Congress, by these rules, or by other rules prescribed by the Supreme Court pursuant to statutory authority. Evidence which is not relevant is not admissible.

Rule 403. Exclusion of Relevant Evidence on Grounds of Prejudice, Confusion, or Waste of Time

Although relevant, evidence may be excluded if its probative value is substantially outweighed by the danger of unfair prejudice, confusion of the issues, or misleading the jury, or by considerations of undue delay, waste of time, or needless presentation of cumulative evidence.

NOTES

1. Does "materiality" have any independent meaning under the Federal Rules?

Rule 401 does not explicitly treat "materiality" as a separate concept. Both traditional requirements of relevance analysis — that evidence must relate to issues that are properly in dispute and that it must shed some light on those issues — are combined into one rule. Thus, the traditional objection that evidence is "irrelevant and immaterial" is no longer correct because materiality is subsumed within the concept of relevance. Whether an issue is properly in dispute is, of course, determined by the applicable substantive law. *See, e.g., Phillips v. Western Co. of N. Am.*, 953 F.2d 923 (5th Cir. 1992) (where substantive law prohibits a setoff for collateral benefits already received by an injury victim, evidence of such benefits has no relevance to the case and is inadmissible).

2. What is the role of circumstantial evidence under Rule 401?

The difficult relevance issues involve circumstantial, as opposed to direct, evidence. If direct eyewitness testimony, for instance, is offered that the defendant in a bank robbery prosecution was the robber, the evidence is clearly relevant, because it relates to a proposition provable in the case. No inferences are required between the proof itself and the ultimate fact to be established. If, however, the testimony proves the robber wore a blue coat and the defendant owns a blue coat, this is circumstantial evidence and the judge must decide whether, if believed, it makes a disputed fact more or less probable. It is here that hard questions arise.

There is no litmus paper test or simple formula for determining whether proffered circumstantial evidence is relevant. Logic and experience together must supply the judge with skills in determining whether a given piece of evidence tends to prove a disputed proposition.[1] Sometimes expert witnesses may be necessary to assist the court in making a relevance determination. And the judge must also consider not only whether the admission of evidence is likely to advance the cause, but also whether its absence might produce negative inferences that would unfairly hurt a party — *i.e.*, the absence of evidence might be probative to a jury that would have expected certain evidence to be presented if it existed. *See, e.g., Blinzler v. Marriott Int'l, 81 F.3d 1148* (1st Cir. 1996) ("When a document relevant to a case is destroyed, the trier of fact sometimes may infer that the party who obliterated it did so out of a realization that the contents were unfavorable.").

All this is not to say that circumstantial evidence is less important or less significant than direct evidence. To the contrary, in some cases circumstantial evidence (*e.g.*, a large amount of trace money from a bank robbery) may have more power than direct evidence (*e.g.*, dubious or fleeting eyewitness testimony). *United States v. Russell*, 919 F.2d 795 (1st Cir. 1990) (circumstantial evidence is not some form of second-rate evidence, and in appropriate cases it may be given as much or more weight than direct evidence).

---

[1] *See, e.g., United States v. Anglin*, 169 F.3d 154 (2d Cir. 1999) (in an armed robbery case, evidence of the defendant's post-robbery cash expenditures was probative circumstantial evidence); *United States v. Grier*, 866 F.2d 908 (7th Cir. 1989) (in a drug conspiracy case, evidence was presented of a note found in the apartment of Harper's codefendant; the note contained Harper's name and telephone number; this was probative of conspiracy between the codefendant and Harper, and admissible under Rules 401 and 402, because it tended "to make Harper's involvement in the conspiracy more probable than it would be without the evidence" even though the note would not be sufficient to convict; the note was circumstantial evidence that "Harper was participating in the conspiracy and aware of its magnitude").

B. ANY TENDENCY

UNITED STATES v. FOSTER
986 F.2d 541 (D.C. Cir. 1993)

RANDOLPH, CIRCUIT JUDGE:

* * *

After a jury trial, James A. Foster was convicted of unlawfully possessing more than 5 grams of crack cocaine with intent to distribute and of committing the offense within 1000 feet of a school. Sergeant Thomas Clark of the U.S. Park Police was the critical witness for the prosecution. His identification of Foster supplied the only evidence directly linking Foster with the cocaine.

The facts, as Sergeant Clark related them, are these. On a clear, sunny August afternoon, Clark settled into his observation post in a District of Columbia neighborhood known for its illicit drug activity. Thirty to forty feet below him and 150 yards away, near an apartment complex, were a parking lot, a basketball court and a playground. Clark was watching this area with 10 × 50 binoculars when he spotted an individual, whom he later identified as Foster, sitting in the front seat of a car in the parking lot.

Events typical of drug dealing then unfolded. Sergeant Clark saw Foster give something to someone in the back seat, leave the car, walk to the basketball court, receive money from another individual, count the bills, hand over a small white object, walk away, take two clear plastic bags from his pocket, put them into a brown paper bag, drop the bag over a chain link fence, pick up the bag again, walk over to the apartment building and drop the paper bag near another fence. Clark radioed a description of Foster. Other officers arrived at the scene. One arrested Foster and found $311 on him. Another officer retrieved the brown bag. It held 51 packets of crack cocaine.

* * *

I

* * *

II

Sergeant Clark testified on direct that he saw Foster pass something to a person seated in the back seat of a car. The first objection came when defense counsel asked Clark if he had been able to observe the features of the other person. The second objection, actually a series of objections, came in response to defense questions posed to Clark and Officer Egan, who had been called to the scene, asking whether Clark had broadcast the description not only of Foster but also of another individual Clark suspected of drug dealing in the same area at the same time.

We think both lines of inquiry sought to elicit relevant evidence and that the district court erred in sustaining the government's objections. The general rule is that relevant evidence is admissible. Rule 402, Fed. R. Evid. Relevant evidence, Rule 401 tells us, is "evidence having any tendency to make the existence of any fact that is of consequence to the determination of the action more probable or less probable than it would be without the evidence." Under this test, there is no such thing as "highly relevant" evidence or, as the government puts it in its brief, "marginally relevant" evidence. Evidence is either relevant or it is not.

"Relevancy is not an inherent characteristic of any item of evidence but exists only as a relation between an item of evidence and a matter properly provable in the case." Advisory Committee's Note to Rule 401, Fed. R. Evid. The initial step in determining relevancy is therefore to identify the "matter properly provable." As Professor James explained in a highly-regarded article, "[t]o discover the relevancy of an offered item of evidence one must first discover to what proposition it is supposed to be relevant." James, *Relevancy, Probability and the Law,* 29 Cal. L. Rev. 689, 696 n. 15 (1941).

Whether Clark could see inside the car on the parking lot well enough to identify its occupants was a matter of consequence at trial. If he could not perceive the features of the person in the back seat this would tend to make it less likely that he was able to recognize the person in the front seat as Foster, and vice versa. Defense counsel's question to Clark about this subject therefore sought relevant evidence and the district court should have allowed it. It is of no moment that a negative answer by Clark would not have conclusively proven that he had misidentified Foster as the person possessing the bag of cocaine. Evaluating all the evidence on a particular issue is for the jury. Each piece of evidence need not be conclusive: "A brick is not a wall." 1 McCormick on Evidence § 185, at 776 (J. Strong ed., 4th ed. 1992); *see* Advisory Committee's Note to Rule 401, Fed. R. Evid.

The questions whether Clark had broadcast the description of another individual suspected of drug dealing also sought relevant evidence. Depending on Clark's response, his answer would have had a tendency to make it more or less probable that he had confused Foster with the other person. In its case-in-chief the government put on evidence that Clark had radioed a description tallying with Foster's — a black male, about 25 years old, 6 feet tall, 150–160 pounds, with a goatee. The relevancy of Clark's and Egan's answers to the questions propounded by defense counsel illustrates Wigmore's principle of "explanation." Wigmore demonstrated that "every evidentiary fact or class of facts may call for two processes and raise two sets of questions: (1) the admissibility of the original fact from the proponent, and (2) the admissibility of explanatory facts from the opponent." 1A J. Wigmore, Evidence § 36, at 1004. It is always open in a criminal case for the defendant to explain away the force of specific items of the government's proof by showing the existence of other hypotheses. "[F]or this purpose other facts affording such explanations are receivable from the [defendant]." *Id.* The district court therefore should have allowed these questions.

For the reasons given, Foster's conviction is reversed and the case is remanded for a retrial in accordance with this opinion.

NOTES

1. What is the distinction between relevance and sufficiency?

See Saltzburg, Martin, and Capra, *Federal Rules of Evidence Manual* (9th ed. 2006):

> The important thing for the Judge and for counsel to remember is that the evidence does not by itself have to prove the ultimate proposition for which it is offered; nor does it have to make that ultimate proposition more probable than not. To be relevant it is enough that the evidence has a *tendency* to make a consequential fact even the least bit more probable or less probable than it would be without the evidence. The question of relevance is thus different from whether evidence is *sufficient* to prove a point.[2]
>
> An example may help to clarify the difference between relevance and sufficiency. Assume that a defendant is charged with an armed robbery committed by someone carrying a handgun. The prosecution wants to offer into evidence testimony that the defendant owned a handgun prior to the time the robbery was committed. Defendant claims the evidence is irrelevant. Certainly this evidence, standing alone, does not make it more probable than not that the defendant committed the crime. Furthermore, it is *a fortiori* not sufficient to prove beyond a reasonable doubt that the defendant committed the crime. The evidence is clearly insufficient on its own to prove the defendant's guilt. But it is a piece of evidence, the existence of which makes it somewhat more likely that the defendant committed the crime than if there were no such evidence. Therefore it is relevant. Thus, relevancy is a threshold admissibility standard to be applied by the Trial Judge. It is up to the trier of fact to weigh the evidence and to determine whether the entirety of the evidence is sufficient to prove a point.

2. Can evidence be excluded on grounds that it is "too remote"?

Occasionally a trial judge will exclude evidence on the basis of remoteness, which is to say that the evidence is too far removed in space or time from the proposition that it is offered to prove. For example, assume a two-car accident where the defendant is trying to prove that the plaintiff was not wearing a seatbelt. If the defendant calls a witness who testifies that he saw the plaintiff driving without a seatbelt a few minutes before the accident, this testimony is undoubtedly relevant; it tends to prove that the plaintiff was not wearing a seatbelt an hour later. *See, e.g., Hill v. Rolleri*, 615 F.2d 886 (9th

---

[2] *See, e.g., Douglass v. Eaton Corp.*, 956 F.2d 1339 (6th Cir. 1992) (Trial Court ruling on whether evidence is relevant may not consider the sufficiency or weight of the evidence; even if the evidence is insufficient to prove the point for which it is offered, the Trial Court "may not exclude the evidence if it has even the slightest probative worth," unless some other Rule such as 403 warrants exclusion); *Smith v. Georgia*, 684 F.2d 729 (11th Cir. 1982) ("Of course, evidence need not prove the proposition for which it is offered to be probative. Rule 401 states that evidence is relevant if it makes the existence of any fact more probable or less probable than it would be without the evidence."). *See also Daubert v. Merrell Dow Pharmaceuticals, Inc.*, 509 U.S. 579 (1993) (Rule 401 relevance standard is "a liberal one").

Cir. 1980) (testimony concerning driver's reckless driving ten minutes before an accident was probative of whether he was engaged in reckless driving at the time of the accident). On the other hand, if the witness testifies that he saw the plaintiff driving without a seatbelt two years before the accident, the trial court is likely to exclude the testimony as too remote. Or assume that the plaintiff must prove icy conditions at 2 a.m. on a road in Montana. Evidence that the road was icy at midnight tends to prove that it was icy two hours later. But evidence that it was icy two weeks before or after the pertinent time is probably too remote, as is evidence of an icy road 20 miles west.

When evidence is excluded as too remote, it is not that it fails to fit the definition of relevant evidence. The definition of relevance in Rule 401 is permissive, to say the least, and the fact that the plaintiff was not wearing a seatbelt two years earlier has at least *some* tendency to prove that he was not wearing one at the time of the accident. Exclusion on grounds of remoteness is better understood as an exercise of the trial court's discretion under Rule 403. That is, the probative value of the evidence is, while not non-existent, at least minimal due to the gap in time and/or space between the fact proffered and the event to be proved. This minimal probative value can be substantially outweighed by the confusion and delay that would result from introducing the evidence. *See, e.g., United States v. Ellzey*, 936 F.2d 492 (10th Cir. 1991) (evidence properly excluded under Rule 403 due to the "remote and tenuous link" between the evidence and the charged crime).

3. What if a fact is only relevant if another fact exists?

By its terms, Rule 401 does not cover the concept of "conditional" relevancy. Evidence is conditionally relevant when its probative value depends upon the existence of another fact. For example, a statement may be probative that a party was aware of a dangerous condition — but only if the party heard the statement.

Rule 104(b) governs conditional relevancy and provides as follows:

> When the relevancy of evidence depends upon the fulfillment of a condition of fact, the court shall admit it upon, or subject to, the introduction of evidence sufficient to support a finding of the fulfillment of the condition.

Under Rule 104(b), the proponent of evidence that is relevant only if a condition is met must provide a foundation that the condition exists. That foundation is stated as "enough evidence to support a finding" of the conditional fact. To take the example of a statement offered to prove notice, the proponent must provide enough proof for a reasonable person to believe that the party heard the statement. Then the relevance of the evidence is considered under Rules 401–403.

Under Rule 104(b), the trial judge has discretion to either require proof of the condition in advance, or to admit the evidence of the fact subject to "connecting up" by later proof of the condition. If the party fails to provide the connection, the trial judge will strike the evidence and in extreme cases a mistrial will be granted or a judgment reversed. *See United States v. Cote,*

744 F.2d 913 (2d Cir. 1984) (admission of prior crimes requires reversal where the government failed to provide evidence connecting them to the defendant; while appreciating "the need for leeway so counsel may select the most persuasive order of proof," the court cautioned that "representations, express or implied, that otherwise irrelevant evidence will be tied to a defendant should not be made without a good faith and objectively reasonable belief that the missing links will in fact be supplied").

4. Can the failure to introduce evidence ever be admissible as relevant evidence?

See United States v. Tory, 52 F.3d 207 (9th Cir. 1995): In a trial for armed bank robbery, the disputed question was whether the defendant had a gun. The bank teller testified that the defendant had a gun stuffed in the waistband of his pants during the robbery. The defendant argued that he was wearing sweatpants during the robbery, and thus he could not have been carrying a gun in his waistband, because it would have fallen from his sweatpants as he ran from the bank. Defense counsel attempted to argue on closing argument that the prosecution had bank surveillance photos in its possession, and that if the prosecution had produced the photos at trial, it would have cleared up the question of whether the defendant was wearing sweatpants during the robbery. Defense counsel contended that he should be permitted to ask the jury to draw a negative inference from the fact that the prosecution had chosen not to introduce the bank photos in its possession. The trial court prohibited defense counsel from referring to the bank photos, but the court of appeals found this to be an abuse of discretion. The court of appeals stated that the defense "should have been allowed to argue that the government's failure to produce relevant evidence within its control gives rise to an inference that the evidence would be unfavorable to it." In light of this and other evidentiary errors, the court reversed the defendant's armed robbery conviction.

C. FACT OF CONSEQUENCE

UNITED STATES v. HALL
653 F.2d 1002 (5th Cir. 1981)

TATE, CIRCUIT JUDGE:

Christopher Hall was tried to a jury on charges of conspiring to distribute and to possess with intent to distribute cocaine (Count I), possessing with intent to distribute cocaine (Count II), and distributing cocaine (Counts III and IV), in violation of 21 U.S.C. §§ 841(a)(1), 846 and 18 U.S.C. § 2. He was convicted of conspiracy and distribution (Counts I, III, and IV) and sentenced to ten years' imprisonment with nine years and nine months suspended and a five year term of probation.

* * *

Because we agree that the court below erred in admitting irrelevant and highly prejudicial opinion testimony by an agent of the federal Drug Enforcement Administration (DEA), we reverse the convictions and remand the case to the district court for a new trial.

I.

The government's case at trial rested primarily upon the testimony of Hall's alleged coconspirators, James Worthy, Jack Beck, and Debbie Ryan, all of whom testified under the auspices of plea bargaining agreements with the government. This testimony was uncorroborated by physical evidence — the government had made no "controlled buy" or seizure of cocaine in connection with any of the transactions covered in the indictment.

Hall stood silent at his trial. The theory of his defense was that the three key government witnesses, in an effort to reap the benefits of cooperation with the government and at the same time to protect their true source of supply, offered him up to federal prosecution as a convenient scapegoat. In support of this theory, Hall sought to impeach the credibility of the witnesses against him by bringing out the details of their plea agreements with the government, their relationships to one another, and their other potential motivations for lying, and by stressing the total absence of any corroborating physical evidence to support their version of the facts.

To bolster its case, the government called its final witness, DEA agent John Donald. Donald did not participate in the investigation leading to Hall's arrest and prosecution, and was in no way connected with the development of the case against Hall. The sole purpose of his testimony was to respond to defense counsel's suggestion that the government had been unable to obtain corroborating physical evidence against Hall because Hall was innocent of the offenses charged. Donald testified in general terms about the various procedures used by the DEA in its narcotics investigations. In sum, Donald described the various investigative techniques and testified that it is not always possible to conduct a "controlled buy" and seizure of narcotics during the course of an investigation, particularly where the conspiracy under investigation has already terminated by the time the investigation is commenced or the subject of the investigation is insulated in the higher echelons of the narcotics conspiracy.

Hall's strenuous objections to this line of testimony were overruled by the district court. On appeal, Hall renews those objections, contending that the testimony of agent Donald should have been excluded as irrelevant or, if relevant, as unfairly prejudicial.

We must agree.

The essential prerequisite of admissibility is relevance. Fed. R. Ev. 402. To be relevant, evidence must have some "tendency to make the existence of any fact that is of consequence to the determination of the action more probable or less probable than it would be without the evidence." Implicit in that definition are two distinct requirements: (1) The evidence must be probative of the proposition it is offered to prove, and (2) the proposition to be proved must be one that is of consequence to the determination of the action. Whether a proposition is of consequence to the determination of the action is a question that is governed by the substantive law. * * *

The governing hypothesis of any criminal prosecution consists of the elements of the offenses charged and the relevant defenses (if any) raised to defeat criminal liability. As characterized by the government, Donald's testimony was offered to show that the DEA routinely utilized procedures other than the controlled buy and seizure method in order to develop criminal narcotics cases. In essence, Donald testified as a kind of quasi-expert on DEA investigative procedures, and his testimony was limited to the general and quite hypothetical descriptions of accepted practice that are typical of the expert witness. He testified to no facts bearing on any manner on the prosecution of Christopher Hall or on the investigation leading to that prosecution. His testimony had no tendency whatsoever to make the existence of any fact of consequence to the government's case in chief either more or less probable than it would have been without his testimony. Clearly, then, in the context of the government's case in chief, agent Donald's opinion testimony lacked substantial relevance to any matter in issue, and was therefore not admissible.

* * *

We conclude, therefore, that the testimony of the DEA agent John Donald lacked substantial relevance to any matters in issue in this case and was improperly admitted. That error was not harmless. The agent's "expert" generalities about the difficulty of making controlled buys and seizures of narcotics from individuals insulated in the higher echelons of drug conspiracies clearly and improperly suggested to the trial jury — in the absence of any substantial evidence to that effect — that Christopher Hall was just such a high-ranking conspirator. The risk of unfair prejudice inherent in such damning generalities — alone enough to warrant reversal, see Fed. R. Ev. 403 — is exacerbated by the nature of the testimony itself. Reduced to its essentials, Donald's testimony constituted little more than a (quasi-) expert commentary on the strength of the government's proof. Its sole purpose was to inform the jury that it need not view the absence of corroborating physical evidence as a weakness in the government's case. Such "evidence" has no place in a criminal trial.

* * *

Reversed and remanded.

NOTE

What is the role of the substantive law in determining whether proffered evidence tends to prove a fact "of consequence"?

Assume that the plaintiff is a mother whose child was run down and killed by a car. Assume further that the plaintiff proffers compelling evidence of emotional distress that she suffered as a result of losing her child. In many states, this evidence is not relevant unless the mother could prove that she was in the "zone of danger" at the time that her child was killed. Where such a state law provides the rule of decision in federal court, the evidence of emotional distress is irrelevant under Rule 401. This is because the mother's emotional distress is not "in dispute" under the state's substantive law unless she was in the zone of danger, and it is the state substantive law which determines the issues in dispute in such cases. *See Garland v. Herrin,* 724 F.2d 16 (2d Cir. 1983) (evidence of parents' emotional distress over the murder of their daughter held irrelevant because "New York law does not permit a bystander to recover for psychic injury for harm inflicted on another"). *See also Phillips v. Western Co. of N. Am.*, 953 F.2d 923 (5th Cir. 1992) (where substantive law prohibits a setoff for collateral benefits already received by an injury victim, evidence of such benefits has no relevance to the case and is inadmissible).

D. SOURCES OF AUTHORITY FOR EXCLUDING RELEVANT EVIDENCE

UNITED STATES v. LOWERY
166 F.3d 1119 (11th Cir. 1999)

CARNES, CIRCUIT JUDGE:

* * * These defendants, in separate criminal cases, prevailed upon the district court to grant their pretrial motions to suppress the testimony of their alleged co-conspirators. That expected testimony had been obtained through plea agreements in which the government promised to consider recommending a lighter sentence in exchange for the alleged co-conspirators' substantial assistance in the prosecution of the remaining defendants, i.e., these appellees.

The district court (the same judge in each case) held that such agreements, although commonplace in the criminal justice system, are prohibited by 18 U.S.C. § 201(c)(2), which makes it a crime to give or promise anything of value for testimony. The court also held that the agreements violated Rule 4–3.4(b) of the Florida Bar Rules of Professional Conduct. It suppressed the testimony obtained through the agreements on both grounds. We reverse.

I. BACKGROUND

We first discuss the procedural facts of each of the three cases.

[In each of these consolidated cases, the defendants moved to exclude the testimony of cooperating witnesses. The testimony was undeniably relevant, but the defendants argued that the testimony had to be excluded because it was in violation of a federal statute prohibiting bribery of witnesses, as well as a state standard of professional responsibility that prohibits a lawyer from giving anything of value to a witness. The defendants argued, and the trial court agreed, that the witnesses received something of value for testifying — specifically a guarantee of a lesser sentence. As to the federal bribery question, the defendants relied on an interpretation of 18 U.S.C. § 201(c)(2) (the federal bribery statute) offered by a panel of the Tenth Circuit in *United States v. Singleton,* 144 F.3d 1343 (10th Cir. 1998), *rev'd en banc,* 165 F.3d 1297 (10th Cir. 1999).]

II. DISCUSSION

* * *

A. 18 U.S.C. § 201(c)(2)

As we have said, this appeal involves what has come to be known as "the *Singleton* issue." The issue is whether plea agreements of the kind found in this case violate the federal prohibition against bribing witnesses contained in 18 U.S.C. § 201(c)(2).

Since the Tenth Circuit panel issued its opinion in *Singleton,* three circuits have rejected its holding that government plea agreements violate § 201(c)(2). The Tenth Circuit itself, sitting en banc, has since reversed the panel decision. *See United States v. Singleton,* 165 F.3d 1297 (10th Cir. 1999). It is not the law of any circuit.

An overwhelming number of the district courts that have considered the issue have also rejected the holding of the panel decision in *Singleton.* * * * In joining the cavalcade — or perhaps we should say stampede — of courts that have considered and rejected the *Singleton* panel's holding, we see no point in going over ground that has been thoroughly trod by the other courts whose decisions we have already cited. But we do wish to discuss the following point, which is not given much attention in those decisions.

The best argument that the defendants can muster in their efforts to bring government plea agreements containing cooperation clauses within the terms of 18 U.S.C. § 201(c)(2) is that the plain meaning of that statutory language requires such a reading. The statute says "Whoever * * *" and that word obviously includes everyone, even the government. Or so the argument goes. The reason this "best" argument is not good enough to carry the day should itself be plain.

The statutory language in question has been on the books since 1962. During the three and a half decades of its existence, what the defendants now claim is the plain meaning of that language has not been plain to the thousands of prosecutors, judges, and defense lawyers who have been involved with testimony for leniency agreements over the decades. * * * These type of agreements have been used extensively in federal prosecutions, both long before and continually since the statutory prohibition in question was enacted. Testimony derived through them is a commonplace feature of trials. * * * If it were plain from the statutory language that entering this type of agreement was a crime, the legions of attorneys who have represented defendants convicted over the years because of testimony dependent upon such illegal agreements would have raised the issue day in and day out in every district court in every circuit in the country. They did not. The sound of their silence is deafening.

Joining all those other courts that have rejected the reasoning and holding of the now-vacated panel decision in *Singleton,* we hold that agreements in which the government trades sentencing recommendations or other official action or consideration for cooperation, including testimony, do not violate 18 U.S.C. § 201(c)(2).

B. FLORIDA BAR RULE OF PROFESSIONAL CONDUCT 4–3.4(B)

The district court also held that the plea agreements with the cooperating co-defendants in these cases violated Rule 4–3.4(b) of the Florida Bar Rules of Professional Conduct, and the resulting testimony was due to be suppressed for that reason. The relevant portion of the Florida rule forbids lawyers from "offer[ing] an inducement to a witness* * * ."

As an initial matter, it is not clear that at the time the plea agreements in this case were negotiated, the Florida Bar Rules of Professional Conduct applied to the conduct of the United States attorneys in this case, though the local rules of the Southern District of Florida do incorporate them. *See* Local Rules of the United States District Court for the Southern District of Florida, Rules Governing Attorney Discipline, Rule I. A (West 1998). Congress has since indicated that state rules of professional conduct should apply to the conduct of federal government attorneys. *See* 28 U.S.C. § 530(b).) ("An attorney for the Government shall be subject to State laws and rules, and local Federal court rules, governing attorneys in each State where such attorney engages in that attorney's duties, to the same extent and in the same manner as other attorneys in that State."). * * * Assuming for present purposes that the rule is violated when a prosecutor promises a witness some consideration regarding charges or sentencing in return for testimony, a state rule of professional conduct cannot provide an adequate basis for a federal court to suppress evidence that is otherwise admissible. Federal law, not state law, determines the admissibility of evidence in federal court. * * * Federal Rule of Evidence 402 provides:

> All relevant evidence is admissible, except as otherwise provided by the Constitution of the United States, by Act of Congress, by these rules, or by other rules prescribed by the Supreme Court pursuant to statutory authority.

That is an exclusive list of the sources of authority for exclusion of evidence in federal court. State rules of professional conduct are not included in the list.

Local rules of federal courts are not listed in Rule 402, either. As a result, otherwise admissible evidence cannot be excluded based upon local rules. For that reason, the Southern District of Florida's adoption of the State of Florida's professional conduct rules does not affect our analysis or the result. Acts of Congress are included in the Rule 402 list, of course, because Congress has the authority to exclude from evidence in federal courts anything it pleases, subject only to the limits placed upon it by the Constitution. The question is whether Congress' recent statutory directive that state laws and rules governing attorney conduct shall apply to federal government attorneys "to the same extent and in the same manner as other attorneys in that State," is aimed at admission of evidence in federal court. In other words, did Congress intend by that enactment to turn over to state supreme courts in every state — and state legislatures, too, assuming they can also enact codes of professional conduct for attorneys — the authority to decide that otherwise admissible evidence cannot be used in federal court? We think not.

There is nothing in the language or legislative history of the Act that would support such a radical notion. Making state prescribed professional conduct rules applicable to federal attorneys is one thing. Letting those rules govern the admission of evidence in federal court is another. If Congress wants to give state courts and legislatures veto power over the admission of evidence in federal court, it will have to tell us that in plain language using clear terms.

III. CONCLUSION

We REVERSE the district court's orders granting the motions to suppress, and REMAND for proceedings consistent with this opinion.

E. RULE 403 BALANCING

McQUEENEY v. WILMINGTON TRUST CO.
779 F.2d 916 (3d Cir. 1985)

BECKER, CIRCUIT JUDGE.

This appeal by the owner and operator of a supertanker from a verdict in favor of plaintiff Francis McQueeney, a seaman aboard the vessel, presents [a question] * * * arising under Fed. R. Evid. 401 and 403, * * * whether evidence from which it might be inferred that McQueeney has suborned perjury of a proffered witness is admissible as substantive evidence that his claim is unfounded even though the witness never testified.* * * The district court excluded the evidence of subornation of perjury, * * * but we conclude that it erred.* * *

I. *Background*

A. *Plaintiff's Accident, His Lawsuit, and the Deposition of Mauro De la Cerda*

Appellee McQueeney was a second officer on the T T WILLIAMSBURG, a supertanker owned by appellant Wilmington Trust Company and operated by Anndep Steamship Corporation. McQueeney claims that on March 20, 1981, while the WILLIAMSBURG was docked at Hounds Point Scotland, he was knocked to the deck while manning a water hose. McQueeney asserts that his fall was caused by both overpressure of the hose and by oil that had been spilled on the deck, making firm footing impossible, and that as a result of his accident, he suffered a herniated cervical disc.* * * The district court conducted a jury trial at the end of which the jury awarded plaintiff a verdict of $305,788.00 against the two defendants. Judgment was entered in the same amount, and the defendants' motions for a new trial and for relief from the judgment were denied. The present appeal followed.

At trial, McQueeney was his only witness on the issue of liability. On the day the trial was scheduled to begin, however, McQueeney's counsel informed the court that he had just located an eyewitness to the accident, a fellow seaman of McQueeney's named Mauro De la Cerda, who was on board a ship in Freeport, Texas, and was therefore not able to appear as a witness. Counsel requested permission to depose De la Cerda.

The district court granted plaintiff's counsel permission to depose De la Cerda on the conditions that (1) defense counsel be given an opportunity to speak with De la Cerda before deciding whether to travel to Texas, and (2) plaintiff pay costs of defense counsel's trip to Texas if defense counsel chose to make the trip. Defense counsel spoke with De la Cerda by telephone that afternoon and chose to go to Houston. The appropriate arrangements were made, trial was recessed, and the next day De la Cerda was deposed in Houston. His testimony corroborated McQueeney's in all significant respects. Defense counsel, claiming to have been surprised by the deposition testimony because De la Cerda had allegedly told him a different version with respect to several significant facts in their telephone conversation, cross-examined De la Cerda about his statements. However, on both direct and then redirect examination at the deposition, De la Cerda either denied making any statements that contradicted his deposition testimony or testified that his statements of the night before were incorrect and that his current statements were accurate. When the parties returned to trial, defense counsel moved for leave to withdraw his appearance so that he could testify and impeach De la Cerda's deposition testimony, which he presumed plaintiff would offer at trial. Defense counsel also listed plaintiff's counsel and his associate as witnesses. After a colloquy in the chambers of the district court, plaintiff's counsel and his associate signed affidavits stating that they had not discussed De la Cerda's testimony with him prior to his deposition. The court thereupon denied the counsel's motion for leave to withdraw.

B. Evidence of the Falsity of De la Cerda's Deposition, Plaintiff's Decision Not to Offer It, and the District Court's Ruling

The trial resumed, and McQueeney took the stand. His testimony lasted several days. During cross-examination, and after court had adjourned for the day, defense counsel received crew lists from his client. The lists reflected that De la Cerda had not joined the crew of the WILLIAMSBURG until three months after the alleged accident. The lists proved, therefore, that De la Cerda's "eyewitness" testimony that he had given at his deposition had been fabricated. The next morning, defense counsel brought this information to the attention of the court in a discussion in chambers. After reviewing the crew lists, plaintiff's counsel immediately stated his intention not to use the deposition. Defense counsel rejoined that he intended to use the deposition to show fraud on the court. Plaintiff's counsel responded that, so long as he was not using the deposition himself, and so long as there was no evidence that McQueeney had perjured himself on the stand, there had been no fraud and the deposition was irrelevant. The district court agreed with plaintiff's counsel and stated that it would not receive the deposition and the crew lists into evidence.

The district court did not articulate the basis for its ruling at trial. However, as appears from the colloquy at the time, the district court felt that so long as the deposition was not introduced by plaintiff, any perjury associated with the deposition was irrelevant to the suit at bar. That this was the court's thinking is evident from its opinion denying defendant's post-trial motion for relief from the judgment or, in the alternative, a new trial. In support of the motion, defendants argued that it was reversible error to bar the deposition and crew lists, but the court ruled that the deposition and crew lists were either irrelevant or only minimally relevant:

> It is questionable if Mr. De la Cerda's testimony is even relevant, since defendant seeks admission for the mere purpose to impeach and not for the substance of the testimony. Certainly, the confusion of a person's recollection brings little to show whether or not a set of facts occurred in a specific manner. Such testimony would confuse and mislead the jury, because what is at issue here is whether Mr. De la Cerda can remember or has such knowledge. To admit such testimony would not be for any probative value but merely to prejudice the jury against the plaintiff. Surely the probative value of such testimony would be minimal at best and is outweighed by the severe prejudice it would cause at the time of trial." Thus the court may fairly be said to have excluded the evidence as either irrelevant under Fed. R. Evid. 401, or as relevant but misleading or unfairly prejudicial, in accordance with Fed. R. Evid. 403.

* * *

II. *Defendants' Proffer that McQueeney had Suborned Perjury*

A. *The Rule 401 Ruling*

* * *

We believe that the district court abused its discretion in excluding the proffered evidence. We base our conclusion on common sense, eminent commentators, case law, and the explicit language of Rule 401.

The intuitive appeal of defendants' proffer is immediate. One who believes his own case to be weak is more likely to suborn perjury than one who thinks he has a strong case, and a party knows better than anyone else the truth about his own case. Thus, subornation of perjury by a party is strong evidence that the party's case is weak. Admittedly the conclusion is not inescapable: parties may be mistaken about the merits or force of their own cases. But evidence need not lead inescapably towards a single conclusion to be relevant, it need only make certain facts more probable than not. The evidence of subornation here does cast into doubt the merits of McQueeney's claim, even if it does not extinguish them.

* * *

Finally, the explicit language of Fed. R. Evid. 401, which defines as relevant evidence that has "any tendency" to make a difference in the case, provides added reason to permit the materials into evidence. The plain meaning of the Rule demonstrates that the scope of relevant evidence is intended to be broad, and the authorities support such a broad reading. *See Carter v. Hewitt*, 617 F.2d 961, 966 (3d Cir. 1980) ("[t]he standard of relevance established by the Federal Rules of Evidence is not high"). Thus, logic, authority, and the clear language of Rule 401 lead us to the conclusion that the deposition and related testimony were relevant and that the district court abused its discretion in excluding it on relevancy grounds.

B. The Rule 403 Balance

That the evidence was relevant does not necessarily mean that it should have been admitted. As noted above, the district court, after voicing its doubts that the evidence had any relevance, ruled that even assuming it was relevant, the evidence should not have been admitted because its prejudicial impact would likely outweigh its probative value* * * . This is a standard Fed. R. Evid. 403 balance which we review with substantial deference. Despite this deferential standard, we find that the district court erred, for it underestimated the probative value of the evidence, and misevaluated its prejudicial impact.

The district court assigned virtually no probative value to the evidence of subornation.* * * It should be clear from what we said above, however, that evidence of subornation of perjury may be quite valuable to the defendant in this case. * * * Evidence that McQueeney suborned perjury might well have made the jurors re-evaluate McQueeney's case. Of course, it is not certain that McQueeney did suborn perjury; De la Cerda may have had other reasons for making up his story. But the circumstances of the case and the correlation between McQueeney's story and De la Cerda's deposition suggest that subornation of perjury by McQueeney is a possibility that the jury should have been allowed to consider.

By contrast, although the district court referred to potential confusion and "severe prejudice," * * * and although there was danger of prejudice — the mere suggestion that McQueeney suborned perjury might have led the jury to reflect on his character in an improper manner — it is unlikely that the evidence would result in the "unfair prejudice" proscribed by Rule 403. *Cf. Dollar v. Long Mfg., N.C. Inc.*, 561 F.2d 613, 618 (5th Cir. 1977) ("'unfair prejudice' as used in Rule 403 is not to be equated with testimony simply adverse to the opposing party. Virtually all evidence is prejudicial or it isn't material. The prejudice must be 'unfair.'"). Moreover, it appears to us that the danger of improper influence was not sufficient to "substantially outweigh[]" the probative value of the evidence, as required by Fed. R. Evid. 403. The court did not articulate any reasons for its finding of prejudice, and this does not appear to us to be the kind of evidence with obvious or overwhelming potential for unfair prejudice. In the absence of a showing of particularized danger of unfair prejudice, the evidence must be admitted. Were we to rule otherwise, evidence could be excluded on an unfounded fear of prejudice and we would effectively preclude all evidence of subornation of perjury.

In sum, the district court misconstrued both elements of the Rule 403 balance hence its balancing exercise was skewed. The court's Rule 403 ruling was thus an abuse of discretion.

* * *

Reversed.

NOTES

1. When is evidence of "consciousness of a weak case" admissible in a civil case?

See Blinzer v. Marriott Int'l, 81 F.3d 1148 (1st Cir. 1996): The court upheld a jury's finding a hotel liable for wrongful death and negligent infliction of emotional damages, resulting from a delay in calling for emergency treatment when a guest had a heart attack. It stated that "[w]hen a document relevant to a case is destroyed, the trier of fact sometimes may infer that the party who obliterated it did so out of a realization that the contents were unfavorable," but added that "[b]efore such an inference may be drawn there must be a sufficient foundation showing that the party who destroyed the document had notice both of the potential claim and the document's potential relevance." The court found a sufficient foundation for admission of evidence that Marriott had destroyed a printout of outgoing calls from its hotel. By contrast, in *Hinkle v. City of Clarksburg*, 81 F.3d 416 (4th Cir. 1996), the estate of a person shot by police officers during an armed standoff brought a civil rights action for excessive force and conspiracy. The events surrounding the shooting were heavily contested, the most hotly disputed point being whether the decedent was shot in the chest or in the back. The plaintiff sought to introduce evidence that a police officer destroyed the decedent's shirt a few days after the shooting, and that when the decedent's body was exhumed for a second autopsy, it was discovered that the bullet wound had been completely excised. The court found no abuse of discretion in the trial court's exclusion of this evidence. It observed that the plaintiff had made no showing that these acts were the result of a deliberate attempt to hide evidence.

2. Is the Rule 403 balancing test tilted toward admissibility or exclusion of relevant but prejudicial evidence?

See Saltzburg, Martin, and Capra, *Federal Rules of Evidence Manual* (9th ed. 2006):

> The drafters of the Rule provided that the probative value must be "substantially" outweighed by these other factors before evidence is excluded. "Substantially" is not defined and there is nothing in the Advisory Committee's Note or in the congressional material that indicates exactly what this word is intended to mean. But the policy of the Rule is that if the balance between probative value and countervailing factors is close, the Judge should admit the evidence. *See, e.g., United States v. Mende*, 43 F.3d 1298 (9th Cir. 1995) (Rule 403 is "an

extraordinary remedy to be used sparingly" and "the danger of prejudice must not merely outweigh the probative value of the evidence, but must *substantially* outweigh it."). In other words, there is a presumption in favor of admitting relevant evidence. In order to overcome this presumption, the negative countervailing factors must be demonstrably greater than the probative value of the evidence. *See, e.g.*, *United States v. Terzado-Madruga*, 897 F.2d 1099 (11th Cir. 1990) (under Rule 403, the balance "should be struck in favor of admissibility"); *United States v. Krenzelok*, 874 F.2d 480 (7th Cir. 1989) (where both probative value and prejudicial effect are high, Rule 403 requires admission). The rationale is that exclusion amounts to a total deprivation of the offeror's probative evidence, while admission may be accompanied by redaction, limiting instruction, or other safeguard by which both the objector and the offeror can ordinarily be accommodated. *See, e.g.*, *United States v. Powers*, 59 F.3d 1460 (4th Cir. 1995) (where the Rule 403 question is close, evidence should be admitted and prejudicial effect should be limited by a strong jury instruction).

PEOPLE OF THE TERRITORY OF GUAM v. SHYMANOVITZ
157 F.3d 1154 (9th Cir. 1998)

REINHARDT, CIRCUIT JUDGE:

In this case we consider whether the prosecution may present testimony regarding the contents of sexually explicit gay adult magazines that are found in the residence of a defendant who is being tried on charges of unlawful sexual activity with minors. John Benjamin Shymanovitz appeals his conviction of multiple counts of criminal sexual conduct involving children, assault, and child abuse, on the ground that his trial was tainted by the admission of such testimony, as well as by the admission of the actual texts of two of the articles. Because we agree that the admission of this evidence constituted prejudicial error, we reverse the convictions.

BACKGROUND

Shymanovitz was a middle-school guidance counselor. He began taking a group of boys who attended the school on outings, such as hiking and camping trips, and sometimes had them sleep over at his home. Shymanovitz was charged with sexually and physically abusing seven of the boys while they were under his supervision. Several months later, he was charged with similar offenses relating to four more boys. The two indictments were then joined.

Prior to trial, the government filed a motion *in limine* requesting permission to introduce into evidence two articles from sexually explicit magazines found in Shymanovitz's residence, on the ground that they were relevant to establishing Shymanovitz's intent to commit the offenses. The court deferred ruling on the motion but at trial permitted a police officer, Winnie Blas, to testify that at Shymanovitz's house she seized, among other things, the following: condoms, a box of surgical gloves, a tube of K-Y Jelly, some children's underwear, a calendar, and six sexually-explicit magazines. Of the six magazines, four were entitled "Stroke"; one was entitled "After Midnight"; and one was entitled "Playboy." Officer Blas testified in great detail, over defense counsel's objections, as to the contents of the four issues of "Stroke"; she told the jury that they contained photos of men masturbating; performing auto-fellatio; ejaculating; using sex toys; wearing "leather equipment"; paddling one another; and having oral and anal sex. She also described two articles from the "Stroke" magazines, which had been the subject of the motion *in limine*. The articles consisted of presumably fictional tales and described two couples engaging in sexual conduct: the first, a father and son; the second, a priest and a young boy. The two articles, the K-Y Jelly, and a page from the calendar were entered directly into evidence.

During her initial closing argument, the prosecutor vigorously argued to the jury that the articles demonstrated that Shymanovitz intentionally engaged in the conduct of which he was accused:

> And the acts that are portrayed in that article are acts that, if you look at what the Defendant himself has done, or what he is charged with, that it goes to his knowledge that he's aware of these kinds of facts, that it goes to his intent to engage in these kinds of acts, that it goes to his motivation to get involved in these types of acts* * * . How does it all go fit in? Again, members of the Jury, it goes to the same thing, that this Defendant knows about these types of facts, that this Defendant was motivated to perform these types of acts.

She recounted the testimony about the content of the "Stroke" magazines in great detail:

> [Officer Blas] talked to you about these magazines. She was asked to describe the contents of these magazines. She told you there were a total of six magazines, four of which were entitled "Stroke," S-T-R-O-K-E, is how she spelled it. She told you about those magazines. She said there was also one "Playboy" and one "After Midnight" magazine. Now in the "Stroke" magazine, she testified that those magazines contained photographs of men ejaculating. When we asked her, "Well, 'ejaculating,' what do you mean?" "Semen coming out of their penis." She talked to you about there are men masturbating, men with men, having oral sex, and anal sex, men's penis being inserted into the anus of another male individual, or an object being inserted into the male anus. She said that it also had photographs of — that depicted the use of mechanisms, and when she was asked, "What do you mean by 'mechanisms,' " she said, "Well, other objects besides a penis and a finger, such as dildos." "Well, what are dildos?" "They're shaped like a penis, rubber-like instrument, dome-like top." She talked about balls on a string; that they're inserted into the anal cavity, and they're pulled out one by one. She also talked about paddles being used on the butt, and so she testified to that. She talked about leather clothing,

people wearing jackets and pants with openings on the penis and the anus, or anal area.

Near the end of her initial closing, the prosecutor emphasized that Shymanovitz and his female roommate were merely friends but not engaged.

Finally, in her rebuttal argument, the prosecutor returned to her theme:

> [D]on't let the fact that these magazines were found in his possession fool you as not being important because I told you what the importance was of those magazines. It's the acts that are depicted in the magazines that Officer [Blas] testified to. The acts — the fellatio, the anal intercourse, the touching — the acts that she described to you are important. That's why it's relevant, because it does go to the Defendant's intent, his motivation; his claim that he doesn't do anything or that he doesn't have any knowledge that certain things might be illegal. The articles are important because they were found in those magazines that were in his possession. Those magazine articles said on the very top how it's illegal to have sex with children* * * . So, it is important and it goes to his intent and motivation.

Aside from the evidence at issue here, the government's case consisted principally of the alleged victims' testimony. Shymanovitz, however, denied any sexual contact with the minors. His counsel argued that the boys and some of the parents had concocted the allegations against him for a number of reasons. He pointed to the testimony of two of the boys who had testified before the grand jury that Shymanovitz abused them but then testified at trial that they had made up the allegations.

The trial lasted three weeks. On the [fifth] day of deliberations, Shymanovitz was convicted on twenty-seven counts and acquitted on eight. He was sentenced to four consecutive terms of life imprisonment for first degree criminal sexual conduct, plus twenty-one years for his convictions on second, third, and fourth degree criminal sexual conduct.

DISCUSSION

Shymanovitz contends that the district court abused its discretion when it permitted the prosecution to adduce oral testimony regarding the contents of the "Stroke" magazines that were seized from his house and to introduce into evidence the texts of the two "Stroke" articles. He further argues that the government's only purpose in doing so was to prejudice the jury by suggesting that he was a homosexual.

We first note that none of the explanations the government proffered during closing arguments for offering the evidence regarding the magazines or introducing the articles is plausible. Although the prosecutor argued primarily that the reading materials in his home proved that Shymanovitz knew that certain forms of sexual conduct were illegal, the defendant never testified at trial that he believed sexual conduct with minors to be legal. Nor was there testimony to indicate that he somehow lacked knowledge of or familiarity with fellatio, anal intercourse, or other general aspects of homosexual sex. Moreover, neither knowledge of the illegality of the conduct of which he was accused nor knowledge of the nature of the specific acts identified by the prosecutor constituted an element of the offense. More important, such knowledge would in no way tend to prove his guilt on any of the charges brought against him.

* * *

There are even more fundamental reasons why the "Stroke" magazines and the fictionalized articles were inadmissible. The mere possession of reading material that describes a particular type of activity makes it neither more nor less likely that a defendant would intentionally engage in the conduct described and thus fails to meet the test of relevancy under Rule 401. * * * Specifically, in this case, neither the defendant's possession of the "Stroke" magazines, nor of any of the articles contained therein, was probative of whether the touching of the alleged victims' genitals was intentional or whether the touching actually was or could be construed as being for sexual purposes. At the very most, Shymanovitz's possession of the sexually-explicit magazines tended to show that he had an interest in looking at gay male pornography, reading gay male erotica, or perhaps even, reading erotic stories about men engaging in sex with underage boys, and not that he actually engaged in, or even had a propensity to engage in, any sexual conduct of any kind. In any event, propensity evidence is contrary to "the underlying premise of our criminal system, that the defendant must be tried for what he did, not who he is." *United States v. Vizcarra-Martinez*, 66 F.3d 1006, 1014 (9th Cir. 1995) (internal citations omitted).

Criminal activity is a wildly popular subject of fiction and nonfiction writing — ranging from the *National Enquirer* to *Les Miserables* to *In Cold Blood*. Any defendant with a modest library of just a few books and magazines would undoubtedly possess reading material containing descriptions of numerous acts of criminal conduct. Under the government's theory, the case against an accused child molester would be stronger if he owned a copy of Nabokov's *Lolita*, and any murder defendant would be unfortunate to have in his possession a collection of Agatha Christie mysteries or even James Bond stories. Woe, particularly, to the son accused of patricide or incest who has a copy of *Oedipus Rex* at his bedside.

In this case the government offered into evidence the text of two out of the dozens of articles from the four "Stroke" magazines and none of the articles from the "Playboy" or "After Midnight" magazines. Undoubtedly there was other reading material in Shymanovitz' residence that was discovered but neither seized nor introduced into evidence. To allow prosecutors to parade before the jury snippets from a defendant's library — the text of two magazine articles and descriptions of four magazines — would compel all persons to choose the contents of their libraries with considerable care; for it is the innocent, and not just the guilty, who are sometimes the subject of good-faith prosecutions.

* * *

Even if anything within the magazines were relevant to Shymanovitz' intent, * * * we would find that the evidence would have been highly improper under Rule 403, which bars evidence when "its probative value is substantially outweighed by the danger of unfair prejudice." Most of the evidence regarding the "Stroke" magazines related to adult gay male sex. Thus, the extensive testimony regarding the publications could easily have caused the jury, rightly or wrongly, to infer that Shymanovitz was a gay man. Generally, "[e]vidence of homosexuality is extremely prejudicial." * * * Evidence implicating Shymanovitz's sexual orientation was particularly prejudicial because he was being tried on numerous sex offense charges: the jury's inference that Shymanovitz was gay could in all likelihood have caused it also to infer that he deviated from traditional sexual norms in other ways, specifically that he engaged in illegal sexual conduct with minors.

Further, the contents of the magazines suggested to the jury that Shymanovitz was far more than a plain and unadorned homosexual — the introduction of this evidence also suggested that he might be interested in or even engage in other sorts of sexual activity that the jurors would perceive as deviant: incest, auto-fellatio, use of sex toys and leather, and sadomasochism. Again, the suggestion of such pursuits is also highly prejudicial to any defendant, and particularly prejudicial to a defendant accused of sexual misconduct or other related misconduct with minors. Accordingly, we conclude that the admission of the evidence regarding the "Stroke" magazines, including the text of two of its articles, was so prejudicial as to outweigh substantially any probative value it could have had.

* * *

CONCLUSION

The government's introduction of highly prejudicial evidence against Shymanovitz tainted the fundamental fairness of his trial. We find it likely that the jury's verdict was materially affected by this improper testimonial and demonstrative evidence. Accordingly, we reverse Shymanovitz' conviction and remand for further proceedings.

NOTES

1. What is the meaning of the term "prejudice" in Rule 403?

See Saltzburg, Martin, and Capra, *Federal Rules of Evidence Manual* (9th ed. 2006):

> Evidence is not "prejudicial" merely because it is harmful to the adversary. After all, if it didn't harm the adversary, it wouldn't be relevant in the first place. Rather, the Rule refers to the negative consequence of "unfair" prejudice.[3] Unfair prejudice is that which could

[3] "As this court has consistently held, unfair prejudice as used in Rule 403 is not to be equated with testimony simply adverse to the opposing party. Virtually all evidence is prejudicial or it isn't material. The prejudice must be unfair. Unfair prejudice within the context of Rule 403 means

lead the jury to make an emotional or irrational decision, or to use the evidence in a manner not permitted by the rules of evidence.[4] Professor Lempert, in *Modeling Relevance*, 75 MICH. L. REV. 1021 (1977), defines prejudicial evidence as "any evidence that influences jury verdicts without relating logically to the issue of guilt or innocence." We would prefer a slightly different definition: "prejudicial evidence is any evidence that affects the trier of fact in a manner not attributable to the permissible probative force of the evidence." This definition makes clear that evidence that strongly relates to the issue of guilt or liability might still be highly prejudicial, and also that evidence that is probative for a permissible use may nonetheless be prejudicial because the jury could use it for an impermissible purpose.

There are, of course, varying degrees of prejudice, and the Trial Court must take that into account when balancing under Rule 403. In a criminal case, any evidence of a defendant's prior criminal activity that is extremely similar to the charges is clearly on the high end of the prejudice scale. The degree of prejudice may well diminish if the evidence might permit some unsavory inferences, and yet does not clearly indicate criminal or highly immoral activity. Thus, in *United States v. Thompson*, 990 F.2d 301 (7th Cir. 1993), the defendant was charged with being a felon in possession of a gun; the gun was found in an apartment in which he was sleeping. He argued that he neither knew of nor exercised control over the gun and was an infrequent guest at the apartment. The Trial Court permitted an agent to testify that officers found $13,000 cash, and expensive jewelry engraved with the defendant's first name, in the bedroom of the apartment. The defendant argued that this testimony should have been excluded under Rule 403, as it prejudiced the jury into thinking the defendant "was a bad guy." The Court of Appeals held that the evidence was properly admitted to show the defendant's control over the premises, and that the probative value was not substantially outweighed by the prejudicial effect because "it is not a crime to keep jewelry or cash in one's bedroom."

---

an undue tendency to suggest a decision on an improper basis, commonly, though not necessarily, an emotional one."

Ballou v. Henri Studios, 656 F.2d 1147 (5th Cir. 1981).

See also Robinson v. Runyon, 149 F.3d 507 (6th Cir. 1998) (evidence of supervisor's use of racial epithets should have been admitted in case charging racial discrimination in employment; the evidence was improperly excluded as prejudicial: "the racially inflammatory nature of the evidence involved here is precisely why it is probative of the racially discriminatory motives alleged in this case").

[4] *See, e.g., United States v. Hands*, 184 F.3d 1322 (11th Cir. 1999) (cocaine-related convictions reversed due to admission of evidence that the defendant abused his wife: "The domestic violence evidence in this case was particularly likely to incite the jury to an irrational decision because it was graphic and arresting."); *United States v. Irvin*, 87 F.3d 860 (7th Cir. 1996) (evidence of gang membership was improperly admitted, since there was no evidence that the gang was involved in the kind of criminal activity charged to the defendant; the evidence had little probative value, and the prejudicial effect was substantial in light of the "negative connotations" that gang evidence arouses and the fact that the government highlighted the "satanic imagery" associated with the gang).

2. How much discretion does a trial court have in balancing the probative value of proffered evidence against the risk of prejudice, confusion, and delay?

Rule 403 provides that evidence "may" be excluded, thus imparting significant discretion to the trial judge. The appellate court will not reverse a Rule 403 decision simply because the appellate judges would have ruled differently from the trial judge. *United States v. Cunningham,* 194 F.3d 1186 (11th Cir. 1999) (trial court did not abuse its discretion in excluding defense-proffered evidence under Rule 403, even though the Court of Appeals judges state that they would probably have admitted the evidence had they been sitting as trial judges). Error will be found only if the trial judge's decision cannot be supported by reasonable argument. *United States v. Awadallah*, 436 F.3d 125 (2d Cir. 2006) (emphasizing that only rarely "and in extraordinarily compelling circumstances" will a trial court's Rule 403 rulings be reversed, and holding that "[b]ecause the testimony, although relevant, indisputably has potential to be highly prejudicial, we cannot say that the district court's limitation on the testimony of grand jurors was arbitrary or irrational"). Appellate courts recognize that the trial judge has a unique vantage point from which to detect and assess the negative factors that might arise from proffered evidence, and from which to balance these factors against the probative value of the evidence. *United States v. Lau*, 828 F.2d 871, 874 (1st Cir. 1987) (trial court is "more directly familiar than a court of appeals with the need for the evidence and its likely effect on the jury"). Appellate courts are also sympathetic to the fact that the trial court must ordinarily conduct its Rule 403 balancing process on the spot, in the heat of the trial; it does not have the luxury of careful balancing. Essentially, appellate courts will check to see that the trial court has *conducted* a balancing process; the *result* of a careful balancing process will not itself be second-guessed. *United States v. Beasley*, 809 F.2d 1273 (7th Cir. 1987) ("although appellate courts cannot often tell whether it was best, all things considered, to let in a given piece of evidence, it may be possible to tell whether the district court and the parties took the right things into account. A flaw in the process is easier to detect than is a flaw in the result.").

On the other hand, the trial judge's discretion under Rule 403 is not unlimited. The following are some general limitations which have been imposed upon the trial judge's discretion:

Power to exclude is to be rarely invoked: Because Rule 403 provides that the negative factors set forth in the rule must *substantially* outweigh the probative value, it follows that the discretionary power to exclude should be used sparingly. *Herrington v. Hiller*, 883 F.2d 411 (5th Cir. 1989) (trial court's power to exclude relevant evidence should be used "sparingly"; abuse of discretion to exclude highly probative evidence where there was no strong indication that it would have been confusing or distracting). Generally speaking, the trial court's decision to exclude evidence is more likely to be found an abuse of discretion than is the trial court's decision to admit evidence.

Credibility questions are for the factfinder: The trial judge may not invoke Rule 403 to exclude evidence merely because he or she finds it unbelievable. Rather, the trial judge must assess the probative value of the evidence if believed by the jury, and balance that against the risk of prejudice, confusion, and delay. *Bowden v. McKenna,* 600 F.2d 282 (1st Cir. 1979) ("Weighing probative value against unfair prejudice under Fed. R. Evid. 403 means probative value with respect to a material fact if the evidence is believed, not the degree the court finds it believable.").

Balancing process must be conducted: A trial court that conducts a balancing process on the record is more likely to be affirmed than a trial court that excludes or admits evidence in a conclusory fashion; at a minimum, as seen in *McQueeney,* remand is a good possibility in the latter instance.

Prejudice must be properly analyzed: As discussed above, evidence is not prejudicial within the meaning of Rule 403 merely because it is harmful to the adversary's case. A trial court that excludes evidence as "prejudicial" merely because it is harmful — as opposed to unfair — runs a substantial risk of reversal.

3. How does the Rule 403 balancing test work in bench trials?

Where the case is tried to a judge, the risk of prejudice is not a proper ground for excluding evidence under Rule 403. It is nonsensical to ask the judge to exclude evidence on the ground that it will prejudice her, because the judge would have to be exposed to the evidence in order to make such a ruling. Moreover, we can fairly presume that trial judges are unlikely to rule emotionally, or to misuse evidence, in the way that juries might. *See, e.g., Gulf States Utils. Co. v. Ecodyne Corp.*, 635 F.2d 517 (5th Cir. 1981) (The portion of Rule 403 referring to prejudice "has no logical application in bench trials. Excluding relevant evidence in a bench trial because it is cumulative or a waste of time is clearly a proper exercise of the judge's power, but excluding relevant evidence on the basis of unfair prejudice is a useless procedure.").

Similarly, an objection on the ground that evidence would be confusing has no place in a bench trial. Nor would it be a good idea even to suggest that the trial judge should exclude evidence because it would confuse the judge. Consequently, in a bench trial the only reason for excluding probative evidence under Rule 403 is that the evidence would be cumulative or a waste of time.

F. COMMON APPLICATIONS OF THE RULE 403 BALANCING TEST

[1] Consciousness of Guilt

[a] Illustration

A police officer is on the stand. After an extensive, two-year investigation, the officer had arrested the defendant for armed robbery. Three thousand dollars was taken in the hold-up.

Prosecution:	Now officer, when you approached the defendant, what did he do?
Officer:	He ran from me and jumped a fence and . . .
Defense:	Objection! That's irrelevant and highly prejudicial.

The court: __________ .

[b] Flight and Escape

UNITED STATES v. HANKINS
931 F.2d 1256 (8th Cir. 1991)

BEAM, CIRCUIT JUDGE:

Larry Wayne Hankins was convicted of armed bank robbery, in violation of 18 U.S.C. § 2113(a), (d) (1988); use of a firearm during a crime of violence, in violation of 18 U.S.C. § 924(c)(1); and escape from federal custody, in violation of 18 U.S.C. § 751(a). He appeals from his convictions, claiming * * * that the district court erred in admitting evidence of his escape. * * *

I. Background

On Monday, April 17, 1989, the Stone County National Bank in Cape Fair, Missouri, was robbed by two people shortly after closing time (3:00 p.m.). [After an investigation, Hankins was arrested and incarcerated pending trial.]

On the morning of April 27, 1989, seven days after being confined in the Greene County jail in Missouri, Hankins escaped from custody. He was found later the same day and returned to custody. In July 1989, a three-count indictment was returned by a federal grand jury, charging Hankins with the robbery, use of a firearm, and escape. Prior to trial, Hankins pleaded guilty to the escape charge. A jury trial began on September 5, 1989, for the remaining two charges and on September 8, 1989, Hankins was found guilty.* * *

II.

Discussion

* * *

* * * [W]e consider Hankins's claim that the district court erred in allowing the admission of evidence relating to his escape from the Greene County jail. Hankins argues that evidentiary rules prohibit the admission of evidence concerning his escape and that the prejudicial effect of its admission was "accentuated" by the extensive testimony and by the lack of overwhelming evidence against him. We disagree and hold that the escape evidence was admissible.

It is widely acknowledged that evidence of flight or escape from custody is often only marginally probative as to the ultimate issue of guilt or innocence. But it is also well established that such evidence is admissible and has probative value as circumstantial evidence of consciousness of guilt. * * * It is for the jury to determine how much weight to give to such evidence.

* * * In *United States v. Peltier*, 585 F.2d 314 (8th Cir. 1978), we explained that the admissibility and probative value of flight evidence

"depends upon the degree of confidence with which four inferences can be drawn: (1) from the defendant's behavior to flight; (2) from flight to consciousness of guilt; (3) from consciousness of guilt to consciousness of guilt concerning the crime charged; and (4) from consciousness of guilt concerning the crime charged to actual guilt of the crime charged."

A court must carefully consider whether there are a sufficient number of evidentiary manifestations to support these inferences. Most of the cases on this subject, like *Peltier*, involve evidence of *flight*, usually from the scene of a crime or from an arresting officer. The present case involves evidence of *escape*, but we see no distinction that would warrant an analytical approach different from that which is used in flight cases. Flight and escape are similar evasive acts.

The second and fourth inferences, it has been said, are often the most difficult to support, and that is true in this case as well. But given the evidentiary manifestations in this case, the district court did not abuse its discretion in admitting evidence of Hankins's escape. One can confidently infer from Hankins's behavior that he was fleeing from custody. One can also confidently infer that Hankins's behavior was related to the armed bank robbery charges. Hankins gave a number of reasons for why he escaped (*e.g.*, he thought he was being framed and he wanted to see his children) and these are all explanations for the jury to consider in weighing the significance of the escape evidence. But there is nothing in the record to suggest that Hankins escaped because he felt guilty about some other offense (*i.e.*, the third inference above). Before his escape, Hankins had been made fully aware of the charges against him. Thus, "there is a sufficient basis in the evidence to warrant the inference that the flight 'was prompted by considerations related to the issue in question.' "

Hankins also argues that an unnecessarily extensive and prejudicial amount of evidence regarding his escape was received by the district court. Given the often marginally probative value of evidence of flight or escape and the risk of its prejudicial effect, district courts should be wary of the amount of evidence permitted on this subject and the way in which it is presented. The evidence of escape in Hankins's trial was not presented in an inflammatory manner, but it is our impression that more testimony than necessary was received by the district court. [At trial, the government presented testimony from the prison guard who saw Hankins escape (including pictures showing the wall Hankins jumped over, the car on which he landed, etc.); testimony from the law enforcement officer who captured him later that same evening (including six photographs of the area where Hankins was hiding from authorities); testimony from an FBI agent regarding a conversation he had with Hankins, during which Hankins admitted planning the escape; and, finally, the government introduced a tape recording of a telephone call Hankins had with a friend after his capture, during which he stated that he planned the escape.] We do not believe, however, that this constitutes an abuse of the district court's discretion.

Hankins's argument that *any* evidence of his escape was too much (or "especially prejudicial") because of the less than overwhelming case against him is without merit. Evidence against a defendant, which is otherwise relevant or admissible, should not be excluded simply because the total evidence is not overwhelming. In fact, the probative value of the evidence is made more significant by the less than overwhelming case and the government's legitimate need for corroborative evidence.

* * *

Affirmed.

NOTES

1. When is evidence of defendant's flight, or other activity to avoid conviction, admissible?

Where a criminal defendant flees prosecution, or bribes a juror, or threatens a witness, or gives a false exculpatory story, this evidence is ordinarily held relevant to the defendant's consciousness of guilt. The inferences work as follows: a person who flees, changes his story, etc., is more likely to believe that he is guilty than a person who has not done any of these things; a person who believes he is guilty is more likely to be guilty than a person who does not; and a person who is guilty is more likely to be guilty of the crime charged than one who is not. *See, e.g., United States v. Tracy,* 989 F.2d 1279 (1st Cir. 1993) (evidence of flight by a defendant is admissible as probative of a "guilty mind" if "there is an adequate factual predicate creating an inference of guilt of the crime charged"; a sufficient factual predicate was established in this case; the defendant was scheduled for trial but left the state and did not appear; independent evidence established his drug dealings); *United States v. Oliver* (6th Cir. 2005) (no error in the admission of evidence that the defendant, while on pretrial release, had left a halfway house and drug treatment program without permission and intending not to return; given the defendant's knowledge of the charges against him, it was not necessary that the flight immediately follow the crime or the defendant's discovery that he was charged in order to show consciousness of guilt); *United States v. Horton*, 873 F.2d 180 (8th Cir. 1989) (no error in admitting the fact that the defendant gave a false name during his pretrial booking interview; "false identification is relevant and admissible to show consciousness of guilt"). Of course, evidence of consciousness of guilt can be prejudicial, and as such is subject to exclusion if the evidence is especially inflammatory and if the probative value of the evidence is diminished by a plausible alternative explanation for the defendant's conduct.

The Federal Judicial Center suggests the following instruction to be given when evidence of consciousness of guilt is admitted: "__________ testified that, after the crime was supposed to have been committed, the defendant [brief description of behavior, such as flight]. If you believe that the defendant [same brief description], you should keep that in mind when deciding whether the government has proved beyond a reasonable doubt that he committed the crime. On the one hand, you may think that what he did at that time indicated that he knew he was guilty and was attempting to avoid punishment. On the other hand, it is sometimes true that an innocent person will [same brief description] in order to avoid being arrested and charged with a crime." Federal Judicial Center Pattern Instruction 43 (1982).

[2] Poverty or Wealth

[a] Illustration

The plaintiff sued the defendant corporation, under a theory of *respondeat superior*, for injuries resulting from an automobile accident. The plaintiff alleges that the defendant corporation's employee drove negligently. There is no claim for punitive damages. The plaintiff subpoenas the defendant's comptroller and calls her to the stand.

Plaintiff:	Who is your employer?
Witness:	The defendant corporation.
Plaintiff:	What is your job?
Witness:	I'm a comptroller.
Plaintiff:	What was the gross revenue of the corporation since the date of this tragic wreck?
Defense:	Objection! Any relevance to liability or damages is substantially outweighed by the prejudicial effect.
The court:	________ .

[b] Punitive Damages

HALL v. MONTGOMERY WARD & CO.

252 N.W.2d 421 (Iowa 1977)

UHLENHOPP, JUSTICE.

This appeal involves a jury award of damages in an action by plaintiff Thomas C. Hall against defendant Montgomery Ward & Company for mental anguish caused by threatening language by Wards' representatives. * * *

Hall, a borderline mental retardate with an intelligence quotient of 69, worked as a maintenance man in Wards' store at Cedar Falls, Iowa. He "borrowed" Wards' floor scrubber to moonlight by cleaning tavern floors, and also took cleaning material for the scrubber. He testified he did not take other items.

A security officer of Wards came from Chicago and, with the local store manager, interrogated Hall in the manager's office. The officer threatened Hall with jail, among other statements, and emerged from the interrogation with four documents signed by Hall. A clinical psychologist testified that some of the words in the documents were beyond Hall's comprehension and that Hall would probably sign anything in a stressful situation to extricate himself. Hall testified he signed the documents because of the threats of jail. The documents were a consent that Wards' representatives could detain and interview Hall on company business as long as they deemed necessary, a list of items Hall allegedly took from the store (such as shorts, knife, belt, brush), a confession to the theft of store merchandise worth $5000, and a promissory note to Wards for $5000. The store manager testified the items listed in the second document as stolen would come to $25 to $35 but the list did not cover everything and the figure $5000 was Hall's estimate.

Hall testified to his mental anguish from the incident. He stated several times that he had recurring dreams from the incident and that the incident affected his relationship with his family. The psychologist testified that Hall reacted as though the incident was "the end of the world," and Wards' officer testified he had to assure Hall at the conclusion of the interrogation that the situation was not the end of the world. Hall did not introduce evidence of physical injury or of financial loss or expense.

Hall testified regarding the pitifully small amount of property possessed by himself and his wife, as tending to show he did not have the property Wards contended he stole. Over Wards' objection of irrelevant, immaterial, and prejudicial, overruled by the trial court, Hall also introduced Wards' balance sheet and operating statement showing *inter alia* assets of $1,964,822,000 and net annual sales of $2,640,122,000.

The trial court overruled a motion for directed verdict by Wards. The jury found for Hall and awarded him $12,500 actual and $50,000 exemplary damages.

Wards moved for judgment notwithstanding verdict and alternatively for a new trial. The trial court overruled the former motion but sustained the latter one on the ground that the court erred in overruling Wards' objection to admission of the exhibit containing the balance sheet and operating statement which, according to the court, Hall's attorney used to make a "devastating" jury argument.

Hall appealed from the new trial award. Wards cross appealed from the court's failure to sustain its motions for directed verdict and for judgment notwithstanding verdict.

* * *

Hall contends that the trial court erred in granting a new trial for admitting Wards' balance sheet and operating statement into evidence. The rule in this jurisdiction has been that with certain exceptions not involved here, a defendant's pecuniary condition may not be shown. * * * This view has the support of a few courts, which state that if pecuniary condition is shown the fact finder will tend to get off on the relative poverty or affluence of the parties; despite trial-court instructions to juries, the issues of liability and damages will become intermixed.

The great weight of authority today, however, holds the other way where the plaintiff seeks and the evidence supports exemplary damages. The rationale employed in these decisions is that the jury needs to know the extent of the defendant's holdings in order to know how large an award of damages is necessary to make him smart. *E.g. Suzore v. Rutherford*, 35 Tenn. App. 678, 684, 251 S.W.2d 129, 131 ("what would be 'smart money' to a poor man would not be, and would not serve as a deterrent, to a rich man").

We are impressed by the large number of courts which have arrived at the conclusion that generally the rule of admissibility is the better one. We are more impressed by the actual need of jurors, in connection with exemplary damages, to have evidence about the defendant's poverty or wealth. We thus * * * hold that the trial court properly admitted the exhibit and erroneously sustained Wards' motion for new trial. In adopting the rule of admissibility, we caution trial courts to confine plaintiffs carefully to the proper use of such evidence — to the issue of the amount of exemplary damages which is necessary to punish the particular defendant.

* * *

Reversed and remanded.

NOTES

1. In a civil case, when is the defendant's net worth admissible following relevancy analysis?

In *Lunsford v. Morris*, 746 S.W.2d 471 (Tex. 1988), the Supreme Court of Texas recognized that "[a]t least forty-three states now allow evidence of net worth to be discovered and admitted for the limited purpose of assessing punitive damages. Substantial federal court authority also supports the proposition that net worth is admissible on punitive damages. The United States Supreme Court recognizes and adheres to the majority view."

2. In a criminal case, when is the defendant's poverty or financial distress admissible?

See United States v. Mullings, 364 F.2d 173 (2d Cir. 1966): "Today when the law has recognized a commitment to the underprivileged to bridge the chasm between 'poor man's' and 'rich man's' justice, courts must be especially alert to prevent a man's rights or liberty from turning on his economic and social status. Thus, while inquiry into an accused's financial background may be relevant to the Government's case, the prosecution must proceed gingerly in its exploration, and the trial judge should permit this inquiry only where there is a proffer that the evidence, in light of other proof, is highly probative." *See also United States v. Weller,* 238 F.3d 1215 (10th Cir. 2001): In a bank manager's trial for embezzlement, the prosecution introduced evidence that the defendant had an empty bank account and "maxed out" credit cards prior to the incident and had substantial cash in the weeks following. The court found no abuse of discretion in admitting the evidence. Ordinarily evidence of poverty is inadmissible to show a motive for a financial crime. However, a significant change in financial status, as in this case, can be quite probative of the commission of the crime.

[3] Similar Occurences

[a] Illustration

The plaintiff sues the defendant for injuries sustained as a result of an automobile accident. The defendant admits that he rear-ended the plaintiff, but argues that he barely nicked the plaintiff's car and could not have injured the plaintiff to the extent that the plaintiff alleges. The plaintiff is on the stand. The defendant cross-examines.

Defendant:	Isn't it true that this is the fifth time you've sued somebody for rear-ending you?
Plaintiff:	Objection! __________ .
Defendant:	__________ .
The court:	__________ .

[b] Substantial Identity

NACHTSHEIM v. BEECH AIRCRAFT CORP.

847 F.2d 1261 (7th Cir. 1988)

RIPPLE, CIRCUIT JUDGE.

The plaintiffs, Edward E. Nachtsheim and Production Tool Corporation (Production Tool), brought this products liability action against the defendant, Beech Aircraft Corporation (Beech). Jurisdiction was based on diversity of citizenship, 28 U.S.C. § 1332. The suit arose from an aircraft accident in which the deceased, William W. Steil, was killed. Mr. Steil was the President of Production Tool. He was piloting a company aircraft on January 8, 1978 when the plane crashed near Tylertown, Mississippi.

The case was tried to a jury on theories of negligence, strict liability, and failure to warn. Mr. Steil's estate sought damages for wrongful death; Production Tool sought damages for the value of the aircraft. After a two-week trial, the jury returned a verdict in favor of the defendant. * * *

In this appeal, the plaintiffs challenge * * * a number of the district court's evidentiary rulings. After reviewing the record and considering each of the challenged rulings, we conclude that there is no basis for granting the requested relief. We therefore affirm the judgment of the district court.

I.

Background

A. *The Crash*

On the afternoon of January 8, 1978, Mr. Steil prepared to fly himself and three passengers from New Orleans, Louisiana to Milwaukee, Wisconsin. Shortly before taking off, he obtained a weather briefing from the New Orleans Flight Service Station. The Flight Service Station informed him that moderate to severe turbulence could be expected between altitudes of 12,000 and 25,000 feet over Louisiana, Mississippi and Tennessee. * * * The Flight Service Station also mentioned the presence of moderate rime icing with mixed freezing drizzle throughout his planned route of flight, as well as ice pellets on the ground in the area of Jackson, Mississippi. * * *

The Steil plane took off from New Orleans at 3:44 p.m. Immediately after takeoff, the airplane began climbing from an initial altitude of 2,000 feet to an altitude of 4,000 feet. Shortly thereafter, Mr. Steil received clearance to climb to 8,000 feet. * * * At approximately 4:12 p.m., Mr. Steil contacted the Houston Air Route Traffic Control Center (Houston Center) and indicated that he was at 7,000 feet and beginning to pick up ice. He requested clearance to ascend over the clouds. * * * Houston Center cleared the Steil craft to an altitude of 11,000 feet, and Mr. Steil acknowledged the clearance. * * * Two minutes later, Houston Center reported that it had lost the airplane on radar. About this time, an eyewitness on the ground sighted the airplane coming out of the clouds. Moments later, the airplane crashed into a forested area, disintegrated and burned. There were no survivors.

B. *The Investigation*

The National Safety Transportation Board (NTSB) conducted an investigation of the crash. Several witnesses to the crash were interviewed. The NTSB accident report summarized the statements of these witnesses:

> Witnesses reported, in essence, that the engines or engine were making a surging or cyclic up and down type sound. The sound was heard before the aircraft came into view below the clouds and continued until the impact sound. The aircraft came out of the overcast in a nosedown wing level dive of about 45 degrees. A steep left bank was observed with the aircraft still descending. The aircraft disappeared behind trees still moving at a high speed before it was heard crashing through trees. The sound of an explosion was heard after the sound of impact with trees.
>
> An eyewitness located about 200 yards southwest of the crash site estimated the cloud ceiling at about 1200–1400 feet and a strong gusty west wind. Prior to the accident it was hazy and about 30–45 minutes after the accident, a light freezing rain started. The weather later cleared from the west and was clear at the accident scene by nightfall.

The NTSB report did not reach any conclusion as to the cause of the crash. However, a separate report filed by a Beech employee who was part of the NTSB investigating team concluded that: "The aircraft lost control due to either ice or pilot inattention. I believe pilot inattention was the problem, because the aircraft had deicing equipment and only light icing was reported." * * *

C. *The Aircraft*

The Steil aircraft was a Beech Baron 58P. * * * The Federal Aviation Agency (FAA) has certified the Baron 58P for flight into known icing conditions * * *.

Nevertheless, the plaintiffs proceeded at trial on the theory that the design of the Baron 58P rendered it unsafe for flight in icing conditions. This theory centered on the elevator, a flight control mechanism located at the rear of the plane. The elevator is a movable control surface which is attached to the fixed, horizontal portion of the tail called the stabilizer. The gap between the elevator and the horizontal stabilizer is called the cove gap. * * * The position of the elevator controls the rise or fall of the nose of the plane in relation to the tail, otherwise known as the plane's pitch.

* * *

The Baron 58P has a pointed elevator horn which is partially shielded from the airstream by the stabilizer portion of the tail. However, when the elevator is moved, its leading edge protrudes from its streamlined position behind the stabilizer. It is then exposed to the airstream.

* * *

D. *The Trial*

The plaintiffs' theory of the case was presented at trial primarily by their expert witness, Professor Donald Kennedy. Professor Kennedy testified that the Steil airplane had stalled. [An aircraft "stalls" when its wings are unable to produce the lift necessary to sustain the plane in the air because of an inordinate angle of attack relative to the airstream.] When an aircraft stalls, the pilot must use the elevator to lower the nose and thereby restore the proper airflow. According to Professor Kennedy, Mr. Steil was unable to recover from the stall because ice had accumulated in the cove gap due to the elevator's exposure to the airstream. The ice buildup prevented Mr. Steil from using the elevator to regain pitch control. * * * In short, Professor Kennedy testified that, in his opinion, the primary cause of the Steil crash was a frozen elevator. * * * He concluded that, because the tail section design of the Beech Baron 58P allows the elevator to become frozen in icing conditions, it is unreasonably dangerous. Additionally, he concluded that the Steil accident could have been prevented had Beech warned Mr. Steil of methods of preventing the elevator from jamming with ice.* * *

Beech contended at trial that the crash was the result of pilot error. Beech agreed with Professor Kennedy that Mr. Steil had stalled the aircraft at about 8,000 feet while attempting to climb to 11,000 feet.* * * However, Beech disagreed about what happened after the stall. According to one of Beech's chief engineers, the Baron 58P cannot be stalled without a movable elevator because the airplane cannot sufficiently change its angle of attack to occasion the stall.* * * Beech thus contended that the crash was not the result of a frozen elevator. Rather, Beech argued that Mr. Steil became spatially disoriented following his loss of control of the airplane. Spatial disorientation is a phenomenon in which a pilot becomes confused as to the actual altitude of his aircraft in relation to the earth by reason of the plane's immersion in the clouds. When spatially disoriented it is very common for a pilot to be in a turn and actually not know it. Upon exiting the clouds, the pilot usually experiences nystagmus and severe confusion whereby he is unable to clearly focus on the instruments. * * * Beech maintained that it was because of this spatial disorientation, and not because of a frozen elevator, that Mr. Steil was unable to recover from the stall.

* * *

III.

Discussion

A. *The St. Anne Accident*

1. *Background*

The plaintiffs' first evidentiary contention is that the district court erroneously excluded evidence of an accident that occurred near St. Anne, Illinois in 1979. The St. Anne crash involved a model 58TC Baron. [For purposes of this case, the parties agree that the model 58TC Baron is identical to the model 58P Baron involved in the Steil crash.] The plane took off at approximately 8:18 p.m. and crashed at 8:39 p.m. There were no survivors. Shortly before the crash occurred, the pilot reported * * * that he was "having a 'problem' with ice." * * * Although the weather report for that evening did not include an ice advisory, a few pilots on the same route had reported some light ice. The NTSB accident report stated that, "[a]lthough it could not be verified, it is suspected [the St. Anne plane] was in instrument, icing, meteorological conditions at the time of occurrence." * * * The St. Anne plane was initially cleared for a cruising altitude of 11,000 feet and was at 15,000 feet when the accident occurred. The aircraft impacted in a 70 or 80 degree nosedown, near-vertical descent and exploded almost immediately upon impact.* * *

The plaintiffs argue that the St. Anne accident was substantially similar to the Steil crash and, therefore, that testimony concerning the St. Anne accident should have been admitted. The plaintiffs submit that the following similarities between the St. Anne accident and the Steil crash justify their position: (1) the parties stipulated to the fact that the St. Anne plane and the Steil plane were identical aircrafts for purposes of this case; (2) both the St. Anne pilot and Mr. Steil were instrument-rated pilots; (3) both the St. Anne flight and the Steil flight "occurred in instrument conditions and, specifically, in an icing environment;" (4) in each case there was a reported accretion of airframe ice; and (5) both planes "were in icing conditions for only a short period of time before control was lost and fatal crashes occurred." * * *

Beech * * * points to several dissimilarities between the two accidents which justify the exclusion of the St. Anne testimony. These include: (1) the St. Anne pilot broke his altitude clearance of 13,000 feet and was detected at 13,800 feet, while the Steil plane crashed before reaching its assigned altitude of 11,000 feet; (2) the St. Anne pilot had a record of pilot problems; (3) the St. Anne pilot indicated that he was having a problem with his autopilot; (4) it cannot be determined how long before the crash the St. Anne plane began to pick up ice, whereas Mr. Steil was "beginning to pick up a little light rime" only three minutes before the impact; and (5) the St. Anne plane crashed in a near-vertical descent, with a 70–80 degree nose-down attitude, whereas the Steil plane appeared flyable when it came out of the clouds, "as evidenced by its impact with the trees at only a three degree nose down attitude."

The district court excluded testimony about the St. Anne accident after balancing the probative value of the testimony against its prejudicial effect pursuant to Federal Rule of Evidence 403. In ruling from the bench, the court stated that:

> '[T]he Court feels that there are so many dissimilar facts and so few established facts to indicate similarity that the probative value of this comparison is outweighed by the fact that it would create an unfair prejudice to the defendant and could in the Court's mind, judging from the arguments here, add to the confusion of this hearing with the state of the record as it is.

* * *

A trial court's balancing under Rule 403 is governed by the abuse of discretion standard and will be accorded "great deference" on appeal. We have reviewed the record carefully. It reveals that the district court fully considered the arguments for and against the admissibility of the St. Anne testimony. "When the district court has given such careful attention to a balancing of prejudice and probative value, we are particularly mindful of our duty not to reverse absent a clear abuse of discretion."

Nevertheless, the plaintiffs argue that, in most airplane crash cases, direct evidence of causation is destroyed in the accident. As a result, there is a special need for circumstantial evidence of the type offered in this case. *Cf. Riordan v. Kempiners*, 831 F.2d 690, 698 (7th Cir. 1987) ("A plaintiff's ability to prove discrimination indirectly, circumstantially, must not be crippled by evidentiary rulings that keep out probative evidence because of crabbed notions of relevance or excessive mistrust of juries."). Because this tension exists between the discretion traditionally accorded to trial courts in this area and the need for circumstantial evidence of causation, we shall discuss in more detail the basis for the district court's ruling.

2. Analysis

a. Similar Accidents Argument

Evidence of other accidents in products liability cases is relevant to show notice to the defendant of the danger, to show existence of the danger, and to show the cause of the accident.* * * However, before such evidence will be admitted, the proponent must show that the other accidents occurred under substantially similar circumstances. (The fact that the St. Anne accident occurred one year *after* the Steil crash does not render the evidence inadmissible. "While only earlier accidents can be relevant to the issue of notice, causation is an issue affected only by the circumstances and the equipment, and is not related to the date of the occurrence." *Uitts v. General Motors Corp.*, 58 F.R.D. 450, 452 (E.D. Pa. 1972)).

The foundational requirement that the proponent of similar accidents evidence must establish substantial similarity before the evidence will be admitted is especially important in cases such as this where the evidence is proffered to show the existence of a dangerous condition or causation.[5] The rationale for this rule is simple. In such cases, the jury is invited to infer from the presence of other accidents (1) that a dangerous condition existed (2) which caused the accident. As the circumstances and conditions of the other accidents become less similar to the accident under consideration, the probative force of such evidence decreases. At the same time, the danger that the evidence will be unfairly prejudicial remains. The jury might infer from evidence of the prior accident alone that ultra-hazardous conditions existed and were the cause of the later accident without those issues ever having been proved. In addition, the costs — in terms of time, distraction and, possibly, prejudice — resulting from such evidence also may weigh against admissibility. Accordingly, even when substantial identity of the circumstances is proven, the admissibility of such evidence lies within the discretion of the trial judge who must weigh the dangers of unfairness, confusion, and undue expenditure of time in the trial of collateral issues against the factors favoring admissibility."

Given these guiding principles, we cannot disturb the district court's conclusion that the plaintiffs have failed to demonstrate sufficient similarity between the St. Anne accident and the Steil crash to justify admission of the disputed testimony. As the district court noted, there are too few *established facts* about the St. Anne accident from which a comparison between the two accidents can be made. Our primary concern is that the plaintiffs have not presented any evidence that the alleged dangerous condition — a frozen elevator — was in any way involved in the St. Anne accident. In contrast, the cases cited by the plaintiffs in support of their position all involve circumstances where the proponent of the evidence was able to establish certain facts about the other accidents that permitted a useful comparison to be made. *See Rimer v. Rockwell Int'l Corp.*, 641 F.2d 450 (6th Cir. 1981) (alleged dangerous condition was a defective fuel cap; other airplane accidents were caused by fuel siphoning in identical planes with similar fuel systems).

Here, the plaintiffs have shown only that both the St. Anne plane and the Steil plane were in some sort of icing environment and that both crashed. There was no evidence that an elevator failure occurred in the St. Anne crash that would provide a link between that accident and the plaintiffs' theory of their case.

Moreover, if the district court had permitted this evidence, the defendant would have had to defend, as a practical matter, not only against the present

[5] The requirement of similarity is less strict when the evidence is sought to be admitted to show notice. "For purposes of proving other accidents in order to show defendants' awareness of a dangerous condition, the rule requiring substantial similarity of those accidents to the accident at issue should be relaxed." *Jackson v. Firestone Tire & Rubber Co.*, 788 F.2d 1070, 1083 (5th Cir. 1986).

suit, but also against the St. Anne crash. The jury would be confronted with additional technical evidence on a collateral issue that would have unnecessarily prolonged the trial and created a risk of confusion of the issues. * * * The district court had good reasons to exclude the testimony and we do not find any abuse of discretion in its ruling.

* * *

Affirmed.

NOTES

1. Is evidence of no accident admissible?

In *Pandit v. Am. Honda Motor Co.*, 82 F.3d 376 (10th Cir. 1996), the plaintiff, who was injured while driving a Honda Accord, brought a product liability action. She objected to evidence proffered by Honda that no similar claim had ever been brought, even though Honda had sold many Accords for many years. The court held that "evidence of the absence of similar accidents or claims is admissible as long as the proponent provides adequate foundation." The proponent must show that a substantially similar product was used in settings and circumstances sufficiently similar to those surrounding the accident in dispute, so that a jury can connect past experience with the disputed accident. The court found no abuse of discretion in the admission of evidence of absence of similar claims involving Honda Accords.

2. Can evidence of other accidents be admissible for some purpose other than to prove how the accident in dispute occurred?

In *Fusco v. Gen. Motors Corp.,* 11 F.3d 259 (1st Cir. 1993), Fusco brought a product liability action arising from an accident in which her car veered out of control over an icy roadway and hit a telephone pole. The major dispute between the parties was whether a key component of the steering system — the front left "ball stud" — had broken from metal fatigue, separated from the tie rod, and caused the accident. General Motors contended that the ball stud had been broken when the car hit the telephone pole and not before, and that at any rate the breaking of a ball stud would not have caused the car to go out of control. To prove this latter point, General Motors proffered two related videotapes. In one tape, a GM expert who testified at trial used a car mounted on a lift to display the function of the ball stud and tie rod and showed how the test vehicle had been altered so that the stud could be deliberately released from inside the car. The test car was a Chevette, the same model driven by Fusco. In the follow-up tape, the expert drove the test car on a test track, and intentionally disconnected the ball stud from the tie rod. The film showed that the car did not veer out of control or hit the track barrier.

Fusco moved to exclude the tapes under Rule 403, on the ground that the test track conditions did not duplicate the road conditions at the time of her accident. GM argued that the dissimilarity went to weight and not admissibility. The trial court excluded the tapes, and the Court of Appeals affirmed.

According to the *Fusco* court, as well as many other courts, the solution for the possibility that jurors may be misled by accident replications is "to call for substantial similarity in conditions, or to stress the great discretion of the trial judge to exclude the evidence where similarity is not shown, or both." The *Fusco* court declared that "the concept of substantial similarity is a flexible one, and ought to be, for the benefits of the demonstration and the dangers of misleading the jury will vary greatly depending on the facts." Accordingly, "the trial judge enjoys great discretion in this area."

Applying these principles to GM's proffered videotapes, the Court of Appeals in *Fusco* concluded that the trial court had not abused its wide discretion in excluding the evidence. The test was done on dry test track, with a driver anticipating that the ball stud would be disengaged, "and with a doctored piece of equipment rather than one that actually broke."

GM responded, however, that the tapes were offered not so much to *recreate* the accident as to explain certain scientific principles to the jury. Indeed, courts have held that where the demonstrative evidence is offered to explain general scientific principles, rather than to prove how the accident occurred, the demonstration need not be made under conditions substantially similar to the accident; all that is required is that the test be properly conducted. As the Tenth Circuit stated in *Gilbert v. Cosco, Inc.*, 989 F.2d 399 (10th Cir. 1993): "[E]xperiments which purport to recreate an accident must be conducted under conditions similar to that accident, while experiments which demonstrate general principles used in forming an expert's opinion are not required to adhere strictly to the conditions of the accident." The *Gilbert* court required no similarity where tests on a product were conducted in order to assist the defendant's expert "in demonstrating physical principles which formed the basis of his expert opinion."

The *Fusco* court responded to GM's argument by expressing doubt as to whether the test was really intended as an abstract demonstration of scientific principles. But even if that were the case, the court concluded that "the critical point is not one of labels." Rather, the issue "is whether the demonstration is sufficiently close in appearance to the original accident to create the risk of misunderstanding by the jury, for it is that risk that gives rise to the special requirement" to show substantially similar conditions. The court found that the test conducted by GM was "rife with misunderstanding" because it looked "very much like a recreation of the event that gave rise to the trial." Accordingly, the trial court did not err in excluding the tapes even as an abstract recreation of scientific principles.

In sum, the *Fusco* court found that GM's taped demonstration was neither fish nor fowl. It was not a legitimate accident replication because the conditions were not substantially similar to the conditions existing at the time of the accident. On the other hand, it was not an admissible demonstration of abstract scientific principles because it looked too much like an attempt to recreate the accident. *See also Finchum v. Ford Motor Co.,* 57 F.3d 526 (7th Cir. 1995) (video of a crash test could not be admitted to illustrate an expert's opinion, because it was "just similar enough to the Finchums' accident to confuse the jury and leave jurors with the prejudicial suggestion that the Finchums flipped over backwards during the crash.").

Gilbert v. Cosco, Inc., *supra*, can be usefully compared to *Fusco*. *Gilbert* was an action against a manufacturer of a child restraint device for injuries resulting in a car accident. The trial court allowed the defendant to present evidence about a test that it had conducted, in which the carseat was placed on a sled and sent down a hill. The *Gilbert* court found that the test was properly admitted solely to demonstrate scientific principles which formed the basis of the conclusions of the defendant's expert. It was clear that the sled test was in no way an attempt to recreate the car accident.

The lesson to defendants from *Fusco* and *Gilbert* is clear: if you want to present demonstrative evidence to prove how an accident occurred, you must conduct the test under conditions that are as identical as reasonably possible to those existing at the time of the accident; sometimes this may be impossible because the accident cannot be sufficiently replicated. On the other hand, if you want to present demonstrative evidence to illustrate general scientific principles, you must conduct the demonstration under circumstances very different from those involved in the accident, so that the jury is not misled.

3. When is evidence of prior claims by the plaintiff admissible?

Generally, evidence of the plaintiff's "litigiousness may have some slight probative value, but that value is outweighed by the substantial danger of jury bias against the chronic litigant." *Raysor v. Port Auth.*, 768 F.2d 34 (2d Cir. 1985). But if a plaintiff has made similar claims that were demonstrably false or fraudulent, most courts will admit the evidence. Thus, in *McDonough v. City of Quincy*, 452 F.3d 8 (1st Cir. 2006), the court, in affirming a judgment for the plaintiff in a Title VII retaliation action, the Court found no error in the exclusion of evidence that the plaintiff had lost a previous lawsuit against the City. Although the City claimed that this showed that the plaintiff was "litigious and had a history of bringing meritless lawsuits," the court noted that "ordinarily proof that the plaintiff filed prior similar lawsuits is admissible to show the plaintiff's litigiousness only if there is also evidence that the prior lawsuits were fraudulently filed." Here, there was only a single lawsuit, and while it was unsuccessful, there was nothing suggesting that it was fraudulently filed.

4. Is evidence of other sales admissible to show the value of a piece of property?

"It is settled law that comparable sales are the best evidence of value. * * * Real property may be unique and the comparable sales too few to establish a conclusive market price, but that does not put out of hand the bearing which the scattered sales may have on what an ordinary purchaser would have paid for the claimant's property." *United States v. Whitehurst*, 337 F.2d 765 (4th Cir. 1964).

[4] Gruesome Visual Presentations

TERRY v. STATE
491 S.W.2d 161 (Tex. Crim. App. 1973)

ODOM, JUDGE.

The jury in this cause found appellant guilty of the offense of murder without malice; the court assessed punishment at five years and this appeal is taken from the conviction.

The evidence shows that the victim of this homicide was the infant son (approximately one month and three days old) of the appellant and her husband.

Appellant complains of the admission in evidence of eight color pictures.

* * *

Photographs are admissible in evidence on the theory that they are pictorial communications of a witness who uses them instead of, or in addition to, some other method of communication. Thus, they are admissible on the same grounds and for the same purposes as are diagrams, maps, and drawings of objects or places, and the same rules of admissibility applicable to objects connected with the crime apply to photographs of such objects. This is true whether they are originals or copies, black and white or colored. So, a photograph, proved to be a true representation of the person, place, or thing which it purports to represent, is competent evidence of those things of which it is material and relevant for a witness to give a verbal description.

* * * Eight color slides were introduced and shown on a screen so the jury could view them. The first three (State's Exhibits 2, 3, and 4) show the nude body of the child depicting many bruises; the next (State's Exhibit 5) is an X-ray showing a broken bone in an arm; the remaining four (State's Exhibits 6, 7, 8, and 9) show areas of the body after an autopsy had been performed. The first three pictures, though gruesome, are admissible as they corroborate the verbal description and bring visibly to the jury the details of the crime by showing the location, nature and extent of the wounds or injuries to the body of the deceased child. Their probative value far outweighs any probable prejudicial effect on the jury. This is especially true since the appellant testified to a single, unintentional act of dropping the child and the pictures show what the jury could reasonably conclude to have been a continual assault.

The X-ray showing the broken arm is admissible. It bears on the degree of the atrociousness of the crime. Such proves a relative issue and enables the jury to better understand the testimony.

Now, we come to the pictures of parts of the body after an autopsy had been performed. State's Exhibit No. 6 shows an incision which exposes the upper interior part of the chest. State's Exhibit No. 7 shows, as described by the expert witness, "* * * the left shoulder, and * * * the flap cut from the chest down the arm * * * to expose the fractured bone." The witness described State's Exhibit No. 8 as, "* * * the head. The bones of a child are not hard;

they are almost rubbery, and to open the head, you reflect the scalp, and you can bend the bones back from the top of the brain. This shows the top of the brain, * * *" State's Exhibit No. 9 shows, "* * * a fracture of the bone in this skull bone, a picture taken of the actual fracture in the skull."

It is apparent from these exhibits that one sees primarily what was done by the person who performed the autopsy rather than that alleged to have been done by appellant. * * *

With this in mind, we must determine if the probative value of these exhibits is sufficient to outweigh their inflammatory aspects * * *. What is shown in these pictures is massive mutilation of the subject matter caused by the surgery in performing the autopsy. The jury, in the absence of the explanation of isolated areas pointed out by the expert witness, sees only severed parts of a human body.

The bruises and injuries to the child had already been shown by verbal descriptions and State's Exhibits 2 through 5. After this was done, what material and relevant issues were necessary to be shown by these photographs taken after an autopsy had been performed? They are, at most, only remotely connected with the crime.

We conclude that the autopsy pictures clearly served to inflame the minds of the jury, and the trial court abused its discretion by not sustaining appellant's objections to their admission.

The judgment is reversed and the cause remanded.

[5] Implicating Another

[a] Illustration

The defendant is charged with rape and has been sitting in jail pending trial. The defendant says someone else did it. At the close of the prosecutor's case, the defendant calls a police officer to the stand.

Defendant:	State your name.
Witness:	Top Cop, Jr.
Defendant:	Do your duties include investigating rape cases?
Witness:	Yes.
Defendant:	The defendant has been in jail for two months. Have any rapes been committed during that time by individuals matching the description of the defendant?
Prosecutor:	Objection! __________ .
The court:	__________ .

[b] Alternative Perpetrator Evidence

UNITED STATES v. McVEIGH
153 F.3d 1166 (10th Cir. 1998)

EBEL, CIRCUIT JUDGE.

Defendant-appellant Timothy J. McVeigh ("McVeigh") was tried, convicted, and sentenced to death on eleven counts stemming from the bombing of the Alfred P. Murrah Federal Building ("Murrah Building") in Oklahoma City, Oklahoma, that resulted in the deaths of 168 people. McVeigh appeals his conviction and sentence * * *. We affirm.

BACKGROUND

At 9:02 in the morning of April 19, 1995, a massive explosion tore apart the Murrah Building in Oklahoma City, Oklahoma, killing a total of 168 people and injuring hundreds more. On August 10, 1995, a federal grand jury returned an eleven-count indictment against McVeigh and Terry Lynn Nichols ("Nichols") charging: one count of conspiracy to use a weapon of mass destruction in violation of 18 U.S.C. § 2332a and 18 U.S.C. § 2(a) & (b); one count of use of a weapon of mass destruction in violation of 18 U.S.C. § 2332a and 18 U.S.C. § 2(a) & (b); one count of destruction by explosives in violation of 18 U.S.C. § 844(f) and 18 U.S.C. § 2(a) & (b); and eight counts of first-degree murder in violation of 18 U.S.C. §§ 1111 & 1114 and 18 U.S.C. § 2(a) & (b). On October 20, 1995, the government filed a Notice of Intent to Seek the Death Penalty. * * *

On February 19, 1996, the district court granted McVeigh's and Nichols' Motion for Change of Venue and transferred the case to Denver, Colorado. On October 25, 1996, the district court granted a Motion for Severance by McVeigh and Nichols and ordered that McVeigh's trial would proceed first. * * *

At the guilt phase of trial, which encompassed twenty-three days of testimony, the government proved the following set of facts. The destruction of the Murrah Building killed 163 people in the building and five people outside. Fifteen children in the Murrah Building day care center, visible from the front of the building, and four children visiting the building were included among the victims. Eight federal law enforcement officials also lost their lives. The explosion, felt and heard six miles away, tore a gaping hole into the front of the Murrah Building and covered the streets with glass, debris, rocks, and chunks of concrete. Emergency workers who reported to the scene made heroic efforts to rescue people still trapped in the building.

The Murrah Building was destroyed by a 3,000–6,000 pound bomb comprised of an ammonium nitrate-based explosive carried inside a rented Ryder truck. In the fall of 1994, McVeigh and Nichols sought, bought, and stole all the materials needed to construct the bomb. First, on September 30, 1994, and October 18, 1994, McVeigh purchased a total of 4,000 pounds of ammonium nitrate from the McPherson branch of the Mid-Kansas Cooperative using the alias "Mike Havens." Second, in October of 1994, McVeigh and Nichols stole seven cases of Tovex explosives and a box of Primadet nonelectric blasting caps from the Martin Marietta rock quarry near Marion, Kansas. Third, on October 21, 1994, McVeigh purchased three drums of nitromethane at a race track outside of Dallas, Texas. Prior to the nitromethane purchase, McVeigh had sought bomb ingredients, including nitromethane, both in person and through the use of a prepaid telephone calling card under the name "Daryl Bridges." Using various aliases, McVeigh and Nichols rented a number of storage lockers in Kansas where they stored the bomb components. In order to fund their conspiracy, McVeigh and Nichols robbed a gun dealer in Arkansas in November of 1994.

In a letter to Michael and Lori Fortier written around September of 1994, McVeigh disclosed that he and Terry Nichols had decided to take some type of positive offensive action against the federal government in response to the government's siege of the Branch Davidians in Waco, Texas in 1993. On a subsequent visit to their home, McVeigh told the Fortiers that he planned to blow up a federal building. McVeigh later informed the Fortiers that he wanted to cause a general uprising in America and that the bombing would occur on the anniversary of the end of the Waco siege. McVeigh rationalized the inevitable loss of life by concluding that anyone who worked in the federal building was guilty by association with those responsible for Waco. * * * McVeigh told the Fortiers that he chose the Murrah Building as the target because he believed that (1) the orders for the attack at Waco emanated from the building, (2) the building housed people involved in the Waco raid, and (3) the building's U-shape and glass front made it an easy target. On a later trip through Oklahoma City, McVeigh showed Michael Fortier the Murrah Building, asking Fortier whether he thought a twenty-foot rental truck would fit in front of the building. * * * The manner in which the bombing was carried out closely tracked several books bought by McVeigh, which he often encouraged his friends to read, describing how to make a powerful bomb mixing ammonium nitrate with nitromethane and romanticizing self-declared patriots who blow up federal buildings. McVeigh was familiar with explosives and had detonated a pipe bomb prior to the attack on the Murrah Building.

* * * During the search of the blast site, the FBI located the rear axle of the Ryder truck used to carry the bomb. The vehicle identification number from the axle matched that of the Ryder truck rented to McVeigh * * * on April 15, 1995, and picked up by McVeigh two days prior to the blast. McVeigh rented the truck under the name "Robert King" using a phony South Dakota drivers license that Lori Fortier had helped McVeigh create.

McVeigh drove to Oklahoma City in the rented Ryder truck, which he had made into a bomb, parking the vehicle in front of the Murrah Building and running to the yellow Mercury that he and Nichols had stashed as a getaway car in a nearby alley a couple of days before the bombing. A Ford key fitting the Ryder truck was found in an alley near where McVeigh had told Michael Fortier that the getaway car would be parked. McVeigh hand-printed a sign inside the yellow Mercury, "Not Abandoned; Please do not tow; will move by April 23 (Needs Battery & Cable)." McVeigh deliberately parked the car so that a building would stand between the car and the blast, shielding McVeigh from the explosion. The bomb then exploded.

Just 77 minutes after the blast, Oklahoma State Trooper Charles Hanger ("Hanger") stopped the yellow Mercury driven by McVeigh because the car had no license tags. The stop occurred between mile markers 202 and 203 on Interstate 35, just before the exit for Billings, Oklahoma, precisely 77.9 miles north of the Murrah Building. Before he was stopped by Hanger, McVeigh was headed northbound away from Oklahoma City towards Kansas. A person driving the posted speed limit would have reached the point of the stop 75 minutes after leaving the Murrah Building. If McVeigh had left the Murrah Building right after the bombing, he would have arrived at the Billings exit around 10:17 a.m., the approximate time of the stop.

Hanger arrested McVeigh upon discovering that he was carrying a concealed, loaded gun. Hanger transported McVeigh to Noble County Jail in Perry, Oklahoma, where McVeigh was booked and incarcerated for unlawfully carrying a weapon and transporting a loaded firearm. Noble County authorities took custody of McVeigh's clothing and property, including earplugs, and issued him prison garb. Two days later, on April 21, 1995, the federal government filed a Complaint against McVeigh for unlawful destruction by explosives. Oklahoma then transferred McVeigh to federal custody on the federal bombing charges. An FBI test performed later found that McVeigh's clothing and the earplugs contained explosives residue, including PETN, EGDN, and nitroglycerine-chemicals associated with the materials used in the construction of the bomb.

A subsequent inventory search of the yellow Mercury uncovered a sealed envelope containing documents arguing that the federal government had commenced open warfare on the liberty of the American people and justifying the killing of government officials in the defense of liberty. Finally, three days after the arrest, Hanger found a Paulsen's Military Supply business card on the floor of his cruiser bearing McVeigh's fingerprints. McVeigh had written on the back of the card, "TNT @ $5/stick Need more" and "Call After 01, May, See if I can get some more."

Closing arguments were made on May 29, 1997, and the district court charged the jury on May 30, 1997. On June 2, 1997, after four days of deliberations, the jury returned guilty verdicts on all eleven counts charged in the Indictment. The penalty phase of trial commenced on June 4, 1997, and concluded with summations and jury instructions on June 12, 1997. The jury deliberated for two days before returning special findings recommending that McVeigh be sentenced to death. After denying McVeigh's motion for a new trial, the district court accepted the jury recommendation on August 14, 1997, sentencing McVeigh to death on all eleven counts. McVeigh filed a timely notice of appeal that same day.

DISCUSSION

* * *

C. EVIDENCE OF ALLEGED ALTERNATIVE PERPETRATORS

McVeigh challenges the district court's decision to exclude two lines of evidence that McVeigh argues would suggest that persons connected with a white-supremacist, anti-government organization in Stillwell, Oklahoma, known as "Elohim City," were involved in the conspiracy to destroy the Murrah Building. McVeigh contends that the district court abused its discretion when it excluded as "not sufficiently relevant" both the proffered testimony from Carol Howe ("Howe"), an undercover government informant at Elohim City, and other proffered evidence that McVeigh argues would have shown the government suspended its independent investigation of Elohim City in the wake of McVeigh's arrest.

McVeigh argues that this ruling was based solely on the relevance standard of Rule 401. The government, however, argues that the court's ruling incorporates both the relevance standard of Rule 401 and the balancing required in Rule 403. The text of the court's ruling appears to favor the government's position, indicating that the court found some "relevance" under Rule 401, but not enough to be "sufficient" under Rule 403.

1. Standard of review

Generally, we review a district court's ruling on the relevance and potential prejudice of proffered evidence under the abuse-of-discretion standard. Furthermore, this circuit has never found a per se abuse of discretion simply because a trial court failed to make explicit, on-the-record findings for a decision under Federal Rule of Evidence 403. * * * Although the trial court should, of course, always make explicit findings to support its Rule 403 rulings, there may be occasions when the record is such that we can do our own *de novo* balancing of the Rule 403 factors without requiring a remand of that issue to the district court. * * *

Here, the district court failed to make an explicit record of its balancing of the Rule 403 factors. However, we may conduct a *de novo* balancing because the record contains a colloquy between the court and counsel that sheds considerable light on how the district court viewed the evidence. We conclude that even if there was probative value to McVeigh's proffered evidence, it was "substantially outweighed by the danger of unfair prejudice, confusion of the issues, or misleading the jury." *See* Fed. R. Evid. 403. Thus, there was no error in excluding such evidence.

2. Background

Near the end of the trial's guilt phase, MeVeigh's defense counsel made an oral proffer during an in-chambers hearing concerning the defense's evidence of alternative perpetrators. This proffer focused on Howe's expected testimony concerning her various visits to Elohim City in 1994-1995.

Howe allegedly would have testified that during her trips to Elohim City, she met Dennis Mahon ("Mahon"), one of Elohim City's leaders, and that Mahon was a violent opponent of the federal government. Howe would have testified that Mahon instructed her in the preparation of napalm and had shown her various bomb components at Elohim City, including a tap, green fuse, black powder, bolts, a funnel, and a grenade shell. Mahon also discussed the availability and cost of the explosive Semtex, as well as his experience in building and exploding a 500-pound ammonium nitrate bomb under a truck in Michigan.

Howe's proffered testimony also promised to discuss Andreas Strassmeir ("Strassmeir"), another leader at Elohim City, who allegedly discussed acquiring bomb components for Elohim City. Howe was to testify that Mahon and Strassmeir had discussed targeting a federal building in either Oklahoma City or Tulsa, or an IRS building. Howe also was to testify about the appearance at Elohim City in the spring of 1995 of James Ellison, who had developed plans to bomb the Murrah Building in 1983 before he was imprisoned on unrelated charges. Furthermore, Howe would have testified about the affinity of the Elohim City members for the people killed in the government's siege of the Branch Davidian compound in Waco, Texas. Finally, two days after the bombing, Howe told federal agents that she allegedly had seen two brothers at Elohim City before the bombing who resembled the composite drawings of "John Doe 1" and "John Doe 2," the suspects originally sought by the government in the immediate aftermath of the bombing.

Separately from Howe's testimony, McVeigh's counsel also offered to introduce copies of FBI and ATF reports that McVeigh argued would establish that the federal investigation into Elohim City was suspended after McVeigh was arrested.

McVeigh contends that this proffered evidence was relevant to two separate propositions: first, that there were other perpetrators of the bombing, and second, that the government's investigation of the bombing was "shoddy and slanted," with investigators allegedly overlooking exculpatory evidence after they became satisfied that McVeigh was the principal perpetrator.

After hearing the proffer, the district court ruled, "Well, we've had a number of disclosures concerning Mahon, Strassmeir, Elohim City and now some additional information from Carol Howe. But my ruling is that it's excluded, not sufficiently relevant to be admissible."

3. Analysis

a. Relevance under Rule 401

Under the Federal Rules of Evidence, "[a]ll relevant evidence is admissible," subject to the limitations provided by the Federal Rules and other laws; any evidence "which is not relevant is not admissible." *See* Fed. R. Evid. 402. Thus, the threshold to admissibility is relevance. The scope of relevancy is bounded only by the liberal standard of Rule 401, which provides that evidence is relevant if it has "any tendency to make the existence of any fact that is of consequence to the determination of the action more probable or less probable than it would be without the evidence." *See* Fed. R. Evid. 401. As commentators have noted, Rule 401's definition of relevancy incorporates notions of both materiality and probativity. *See* 1 Kenneth S. Broun, et al., McCormick on Evidence § 185, at 774–75 (John William Strong ed., 4th ed.1992).

As for materiality, under Rule 401 a fact is "of consequence" when its existence would provide the fact-finder with a basis for making some inference, or chain of inferences, about an issue that is necessary to a verdict. As for the degree of probative value required under Rule 401, the rule sets the bar very low. The rule establishes that even a minimal degree of probability — i.e., "any tendency" — that the asserted fact exists is sufficient to find the proffered evidence relevant. *See* Fed. R. Evid. 401. The Advisory Committee explained that the "any tendency" language establishes that the "standard of probability under the rule is 'more probable than it would be without the evidence.' "

b. Balancing under Rule 403

Even though evidence may meet the relevancy standard of Rule 401, a trial court still may exclude it on the grounds that its probative value — the evidence's probability of establishing a fact of consequence — is "substantially outweighed" by certain negative factors. *See* Fed. R. Evid. 403. Those factors include "unfair prejudice," "confusion of the issues," and "misleading the jury."

The danger of "unfair prejudice" under Rule 403 is not simply the tendency of evidence to undermine a party's position. Rather, the prejudice that is "unfair" is prejudice arising from the tendency of proffered evidence to suggest to the jury that it should render its findings "on an improper basis, commonly, though not necessarily, an emotional one." *See* Fed. R. Evid. 403, Adv. Comm. Notes (1972 Proposed Rules).

The danger of "confusion of the issues" and "misleading the jury" arises when circumstantial evidence would tend to sidetrack the jury into consideration of factual disputes only tangentially related to the facts at issue in the current case. The classic explanation of this danger comes from Dean Wigmore: "The notion here is that, in attempting to dispute or explain away the evidence thus offered, new issues will arise as to the occurrence of the instances and the similarity of conditions, [and] new witnesses will be needed whose cross examination and impeachment may lead to further issues." 2 John Henry Wigmore, Evidence § 443, at 528–29 (James H. Chadbourn rev., 1979).

In the course of weighing probative value and adverse dangers, courts must be sensitive to the special problems presented by "alternative perpetrator" evidence. Although there is no doubt that a defendant has a right to attempt to establish his innocence by showing that someone else did the crime, a defendant still must show that his proffered evidence on the alleged alternative perpetrator is sufficient, on its own or in combination with other evidence in the record, to show a nexus between the crime charged and the asserted "alternative perpetrator." It is not sufficient for a defendant merely to offer up unsupported speculation that another person may have done the crime. Such speculative blaming intensifies the grave risk of jury confusion, and it invites the jury to render its findings based on emotion or prejudice.

Finally, after identifying the degree of probative value and adverse danger, courts exclude relevant evidence if the adverse dangers "substantially outweigh" the probative value. *See* Fed. R. Evid. 403.

c. Admissibility of Carol Howe's proffered testimony

Even if we assume that the proffered evidence had some marginal relevance, the Howe testimony cannot survive the balancing under Rule 403. First, we conclude that the probative value of such proffered testimony was slight because of its highly generalized and speculative nature. The fact that another group held similar anti-government views as did McVeigh and that some of its members expressed vague threats to bomb a variety of potential targets in Oklahoma, possibly including a federal building in Oklahoma City, says very little about whether this group actually bombed the Murrah Building. That others shared McVeigh's political views is a slender reed upon which to vault the dangers of unfair prejudice and jury confusion. Howe's alleged identification of "John Doe 1" and "John Doe 2" arguably increases the probative value of her other testimony. However, the composite sketches included no particular identifying features that would strengthen the significance of Howe's allegation of two matches. In fact, there are undoubtedly thousands of men across America who resembled the government's composite sketches. Finally, there was no evidence in this proffer, or in the record, that would establish a probative nexus between the alleged Elohim City conspiracy and the bombing of the Murrah Building.

In the face of the speculative probative value of Howe's testimony, we must confront the very real dangers of unfair prejudice and confusion of the issues. The Howe testimony presented a great threat of "confusion of the issues" because it would have forced the government to attempt to disprove the nebulous allegation that Elohim City was involved in the bombing. This side trial would have led the jury astray, turning the focus away from whether McVeigh — the only person whose actions were on trial — bombed the Murrah Building. It also presented a threat of "unfair prejudice" as it would invite the jury to blame absent, unrepresented individuals and groups for whom there often may be strong underlying emotional responses.

Thus, the district court did not err in excluding this testimony.

d. Admissibility of suspension of Elohim City investigation

McVeigh's additional claim of error involves the exclusion of FBI and ATF reports pertaining to the activities of the Elohim City group. McVeigh contends that the reports show that the government's investigation of Elohim City was "shoddy" and "slanted" because they allegedly show that the government failed to investigate other potential suspects once it focused on McVeigh.

McVeigh's argument runs aground on both his factual and legal premises. Factually, these reports simply do not support his claim that the government's investigation of Elohim City was shoddy or that the government prematurely terminated the investigation. To the contrary, the proffered reports suggest that the government actively pursued the potential connection between Elohim City and the bombing, and that this aspect of the bombing investigation remained open well after McVeigh became the primary focus. The reports suggest that the government was unwilling to send Howe back into Elohim City, as a confidential informant, because leaders of that group had begun to suspect her status and she had received warnings that she would be in danger if she returned to Elohim City. These details in the ATF and FBI reports do not in the slightest offer any probative evidence for McVeigh's unfounded speculation that the government's investigation was shoddy or prematurely terminated.

The legal premise of McVeigh's claim — that the quality of the government's investigation was material to his defense — also founders. Admittedly, the quality or bias of a criminal investigation occasionally may affect the reliability of particular evidence in a trial, and hence, the facts surrounding the government's investigation may become relevant. However, in McVeigh's case, he failed to establish the requisite connection between the allegedly "shoddy" and "slanted" investigation and any evidence introduced at trial. There was no trial evidence whose reliability would have been undercut had McVeigh been able to prove his contentions about the Elohim City investigation. To have allowed McVeigh to put the government on trial because there might have been something more the government perhaps could have done with respect to the activities of the Elohim City group would inevitably divert the jury's attention from the issues of the trial. *See United States v. Veal*, 23 F.3d 985, 989 (6th Cir. 1994) (upholding a trial court's refusal to allow a defendant to show that the government's investigation had been "sloppy" because "the jury would not be called upon to determine whether the government's investigation had been good or bad").

Under our system of criminal justice, the issue submitted to the jury is whether the accused is guilty or not guilty. The jury is not asked to render judgment about non-parties, nor is it normally asked to render a verdict on the government's investigation. The district court did not abuse its discretion, but rather is to be commended, in keeping the focus of the trial upon the issues properly before the jury.

* * *

CONCLUSION

For the foregoing reasons, Timothy McVeigh's conviction and sentence are AFFIRMED.

---

[c] Alternative Perpetrator Evidence and the Constitutional Right to an Effective Defense

In the following case, the Court finds that exclusion of evidence, offered by a criminal defendant to prove that another person did it, can violate the defendant's constitutional right to an effective defense. The case certainly does not invalidate the use of Rule 403 and similar exclusionary rules, but it does establish that there are constitutional limits on excluding evidence proffered by a criminal defendant.

HOLMES v. SOUTH CAROLINA
547 U.S. 319 (2006)

JUSTICE ALITO delivered the opinion of the Court.

This case presents the question whether a criminal defendant's federal constitutional rights are violated by an evidence rule under which the defendant may not introduce proof of third-party guilt if the prosecution has introduced forensic evidence that, if believed, strongly supports a guilty verdict.

I

On the morning of December 31, 1989, 86-year-old Mary Stewart was beaten, raped, and robbed in her home. She later died of complications stemming from her injuries. Petitioner was convicted by a South Carolina jury of murder, first-degree criminal sexual conduct, first-degree burglary, and robbery, and he was sentenced to death. The South Carolina Supreme Court affirmed his convictions and sentence, and this Court denied certiorari. Upon state postconviction review, however, petitioner was granted a new trial.

At the second trial, the prosecution relied heavily on the following forensic evidence:

> (1) [Petitioner's] palm print was found just above the door knob on the interior side of the front door of the victim's house; (2) fibers consistent with a black sweatshirt owned by [petitioner] were found on the victim's bed sheets; (3) matching blue fibers were found on the victim's pink nightgown and on [petitioner's] blue jeans; (4) microscopically consistent fibers were found on the pink nightgown and on [petitioner's] underwear; (5) [petitioner's] underwear contained a mixture of DNA from two individuals, and 99.99% of the population other than [petitioner] and the victim were excluded as contributors to that mixture; and (6) [petitioner's] tank top was found to contain a mixture of [petitioner's] blood and the victim's blood.

In addition, the prosecution introduced evidence that petitioner had been seen near Stewart's home within an hour of the time when, according to the prosecution's evidence, the attack took place.

As a major part of his defense, petitioner attempted to undermine the State's forensic evidence by suggesting that it had been contaminated and that certain law enforcement officers had engaged in a plot to frame him. Petitioner's expert witnesses criticized the procedures used by the police in handling the fiber and DNA evidence and in collecting the fingerprint evidence. Another defense expert provided testimony that petitioner cited as supporting his claim that the palm print had been planted by the police.

Petitioner also sought to introduce proof that another man, Jimmy McCaw White, had attacked Stewart. At a pretrial hearing, petitioner proffered several witnesses who placed White in the victim's neighborhood on the morning of the assault, as well as four other witnesses who testified that White had either acknowledged that petitioner was "'innocent'" or had actually admitted to committing the crimes. One witness recounted that when he asked

White about the "word * * * on the street" that White was responsible for Stewart's murder, White "put his head down and he raised his head back up and he said, well, you know I like older women." According to this witness, White added that "he did what they say he did" and that he had "no regrets about it at all." Another witness, who had been incarcerated with White, testified that White had admitted to assaulting Stewart, that a police officer had asked the witness to testify falsely against petitioner, and that employees of the prosecutor's office, while soliciting the witness' cooperation, had spoken of manufacturing evidence against petitioner. White testified at the pretrial hearing and denied making the incriminating statements. He also provided an alibi for the time of the crime, but another witness refuted his alibi.

The trial court excluded petitioner's third-party guilt evidence citing *State v. Gregory,* 198 S. C. 98, 16 S. E. 2d 532 (1941), which held that such evidence is admissible if it "raises a reasonable inference or presumption as to [the defendant's] own innocence" but is not admissible if it merely "casts a bare suspicion upon another" or "raises a conjectural inference as to the commission of the crime by another." On appeal, the South Carolina Supreme Court found no error in the exclusion of petitioner's third-party guilt evidence. Citing both *Gregory* and its later decision in *State v. Gay,* 343 S. C. 543, 541 S. E. 2d 541 (2001), the State Supreme Court held that "where there is strong evidence of an appellant's guilt, especially where there is strong forensic evidence, the proffered evidence about a third party's alleged guilt does not raise a reasonable inference as to the appellant's own innocence." Applying this standard, the court held that petitioner could not "overcome the forensic evidence against him to raise a reasonable inference of his own innocence." We granted certiorari.

II

"State and federal rulemakers have broad latitude under the Constitution to establish rules excluding evidence from criminal trials." *United States v. Scheffer,* 523 U.S. 303, 308 (1998); see also *Crane v. Kentucky*, 476 U.S. 683, 689–690 (1986); *Chambers v. Mississippi*, 410 U.S. 284, 302–303 (1973). This latitude, however, has limits. "Whether rooted directly in the Due Process Clause of the Fourteenth Amendment or in the Compulsory Process or Confrontation clauses of the Sixth Amendment, the Constitution guarantees criminal defendants 'a meaningful opportunity to present a complete defense.' " *Crane, supra*, 476 U.S. at 690 (quoting *California v. Trombetta*, 467 U.S. 479, 485 (1984). This right is abridged by evidence rules that "infringe upon a weighty interest of the accused" and are "arbitrary or disproportionate to the purposes they are designed to serve." *Scheffer, supra,* 523 U.S. at 308 (quoting *Rock v. Arkansas,* 483 U.S. 44, 58, 56 (1987)).

This Court's cases contain several illustrations of "arbitrary" rules, *i.e.*, rules that excluded important defense evidence but that did not serve any legitimate interests. In *Washington v. Texas*, 388 U.S. 14 (1967), state statutes barred a person who had been charged as a participant in a crime from testifying in defense of another alleged participant unless the witness had been acquitted. As a result, when the defendant in *Washington* was tried for murder, he was precluded from calling as a witness a person who had been charged and previously convicted of committing the same murder. Holding that the defendant's right to put on a defense had been violated, we noted that the rule embodied in the statutes could not "even be defended on the ground that it rationally sets apart a group of persons who are particularly likely to commit perjury" since the rule allowed an alleged participant to testify if he or she had been acquitted or was called by the prosecution.

A similar constitutional violation occurred in *Chambers v. Mississippi, supra.* A murder defendant called as a witness a man named McDonald, who had previously confessed to the murder. When McDonald repudiated the confession on the stand, the defendant was denied permission to examine McDonald as an adverse witness based on the State's "voucher' rule," which barred parties from impeaching their own witnesses. In addition, because the state hearsay rule did not include an exception for statements against penal interest, the defendant was not permitted to introduce evidence that McDonald had made self-incriminating statements to three other persons. Noting that the State had not even attempted to "defend" or "explain [the] underlying rationale" of the "voucher rule," this Court held that "the exclusion of [the evidence of McDonald's out-of-court statements], coupled with the State's refusal to permit [the defendant] to cross-examine McDonald, denied him a trial in accord with traditional and fundamental standards of due process."

Another arbitrary rule was held unconstitutional in *Crane v. Kentucky, supra.* There, the defendant was prevented from attempting to show at trial that his confession was unreliable because of the circumstances under which it was obtained, and neither the State Supreme Court nor the prosecution "advanced any rational justification for the wholesale exclusion of this body of potentially exculpatory evidence."

In *Rock v. Arkansas, supra*, this Court held that a rule prohibiting hypnotically refreshed testimony was unconstitutional because "wholesale inadmissibility of a defendant's testimony is an arbitrary restriction on the right to testify in the absence of clear evidence by the State repudiating the validity of all post-hypnotic recollections." By contrast, in *United States v. Scheffer, supra*, we held that a rule excluding all polygraph evidence did not abridge the right to present a defense because the rule "served several legitimate interests in the criminal trial process," was "neither arbitrary nor disproportionate in promoting these ends," and did not "implicate a sufficiently weighty interest of the defendant."

While the Constitution thus prohibits the exclusion of defense evidence under rules that serve no legitimate purpose or that are disproportionate to the ends that they are asserted to promote, well-established rules of evidence permit trial judges to exclude evidence if its probative value is outweighed by certain other factors such as unfair prejudice, confusion of the issues, or potential to mislead the jury. *See, e.g.,* Fed. Rule Evid. 403. Plainly referring to rules of this type, we have stated that the Constitution permits judges "to exclude evidence that is repetitive * * *, only marginally relevant or poses an undue risk of harassment, prejudice, [or] confusion of the issues." *Crane, supra,* 476 U.S. at 689–690.

A specific application of this principle is found in rules regulating the admission of evidence proffered by criminal defendants to show that someone else committed the crime with which they are charged. *See, e.g.,* 41 C. J. S., Homicide § 216, pp. 56–58 (1991) ("Evidence tending to show the commission by another person of the crime charged may be introduced by accused when it is inconsistent with, and raises a reasonable doubt of, his own guilt; but frequently matters offered in evidence for this purpose are so remote and lack such connection with the crime that they are excluded"); 40A Am. Jur. 2d, Homicide § 286, pp. 136–138 (1999) ("The accused may introduce any legal evidence tending to prove that another person may have committed the crime with which the defendant is charged * * * . [Such evidence] may be excluded where it does not sufficiently connect the other person to the crime, as, for example, where the evidence is speculative or remote, or does not tend to prove or disprove a material fact in issue at the defendant's trial."). Such rules are widely accepted, and neither petitioner nor his *amici* challenge them here.

In *Gregory*, the South Carolina Supreme Court adopted and applied a rule apparently intended to be of this type, given the court's references to the "applicable rule" from Corpus Juris and American Jurisprudence:

> Evidence offered by accused as to the commission of the crime by another person must be limited to such facts as are inconsistent with his own guilt, and to such facts as raise a reasonable inference or presumption as to his own innocence; evidence which can have (no) other effect than to cast a bare suspicion upon another, or to raise a conjectural inference as to the commission of the crime by another, is not admissible * * * . Before such testimony can be received, there must be such proof of connection with it, such a train of facts or circumstances, as tends clearly to point out such other person as the guilty party.

198 S. C., at 104–105, 16 S. E. 2d, at 534–535 (quoting 16 C. J., Criminal Law § 1085, p. 560 (1918) and 20 Am. Jur., Evidence § 265, p. 254 (1939).

In *Gay* and this case, however, the South Carolina Supreme Court radically changed and extended the rule. In *Gay*, after recognizing the standard applied in *Gregory*, the court stated that "in view of the strong evidence of appellant's guilt — especially the forensic evidence — * * * the proffered evidence * * * did not raise a reasonable inference as to appellant's own innocence." Similarly, in the present case, as noted, the State Supreme Court applied the rule that "where there is strong evidence of [a defendant's] guilt, especially where there is strong forensic evidence, the proffered evidence about a third party's alleged guilt" may (or perhaps must) be excluded.

Under this rule, the trial judge does not focus on the probative value or the potential adverse effects of admitting the defense evidence of third-party guilt. Instead, the critical inquiry concerns the strength of the prosecution's case: If the prosecution's case is strong enough, the evidence of third-party guilt is excluded even if that evidence, if viewed independently, would have great probative value and even if it would not pose an undue risk of harassment, prejudice, or confusion of the issues.

Furthermore, as applied in this case, the South Carolina Supreme Court's rule seems to call for little, if any, examination of the credibility of the prosecution's witnesses or the reliability of its evidence. Here, for example, the defense strenuously claimed that the prosecution's forensic evidence was so unreliable (due to mishandling and a deliberate plot to frame petitioner) that the evidence should not have even been admitted. The South Carolina Supreme Court responded that these challenges did not entirely "eviscerate" the forensic evidence and that the defense challenges went to the weight and not to the admissibility of that evidence. Yet, in evaluating the prosecution's forensic evidence and deeming it to be "strong" — and thereby justifying exclusion of petitioner's third-party guilt evidence — the South Carolina Supreme Court made no mention of the defense challenges to the prosecution's evidence.

Interpreted in this way, the rule applied by the State Supreme Court does not rationally serve the end that the *Gregory* rule and its analogues in other jurisdictions were designed to promote, *i.e.*, to focus the trial on the central issues by excluding evidence that has only a very weak logical connection to the central issues. The rule applied in this case appears to be based on the following logic: Where (1) it is clear that only one person was involved in the commission of a particular crime and (2) there is strong evidence that the defendant was the perpetrator, it follows that evidence of third-party guilt must be weak. But this logic depends on an accurate evaluation of the prosecution's proof, and the true strength of the prosecution's proof cannot be assessed without considering challenges to the reliability of the prosecution's evidence. Just because the prosecution's evidence, *if credited*, would provide strong support for a guilty verdict, it does not follow that evidence of third-party guilt has only a weak logical connection to the central issues in the case. And where the credibility of the prosecution's witnesses or the reliability of its evidence is not conceded, the strength of the prosecution's case cannot be assessed without making the sort of factual findings that have traditionally been reserved for the trier of fact and that the South Carolina courts did not purport to make in this case.

The rule applied in this case is no more logical than its converse would be, *i.e.*, a rule barring the prosecution from introducing evidence of a defendant's guilt if the defendant is able to proffer, at a pretrial hearing, evidence that, if believed, strongly supports a verdict of not guilty. In the present case, for example, the petitioner proffered evidence that, if believed, squarely proved that White, not petitioner, was the perpetrator. It would make no sense, however, to hold that this proffer precluded the prosecution from introducing its evidence, including the forensic evidence that, if credited, provided strong proof of the petitioner's guilt.

The point is that, by evaluating the strength of only one party's evidence, no logical conclusion can be reached regarding the strength of contrary evidence offered by the other side to rebut or cast doubt. Because the rule applied by the State Supreme Court in this case did not heed this point, the rule is "arbitrary" in the sense that it does not rationally serve the end that the *Gregory* rule and other similar third-party guilt rules were designed to further. Nor has the State identified any other legitimate end that the rule serves. It follows that the rule applied in this case by the State Supreme Court violates a criminal defendant's right to have "a meaningful opportunity to present a complete defense." *Crane*, 476 U.S., at 690.

III

For these reasons, we vacate the judgment of the South Carolina Supreme Court and remand the case for further proceedings not inconsistent with this opinion.

It is so ordered.

NOTE

To be admissible, what must evidence incriminating others tend to prove?

The court in *State v. Woods*, recognized that "[e]vidence that another person had an opportunity or motive for committing the crime for which the defendant is on trial is not admissible absent proof that the other person committed some act directly connecting him with the crime." 508 S.W.2d 297 (Mo. 1974). In other words, "The evidence, to be admissible, must be such proof as directly connects the other person with the *corpus delicti*, and tends clearly to point out someone besides accused as the guilty person. Disconnected and remote acts outside the crime itself cannot be separately proved for such purpose; and evidence which can have no other effect than to cast a bare suspicion on another, or to raise a conjectural inference as to the commission of the crime by another, is not admissible."

In *United States v. DeNoyer*, the defendant was convicted of committing involuntary sodomy against his five-year-old son. The trial court excluded the defendant's "offers to prove that his wife's brother undressed a five-year-old girl at a prayer meeting; that a neighbor two houses away from the DeNoyer dwelling had committed sodomy a year previous to the incident in the case at bar; and that other deviant sex offenders were operating in the community." 811 F.2d 436 (8th Cir. 1987). The court of appeals held that "[t]his sort of evidence was properly excluded as remote and speculative. Such efforts to cast suspicion elsewhere fall far short of establishing a 'Perry Mason defense.' The proferred testimony was pure 'red herring' and had no probative value in establishing the culpability of any party other than the defendant with respect to the offense involved in the case at bar." For a different outcome, see *United States v. Stevens*, 935 F.2d 1380 (3d Cir. 1991), where the court allowed the testimony that someone other than the defendant committed the crime, given the numerous similarities between the crime committed by the other person and the one with which the defendant was charged.

G. EVIDENTIARY ALTERNATIVES AND STIPULATIONS

OLD CHIEF v. UNITED STATES
519 U.S. 172 (1997)

JUSTICE SOUTER delivered the opinion of the Court.

Subject to certain limitations, 18 U.S.C. § 922(g)(1) prohibits possession of a firearm by anyone with a prior felony conviction, which the Government can prove by introducing a record of judgment or similar evidence identifying the previous offense. Fearing prejudice if the jury learns the nature of the earlier crime, defendants sometimes seek to avoid such an informative disclosure by offering to concede the fact of the prior conviction. The issue here is whether a district court abuses its discretion if it spurns such an offer and admits the full record of a prior judgment, when the name or nature of the prior offense raises the risk of a verdict tainted by improper considerations, and when the purpose of the evidence is solely to prove the element of prior conviction. We hold that it does.

I

In 1993, petitioner, Old Chief, was arrested after a fracas involving at least one gunshot. The ensuing federal charges included not only assault with a dangerous weapon and using a firearm in relation to a crime of violence but violation of 18 U.S.C. § 922(g)(1). This statute makes it unlawful for anyone "who has been convicted in any court of, a crime punishable by imprisonment for a term exceeding one year" to "possess in or affecting commerce, any firearm." * * *

The earlier crime charged in the indictment against Old Chief was assault causing serious bodily injury. Before trial, he moved for an order requiring the Government "to refrain from mentioning — by reading the Indictment, during jury selection, in opening statement, or closing argument — and to refrain from offering into evidence or soliciting any testimony from any witness regarding the prior criminal convictions of the Defendant, *except* to state that the Defendant has been convicted of a crime punishable by imprisonment exceeding one (1) year." He said that revealing the name and nature of his prior assault conviction would unfairly tax the jury's capacity to hold the Government to its burden of proof beyond a reasonable doubt on current charges of assault, possession, and violence with a firearm, and he offered to "solve the problem here by stipulating, agreeing and requesting the Court to instruct the jury that he has been convicted of a crime punishable by imprisonment exceeding one (1) year." He argued that the offer to stipulate to the fact of the prior conviction rendered evidence of the name and nature of the offense inadmissible under Rule 403 of the Federal Rules of Evidence, the danger being that unfair prejudice from that evidence would substantially outweigh its probative value. * * *

The Assistant United States Attorney refused to join in a stipulation, insisting on his right to prove his case his own way, and the District Court agreed, ruling orally that, "If he doesn't want to stipulate, he doesn't have to." At trial, over renewed objection, the Government introduced the order of judgment and commitment for Old Chief's prior conviction. This document disclosed that on December 18, 1988, he "did knowingly and unlawfully assault Rory Dean Fenner, said assault resulting in serious bodily injury," for which Old Chief was sentenced to five years' imprisonment. The jury found Old Chief guilty on all counts, and he appealed. [The Ninth Circuit affirmed, holding that regardless of the defendant's offer to stipulate, the government is entitled to prove a prior felony offense through introduction of probative evidence."] We now reverse the judgment of the Ninth Circuit.

II

A

As a threshold matter, there is Old Chief's erroneous argument that the name of his prior offense as contained in the record of conviction is irrelevant to the prior-conviction element, and for that reason inadmissible under Rule 402 of the Federal Rules of Evidence. Rule 401 defines relevant evidence as having "any tendency to make the existence of any fact that is of consequence to the determination of the action more probable or less probable than it would be without the evidence." To be sure, the fact that Old Chief's prior conviction was for assault resulting in serious bodily injury rather than, say, for theft was not itself an ultimate fact, as if the statute had specifically required proof of injurious assault. But its demonstration was a step on one evidentiary route to the ultimate fact, since it served to place Old Chief within a particular subclass of offenders for whom firearms possession is outlawed by § 922(g)(1). A documentary record of the conviction for that named offense was thus relevant evidence in making Old Chief's § 922(g)(1) status more probable than it would have been without the evidence.

Nor was its evidentiary relevance under Rule 401 affected by the availability of alternative proofs of the element to which it went, such as an admission by Old Chief that he had been convicted of a crime "punishable by imprisonment for a term exceeding one year" within the meaning of the statute. The 1972 Advisory Committee Notes to Rule 401 make this point directly:

> The fact to which the evidence is directed need not be in dispute. While situations will arise which call for the exclusion of evidence offered to prove a point conceded by the opponent, the ruling should be made on the basis of such considerations as waste of time and undue prejudice (see Rule 403), rather than under any general requirement that evidence is admissible only if directed to matters in dispute." Advisory Committee's Notes on Fed. Rule Evid. 401.

If, then, relevant evidence is inadmissible in the presence of other evidence related to it, its exclusion must rest not on the ground that the other evidence has rendered it "irrelevant," but on its character as unfairly prejudicial, cumulative or the like, its relevance notwithstanding.

B

The principal issue is the scope of a trial judge's discretion under Rule 403, which authorizes exclusion of relevant evidence when its "probative value is substantially outweighed by the danger of unfair prejudice, confusion of the issues, or misleading the jury, or by considerations of undue delay, waste of time, or needless presentation of cumulative evidence." Old Chief relies on the danger of unfair prejudice.

1

The term "unfair prejudice," as to a criminal defendant, speaks to the capacity of some concededly relevant evidence to lure the factfinder into declaring guilt on a ground different from proof specific to the offense charged. * * * Such improper grounds certainly include the one that Old Chief points to here: generalizing a defendant's earlier bad act into bad character and taking that as raising the odds that he did the later bad act now charged (or, worse, as calling for preventive conviction even if he should happen to be innocent momentarily). As then-Judge Breyer put it, "Although * * * 'propensity evidence' is relevant, the risk that a jury will convict for crimes other than those charged — or that, uncertain of guilt, it will convict anyway because a bad person deserves punishment — creates a prejudicial effect that outweighs ordinary relevance." *United States v. Moccia,* 681 F.2d 61, 63 (C.A.1 1982). * * * There is, accordingly, no question that propensity would be an "improper basis" for conviction and that evidence of a prior conviction is subject to analysis under Rule 403 for relative probative value and for prejudicial risk of misuse as propensity evidence.

As for the analytical method to be used in Rule 403 balancing, two basic possibilities present themselves. An item of evidence might be viewed as an island, with estimates of its own probative value and unfairly prejudicial risk the sole reference points in deciding whether the danger substantially outweighs the value and whether the evidence ought to be excluded. Or the question of admissibility might be seen as inviting further comparisons to take account of the full evidentiary context of the case as the court understands it when the ruling must be made. This second approach would start out like the first but be ready to go further. On objection, the court would decide whether a particular item of evidence raised a danger of unfair prejudice. If it did, the judge would go on to evaluate the degrees of probative value and unfair prejudice not only for the item in question but for any actually available substitutes as well. If an alternative were found to have substantially the same or greater probative value but a lower danger of unfair prejudice, sound judicial discretion would discount the value of the item first offered and exclude it if its discounted probative value were substantially outweighed by unfairly prejudicial risk. As we will explain later on, the judge would have to make these calculations with an appreciation of the offering party's need for evidentiary richness and narrative integrity in presenting a case, and the mere fact that two pieces of evidence might go to the same point would not, of course, necessarily mean that only one of them might come in. It would only mean that a judge applying Rule 403 could reasonably apply some discount to the probative value of an item of evidence when faced with less risky alternative proof going to the same point. Even under this second approach, as we explain below, a defendant's Rule 403 objection offering to concede a point generally cannot prevail over the Government's choice to offer evidence showing guilt and all the circumstances surrounding the offense.

The first understanding of the Rule is open to a very telling objection. That reading would leave the party offering evidence with the option to structure a trial in whatever way would produce the maximum unfair prejudice consistent with relevance. He could choose the available alternative carrying the greatest threat of improper influence, despite the availability of less prejudicial but equally probative evidence. The worst he would have to fear would be a ruling sustaining a Rule 403 objection, and if that occurred, he could simply fall back to offering substitute evidence. This would be a strange rule. It would be very odd for the law of evidence to recognize the danger of unfair prejudice only to confer such a degree of autonomy on the party subject to temptation, and the Rules of Evidence are not so odd.

Rather, a reading of the companions to Rule 403, and of the commentaries that went with them to Congress, makes it clear that what counts as the Rule 403 "probative value" of an item of evidence, as distinct from its Rule 401 "relevance," may be calculated by comparing evidentiary alternatives. The Committee Notes to Rule 401 explicitly say that a party's concession is pertinent to the court's discretion to exclude evidence on the point conceded. Such a concession, according to the Notes, will sometimes "call for the exclusion of evidence offered to prove [the] point conceded by the opponent* * * ." As already mentioned, the Notes make it clear that such rulings should be made not on the basis of Rule 401 relevance but on "such considerations as waste of time and undue prejudice (see Rule 403)* * * ." The Notes to Rule 403 then take up the point by stating that when a court considers "whether to exclude on grounds of unfair prejudice," the "availability of other means of proof may * * * be an appropriate factor." * * * Thus the notes leave no question that when Rule 403 confers discretion by providing that evidence "may" be excluded, the discretionary judgment may be informed not only by assessing an evidentiary item's twin tendencies, but by placing the result of that assessment alongside similar assessments of evidentiary alternatives. *See* 22 C. Wright & K. Graham, Federal Practice and Procedure § 5250, pp. 546–547 (1978) ("The probative worth of any particular bit of evidence is obviously affected by the scarcity or abundance of other evidence on the same point").

2

In dealing with the specific problem raised by § 922(g)(1) and its prior-conviction element, there can be no question that evidence of the name or nature of the prior offense generally carries a risk of unfair prejudice to the defendant. That risk will vary from case to case, for the reasons already given, but will be substantial whenever the official record offered by the Government would be arresting enough to lure a juror into a sequence of bad character reasoning. Where a prior conviction was for a gun crime or one similar to other charges in a pending case the risk of unfair prejudice would be especially obvious, and Old Chief sensibly worried that the prejudicial effect of his prior assault conviction, significant enough with respect to the current gun charges alone, would take on added weight from the related assault charge against him.

The District Court was also presented with alternative, relevant, admissible evidence of the prior conviction by Old Chief's offer to stipulate, evidence necessarily subject to the District Court's consideration on the motion to exclude the record offered by the Government. * * * Old Chief's proffered admission would, in fact, have been not merely relevant but seemingly conclusive evidence of the element. The statutory language in which the prior-conviction requirement is couched shows no congressional concern with the specific name or nature of the prior offense beyond what is necessary to place it within the broad category of qualifying felonies, and Old Chief clearly meant to admit that his felony did qualify, by stipulating "that the Government has proven one of the essential elements of the offense." As a consequence, although the name of the prior offense may have been technically relevant, it addressed no detail in the definition of the prior-conviction element that would not have been covered by the stipulation or admission. Logic, then, seems to side with Old Chief.

3

There is, however, one more question to be considered before deciding whether Old Chief's offer was to supply evidentiary value at least equivalent to what the Government's own evidence carried. In arguing that the stipulation or admission would not have carried equivalent value, the Government invokes the familiar, standard rule that the prosecution is entitled to prove its case by evidence of its own choice, or, more exactly, that a criminal defendant may not stipulate or admit his way out of the full evidentiary force of the case as the Government chooses to present it. The authority usually cited for this rule is *Parr v. United States,* 255 F.2d 86 (5th Cir. 1958), in which the Fifth Circuit explained that the "reason for the rule is to permit a party to present to the jury a picture of the events relied upon. To substitute for such a picture a naked admission might have the effect to rob the evidence of much of its fair and legitimate weight."

This is unquestionably true as a general matter. The "fair and legitimate weight" of conventional evidence showing individual thoughts and acts amounting to a crime reflects the fact that making a case with testimony and tangible things not only satisfies the formal definition of an offense, but tells a colorful story with descriptive richness. Unlike an abstract premise, whose force depends on going precisely to a particular step in a course of reasoning, a piece of evidence may address any number of separate elements, striking hard just because it shows so much at once; the account of a shooting that establishes capacity and causation may tell just as much about the triggerman's motive and intent. Evidence thus has force beyond any linear scheme of reasoning, and as its pieces come together a narrative gains momentum, with power not only to support conclusions but to sustain the willingness of jurors to draw the inferences, whatever they may be, necessary to reach an honest verdict. This persuasive power of the concrete and particular is often essential to the capacity of jurors to satisfy the obligations that the law places on them. Jury duty is usually unsought and sometimes resisted, and it may be as difficult for one juror suddenly to face the findings that can send another human being to prison, as it is for another to hold out conscientiously for acquittal. When a juror's duty does seem hard, the evidentiary account of what a defendant has thought and done can accomplish what no set of abstract statements ever could, not just to prove a fact but to establish its human significance, and so to implicate the law's moral underpinnings and a juror's obligation to sit in judgment. Thus, the prosecution may fairly seek to place its evidence before the jurors, as much to tell a story of guiltiness as to support an inference of guilt, to convince the jurors that a guilty verdict would be morally reasonable as much as to point to the discrete elements of a defendant's legal fault.

But there is something even more to the prosecution's interest in resisting efforts to replace the evidence of its choice with admissions and stipulations, for beyond the power of conventional evidence to support allegations and give life to the moral underpinnings of law's claims, there lies the need for evidence in all its particularity to satisfy the jurors' expectations about what proper proof should be. Some such demands they bring with them to the courthouse, assuming, for example, that a charge of using a firearm to commit an offense will be proven by introducing a gun in evidence. A prosecutor who fails to produce one, or some good reason for his failure, has something to be concerned about. "If [jurors'] expectations are not satisfied, triers of fact may penalize the party who disappoints them by drawing a negative inference against that party." Saltzburg, A Special Aspect of Relevance: Countering Negative Inferences Associated with the Absence of Evidence, 66 Calif. L.Rev. 1011, 1019 (1978). Expectations may also arise in jurors' minds simply from the experience of a trial itself. The use of witnesses to describe a train of events naturally related can raise the prospect of learning about every ingredient of that natural sequence the same way. If suddenly the prosecution presents some occurrence in the series differently, as by announcing a stipulation or admission, the effect may be like saying, "never mind what's behind the door," and jurors may well wonder what they are being kept from knowing. A party seemingly responsible for cloaking something has reason for apprehension, and the prosecution with its burden of proof may prudently demur at a defense request to interrupt the flow of evidence telling the story in the usual way.

In sum, the accepted rule that the prosecution is entitled to prove its case free from any defendant's option to stipulate the evidence away rests on good sense. A syllogism is not a story, and a naked proposition in a courtroom may be no match for the robust evidence that would be used to prove it. People who hear a story interrupted by gaps of abstraction may be puzzled at the missing chapters, and jurors asked to rest a momentous decision on the story's truth can feel put upon at being asked to take responsibility knowing that more could be said than they have heard. A convincing tale can be told with economy, but when economy becomes a break in the natural sequence of narrative evidence, an assurance that the missing link is really there is never more than second best.

4

This recognition that the prosecution with its burden of persuasion needs evidentiary depth to tell a continuous story has, however, virtually no application when the point at issue is a defendant's legal status, dependent on some judgment rendered wholly independently of the concrete events of later criminal behavior charged against him. As in this case, the choice of evidence for such an element is usually not between eventful narrative and abstract proposition, but between propositions of slightly varying abstraction, either a record saying that conviction for some crime occurred at a certain time or a statement admitting the same thing without naming the particular offense. The issue of substituting one statement for the other normally arises only when the record of conviction would not be admissible for any purpose beyond proving status, so that excluding it would not deprive the prosecution of evidence with multiple utility; if, indeed, there were a justification for receiving evidence of the nature of prior acts on some issue other than status (*i.e.,* to prove "motive, opportunity, intent, preparation, plan, knowledge, identity, or absence of mistake or accident," Fed. Rule Evid. 404(b)), Rule 404(b) guarantees the opportunity to seek its admission. Nor can it be argued that the events behind the prior conviction are proper nourishment for the jurors' sense of obligation to vindicate the public interest. The issue is not whether concrete details of the prior crime should come to the jurors' attention but whether the name or general character of that crime is to be disclosed. Congress, however, has made it plain that distinctions among generic felonies do not count for this purpose; the fact of the qualifying conviction is alone what matters under the statute. The most the jury needs to know is that the conviction admitted by the defendant falls within the class of crimes that Congress thought should bar a convict from possessing a gun, and this point may be made readily in a defendant's admission and underscored in the court's jury instructions. Finally, the most obvious reason that the general presumption that the prosecution may choose its evidence is so remote from application here is that proof of the defendant's status goes to an element entirely outside the natural sequence of what the defendant is charged with thinking and doing to commit the current offense. Proving status without telling exactly why that status was imposed leaves no gap in the story of a defendant's subsequent criminality, and its demonstration by stipulation or admission neither displaces a chapter from a continuous sequence of conventional evidence nor comes across as an officious substitution, to confuse or offend or provoke reproach.

Given these peculiarities of the element of felony-convict status and of admissions and the like when used to prove it, there is no cognizable difference between the evidentiary significance of an admission and of the legitimately probative component of the official record the prosecution would prefer to place in evidence. For purposes of the Rule 403 weighing of the probative against the prejudicial, the functions of the competing evidence are distinguishable only by the risk inherent in the one and wholly absent from the other. In this case, as in any other in which the prior conviction is for an offense likely to support conviction on some improper ground, the only reasonable conclusion was that the risk of unfair prejudice did substantially outweigh the discounted probative value of the record of conviction, and it was an abuse of discretion to admit the record when an admission was available. What we have said shows why this will be the general rule when proof of convict status is at issue, just as the prosecutor's choice will generally survive a Rule 403 analysis when a defendant seeks to force the substitution of an admission for evidence creating a coherent narrative of his thoughts and actions in perpetrating the offense for which he is being tried.

The judgment is reversed, and the case is remanded to the Ninth Circuit for further proceedings consistent with this opinion.

[The dissenting opinion of Justice O'Connor, joined by Chief Justice Rehnquist and Justices Scalia and Thomas, is omitted.]

NOTES

1. After *Old Chief*, how does the court analyze evidence that is offered as relevant to the "moral reasonableness" of a guilty verdict?

See Saltzburg, Martin and Capra, *Federal Rules of Evidence Manual* (9th ed. 2006):

> One passage in *Old Chief* indicates that the prosecution should be unfettered by a proffered stipulation because a stipulation would deprive the government of an opportunity "to convince the jurors that a guilty verdict would be morally reasonable as much as to point to the discrete elements of a defendant's legal fault." This would seem to mean that the government could proffer evidence beyond the actual facts in dispute, in order to provide a broader perspective on the morality of the defendant's conduct or the morality of the government's objectives. Thus, one reading of *Old Chief* is that evidence can be relevant on broader issues of morality, even if those issues are not contested by the parties. Professor Todd Pettys refers to this reading of *Old Chief* as adopting an "Enhanced Relevance Model." Todd Pettys, *Evidentiary Relevance, Morally Reasonable Verdicts, and Jury Nullification*, 86 Iowa L. Rev. 467 (2001).
>
> Professor Pettys demonstrates the disastrous consequences that flow from the view that evidence is relevant to prove the moral reasonableness of a litigant's position:
>
>> Imagine two jurors who have conflicting notions of moral behavior. The jurors are asked to determine whether the defendant, an African-American male, is guilty of possessing crack cocaine with the intent to distribute. Juror One believes that recreational drug use is morally neutral behavior — it is neither blameworthy nor praiseworthy — and that racist prosecutors use the nation's drug laws to incarcerate as many young African-American males as possible. Juror Two, on the other hand, believes that possessing or distributing illegal drugs is always morally wrong because those drugs might wind up in the hands of people who lack the knowledge

to use them responsibly and innocent people might be harmed. The prosecutor offers the testimony of a witness who will say that, one week before the defendant's arrest, she saw the defendant sell several small bags of crack cocaine to another man, who in turn gave the cocaine to children. Though the Government never charged the defendant in connection with that alleged incident, the prosecutor argues that the testimony is relevant because it tends to show that the defendant intended to distribute the small bags of crack cocaine he was carrying at the time of his arrest. The defendant objects under Rule 403, arguing that the jury is likely to conclude that he is a dangerous person who should be sent to prison regardless of whether he is guilty of the charged offense.

Might the Enhanced Relevance Model tip the balance more decisively in favor of admission? That is, might the probative weight of the evidence be further increased by its tendency to show that it would be morally reasonable to convict the defendant, thereby increasing the degree of prejudicial risk required to render the evidence inadmissible under Rule 403? The answer depends on the moral premises employed in the analysis. In the eyes of Juror One, the testimony might carry little moral weight, while Juror Two might regard the testimony as morally significant. In the language of *Old Chief*, the evidence might provide Juror Two with "concrete and particular" details that "give life to the moral underpinnings of the law's claims." The testimony might confirm for Juror Two that it makes good moral sense to prohibit the possession and distribution of controlled substances, since those dangerous substances might find their way into the hands of youths.

Before one can determine whether evidence tends to establish the moral reasonableness of a guilty verdict in any given case, then, one must identify the moral criteria that describe the conditions when, in fact, it would be morally appropriate to convict. The difficulties one encounters when trying to identify those criteria are so daunting that the very notion of assigning weight to evidence in accordance with its moral probity should probably be abandoned. If the Enhanced Relevance Model requires agreement upon a general moral theory, it is surely doomed. While jurors undoubtedly do sometimes render verdicts that best comport with their own notions of morality, those basic conceptions of morality just as surely vary from juror to juror. * * *

Besides the problems of moral relativism, Professor Pettys also notes that the "enhanced relevance" view of *Old Chief* might permit defense counsel to present counteractive evidence with a goal toward jury nullification.

At least three consequences would flow from holding, in any given case, that an item of evidence's probative weight is increased because the evidence tends to show that a guilty verdict would be morally reasonable. First, the Court might have to give the defendant increased leeway to present evidence that a guilty verdict

> would be morally unreasonable, in order both to ensure that jurors are able wisely to evaluate the Government's implicit moral argument and to preserve the appearance of fairness within the criminal justice system. Second, the defendant would have a limited right, under the Fifth and Sixth Amendments, to contend in his closing argument that the Government's evidence fails to show that it would be morally reasonable to convict. Third, the defendant would be entitled to a jury instruction that states, at a minimum, that evidence has been admitted in part for the purpose of persuading the jury that a guilty verdict would be morally reasonable.

For all the reasons given by Professor Pettys, it is profoundly hoped that the Court will not take an expansive, "moral reasonableness" view of relevance. The Enhanced Relevance view of *Old Chief* leads to an indeterminate system of evidence, a system that will result in less accurate determination of the facts that are legally in dispute between the parties."

2. Why is the Court in *Old Chief* so reluctant to require the prosecution to accept a proffered stipulation from the defendant?

The *Old Chief* Court was rightfully wary about an opponent's attempts to stipulate away relevant evidence. There is a real danger that the proponent of relevant evidence can be "sandbagged" by an opponent who proffers a stipulation. The proffered stipulation may well be crafted with the intent to deny the proponent the fair effect of the evidence. One problem with forced stipulations is that it is rare for relevant evidence to be offered to prove only a single point in dispute in a trial. (*Old Chief* was an unusual case in which proof of a prior conviction was offered on a single point — the defendant's status as a felon for purposes of a felon-firearm-possession charge. But as the Court in *Old Chief* noted, most relevant evidence cannot be so easily confined to a single issue.) An item of evidence often proves more than one disputed point. A common risk of stipulations is that the opponent will offer to stipulate in such a way that the stipulation is probative on only one of the multiple points on which the evidence is actually relevant. If the proponent is forced to accept that stipulation, then the stipulation will deprive the proponent of the rightful weight of the evidence. To take an easy example: eyewitness testimony that the defendant shot the victim will usually prove a number of points in issue — the bare fact of shooting proves the act of shooting, but the *circumstances* of the shootings as seen by the eyewitness will usually be evocative of the defendant's intent, absence of mistake, etc. Assume that the defendant offers to stipulate that he shot the victim. The Court in *Old Chief* is right to declare that the government should not be forced to accept that stipulation; to do so would rob the evidence of its fair weight in proving intent. And this is not to speak of all the other deleterious consequences of forced stipulations mentioned by the Court in *Old Chief*, e.g., depriving the jury of traditional means of proof and a full narrative.

Another problem with stipulations is that the opponent has an incentive to frame the stipulation in such a way as to give away as little ground as possible. Lawyers being as they are, there is a possibility that a stipulation does not even concede the point on which the evidence is offered. For example, in *United States v. Colon*, 880 F.2d 650 (2nd Cir. 1989), the defendant was charged with intent to distribute narcotics, specifically that he was operating as a "steerer" in a drug transaction (i.e., a conspirator who "steered" prospective buyers to the conspirator holding the drugs). The government planned to offer the defendant's prior steering convictions to prove intent. Defense counsel sought to head this off by proffering a stipulation. He offered to stipulate that if the government proved that Colon knew the drug seller and was in fact directing the undercover buyer specifically to that drug seller, "then I will acknowledge that he intended to violate the federal narcotics law and intended to aid in the sale of drugs." But this stipulation was rightly rejected, because in effect, the stipulation said, "if you can prove intent, then I admit intent." The court concluded that defense counsel's offer "stipulated nothing." Tactics like these indicate that the *Old Chief* Court was rightfully reluctant to hold that a defendant can control the government's choice of proof by way of stipulation.

PROBLEM 4-1

Plaintiff, Hurt Badly, sues defendant, Poor Driver, for injuries sustained when plaintiff was hit by a car. Plaintiff alleges the defendant owned and used the car that hit him. Defendant denies owning the car or using it. Plaintiff further alleges that as a result of his physical injuries he sustained serious emotional damage.

Plaintiff calls a ship's captain to the stand.

Plaintiff:	State your name.
Captain Good:	Captain Good.
Plaintiff:	Do you know the defendant?
Captain Good:	Yes.
Plaintiff:	Did you sell him passage on your ship from England to France?
Defendant:	Objection! That's irrelevant!
The court:	Why?
Defendant:	(1) ________ .
The court:	(2) ________ .
Plaintiff:	Your honor, I'm offering the evidence to show the defendant actually sailed to France.
Defendant:	(2) Objection! That's irrelevant.
The court:	Why?
Defendant:	(3) ________ .
The court:	(4) ________ .

Later in the trial the defendant calls a psychiatrist to the stand who interviewed the plaintiff on defendant's behalf. After being duly qualified and laying a foundation, the following ensued:

Defendant:	Do you have an opinion whether plaintiff suffered any emotional damage as a result of the car incident?
Psychiatrist:	Yes, I do.
Defendant:	What is your opinion?
Psychiatrist:	He did not.
Defendant:	Then do you have an opinion why plaintiff is suffering emotional trauma at this time if any?
Psychiatrist:	Yes, I do.
Defendant:	What is your opinion?
Psychiatrist:	Plaintiff is suffering some personal stress in his life right now because he is separated from his wife and children and is living with another woman, his eighteen-year-old maid.
Plaintiff:	(6) Objection and move to strike!
The court:	On what grounds?
Plaintiff:	None of those facts have any tendency to make any fact in dispute more or less probable.
Defendant:	(5) ________ .
The court:	(6) ________ .
Plaintiff:	Well then, your honor, any fact which may be made more probable is not of consequence to the case.
Defendant:	(7) ________ .
The court:	(8) ________ .
Plaintiff:	OK, the statement as a whole and each subpart is unduly prejudicial.
The court:	Let's break the statement up. The first part is "he is separated from his wife and children* * * ." Defense, what is your argument that this statement is admissible?
Defendant:	(9) ________ .
Plaintiff:	(10) ________ .
The court:	Alright, the second part of the statement is "* * * and he's living with another woman* * * ." Defense?
Defendant:	(11) ________ .
Plaintiff:	(12) ________ .
The court:	The last part was, I believe, "* * * his eighteen-year-old maid." Defense?
Defendant:	(13) ________ .
Plaintiff:	(14) ________ .
The court:	(15) ________ .

Because Defendant offered medical testimony that Plaintiff's injuries were not as severe as Plaintiff claims, Plaintiff asks the court for permission to walk to the jury box, to show the jury the scars on his hands and arms, and to have the jurors touch the scars to see how they feel.

Defendant: Objection! This is impermissible. It is extremely prejudicial. Plaintiff can testify to his condition. Moreover, how the scars feel is irrelevant.

Plaintiff: Defendant has called these injuries into question. The best evidence of the scope of injury is the injuries themselves. And, the scars are relevant because every time Plaintiff's children, or his good friend touch the scars they react in a certain way. The jury should know how people react by seeing how they would react.

The court: (16) __________ .

Plaintiff offers into evidence a film showing his children approaching him, kissing him, touching his hands, and crying.

Defendant: Objection! Irrelevant.

Plaintiff: It shows the impact that the accident has had on Plaintiff and his family.

The court: (17) __________ .

Defendant: Further Objection! This is unduly prejudicial and may confuse the jury.

Plaintiff: It is important to show the impact that the accident has had on Plaintiff and his family.

The court: (18) __________ .

Chapter 5

RELEVANCE — SPECIAL RULES

A. SUBSEQUENT REMEDIAL MEASURES

[1] Federal Rule 407

Subsequent Remedial Measures.

When, after an injury or harm allegedly caused by an event, measures are taken that, if taken previously, would have made the injury or harm less likely to occur, evidence of the subsequent measures is not admissible to prove negligence, culpable conduct, a defect in a product, a defect in a product's design, or a need for a warning or instruction. This rule does not require the exclusion of evidence of subsequent measures when offered for another purpose, such as proving ownership, control, or feasibility of precautionary measures, if controverted, or impeachment.

[2] Committee Note to 1997 Amendment to Rule 407

The amendment to Rule 407 makes two changes in the rule. First, the words "an injury or harm allegedly caused by" were added to clarify that the rule applies only to changes made after the occurrence that produced the damages giving rise to the action. Evidence of measures taken by the defendant prior to the "event" causing "injury or harm" do not fall within the exclusionary scope of Rule 407 even if they occurred after the manufacture or design of the product. *See Chase v. General Motors Corp.*, 856 F.2d 17, 21-22 (4th Cir. 1988).

Second, Rule 407 has been amended to provide that evidence of subsequent remedial measures may not be used to prove "a defect in a product or its design, or that a warning or instruction should have accompanied a product." This amendment adopts the view of the majority of the circuits that have interpreted Rule 407 to apply to products liability cases. *See Raymond v. Raymond Corp.*, 938 F.2d 1518, 1522 (1st Cir. 1991); *In re Joint Eastern District and Southern District Asbestos Litigation v. Armstrong World Industries, Inc.*, 995 F.2d 343 (2d Cir. 1993); *Cann v. Ford Motor Co.*, 658 F.2d 54, 60 (2d Cir. 1981), *cert. denied,* 456 U.S. 960 (1982); *Kelly v. Crown Equipment Co.*, 970 F.2d 1273, 1275 (3d Cir. 1992); *Werner v. Upjohn, Inc.*, 628 F.2d 848 (4th Cir. 1980), *cert. denied,* 449 U.S. 1080 (1981); *Grenada Steel Industries, Inc., v. Alabama Oxygen Co., Inc.*, 695 F.2d 883 (5th Cir. 1983); *Bauman v. Volkswagenwerk Aktiengesellschaft,* 621 F.2d 230, 232 (6th Cir. 1980); *Flaminio v. Honda Motor Company, Ltd.*, 733 F.2d 463, 469 (7th Cir. 1984); *Gauthier v. AMF, Inc.*, 788 F.2d 634, 636-37 (9th Cir. 1986).

Although this amendment adopts a uniform federal rule, it should be noted that evidence of subsequent remedial measures may be admissible pursuant to the second sentence of Rule 407. Evidence of subsequent remedial measures that is not barred by Rule 407 may still be subject to exclusion on Rule 403 grounds when the dangers of prejudice or confusion substantially outweigh the probative value of the evidence.

[3] Illustration

The defendant invented and marketed the wheel. The plaintiff bought one and, while wheeling at a rapid pace, fell off. The plaintiff sued the defendant for negligent design. The defendant's sole defense is that the plaintiff was wheeling faster than the instruction manual allowed. The plaintiff calls the defendant's chief of design:

Plaintiff:	State your name.
Witness:	Chief Engineer.
Plaintiff:	Did you participate in design decisions made about the wheel?
Witness:	Yes.
Plaintiff:	Did the defendant change the design of the wheel shortly after the plaintiff's accident?
Defendant:	Objection! ________.

[4] Strict Liability, Feasibility, and Control

CAMERON v. OTTO BOCK ORTHOPEDIC INDUSTRY, INC.

43 F.3d 14 (1st Cir. 1994)

BOUDIN, CIRCUIT JUDGE:

In March of 1990, William Cameron, whose left leg had been amputated below the knee in 1965, was fitted with a prosthetic leg. The prosthesis was assembled by Mr. Cameron's prosthetist from components originally sold by various suppliers, including Otto Bock Orthopedic Industry, Inc. ("Otto Bock"). Specifically, the artificial limb featured an Otto Bock pylon, which is an aluminum tube that substitutes for the missing portion of the leg, and an Otto Bock clamp, which attaches the pylon to an artificial foot manufactured and sold by another company.

On May 28, 1991, Mr. Cameron fell when the Otto Bock pylon in his artificial leg broke into two pieces. Cameron alleged that he suffered a fractured pelvis and emotional damage as a result of the fall. Based on diversity jurisdiction, Mr. Cameron sued Otto Bock in federal court, charging negligence and breach of warranty. His wife, Kay Cameron, claimed loss of consortium.

The case was tried by a jury in 1993. Each side attributed the failure of the leg to a different cause. The Camerons claimed that the pylon and clamp had been negligently and defectively designed. Otto Bock's expert testified that the prosthesis broke because the screw that fastened the pylon to the clamp had been "overtorqued," or screwed too tightly, by the prosthetist, despite a warning against overtightening by Otto Bock. The Camerons said that the instructions should have been more detailed. The jury found in favor of Otto Bock and the Camerons appeal.

* * *

2. The Camerons * * * challenge * * * the trial judge's exclusion of letters sent by Otto Bock to its prosthetist customers after Mr. Cameron's fall. These "Dear Customer" letters specified, inter alia, the specific torque levels that should be observed in screwing the pylon to the clamp in prosthetic limbs like Mr. Cameron's. Arguably these letters, if sent earlier, would have prevented Mr. Cameron's accident. The Camerons contend that such letters are evidence that Otto Bock breached its warranties of merchantability and fitness for a particular purpose.

The trial judge excluded the letters on the ground that the furnishing of precise torque measurements was a safety measure undertaken after the accident, and thus inadmissible under Federal Rule of Evidence 407 * * *.

The Camerons argue first that the Dear Customer letters should have been admitted to show the feasibility of providing the torque measurements earlier and to show the control Otto Bock exerted over its prosthetist customers. These exceptions apply, however, only "if" feasibility or control are "controverted." The feasibility of giving the torque measurements was certainly not controverted. The defense offered to stipulate to feasibility; and when the Camerons rejected the offer, apparently for tactical reasons, the district court instructed the jury that the further information could feasibly have been distributed.

"Control" is also a non-issue. Otto Bock never disputed that it provided advice to the prosthetists who assembled its products. Nor did it deny that providing more detailed measurements might have avoided the accident; indeed, its position was that the screw was overtightened and it had never provided specific numbers prior to the accident. If the Camerons justify the introduction of the letters in order to show causation, as their brief implies, then we think that the "if controverted" condition is not satisfied.

The Camerons do not appear to be claiming that the prosthetists were effectively employees of Otto Bock so that it might be vicariously liable for the negligence of Cameron's own prosthetist on a master-servant theory. Even if the Camerons had advanced such a claim, the raw fact that Otto Bock provided directions for the use of its product was undisputed and that is the most that the Camerons would be entitled to derive from the letters. There may also be some doubt whether "control" in the master-servant sense is what the drafters of Rule 407 had in mind, but we need not explore this interesting issue.

The Camerons also argue that the Dear Customer letters should have been admitted as direct evidence of breach of warranty — *i.e.*, as evidence that the Otto Bock components were defective — because, under Massachusetts law, such evidence might be admissible in a state trial. This circuit, however, has long held that the Federal Rules of Evidence, and specifically Rule 407, apply in diversity proceedings, because they "address procedural matters, [were] duly passed by Congress, [and] shall be presumed constitutionally valid unless they cannot rationally be characterized as rules of procedure." *McInnis v. A.M.F., Inc.*, 765 F.2d 240, 244 (1st Cir. 1985). Compare Fed. R. Evid. 501 (providing that state privilege law governs in diversity cases).

* * *

Affirmed.

NOTES

1. What is the rationale behind Rule 407?

The principal argument made in favor of the Rule is based in social policy: that without the Rule, remedial measures would not be taken after an injury or harm, for fear that such measures could be used as an admission of fault, culpability, defective design, etc., on the part of the defendant. Thus, the Rule is a response to the negative social consequences that would allegedly arise in the *absence* of an exclusionary rule.

Yet, a strong argument can be made that the articulated social policy does not justify the Rule. First, the policy argument presumes that a person or organization would know if there is no exclusionary rule for subsequent remedial measures in the relevant jurisdiction, and would also know that in the absence of such a rule, a subsequent remedial measure could constitute an admission that could be used at a trial that has not yet begun. Second, even if the informed defendant assumption is correct, a defendant with that kind of knowledge of the rules of evidence would also know that the failure to correct a situation in which an accident occurred could be admissible if a subsequent injury were to occur, with far more serious consequences to the defendant. That is, if a remedial action is not undertaken, and *another* accident occurs, the well-informed defendant would know that there would be a strong case of gross negligence or recklessness, and even the possibility of punitive damages. The defendant would balance the relatively contained cost of remedying the condition (use of that evidence against the defendant in the case arising from the past accident) against the potentially dramatic cost of not remedying the condition (use of that evidence against the defendant in all cases arising from future accidents). So a well-informed defendant, even in the absence of a rule such as Rule 407, would be very likely to take corrective measures in order to avoid more serious liability for future accidents. It follows that the social policy argument behind Rule 407 is flawed. If the policy of promoting safety were the only basis for the Rule, then Rule 407 would be nothing more than a windfall for defendants, who would probably take corrective action even in the absence of any exclusionary Rule.

Judge Posner, however, disagrees with this analysis. He argues as follows:

> One might think it not only immoral but reckless for an injurer, having been alerted by the accident to the existence of danger, not to take steps to correct the danger. But accidents are low-probability events. The probability of another accident may be much smaller than

> the probability that the victim of the accident that has already occurred will sue the injurer and, if permitted, will make devastating use at trial of any measures that the injurer may have taken since the accident to reduce the danger.

Flaminio v. Honda Motor Co., 733 F.2d 463, 470 (7th Cir. 1984).

But even if a future accident is considered unlikely, most defendants would rationally conclude that the risk of substantially higher liability resulting from an uncorrected condition would be too great to bear, should the low-probability event ever come to pass. The defendant must factor in not only the likelihood of injury but the amount of liability should an accident occur. And if the defendant is aware of a dangerous condition but does nothing to correct it, the amount of liability for future accidents is bound to be high.

The more persuasive basis for the Rule is that subsequent remedial measures are of marginal relevance in assessing the defendant's liability, and that this limited relevance is almost always substantially outweighed by the risk of jury confusion created by the introduction of a subsequent remedial measure. *See, e.g.*, *In re Air Crash Disaster*, 86 F.3d 498, 529 (6th Cir. 1996) ("Independent of its effect on safety upgrades by alleged tortfeasors, the rule bars a class of evidence that is very poor proof of negligence or defectiveness."); *Grenada Steel Indus. v. Alabama Oxygen Co.*, 695 F.2d 883 (5th Cir. 1983) (in a product liability case, "evidence of subsequent repair or change has little relevance to whether the product in question was defective at some previous time," and such evidence "threatens to confuse the jury by diverting its attention from whether the product was defective at the relevant time to what was done later"). The balance so often favors exclusion that it may make sense to impose a generalized rule of exclusion rather than to rely initially on a case-by-case approach under Rule 403. What Rule 407 does is to keep the jury's attention on the defendant's information and conduct at the relevant time — i.e., prior to the accident.

2. How does Rule 407 apply in product liability cases?

Up until 1997, courts had been divided on whether Rule 407 was applicable to product liability cases. Before that time, the Rule prohibited evidence of subsequent remedial measures only if offered to prove negligence or culpable conduct. Despite the language of the Rule, however, most courts had held that Rule 407 excluded subsequent remedial measures when offered to prove defective manufacture, defective design, or failure to warn in product liability cases. Some of these courts reasoned that the social policy basis of the Rule is as applicable to defendants in product liability cases as it is in negligence cases. Other courts reasoned that the relevance-based aspects of the Rule are equally applicable to strict liability cases and negligence cases. In 1997, Rule 407 was amended to specify that subsequent remedial measures are not admissible to prove "a defect in a product, a defect in a product's design, or a need for a warning or instruction."

3. When is feasibility "controverted" so that a subsequent remedial measure would be admissible?

See Saltzburg, Martin, and Capra, *Federal Rules of Evidence Manual* (9th ed. 2006):

> Rule 407 by its terms is not applicable if the feasibility of making a suggested change to a product or condition is controverted by the defendant. For example, assume that the plaintiff has been injured by a product and claims that it was defectively designed. Ordinarily, to prove defective design, the plaintiff will have to suggest some alternative design that would have made the product less dangerous. If the defendant claims that the alternative suggested was not feasible — either because it would have been prohibitively expensive, or that it was not within the state of the art at the time of manufacture — then feasibility is controverted and the Rule does not prevent the admission of subsequent changes to the product or condition made by the defendant, offered solely to prove feasibility. Of course, the defendant is entitled to a limiting instruction as to the permissible use of the evidence; and in rare cases, the probative value of the subsequent remedial measure as proof of feasibility might be substantially outweighed by the risk of prejudice and confusion, so that the evidence could still be excluded under Rule 403. But exclusion under Rule 403 in this scenario would be rare because the defendant is affirmatively contesting feasibility, and the plaintiff is simply providing a fair response.
>
> The feasibility "exception" to Rule 407 is rarely applicable, however, because feasibility is a weak defense if the defendant has in fact made a change to the product or condition after the plaintiff's injury. It is difficult, if not foolhardy, to argue that a suggested change was prohibitively expensive or beyond the state of the art when the change was in fact made after the injury. Consequently, most defendants concede feasibility when subsequent remedial measures have been taken. Such a concession prevents the plaintiff from arguing that feasibility is in controversy, and therefore precludes the use of subsequent remedial measures on that point.[1]
>
> The defendant remains free to defend on the ground that the suggested change, while feasible, would not have made the condition significantly safer, or would have resulted in other disadvantages such

---

[1] *See, e.g., Mills v. Beech Aircraft Corp.*, 886 F.2d 758, 764 (5th Cir. 1989) (revised manual, offered to show the feasibility of providing a better installation instruction, held properly excluded under Rule 407: "The feasibility exception to Rule 407 does not apply when feasibility is not in controversy. The defendants in the present case did not contest the feasibility of a better installation instruction, but rather maintained that the instructions in the [original] manual were acceptable."); *Middleton v. Harris Press & Shear, Inc.*, 796 F.2d 747 (5th Cir. 1986) (in a product liability suit where the plaintiff claimed that the product was defectively designed by failing to include a circuit interrupt device, a design change by the defendant to include such a device was not admissible to prove feasibility: "Though Harris contended that circuit interrupt devices were unreliable and not a safety device of first choice, the feasibility of installing them was not called into dispute," since the defendant stipulated that the change was feasible "in the sense of being physically possible").

that the defendant's original conduct was reasonable. As one Court has put it, "where a defendant argues about the trade-offs involved in taking precautionary measures, it is not placing *feasibility* in issue."

4. What constitutes a "remedial measure"?

Obviously, a repair to a defective condition constitutes a remedial measure. *Stanley v. Amoco Oil Co.*, 965 F.2d 203 (7th Cir. 1992). A design change also meets the definition. *Cann v. Ford Motor Co.*, 658 F.2d 54 (2d Cir. 1981). The firing of a negligent employee after an accident has been held to be a remedial measure. *Specht v. Jensen*, 863 F.2d 700 (10th Cir. 1988). In addition, a change in rules or policies may be covered by the definition. *Ford v. Schmidt*, 577 F.2d 408 (7th Cir. 1978).

In *Prentiss & Carlisle v. Koehring-Waterous*, 972 F.2d 6 (1st Cir. 1992), a product liability case in which the product caught fire and injured the plaintiff, the defendant company sent employees to the site to investigate. The investigators prepared a report essentially stating that the fire was caused by a defect in the product. These reports were held not excluded by Rule 407, because they were not remedial measures: "It would strain the spirit of the remedial measure prohibition in Rule 407 to extend its shield to evidence contained in post-event tests or reports." The fact that a product analysis or post-accident report might lead to remedial measures being taken did not mean that evidence of the analysis is excluded.

5. Does Rule 407 apply to remedial measures taken before the plaintiff's injury?

Suppose the plaintiff bought a snowblower in January 1991. Then in November 1991, the defendant changed the design of the snowblower. Then in January 1992, the plaintiff was injured when using his (unmodified) snowblower. The modification would have made the accident less likely to occur. Is the modification excluded under Rule 407 if offered to prove that the initial product was defectively designed?

Before the 1997 amendment to the Rule, the courts were in dispute as to whether a defendant's pre-accident design change was excluded by Rule 407. The pre-1997 Rule applied to measures taken "after an event" that would have made the event less likely to occur. This created confusion as to whether the relevant "event" was the sale or creation of a product, or rather the accident or injury. Most courts refused to exclude pre-accident remedial measures under the Rule, arguing that the social policy basis of the Rule was inapplicable to safety measures taken before an accident. The reasoning was that a manufacturer will not be deterred from making safety improvements before an accident has even occurred: if the defendant is concerned about the use of a remedial measure in some hypothetical future case, then it can "limit its liability by recalling the unimproved product." *Traylor v. Husqvarna Motor Co.*, 988 F.2d 729, 733 (7th Cir. 1993) (expressing "doubt that a producer will often be deflected from making improvements by fear about the consequences to his litigating position in hypothetical future cases — cases especially hypothetical because no accident has yet occurred").

The 1997 amendment to the Rule limits exclusion to measures taken "after an injury or harm." This clarifies that the Rule applies only to changes made after the occurrence that produced the damages giving rise to the action. Evidence of measures taken by the defendant prior to the "event" causing the plaintiff's "injury or harm" does not fall within the exclusionary scope of Rule 407 even if the measures were taken after the manufacture or design of the product.

It must be remembered that a Court has the discretion to exclude pre-accident design changes under Rule 403 when their probative value as proof of defective design or failure to warn is substantially outweighed by the risk of prejudice and jury confusion; and this might be the case where the design change is unresponsive to any indication of a problem with the product. *See Trull v. Volkswagen of Am., Inc.*, 187 F.3d 88 (1st Cir. 1999) (pre-accident design change was properly excluded; while measures taken before the plaintiff's accident do not fall within the prohibition of Rule 407, the trial court properly exercised its discretion to exclude the evidence under Rule 403; there was no indication that the alternative design was employed to remedy any defects in the model in which the plaintiff was injured).

6. Under what circumstances does the impeachment exception apply?

See Saltzburg, Martin and Capra, *Federal Rules of Evidence Manual* (9th ed. 2006):

> Impeachment of witnesses is specifically listed as a permissible purpose for admitting subsequent remedial measures. Presumably, the mode of impeachment contemplated is that of contradiction — the subsequent remedial measure may be relevant to contradict testimony from the defendant's witness, thus making that witness less credible before the jury.
>
> The problem is that almost any testimony given by defense witnesses could be contradicted at least in some minimal way by a subsequent remedial measure. If the defendant's expert testifies that the product was safe, a subsequent remedial measure could be seen as contradicting that testimony. If the defendant is asked on cross-examination whether the defendant thinks that all reasonable safety precautions had been taken at the time of the accident, and answers in the affirmative, then a subsequent remedial measure can be seen as contradicting that testimony.
>
> If "impeachment" means simple contradiction, then the impeachment exception to Rule 407 would threaten to swallow the Rule itself. *See, e.g., Harrison v. Sears, Roebuck & Co.*, 981 F.2d 25 (1st Cir. 1992) ("Rule 407's impeachment exception must not be used as a subterfuge to prove negligence or culpability"; a desire merely to undercut an expert's qualifications cannot be sufficient to trigger the impeachment exception, or else the exception could swallow the rule of exclusion).
>
> Accordingly, most courts have held that a subsequent remedial measure is not admissible for impeachment if it is offered for simple contradiction of a defense witness's testimony. *See, e.g., Kelly v. Crown Equip. Co.*, 970 F.2d 1273 (3d Cir. 1992) (the impeachment exception does not apply merely because the expert testified that the product

was of an excellent and proper design; if the impeachment exception applied to simple contradiction, the exception would swallow the rule); *Flaminio v. Honda Motor Co.*, 733 F.2d 463 (7th Cir. 1984) (no impeachment with subsequent remedial measures was permissible where defense witnesses merely testified to the safety of the product under normal circumstances). In those circumstances, the limited probative value of the evidence for impeachment is substantially outweighed by the risk of prejudice and confusion resulting from the possible misuse of the subsequent remedial measure by the jury. If the defense witness simply testifies that a product was safe, a subsequent remedial measure does contradict that testimony, but not very much so — there could be many reasons, other than a recognition of safety concerns, for the decision to change a product or condition after an accident.

On the other hand, if the defendant's witnesses testify in superlatives — e.g., "this is the safest product on the market" — then the evidence of a subsequent remedial measure provides more than simple contradiction. It shows that the witness puffed and exaggerated while on the stand. As such, the remedial measure provides a more direct and probative form of impeachment, which justifies a limited exception to the Rule. *See, e.g.*, *Wood v. Morbark Indus.*, 70 F.3d 1201 (11th Cir. 1995) (post-accident change to the design of a woodchipper was admissible for impeachment where the president of the corporate defendant testified that the woodchipper contained "the safest length chute you could possibly put on the machine"); *Muzyka v. Remington Arms Co.*, 774 F.2d 1309 (5th Cir. 1985) (subsequent remedial measures, offered for impeachment purposes, were erroneously excluded where defense witnesses testified that the product "embodied the ultimate in gun safety" and that it was "*the* best and *the* safest rifle of its kind on the market"; the jury was improperly denied "evidence in impeachment of the experts who spoke in those superlatives").

Likewise, if defense witnesses testify that the product or condition has not been changed since the accident, then evidence of subsequent remedial measures provides a more direct and probative, and hence a permissible, form of impeachment through contradiction. *See, e.g.*, *Harrison v. Sears, Roebuck & Co.*, 981 F.2d 25, 31 (1st Cir. 1992) ("A more direct impeachment use of subsequent remedial measure evidence would exist if Appellees' witness stated that he did not change the product after the alleged accident was brought to his employer's attention.").

7. If the subsequent remedial measure is taken by someone other than the defendant, does Rule 407 apply?

In *Dixon v. International Harvester Co.*, 754 F.2d 573 (5th Cir. 1985), the plaintiff was injured while working on a tractor, after an object entered the tractor cab through an open area between the support bar and the dashboard. After the accident, the owner of the tractor added screening and a metal plate to close off this open area of the tractor cab. The plaintiff sued International

Harvester, alleging defective design. Harvester sought to exclude the tractor owner's remedial measure, but the Court held that Rule 407 was inapplicable. The Court relied on the policy basis for the Rule, which is "to avoid discouraging defendants from making necessary repairs or changes to products or dangerous conditions." It concluded that since the remedial measure "was made by a non-defendant, Rule 407 does not bar the evidence." *See also Diehl v. Blaw-Knox*, 360 F.3d 426 (3d Cir. 2004) (admitting evidence of third-party repairs is consistent with the policy of Rule 407, which is to prevent repairs from being used as proof of an admission of fault; a party's fault cannot be "admitted" by a third party).

8. Is evidence always admitted once it has passed the Rule 407 analysis?

"Rule 407 prohibits the admission of evidence of subsequent remedial measures when the evidence is offered to prove negligence or culpable conduct. However, the rule expressly does not require the exclusion of such evidence when offered for another purpose. Of course, to be admissible any evidence not excluded by rule 407 must still be relevant (Fed. R. Evid. 402) and its probative value must not be substantially outweighed by any dangers associated with its admission (Fed. R. Evid. 403)." *Anderson v. Malloy*, 700 F.2d 1208, 1213 (8th Cir. 1983). *See also Middleton v. Harris Press & Shear, Inc.*, 796 F.2d 747 (5th Cir. 1986) (remedial measure not excluded under Rule 407 because it was made by someone other than the defendant; however, exclusion of the evidence was proper under Rule 403 due to its tendency to divert the jury's attention away from the defendant's conduct at the time of manufacture).

B. COMPROMISE AND OFFER OF COMPROMISE

[1] Federal Rule 408

Rule 408. Compromise and Offers to Compromise

(a) Prohibited uses. — Evidence of the following is not admissible on behalf of any party, when offered to prove liability for, invalidity of, or amount of a claim that was disputed as to validity or amount, or to impeach through a prior inconsistent statement or contradiction:

(1) furnishing or offering or promising to furnish — or accepting or offering or promising to accept — a valuable consideration in compromising or attempting to compromise the claim; and

(2) conduct or statements made in compromise negotiations regarding the claim, except when offered in a criminal case and the negotiations related to a claim by a public office or agency in the exercise of regulatory, investigative, or enforcement authority.

(b) Permitted uses. — This rule does not require exclusion if the evidence is offered for purposes not prohibited by subdivision (a). Examples of permissible purposes include proving a witness's bias or prejudice; negating a contention of undue delay; and proving an effort to obstruct a criminal investigation or prosecution.

[2] Committee Note to 2006 Amendment to Rule 408

Rule 408 has been amended to settle some questions in the courts about the scope of the Rule, and to make it easier to read and apply. First, the amendment provides that Rule 408 does not prohibit the introduction in a criminal case of statements or conduct during compromise negotiations regarding a civil dispute by a government regulatory, investigative, or enforcement agency. *See, e.g., United States v. Prewitt*, 34 F.3d 436, 439 (7th Cir. 1994) (admissions of fault made in compromise of a civil securities enforcement action were admissible against the accused in a subsequent criminal action for mail fraud). Where an individual makes a statement in the presence of government agents, its subsequent admission in a criminal case should not be unexpected. The individual can seek to protect against subsequent disclosure through negotiation and agreement with the civil regulator, or an attorney for the government.

Statements made in compromise negotiations of a claim by a government agency may be excluded in criminal cases where the circumstances so warrant under Rule 403. For example, if an individual was unrepresented at the time the statement was made in a civil enforcement proceeding, its probative value in a subsequent criminal case may be minimal. But there is no absolute exclusion imposed by Rule 408.

In contrast, statements made during compromise negotiations of other disputed claims are not admissible in subsequent criminal litigation, when offered to prove liability for, invalidity of, or amount of those claims. When private parties enter into compromise negotiations they cannot protect against the subsequent use of statements in criminal cases by way of private ordering. The inability to guarantee protection against subsequent use could lead to parties refusing to admit fault, even if by doing so they could favorably settle private matters. Such a chill on settlement negotiations would be contrary to the policy of Rule 408.

The amendment distinguishes statements and conduct (such as a direct admission of fault) made in compromise negotiations of a civil claim by a government agency from an offer or acceptance of a compromise of such a claim. An offer or acceptance of a compromise of a civil claim is excluded under the Rule if offered against the defendant as an admission of fault. In that case, the predicate for the evidence would be that the defendant, by compromising with the government agency, has admitted the validity and amount of the civil claim, and that this admission has sufficient probative value to be considered as proof of guilt. But unlike a direct statement of fault, an offer or acceptance of a compromise is not very probative of the defendant's guilt. Moreover, admitting such an offer or acceptance could deter defendants from settling a civil regulatory action, for fear of evidentiary use in a subsequent criminal action. *See, e.g.*, Fishman, *Jones on Evidence, Civil and Criminal*, § 22:16 at 199, n.83 (7th ed. 2000) ("A target of a potential criminal investigation may be unwilling to settle civil claims against him if by doing so he increases the risk of prosecution and conviction.").

The amendment retains the language of the original rule that bars compromise evidence only when offered as evidence of the "validity", "invalidity", or "amount" of the disputed claim. The intent is to retain the extensive case law finding Rule 408 inapplicable when compromise evidence is offered for a purpose other than to prove the validity, invalidity, or amount of a disputed claim. *See, e.g., Athey v. Farmers Ins. Exchange,* 234 F.3d 357 (8th Cir. 2000) (evidence of settlement offer by insurer was properly admitted to prove insurer's bad faith); *Coakley & Williams v. Structural Concrete Equip.,* 973 F.2d 349 (4th Cir. 1992) (evidence of settlement is not precluded by Rule 408 where offered to prove a party's intent with respect to the scope of a release); *Cates v. Morgan Portable Bldg. Corp.,* 708 F.2d 683 (7th Cir. 1985) (Rule 408 does not bar evidence of a settlement when offered to prove a breach of the settlement agreement, as the purpose of the evidence is to prove the fact of settlement as opposed to the validity or amount of the underlying claim); *Uforma/Shelby Bus. Forms, Inc. v. NLRB,* 111 F.3d 1284 (6th Cir. 1997) (threats made in settlement negotiations were admissible; Rule 408 is inapplicable when the claim is based upon a wrong that is committed during the course of settlement negotiations). So for example, Rule 408 is inapplicable if offered to show that a party made fraudulent statements in order to settle a litigation.

The amendment does not affect the case law providing that Rule 408 is inapplicable when evidence of the compromise is offered to prove notice. *See, e.g., United States v. Austin,* 54 F.3d 394 (7th Cir. 1995) (no error to admit evidence of the defendant's settlement with the FTC, because it was offered to prove that the defendant was on notice that subsequent similar conduct was wrongful); *Spell v. McDaniel,* 824 F.2d 1380 (4th Cir. 1987) (in a civil rights action alleging that an officer used excessive force, a prior settlement by the City of another brutality claim was properly admitted to prove that the City was on notice of aggressive behavior by police officers).

The amendment prohibits the use of statements made in settlement negotiations when offered to impeach by prior inconsistent statement or through contradiction. Such broad impeachment would tend to swallow the exclusionary rule and would impair the public policy of promoting settlements. *See McCormick on Evidence* at 186 (5th ed. 1999) ("Use of statements made in compromise negotiations to impeach the testimony of a party, which is not specifically treated in Rule 408, is fraught with danger of misuse of the statements to prove liability, threatens frank interchange of information during negotiations, and generally should not be permitted."). *See also EEOC v. Gear Petroleum, Inc.*, 948 F.2d 1542 (10th Cir.1991) (letter sent as part of settlement negotiation cannot be used to impeach defense witnesses by way of contradiction or prior inconsistent statement; such broad impeachment would undermine the policy of encouraging uninhibited settlement negotiations).

The amendment makes clear that Rule 408 excludes compromise evidence even when a party seeks to admit its own settlement offer or statements made in settlement negotiations. If a party were to reveal its own statement or offer, this could itself reveal the fact that the adversary entered into settlement negotiations. The protections of Rule 408 cannot be waived unilaterally because the Rule, by definition, protects both parties from having the fact of negotiation disclosed to the jury. Moreover, proof of statements and offers made in settlement would often have to be made through the testimony of attorneys, leading to the risks and costs of disqualification. *See generally Pierce v. F.R. Tripler & Co.*, 955 F.2d 820, 828 (2d Cir. 1992) (settlement offers are excluded under Rule 408 even if it is the offeror who seeks to admit them; noting that the "widespread admissibility of the substance of settlement offers could bring with it a rash of motions for disqualification of a party's chosen counsel who would likely become a witness at trial").

The sentence of the Rule referring to evidence "otherwise discoverable" has been deleted as superfluous. *See, e.g.,* Advisory Committee Note to Maine Rule of Evidence 408 (refusing to include the sentence in the Maine version of Rule 408 and noting that the sentence "seems to state what the law would be if it were omitted"); Advisory Committee Note to Wyoming Rule of Evidence 408 (refusing to include the sentence in Wyoming Rule 408 on the ground that it was "superfluous"). The intent of the sentence was to prevent a party from trying to immunize admissible information, such as a pre-existing document, through the pretense of disclosing it during compromise negotiations. *See Ramada Development Co. v. Rauch,* 644 F.2d 1097 (5th Cir. 1981). But even without the sentence, the Rule cannot be read to protect pre-existing information simply because it was presented to the adversary in compromise negotiations.

[3] Illustration

Tree Doc sues the defendant for failure to pay a bill for removing diseased elm trees from the defendant's property. The only issue is the reasonable value of the service. The defendant claims Tree Doc gave him an oral estimate of $1000. The final bill was $3000. The defendant is on the stand and Tree Doc cross-examines:

Plaintiff:	Now you just testified that there was an oral estimate of $1000 and that $1000 was the fair value of the service, isn't that true?
Witness:	Yes, that's exactly right.
Plaintiff:	Then why would you have offered to settle this case for $2500?
Defendant:	Objection! ________.

[4] Disputes, Waiver, and Other Purposes

ALPEX COMPUTER CORP. v. NINTENDO CO., LTD.

United States District Court, S.D. New York, 1991

770 F.Supp 161

KIMBA M. WOOD, DISTRICT JUDGE:

Plaintiff Alpex Computer Corporation ("Alpex") moves for an order pursuant to Federal Rules of Evidence 408 precluding defendants Nintendo Company, Ltd. and Nintendo of America ("Nintendo") from introducing any evidence concerning plaintiff's efforts to compromise disputed claims regarding the 555 patent and the amounts involved in those efforts to compromise. For the reasons set forth below, the court grants plaintiff's motion.

Background

This case arises from a dispute over the validity and alleged infringement of U.S. Patent No. 4,026,555 (the 555 patent), a patent that involves the earliest video games.

* * *

After receiving the right to sue for past infringement of the 555 patent from Fairchild Camera & Instrument Co., the original licensee of the patent, Alpex embarked on a program to combat what it viewed as widespread infringement of the patent. As part of this program, outside counsel for Alpex wrote letters to a number of companies in the video game industry in December 1979 notifying them of Alpex's view that they were infringing the 555 patent. The letter to Atari, one of the leaders in the video game industry at the time, is illustrative. Alpex's counsel informed Atari that "[a] number of the TV games which Atari is manufacturing and selling under the name PONG clearly infringe the 555 patent." The letter concluded with Alpex offering "to extend a non-exclusive license under its patents on a royalty basis." This notice led to "extended negotiations," and eventually a settlement between Alpex and Atari under which Atari paid for and received a non-exclusive license. Alpex's counsel sent similar letters to Mattel and Bally. As was the case with Atari, the notice to Mattel resulted in extended negotiations, a settlement, and a license. Nintendo seeks to designate as trial exhibits a variety of documents from these two negotiations, including letters between the parties describing the negotiations over the license price, news articles about the Atari settlement, Bankruptcy Court pleadings describing the Mattel settlement, and the actual license agreements.

In 1983, after the settlement with Atari and another with Magnavox, counsel for Alpex sent infringement letters to approximately 70 companies. These letters announced that Alpex had recently granted licenses under the patent to Atari and Magnavox, and stated that Alpex had "recently obtained information indicating that your company manufactures and/or sells video game cartridges and/or consoles which may infringe the subject patent." "We would prefer to resolve this matter without litigation," the letters continued, "and the purpose of this letter is to advise you that our client is prepared to extend a nonexclusive license under the 555 patent on a paid-up or royalty basis."

As a result of Alpex's efforts, as expressed in these and subsequent letters, six companies entered into license agreements with Alpex without litigation * * *. From the course of the negotiations leading to these licenses, defendants seek to designate as trial exhibits numerous documents that discuss the history of the negotiations, disputes over the size of the settlement offers, the license agreements themselves, and bankruptcy court documents describing and approving the agreements.

As part of its campaign, Alpex sued six companies alleged to have sold or manufactured products that infringed on its patent. The first suit filed was against Magnavox in 1981 and was settled, with Magnavox receiving a non-exclusive license, in December 1982. Several years later, Alpex brought suit against five additional companies: Activision, Coleco, Commodore, Tandy, and Parker Brothers. Alpex has agreed to settle with four of the companies; the action against Parker Brothers has been stayed pending the outcome of this case. Nintendo wishes to designate as trial exhibits a variety of documents that pertain to these actions, including documents setting forth the terms of settlement and various letters between Alpex and the prospective licensees.

Discussion

I. Preclusion Under Rule 408

Alpex argues simply that the same considerations that led to the enactment of [Rule 408], namely "the promotion of the public policy favoring the compromise and settlement of disputes," F.R.Evid. 408 advisory committee's note, compel the granting of this motion. Faced with widespread infringement of its patent over a long period of time, Alpex contends, the company followed a reasonable course of action in alerting companies it believed were infringing the patent and then attempting to negotiate a settlement or filing suit or both, as the circumstances warranted.

A. Evidence of Unsuccessful Offers to License the Patent

Nintendo counters with several different arguments. It argues first that, as to the documents relating to Alpex's licensing offers that did not result in a completed agreement, Rule 408 does not apply because no actual dispute existed at the time. Nintendo characterizes Alpex's offers to license the patent as merely the "opening gambit" in an expected negotiation and thus not protected by the privilege afforded offers to compromise. Because some of those licensing offers never received a response, Nintendo argues, no dispute could possibly have existed, and Rule 408 does not bar the admission of these offers.

Nintendo's reading of this requirement of Rule 408, however is too narrow. All that is needed for Rule 408 to apply is an actual dispute, or at least an apparent difference of opinion between the parties as to the validity of a claim. At the time it began its efforts to license the 555 and related patents, Alpex believed that many companies in the industry sold or manufactured products that infringed the patents. It is reasonable to assume that the alleged infringers believed either (1) that their products did not infringe the patent in question, or (2) that even if they did, the patent was not valid, or (3) that they could somehow get away with infringing. Alpex's offers to license the patent were sent only to those it believed were infringing on the patent. * * * By infringing on the patent, or at least selling products that Alpex reasonably believed were infringing on the patent, the infringers signaled that they held an opinion at variance with Alpex's position. The dispute or difference of opinion begins with the act of infringement; Alpex's letters — those that provoked responses as well as those that did not — were offers to compromise that dispute and thus fall within the ambit of Rule 408.

* * *

B. Evidence Relating to Licenses Agreed to Without Litigation

Nintendo argues that none of the license agreements agreed to by Alpex without litigation is barred by Rule 408. In its view, "none of the these licenses was agreed to during litigation and none was the result of threats of imminent litigation." Rather, Nintendo argues, these licenses represent the results of ordinary business negotiations in an industry-wide licensing program, and thus Rule 408 does not apply. * * * Here, none of the parties that entered into a licensing agreement with Alpex did so without the threat of litigation from Alpex. For example, in writing to outside counsel for Alpex, patent counsel for Texas Instruments summarized the history of licensing negotiations between the two companies, and denied that any Texas Instruments products infringed upon Alpex's patents, but concluded that when "faced with your indication of Alpex's willingness to bring suit against Texas Instruments under the 555 Patent, and recognizing the costs and inconvenience of litigation," an "offer to settle this matter" was warranted. * * * It is clear that this entire category of documents that Nintendo seeks to designate as trial exhibits was generated only under the threat of litigation from Alpex, [and therefore Rule 408 is applicable].

C. Evidence Relating to License Agreements Reached During Litigation

The final category of documents Alpex seeks to preclude Nintendo from offering at trial pertain to the licensing agreements reached between Alpex and four other companies during ongoing litigation. Numerous Federal Circuit decisions have held that offers to license patents made during pending litigation are inadmissible under Rule 408, a fact that Nintendo concedes. * * * Nevertheless, Nintendo argues that the unique facts of this case, in which Alpex made "repeated industry-wide offers to license the patent at a standard price," and then adhered to those terms even when forced to litigate its claims, compel a different result. Nintendo's argument is unavailing. The mere fact that Alpex offered to settle with a large number of companies does not render the protection afforded such offers under Rule 408 any less applicable. As discussed, *supra*, Alpex accused every corporation to which it offered a license (except Fairchild) of infringing on its patents. It threatened most of them with litigation. * * * That Alpex offered the same terms to those companies it threatened with litigation early in its licensing efforts as it did to those it actually sued is immaterial. Regardless of the terms of the settlements between Alpex and Magnavox, Activision, Tandy, and Coleco, the agreements were made in settlement of litigation; any documents or other evidence relating to these agreements thus plainly fall within the protection of Rule 408.

II. Waiver of the Rule 408 Privilege

Nintendo also argues that even if the licenses granted by Alpex during ongoing litigation fall within the scope of Rule 408, Alpex has deliberately waived the protection generally afforded under the rule by disclosing the fact and the terms of its settlements outside the context of this litigation. More specifically, Nintendo contends that Alpex waived the rule by disclosing information regarding the terms of previous settlements in letters to other companies Alpex alleged were infringing its patents, and with whom it hoped to reach similar settlements. In addition, Nintendo suggests that the fact that the press published details of several of the licensing agreements destroys whatever protection those agreements might have once enjoyed, and thus enables Nintendo offer those details as evidence in this case.

* * *

* * * Rule 408 is designed to promote "the public policy favoring the compromise and settlement of disputes." F.R.Evid. 408 advisory committee's note. It is true that complete confidentiality of settlements may promote this goal. But Rule 408 is merely a rule of evidence, which promotes compromise in one limited way — it provides that evidence of compromise is not admissible to show invalidity of a claim or its amount. * * * Accordingly, the rule "limits a document's relevance *at trial*, not its disclosure for other purposes." *Center for Auto Safety v. Department of Justice*, 576 F. Supp. 739, 749 (D.D.C.1983) (emphasis added). The issue of whether a party to a settlement agreement has publicized the existence or the terms of that agreement outside the context of the trial at hand does not enter into a court's decision under Rule 408.

* * *

Conclusion

For the reasons set forth above, the court grants plaintiff's motion *in limine* to preclude defendants from introducing any evidence concerning Alpex's efforts to compromise disputed claims regarding its patent.

SO ORDERED.

NOTES

1. When is evidence of a compromise or offer of compromise admissible to show the bias or prejudice of a witness?

In *John McShain, Inc. v. Cessna Aircraft Co.*, 563 F.2d 632 (2d Cir. 1977), after two crashes caused by landing-gear collapse, McShain brought action against Cessna alleging defective design in the landing gear of his Cessna aircraft. Cessna joined Butler Aviation-Friendship, McShain's mechanic, as a third-party defendant on the theory that the second collapse was the result of inept repairs. The judge allowed into evidence the fact that McShain "signed an agreement releasing Butler from any liability for the accident in exchange for $10 and the right to engage as a consultant Ralph Harmon, who was at the time an employee of Butler's sister corporation, Mooney Aircraft Corp." Because McShain retained Harmon, and Harmon testified as an expert witness in support of the design-defect contention, the Court of Appeals decided that the trial judge "did not commit reversible error in admitting the agreement and in allowing comments upon it. The fact that a sister corporation of Harmon's employer had been released from liability in exchange for Harmon's testimony cast doubt upon Harmon's impartiality." Thus, evidence of the compromise was admissible to impeach the witness by showing his bias and prejudice.

2. When may compromise negotiations be admissible to negate a contention of undue delay?

In *Freidus v. First National Bank of Council Bluffs*, 928 F.2d 793 (8th Cir. 1991), the plaintiffs sued the defendant bank on the theory that the bank unreasonably withheld its approval of the plaintiff's assignment of property subject to the bank's mortgage. When the new purchaser refused to close the transaction due to delay in the negotiations between plaintiff and the bank, plaintiff instituted this suit. In order to show that the bank's position was reasonable and that it did not delay the transaction between the plaintiff and the purchaser, the bank offered evidence of letters which were part of the ongoing negotiations between it and the plaintiff. The court ruled that Fed. R. Evid. 408 permitted this use of compromise negotiations to negate a contention of undue delay.

3. May evidence of a compromise be admitted to show breach of the settlement agreement?

In *Cates v. Morgan Portable Building Corp.*, 780 F.2d 683 (7th Cir. 1985), motel owners bought defective portable building units from the manufacturer. Subsequently, the motel owners brought a breach of contract action against the manufacturer. Trial began but was adjourned on the basis of a settlement agreement. In an order signed by the judge, the parties stipulated that Morgan would make repairs on the defective building units. The repairs did not meet the motel owners' satisfaction and the trial eventually resumed. After trial, the judge used the stipulation to fix liability for consequential damages incurred thereafter. Morgan argued that this use of the stipulation agreement violated Fed. R. Evid. 408. The Court held that while statements made during negotiations could not be used to establish liability for breach of the original contract or to fix liability for that breach, the "settlement agreement is admissible to prove the parties' undertakings in the agreement, should it be argued that a party broke the agreement."

4. When evidence of compromise negotiations is being offered for a permissible purpose, is an additional 403 analysis required?

See Meyer v. Pennzoil Co., 889 F.2d 1457 (5th Cir. 1989) (trial court did not abuse its discretion in excluding compromise evidence offered to impeach witnesses for bias, where trial court determined that the probative value of the evidence as to bias was substantially outweighed by the risk of prejudice and confusion).

5. If a civil defendant enters into a settlement admitting fault, is that settlement admissible against the defendant in a subsequent criminal prosecution?

The 2006 amendment to Rule 408 resolved a conflict in the courts on whether evidence of a civil compromise is admissible in a subsequent criminal prosecution. The Rule now provides that a civil settlement is inadmissible to prove a defendant's guilt. The policy basis for that result is that if the settlement were admissible, defendants in civil cases would be less likely to settle — a consequence that would be contrary to the basic policy of Rule 408. The Rule as amended does provide, however, that if a defendant makes a statement admitting fault to a public officer conducting a regulatory investigation, that statement is not barred in a subsequent criminal prosecution. The policy reason for that result is that it would be contrary to justice to allow a person to make a statement to a public officer admitting guilt, and then to hide behind Rule 408 in a criminal prosecution. See the Advisory Committee Note to the 2006 amendment for a more detailed explanation.

C. PAYMENT OF MEDICAL OR SIMILAR EXPENSES

[1] Federal Rule 409

Rule 409. Payment of Medical and Similar Expenses

Evidence of furnishing or offering or promising to pay medical, hospital, or similar expenses occasioned by an injury is not admissible to prove liability for the injury.

[2] Illustration

The plaintiff sues the defendant for injuries arising out of a slip and fall at the defendant's shop. The defendant denies he had any prior knowledge of the candy wrapper that plaintiff says made her fall. The nurse who attended the plaintiff at the emergency room takes the stand on behalf of the plaintiff.

Plaintiff:	State your name.
Witness:	Nurse Ratchett.
Plaintiff:	Were you at the hospital when the plaintiff was admitted?
Witness:	Yes.
Plaintiff:	Did the defendant show up there as well?
Witness:	Yes, he came in about 15 minutes later.
Plaintiff:	Did you hear him say anything to the plaintiff?
Witness:	Yes.
Plaintiff:	What?
Witness:	"I'll be happy to pay all your medical bills. I should have picked up that wrapper before you got to the shop."
Defendant:	Objection! __________.
Plaintiff:	__________.

The court: __________.

[3] Admission of Fault

GALARNYK v. HOSTMARK MANAGEMENT, INC.
55 F. App'x. 763 (7th Cir. 2003)

Order:

* * *

Timothy Galarnyk fell in the bathroom of the Holiday Inn Mart Plaza in Chicago, converting gravitational energy to kinetic energy with such effectiveness that he punched a hole in the wall. Galarnyk did not seek medical attention at the time but says that he began to experience excruciating pain while driving home. His theory of recovery is that the hotel negligently failed to ensure that a bath mat was properly secured, and that it gave way when he stepped into the tub. Galarnyk testified in his deposition that he did not notice a mat before entering the tub, but that after the fall he saw a mat that was loose on one end. Belia Valenciano, the attendant who had cleaned the room before Galarnyk checked in, testified that she inspected bath mats as part of her routine, that she did so in this case, and that the mat was properly secured. Dan Sapp, who inspected the room after the fall, testified that the mat *still* was properly secured "except for a little small inch of the tub." The hotel's theory is that the mat had nothing to do with the fall — and that, if it was loose (as Galarnyk says) that this was a consequence rather than a cause of the accident. The district court granted summary judgment to the hotel. It held that, even taking all evidence in the light most favorable to Galarnyk, a reasonable trier of fact could not conclude that the hotel knew, or had cause to suspect, that a problem had cropped up with the mat in this room; and if, despite taking appropriate precautions, the hotel lacked knowledge that its equipment had begun to fail, it could not be liable under Illinois law.

Galarnyk insists that this is beside the point, because both the hotel and its insurance carrier admitted liability by offering to pay his medical expenses. Such an offer, in the nature of a settlement proposal (or perhaps just a gesture to maintain goodwill), differs from an admission of liability, for damages in tort often greatly exceed medical expenses. Federal law makes this clear: "Evidence of furnishing or offering or promising to pay medical, hospital, or similar expenses occasioned by an injury is not admissible to prove liability for the injury." Fed. R. Evid. 409. The offers were accompanied by expressions of regret and dismay, which likewise differ from admissions of liability. * * * None of the statements constitutes an admission of liability that pretermits further inquiry.

* * *

* * * All a jury could find on this record is that Galarnyk fell, and that after the fall part of the mat was loose. That is not enough to support a conclusion that the hotel was negligent.

AFFIRMED.

NOTE

Why does the treatment of offers of compromise under Fed. R. Evid. 408 differ from the treatment of offers to pay medical expenses under Fed. R. Evid. 409?

The Advisory Committee's Note to Fed. R. Evid. 409 states that "[c]ontrary to Rule 408, dealing with offers of compromise, [Rule 409] does not extend to conduct or statements not a part of the act of furnishing or offering or promising to pay. This difference in treatment arises from fundamental differences in nature. Communication is essential if compromises are to be effected, and consequently broad protection of statements is needed. This is not so in cases of payments of offers or promises to pay medical expenses, where factual statements may be expected to be incidental in nature."

Professors Saltzburg, Martin and Capra, *Federal Rules of Evidence Manual* (9th ed. 2006), distinguish Rule 409 from Rule 408 as follows:

> It is important to note, however, that unlike Rule 408, this Rule does not exclude opinions or admissions of liability when made in connection with an offer to pay hospital or other expenses covered by this Rule. It is only the offer and the payment itself that are protected. The Advisory Committee and the Congress apparently felt that exclusion of statements beyond the offer or payment itself was not necessary, because any further statements need not be made in connection with the kind of offer or action covered by this Rule. They are not necessary in the same way that factual statements are necessary for the negotiations covered by Rule 408.
>
> It would seem, however, that if offers of payment covered by this Rule are made as part of a settlement offer, Rule 408 should govern, and statements made in connection with the offers should be excluded as well. Also, statements that are "a part of the act" covered by the Rule may be protected, according to the second paragraph of the Advisory Committee's Note. In deciding what is part of an act, Courts may have to fall back on cases involving offers to compromise that protected, prior to enactment of Rule 408, statements inextricably bound up with settlement offers.
>
> Unlike Rule 408, Rule 409 is not limited to offers or promises related to a disputed claim. Any offer, promise, or actual payment is inadmissible whether or not a dispute over obligation to pay had arisen at the time of the humane gesture.

D. PLEAS AND DISCUSSIONS

[1] Federal Rule 410

Rule 410. Inadmissibility of Pleas, Plea Discussions, and Related Statements

Except as otherwise provided in this rule, evidence of the following is not, in any civil or criminal proceeding, admissible against the defendant who made the plea or was a participant in the plea discussions:

(1) a plea of guilty which was later withdrawn;

(2) a plea of nolo contendere;

(3) any statement made in the course of any proceedings under Rule 11 of the Federal Rules of Criminal Procedure or comparable state procedure regarding either of the foregoing pleas; or

(4) any statement made in the course of plea discussions with an attorney for the prosecuting authority which do not result in a plea of guilty or which result in a plea of guilty later withdrawn.

However, such a statement is admissible (i) in any proceeding wherein another statement made in the course of the same plea or plea discussion has been introduced and the statement ought in fairness be considered contemporaneously with it, or (ii) in a criminal proceeding for perjury or false statement if the statement was made by the defendant under oath, on the record and in the presence of counsel.

Editor's Note: Rule 410 originally replicated the language of Fed. R. Crim. P. 11(e)(6). When the Federal Rules of Criminal Procedure were restylized in 2005, Criminal Rule 11(e)(6) was amended to provide simply that the admissibility of statements and offers made in plea negotiations is governed by Fed. R. Evid. 410. Cases before 2005 (such as the cases set forth below) often refer to both the Evidence Rule and the Criminal Rule. That is no longer necessary or useful, and so the cases have been edited to delete references to former Criminal Rule 11(e)(6).

[2] Illustration

The defendant pled guilty to second degree murder after plea negotiations with the District Attorney reduced the charge from first degree. The defendant discharged his first attorney and was later allowed to withdraw his plea and proceed to trial. The defendant defends against the 1st degree charges on the theory that the gun accidentally discharged while the defendant was cleaning it. The state calls the defendant's former attorney to the stand:

Prosecutor: Were you with the defendant when he was talking to the D.A. about reducing the charges in this case?

Witness: Yes.

Prosecutor: What did he say?

Defendant: Objection! __________.

The court:	(Interrupting) Let me hear the answer, then I'll rule.
Witness:	Well, at that point he said "Yeah, I shot him and it was because I was mad at him. I certainly didn't plan it."

[3] Use of Pleas for Impeachment

UNITED STATES v. UDEAGU
United States District Court, E.D. New York, 1986
110 F.R.D. 172

WEINSTEIN, CHIEF JUDGE.

FACTS

Defendant was charged with the knowing and intentional importation of heroin and of possession with intent to distribute. On March 10, 1986, he pled guilty to one count of illegal importation of heroin. At the time of his plea, pursuant to Rule 11 of the Federal Rules of Criminal Procedure, defendant, under oath with his counsel present and advising him, freely admitted his guilt and described his participation in detail on the record.

On April 15, 1986, defendant moved to withdraw his guilty plea, principally on the ground that he was not in fact guilty. This motion was granted.

Defendant has moved for a ruling *in limine* on whether the government, to impeach the credibility of defendant should he take the stand, can use the statements made by him during his plea allocution. Such evidence would be introduced by the government on cross-examination should defendant elect to take the stand in his own defense since his testimony would have to be inconsistent with his admission under oath at the time his guilty plea was received.

LAW

* * *

Evidence of incriminating statements made in connection with a plea of guilty which is later withdrawn may not be used against defendant at trial as part of the government's case-in-chief as evidence of his guilt. The reason is clear: the incriminatory admissions would make withdrawal of the plea nugatory since conviction would almost surely result from a trial.

* * *

[Rule] 410 [is] designed to encourage unrestrained candor necessary to produce effective plea discussions and pleas. Rule 410 was originally promulgated with the proviso that it would not apply to "voluntary and reliable statements made in court on the record in connection with [an offer to plead guilty] when offered for impeachment purposes * * * ." [but subsequently] the impeachment proviso was eliminated. This legislative history establishes Congress' explicit intention to preclude use of statements made in plea negotiations for impeachment purposes. *United States v. Lawson*, 683 F.2d 688, 693 (2d Cir.1982).

There is even less reason to allow the use of the statements for impeachment in this case than in *Lawson*. In the first place, here the court itself impliedly promised defendant that his statements could be used only in a perjury or false statement proceedings. Second, should the defendant elect to take the witness stand during his trial and testify contrary to the inculpatory statements made under oath at his plea allocution, there are prima facie grounds for a prosecution for perjury. This threat is sufficient to ensure truthfulness in almost all cases. Additionally, the distinct possibility that the court will consider perjury in sentencing precludes all but the most foolish defendant from lying under these circumstances.

CONCLUSION

The statements of defendant given in open court under oath in the presence of counsel under Rule 11 when admitting details of guilt may not be used at defendant's trial after the plea of guilty is withdrawn.

So ordered.

NOTE

With regard to Fed. R. Evid. 410, what is the difference between a plea and a confession?

Defendants have sometimes tried to argue that confessions made to police officers are covered by Rule 410 because a confession is tantamount to a guilty plea. But by the terms of the Rule, the protections of Rule 410 do not apply to statements made to police officers. The Rule covers statements made in "plea discussions with an attorney for the prosecuting authority." But some courts have extended the protections of the Rule to the rather unusual situation in which the police obtain authority from the prosecutor to negotiate a plea agreement as part of custodial interrogation. *United States v. Sitton*, 968 F.2d 947 (9th Cir. 1992) (stating that conversations between accused and police officers can constitute plea bargaining where the police obtain authority from the government attorney to negotiate; no such showing on the facts of this case). Compare *United States v. Olson*, 450 F.3d 655 (7th Cir. 2006) (the defendant's statements to police officials at a meeting were not covered by Rule 410 where the agent "made clear that he could, at most recommend a plea agreement"; nothing the agent did or said could have led the defendant "to reasonably believe" that the meeting was a plea discussion).

[4] Can the Protection be Waived?

UNITED STATES v. MEZZANATTO
513 U.S. 196 (1995)

JUSTICE THOMAS delivered the opinion of the Court:

Federal Rule of Evidence 410 [provides] that statements made in the course of plea discussions between a criminal defendant and a prosecutor are inadmissible against the defendant. The court below held that these exclusionary provisions may not be waived by the defendant. We granted certiorari to resolve a conflict among the Courts of Appeals, and we now reverse.

I

On August 1, 1991, San Diego Narcotics Task Force agents arrested Gordon Shuster after discovering a methamphetamine laboratory at his residence in Rainbow, California. Shuster agreed to cooperate with the agents, and a few hours after his arrest he placed a call to respondent's pager. When respondent returned the call, Shuster told him that a friend wanted to purchase a pound of methamphetamine for $ 13,000. Shuster arranged to meet respondent later that day.

At their meeting, Shuster introduced an undercover officer as his "friend." The officer asked respondent if he had "brought the stuff with him," and respondent told the officer it was in his car. The two proceeded to the car, where respondent produced a brown paper package containing approximately one pound of methamphetamine. Respondent then presented a glass pipe (later found to contain methamphetamine residue) and asked the officer if he wanted to take a "hit." The officer indicated that he would first get respondent the money; as the officer left the car, he gave a pre-arranged arrest signal. Respondent was arrested and charged with possession of methamphetamine with intent to distribute.

On October 17, 1991, respondent and his attorney asked to meet with the prosecutor to discuss the possibility of cooperating with the Government. The prosecutor agreed to meet later that day. At the beginning of the meeting, the prosecutor informed respondent that he had no obligation to talk, but that if he wanted to cooperate he would have to be completely truthful. As a condition to proceeding with the discussion, the prosecutor indicated that respondent would have to agree that any statements he made during the meeting could be used to impeach any contradictory testimony he might give at trial if the case proceeded that far. Respondent conferred with his counsel and agreed to proceed under the prosecutor's terms.

Respondent then admitted knowing that the package he had attempted to sell to the undercover police officer contained methamphetamine, but insisted that he had dealt only in "ounce" quantities of methamphetamine prior to his arrest. Initially, respondent also claimed that he was acting merely as a broker for Shuster and did not know that Shuster was manufacturing methamphetamine at his residence, but he later conceded that he knew about Shuster's laboratory. Respondent attempted to minimize his role in Shuster's operation by claiming that he had not visited Shuster's residence for at least a week before his arrest. At this point, the Government confronted respondent with surveillance evidence showing that his car was on Shuster's property the day before the arrest, and terminated the meeting on the basis of respondent's failure to provide completely truthful information.

Respondent eventually was tried on the methamphetamine charge and took the stand in his own defense. He maintained that he was not involved in methamphetamine trafficking and that he had thought Shuster used his home laboratory to manufacture plastic explosives for the CIA. He also denied knowing that the package he delivered to the undercover officer contained methamphetamine. Over defense counsel's objection, the prosecutor cross-examined respondent about the inconsistent statements he had made during the October 17 meeting. Respondent denied having made certain statements, and the prosecutor called one of the agents who had attended the meeting to recount the prior statements. The jury found respondent guilty, and the District Court sentenced him to 170 months in prison.

A panel of the Ninth Circuit reversed, over the dissent of Chief Judge Wallace. 998 F.2d 1452 (1993). The Ninth Circuit held that respondent's agreement to allow admission of his plea statements for purposes of impeachment was unenforceable and that the District Court therefore erred in admitting the statements for that purpose. * * *

II

The Ninth Circuit's analysis is directly contrary to the approach we have taken in the context of a broad array of constitutional and statutory provisions. Rather than deeming waiver presumptively unavailable absent some sort of express enabling clause, we instead have adhered to the opposite presumption. A criminal defendant may knowingly and voluntarily waive many of the most fundamental protections afforded by the Constitution. *See, e.g., Boykin v. Alabama*, 395 U.S. 238, 243 (1969) (knowing and voluntary guilty plea waives privilege against compulsory self-incrimination, right to jury trial, and right to confront one's accusers); *Johnson v. Zerbst*, 304 U.S. 458, 465 (1938) (Sixth Amendment right to counsel may be waived). Likewise, absent some affirmative indication of Congress' intent to preclude waiver, we have presumed that statutory provisions are subject to waiver by voluntary agreement of the parties. *See, e.g., Evans v. Jeff D.*, 475 U.S. 717, 730-732 (1986) (prevailing party in civil-rights action may waive its statutory eligibility for attorney's fees).

* * *

The presumption of waivability has found specific application in the context of evidentiary rules. Absent some "overriding procedural consideration that prevents enforcement of the contract," courts have held that agreements to waive evidentiary rules are generally enforceable even over a party's subsequent objections. Courts have "liberally enforced" agreements to waive various exclusionary rules of evidence. Thus, at the time of the adoption of the Federal Rules of Evidence, agreements as to the admissibility of documentary evidence were routinely enforced and held to preclude subsequent objections as to authenticity. And although hearsay is inadmissible except under certain specific exceptions, we have held that agreements to waive hearsay objections are enforceable.

Indeed, evidentiary stipulations are a valuable and integral part of everyday trial practice. Prior to trial, parties often agree in writing to the admission of otherwise objectionable evidence, either in exchange for stipulations from opposing counsel or for other strategic purposes. * * *

III

Because the plea-statement Rules were enacted against a background presumption that legal rights generally, and evidentiary provisions specifically, are subject to waiver by voluntary agreement of the parties, we will not interpret Congress' silence as an implicit rejection of waivability. Respondent bears the responsibility of identifying some affirmative basis for concluding that the plea-statement Rules depart from the presumption of waivability.

Respondent offers three potential bases for concluding that the Rules should be placed beyond the control of the parties. We find none of them persuasive.

A

Respondent first suggests that the plea-statement Rules establish a "guarantee [to] fair procedure" that cannot be waived. We agree with respondent's basic premise: there may be some evidentiary provisions that are so fundamental to the reliability of the fact-finding process that they may never be waived without irreparably "discrediting the federal courts." *See United States v. Josefik*, 753 F.2d 585, 588 (CA7 1985) ("No doubt there are limits to waiver; if the parties stipulated to trial by 12 orangutans the defendant's conviction would be invalid notwithstanding his consent, because some minimum of civilized procedure is required by community feeling regardless of what the defendant wants or is willing to accept"). But enforcement of agreements like respondent's plainly will not have that effect. The admission of plea statements for impeachment purposes enhances the truth-seeking function of trials and will result in more accurate verdicts. Under any view of the evidence, the defendant has made a false statement, either to the prosecutor during the plea discussion or to the jury at trial; making the jury aware of the inconsistency will tend to increase the reliability of the verdict without risking institutional harm to the federal courts.

* * *

B

Respondent also contends that waiver is fundamentally inconsistent with the Rules' goal of encouraging voluntary settlement. Because the prospect of waiver may make defendants "think twice" before entering into any plea negotiation, respondent suggests that enforcement of waiver agreements acts "as a brake, not as a facilitator, to the plea-bargain process." The Ninth Circuit expressed similar concerns, noting that [the plea-statement Rules] "aid in obtaining the cooperation" that is often necessary to identify and prosecute the leaders of a criminal conspiracy and that waiver of the protections of the Rules "could easily have a chilling effect on the entire plea bargaining process." According to the Ninth Circuit, the plea-statement Rules "permit the plea bargainer to maximize what he has 'to sell' " by preserving "the ability to withdraw from the bargain proposed by the prosecutor without being harmed by any of his statements made in the course of an aborted plea bargaining session."

We need not decide whether and under what circumstances substantial "public policy" interests may permit the inference that Congress intended to override the presumption of waivability, for in this case there is no basis for concluding that waiver will interfere with the Rules' goal of encouraging plea bargaining. The court below focused entirely on the defendant's incentives and completely ignored the other essential party to the transaction: the prosecutor. Thus, although the availability of waiver may discourage some defendants from negotiating, it is also true that prosecutors may be unwilling to proceed without it.

Prosecutors may be especially reluctant to negotiate without a waiver agreement during the early stages of a criminal investigation, when prosecutors are searching for leads and suspects may be willing to offer information in exchange for some form of immunity or leniency in sentencing. In this "cooperation" context, prosecutors face "painfully delicate" choices as to "whether to proceed and prosecute those suspects against whom the already produced evidence makes a case or whether to extend leniency or full immunity to some suspects in order to procure testimony against other, more dangerous suspects against whom existing evidence is flimsy or nonexistent." Hughes, *Agreements for Cooperation in Criminal Cases*, 45 Vand. L. Rev. 1, 15 (1992). Because prosecutors have limited resources and must be able to answer "sensitive questions about the credibility of the testimony" they receive before entering into any sort of cooperation agreement, prosecutors may condition cooperation discussions on an agreement that the testimony provided may be used for impeachment purposes. If prosecutors were precluded from securing such agreements, they might well decline to enter into cooperation discussions in the first place and might never take this potential first step toward a plea bargain.

Indeed, as a logical matter, it simply makes no sense to conclude that mutual settlement will be encouraged by precluding negotiation over an issue that may be particularly important to one of the parties to the transaction. A sounder way to encourage settlement is to permit the interested parties to enter into knowing and voluntary negotiations without any arbitrary limits on their bargaining chips. To use the Ninth Circuit's metaphor, if the prosecutor is interested in "buying" the reliability assurance that accompanies a waiver agreement, then precluding waiver can only stifle the market for plea bargains. A defendant can "maximize" what he has to "sell" only if he is permitted to offer what the prosecutor is most interested in buying. And while it is certainly true that prosecutors often need help from the small fish in a conspiracy in order to catch the big ones, that is no reason to preclude waiver altogether. If prosecutors decide that certain crucial information will be gained only by preserving the inadmissibility of plea statements, they will agree to leave intact the exclusionary provisions of the plea-statement Rules.

In sum, there is no reason to believe that allowing negotiation as to waiver of the plea-statement Rules will bring plea bargaining to a grinding halt; it may well have the opposite effect. Respondent's unfounded policy argument thus provides no basis for concluding that Congress intended to prevent criminal defendants from offering to waive the plea-statement Rules during plea negotiation.

C

Finally, respondent contends that waiver agreements should be forbidden because they invite prosecutorial overreaching and abuse. Respondent asserts that there is a "gross disparity" in the relative bargaining power of the parties to a plea agreement and suggests that a waiver agreement is "inherently unfair and coercive." Because the prosecutor retains the discretion to "reward defendants for their substantial assistance" under the Sentencing Guidelines, respondent argues that defendants face an "incredible dilemma" when they are asked to accept waiver as the price of entering plea discussions.

The dilemma flagged by respondent is indistinguishable from any of a number of difficult choices that criminal defendants face every day. The plea bargaining process necessarily exerts pressure on defendants to plead guilty and to abandon a series of fundamental rights, but we have repeatedly held that the government may encourage a guilty plea by offering substantial benefits in return for the plea. * * *

The mere potential for abuse of prosecutorial bargaining power is an insufficient basis for foreclosing negotiation altogether. * * * Instead, the appropriate response to respondent's predictions of abuse is to permit case-by-case inquiries into whether waiver agreements are the product of fraud or coercion. We hold that absent some affirmative indication that the agreement was entered into unknowingly or involuntarily, an agreement to waive the exclusionary provisions of the plea-statement Rules is valid and enforceable.

IV

Respondent conferred with his lawyer after the prosecutor proposed waiver as a condition of proceeding with the plea discussion, and he has never complained that he entered into the waiver agreement at issue unknowingly or involuntarily. The Ninth Circuit's decision was based on its per se rejection of waiver of the plea-statement Rules. Accordingly, the judgment of the Court of Appeals is reversed.

JUSTICE GINSBURG, with whom JUSTICE O'CONNOR and JUSTICE BREYER join, concurring.

The Court holds that a waiver allowing the Government to impeach with statements made during plea negotiations is compatible with Congress's intent to promote plea bargaining. It may be, however, that a waiver to use such statements in the case-in-chief would more severely undermine a defendant's incentive to negotiate, and thereby inhibit plea bargaining. As the Government has not sought such a waiver, we do not here explore this question.

JUSTICE SOUTER, with whom JUSTICE STEVENS joins, dissenting.

* * *

The unlikelihood that Congress intended the modest default rule that the majority sees in [Rule] 410 looms all the larger when the consequences of the majority position are pursued. The first consequence is that the Rules will probably not even function as default rules, for there is little chance that they will be applied at all. Already, standard forms indicate that many federal prosecutors routinely require waiver of [Rule 410] rights before a prosecutor is willing to enter into plea discussions. *See also United States v. Stevens*, 935 F.2d 1380, 1396 (CA3 1991) ("Plea agreements * * * commonly contain a provision stating that proffer information that is disclosed during the course of plea negotiations is * * * admissible for purposes of impeachment"). As the Government conceded during oral argument, defendants are generally in no position to challenge demands for these waivers, and the use of waiver provisions as contracts of adhesion has become accepted practice. Today's decision can only speed the heretofore illegitimate process by which the exception has been swallowing the Rules. * * *

The second consequence likely to emerge from today's decision is the practical certainty that the waiver demanded will in time come to function as a waiver of trial itself. It is true that many (if not all) of the waiver forms now employed go only to admissibility for impeachment. But although the erosion of the Rules has begun with this trickle, the majority's reasoning will provide no principled limit to it. The Rules draw no distinction between use of a statement for impeachment and use in the Government's case in chief. If objection can be waived for impeachment use, it can be waived for use as affirmative evidence, and if the government can effectively demand waiver in the former instance, there is no reason to believe it will not do so just as successfully in the latter. When it does, there is nothing this Court will legitimately be able to do about it. * * * Just what the traffic may bear is an open question, but what cannot be denied is that the majority opinion sanctions a demand for waiver of such scope that a defendant who gives it will be unable even to acknowledge his desire to negotiate a guilty plea without furnishing admissible evidence against himself then and there. In such cases, the possibility of trial if no agreement is reached will be reduced to fantasy. The only defendant who will not damage himself by even the most restrained candor will be the one so desperate that he might as well walk into court and enter a naked guilty plea. It defies reason to think that Congress intended to invite such a result, when it adopted a Rule said to promote candid discussion in the interest of encouraging compromise.

UNITED STATES v. BURCH

156 F.3d 1315 (D.C. Cir. 1998)

WALD, CIRCUIT JUDGE:

On December 6, 1995, a jury convicted Larry Burch ("Burch") of possession with intent to distribute more than 50 grams of cocaine base in violation of 21 U.S.C. §§ 841(a)(1) and 841(b)(1)(A)(iii) (1994), while acquitting him on a charge of conspiracy to distribute and to possess with intent to distribute cocaine base in violation of 21 U.S.C. § 846 (1994). * * *

[T]he defendant challenges his conviction on the basis of alleged errors made by the district court in (1) holding that the defendant had made a knowing and voluntary waiver of his rights under * * * Rule 410 of the Federal Rules of Evidence, such that statements made during his plea hearing and subsequent debriefing could be offered into evidence by the prosecution; * * *. Finding no merit in any of these claims, we affirm the conviction * * *.

I. BACKGROUND

* * *

Following his arrest, Burch entered into plea negotiations with members of the United States ("U.S.") Attorney's Office, culminating in an October 25, 1995 agreement in which he pled guilty to possession with intent to distribute more than 50 grams of crack cocaine, count two of his four-count indictment. Burch also agreed to assist law enforcement authorities whenever and in whatever form the U.S. Attorney's Office deemed appropriate. In return, the government agreed to request the dismissal of the other three counts of the indictment, to allow the defendant's presentence release into the community to assist in undercover operations, and to inform the U.S. Attorney's Departure Guideline Committee of the nature and extent of the defendant's cooperation. Should the Departure Committee determine that the defendant had rendered substantial assistance to the investigation and prosecution of another individual, it would file a motion pursuant to 18 U.S.C. § 3553(e) (1994) in order to allow the sentencing judge to depart downwards from the federal sentencing guidelines.

Burch, however, did not prove particularly cooperative, despite being informed by the trial judge on several occasions that he faced a mandatory minimum sentence of twenty years if he did not provide some opening for a downward departure by assisting the government. He did outline the history of his involvement in narcotics distribution in a debriefing session with the Drug Enforcement Agency ("DEA"), discussing the identity of his sources as well as the quantities of crack cocaine that he typically purchased from them, but not much more. The defendant's name came up in relation to a homicide in May and June of 1996 and, at the government's request, the court revoked his bond and detained him pending sentencing. When questioned about the homicide, Burch was not forthcoming, and told a story which he subsequently recanted. On July 22, 1996, the Assistant U.S. Attorney supervising the case filed a memorandum with the Departure Committee outlining the limited nature of Burch's cooperation. Eight days later, the defendant's trial counsel filed a motion seeking to withdraw the guilty plea and alleging Burch's innocence of the underlying narcotics offense. In the motion, as well as in an August 1, 1996 letter addressed to the trial judge, Burch [proclaimed his innocence and contended that he only pleaded guilty after threats from the real drug dealer].

After a hearing, the trial court judge ultimately allowed Burch to withdraw his plea pursuant to Rule 32(e) of the Federal Rules of Criminal Procedure. "Implausible as Mr. Burch's belated claim of innocence may seem, the Court will give Mr. Burch his day in court." However, as part of its decision, the court stated that it would not allow him to benefit from * * * Evidence Rule 410's restriction on the admissibility of statements made pursuant to a withdrawn plea. In his plea agreement, as well as in a Rule 11 colloquy with the trial judge prior to entering the plea, Burch specifically had waived his rights under [Rule] 410. In allowing him to withdraw the plea, the trial court announced its intention to hold the defendant to this part of the agreement. The court ultimately ruled that statements made by appellant during the October 25, 1995 plea hearing and a January 22, 1996 debriefing with the DEA could be used as part of the prosecution's case-in-chief, while those made during plea negotiations taking place on October 24, 1995 could only be used for rebuttal or impeachment purposes should the defendant contradict them while on the witness stand.

* * *

II. DISCUSSION

A. Appellant's Evidentiary Challenges

1. The Withdrawn Plea

a. Waiver

* * *

Although we face here the additional question of whether a defendant's Rule 11(e)(6) rights can be waived for purposes of the prosecution's case-in-chief, our inquiry still begins with *Mezzanatto*. Justice Thomas' opinion paints with broad brush strokes, and its reasoning resonates beyond the precise question upon which it ruled. In a one paragraph concurring opinion, Justice Ginsburg, joined by Justices O'Connor and Breyer, cautioned that the *Mezzanatto* decision did not address the question of whether a waiver of Rule [410] for purposes of the prosecution's case-in-chief would be valid. * * *

On reflection, * * * we cannot discern any acceptable rationale for not extending the majority opinion in *Mezzanatto* to this case. Justice Thomas' opinion rests on three principles. First, it finds that in the absence of an affirmative indication that Congress intended to preclude or to limit the waiver of statutory protections, including evidentiary rules, voluntary agreements to waive these protections are presumptively enforceable. Second, the opinion rejects the argument that [Rule 410 expresses] congressional disfavor towards waivability. Finally, the opinion stresses that in weighing whether to override a presumption of waivability, a court should assess the public policy justifications, if any, which counsel in favor of departing from that norm. Cumulatively, we believe these principles do not countenance drawing any distinction in this case between permitting waivers for purposes of impeachment or rebuttal and permitting waivers for the prosecution's case-in-chief.

There are two arguments in favor of restricting the reach of *Mezzanatto* to rebuttal and impeachment. They go like this: First, in enacting [Rule] 410, Congress has signaled an intent to create rights that benefit both the accused and the federal judicial system. * * * If extending *Mezzanatto* would undermine Congress' attempt to promote candid plea discussions, deference to congressional intent could counter the presumption of waivability. We think that there is a ready answer to this argument: the *Mezzanatto* Court declined to read the [Rule] as mandating any default rule against waiver, a position that Justice Souter staked out in dissent. * * * Since the Supreme Court has already rejected congressional intent to promote candor as a justification for refusing to enforce voluntary waivers of [Rule 410] in rebuttal, any argument relying on that intent is too weak to justify refusing to allow use of the plea statement in the government's case-in-chief. In any event, the waiver in this case was part of the plea agreement; it resulted from successful plea negotiations. During the negotiations, the defendant was protected by [Rule] 410. Thus, it is difficult to see how the waiver in this case could have reduced the "zone of unrestrained candor" during negotiations, as the waiver in *Mezzanatto*, which was secured by the prosecutor at the start of bargaining, arguably did.

Second, while it is conceivable that sanctioning waivers for the use of statements made during plea proceedings in the prosecution's case-in-chief, as opposed to impeachment or rebuttal, could have a markedly greater impact on the willingness of defendants to participate in such negotiations, the three-Justice concurrence in *Mezzanatto* presents no reason why that would be the case. Nor has the appellant. Lacking any evidence to the contrary, it seems unlikely to us that most defendants would draw fine distinctions as to whether statements made in the course of or after the plea proceeding could be used in the government's case-in-chief or only in rebuttal. It is true that the three concurring Justices in *Mezzanatto*, whose votes were necessary for the majority, expressed concern that admitting plea negotiation statements in the case-in-chief would too severely undermine the defendant's incentives to negotiate. Such concern is far less warranted with respect to a waiver, like the one in this case, which is executed as a result of plea negotiations, rather than as a condition for such negotiations. In any event, allowing the government to bargain for a waiver during plea negotiations certainly does not undermine the reliability of the fact-finding process, the only institutional concern cited by *Mezzanatto* as a potential counterweight to the presumption in favor of waivability. * * *

b. Knowing and Voluntary

Having decided that a defendant can affirmatively waive his rights under [Rule] 410 to allow his plea statement to be admitted into evidence, we move on to appellant's more basic contention that his waiver was involuntary. Before any waiver can be deemed unenforceable, *Mezzanatto* held that a trial judge must find "some affirmative indication that the agreement was entered into unknowingly or involuntarily." For this indication, appellant relies on the district court's decision to permit him to withdraw his plea, alleging that it represents an implicit finding of involuntariness. The district court, however, gave no such indication. It characterized appellant's belated assertion of innocence as both "implausible" and "hard to accept," and decided to grant him the opportunity to present his case before a jury primarily because a trial represented appellant's "only chance to avoid the draconian sentence adopted by Congress for possession of crack cocaine by one previously convicted of a drug offense." Moreover, it specifically warned him that it would allow all of appellant's plea statements into evidence for impeachment, rebuttal, or the case-in-chief in any future trial, an act that belies any view that the plea or the waiver were coerced.

* * * Neither the Rule 11 plea colloquy between the trial judge and appellant, nor the judge's order permitting appellant to withdraw the plea, support in any way appellant's contention that the plea itself was entered into involuntarily. The trial court asked the appellant "has anybody threatened you or forced you in any way to enter this plea of guilty?" "And are you pleading guilty voluntarily and because you are guilty?" Appellant answered both questions in the affirmative. The trial judge also went through the specific terms of the plea agreement with appellant, including the provision in which he waived his rights under [Rule] 410. When subsequently challenged, the judge characterized appellant's waiver of his rights under [Rule] 410 as "knowing and voluntary," and rejected the defendant's motion to suppress on the grounds that "[t]here was nothing wrong with the plea proceeding. * * *" The extensive colloquy conducted by the trial court clearly supports this determination that appellant knowingly and voluntarily waived his rights under [Rule] 410. In no way could such a decision to permit the plea statement and the debriefings into evidence constitute an abuse of discretion.

* * *

III. CONCLUSION

For reasons explained, we reject all of Burch's contentions and affirm his conviction. * * *

E. LIABILITY INSURANCE

[1] Federal Rule 411

Rule 411. Liability Insurance

Evidence that a person was or was not insured against liability is not admissible upon the issue whether the person acted negligently or otherwise wrongfully. This rule does not require the exclusion of evidence of insurance against liability when offered for another purpose, such as proof of agency, ownership, or control, or bias or prejudice of a witness.

[2] Illustration

Plaintiff sues defendant, Deep Shaft, for injuries that plaintiff sustained when he fell into a mine shaft while hunting on government property. The defendant denies any responsibility, alleging he had no ownership of or control over the old shaft. At a pretrial conference the plaintiff offers an insurance policy by which Deep Shaft maintains liability insurance on the mine.

How would Deep Shaft object to the introduction of the insurance policy?

How would the plaintiff respond?

[3] Permissible Uses of Liability Insurance

BERNIER v. BOARD OF COUNTY ROAD COMMISSIONERS

581 F. Supp 71 (W.D. Mich. 1983)
Opinion Re Pending Motions

HILLMAN, DISTRICT JUDGE:

This is a diversity action for wrongful death. Plaintiff's decedent was her 17-year-old son, Michael Moon, who was killed when the vehicle he was driving was struck at the intersection of Stedman Road and Woods Road in Ionia County, Michigan. Plaintiff contends that the accident was caused by the county's failure to properly mark the intersection, and sues in her individual and representative capacities.

* * *

II. MOTIONS IN LIMINE

Defendant has asserted an affirmative defense that it did not have sufficient funds to properly maintain the intersection.

* * *

Defendant argues that under Michigan law evidence that it lacked sufficient funds to do more than was done under the circumstances of this case is highly relevant on the issue of whether defendant met its statutory duty to keep roads in "reasonable repair" and in a "reasonably safe condition."

* * *

Plaintiff * * * argues that the message implicit in the defendant's so-called "lack of funds" defense is that defendant would be unable to pay a substantial judgment rendered against it by the jury. To rebut such an inference, plaintiff maintains that she should be allowed to introduce evidence that defendant has liability insurance. Defendant argues that evidence of its liability insurance is prohibited by Fed. R. Evid. 411, and that its probative value is outweighed by its prejudicial impact, pursuant to Fed. R. Evid. 403.

* * *

Rule 411 excludes evidence that a party is covered by liability insurance when offered to show that the insured acted "negligently or otherwise wrongfully." 23 Wright & Miller, *Federal Practice and Procedure*, § 5364 at 448-49 (1st ed. 1980). The list of exceptions to Rule 411 is not exclusive but illustrates those exceptions which courts have generally held as admissible to prove a fact relevant to a material issue other than negligence.

* * * I shall defer a ruling on plaintiff's proffered evidence that defendant has liability insurance, until after the close of defendant's case-in-chief. I am not persuaded that defendant's proposed defense that it had limited resources and was therefore required to use discretion in determining which intersections were most in need of maintenance "opens the door" for plaintiff's introduction of liability insurance. Defendant should keep in mind, however, that should the nature of defendant's proofs be such that the jury might infer defendant's inability to pay a judgment, evidence that defendant has liability insurance may become admissible as an exception to the general prohibition of insurance evidence contained in Fed. R. Evid. 411.

* * *

IT IS SO ORDERED.

NOTES

1. As an exception to the rule of exclusion under Fed. R. Evid. 411, when is evidence of liability insurance admissible to show agency, ownership, or control?

In *Dobbins v. Crain Brothers, Inc.,* an action against a barge owner for personal injuries suffered in a fall on the barge's deck, the court recognized that "[t]he concept of ownership, hotly contested at earlier stages of this trial relates to ownership, possession, custody and control of a barge. The existence of insurance is some evidence of such ownership and control which may properly be considered by the jury under the exception clause to Rule 411 of the Federal Rules of Evidence." 432 F. Supp. 1060, 1069 (W.D. Pa. 1976).

2. As an exception to the rule of exclusion under Fed. R. Evid. 411, when is evidence of liability insurance admissible to impeach a witness?

In *Charter v. Chleborad*, a medical malpractice action, the court recognized that liability insurance is admissible when offered to prove the bias or prejudice of a witness. 551 F.2d 246 (8th. Cir. 1977). The Court of Appeals held that "the fact that defendant's insurer employed [defendant's impeaching witness] was clearly admissible to show possible bias of that witness."

PROBLEM 5-1

An investor sued her securities broker and his firm for breach of fiduciary duty by "churning" her account. The investor claims that the broker made numerous unnecessary trades over a two-year period which made no profit for her but generated considerable commissions for the broker and his firm. The broker and firm deny any wrongdoing and defend on the ground that the investor, a 40-year-old woman, has considerable business background and consented to the trades.

Investor calls the broker as a witness for the plaintiff. Because the broker is an adverse party, the court rules that leading questions are permitted.

Plaintiff: You were the broker for the plaintiff for 7 years?

Broker: Yes I was.

Plaintiff: For the first five of the seven years, you made approximately 8 trades a year in the plaintiff's account?

Broker: Yes.

Plaintiff: During the last two years you made more than a hundred trades a year in her account?

Defendant: Objection! Rule 407. Subsequent remedial measure.

The court: (1) __________.

Plaintiff: Each time you make a trade in the plaintiff's account, you earn a commission?

Broker: Yes.

Plaintiff: You reduced your commission after the plaintiff sued you?

Defendant: Objection! Rule 407. Subsequent remedial measure.

Plaintiff: Your Honor, there is no event here; this is not a negligence case.

The court: (2) __________.

Plaintiff: You remember that the plaintiff called you late last year and said she had been going over her books and was very upset at the number of trades you had made?

Broker: Yes.

Plaintiff: Didn't you offer to return some of your commissions at that time?

Defendant: Objection! Rule 408. Settlement discussion.

Plaintiff: Your Honor, no dispute had yet arisen.

The court: (3) ________.

Plaintiff: Didn't the district attorney investigate you and your firm for alleged violations of state securities laws involving churning?

Broker: Yes.

Plaintiff: Didn't you make an unsuccessful offer to plead nolo contendere to a misdemeanor involving churning?

Defendant: Objection! Rule 410.

Plaintiff: Your Honor, this is a civil case.

The court: (4) ________.

Plaintiff: You reduced your commission after the plaintiff sued you?

Defendant: Objection! Rule 407. Subsequent measure.

Plaintiff: Your Honor, there is no event here; this is not a negligence case.

The court: (5) ________.

Plaintiff: Does your firm carry liability insurance to protect its brokers?

Defendant: Objection! Rule 411.

Plaintiff: Your Honor, this is a not a negligence or product case. It goes to his incentive to take care in his fiduciary relationship.

The court: (6) ________.

Plaintiff: Your firm is a member of a national association of securities dealers?

Broker: Yes.

Plaintiff: That association makes available arbitration of securities disputes?

Broker: Yes.

Plaintiff: Shortly before the plaintiff filed this suit, you called her and said that you and your firm would be willing to arbitrate any claim she wanted to make?

Defendant: Objection! Rule 408.

Plaintiff: Your Honor, this is a fact. Facts are not protected.

The court: (7) ________.

Plaintiff: In fact, didn't you offer to pay for the costs of arbitration for the plaintiff?

Defendant: Objection! Rule 408.

Plaintiff: Your Honor, I'm not asking about this case, but about a proposed arbitration.

The court: (8) ________.

Plaintiff: Your firm actually pled guilty to the misdemeanor improper churning, didn't it?

Defendant: Objection! Rule 410.
The court: (9) ________.
Plaintiff: You made a statement to the court at the time of the misdemeanor plea saying that "we did not do our duty," right?
Defendant: Objection! Rule 410.
The court: (10) ________.
Plaintiff: After the plaintiff sued you, your firm required that you note in your records client approval for each trade that you make?
Defendant: Objection! Rule 407.
Plaintiff: Your Honor, this is not any sort of repair.
The court: (11) ________.
Plaintiff: Isn't it true that several years before this suit was filed, another client sued your firm for churning and the firm reacted by issuing a written policy statement warning against churning?
Defendant: Objection! Rule 407.
Plaintiff: Your Honor, this is not a subsequent measure at all.
The court: (12) ________.
Plaintiff: Isn't it true that your firm issued a written policy statement warning against churning because your liability carrier insisted upon it.
Defendant: Objection! Rule 411.
Plaintiff: Your Honor, this is another fact.
The court: (13) ________.
Plaintiff: Isn't it true that just yesterday the association of securities dealers to which your firm belongs issued a recommendation that brokers should be required to record client permission for each trade contemporaneously with the trade?
Defendant: Objection! Rule 407.
Plaintiff: Your Honor, this is not any sort of action by the defendants.
The court: (14) ________.

PROBLEM 5-2

Jan Smith brings a lawsuit against Hercules Trucking Co. seeking compensatory and punitive damages arising from an accident in which the driver of a Hercules tractor-trailer fell asleep and thereby permitted his large vehicle to swerve into Smith's. The collision forced Smith's car off the road, knocked it over the protective barrier on a bridge and caused it to fall 15 feet to the ground causing Smith permanent injuries.

Smith calls as a witness the President of Hercules Trucking Co. Because the President is identified with an adverse party, the court rules that leading questions are permitted.

Plaintiff:	The driver of the tractor-trailer that crashed into Smith's car had worked for your company for five years?
President:	Yes.
Plaintiff:	Three years before the accident with Smith, did you suspend the driver for two weeks because he had been in an accident?
Defendant:	Objection! Rule 407. This is a classic subsequent measure.
The court:	(1) ________.
Plaintiff:	You suspended the driver for three weeks after this accident?
Defendant:	Objection! Rule 407. Once again this is barred by the rule.
The court:	(2) ________.
Plaintiff:	After the accident, you offered to pay Smith's medical bills?
Defendant:	Objection! Rule 409.
Plaintiff:	This is not a settlement offer, Your Honor.
The court:	(3) ________.
Plaintiff:	After the accident, you did in fact pay Smith's medical bills?
Defendant:	Objection! Rule 409.
Plaintiff:	This not disputed, Your Honor.
The court:	(4) ________.
Plaintiff:	After the accident, when you offered to pay Smith's medical bills, you phoned Smith in the hospital and said that the accident involved horrendous conduct on the part of your driver?
Defendant:	Objection! Rule 409.
Plaintiff:	This is not a settlement offer, Your Honor.
The court:	(5) ________.
Plaintiff:	Smith's attorney contacted you and said that Smith was contemplating filing a suit?
President:	Yes.
Plaintiff:	You offered Smith $250,000 in exchange for waiving all claims?
Defendant:	Objection! Rule 408. Settlement discussion
Plaintiff:	Your Honor, no case had been filed.
The court:	(6) ________.
Plaintiff:	You actually sat down with Smith's lawyer before the suit was filed?
President:	Yes.
Plaintiff:	Didn't you say in that conversation that you were as shocked by the appalling driving as Smith?

Defendant: Objection! Rule 408.
Plaintiff: Your Honor, this is an admission.
The court: (7) ________.
Plaintiff: After the driver had his first accident three years before the one we are concerned with, you increased your liability insurance?
Defendant: Objection! Rule 411.
The court: (8) ________.
Plaintiff: The local prosecutor investigated your company and the driver after the accident?
President: Yes, but she decided not to bring charges.
Plaintiff: Didn't you say to her that you recognized that the accident should never have happened and that the driver's actions were inexcusable in the course of persuading her not to bring charges?
Defendant: Objection! Rule 410.
Plaintiff: Your Honor, no charges were brought.
The court: (9) ________.
Plaintiff: In fact, didn't the driver go with you to meet with the prosecutor and confess to her that he knew his actions were horrible?
Defendant: Objection! Rule 410.
Plaintiff: Your Honor, the driver is not a defendant in this case.
The court: (10) ________.
Plaintiff: Didn't your company make an announcement to the public after Smith's accident that it was going to provide additional training for all of its over-the-road drivers?
Defendant: Objection! Rule 407.
Plaintiff: Your Honor, this is an announcement we are talking about, not anything else.
The court: (11) ________.
Plaintiff: Didn't you tell Driver after the accident that you would fire him if he got into another accident?
Defendant: Objection! Rule 407.
Plaintiff: Your Honor, this is a warning, nothing else.
The court: (12) ________.
Plaintiff: It's true, isn't it, that you have a million dollars of insurance in this case?
Defendant: Objection! Rule 411.
Plaintiff: Your Honor, this goes to punitive damages.
The court: (13) ________.

Chapter 6

CHARACTER EVIDENCE, PRIOR BAD ACTS, AND HABIT

A. INTRODUCTION

Character is defined in *Black's Law Dictionary* as "the aggregate of the moral qualities which belong to and distinguish an individual person; * * * A person's fixed disposition or tendency, as evidenced to others by his habits of life, through the manifestation of which his general reputation for the possession of a character, good or otherwise, is obtained." For purposes of evidence law, character evidence is generally used to show the nature of a person as it pertains to a particular trait, *i.e.*, reckless, careful, hot-tempered, peaceful, violent, calm, etc.

A quick reading of Federal Rule of Evidence 404(a) would lead one to believe that there is a broad prohibition against the use of character evidence, subject only to the three exceptions set forth in subparagraphs (1), (2), and (3). However, as will become apparent as we attempt to untangle the mass of decisions relating to character evidence, the rule is so riddled with exceptions that even judges and experienced lawyers find themselves confused by the maze. Therefore, we begin with a simplified view of some preliminary issues which must be addressed in a character evidence analysis.

Distinguishing substantive character evidence from impeachment by the use of character evidence

Character evidence may be divided into two primary categories based on how the evidence is used:

> **Substantive character evidence.** When a trait of a person's character is offered to prove a disputed issue in the case, evidence of that character trait is substantive. For example, in a homicide case the defendant may wish to show that the victim was the initial aggressor. In that case, the aggressive character of the victim is offered as substantive evidence.
>
> **Impeachment use of character evidence.** Impeachment has nothing to do with the issues in the case. Rather impeachment is an attempt to discredit the witness or the witness's testimony so that the judge or jury will find it unworthy of belief. For example, in a criminal prosecution for murder, assume the prosecution's principal witness has several convictions for perjury. Evidence of the convictions has nothing to do with the issues in the criminal trial for murder. However, defense counsel would definitely want to introduce those perjury convictions to impeach the witness, i.e., to undermine the witness's

testimony by showing the factfinder that the witness is not a truthteller and is therefore not credible. Use of character testimony for impeachment purposes is the third exception to the nonadmissibility of character testimony provided by Rule 404(a).

Keeping these two concepts analytically distinct is not always an easy task; however, it is critical if one is to master the rules of evidence relating to character evidence. This chapter deals only with substantive character evidence and the related concern of whether the evidence meets the relevancy requirements of the federal rules. The use of character evidence for impeachment is covered in Chapter 17.

Distinguishing circumstantial use of character evidence from character "in issue"

After one makes the determination that the use of character evidence is for a substantive purpose, i.e., the character evidence is offered to prove a disputed issue in the case, then substantive character evidence can be roughly divided into two categories of use:

Character in issue. Character is in issue when a person's character is an element of proof under the substantive law. For example, in a defamation case when truth is a defense, character is said to be in issue because evidence of the plaintiff's character will lead the factfinder to determine whether the defendant defamed the plaintiff or, on the other hand, whether the defendant published a true statement about the plaintiff's character. The determination of the plaintiff's character will decide the case. Negligent entrustment cases are another example of cases in which character is in issue. In a negligent entrustment action the plaintiff alleges that the defendant allowed an unfit person to use a car or other dangerous object. Thus, the issue is whether the defendant knew or should have known that the person to whom the vehicle was entrusted had the character trait of being a bad driver. When character is in issue, it falls outside the limitations of Rule 404(a) and its admissibility is governed by the more general rules, 401-403.

Circumstantial use of character evidence. In most cases the substantive law does not require proof of a person's character. For example, in a bank robbery prosecution, the government has to prove that the defendant intended to rob the bank and did so; it doesn't have to prove that the defendant is a certain kind of person, e.g., violent, crime-prone, etc. Where character is not in issue, parties often attempt to introduce evidence of a person's character to show that on a particular occasion the person acted in conformity with his character. This use of character is generally referred to as circumstantial use of character evidence. Circumstantial use of character evidence is demonstrated by the criminal battery case when there is an issue as to who was the first aggressor. In such a case, the character evidence is used to support an inference that an individual in a specific situation acted consistently with the proven trait, i.e., that an aggressive "victim" attacked first, or that a peaceable defendant did not attack first. As you will learn in this chapter, the circumstantial use of character evidence as a general matter is disallowed by Federal Rule of Evidence 404(a).

The three subsections of Fed. R. Evid. 404(a) provide exceptions to this general rule. Thus, under certain circumstances, circumstantial character evidence relating to an accused and a victim may be admissible provided it can be made to fit one of the Rule 404(a) exceptions.

Methods of proof

After a determination has been made that the character evidence is admissible, one must refer to Rule 405 to determine what method of proof can be used to present such evidence to the court. There are three ways to present substantive character evidence: reputation testimony, opinion testimony, and specific instances of conduct. As will be seen in this chapter, the available methods of proof vary depending upon the purpose for which the character evidence is offered.

B. FEDERAL RULES 404, 405, AND 406

Rule 404. Character Evidence Not Admissible to Prove Conduct; Exceptions; Other Crimes

(a) Character evidence generally. Evidence of a person's character or a trait of character is not admissible for the purpose of proving action in conformity therewith on a particular occasion, except:

(1) Character of accused. In a criminal case, evidence of a pertinent trait of character offered by an accused, or by the prosecution to rebut the same; or if evidence of a trait of character of the alleged victim of the crime is offered by an accused and admitted under Rule 404(a)(2), evidence of the same trait of character of the accused offered by the prosecution;

(2) Character of alleged victim. In a criminal case, and subject to the limitations imposed by Rule 412, evidence of a pertinent trait of character of the alleged victim of the crime offered by an accused, or by the prosecution to rebut the same, or evidence of a character trait of peacefulness of the alleged victim offered by the prosecution in a homicide case to rebut evidence that the alleged victim was the first aggressor;

(3) Character of witness. Evidence of the character of a witness as provided in rules 607, 608, and 609.

(b) Other crimes, wrongs, or acts. Evidence of other crimes, wrongs, or acts is not admissible to prove the character of a person in order to show action in conformity therewith. It may, however, be admissible for other purposes, such as proof of motive, opportunity, intent, preparation, plan, knowledge, identity, or absence of mistake or accident, provided that upon request by the accused, the prosecution in a criminal case shall provide reasonable notice in advance of trial, or during trial if the court excuses pretrial notice on good cause shown, of the general nature of any such evidence it intends to introduce at trial.

Rule 405. Methods of Proving Character

(a) Reputation or opinion. In all cases in which evidence of character or a trait of character of a person is admissible, proof may be made by testimony as to reputation or by testimony in the form of an opinion. On cross-examination, inquiry is allowable into relevant specific instances of conduct.

(b) Specific instances of conduct. In cases in which character or a trait of character of a person is an essential element of a charge, claim, or defense, proof may also be made of specific instances of that person's conduct.

Rule 406. Habit; Routine Practice

Evidence of the habit of a person or of the routine practice of an organization, whether corroborated or not and regardless of the presence of eyewitnesses, is relevant to prove that the conduct of the person or organization on a particular occasion was in conformity with the habit or routine practice.

C. COMMITTEE NOTE TO 2006 AMENDMENT TO RULE 404

The Rule has been amended to clarify that in a civil case evidence of a person's character is never admissible to prove that the person acted in conformity with the character trait. The amendment resolves the dispute in the case law over whether the exceptions in subdivisions (a)(1) and (2) permit the circumstantial use of character evidence in civil cases. *Compare Carson v. Polley*, 689 F.2d 562, 576 (5th Cir. 1982) ("when a central issue in a case is close to one of a criminal nature, the exceptions to the Rule 404(a) ban on character evidence may be invoked"), *with SEC v. Towers Financial Corp.*, 966 F. Supp. 203 (S.D.N.Y. 1997) (relying on the terms "accused" and "prosecution" in Rule 404(a) to conclude that the exceptions in subdivisions (a)(1) and (2) are inapplicable in civil cases). The amendment is consistent with the original intent of the Rule, which was to prohibit the circumstantial use of character evidence in civil cases, even where closely related to criminal charges. *See Ginter v. Northwestern Mut. Life Ins. Co.*, 576 F.Supp. 627, 629-30 (D. Ky.1984) ("It seems beyond peradventure of doubt that the drafters of F.R.Evi. 404(a) explicitly intended that all character evidence, except where 'character is at issue' was to be excluded" in civil cases).

The circumstantial use of character evidence is generally discouraged because it carries serious risks of prejudice, confusion and delay. *See Michelson v. United States,* 335 U.S. 469, 476 (1948) ("The overriding policy of excluding such evidence, despite its admitted probative value, is the practical experience that its disallowance tends to prevent confusion of issues, unfair surprise and undue prejudice."). In criminal cases, the so-called "mercy rule" permits a criminal defendant to introduce evidence of pertinent character traits of the defendant and the victim. But that is because the accused, whose liberty is at stake, may need "a counterweight against the strong investigative and prosecutorial resources of the government." C. Mueller & L. Kirkpatrick, *Evidence: Practice Under the Rules*, pp. 264-5 (2d ed. 1999). *See also* Richard Uviller, *Evidence of Character to Prove Conduct: Illusion, Illogic, and Injustice in the Courtroom*, 130 U. Pa. L. Rev. 845, 855 (1982) (the rule prohibiting circumstantial use of character evidence "was relaxed to allow the criminal defendant with so much at stake and so little available in the way of conventional proof to have special dispensation to tell the factfinder just what sort of person he really is"). Those concerns do not apply to parties in civil cases.

The amendment also clarifies that evidence otherwise admissible under Rule 404(a)(2) may nonetheless be excluded in a criminal case involving sexual misconduct. In such a case, the admissibility of evidence of the victim's sexual behavior and predisposition is governed by the more stringent provisions of Rule 412.

Nothing in the amendment is intended to affect the scope of Rule 404(b). While Rule 404(b) refers to the "accused", the "prosecution" and a "criminal case", it does so only in the context of a notice requirement. The admissibility standards of Rule 404(b) remain fully applicable to both civil and criminal cases.

D. THE 11 RULES OF SUBSTANTIVE CHARACTER EVIDENCE, SIMILAR ACTS, AND HABIT

RULE #1: THE CIRCUMSTANTIAL USE OF CHARACTER EVIDENCE IS NOT PERMITTED IN A CIVIL CASE.

[1] Illustration

Perry Wilson sues Robin Rich for negligent driving alleging that Robin ran him over. As a result Wilson alleges that he sustained grievous injuries.

Brian Jones takes the stand on behalf of Wilson.

Plaintiff::	Please state your name.
Witness:	Brian Jones.
Plaintiff:	Do you know the plaintiff, Perry Wilson?
Witness:	Yes, for many years in many ways, and I know many others who know him as well.
Plaintiff:	Does he have a reputation of having a good moral character?
Defendant:	Objection! ________.
The court:	________.
Plaintiff:	Well then, is he an honest man?
Defendant:	Objection! ________.
The court:	________.
Plaintiff:	Well, in your opinion is he a safe driver?
Defendant:	Objection! ________.
The court:	________.
Plaintiff:	To your knowledge, has he ever been involved in any kind of accident in the past?

Defendant: Objection! ________.
The court: ________.

[2] General Rule

GINTER v. NORTHWESTERN MUTUAL LIFE INS. CO.
576 F. Supp. 627 (E.D. Ky. 1984)

BERTELSMAN, DISTRICT JUDGE:

This matter is before the court on a motion for a pretrial evidentiary ruling on the question of whether character evidence is admissible in a civil case under Fed. R. Evid. 404(a).

FACTS

This is an action by the beneficiary of a life insurance policy against the insurance company which issued the policy. There is no dispute that the plaintiff's deceased husband took out a policy on his life with the defendant insurance company and that the premiums were properly paid. However, the insurance company defends on the ground that there were material omissions from the application. More particularly, the insurance company contends that the insured decedent failed to disclose that he was under treatment by a psychiatrist for depression. Plaintiff responds that the application was completely answered and that any inaccuracies were not a material consideration in the issuance of the policy.

The plaintiff in the pending motion has requested a ruling from the court that evidence is admissible from witnesses who would testify that the deceased insured was a man of good character who would be unlikely to submit a fraudulent or erroneous application.

ANALYSIS

* * *

[T]he drafters of Fed. R. Evid. 404(a) explicitly intended that all character evidence, except where "character is at issue" was to be excluded. After an extensive review of the various points of view on this issue, the Advisory Committee expressly stated, "[i]t is believed that those espousing change (from the view of excluding character evidence in civil cases) have not met the burden of persuasion." This language leads to the inevitable conclusion that the use in Rule 404(a) of the terms applicable only to criminal cases was not accidental.

* * *

This court believes that the language of the rule, as originally drafted by the Advisory Committee and ultimately approved by Congress, has the effect of a statute in excluding the profferred evidence here, even though the case may be considered as analogous to a criminal prosecution. (Here some of the elements of mail fraud or larceny by trick are arguably present.) The court regards itself as not having any discretion in this matter by reason of the explicit language of the rule, since it is clear that this case is not one where character is at issue.

Therefore, the preliminary motion seeking admissibility of the evidence must be denied. The proffered evidence will be excluded at trial.

ORDER ACCORDINGLY.

NOTE

Why do the Federal Rules of Evidence permit the circumstantial use of character evidence in some criminal cases and not in civil cases?

The Advisory Committee's Note to the 2006 Amendment to Rule 404 — which codifies the result in *Ginter*, that the circumstantial use of character evidence is never permitted in a civil case — explains the difference in the character evidence rules in civil and criminal cases:

> The circumstantial use of character evidence is generally discouraged because it carries serious risks of prejudice, confusion and delay. *See Michelson v. United States,* 335 U.S. 469, 476 (1948) ("The overriding policy of excluding such evidence, despite its admitted probative value, is the practical experience that its disallowance tends to prevent confusion of issues, unfair surprise and undue prejudice."). In criminal cases, the so-called "mercy rule" permits a criminal defendant to introduce evidence of pertinent character traits of the defendant and the victim. But that is because the accused, whose liberty is at stake, may need "a counterweight against the strong investigative and prosecutorial resources of the government." C. Mueller & L. Kirkpatrick, *Evidence: Practice Under the Rules*, pp. 264-5 (2d ed. 1999). *See also* Richard Uviller, *Evidence of Character to Prove Conduct: Illusion, Illogic, and Injustice in the Courtroom*, 130 U. Pa. L. Rev. 845, 855 (1982) (the rule prohibiting circumstantial use of character evidence "was relaxed to allow the criminal defendant with so much at stake and so little available in the way of conventional proof to have special dispensation to tell the factfinder just what sort of person he really is"). Those concerns do not apply to parties in civil cases."

RULE #2: WHEN CHARACTER IS IN ISSUE IN A CIVIL CASE, EVIDENCE OF THE PERTINENT CHARACTER TRAIT IS ADMISSIBLE AND MAY BE PROVEN BY REPUTATION, OPINION, AND SPECIFIC INSTANCES OF CONDUCT.

[1] Character in Issue

SCHAFER v. TIME, INC.
142 F.3d 1361 (11th Cir. 1998)

BIRCH, CIRCUIT JUDGE:

* * *

This appeal * * * presents a number of evidentiary questions, most notably whether specific instances of misconduct are admissible to prove character under Federal Rule of Evidence 405(b) in an action for libel under Georgia law. The plaintiff-appellant challenges the district court's decision to admit character evidence * * *.

BACKGROUND

On December 21, 1988, Pan Am Flight 103 exploded in mid-flight over Lockerbie, Scotland, causing the death of everyone on board. A terrorist's bomb was then, and is now, widely suspected to be the source of that explosion. On April 20, 1992, defendant-appellee, Time, Inc. ("Time"), published a cover story entitled "The Untold Story of Pan Am 103." The article purported to debunk the then-prevailing theory that the government of Lybia had sponsored the attack on Pan Am 103. Instead, the article posited that a Palestinian group, with connections to Syrian drug traffickers, had targeted Pan Am 103 to eliminate several of the passengers who were members of a United States counter-terrorism team attempting to rescue United States hostages in Lebanon. The article claims that these passengers had discovered an unsavory, covert relationship between the Syrian drug traffickers and a unit of the United States Central Intelligence Agency and intended to expose it upon their return to the United States.

The article further stated that an American agent, David Lovejoy, had become a double agent and had leaked information regarding the team's travel plans to forces hostile to the United States. The article included a photograph of a man identified by the following caption:

> David Lovejoy, a reported double agent for the U.S. and Iran, is alleged to have told Iranian officials that McKee [one of the U.S. agents] was booked on Flight 103.

The article went on to imply that the information Lovejoy disclosed to hostile forces led to the attack on Pan Am 103.

* * * The man in the photograph, however, is Michael Schafer, the plaintiff-appellant in this case. Time's article, therefore, erroneously identified Schafer,

then working in his family's janitorial business in Austell, Georgia, both as a traitor to the United States government and a player in the bombing of Pan Am 103.

Upon discovering his picture in the magazine, Schafer demanded and eventually received a retraction from Time. Schafer filed suit against Time, making claims under Georgia's libel laws. A jury returned a verdict in Time's favor, finding no liability for the error. * * *

DISCUSSION

* * *

II. Evidentiary Issues

Schafer also argues that the district court committed reversible error by permitting Time's counsel to question Schafer regarding a number of "specific acts of misconduct" during cross-examination * * *.

A. Specific Acts of Misconduct

Evidence of a person's character is viewed with some suspicion under the law and generally is disfavored in the Federal Rules of Evidence. *See* Fed. R. Evid. 404 (character evidence generally inadmissible to prove conforming conduct). In an action for defamation or libel, however, the issue of the plaintiff's reputation and character scarcely can be avoided because the plaintiff typically seeks to recover compensation for damage to his or her reputation. Even in such cases, however, the rules of evidence prescribe particular methods for broaching the issue of character. *See* Fed. R. Evid. 405 ("Methods of Proving Character").

Before trial, the district court instructed the parties that Time would not be permitted to introduce and explore a number of specific acts and events in Schafer's life as they were irrelevant to the issues before the jury. At that time, however, the district court warned both parties that the court would revisit the character issue to the extent that particular acts and events were shown to be relevant to the question of damages or how Schafer's picture might have become associated with the Pan Am case. During the course of the trial, the district court made a preliminary ruling permitting Time to explore selective incidents and acts in Schafer's background but excluding evidence of others. Specifically, the district court ruled that Time would be permitted to question Schafer about a felony conviction, a possible violation of his subsequent parole, convictions for driving under the influence, an arrest for writing a bad check, failure to file tax returns, failure to pay alimony and child support, and evidence concerning Schafer's efforts to change his name and social security number. Schafer attacks the district court's ruling and argues that these specific acts were inadmissible.

The Federal Rules of Evidence detail the circumstances under which character evidence is admissible and the methods available for presenting such evidence. In all cases in which character evidence is admissible a party may offer reputation or opinion testimony on the issue of a person's character. *See* Fed. R. Evid. 405(a). Only in cases in which a person's character is "an essential element of a charge, claim or defense," however, may a party offer evidence of specific instances of conduct. *See* Fed. R. Evid. 405(b).

Character evidence does not constitute an "essential element" of a claim or charge unless it alters the rights and liabilities of the parties under the substantive law. Our determination of whether character constitutes an essential element requires us to examine the "authoritative statutory or common law statement of the elements of the prima facie case and defenses." The advisory committee's notes to the Federal Rules of Evidence provide two examples in which character evidence constitutes such an essential element: "[1] the chastity of a victim under a statute specifying her chastity as an element of the crime of seduction, or [2] the competency of the driver in an action for negligently entrusting a motor vehicle to an incompetent driver." Fed. R. Evid. 404(a) adv. comm. note (explaining that Rule 404 does not exclude such evidence because it is not offered to prove conduct consistent with character). In addition to these examples, a charge of defamation or libel commonly makes damage to the victim's reputation or character an essential element of the case. Georgia law confirms that an assertion of damage to reputation in a libel case makes the plaintiff's character an issue under the substantive law. Since the plaintiff's character is substantively at issue in a libel case under Georgia law, Rule 405(b) permits the admission of evidence regarding specific instances of the plaintiff's conduct on that issue. * * * Given the plain language of Rule 405(b), Schafer's arguments that specific acts remain inadmissible to prove character in an action for libel are unpersuasive.

[The Court reversed and remanded on other grounds.]

[2] Illustration

Perry Wilson sues Robin Rich for personal injuries alleging that Robin allowed his friend Bob Tuck to drive Robin's car, and that Bob ran over Wilson. The basis of the claim against Robin is negligent entrustment. The defense is that the plaintiff was not paying attention. Wilson takes the stand and after describing the accident and his injuries and certifying that the car was licensed to one R. Rich, testifies as follows:

Wilson on direct examination:

Plaintiff:	Do you know Bob well?
Wilson:	For many years, in many ways and I know many others who know him in the community, and we've talked about him.
Plaintiff:	What is his reputation as a safe driver?
Defendant:	Objection! Character evidence is inadmissible in civil cases.
Plaintiff:	(1) ________.
The court:	(2) ________.
Plaintiff:	I'll ask the question again. What is Bob's reputation as a safe driver?
Wilson:	A truly dangerous man.
Plaintiff:	What is your own opinion about his ability to safely drive a car?

Defendant:	Objection! Only reputation evidence is admissible.
Plaintiff:	(3) ________.
The court:	(4) ________.
Plaintiff:	Once again, what is your opinion about his ability to safely drive a car?
Wilson:	I think he is an unsafe driver.
Plaintiff:	Are you aware of any specific instances where Bob has carelessly driven a car?
Defendant:	Objection! Improper character evidence.
Plaintiff:	(5) ________.
The court:	(6) ________.
Plaintiff:	I'll ask again, are you aware of any specific instances where Bob Tuck has carelessly driven a car?
Wilson:	Yes, I have personally seen him hit telephone poles on four separate occasions.

The Plaintiff rests and Terry Porter is called to the stand by Robin Rich.

Terry Porter on direct examination:

Defendant:	State your name.
Witness:	Terry Porter.
Defendant:	Do you know Bob well?
Witness:	No, I've been away for a while, but I sure know all about Perry Wilson.
Defendant:	Is he a safe and careful pedestrian when walking the streets around town?
Plaintiff:	Objection! (7) ________.
The court:	(8) ________.

RULE #3: IN A CRIMINAL CASE, THE PROSECUTION MAY NOT OFFER CHARACTER EVIDENCE CONCERNING THE DEFENDANT IN ITS CASE IN CHIEF.

UNITED STATES v. WILLIAMS

739 F.2d 297 (7th Cir. 1984)

FLAUM, CIRCUIT JUDGE.

This is an appeal from a conviction following a jury trial in which the defendant was found guilty on four counts of transporting stolen motor vehicles in interstate commerce in violation of the Dyer Act, 18 U.S.C. § 2312 (1982) and of aiding and abetting the commission of Dyer Act violations, 18 U.S.C. § 2 (1982). The defendant alleges several trial errors that he says deprived him of a fair trial. For the reasons stated below, we agree that the defendant did not receive a fair trial, and we vacate the defendant's conviction and remand for a new trial.

I.

Several years ago, the Federal Bureau of Investigation (FBI) established an undercover business in southern Missouri. This business purchased salvaged wrecked automobiles from insurance companies and sold the public Vehicle Identification Number (VIN) tags to persons who then used them to retag stolen automobiles and sell them. The purpose of the FBI operation was to investigate and identify persons involved in the retagging of stolen automobiles in the St. Louis, Missouri, area. As a result of this FBI investigation, the defendant was implicated in a scheme involving the theft, retagging, and resale of four automobiles.

At the defendant's trial, four witnesses testified that they had purchased an automobile from the defendant and had taken delivery from him in Illinois some time in 1981 or early 1982. Evidence then was introduced to show that each of these automobiles delivered by the defendant had been stolen a short time earlier from individuals living in St. Louis. Each of these stolen automobiles contained a VIN tag sold by the FBI's undercover business to two suspected dealers of stolen automobiles, L.C. Kirkwood and Lee Morgan. The prosecution's theory was that the defendant had acted as a middleman between Kirkwood and Morgan and the purchasers of the stolen automobiles. The defendant admitted to working as a delivery man for Kirkwood and Morgan, but claimed that he did not know that the vehicles that he was delivering were stolen. Thus, the defendant's state of mind was the key issue in the case.

After a three-day jury trial, the defendant was found guilty on all four counts charged in his indictment. His post-trial motions were denied and he was sentenced to a total of six years in prison. He then brought this appeal.

II.

Although the defendant makes several arguments on appeal, we find two sufficiently persuasive in this factual context to warrant reversal. * * * The second error alleged by the defendant occurred during the testimony of one of the prosecution's witnesses, a detective with the St. Louis Police Department. The prosecutor asked the detective whether the defendant was known by any aliases. The defense counsel objected, but the trial court permitted the detective to state that he knew the defendant as "Fast Eddie." The defendant contends that this testimony caused him undue prejudice and should not have been permitted.

* * *

The defendant argues not only that "Fast Eddie" is a nickname suggesting a bad character, but also that the fact that a police detective stated that he knew the defendant as "Fast Eddie" intimated to the jury that the defendant was known to be involved in criminal activity. Thus, the defendant argues, the detective's statement should have been excluded from evidence as more prejudicial than probative under Rule 403 of the Federal Rules of Evidence. The government responds by contending that "Fast Eddie" is a "neutral" name that did not suggest that the defendant had a criminal reputation or background, and that even if it did suggest this, its introduction into evidence does not constitute reversible error.

We find it self-evident that the testimony of a police detective stating that he knew the defendant as "Fast Eddie" might suggest to the jury that the defendant had some sort of history of or reputation for unsavory activity. We also agree with the defendant that the detective's testimony should have been excluded from evidence as more prejudicial than probative. As many courts have recognized, a prosecutor may introduce evidence of a defendant's alias or nickname if this evidence aids in the identification of the defendant or in some other way directly relates to the proof of the acts charged in the indictment. *See, e.g., United States v. Kalish*, 690 F.2d 1144, 1155 (5th Cir. 1982) (defendant's alias admissible where it was used to conceal identity from arresting officer). * * * In the instant case, however, the detective's testimony about the defendant's nickname was completely unrelated to any of the other proof against the defendant. The prosecution's only possible purpose in eliciting the testimony was to create an impression in the minds of the jurors that the defendant was known by the police to be an unsavory character or even a criminal. Thus, the detective's statement was tantamount to testimony about a defendant's character that is proffered to show the probability that the defendant acted in conformity with that character in a particular case. This type of evidence, of course, is not permitted in the prosecution's case-in-chief, on the theory that it causes defendants undue prejudice and denies defendants the opportunity to defend against the particular charges against them. Fed. R. Evid. 404(a). Therefore, it was improper for the prosecutor to elicit the gratuitous testimony about the defendant's nickname, and the testimony should not have been permitted.

Having found error in the defendant's trial, we must consider the question of prejudice. * * * Whenever the prosecution improperly introduces evidence relating to a defendant's bad character, there is always a danger that the evidence will cause the defendant undue prejudice. In this case, the detective's statement seems particularly prejudicial, since the defendant's only defense was that he did not know that the vehicles that he was transporting were stolen. It is quite possible that this would be viewed as an unlikely story when told by someone known to the police as "Fast Eddie." The testimony also was particularly prejudicial because no other evidence relating to the defendant's character, reputation, or criminal past was introduced at trial. * * * Thus, by the time the case was submitted to the jury, the detective's testimony about "Fast Eddie" had gained significance as the only evidence relating to the defendant's character, reputation, or background.

If the properly admitted evidence of the defendant's guilt had been very strong, we might find the errors in this case to be harmless. * * * However, that was not the case here. The prosecution presented only slight evidence that the defendant actually knew he was transporting stolen vehicles. * * * Under such circumstances, the errors discussed herein cannot be considered harmless. Accordingly, we vacate the defendant's conviction and remand for a new trial.

NOTE

Under what circumstances can a defendant's prejudicial alias be admitted?

Williams can be compared usefully with *United States v. Delpit*, 94 F.3d 1134 (8th Cir. 1996). Delpit was charged in a drug conspiracy. Much of the evidence of conspiracy consisted of electronically intercepted conversations among the conspirators. In many of these conversations, the conspirators referred to "Monster" as a major player in the conspiracy. The trial court allowed the prosecution to admit evidence that the defendant's nickname was "Monster." The court of appeals found no error, distinguishing *Williams* as a case in which the prejudicial reference to the defendant's nickname was a gratuitous attempt to interject the defendant's bad character into the case. In contrast, there was no way for the government to introduce the tapes and have the jury make sense of them without letting the jury know that the defendant had the unfortunate sobriquet, Monster. Thus, the nickname evidence was admitted for a proper purpose, not to show the defendant's bad character.

RULE #4: IN A CRIMINAL CASE, CHARACTER EVIDENCE OF A PERTINENT TRAIT OF THE DEFENDANT IS ADMISSIBLE IF OFFERED BY THE DEFENDANT, AFTER WHICH THE STATE MAY OFFER REBUTTAL EVIDENCE. PROOF MAY BE MADE ONLY BY REPUTATION AND OPINION.

MICHELSON v. UNITED STATES
335 U.S. 469 (1948)

JUSTICE JACKSON delivered the opinion of the Court.

In 1947 petitioner Michelson was convicted of bribing a federal revenue agent. The Government proved a large payment by accused to the agent for the purpose of influencing his official action. The defendant, as a witness on his own behalf, admitted passing the money but claimed it was done in response to the agent's demands, threats, solicitations, and inducements that amounted to entrapment. It is enough for our purposes to say that determination of the issue turned on whether the jury should believe the agent or the accused.

* * *

Defendant called five witnesses to prove that he enjoyed a good reputation. Two of them testified that their acquaintance with him extended over a period of about thirty years and the others said they had known him at least half that long. A typical examination in chief was as follows:

Q. Do you know the defendant Michelson?

A. Yes.

Q. How long do you know Mr. Michelson?

A. About 30 years.

Q. Do you know other people who know him?

A. Yes.

Q. Have you have occasion to discuss his reputation for honesty and truthfulness and for being a law-abiding citizen?

A. It is very good.

Q. You have talked to others?

A. Yes.

Q. And what is his reputation?

A. Very good.

* * *

To four of these witnesses the prosecution also addressed the question the allowance of which, over defendant's objection, is claimed to be reversible error:

"Did you ever hear that on October 11th, 1920, the defendant, Solomon Michelson, was arrested for receiving stolen goods?"

None of the witnesses appears to have heard of this.

The trial court asked counsel for the prosecution, out of presence of the jury, "Is it a fact according to the best information in your possession that Michelson was arrested for receiving stolen goods?" Counsel replied that it was, and to support his good faith exhibited a paper record which defendant's counsel did not challenge.

The judge also on three occasions warned the jury, in terms that are not criticized, of the limited purpose for which this evidence was received.

Defendant-petitioner challenges the right of the prosecution so to cross-examine his character witnesses. The Court of Appeals held that it was permissible. The opinion, however, points out that the practice has been severely criticized and invites us, in one respect, to change the rule. Serious and responsible criticism has been aimed, however, not alone at the detail now questioned by the Court of Appeals but at common-law doctrine on the whole subject of proof of reputation or character. It would not be possible to appraise the usefulness and propriety of this cross-examination without consideration of the unique practice concerning character testimony, of which such cross-examination is a minor part.

Courts that follow the common-law tradition almost unanimously have come to disallow resort by the prosecution to any kind of evidence of a defendant's evil character to establish a probability of his guilt. Not that the law invests the defendant with a presumption of good character, * * * but it simply closes the whole matter of character, disposition and reputation on the prosecution's case-in-chief. The State may not show defendant's prior trouble with the law, specific criminal acts, or ill name among his neighbors, even though such facts might logically be persuasive that he is by propensity a probable perpetrator of the crime. The inquiry is not rejected because character is irrelevant; on the contrary, it is said to weigh too much with the jury and to so over persuade them as to prejudge one with a bad general record and deny him a fair opportunity to defend against a particular charge. The overriding policy of excluding such evidence, despite its admitted probative value, is the practical experience that its disallowance tends to prevent confusion of issues, unfair surprise and undue prejudice.

But this line of inquiry firmly denied to the State is opened to the defendant because character is relevant in resolving probabilities of guilt. He may introduce affirmative testimony that the general estimate of his character is so favorable that the jury may infer that he would not be likely to commit the offense charged. This privilege is sometimes valuable to a defendant for this Court has held that such testimony alone, in some circumstances, may be enough to raise a reasonable doubt of guilt and that in the federal courts a jury in a proper case should be so instructed. * * *

* * *

Thus the law extends helpful but illogical options to a defendant. Experience taught a necessity that they be counterweighted with equally illogical conditions to keep the advantage from becoming an unfair and unreasonable one. The price a defendant must pay for attempting to prove his good name is to throw open the entire subject which the law has kept closed for his benefit and to make himself vulnerable where the law otherwise shields him. The prosecution may pursue the inquiry with contradictory witnesses to show that damaging rumors, whether or not well-grounded, were afloat-for it is not the man that he is, but the name that he has which is put in issue. Another hazard is that his own witness is subject to cross-examination as to the contents and extent of the hearsay on which he bases his conclusions, and he may be required to disclose rumors and reports that are current even if they do not affect his own conclusion. It may test the sufficiency of his knowledge by asking what stories were circulating concerning events, such as one's arrest, about which people normally comment and speculate. Thus, while the law gives defendant the option to show as a fact that his reputation reflects a life and habit incompatible with commission of the offense charged, it subjects his proof to tests of credibility designed to prevent him from profiting by a mere parade of partisans.

* * *

In this case the crime inquired about was receiving stolen goods; the trial was for bribery. The Court of Appeals thought this dissimilarity of offenses too great to sustain the inquiry in logic, though conceding that it is authorized by preponderance of authority. It asks us to substitute the Illinois rule which allows inquiry about arrest, but only for very closely similar if not identical charges, in place of the rule more generally adhered to in this country and in England. We think the facts of this case show the proposal to be inexpedient.

The good character which the defendant had sought to establish was broader than the crime charged and included the traits of "honesty and truthfulness" and "being a law-abiding citizen." Possession of these characteristics would seem as incompatible with offering a bribe to a revenue agent as with receiving stolen goods. The crimes may be unlike, but both alike proceed from the same defects of character which the witnesses said this defendant was reputed not to exhibit. It is not only by comparison with the crime on trial but by comparison with the reputation asserted that a court may judge whether the prior arrest should be made subject of inquiry. By this test the inquiry was permissible. It was proper cross-examination because reports of his arrest for receiving stolen goods, if admitted, would tend to weaken the assertion that he was known as an honest and law-abiding citizen. The cross-examination may take in as much ground as the testimony it is designed to verify. To hold otherwise would give defendant the benefit of testimony that he was honest and law-abiding in reputation when such might not be the fact; the refutation was founded on convictions equally persuasive though not for crimes exactly repeated in the present charge.

The inquiry here concerned an arrest twenty-seven years before the trial. Events a generation old are likely to be lived down and dropped from the present thought and talk of the community and to be absent from the knowledge of younger or more recent acquaintances. The court in its discretion may well exclude inquiry about rumors of an event so remote, unless recent misconduct revived them. But two of these witnesses dated their acquaintance with defendant as commencing thirty years before the trial. Defendant, on direct examination, voluntarily called attention to his conviction twenty years before. While the jury might conclude that a matter so old and indecisive as a 1920 arrest would shed little light on the present reputation and hence propensities of the defendant, we cannot say that, in the context of this evidence and in the absence of objection on this specific ground, its admission was an abuse of discretion.

We do not overlook or minimize the consideration that "jury almost surely cannot comprehend the Judge's limiting instructions," which disturbed the Court of Appeals. The refinements of the evidentiary rules on this subject are such that even lawyers and judges, after study and reflection, often are confused, and surely jurors in the hurried and unfamiliar movement of a trial must find them almost unintelligible. However, limiting instructions on this subject are no more difficult to comprehend or apply than those upon various other subjects; for example, instructions that admissions of a co-defendant are to be limited to the question of his guilt and are not to be considered as evidence against other defendants, and instructions as to other problems in the trial of conspiracy charges. A defendant in such a case is powerless to prevent his cause from being irretrievably obscured and confused; but, in cases such as the one before us, the law foreclosed this whole confounding line of inquiry, unless defendant thought the net advantage from opening it up would be with him. Given this option, we think defendants in general and this defendant in particular have no valid complaint at the latitude which existing law allows to the prosecution to meet by cross-examination an issue voluntarily tendered by the defense.

* * *

We concur in the general opinion of courts, textwriters and the profession that much of this law is archaic, paradoxical and full of compromises and compensations by which an irrational advantage to one side is offset by a poorly reasoned counter-privilege to the other. But somehow it has proved a workable even if clumsy system when moderated by discretionary controls in the hands of a wise and strong trial court. To pull one misshapen stone out of the grotesque structure is more likely simply to upset its present balance between adverse interests than to establish a rational edifice.

* * *

The judgment is Affirmed.

* * *

[Dissent omitted]

NOTES

1. What is a pertinent character trait?

"Evidence of a pertinent character trait of an accused is admissible to prove action in conformity with that trait. Fed. R. Evid. 404(a)(1). As used in this context, 'pertinent' is synonymous with 'relevant.'" *United States v. Roberts*, 887 F.2d 534, 536 (5th Cir. 1989). In *Hawaii v. Rabe*, 687 P.2d 554, 562 (Haw. App. 1984), the court noted:

> Notwithstanding the choice of a different word, the prevailing view is that the word "pertinent" as used in Rule 404(a)(1) is generally synonymous with the word "relevant," which is defined in Rule 401 as "having any tendency to make the existence of any fact that is of consequence to the determination of the action more probable or less probable than it would be without the evidence."

2. Is good moral character a pertinent trait in criminal actions?

In *United States v. Cylkouski*, the court held that good moral character is a pertinent trait in criminal actions. The court noted "such testimony alone, in some circumstances, may be enough to raise a reasonable doubt of guilt." 556 F.2d 799, 801-02 (6th Cir. 1977) (quoting *Michelson*, 335 U.S. 469 (1948)).

3. Is being law-abiding a pertinent trait?

The government has often argued that "being prone to law-abiding conduct" is not an "actual" character trait but is rather a conclusion that must be drawn from other character traits such as honesty, reliability, and rectitude. However, the courts have generally held that "character traits admissible under Rule 404(a)(1) need not constitute specific traits of character but may include general traits such as lawfulness and law-abidingness." *United States v. Diaz*, 961 F.2d 1417, 1419 (9th Cir. 1992).

This does not mean, however, that the defendant has unmitigated freedom to define a character trait. For example, in *United States v. Diaz*, *supra*, the defendant was charged with possession with intent to distribute more than 500 grams of cocaine. Defense counsel tried to ask a defense witness whether Diaz had a "character trait for being prone to large-scale drug dealing." The prosecution objected and the objection was sustained. The court of appeals found no error because a defendant's propensity (or lack thereof) to engage in large-scale drug-dealing "is not an admissible character trait." The proposed testimony was not the same as testimony that the defendant was law-abiding, because it was in effect too specific, i.e., that the defendant was not prone to violate a very specific law. The court reasoned that an inquiry into a propensity to engage in large-scale drug-dealing "would be misleading if addressed to a defendant with a record of criminal offenses other than drug-dealing: If answered in the negative [as the defendant in *Diaz,* of course, anticipated] the impression may be given that the defendant is a law-abiding person although he has a record of other crimes."

4. When is honesty a pertinent trait?

Michelson notes that the trait of honesty is pertinent to both bribery and receiving-stolen-goods charges. 335 U.S. at 483. Honesty is not, however, a pertinent trait in all crimes. *See United States v. Elmer*, 21 F.3d 331, 335 (9th Cir. 1994) (holding that honesty is not a pertinent trait in a case charging a border patrol agent with ten counts of aggravated assault for shooting at aliens).

Honesty is typically held to be not pertinent to drug possession charges. Thus, in *Spector v. State*, 746 S.W.2d 946 (Tex. Ct. App. 1988), the court held that honesty and truthfulness are not pertinent traits in the offense of possession of marijuana.

5. What methods of proof are available to show the character of a defendant as circumstantial evidence in a criminal case?

Michelson notes the common-law rule that character evidence may only be shown by reputation.Federal Rule 405, however, also allows opinion testimony regarding a defendant's character traits. Thus, in *United States v. Roberts*, 887 F.2d 534 (5th Cir. 1989), the Court held it was error to exclude a psychologist's opinion testimony that the accused's personality was consistent with that of a person who might engage in a private undercover operation to catch drug dealers.

However, character cannot be proven through specific acts of the defendant. *United States v. Hill*, 40 F.3d 164 (3d Cir. 1994) (in a prosecution for stealing and cashing a check, the trial judge properly excluded evidence that the defendant did not steal three "test letters" several months after the charged embezzlement: "the proper method of proof would have been by reputation or opinion testimony.").

RULE #5: IN A CRIMINAL CASE, CHARACTER EVIDENCE OF A PERTINENT TRAIT OF A VICTIM IS ADMISSIBLE IF FIRST OFFERED BY THE DEFENDANT, AFTER WHICH THE STATE MAY OFFER REBUTTAL EVIDENCE AS TO THE VICTIM AS WELL AS ON THE SAME TRAIT OF THE DEFENDANT. PROOF MAY BE MADE ONLY BY REPUTATION AND OPINION.

UNITED STATES v. KEISER
57 F.3d 847 (9th Cir. 1995)

CYNTHIA HOLCOMB HALL, CIRCUIT JUDGE:

Ronald Keiser shot Victor Romero, paralyzing him from the waist down. The shooting occurred inside the boundaries of Fort Peck Indian Reservation in Montana. Keiser was indicted and convicted of violating 18 U.S.C. § 113(f) (assault resulting in serious bodily injury). He is currently serving a prison term of 71 months.

* * *

[Defendant's] theory at trial was that he had acted in defense of his brother, who he reasonably believed was in danger because of the assault by three armed and angry men.

During the second day of trial, the defense called the defendant's brother, Randy Keiser. Defense counsel began to ask Randy about an incident that had occurred the day prior in the lobby outside the courtroom. The prosecutor objected to the line of questioning as irrelevant and the court sustained the objection.

Counsel then approached the bench and defense counsel made an offer of proof:

> My purpose in this was not — yesterday afternoon Victor Romero [the victim] was with his family and friends in the presence of court security. He looked at this witness and he said words to the effect, there he is, that's the fucker's brother. And I want you to remember his face, remember his face.
>
> And he had to be taken out of there, he was screaming. I think that's indicative of he wanted to get revenge, it is indicative of his actions on the night in question. This is not the sympathetic individual that comes in here and says he was very calm and collected. And I think it is indicative of his state of mind now and his state of mind at the time. I think it is relevant.

* * * The court again sustained the objection. Keiser was convicted on May 11, 1993 and is incarcerated for a term of 71 months.

* * *

Keiser's only defense in this case was that he was justified in shooting * * * because he was acting in defense of his brother, whom Romero was assaulting at the time of the shooting. Keiser sought to introduce testimony about this incident outside the courtroom in order to bolster his self-defense claim. He argues on appeal that the incident "tend[s] to show the character of Mr. Romero for anger and violence." Admission of Randy Keiser's testimony regarding the incident would have "show[n] the jury the true nature of the 'victim.'" The government responds that the testimony "would have added absolutely nothing material to the trial," because "the appellant did not personally know the victim, nor did he therefore have personal knowledge of the victim's character." We think that neither party has properly addressed the legal questions this proffered testimony raises.

The question whether defendants may introduce specific violent or aggressive acts of the victim in order to bolster a claim of self-defense has begotten a host of written opinions, both in the federal courts and in state courts interpreting analogs to the Federal Rules of Evidence. The analytic approaches, as well as the answers these approaches have yielded, are myriad. Some courts have reasoned that a victim's volent nature is an essential element of a claim of self-defense and that defendants should therefore be allowed to introduce evidence of specific acts in order to prove that character. Some have concluded that the victim's violent nature is not essential to the claim of self-defense, and therefore limit the defendant to the use of reputation or opinion evidence to show the victim's character for violence. Others, on the other hand, have refused to admit specific acts on the rationale that their use would be circumstantial rather than direct. Others still admit specific acts under the theory that the acts themselves bear on the defendant's state of mind and the reasonableness of his use of force in self-defense. At least one court admits specific acts under the theory that the victim's character is an essential element of self-defense, but limits the acts to those of which the defendant had personal knowledge at the time of the crime, and another admits specific acts as character evidence because the acts are essential to determining the defendant's state of mind. This Court has not yet addressed this question.

Our task, therefore, is not simple. It is made significantly easier, however, by clarification of what this case is *not* about. Keiser makes no claim on appeal that the incident outside the courtroom — which obviously occurred after the shooting — was relevant to his state of mind at the time of the shooting or the reasonableness of his belief that force in self-defense was necessary. Thus, we need not, and do not, reach the question whether specific acts are admissible to bolster the assertion that the defendant's belief in the need for force was reasonable. Instead, we need only decide whether testimony regarding this incident should have been admitted *as character evidence, i.e.*, as evidence from which the jury could infer that the victim, at the time of the shooting, was likely to be behaving in accordance with his violent character.

Put another way, introduction of specific acts as victim character evidence would support the proposition that the victim was in fact using unlawful force, whereas introduction of specific acts to prove the defendant's state of mind would support the proposition that the defendant's belief that force was necessary was reasonable. These two propositions are separate elements of the defense of self-defense or defense of another.

A. *Relevance of the excluded testimony*

The Federal Rules of Evidence provide an exception to the general rule against character evidence as propensity evidence in the case of "[e]vidence of a pertinent trait of character of the victim of the crime offered by an accused." Fed. R. Evid. 404(a)(2). The advisory committee's note to this rule indicates that a victim's "violent disposition" is exactly the sort of evidence this rule was intended to encompass. *See* Fed. R. Evid. 404 advisory committee's note ("Illustrations are: evidence of a violent disposition to prove that the person was the aggressor in an affray * * * .").

Thus, whether Romero is a violent and angry person is certainly relevant to the defendant's claim that he was acting in defense of his brother: Romero's violent character makes it more likely that his behavior on the night of the shooting was violent — which supports the defendant's defense that he was shooting to protect his brother — than it would be if Romero were peaceable.

The government, however, argues that because the incident occurred *after* the shooting, it has no bearing on whether the defendant acted reasonably at the time of the shooting. It reasons that, at the time of the shooting, the defendant did not "have personal knowledge of the victim's character."

This argument misapprehends the purpose of presenting testimony regarding the victim's character. Rule 404(a)(2) provides one of the few instances in which character evidence *is* admissible to allow the jury to infer that a person acted on a specific occasion in conformity with his character. The rule does not contemplate that the character evidence will somehow reveal the defendant's state of mind at the time he acted in self-defense.

The structure of the rule supports this conclusion. Section 404(a) establishes the general prohibition: "Evidence of a person's character or a trait of his character is not admissible *for the purpose of proving that he acted in conformity therewith on a particular occasion* * * * ." Fed. R. Evid. 404(a) (emphasis added). The rule then provides three exceptions to the prohibition, one of which is the exception for character of the victim provided in section 404(a)(2). The fact that section 404(a)(2) is an exception to the rule against introducing character evidence to imply that a person acted in conformity with that character on a particular occasion suggests that the very purpose of victim character evidence is to suggest to the jury that the victim did indeed act in conformity with his violent character at the time of the alleged crime against him. The purpose is not to provide insight into the reasonableness of the thought processes of the defendant. Thus, whether the defendant knew of the victim's character at the time of the crime has no bearing on whether victim character evidence should come in under section 404(a)(2).

* * * We therefore hold that Romero's violent nature is relevant to Keiser's theory of defense of his brother.

B. *Form of the excluded testimony*

Despite its relevance, the testimony regarding the altercation outside the courtroom was properly excluded. Under the Federal Rules of Evidence, only reputation or opinion evidence is proper to show that the victim of an assault had a propensity toward violence. The excluded testimony, on the other hand, would have constituted paradigmatic "specific act" evidence.

After a court determines that character evidence is admissible under Rule 404, it must next turn to Rule 405 to determine what *form* that evidence may take. *See United States v. Talamante*, 981 F.2d 1153, 1156 (10th Cir. 1992) ("Federal Rule of Evidence 405 establishes the permissible methods of proving character under Rule 404(a)(2)."). * * * The relevant question should be: would proof, or failure of proof, of the character trait by itself actually satisfy an element of the charge, claim, or defense? If not, then character is not essential and evidence should be limited to opinion or reputation.

Our object in this case, therefore, is to determine whether Romero's violent character is an "essential element" of Keiser's defense. We conclude * * * that Romero's violent character does not constitute an essential element of Keiser's claim that the shooting was justified because he was acting in defense of his brother. Even had Keiser proven that Romero is a violent person, the jury would still have been free to decide that Romero was not using or about to use unlawful force, or that the force Romero was using was not likely to cause death or great bodily harm, or that Keiser did not reasonably believe force was necessary, or that he used more force than appeared reasonably necessary. On the other hand, a successful defense in no way depended on Keiser's being able to show that the Romero has a propensity toward violence. A defendant could, for example, successfully assert a claim of self-defense against an avowed pacifist, so long as the jury agrees that the defendant reasonably believed unlawful force was about to be used against him. Thus, even though relevant, Romero's character is not an essential element of Keiser's defense.

Thus, exclusion of the proffered testimony regarding the verbal altercation outside the courtroom was proper because the victim's violent nature is not essential to a successful claim of self-defense. Keiser's claim of self-defense neither rises nor falls on his success in proving that Romero has a penchant for violent outbursts. Thus, Keiser had no right to introduce evidence of the incident outside the courtroom to buttress his defense. We therefore affirm the district court's exclusion of the testimony.

* * *

AFFIRMED.

NOTES

1. Is the victim's character trait for aggressiveness always relevant in a homicide case?

In *United States v. Martinez,* 988 F.2d 685 (7th Cir. 1993), defendants were charged with murder arising from a prison conflagration. Evidence of the violent character of the victims was held properly excluded as not relevant where there was no viable self-defense claim. The evidence showed that the victims were rendered defenseless and were repeatedly stabbed while lying motionless on the ground. The defendants argued that they were acting in self-defense at the beginning of the fight; but this was not relevant to the subsequent conduct that was at the heart of the murder charge.

2. If the defendant offers evidence of the victim's pertinent character trait, does this open the door to proof of the defendant's character traits?

The Committee Note to the 2001 Amendment to Federal Rule of Evidence 404(a)(1) explains the risk that the defendant runs in offering evidence of the victim's character:

> Rule 404(a)(1) has been amended to provide that when the accused attacks the character of an alleged victim under subdivision (a)(2) of this Rule, the door is opened to an attack on the same character trait of the accused. Current law does not allow the government to introduce negative character evidence as to the accused unless the accused introduces evidence of good character. *See, e.g., United States v. Fountain,* 768 F.2d 790 (7th Cir. 1985) (when the accused offers proof of self-defense, this permits proof of the alleged victim's character trait for peacefulness, but it does not permit proof of the accused's character trait for violence).
>
> The amendment makes clear that the accused cannot attack the alleged victim's character and yet remain shielded from the disclosure of equally relevant evidence concerning the same character trait of the accused. For example, in a murder case with a claim of self-defense, the accused, to bolster this defense, might offer evidence of the alleged victim's violent disposition. If the government has evidence that the accused has a violent character, but is not allowed to offer this evidence as part of its rebuttal, the jury has only part of the information it needs for an informed assessment of the probabilities as to who was the initial aggressor.* * *
>
> The amendment does not permit proof of the accused's character if the accused merely uses character evidence for a purpose other than to prove the alleged victim's propensity to act in a certain way. *See United States v. Burks,* 470 F.2d 432, 434-5 (D.C. Cir. 1972) (evidence of the alleged victim's violent character, when known by the accused, was admissible "on the issue of whether or not the defendant reasonably feared he was in danger of imminent great bodily harm"). Finally, the amendment does not permit proof of the accused's character when the accused attacks the alleged victim's character as a witness under Rule 608 or 609.

* * *

PROBLEM 6-1

Assume a criminal defendant calls a character witness to testify that the victim has a reputation as an aggressive person. Also assume the defendant does not call a witness to testify that the defendant is peaceful. Could the prosecution properly call a witness to testify:

(1) The victim has a reputation as a peaceful person.

(2) One witness has an opinion the victim is peaceful.

(3) The victim once stopped a bar fight by calming the participants.

(4) The defendant has a reputation as an aggressive person.

(5) The defendant has beaten his spouse.

RULE #6: IN A HOMICIDE CASE, IF THE DEFENDANT OFFERS ANY EVIDENCE THAT THE DECEASED WAS THE FIRST AGGRESSOR, THEN THE PROSECUTION MAY OFFER REBUTTAL EVIDENCE OF THE PEACEFULNESS OF THE VICTIM. PROOF MAY BE MADE ONLY BY REPUTATION AND OPINION.

STATE v. HICKS
649 P.2d 267 (Ariz. 1982)

HOLOHAN, CHIEF JUSTICE:

Appellant, Ernest Floyd Hicks, was convicted after trial by a jury of first degree murder. Appellant was sentenced to life imprisonment. * * * We affirm.

[The defendant was charged with killing the victim in a fight outside a bar. He pleaded not guilty and did not specifically interpose an affirmative defense of self-defense.]

* * *

EVIDENCE OF VICTIM'S CHARACTER

The appellant claims that there was error in the admission of evidence showing the peacefulness of the victim. The state argues that objection to the evidence was waived and the defense raised the issue initially.

Defense counsel did remark to the jury in his opening statement that: "Cathy Barrow knew [the victim], had had problems with him in the past. He was a loudmouth. She characterized him as obnoxious, a cutting-type person."

The prosecution apparently sought to anticipate a defense of self-defense. The prosecutor asked four witnesses, all patrons or employees of the Club 37, whether the witnesses had ever seen the victim quarrel or engage in physical violence with anyone at the bar. Defense counsel allowed all but the third inquiry to pass without objection, and his relevancy objection to the third inquiry was overruled. All of the witnesses testified that they had never seen the victim become physically violent, and only one witness had seen him argue with people in the bar.

The defense counsel's objection to the testimony of the third witness concerning the character of the victim should have been sustained. * * *

In the instant case, the defense had introduced no evidence of the victim's character for the state to rebut. Whatever the defense counsel had in mind by the reference to the victim's nature was never developed in the defense case. We do not believe this remark opened the door for the state to present evidence on the issue. The defense did not follow up with any evidence tending to support the remark in the opening statement. Self-defense was not raised at trial and there was no evidence that the victim was the first aggressor. We therefore hold that it was error to permit the prosecution to present evidence of the victim's peaceful character.

The state urged that the defense waived its objection because on cross-examination, defense counsel asked the fourth witness whether she had ever seen the victim or the defendant fight or argue with anyone at the bar. The state contends that this question waived the previous objection. We disagree. Once an objection has been made and overruled, defense counsel must attempt as best he can to minimize any harm that might flow from the erroneous admission of unfavorable evidence. To do so by asking a question concerning the objected-to evidence does not thereby waive the objection. * * *

Although the testimony was irrelevant and should have been excluded pursuant to rule 404(a), we do not believe that any prejudice to appellant resulted from admission of the testimony. The first two witnesses who testified on the issue did so without objection, so the evidence came before the jury in the first instance without defense objection. We do not believe that the additional evidence from the later witnesses caused any prejudice. In fact, defense counsel used the questioned evidence to appellant's advantage during closing argument. The state's argument, on the other hand, made no reference to the testimony. Furthermore, the testimony was not such that it was likely to evoke sympathy from the jurors.

* * *

The judgment of conviction and sentence is affirmed.

PROBLEM 6-2

Assume the criminal defendant in a battery case testifies the victim was the first aggressor, but does not call a character witness to testify the victim has a reputation as aggressive. Could the prosecution properly call witnesses to testify:

(1) The victim has a reputation as a peaceful person.

(2) The victim once stopped a bar fight by calming the participants.

(3) The defendant has a reputation for aggression.

(4) The defendant beats his spouse.

Assume the criminal defendant in a homicide case testifies the victim was the first aggessor, but does not call a character witness to testify the victim has a reputation as aggressive. Could the prosecution properly call witnesses to testify:

(1) The victim has a reputation as a peaceful person.

(2) The victim once stopped a bar fight.

(3) The defendant has a reputation for aggression.

(4) The defendant beats his spouse.

RULE #7: IN A CRIMINAL CASE, WHEN CHARACTER IS AN ESSENTIAL ELEMENT OF A CHARGE, CLAIM, OR DEFENSE, PROOF MAY BE MADE BY REPUTATION, OPINION, AND SPECIFIC INSTANCES OF CONDUCT.

There is at least one recognized instance of essential element cases in the criminal context. The Advisory Committee's Notes to Rule 404 give the often quoted example of "the chastity of the victim under a statute specifying her chastity as an element of the crime of seduction * * * ." This example is almost always quoted to show why the case at hand is not an essential element case.

The impact of the essential element rule, rare as it is in the criminal context, is in the methods of proof available. When a character trait is an essential element of a criminal charge, it is provable by all three methods of proof. Fed. R. Evid. 405(a) & (b).

RULE #8: ANY CHARACTER WITNESS MAY BE CROSS-EXAMINED CONCERNING THAT WITNESS'S KNOWLEDGE OF SPECIFIC INSTANCES OF PERTINENT BAD ACTS COMMITTED BY THE PERSON WHOSE CHARACTER THAT WITNESS HAS ENDORSED; THE CROSS-EXAMINER MUST HAVE GOOD FAITH PROOF THAT THE ACTS OCCURRED.

UNITED STATES v. HOLT

170 F.3d 698 (7th Cir. 1999)

ILANA DIAMOND ROVNER, CIRCUIT JUDGE:

Kevin Holt and Kent Buckner were indicted for conspiracy to knowingly and intentionally transfer an automatic weapon in violation of 18 U.S.C. §§ 371 & 922(o). A jury found Holt guilty of violating 18 U.S.C. § 371, but acquitted Buckner on both charges. Holt was sentenced to imprisonment for thirty-three months, followed by two years of supervised release. Holt now appeals that conviction and sentence. * * * Holt was a part-time police officer for the Village of Glassford and owned a gun shop called the Patriot Arms. He often attended gun shows at which he set up a booth for his shop. At one of these gun shows, Kent Buckner offered to sell him an M-14 rifle for approximately $1200. Some testimony indicated that a rifle which operated only as a semi-automatic would only be worth $600 to $700 dollars. The M-14 had a selector switch that allowed the rifle to operate in semi-automatic or fully automatic mode, and Holt and Buckner discussed the automatic capabilities of the weapon. At one point, Holt covered the selector switch with his hand, and stated "I can't let anybody see this." * * * Holt claimed at trial that he was not aware that the rifle was fully automatic * * *. The jury rejected Holt's contention at trial that he was unaware that the M-14 was fully automatic when he purchased it.

I

Holt first argues that the district court erred in denying his Motion for a New Trial. The basis for his motion is that the government improperly introduced irrelevant character evidence * * *. No objection was made to any of this testimony, so we review its admission only for plain error. As a result, we will reverse only if the error seriously affects the fairness, integrity or public reputation of judicial proceedings.

As part of his defense, Holt introduced a number of character witnesses who testified as to his reputation as an honest and law-abiding individual. In cross-examination of those witnesses, the government asked whether they were familiar with allegations that he was behind on child support payments and with allegations of sexual harassment against Holt at his workplace. Those questions were relevant to determine the extent of the witness' familiarity with Holt's reputation and character. In *Michelson v. United States*, 335 U.S. 469 (1948), the Supreme Court declared that [a defendant's character witness] "is subject to cross-examination as to the contents and extent of the hearsay on which he bases his conclusions, and he may be required to disclose rumors and reports that are current even if they do not affect his own conclusion." Rule 405 codifies that common law rule, explicitly allowing cross-examination of character witnesses by prior instances of specific conduct. Therefore, by calling witnesses to testify regarding his reputation as law-abiding, Holt opened the door for the prosecution to examine the witness' familiarity with his reputation. Holt does not now allege that the government lacked a good faith basis for the allegations. In fact, Holt acknowledged that he was in arrearage in his child support payments, and that there were rumors circulating that he was involved in sexual harassment at his workplace. Thus, this is not a case of a prosecutor "merely taking a random shot at a reputation imprudently exposed or asking a groundless question to waft an unwarranted innuendo into the jury box." *Michelson*, 335 U.S. at 480. The district court did not err in permitting the questions.

CONVICTION AFFIRMED.

UNITED STATES v. BRUGUIER
161 F.3d 1145 (8th Cir. 1998)

RICHARD S. ARNOLD, CIRCUIT JUDGE:

Merlin J. Bruguier, Sr., was charged with aggravated sexual abuse, in violation of 18 U.S.C. §§ 1153, 2241(c), and 2246(2)(A). He was convicted by the jury and sentenced to 25 years and 10 months in prison, to be followed by five years of supervised release. * * * This appeal followed. The defendant contends, among other things, that the District Court erred in allowing testimony about various uncomplimentary aspects of his past life. We affirm, finding no error sufficiently serious to justify reversal. * * *

I.

* * * The case arises out of an incident in which M.M.B., Bruguier's 17-month old daughter, suffered injuries in August of 1996. The baby's thigh bone and one leg were injured, and her perineum, the area between the vagina and the anus, was seriously torn. The defendant contends that the injuries occurred when the family car accidentally rolled over M.M.B. The case was hotly contested at trial and could have gone either way, but there was unquestionably evidence from which a reasonable jury could find the defendant guilty beyond a reasonable doubt. Among other things, defense witnesses had told conflicting stories about what happened, most of the medical testimony at trial was to the effect that it was extremely unlikely that all of the baby's injuries could have been caused by the car, and at least one sperm cell was found in material taken from M.M.B.'s person. In addition, defendant made a statement during an interview with an FBI agent in which he admitted "inappropriate sexual contact" between himself and the child.

II.

The issues we have found most difficult have to do with defendant's claim that the District Court allowed a number of irrelevant and prejudicial items of evidence to be introduced against him. We address in turn the specific evidentiary points that seem to us substantial. Bruguier's mother-in-law, Colette Iron Hawk, testified for the defense that Bruguier was a good father and that she had never known him to discipline the children physically or to abuse them sexually. On cross-examination the government asked about prior findings that the Bruguiers had neglected their children:

Q: You say the defendant has been a good father?

A: Yes, he has.

Q: Can you explain why in January 1990 he and Rhene were found neglectful by the Department of Social Service?

A: When is this?

Q: Neglect of their children in 1990?

A: I don't recall that.

Q: You are not aware they were?

Defense: Objection, Your Honor. I object to this. First of all, I have never been provided this information. Secondly, it's irrelevant unless we have some kind of identification other than his unsupported allegation.

The Court: Are you in a position to establish what you're talking about?

Government: Yes.

The Court: Overruled. If she doesn't know anything about it, that ends it.

A: I don't know.

(Government): Were you aware that they were — for two years they were supervised by Child Protection Services?

A: No, I was not aware.

Violet Good Bear, a community health representative, also testified that Bruguier was a good father. She explained that she had observed Bruguier interacting well with his children hundreds of times during her home visits with the Bruguiers. On cross-examination, the government asked her: "In 1990 there was a finding of substantial neglect by the Bruguiers. Were you aware of that, by the tribal social services?" Ms. Good Bear responded that she was unaware of such a finding. The government continued, "Were you aware that for two years they were supervised by tribal social services?" Again, the witness responded "no."

We hold that the District Court did not err in allowing this testimony. Under Rule 404(a)(1), evidence of a person's character or a trait of character is generally not admissible for the purpose of proving action in conformity therewith on a previous occasion. An accused, however, may offer evidence of a pertinent trait of character (here, that he was a good father), and, if he does, the prosecution may offer evidence in rebuttal. Further, under Rule 405(a), if evidence of character or a trait of character is admissible, "proof may be made by testimony as to reputation or by testimony in the form of an opinion." Here, Ms. Iron Hawk and Ms. Good Bear testified in the form of an opinion. They gave their opinion that the defendant was a good father. We think it was proper cross-examination for the government to explore the witnesses' basis for holding such an opinion. If, for example, a finding of child neglect had been made with respect to Mr. Bruguier, and if the witnesses knew that, any grounds for their believing that Mr. Bruguier was a good father would be undermined. And if, on the other hand, the witnesses were not aware of such a finding, a jury might believe that their acquaintance with the defendant was not thorough enough to justify their opinion.

So we think the fact inquired about — whether the witnesses knew of a finding that the defendant and his wife had neglected their children — was relevant. The real difficulty with the government's conduct here is that it was allowed to state, in the presence of the jury, that such a finding had in fact been made, or, at least, that there was a reasonable basis for the government's belief that it had been made. This was not the procedure that should have been followed, and government counsel ought to have known it. When this sort of "did you know" question is asked, and the fact inquired about would be injurious to defendant's character and is not otherwise in evidence, preliminary proceedings outside the presence of the jury should be conducted first. At these proceedings, either in camera or at the bench, the government could privately state its evidence that a finding of neglect had been made, defense counsel could argue with the evidence or attempt to rebut it in some way, and the Court could satisfy itself that the government had a reasonable, good-faith basis for asking its question. That did not happen here. What we said in *United States v. Krapp*, 815 F.2d 1183 (8th Cir.1987), fits the present case.

> However, we admonish the Assistant United States Attorney for asking Krapp's character witness about the Krapps' tax returns in front of the jury

without first raising the matter with the trial judge. Before an attempt at impeachment of a character witness with "did you know" type questions such as this, the trial judge should have the opportunity, out of the hearing of the jury, to rule on the propriety of the questions. By failing to raise the matter first with the trial judge, the Assistant United States Attorney created the risk of mistrial after substantial time had been invested in the trial.

* * *

In the present case, defense counsel duly objected to the question when it was put to Ms. Iron Hawk. He stated that the information about a finding of neglect would be "irrelevant unless we have some kind of identification other than his unsupported allegation." Counsel was making the point that the government ought not to be allowed to ask such a question unless it had some support for the claim that defendant had been found to have neglected his children. It was then that the Court asked whether the government was in a position to establish what it was talking about, to which question counsel for the government answered yes. The Court then overruled the objection. Defense counsel did not ask that the matter be taken up in chambers; he did not move for a mistrial; and he did not ask for an instruction that would tell the jury that government counsel's statement could not itself be regarded as evidence. The Court could well have instructed counsel, on its own motion, to repair to chambers so the matter could be explored in the proper fashion, and indeed, we believe that it should have done so. Absent a more specific objection from counsel, however, and in the particular circumstances of this case, we are not persuaded that the error worked any substantial prejudice. If a chambers conference on the matter had been held, we have no reason to think that government counsel could not have backed up his assertion. If he had done so, it would then have been proper for the proceedings to have returned to the presence of the jury, and for the witnesses to be allowed to answer the question.

* * *

On the whole, we are convinced that what occurred here did not adversely affect Bruguier's substantial rights. The procedure that was followed left something to be desired, for reasons we have tried to explain, but we see no reversible error.

* * *

NOTES

1. Are any procedural safeguards required before inquiring into prior specific bad conduct in order to impeach a character witness?

The procedural requirements for introducing bad acts to impeach character witnesses are discussed in *United States v. Monteleone*, 77 F.3d 1086 (8th Cir. 1996). Monteleone was convicted for disposing of a firearm to a convicted felon. At trial, the defendant called a character witness who testified that Monteleone had a good reputation in the community for truthfulness and lawfulness. During cross-examination, over defense objections, the prosecutor asked whether the witness had heard that Monteleone had perjured himself before a federal grand jury twenty-five years earlier.

The court of appeals held that the trial court committed reversible error in permitting this question to be asked. The court emphasized the danger of prejudice inherent in inquiry into specific bad acts of the defendant on cross-examination of a character witness. Accordingly, the government must meet two important requirements before utilizing this type of questioning: "First, the Government must demonstrate a good faith factual basis for the incidents raised during cross-examination of the witness. Secondly, the incidents inquired about must be relevant to the character traits at issue in the case."

The government in *Monteleone* argued that both requirements were met because there was good faith proof that Monteleone perjured himself, and his act of perjury was obviously relevant to the character trait of truthfulness attested to by the witness. But the court found a fundamental flaw in the government's argument. The only legitimate reason for inquiring into specific acts on cross-examination is to test the knowledge and credibility of the character witness. Therefore, the prosecution must not only have good faith belief that the specific acts occurred. It must also have a good faith belief that the specific acts are of the type that the witness should have known about (if he is an opinion witness) or that the community should have known about (if he is a reputation witness). Thus, if the specific acts are essentially private in nature, they "cannot possibly be intended to test the accuracy, reliability, or credibility" of the character witness.

Applying these principles to Monteleone's perjury before the grand jury, the court held that the prosecution lacked a good faith basis for believing that the act was of such a type as to be known by the witness or by the community. The court noted that grand jury testimony is protected by an obligation of secrecy, and that the only person who could have disclosed the perjury legitimately would have been Monteleone himself. The court doubted that Monteleone would "blazon his own prevarication." Obviously, the result in the case would have been different if Monteleone had been convicted of perjuring himself before the grand jury, since the conviction would be a public matter.

2. Can the prosecutor ask questions of character witnesses that assume the defendant's guilt of the crime charged?

In *United States v. Smith-Bowman*, 76 F.3d 634 (5th Cir. 1996), the defendant was charged with mail fraud resulting from use of her employer's credit card for personal purchases. A defense witness testified to the defendant's reputation for honesty in the community. On cross-examination, the prosecutor asked whether the witness had heard that the defendant used her employer's credit card to rent a motel room under an assumed name, in order to have a rendezvous with her boyfriend. The prosecutor also asked whether the witness had heard that the defendant had used her employer's credit card to buy jewelry for herself. These credit card usages formed the basis of the prosecution's charges against the defendant.

The *Smith-Bowman* Court recognized, as most courts have, that it is impermissible to ask guilt-assuming hypotheticals of a witness who has testified about the defendant's good character. As Judge Mansfield put it in *United States v. Morgan*, 554 F.2d 31 (2d Cir. 1977): "Since character evidence is admitted only as bearing upon guilt or innocence, an opinion based upon the assumption that the defendant is guilty cannot have any probative value in deciding that issue." And of course the defendant is likely to suffer prejudice if guilt is assumed, albeit hypothetically, by both the prosecution and the defense witness. Such a hypothetical comes perilously close to treading on the presumption of innocence. *See United States v. Candelaria-Gonzalez*, 547 F.2d 291 (5th Cir. 1977) (guilt-assuming hypotheticals are improper because they strike at the very heart of the presumption of innocence).

However, the limitation on guilt-assuming hypotheticals is not triggered if the question put to the character witness only assumes facts that are already admitted by the defendant. The court in *Smith-Bowman* held that the prosecutor's question did not present a guilt-assuming hypothetical, because the defendant admitted that she used the credit card for personal purchases; her defense was that the use was authorized by the employer and that she had planned to reimburse her employer for the expenses. If the prosecutor had asked the witness to assume that the defendant never had an intent to reimburse the employer, or to assume that the use of the credit card was unauthorized, then the questions would have been improper. *See also United States v. Velasquez*, 980 F.2d 1275 (9th Cir. 1992) (proper to ask character witnesses whether their opinion would change if it were established that the defendant had taken a grenade into the bank and inquired about money; defendant admitted this act, and merely denied that he had the intent to rob the bank).

3. When is a witness treated as a character witness?

If defense counsel decides that the benefit of character evidence is not worth the risk of rebuttal, then counsel must guard against presenting any testimony which could be interpreted as character evidence. The character door can be deemed opened by means less obvious than calling a witness who testifies explicitly to a person's character trait. For example, in *United States v. Dahlin,* 734 F.2d 393 (8th Cir. 1984), the defendant was charged with robbery; his alibi was that he was babysitting his sister's infant child at the time of the robbery. The prosecution argued that Dahlin could still have committed the robbery, by leaving the infant at home, unattended, for a period of time. Dahlin took the stand and testified that he was deeply devoted to his niece and that he never left the child alone. The prosecution rebutted this claim of Dahlin's family devotedness by questioning Dahlin about a knife fight that he had had with his father. The Court of Appeals held that Dahlin had opened the door to this evidence because he had "put at issue his reliability, responsibility and familial devotion, which were traits pertinent to the jury's appraisal of his defense." *See also United States v. McHorse,* 179 F.3d 889 (10th Cir. 1999) (in a prosecution for child sexual abuse, the defendant's son testified that the defendant "couldn't do anything bad to anyone" and "would not do anything like" the conduct he was charged with; by this testimony, the defendant's son became a character witness, opening the door to impeachment with the defendant's relevant bad acts).

RULE #9: SPECIFIC INSTANCES OF CONDUCT ARE ADMISSIBLE TO PROVE INTENT, MOTIVE, PLAN, DESIGN, OR ANY PURPOSE OTHER THAN CHARACTER, UNLESS THE PROBATIVE VALUE OF THE EVIDENCE AS TO ITS NOT-FOR-CHARACTER PURPOSE IS SUBSTANTIALLY OUTWEIGHED BY THE RISK OF PREJUDICE, CONFUSION, AND UNDUE DELAY.

[1] Federal Rule 404

Rule 404. Character Evidence Not Admissible to Prove Conduct; Exceptions; Other Crimes

* * *

(b) Other crimes, wrongs or acts. Evidence of other crimes, wrongs, or acts is not admissible to prove the character of a person in order to show action in conformity therewith. It may, however, be admissible for other purposes, such as proof of motive, opportunity, intent, preparation, plan, knowledge, identity, or absence of mistake or accident, provided that upon request by the accused, the prosecution in a criminal case shall provide reasonable notice in advance of trial, or during trial if the court excuses pretrial notice on good cause shown, of the general nature of any such evidence it intends to introduce at trial.

[2] Plan and Identity

UNITED STATES v. CARROLL
207 F.3d 465 (8th Cir. 2000)

BOWMAN, CIRCUIT JUDGE:

Gerald Carroll was convicted by a jury of armed robbery of a federally insured credit union and a related firearms charge, and was sentenced by the District Court to life in prison plus twenty years. * * * Carroll argues that evidence of a prior conviction was improperly admitted. * * *

I.

Carroll has been convicted of armed robbery previously. In 1988, he robbed a bank using a firearm. He pleaded guilty in 1989 and was sentenced to a substantial prison term. He entered supervised release on September 6, 1996. On July 30, 1998, Carroll and an accomplice, Kevin Carroll, robbed the St.

Louis Community Credit Union, the crime at issue in this appeal. During Gerald Carroll's trial, the United States sought to introduce evidence of his prior conviction under Federal Rule of Evidence 404(b), which prohibits the admission of evidence of "other crimes, wrongs, or acts * * * to prove the character of a person in order to show action in conformity therewith." But such evidence is admissible "for other purposes," including "plan, knowledge, [or] identity." Like all other evidence, evidence admissible under Rule 404(b) is still subject to analysis under Rule 403, which allows admission unless the evidence's unfair prejudice substantially outweighs its probative value. *United States v. LeCompte*, 99 F.3d 274, 277 (8th Cir. 1996). Over objection, the District Court determined that the evidence of Carroll's prior conviction was "admissible for purposes of showing a plan or pattern * * * a melding basically of that, plus identity." The District Court instructed the jury that it could use the Rule 404(b) evidence "to help [it] decide whether the similarity between the acts previously committed and the ones charged in this case suggest that the same person committed all of them." * * *

The case law discusses two circumstances in which prior bad acts can be used to show a "plan or pattern." In some circumstances, a defendant's prior bad acts are part of a broader plan or scheme relevant to the charged offense. "For example, when a criminal steals a car to use it in a robbery, the automobile theft can be proved in a prosecution for the robbery." 1 McCormick on Evidence § 190, at 660-61 (John W. Strong ed., 5th ed. 1999). If the evidence merely shows the full context of the charged crime, it is "intrinsic evidence" not governed by Rule 404(b). *See United States v. Rolett*, 151 F.3d 787, 790 (8th Cir. 1998). Evidence of past acts may also be admitted under Rule 404(b) as direct proof of a charged crime that includes a plan or scheme element, or evidence might serve both intrinsic and direct-proof purposes. In other circumstances, where the "pattern and characteristics of the crimes [are] so unusual and distinctive as to be like a signature," 1 McCormick on Evidence § 190, at 663, evidence of a defendant's prior crimes is admissible to prove that it was indeed the defendant that committed the charged crime. In these cases, the evidence goes to identity. These "plan" and "identity" uses of Rule 404(b) evidence are distinct from each other and from use of prior acts to show knowledge and intent. In drug distribution cases, for example, knowledge and intent are often contested facts proven in part through prior bad acts.

We reject the theory that Carroll's ten-year-old conviction was admissible as part of a broad criminal undertaking including both the prior offense and the charged offense. "The victims were different, and the events were far apart in time. Absent more specific linkage, such evidence is relevant to 'plan' or 'preparation' only insofar as it tends to prove a propensity to commit crimes, which Rule 404(b) prohibits." *LeCompte*, 99 F.3d at 278. The fact that Carroll was incarcerated in the interim period only reinforces the conclusion that the events are not part of the same criminal undertaking.

The District Court's jury instruction demonstrates that the evidence was admitted to show identity. If the conduct underlying Carroll's prior conviction and his current charged offense both involved a unique set of "signature facts," then his prior conviction would be admissible to show that the same person committed both crimes. But unless the robberies are "sufficiently idiosyncratic" to make them "clearly distinctive from the thousands of other bank robberies committed each year," evidence of the prior crime is "nothing more than the character evidence that Rule 404(b) prohibits." *United States v. Smith*, 103 F.3d 600, 603 (7th Cir. 1996); 2 Weinstein's Federal Evidence § 404.22[5][c], at 404-119 (Joseph M. McLaughlin ed., 2nd ed. 1999) (noting that where alleged modus operandi is really just "garden variety criminal act" any inference of identification would be based on "forbidden inference of propensity").

In sum, in order to admit Rule 404(b) identity evidence on the signature facts or *modus operandi* theory, the District Court must make a threshold determination that, based solely on the evidence comparing the past acts and the charged offense, a reasonable juror could conclude that the same person committed both crimes. Two factors are relevant in analyzing the question. The first is the distinctiveness of the facts that make the crimes unique and the second is the proximity of the crimes in space and time. After reviewing the evidence in this case, we believe that the prior bank robbery and the credit union robbery charged here are too generic and remote from one another to permit a reasonable inference of identity.

First, the characteristics shared by the two robberies are too common to form a modus operandi that uniquely identifies Carroll as the perpetrator. All the United States can argue is that, in both crimes, the perpetrator wore a nylon stocking mask, carried a gun, and vaulted over the counter to put the bank's money in a bag. We must initially determine the frame of reference against which to measure the uniqueness of the crimes. As the question of how often a particular crime is committed in a particular way is ultimately factual, it might be appropriate, in some cases, for the District Court to take evidence on the matter in, for example, deciding a motion *in limine*. In other cases, the modus operandi or other characteristics of the prior crime and the crime currently charged may be so distinctive as to self-evidently permit a reasonable inference of identity between the perpetrator of the first and the perpetrator of the second. In the present case, we simply use a set of data readily before us. Based merely on the descriptions of bank robberies available in the published federal appellate reporters, which are incomplete in detail and refer only to a subset of all bank robberies committed, it is amply clear that the signature facts relied upon by the government in this case occur frequently, even in combination. The bank robbery cases finding signature facts have reported much less common features, such as distinguishing costumes or equipment, see, e.g., *United States v. Robinson*, 161 F.3d at 468 (orange ski mask and "distinctive" duffel bag), unusual methods, see, e.g., *United States v. Moore*, 115 F.3d 1348, 1355 (7th Cir. 1997) (robbers entered bank thirty to sixty minutes before robbery and politely asked for a job application or directions), or distinctive use of a weapon, see, e.g., *United States v. Smith*, 103 F.3d at 603 (robbers brandished knives and held them vertically during robbery).

Further, examination of the closeness of the robberies, geographically and in time, supports the conclusion that the crimes are not sufficiently related to allow an inference of identity. The two financial institutions here, while not in the same neighborhood, are both in the St. Louis area, relatively close to each other. But the crimes occurred ten years apart. This is not a case, as in *Robinson,* 161 F.3d at 468 (ten days apart), *Smith*, 103 F.3d at 603 (one month apart), or *Moore*, 115 F.3d at 1355 ("a few months" apart), where it could be inferred from the temporal and geographic proximity of the two robberies, along with other facts, that the same individuals committed them both. The government, citing *United States v. Alaniz*, 148 F.3d 929 (8th Cir. 1998), asserts that the intervening period is irrelevant because Carroll was incarcerated for most of that time. *Alaniz* dealt with the use of prior drug crimes to show the defendant's mental state with respect to a new drug conspiracy, a much different use from the signature-facts identity theory advanced in this case. Perhaps Carroll's incarceration undercuts the significance of the ten-year delay to some extent, but certainly not enough to permit an inference of identity.

Based on the generic nature of the crimes and on the ten years that passed between them, we conclude that the prior conviction was not relevant to prove identity through *modus operandi* because no substantial inference of identity reasonably could be made. Our criminal justice system has long forbidden juries from convicting an individual, not for facts which prove the charged offense, but for prior acts that, at best, show a criminal propensity. It was therefore an abuse of discretion to admit evidence of the prior bank robbery committed by Carroll, for that robbery is not relevant to any question other than Carroll's propensity to rob banks.

[The Court found the error to be harmless and affirmed the convictions.]

NOTE

Are bad acts probative of identity only when they are offered to prove a *modus operandi* tantamount to a "signature crime"?

In *United States v. Muniz*, 60 F.3d 65 (2d Cir. 1995), the court affirmed the defendant's conviction for possession of heroin with intent to distribute. Police found the heroin in a mailbox, to which both the defendant and his mother had access. The police also found a large number of empty glassine envelopes in the bedroom where the defendant was arrested. The defendant argued that the trial court erred in admitting the empty glassines. But the Court reasoned that the defendant's possession of the tools of the heroin trade at the time heroin was found in his mailbox "increases the likelihood that it was he, rather than another person having possible access, who in fact controlled the drugs in the mailbox."

In *United States v. White*, 368 F.3d 911 (2004), the court affirmed a conviction for felon firearm possession, holding that evidence of numerous customer invoice forms from the newspaper where the defendant had worked, which were seized from the defendant's residence and tended to prove identity theft, was properly admitted to prove that the defendant kept his belongings in the dresser where the guns were found. The Court noted that the evidence was "highly probative of White's identity" and that the bad act of identity theft "was not of the type which typically arouses strong passions in jurors."

[3] Motive

UNITED STATES v. POTTER
616 F.2d 384 (9th Cir. 1979)

JAMESON, DISTRICT JUDGE:

A jury found appellant, James Dell Potter, a Nevada physician, guilty on 54 counts of unlawfully distributing controlled substances in violation of 21 U.S.C. § 41(a)(1). We affirm the judgment of conviction.

Factual Background

Appellant is licensed to practice medicine in the State of Nevada and at the time of trial was registered with the Drug Enforcement Administration to prescribe and dispense controlled substances for legitimate medical purposes. In a 54 count indictment he was charged with prescribing controlled substances for five persons, "not in the usual course of professional practice" and "not for a legitimate medical purpose". The testimony of these five persons, including an employee of the Nevada Division of Investigation and Narcotics, provided the factual basis for the Government's case.

* * *

Dawn Marie Campbell, a 22 year old dancer, visited the doctor initially in March, 1977, to obtain a prescription for quaalude and to be treated for a bronchial condition. After giving her a medical examination, Dr. Potter prescribed penicillin for her bronchitis. He also wrote two prescriptions for quaalude when she complained that she was having difficulty sleeping. He told her to have the prescriptions filled at different pharmacies.

Campbell testified that after her bronchitis had subsided she again visited Dr. Potter at his office. She again requested quaalude. Potter then asked her to perform fellatio on him and while the sexual act was being performed, he wrote a prescription for quaalude. On several subsequent visits Potter prescribed both quaalude and other controlled substances. Campbell testified that on two occasions she again engaged in oral sex at the doctor's request and each time received double prescriptions. Often when Dr. Potter wrote double prescriptions he wrote one in the name of "Dawn Campbell" and the other in the name of "Marie Campbell".

Sheri Cosner, a 22 year old prostitute, testified that she visited appellant's office several times between 1975 and 1977 and received prescriptions for controlled substances. She testified that during several visits she performed oral sex for appellant at his request and at the same time received prescriptions for drugs. On one of these occasions, she and her girl friend performed oral sex for him together. She testified that the doctor would use different names when writing more than one prescription and that she told him that she was giving some of the drugs to her friends.

* * *

Dr. Potter testified in his defense that he had never had sexual relations with anyone in his office and denied all allegations of improper conduct in the examination and treatment of the Government witnesses.

Contentions on Appeal

Appellant contends that the trial court erred in * * * permitting testimony that the defendant had sexual relations with his patients * * *.

I. *Evidence of Sexual Conduct*

Appellant contends that testimony concerning repeated occurrences of oral sex in his office with the various Government witnesses should have been excluded as irrelevant under Fed. R. Evid. 404(b), and even if relevant, as unfairly prejudicial under Rule 403. We disagree. * * * Here the evidence was not offered to impugn character, as appellant argues, but rather to prove motive and lack of good faith intent in failing to comply with usual "professional practices" and "legitimate medical purposes".

Rule 404(b) is "one of inclusion which admits evidence of other crimes or acts relevant to an issue in the trial, except where it tends to prove *only* criminal disposition". *United States v. Rocha*, 553 F.2d 615, 616 (9 Cir. 1977). This "inclusionary rule", however, is subject to the balancing test of Rule 403.

The record contains substantial evidence that there was often no legitimate medical purpose for appellant's dispensing of controlled substances. The motive for his prescribing the controlled substances was unclear. From the evidence that the doctor engaged in sexual activities with his patients simultaneously with the writing of prescriptions the jury could properly infer that the granting of sexual favors provided at least some incentive for his actions. It was not necessary, as appellant argues, for the Government to prove that the issuance of the prescriptions was conditioned upon the granting of sexual favors. It was sufficient that the sexual favors provided an inducement to prescribe controlled substances without legitimate medical purpose. The sexual acts were clearly connected with the illegal transactions.

* * *

Affirmed.

NOTES

1. What other kinds of bad acts are probative of motive?

See United States v. Santiago, 46 F.3d 885 (9th Cir. 1995): Affirming the defendant's conviction for murder of a fellow prisoner, the Court held that evidence of the defendant's affiliation with the Mexican Mafia, a prison gang, was properly admitted where the evidence showed that the defendant committed the murder in order to gain entry into the gang. The Court concluded that the gang-related evidence "was necessary to explain the reason that Santiago would kill a stranger — to be accepted into the gang — and to show how and why other inmates assisted him in obtaining the weapon."

2. What limitations exist on using uncharged misconduct as proof of motive?

See United States v. Varoudakis, 233 F.3d 113 (1st Cir. 2000): The Court reversed a defendant's convictions for arson and conspiracy to commit arson arising from the burning of his restaurant. It held that the trial judge erred in admitting evidence of the defendant's burning of a leased car 16 months earlier to prove motive. The Court observed that a trial judge must be on guard when prior bad act evidence is offered to prove motive, because it is possible that "motive" is a smokescreen to introduce forbidden evidence of propensity to the jury. In this case, the argument that the car fire testimony was probative of a motive to burn the restaurant "involves an inference of propensity as a necessary link in the inferential chain." The Court explained the difference between admissible and inadmissible motive evidence:

> Put most simply, the government argues that Varoudakis's commission of the car fire arson in response to financial stress makes it more likely that he committed the restaurant arson in response to financial stress. Contrast this forbidden inference with the permissible inference to be drawn in a case in which the prior bad act — say, a botched robbery by the defendant that was frustrated by the ineptitude of his cohort — provided the motive for the defendant's subsequent assault on his cohort. There the prior bad act would provide circumstantial evidence of the commission of the assault without the involvement of any propensity inference.

3. Can the defendant's drug use be offered as proof of motive where the goal of the charged crime is to obtain money?

In *United States v. Sutton*, 41 F.3d 1257 (8th Cir. 1994), a prosecution for bank robbery, the Court held that the trial judge improperly admitted evidence of prior drug use. The Court stated that "[t]he government simply asked the jury to draw a raw inference about the defendant's motive from the fact that he used drugs," and "[w]e decline to approve such a tenuous link." The Court dismissed the probative value of the evidence to prove motive because "it could hardly come as a surprise to the jury that Mr. Sutton was robbing a bank because he needed money for *some* reason."

See also United States v. Madden, 38 F.3d 747 (4th Cir. 1994): The Court reversed the defendant's conviction for bank robbery, finding harmful error when the prosecution was allowed to call a witness to testify to the defendant's use of cocaine. The government argued that the defendant's cocaine use was probative of motive, i.e., it tended to establish his financial need, even though the government conceded that the defendant and his wife were gainfully employed. The Court responded that "there are limits" to the drugs-as-financial-motive argument:

> Contrary to the implied suggestion in the government's position that *any* drug use should be admitted in a bank robbery prosecution * * * it is not drug use *per se* that supports the underlying inference of financial need that makes the evidence relevant under Rule 401, but rather a demonstration by the government both that the accused has a significant drug habit or addiction and that he did not have the financial means to support it that makes such evidence of drug use relevant to establish a motive.

In the instant case, the Court found that the government had introduced "highly imprecise evidence of drug usage with no corresponding evidence of financial need."

[4] Intent or Knowledge

UNITED STATES v. HEARST
563 F.2d 1331 (9th Cir. 1977)

PER CURIAM:

Appellant was tried under a two-count indictment charging her with armed robbery of a San Francisco bank in violation of 18 U.S.C. §§ 2113(a), (d) and 924(c)(1). The government introduced photographs and testimony descriptive of appellant's role in the robbery. Appellant raised the defense of duress, contending her co-participants compelled her to engage in the criminal activity. The jury found appellant guilty. The district court sentenced her to seven years in prison on one count and two years on the other, the sentences to be served concurrently.

* * * We conclude on the basis of well established principles that no reversible error occurred and that the judgment must be affirmed.

I. *Evidence of Subsequent Crimes*

During its case-in-chief the government introduced evidence connecting appellant with criminal activity at a sporting goods store and with a kidnapping and theft. These incidents occurred in the Los Angeles area approximately one month after the San Francisco bank robbery. The evidence showed that appellant accompanied William and Emily Harris to Mel's Sporting Goods Store in Los Angeles, that the Harrises entered the store and left appellant outside in a truck, that a store clerk saw William Harris shoplifting and attempted to arrest him, and that appellant discharged an automatic rifle at the store, enabling Harris to escape. The evidence further showed that on the same day appellant and the Harrises stole a van and kidnapped its owner, Thomas Matthews. Matthews testified that during this incident the Harrises were outside the van and appellant had an opportunity to escape or give Matthews a message but did not do so.

Appellant * * * asserts the evidence was irrelevant for any purpose except the improper one of convincing the jury that appellant acted in accordance with a criminal disposition. She argues that even if the evidence were relevant to the issue of intent, as the district court held, the incidents were so dissimilar to the bank robbery that its probative value was minimal and outweighed by its prejudicial effect. * * *

Evidence of other criminal acts may be persuasive that the accused is by propensity a probable perpetrator of the crime charged. Nonetheless, it is excluded when offered for this purpose because it may unduly influence the jury and deny the accused a fair opportunity to defend against the particular charge. *Michelson v. United States*, 335 U.S. 469 (1948).

Evidence of other criminal acts may be admitted for purposes other than proving criminal predisposition, however. It may be received, for example, to prove knowledge, motive, and intent. Fed. R. Evid. 404(b). The government contends that the evidence of appellant's criminal acts in Los Angeles a month after the bank robbery was relevant to the issue of appellant's intent when she participated in the San Francisco bank robbery, and to whether appellant was acting under duress.

Appellant raised the defense of duress at trial and offered substantial evidence to support it. To convict appellant, therefore, the government was required to show appellant was not acting under duress when she participated in the San Francisco robbery. The evidence of appellant's involvement in the Los Angeles activity was relevant to this issue because it tended to show appellant willingly engaged in other criminal activity with persons of the same group at a time not unduly remote.

Appellant correctly points out that though relevant, evidence of other criminal conduct by the accused should be excluded if its probative value is outweighed by its prejudicial impact upon the accused. Fed. R. Evid. 403. This determination is largely a matter for the discretion of the district court. Appellant challenges the discretionary determination made by the district court in this instance.

Appellant points out that the Los Angeles offenses were not similar to the San Francisco robbery with which she was charged. Because the events were so dissimilar, she contends, they offer little insight into her state of mind during the robbery. But to justify admission of evidence of other crimes, the crimes must be "similar" to the offense charged only if it is the similarity of the crimes that underlies the relevance of the evidence. Here the relevance of the evidence did not depend on the similarity of the Los Angeles crimes to the bank robbery but on the circumstances surrounding the occurrence of the Los Angeles crimes, which indicated appellant had not acted under duress when she participated in the bank robbery. The tendency of the evidence regarding the Los Angeles crimes to prove appellant was not coerced when she participated in the San Francisco robbery is not diminished by the lack of similarity between the Los Angeles and San Francisco offenses.

Appellant also argues that the sequence of the San Francisco and Los Angeles events undermines the relevance of the latter to her state of mind during the San Francisco robbery. Absence of duress in the later Los Angeles incidents would not be probative of her state of mind during the San Francisco robbery, she contends, because the robbery itself made her an outlaw and a fugitive. This fact may have caused her to participate willingly in the Los

Angeles events, she asserts, even if she were under duress during the earlier robbery.

Appellant's hypothesis does bear upon the probative value of the evidence, and it is an appropriate consideration in determining whether on balance the evidence should have been admitted. It is, however, only a hypothesis, and a highly speculative one. The mere assertion of this hypothesis does not so undermine the probative worth of the evidence of the Los Angeles incidents in establishing appellant's state of mind during the San Francisco robbery as to render admission of the evidence an abuse of discretion. The jury could well reject appellant's theory and conclude that if appellant had been forced to participate in the bank robbery against her will she would have refrained from criminal activity in Los Angeles or seized the opportunity to escape.

The trial judge was called upon to balance the need for the evidence in the search for the truth against the possibility that the jury would be prejudiced against appellant because the evidence revealed she had participated in other conduct that was criminal. The district court acted well within its discretion in admitting the evidence. Appellant's state of mind during the San Francisco robbery was the central issue in the case. State of mind is usually difficult to prove, and the evidence on the issue was sharply divided. The timing and other circumstances of the Los Angeles incidents made evidence of them highly probative on this critical issue. Though criminal, the incidents were not of a kind likely to inflame the jury. The prejudice to appellant arose primarily from the light the evidence cast on appellant's state of mind during the San Francisco robbery and not from the incidental circumstance that it revealed appellant's involvement in other criminal acts.

* * *

Affirmed.

UNITED STATES v. MARTINEZ

182 F.3d 1107 (9th Cir. 1999)

KLEINFELD, CIRCUIT JUDGE:

* * *

FACTS

Martinez and Serrano smuggled methamphetamine from San Francisco into Hawaii. Their courier, Crystal York, got caught in the airport. She agreed to help the police catch her boyfriend, Serrano, and the person to whom he was delivering the methamphetamine, Martinez. Crystal then called Serrano on the telephone, with the police taping the call. He was angry that she had been in Hawaii for five hours without calling him, and complained about all the effort and money he had spent trying to find out if she got in all right. Crystal said "I was going to surprise you," "I love you," and explained that the reason for the delay was that "one of the pac — the things, you know * * * . [w]as jabbing me in the back, so I was messing with it. And the package broke. And then this stuff coming out, so I been * * * sitting here in the bathroom trying to do it." Crystal had five pounds of methamphetamine taped to her body under her loosely fitting dress, but she never said in so many words what, exactly, was jabbing her in the back or coming out. The closest she came was "I'm * * * scared, dude, I've been * * * carrying this shit * * * ." Her boyfriend Serrano did not have a car, just a motorcycle, so he got a ride to the airport from Martinez, to whom he was to transfer the methamphetamine. Serrano went inside the terminal and was arrested. Martinez was detained, and when Crystal identified Martinez to the police as a man to whom Serrano had previously delivered drugs, he was arrested.

ANALYSIS

* * *

Martinez argues that his heroin importing conviction should have been excluded from evidence, because it was too old, ten years, and for a different drug, heroin rather than methamphetamine. His theory is that the conviction was not relevant to anything permitted to be proved under Federal Rule of Evidence 404(b), and that unfair prejudice outweighed any probative value under Rule 403.

Our review of admission of evidence against Rule 403 and 404 objections is for abuse of discretion. The trial judge carefully considered the evidence, and admonished the jury that it could not infer guilt from the prior conviction, but only use the evidence insofar as it bore on knowledge, intent and so forth * * *.

The reason why the judge let the prior conviction in was, as he explained, that he anticipated a defense of lack of knowledge. He expected Martinez's defense to be that he was simply driving someone to the airport, and did not know that the purpose of the trip was to import narcotics. The judge anticipated that Serrano would defend on the basis that the government could not prove that he knew what, exactly, Crystal was bringing to Hawaii, and that the evidence showed merely that he was picking up his girlfriend at the airport when she arrived to surprise him for his birthday. Without knowledge, there was no conspiracy and no aiding and abetting, so there was no crime.

The judge's prediction was correct. The theory of the defenses was lack of proof of guilty knowledge. Serrano's lawyer established with Crystal's girlfriend that even though they lived together and shopped for the loose fitting dress together, she thought Crystal was just going to Hawaii to be with Serrano on his birthday, and did not know she was bringing in drugs. He established that Crystal was not the "goodie two-shoes" she pretended to be, and that Serrano had been trying to get her to stop using drugs. He argued in his opening statement that the evidence would show that another man, not a defendant, was the person for whom Crystal was importing the methamphetamine, and that Crystal's "I just wanted to surprise you honey" was basically true, that Crystal was surprising Serrano with a trip he did not know she was going to make for a purpose he did not know she had. He did not even have a car available to go to the airport and get her. Martinez's lawyer said that all the evidence would prove was that Martinez gave Serrano a ride to the airport, without even knowing Serrano's last name, and without any knowledge of a drug importation scheme.

The judge * * * examined the exact words of Crystal's phone call to Serrano, and noted that she never expressly referred to "meth" or "ice," but that prior criminal activity regarding narcotics would make Crystal's references to what she was carrying comprehensible, and thereby show knowledge. Though the prior offenses were for different drugs, cocaine and heroin, the fact that distribution quantities were involved made the crimes similar enough to bear on Serrano's and Martinez's knowledge. The judge kept out a Martinez conviction because it was too old, but admitted a 1993 final conviction based on 1986 conduct (trial was in 1996). He considered the age to be somewhat offset by Martinez's inability to complete more recent crimes because he was in prison for most of the intervening time.

The trial judge was within his discretion. Of course the government may not, under Rule 404(a), prove that the defendant is a bad person, simply to show that in all likelihood he acted criminally on the occasion at issue. But it may prove that the defendant previously committed a crime in order to prove that the defendant had knowledge relevant to the crime at issue. * * * That is what the evidence was admitted for. The judge carefully considered the risk of unfair prejudice, but reasonably concluded that it was outweighed by the probative value of the evidence.

Similarity of the crimes, identity of the narcotics, age of the prior offense, and other factors all may bear on whether the prior criminal or wrongful act really proves anything except that the defendant is a bad person. * * * Sometimes the prior bad act evidence does not prove any element of the crime, just background of the defendant, which is to say bad character from which the government hopes for an inference of conduct consistent with bad character, so the evidence is excluded.

Thus the question in a prior bad acts case is whether the proffered evidence really does tend to prove something material by a means other than bad character. In this case, was there a logical connection between the knowledge that would have been gained from the prior crime and the knowledge at issue in this case? There was. The government had to prove that Serrano knew what Crystal was bringing him, and that Martinez knew what he was bringing Serrano to the airport to accomplish. The defense theory was that it could not prove such knowledge beyond a reasonable doubt. As to Serrano, the trial judge pointed out the indeterminacy of Crystal's words on the telephone. She did not say she had methamphetamine with her and wanted to be picked up so that she could deliver it to Serrano for a handoff to Martinez. She said that a package of "stuff" was "jabbing me in my back" and referred to it as "shit" rather than methamphetamine. She also said "I love you" and "I was going to surprise you." A man ignorant of the narcotics trade might respond to "I love you" and "I was going to surprise you" by going to the airport and getting the woman who said these things. The ignorant man might respond to the sweet words without asking, "What in the world are you talking about?"

regarding whatever was jabbing the woman in the back. But prior drug crime would make the references to what she was carrying and the physical discomfort and packaging failure much more comprehensible. The prior conviction genuinely did tend to prove that Serrano knew what Crystal was talking about, so that he knew he was going to the airport to import drugs and not merely to pick up a woman who told him she loved him and had wanted to surprise him for his birthday.

As to Martinez, the case is closer, because he was not on the telephone with Crystal. The court had to consider what he would know, as a result of his prior drug importing conviction, relevant to a material proposition in this case. It is not enough to show that a defendant has knowledge of something not probative of some proposition material to the charges. The court needs a "focused determination of relevance." It had one. Without any other evidence, what the jury had was Martinez driving Serrano to the airport for what Serrano knew was narcotics importing. The question, the only salient question, was whether Martinez knew what Serrano was going there for. Crystal testified that Serrano had transferred narcotics to Martinez before. But Crystal was a person of quite limited credibility. The jury had to decide whether what she testified to, that Martinez was in on the deal, was true. Martinez's prior convictions for importing drugs tend to prove knowledge of how drugs are imported, a specialized sort of knowledge most people lack. That might include packaging, transfer to one or more individuals, transporting, avoiding apprehension during the drive, and other knowledge gained from experience. Also, as to whether Martinez would realize he was driving Serrano to the airport to pick up drugs, not just to pick up his girlfriend, the prior would tend to show "he would know [such crime] when he sees it." An important kind of knowledge experts have, gained from experience, is recognition of patterns; experience in crime may tend to prove expertise in pattern recognition for materially similar crimes.* * *

Though Martinez argues that his prior conviction for heroin importation has no bearing on his knowledge relating to this methamphetamine importation, we cannot see why not. For some drug cases, the specialized knowledge might not carry over, so, for example, a conviction for carrying a backpack of marijuana across the border might not tend to show knowledge of heroin in a car one was driving across a border. Prior sale of heroin might not tend to prove knowledge of how to "rock up" cocaine into crack, or how to cook methamphetamine from precursor chemicals. But there must be a lot of knowledge of smuggling that would carry over from one compact, relatively odorless, extremely expensive, illegal powder to another. A prior conviction may be sufficiently probative of something material, even though dissimilar, when it makes the "existence of the defendant's knowledge more probable than it would be without the evidence." The judge was within his discretion in concluding that it did in this case.

* * *

UNITED STATES v. JONES
455 F.3d 800 (7th Cir. 2006)

RIPPLE, CIRCUIT JUDGE:

After a jury trial, Keefer Jones was found guilty of possession with intent to distribute five or more grams of cocaine base ("crack"). * * * Mr. Jones now appeals his conviction and sentence. For the reasons set forth in the following opinion, we affirm the judgment of the district court.

I

BACKGROUND

A. Facts

[Police officers conducting a search found crack cocaine in a house at 940 Main Street. Jones was arrested and drafted a written confession. It stated:

> I've been staying at 940 Main Street for about three to four weeks and have been dealing drugs. About a couple thousand worth of the drugs were mine that were seized at that apartment in a raid (crack cocaine).]

B. District Court Proceedings

* * *

At the close of the prosecution's case, the Government asked the court to take judicial notice of Mr. Jones' prior conviction on February 15, 1994, for the unlawful delivery of a controlled substance in Macon County, Illinois. The district court also gave the jury a limiting instruction, based on Pattern Criminal Federal Jury Instructions for the Seventh Circuit 3.04, which instructed the jury to consider the prior conviction only for the purpose of establishing intent.

Mr. Jones testified on his own behalf. He denied living at 940 North Main Street, denied making either an oral or a written statement to Detective Ramey and denied that any of the crack cocaine found in the apartment had belonged to him. He admitted that he had a 1994 conviction for selling cocaine, but testified that he had "pretty much" forgotten how to sell drugs since that conviction. * * * After closing arguments, the jury returned a verdict of guilty.

* * *

II

DISCUSSION

* * *

B. Admission of Mr. Jones' Prior Conviction

Mr. Jones submits that the district court erred in admitting his 1994 conviction into evidence under Federal Rule of Evidence 404(b). We review a district court's decision to admit evidence under Rule 404(b) for an abuse of discretion; we ask whether:

> (1) the evidence is directed toward establishing a matter in issue other than the defendant's propensity to commit the crime charged, (2) the evidence shows that the other act is similar enough and close enough in time to be relevant to the matter in issue, (3) the evidence is sufficient to support a jury finding that the defendant committed the similar act, and (4) the probative value of the evidence is not substantially outweighed by the danger of unfair prejudice.

United States v. Toro, 359 F.3d 879, 884 (7th Cir. 2004).

The third prong of the test is not at issue in this appeal; we have stated that a conviction is sufficient to support a jury finding that a defendant committed a similar act. *See United States v. Best*, 250 F.3d 1084, 1092 (7th Cir. 2001). Mr. Jones had filed a motion in limine requesting that his prior conviction not be entered into evidence. He contended that the conviction was "not relevant to proving any fact in issue other than [his] propensity to commit the crime charged," that it was too remote in time to be admissible and that any probative value would be outweighed by the prejudice that it would cause him. In response, the Government argued that the prior conviction was admissible to that show Mr. Jones possessed the intent to distribute the crack because possession with intent to distribute is a specific intent crime.

In assessing this issue, the district court employed the four-part test set forth above and discussed each part of that test in reaching the conclusion that the 1994 conviction was admissible. As to the first prong, the district court stated that "it is proper to admit this evidence on the issue of intent." Turning to the second prong, the district court held that an eight-year-old conviction is not too old to be admissible. It relied upon *United States v. Tringali*, 71 F.3d 1375, 1379 (7th Cir. 1995), which upheld the admission of a nine-year-old conviction. The district court further held that, under the fourth prong, the conviction was not more prejudicial than probative. Nevertheless, the court agreed to give a cautionary instruction to the jury.

On appeal, Mr. Jones * * * submits that it would have been more appropriate to introduce the evidence if he had admitted possession but had denied the intent to distribute the drugs. Focusing on the second prong, Mr. Jones further contends that the prior conviction was too dissimilar to be admissible because it was for possession of cocaine, not crack. He also submits that the earlier conviction was too remote in time to be admissible. Finally, Mr. Jones argues that this evidence was more prejudicial than it was probative and that the limiting instruction was not sufficient to safeguard his right to a fair trial.

First, we must determine whether evidence of the previous conviction was relevant and probative on the issue of intent. Although we must give great deference to the district court's decision to admit the evidence, we pause to point out that our examination of the record in this case reveals that the district court's consideration of the matter does not appear to reflect the sort of critical evaluation of the issue that we believe ought to be undertaken in determining whether, in an exercise of discretion, such evidence ought to be admitted on the issue of intent. As far as we can ascertain from the cold record, in deciding the matter, the court recited the governing principles from our case law, but otherwise revealed little in the way of critical analysis as to how those principles ought to apply to the facts of this particular case. This lapse well maybe attributable, in part at least, to our own treatment of such matters on occasion; our cases have not always reflected a critical application of the principles reflected in the case law to the facts of the individual case. The district court also was not aided by the conclusory nature of Mr. Jones' motion in limine that simply claimed that admission of the evidence was sought simply to establish propensity to commit the charged offense. Similarly, the Government's reply added little to aid the court in its decision.

The most obvious justifiable situation in which prior convictions are admissible in drug prosecutions on the issue of intent are in those situations in which the defendant, while admitting possession of the substance, denies the intent to distribute it. In such a context, the matter of intent is placed squarely before the jury, and previous convictions generally are relevant and probative on the issue of intent. Our case law also has recognized that evidence of earlier drug trafficking convictions also can be relevant and probative when the defendant flatly contests all elements of the charge of possession with intent to distribute. * * * Here too, the issue of intent must be established by the Government and evidence of prior convictions for drug trafficking may be helpful. * * *

The Government's argument before this court, had it been made to the district court, would have been of significant assistance to that court, as it has been to us. An examination of the record reveals that, at trial, counsel for the defendant argued to the jury that only a small amount of cocaine was near the defendant's identification card and that the remainder of the cocaine, a larger amount, was situated in another place in the house. Counsel also emphasized the presence of others at the scene at the time that the search warrant was executed. A fair reading of counsel's argument is that Mr. Jones did not control the larger amount and that the lesser amount was held for personal use rather than resale. In this context, an earlier conviction for drug trafficking was certainly relevant and probative on, among other things, the issue of Mr. Jones' intent. It evidenced his knowledge of the drug trade and the practices of drug dealers in selling their deadly wares. It also was relevant and probative with respect to the defendant's knowledge of the commercial value of even small amounts of the drug and therefore of his intent to sell the lesser amount. Accordingly, it certainly was in the sound discretion of the district court to determine, given the facts and circumstances presented by this case, that this evidence was relevant and probative on the issues placed into contention by Mr. Jones.

Next, the district court acted within its discretion in deciding that the prior conviction was close enough in time and sufficiently similar in circumstances to be relevant to the issue of intent. Mr. Jones' prior conviction occurred six years before the charged offense; the district court correctly noted that we have allowed similar prior convictions that were even more temporally distant from the charged conduct. We also have held that a prior conviction for distribution of crack is admissible in a case where the charged act involves distribution of cocaine, as the distinction between the two drugs is a "*distinction without substance*" as "[b]oth crimes involve the possession with intent to distribute a chemical composition of cocaine." *United States v. Puckett*, 405 F.3d 589, 597 (7th Cir. 2005) (emphasis in original).

Finally, the district court certainly did not abuse its discretion in determining that the prior conviction was not more prejudicial than probative. Any probative evidence of prior convictions will be prejudicial; however, we must determine if it was *unfairly* prejudicial. Here, the trial court offered a limiting instruction, and we have held that such instructions "are effective in reducing or eliminating any possible unfair prejudice from the introduction of Rule 404(b) evidence." After analyzing each of the relevant factors, we cannot say that the district court abused its discretion.

* * *

Conclusion

For the reasons set forth in this opinion, the judgment of the district court is affirmed.

EASTERBROOK, CIRCUIT JUDGE, concurring.

Although I join the court's opinion, a few extra words are in order about the introduction of Jones's prior drug conviction.

Rule 404(b) provides that evidence of prior bad acts (including convictions) is inadmissible to show character or propensity but may be admissible to show intent, motive, or some other subject material to the trial. In this prosecution, as in quite a number of others we have seen in recent years, the parties and district judge alike treated the rule's second sentence as if it were a rule of admissibility. It is not; it says that evidence "may" be admissible for a given purpose, not that it is automatically admissible. Allowing the jury to learn about the defendant's criminal history, with or without a *pro forma* limiting instruction, invites the impermissible inference. Whether a conviction (or other bad act) is admissible depends not on Rule 404(b) but on whether it is relevant (*Rule 402*) and whether its probative value outweighs the considerable potential for prejudice (*Rule 403*).

Although intent always is at issue in a drug-distribution case — for a plea of not guilty puts the prosecution to its proof on every element of the offense

— a conviction or other bad act may or may not be relevant to that topic. I have grave doubts about the prosecution's theory of relevance in this prosecution. Jones argued that he did not own the distribution-size cache of drugs that investigators found; he admitted only to the personal-use-size cache that was in a different location. According to the prosecutor Jones's conviction shows that he had learned to separate stocks of drugs in order to throw the hounds off the scent. Yet *how* does the conviction show this? Is it that every drug dealer knows this trick of the trade? Of that there is no evidence, and it is not something that a jury could find without proof. Is it that Jones's conviction shows that his former strategy had flopped, so he hit upon this as something new? Of that there is no evidence either; we don't know the facts underlying the 1994 conviction. Thus the prosecutor's theory boils down to a belief that a drug conviction always is relevant in any later drug prosecution, and *Beasley* disapproves that perspective.

Maybe the prosecutor could have supplied the subsidiary facts needed to make this theory of relevance fly. We will never know, because in the district court neither the litigants nor the district judge discussed this subject on the record. The defense's objection was based not on Rule 402 but on a theory that the conviction was old and therefore "stale" — as if convictions were breakfast pastries left too long in a shop's display case. That's a bad objection: if Jones's prior acts do imply something about his intent or method of operation, it is unlikely that he would have forgotten his knowledge of the drug trade during his time behind bars. Jones's counsel confused Rule 609(b), which makes the passage of time pertinent when a conviction is used for impeachment, with Rules 402 and 403. Because the objection was off target, the judge never concentrated on what really matters to the proper use of convictions under the Rules of Evidence.

Prosecutors sometimes argue that we need not worry because district judges give limiting instructions. Most of these are formulaic, however, and of little help — and they may make things worse. Telling juries not to infer from the defendant's criminal record that someone who violated the law once is likely to do so again is like telling jurors to ignore the pink rhinoceros that just sauntered into the courtroom. Often judges just recite the language of Rule 404(b), instructing jurors that the conviction may be used "as proof of motive, opportunity, intent, preparation, plan, knowledge, identity, or absence of mistake or accident". Jurors are likely to hear this as so much mumbo-jumbo. The Federal Rules of Evidence speak to the bench and bar; for jurors, translation is essential.

Here the district judge avoided that pitfall by using instruction 3.04 from the Pattern Criminal Federal Jury Instructions for the Seventh Circuit. This pattern instruction is:

> You have heard evidence of acts of the defendant other than those charged in the indictment. You may consider this evidence only on the question of . You should consider this evidence only for this limited purpose.

The judge filled in the blank with "intent." That's a good start but leaves the jury at sea. *How* would a conviction show "intent"? The prosecutor's argument on appeal is that it shows not intent but knowledge of an avoidance technique (separating commercial from personal supplies). This "limiting" instruction is so general that it does not effectively distinguish appropriate from inappropriate inferences. A good limiting instruction needs to be concrete so that the jury understands what it legitimately may do with the evidence.

The risk that jurors will draw the forbidden propensity inference from prior convictions makes it prudent for the court to exclude them under Rule 403 unless in opening argument the defendant's lawyer makes an argument (such as the defendant's supposed inability to recognize a white powder as cocaine) that highlights intent, knowledge, or some other appropriate use of bad acts. If the evidence is excluded during the opening presentation, and something unexpected comes up during the defense case, the prosecutor can wheel out the conviction during rebuttal; by then its relevance (or irrelevance) should be apparent. Allowing a prosecutor routinely to introduce drug convictions in the case in chief without demonstrating relevance to some concrete dispute between the litigants creates needless risk that a conviction will rest on the forbidden propensity inference.

NOTE

What other kinds of bad acts are probative of a criminal defendant's intent or knowledge?

See United States v. Mejia-Uribe, 75 F.3d 395 (8th Cir. 1996): Although the Court affirmed a defendant's cocaine-related convictions, it found that the trial judge erred (harmlessly) in admitting the defendant's 15-year-old conviction for another cocaine offense. The government offered the prior conviction to prove intent, but the Court reasoned that the prior conviction was not admissible because it was (1) too remote in time, and (2) involved a single sale, while the instant case involved a large scale, ongoing operation. It concluded that the prior conviction "offered little, if any, probative value beyond the tendency to show that Uribe was the type of person with a propensity to commit this type of crime." *See also United States v. Peters*, 283 F.3d 300 (5th Cir. 2002) (affirming convictions for crack cocaine offenses, the Court held that evidence that a defendant operated a crack house and sold cocaine 10 years earlier was admissible to prove knowledge and experience with cocaine and his continuing intent to sell crack cocaine); *United States v. Wynn,* 987 F.2d 354 (6th Cir. 1993) (defendant's prior threats and acts of violence against his wife are admissible to show intent to have his wife killed); *United States v. Robichaux,* 995 F.2d 565 (5th Cir. 1993) (prior fraudulent transaction properly admitted to rebut the defendant's claim that he did not know "what was going on" in the transaction for which he was charged); *United States v. Arambula-Ruiz*, 987 F.2d 599 (9th Cir. 1993) (prior conviction for possession of heroin with intent to distribute is probative of knowledge where defendant is charged with conspiring to possess heroin, and claims that he was an innocent bystander in the wrong place at the wrong time; however, prior arrests for being an undocumented alien and for illegal possession of a firearm "do not tend to prove a material issue of the drug conspiracy and possession charges" and were only offered to show the defendant's propensity to commit criminal acts).

[5] Other Not-For-Character Uses for Uncharged Acts of Misconduct

UNITED STATES v. WOODS
484 F.2d 127 (4th Cir. 1973)

WINTER, CIRCUIT JUDGE:

Martha L. Woods was found guilty by a jury of murder in the first degree and seven other charges of assault with intent to murder, attempt to murder, and mistreatment of her eight-month-old pre-adoptive foster son, Paul David Woods. She had also been indicted and went to trial on three counts of assault, attempt to murder, and mistreatment of Judy Woods, her two-year-old adopted daughter, but the district court granted a judgment of acquittal on these charges. Mrs. Woods was sentenced to life imprisonment on the conviction of first degree murder, and she received various sentences on the other convictions, some to run concurrently with one another, and others to run consecutively.

* * *

I.

The issues before us arise from the manner in which the government, by necessity, undertook to prove its case. The government showed that Paul was born February 9, 1969, and that he spent the first five months of his life in a foster home. During that time his physical health was uneventful and he never suffered from any breathing problems or cyanosis (a blue color, principally around the lips, due to a lack of oxygen). At the time he was placed in Mrs. Woods' home, he was a normal, healthy baby.

Beginning August 4, 1969, a bizarre series of events occurred. Twice on that date, and once again on August 8, August 13, and August 20, Paul suffered instances of gasping for breath and turning blue from lack of oxygen. Each time he responded to mouth-to-mouth resuscitation, except on August 20, when he went into a coma which persisted until September 21, when he died at an age of slightly more than seven months. On each of these occasions the evidence indicated that Paul had been in Mrs. Woods' custody, and only Mrs. Woods had had access to him. On each occasion prior to August 20, Paul was taken to the hospital. On the first occasion, he was immediately released because an examination disclosed that he was apparently well. On the other occasions, even after several days' observation, no reason for his cyanosis or respiratory difficulties could be discovered.

To prove that Paul's death was neither accidental nor the result of natural causes, the government presented the testimony of a forensic pathologist, Dr. DiMaio, who, based upon Paul's medical history, the records of his various hospitalizations, and the results of an autopsy which the pathologist had performed after Paul's death stated that Paul's death was not suicide or accident and that he found no evidence of natural death. Dr. DiMaio expressed his opinion as one of seventy-five percent certainty that Paul's death was homicide caused by smothering. Dr. DiMaio explained his twenty-five percent degree of doubt as being the possibility that Paul died naturally from a disease currently unknown to medical science, and he agreed that his doubt was a "reasonable doubt" within the standard definition given by the court.

Next, the government showed that beginning in 1945 Mrs. Woods had had custody of, or access to, nine children who suffered a minimum of twenty episodes of cyanosis. Seven children died, while five had multiple episodes of cyanosis. Three of the children were her own natural born children; two were children she had adopted; one was a niece; one was a nephew; and two were children of friends.

* * *

II.

* * *

A. *General.* * * * The evidence of what happened to the other children was not, strictly speaking, evidence of other crimes. There was no evidence that defendant was an accused with respect to the deaths or respiratory difficulties of the other children, except for Judy. Simultaneously with her trial for crimes alleged against Paul, defendant was being tried for crimes alleged against Judy, but there was no direct proof of defendant's guilt and the district court ruled that the circumstantial evidence was insufficient for the government to have proved its case. Thus, with regard to no single child was there any legally sufficient proof that defendant had done any act which the law forbids. Only when all of the evidence concerning the nine other children and Paul is considered collectively is the conclusion impelled that the probability that some or all of the other deaths, cyanotic seizures, and respiratory deficiencies were accidental or attributable to natural causes was so remote, the truth must be that Paul and some or all of the other children died at the hands of the defendant. We think also that when the crime is one of infanticide or child abuse, evidence of repeated incidents is especially relevant because it may be the only evidence to prove the crime. A child of the age of Paul and of the others about whom evidence was received is a helpless, defenseless unit of human life. Such a child is too young, if he survives, to relate the facts concerning the attempt on his life, and too young, if he does not survive, to have exerted enough resistance that the marks of his cause of death will survive him. Absent the fortuitous presence of an eyewitness, infanticide or child abuse by suffocation would largely go unpunished.

B. *Admissibility of Evidence Generally.* The government and the defendant agree that evidence of other crimes is not admissible to prove that an accused is a bad person and therefore likely to have committed the crime in question. * * * Defendant argues that while there are certain recognized exceptions to this rule, the instant case cannot be fitted into any of them, emphasizing that corpus delicti is not an exception. The government, in meeting this approach, contends that the evidence was admissible on the theory that it tended to prove (a) the existence of a continuing plan, (b) the handiwork or signature exception, (c) that the acts alleged in the indictment were not inadvertent, accidental, or unintentional, and (d) the defendant's identity as the perpetrator of the crime. We are inclined to agree with the defendant that the evidence was not admissible under the scheme or continuing plan exception because there was no evidence that defendant engaged in any scheme or plan, or, if so, the objective or motive. The evidence may have been admissible under the lack of accident exception, although ordinarily that exception is invoked only where an accused admits that he did the acts charged but denies the intent necessary to constitute a crime, or contends that he did the acts accidentally. * * *

The handiwork or signature exception is the one which appears most applicable, although defendant's argument that cyanosis among infants is too common to constitute an unusual and distinctive device unerringly pointing to guilt on her part would not be without force, were it not for the fact that so many children at defendant's mercy experienced this condition. In the defendant's case, the "commonness" of the condition is outweighed by its frequency under circumstances where only defendant could have been the precipitating factor.

While we conclude that the evidence was admissible generally under the accident and signature exceptions, we prefer to place our decision upon a broader ground. Simply fitting evidence of this nature into an exception heretofore recognized is, to our minds, too mechanistic an approach.

* * *

[E]vidence of other offenses may be received, if relevant, for any purpose other than to show a mere propensity or disposition on the part of the defendant to commit the crime, provided that the trial judge may exclude the evidence if its probative value is outweighed by the risk that its admission will create a substantial danger of undue prejudice to the accused.

As we stated at the outset, we think that the evidence would prove that a crime had been committed because of the remoteness of the possibility that so many infants in the care and custody of defendant would suffer cyanotic episodes and respiratory difficulties if they were not induced by the defendant's wrongdoing, and at the same time, would prove the identity of defendant as the wrongdoer. Indeed, the evidence is so persuasive and so necessary in case of infanticide or other child abuse by suffocation if the wrongdoer is to be apprehended, that we think that its relevance clearly outweighs its prejudicial effect on the jury. We reject defendant's argument that the proof was not so clear and convincing that its admissibility should not be sustained. As we stated at the outset, if the evidence with regard to each child is considered separately, it is true that some of the incidents are less conclusive than others; but we think the incidents must be considered collectively, and when they are, an unmistakable pattern emerges. That pattern overwhelmingly establishes defendant's guilt.

* * *

Affirmed.

[The dissenting opinion of Judge Weidener is omitted].

[6] The Effect of Stipulation

UNITED STATES v. CROWDER
141 F.3d 1202 (D.C. Cir. 1998)(en banc)

RANDOLPH, CIRCUIT JUDGE:

The principal question in these cases is whether a criminal defendant may, over the government's objection, offer to concede an element of an offense (such as knowledge or intent) and thereby (1) preclude the government from introducing evidence under Rule 404(b), Fed. R. Evid., to prove that element, and (2) obtain an instruction that the jury need not consider or decide that element. When we first heard these cases en banc, a divided court answered the question this way: whenever there is "a defendant's offer to concede knowledge and intent combined with an explicit jury instruction that the Government no longer needs to prove either element," Rule 404(b) renders the bad acts evidence inadmissible. *United States v. Crowder (Crowder I),* 87 F.3d 1405, 1410 (D.C. Cir. 1996). On the government's petition for a writ of certiorari, the Supreme Court granted the writ, vacated our judgment and remanded the cases for reconsideration in light of the intervening decision in *Old Chief v. United States*, 519 U.S. 172 (1997) [*Old Chief* is set forth in Chapter 5, *supra*]. We now hold that despite a defendant's unequivocal offer to stipulate to an element of an offense, Rule 404(b) does not preclude the government from introducing evidence of other bad acts to prove that element.

I

A

* * * In separate jury trials, both defendants were convicted of drug offenses, Crowder for possessing heroin and crack cocaine with intent to distribute, Davis for distributing crack cocaine and for possessing crack with intent to distribute.

Crowder. Police officers driving along the 1300 block of Newton Street, N.W., Washington, D.C., saw Crowder engage in what appeared to be a drug transaction, exchanging a small object for cash. The officers stopped their car and gestured for Crowder to approach. Crowder started to come closer but then turned and ran. During the ensuing chase Crowder discarded a brown paper bag containing 93 ziplock bags of crack cocaine and 38 wax-paper packets of heroin. When the officers caught up with him, they found that he was carrying a beeper and $988 in small denominations.

Crowder's first trial ended in a mistrial. Before the retrial, the government gave notice that it would seek to prove Crowder's knowledge, intent and modus operandi by introducing evidence to show that Crowder sold crack cocaine to an undercover officer on the same block on Newton Street seven months after his arrest in this case. Crowder objected to the evidence, partly on the basis that he was willing to stipulate that the amounts of drugs "seized [by the police in this case] were consistent with distribution" so that "anybody who possessed those drugs possessed them with the intent to distribute."

The district court took the matter under advisement. After the government presented its case-in-chief, Crowder mounted a defense based on the theory that the police had framed him. Through nine witnesses, including his nephew, his father, the mother of his child, and Newton Street neighbors, he tried to show that the officers came looking for him to enlist his aid in a homicide investigation, that the transaction the officers observed consisted merely of the passing of a cigarette, that he had the $988 to pay for repairs to his family's house, and that his child's mother had loaned him the beeper so that he could keep in touch with her.

At the close of the defense case, the government renewed its effort to introduce the evidence of Crowder's other drug offense. As to Crowder's pretrial offer to stipulate, the government argued that Crowder had now contested his intent to distribute, and that the evidence of his other drug deal had legitimate probative value apart from its bearing on intent, which is all the proposed stipulation addressed.

The district court first took up Rule 404(b):

> It seems to the court that the first question is whether or not this evidence is probative of anything in the case, and it seems to the court that this evidence is probative, because Mr. Crowder is trying to suggest in his defense and I think, if we look at the evidence in the defense, not just Mr. Crowder's testimony, that all of this was just a coincidence, it was a coincidence that he had the $900 in his possession, it's a coincidence that he had a beeper in his possession, and that everything else took place, presumably, the running away and the officer chasing him, and the officer finding a large quantity of drugs in the alley, had nothing at all to do with Mr. Crowder. So, to me, that raises an issue of intent, raises an issue of knowledge, perhaps raises an issue, as was raised in the Watson case, of his knowledge of even the drug trade. It seems to me, based upon that evidence, that the 404(b) evidence is probative.

Having found the evidence probative for a proper purpose under Rule 404(b), the court turned to Federal Rule of Evidence 403 and concluded that the probative value of Crowder's other drug crime was not substantially "outweighed by potential undue prejudice to Mr. Crowder." The court noted the highly probative nature of the evidence to prove intent and knowledge, particularly in view of Crowder's defense that "he doesn't know anything about it * * * [and] this is all a setup by the police." When the court admitted the evidence in the government's rebuttal case, it gave a limiting instruction, which it repeated during its jury charge.

Davis. An undercover officer purchased a rock of crack cocaine from Horace Lee Davis on the 900 block of 5th Street, N.W. Davis had obtained the crack from a man sitting in a nearby car. After the transaction, the undercover officer left the scene and broadcast a description of Davis and the other man. Both were stopped a short time later and positively identified by the undercover officer. The police apprehended Davis as he was opening the door to the car from which he had obtained the rock. A search of the car uncovered more than 20 grams of crack as well as $40 in cash. The cash included pre-recorded bills the officer had used to buy the rock from Davis.

Davis put on a defense of misidentification. He explained that he had purchased a beer from a nearby liquor store and had simply walked out of the store just before his arrest. Before trial, the government gave notice that it intended to introduce evidence of three prior cocaine sales by Davis, all in the vicinity of a shelter at 425 2nd Street, N.W., only a few blocks from the site of the charged offense. The government sought to introduce these prior acts to prove essential elements of Davis's crime — knowledge and intent. Davis objected, in part on the basis of his proposed stipulation "that the person who sold the undercover officer the drugs in this case had the intent to distribute any and all drugs recovered by the police, both through their purchase and through the seizure from [the] car, and that that individual also knew of the drugs recovered from [the] car." The district court ruled that the government did not have to accept Davis's concession and could prove the required elements of knowledge and intent through evidence of Davis's prior acts. When the court admitted evidence of the prior acts, it gave a limiting instruction, and reiterated the instruction in its jury charge.

B

While the government's certiorari petition in these cases was pending, the Supreme Court handed down *Old Chief v. United States.* * * *

* * *

II

* * *

Our original en banc decision rested on the following theory: "a defendant's offer to concede knowledge and intent combined with an explicit jury instruction that the Government no longer needs to prove either element" results in the other crimes evidence having, as "its only purpose," proof of the defendant's propensity, which Rule 404(b) forbids. The idea was that the proposed stipulation (and instruction) "completely removed" knowledge and intent from the trial; that evidence of the defendant's other crimes therefore could no longer be considered relevant to those elements; and that if the evidence had no other nonpropensity purpose, its only function would be to prove what Rule 404(b) barred.

Tested against the Supreme Court's *Old Chief* decision, the theory of *Crowder I* fails. *See* 1 Stephen A. Saltzburg, Michael M. Martin & Daniel J. Capra, Federal Rules of Evidence Manual 385-86 (7th ed. 1998). *Old Chief's* holding ultimately rested on Federal Rule of Evidence 403, which authorizes trial courts to exclude evidence if its "probative value is substantially outweighed by the danger of unfair prejudice * * * ." But before getting to Rule 403, the Court had to dispose of a preliminary question, a question that bears directly on the *Crowder I* theory. The defendant in *Old Chief* claimed, as *Crowder I* held, that a defense stipulation to an element of a crime completely removes the element from trial, thereby rendering other evidence of the element irrelevant and thus inadmissible. The Supreme Court rejected this argument. A defendant's offer to stipulate or concede an element of an offense, the Court concluded, does not deprive the government's evidence of relevance. There does not have to be an "actual issue" about the facts sought to be proven. As the Court put it, "evidentiary relevance under Rule 401 [is not] affected by the availability of alternative proofs of the element," such as a defendant's concession or offer to stipulate. In support, the Court quoted the statement in the advisory committee notes to Rule 401 that the "fact to which the evidence is directed need not be in dispute." * * *

From this aspect of *Old Chief*, several propositions necessarily follow. First, if the government's other crimes evidence would have been relevant under Rule 401 — if it would have made it more likely with the evidence than without it that the defendants had the requisite knowledge or intent — the evidence remained relevant despite the defendants' offers to stipulate. Second, the government therefore could offer this evidence for the purpose of proving something Rule 404(b) expressly permits, namely, the defendants' knowledge or intent. * * * In other words, properly viewed, the first sentence of Rule 404(b) bars not evidence as such, but a theory of admissibility. Third, compliance with Rule 404(b) does not assure admission of the other crimes evidence. *Old Chief* stated that if "there were a justification for receiving evidence of the [defendant's felony conviction] on some issue other than status [such as knowledge or intent], Rule 404(b) guarantees the opportunity to seek its admission." The "opportunity," not the "admission," is what Rule 404(b) "guarantees." But if a trial court were to exclude the government's evidence of bad acts, the court could not do so "on the ground that the other evidence" — the proposed stipulation backed up by a jury instruction — "rendered it 'irrelevant,' " Instead, * * * exclusion would have to be on the basis that the evidence is "unfairly prejudicial, cumulative or the like, its relevance notwithstanding."

In other important ways, *Old Chief* stands at odds with our original decision in these cases. According to *Crowder I*, the government may not introduce its bad acts evidence because a "defendant's concession of intent and knowledge deprives the evidence of any value * * * ." There are several problems lurking within this formulation. For one thing, it hands to criminal defendants the ability to control the government's presentation of its case. Yet all nine Justices in *Old Chief* agreed with "the familiar, standard rule that the prosecution is entitled to prove its case by evidence of its own choice, or, more exactly, that a criminal defendant may not stipulate or admit his way out of the full evidentiary force of the case as the government chooses to present it."

For another thing, every Justice disagreed with the notion that a stipulation has the same evidentiary value as the government's proof. * * * There is, in short, a "need for evidence in all its particularity to satisfy the jurors' expectations about what proper proof should be," and so to prevent nullification or unjustified acquittal.

The Supreme Court made these points to distinguish between "stipulations to the status element of a crime, which can be forced upon the prosecution, and stipulations to other elements of a crime, which the prosecution should remain free to reject." 1 Saltzburg, *supra*, at 385. Proof of status, the Court said, concerns an element that is "wholly independent[] of the concrete events" of the charged crime. In contrast, the elements of intent and knowledge are at the core of the offenses charged in the cases before us. Replacing proof of these elements with stipulations creates "a gap in the story of a defendant's subsequent criminality." To be sure, other crimes evidence will typically relate to events more or less removed in time from the charged offense. But that is true of many other kinds of evidence. A husband's prior physical abuse of his wife while he was in a jealous rage may suggest his motive for murdering her; an incriminating statement made after the offense may reveal intent; tangible evidence found later may suggest identity. Evidence about what the defendant said or did at other times can be a critical part of the story of a crime, and may be introduced to prove what the defendant was thinking or doing at the time of the offense. This is true regardless whether the defendant's actions on those other occasions were in themselves criminal. *Old Chief* establishes that the prosecution cannot be forced to stipulate away the force of such evidence.

The Supreme Court also distinguished Old Chief's case on the ground that there was "no cognizable difference" between the proof the prosecution sought to present — a document reflecting the prior conviction — and the stipulation the defendant offered. As to the stipulation, Old Chief was willing to concede that he personally had the requisite prior felony conviction.

The stipulations Crowder and Davis proposed were of an entirely different sort. Both were of uncertain and doubtful significance. Crowder was willing to stipulate only that "anybody who possessed those drugs possessed them with the intent to distribute." But "anybody" was not on trial. Crowder was. And it was Crowder's intent, not "anybody's," that the prosecution had to establish to the jury's satisfaction. The stipulation Davis offered is of a piece. It mentioned only some hypothetical drug dealer, some "person." Yet the prosecution's evidence of Davis's prior crack cocaine sales — sales close in time and place to those charged in the indictment — was not meant to show that someone had intent and knowledge. The evidence was introduced to prove that Davis had the intent to distribute the crack and that Davis knew what he was possessing. Davis's proposed stipulation could not possibly have substituted for such proof. It did not even mention him by name. Far from a choice between "propositions of slightly varying abstraction," the choice in these cases was between concrete evidence of the defendants' actions giving rise to natural and sensible inferences, and abstract stipulations about hypothetical persons not on trial.

The government's proof of Crowder's other crime also had legitimate probative force with respect to matters beyond those encompassed in his proposed stipulation. * * * Rule 404(b) evidence will often have such multiple utility, showing at once intent, knowledge, motive, preparation and the like. * * * In proving that a defendant intended to distribute crack cocaine, for instance, the government might simultaneously be showing the defendant's motive to possess the crack, which Rule 404(b) permits. Intent would thereby serve as an intermediate fact from which the jury could infer another intermediate fact-motive from which it could in turn infer the element of possession. Thus, other-offense evidence of intent would have probative value not just on the intent element, but also on the possession element of the offense.

The multiple utility of Rule 404(b) evidence is illustrated in Crowder's case. The trial court permitted the prosecution to introduce evidence of Crowder's other crime to prove not only his intent to distribute, but also his "knowledge of the substance within his possession." One of the charges against Crowder was possessing with intent to distribute crack cocaine. Crowder threw away a brown paper bag as he ran from the police to avoid arrest. The paper bag contained wax-paper packets of heroin and ziplock bags of crack. Some of the ziplock bags were clear; others were dark. The clear bags contained a larger amount of crack than the dark bags. The government's other-offense evidence showed that several months after his arrest in this case, the police caught Crowder selling crack cocaine on the same block. Crowder held up two ziplock bags to an undercover officer. One bag was clear; he offered it for $20. The other bag was dark; it contained a smaller amount of crack of less purity; he offered it for $10. As the government told the court, Crowder's other offense was thus probative of several matters "of consequence" at trial. *See* Fed. R. Evid. 401. In terms of Rule 401, it was more probable with the evidence than without it that Crowder intended to distribute the crack cocaine in the brown paper bag. On the other occasion when he had crack cocaine in his possession, he sold it. It was more probable with the evidence than without it that Crowder knew the material in the ziplock bags was crack cocaine, just as he knew the substance in the ziplock bag he sold to the undercover officer was crack cocaine. And it was more probable with the evidence than without it that Crowder knowingly possessed the crack cocaine recovered from the brown paper bag. Crowder's offer to stipulate dealt only with someone's intent and therefore did not even come close to covering everything the government's Rule 404(b) evidence legitimately proved against him.

* * *

For all of these reasons, upon reconsideration of our earlier decision in light of *Old Chief* we hold that a defendant's offer to stipulate to an element of an offense does not render the government's other-crimes evidence inadmissible under Rule 404(b) to prove that element, even if the defendant's proposed stipulation is unequivocal, and even if the defendant agrees to a jury instruction of the sort mentioned in our earlier opinion. Other rules of evidence may bear on the admissibility of evidence satisfying Rule 404(b) and we will get to them next. For now it is enough to repeat the words of the advisory committee on Rule 404(b): if evidence is offered for a purpose Rule 404(b) permits, such as proving knowledge or intent, Rule 404(b) "does not require that the evidence be excluded."

III

While Rule 404(b) does not require the exclusion of bad acts evidence offered for a purpose the rule recognizes as legitimate, other evidentiary rules might. For instance, offering the evidence for a proper purpose will satisfy Rule 404(b), but it will not in itself satisfy the relevancy standards of Rules 401 and 402. * * * The government must identify which of the matters listed in Rule 404(b) * * * it is intending to prove by the other crimes evidence. If the defense objects, the court must then satisfy itself that the evidence is relevant to that matter.

In the cases before us, neither defendant contested the relevancy of the other crimes evidence to his intent, except on the basis that their proposed stipulations took intent out of the case. * * * And so we move on to another hurdle, Rule 403.

* * * In these cases, the concern about "prejudice" focused on the danger of the jury using the other crimes evidence in a way the rules do not permit — to conclude that because the defendant committed some other crime, he must have committed the one charged in the indictment. This danger, of course, will be present in every Rule 404(b) case. But that alone cannot give rise to a per se rule of exclusion, as Crowder and Davis argued when we first heard their cases en banc. As to Rule 403, each case will turn on the discretionary judgment of the trial court and its assessment, not of relevance, but of the evidentiary value of the government's Rule 404(b) evidence. On the same side of the balance, the trial court will take into account the effect of a limiting jury instruction to protect the rights of the accused.

Crowder and Davis maintained, however, that whenever a defendant offers to stipulate to intent, as both purported to do here, the Rule 403 balance will always tip in favor of exclusion. We agree that trial courts may take offers to stipulate into account in making their Rule 403 determinations. But we do not agree that the existence of the offer will necessarily be decisive. Here the proposed stipulations were ambiguous, conditional and tentative. Neither mentioned the defendant directly. At no point in their trials did either defendant propose a jury instruction requiring the jury to find the conceded element of intent. * * *

In short, the Rule 403 inquiry in each case involving Rule 404(b) evidence will be case-specific. There can be no "mechanical solution," no per se rule of the sort Crowder and Davis advocate.

We have considered the defendants' other arguments and reject them. The convictions are affirmed.

TATEL, CIRCUIT JUDGE, with whom EDWARDS, CHIEF JUDGE, WALD, and SILBERMAN, CIRCUIT JUDGES, join, dissenting:

* * *

As the court now interprets Rule 404(b), the Rule's first sentence never comes into play unless the government is careless enough to confess that its only motive for introducing the evidence is to prove the defendant's bad character. The clear implication of today's decision is that Rule 404(b) is satisfied if propensity evidence is remotely relevant to any issue, even a conceded issue that the government need never prove. Rule 404(b) requires more. It imposes an affirmative burden on prosecutors to articulate — and on courts to approve — material, non-propensity purposes for admitting bad acts evidence. * * * This burden constitutes the defendant's first and most important protection against the harmful effects of character evidence. Once that threshold is passed, the evidence's relevance will often tip Rule 403's scales in the government's favor, and once the evidence is admitted the curative effects of limiting jury instructions are an "unmitigated fiction."

* * *

The court [reiterates] *Old Chief*'s point that intrinsic evidence may be essential to "creat[e] a coherent narrative of [a defendant's] thoughts and actions in perpetrating the offense for which he is being tried." By their very nature, however, "other bad acts" are separate from, not integral to, "the offense * * * being tried." In Davis's case, the other bad acts evidence concerned events that took place before the offense with which he was charged. The bad acts in Crowder's case occurred after his first trial. In neither case, therefore, did the evidence have any place in the government's narrative about what actually happened on the dates of the alleged crimes for which the defendants were on trial, unless, of course, the government were permitted to argue based on propensity. But Rule 404(b) requires the prosecution to produce some reason other than propensity to connect a defendant's prior or subsequent acts with the "narrative" of the charged offense. Absent such a connection, excluding the bad acts evidence does not detract from the prosecution's story in any way, except by forbidding tales of defendants' bad character. * * *

* * *

The court worries that a confused jury may decline to convict, but Crowder's and Davis's willingness to accept a "must convict" jury instruction removes this danger. The instruction also answers the court's concern that the stipulations were unclear because they failed to refer to defendants by name. The offered instruction makes abundantly clear that possession, not knowledge or intent, remains the only issue in dispute. * * *

As *Crowder I* also explained, the instruction itself promotes clarity. Unlike limiting jury instructions that are used when character evidence is admitted and that require juries to ignore the obvious implication of bad acts evidence, a "must convict" instruction would not require the jury to perform "'mental gymnastic[s].'" Rather, the trial court simply instructs the jury that to convict it need find only possession beyond a reasonable doubt. Hardly confusing, this approach protects defendants from the prejudice of bad acts evidence while preserving the government's ability to prove its case.

Aside from depriving the government of the ability to introduce character evidence, Crowder's and Davis's concessions and proposed jury instructions would have made the government's task easier — in effect transforming these distribution cases into simple possession cases. Why, then, does the government decline the offer? The answer is this: Bad acts evidence is so prejudicial that by using it, the government is more likely to convict, even with the burden of proving all three elements of the crime, than if it need prove only possession but cannot use the evidence. * * *

[7] Standard of Proof for Acts of Uncharged Misconduct

HUDDLESTON v. UNITED STATES
485 U.S. 681 (1988)

CHIEF JUSTICE REHNQUIST delivered the opinion of the Court.

* * *

This case presents the question whether [under Rule 404(b)] the district court must itself make a preliminary finding that the Government has proved the "other act" by a preponderance of the evidence before it submits the evidence to the jury. We hold that it need not do so.

Petitioner, Guy Rufus Huddleston, was charged with one count of selling stolen goods in interstate commerce, 18 U.S.C. § 2315, and one count of possessing stolen property in interstate commerce, 18 U.S.C. § 659. The two counts related to two portions of a shipment of stolen Memorex videocassette tapes that petitioner was alleged to have possessed and sold, knowing that they were stolen. The evidence at trial showed that a trailer containing over 32,000 blank Memorex videocassette tapes with a manufacturing cost of $4.53 per tape was stolen from the Overnight Express yard in South Holland, Illinois, sometime between April 11 and 15, 1985. On April 17, 1985, petitioner contacted Karen Curry, the manager of the Magic Rent-to-Own in Ypsilanti, Michigan, seeking her assistance in selling a large number of blank Memorex videocassette tapes. After assuring Curry that the tapes were not stolen, he told her he wished to sell them in lots of at least 500 at $2.75 to $3 per tape. Curry subsequently arranged for the sale of a total of 5,000 tapes, which petitioner delivered to the various purchasers — who apparently believed the sales were legitimate.

There was no dispute that the tapes which petitioner sold were stolen; the only material issue at trial was whether petitioner knew they were stolen. The District Court allowed the Government to introduce evidence of "similar acts" under Rule 404(b), concluding that such evidence had "clear relevance as to [petitioner's knowledge]." The first piece of similar act evidence offered by the Government was the testimony of Paul Toney, a record store owner. He testified that in February 1985, petitioner offered to sell new 12" black and white televisions for $28 apiece. According to Toney, petitioner indicated that he could obtain several thousand of these televisions. Petitioner and Toney eventually traveled to the Magic Rent-to-Own, where Toney purchased 20 of the televisions. Several days later, Toney purchased 18 more televisions. * * *

Petitioner testified that the Memorex tapes, the televisions, and the appliances had all been provided by Leroy Wesby, who had represented that all of the merchandise was obtained legitimately. Petitioner stated that he had sold 6,500 Memorex tapes for Wesby on a commission basis. Petitioner maintained that all of the sales for Wesby had been on a commission basis and that he had no knowledge that any of the goods were stolen.

In closing, the prosecution explained that petitioner was not on trial for his dealings with the appliances or the televisions. The District Court instructed the jury that the similar acts evidence was to be used only to establish petitioner's knowledge, and not to prove his character. The jury convicted petitioner on the possession count only. * * *

We granted certiorari, to resolve a conflict among the Courts of Appeals as to whether the trial court must make a preliminary finding before "similar act" and other Rule 404(b) evidence is submitted to the jury. We conclude that such evidence should be admitted if there is sufficient evidence to support a finding by the jury that the defendant committed the similar act.

Federal Rule of Evidence 404(b) — which applies in both civil and criminal cases — generally prohibits the introduction of evidence of extrinsic acts that might adversely reflect on the actor's character, unless that evidence bears upon a relevant issue in the case such as motive, opportunity, or knowledge. Extrinsic acts evidence may be critical to the establishment of the truth as to a disputed issue, especially when that issue involves the actor's state of mind and the only means of ascertaining that mental state is by drawing inferences from conduct. The actor in the instant case was a criminal defendant, and the act in question was "similar" to the one with which he was charged. Our use of these terms is not meant to suggest that our analysis is limited to such circumstances.

Before this Court, petitioner argues that the District Court erred in admitting Toney's testimony as to petitioner's sale of the televisions. The threshold inquiry a court must make before admitting similar acts evidence under Rule 404(b) is whether that evidence is probative of a material issue other than character. The Government's theory of relevance was that the televisions were stolen, and proof that petitioner had engaged in a series of sales of stolen merchandise from the same suspicious source would be strong evidence that he was aware that each of these items, including the Memorex tapes, was stolen.

As such, the sale of the televisions was a "similar act" only if the televisions were stolen. Petitioner acknowledges that this evidence was admitted for the proper purpose of showing his knowledge that the Memorex tapes were stolen. He asserts, however, that the evidence should not have been admitted because the Government failed to prove to the District Court that the televisions were in fact stolen.

Petitioner argues from the premise that evidence of similar acts has a grave potential for causing improper prejudice. For instance, the jury may choose to punish the defendant for the similar rather than the charged act, or the jury may infer that the defendant is an evil person inclined to violate the law. Because of this danger, petitioner maintains, the jury ought not to be exposed to similar act evidence until the trial court has heard the evidence and made a determination under Federal Rule of Evidence 104(a) that the defendant committed the similar act. Rule 104(a) provides that "[p]reliminary questions concerning the qualification of a person to be a witness, the existence of a privilege, or the admissibility of evidence shall be determined by the court, subject to the provisions of subdivision (b)." According to petitioner, the trial court must make this preliminary finding by at least a preponderance of the evidence.

We reject petitioner's position, for it is inconsistent with the structure of the Rules of Evidence and with the plain language of Rule 404(b). * * * Rule 404(b) * * * protects against the introduction of extrinsic act evidence when that evidence is offered solely to prove character. The text contains no intimation, however, that any preliminary showing is necessary before such evidence may be introduced for a proper purpose. If offered for such a proper purpose, the evidence is subject only to general strictures limiting admissibility such as Rules 402 and 403.

We conclude that a preliminary finding by the court that the Government has proved the act by a preponderance of the evidence is not called for under Rule 104(a).

This is not to say, however, that the Government may parade past the jury a litany of potentially prejudicial similar acts that have been established or connected to the defendant only by unsubstantiated innuendo. Evidence is admissible under Rule 404(b) only if it is relevant. * * * In the Rule 404(b) context, similar act evidence is relevant only if the jury can reasonably conclude that the act occurred and that the defendant was the actor. In the instant case, the evidence that petitioner was selling the televisions was relevant under the Government's theory only if the jury could reasonably find that the televisions were stolen.

Such questions of relevance conditioned on a fact are dealt with under Federal Rule of Evidence 104(b). Rule 104(b) provides: "When the relevancy of evidence depends upon the fulfillment of a condition of fact, the court shall admit it upon, or subject to, the introduction of evidence sufficient to support a finding of the fulfillment of the condition."

In determining whether the Government has introduced sufficient evidence to meet Rule 104(b), the trial court neither weighs credibility nor makes a finding that the Government has proved the conditional fact by a preponderance of the evidence. The court simply examines all the evidence in the case and decides whether the jury could reasonably find the conditional fact — here, that the televisions were stolen — by a preponderance of the evidence. The trial court has traditionally exercised the broadest sort of discretion in controlling the order of proof at trial, and we see nothing in the Rules of Evidence that would change this practice. Often the trial court may decide to allow the proponent to introduce evidence concerning a similar act, and at a later point in the trial assess whether sufficient evidence has been offered to permit the jury to make the requisite finding. If the proponent has failed to meet this minimal standard of proof, the trial court must instruct the jury to disregard the evidence.

We emphasize that in assessing the sufficiency of the evidence under Rule 104(b), the trial court must consider all evidence presented to the jury. "[I]ndividual pieces of evidence, insufficient in themselves to prove a point, may in cumulation prove it. The sum of an evidentiary presentation may well be greater than its constituent parts." *Bourjaily v. United States*, 483 U.S. 171 (1987). In assessing whether the evidence was sufficient to support a finding that the televisions were stolen, the court here was required to consider not only the direct evidence on that point — the low price of the televisions, the large quantity offered for sale, and petitioner's inability to produce a bill of sale — but also the evidence concerning petitioner's involvement in the sales of other stolen merchandise * * * such as the Memorex tapes * * *. Given this evidence, the jury reasonably could have concluded that the televisions were stolen, and the trial court therefore properly allowed the evidence to go to the jury.

We share petitioner's concern that unduly prejudicial evidence might be introduced under Rule 404(b). We think, however, that the protection against such unfair prejudice emanates not from a requirement of a preliminary finding by the trial court, but rather from four other sources: first, from the requirement of Rule 404(b) that the evidence be offered for a proper purpose; second, from the relevancy requirement of Rule 402 — as enforced through Rule 104(b); third, from the assessment the trial court must make under Rule 403 to determine whether the probative value of the similar acts evidence is substantially outweighed by its potential for unfair prejudice; and fourth, from Federal Rule of Evidence 105, which provides that the trial court shall, upon request, instruct the jury that the similar acts evidence is to be considered only for the proper purpose for which it was admitted.

Affirmed.

NOTES

1. Does acquittal preclude the admission of prior bad acts under 404(b)?

In *Dowling v. United States*, 493 U.S. 342, 343 (1990), the Court strongly suggested that a prior bad act could be admissible under Rule 404(b) even though the defendant was acquitted of the act. Dowling was charged with bank robbery. The perpetrator wore a ski mask and carried a gun. The trial court allowed a witness to testify that Dowling and a man named Christian assaulted her two weeks after the bank robbery, and that during the assault Dowling was wearing a ski mask and carrying a handgun. Dowling was acquitted of charges arising from the assault; the government offered and the trial court admitted the assault victim's testimony to strengthen the identification of Dowling as the masked, gun-toting bank robber, and to link Dowling with Christian, who was the getaway driver for the bank robbery. The Third Circuit held that this was error (though harmless) because, among other things, Rule 404(b) could not apply to conduct for which the defendant had been acquitted.

The Rule 404(b) question was not raised in the Supreme Court in *Dowling*. Rather, Dowling argued that the collateral estoppel component of the Double

Jeopardy Clause prohibited the proof of conduct for which he had been acquitted. In rejecting that claim, the Court relied heavily on the fact that the standard of proof governing the admissibility of Rule 404(b) evidence was considerably less than the beyond a reasonable doubt standard applied at a criminal trial. The Court noted that after *Huddleston,* the prosecution need only provide evidence sufficient to support a finding by a preponderance of the evidence that the defendant committed the prior bad act. Therefore, when the government offered evidence of the assault at the bank robbery trial, the government was not trying to relitigate the question of whether Dowling had committed the assault beyond a reasonable doubt: "Because a jury might reasonably conclude that Dowling was the masked man who entered Henry's home, even if it did not believe beyond a reasonable doubt that Dowling committed the crimes charged at the first trial, the collateral estoppel component of the Double Jeopardy Clause is inapposite."

Dowling is not technically a Rule 404(b) case. But the Court's rationale leads to the conclusion that bad acts are not inadmissible under Rule 404(b) simply because the defendant has been acquitted of those acts. An acquittal is not dispositive given the significantly lower standard of proof applied to Rule 404(b) evidence after *Huddleston*. However, the defendant should be prepared to argue that the probative value of the bad act is diminished in light of the acquittal. As the Court stated in *Huddleston,* "the strength of the evidence establishing the similar act is one of the factors the court may consider when conducting the Rule 403 balancing."

2. Is evidence of a prior arrest admissible as a bad act under Rule 404(b)?

United States v. Robinson, 978 F.2d 1554 (10th Cir. 1992), was a narcotics case, where conspiracy and intent were contested issues. The government offered, and the trial court admitted, evidence that two of the defendants had been previously arrested for narcotics violations. The Court of Appeals held that the mere evidence of arrest, without any showing of the underlying act or circumstances, was not probative of intent, knowledge, or any other of the permissible purposes for bad act evidence under Rule 404(b). It concluded: "Rule 404(b) allows evidence concerning the prior activity of a particular defendant, not simply testimony that records indicate an arrest took place." Put another way, the mere fact of arrest did not show sufficiently, under *Huddleston,* that the bad act was committed and that the defendant committed it. In contrast, officers in *Robinson* testified with respect to another defendant not merely about prior arrests but also about specific acts of the defendant and the circumstances that culminated in the arrest (i.e., that drugs were found in the apartment and that the defendant was apprehended while trying to jump from a second-story window). This evidence was found properly admitted because it was probative on the subject of intent and knowledge, and because the prosecution provided enough evidence to support a finding that the act was committed and that the defendant committed it.

[8] Procedural Issues Raised by Rule 404(b)

[a] Acts That Are Inextricably Intertwined with the Crime Charged

In a criminal case, Rule 404(b) operates to assure that the jury, when it convicts, does so for the offense charged, and not for general bad character. But it is sometimes difficult to determine which acts are part of the offense charged, and which are uncharged acts subject to Rule 404(b). The test used by the courts is whether the acts that are the subject of the proof are "inextricably intertwined" with the basic elements of the crime charged. If so, Rule 404(b) is inapplicable and there is no need to articulate a "not-for-character" purpose for the evidence. Of course, Rule 403 will still apply to the evidence. But it would be the rare case in which proof of an inextricably intertwined act could be considered so prejudicial as to justify exclusion under Rule 403.

One of the clearest cases of "intertwined" evidence arises in conspiracy cases where the government proffers evidence of an act committed during the course and in furtherance of a conspiracy. For example, in *United States v. Pace*, 981 F.2d 1123 (10th Cir. 1992), the Court held that Rule 404(b) did not prohibit the admission of evidence of the distribution of drugs by the defendant's co-conspirator. The distribution occurred while the charged conspiracy was ongoing. The Court stated that "conduct during the life of the conspiracy that is evidence of the conspiracy is not Rule 404(b) evidence."

A more difficult case is one such as *United States v. Hilgeford,* 7 F.3d 1340 (7th Cir. 1993). Hilgeford was charged with, among other things, wilfully filing a false tax return. He claimed various deductions from two farms. However, these properties had been subject to foreclosure actions by a bank and by the United States respectively. In the years prior to the challenged tax returns, Hilgeford had generated "a blizzard of complicated and groundless litigation, primarily involving his fruitless attempts to regain his two farms." Evidence of these frivolous proceedings was introduced at Hilgeford's trial. The Court of Appeals held that Rule 404(b) was not applicable to this evidence, because it was "intricately related to the fact of the case at hand." The Court explained as follows:

> The government argues that the record of defendant's failed litigation proves that he knew that the returns, premised as they are on his ownership of the property, were false. * * * Evidence demonstrating that a defendant knew he did not own certain property, when he submitted a tax return premised on a claim that he did own the property, goes directly to [the element of wilfulness]. * * * The evidence of defendant's prior conduct is "intricately related" or "inextricably tied" to the facts in this case. It is therefore not subject to Rule 404(b).

On the Rule 403 question, the *Hilgeford* Court found no error in admitting the evidence of frivolous litigation, given the already-determined crucial nature of the evidence in proving wilfulness.

Cases such as *Hilgeford* are more difficult than the conspiracy cases discussed above, because the bad act in *Hilgeford* was not encompassed in the indictment. The fact that the act was probative of an element of the prosecution's case does not distinguish it from bad act evidence covered by Rule 404(b); all evidence offered by the prosecution in a criminal trial must be somehow probative of an element of the crime, otherwise it must be excluded as irrelevant. The difference between the evidence in *Hilgeford* and that in *Huddleston,* where the Supreme Court held that Rule 404(b) was applicable when a prior act was offered to show the knowledge element as to the charged crime, is at best one of degree rather than kind.

It must be noted that there is no significant cost to requiring a Rule 404(b) analysis; all the prosecution must do is establish a not-for-character purpose for the bad acts evidence, and give pretrial notice, as discussed below. Nor does avoiding Rule 404(b) absolve the court of the duty, upon request, to provide a limiting instruction. Therefore, the better result is that Rule 404(b) should apply to all specific bad acts proffered by the prosecution, unless such acts occurred in the time period covered by the indictment and are substantively related to the charges. For an application of the "inextricably intertwined" test in accordance with this suggestion, see *United States v. Stotts,* 792 F.2d 1318 (5th Cir. 1986) (no error to compare handwriting exemplars with extortion letters written by the defendants; Rule 404(b) was not applicable because the extortion letters were specifically described in the indictment: "There was no crime not alleged in the indictment which was testified to by the handwriting expert."). *See also United States v. Vizcarra-Martinez*, 66 F.3d 1006 (9th Cir. 1995) (defendant charged with conspiring to possess and for possessing a listed chemical knowing it was to be used to manufacture methamphetamine; the government offered evidence that when the defendant was arrested, he was carrying a small amount of methamphetamine on his person; admission of this evidence was reversible error; the evidence was not "inextricably intertwined" with the charged crime, because possession of the substance was not "part of the transaction" with which the defendant was charged).

[b] Applicability of Rule 403

Bad act evidence is not automatically admissible simply because the proponent has articulated a not-for-character purpose to which the evidence could be put. The Supreme Court, in *Huddleston v. United States*, *supra*, stated that the decision to admit evidence under Rule 404(b) depends on "whether the danger of unfair prejudice outweighs the probative value of the evidence in view of the availability of other means of proof and other factors appropriate for making decisions of this kind under Rule 403." Thus, the Court has recognized that the probative value of the bad act, in proving the permissible, not-for-character purpose, may be substantially outweighed by the risk that the jury would misuse the evidence as proof of bad character. Most courts have consequently applied a four-part test in assessing bad acts evidence. As stated by the Court in *United States v. Rackstraw,* 7 F.3d 1476, 1479 (10th Cir. 1993), the test is as follows:

(1) the evidence must be offered for a proper [not-for-character] purpose; (2) the evidence must be relevant [for that purpose]; (3) the trial court must make a Rule 403 determination of whether the probative value of the [bad] acts is substantially outweighed by its potential for unfair prejudice; and (4)

pursuant to Fed. R. Evid. 105, the trial court shall, upon request, instruct the jury that the evidence of similar acts is to be considered only for the proper purpose for which it was admitted.

A slightly different four-pronged test is applied by some circuits. For example, the court in *United States v. Kern*, 12 F.3d 122 (8th Cir. 1993), set forth the following test for assessing bad acts evidence offered under Rule 404(b):

To properly admit Rule 404(b) evidence for purposes other than to prove propensity, it must (1) be relevant to a material issue raised at trial, (2) be similar in kind and close in time to the crime charged, (3) be supported by sufficient evidence to support a finding by a jury that the defendant committed the other act, and (4) not have a prejudicial value that substantially outweighs its probative value.

Under the Rule 403 test, evidence of serious criminal activity other than that charged should be examined very carefully. The more heinous the other acts by a defendant, the more likely the jury is to misuse the evidence and treat the defendant as a generally bad person, something the Rule does not permit. Also, the more similar the bad act is to the act charged, the more likely the jury is to draw the impermissible inference that the defendant has a propensity to commit such acts. Recognition of these dangers is not inconsistent with also recognizing the intent of Congress that probative evidence should be admitted if it is not unduly prejudicial.

One thing should be clear: under Rules 403 and 404(b) the decision should be made to allow the evidence to be introduced when the balance between probative value and prejudicial effect is close. *See, e.g., United States v. Clark*, 988 F.2d 1459 (6th Cir. 1993) (where the defendant was charged with killing a witness to a crime the defendant committed, evidence of the underlying crime, even though highly prejudicial, is admissible under Rule 404(b) and Rule 403 to prove motive). Equally clear, however, is that where the evidence is plainly prejudicial and is not very important to the government's case, it should be excluded. *See, e.g., United States v. Gordon,* 987 F.2d 902 (2d Cir. 1993) (prior minor drug transaction is not sufficiently probative of the defendant's participation in a major drug conspiracy; none of the alleged co-conspirators were participants in the prior transaction; evidence should have been excluded under Rule 403). The trial court must take into account whether the same point can be proven with evidence that does not refer to uncharged bad acts; the cost of admitting prejudicial evidence is unacceptable if equally probative and less prejudicial evidence is reasonably available. For example, it may be necessary in many cases to introduce the defendant's handwriting exemplar; but it is not necessary to do so by way of a document that refers to the defendant's uncharged crimes. As the Supreme Court noted in *Old Chief*, the relevance of evidence cannot be considered in a vacuum; if the proponent has evidentiary alternatives that are equally probative and less prejudicial than the proffered evidence, then the proponent should use those alternatives.

[c] Rule 404(b) and Civil Cases

While bad acts evidence is mostly offered in criminal cases, Rule 404(b) can be used in a civil case, thereby allowing a party to get out from under the exclusionary rules as to character. For example, *Dillon v. Nissan Motor Co., Ltd.*, 986 F.2d 263 (8th Cir. 1993), was a personal injury action, where the plaintiff claimed emotional injuries as a result of the accident. Plaintiff's drug use was held properly admitted for the not-for-character purpose of providing an alternative explanation for his emotional turmoil. *See also Heyne v. Caruso*, 69 F.3d 1475 (9th Cir. 1995): In a quid pro quo sexual harassment case, the Court reversed a judgment for the employer, holding that the trial judge erred in excluding testimony concerning the employer's alleged harassment of other female employees. Analyzing the evidence as proof of motive and intent which is permissible under Rule 404(b), the Court reasoned as follows: "It is clear that an employer's conduct tending to demonstrate hostility towards a certain group is both relevant and admissible where the employer's general hostility towards that group is the true reason behind firing an employee who is a member of that group."

[d] The Notice Requirement

Rule 404(b) requires the prosecution, upon request of the accused, to give the accused notice of the general nature of the bad act evidence it intends to offer under Rule 404(b). The purpose of the notice requirement in Rule 404(b) is to prevent unfair surprise and to make it easier for the accused to obtain a pretrial *in limine* ruling on bad acts evidence. The Rule provides that the notice requirement is to be flexibly applied. No specific time limits are set, and the Rule permits notice to be given as late as during trial upon a showing of good cause. As to the substance of the notice, the prosecution need only disclose the "general nature" of the bad acts evidence. However, it is not enough simply to inform defense counsel that the government's files are open for counsel's perusal. As one court put it: "making available mountains of documents without specifying which will likely be submitted has elements of unfairness causing needless expense to the defendant." *United States v. Swinton*, 75 F.3d 374 (8th Cir. 1996) (notice requirement not complied with when the government, after receiving a request for Rule 404(b) material, responded that its files were open and the Rule 404(b) evidence could be found in those files). Notably, however, the *Swinton* Court found that most of the evidence requested was not Rule 404(b) material in the first place — rather, it was evidence concerning acts "inextricably intertwined" with the crime charged, rendering Rule 404(b) and its notice requirement inapplicable.

There is no requirement that the notice be in writing.

Note that the notice requirement is a one-way street. Although criminal defendants may use Rule 404(b) to introduce other act evidence in their favor, the Rule does not provide the government with any discovery right. The difference in treatment of prosecutors and defendants reflects the different degrees of prejudice that might be anticipated when the defendant's personal acts are admitted as evidence (raising the possibility that they might be misused as propensity evidence) and when acts of persons not on trial are admitted (which are unlikely to be misused, because the propensity of these persons to commit crimes is typically not relevant).

The notice requirement is inapplicable in civil cases. However, other discovery provisions in the Federal Rules of Civil Procedure might well require pretrial disclosure.

RULE #10: HABIT — EVIDENCE OF HABIT IS ADMISSIBLE TO SHOW THAT CONDUCT CONFORMED TO HABIT.

[1] Introduction

In order for conduct to be admissible as habit evidence it must meet two requirements. First, the evidence must meet the definition of habit. Habit is typically defined as a regular response to a certain repeated situation. Second, the habit must be tied specifically to conduct in the case.

Two common-law requirements are expressly excluded from the Federal Rule. The requirement that evidence of the routine practice of an organization be corroborated as a condition precedent to its admission into evidence is rejected. The reasoning is that corroboration relates to the sufficiency of the evidence rather than its admissibility. Additionally, the requirement of the absence of eyewitnesses is rejected. The possible bias of eyewitnesses is one rationale for abandoning this common-law requirement. *See* M.C. Slough, *Relevancy Unraveled, Part II*, 5 Kan. L. Rev. 404, 447 (1957).

Distinguishing character and habit:

As will be seen from the court's opinion in *Perrin v. Anderson* below, even experienced judges have difficulty in drawing the line between habit and character evidence. The Advisory Committee's Note to Rule 406 quotes a helpful passage from McCormick that describes habit and contrasts it with character:

> Character and habit are close akin. Character is a generalized description of one's disposition, or of one's disposition in respect to a general trait, such as honesty, temperance, or peacefulness. "Habit," in modern usage, both lay and psychological, is more specific. It describes one's regular response to a repeated specific situation. If we speak of character for care, we think of the person's tendency to act prudently in all the varying situations of life, in business, family life, in handling automobiles and in walking across the street. A habit, on the other hand, is the person's regular practice of meeting a particular kind of situation with a specific type of conduct, such as the habit of going down a particular stairway two stairs at a time, or of giving the hand-signal for a left turn, or alighting from railway cars while they are moving. The doing of the habitual acts may become semi-automatic.

The rationale for admitting evidence of habit and not of character is based mostly on a differentiation of probative value. It is not always, or even often, the case, that a person acts in accordance with a character trait. Violent people, for example, do not act violently on every conceivable occasion. In contrast, the specificity and consistency attendant to habit give increased confidence that a person acted in accordance with habit on a specific occasion. *See Jones v. Southern Pacific R.R.*, 962 F.2d 447, 449 (5th Cir. 1992) ("Habit evidence is superior to character evidence because the uniformity of one's response to habit is far greater than the consistency with which one's conduct conforms to character."). If a person has a habit of wearing a seatbelt, for example, this is much more probative evidence of his wearing a seatbelt on a certain occasion than is evidence that he is generally a safety-oriented person.

[2] Federal Rule 406

Rule 406. Habit; Routine Practice

Evidence of the habit of a person or of the routine practice of an organization, whether corroborated or not and regardless of the presence of eyewitnesses, is relevant to prove that the conduct of the person or organization on a particular occasion was in conformity with the habit or routine practice.

UNITED STATES v. ANGWIN

271 F.3d 786 (9th Cir. 2001)

BREYER, DISTRICT JUDGE:

The appellants Ted Stevenson Angwin and Christine Khamis ("the defendants") were stopped by United States Border Patrol ("USBP") agents at a checkpoint near Niland, California. The agents inspected the motorhome the defendants were driving and found fourteen illegal aliens hiding throughout the vehicle. The defendants were indicted and, after a joint jury trial, convicted. This is an appeal from the district court's orders: * * * (2) excluding Angwin's proposed habit evidence * * * . We have jurisdiction pursuant to 28 U.S.C. § 1291, and we affirm.

I. BACKGROUND

A. Factual Background

On October 24, 1999, Angwin, Khamis, and their dog were traveling north on Highway 111 in a motorhome. USBP agents stopped them at the checkpoint near Niland, California, approximately forty miles north of the United States-Mexico border. Angwin was driving, and Khamis was the only visible passenger.

When the defendants arrived at the checkpoint, USBP Agent Michael Mikuski asked if they were citizens of the United States. Angwin replied that they were. Mikuski asked Khamis if she was an American citizen, to which she replied in the affirmative without looking at Mikuski. Mikuski then asked if they were the only occupants of the vehicle. Angwin responded that it was just the two of them and the dog. While speaking to Angwin, Mikuski "noticed that his hands had a slight tremble, which indicated nervousness, and he * * * kept breaking eye contact with me." Mikuski also noticed that Khamis "never looked my way, even when I was talkin' to her."

Mikuski then asked the defendants if he could inspect the motorhome, and Angwin consented. Mikuski directed Angwin to the secondary inspection area, where USBP Agent James Beresovoy asked Angwin and Khamis to exit the vehicle. The defendants waited near a checkpoint building while Beresovoy searched the vehicle. Upon entering the motorhome, Beresovoy discovered two Mexican citizens hiding under a table covered by a cloth. Agents Beresovoy and Mikuski eventually found a total of fourteen individuals hiding throughout the motorhome, including in the shower, in the bathroom, in a closet, and even lying in a small compartment under the bed. The agents learned that all fourteen of the individuals were Mexican citizens who were in the United States illegally.

Mikuski thereupon asked Angwin if there was anything he wanted to tell the agents about the inside of the motorhome. Angwin hesitated and stuttered, and then said that he had seen a van parked on the side of the road and that he had stopped to offer assistance. Angwin told Mikuski that when he stopped, several people climbed into the back of the motorhome. Angwin also indicated that he intended to take the people to the checkpoint and turn them over to the USBP.

At trial, Angwin testified that he acted under duress. Angwin asserted that he had pulled over so that the dog could walk around and relieve itself. Angwin stated that while Khamis walked the dog, he walked around the motorhome to inspect the tires. According to Angwin, two Latino men who were standing by a parked van on a nearby dirt road approached him and spoke to him in Spanish. One of the men turned toward the van and yelled, and the group of fourteen aliens, who had been hiding in the underbrush, ran toward the motorhome. Angwin testified that he tried unsuccessfully to stop the aliens from entering the vehicle. He claimed that one of the men who had approached him pushed him in a threatening manner and had a knife sheath on his belt. Angwin claimed that he believed that the wisest course of action was to drive to the upcoming USBP checkpoint. When the prosecutor asked Angwin why he did not reveal his version of the events to the USBP agents before they inspected the motorhome, Angwin stated, "I tried to answer, but I was a nervous wreck at that point and my mouth was dry and I'll never forget this; my tongue stuck to the top of my mouth and even the sides of it were sticking. And I couldn't get any words out."

While Khamis did not testify at trial, she did give a statement on October 24 to USBP Agent John Searle. According to Searle, Khamis indicated that the defendants had pulled off to the side of the road to let the dog walk around. After walking the dog briefly, Khamis allegedly told Searle that she saw Angwin off to one side of the motorhome speaking with an unidentified man. Angwin then asked her to get back into the motorhome, to sit in the passenger seat, and not to say anything. Khamis told Searle that she got back into the motorhome and heard and felt others entering the home as well. Khamis refused to sign a summation of her statement that Searle had prepared based on his notes from the interview, however.

Two aliens who were found in the motorhome, Hilario and Juan Vincente-Morales, were detained as material witnesses. Hilario Vincente-Morales testified at trial that he and his brother Juan had traveled from Mexico City to Tijuana to be smuggled to Los Angeles, where he understood that he would work to pay for his travel. He indicated that a guide led them to the area by the side of the road where they hid to await the motorhome. Vincente-Morales stated that approximately fifteen minutes after they arrived, the motorhome pulled up and he saw a person who was not a member of their group wave towards the group as if to signal them. While he could not tell whether the person waving was a man or a woman, he said that the person was located toward the front of the vehicle on the passenger side.

B. Procedural History

* * *

On February 8, 2000, the district court commenced a jury trial. At trial, Angwin attempted to introduce evidence to show that his reactions both when the aliens entered the motorhome and at the checkpoint were consistent with his training and experience with rescuing distressed ships while serving in the Coast Guard Auxiliary. The United States objected that the evidence was not relevant, and the district court sustained the Government's objection, finding that the evidence lacked probative value since Angwin's rescue of people on the high seas was not parallel to the situation at issue in the trial.

On February 14, 2000, the jury found Angwin guilty on all four Counts but found Khamis guilty only on Counts Two and Four. * * *

II. DISCUSSION

* * *

B. The Exclusion of Angwin's Proposed Habit Evidence

Angwin * * * asserts that the district court erred by excluding testimony regarding his training and experience in the Coast Guard Auxiliary as habit evidence under Federal Rule of Evidence 406. According to Angwin, that evidence would have shown that his reactions when the aliens entered the motorhome and at the USBP checkpoint were consistent with his training and experience in the Auxiliary, which, he claims, had taught Angwin to take the least confrontational course of action in potentially dangerous situations. Angwin interprets the district court's remarks in excluding the evidence as doing so because the defendant intended to introduce multiple examples of his training as opposed to one example. In Angwin's view, that was a misapplication of Rule 406.

A district court's evidentiary rulings during trial are typically reviewed for an abuse of discretion. We will only reverse if an erroneous evidentiary ruling more likely than not affected the verdict. However, evidentiary rulings which raise predominantly legal questions regarding the interpretation of the Federal Rules of Evidence are reviewed de novo.

A district court's ruling on whether proffered evidence qualifies as habit evidence under Federal Rule of Evidence 406 is highly fact-specific. *See Mathes v. The Clipper Fleet*, 774 F.2d 980, 984 (9th Cir. 1985) (noting that examples of conduct submitted for the purpose of establishing habit must be "carefully scrutinized" to ensure that they are numerous enough to justify an inference of systematic conduct). Because factual matters predominate in determining whether certain evidence sought to be introduced at trial qualifies as habit under Rule 406, we will employ an abuse of discretion standard.

* * * In deciding whether certain conduct constitutes habit, courts consider three factors: (1) the degree to which the conduct is reflexive or semi-automatic as opposed to volitional; (2) the specificity or particularity of the conduct; and (3) the regularity or numerosity of the examples of the conduct. These elements are not meant to be three discrete components, each of which must be fully satisfied for evidence to qualify under Rule 406. Instead, a district court must consider the overall reliability of the evidence, using these factors as guides. The burden of establishing that certain conduct qualifies as evidence of habit falls on the party wishing to introduce the evidence. Rule 406 is an exception to the general exclusion of character evidence under the Federal Rules, so courts are somewhat cautious in admitting the evidence.

Angwin asserts that the district court excluded Angwin's proffered evidence regarding his training with the Auxiliary on the ground that Angwin wanted to present multiple examples of his conduct. In Angwin's view, the district court's rationale for excluding the evidence is diametrically opposed to the basis on which habit evidence is probative, which is that the conduct is done so repeatedly that it is reflexive or instinctual and therefore suggestive that the person acted in conformity with the habit during the event in question. Angwin is correct as a matter of applying the rule; the more frequently that someone has engaged in certain conduct, the more likely it is that the conduct will qualify as evidence of habit. However, Angwin has misinterpreted the district court's ruling and has failed to establish that his conduct constituted evidence of habit.

First, the district court did not reject Angwin's proffered evidence on the ground that Angwin wanted to show too many examples of his conduct and training. Instead, the court found that his training simply was not sufficiently parallel to his conduct on the day of the crime. The district court's comment that Angwin's Auxiliary training was not parallel implies that the court was skeptical about the probative value of the evidence, not that the court misinterpreted Rule 406. In other words, as the United States explains, the district court was not objecting to the quantity of Angwin's evidence but its quality. Because Angwin's experience in rescuing distressed boats at sea is not particularly similar to the factual context of his crime, see infra, the district court did not abuse its discretion in finding that Angwin's proffered evidence of habit was not relevant.

Second, even if the district court did employ a flawed understanding of the rule, the record is inadequate for Angwin to meet his burden of showing that his training and experience in the Auxiliary qualified as evidence of habit. Angwin's proffered evidence of his training was not sufficiently reflexive and specific to constitute habit evidence. His response to dangerous situations — prudently taking the least confrontational course of action — is hardly reflexive or semi-automatic. The defendant testified that he considered a variety of factors in deciding what to do once the aliens approached the motorhome, including the ages and physical condition of the Latino men who threatened him, the proximity of nearby towns as opposed to the USBP checkpoint, and other criteria. By its very nature, such calculation is volitional, a "deliberate assessment[]of a crisis before choosing a safe route of escape." While specialized training might in some instances become habit, acting with particular care is distinguished from habit in the advisory notes to Rule 406. *See* Fed. R. Evid. 406 advisory committee note (distinguishing "character for care" and a "person's tendency to act prudently" from a "regular practice of meeting a particular kind of situation with a specific type of conduct").

In addition, Angwin's proffered conduct lacks the specificity required of habit evidence. Merely indicating that he takes a non-confrontational course of action in dangerous situations in general does not describe his conduct with sufficient particularity to be probative of whether he acted in conformity with that general practice on this particular occasion.

Thus, the district court did not abuse its discretion in excluding Angwin's proffered conduct evidence, as his training and experience in the Auxiliary did not qualify as evidence of habit under Rule 406.

* * *

Affirmed.

NOTES

1. How should a court draw the line between character and habit?

See Saltzburg, Martin, and Capra, *Federal Rules of Evidence Manual* (9th ed. 2006):

> Courts have generally proceeded cautiously in permitting the admission of a pattern of conduct as habit, "because it necessarily engenders the very real possibility that such evidence will be used to establish a party's propensity to act in conformity with its general character, thereby thwarting Rule 404's prohibition against the use of character evidence except for narrowly prescribed purposes." *Simplex, Inc. v. Diversified Energy Systems, Inc.*, 847 F.2d 1290, 1293 (7th Cir. 1988). That is, courts are concerned that the rule admitting habit evidence will swallow the rule excluding character evidence. *United States v. Mascio,* 774 F.2d 219 (7th Cir. 1985) (there is no such thing as a habit of committing insurance fraud, because evidence of such "habits" "would be identical to the kind of evidence that is the target of the general rule against character evidence").
>
> Although it is difficult to delineate the difference between character and habit, generally it may be said that the more particular and the more regular the performance of an act, the more likely it is to be regarded as habit. In other words, the easier it is to describe with particularity what it is that someone does and the more routine the action, the more likely a court is to hold the activity to be a habit. Another factor is the degree of volition required for the activity; the more thought and planning required for the act, the less likely it will

be found to be a habit; the more reflexive and automatic the conduct, the more likely it will be found to be habit. *See Becker v. ARCO Chem. Co.*, 207 F.3d 176 (3d Cir. 2000) (the fabrication of reasons to justify the dismissal of employees is not the sort of automatic, non-volitional, situation-specific conduct admitted as habit under Rule 406).

One court has stated the test for habit as follows: "To offer evidence of a habit, a party must at least demonstrate a regular practice of meeting a particular kind of situation with a specific type of response." *Jones v. Southern Pacific R.R.*, 962 F.2d 447, 449 (5th Cir. 1992). Another court has added that "habit refers to the type of non-volitional activity that occurs with invariable regularity. It is the non-volitional character of habit evidence that makes it probative." *Weil v. Seitzer,* 873 F.2d 1453, 1460 (D.C. Cir. 1989). Thus, activity that is extremely complicated is unlikely to be considered as habit, since such activity would ordinarily be dependent on a significant thought process, and a number of contingencies, and all of this is inconsistent with the notion of habit as reflexive and semi-automatic. *United States v. Troutman,* 814 F.2d 1428 (10th Cir. 1987) (evidence of past official conduct not admissible as habit because "extortion or refraining from extortion is not a semi-automatic act and does not constitute habit"). Also, activity that is dependent on cooperation from other individuals, or that is dependent on a number of instrumentalities, is unlikely to be considered as habit, because the circumstances will ordinarily be subject to too much variation. *See, e.g.*, *Halloran v. Virginia Chemicals Inc.*, 41 N.Y.2d 386, 393 N.Y.S.2d 341 (1977) ("On no view * * * can conduct involving not only oneself but particularly other persons or independently controlled instrumentalities produce a regular usage because of the likely variation of the circumstances in which such conduct will be indulged.").

2. When is evidence of conduct within an organization admissible under Rule 406?

When proof of organizational practice is offered under Rule 406, greater emphasis is placed on the routine nature of the activity than on its particularity; there is not the same problem of drawing a line between general and specific qualities that exists with natural persons. Because the line between habit and character is not so problematic with respect to organizations, courts admit routine organizational practice more liberally, noting that there is significant probative value in the routinized aspects of organizational activity. *See, e.g.*, *Rosenburg v. Lincoln American Life Ins. Co.*, 883 F.2d 1328 (7th Cir. 1989) (evidence that insurance company waived certain standard conditions when issuing a policy was admissible as evidence of routine practice); *Garvey v. Dickinson College*, 763 F. Supp. 799 (M.D.Pa. 1991) (in Title VII action, evidence of a college's routine procedures for screening faculty applicants, processing applications and reviewing candidates for tenure were admissible under Rule 406).

However, in order to invoke the more liberal admissibility requirements attendant to organizational activity, the proponent must show that the activity is that of a structured organization; a loose-knit, ad hoc alliance of individuals does not give rise to the same inference of routinized activity. Thus, in *United States v. Rangel-Arreola,* 991 F.2d 1519 (10th Cir. 1993), the defendant was a trucker who was found with a large amount of marijuana in the fuel tank of the truck he was driving. He objected to exclusion of evidence that it was common practice for truck drivers to accept jobs without checking the fuel tanks. This activity, or rather non-activity, was considered too volitional to constitute habit evidence. Nor could it be admitted as evidence of organizational practice. A loose-knit group such as freelance truck drivers did not form a cohesive organization with a structure and routinized practice.

[3] Distinguishing between Character and Habit

PERRIN v. ANDERSON

784 F.2d 1040 (10th Cir. 1986)

LOGAN, CIRCUIT JUDGE.

* * *

This is a 42 U.S.C. § 1983 civil rights action for compensatory and punitive damages arising from the death of Terry Kim Perrin. Plaintiff, administratrix of Perrin's estate and guardian of his son, alleged that defendants, Donnie Anderson and Roland Von Schriltz, members of the Oklahoma Highway Patrol, deprived Perrin of his civil rights when they shot and killed him while attempting to obtain information concerning a traffic accident in which he had been involved. The jury found in favor of defendants.

In this appeal plaintiff contends that the district court erred in admitting * * * testimony by four police officers recounting previous violent encounters they had had with Perrin. * * *

A simple highway accident set off the bizarre chain of events that culminated in Perrin's death. The incident began when Perrin drove his car into the back of another car on an Oklahoma highway. After determining that the occupants of the car he had hit were uninjured, Perrin walked to his home, which was close to the highway.

Trooper Von Schriltz went to Perrin's home to obtain information concerning the accident. He was joined there by Trooper Anderson. They knocked on and off for ten to twenty minutes before persuading Perrin to open the door. Once Perrin opened the door, the defendant officers noticed Perrin's erratic behavior. The troopers testified that his moods would change quickly and that he was yelling that the accident was not his fault. Von Schriltz testified that he sensed a possibly dangerous situation and slowly moved his hand to his gun in order to secure its hammer with a leather thong. This action apparently provoked Perrin who then slammed the door. The door bounced open and Perrin then attacked Anderson. A fierce battle ensued between Perrin and the two officers, who unsuccessfully applied several chokeholds to Perrin in an attempt to subdue him. Eventually Anderson, who testified that he feared he was about to lose consciousness as a result of having been kicked repeatedly in the face and chest by Perrin, took out his gun, and, without issuing a warning, shot and killed Perrin. Anderson stated that he was convinced Perrin would have killed both officers had he not fired.

I

At trial the court permitted four police officers to testify that they had been involved previously in violent encounters with Perrin. These officers testified to Perrin's apparent hatred or fear of uniformed officers and his consistently violent response to any contact with them. For example, defendants presented evidence that on earlier occasions Perrin was completely uncontrollable and violent in the presence of uniformed officers. On one occasion he rammed his head into the bars and walls of his cell, requiring administration of a tranquilizer. Another time while barefoot, Perrin kicked loose a porcelain toilet bowl that was bolted to the floor. One officer testified that he encountered Perrin while responding to a public drunk call. Perrin attacked him, and during the following struggle Perrin tried to reach for the officer's weapon. The officer and his back-up had to carry Perrin handcuffed, kicking and screaming, to the squad car, where Perrin then kicked the windshield out of the car. Another officer testified that Perrin attacked him after Perrin was stopped at a vehicle checkpoint. During the ensuing struggle three policemen were needed to subdue Perrin, including one 6'2" officer weighing 250 pounds and one 6'6" officer weighing 350 pounds.

Defendants introduced this evidence to prove that Perrin was the first aggressor in the fight — a key element in defendants' self-defense claim. The court admitted the evidence over objection * * * . Plaintiff contends this was error.

A

* * *

B

Character and habit are closely akin. The district court found * * * that the testimony recounting Perrin's previous violent encounters with police officers was admissible as evidence of a habit under Fed. R. Evid. 406. Here, we concur. * * * The limitations on the methods of proving character set out in Rule 405 do not apply to proof of habit. Testimony concerning prior specific incidents is allowed. This court has defined "habit" as "a regular practice of meeting a particular kind of situation with a certain type of conduct, or a reflex behavior in a specific set of circumstances." The advisory committee notes to Rule 406 state that, "[w]hile adequacy of sampling and uniformity of response are key factors, precise standards for measuring their sufficiency for evidence purposes cannot be formulated." Fed. R. Evid. 406 advisory committee note. That Perrin might be proved to have a "habit" of reacting violently to uniformed police officers seems rather extraordinary. We believe, however, that defendants did in fact demonstrate that Perrin repeatedly reacted with extreme aggression when dealing with uniformed police officers.

Four police officers testified to at least five separate violent incidents, and plaintiff offered no evidence of any peaceful encounter between Perrin and the police. Five incidents ordinarily would be insufficient to establish the existence of a habit. *See Reyes v. Missouri Pacific Railway Co.,* 589 F.2d 791, 794-95 (5th Cir. 1979) (four convictions for public intoxication in three and one-half years insufficient to prove habit). But defendants here had made an offer of proof of testimony from eight police officers concerning numerous different incidents. To prevent undue prejudice to plaintiff, the district court permitted only four of these witnesses to testify, and it explicitly stated that it thought the testimony of the four officers had been sufficient to establish a habit. We hold that the district court properly admitted this evidence pursuant to Rule 406. There was adequate testimony to establish that Perrin invariably reacted with extreme violence to any contact with a uniformed police officer.

* * *

AFFIRMED.

NOTE

What constitutes sufficient proof of habit?

The draft of Rule 406 that was approved by the Supreme Court provided that habit or routine practice could be proved by testimony in the form of an opinion or by specific instances of conduct sufficient in number to warrant a finding that a habit existed or that a practice was routine. This provision was deleted by Congress, however. Apparently, Congress wished to allow courts to develop and consider methods of proof of habit on a case-by-case basis. Certainly one way to prove habit is to show that someone acted in a particular way at specific and frequent instances, and also that the person did not act otherwise at other similar instances. *Simplex, Inc. v. Diversified Energy Systems, Inc.,* 847 F.2d 1290, 1294 (7th Cir. 1988) (the Rule 406 inquiry "necessitates some comparison of the number of instances in which any such conduct occurs with the number in which no such conduct took place"; evidence of late performance of contracts was not admissible under Rule 406 where the proponent made no attempt at "a comparison of the number of late and defectively performed contracts relative to those without such inadequacies"). Probably the best testimony will be by a witness who has personal knowledge of the conduct of the relevant actor on numerous separate occasions.

Whatever the mode of proof, the touchstone of admissibility is to provide an "adequacy of sampling and uniformity of response" in specific circumstances. *Thompson v. Boggs,* 33 F.3d 847 (7th Cir. 1994) (plaintiff was properly precluded from offering evidence that the defendant had a habit of using excessive force while making arrests; evidence of five arrests employing excessive force was insufficient where the plaintiff offered no evidence of the total number of arrests that the defendant had performed; plaintiff "failed to establish that the requisite regularity is tested by the ratio of reaction to situations."). The burden of proving habit is on the proponent of the evidence. *Weil v. Seltzer*, 873 F.2d 1453 (D.C. Cir. 1989) (fact that evidence of specific instances was uncontradicted held not dispositive, since "the admissibility of habit evidence under Rule 406 does not hinge on the ability of the party seeking exclusion of the evidence to disprove the habitual character of the evidence. Rather, the burden of establishing the habitual nature of the evidence rests on the proponent of the evidence."). So if only a few instances are shown, and the conduct has occurred over the course of a long period of time, it is unlikely that sufficient evidence of habit will be found; and this is especially so if the instances of conduct are not exactly identical in detail. *Jones v. Southern Pacific R.R.*, 962 F.2d 447 (5th Cir. 1992) (in a negligence action arising out of a train accident, plaintiff offered evidence of prior safety infractions of the conductor; these were not admissible as habit evidence because the plaintiff had not demonstrated a regular practice of meeting a particular kind of situation with a specific type of conduct; the conductor was cited for nine safety infractions over a twenty-nine year period, and the infractions were varied). Conversely, habit is more likely to be found if the proponent can provide multiple instances of specific, identical conduct over a relatively short period of time.

PROBLEM 6-3

The prosecution has charged the defendant with the armed robbery of two people outside the football stadium at State University on November 1st of last year. The prosecution has made an opening statement and indicated that it would prove that the defendant was carrying a rifle as he approached each victim, demanded money, and obtained money from each victim. Defense counsel stated in her opening statement that the defendant was standing outside the stadium, having returned from hunting, and was asking for contributions for the Save the Speckled Bird Society, and that everyone who gave the defendant money made a voluntary contribution.

As the first witness, the prosecution calls one of the alleged victims to testify.

Prosecution: Calling your attention to November 1 of last year, did you go to a football game at State University?

First Victim: Yes I did.

Prosecution: Did anything unusual happen?

First Victim: I was robbed at rifle point as I entered the stadium.

Prosecution: Did you get a good look at the robber?

First Victim: Sure did.

Prosecution: Do you see him in the courtroom?

First Victim: Most certainly, that's him (pointing to a defendant) sitting over there.

Prosecution: Did the defendant say anything to you when you encountered him on November 1 of last year?

First Victim: Yes he did. He said he wanted my money.
Prosecution: Did you give it to him?
First Victim: Sure did, fifty-five dollars worth.
Prosecution: Did you know the defendant prior to November 1 of last year?
First Victim: I had seen him around but I personally did not know him well.
Prosecution: Had you heard others speak of the defendant prior to November 1 of last year?
First Victim: On many occasions. I know a bunch of people who know the defendant well and they spoke to me about him so much that I felt like I knew him well although I didn't, of course.
Prosecution: Based on your many conversations with those who knew the defendant would you tell us, please, what is the defendant's reputation in the community for good moral character?
Defendant: (1) Objection. __________.
The court: (2) __________.
Prosecution: Tell us whether, in your opinion based on what you heard, he is an honest man?
Defendant: Objection. Your Honor, this also is improper character evidence, and there is no basis for any opinion.
The court: (3) __________.
Prosecution: Where did defendant have the rifle when he said he wanted your money?
First Victim: He was pointing it at me.
Prosecution: Had you seen him beat his wife on a previous occasion?
Defendant: (4) Objection. __________.
The court: (5) __________.

The prosecution calls the second alleged victim to testify.

Prosecution: Did you go to a football game at State University on November 1 of last year?
Second Victim: Yes I did.
Prosecution: Did anything unusual happen?
Second Victim: I was robbed at rifle point as I entered the stadium.
Prosecution: Did you get a good look at the robber?
Second Victim: I did.
Prosecution: Do you see him in the courtroom?
Second Victim: Yup, that's him (pointing to defendant) sitting over there.
Prosecution: Did the defendant say anything to you at the time he robbed you?
Second Victim: He said to hand over my money.
Prosecution: Did you give it to him?
Second Victim: I gave him a hundred dollars.

Prosecution:	Did you know the defendant prior to November 1st of last year?
Second Victim:	I did not know him.
Prosecution:	Why did you give the defendant the money?
Second Victim:	I was scared.
Prosecution:	Why were you scared?
Second Victim:	Well, he had the rifle, and I had previously been warned that the defendant was a dangerous and violent man.
Defendant:	I object and move to strike everything after the word "rifle" as improper character evidence.
Prosecution:	We are not offering this as character evidence but to explain fear.
Defendant:	Then it's not relevant.
The court:	(6) ________.
Prosecution:	Is there any other reason you were scared?
Second Victim:	Well, the defendant is a big guy and he had a menacing look on his face.
Defendant:	I object and move to strike. This is nothing but character evidence.
The court:	(7) ________.

The prosecution's third witness claims to have been robbed by the defendant a week before the robberies charged in this case.

Prosecution:	Did anything unusual happen to you on October 25th last year?
Prior Victim:	I was robbed as I was entering the football stadium.
Prosecution:	Who was it that robbed you?
Defendant:	Objection. Impermissible specific act evidence.
Prosecution:	We shall prove, your Honor, that the defendant pointed a rifle at the witness and demanded money. It proves intent.
Defendant:	It's character evidence and inadmissible.
The court:	(8) ________.

The prosecution rests and defendant calls his roommate to the stand.

Defendant:	How do you know the defendant?
Roommate:	For three years we have roomed together, and I have seen him in many different roles in the community in which we both live. I know many others who know him as well, and we've discussed the defendant frequently.
Defendant:	What is his reputation for good moral character?
Prosecution:	Objection. Improper character evidence.
The court:	(9) ________.
Defendant:	In your opinion, is he a law-abiding man?
Prosecution:	Objection! Improper character evidence.
The court:	(10) ________.

Defendant: Are you aware of any specific examples that demonstrate that the defendant is a law-abiding person?
Roommate: I sure am.
Defendant: Can you give us an example?
Prosecution: Objection. Improper character evidence.
The court: (11) __________.
Defendant: Do you and the defendant belong to any clubs?
Roommate: Yes, we each belong to the Save the Speckled Bird Society.
Defendant: Have you ever been with the defendant when he solicits funds for the Society?
Roommate: Yes, we've done that together six or seven times.
Defendant: Approximately when did you do the soliciting?
Roommate: We always did it before football games.
Defendant: Did the defendant ever have a rifle with him?
Roommate: Every time. He always went hunting before the games and arrived to solicit funds carrying his rifle.
Defendant: Did he every point his rifle at anyone while soliciting?
Prosecution: Objection. These other instances establish nothing.
Defendant: Your Honor, the witness is going to say that on each occasion the defendant deliberately and carefully put his rifle on the ground while soliciting. It's admissible as (12) __________.
The court: (13) __________.
Defendant: Based on your knowledge of the defendant, what is your opinion of his character for truthfulness?
Prosecution: Objection. Improper character evidence.
The court: (14) __________.
Defendant: Based on your knowledge of the defendant, do you believe that he pointed his rifle at these alleged victims and robbed them?
Prosecution: Objection. Improper character and opinion evidence.
The court: (15) __________.
Defendant: Have you ever had any conversations with the defendant about use of force?
Roommate: We have had several conversations.
Defendant: What did the defendant say to you about the use of force?
Prosecution: Objection. This is not proper character evidence.
The court: (16) __________.
Defendant: No further questions.

Cross-examination by the prosecution.

Prosecution: Have you heard that defendant was arrested on four prior occasions for armed robbery?
Defendant: Objection! Improper character evidence.
The court: (17) ________.
Prosecution: In fact, you yourself know that defendant was arrested on four prior occasions for armed robbery?
Defendant: Objection! Improper character evidence.
The court: (18) ________.
Prosecution: Isn't it true that you were aware that the defendant had sexual relations with a 15-year-old?
Defendant: Objection. Improper cross-examination as to character and unduly prejudicial.
The court: (19) ________.
Prosecution: No further questions.

The prosecution calls a police officer to the stand during rebuttal.

Prosecution: Do you know the defendant?
Officer: Yes. I have known him for many years.
Prosecution: What about First Victim and Second Victim.
Officer: Yes. I also have known them for many years.
Prosecution: What is your opinion as to the defendant's character for law abidingness?
Defendant: Objection. Improper character evidence.
The court: (20) ________.
Prosecution: What is your opinion as to First Victim's moral character?
Defendant: Objection! Improper character evidence.
The court: (21) ________.
Prosecution: Who is more law abiding in your opinion, Second Victim or the defendant?
Defendant: Objection! Improper character evidence.
The court: (22) ________.

PROBLEM 6-4

The plaintiff in a personal injury case arising out of a two-car automobile accident sues the defendant, claiming that the defendant was speeding and failed to maintain a proper lookout at the time of the accident. The defendant denies liablity and alleges that the plaintiff was negligent and caused the accident. The defendant also alleges that the plaintiff failed to wear her seatbelt, and that she would not have been injured if she had been wearing the belt.

The plaintiff calls defendant's neighbor to testify.

Plaintiff:	Have you spoken with others in the community about the defendant so that you know his reputation?
Neighbor:	Yes.
Plaintiff:	Would you tell us then what his reputation for careless or careful driving is?
Defendant:	Objection. Improper character evidence.
The court:	(1) ________.
Plaintiff:	Have you ridden with the defendant while he was driving his car?
Neighbor:	Yes.
Plaintiff:	What is your opinion of his carelessness or carefulness as a driver?
Defendant:	Objection. Improper character evidence
The court:	(2) ________.
Plaintiff:	Has the defendant ever exceeded the speed limit while you were in the defendant's car?
Defendant:	Objection Improper character evidence.
The court:	(3) ________.
Plaintiff:	Does the defendant like to drive fast, in your opinion?
Defendant:	Objection. Improper character evidence.
The court:	(4) ________.
Plaintiff:	Was defendant ever ticketed for speeding while you were driving with him?
Defendant:	Objection. Improper character evidence.
The court:	(5) ________.
Plaintiff:	Has the defendant ever daydreamed while you were riding with him?
Defendant:	Objection. Improper character evidence.
The court:	(6) ________.
Plaintiff:	Did the defendant ever fall asleep while driving to your knowledge?
Defendant:	Objection. Improper character evidence.
The court:	(7) ________.
Plaintiff:	Did the defendant admit to you that he fell asleep and caused an accident last year?
Defendant:	Objection. Improper character evidence.
The court:	(8) ________.
Plaintiff:	Haven't you said that the defendant is the worst driver you ever saw?
Neighbor:	Objection. Improper character evidence.
The court:	(9) ________.

Defendant calls the plaintiff's former husband.

Defendant:	How careful would you say your former spouse is?
Plaintiff:	Objection improper character evidence.
The court:	(10) ________.

Defendant: Does the car your ex-wife was driving when the accident occurred have an automatic transmission?

Ex-Husband: No, it is a stick shift.

Defendant: Isn't it true that she cannot drive a stick shift and has always had problems driving a car without automatic transmission?

Plaintiff: Objection. Improper character evidence.

The court: (11) ________.

Defendant: Was your ex-wife ever convicted of reckless driving?

Plaintiff: Objection. Improper character evidence.

The court: (12) ________.

Defendant: Was your ex-wife's license ever suspended for traffic infractions?

Plaintiff: Objection. Improper character evidence.

The court: (13) ________.

The plaintiff cross-examines.

Plaintiff: How many times have you ridden in a car driven by your ex-wife?

Ex-husband: Hundreds of times.

Plaintiff: How many of those hundreds of times did she fasten her seat belt?

Defendant: Objection. Improper character evidence.

The court: (14) ________.

RULE #11: THE RULES ON CHARACTER AND BAD ACT EVIDENCE ARE APPLIED DIFFERENTLY IN CASES INVOLVING RAPE OR SEXUAL ABUSE — EVIDENCE OF THE VICTIM'S PRIOR SEXUAL ACTIVITY IS MORE STRICTLY REGULATED, WHILE EVIDENCE OF THE DEFENDANT'S PRIOR BAD ACTS IS MORE PERMISSIVELY TREATED.

[1] Federal Rule 412

Rule 412. Sex Offense Cases; Relevance of Alleged Victim's Past Sexual Behavior or Alleged Sexual Predisposition

(a) EVIDENCE GENERALLY INADMISSIBLE — The following evidence is not admissible in any civil or criminal proceeding involving alleged sexual misconduct except as provided in subdivisions (b) and (c):

(1) Evidence offered to prove that any alleged victim engaged in other sexual behavior.

(2) Evidence offered to prove any alleged victim's sexual predisposition.

(b) EXCEPTIONS —

(1) In a criminal case, the following evidence is admissible, if otherwise admissible under these rules:

(A) evidence of specific instances of sexual behavior by the alleged victim offered to prove that a person other than the accused was the source of semen, injury or other physical evidence;

(B) evidence of specific instances of sexual behavior by the alleged victim with respect to the person accused of the sexual misconduct offered by the accused to prove consent or by the prosecution; and

(C) evidence the exclusion of which would violate the constitutional rights of the defendant.

(2) In a civil case, evidence offered to prove the sexual behavior or sexual predisposition of any alleged victim is admissible if it is otherwise admissible under these rules and its probative value substantially outweighs the danger of harm to any victim and of unfair prejudice to any party. Evidence of an alleged victim's reputation is admissible only if it has been placed in controversy by the alleged victim.

(c) PROCEDURE TO DETERMINE ADMISSIBILITY —

(1) A party intending to offer evidence under subdivision (b) must —

(A) file a written motion at least 14 days before trial specifically describing the evidence and stating the purpose for which it is offered unless the court, for good cause requires a different time for filing or permits filing during trial; and

(B) serve the motion on all parties and notify the alleged victim or, when appropriate, the alleged victim's guardian or representative.

(2) Before admitting evidence under this rule the court must conduct a hearing *in camera* and afford the victim and parties the right to attend and be heard. The motion, related papers, and the record of the hearing must be sealed and remain under seal unless the court orders otherwise.

[2] Rape Shield Protection and the Defendant's Constitutional Rights

UNITED STATES v. BEAR STOPS
997 F.2d 451 (8th Cir. 1993)

HANSEN, CIRCUIT JUDGE:

Kermit Oris Bear Stops appeals his conviction of aggravated sexual abuse of P.M. (count I); his conviction of aggravated sexual abuse of his son (count II); and his conviction of abusive sexual contact with B.B. (count III). Bear Stops challenges several evidentiary rulings made during the seven-day trial and claims that the district court erred in refusing to declare a mistrial. We reverse the conviction of Bear Stops on count I of the indictment and affirm the conviction of Bear Stops on counts II and III.

I.

Bear Stops lived with T.M. and her son, P.M., periodically from approximately 1984 until February of 1990. During this time, B.B. was born.

Depending on the state of Bear Stops and T.M's unstable relationship, T.M. and her children, P.M., B.B., and a younger daughter, S.B., lived either in Fort Yates, North Dakota, or in the Red Scaffold/Cherry Creek area on the Cheyenne River Indian reservation in South Dakota. Bear Stops's family lived in the Red Scaffold/Cherry Creek area, and T.M.'s parents lived in Fort Yates.

In September of 1989, P.M. was living with his grandparents in Fort Yates. When doing dishes by the sink with his grandmother, P.M. told her that he had been sexually abused by Bear Stops, and she then relayed this information to T.M. T.M. confronted Bear Stops and a fight ensued. T.M. left Bear Stops, taking B.B. with her, and went to stay in a woman's shelter in South Dakota. Once they were no longer living with Bear Stops, B.B. told T.M. that Bear Stops had sexually abused him also.

* * *

Bear Stops denied that he sexually assaulted P.M., presented an alibi defense for the few days surrounding the approximate date listed in the indictment, introduced testimony demonstrating inconsistencies between the description of the assault given by P.M., and attempted to submit evidence regarding prior sexual assaults of P.M. by other persons. The evidence regarding the prior sexual assaults was largely excluded by the district court. With respect to counts II and III, the government presented the testimony of the child victim B.B., as well as the testimony of his mother, of a social worker, and of a pediatrician. The expert testimony presented regarding the symptoms of a sexually abused child also pertained to the counts involving B.B. Bear Stops denied the allegations with respect to B.B.

* * * Bear Stops raises several evidentiary issues, most challenging the exclusion of evidence indicating that P.M. had been assaulted by other persons.

II.

Bear Stops moved pursuant to Federal Rule of Evidence 412 to introduce evidence of sexual abuse of P.M. committed by persons other than Bear Stops. Bear Stops made numerous offers of proof during trial regarding that evidence. The district court excluded the evidence in large part based upon Federal Rule of Evidence 403. Bear Stops's motion for mistrial because of the exclusion was denied. On appeal, Bear Stops argues that the exclusion of such evidence violated his Sixth Amendment right to effective confrontation and cross-examination and his due process rights under the Fifth Amendment. Bear Stops specifically argues that the evidence of sexual abuse of P.M. by persons other than Bear Stops is constitutionally required to be admitted (1) to provide an alternative explanation for the characteristics identified as frequently observed in sexually abused children and exhibited by P.M.; (2) to provide an alternative explanation to testimony regarding P.M.'s alleged bloody underwear; (3) to establish an alternative source for P.M.'s sexual knowledge; (4) to challenge the accuracy of the child's identification of the perpetrator; and (5) to challenge the credibility of P.M. The government contends that Rules 403 and 412 precluded the admission of such evidence. We agree with Bear Stops but only for the first two reasons.

A.

Bear Stops offered uncontroverted evidence of an incident in 1988, when P.M. was six years old and staying with Bear Stops's sister, Delores Cook, at Red Scaffold, South Dakota, in which P.M. was taken under a bridge and sexually assaulted, specifically anal penetration by the penis, by three older boys ages nine, ten, and twelve. The assault by the three older boys occurred approximately during the same time period as count I's alleged sexual abuse by Bear Stops.

At trial, Debra Baune, a licensed clinical social worker, testified that sexually abused children often exhibit regressive behaviors, such as bed wetting after being potty trained, hyperactivity, aggressiveness, and nightmares, and the children may also act out sexually as a result of the emotional trauma caused by the abuse. Dr. Bean, a licensed psychiatrist, testified likewise. P.M.'s grandparents and mother each testified that P.M. had shown such behaviors after he had been in Red Scaffold. Bear Stops asserts that because of the government's evidence that P.M. exhibited the symptoms of a sexually abused child, the jury determined that P.M. must have been sexually abused. Bear Stops concludes that the jury assumed that the perpetrator of the sexual abuse must have been Bear Stops unless he can put forth an alternative explanation for P.M.'s symptoms by submitting evidence of the uncontroverted sexual assault inflicted by the three boys. Bear Stops argues that the exclusion of this evidence denied him his constitutional right to a fair trial.

* * * The Supreme Court has stated that "the right to present relevant testimony is not without limitation." *Michigan v. Lucas*, 111 S. Ct. 1743, 1746 (1991). "The right 'may, in appropriate cases, bow to accommodate other legitimate interests in the criminal trial process.' " *Rock v. Arkansas,* 483 U.S. 44, 55. * * * "Restrictions on criminal defendant's rights to confront adverse witnesses and to present evidence 'may not be arbitrary or disproportionate to the purposes they are designed to serve.' "

The district court acknowledged that the proffered evidence, when offered to establish an alternative explanation for why P.M. exhibited the behavioral manifestations of a sexually abused child, was relevant and probative on that point. Fed. R. Evid. 402. We agree. This point was an important one at trial because little physical evidence of the alleged sexual assault was presented and because P.M. had been somewhat inconsistent in describing the details regarding the alleged assault or assaults by Bear Stops. With the proof that P.M. exhibited the symptoms of a sexually abused child and without an alternative explanation, the jury may have been led directly to the conclusion that Bear Stops was the perpetrator of the sexual abuse and convicted him on count I largely on that basis.

The district court limited the admission of the evidence regarding the incident with the three older boys relying on Federal Rules of Evidence 403 and 412. Rule 412 generally prohibits "evidence of an alleged victim's past sexual behavior" with an exception for evidence that is "constitutionally required." * * * In our judgment, the fact that P.M. was sexually assaulted by the three older boys was constitutionally required to be admitted.

The district court, however, rigorously limited the admission of the evidence after carefully balancing the probative value against its negative effects. * * *

The district court expressed its grave concern about subjecting P.M., a child who has been victimized by other persons in a sexual manner, to further difficult questioning regarding such sensitive matters. The court stated that the "inevitable effect of admitting such evidence" would be the harassment of P.M., albeit unintentional, and an "unwarranted intrusion into his private life — effects that Rule 412 was designed to prevent." The court further expressed the concern that the incident with the three older boys was a collateral matter and that evidence regarding the incident may confuse and distract the jury and could be misused by the jury.

We share the concerns expressed by the district court and determine that the "restrictions on criminal defendant's rights to confront adverse witnesses and to present evidence" in this case were not arbitrary. We do conclude, however, that the restrictions placed on Bear Stops's rights to confront adverse witnesses and to present evidence were "disproportionate to the purposes they are designed to serve." As noted by the district court, the admission of evidence may be limited, in accordance with the constitution, to only a sanitized version of the sexual assault sufficient to effectuate the purpose for which the evidence was offered. The version allowed in this case, however, was so sanitized that it was insufficient to support the purpose for which it was offered. During the seven-day trial, the only evidence admitted pertaining to the sexual assault by the three older boys was the testimony of P.M.'s grandmother, E.M.; the testimony of Dr. Peter C. Peterson, a clinical psychologist in North Dakota who treated P.M.; and the testimony of Bear Stops's expert witness, Dr. Bean.

On the second day of trial during the grandmother's testimony on direct examination, the following exchange took place:

Q: Do you ever bring up the subject [of sexual abuse] with him [P.M.], or how does it come up?

A: [by E.M.]: Well, the first time at the sink, well, I brought up the subject. But, then, to my knowledge, that case — the social worker in Eagle Butte told me that he [P.M.] was molested by three older boys. Then that's when — that's when he told me that Oris [Bear Stops] got to him first before them three boys.

Q: And were you aware of whether that first — or, that incident with the three boys was investigated?

A: I wasn't aware of it until I talked to the social worker and he [P.M.] was turned over to me.

Also on that same day of trial, Dr. Peterson testified on cross-examination that one of the reasons that P.M. was brought to him for treatment was because P.M. had been sexually acting out.

Q: Did they tell you with whom he was sexually acting out?

A: My recollection was that — now, this didn't come from the [M.]s. This came through hospital staff and input from school staff, that he was inappropriately touching other students and, apparently, there had been some of that going the other way.

Q: What do you mean by that?

A: My understanding was that he was allegedly molested by some other kids.

On the final day of trial, a deposition of Dr. Bean, a licensed psychiatrist, was admitted as testimony of an expert witness for Bear Stops.

Q: * * * I'm going to ask a hypothetical now. Assume for the purposes of this question that a six-year-old boy was the subject of a violent sexual assault, including sodomy, perpetrated by three boys between the ages of 10 and 13 years. Would that six-year-old boy be likely or not be likely to exhibit the symptoms you described?

A: Well, all things being equally would be likely to show symptomatology of some traumatic event. And that would be a likely traumatic event that would result in the symptoms that we have previously discussed.

Q: Doctor, I need to ask another hypothetical. For the purposes of this question assume that a six-year-old boy is sexually assaulted, which assault includes sodomy, by three older and stronger boys. Now, would that six-year-old boy be likely or not be likely to exhibit the symptoms that you have described?

A: He would be likely to exhibit symptoms also.

Q: Okay. And one final hypothetical, Doctor. Assume a six-year-old boy is sexually molested by three boys. Based on those facts are you able to form an opinion as to whether or not that six-year-old boy would be likely to exhibit the symptoms you have described?

A: I guess I'm not certain what you mean by sexual molestation at this time. Do you mean with sodomy again? Is that the same hypothetical?

Q: Those are the only facts I can give you for this hypothetical, Doctor, and I need to have you tell me if you can form an opinion based on those?

A: Well, it really depends on the nature of the sexual molestation. If it includes severe physical abuse with sexual aggressive activity including sodomy, then, again, my answer is very likely. If the sexual molestation is very minor the child may not show symptomatology. Really, the nature and degree of symptom formation in children and adults following emotionally traumatic events is related to the degree, intensity, duration of these events. That is, the greater the degree the greater duration, the greater the intensity the greater the symptom findings.

As demonstrated by Dr. Bean's response to the last hypothetical, the testimony of E.M. and of Dr. Peterson regarding the assault by the three older boys was too vague to provide even a potential alternative explanation for why P.M. exhibited the symptoms of a sexually abused child. No information was before the jury that the assault by the three older boys was the same type of sexual abuse as allegedly perpetrated by Bear Stops. In fact, Dr. Peterson's testimony seems to imply the "sexual molestation" by the three older boys was only inappropriate touching rather than anal penetration by a penis. The jury was also not presented with any evidence indicating that the events occurred approximately during the same time period as the alleged assault by Bear Stops. Without sufficient information to determine whether a potential alternative explanation for P.M.'s behavior existed, the serious risk of a conviction on erroneous reasoning identified by the trial court remained. The basic information of the undisputed assault by the three boys (the type of sexual assault and the time period during which it occurred) was constitutionally required for Bear Stops to receive a fair trial.

The district court's concerns regarding the admission of the evidence were valid. Restricting the testimony regarding the sexual assault by the three boys to only the references volunteered by the grandmother and Dr. Peterson, and the hypotheticals asked of Dr. Bean, was, however, disproportionate to those concerns. Because the evidence about the incident with the three older boys was uncontroverted, the potential for jury confusion and for a distracting "mini-trial" about the event was minimal. To avoid the intrusion on P.M.'s privacy, testimony about the basic facts of the incident could have been introduced through P.M.'s mother who discovered the sexual assault by the three older boys and stopped it, or through any other witness other than P.M. who had knowledge about it. Because of both its relevance and its uncontroverted nature, the evidence would also be a likely candidate for stipulation. Accordingly, we hold that the district court abused its discretion and erred when it refused to admit thc basic factual details (time, place, age and sex of the perpetrators, the type of sexual assault, etc.) when that evidence was offered to provide an alternative explanation for the prosecution's persuasive evidence about P.M.'s behavioral manifestations of a sexually abused child.

B.

Bear Stops argues that proffered testimony regarding alleged bloody underwear of P.M. should not have been excluded. At trial, the child victim, P.M., after describing an incident of sexual abuse by Bear Stops, testified as follows:

> Q: All right. And can you tell the jury before that happened what you were doing, or where you were at, or some things that happened right before that?
>
> A: I was at Delores'.
>
> Q: You were at Delores'. And that is Delores Bear Stops [Cook]?

(Nodded head up-and-down).

P.M. also testified that Delores told P.M. "not to tell" about the sexual assault by Bear Stops. Agent McConaghy testified that he interviewed P.M. and P.M. described the sexual assault by Bear Stops.

> Q: Did [P.M.] indicate what had occurred, what happened after that event?
>
> A: He stated when Oris [Bear Stops] was done he had fallen asleep, when he woke up Oris was gone. He advised his rectum area was bleeding and there was blood coming from his rectum area. He advised that there was no one else being in the house he went to his Aunt Delores' which was close by and she washed him up, gave him a bath, and put him to sleep.

Following her testimony about confronting Bear Stops regarding the alleged abuse, P.M.'s mother, T.M., testified as follows:

A: When [P.M.] stayed with Delores I went to her house and collected his clothing. And I found his shorts and they had blood on them.

Q: In what part of the shorts?

A: In the anal part.

Q: Did you say or do anything, or what was going through your mind at that time when you discovered that?

A: I had a feeling that something had happened to him.

In an offer of proof, Bear Stops sought permission to cross-examine T.M. about the incident involving the three older boys and to then call Kay Traversie, a social worker at State Social Services in South Dakota during the relevant times, to testify that the sexual abuse report she prepared indicates that T.M. reported finding P.M.'s underwear hidden at Cook's house and that T.M. associated it with the assault by the three older boys.

The alleged bloody underwear is the only physical evidence of a sexual assault of P.M. The alleged sexual assault by Bear Stops and the uncontroverted sexual assault by the three older boys occurred in approximately the same time period. Absent any proof of the type of and the timing of the sexual assault by the three older boys, the jury likely concluded that the alleged bloody underwear could only be the result of sexual abuse of P.M. by Bear Stops. Precluding Bear Stops from cross-examining P.M.'s mother on this point and offering a potential alternative explanation for the bloody underwear was a denial of his Sixth Amendment right. Evidence regarding the facts of the sexual assault by the three older boys should have been admitted for the purpose of providing an alternative explanation for the bloody underwear. As explained in the preceding section, however, the district court may control the manner in which the testimony on this matter is presented and the amount of evidence introduced on the subject.

Because the basic evidence about the assault by the three older boys was constitutionally required, and its exclusion was not harmless error, the conviction of Bear Stops on count I must be reversed.

* * *

For the reasons stated above, we reverse the conviction of Bear Stops on count I of the indictment and affirm the conviction of Bear Stops on counts II and III.

NOTES

1. Is Rule 412 applicable to civil cases?

As amended by Congress in 1994, Rule 412 applies in all civil and criminal cases "involving alleged sexual misconduct." This term is left undefined.

Clearly it applies to cases alleging rape and sexual abuse, whether civil or criminal. But the breadth of the term "involving alleged sexual misconduct" has also been held to cover claims such as for sexual harassment in employment. As such, the amended Rule is far broader that the original Rule, which was limited to criminal cases in which a sex crime was charged. For civil cases, subdivision (c) of Rule 412 permits any type of evidence of the victim's sexual behavior (e.g., reputation, opinion and specific acts), but only so long as the probative value of the evidence substantially outweighs the danger of harm to any victim and the danger of prejudice to any party. Subdivision (c) mandates a "Areverse 403" test, but with one variation: harm to the victim is specifically weighed together with prejudice to a party on the exclusionary side of the scale. The balancing test set forth in subdivision (c) consequently provides for a strong presumption of exclusion of evidence of the plaintiff's sexual behavior — in contrast to Rule 403, which provides for a strong presumption of admissibility.

Interestingly, in a criminal case, if a specific sexual act is offered for one of the two limited purposes provided in the Rule (i.e. an alternative source for the injury, or prior activity between the victim and the defendant bearing on consent), the act is admissible so long as it also satisfies Rule 403. That is, there is no heightened exclusionary balancing test applied. This makes sense, because if the evidence is narrow enough to fit one of the limited exceptions to subdivision (b), there is little reason to filter it further through a strict exclusionary balancing test.

2. How does Rule 412 apply if the complainant has made prior false claims of rape?

See Saltzburg, Martin, and Capra, *Federal Rules of Evidence Manual* (9th ed. 2006):

> Suppose the victim has made previous allegations of rape that turned out to be false. Does the rape shield law exclude evidence of prior false allegations of rape? This depends in part on whether a false allegation of rape is "sexual behavior" within the meaning of the Rule. The Advisory Committee Note to the amended Rule states flatly that "[e]vidence offered to prove allegedly false prior claims by the victim is not barred by Rule 412," though it might be barred by Rules 404 and 403. Yet the Advisory Committee Note also describes the sexual behavior excluded by the Rule quite broadly. It states that the word "behavior" "should be construed to include activities of the mind, such as fantasies or dreams." It could certainly be argued that false allegations are related to activities of the mind of a sexual nature, and so are covered by the exclusionary language of Rule 412. There is something to the government's argument in *United States v. Cournoyer*, 118 F.3d 1279 (8th Cir. 1997), that evidence of prior false rape allegations is "inseparable from evidence of the victim's past sexual behavior, which Rule 412 was designed to exclude."
>
> In the end, however, we believe that prior false rape allegations are sufficiently distinguishable from sexual activity that they should not be covered by Rule 412. Evidence of a false rape allegation does not intrude into the zone of private and personal activity that the Rule

is trying to protect. Moreover, such evidence clearly goes to an important matter of credibility, independent of its sexual content. It is one thing to argue that a rape complainant is not credible because she has engaged in sexual activity — this is clearly prohibited by the Rule. But it is another thing to argue that she is not credible because she has falsely accused someone of a crime. Professor Clifford Fishman, in *Consent, Credibility, and the Constitution: Evidence Relating to a Sex Offense Complainant's Past Sexual Behavior,* 44 Cath. L. Rev. 711, 770 (1995), puts the argument this way:

> Rape shield legislation should not exclude evidence that the complainant previously made false sex offense accusations. * * * Rape shield legislation is designed to protect a complainant from exposure of her prior sexual conduct. A prior false accusation is not "sexual conduct," thus the statute should not protect the complainant from exposure of prior lies or falsehoods. * * * It is appropriate for the law to protect a woman's decision to have sex with other men from unnecessary exposure because, among other reasons, it has only minimal probative value as to whether or not she consented with the defendant. A false accusation of rape, by contrast, reveals flaws in character — a ruthless disregard of the truth and a willingness to use sexual allegations unjustly — which are highly relevant as to whether she has falsely accused the defendant. Such conduct deserves exposure, not protection.

See also Christopher Bopst, *Rape Shield Laws and Prior False Accusations of Rape: The Need for Meaningful Legislative Reform*, 24 J. Legis. 125, 145 (1998) (arguing that "prior false rape accusations represent evidence of lies, not sex, and do not fall within the protections of the rape shield statutes"); Hon. Denise Johnson, *Prior False Allegations of Rape: Falsus in Uno, Falsus in Omnibus?* 7 Yale J. L. and Feminism 243 (1995) (arguing that false claims of rape should be treated the same as any other false claim when offered for impeachment).

The *Cournoyer* Court ultimately found it unnecessary to decide whether prior false rape allegations "must survive the rigors of Rule 412 scrutiny." It reasoned that even if Rule 412 did not apply, the evidence of false allegations would have to pass muster under Rules 404 and 403. In *Cournoyer*, the evidence of false allegations was to be brought in through an opinion witness, but the defense made no effort to establish a foundation for the witness' testimony. Given "defense counsel's failure to follow up, for example, with foundation testimony to support an opinion as to reputation, or with an offer of proof to show relevant, specific prior conduct," the evidence was properly excluded. A number of other courts, without mentioning the Advisory Committee Note to Rule 412, have held that the Rule excludes false accusations of rape.

3. What kind of conduct is "sexual behavior" within the meaning of Rule 412?

While a false allegation of rape probably should not be considered "sexual behavior" within the meaning of the Rule, the term "sexual behavior" is clearly intended to mean more than actual participation in actual sexual activity. A good example of the proper breadth of the term "sexual behavior" is found in *Wolak v. Spucci*, 217 F.3d 157 (2d Cir. 2000). The plaintiff, a female police officer, alleged a hostile work environment. The plaintiff claimed among other things that fellow officers placed pornography throughout the police station — often just before she came to work. A jury found that there was a hostile work environment but that it did not injure the plaintiff. The trial court had permitted the defendants to introduce the fact that the plaintiff had watched sex acts and pornographic videos at several parties. The articulated purpose was to show that the plaintiff could not have been as upset about the pornography in the workplace as she claimed. The defendants argued that Rule 412 did not apply, because the plaintiff's viewing of sex acts did not constitute "sexual behavior" within the meaning of the Rule. But the Court rejected this argument, noting that the Advisory Committee Note to the amendment explains that the term "sexual behavior" encompasses "activities of the mind, such as fantasies," and concluding that because "viewing pornography falls within Rule 412's broad definition of behavior, defendants' extensive questions were subject to the Rule." In the context of a civil case, this meant that the special exclusionary balancing test applied to the evidence. The Court held that the Trial Court abused its discretion in admitting the evidence, because its probative value did not substantially outweigh the risk of prejudice and harm to the victim."

[3] Federal Rules 413, 414, and 415

[a] The Congressional Enactments

Rule 413. Evidence of Similar Crimes in Sexual Assault Cases

(a) In a criminal case in which the defendant is accused of an offense of sexual assault, evidence of the defendant's commission of another offense or offenses of sexual assault is admissible, and may be considered for its bearing on any matter to which it is relevant.

(b) In a case in which the Government intends to offer evidence under this rule, the attorney for the Government shall disclose the evidence to the defendant, including statements of witnesses or a summary of the substance of any testimony that is expected to be offered, at least fifteen days before the scheduled date of trial or at such later time as the court may allow for good cause.

(c) This rule shall not be construed to limit the admission or consideration of evidence under any other rule.

(d) For purposes of this rule and Rule 415, "offense of sexual assault" means a crime under Federal law or the law of a State (as defined in section 513 of title 18, United States Code) that involved —

(1) any conduct proscribed by chapter 109A of title 18, United States Code;

(2) contact, without consent, between any part of the defendant's body or an object and the genitals or anus of another person;

(3) contact, without consent, between the genitals or anus of the defendant and any part of another person's body;

(4) deriving sexual pleasure or gratification from the infliction of death, bodily injury, or physical pain on another person; or

(5) an attempt or conspiracy to engage in conduct described in paragraph (1)-(4).

Rule 414. Evidence of Similar Crimes in Child Molestation Cases

(a) In a criminal case in which the defendant is accused of an offense of child molestation, evidence of the defendant's commission of another offense or offenses of child molestation is admissible, and may be considered for its bearing on any matter to which it is relevant.

(b) In a case in which the Government intends to offer evidence under this rule, the attorney for the Government shall disclose the evidence to the defendant, including statements of witnesses or a summary of the substance of any testimony that is expected to be offered, at least fifteen days before the scheduled date of trial or at such later time as the court may allow for good cause.

(c) This rule shall not be construed to limit the admission or consideration of evidence under any other rule.

(d) For purposes of this rule and Rule 415, "child" means a person below the age of fourteen, and "offense of child molestation" means a crime under Federal law or the law of a State (as defined in section 513 of title 18, United States Code) that involved —

(1) any conduct proscribed by chapter 109A of title 18, United States Code, that was committed in relation to a child;

(2) any conduct proscribed by chapter 110 of title 18, United States Code;

(3) contact between any part of the defendant's body or an object and the genitals or anus of a child;

(4) contact between the genitals or anus of the defendant and any part of the body of a child;

(5) deriving sexual pleasure or gratification from the infliction of death, bodily injury, or physical pain on a child; or

(6) an attempt or conspiracy to engage in conduct described in paragraph (1)-(5).

Rule 415. Evidence of Similar Acts in Civil Cases Concerning Sexual Assault or Child Molestation

(a) In a civil case in which a claim for damages or other relief is predicated on a party's alleged commission of conduct constituting an offense of sexual assault or child molestation, evidence of that party's commission of another offense or offenses of sexual assault or child molestation is admissible and may be considered as provided in Rule 413 and Rule 414 of these rules.

(b) A party who intends to offer evidence under this Rule shall disclose the evidence to the party against whom it will be offered, including statements of witnesses or a summary of the substance of any testimony that is expected to be offered, at least fifteen days before the scheduled date of trial or at such later time as the court may allow for good cause.

(c) This rule shall not be construed to limit the admission or consideration of evidence under any other rule.

[b] Scope of the Rules Permitting Use of the Defendant's Prior Sex Offenses

Rules 413, 414, and 415 were enacted directly by Congress. They did not go through the usual route of proposal by the Judicial Conference and approval by the Supreme Court. The rules are substantively identical. The goal of these rules is to provide for more liberal admissibility of the defendant's prior sex offenses in a case involving alleged rape or sexual abuse. Rule 413 applies to criminal cases involving sexual assault. Rule 414 applies to criminal cases involving child molestation. Rule 415 applies to civil cases involving sexual assault or child molestation.

These rules create an exception to Rule 404(b) in sexual assault cases, where the prosecution or plaintiff wishes to offer a previous act of sexual assault committed by the defendant. Under Rule 404(b), for example, the prosecution would have to articulate a not-for-character purpose for a prior act of sexual assault, such as intent or motive. The prosecution would be prohibited by Rule 404(b) from offering the prior sexual assault simply to prove that the defendant has a propensity to commit sex crimes. Under Rule 413, however, it appears that the prosecution can offer a prior act of sexual assault explicitly to prove the defendant's bad character. A limiting instruction is not required, because the jury is free to use the prior act of sexual misconduct as evidence that the defendant has a propensity to commit sex crimes.

Rule 413 singles out sexual assault crimes for special treatment. This can lead to unusual results. Assume that a defendant is being tried for a rape-murder, and has two different prior bad acts in his past — a rape and a murder. Under the Rule, the prior rape can be admitted even if it is offered solely to prove propensity, while the murder cannot be admitted without the articulation of a not-for-propensity purpose.

One justification for this differentiation, however, is that sexual assault crimes pose unique difficulties of proof. Often there is no physical evidence that ties the defendant to the charged crime; often the jury must make a credibility determination between the victim and the defendant.

[c] Constitutional Challenges and the Applicability of Rule 403 to Uncharged Acts of Sexual Misconduct

UNITED STATES v. LEMAY

260 F. 3d 1018 2001 (9th Cir. 2001)

Trott, Circuit Judge:

Fred LeMay appeals his convictions for two counts of child molestation in violation of 18 U.S.C. §§ 2241 and 3231. We must decide whether admission of his prior acts of child molestation under Rule 414 of the Federal Rules of Evidence violated his constitutional right to due process. We agree with numerous other courts that Rule 403 remains applicable to evidence introduced under Rule 414, and, if conscientiously applied, will protect defendants from propensity evidence so inflammatory as to jeopardize their right to a fair trial. We therefore conclude that Rule 414 is constitutional.

In so holding, we emphasize that Rule 414 is not a blank check entitling the government to introduce whatever evidence it wishes, no matter how minimally relevant and potentially devastating to the defendant. We also emphasize that district courts must apply the balancing test of Rule 403 in a manner that allows for meaningful appellate review. We conclude that the district judge in this case applied Rule 403 conscientiously and did not abuse his discretion in finding that LeMay's prior acts of child molestation were not so prejudicial as to outweigh their probative value. Thus, we can find no constitutional error or abuses of discretion. We therefore AFFIRM LeMay's convictions.

BACKGROUND

Fred LeMay is a twenty-four-year-old Native American and a member of the Fort Peck Indian tribe. The charges in this case arose from an incident that occurred during the summer of 1997 in Poplar, Montana, on the Fort Peck Indian Reservation. LeMay lived on the Fort Peck Reservation from 1991 to 1998, and intermittently resided at the home of his sister, Justine Shields, and her husband, Daniel Renz. Shields and Renz had several young children, for whom LeMay often babysat. One such instance occurred during the summer of 1997. Shields and Renz had gone out for the evening, leaving LeMay to watch their children D.R. and A.R., two boys ages five and seven.

LeMay made both children orally copulate with him while their parents were away and threatened to beat them up if they told anyone. Undeterred, the boys informed their mother of the abuse the next morning. Although Shields refused to let LeMay babysit for her children after that, she did not report the incident, look for evidence, or take the boys to a doctor or a counselor. Two years later, however, law enforcement authorities got wind of LeMay's abuse of the children and investigated the allegations. LeMay was eventually arrested and charged with child molestation.

Before trial, the prosecutor gave notice of her intent to introduce evidence of LeMay's prior acts of sexual misconduct under Rule 414 of the Federal Rules of Evidence. The evidence consisted of a juvenile rape conviction arising from events that had occurred in 1989, when LeMay was just twelve years old. At that time, LeMay resided with his aunt, Francine LeMay, in Gresham, Oregon. Francine LeMay had two daughters, who in the summer of 1989 were two years and eight months old, respectively.

As in the 1997 incident for which LeMay was charged, LeMay sexually abused the children while babysitting for them. * * * In a subsequent juvenile adjudication, LeMay was found guilty of rape.

LeMay opposed the prosecution's attempt to introduce this evidence, mounting both a facial and an "as-applied" challenge to the constitutionality of Rule 414. He also claimed that the evidence was not admissible under Rule 403, arguing that its potential for prejudice far outweighed its probative value. After an extensive pretrial hearing, the district judge rejected LeMay's facial constitutional challenge. The judge reserved the "as applied" and Rule 403 challenges until trial, in order to be able to determine more accurately whether the prosecution's proffered evidence would be relevant. The judge observed that "[a] full evaluation of all the evidence and the appropriate balancing test to be applied in this case is best left for trial."

At trial, the prosecution called both A.R. and D.R., who by that time were seven and nine years old. Both boys remembered the incidents and testified consistently. The prosecution also called the boys' mother, Justine Shields. Because Shields had not informed anyone that LeMay had molested her children, the prosecution was unable to offer any forensic, medical, or psychological evidence that the boys had been abused, and the case therefore rested on their testimony.

LeMay took advantage of this lack of evidence in his opening statement, arguing that no eyewitnesses or medical or scientific experts would corroborate the testimony of A.R. and D.R. Further, in cross-examining the boys, LeMay's counsel attempted to call into question their ability to remember events accurately. He also suggested that the boys might have a motive to lie because they were currently in foster care, and that they might have thought that accusing LeMay of molesting them would be a way to be reunited with their parents.

After A.R., D.R., Shields, and the investigator testified, the judge decided the remaining Rule 414 issues. He determined that Rule 403 did not otherwise preclude the introduction of the prior acts of molestation, and that Rule 414 was not unconstitutional as applied to LeMay. In conducting the Rule 403 balancing test, the judge stated: "On examination of each of the boys in question, there [have] been substantial issues raised concerning their credibility * * * There's a substantial issue that goes to the credibility of all of the persons involved in the care of these children. And I find that the evidence proffered by the government is relevant to issues of credibility. It is also relevant in rebutting the suggestion that there's no proof that this happened, which was made by the defendant in his opening statement, and that there would be no witnesses, medical, psychological, or eyewitnesses called. And, consequently, I am going to admit the evidence over the objection of the defendant."

Before allowing the prosecution to present its prior act evidence, however, the judge gave the jury the following limiting instruction:

> You are going to hear testimony from this witness and this testimony has a limited purpose. The limited purpose is as it may bear on the credibility of witnesses from whom you have already heard testimony. The evidence you are about to hear is not evidence of guilt in this case of the defendant, per se, it is evidence that can be considered by you for any purpose to which it is relevant in terms of the issues in this case.

After this instruction, the prosecutor called her last two witnesses. She first called Francine LeMay, who testified about the defendant's abuse of her children in Oregon in 1989. Ms. LeMay, who began her testimony in tears, described generally how she had discovered that LeMay had abused her daughters and how she had gotten him to admit to that abuse. The prosecution's final witness established that LeMay had been found guilty of rape in a juvenile adjudication. After these witnesses, the prosecution closed its case.

When both sides had rested, the district court reminded the jury that LeMay was on trial for the acts charged in the indictment, and not for the acts of molestation that occurred in 1989. Over LeMay's objection, the judge instructed that "the defendant is not on trial for any conduct or offense that is not charged in the indictment. You should consider any evidence about other acts of the defendant that you have heard * * * only as those acts may bear on the matter that is relevant in this case."

The jury found LeMay guilty of both counts of molestation, and the district judge sentenced him to 405 months in prison.

DISCUSSION

* * *

B. Due Process

* * * LeMay contends that Rule 414 violates due process principles by removing the longstanding ban on propensity evidence in criminal trials. He argues that the traditional rule precluding the use of a defendant's prior bad acts to prove his disposition to commit the type of crime charged is so ingrained in Anglo-American jurisprudence as to be embodied in the due process clause of the Constitution. LeMay has a very high burden in proving this assertion, and we conclude he has not met it.

* * *

We conclude that there is nothing fundamentally unfair about the allowance of propensity evidence under Rule 414. As long as the protections of Rule 403 remain in place to ensure that potentially devastating evidence of little probative value will not reach the jury, the right to a fair trial remains adequately safeguarded.

Although this court has never squarely addressed the issue of whether Rule 414 and its companion rules are constitutional, we have recently held that the balancing test of Rule 403 continues to apply to those rules, and that district judges retain the discretion to exclude evidence that is far more prejudicial than probative. *See Doe by Rudy-Glanzer v. Glanzer*, 232 F.3d 1258, 1268 (9th Cir. 2000) (rejecting claim that Rule 415, which allows for introduction of prior sexual misconduct in civil sexual assault or child molestation cases, eliminates balancing protections of Rule 403).

With the protections of the Rule 403 balancing test still in place, LeMay's due-process challenge to Rule 414 loses much of its force. The evidence that he had sexually molested his cousins in 1989 was indisputably relevant to the issue of whether he had done the same thing to his nephews in 1997. The introduction of relevant evidence, by itself, cannot amount to a constitutional violation.

Likewise, the admission of prejudicial evidence, without more, cannot be unconstitutional. All evidence introduced against a criminal defendant might be said to be prejudicial if it tends to prove the prosecution's case. Moreover, evidence that a defendant has committed similar crimes in the past is routinely admitted in criminal prosecutions under Rule 404(b) to prove preparation, identity, intent, motive, absence of mistake or accident, and for a variety of other purposes.

The introduction of such evidence can amount to a constitutional violation only if its prejudicial effect far outweighs its probative value. * * * Potentially devastating evidence of little or no relevance would have to be excluded under Rule 403. Indeed, this is exactly what Rule 403 was designed to do. We therefore conclude that as long as the protections of Rule 403 remain in place so that district judges retain the authority to exclude potentially devastating evidence, Rule 414 is constitutional.

* * *

C. Rule 403

LeMay also argues that even if Rule 414 is facially constitutional, it is unconstitutional as applied to him, and that the district judge abused his discretion in admitting the evidence under Rule 403. If the prior acts of molestation were properly admitted under Rule 403, there can have been no as-applied constitutional violation. We therefore first address whether admitting the evidence was an abuse of discretion. We conclude that it was not.

Rule 403 provides that relevant evidence may be excluded, among other reasons, if "its probative value is substantially outweighed by the danger of unfair prejudice." In *United States v. Glanzer*, we stated that "because of the inherent strength of the evidence that is covered by [Rule 414], when putting this type of evidence through the [Rule 403] microscope, a court should pay careful attention to both the significant probative value and the strong prejudicial qualities of that evidence." *Glanzer*, 232 F.3d at 1268. We also articulated several factors that district judges must evaluate in determining whether to admit evidence of a defendant's prior acts of sexual misconduct. These factors are: (1) "the similarity of the prior acts to the acts charged," (2) the "closeness in time of the prior acts to the acts charged," (3) "the frequency of the prior acts," (4) the "presence or lack of intervening circumstances," and (5) "the necessity of the evidence beyond the testimonies already offered at trial." We also stated that this list of factors is not exclusive, and that district judges should consider other factors relevant to individual cases.

[The trial judge] held an extensive pre-trial hearing, at which he grilled the prosecutor about all aspects of Rule 414, and questioned her as to why she needed the prior acts evidence and how she intended to introduce it. The judge also reserved the Rule 403 decision until after the prosecution had introduced all its other evidence, in order to get a feel for the evidence as it developed at trial before ruling on whether LeMay's prior acts of child molestation could come in. After hearing the opening statements and the prosecutor's case, the judge concluded that the prior molestations were relevant to bolster the credibility of D.R. and A.R., and to rebut the suggestion that there was no evidence to corroborate their testimony. Finally, the district court reminded the jury in its final instructions that, while it could consider the prior acts evidence for any matter which it deemed relevant, it could only convict LeMay for the charged crimes. In short, * * * the record reveals that he exercised his discretion to admit the evidence in a careful and judicious manner.

We also conclude that admitting LeMay's prior acts of molestation was proper in light of the factors we discussed in *Glanzer* and others relevant to this particular case. We begin by noting, as the district judge did, that the evidence of LeMay's prior acts of child molestation was highly relevant. The 1989 molestations were very similar to the charged crimes. Each case involved forced oral copulation. In each case the victims were young relatives of LeMay, and each instance occurred while LeMay was babysitting them.

Moreover, as the district judge suggested, the prior acts evidence was relevant to bolster the credibility of the victims after LeMay suggested they could be fabricating the accusations. The evidence also countered LeMay's claim that there was no evidence corroborating the testimony of D.R. and A.R.

* * *

Additionally, the evidence of LeMay's prior abuse of his cousins was also highly reliable. LeMay had been convicted of at least one of the rape charges arising from the incidents in Oregon. * * * To the extent that allowing the evidence permitted a propensity inference, it was an inference based on proven facts and LeMay's own admissions, not rumor, innuendo, or prior uncharged acts capable of multiple characterizations. Thus, although we do not suggest that district courts may only introduce prior acts of molestation for which a defendant has been tried and found guilty, we hold that the extent to which an act has been proved is a factor that district courts may consider in conducting the Rule 403 inquiry.

We must also consider the remoteness in time of LeMay's prior acts of molestation, the frequency of prior similar acts, and whether any intervening events bear on the relevance of the prior similar acts. The "intervening events" factor seems to have little relevance in the present case, and the other two cut in favor of the government. About eleven years had passed between LeMay's abuse of his nieces and his trial for the abuse of D.R. and A.R. We have held, in the context of Rule 404(b), that the lapse of twelve years does not render the decision to admit relevant evidence of similar prior acts an abuse of discretion. The "frequency of events" factor discussed in *Glanzer* also cuts in favor of the government. Although it was not introduced at trial, the government also had evidence of a third incident in which LeMay had sexually abused his young relatives. True, this incident occurred even before the 1989 abuse of his cousins when LeMay himself was extremely young, and, as the prosecutor noted, was "triple hearsay." However, that there was evidence of a third similar incident suggests that LeMay's abuse of his cousins in 1989 was not an isolated occurrence.

Glanzer also instructs that courts must consider whether the prior acts evidence was necessary to prove the case. This factor also supports the government's position and indicates that the district judge did not abuse his discretion in admitting the evidence. The prosecution's case rested on the testimony of A.R. and D.R. No other scientific, forensic, medical, or psychological witness was available. LeMay had attacked the credibility of the boys and capitalized on the lack of eyewitness and expert testimony. That the prosecutor claimed that she could get a conviction without introducing LeMay's prior acts of molestation does not suggest that the evidence was not "necessary." Prior acts evidence need not be absolutely necessary to the prosecution's case in order to be introduced; it must simply be helpful or practically necessary.

Finally, Francine LeMay's testimony was necessary to establish that LeMay's 1989 molestations were very similar, and thus relevant, to the charged crimes. We reject the idea that the district court should have limited the prosecution to merely proving that LeMay had been convicted of rape eleven years before. The relevance of the prior act evidence was in the details. * * *

Several factors do admittedly favor LeMay. LeMay himself was only twelve years old at the time of the 1989 molestations. And foremost, of course, is the emotional and highly charged nature of Francine LeMay's testimony. Although we, as an appellate court, are not in a position to evaluate how great an effect Francine LeMay's testimony had on the jury, we do not doubt that it was powerful. Francine LeMay began her testimony in tears, and certainly, her suggestion that LeMay had raped her infant daughter would have been particularly shocking. However, evidence of a defendant's prior acts of molestation will always be emotionally charged and inflammatory, as is the evidence that he committed the charged crimes. Thus, that prior acts evidence is inflammatory is not dispositive in and of itself. Rather, district judges must carefully evaluate the potential inflammatory nature of the proffered testimony, and balance it with that which the jury has already heard, the relevance of the evidence, the necessity of introducing it, and all the other relevant factors discussed above. The record here shows that the district judge did just that. Therefore, admitting LeMay's prior acts of molestation was not an abuse of discretion.

All in all, the record shows that the district judge struck a careful balance between LeMay's rights and the clear intent of Congress that evidence of prior similar acts be admitted in child molestation prosecutions.

D. Equal Protection

LeMay also argues that Rule 414 violates his right to equal protection. LeMay proffers various theories to support this claim. We reject these arguments.

First, Rule 414 does not discriminate against any group of individuals on the basis of a suspect or quasi-suspect class. Sex offenders are not a suspect class. LeMay, however, argues that Rule 414 has a far greater impact on Native Americans because they are far more likely than members of other races to be prosecuted federally for child molestation. LeMay may be correct that a disproportionately large number of federal child molestation prosecutions involve Indian defendants. But this disproportion, if true, would arise simply because the federal government only has jurisdiction over crimes such as child molestation when they arise on Indian Reservations, military bases, or other federal enclaves. There is no evidence of any intent on the part of Congress to discriminate against Native Americans, and LeMay's claim therefore is without merit.

LeMay also argues that Rule 414 violates equal protection principles because it deprives child molesters of a "fundamental right" enjoyed by other criminal defendants. This claim also fails. As discussed above, LeMay has no fundamental right to have a trial free from relevant propensity evidence that is not unduly prejudicial. Although the right to a fair trial may in some instances preclude the introduction of highly inflammatory evidence completely out of proportion to its probative value, Rule 403 ensures that evidence which is so prejudicial as to jeopardize a defendant's right to a fair trial will be excluded. Thus, the claim that Rule 414 unfairly impinges on sex offenders' fundamental right to a fair trial also fails.

* * *

E. Remaining Arguments

LeMay also argues that Rule 414 undermines the presumption of innocence and permits irrational evidentiary inferences. Rule 414 does neither of these things. To support these contentions, LeMay relies on Supreme Court cases that deal with unconstitutional evidentiary presumptions. Rule 414 does not create a presumption that a defendant is guilty because he has committed similar acts in the past; it merely allows the jury to consider prior similar acts along with all other relevant evidence. Moreover, although the inference that because a person has done something once, he might be more likely to have done it again has until recently been impermissible, it is certainly not irrational.

LeMay also contends that Rule 414 violates the "due process reciprocity requirement" because it would, as he puts it, prevent him "from introducing the exact type of evidence regarding the alleged victim that Rule 414 permits the Government to introduce against the defendant." Given the age of LeMay's chosen victims, this claim is nonsensical.

Finally, LeMay contends that the rule violates the Eighth Amendment ban on cruel and unusual punishment. This argument fails. * * * [Rule 414] does not impose criminal punishment at all; it is merely an evidentiary rule. * * * For the defendant to be correct that Rule 414 punishes one's status as a sex offender juries would have to ignore courts' instructions to them that they consider only the crime charged in deciding whether to convict. The prosecution's other witnesses provided enough evidence that we are convinced that LeMay was not convicted for his status as a sex offender.

Conclusion

In sum, we hold that Rule 414 is constitutional and does not violate due process, equal protection, or any other constitutional guarantee. Rule 403 adequately safeguards the right to a fair trial. We emphasize, however, that evidence of a defendant's prior sex crimes will always present the possibility of extreme prejudice, and that district courts must accordingly conduct the Rule 403 balancing inquiry in a careful, conscientious manner that allows for meaningful appellate review of their decisions. District courts should also examine the relevant factors we discussed in *Glanzer*, those we articulated here, and any others that might have relevance to a particular case. Because the record before us shows that the district judge's decision to admit the evidence under Rule 403 was conducted in a careful and conscientious manner, we can find no abuse of discretion. We therefore AFFIRM LeMay's convictions.

Paez, Circuit Judge, concurring in part and dissenting in part:

* * *

Rules 413, 414, and 415 were extraordinarily controversial at the time of their passage. The Judicial Conference Advisory Committee on Evidence Rules and the Judicial Conference Committee on Rules of Practice and Procedure both voted overwhelmingly to oppose the rules because they "would permit the introduction of unreliable but highly prejudicial evidence * * * ." The report submitted by the Judicial Conference to Congress expressed "significant concern" about the "danger of convicting a criminal defendant for past, as opposed to charged, behavior or for being a bad person."

Nevertheless, there are benefits to these rules. As members of Congress repeatedly recognized, "in most rape or molestation cases, it is the word of the defendant against the word of the victim. If the defendant has committed similar acts in the past, the claims of the victim are more likely to be considered truthful if there is substantiation of other assaults." 140 Cong. Rec. H5437-03, *H5439 (daily ed. June 29, 1994) (statement of Rep. Kyl). This case, with two child victims and no other witnesses, is precisely the type of case for which Fed. R. Evid. 414 was designed.

As courts, we are left to balance the public's interest in convicting those charged with sexual abuse crimes, as expressed in these evidentiary rules, with the right of the accused to be convicted only for the crime charged, and not his previous acts. LeMay served his sentence for his previous criminal acts, and he may not be punished again, unless the government can prove that he committed new crimes as well. The best way for district courts to balance these competing interests is to conduct the Rule 403 analysis on the record, carefully considering each of the factors, and others as necessary, identified by this court in *Glanzer*.

* * *

In this case, the district court made no record of its Rule 403 analysis at all. Unlike *Glanzer*, there was much more the district court could — and should — have done. In fact, the district court did not even identify the probative value of the evidence, only describing it as "relevant." There is a marked difference between describing evidence as relevant and describing it as having probative value significant enough to outweigh any unfair prejudicial effect. * * *

In this case, the district court found that evidence of LeMay's prior conviction was "relevant" to bolstering the child witnesses' credibility and to rebutting the suggestion that there was no proof that a crime actually occurred. But the district court later made an explicit factual finding that the two victims were "extremely credible," that their testimony was clear, and that they testified with certitude and impressive demeanor. This, combined with the prosecution's own assertion that the children's testimony alone was sufficient for a conviction, suggests that the prior acts evidence had minimal probative value. That minimal probative value should have been weighed against the risk of unfair prejudice to LeMay.

Because the district court did not conduct the 403 balancing on the record and consider the *Glanzer* factors, I would find that it abused its discretion. * * *

PROBLEM 6-5

Phyllis Partrin filed a timely complaint with the EEOC alleging sexual harassment after she was fired by the Nuveal Equipment Company, a Philadelphia company, three years ago. She has followed up on her complaint by filing a timely law suit against the Company in federal district court, relying on Title VII. Phyllis was hired as a secretary for the President of the company, Dennis Dunston, but was fired later the same year. She claims that she was fired because she refused to have sex with Dunston. According to Phyllis, about a month after she was hired, Dunston had a meeting in Chicago, told Phyllis that he needed to have a secretary at the meeting, took Phyllis with him to an airport hotel in Chicago, told Phyllis to come to his room for dictation, threw her on the bed and attempted to force himself on her, she resisted and slapped his face, went back to her own room, attended a meeting in the hotel the next day with Dunston, and returned to Philadelphia. Phyllis was fired a month later. Nuveal defends on the ground that Phyllis was fired because her work performance was not up to par.

Phyllis calls as a witness Mary Burton.

Plaintiff: When did you begin working for the Company?

Burton: Nine years ago.

Plaintiff: For whom did you work?

Burton: As officer manager, first for the President, Ernie Evin, then for his successor, Dennis Dunston.

Plaintiff: What kind of evaluations did you get?

Burton: At the beginning I got great evaluations, but that changed.

Plaintiff: What happened?

Burton: In 1995, Ernie Evin retired and was replaced by Dunston, who previously had been President of a competitor. Shortly after Dunston became President of Nuveal, he called me into his office and told me that I was an attractive, mature woman who seemed to know how business worked. Dunston then grabbed me, put his hands under my dress, and tried to grab me inappropriately. I resisted, pushed him away, and told him that I was happily married and had no interest in an office romance.

Defendant: Objection. Improper character evidence. Move to strike.

The court: (1) ________.

Plaintiff: Was that the only time that Dunston made sexual advances?

Burton: No, not long thereafter, I received an evaluation that was partly positive and partly negative. It was signed by Dunston. I arranged for an appointment to see him to discuss the evaluation. During our meeting, Dunston claimed to have something in his eye and asked if I could help him get it out. I stood over Dunston as he sat in his chair, looked into Dunston's eye, and Dunston grabbed my breasts and pulled me onto him on the chair. Completely off balance, I fell onto Dunston who kissed me and moved one hand under my dress. Once I regained my balance, I pushed away from the chair. Dunston said, "that's a little better." I fled from the office crying.

Defendant: Objection. Improper character evidence. Move to strike.

The court: (2) ________.

Plaintiff: Did Dunston hire a secretary to work with you?

Burton: Yes, he hired a new secretary, Amy Harkin.

Plaintiff: Did she have any problems with harassment from Dunston?

Burton: On three separate occasions, I saw Harkin emerge from Dunston's office with her lipstick smeared, her hair messed, and her dress not quite right. On the third occasion, I approached Harkin and said, "You know, he hit on me too. You don't have to let him do anything." Harkin, trembling, replied, "He just grabbed me and wouldn't let me go until I agreed to oral sex. Then he told me I wouldn't be sorry."

Defendant: Objection Improper character evidence. Move to strike.

The court: (3) __________.

Plaintiff: Did you experience any other harassment from Dunston?

Burton: During the office Christmas party four years ago, Dunston entered my office while I was on the phone and demanded that I perform oral sex. I refused, and Dunston said, "Well, you're going to be sorry." Within two months, Dunston transferred me to a Delaware subsidiary where I became office administrator, and Dunston made Harkin office manager.

Defendant: Objection Improper character evidence. Move to strike.

The court: (4) __________.

The defendant calls the President of Germantown Shoe, a sporting goods company for whom Phyllis worked for three years before joining Nuveal.

Defendant: Did the plaintiff work for your company?

President: Yes, she did.

Defendant: Were there any problems with her while she was there?

President: I was told by our Chief Operating Officer that Phyllis had been having an affair with our Sales Manager. We did an investigation, and found out it was true. I told both the Manager and Phyllis that it was unacceptable, and shortly thereafter Phyllis left the company.

Plaintiff: Objection. Improper character evidence. Move to strike.

The court: (5) __________.

Chapter 7

FOUNDATIONAL REQUIREMENTS

A. REAL EVIDENCE

[1] Federal Rule of Evidence 901

Rule 901. Requirement of Authentication or Identification

(a) General Provision. The requirement of authentication or identification as a condition precedent to admissibility is satisfied by evidence sufficient to support a finding that the matter in question is what its proponent claims.

(b) Illustrations. By way of illustration only, and not by way of limitation, the following are examples of authentication or identification conforming with the requirements of this rule:

(1) Testimony of witness with knowledge. Testimony that a matter is what it is claimed to be.

. . . .

(4) Distinctive characteristics and the like. Appearance, contents, substance, internal patterns, or other distinctive characteristics, taken in conjunction with circumstances.

[2] Illustration

Prosecutor:	Were you the arresting officer of the defendant in this case?
Officer:	Yes, I was.
Prosecutor:	Did you take anything from his person?
Officer:	Yes, a .32 caliber semi-automatic pistol.
Prosecutor:	What did you do with the gun?
Officer:	I marked my initials on the gun and turned it over to the evidence officer at the police station.
Prosecutor:	Now I'd like to hand you what has been marked for identification as State's Exhibit #5. Can you identify the gun?
Officer:	Yes, it has my initials on it. It's the gun I took from the defendant.
Prosecutor:	Your honor, we offer State's Exhibit #5.
Defendant:	Objection! Lack of foundation. Failure to establish chain of custody.

[3] Chain of Custody

LOCKHART v. McCOTTER
782 F.2d 1275 (5th Cir. 1986)

JOHNSON, CIRCUIT JUDGE:

Thaddeus Michael Lockhart appeals the federal district court's denial of Lockhart's petition for *habeas corpus* relief. Lockhart contends that he is entitled to *habeas corpus* relief on the grounds that he was deprived of effective assistance of counsel both at trial and on appeal. Perceiving no reversible error in the federal magistrate's findings and recommendations, which were adopted by the district court, we affirm.

Background

Lockhart was arrested and ultimately convicted of aggravated robbery in Dallas, Texas. On the day of his arrest, April 2, 1976, Lockhart had worked distributing hand circulars and been paid $18.00. After work, Lockhart spent several hours at the Stop-In Cafe in North Dallas. Lockhart testified at trial that he left the cafe at approximately 11:00 p.m. following an argument with a prostitute.

At approximately the same time that Lockhart left the Stop-In Cafe and in that same neighborhood, James Hall, who had also just left the Stop-In Cafe, was robbed. According to Hall, a man put a knife to Hall's throat and demanded Hall's money. After giving the man his wallet, which contained $30.00, Hall was released. Hall immediately ran to a pay phone and called the police.

When police officers arrived, Hall told the officers that his assailant was about 5 feet, 11 inches tall, weighed 170 pounds, and was wearing a red windbreaker and blue pants. Hall then accompanied the officers to search for the robber. Approximately one block from the Stop-In Cafe, the police encountered Lockhart, who was wearing a red windbreaker and blue trousers, walking along the street. The police officer who spotted Lockhart asked Hall, "Is that him?" In response, Hall identified Lockhart as the robber and, after Lockhart had been stopped and searched, identified a knife taken from Lockhart as the one used in the robbery. Although the police found $12.00 in Lockhart's pants, they could not recall whether they had also discovered Hall's stolen wallet at the time of Lockhart's arrest.

The police took Lockhart to the Dallas City Jail where he was strip searched and booked. After Lockhart was searched, a "purse", keys, two necklaces and $1.06 were inventoried and placed in a personal property envelope to be held for Lockhart. Two knives along with $12.00 in cash which had also been found on Lockhart when he was searched were held by the police as evidence.

Several months after Lockhart's arrest and subsequent transfer to the Dallas County Jail, Dallas County prosecutor Rider Scott asked police investigator William C. Kelley to search Lockhart's personal property envelope. Scott had noticed that a "purse" had been taken from Lockhart and speculated that the inventoried "purse" could be the wallet taken in the robbery. Officer Kelley searched Lockhart's personal property envelope and located a wallet which was in fact later identified at trial as belonging to the robbery victim James Hall.

On May 10, 1976, Lockhart was indicted by a Dallas County Grand Jury for aggravated robbery. Three days later, Dallas attorney Don G. Smith was appointed to represent Lockhart. Smith was unsuccessful in persuading Lockhart to accept a plea bargain and on January 5, 1977, Lockhart's trial was held.

At trial, the State produced three witnesses. First, the robbery victim James Hall testified identifying Lockhart as the man who had robbed Hall on April 2, 1976. The arresting officer, Larry Davis, also testified giving a detailed account of the events which had occurred after he was called to investigate Hall's robbery. Davis also identified the two knives taken from Lockhart at the time of the arrest. The final prosecution witness, Officer Kelley, produced the wallet recovered from Lockhart's personal property envelope. The State recalled James Hall who identified the wallet and two pictures, one of Hall's girlfriend and the other of her children, which were contained in the wallet.

* * *

Failure to Object to Introduction of Hall's Wallet into Evidence

Lockhart contends that had his trial counsel raised a chain of custody objection to the State's introduction of the wallet, the wallet would have been excluded from evidence. To establish a proper chain of custody as a predicate to introducing the wallet, the State should have introduced testimony (1) tracing the wallet from the arrest to Lockhart's property envelope; (2) establishing the security of and limited access to the envelope; and (3) tracing the wallet from the property envelope to the court. However, the State only introduced testimony tracing the wallet from Lockhart's property envelope to the court. Moreover, the State failed to establish the security of the wallet once it had been removed from Lockhart's personal property envelope.

* * *

Without deciding whether Lockhart's attorney rendered deficient representation, this Court agrees with the federal magistrate that Lockhart was not prejudiced by his counsel's failure to assert a chain of custody objection. Tangible objects involved in a crime, such as the wallet in the instant case, are admissible in evidence only when identified and shown to be in materially the same condition as at the time of the crime. When the object has passed through several hands before being produced in court, it often is necessary to establish a chain of custody in order to prove either identity or lack of alteration.

However, when an object cannot be easily altered or substituted, establishing a continuous chain of custody is not as important. *See* McCormick's Handbook of the Law of Evidence 527 (E. Cleary 2d ed. 1972) ("If the offered item possesses characteristics which are fairly unique and readily identifiable, and if the substance of which the item is composed is relatively impervious to change, the trial court is viewed as having broad discretion to admit merely on the basis of testimony that the item is the one in question and is in a substantially unchanged condition."). Absent evidence of substitution or alteration, the failure to establish a chain of custody will generally go only to the weight of the evidence rather than its admissibility. Moreover, when the object is expressly identified at trial as the object involved in the crime, establishing a chain of custody is not necessary for the object to be admissible. *United States v. Mahone*, 537 F.2d 922, 930 (7th Cir. 1976) ("The chain of custody is not relevant when a witness identifies the object as the actual object about which he has testified.").

In the instant case, the wallet, containing pictures of the robbery victim's girlfriend and her children, was readily identifiable and not subject to undetectable alteration. At trial, the robbery victim specifically identified the wallet as the wallet which had been taken during the robbery. Moreover, Officer Kelley identified the wallet as the same wallet Kelley had removed from Lockhart's personal property envelope. In these circumstances, a chain of custody objection by Lockhart's attorney would not have resulted in exclusion of the wallet.

* * *

Conclusion

For the foregoing reasons, the judgment of the district court is AFFIRMED.

NOTES

1. Would the *Lockhart* analysis be employed under the Federal Rules?

According to *United States v. Collado*, 957 F.2d 38 (1st Cir. 1992), the unique characteristics approach to authentication of real evidence is provided for by Federal Rule 901(b)(4) and the chain of custody analysis by Rule 901(b)(1).

2. When chain of custody is required, does one break in the chain preclude admissibility?

See Saltzburg, Martin, and Capra, *Federal Rules of Evidence Manual* (9th ed. 2006):

> In criminal cases a question of authenticity arises if something is seized from the defendant and then introduced at trial, and the defendant disputes that it is his or argues that the thing has been altered in some way. One way for the prosecution to authenticate the evidence in these circumstances is to establish a chain of custody. (Of course, a chain of custody can establish authenticity in civil cases as well, though it happens far less frequently.) Most Courts have been very permissive in determining whether the government has established a sufficient chain of custody. The standard line is that gaps in the

chain of custody go to weight and not admissibility. *See, e.g., United States v. Dent*, 149 F.3d 180 (3d Cir. 1998) (prosecution sufficiently established a chain of custody for seized drugs, despite the fact that there was a tear in the plastic bag holding the drugs that was not present when the drugs were tested and weighed); *United States v. Miller*, 994 F.2d 441 (8th Cir. 1993) (a one-year gap in the chain of custody for contraband goes to the weight and not the admissibility of the evidence; there was no showing of bad faith on the part of government officials, who are entitled to a presumption that they did not alter the proffered evidence); *United States v. Hon*, 904 F.2d 803 (2d Cir. 1990) (the defendant pointed to defects in the chain of custody including an incorrectly labeled evidence bag, a bag carried by a witness who did not testify, bags that were left open for a couple of months, and a lack of written records; the Court concluded that these deficiencies went to weight and not admissibility); *United States v. Shaw*, 920 F.2d 1225 (5th Cir. 1991) (no abuse of discretion to admit contraband evidence against the defendant, even though the custodian of the search team could not remember who delivered the contraband for analysis or whether it was delivered by hand or placed in the analyst's night deposit box; there was sufficient evidence to support a finding that the drugs introduced at trial were the drugs found in the defendant's motel room, and any gaps or deficiencies went to weight and not admissibility).

Moreover, if evidence is in official custody at all times, there is a presumption that it has been handled properly and not altered or fabricated. *See, e.g., United States v. Thomas*, 294 F.3d 899 (7th Cir. 2002) (tape recording properly authenticated as it was clear that the tape was in police custody at all times and this creates "a presumption that the tapes were handled properly").

In our view, the strictness with which a chain of custody requirement is applied should depend on the importance of the evidence, the likelihood that it can be changed, and the extent to which its probative value depends on its unchanged condition. A unitary, conditional relevance approach is not appropriate because the trial court must also be concerned with prejudice and unreliability of evidence under Rule 403. So, for example, in the usual drug case, the most important chain of custody is the one from the original seizure of the evidence to the analysis of the substance. Given the fungibility of drugs, it is essential to make a connection between the substance seized from the defendant and the substance actually tested. We think that any substantial gap in this chain of custody or any indication of alteration should be treated as fatal, because otherwise there is an unacceptable risk that the test does not reflect the contents of the substance seized. *See, e.g., United States v. Casamento*, 887 F.2d 1141 (2d Cir. 1989) (there was insufficient authentication that a bag tested by a chemist came from the defendant's garage; the officer who seized property in the garage could not remember whether he seized a bag, and the bag was not mentioned on the inventory list of property seized from the garage).

A gap in the chain occurring after testing can be treated much more permissively, given the admissibility of the test itself and the fact that the only purpose for introducing the substance in court is to illustrate the testimony of government witnesses. This function could be performed by any package wrapped identically to that originally found by the officer. *See, e.g., United States v. Price*, 265 F.3d 1097 (10th Cir. 2001) (chain of custody attack concerning drugs after they were tested was "off-target because the actual drugs were never admitted into evidence"); *United States v. Kelly*, 14 F.3d 1169 (7th Cir. 1994) (chain of custody was sufficiently established where seals on the evidence bags remained intact until broken by the chemist for laboratory analysis; subsequent loss of the evidence was not fatal because "the government is not required to introduce narcotics in evidence in order to obtain a narcotics conviction"). Thus, an intact chain of custody after testing is not essential.

Moreover, the degree of proof necessary to support a chain of custody will also properly depend on the nature of the evidence proffered. If the evidence is unique and resistant to change (e.g., an ancient pearl-handled scimitar), then the chain of custody is relatively unimportant. *See United States v. Humphrey*, 208 F.3d 1190 (10th Cir. 2000) (gap in chain of custody of several weeks did not render documents inadmissible, because the documents were not "fungible evidence, such as drugs or cash, where absent a reliable chain of custody there would be a relatively high risk that the original item had been contaminated or tampered with").

On the other hand, "if the evidence is open to alteration or tampering, or is not readily identifiable, the trial court requires a more elaborate chain of custody to establish that the evidence has not been tampered with or altered." *United States v. Clonts*, 966 F.2d 1366 (10th Cir. 1992).

3. Who determines authenticity?

Rule 901 provides that the proponent must provide evidence sufficient to support a finding that the proffered material is what the proponent says it is. Under the rule, the question of authenticity is considered one of conditional relevance — a document or other piece of evidence is not relevant unless it is what the proponent purports it to be. As a question of conditional relevance, the admissibility standard under Rule 901 is the same as that provided by Rule 104(b): has the proponent offered a foundation from which the jury could reasonably find that the evidence is what the proponent says it is? This is a liberal standard favorable to admitting the evidence. The drafters of the rule apparently believed that authenticity should generally be a jury question, subject to the limitation that there is no reason to bother the jury with evidence that clearly is not what the proponent claims it to be.

[4] Evidence of Tampering

UNITED STATES v. EDWARDS
235 F.3d 1173 (9th Cir. 2000)

PER CURIAM:

Troy Anthony Edwards appeals his conviction from his second trial on one count of possession of cocaine with intent to distribute. Because we find that the admission of certain evidence denied Edwards the right to a fair trial, we reverse.

The prosecution of Edwards has been troubled from the beginning. At the first trial, the court admitted a bail receipt linking Edwards to the black bag that contained the cocaine after the bag, which had been introduced as evidence, was removed from the courtroom by a government attorney in violation of Local Rule CR 79(g). At the second trial, the government called a key witness despite repeatedly telling Edwards's attorney and the district court that the witness had refused to testify, and, in any case, could not be found.

I. FACTUAL AND PROCEDURAL BACKGROUND

In January 1995, the Tacoma Police responded to the scene of a domestic dispute. The victim, Carbeania Grimes, was bleeding from her forehead and was very upset. She told the officers that her boyfriend, Edwards, had struck her in the head with a gun. Grimes apparently also told the officers that Edwards had left the house with the gun and a black nylon bag. Four officers interviewed Grimes; one of the officers made a tape recording of his interview.

An officer at the scene observed Edwards drive a gray BMW out of an alley that ran next to Edwards's house and back the car into a parking space. Edwards was arrested on the suspicion of assault. Based on the interviews with Grimes, the police impounded the BMW, which was not registered to Edwards. The officers then obtained a warrant to search the car for the gun. Inside the trunk, they found clothes, paperwork, and a black nylon bag. The police opened the bag, which contained no indicia of ownership, and saw baggies of what appeared to be crack cocaine. They closed the bag and then obtained a second search warrant to search it. The search revealed eight baggies of crack cocaine and nearly seven kilograms of cocaine. In the front seat of the car, the police found a folder of legal papers belonging to Edwards, two cellular phones, and material used to package the cocaine. They also found various shopping bags with receipts containing Edwards's name. Neither the receipts nor Edwards's legal papers were ever inventoried by police. They never found the gun.

Edwards was charged with possession of cocaine with intent to distribute in violation of 21 U.S.C. §§ 841(a)(1) & (b)(1)(A). He initially pleaded guilty, but later moved to withdraw his plea. The district court denied his motion to withdraw the guilty plea, and sentenced Edwards to 240 months in prison. In 1997, the Ninth Circuit vacated Edwards's guilty plea and remanded the case to the district court for trial. *See United States v. Edwards*, No. CR-95-05021-1-JET, 1997 WL 8579 (9th Cir. 1997) (unpublished opinion).

A. First Trial

At Edwards's first trial on May 5 and 6, 1997, the defense argued that the government had insufficient proof that the black nylon bag containing cocaine belonged to Edwards. During pretrial proceedings, the district court excluded as inadmissible hearsay the statements made by Grimes in her interviews with the police. Because Grimes refused to testify at the first trial, her hearsay statements to the police were the government's only evidence linking Edwards to the black nylon bag found in the trunk of the car.[1]

The government introduced the black nylon bag into evidence on the first day of the trial. Neither the bag nor its contents contained any fingerprints. A police officer who had searched the car testified that there was nothing in the black nylon bag that established the identity of its owner. The bag and the cocaine were separate exhibits but were contained in a single box, which had been sealed before it was opened and the evidence was introduced. At the end of the first day of trial, the prosecutor instructed another officer to take the black nylon bag out of the courtroom and into the U.S. Attorney's office. This conduct violated Local Rule CR 79(g), which states that "after being marked for identification, all exhibits, except weapons or other sensitive material, shall be placed in the custody of the clerk during the duration of the trial, unless otherwise ordered by the court." For safety and security reasons, this local rule gives parties custody, during the trial, of "any weapons or other sensitive exhibits." The cocaine was unquestionably a sensitive exhibit, but the bag was not.

At the U.S. Attorney's office, the prosecutor examined the empty bag in the presence of two officers. In examining the bag, he removed a cardboard stiffener in the bottom of the bag. Beneath the cardboard stiffener, he allegedly discovered a wadded up piece of paper. The paper was a bail receipt from the Tacoma Municipal Court with Edwards's name on it. The bag had been in the possession of the Tacoma Police for two years, but the receipt was not discovered until the first day of trial. That evening, the prosecutor called Edwards's counsel and informed him that the government would be introducing the bail receipt.

The next day, Edwards's counsel moved to exclude the bail receipt and asked for a mistrial. Defense counsel claimed that his case had been unfairly prejudiced by the alleged discovery of the receipt because the defense theory depended entirely on the contention that there was no evidence linking Edwards to the black nylon bag. Counsel also argued that the prosecutor was injecting himself into the case as the government's chief witness. The district court denied the motion. At the suggestion of the trial judge, a police officer then testified about the bail receipt, acting as if he were discovering it for the first time in the courtroom. On cross-examination, the officer admitted that the prosecutor had found the bail receipt the night before. On redirect, when the officer was again asked about how the bail receipt had been discovered, he insisted that no one had tampered with the black bag.

---

[1] The district court subsequently admitted Grimes's hearsay statements in the first trial, ruling that the defense had "opened the door," on cross examination. *United States v. Edwards*, 154 F.3d 915, 918 (9th Cir. 1998).

The prosecutor did not testify. Neither did Grimes. The prosecutor told the court that Grimes was living in Las Vegas, had been subpoenaed, but was reluctant to testify. The court denied a continuance that would have allowed the government to secure Grimes's testimony. The police conceded on cross-examination that they failed to inventory the legal documents contained in the manila folder found in the front seat of the BMW. The failure to inventory those documents raised additional questions about the origins of the bail receipt purportedly discovered in the bottom of the black bag. During closing argument, the prosecutor denied that the black nylon bag had been tampered with and argued that the bail receipt was "the closest thing to a smoking gun that ties the defendant to the bag." The jury convicted Edwards, and the trial judge sentenced him to 262 months in prison.

On June 23, 1998, the Ninth Circuit reversed Edwards's conviction, finding that "the prosecutor's continued performance of his role as prosecutor in this case violated the principles upon which both the rule against prosecutorial vouching and the advocate-witness rule are based." Because the court declined to address the other issues raised, it did not rule on Edwards's argument that the bail receipt should have been suppressed. The court concluded "that the prosecutorial vouching in this case warrants reversal of Edwards's conviction because the error cannot be characterized as harmless." Following this discussion of the vouching rule and the basis for reversal, the panel noted that it did not view the prosecutor's conduct as unethical or improper.

B. Second Trial

A new judge presided over the second trial. The case was re-assigned to an out-of-district prosecutor. Edwards renewed his motion to suppress the bail receipt. At a pre-trial conference on January 8, 1999, Edwards's attorney argued that the bail receipt should be excluded because: (1) the evidence had been illegally obtained in direct violation of Local Rule CR 79(g); (2) it was inherently unreliable; and (3) suppression was an appropriate sanction for government misconduct in the first trial. The district court denied the motion and instructed both parties to prepare a list of witnesses they intended to call. The government left Grimes's name off the witness list and repeatedly informed both the judge and defense that she would not be testifying.

The defense attorney's opening statement at the retrial focused on the bail receipt:

> The government wants you to think that this case is about a big bag of dope, but what this case is really about is a little piece of paper. A little piece of paper like this crumpled up. A little piece of paper with Troy Edwards' name on it that was planted in that big bag of dope by the government to fake the evidence that the government didn't have. A little crumpled up piece of paper that says you must acquit Troy Edwards.

The defense explained that the prosecutor at the last trial described the bail receipt as "the smoking gun," and that absent this tainted evidence the government had no way of determining that the bag belonged to Edwards. Edwards's defense focused on discrediting the government's witnesses who handled the black nylon bag and who allegedly found the bail receipt. The former prosecutor testified that none of the documents from Edwards's car had been inventoried. He admitted that, during the first trial, he had told one of the officers to remove the black nylon bag from the courtroom after it had been admitted into evidence and bring it back to the U.S. Attorney's Office. He also recounted how he allegedly discovered the bail receipt by removing the bag's cardboard stiffener.

Before the second day of the retrial, the government announced that Grimes would testify. The court denied Edwards's motion to exclude Grimes's testimony or to declare a mistrial. During his direct examination of Grimes, the prosecutor asked numerous questions about the black bag:

> Q: Ma'am, did you in fact see the defendant with a black bag as he left the residence.
>
> A: I seen him with something.
>
> Q: Did it look like a black bag, ma'am?
>
> A: Yes, it was a dark colored bag.
>
> A: Grimes could not remember what she told police officers about the bag on the night of the incident:
>
> Q: Do you remember telling them you saw the defendant leave with a black bag?
>
> A: No, I don't remember telling them that, but if that's what I told them —
>
> Q: Do you remember looking at photographs at that time of the black bag?
>
> A: No, I don't remember.

Although Grimes acknowledged that either she or Edwards had purchased the bag in question, she would not testify that she saw Edwards carrying a black bag that night.

On cross-examination, Grimes admitted that she was drunk, that she had been crying, and that she had a difficult time seeing that night. She also attempted to clarify her testimony on direct examination:

> Q: It's also true, isn't it, that you saw Troy leave the house, but you didn't see exactly what he was carrying isn't that correct?
>
> A: No, I didn't see exactly what he was carrying.
>
> Q: In fact, you weren't sure about the what color any bag he might have been carrying was, isn't that correct?
>
> A: No, I just know it was a dark bag. I didn't know the exact description of the bag.
>
> Q: And you had a number of pieces of luggage, did you not?
>
> A: We had three sets.

Grimes's inability to identify the bag on cross-examination is corroborated by what she told police at the scene. In a transcript of Grimes's taped interview with one of the police officers, Grimes told the officer, "so I knew he took a bag and the officer asked me what color it was, and I told him I didn't know, I knew it was a bag, because it was over his shoulder * * *."

In its closing argument, the government argued that Grimes's testimony was the new "smoking gun" that obliterated the defense's theory of the case:

> The receipt is a moot point at this point in time. It's nice. It's corroborative. It's helpful to have. But what was that receipt. That receipt was circumstantial evidence, basically, of the ownership of this bag. It was circumstantial evidence of what Ms. Grimes has now confirmed to you with direct testimony based upon her personal knowledge.
>
> It wasn't a comfortable thing to do. You could see her looking at this and saying, "Yeah, I do recognize that." Whatever the receipt was in the last trial, the receipt is not the smoking gun in this trial. The smoking gun is Ms. Grimes saying, "I recognize that bag."

The following day, the jury convicted Edwards. On March 12, 1999, the district court heard oral argument and denied Edwards's renewed motion for a new trial. On April 23, 1999, Edwards was sentenced to 240 months in prison. Edwards timely appeals.

II. SUPPRESSION OF THE BAIL RECEIPT

Edwards argues that the bail receipt should have been excluded at the second trial because at the first trial the government had removed the black bag from the courtroom in violation of the local rule, because the government tampered with the bag, and because the evidence was inherently unreliable.

We review the district court's decision to admit or exclude evidence for an abuse of discretion. *See United States v. Leon-Reyes*, 177 F.3d 816, 819 (9th Cir. 1999). Such decisions will be reversed for an abuse of discretion only if such nonconstitutional error more likely than not affected the verdict. *See United States v. Ramirez*, 176 F.3d 1179, 1182 (9th Cir. 1999) (citations omitted).

"The authentication of evidence is 'satisfied by evidence sufficient to support a finding that the matter in question is what its proponent claims.' " *United States v. Harrington*, 923 F.2d 1371, 1374 (9th Cir. 1991) (quoting Fed. R. Evid. 901(a)). The burden is on the government to "introduce sufficient proof so that a reasonable juror could find that [the evidence is] in 'substantially the same condition' as when [it] was seized." *Id.* (quoting *Gallego v. United States*, 276 F.2d 914, 917 (9th Cir. 1960)).

Local Rule 79(g) mandates that "all exhibits, except weapons and other sensitive material, shall be placed in the custody of the clerk during the duration of the trial * * * ." As a witness in the second trial, the prosecutor admitted on direct and on cross-examination that the empty bag did not fall into the category of "sensitive material" contemplated by the rule. "Under normal procedures," he testified, the bag would have been marked separately and kept in the clerk's custody until the end of the trial. Local Rule 79(g) is designed to protect the integrity of the evidence. The fact that the bag was removed from evidence and the particular circumstances of the discovery of the bail receipt undermine the reliability of the evidence.

Under the unique circumstances present in this case, including the failure of the police to conduct a thorough initial search of the bag, the failure to inventory numerous papers belonging to Edwards that were seized from the car, the removal of the bag from the courtroom and the timing and circumstances of the discovery of the bail receipt, we conclude that the evidence is inherently unreliable and that the bail receipt should have been excluded at the second trial.

Our conclusion that the bail receipt should have been suppressed does not end our inquiry. We also must address the harmless error standard. We are guided by the rule that evidentiary decisions will be reversed for an abuse of discretion only if such nonconstitutional error more likely than not affected the verdict. *See Ramirez*, 176 F.3d at 1182 (citations omitted).

We hold that the admission of the bail receipt was not harmless error because Grimes's equivocal testimony, standing alone, is insufficient to support a conviction beyond a reasonable doubt. Grimes never linked Edwards to the black nylon bag containing cocaine, nor could she identify the bag she saw Edwards carrying when he left the house, other than to provide a vague description that it was a "dark colored bag." Furthermore, Grimes admitted that she was drunk that night, couldn't see that well, and that she and Edwards owned three different sets of luggage.

During closing argument, the government conceded that the bail receipt "corroborated" Grimes's testimony. But the bail receipt did more than that — it provided a degree of certainty regarding ownership of the bag that Grimes's testimony could not supply. Because the bail receipt more likely than not affected the outcome of the trial, we hold that its admission was not harmless error.

III. CONCLUSION

We reverse and remand for further proceedings not inconsistent with the views expressed in this opinion.

B. ILLUSTRATIVE EVIDENCE

[1] Illustrative Evidence Defined

SMITH v. OHIO OIL CO.

134 N.E.2d 526 (Ill. Ct. App. 1956)

SCHEINEMAN, JUSTICE:

Plaintiff, W. R. Smith, suffered personal injuries when his truck was run into by a truck of the Ohio Oil Company, driven by its employee, Maurice M. Smedley. In a suit against these parties, plaintiff recovered a judgment on a verdict of $50,000 and the defendants have appealed.

The collision occurred about 8:30 A.M. on a clear day. Plaintiff was driving westerly on U.S. Route 460. Smedley was driving south on a gravel road in a truck with defective brakes. Upon approaching the stop sign at U.S. 460, the brakes would not hold and he ran into the rear wheels of plaintiff's truck as it was passing the side road, resulting in an upset, and injuries to plaintiff.

* * *

During the testimony of a medical witness for plaintiff, the court permitted the use of a plastic model of a human skeleton to assist the explanations. This is assigned as error on the ground that it was unnecessary to an understanding of the issues, was gruesome, and tended only to arouse emotion rather than explain anything.

The use of physical objects before a jury falls into two categories: 1, real evidence, which Wigmore calls "autoptive," and 2, demonstrative evidence. The tests for the proper use of either are substantially similar, *i.e.*, the object must be relevant to some issue in the case, and it must also be actually explanatory of something which it is important for the jury to understand. If these tests are met, the courts do not seem to be greatly concerned with the question whether the object is gruesome.

Real evidence involves the production of some object which had a direct part in the incident, and includes the exhibition of injured parts of the body.

* * *

Demonstrative evidence (a model, map, photograph, X-ray, etc.) is distinguished from real evidence in that it has no probative value in itself, but serves merely as a visual aid to the jury in comprehending the verbal testimony of a witness. It is said its great value lies in the human factor of understanding better what is seen than what is heard.* * * The limitations are: that the evidence must be relevant and the use of the object actually explanatory. Sometimes the question of accuracy of an exhibit is pertinent, but this seems to be a phase of its explanatory function, since it may be misleading if inaccurate.

* * *

This court holds that the determination of relevancy and explanatory value of demonstrative evidence is primarily within the discretion of the trial court, but, to curtail abuses, is subject to review as to the actual use made of the object. If it appears that the exhibit was used for dramatic effect, or emotional appeal, rather than factual explanation useful to the reasoning of the jury, this should be regarded as reversible error, not because of abuse of discretion, but because actual use proved to be an abuse of the ruling.

Applying these tests to the actual use in the case at bar, it appears that the model was not used at all during the physician's testimony as to injuries he found, operations performed, methods of treatment, etc. Not until he proceeded to describe the present condition of plaintiff was the model exhibited. This involved the pelvic area, which is probably the part of the body most difficult for the average person to visualize.

In reply to questions by the court, the witness stated the model would assist his explanation, and that it was an excellent reproduction of a normal human skeleton. Permission was given to use the model. The witness then pointed to displacement of bones of the pelvis in a recent X-ray of plaintiff, and pointed to the model to illustrate normal alignment. The witness also explained the muscular arrangement and how the weight of the upper torso is transmitted to the lower extremities. He pointed out where excess strain would occur because of damaged ligaments and bone displacement, and how this would affect the ability to balance, or to stoop over. This was important as an explanation of the doctor's statement that a built-up shoe would not remedy the condition.

From consideration of testimony of the witness, this court concludes that the explanation was relevant, legitimate and helpful, and contained nothing emotional or dramatic in character. The rulings of the court thereon were correct.

* * *

Judgment affirmed.

---

[2] Limits on Use of Illustrative Evidence

CARSON v. POLLEY
689 F.2d 562 (5th Cir. 1982)

JERRE S. WILLIAMS, CIRCUIT JUDGE:

Arthur Carson brought this civil rights action under 42 U.S.C. § 1983 against the Dallas County Sheriff and four of his deputies and a Dallas County Constable and three of his deputies. Carson alleged that he suffered injuries because the defendants used excessive force when arresting him and booking him into jail. * * * In the first trial of this case, Carson recovered a verdict of $31,725.00. On motion of the defendants, the district court granted a new trial because the jury had considered several exhibits that had been ruled inadmissible and because of an erroneous evidentiary ruling. The second trial resulted in a jury verdict in favor of all defendants. Carson appeals from this judgment, arguing that * * * evidentiary errors attending the second trial require that we order a third trial in this case.

* * *

I. Facts

The events of Carson's arrest were hotly disputed at trial. We present the facts as asserted by Carson without purporting to resolve the conflicts. On Friday, February 10, 1978, Arthur Carson, while on his way to visit his mother-in-law, took a short-cut through the parking lot behind a precinct police station in Dallas, Texas. Earlier that day, police officers had observed someone tampering with a car in the station's parking lot. Mistaking Carson for this person, two plain clothes officers emerged from an unmarked car and told Carson he was under arrest. Because neither officer identified himself or informed Carson of the charges, Carson walked off. One of the officers then grabbed Carson's wrist and twisted it behind his back. The two tumbled to the ground as Carson attempted to free his arm. At this point, help in the form of three or four more officers emerged from the precinct station. The officers apprehended Carson and subdued him. On Carson's account, they did so by repeatedly hitting and kicking him.

Handcuffs were placed on Carson's wrists and ankles. The officers carried him into the station house where the two sets of cuffs were connected behind his back with a third set of handcuffs. Thus bound, Carson was left face down in an empty room. Three defendants — Deputy Constables Flatt and Crow, and Assistant Chief Deputy Constable Jack Thomas, were among the officers who participated in the arrest. A fourth defendant, Constable Vines, was the official in charge of the precinct station.

Carson was then transported to the Dallas County Jail. During the trip, Carson maintains, one of the officers grabbed him from behind and choked him into unconsciousness. On arrival at the jail, Carson was pushed out of the car and landed on his face on the parking lot. The officers carried Carson into the jail, using the third set of handcuffs as a handle and transporting him like a suitcase.

In the jail, sheriff's department personnel took charge of Carson. Carson's handcuffs were removed and he was taken to the book-in center, also known as the "shakedown" room. There, Carson testified, Deputy Sheriff Polley approached Carson and pushed him towards the back of the room. Carson requested to use a phone, but Polley's only response was to throw him jail coveralls and to tell him to "shut up". Carson still did not know why he had been arrested. Carson testified that Polley then struck him three times in the eye, knocking him over a bench. More officers then entered and kicked and hit Carson. Carson was again choked into unconsciousness. When Carson awoke, he was in solitary confinement. But for one visit to a nurse, Carson was left incommunicado in solitary confinement for three days until the following Monday. In addition to Polley, Carson alleged that Deputy Sheriffs Holley, Ingram, and Ellis were involved in the jail house events. Another defendant, Sheriff Carl Thomas, was the official responsible for the Dallas County Jail.

In July 1978, Carson pleaded guilty to two counts of aggravated assault for his conduct in the arrest. In August 1978, Carson filed this suit pro se [alleging] three separate causes of action under § 1983. First, Carson alleged that he was arrested without probable cause and subsequently assaulted without cause, by Deputy Constables J. Thomas, Crow, and Flatt. Second, Carson alleged that he was assaulted during the book-in process at the jail by defendants Ellis, Holley, Polley, and Ingram, all deputy sheriffs. Third, Carson alleged that he was cruelly and unusually punished by subjection to solitary confinement by Deputy Sheriffs Ingram and Ellis. * * * After a trial at which the jury awarded Carson $31,750, the district court granted the defendants' motion for a new trial. Because the jury had reached a verdict in favor of two defendants in the first trial, Sheriff Thomas and Constable Vines, the district court ordered that these defendants not be retried. At the second trial, the jury returned a verdict in favor of all of the remaining defendants. Carson's motion for a new trial was denied, and this appeal followed.

* * *

III. The Second Trial

Carson argues that he is entitled to a new, third trial because the district court at the second trial erroneously excluded certain exhibits offered by Carson and also erroneously admitted an exhibit against him. * * * We agree that evidentiary error at the second trial forces us to order a third trial in this case.

* * *

B. Carson's Alleged Knife

Carson * * * objects to the district court's decision to admit into evidence a knife as "similar" to a knife allegedly found on Carson's person when he was arrested. Deputy Constable Jack Thomas testified that he confiscated a knife from Carson at Carson's arrest. Thomas also stated that the knife was visible as a bulge in Carson's pants pocket before the arrest was made. Carson fully denied having a knife in his possession during the arrest, and specifically denied that the knife identified by Thomas belonged to him.

The knife was relevant to two issues in the case. First, Carson charged that the deputy constables had arrested him without probable cause. The constables asserted that Carson was seen with a tool in his hand that they believed was used to open locked car doors, which tool later turned out to the knife. Carson's possession of the knife thus had relevance to the officers' probable cause to arrest Carson for supposedly breaking into a car on the precinct station parking lot. Second, Carson contended that the officers used excessive force in subduing him after the arrest. That a knife was seen on Carson's person during the arrest had relevance to the amount of force the constables could reasonably employ.

While the court purported to admit the knife in evidence as a "similar" knife, the transcript reveals that it was by no means made clear to the jury that the knife as admitted had absolutely no connection with the knife alleged to be in Carson's possession except that it was a look-alike. The careful review of the transcript is important on this point. Assistant Chief Deputy Thomas is testifying:

> Q: Officer Thomas, I will show you what has been marked as Defendants' Exhibit Number 2, and I will ask you if you have ever seen that knife before?
>
> A: Yes.
>
> Q: Tell the members of the Jury, if you would, where you have seen that knife.
>
> A: It was protruding through the right pants leg of Arthur Wayne Carson.

Q: You say the right pants leg?

A: Yes.

Q: Now, what happened to that knife, if you know, Officer Thomas, after it was taken off of Mr. Carson's person on February the 10th?

A: It was given to me.

Q: And what, if anything, did you do with that?

A: I put it in the property room.

Q: Now, when you say "property room" explain to the Jury exactly what you mean by that.

A: This is a room that we — it's a locked room. There's only my boss and one secretary has a key to this. It's a room where we store weapons. No one else has access except those two.

Q: Q. Do you put all of a prisoner's personal property into that particular property room?

Q: No.

A: If you would, explain if there's a difference in your putting some there and taking some somewhere else; what that procedure is.

Q: In the normal case this knife would have been taken to the County Jail and placed with his property at the book-in section. But on this particular instance there was another charge of burglary of a vehicle that was filed, and this would be used in evidence. Had Mr. Carson been released on bond, the knife would have gone with him and we wouldn't have had it for evidence if we had a case of burglary of a vehicle. And that was the reason it was retained in our office.

A: Was it retained as physical evidence in a case, as opposed to just the suspect's personal property that would be later released to him?

Q: That's correct.

After the defendants offered the knife in evidence, Carson's attorney, Mr. Cunningham, took Officer Thomas on voir dire:

Q: Mr. Thomas, are you saying that you can identify Plaintiff's Exhibit Number 2 as being the knife, you recognize this knife, or you just recognize it because Ms. Lagarde (defendants' attorney) showed you a knife that came out of that folder up there?

A: No, sir.

Q: You cannot identify this —

A: Yes, I can.

Q: You can tell this knife from another Old Timer?

A: I remember it being brown and white, and the trade name or brand name was Old Timer.

Q: Can you identify this as the knife taken from the — from Arthur Wayne Carson that day?

A: It was that type knife.

Q: Is that all you're able to say, it was this type knife?

A: That's the knife.

Q: Okay. Can you say it was this knife? If I showed you another Old Timer you could tell me it was this knife as opposed to another Old Timer?

A: If that's the knife that was here on the other hearing.

Q: That's the only way —

A: Yes, sir.

Q: — isn't it, Mr. Thomas?

MR. CUNNINGHAM: Your Honor, we'll object to the introduction of Defendants' Exhibit 2 if he can't identify it. There's no chain of custody been established.

THE COURT: Well, I'll admit it for the purpose of showing that it was a similar knife.

MR. CUNNINGHAM: Well, Your Honor, for the record, we'll object to the introduction of a similar type knife because it's irrelevant.

THE COURT: I'll overrule.

Later, the defendants undertook to introduce in evidence an envelope in which the knife purportedly had been kept. The transcript reads:

Q: I'll show you what has been marked for purposes of identification as Defendants' Exhibit 3, and ask you if you recognize that document?

A: Yes, I do.

Q: And what is that, please?

A: It's a package that I put the knife in before it was placed in the property room.

Q: And where have you seen that before?

A: At the other hearing.

Q: Did you see it on February the 10th of 1978?

A: Yes.

Q: Did you have occasion to prepare that yourself or have someone under your supervision prepare that?

A: Had a secretary, Coleen Reed, type it up.

Q: After that was typed up what was done with that?

A: She placed it in our secure property room.

Q: Was there any other item placed in this envelope before it was placed in the property room?

A: No.

Q: What about the knife?

A: Just the knife, is all that was placed in it.

Q: And did it remain there?

MR. LOEWINSOHN (plaintiff's co-counsel): I'm sorry, I can't hear back here. Excuse me.

THE COURT: Yes. He said just the knife was placed in it.

Q: Mr. Thomas, after February 10th of 1978 did you have occasion at some point in time to bring Defendants' Exhibits Number 2 and 3 somewhere?

A: To the last hearing.

MS. LAGARDE: We would offer into evidence Defendants' Exhibit Number 3.

MR. CUNNINGHAM: We'll object to Defendants' Exhibit Number 3, Your Honor, insofar as it's hearsay, and it does not prove the facts reflected on the exhibit itself.

THE COURT: I'll overrule the objection. I'll admit 3.

Thus the envelope in which the knife, admitted solely as a "similar" knife, was purportedly kept was admitted in evidence. Counsel for Carson on cross-examination then asked Officer Thomas:

Q: Mr. Thomas, can you sit here and swear that the knife that sits before you is the knife that was placed in Defendant's Exhibit 3?

A: Yes.

Q: You can testify that just because Ms. Lagarde handed that to you. You couldn't tell that Old Timer from any Old Timer, could you?

A: If the knife's been in the Court's possession.

Q: Do you know where the knife's been?

A: It's been left with the Court.

Q: Do you know that of your own personal knowledge?

A: Yes.

Q: You do?

A: I was advised of that.

Q: Do you know that of your own personal knowledge?

THE COURT: No, he doesn't.

MR. CUNNINGHAM: Your Honor, on the basis of them still being unable to establish a chain of custody, we still object to Defendant's Exhibit Number 3, or the introduction of it.

THE COURT: I'll overrule the objection.

This record reveals a far greater authentication of the knife than should have been the effect of the court's limited admission of the knife solely because it was "similar." After the knife was admitted as similar, Thomas was allowed to testify that it was "the knife" which had been in police custody in the exhibit 3 envelope throughout, and he was permitted on the basis solely of unattributed hearsay to authenticate the exhibit 3 envelope as having been in police custody throughout the entire alleged custodial period and as having contained the exhibit 2 knife.

Concededly, this knife could have been admitted in evidence as illustrative or demonstrative evidence. Trial courts have great discretion in this area. *Gaspard v. Diamond M Drilling Co.*, 593 F.2d 605, 607 (5th Cir. 1979); *Wright v. Redman Mobile Homes, Inc.*, 541 F.2d 1096, 1097 (5th Cir. 1976). Illustrative evidence is admitted solely to help the witness explain his or her testimony. Illustrative evidence has no probative force beyond that which is lent to it by the credibility of the witness whose testimony it is used to explain. 22 Wright & Graham, Fed. Prac. & Pro. § 5174 p. 134 (1978).

Because it is tangible, however, illustrative evidence tends to have a strong effect in bolstering the credibility of the witness who identifies the illustrative exhibit. In the words of one treatise,

> Real proof often has an enormous apparent probative value because the lay trier may lose sight of the fact that its connection to a party may depend upon the credibility of an authenticating witness. Particularly since such proof is often taken into the jury room it continues to "speak" long after the witnesses have departed. Even the most unbelievable statements tend to take on an air of verity when they are connected to a tangible object.

See 5 Weinstein & Berger, *Weinstein's Evidence*, para. 901(a) [01], p. 17 (1978).

But what is crucial in this case is the fact that the record shows that ultimately it was not made clear to the jury that the knife was admitted solely for illustrative purposes. After admission only as a "similar" knife, Thomas reiterated that it was "the knife" which had been in police custody. This testimony occurred in connection with the admission of the envelope in which the knife was alleged to have been kept. It gave far more strength to the knife as an exhibit than was proper under the limited admission. The court gave no further instruction to the jury than is found in the transcript above. While no further specific instruction was requested by Carson, the precise and specific objections to the admission of the knife in evidence and to the admission of the envelope were clear.

Further, the knife was one of the exhibits taken to the jury room. It rarely is error to have such illustrative evidence introduced in the jury room, but in general: "Just as the testimony of witnesses is not sent to the jury room, so illustrative objects should be left behind when the jury retires to deliberate. This practice will reduce the likelihood that jurors will use the object as a source of original inference. Moreover, it will eliminate any incentive for counsel to use illustrative objects solely as a method of smuggling argument into the jury room." 22 Wright & Graham, Fed.Prac. & Pro. § 5174 p. 137. Under these particular circumstances, sending the knife into the jury room was an additional strengthening of its force as an exhibit.

Under all these circumstances, we must conclude that the record reveals the district court was in error in admitting in evidence the knife under the ambiguous posture which resulted. Such error clearly was prejudicial in view of the bitterly disputed factual issue concerning the alleged possession of a knife by Carson and the role that the alleged possession would play in justifying the force which the police officers used against Carson in effecting the arrest. This prejudicial error also justifies remanding the case for a new trial.

C. PHOTOGRAPHS, VIDEOTAPES, AND RECORDINGS

[1] Illustration

In order to show where a stop sign is located, plaintiff wants admitted into evidence a picture of the scene of the accident. Plaintiff's wife takes the stand.

Plaintiff:	Did you take this picture?
Wife:	No.
Plaintiff:	Do you know who did?
Wife:	No.
Plaintiff:	Were you at the scene when the accident took place?
Wife:	No.
Plaintiff:	Well, have you ever been at the scene?
Wife:	Oh yes, I go by it every day.
Plaintiff:	Has the stop sign always been in the same place?
Wife:	Yes, since before the accident.
Plaintiff:	I show you what has been labeled plaintiff's exhibit #1. Does it accurately reflect the location of the stop sign?
Defendant:	Objection! Your honor, a total lack of foundation. She wasn't there that day, didn't take the picture and doesn't even know who did.
Plaintiff:	________.

[2] Foundation

BROWN v. BARNES
290 S.E.2d 483 (Ga. Ct. App. 1982)

BIRDSONG, JUDGE.

This case involves an automobile collision which occurred when the appellee's vehicle ran a stop sign which the appellee contended she did not see because the sign was hidden from her view by a large truck parked at the roadside. The jury returned a verdict for the appellee, who was the defendant below. The plaintiff Johnny D. Brown appeals.

* * *

The trial court did not err in admitting photographs which the appellant contends were not properly identified and did not accurately depict the scene of the collision.

These photographs admittedly were taken a year after the accident by an unknown photographer whom the appellee did not know; they purport to show a view of the rather cluttered city intersection as approached by the appellee in the collision. A large truck parked on the right-hand roadside obscures the view of any stop sign. While ordinarily such evidence ought to be received cautiously admission in this case was not reversible error. The appellee identified the photographs as depicting the intersection where the collision occurred, and testified that the truck in the picture was parked in the approximate position that the truck which obscured her vision of the stop sign, and that the truck in the picture was similar to the one actually parked on the street at the time of the collision, and that the pictures showed essentially the same view of the intersection as she had on that day. These photographs were admissible.

* * *

Judgment affirmed.

NOTES

1. Must a witness who authenticates a photo have an independent recollection of the scene?

In *State v. Madison*, 345 So. 2d 485 (La. 1977), the defendant argued that there was a lack of foundation for five photographs of his automobile that were introduced against him at trial. During trial, a police detective "testified that he had taken the pictures at the pipeyard where defendant abandoned his car within an hour of the arrest. Each photograph bore [the detective's signature] on the reverse side and was marked for identification with the case number and the date of the incident. [The detective] stated that the photographs were faithful and accurate depictions of the scenes reproduced, but because he admitted that he would be unable to swear to their authenticity without the identifying stamp, defendant claims they were inadmissible." The court held that "[t]he law does not require as a prerequisite to the admissibility of photographs that the photographer have an independent recollection of the scenes depicted in them. The pictures themselves serve as an aid to the memory and there is no reason why the photographer may not rely upon a label as a further aid to their identification. [The detective's] positive visual identification of the photographs as being those he had taken on the night of the crime, and had developed and printed himself established a sufficient foundation for their admission."

2. Are pictures taken by surveillance cameras admissible if no one was present at the scene of the crime?

Surveillance cameras are often used to take pictures and to monitor areas where people cannot always be present. This is a common practice for banks, automatic teller machines, and retail stores. An admissibility problem arises when no one can truthfully testify that the pictures accurately and fairly depict the scene.

In *United States v. Taylor*, 530 F.2d 639 (5th Cir. 1976), a surveillance camera took pictures of a bank lobby during a robbery while all the employees of the bank were locked in the vault. The court noted that "[t]he only testimony offered as foundation for the introduction of the photographs was by government witnesses who were not present during the actual robbery. These witnesses, however, testified as to the manner in which the film was installed in the camera, how the camera was activated, the fact that the film was removed immediately after the robbery, the chain of its possession, and the fact that it was properly developed and contact prints made from it." The court held that under the circumstances of the case, "such testimony furnished sufficient authentication for the admission of the contact prints into evidence. Admission of this type of photographic evidence is a matter largely within the discretion of the court, * * * and it is clear that the district court did not abuse its discretion here."

3. What happens when one witness testifies that a photo is not a fair and accurate depiction of the scene?

Conflicting opinions of whether a photograph fairly and accurately depicts the scene go to the weight of the evidence and not to the admissibility. As long as one witness testifies that the photo is a fair and accurate depiction, the photo should be admitted, because a reasonable juror could believe that the photograph is what the proponent says it is — and that is the standard of proof necessary for authentication. *United States v. Soto-Beniquez,* 356 F.3d 1 (1st Cir. 2003) (photo sufficiently authenticated by police officer's testimony that it was accurate).

4. What are the requirements for the authentication of a videotape or film?

Authentication of a video ape is very similar to authentication of a photograph. A witness must testify that the videotape is a fair and accurate depiction of the scene shown. *State v. Thurman*, 498 P.2d 697, 700 (N.M. Ct. App. 1972).

5. What are the requirements for authentication of a sound recording?

United States v. Branch, 970 F.2d 1368 (4th Cir. 1992), is exemplary of the approach taken toward tape recordings in most federal courts. In that case, the defendant objected to the introduction of tape recordings on authenticity grounds. The court looked to seven factors, recognizing that not all had to be met, given the liberal admissibility standards of Rule 901. The court held that the proponent was generally required to show that:

i. the recording device was capable of recording the conversation.
ii. the operator was competent to operate the machine.
iii. the recording is a correct rendition of the occurrence.
iv. no changes, additions or deletions have been made.
v. the recording has been preserved in a manner shown to the court.
vi. the speakers are identified.

The court in *Branch* found that there was sufficient evidence of authenticity where an agent described the implementation and operation of the wiretaps; described how the extracted tape recordings were prepared for trial; stated that he was familiar with the voices on the tapes and identified them; and stated that the recording machine was in good working order and that the tapes had not been altered.

See also United States v. Brown, 136 F.3d 1176 (7th Cir. 1998) (tape of surreptitiously recorded transactions was properly authenticated by the following: 1) the confidential informant testified that the transactions recorded on the tape actually occurred; 2) the CI testified that the speakers on the tape were himself and the defendants; 3) the CI testified that the tapes were in the same condition as when he last saw them; and 4) the agent who monitored the taped conversations testified that he listened to the conversations during each transaction and that he personally observed one transaction); *United States v. DeJohn*, 368 F.3d 533 (6th Cir. 2004) (audio tape recordings of conspirators' conversations were properly authenticated; an agent testified that the recording devices were operative, the agent monitored the conversations and made a log of them, and could identify the voices on the tape).

[3] X-Rays

[a] Federal Rule of Evidence

Rule 901. Requirement of Authentication or Identification

* * *

(b) Illustrations. By way of illustration only, and not by way of limitation, the following are examples of authentication or identification conforming with the requirements of this rule:

* * *

(9) Process or system. Evidence describing a process or system used to produce a result and showing that the process or system produces an accurate result.

* * *

[b] Illustration

Plaintiff sues defendant for personal injuries sustained when a barrel fell out of defendant's window and hit plaintiff in the head. Defendant disputes the extent of plaintiff's injuries. Defendant's expert witness, Dr. No Injury is on the stand.

Defendant:	Doctor, in reaching your opinion on the extent of the plaintiff's injuries, did you review any of the plaintiff's x-rays?
Doctor:	Yes.
Defendant:	I hand you what has been marked as defendant's exhibits A and B. Where did you get them?
Doctor:	From the plaintiff's treating physician. They came in the mail.

Defendant:	Do you know who took the x-rays?
Doctor:	No.
Defendant:	How do you know they are x-rays of the plaintiff?
Doctor:	It says so right on the x-ray. It also gives the date, time, place, the name of the x-ray technician, and the name of the plaintiff's treating physician.
Defendant:	I offer defendant's exhibits A and B.
Plaintiff:	Objection! ________.
Defendant:	________.
The court:	________.

[c] Foundation

KING v. WILLIAMS
279 S.E.2d 618 (S.C. 1981)

LITTLEJOHN, JUSTICE:

Defendant Eston E. Williams, Jr., a general practitioner of medicine at Loris, South Carolina, appeals the jury verdict of $40,000 actual damages against him for his negligent diagnosis and treatment of plaintiff Joe D. King. We affirm.

In February, 1974, King suffered various scrapes, bruises and injuries after losing control of his vehicle and hitting several trees. The following day he entered Loris Community Hospital where he was examined and treated by Dr. Williams.

Among other injuries, King suffered a painful and swollen left foot. Dr. Williams ordered x-rays of only the ankle region and personally observed and manipulated the foot. Based upon his reading of the x-rays, as well as the report of the radiologist, Dr. Williams diagnosed and treated the injury as a severe ankle sprain; he expected the pain and swelling to subside in about one month. King was released in early March and allowed to walk on the foot using a walking cast.

When the cast was removed in late March, the foot remained swollen and blue. Dr. Williams considered this condition to be normal and continued the same treatment. Over the next nine months, the foot did not heal; instead, King suffered ongoing agony, discomfort, and inconvenience from the extreme pain in his foot. Additional x-rays of the ankle region were ordered and read by Dr. Williams during this interval, but his evaluation and treatment remained unchanged. Continued pain medication was prescribed in addition to the use of an ace bandage and arch support.

In January, 1975, at the insistence of King and his wife, Dr. Williams referred King to orthopedic specialists in Myrtle Beach and Columbia. The specialists x-rayed the entire foot, including areas other than the ankle. Each diagnosed a fracture-dislocation of the foot, and corrective surgery was subsequently performed in June, 1975. King suffered a 30% disability.

At trial, Dr. Harry Rein of Orlando, Florida, testified on King's behalf, over objections, to the following:

1. that the injury to King's foot was a common one treated similarly by all physicians throughout the country;
2. that he was generally familiar with the standard of medical care in Loris, S.C.; and
3. that Dr. Williams failed to meet the standard of care in Loris or similar localities in his diagnosis and treatment of King's foot (*e.g.*, failure to order proper x-rays or diagnose the injury; failure to consult other physicians; failure to earlier refer the patient to a specialist).

* * *

Counsel for Dr. Williams objected strenuously at trial to the introduction of x-rays purportedly of King's foot on the ground that they were not properly authenticated. Authentication involves verification and identification by someone who has knowledge that the x-rays are what they purport to be, such as the technician taking them or the physician ordering them. In this instance, the technician who made the x-rays had moved away, and the physician who ordered them, Dr. Williams, was advised by his counsel to refuse to respond to any questions concerning authentication. The x-rays, each inscribed with King's name, the date taken, and the name of Loris Community hospital, were admitted after the chain of possession was established. Additionally, Dr. Williams himself testified at one point that he had seen the x-rays "many times." We find no abuse of discretion in their admittance. Furthermore, we are aware of no authority which gives a witness in a civil trial the right to remain silent (as Dr. Williams was instructed by his counsel) absent the claim that the answer might subject the witness to *criminal responsibility*.

The exceptions are without merit; the defendant received a fair trial and the judgment of the lower court is

Affirmed.

NOTE

How are X-rays usually authenticated?

Since the taker of an X-ray can not confirm its accuracy by his own vision, more is usually required to authenticate an X-ray than a normal picture. Thus, X-rays are usually authenticated applying the analysis of Federal Rule 901(b)(9), requiring a foundation that the *process* leads to accurate results. This may require extensive testimony concerning, among other things, the acceptability of the equipment used and the qualifications of the technicians.

D. VOICE IDENTIFICATION AND PHONE CALLS

[1] Federal Rule of Evidence 901

Rule 901. Requirement of Authentication or Identification

* * *

(b) **Illustrations.** By way of illustration only, and not by way of limitation, the following are examples of authentication or identification conforming with the requirements of this rule:

(4) **Distinctive characteristics and the like.** Appearance, contents, substance, internal patterns, or other distinctive characteristics, taken in conjunction with circumstances.

(5) **Voice identification.** Identification of a voice, whether heard firsthand or through mechanical or electronic transmission or recording, by opinion based upon hearing the voice at any time under circumstances connecting it with the alleged speaker.

(6) **Telephone conversations.** Telephone conversations, by evidence that a call was made to the number assigned at the time by the telephone company to a particular person or business, if (A) in the case of a person, circumstances, including self-identification, show the person answering to be the one called, or (B) in the case of a business, the call was made to a place of business and the conversation related to business reasonably transacted over the telephone.

* * *

[2] Advisory Committee's Note to Rule 901

ADVISORY COMMITTEE's NOTE
56 F.R.D. 183, 332

* * *

Example (5). Since aural voice identification is not a subject of expert testimony, the requisite familiarity may be acquired either before or after the particular speaking which is the subject of the identification, in this respect resembling visual identification of a person rather than identification of handwriting.

* * *

Example (6). The cases are in agreement that a mere assertion of his identity by a person talking on the telephone is not sufficient evidence of the authenticity of the conversation and that additional evidence of his identity is required.

The additional evidence need not fall in any set pattern. Thus the content of his statements or the reply technique * * * or voice identification under Example (5), may furnish the necessary foundation. Outgoing calls made by the witness involve additional factors bearing upon authenticity. The calling of a number assigned by the telephone company reasonably supports the assumption that the listing is correct and that the number is the one reached. If the number is that of a place of business, the mass of authority allows an ensuing conversation if it relates to business reasonably transacted over the telephone, on the theory that the maintenance of the telephone connection is an invitation to do business without further identification. Otherwise, some additional circumstance of identification of the speaker is required. The authorities divide on the question whether the self-identifying statement of the person answering suffices. Example (6) answers in the affirmative on the assumption that usual conduct respecting telephone calls furnish adequate assurances of regularity, bearing in mind that the entire matter is open to exploration before the trier of fact.

* * *

[3] Voice Identification

[a] Illustration

Defendant is charged with the hold-up of a bank. The teller is on the stand.

Prosecutor:	Can you identify the defendant in this courtroom?
Teller:	No, he was wearing a mask.
Prosecutor:	Did he say anything to you at the bank?
Teller:	Yes.
Prosecutor:	What?
Teller:	He said, "This is a stick-up. Your money or your life."
Prosecutor:	Did you go to a line-up?
Teller:	Yes.
Prosecutor:	What happened?
Teller:	Several men were there and each was asked to say, "This is a stick-up. Your money or your life."
Prosecutor:	And * * * .
Teller:	I recognized the defendant's voice.
Defendant:	Objection! Lack of authentication. The witness had never heard the voice before the stick-up. This identification was in preparation for trial.
Prosecutor:	__________.
The court:	__________.

[b] Identification at Any Time

UNITED STATES v. WATSON

594 F.2d 1330 (10th Cir. 1979)

HOLLOWAY, CIRCUIT JUDGE:

[Defendants appeal drug and related convictions.] Appellants' major contentions are that tape recordings of intercepted telephone conversations and transcripts thereof were improperly permitted to be used against them * * * The conspiracy involved a California supplier, "Pete" Anderson, a Tulsa wholesaler, John Thompson, assisted by one Karen Brooks, and several retailers or street dealers, including appellants Watson, Maxwell, and Brown.

* * *

I

Appellants Brown and Watson strenuously argue that there was error in not suppressing tape recordings of certain intercepted telephone communications, in not suppressing transcripts of certain intercepted phone communications, and in permitting transcripts of the tape recordings of the telephone conversations to be used by the jurors.

The admission of tape recordings in evidence is subject to the rules of evidence generally. This means that a proper foundation must be laid for their admission, and that they must be relevant and not privileged. In addition, the Federal Rules of Evidence provide that the original tape recordings be used, if possible, Rule 1002, and that when telephone conversations are involved, evidence be offered as to the correct telephone number, Rule 901(b)(6). Appellants here make several specific challenges to the foundation laid for playing of the tapes which we will consider.

First, appellant Brown argues that there was improper and inadequate identification of the speakers on certain tapes for which agent Bell provided the voice identification. This challenge is based on the claim that agent Bell did not have sufficient opportunity to become acquainted with appellant Brown's voice in order to authenticate tapes introduced at trial. Furthermore, it is claimed that agent Bell's familiarity with Brown's voice was developed after the conversations in question transpired.

Rule 901(b)(5), F.R.E., provides one example of acceptable voice identification as follows:

> (5) Voice identification. Identification of voice, whether heard firsthand or through mechanical or electronic transmission or recording, by opinion based upon hearing the voice *at any time* under circumstances connecting it with the alleged speaker. (emphasis added).

As the Rule plainly says, familiarity with another's voice may be acquired either before or after the particular speaking which is the subject of the identification.* * * Thus, the fact that Bell did not speak with appellant Brown until after the date of the telephone intercept did not prevent him from authenticating Brown's voice on a tape introduced at trial.* * * Furthermore, we find that the record reflects that Bell had ample time in which to become acquainted with Brown's voice. He had face-to-face conversations with her on three occasions, and one of these conversations extended over half an hour. Any doubts about Bell's powers of recall were properly questions for the jury to determine.* * * We reject appellant Brown's argument * * * that the court improperly gave the authentication question to the jury. The trial judge properly took evidence on the threshold question whether Bell had any basis for identifying the voice and then left all questions of weight and credibility for the jury.

Second, all appellants challenge the use of the tapes on the ground of unintelligibility. Where a tape recording is objected to as unintelligible or inaudible, its admissibility is within the sound discretion of the trial judge.* * * Unless the unintelligible portions are so substantial as to render the recording as a whole untrustworthy, it may be admitted.* * * The trial judge held a pre-trial hearing at which he considered the issue of intelligibility and exercised his discretion on this issue. From our independent hearing of the tapes we conclude that there was no abuse of the trial court's discretion and no substantial unintelligibility productive of untrustworthiness.

Third, appellants argue that it was prejudicial error to provide the jury with transcripts of the tapes during the playing of the tapes. *See generally United States v. Gerry*, 515 F.2d 130, 143-44 (2d Cir.) (use of transcripts upheld because trial judge had difficulty understanding them). Proof was offered of accuracy of the transcripts at a pre-trial hearing, and the court permitted their use during the playing of the tapes to permit clear identification of the voices. The trial judge, however, did not admit the transcripts in evidence. Instead he gave a limiting instruction, which he repeated several times during the trial, instructing the jury to use the transcripts only to assist them in listening to the tapes and not to consider the transcripts as evidence. In the sound discretion of the trial judge, which was properly exercised here, such limited use of transcripts is permissible.

* * *

We have considered all the contentions regarding the playing of the tapes and the use of the transcripts and are satisfied there was no reversible error. Our hearing of the tapes persuades us that they are substantially accurate and intelligible and that the transcripts are substantially accurate as well. Therefore, with respect to the rights of these three appellants there was no prejudicial error and no abuse of discretion by the trial court in the procedure followed regarding the tapes and the transcripts.

* * *

Affirmed.

NOTE

How much familiarity must a witness have with a person's voice in order to establish a foundation for voice identification?

In *United States v. Saulter*, 60 F.3d 270 (7th Cir. 1995), the court found no error in a government witness's identification of two coconspirators on a tape recording. The witness's familiarity with one of the coconspirators was limited to having purchased narcotics from him on two occasions. Nonetheless, the court held that "minimal familiarity is sufficient for admissibility purposes," and that two meetings formed a sufficient basis for a voice identification. Similarly, in *United States v. Bush*, 405 F.3d 909 (10th Cir. 2005) the court found no error in allowing an undercover officer to testify as a lay witness that it was the defendant's voice in an incriminating conversation that was surreptitiously recorded and played at trial. The witness had sufficient familiarity with the defendant's voice from speaking to him in person and numerous times on the phone. A voice identification "need only rise to the level of minimal familiarity" and once that standard has been satisfied, "it is for the jury to assess any issues regarding the extent of the witness' familiarity with the voice."

[4] Incoming Telephone Calls

[a] Illustration

Plaintiff sues defendant, Bad Driver, for injuries sustained in an accident at an uncontrolled intersection. The case is very close on the negligence issue. The plaintiff is on the stand.

Plaintiff's counsel:	Did you talk to the defendant after the accident?
Plaintiff:	Yes I did. He called me on the phone.
Plaintiff's counsel:	How do you know it was the defendant?
Plaintiff:	He said, "Hi, I'm Bad Driver, the guy who failed to yield to you a couple of weeks ago. I'm real sorry."
Defendant:	Objection! _________.
Plaintiff's counsel:	_________.
The court:	_________.

[b] Context of the Statements

UNITED STATES v. PARKER

133 F.3d 322 (5th Cir. 1998)

EMILIO M. GARZA, CIRCUIT JUDGE:

Joann A. Parker ("Mrs. Parker") appeals her conviction and sentence for conspiracy to commit public bribery and five counts of public bribery * * *. Ralph Parker ("Mr. Parker") appeals his conviction for conspiracy to commit public bribery and three counts of public bribery * * *. We affirm.

I

The Social Security Administration ("SSA") Office of Hearings and Appeals employed Mrs. Parker as a clerk to Administrative Law Judge ("ALJ") John Aronson. She led a group that helped certain individuals to fraudulently obtain Supplemental Security Income ("SSI") benefits in return for money. The scheme began when Mrs. Parker met Niknitta Simmons ("Simmons") at a hearing where Simmons was appealing the denial of SSI benefits for her son, Kevin Simmons. ALJ Aronson advised Simmons that additional documentation would be necessary for a favorable ruling on Kevin's claim. Mrs. Parker approached Simmons after the hearing and offered to help. A few days later, Mrs. Parker gave Simmons a letter approving Kevin's benefits. Mrs. Parker thereafter called Simmons and demanded money for her help. Simmons refused to pay, and Kevin's benefits were terminated. Mrs. Parker advised Simmons that Kevin's benefits would be reinstated if Simmons paid her.

Simmons went to several SSA offices and reported Mrs. Parker's demands. Investigators from the SSA and FBI contacted Simmons, and she agreed to assist them by permitting FBI Agent Karen Jenkins to record her telephone conversations with Mrs. Parker. In multiple recorded conversations, Mrs. Parker demanded payment for having Kevin's benefits approved initially and for having those benefits reinstated. At a meeting at Simmons' home, Mrs. and Mr. Parker took $ 500, as captured on videotape by the FBI. Mrs. Parker thereafter demanded more money, which Simmons paid, and Mrs. Parker gave Simmons a letter purportedly bearing ALJ Aronson's signature reinstating Kevin's benefits.

Agent Jenkins and a SSA agent interviewed Mrs. Parker about her contacts with Simmons. The agents advised Mrs. Parker of her rights and she signed a written waiver before confessing to fraudulently approving benefits for Kevin Simmons, Raymond Henry, Georgette Lemon, Yvette Scott, and Karen Johnson. Mrs. Parker stated that two other SSA employees had assisted her and implicated Mr. Parker. Mrs. Parker admitted that she had approved benefits by taking letters addressed to different persons, changing the names and dates of those letters to match those of the applicants who had paid her money, and forging the signature of ALJ Aronson.

II

* * *

D

Mr. Parker argues that the district court abused its discretion on two evidentiary rulings.

* * *

In the second ruling, Peggy Kelly testified about a telephone conversation she had with a man who referred to Mrs. Parker as his "old lady" and who threatened Kelly. Kelly stated that she thought that the man on the telephone was Mr. Parker and her reasons for so thinking, but admitted that she could not identify his voice and that she had never previously met him. Mr. Parker argues that the government therefore failed to properly establish the evidentiary foundation for the telephone conversation. "While a mere assertion of identity by a person talking on the telephone is not in itself sufficient to authenticate that person's identity, some additional evidence, which 'need not fall into any set pattern,' may provide the necessary foundation." *United States v. Khan*, 53 F.3d 507, 516 (2nd Cir. 1995).

Here, the trial court found sufficient circumstantial evidence to indicate that the man on the telephone was Mr. Parker because Mrs. Parker placed the call to Kelly, and, thereafter, a man interrupted the telephone conversation and stated that Mrs. Parker was his "old lady." Based on this circumstantial evidence, we affirm the district court's finding that the government established a foundation for the conversation. Once the government established this foundation, it became the province of the jury to decide whether Mr. Parker was indeed the man on the phone and whether he made the threats; as the conversation was relevant to this determination, it was properly admissible under Fed. R. Evid. 401. Accordingly, we reject Mr. Parker's argument.

* * *

AFFIRMED.

[5] Outgoing Telephone Calls

[a] Illustration

Plaintiff, Easy Money, sues defendant, No Credit, Inc., claiming that the defendant failed to deliver ordered goods in a timely fashion. Easy Money takes the stand.

Plaintiff's counsel:	How did you place the order?
Easy Money:	Well, I looked up the number of No Credit in the yellow pages and called the number.
Plaintiff's counsel:	What happened?
Easy Money:	Well, the person that answered the phone said, "No Credit, may I help you?" Then I placed my order.
Plaintiff's counsel:	And what did they say?
Defendant:	Objection! Lack of authentication.
Plaintiff's counsel:.	________.

[b] Calls to Businesses

BARRICKMAN v. NATIONAL UTILITIES CO.
191 S.W.2d 265 (Mo. Ct. App. 1945)

HUGHES, PRESIDING JUDGE:

The suit was instituted by respondent against appellant to recover for personal injuries alleged to have been sustained from an explosion of gas in the basement of his home. The allegation as to negligence being, "defendant wholly failing to use a high degree of care in the control, distribution and delivery of said gas to plaintiff at said above described dwelling house and premises, negligently and carelessly permitted large quantities of said gas to escape from the pipes, mains, conduits, connections, meter, valves of jets, and to accumulate, permeate and impregnate the air in the basement of said dwelling house them and there occupied by plaintiff as aforesaid, which said fact defendant knew or by the exercise of a high degree of care on the part of defendant should have known," etc. The answer admits that appellant furnished gas to respondent in his home, denies the other allegations of the petition and alleges contributory negligence in that respondent carelessly ignited gas in the basement of his dwelling when he had knowledge of the fact that gas was escaping from the connection to the hot water heater in the basement.

The evidence of the respondent discloses that on September 11, 1944, he went to the basement of his house for the purpose of lighting his hot water heater, stooped down before the heater, lit a match, and an explosion ensued. He received burns and injuries therefrom.

* * *

Respondent's wife, Ruth Barrickman, testified that on August 29, 1944, prior to the explosion she went to the basement for the purpose of lighting the water heater, and that when she lit a match, flames rushed around on the floor. She was then asked if she made an effort to advise the appellant of the fact of that occurrence, to which objection was made on the ground that * * * the purported notice was given by telephone and that the witness did not know to whom she spoke * * *. The objection was sustained, and respondent made a proffer of proof that on the morning of August 30, 1944, the witness placed a telephone call through the operator who answered her when she took down the receiver; that she gave the number listed for the business office of the National Utilities Company and immediately thereafter a man's voice answered, "National Utilities Company"; that she then told the party who had so answered the telephone that she was Mrs. Barrickman of 602 South Florence Street, and that something was wrong with the gas appliances or pipes in the basement of their home; that a flash and explosion had occurred when she had struck a match in the basement, and she wished they would send someone to find the difficulty and repair it, and the man replied that it would be given immediate attention.* * * Objection to the proffer was sustained.

* * *

The determinative question presented in the appeal is whether or not the testimony sought to be elicited from Mrs. Barrickman with reference to a telephone conversation with someone at the business office of the defendant was admissible for the purpose of bringing notice to the defendant that on August 29th prior to the explosion on September 11th, when plaintiff was injured, gas was escaping in plaintiff's basement.* * * The general rule is that statements made by a person answering a telephone call to a place of business in the course of negotiations relating to and in the transaction of ordinary business of the company called are admissible, although no personal identification is made of such person answering the call; the presumption being that such person is authorized to transact such business for the company.

* * *

NOTE

Is there a short-cut method to authenticate several phone calls from the same person?

Remember that if the witness can identify the voice on the other end of the line, the phone call is sufficiently authenticated. Therefore, after authenticating one phone call under Rule 901(b)(6) (for example, calling a listed phone number coupled with self-identification), all other phone calls to that person may be authenticated under Rule 901(b)(5). *See Bear Stearns & Co., Inc. v. Nanos*, 1987 W.L. 5238 (N.D. Ill.).

E. HANDWRITING AND WRITINGS

[1] Federal Rule of Evidence 901

Rule 901. Requirement of Authentication or Identification

* * *

(b) Illustrations. By way of illustration only, and not by way of limitation, the following are examples of authentication or identification conforming with the requirements of this rule:

* * *

(2) Non-expert opinion on handwriting. Non-expert opinion as to the genuineness of handwriting, based upon familiarity not acquired for purposes of the litigation.

(3) Comparison by trier or expert witness. Comparison by the trier of fact or by expert witnesses with specimens which have been authenticated.

(4) Distinctive characteristics and the like. Appearance, contents, substance, internal patterns, or other distinctive characteristics, taken in conjunction with circumstances.

* * *

[2] Handwriting

[a] Illustration

Plaintiff's counsel:	On what do you base your contention that the defendant accepted your offer to sell him two hundred Rough Rider Surf Boards?
Plaintiff:	Why, on the letter he sent back to me.
Plaintiff's counsel:	I hand you what has been marked as Plaintiff's Exhibit #1. Can you identify it?
Plaintiff:	Yes, this is the letter. It's his signature at the bottom.
Plaintiff's counsel:	I offer Plaintiff's Exhibit #1.
Defendant:	Objection! Lack of foundation. Failure to properly authenticate.
Plaintiff's counsel:	__________.

[b] Extent and Timing of Perception

IN RE DIGGINS' ESTATE
34 A. 696 (Vt. 1896)

Ross, C. J.

The appellee contends * * * that the referee erroneously allowed certain witnesses who had seen the intestate write his name to testify whether the signature to a note in controversy was the genuine signature of the intestate. A witness who has seen a person write but once, and then only his name, is deemed competent to testify to the genuineness of that person's signature. That he has seen him write only a little goes to the weight to be given to his testimony, and not to the competency of the witness. If such witness says he has no opinion in regard to whether the proposed signature is that of the claimed writer, it is not error to exclude him from testifying. But if the witness is permitted to answer that he can form, and has, no opinion in regard to the genuineness of the proposed signature, if error, it is harmless error; for his testimony throws doubt upon, rather than tends to establish, the genuineness of the signature. Hence there was no reversible error in receiving the testimony of witness Wright. He had seen the intestate write, and sign his name, some 20 years before. After the lapse of such a period, unless the signature of the intestate had marked peculiarities, or the witness had an exceptional recollection, — all of which was addressed to the judgment of the triers, — his opinion, if given, would have slight probative force. But when the witness said he was in doubt, and could not swear one way or the other, his testimony could not harm the party contesting the genuineness of the intestate's signature. The witness Blanchard had seen the intestate write. From this the referee could find that he was competent to give his opinion in regard to the genuineness of the contested signature, although he did not then recall having seen him write his name. That he subsequently recalled that he had seen him write his name only added to the probative force of his testimony. This objection to the report of the referee was properly overruled. Judgment affirmed.

NOTE

Does it matter when or how the witness became familiar with the handwriting?

Unlike voice identification, a lay witness may not become familiar with a person's handwriting solely for the purpose of litigation. In *United States v. Pitts*, the Fifth Circuit Court of Appeals, in commenting on a lay witness's opinion, noted that the lay witness "obtained his 'familiarity' solely by comparing the signature on the purported car sales receipt to another sample of [the] signature. Such one-shot comparisons made for purposes of the litigation lack the extent of familiarity contemplated by Rule 901(b)(2). In light of this 901(b)(2) standard and the absence of any other evidentiary predicate that indicated justifiable reliability for this opinion, the trial judge properly excluded [the lay witness'] opinion on the genuineness of [the] signature." 569 F.2d 343, 348 (5th Cir. 1978). Recognize that an expert witness, by virtue of his or her role as an expert, is not subject to the same restrictions.

[3] Comparisons by the Jury

[a] Illustration

Plaintiff, Small Town Bank, sues defendant, Hot Checks, for recovery on a $500 bad check drawn on Hot Checks' account. Hot Checks claims the check was forged. Small Town Bank cannot afford a handwriting expert for such a small case. Plaintiff has already introduced into evidence the signature card, including Hot Checks' signature, from the defendant's account. The president of Small Town Bank is on the stand.

Plaintiff:	I hand you what has been marked as Plaintiff's Exhibit #2. Can you identify it?
President:	Yes, this is the $500 check that was cashed at our bank. The defendant claims it was forged.
Plaintiff:	Do you recognize the defendant's signature?
President:	No, I'm afraid I've never seen it before.
Plaintiff:	Your honor, I'd like to admit the check so the jury can compare the signature on the check with the one on the signature card.
Defendant:	Objection! Lack of authentication.
The court:	__________.

[b] Genuine Example

UNITED STATES v. RANTA
482 F.2d 1344 (8th Cir. 1973)

PER CURIAM:

Defendant Arnold Marvin Ranta was charged with two counts of violating 18 U.S.C. § 1708: (1) stealing a letter from the United States mail; and (2) knowing possession of a United States Treasury check unlawfully taken from the mail. A jury found Ranta guilty of the second count and he appeals his conviction. We affirm.

* * * Clayton Amundson, a disabled Vietnam veteran, was to receive "training allowance" checks from the United States Treasury while attending the University of Minnesota, Duluth Branch. At the University, Amundson lived in a two-bedroom trailer unit with three other students, defendant-Ranta, Hoene, and Trachsel. Ranta roomed with Amundson. Each of the four students had access to a single mailbox.

After failing to receive either his May or June Treasury checks, Amundson reported the losses. An investigation by the Secret Service disclosed that the May check had been cashed at a business establishment in Superior, Wisconsin, a city adjacent to Duluth. Amundson's signature had been forged as an endorsement on this check. According to the manager of the business establishment, the check had been cashed by a University of Minnesota, Duluth, student. A Secret Service Identification Specialist identified defendant's fingerprint on the May check.

Hoene, one of the other occupants of the trailer, when called as a witness for the prosecution, testified that he had forged the subsequent June Treasury check in Ranta's presence and had discussed with Ranta the possible ways of cashing a government check owned by someone else.

The Secret Service agent investigating the case took handwriting exemplars from Amundson's three roommates, including five pages of defendant-Ranta's handwriting. According to a Secret Service report, the government handwriting expert could not determine conclusively that Ranta's handwriting was the same as that found on the forged check, nor could he exclude Ranta as the forger. Neither the prosecutor nor counsel for the defendant called the handwriting expert. Over defense objections, Ranta's exemplars were submitted to the jury, and the jury was asked to compare them with the forged endorsement.

On this appeal Ranta contends that his handwriting exemplars should not have been admitted into evidence. The thrust of defendant's argument is that admission of the exemplars was error because the jury should not be permitted to do that which the government's handwriting expert could not do, *i.e.*, reach the conclusion that the forged signature on the check was Ranta's handwriting by comparing the signature with the exemplars. Defendant further alleges that the error was compounded by the prosecutor's remarks to the effect that if the handwriting expert could have exculpated Ranta, defendant's counsel would have called him. Ranta relies on several state cases to support his proposition that the exemplars were inadmissible.

* * * This circuit and other circuits have permitted the introduction of a defendant's handwriting for purposes of comparison with handwriting attributed to him.* * * The existence of Ranta's fingerprint on the missing check sufficiently connected him with the forged endorsement contained thereon and provided adequate foundation to permit the jury to make the handwriting comparison.* * * Additionally, we do not think that the government has engaged in any unfair conduct by its failure to call the handwriting expert to the stand since the expert could have been called by the defense counsel if he had not chosen to forego that opportunity as a matter of trial strategy. The government had made arrangements to have this witness available for use by the defendant.

* * *

Affirmed.

NOTE

With respect to the handwriting sample used for comparison by the jury or expert, what special considerations should an attorney keep in mind?

An attorney must establish that the sample, or exemplar, is genuine. The simplest method is to have the person whose handwriting is in question submit a sample of their writing and testify that it is genuine. Some courts have been reluctant to allow a defendant to use a sample prepared after proceedings begin, finding that the defendant "has a strong motive to alter his writing so as to render it dissimilar to an incriminating document alleged by the prosecution to be in his hand." *United States v. Pastore*, 537 F.2d 675, 678 (2d Cir. 1976). In any case, the decision whether the sample is genuine and should be admitted for comparison belongs to the judge and not the jury. *United States v. Alvarez-Farfan*, 338 F.3d 1043 (9th Cir 2003).

[4] Circumstantial Evidence

UNITED STATES v. McMAHON
938 F.2d 1501 (1st Cir. 1991)

COFFIN, SENIOR CIRCUIT JUDGE:

Appellant, Charles McMahon, was convicted of conspiracy to commit extortion, attempt to commit extortion, several counts of using a facility in interstate commerce (the telephone) to promote unlawful activity, and making false material declarations before a grand jury * * *. We affirm.

Background

In 1985, James Proko sought approval of his proposed Honda dealership from the Salem, New Hampshire planning board. Prior to the meeting at which the plan was to be discussed, Proko was contacted by William Hicks, a wealthy retired car dealer. Hicks claimed to control the votes of the planning board and demanded $10,000 from Proko to assure approval of the site. Proko called the FBI.

Under FBI supervision, Proko continued to engage in negotiations with Hicks and attempted to get Hicks to reveal the identities of those board members whose votes he allegedly controlled. Hicks never singled out any person. He eventually was tried and convicted of extortion, and his conviction was affirmed on appeal. At the time of his incarceration, Hicks finally implicated McMahon, a member of the planning board who used to work for Hicks, alleging that McMahon had needed money and had planned the whole affair. The grand jury returned a seventeen-count indictment against McMahon.

Hicks claimed that McMahon had asked him to approach Proko and had consulted with Hicks on the ensuing negotiations. Telephone toll records reflected multiple telephone calls between Hicks and McMahon during the two weeks between May 28 and June 12, 1985. On June 11, during the meeting to approve the plan, McMahon raised multiple objections to the proposed plan. At the last minute, after a motion to approve the plan had been made, he suddenly claimed to remember the potential applicability of a Salem ordinance requiring that sellers of used cars not be located within 2,000 feet of one another. McMahon noted that Rogers' service station, which was principally located in the next township of Windham but straddled the Windham/Salem town line, sold some used cars. McMahon questioned whether the ordinance would be applicable if the cars were sold from that portion of the land located in Salem. He ultimately proposed approving the plan, contingent on the outcome of the township attorney's review. Ten days later, the township attorney issued his opinion that the ordinance was inapplicable.

Although McMahon claimed to have remembered the ordinance only at the end of the meeting, the government introduced testimony from the planning director, Ross Moldoff, that immediately before the meeting he had overheard McMahon attempt to recruit another board member, George Salisbury, to help him block the plan. Another board member also testified to the content of a note he observed McMahon pass to Salisbury at the beginning of the meeting that referred to blocking the plan based on the 2,000-foot ordinance.

McMahon eventually was convicted on all but one count of the indictment. On appeal, he * * * suggests that evidence of the contents of the note that he allegedly passed at the planning board meeting was improperly admitted.

* * *

Admission of Contents of the Note

McMahon contends that the district court improperly allowed testimony about the contents of a note that he allegedly passed to George Salisbury. [The note stated "I need your help to stop the Proko plan. I believe it's within 2,000 feet of another dealer."] McMahon objected on the ground that there was nothing to demonstrate that McMahon was the author of the note * * *. Under the Federal Rules of Evidence, the authentication of evidence is a condition precedent to its admissibility. *See* Fed. R. Evid. 901(a). In order to authenticate a document under the federal rules, there must be "evidence sufficient to support a finding that the evidence is what the proponent claims it to be." *United States v. Arboleda*, 929 F.2d 858, 869 (1st Cir. 1991). The determination of whether a proper foundation has been laid for the introduction of evidence lies within the sound discretion of the district court.

McMahon contends on appeal that no adequate basis was offered by the government to support the district court's finding that he authored the note. McMahon rests his argument on the failure of the government's witness, Laurence Belair, to testify that he recognized the handwriting as McMahon's. *See* Fed. R. Evid. 901(b)(2) (allowing authentication by opinion of lay witness as to handwriting).

We reject this conclusion. Rule 901(b)(2) is provided as only one example of a means by which a document may be authenticated, not as a precondition to admissibility in and of itself. *See* Fed. R. Evid. 901(b) (providing "illustrations" of means of authentication or identification, not intended "by way of limitation" to constrain the authentication of a document). In this case, the district court was well within its discretion in determining that there was sufficient evidence to conclude that the document was a party admission. McMahon was observed passing the note. The document repeated nearly verbatim the content of a conversation conducted between McMahon and Salisbury in a "soft tone of voice" and overheard only moments before by a different board member. Salisbury was hard of hearing, so there was some basis for thinking that the conversation needed repeating. The handwritten note twice employed the personal pronoun "I," saying "*I* need your help" and "*I* believe," suggesting in the absence of a signature that the passer of the note was its author. The note described the planned Proko site as within 2,000 feet of another dealership, an issue raised by McMahon later in the meeting. Finally, there was no basis for thinking the note originated with any other author, in part because no one else raised the issue of the 2,000-foot ordinance, and in part because McMahon allegedly passed the note himself and never contended that he merely passed a note authored by another; he instead denied the existence of any note.

This evidence amply supports a reasonable conclusion that the note was written by McMahon, and thus was admissible as a party admission. *See* Fed. R. Evid. 901(b)(4) (evidence may be authenticated by "[a]ppearance, contents, substance, internal patterns, or other distinctive characteristics, taken in conjunction with circumstances"); *United States v. Newton*, 891 F.2d 944, 947 (1st Cir. 1991) (document contained sufficient connections to personally known information to be authentic, and therefore was admissible as party admission); *United States v. Ingraham*, 832 F.2d 229, 236 (1st Cir. 1987) ("Like a wide array of other phenomena, telephone calls may be authenticated by exclusively circumstantial evidence."). While the jury was entitled to disbelieve the authorship or existence of the document, the note clearly was sufficiently authenticated to be admissible by the district court.

* * *

Affirmed.

NOTE

Are there other ways to authenticate writings?

There are many ways to authenticate a writing besides showing similarities (or dissimilarities) to a known sample. Courts accept many types of circumstantial evidence to indicate the author of a writing. An interesting example of circumstantial proof of authenticity is found in *United States v. McGlory,* 968 F.2d 309 (3d Cir. 1992), a drug conspiracy case, where the government sought to admit notes indicative of drug activity against the defendant. The government relied on the following circumstances to establish authentication: the notes were seized from the trash outside from where McGlory lived during the course of the conspiracy; they were torn from a notebook found inside his house; they were contained in the same trash bag as other papers clearly identified with McGlory; the government's handwriting expert testified that the handwriting on the notes was similar to McGlory's, although he could not be conclusive; finally, the notes were similar in form and contained similar amounts and initials of persons listed in McGlory's private telephone books, who were known to associate with him. The court found that all this together was sufficient circumstantial evidence upon which a juror could find that the notes were McGlory's. Similarly, authentication has often been accomplished by showing that the information contained in the writing could only have been known to the alleged author.

F. PUBLIC RECORDS

[1] Federal Rules of Evidence 901 and 902

Rule 901. Requirement of Authentication or Identification

* * *

(b) Illustrations. By way of illustration only, and not by way of limitation, the following are examples of authentication or identification conforming with the requirements of this rule:

* * *

(7) Public records or reports. Evidence that a writing authorized by law to be recorded or filed and in fact recorded or filed in a public office, or a purported public record, report, statement, or data compilation, in any form, is from the public office where items of this nature are kept.

* * *

Rule 902. Self-Authentication

Extrinsic evidence of authenticity as a condition precedent to admissibility is not required with respect to the following:

* * *

(4) Certified copies of public records. A copy of an official record or report or entry therein, or of a document authorized by law to be recorded or filed and actually recorded or filed in a public office, including data compilations in any form, certified as correct by the custodian or other person authorized to make the certification, by certificate complying with paragraph (1), (2), or (3) of this rule or complying with any Act of Congress or rule prescribed by the Supreme Court pursuant to statutory authority.

* * *

NOTES

1. Does the custodian of the records need to appear in court?

Rule 902 provides that certain records are self-authenticating — no witness is required to appear in court to establish authenticity. The rationale is that certain records in themselves establish to a reasonable juror that they are not forgeries, e.g., a public record under seal.

2. Is authentication the only step to admissibility?

Authenticity is only one of the foundational steps toward admissibility. The Advisory Committee's Note to Federal Rule of Evidence 901(b) contains a specific reminder that "compliance with requirements of authentication or identification by no means assures admission of an item into evidence, as other bars, hearsay for example, may remain."

G. BUSINESS RECORDS

[1] Federal Rule of Evidence 902 (11) and (12)

Rule 902. Self-authentication

Extrinsic evidence of authenticity as a condition precedent to admissibility is not required with respect to the following:

* * *

(11) Certified domestic records of regularly conducted activity. The original or a duplicate of a domestic record of regularly conducted activity that would be admissible under Rule 803(6) if accompanied by a written declaration of its custodian or other qualified person, in a manner complying with any Act of Congress or rule prescribed by the Supreme Court pursuant to statutory authority, certifying that the record —

(A) was made at or near the time of the occurrence of the matters set forth by, or from information transmitted by, a person with knowledge of those matters;

(B) was kept in the course of the regularly conducted activity; and

(C) was made by the regularly conducted activity as a regular practice.

A party intending to offer a record into evidence under this paragraph must provide written notice of that intention to all adverse parties, and must make the record and declaration available for inspection sufficiently in advance of their offer into evidence to provide an adverse party with a fair opportunity to challenge them.

(12) Certified foreign records of regularly conducted activity. In a civil case, the original or a duplicate of a foreign record of regularly conducted activity that would be admissible under Rule 803(6) if accompanied by a written declaration by its custodian or other qualified person certifying that the record —

(A) was made at or near the time of the occurrence of the matters set forth by, or from information transmitted by, a person with knowledge of those matters;

(B) was kept in the course of the regularly conducted activity; and

(C) was made by the regularly conducted activity as a regular practice.

The declaration must be signed in a manner that, if falsely made, would subject the maker to criminal penalty under the laws of the country where the declaration is signed. A party intending to offer a record into evidence under this paragraph must provide written notice of that intention to all adverse parties, and must make the record and declaration available for inspection sufficiently in advance of their offer into evidence to provide an adverse party with a fair opportunity to challenge them.

[2] Committee Note to 2000 Amendment to Rule 902

The amendment adds two new paragraphs to the rule on self-authentication. It sets forth a procedure by which parties can authenticate certain records of regularly conducted activity, other than through the testimony of a foundation witness. See the amendment to Rule 803(6). 18 U.S.C. § 3505 currently provides a means for certifying foreign records of regularly conducted activity in criminal cases, and this amendment is intended to establish a similar procedure for domestic records, and for foreign records offered in civil cases.

A declaration that satisfies 28 U.S.C. § 1746 would satisfy the declaration requirement of Rule 902(11), as would any comparable certification under oath.

The notice requirement in Rules 902(11) and (12) is intended to give the opponent of the evidence a full opportunity to test the adequacy of the foundation set forth in the declaration.

[3] Translation Issues

KASSIM v. CITY OF SCHENECTADY
415 F.3d 246 (2d Cir. 2005)

LEVAL, CIRCUIT JUDGE:

Plaintiff Khaled Kassim appeals from two judgments in his favor, one for damages, one for attorney's fees, which plaintiff contends were insufficient. Kassim brought this suit under 42 U.S.C. § 1983 against the City of Schenectady ("City") and its corporation counsel, Michael T. Brockbank (collectively "defendants"), alleging that defendants violated his due process rights under the Fourteenth Amendment by evicting him from a property where he operated a convenience store, without prior notice or opportunity to be heard.

The United States District Court for the Northern District of New York (David N. Hurd, *J.*) granted Kassim's motion for partial summary judgment as to defendants' liability and ordered a jury trial to determine damages. On the trial of damages, the jury awarded compensatory damages of $ 2500 and denied punitive damages. On appeal, Kassim contests principally a court ruling limiting the scope of damages and an evidentiary ruling that limited the use of some of his evidence.

* * *

As for the award of damages, we reject Kassim's contentions.

* * *

BACKGROUND

Kassim operated a convenience store, called Victory Market, in rented space at 605 Craig Street in Schenectady, New York. Kassim's lease was not recorded. Because the owner of the property was delinquent in paying $ 11,827.78 in taxes, the City instituted foreclosure proceedings. Although defendant Brockbank, the City's corporation counsel, was aware of the Victory Market, notice of the foreclosure proceeding was sent only to the owner; no notice was given to Kassim. A default judgment of foreclosure was entered on April 7, 2001, awarding the City possession of 605 Craig Street. *Id.*

On April 23, 2001, City officials (including defendant Brockbank, a city carpenter, and police officers) arrived at the Victory Market with a notice to vacate. This was the "first and only notice plaintiff received to vacate the premises." Kassim left the premises that day with cash, lottery tickets, and cigarettes, and was told that he had thirty days to remove the remainder of his property.

* * *

* * * During the trial, Kassim attempted to introduce an English translation of notebooks written in Arabic, which were kept in Kassim's store and contained daily entries from February 2001 to April 23, 2001 (the day of eviction), showing receipts and expenditures. Defendants objected to the introduction of the exhibit. The court admitted the books, but only "for the limited purpose of showing * * * that this was a going business at the time and it was in operation." The notations of receipts and expenditures were thus excluded for the purpose of showing lost profits.

The jury awarded $ 2500 in compensatory damages for lost profits, but awarded nothing for loss and/or damage to property and denied punitive damages. The court denied plaintiff's motion to set aside the jury verdict.

* * *

DISCUSSION

1. The Amount of Damages

Kassim's appeal from the judgment awarding only $ 2500 in compensatory damages is clearly without merit and easily answered.

* * *

b. Exclusion of Business Records

Kassim contends the district court committed prejudicial error in refusing to receive an English translation of notes made by plaintiff in Arabic to show the daily receipts and expenditures of the store for the purpose of demonstrating lost profits. We find no error in the court's ruling, although we do not agree with the reasons given for it by the district court.

The reasons given by the court for the exclusion were not entirely clear. An explanation for the exclusion was based on the document's seeming inconsistency with Kassim's recent tax returns, which apparently showed lower profits than the notebooks. The court stated:

> You can't have it both ways. He can't be claiming to this jury that he's making a net profit of hundreds of dollars each day and then claiming income tax returns in which he either takes a loss or makes a minimal profit of a hundred dollars for the whole year.

In refusing to allow the notes to be presented to the jury, the court seemed to be saying one of two things: (i) as between a party's two inconsistent statements, the court may decide which was more reliable and allow only that one to be presented to the jury, or (ii) where a U.S. taxpayer declares low earnings on his tax return in order to get the benefit of low taxes, the taxpayer is estopped from inconsistently claiming higher earnings in a separate civil proceeding against a private party in which a claim of higher earnings would be advantageous. We think neither explanation would justify the court's ruling.

Where a party has made a prior statement inconsistent with the one the party seeks to advance at trial, a question of credibility arises, which is for the jury, not the judge, to assess. *See* Fed. R. Evid. 607, 613. Nor is there a rule of estoppel, based on fealty to the United States Treasury, that one who has claimed low earnings on tax returns in order to secure a low tax burden is estopped from inconsistently claiming higher earnings in a civil proceeding against a private party. The credibility of plaintiff's evidence of his business profits, in light of its inconsistency with his tax return, was for the jury to assess.

Nonetheless, the exhibit offered by plaintiff was properly excluded. The exhibit was purportedly a translation from Arabic prepared by Marcia Parker. Parker, however, admitted in her testimony she neither speaks nor reads Arabic and that her so-called translation consisted of what plaintiff told her to write. Parker did not testify that she had accurately translated the notes. Nor did Kassim testify that he had done so. There was no foundation to establish that the exhibit was a competent translation of the Arabic notes. The exhibit and testimony failed to satisfy the requirement of Federal Rules of Evidence 602, 702, and 901(a). Defendants' objection to the exhibit was properly sustained.

* * *

CONCLUSION

The judgment awarding plaintiff $ 2500 in damages is affirmed.

* * *

NOTE

What does it mean for a record to be "self-authenticating"?

"Self-authentication" means that no evidence other than the document or item itself is needed to authenticate it. Note, though, that just because evidence is authenticated does not mean that it must be accepted as valid by a factfinder. Authentication signifies only that the proponent of the evidence has done enough to identify or to explain the evidence for the trier to be justified in finding that the evidence is what the proponent claims. After the item is admitted an opposing party can offer evidence attacking its authenticity and the factfinder may accept that as true. Thus, self-authentication lifts some of the usual burden in introducing evidence from its proponent without inhibiting an opponent from offering conflicting evidence. *See, e.g.*, *United States v. McIntosh,* 200 F.3d 1168 (8th Cir. 2000) (no error in admitting certified court documents under Rule 902(4); the Court notes that the opponent could attack the authenticity of the records at trial).

H. E-MAIL AND INTERNET

UNITED STATES v. SAFAVIAN
435 F. Supp. 2d 36 (D.D.C. 2006)

PAUL L. FRIEDMAN, DISTRICT JUDGE

[The defendant was an associate of the disgraced lobbyist Jack Abramoff. He was charged with making false statements and obstruction of justice during the investigation of Abramoff.]

* * * These motions all make arguments regarding the admissibility of approximately 260 e-mails that the government seeks to admit in its case against the defendant.

A. Authentication of E-mails

Authentication is an aspect of relevancy. Advisory Committee Note, Fed. R. Evid. 901(a) (citations omitted); 31 Wright & Gold, Federal Practice and Procedure: Evidence § 7102 at 13 (2000). "The requirement of authentication or identification as a condition precedent to admissibility is satisfied by evidence sufficient to support a finding that the matter in question is what its proponent claims." Fed. R. Evid. 901(a). *See* 5 Saltzburg, Martin & Capra, Federal Rules of Evidence Manual § 901.02[1] at 901-5 (8th ed. 2002). The threshold for the Court's determination of authenticity is not high. *See, e.g.*, *United States v. Reilly*, 33 F.3d 1396, 1404 (3d Cir. 1994) ("the burden of proof for authentication is slight"); *United States v. Holmquist*, 36 F.3d 154, 168 (1st Cir. 1994) ("the standard for authentication, and hence for admissibility, is one of reasonable likelihood"); *United States v. Coohey*, 11 F.3d 97, 99 (8th Cir. 1993) ("the proponent need only demonstrate a rational basis for its claim that the evidence is what the proponent asserts it to be"). The question for the Court under Rule 901 is whether the proponent of the evidence has "offered a foundation from which the jury could reasonably find that the evidence is what the proponent says it is." 5 Federal Rules of Evidence Manual § 901.02[1] at 901-5 -901-6. The Court need not find that the evidence is necessarily what the proponent claims, but only that there is sufficient evidence that the jury ultimately might do so.

1. Rule 902(11)

Rule 902 of the Federal Rules of Evidence lists those documents that are self-authenticating — that is, those that do not require extrinsic evidence of authenticity as a condition precedent to admissibility. Rule 902(11) is intended to set forth "a procedure by which parties can authenticate certain records of regularly conducted activity, other than through the testimony of a foundation witness." Advisory Committee Note, Fed. R. Evid. 902. Similarly, the Advisory Committee Notes to Rule 803 state that Rule 902(11) "provides that the foundation requirements of Rule 803(6) can be satisfied under certain circumstances without the expense and inconvenience of producing time-consuming foundation witnesses." Advisory Committee Note, Fed. R. Evid. 803. These comments to each Rule make clear that they were intended to go "hand in hand." *Rambus, Inc. v. Infineon Technologies AG*, 348 F. Supp. 2d 698, 701 (E.D. Va. 2004) ("Rule 902(11) is * * * the functional equivalent of testimony offered to authenticate a business record tendered under Rule 803(6)").

Pursuant to Rule 902(11), the government submitted a certification from Jay Nogle, the official custodian of records for Greenberg Traurig, LLP, the law firm that once employed Jack Abramoff. Mr. Nogle stated that in his capacity as official custodian he could certify that 467,747 e-mails had been produced by Greenberg Traurig to the United States and that those e-mails comport with the requirements of Rule 902(11), in part because the e-mails "would be admissible under Fed. R. Evid. 803(6) if accompanied by a written declaration of [their] custodian or other qualified person." The government does not, however, seek to admit these e-mails pursuant to the business records exception to the hearsay rule in Rule 803(6), but offers other hearsay exceptions and non-hearsay arguments as bases for admission. The defendant objects to the authentication of the Greenberg Traurig e-mails pursuant to Mr. Nogle's Rule 902(11) certification. Because Rule 902(11) was intended as a means of authenticating only that evidence which is being offered under the business records exception to the hearsay rule, the Court will not accept the proffered Rule 902(11) certification of Mr. Nogle with reference to the Greenberg Traurig e-mail exhibits.

2. Rule 901

Because it is not appropriate for these e-mails to be admitted as self-authenticating under Rule 902 of the Federal Rules of Evidence, the Court turns to the authentication requirements set forth in Rule 901. The question under Rule 901 is whether there is sufficient evidence "to support a finding that the matter in question is what its proponent claims," Fed. R. Evid. 901(a) — in this case, e-mails between Mr. Safavian, Mr. Abramoff, and other individuals. As noted, the Court need not find that the e-mails are necessarily what the proponent claims, only that there is evidence sufficient for the jury to make such a finding. *See* 5 Federal Rules Of Evidence Manual § 901.02[1] at 901-5 -901-6 (8th ed. 2002); id. at 901-14 ("Evidence is sufficient for authentication purposes if the foundation for particular evidence warrants the trier of fact in finding that it is what the proponent claims."). Rule 901(b) sets forth illustrations of how evidence may be authenticated or identified; it emphasizes, however, that these are "illustration(s) only" and are not intended to be the only methods by which the Court may determine that the e-mails are what the government says they are. *See United States v. Dean*, 989 F.2d 1205, 1210 n. 7 (D.C. Cir. 1993) ("The rule contains an illustrative, but not exhaustive, list of suggested methods of identification.").[2] For the reasons that follow, the Court finds that there is ample evidence for the jury to find that these exhibits are, in fact, e-mail exchanges between Mr. Safavian, Mr. Abramoff, and other individuals.

[2] The first method identified by the Rule is testimony of a witness with knowledge that the matter is what it is claimed to be. Fed. R. Evid. 901(b)(1). Apparently, however, the government has decided not to call the one witness who could authenticate almost every one of the proffered e-mails, Jack Abramoff.

One method of authentication identified under Rule 901 is to examine the evidence's "distinctive characteristics and the like," including "[a]ppearance, contents, substance, internal patterns, or other distinctive characteristics, taken in conjunction with circumstances." Fed. R. Evid. 901(b)(4). Most of the proffered exhibits can be authenticated in this manner. The e-mails in question have many distinctive characteristics, including the actual e-mail addresses containing the "@" symbol, widely known to be part of an e-mail address, and certainly a distinctive mark that identifies the document in question as an e-mail. In addition, most of the e-mail addresses themselves contain the name of the person connected to the address, such as "abramoffj@gtlaw.com," "David.Safavian@mail.house.gov," or "david.safavian@gsa.gov." Frequently these e-mails contain the name of the sender or recipient in the bodies of the e-mail, in the signature blocks at the end of the e-mail, in the "To:" and "From:" headings, and by signature of the sender. The contents of the e-mails also authenticate them as being from the purported sender and to the purported recipient, containing as they do discussions of various identifiable matters, such as Mr. Safavian's work at the General Services Administration ("GSA"), Mr. Abramoff's work as a lobbyist, Mr. Abramoff's restaurant, Signatures, and various other personal and professional matters.[3]

Those e-mails that are not clearly identifiable on their own can be authenticated under Rule 901(b)(3), which states that such evidence may be authenticated by comparison by the trier of fact (the jury) with "specimens which have been [otherwise] authenticated" — in this case, those e-mails that already have been independently authenticated under Rule 901(b)(4). For instance, certain e-mails contain the address "MerrittDC@aol.com" with no further indication of what person uses that e-mail address either through the contents or in the e-mail heading itself. This e-mail address on its own does not clearly demonstrate who was the sender or receiver using that address. When these e-mails are examined alongside Exhibit 100 (which the Court finds is authenticated under Rule 901(b)(4) by its distinctive characteristics), however, it becomes clear that MerrittDC@aol.com was an address used by the defendant. Exhibit 100 is also an e-mail sent from that address, but the signature within the e-mail gives the defendant's name and the name of his business, Janus-Merritt Strategies, L.L.C., located in Washington, D.C. (as well as other information, such as the business' address, telephone and fax numbers), thereby connecting the defendant to that e-mail address and clarifying the meaning of both "Merritt" and "DC" in it. The comparison of those e-mails containing MerrittDC@aol.com with Exhibit 100 thereby can provide the jury with a sufficient basis to find that these two exhibits are what they purport to be — that is, e-mails to or from Mr. Safavian. The Court will not perform this exercise with respect to each exhibit. Suffice it to say that the Court has examined each of these e-mails and found that all those that the Court is admitting in whole or in part meet the requirements for authentication under Rule 901.

The defendant argues that the trustworthiness of these e-mails cannot be demonstrated, particularly those e-mails that are embedded within e-mails

---

[3] Presumably, a person with personal knowledge will testify that Mr. Safavian worked at GSA, and that Mr. Abramoff worked as a lobbyist and owned a restaurant named Signatures.

as having been forwarded to or by others or as the previous e-mail to which a reply was sent. The Court rejects this as an argument against authentication of the e-mails. The defendant's argument is more appropriately directed to the weight the jury should give the evidence, not to its authenticity. While the defendant is correct that earlier e-mails that are included in a chain — either as ones that have been forwarded or to which another has replied — may be altered, this trait is not specific to e-mail evidence. It can be true of any piece of documentary evidence, such as a letter, a contract or an invoice. Indeed, fraud trials frequently center on altered paper documentation, which, through the use of techniques such as photocopies, white-out, or wholesale forgery, easily can be altered. The possibility of alteration does not and cannot be the basis for excluding e-mails as unidentified or unauthenticated as a matter of course, any more than it can be the rationale for excluding paper documents (and copies of those documents). We live in an age of technology and computer use where e-mail communication now is a normal and frequent fact for the majority of this nation's population, and is of particular importance in the professional world. The defendant is free to raise this issue with the jury and put on evidence that e-mails are capable of being altered before they are passed on. Absent specific evidence showing alteration, however, the Court will not exclude any embedded e-mails because of the mere possibility that it can be done.

The defendant does raise some noteworthy points regarding the limits of what the government can show regarding these e-mails and what they purport to be. The Court notes that it is possible to authenticate these e-mails through examination of the contents, distinctive characteristics, and appearance, and others by comparison to authenticated e-mails, and the jury is free to make its own examinations and conclusions. But the Court has been aided in reaching its conclusions by the proffers of government lawyers. The government will not, of course, be permitted to make such proffers to the jury nor may government witnesses testify to facts beyond their personal knowledge concerning these e-mails. For instance, the F.B.I. agent through whom the government plans to offer these e-mails cannot testify from personal knowledge as to whether MerrittDC@aol.com is, in fact, Mr. Safavian's e-mail address. He may testify only that Exhibit 100 contains that e-mail address in the From: section of the heading, and that the Exhibit has a signature section that contains Mr. Safavian's name. Similarly, an F.B.I. agent will not be permitted to testify to the meaning of Greenberg Traurig internal e-mail codes (such as the "DIRDC-Gov" designation next to Jack Abramoff's name, which the government proffered at the May 16, 2006 hearing means that Mr. Abramoff was the Director of the Governmental Affairs Division of Greenberg Traurig's D.C. office).

Some of the e-mail addresses do not appear in full in any part of an exhibit. Rather the "To:" and "From:" parts of the heading contain full names with no e-mail address containing the @symbol. Jay Nogle, the official custodian of records for Greenberg Traurig, explained in his Rule 902(11) certification that the "To:" and "From:" sections of these e-mails denoted that a Greenberg Traurig employee had sent or received the e-mail. Certainly, if Mr. Nogle, or another Greenberg Traurig employee with knowledge of these codes, is called to testify, he or she may testify to their meaning. An F.B.I. agent may not.

In certain e-mails, Mr. Safavian appears to have replied to Mr. Abramoff's e-mails in an atypical manner. Whereas most e-mail chains appear in reverse chronological order, the most recent of the e-mails appearing first, Mr. Safavian's responses to Mr. Abramoff's e-mails sometimes come after the e-mail from Mr. Abramoff. Further complicating the matter, this reversal of the order is not designated by the "To:" and "From:" section that normally denotes the start of a separate e-mail. The result is that the text of separate e-mails appears next to one another without a clear division between the end of one and the start of the next. Having examined these e-mails in comparison to one another, the Court has determined that it is apparent that some parts of the text are questions that lead to responses, and therefore the contents and substance serve to identify the exhibit as an exchange of e-mails. A jury, using its own knowledge of how e-mail exchanges work, and considering any testimony that may be offered by those with personal knowledge of these e-mails, may determine which persons, identified in the e-mail through their addresses and names, wrote which portions. No F.B.I. agent, however, may testify to these conclusions nor state which sections of these e-mails have been written by whom. It is beyond his or her personal knowledge and would be wholly speculative.

The jury may draw whatever reasonable conclusions and inferences it chooses to from these e-mails and determine how to consider them, but the Court will not permit any testimony beyond the bare fact of what words appear on a particular e-mail by a case agent or summary witness who neither composed nor received these e-mails. Should the government choose to call Mr. Abramoff or any other of the authors of these e-mails (other than, of course, the defendant, whom the government is not permitted to call as a witness), that witness may testify as to his or her personal knowledge of any particular e-mails he or she sent or received, and to any personal knowledge of e-mail addresses of persons with whom he or she has exchanged e-mails, even if not the specific ones in evidence.

* * *

ORDERED that defendant's motion in limine to deny the government's Rule 902(11) certifications [68] is GRANTED with respect to Jay Nogle's certification, and DENIED with respect to all other Rule 902(11) certifications submitted by the government.

Internet and Email Evidence

By Gregory P. Joseph, Esq.

Editors' Note: Mr. Joseph is the former chair of the ABA Section of Litigation, a former member of the Judicial Conference Advisory Committee on Evidence Rules, and the foremost expert on authenticating electronic evidence. We are grateful for his contribution. His article is edited so as to focus on the authenticity issues presented by electronic evidence.

The explosive growth of the Internet and burgeoning use of electronic mail are raising a series of novel evidentiary issues. The applicable legal principles are familiar — this evidence must be authenticated and, to the extent offered for its truth, it must satisfy hearsay concerns. The novelty of the evidentiary issues arises out of the novelty of the media — thus, it is essentially factual. These issues can be resolved by relatively straightforward application of existing principles in a fashion very similar to the way they are applied to other computer-generated evidence and to more traditional exhibits.

I. Internet Evidence

There are primarily three forms of Internet data that are offered into evidence — (1) data posted on the website by the owner of the site ("website data"); (2) data posted by others with the owner's consent (a chat room is a convenient example); and (3) data posted by others without the owner's consent ("hacker" material). The wrinkle for authenticity purposes is that, because Internet data is electronic, it can be manipulated and offered into evidence in a distorted form.

* * *

A. Authentication

Website Data. Corporations, government offices, individuals, educational institutions and innumerable other entities post information on their websites that may be relevant to matters in litigation. Alternatively, the fact that the information appears on the website may be the relevant point. Accordingly, courts routinely face proffers of data (text or images) allegedly drawn from websites. The proffered evidence must be authenticated in all cases, and, depending on the use for which the offer is made, hearsay concerns may be implicated.

The authentication standard is no different for website data or chat room evidence than for any other. Under Rule 901(a), "The requirement of authentication * * * is satisfied by evidence sufficient to support a finding that the matter in question is what its proponent claims." *United States v. Simpson*, 152 F.3d 1241, 1249 (10th Cir. 1998)

In applying this rule to website evidence, there are three questions that must be answered, explicitly or implicitly:

1. What was actually on the website?
2. Does the exhibit or testimony accurately reflect it?
3. If so, is it attributable to the owner of the site?

In the first instance, authenticity can be established by the testimony of any witness that the witness typed in the URL associated with the website (usually prefaced with www); that he or she logged on to the site and reviewed what was there; and that a printout or other exhibit fairly and accurately reflects what the witness saw. This last testimony is no different than that required to authenticate a photograph, other replica or demonstrative exhibit. The witness may be lying or mistaken, but that is true of all testimony and a principal reason for cross-examination. Unless the opponent of the evidence raises a genuine issue as to trustworthiness, testimony of this sort is sufficient to satisfy Rule 901(a), presumptively authenticating the website data and shifting the burden of coming forward to the opponent of the evidence. It is reasonable to indulge a presumption that material on a web site (other than chat room conversations) was placed there by the owner of the site.

The opponent of the evidence must, in fairness, be free to challenge that presumption by adducing facts showing that proffered exhibit does not accurately reflect the contents of a website, or that those contents are not attributable to the owner of the site. First, even if the proffer fairly reflects what was on the site, the data proffered may have been the product of manipulation by hackers (uninvited third parties). *See, e.g., Wady v. Provident Life & Accident Ins. Co. of Am.,* 216 F. Supp. 2d 1060, 1064-1065 (C.D. Cal. 2002) ("Defendants have objected on the grounds that [counsel] has no personal knowledge of who maintains the website, who authored the documents, or the accuracy of their contents" — objections sustained). Second, the proffer may not fairly reflect what was on the site due to modification — intentional or unintentional, material or immaterial — in the proffered exhibit or testimony.

Detecting modifications of electronic evidence can be very difficult, if not impossible. That does not mean, however, that nothing is admissible because everything is subject to distortion. The same is true of many kinds of evidence, from testimony to photographs to digital images, but that does not render everything inadmissible. It merely accentuates the need for the judge to focus on all relevant circumstances in assessing admissibility under Fed. R. Evid. 104(a) — and to leave the rest to the jury, under Rule 104(b).

In considering whether the opponent has raised a genuine issue as to trustworthiness, and whether the proponent has satisfied it, the court will look at the totality of the circumstances, including, for example:

The length of time the data was posted on the site.

Whether others report having seen it.

Whether it remains on the website for the court to verify.

Whether the data is of a type ordinarily posted on that website or websites of similar entities (e.g., financial information from corporations).

Whether the owner of the site has elsewhere published the same data, in whole or in part.

Whether others have published the same data, in whole or in part.

Whether the data has been republished by others who identify the source of the data as the website in question.

A genuine question as to trustworthiness may be established circumstantially. For example, more by way of authentication may be reasonably required of a proponent of Internet evidence who is known to be a skilled computer user and who is suspected of possibly having modified the proffered website data for purposes of creating false evidence. *See, e.g., United States v. Jackson,* 208 F.3d 633, 637 (7th Cir. 2000) ("Jackson needed to show that the web postings in which the white supremacist groups took responsibility for the racist mailing actually were posted by the groups, as opposed to being slipped onto the groups' web sites by Jackson herself, who was a skilled computer user.").

In assessing the authenticity of website data, important evidence is normally available from the personnel managing the website ("webmaster" personnel). A webmaster can establish that a particular file, of identifiable content, was placed on the website at a specific time. This may be done through direct testimony or through documentation, which may be generated automatically by the software of the web server. It is possible that the content provider — the author of the material appearing on the site that is in issue — will be someone other than the person who installed the file on the web. In that event, this second witness (or set of documentation) may be necessary to reasonably ensure that the content which appeared on the site is the same as that proffered.

Self-Authentication. Government offices publish an abundance of reports, press releases and other information on their official web sites. Internet publication of a governmental document on an official website constitutes an "official publication" within Federal Rule of Evidence 902(5).

Fed. R. Evid. 902(5) provides that the following are self-authenticating:

> *Official publications.* — Books, pamphlets, or other publications purporting to be issued by public authority. Under Rule 902(5), official publications of government offices are self-authenticating.

See, e.g., Sannes v. Jeff Wyler Chevrolet, Inc., 1999 U.S. Dist. LEXIS 21748 at *10 n. 3 (S.D. Ohio March 31, 1999) ("The FTC press releases, printed from the FTC's government world wide web page, are self-authenticating official publications under Rule 902(5) of the Federal Rules of Evidence")

Chat Room Evidence. A proffer of chat room postings generally implicates the same authenticity issues discussed above in connection with website data, but with a twist. While it is reasonable to indulge a presumption that the contents of a website are fairly attributable to the site's owner, that does not apply to chat room evidence. By definition, chat room postings are made by third parties, not the owner of the site. Further, chat room participants usually use screen names (pseudonyms) rather than their real names.

Since chat room evidence is often of interest only to the extent that the third party who left a salient posting can be identified, the unique evidentiary issue concerns the type and quantum of evidence necessary to make that identification — or to permit the finder of fact to do so. Evidence sufficient to attribute a chat room posting to a particular individual may include, for example:

> Evidence that the individual used the screen name in question when participating in chat room conversations (either generally or at the site in question).
>
> Evidence that, when a meeting with the person using the screen name was arranged, the individual in question showed up.
>
> Evidence that the person using the screen name identified him — or herself as the individual (in chat room conversations or otherwise), especially if that identification is coupled with particularized information unique to the individual, such as a street address or email address.
>
> Evidence that the individual had in his or her possession information given to the person using the screen name (such as contact information provided by the police in a sting operation).
>
> Evidence from the hard drive of the individual's computer reflecting that a user of the computer used the screen name in question.

See generally United States v. Tank, 200 F.3d 627, 630-31 (9th Cir. 2000); *United States v. Simpson*, 152 F.3d 1241, 1249-50 (10th Cir. 1998); *Perfect 10, Inc. v. Cybernet Ventures, Inc.*, 213 F. Supp. 2d 1146, 1154 (C.D. Cal. 2002).

* * *

Judicial Skepticism. As they were with computerized evidence prior to the mid-1990s, some judges remain skeptical of the reliability of anything derived from the Internet. *See, e.g., St. Clair v. Johnny's Oyster & Shrimp, Inc.*, 76 F. Supp. 2d 773, 774-75 (S.D. Tex. 1999) ("While some look to the Internet as an innovative vehicle for communication, the Court continues to warily and wearily view it largely as one large catalyst for rumor, innuendo, and misinformation * * * . Anyone can put anything on the Internet. No web-site is monitored for accuracy and nothing contained therein is under oath or even subject to independent verification absent underlying documentation. Moreover, the Court holds no illusions that hackers can adulterate the content on any web-site from any location at any time. For these reasons, any evidence procured off the Internet is adequate for almost nothing * * *."). While there is no gainsaying a healthy judicial skepticism of any evidence that is subject to ready, and potentially undetectable, manipulation, there is much on the web which is not subject to serious dispute and which may be highly probative. As with so many of the trial judge's duties, this is a matter that can only be resolved on a case-by-case basis.

II. Email Evidence

Like Internet evidence, email evidence raises both authentication and hearsay issues. The general principles of admissibility are essentially the same since email is simply a distinctive type of Internet evidence — namely, the use of the Internet to send personalized communications.

Authentication. The authenticity of email evidence is governed by Federal Rule of Evidence 901(a), which requires only "evidence sufficient to support a finding that the matter in question is what its proponent claims." Under Fed. R. Evid. 901(b)(4), email may be authenticated by reference to its "appearance, contents, substance, internal patterns, or other distinctive characteristics, taken in conjunction with circumstances." *See generally United States v. Siddiqui,* 215 F.3d 1318, 1322 (11th Cir. 2000).

If email is produced by a party from the party's files and on its face purports to have been sent by that party, these circumstances alone may suffice to establish authenticity. Authenticity may also be established by testimony of a witness who sent or received the emails — in essence, that the emails are the personal correspondence of the witness.

It is important, for authentication purposes, that email generated by a business or other entity on its face generally reflects the identity of the organization. The name of the organization, usually in some abbreviated form, ordinarily appears in the email address of the sender (after the @ symbol). This mark of origin has been held to self-authenticate the email as having been sent by the organization, under Fed. R. Evid. 902(7), which provides for self-authentication of: "Trade inscriptions and the like. — Inscriptions, signs, tags, or labels purporting to have been affixed in the course of business and indicating ownership, control, or origin." Where the email reflects the entire email name of a party (and not just the mark of origin), it has been held to comprise a party admission of origin.

Independently, circumstantial indicia that may suffice to establish that proffered email were sent, or were sent by a specific person, include evidence that:

A witness or entity received the email.

The email bore the email address of a particular individual.

This email contained the typewritten name or nickname of this individual in the body of the email.The email recited matters that would normally be known only to the individual who is alleged to have sent it (or to a discrete number of persons including this individual).

Following receipt of the email, the recipient witness had a discussion with the individual who purportedly sent it, and the conversation reflected this individual's knowledge of the contents of the email.

* * *

There are a variety of technical means by which email transmissions may be traced. *See, e.g., Clement v. California Dep't of Corrections*, 2002 U.S. Dist. LEXIS 17426 at *32 (N.D. Cal. Sept. 9, 2002) ("major e-mail providers include a coded Internet Protocol address (IP address) in the header of every e-mail * * *. The IP address allows the recipient of an e-mail to identify the sender by contacting the service provider"). Therefore, if serious authentication issues arise, a technical witness may be of assistance. This may become important, for example, in circumstances where a person or entity denies receipt of an email and has not engaged in conduct that furnishes circumstantial evidence of receipt (such as a subsequent communication reflecting knowledge of the contents of the email). *See, e.g.*, *Ellison v. Robertson,* 189 F. Supp. 2d 1051, 1057 n.7 (C.D. Cal. 2002) ("Plaintiff has provided no evidence that AOL actually did receive the email. To the contrary, Plaintiff's former counsel states that while she received an acknowledgment of receipt for her April 17, 2000, email from [a local Internet provider], no such acknowledgment came from AOL"); *Carafano v. Metrosplash.com, Inc.*, 207 F. Supp. 2d 1055, 1072 (C.D. Cal. 2002) ("Plaintiff provides no evidence that [defendant Internet service] ever received the reply email in response to its welcome confirmation email").

* * *

PROBLEM 7-1

Maggy Murdick sues Helen Tracson, a gossip columnist for the *New York Finesse*, a weekly publication, for libel and slander. Maggy claims that at a series of cocktail parties a year ago Helen made comments indicating that Maggy, who is married and the mother of three children, was having an affair with the City Manager, her boss. Maggy also claims that Helen's column, "Hear Ye, Hear Ye," slandered her when it reported that "an attractive wife and mother working in a key City office seems to be sleeping more with her boss than at home." Maggy claims that the article was understood by many to refer to her, especially because of the rumors that Helen spread orally before and after the article was printed. Helen denies spreading rumors and claims that the story was not about Maggy but about someone else, although she also claims that the story turns out to be true.

At trial, Maggy calls Geoffrey Jetson as her first witness.

Direct Examination by Plaintiff's Counsel:

Q: Mr. Jetson, were you present at a cocktail party on June 3 of last year?
A: Yes, I was.
Q: Where was it?
A: At State Senator Stone's house.
Q: Prior to the party, had you ever met the defendant, Helen Tracson?
A: No.
Q: Did you meet her at the party?
A: No.
Q: Did you see her at the party?
A: No.
Q: Did you hear anyone say anything at the party about Maggy Murdick?
A: Yes, I heard the defendant * * *
Defendant: Your Honor, I object. There is nothing to tie anything said to the defendant.

Plaintiff: Your Honor, let me withdraw the question and ask another. At some point prior to today, have you become familiar with the defendant's voice?
A: Yes.
Q: How did that occur?
A: I saw her interviewed on Larry King and I heard her voice.
Q: When was that?
A: About two months ago.
Q: Now, had you ever heard that voice before?
A: Yes, at Senator Stone's party.
Q: What did you hear that voice say at Senator Stone's party?
Defendant: I object. This is not a proper foundation.
Plaintiff: Sure it is.
Court: Well, outside the presence of the jury, tell me what the answer is going to be.
Plaintiff: The witness will say that he heard the defendant say in a loud voice that "Maggy Murdick is sleeping with her boss, the City Manager, and she's doing it quite often with no sense of discretion or propriety. She ought to be ashamed."
Court: (1) __________.
Q: Can you identify in this courtroom the person you saw on Larry King?
Defendant: I object. This is not proper identification.
Court: (2) __________.
Q: I show you what has been marked for identification as Plaintiff's Exhibit 1. Can you identify it?
A: Yes. It is a tape-recording of the deposition taken of the defendant in this case.
Q: Now, did you listen to the tape?
A: Yes, I did. I listened to it yesterday.
Q: Was there any voice on the tape that you had heard before?
A: I object. The witness was not at the deposition. He has no idea what occurred, and he is not a proper witness to identify voices on this tape. Furthermore, the witness did not listen to the tape until yesterday and his testimony relates to something that occurred a year ago.
Court: (3) __________.

Cross-examination by Defense Counsel:

Q: I want to play a tape for you, sir. Are you ready?
Plaintiff: What's going on here? What is this tape?
Defendant: Your Honor, this is a tape of voices. We have a witness who made the tape and who will testify as to whose voices are on the tape. We simply want to ask this witness whether he can identify the defendant's voice on this tape.

Plaintiff: I object. They could have altered or modified the voices on that tape. This is a trick and has no bearing on what the witness has testified about.

Court: (4) __________.

Maggy calls Pen Prosper as her second witness.

Direct Examination by Plaintiff's Counsel:

Q: Do you know the defendant in this case?

A: Yes, I've known her for 10 years.

Q: Were you present at any cocktail parties a year or so ago when the defendant made comments about the plaintiff?

A: Yes I was.

Q: How many parties were you at where the defendant made comments about the plaintiff?

A: I believe three.

Q: Can you recall the dates and places of these parties?

A: I really can't. I didn't save my calendar from last year, and the parties get to be a blur after a while.

Q: Tell us what you heard the defendant say about the plaintiff?

Defendant: I object. There is no foundation about time or place.

Plaintiff: Your Honor, she will say that on three different occasions, she heard the defendant say that the plaintiff was sleeping with the City Manager and that the defendant was shouting it out for all to hear. This is important.

Defendant: It may be important, but there is no foundation.

Court: (5) __________.

Q: Did there come a time when you saw a column by the defendant that caught your eye?

A: Yes. After the parties that I was at, I saw the defendant's column in the weekly in which she wrote about an attractive wife and mother working in a key City office who was sleeping with her boss.

Q: I show you Plaintiff's Exhibit 7. Can you identify it?

A: That is a copy of the article in the weekly that I saw.

Plaintiff: We move its admission.

Defendant: Objection. The article makes no mention of the plaintiff, and thus there is no foundation.

Court: (6) __________.

Q: When you read this article, did you have any idea of whom the defendant was writing about?

Defendant: Objection. She cannot possibly know what was in the defendant's mind.

Plaintiff: That was not my question. She is entitled to say that she immediately thought that the defendant was putting in writing what she had been saying out loud.

Court: (7) __________.

Defendant calls Cyd Dirksel as her first witness.

Direct Examination by Defense Counsel:

Q: Where do you work?
A: Hollow Springs Motel.
Q: What is your job?
A: Manager.
Q: I show you Defendant's Exhibit 1. Can you identify it?
A: Yes, it is our sign-in book.
Q: Looking back approximately a year ago, can you identify any sign-ins by the City Manager?
Plaintiff: I object. May I ask two questions?
Court: Yes.
Plaintiff: Were you present when the sign-ins occurred?
A: No.
Q: Had you ever seen the City Manager's signature before the sign-ins?
A: No.
Plaintiff: I object. Lack of foundation.
Defendant: Your Honor, he's the manager. Certainly he can say that the City Manager's signature appears on 12 different occasions.
Court: (8) __________

Defendant calls Zack Yand as her second witness.

Direct Examination by Defense Counsel:

Q: Where do you work?
A: Benedict Arnold Law School.
Q: What is your job?
A: Dean of Admissions.
Q: I show you Defendant's Exhibit 1, and call your attention specifically to 12 signatures that I have marked with an x. Can you identify them?
A: Yes, I can.
Q: How can you identify them?
A: I have a certificate of achievement in my office signed by the City Manager and dated two years ago.
Plaintiff: I object. May I ask two questions?
Court: Yes.
Plaintiff: Were you present when the certificate of achievement was signed?
A: No.
Q: Had you ever seen the City Manager's signature before you received the certificate of achievement?
A: No.
Plaintiff: I object. Lack of foundation.
Defendant: Your Honor, he can recognize the signature.
Court: (9) __________.

Defendant calls Zeke Clamm as her third witness.

Direct Examination by Defense Counsel:

Q:	Where do you work?
A:	Hollow Springs Motel.
Q:	What is your job?
A:	Desk Clerk.
Q:	I show you Defendant's Exhibit 1, and call your attention specifically to 12 signatures that I have marked with an x. Can you identify them?
A:	Yes, I can.
Q:	How can you identify them?
A:	I saw the man who signed them.
Q:	Who was it?
Plaintiff:	I object. There is no proper foundation here.
Defendant:	Let me ask another question. Do you know the person who you saw sign his name?
A:	Yes.
Q:	Who was it?
A:	I object. The witness has not indicated any familiarity with the signature.
Court:	(10) __________.
Q:	Do you recall whether the City Manager was alone when he signed in?
A:	Yes. He was not alone; he was with a woman.
Q:	Is that woman present in the courtroom?
Plaintiff:	I object. May I ask a question?
Court:	Yes.
Plaintiff:	Had you ever seen the woman with the City Manager before he signed in?
A:	No.
Plaintiff:	I object. He has no basis for making any identification.
Defendant:	He does not have to have seen the plaintiff before the sign-ins occurred to identify her now.
Court:	(11) __________.

Plaintiff, who testified during her case-in-chief, is recalled for rebuttal.

Direct Examination by Plaintiff's Counsel:

Q:	I show you Defendant's Exhibit 1 in Evidence, and I want you to look at the signatures that the defendant has marked with an X. Do you see them?
A:	Yes.
Q:	Calling your attention to the first date, where were you on that day?
A:	I was 100 miles away in New York City that day and night.
Q:	I show you what has been marked for identification as Plaintiff's Exhibit 12. Can you identify it?
A:	Yes, that it is the receipt I received from the New York Center showing that I stayed there that night and paid my bill.

Defendant: I object and move to strike. This witness does not work for the New York Center and cannot lay a foundation for documents allegedly produced by that hotel.

Court: (12) __________.

Q: I show you what has been marked for identification as Plaintiff's Exhibit 13. Can you identify it?

A: Sure. That is my husband and my home telephone bill for one month last year.

Q: Calling your attention to the fifth long-distance number on that bill, can you explain that?

A: Yes. The number is that of the New York Center. My husband called me that night to talk with me. We spoke for about 10 minutes as the bill reflects.

Defendant: I object and move to strike. The witness claims to have been in New York. She could not have dialed the phone or placed the call. Thus, she cannot lay a foundation for this document.

Court: (13) __________.

Q: I show you what has been marked for identification as Plaintiff's Exhibit 14. Can you identify it?

A: Yes. It is a picture of the New York Center.

Q: Is it a fair and accurate depiction of the New York Center?

Defendant: I object. This picture shows a date stamp at the bottom of January 1 of this year. The witness claims to have been there a year ago. This picture cannot be a fair and accurate depiction of what she saw when she was there, because it was taken at a totally different time.

Court: (14) __________.

PROBLEM 7-2

The defendant was stopped for speeding by a state trooper on January 2 of this year. The trooper asked for permission to search the car, which the defendant granted. The trooper found three pounds of marijuana in a suitcase in the trunk. He arrested the defendant who is now charged with possession of marijuana with intent to distribute.

The prosecution calls the trooper as its first witness.

Direct Examination by the Prosecutor:

Q: Trooper, I show you what has been marked for identification as Government Exhibit 1. Can you identify it?

A: Yes, I can. That is the suitcase that I found in the defendant's car.

Defendant: I object. May I ask a question?

Court: Yes.

Defendant: Did you put any mark of any sort on the suitcase?

A: No.

Defendant: I object on the ground that there is no way he can identify a suitcase that has no mark on it.

Court: (1) __________.

Q: I show you what has been marked for identification as Government Exhibit 2. Can you identify it?

A: Yes, it is three pounds of marijuana which I found in an Office Deposit sack.

Defendant: I object. May I ask a question?

Court: Yes.

Defendant: Did you put any mark of any sort on the sack?

A: No.

Defendant: I object on the ground that there is no way he can identify the sack that has no mark on it.

Court: (2) __________.

Q: I show you what has been marked for identification as Government Exhibit 4. Can you identify it?

A: It's the finding of the FBI lab in Washington, D.C. that the fingerprints on the sack matched fingerprints of the defendant on file with the FBI.

Defendant: I object. May I ask two questions?

Court: Yes.

Defendant: You did not do a fingerprint analysis?

A: No.

Defendant: And you were not present when the FBI purported to do an analysis?

A: No, I was not.

Defendant: I object on the ground that there is no way he can lay the foundation for this exhibit.

Court: (3) __________.

Q: Were you present during a search of the defendant's house conducted after his arrest?

A: Yes.

Q: I show you what has been marked for identification as Government Exhibit 5. Can you identify it?

A: It's a notebook we found in the defendant's house during the search.

Q: Turning your attention to the fifteenth page of the notebook, do you see what it says?

A: Yes, it says "3 lbs M — $10,000."

Prosecutor: Move its admission.

Defendant: I object. May I ask a question?

Court: Yes.

Defendant: Do you have any personal knowledge what the writing on that page of the notebook means?

A: No.

Defendant: I object. There is no foundation here.

Court: (4) __________.

Chapter 8
BEST EVIDENCE RULE

A. DEFINITION

[1] Federal Rules of Evidence 1001–1008

Rule 1001. Definitions

For purposes of this article the following definitions are applicable:

(1) Writings and recordings. "Writings" and "recordings" consist of letters, words, or numbers, or their equivalent, set down by handwriting, typewriting, printing, photostating, photographing, magnetic impulse, mechanical or electronic recording, or other form of data compilation.

(2) Photographs. "Photographs" include still photographs, X-ray films, video tapes, and motion pictures.

(3) Original. An "original" of a writing or recording is the writing or recording itself or any counterpart intended to have the same effect by a person executing or issuing it. An "original" of a photograph includes the negative or any print therefrom. If data are stored in a computer or similar device, any printout or other output readable by sight, shown to reflect the data accurately, is an "original."

(4) Duplicate. A "duplicate" is a counterpart produced by the same impression as the original, or from the same matrix, or by means of photography, including enlargements and miniatures, or by mechanical or electronic re-recording, or by chemical reproduction, or by other equivalent technique which accurately reproduces the original.

Rule 1002. Requirement of Original

To prove the content of a writing, recording, or photograph, the original writing, recording, or photograph is required, except as otherwise provided in these rules or by Act of Congress.

Rule 1003. Admissibility of Duplicates

A duplicate is admissible to the same extent as an original unless (1) a genuine question is raised as to the authenticity of the original or (2) in the circumstances it would be unfair to admit the duplicate in lieu of the original.

Rule 1004. Admissibility of Other Evidence of Contents

The original is not required, and other evidence of the contents of a writing, recording, or photograph is admissible if —

(1) Originals lost or destroyed. All originals are lost or have been destroyed, unless the proponent lost or destroyed them in bad faith; or

(2) Original not obtainable. No original can be obtained by any available judicial process or procedure; or

(3) Original in possession of opponent. At a time when an original was under the control of the party against whom offered, that party was put on notice, by the pleadings or otherwise, that the contents would be a subject of proof at the hearing, and that party does not produce the original at the hearing; or

(4) Collateral matters. The writing, recording, or photograph is not closely related to a controlling issue.

Rule 1005. Public Records

The contents of an official record, or of a document authorized to be recorded or filed and actually recorded or filed, including data compilations in any form, if otherwise admissible, may be proved by copy, certified as correct in accordance with rule 902 or testified to be correct by a witness who has compared it with the original. If a copy which complies with the foregoing cannot be obtained by the exercise of reasonable diligence, then other evidence of the contents may be given.

Rule 1006. Summaries

The contents of voluminous writings, recordings, or photographs which cannot conveniently be examined in court may be presented in the form of a chart, summary, or calculation. The originals, or duplicates, shall be made available for examination or copying, or both, by other parties at reasonable time and place. The court may order that they be produced in court.

Rule 1007. Testimony or Written Admission of Party

Contents of writings, recordings, or photographs may be proved by the testimony or deposition of the party against whom offered or by that party's written admission, without accounting for the nonproduction of the original.

Rule 1008. Functions of Court and Jury

When the admissibility of other evidence of contents of writings, recordings, or photographs under these rules depends upon the fulfillment of a condition of fact, the question whether the condition has been fulfilled is ordinarily for the court to determine in accordance with the provisions of rule 104. However, when an issue is raised (a) whether the asserted writing ever existed, or (b) whether another writing, recording, or photograph produced at the trial is the original, or (c) whether other evidence of contents correctly reflects the contents, the issue is for the trier of fact to determine as in the case of other issues of fact.

[2] Illustration

The defendant is accused of hitting the victim over the head with a beer bottle. The victim is on the stand.

Prosecution:	Now I'd like to hand you this beer bottle. Is it similar to the one that you were hit with at the bar?
Defendant:	Objection, best evidence! The original bottle should be introduced.
The court:	________ .
Prosecution:	Is the person who hit you seated in the courtroom?
Defendant:	Objection! The witness's back was turned when he was hit. Other witnesses had a better view. This violates the best evidence rule.
The court:	________ .

B. GENERAL RULE — PROVING THE CONTENTS OF A WRITING OR RECORDING

[1] Proving the Contents of a Writing

DEMARCO v. OHIO DECORATIVE PRODUCTS, INC.
19 F.3d 1432 (6th Cir. 1994)

RALPH B. GUY, JR., CIRCUIT JUDGE:

In this diversity action, plaintiff, a former sales representative for defendants, alleged that he had orally agreed to a "life-of-the-part" contract term with defendants entitling him to post-termination commissions on sales he had procured prior to his termination. Defendants' failure to honor their commitment to pay these commissions, in part, precipitated this suit. A jury found in favor of plaintiff and awarded him approximately $850,000 on his breach of contract claim.

* * *

Ohio Decorative Products, Inc. ("Ohio Dec"), along with its subsidiaries Edgerton Metal Products, Inc., and Ken-Dec, Inc., form the Ohio Dec Metal Group ("the Group"). In 1965, Ohio Dec and Edgerton were primarily engaged in the business of manufacturing specialized metal die cast products for the appliance industry. In the fall of 1965, Robert DeMarco began negotiations with Ohio Dec concerning possible employment with the company.

DeMarco's first contact with Ohio Dec actually came in 1964. At the time, Ohio Dec was performing a trial run on a die for Chevrolet Bay City, and DeMarco was an industrial engineer at General Motors, a position he had held for the previous ten years. During this trial run, DeMarco worked with Charles Neumann, Ohio Dec's chief engineer. After DeMarco approached Neumann about a sales representative position, Neumann introduced DeMarco to Charles Moeller, Ohio Dec's president. Although DeMarco had no experience as a manufacturer's representative, DeMarco felt that he could help expand the Group's business into an area it had yet to exploit: the automotive industry.

Concerned about the risk he was facing in leaving a secure position at GM, DeMarco sought advice from several unidentified GM sales representatives before negotiating the specific terms of his prospective employment. DeMarco claims these representatives suggested that he protect himself by obtaining a "life-of-the-part" commissioning agreement. Such an agreement earns a sales representative commissions on sales of every part for which he obtains the first purchase order. Thus, until the parts in question become obsolete, a life-of-the-part agreement entitles a representative not only to commissions generated during his tenure, but also to commissions made after the representative's employment has been terminated.

In September of 1965, Moeller and DeMarco met at Ohio Dec's corporate offices in Spencerville, Ohio, to discuss the terms of DeMarco's employment. Subject to the execution of a mutually satisfactory written contract, the parties agreed on a five-year fixed term during which DeMarco would be Ohio Dec's and Edgerton's exclusive representative to the automotive industry. The parties further agreed that DeMarco would receive a five percent commission for the first three years under the agreement and a four percent commission for the remaining two years.

Finally, DeMarco and Moeller discussed "post-termination" commissions. Here, however, the parties seem to have misunderstood each other. DeMarco claims that the parties agreed "that DeMarco would receive commissions on the parts placed with the Metal Group as long as the Group made the part." DeMarco evidently took this to mean that they had settled on a "life-of-the-part" agreement. Moeller, on the other hand, disputes that such an arrangement was reached. He notes that the term "life-of-the-part" was never used during their negotiations and that they never discussed the payment of commissions beyond the first year after termination.

After the meeting, DeMarco, according to his testimony, met with a Flint, Michigan, attorney whom he had hired to draft the contract. Upon reviewing the contract and finding it to his liking, DeMarco returned to Ohio Dec's corporate offices, where both he and Moeller executed triplicate originals. DeMarco retained one copy, left another with Moeller, and hand-delivered the third to his attorney in Flint.

* * *

Defendants claim that the district court erred in admitting [testimony concerning the terms of the contract] in contravention of the best evidence rule. * * * The best evidence rule * * * is something of a misnomer. The rule is perhaps more accurately dubbed the original document rule, for instead of requiring the "best" evidence in every case, the rule actually requires the production of an original document rather than a copy.* * * By its own terms, the rule is implicated only in instances where the contents of a writing, recording, or photograph are at issue.

* * *

Although we agree with defendants that DeMarco's suit for commissions rests ultimately on the contents of the 1965 written contract and, therefore, that the best evidence rule does apply here, we conclude that this action fits squarely within the exception provided for by Rule 1004(1). "Rule 1004 does not contain an independent requirement that a search be conducted; rather, the concept of a diligent search is an avenue by which the larger issue of the document's destruction may be proved." *United States v. McGaughey*, 977 F.2d 1067, 1071 (7th Cir. 1992). Here, we are persuaded that DeMarco conducted, in good faith, a reasonably diligent search for the original copies of the 1965 written contract. That his search turned out to be futile, in our estimation, provides sufficient proof that all copies were either lost or destroyed. The 1004(1) exception to the best evidence rule therefore applies, and for this reason, defendants' challenge to the district court's admission of secondary evidence concerning DeMarco's right to post-termination commissions must fail.

* * *

NOTES

1. In *DeMarco*, the content of a contract was in issue. In what other cases are the content of writings in issue?

As a general rule, to prove the terms of a conveyance of real estate, the deed is required; to prove the outcome of a court proceeding, the judgment must be produced; and to establish the terms of a will, the will is necessary.

On the other hand, a marriage may be proven without resort to the marriage certificate, *Lopez v. Mo., Kan. & Tex. R.R.*, 222 S.W. 695 (Tex. Civ. App. 1920); payment without proof of the check or receipt, *Kendall v. Hargrave*, 349 P.2d 993 (Colo. 1960); or salary without the books of account, *D'Angelo v. United States*, 456 F. Supp 127 (D. Del. 1978). The question whether a document is essential to proving something is a question of substantive law rather than one of evidence.

2. When is a party trying to prove the contents of a document?

In *United States v. Hernandez-Fundora*, 58 F.3d 802 (2d Cir. 1995), the defendant, who beat up a fellow inmate at Raybrook penitentiary, was convicted of assault committed within the special territorial jurisdiction of the United States. The court held that the jurisdictional component was properly proved through the testimony of a witness who saw the deed establishing Raybrook's federal status — the actual deed did not have to be proffered. In the court's view, Rule 1002 did not require that the deed be placed in evidence, because it was the fact of federal status that was relevant, not the terms of the deed establishing that status. For the court to be correct, the witness presumably would be able to testify to some fact that would prove federal status independent of the contents of the document. If the witness was aware that the workers at Raybrook were paid by the federal government, this might be admissible testimony that would prove federal status without reference to the deed. If the witness was relying on the deed, however, it is difficult to see why the best evidence rule was not violated by the testimony.

It is easier to see why the best evidence rule was no bar to testimony in *United States v. Sliker*, 751 F.2d 477 (2d Cir. 1984). In this case, the court of appeals affirmed convictions arising out of a scheme to defraud a bank by cashing fraudulent checks. The court held that the government could prove that the bank was federally insured through testimony, without producing a writing documenting the insurance. The fact to be proved was the existence of insurance, not the contents of the writing. Witnesses may well have personal knowledge of federal insurance.

3. Does the existence of a document bar testimony on a subject?

Generally, a party may use a document to prove a fact, prove that fact through testimony that is independent of the document, or offer both the document and testimony. The best evidence rule is triggered only when a party wants to prove the contents of the document, not when a document is relevant for other reasons.

Since the content of the writing is not being proven when one only wishes to establish its existence, *Fish v. Fleishman*, 391 P.2d 344 (Idaho 1964), execution, *Redwine v. King*, 366 P.2d 921 (Okla. 1961), or delivery, *Higgins v. Ariz. Sav. and Loan Assoc.*, 365 P.2d 476 (Ariz. 1961), the original writing rule is not implicated in these circumstances.

In *United States v. Jones*, 958 F.2d 520 (2d Cir. 1992), a prosecution for failing to file 1984-87 tax returns, the defendant asserted that she did not file because she believed that a taxpayer could not file without paying the taxes due. The government offered a summary of her 1982 transactions indicating she had filed that year without paying. The court held that the original of her 1982 return was not required, as the summary was being introduced to demonstrate conduct inconsistent with her stated belief, not to prove the contents of her 1982 return.

In *United States v. Mayans*, 17 F.3d 1174 (9th Cir. 1994), the court found that it was error to sustain best evidence objections when the defendant attempted to cross-examine codefendant witnesses about their understanding of their plea agreements. Both the terms of the agreements and the witnesses' understanding of those terms were relevant.

[2] Writings Defined

SEILER v. LUCASFILM, LTD.

797 F.2d 1504 (9th Cir. 1986)

Farris, Circuit Judge:

Lee Seiler, a graphic artist and creator of science fiction creatures, alleged copyright infringement by George Lucas and others who created and produced the science fiction movie *The Empire Strikes Back*. * * *

Facts

Seiler contends that he created and published in 1976 and 1977 science fiction creatures called Garthian Striders. In 1980, George Lucas released *The Empire Strikes Back*, a motion picture that contains a battle sequence depicting giant machines called Imperial Walkers. In 1981 Seiler obtained a copyright on his Striders, depositing with the Copyright Office "reconstructions" of the originals as they had appeared in 1976 and 1977.

Seiler contends that Lucas' Walkers were copied from Seiler's Striders which were allegedly published in 1976 and 1977. Lucas responds that Seiler did not obtain his copyright until one year after the release of *The Empire Strikes Back* and that Seiler can produce no documents that antedate *The Empire Strikes Back*.

Because Seiler proposed to exhibit his Striders in a blow-up comparison to Lucas' Walkers at opening statement, the district judge held an evidentiary hearing on the admissibility of the "reconstructions" of Seiler's Striders. Applying the "best evidence rule," Fed. R. Evid. 1001–1008, the district court found at the end of a seven-day hearing that Seiler lost or destroyed the originals in bad faith under Rule 1004(1) and that consequently no secondary evidence, such as the post-*Empire Strikes Back* reconstructions, was admissible. In its opinion the court found specifically that Seiler testified falsely, purposefully destroyed or withheld in bad faith the originals, and fabricated and misrepresented the nature of his reconstructions. The district court granted summary judgment to Lucas after the evidentiary hearing.

* * *

Discussion

1. *Application of the Best Evidence Rule*

The best evidence rule embodied in Rules 1001–1008 represented a codification of longstanding common law doctrine. Dating back to 1700, the rule requires not, as its common name implies, the best evidence in every case but rather the production of an original document instead of a copy. Many commentators refer to the rule not as the best evidence rule but as the original document rule.

Rule 1002 states: "To prove the content of a writing, recording, or photograph, the original writing, recording, or photograph is required, except as otherwise provided in these rules or by Act of Congress." Writings and recordings are defined in Rule 1001 as "letters, words, or numbers, or their equivalent, set down by handwriting, typewriting, printing, photostating, photographing, magnetic impulse, mechanical or electronic recording, or other form of data compilation."

The Advisory Committee Note supplies the following gloss:

> Traditionally the rule requiring the original centered upon accumulations of data and expressions affecting legal relations set forth in words and figures. This meant that the rule was one essentially

> related to writings. Present day techniques have expanded methods of storing data, yet the essential form which the information ultimately assumes for usable purposes is words and figures. Hence the considerations underlying the rule dictate its expansion to include computers, photographic systems, and other modern developments * * *

We hold that Seiler's drawings were "writings" within the meaning of Rule 1001(1); they consist not of "letters, words, or numbers" but of "their equivalent." To hold otherwise would frustrate the policies underlying the rule and introduce undesirable inconsistencies into the application of the rule.

In the days before liberal rules of discovery and modern techniques of electronic copying, the rule guarded against incomplete or fraudulent proof. By requiring the possessor of the original to produce it, the rule prevented the introduction of altered copies and the withholding of originals. The purpose of the rule was thus long thought to be one of fraud prevention, but Wigmore pointed out that the rule operated even in cases where fraud was not at issue, such as where secondary evidence is not admitted even though its proponent acts in utmost good faith. Wigmore also noted that if prevention of fraud were the foundation of the rule, it should apply to objects as well as writings, which it does not.

The modern justification for the rule has expanded from prevention of fraud to a recognition that writings occupy a central position in the law. When the contents of a writing are at issue, oral testimony as to the terms of the writing is subject to a greater risk of error than oral testimony as to events or other situations. The human memory is not often capable of reciting the precise terms of a writing, and when the terms are in dispute only the writing itself, or a true copy, provides reliable evidence. To summarize then, we observe that the importance of the precise terms of writings in the world of legal relations, the fallibility of the human memory as reliable evidence of the terms, and the hazards of inaccurate or incomplete duplication are the concerns addressed by the best evidence rule.

* * * * * *

The contents of Seiler's work are at issue. There can be no proof of "substantial similarity" and thus of copyright infringement unless Seiler's works are juxtaposed with Lucas' and their contents compared. Since the contents are material and must be proved, Seiler must either produce the original or show that it is unavailable through no fault of his own. Rule 1004(1). This he could not do.

The facts of this case implicate the very concerns that justify the best evidence rule. Seiler alleges infringement by *The Empire Strikes Back*, but he can produce no documentary evidence of any originals existing before the release of the movie. His secondary evidence does not consist of true copies or exact duplicates but of "reconstructions" made after *The Empire Strikes Back*. In short, Seiler claims that the movie infringed his originals, yet he has no proof of those originals.

The dangers of fraud in this situation are clear. The rule would ensure that proof of the infringement claim consists of the works alleged to be infringed.

Otherwise, "reconstructions" which might have no resemblance to the purported original would suffice as proof for infringement of the original. Furthermore, application of the rule here defers to the rule's special concern for the contents of writings. Seiler's claim depends on the content of the originals, and the rule would exclude reconstituted proof of the originals' content. Under the circumstances here, no "reconstruction" can substitute for the original.

Seiler argues that the best evidence rule does not apply to his work, in that it is artwork rather than "writings, recordings, or photographs." He contends that the rule both historically and currently embraces only words or numbers. Neither party has cited us to cases which discuss the applicability of the rule to drawings.

To recognize Seiler's works as writings does not, as Seiler argues, run counter to the rule's preoccupation with the centrality of the written word in the world of legal relations. Just as a contract objectively manifests the subjective intent of the makers, so Seiler's drawings are objective manifestations of the creative mind. The copyright laws give legal protection to the objective manifestations of an artist's ideas, just as the law of contract protects through its multifarious principles the meeting of minds evidenced in the contract. Comparing Seiler's drawings with Lucas' drawings is no different in principle than evaluating a contract and the intent behind it. Seiler's "reconstructions" are "writings" that affect legal relations; their copyrightability attests to that.

A creative literary work, which is artwork, and a photograph whose contents are sought to be proved, as in copyright, defamation, or invasion of privacy, are both covered by the best evidence rule. We would be inconsistent to apply the rule to artwork which is literary or photographic but not to artwork of other forms. Furthermore, blueprints, engineering drawings, architectural designs may all lack words or numbers yet still be capable of copyright and susceptible to fraudulent alteration. In short, Seiler's argument would have us restrict the definitions of Rule 1001(1) to "words" and "numbers" but ignore "or their equivalent." We will not do so in the circumstances of this case.

Our holding is also supported by the policy served by the best evidence rule in protecting against faulty memory. Seiler's reconstructions were made four to seven years after the alleged originals; his memory as to specifications and dimensions may have dimmed significantly. Furthermore, reconstructions made after the release of *The Empire Strikes Back* may be tainted, even if unintentionally, by exposure to the movie. Our holding guards against these problems.

2. Rule 1008

As we hold that the district court correctly concluded that the best evidence rule applies to Seiler's drawings, Seiler was required to produce his original drawings unless excused by the exceptions set forth in Rule 1004.* * *

In the instant case, prior to opening statement, Seiler indicated he planned to show to the jury reconstructions of his "Garthian Striders" during the opening statement. The trial judge would not allow items to be shown to the jury until they were admitted in evidence. Seiler's counsel reiterated that he needed to show the reconstructions to the jury during his opening statement.

Hence, the court excused the jury and held a seven-day hearing on their admissibility. At the conclusion of the hearing, the trial judge found that the reconstructions were inadmissible under the best evidence rule as the originals were lost or destroyed in bad faith. This finding is amply supported by the record.

Seiler argues on appeal that regardless of Rule 1004(1), Rule 1008 requires a trial because a key issue would be whether the reconstructions correctly reflect the content of the originals.* * *

Seiler's position confuses admissibility of the reconstructions with the weight, if any, the trier of fact should give them, after the judge has ruled that they are admissible. Rule 1008 states, in essence, that when the *admissibility* of evidence other than the original depends upon the fulfillment of a condition of fact, the trial judge generally makes the determination of that condition of fact. The notes of the Advisory Committee are consistent with this interpretation in stating: "Most preliminary questions of fact in connection with applying the rule preferring the original as evidence of contents are for the judge * * * [t]hus the question of. . . fulfillment of other conditions specified in Rule 1004 * * * is for the judge." In the instant case, the condition of fact which Seiler needed to prove was that the originals were not lost or destroyed in bad faith. Had he been able to prove this, his reconstructions would have been admissible and then their accuracy would have been a question for the jury. In sum, since admissibility of the reconstructions was dependent upon a finding that the originals were not lost or destroyed in bad faith, the trial judge properly held the hearing to determine their admissibility.

* * *

AFFIRMED

---

[3] Physical Evidence

UNITED STATES v. DUFFY

454 F.2d 809 (5th Cir. 1972)

WISDOM, CIRCUIT JUDGE:

The defendant-appellant James H. Duffy was convicted by a jury of transporting a motor vehicle in interstate commerce from Florida to California knowing it to have been stolen in violation of 18 U.S.C. § 2312. He was sentenced to imprisonment for a term of two years and six months* * *.

At the trial, the Government established that Duffy was employed in the body shop of an automobile dealership in Homestead, Florida; that the stolen vehicle was taken by the dealership as a trade-in on the purchase of a new car; that the vehicle was sent to the body shop for repair; and that the vehicle and the defendant disappeared over the same weekend. The Government also presented testimony as to the discovery of the car in California including the testimony of 1) a witness who was found in possession of the vehicle and arrested and who testified he had received the vehicle from the defendant, 2) a San Fernando, California police officer who made the arrest and recovered the automobile, and 3) an F.B.I. agent who examined the vehicle, its contents, and the vehicle identification number. The defense stipulated to the authenticity of fingerprints, identified as Duffy's found on the rear-view mirror of the vehicle. The defense sought, through the testimony of three witnesses including the defendant, to establish that Duffy had hitchhiked to California and that, although he had worked on the stolen vehicle in the automobile dealership in Florida, he had not stolen it and had not transported it to California.

Both the local police officer and the F.B.I. agent testified that the trunk of the stolen car contained two suitcases. Found inside one of the suitcases, according to the witnesses, was a white shirt imprinted with a laundry mark reading "D-U-F". The defendant objected to the admission of testimony about the shirt and asked that the government be required to produce the shirt. It is undisputed that the shirt was available to be produced and that there was no reason for failure to produce the shirt. The trial judge overruled the objection and admitted the testimony. This ruling is assigned as error.

The appellant argues that the admission of the testimony violated the "Best Evidence Rule". According to his conception of the "Rule", the Government should have been required to produce the shirt itself rather than testimony about the shirt. This contention misses the import of the "Best Evidence Rule." * * * Although the phrase "Best Evidence Rule" is frequently used in general terms, the "Rule" itself is applicable only to the proof of the contents of a writing. * * * McCormick summarizes the policy-justifications for the rule preferring the original writing:

> (1) * * * precision in presenting to the court the exact words of the writing is of more than average importance, particularly as respects operative or dispositive instruments, such as deeds, wills and contracts, since a slight variation in words may mean a great difference in rights, (2) * * * there is a substantial hazard of inaccuracy in the human process of making a copy by handwriting or typewriting, and (3) as respects oral testimony purporting to give from memory the terms of a writing, there is a special risk of error, greater than in the case of attempts at describing other situations generally. In the light of these dangers of mistransmission, accompanying the use of written copies or of recollection, largely avoided through proving the terms by presenting the writing itself, the preference for the original writing is justified.

The "Rule" is not, by its terms or because of the policies underlying it, applicable to the instant case. The shirt with a laundry mark would not, under ordinary understanding, be considered a writing and would not, therefore, be covered by the "Best Evidence Rule." When the disputed evidence, such as the shirt in this case, is an object bearing a mark or inscription, and is, therefore, a chattel *and* a writing, the trial judge has discretion to treat the evidence as a chattel or as a writing. In reaching his decision, the trial judge should consider the policy-consideration behind the "Rule". In the instant case, the trial judge was correct in allowing testimony about the shirt without requiring the production of the shirt. Because the writing involved in this case was simple, the inscription "D-U-F", there was little danger that the witness would inaccurately remember the terms of the "writing". Also, the terms of the "writing" were by no means central or critical to the case against Duffy. The crime charged was not possession of a certain article, where the failure to produce the article might prejudice the defense. The shirt was collateral evidence of the crime. Furthermore, it was only one piece of evidence in a substantial case against Duffy.

* * *

Affirmed.

NOTE

When might the best evidence rule be relevant to physical evidence?

In *United States v. Stockton*, 968 F.2d 715 (8th Cir. 1992), a prosecution for conspiring to manufacture methamphetamine, the government offered photographs of miscellaneous papers seized at a coconspirator's house. Rejecting the government's argument that the best evidence rule does not apply to photographs of demonstrative evidence, the court held that the contents of the photographs were at issue in this case because a DEA agent testified to the contents of the photographs and specifically read from them. The court also found, however, that there was no error in admitting the photographs in lieu of the originals, because they were "duplicates" admissible under Rule 1003. This case is a reminder that when a party offers documents as part of proof, even in a case that does not involve documents as an element of a claim or defense, the best evidence rule becomes relevant if the party wishes to prove the contents of the documents as a part of its evidence.

[4] Tape Recordings

UNITED STATES v. HOWARD
953 F.2d 610 (11th Cir. 1992)

PER CURIAM:

* * *

Facts

The record demonstrates that in April 1990, Howard approached his long-time friend and fellow resident of Cedartown, Georgia, Richard Landrum ("Landrum"), and asked him for help in obtaining fifty-one hundred pounds of marijuana. At the time of the inquiry, Howard was aware that Landrum had recently been arrested on narcotics charges in Alabama. Landrum referred this information to the Drug Enforcement Agency ("DEA"). Landrum was subsequently introduced to DEA agent Mike Dolan ("Dolan"). After debriefing Landrum with DEA agent Jack Harvey ("Harvey"), Dolan instructed Landrum to make a monitored telephone call to Howard later that same day to discuss the marijuana deal. Prior to making the call, Dolan told Landrum that the scenario would be that an individual by the name of "Mike" would be bringing the marijuana in from Texas. As originally planned, Dolan was to pose as "Mike."

Numerous monitored telephone conversations between Landrum and Howard were recorded. During one of the conversations, Howard stated that a portion of the purchase money would be provided by a third party. Howard's side of the taped conversation was only partially audible, so the district court, after having the tape played for the jury, permitted, over objection, the monitoring agent, Harvey, to testify as to its contents. According to Harvey, Howard made references during the call to an earlier attempt on his part to purchase marijuana and to the manner and price at which he planned to resell the marijuana about to be purchased.

* * *

Discussion

Howard argues that agent Harvey should not have been permitted to testify as to recorded statements made by Howard which he overheard, even though, as Howard concedes, the tape was only partially audible. Howard relies on the "best evidence rule" in support of his contention that Harvey's testimony was inadmissible. The best evidence rule, however, requires the introduction of original recordings, if at all, only when the content of the recording itself is a factual issue relevant to the use. Since the proffered testimony was offered not to prove the content of the tapes, but rather, the content of the conversations, the best evidence rule does not apply, and agent Harvey's testimonial recollection of the conversation was properly admitted.

The tape in issue concerned a May 7, 1990, conversation between Landrum and Howard, which was monitored by Harvey. Harvey testified that, although much of the tape was inaudible, he was able to hear both sides of the conversation while it was taking place as though he was participating in it. At trial, Howard did not contend that the transmitting equipment was not working properly, only that the tape recording was the best and only evidence of the conversation which should have been admitted. We disagree.

* * *

The best evidence rule presupposes the existence at one time of a decipherable original, and is intended to prevent fraud in proving the contents of documents and/or recordings. In the present case, this underlying purpose would not have been furthered by the exclusion of the agent's testimony since no audible original ever existed. Moreover, the monitoring agent testified at trial giving Howard ample opportunity to challenge through cross-examination the agent's ability to hear and recollect the substance of the conversation.

In conclusion, we are persuaded that, since the prosecution was attempting to prove the contents of the recorded conversation and not the contents of the disputed tape, the district court acted within its discretion in permitting the testimony of the listening agent. Accordingly, we affirm Howard's conviction.

NOTES

1. If a tape exists, must it be offered?

In *United States v. Fagan*, 821 F.2d 1002 (5th Cir. 1987), the Court held that the best evidence rule was not violated when testimony was admitted concerning a conversation, even though a tape was available. The Court reasoned, as in *Howard, supra,* that the testimony was offered to prove the content of the conversation, not the content of the tape. There is no requirement that a party that has a tape must offer it before eliciting testimony. Participants in conversations may testify to what they said and heard without offering a tape. For strategic reasons, however, a party may want to offer a tape before eliciting testimony. This is an option, not a requirement.

2. Does the best evidence rule apply to transcripts of oral testimony?

The analysis of conversations also applies to transcripts of events or testimony. The fact that a transcript is made does not preclude a witness who was present from relating the testimony. *Meyers v. United States*, 171 F.2d 800 (D.C. Cir. 1949).

[5] Pictures, Films, and X-Rays

UNITED STATES v. LEVINE
546 F.2d 658 (5th Cir. 1977)

CLARK, CIRCUIT JUDGE:

Defendants, Sidney Levine and MPD Film Productions, Inc. (MPD), appeal from judgments of conviction and sentences entered by the district court for conspiracy and interstate shipment of obscene films. Because the indictment charged separate, distinct, and unrelated offenses by different defendants in contravention of Federal Rule of Criminal Procedure 8(b), we reverse and remand for a new trial. Since the cause must be tried again, we also reach and decide other assignments of error likely to recur.

* * *

To understand the evidentiary objections raised by defendants, a brief explication of the film-making process proof introduced in this case is necessary. Upon shooting a 16 millimeter film for Levine, Harvard would ship the initial negative material to Radiant in New York for processing. This footage was processed and developed by Radiant into footage called "dailies." Radiant returned the dailies to Harvard who cut, edited, and prepared what is called the "cut negative." Music and sound were then synchronized with the scenes in the cut negative and applied to the film. The resulting product is called a "work print." Harvard then shipped the work print of each film to Radiant for the making of what is called the "answer print." In New York, Levine would approve the answer print from which "release prints" were made for distribution of the final version of the film.

After a release print of *Ball and Chain* was exhibited to the jury in November, 1975, Harvard was asked whether he could testify that the scenes from the release print were identical to those contained in the work print he had shipped to Radiant in November, 1972. Although he admitted that it would be impossible for him to establish the two as identical in every respect, Harvard stated that he knew it was the film he had made in November, 1972. He knew this from the film's title, credits, participants, props, and the fact that each of his films made for Levine had a joke or gag which served as the film's "story." The telling of the joke comprised 10 percent of the action with the remainder being explicit sex. A special agent of the FBI testified that he saw *Ball and Chain* in December, 1972 and that the film shown in the courtroom in November, 1975 was the same. At trial, defendants objected to the authentication of *Ball and Chain* as violating the best evidence rule. The objection was overruled.

Defendants now argue that since Counts IV and V charged shipment of the *Ball and Chain* work print from Florida to New York in November, 1972, admission and viewing a release print of the film violated the best evidence rule. They argue that the best evidence that the 1972 work print is obscene is the work print itself. They contend that the government's failure to account for not introducing the 1972 work print precluded the introduction of the release print of *Ball and Chain* which is merely secondary evidence.

* * *

Federal Rule of Evidence 1002 provides: "To prove the content of a writing, recording, or photograph, the original writing, recording, or photograph is required, except as otherwise provided in [the Federal Rules of Evidence] or by Act of Congress." Motion pictures are within the ambit of the definition of photograph, and an original of the motion picture "includes the negative or any print therefrom." Fed. R. Evid. 1001(3). Accordingly, under the Federal Rules of Evidence, the 1972 work print or cut negative as well as the answer prints and release prints are regarded as originals of the film *Ball and Chain*. Whether a motion picture film is obscene must be adjudged upon viewing it in its entirety. *Roth v. United States*, 354 U.S. 476, 489 (1956). The contents of the film are what is sought to be proved. Thus, the "best evidence" standard embodied in rule 1002 applies to the introduction of the film. Harvard's testimony that the release print of *Ball and Chain* viewed during trial was substantially the same as the work print he shipped to Radiant in New York in November, 1972, provided sufficient authentication. Fed. R. Evid. 901(a), (b)(1); *see id.* 104(b).

NOTES

1. When is the best evidence rule inapplicable to films?

Generally, the best evidence rule will not apply to films or videotapes that are created to illustrate how an event occurred, but that are not offered as evidence of the actual event. In *Persian Galleries, Inc. v. Transcontinental Ins. Co.*, 38 F.3d 253 (6th Cir. 1994), the court affirmed a judgment for the plaintiff rug dealer in an action against its insurer for the alleged theft of oriental rugs from its store. The court held there was no abuse of discretion in admitting a videotaped reenactment of the theft, where the experiment and the actual conditions at the scene were substantially similar, even though not identical. In this kind of case, any version of the film will not involve best evidence issues; however, concerns about relevance and possible unfairness may arise.

2. Are X-rays treated differently from regular photographs?

The Advisory Committee's Note to Federal Rule of Evidence 1002 points out that "[t]he usual course is for a witness on the stand to identify the photograph or motion picture as a correct representation of events which he saw or of a scene with which he is familiar. In fact he adopts the picture as his testimony, or, in common parlance, uses the picture to illustrate his testimony. Under these circumstances, no effort is made to prove the contents of the picture, and the rule is inapplicable."

X-rays, on the other hand, are generally subject to the best evidence rule. Consider that when a doctor or radiologist testifies, he or she is often called to prove the condition of a patient's internal organs. To do this, the doctor or radiologist typically testifies to information gained from X-rays. Here, the contents of the X-rays — the condition of a patient — are in issue; therefore, the best evidence rule must apply. The following, however, is an excerpt from the Advisory Committee's Note to Rule 1002 which contains an exception to this general rule:

> It should be noted, however, that Rule 703, *supra*, allows an expert to have an opinion based on matters not in evidence, and the present rule must be read as being limited accordingly in this application. Hospital records which may be admitted as business records under Rule 803(6) commonly contain reports interpreting X-rays by the staff radiologist, who qualifies as an expert, and these reports need not be excluded from the records by the instant rule.

Note, however, that the X-ray will not be admissible under Rule 703 unless its probative value in illustrating the expert's opinion substantially outweighs the risk that the jury will use the X-ray as substantive evidence. See the discussion of Rule 703 in Chapter Nine, *supra*.

3. What is the first step in every best evidence analysis?

As the examples so far illustrate, the first step in any best evidence analysis is to ask whether, when a best evidence objection is made, the proponent of the challenged evidence is offering: (a) a writing or recording; (b) to prove the contents thereof. If the evidence does not constitute a writing or recording or if the proponent is not attempting to prove the contents of a writing or recording, the best evidence objection will be overruled.

C. DUPLICATES AND SECONDARY EVIDENCE

[1] Duplicates

RAILROAD MANAGEMENT COMPANY LLC v. CFS LOUISIANA MIDSTREAM CO.

428 F.3d 214 (5th Cir. 2005)

Emilio M. Garza, Circuit Judge:

Strong Capital I, L.P. and its agent, Railroad Management Co., L.L.C. (collectively "Strong"), appeal the district court's order granting summary judgment for the defendant CFS Louisiana Midstream Co. ("CFS"). The issues on appeal are whether the district court abused its discretion in excluding evidence proffered by Strong that it had been assigned the right to collect payments from CFS pursuant to a licensing agreement, and whether the district court erred in holding as a matter of law that the parties had not entered into an implied contract.

I

In 1973, Enterprise Pipeline Company ("Enterprise") and Southern Pacific Transportation Company ("Southern Pacific") entered into a licensing agreement that permitted Enterprise to build a pipeline across Southern Pacific's land. In exchange, Enterprise agreed to pay an annual fee. Through a series of assignments, CFS became liable for making the annual payment and Union Pacific Railroad Company ("Union Pacific") became entitled to receipt of those payments. Strong contends that Union Pacific assigned its rights to it in 2001. Accordingly, Strong sent CFS bills requesting that either the annual payment be made or the pipeline removed. CFS failed to do either. Strong and its agent, Railroad Management, subsequently commenced this action, alleging a claim for breach of contract.

During the course of the litigation, CFS served a discovery request on Railroad Management for a copy of the assignment agreement between Union Pacific and Strong, and filed a motion for summary judgment on the grounds that there was no evidence that Union Pacific ever assigned its interests to Strong. Strong objected to the discovery request on the ground that the agreement contained proprietary information. Following a discovery conference, the district court ordered Railroad Management to produce the assignment agreement in a redacted form that eliminated the amount that Strong paid Union Pacific for the assignment and the names of other property owners affected by the transaction. Strong cross-moved for summary judgment.

Strong failed to submit a complete copy of the assignment agreement either in opposition to CFS's motion or in support of its own. Instead, it submitted: (1) affidavits of Howard L. Armistead III, Railroad Management's manager, and Greg Pinker, Union Pacific's director of commerce, stating that Union Pacific assigned its rights to Strong; (2) a four-page excerpt of the assignment agreement; and (3) what appeared to the district court to be a retyped version of the assignment agreement, omitting the proprietary information as provided for in the district court's discovery ruling. The district court held that none of this evidence was admissible to prove Strong's right to collect the licensing fees. After finding no evidence of an actual or implied contract between CFS and Strong, the district court granted summary judgment for CFS. Strong appealed.

II

Strong first contends that the district court abused its discretion in excluding the affidavits of Armistead and Pinker, submitted to prove the existence of an assignment agreement between Union Pacific and Strong, and Strong's rights thereunder. We review a district court's exclusion of evidence for an abuse of discretion. Resolution of preliminary factual questions concerning the admissibility of evidence are reviewed for clear error.

A

Pursuant to Federal Rule of Evidence 1002, the district court ruled that the Pinker and Armistead affidavits would be considered for the purpose of proving the existence of an agreement between Strong and Union Pacific, but not to prove the terms of that agreement, one of which was the assignment of the proceeds of the lease to CFS. Strong contends that Pinker's and Armistead's affidavits were not submitted "to prove the content of" the assignment, but instead merely to prove that an assignment of the relevant rights occurred.

Federal Rule of Evidence 1002, commonly called the "best evidence rule", provides "to prove the content of a writing, recording, or photograph, the original writing, recording, or photograph is required, except as otherwise provided in these rules or by Act of Congress." But where the writing is not "closely related to a controlling issue," the Rules of Evidence deem the matter "collateral" and "other evidence of the contents of [the] writing" is admissible. Fed. R. Evid. 1004(4).

Difficulty applying the rule commonly arises in situations such as this, where the party proffering the affidavit or testimony contends that it is not intended to "prove the content" of the document it discusses, but merely its "existence." The Rules do not define the difference, but in practice "testimony about a document cannot go very far without referring to its terms." 4 Wigmore on Evidence § 1242 (Chadbourne rev. 1972). The distinction requires careful consideration of the facts of each case to avoid descent into mere "logical subtlety and verbal quibbling. "*Id.*; *see* McCormick on Evidence § 233 (John W. Strong ed., 5th ed. 1999) (discussing difficulty); 31 Wright & Gold, Federal Practice and Procedure § 7184 (2000) (same). Although there are cases from this court differentiating between the content of a writing and the existence of the writing, they generally address the issue in a conclusory fashion and provide little guidance. *See, e.g., Dalton v. Fed. Deposit Ins. Corp.*, 987 F.2d 1216, 1223 (5th Cir. 1993) (in suit on defaulted promissory note, plaintiff need not produce documents that show precise payments made by the defendant and amounts owed in lieu of affidavit of bank officer); *United States v. Yamin*, 868 F.2d 130, 134 (5th Cir. 1989) (to prove that trademark on watch was counterfeit, prosecution need not produce actual watch even though "it may be argued that it is the content of [the writing on the watch] that must be proved"); *United States v. Carlock*, 806 F.2d 535, 551 (5th Cir. 1986) (testimony that union officials deviated from an "out-of-work list" used to assign jobs admissible in lieu of the actual list because the purpose of the testimony was not to prove contents of the list, but only to prove that it was not followed). The authorities from other jurisdictions appear to be in conflict.

In any event, because application of the best evidence rule generally depends on the "particular state of facts presented in each case and changing slightly in each instance, * * * rulings are generally of little profit as precedents." 4 Wigmore, *supra* at § 1242; *see* 31 Wright & Gold, *supra* at 7184 ("Rule 1002 is deceptive in its apparent simplicity and * * * its application frequently requires a careful consideration of the facts in each case."); Comment, The Best Evidence Rule, 14 Ark. L. Rev. 153, 158–59 (1960) (cautioning against "the danger that particular cases will solidify into unalterable rules and thus be applied when the circumstances of the case would not merit such requirements").

The purpose, flexibility, and fact-intensive nature of the application of the best evidence rule persuade us that the following factors are appropriately considered when distinguishing between whether it is the content of the document or merely its existence that a witness intends to testify concerning:

> (a) the relative importance of content in the case, (b) the simplicity or complexity of content and consequent risk of error in admitting a testimonial account, (c) the strength of the proffered evidence of content, taking into account corroborative witnesses or evidence and the presence or absence of bias or self-interest on the part of the witnesses, (d) the breadth of the margin for error within which mistake in a testimonial account would not undermine the point to be proved, (e) the presence or absence of an actual dispute as to content, (f) the ease or difficulty of producing the writing, and (g) the reasons why the proponent of other proof of its content does not have or offer the writing itself.

5 Christopher B. Mueller & Laird C. Kirkpatrick, Federal Evidence § 570 (2d ed. 1994); *see also* McCormick, *supra* at § 233 (arguing that application of the rule should turn "upon the trial judge's determination of such factors as the centrality of the writing to the litigation, the importance of bringing the precise words of the writing before the trier, and the danger of mistransmission or imposition in the absence of the original"). Although a court must be careful in applying these factors so as not "to hamper the inquiry without at all advancing the cause of truth," *United States v. Manton*, 107 F.2d 834, 845 (2d Cir. 1939) (Sutherland, J., sitting as circuit judge), we are persuaded that in this case the district court did not abuse its discretion in excluding the affidavits.

The affidavits in the present case were submitted to prove: 1) that an agreement between Union Pacific and Strong existed; 2) that it concerned the assignment of certain rights in land; 3) that one such right was to collect payments on the license agreement with CFS; and 4) the date upon which that agreement was effective. It is not disputed that Strong had the assignment agreement at its disposal, and it has provided no justification for its failure to submit admissible copies of them. Nor is it disputed that the fact of assignment and the relevant time periods are facts critical and central to this litigation. The assignment agreement in question could not have been identified as such without reference to its content. Under these circumstances, it was not an abuse of discretion to exclude oral testimony of the transaction.

B

Strong also contends that the district court erred when it excluded Exhibit D, a four-page excerpt of the assignment agreement between Strong and Union Pacific. The district court held that Strong had failed to authenticate the exhibit and that it was an inadmissible duplicate of the original contract.

Federal Rule of Evidence 901(a) states that "the requirement of authentication or identification as a condition precedent to admissibility is satisfied by evidence sufficient to support a finding that the matter in question is what its proponent claims." The district court noted that neither Pinker nor Armistead referred to the excerpt in their affidavits and that there was no other evidence on record that served to authenticate the document. Strong relies on *McConathy v. Dr. Pepper/Seven Up Corp.*, 131 F.3d 558 (5th Cir. 1998), for the proposition that because it had previously produced the excerpt in response to a discovery request, the exhibit was properly authenticated. In *McConathy*, a wrongful termination case, the district court admitted the plaintiff's application for social security benefits for the purpose of demonstrating that she was judicially estopped from denying the information she had provided in that form. We held that the district court had not abused its discretion in concluding that the exhibit was properly authenticated where: "(1) [the plaintiff] produced the document in response to a discovery request, (2) the document bore [the plaintiff's] signature, (3) [the plaintiff] did not claim that the document is not authentic or that her signature is a forgery, and (4) [the plaintiff] acknowledged in her response to [the defendant's] motion for summary judgment that she requested total disability benefits for certain time periods."

None of these criteria apply to the case at bar. Exhibit D was produced during discovery by Strong, the party seeking to benefit from the inference it provides. The document does not bear the signature of any of CFS's agents. Further, Strong does not indicate any place in the record where CFS has acknowledged the existence of any facts that would tend to authenticate the exhibit. Accordingly, it was not an abuse of discretion to exclude the exhibit pursuant to Federal Rule of Evidence 901.

C

Strong argues that the district court abused its discretion when it excluded Exhibit G, a redacted version of the assignment agreement, pursuant to

Federal Rule of Evidence 1003. Rule 1003 provides, "A duplicate is admissible to the same extent as an original unless (1) a genuine question is raised as to the authenticity of the original or (2) in the circumstances it would be unfair to admit the duplicate in lieu of the original." For a document to be a "duplicate," however, it must be "a counterpart produced by the same impression as the original, or from the same matrix, or by means of photography, including enlargements and miniatures, or by mechanical or electronic re-recording, or by chemical reproduction, or by other equivalent techniques which accurately reproduces the original." Fed. R. Evid. 1001(4).

The district court concluded that the redacted version of the agreement was neither the original writing nor a duplicate. Instead, based on physical inconsistencies between Exhibit G and Exhibit D, which Strong argued were duplicates of the same contract, the district court concluded that there was insufficient evidence to support a conclusion that Exhibit G was either an original or a duplicate of the assignment agreement. The page numbering of the two exhibits do not correspond to each other, and the two documents have different identifying marks in their lower left-hand corners. *Cf.* 31 Wright & Gold, *supra* at § 7167 ("In determining whether the copy is an accurate reproduction, the court may consider, amongst other evidence, the appearance of the very item in question."). We therefore cannot conclude that the district court's finding that Exhibit D was not a duplicate was clearly erroneous.

* * *

IV

For the above stated reasons, we AFFIRM the judgment of the district court

---

NOTES

1. Why are duplicates readily admissible?

Rule 1003 is clearly intended to do away with technical best evidence objections, in recognition of the highly reliable way in which many copies of writings and recordings are made in an era of high technology. The thrust of the Federal Rules is to limit best evidence issues to situations in which a party raises a genuine issue of the authenticity of a writing or recording. Some evidence of this is found in Rule 1007, which does not require an original or a duplicate where a party has conceded under certain circumstances the genuineness of a writing or recording. *See, e.g., United States v. Westmoreland*, 312 F.3d 302 (7th Cir. 2002) (holding that that four tapes of incriminating conversations between the defendant and a co-conspirator were properly admitted; the "first generation copies" were admissible as duplicates under Rule 1003; the defendant had the opportunity to have the tapes tested and pointed to no reason to believe that they were not authentic).

2. When is a genuine question of authenticity raised?

In *United States v. Haddock*, 956 F.2d 1534 (10th Cir. 1992), a bank fraud prosecution, the court held there was no error in excluding photocopies of six documents offered by the defendant, as only the defendant could recall ever seeing either the original or a copy of these documents, persons who allegedly typed or received the documents were not familiar with their contents, and witnesses testified the documents bore markings and included statements that did not comport with similar documents prepared by the purported sources in the ordinary course of business.

In *Amoco Prod. Co. v. United States*, 619 F.2d 1383 (10th Cir. 1980), the court approved exclusion of a duplicate file copy of a deed under Rule 1003, because the most critical part of the original conformed copy was not completely reproduced in the duplicate.

3. What is the second step in any best evidence analysis?

Under the Federal Rules, if it is clear in response to an objection that a party is trying to prove the contents of a writing or recording, the second step is to see whether the party is offering a duplicate that is presumptively admissible. If the party is offering a duplicate, the objecting party will have to show that there is a genuine dispute about authenticity in order to pursue a best evidence point.

[2] Secondary Evidence

NEVILLE CONSTRUCTION CO. v. COOK PAINT AND VARNISH

671 F.2d 1107 (8th Cir. 1982)

BRIGHT, CIRCUIT JUDGE:

Cook Paint and Varnish Company (Cook) appeals from a judgment entered upon a jury verdict awarding $80,000 in damages to Neville Construction Company (the Nevilles) in this action based on negligence and breach of warranty. We affirm.

* * *

I. *Background.*

In 1962, Cook Paint and Varnish Company began marketing polyurethane foam insulation products under the brand name "Coro-foam." In the spring of 1970, Cook sold "Coro-foam 340" insulation to Thomas Kreis, who was in the business of selling and installing insulation. Shortly thereafter, Kreis contracted with the Nevilles to apply the Coro-foam insulation with a spray applicator to the inside walls and ceiling of the vehicle repair shop owned by the Nevilles.

Before making the sale, Kreis gave the Nevilles a brochure from Cook describing the properties of Coro-foam insulation. Kreis also conducted a demonstration to show the Nevilles flame retardant characteristics of the insulation. Neither Kreis nor the brochure from Cook indicated that the insulation should be covered by paneling or other building material.

On July 30, 1976, fire destroyed the Nevilles' building when sparks or a hot metal slag from a welder used in their vehicle repair shop ignited the Coro-foam insulation. The fire spread rapidly throughout the building destroying it in a matter of minutes.

The Nevilles instituted this action to recover the property loss they suffered as a result of the fire. The parties stipulated damages at $80,000, and the court submitted the case to the jury on theories of negligence and express warranty. The jury returned a verdict for the Nevilles in the amount of $60,000 on their negligence theory, having reduced the award by twenty-five percent because of the Nevilles' contributory negligence, and in the amount of $80,000 on their express warranty theory. Following entry of judgment for the Nevilles in the amount of $80,000, Cook Paint and Varnish Company moved for judgment notwithstanding the verdict and, in the alternative, for a new trial. The court denied these motions and Cook appealed.

II. *Discussion.*

Express Warranty.

Secondary Evidence.

Cook contends that the trial court should not have permitted Dennis Neville to testify regarding the contents of Cook's brochure describing the characteristics of Coro-foam insulation. Neville testified that the fire destroyed the brochure supplied by Kreis. The Nevilles attempted to introduce a similar brochure distributed by Cook; however, the court sustained Cook's objection to admissibility of the brochure on the ground that the exhibit had not been included on the pretrial exhibit list. Dennis Neville then testified that Kreis had given him literature on Coro-foam insulation which he had glanced through before deciding to buy the insulation. Neville testified, over objection, that the literature described Coro-foam's fire retardance.

Cook maintains that Neville's testimony was not the best evidence to prove the contents of Cook's brochure. Cook contends that because the witness had identified a brochure similar to the one destroyed in the fire it was incumbent upon the Nevilles to introduce that brochure as a duplicate.

Cook's argument lacks merit. Because Cook successfully objected to the admission of the similar brochure, it now cannot complain that that document provided the only proper evidence of the contents of the brochure destroyed in the fire. Moreover, the Federal Rules of Evidence recognize no degrees of secondary evidence to prove the contents of a writing that has been lost or destroyed. * * * The court, therefore, properly admitted the testimony of Dennis Neville as secondary evidence of the contents of the brochure destroyed in the fire.

NOTES

1. What is the third step in any best evidence analysis?

If a party is offering a writing or recording to prove the contents thereof and does not present an original or a duplicate, the party must justify the non-production of the original. Rule 1004 sets forth the common reasons why a party will not or cannot produce an original. A party who satisfies Rule 1004 may offer any form of secondary evidence that otherwise is admissible. As a matter of tactics rather than a matter of evidence law, a party generally will offer the most reliable and persuasive secondary evidence that is available.

2. What kind of showing must be made under Rule 1004?

The trial judge has considerable discretion in deciding whether a party has done enough to satisfy the rule. The circumstances of any particular case, including the investigatory options available to the party proffering secondary evidence, may vary considerably and affect a trial judge's willingness to admit secondary evidence.

In *Cartier v. Jackson*, 59 F.3d 1046 (10th Cir. 1995), the plaintiff, suing for infringement of a copyrighted song, alleged that the defendant had had access to a "demo tape" version of her song, but because she no longer had any of the demo tapes, she sought to introduce secondary evidence to prove the contents of the missing cassettes. The court of appeals held the trial judge did not abuse his discretion in excluding the secondary evidence; even though the plaintiff carefully searched among her possessions and called friends and former colleagues, she had not subpoenaed record companies to which she had sent demo tapes.

Contrast *Malkin v. United States*, 243 F.3d 120 (2d Cir. 2001), in which a taxpayer sued for a refund on the ground that the statute of limitations had run prior to the assessment of a deficiency. The IRS claimed that he had timely consented to extension of the limitations period, but the IRS file on the taxpayer, which contained the original extension form, had been lost or destroyed before the time of trial. Affirming a judgment for the government, the Court held there was no abuse of discretion in admitting the IRS computer reports that indicated when items in the file had been entered, as there was no evidence that the unavailability of the original documents was anything other than inadvertent and the secondary evidence was shown to be reliable.

In *United States v. Marcantoni*, 590 F.2d 1324 (5th Cir. 1979), the court held that a police officer who had seen several $10 bills in the defendant's home, but who could not find them when he returned with a search warrant, could testify as to the serial numbers of the bills, because it was obvious they were not available to the government.

D. SUMMARIES

UNITED STATES v. NORTH AMERICAN REPORTING, INC.
740 F.2d 50 (D.C. Cir. 1984)

WALD, CIRCUIT JUDGE:

In this case, North American Reporting, Inc. and Richard Lee Boyd appeal convictions on eight counts of mail fraud, in violation of 18 U.S.C. § 1341, and eight counts of making false statements, in violation of 18 U.S.C. § 1001. Appellants * * * contend that the district judge improperly excluded from evidence a summary chart proffered by the defense.* * *

North American Reporting, Inc. (North American) is a corporation that provides stenographical services. Richard Lee Boyd is the president of North American. From November 1, 1979 to October 31, 1981, North American provided court reporting services to the White House under two year-long contracts.

Under these contracts, North American was paid on the basis of the number of hours worked by its employees. The company submitted vouchers to the government every month listing the hours worked during the previous month, and breaking down the hours to show the time worked by each individual employee on each particular day. The government then paid North American in accordance with the hours represented on the vouchers.

North American's employees were also paid by the hour. Each employee would submit a time sheet to the company twice a month, and would receive compensation on the basis of the hours noted on the time sheet.

The prosecution alleged that Boyd, through the company, deliberately submitted false vouchers that overstated the hours worked by the company's employees. To prove the deliberate overbillings, the prosecution presented numerous former employees who authenticated their time sheets. A summary witness, Federal Bureau of Investigation (FBI) Special Agent Richard D. Coy, then presented a summary chart that compared the hours submitted by the employees on the time sheets and the hours submitted by Boyd on the vouchers. Coy testified that he had found 38.5% of the voucher entries he examined to be in excess of the hours represented on the employees' time sheets. He also identified 3.6% of the entries as understating the number of hours represented on the time sheets. To aid Coy's summary testimony, the prosecution entered into evidence a chart that listed the relevant entries from the vouchers and from the time sheets, and calculated the differences between the two for each particular employee.

* * *

To counter the prosecution's case, the defense argued that "any discrepancies between the employee time sheets and the vouchers resulted from legitimate rounding off of hours, different contractual interpretations by the employees and North American Reporting as to what hours could be billed, and honest mistakes." To support this theory, Boyd testified that, instead of referring to employees' time sheets to prepare the vouchers, he relied upon various sources, including his own memory, the President's schedule, typed transcripts, and employee sign-in sheets (so-called "wall sheets"), in order to reconstruct the time worked by his employees and himself.

To aid Boyd's testimony, the defense attempted to introduce into evidence a chart purporting to summarize, in the same manner as the prosecution's summary chart, numerous instances in which Boyd contends he underbilled the hours actually worked in his vouchers submitted to the government. After objection by the prosecution, however, the district court excluded the chart on the grounds that it was "terribly confusing" and "absolutely baffling to the court [and] * * * to the jury."

At the conclusion of the seven day trial, the jury convicted appellants on all counts. * * * This appeal ensued.

II. *The Exclusion of Defendants' Exhibit No. 24*

During Richard Boyd's testimony, the defense attempted to introduce Defendants' Exhibit No. 24 into evidence. This exhibit purported to be a calendar of the defendants' underbillings, and was designed to counter the prosecution's case as to deliberate overbillings by Boyd. Designed with a format similar to the government's summary chart, the defendants' exhibit listed, day by day, the hours Boyd claimed to have underbilled the government.

However, unlike the prosecution's summary chart — which relied primarily upon the authenticated time sheets of employees — the defendants' exhibit relied upon a hodge-podge collection of personal memory, unauthorized evidence, surmise, and post hoc contract interpretation. For example, seventeen entries on the defendant's exhibit relied entirely on Boyd's undocumented assertion that he was working on a given day, but did not bill for the time worked. Boyd testified that he assumed he worked on some of those days because he and Carol DeHaven, who married Boyd in September 1981, were "inseparable," and since Ms. DeHaven was working on those days, he "would have been there" also. In another entry, Boyd listed overtime for three employees because a fourth employee worked overtime that day, and Boyd "presumed [that the other three were] in also." However, the authenticated time sheet for at least one of those employees shows that the employee worked a normal eight hours that day. Moreover, the voucher submitted by Boyd for that day shows a normal workday for all four employees.

Moreover, a vast number of the entries in the defendants' chart rely upon a highly questionable interpretation of North American's White House contract. At trial, Boyd maintained that he would have been entitled to bill the government for overtime, in addition to the regular contract amount for a workday, whenever an employee began work before 10 a.m. or left work after 7 p.m., regardless of whether the total hours worked by the employee exceeded the nine hour period specified in the contract. While none of the government administrators who testified at trial supported this interpretation, and Boyd himself failed to submit vouchers that adhere to this interpretation, the defendants' chart employed this interpretation in order to create the preponderance of the supposed underbillings.

For these, and additional, reasons, we believe that the district judge had ample basis for excluding the defendants' chart on the ground that it was confusing. Evidence may be excluded, although it is relevant, if "its probative value is substantially outweighed by the danger of unfair prejudice, confusion of the issues, or misleading the jury." Fed. R. Evid. 403. * * * Defendants' Exhibit No. 24 presents a frequently observed danger associated with summary charts: the jury might "treat the summary as additional evidence or as corroborative of the truth of the underlying testimony." * * * When, as here, the "evidence" summarized derives from such diverse sources, of various shades of unreliability, including mere surmise, undocumented recollection and questionable assumptions, we do not think the district judge abused her discretion in preventing the exhibit from influencing the jury.

Finally, we note that the district judge permitted Boyd to testify as to the matters presented by the chart. The defense therefore was not deprived of the opportunity to make its case regarding its underbilling theory. By excluding the defendants' exhibit, the district judge simply assured that the jury would not be confused by the chart which, on its face, appeared to summarize "facts," but which, in actuality, collected the results of the jumble of the defendants' wishes, guesses and undocumented recollections. Accordingly, we find no error in the district judge's decision to exclude the chart from evidence.

* * *

AFFIRMED

NOTES

1. What foundation is required for summaries?

Before offering a summary under Rule 1006, the proponent will have to lay a proper foundation for the admission of the originals. *See, e.g.*, *United States v. Samaniego*, 187 F.3d 1222 (10th Cir. 1999) (reversing drug convictions because the government had introduced summaries of telephone records without making any effort to establish a foundation for the admissibility of the underlying records); *SEC v. Hughes Capital Corp.*, 124 F.3d 449 (3d Cir. 1997) (summary of the information contained on check stubs was properly excluded where the proponent failed to establish that the check stubs were admissible). Once the originals are authenticated, the summary must be authenticated.

If the data or material that is used as the basis for a summary or chart would not be accepted at trial (even to illustrate the basis for the testimony of an expert under Rule 703), the summary or chart itself is not admissible in evidence. For example, in *United States v. Pelullo*, 964 F.2d 193 (3d Cir. 1992), a government agent in a RICO prosecution summarized his analysis of the defendant's financial activity. The summary was based in part on interviews with people who engaged in suspect financial transactions with the defendant, and also upon information obtained from bank documents describing wire transfers. The court held that the summary was inadmissible under Rule 1006, because the underlying materials upon which the summary was based were out-of-court statements that the witness used for their truth in making the conclusions set forth in the summary. The court stated that "the schedules are inadmissible not because [the witness] merely interviewed people during the course of his investigation, but because the schedules were predicated upon inadmissible evidence. Rule 1006 does not permit such a result." *See also Johnson v. Ford Motor Co.*, 988 F.2d 573 (5th Cir. 1993) (summary of pending claims, lawsuits and complaints against Ford is "nothing more than a summary of allegations by others which constitute hearsay").

It should be noted that Rule 1006 requires only that the underlying evidence be admissible and made available to the adversary; the underlying evidence need not actually have been admitted at trial. *See, e.g., United States v. Strissel*, 920 F.2d 1162 (4th Cir. 1990) (it is not necessary that all the information upon which a summary is based must be in evidence; Rule 1006 requires only that the underlying evidence be admissible and available to the opponent for purposes of cross-examination).

The *Pelullo* Court noted that "the schedules were not pedagogical devices used to summarize or organize testimony or documents that have been admitted into evidence," in which case Rule 1006 would have been inapplicable and there would have been no need for the underlying information to satisfy independent admissibility requirements. Thus there is an important distinction between a summary of voluminous admissible evidence, governed by Rule 106, and summaries of the evidence already presented in the case. The latter summaries are not evidence at all, but rather pedagogical devices, and their use is regulated by Rule 611(a). See the discussion in point 2 below.

2. Are summaries of trial evidence admissible?

Many courts cite Rule 1006 in approving the admission of summaries of trial evidence. It should be obvious from the text of the Rule that these types of summaries are not compilations of evidence too voluminous to be produced, because the evidence *has* been produced. Rule 1006 allows admission of summaries in lieu of having the voluminous originals presented at trial. This use of summaries as evidence must be distinguished from charts and summaries used only for demonstrative purposes to clarify argument based on evidence that has already been admitted. For example, a government agent in a tax evasion trial may use a chart to help the jury see how hundreds of business records admitted as exhibits show that the defendant's tax returns understated his income. Although some courts have treated such charts and summaries under Rule 1006, the rule is really not applicable because they are not evidence, but only demonstrative aids governed by Rule 611.

In *White Indus. v. Cessna Aircraft Co.*, 611 F. Supp. 1049 (W.D. Mo. 1985), the district judge noted in a Robinson-Patman Act case that "there is a distinction between a Rule 1006 summary and a so-called 'pedagogical' summary. The former is admitted as substantive evidence, without requiring that the underlying documents themselves be in evidence; the latter is simply a demonstrative aid which undertakes to summarize or organize other evidence already admitted." The judge added, however, "that a pedagogical summary can itself be admitted in evidence where the trier of fact will find it helpful and will not be unduly influenced thereby."

Not all courts are so careful to distinguish between Rule 1006 summaries and pedagogical summaries. In *United States v. Lemire*, 720 F.2d 1327 (D.C. Cir. 1983), the court affirmed convictions for wire fraud and other offenses. The court held that an FBI agent properly used four charts, which summarized the testimony of government witnesses, to explain to the jury how cash flowed through certain companies. The court concluded that Rule 1006 permitted a summary of evidence already before the jury. The court did express concern about the possible misuse of summaries — *e.g.*, a jury might erroneously view a summary as additional or corroborative evidence, a summary might incorporate inadmissible evidence, and it might be used as an extra summation — but it found that the charts were not misused in the instant case.

3. What types of summaries are admitted?

Virtually every kind of complex or lengthy set of records can be presented in summary form, so long as the summary is fairly representative of the underlying information.

In *Martin v. Funtime, Inc.*, 963 F.2d 110 (6th Cir. 1992), the court held that summaries of the employer's personnel records introduced by the Department of Labor were properly admitted, as the original records were voluminous and admissible under Rule 803(6).

In *United States v. Campbell*, 845 F.2d 1374 (6th Cir. 1988), a prosecution for Medicare fraud, the court held that a summary chart based on the defendant's medical files was admissible, since without the chart the jury would have had to read hundreds of pages of technical information.

In *United States v. Meyers*, 847 F.2d 1408 (9th Cir. 1988), the court held that a chart summarizing long distance phone calls and surveillance logs of FBI teams was properly admitted.

In *United States v. Robinson*, 774 F.2d 261 (8th Cir. 1985), the court affirmed mail fraud convictions arising out of a bogus loan scheme, holding there was no abuse of discretion in admitting a summary and chart listing 105 loan applications.

PROBLEM 8-1

Plaintiff, Green Acres, sues defendant, Walk About, for trespass, alleging that the defendant walked across his property in spite of "No Trespassing" signs and cut down several small trees. Defendant admits walking across the property but defends on the theory that he has an easement. Defendant denies cutting down the trees. Plaintiff alleges that the trees were cut with a unique saber cut saw and has a witness who will testify that defendant owns such a saw.

Green Acres takes the stand.

Plaintiff's counsel: State your name.
Green Acres: Green Acres.
Plaintiff's counsel: Do you own Green Acres Manor?
Defense counsel: Objection! Best evidence. Ownership requires a deed.
Plaintiff's counsel: This is a matter of personal knowledge.
The court: (1) __________ .
Plaintiff's counsel: I'll ask you again. Do you own Green Acres Manor?
Green Acres: Yes.
Plaintiff's counsel: Do you know the defendant?
Green Acres: Yes.
Plaintiff's counsel: Have you seen him walking across your property?
Defense counsel: (2) Objection! Best evidence. Discovery has disclosed two witnesses who were much closer to the alleged trespasser than the plaintiff.
Plaintiff's counsel: (3) __________ .
The court: (4) __________ .
Plaintiff's counsel: Once again, have you seen him walking across your property?
Green Acres: Yes.
Plaintiff's counsel: I hand you what has been marked Plaintiff's Exhibit 1. Can you identify this saw?
Green Acres: Yes, it's similar to the one he had with him.
Defense counsel: Objection! Best evidence.
Plaintiff's counsel: (5) __________ .
The court: (6) __________ .
Plaintiff's counsel: Did he have your permission to enter your land?
Green Acres: No, and he certainly didn't have my permission to cut down several small trees. I saw him do it.
Plaintiff's counsel: Do you have any pictures of the damage to the trees?
Green Acres: Yes, I do.
Plaintiff's counsel: What do they show?
Defense counsel: Objection! This is not the best evidence.
The court: (7) __________ .
Plaintiff's counsel: Did you see the damage?
Green Acres: Yes.
Plaintiff's counsel: Please describe it.
Green Acres: It was a mess. Three trees were destroyed.
Plaintiff's counsel: Did you have a sign posted, if so, what did it say?
Defense counsel: Objection! This is not the best evidence.
Plaintiff's counsel: (8) __________ .
The court: (9) __________ .

Plaintiff's counsel: No further questions.

Later in the trial, Walk About is called to the stand by the defense.

Defense counsel: State your name.
Walk About: Walk About.
Defense counsel: Did you enter into a contract with plaintiff to purchase an easement over Green Acres Manor?
Plaintiff's counsel: Objection! Best evidence.
Defense counsel: (10) __________ .
The court: (11) __________ .
Defense counsel: You may answer the question.
Walk About: Yes, we had a contract. It was in writing.
Defense counsel: What did it provide?
Plaintiff's counsel: (12) Objection! __________ .
The court: (13) __________ .
Defense counsel: Where is it now?
Walk About: I lost my only copy a long time ago.
Defense counsel: What did it say?
Plaintiff's counsel: Objection! Best evidence.
Defense counsel: (14) __________ .
The court: (15) __________ .
Defense counsel: Again, what did the contract say?
Walk About: For $500 I got the right to walk across Green Acres to fish in Green Acres Pond.
Defense counsel: Was an easement ever written up?
Plaintiff's counsel: Objection! Best evidence.
Defense counsel: (16) __________ .
The court: (17) __________ .
Defense counsel: You may answer the question.
Walk About: Yes, an easement was written up.
Defense counsel: Was it delivered to you?
Plaintiff's counsel: Objection! Best evidence.
Defense counsel: (18) __________ .
The court: (19) __________ .
Defense counsel: Was it delivered to you?
Walk About: Yes.
Defense counsel: What did it say?
Plaintiff's counsel: (20) Objection! __________ .
The court: (21) __________ .
Defense Counsel: Did you file it at the courthouse?
Plaintiff's counsel: Objection! Best evidence.
Defense counsel: (22) __________ .
The court: (23) __________ .
Defense counsel: Please answer the question.
Walk About: Yes, I filed it.
Defense counsel: What does it say?
Plaintiff's counsel: (24) Objection! __________ .
The court: (25) __________ .
Defense counsel: Do you know what happened to the easement document at the courthouse?

Walk About:	Yes, the courthouse burned down and all the documents were lost.
Defense counsel:	What did the easement say?
Plaintiff's counsel:	Objection! Best evidence.
The court:	(26) __________ .
Defense counsel:	What did the easement say?
Walk About:	I could walk across the property to fish at the pond.
Defense counsel:	Did you pay for the easement?
Plaintiff's counsel:	Objection! Best evidence.
Defense counsel:	(27) __________ .
The court:	(28) __________ .
Defense counsel:	Once again, did you pay for the easement?
Walk About:	Yes, I paid $500.
Defense counsel:	Are you married?
Plaintiff's counsel:	Objection! Best evidence.
Defense counsel:	(29) __________ .
The court:	(30) __________ .
Defense counsel:	You may answer the question.
Walk About:	Yes, I'm married to the plaintiff's ex-wife.
Defense counsel:	Did you have a conversation with the plaintiff the day after this alleged incident?
Walk About:	Yes.
Defense counsel:	Did you tape-record the conversation?
Walk About:	Yes.
Defense counsel:	What did the plaintiff say?
Plaintiff's counsel:	Objection! Best evidence.
Defense counsel:	(31) __________ .
The court:	(32) __________ .
Defense counsel:	What did the plaintiff say?
Walk About:	The plaintiff said that I had an easement.

Chapter 9
OPINION TESTIMONY

A. LAY OPINIONS

[1] Illustration

Eye Witness is the only witness to a fight between Hurt Bad and Bad Hurt that took place outside the Blue Book Inn in the land of Oz. Bad Hurt is charged with battery and depends on the theory of self-defense. In Oz, battery is defined as "an unprovoked physical attack on another."

Eye Witness takes the stand for the prosecution.

Prosecution: State your name.
Witness: Eye Witness.
Prosecution: Were you at the Blue Book Inn on January 8?
Witness: Yes, I was.
Prosecution: What were you doing there?
Witness: Taking a study break.
Prosecution: Did you see the defendant or the victim inside the Inn?
Witness: No.
Prosecution: When did you leave the Inn?
Witness: About 1:00 a.m.
Prosecution: Did you see the defendant and the victim outside the Inn?
Witness: Yes, as I was going to my car I heard some shouting and I stopped to watch.
Prosecution: Did you see a fight?
Witness: Yes.
Prosecution: How long were you watching the defendant and the victim before the fight started?
Witness: Oh, about five minutes.
Defendant: Objection! Unless he was timing the event with his watch, that is an objectionable opinion.
Prosecution: (1) __________.
The court: (2) __________.
Prosecution: Could you describe the demeanor of the defendant?
Witness: Sure, he was real drunk and * * *.
Defendant: Objection! That's an opinion.
Prosecution: (3) __________.
The court: (4) __________.
Prosecutor: Please continue.
Witness: * * * and he was real angry.
Defendant: Objection! That's an opinion.
Prosecution: (5) __________.
The court: (6) __________.

Prosecution:	Who started the fight?
Defendant:	Objection! That's an opinion.
Prosecution:	(7) ________.
The court:	(8) ________.
Prosecution:	Let me rephrase the question. Who threw the first punch?
Witness:	The defendant.
Prosecution:	Do you have an opinion as to what happened inside the bar to trigger the attack?
Defendant:	(9) ________.
The court:	(10) ________.
Prosecution:	Was the physical attack by the defendant unprovoked?
Defendant:	(11) Objection! ________.
Prosecution:	(12) ________.
The court:	(13) ________.

[2] Federal Rules of Evidence 701 and 704

Rule 701. Opinion Testimony by Lay Witnesses

If the witness is not testifying as an expert, the witness' testimony in the form of opinions or inferences is limited to those opinions or inferences which are (a) rationally based on the perception of the witness, (b) helpful to a clear understanding of the witness' testimony or the determination of a fact in issue, and (c) not based on scientific, technical, or other specialized knowledge within the scope of Rule 702.

Rule 704. Opinion on Ultimate Issue

(a) Except as provided in subdivision (b), testimony in the form of an opinion or inference otherwise admissible is not objectionable because it embraces an ultimate issue to be decided by the trier of fact. (b) No expert witness testifying with respect to mental state or condition of a defendant in a criminal case may state an opinion or inference as to whether the defendant did or did not have the mental state or condition constituting an element of the crime charged or of a defense thereto. Such ultimate issues are matters for the trier of fact alone.

[3] Rationally Based on Perception

UNITED STATES v. HOFFNER
777 F.2d 1423 (10th Cir. 1985)

Barrett, Circuit Judge:

Mary Hoffner, M.D., (Appellant or Dr. Hoffner), was convicted of * * * distributing controlled substances (Schedule II), pursuant to prescriptions not issued for a legitimate medical purpose. Dr. Hoffner was acquitted on two counts of the indictment, but convicted on fifteen counts by virtue of a jury verdict rendered September 6, 1984. She appeals from the judgment of conviction.

Facts

In November of 1983, during a survey of pharmacies in the Fort Collins, Colorado, area DEA investigators were alerted to large numbers of Schedule II prescriptions being written by Dr. Hoffner. At that time a special DEA agent was assigned to the case to pose as a patient who needed diet pills. The agent was issued prescriptions by Dr. Hoffner for large amounts of Seconal, Biphetamine, and Valium over a short period of time.

At trial, the government established its case against Dr. Hoffner through the testimony of the special DEA agent, several expert witnesses, and a former patient of Dr. Hoffner's who also had been issued prescriptions for large quantities of Quaalude and Ritalin. It was determined that Dr. Hoffner was charging $100.00 per visit to those who had received prescriptions for large quantities of drugs while regular patients were charged only $30.00. Patients who had received the large quantity prescriptions were also told to go to different pharmacies when filling their prescriptions to avoid suspicion. Dr. Hoffner told these patients the names of diseases for which they could say they were being treated if a druggist should ask. Dr. Hoffner testified, though, that these patients did not actually suffer from these ailments.

* * *

I. *The Lay Opinion Testimony*

Dr. Hoffner argues that the trial court committed reversible error when it did not allow three lay witnesses to answer the following question, "whether, in your opinion, Dr. Hoffner intended to issue these particular prescriptions for a legitimate medical purpose?" The three witnesses were offered as lay witnesses although one was a medical doctor and two were nurses and long-time employees of Dr. Hoffner. In each instance, as defense counsel tried to elicit this lay opinion testimony the government made a timely objection which was sustained by the court.

* * *

* * * F.R.E. 701 permits the admission of lay opinion testimony provided that it meets two criteria: (1) it must be rationally based on the perception of the witness, and (2) it must be helpful to a clearer understanding of the witness' testimony or the determination of a fact in issue. The perception requirement stems from F.R.E. 602 which requires a lay witness to have first-hand knowledge of the events he is testifying about so as to present only the most accurate information to the finder of fact.

* * *

Although most courts opt for the broad admissibility of lay opinion, that does not mean that all such testimony ought to be indiscriminately admitted.

Determination of the preliminary questions of perception and helpfulness are within the discretion of the trial court. Here the court accepted offers of proof outside of the hearing of the jury to determine these preliminary matters. After learning that none of the witnesses had been present in the examining room when any of the patients who had received the improper prescriptions were with Dr. Hoffner, the court concluded that their opinions as to the doctor's intent were not based on any rational perceptions or observations. We agree. These witnesses did not overhear any conversations between the patients and Dr. Hoffner, nor did they witness any physical examinations or the actual writing of these prescriptions. Their opinions could not have been based on any concrete facts but amount only to speculative conclusions.

* * *

Dr. Hoffner also protests that government experts were allowed to testify as to their opinions about whether the prescriptions were issued for a legitimate medical purpose and therefore, Dr. Hoffner's lay witnesses' testimony on this issue should be admissible. We need not expand on the proposition that the admissibility of expert opinion testimony and lay opinion testimony is governed by different standards. *See* F.R.E. 701, 702, and 703. Admitting certain expert testimony does not provide Dr. Hoffner with *carte blanche* to introduce any and all lay testimony to counter the government's evidence. The rules of evidence were correctly applied by the trial court in excluding the lay opinion testimony.

* * *

Affirmed.

NOTE

When does a lay witness have sufficient personal knowledge?

In *Gorby v. Schneider Tank Lines, Inc.*, 741 F.2d 195 (7th Cir. 1984), the court held that a driver with twenty-nine years of experience who witnessed an accident could not opine that the driver of a truck did everything possible to avoid an accident because, among other reasons, the witness was not in the truck at the time to see what the truck driver was doing nor did the witness have personal knowledge of the safety features in the truck for emergency stops. In *United States v. Gibson*, 636 F.2d 761 (D.C. Cir. 1980), the court refused to allow a witness who had looked out a window into a car to testify what the witness could or could not have seen had he had binoculars. In *United States v. Glenn*, 312 F.3d 58 (2d Cir. 2002), the Court reversed a murder conviction partly because a cooperating witness, a drug dealer like the defendant, was improperly permitted to testify about the manner in which drug dealers carry handguns and then to opine that, based on his experience, the bulge he observed, from a distance of five or six house-widths, at the defendant's waist, was caused by a gun and could not have been caused by a pager or any other item. The Court held that the witness "clearly lacked sufficient 'first-hand knowledge or observation' to enable him to reach this conclusion," and to the extent the opinion was based on specialized knowledge, the witness was not qualified as an expert using reliable principles and methods.

But in *United States v. Rivera*, 22 F.3d 430 (2d Cir. 1994), the court held that a lay person could testify to the meaning of the records of an illegal drug operation even though she did not prepare all of them because she had prepared some of them and had been trained by one of the bosses in the organization on how to prepare records.

[4] Helpful to the Jury

[a] Short-Hand Rendition

UNITED STATES v. YAZZIE
976 F.2d 1252 (9th Cir. 1992)

Reinhardt, Circuit Judge:

Johnny Yazzie, Jr., appeals his conviction for sexual abuse of a minor (statutory rape) * * *. Because we conclude that the district court improperly excluded lay witnesses' testimony that the minor appeared to be at least sixteen years old when the alleged sexual abuse occurred, we reverse.

I.

Johnny Yazzie, Jr., was charged with aggravated sexual abuse (forcible rape) * * *, and with sexual abuse of a minor (statutory rape) * * *. Both charges stemmed from an incident involving Yazzie and a female minor that occurred on a Navajo Indian reservation on July 19, 1989, one month before Yazzie's twenty-first birthday and not quite six months before the sixteenth birthday of the minor.

Yazzie admitted that he had sexual intercourse with the minor on the night in question. His defense to the charge of forcible rape was that the intercourse was consensual. The jurors acquitted Yazzie of forcible rape but convicted him of statutory rape.

Yazzie's sole defense to the statutory rape charge was an affirmative defense permitted under 18 U.S.C. § 2243(c): that at the time of the incident, he reasonably believed that the minor, who was then fifteen-and-a-half years old, was at least sixteen. *See* 18 U.S.C. § 2243(c) ("[I]t is a defense * * * that the defendant reasonably believed that the other person had attained the age of 16 years.").

To establish his belief as to the minor's age, Yazzie testified that on the night of the incident, he believed that the minor was at least sixteen years old. To establish the reasonableness of his belief, he testified that at the time of the incident, the minor smoked cigarettes, drove a car, used makeup, and looked "mature" enough to be at least sixteen. He testified that he knew the minor because he had previously dated her older sister, but that the minor never told him her age.

To further establish the reasonableness of his belief, Yazzie called several witnesses who offered to testify that as of the date of the alleged sexual abuse, their observations caused them to believe the minor to be between sixteen and twenty years old. The district court excluded this testimony, ruling that defense witnesses were permitted to testify to their perceptions of the minor's physical appearance and behavior at the time of the incident but were barred from stating their opinion that the minor was at least sixteen years of age. The reason for the ruling, the court explained, was that a witness' belief as to the minor's age was "subjective and has nothing to do with what [Yazzie] might have believed."

In accordance with the district court's ruling, Yazzie's witnesses did not testify as to their beliefs regarding the minor's age. Instead, three of Yazzie's witnesses confirmed his claim that the minor smoked cigarettes on the night in question; two testified that they had seen her drive a car before the alleged sexual abuse took place; and two testified that she wore makeup at the time of the incident. Further, three witnesses testified that the minor appeared sexually mature at the time of the alleged sexual abuse. One stated that the minor "was tall and appeared to be a lady * * * a lady like she was full, how do you say, she was fully developed," and that "she was mainly filled out, she was very tall." Another testified that the minor's body shape made her look "[l]ike an older person." A third stated that the minor "was well into her womanhood, well developed * * * [and] had her curves and was into her maturity." In addition, one witness testified that the minor drank beer on the night of the incident.

The minor testified regarding her age and her date of birth, but did not state that she had told Yazzie how old she was or that she had reason to believe that Yazzie knew at the time of the incident that she was not yet sixteen. She did not deny that she occasionally drank beer and smoked cigarettes; indeed, she testified that she did both on the night in question.

To refute Yazzie's claim that he reasonably believed the minor to be at least sixteen years old, the prosecution introduced evidence that Yazzie lived down the street from the minor; that he had dated her sister for several months, up until about ten weeks before the incident occurred; that during the time he dated her sister he went on walks with the minor and helped her with her math homework; and that on the night of the incident, the minor did not wear sophisticated clothing but rather high-top athletic shoes, tube socks, jean shorts over bicycle tights, and a tee shirt. Yazzie denied none of these contentions, but he continued to insist that the minor never said anything to him about her age, that he did not know what school she attended or what grade she was in, and that he thought that she was at least sixteen. When the prosecutor attempted to imply (without offering any supporting evidence) that Yazzie had attended the minor's fifteenth birthday party, which had been held during the time that Yazzie was dating the minor's sister, he denied that he had done so. The prosecution also introduced substantial evidence that people under the age of sixteen commonly drove on the reservation.

II.

* * *

> We understand Rule 701 to mean that [o]pinions of non-experts may be admitted where the facts could not otherwise be adequately presented or described to the jury in such a way as to enable the jury to form an opinion or reach an intelligent conclusion. If it is impossible or difficult to reproduce the data observed by the witnesses, or the facts are difficult of explanation, or complex, or are of a combination of circumstances and appearances which cannot be adequately described and presented with the force and clearness as they appeared to the witness, the witness may state his impressions and opinions based upon what he observed. It is a means of conveying to the jury what the witness has seen or heard.

United States v. Skeet, 665 F.2d 983, 985 (9th Cir. 1982).

Here, the * * * testimony helps in the understanding of the witnesses' descriptive testimony and in determining a critical fact at issue — whether it was reasonable for Yazzie to believe that the minor was sixteen or older.

In the case before us, the jurors could not themselves assess how old the minor looked at the time of the incident: by the time of the trial, the minor was almost seventeen years old, and her appearance was undoubtedly substantially different than it had been on the night in question, a year and a half earlier. Thus, the jurors were wholly dependent on the testimony of witnesses. Yet the witnesses were permitted to testify only to the minor's describable features and behavior. Their testimony was no substitute for a clear and unequivocal statement of their opinions. It did not tell the jury that these witnesses believed the minor to be at least sixteen years old at the time of the incident.

Our finding that the trial judge erred in not admitting the opinions of Yazzie's witnesses as to the minor's age is supported by all of the considerations that underlie Rule 701's authorization of the use of lay opinion testimony. First, it is difficult to distinguish a fifteen-and-a-half-year-old from a sixteen-year-old, and it is still more difficult to put into words why one believes that a person is one age and not the other. There is a certain intangible element involved in one's conclusions on such a question. We form an opinion of a person's age from "a combination of circumstances and appearances which cannot be adequately described and presented with the force and clearness as they appear" to us. *Skeet*, 665 F.2d at 985. Mannerisms and facial features are notoriously difficult to describe accurately, and one's reasons for concluding that a person is a particular age are both too complex and too indefinable to set out fully.

In addition, a witness may not know, let alone be able to report precisely, what factors induced his or her conclusion. In such a case, the fact that the witness reached the conclusion is the important part of the testimony, not the largely undeterminable or inexplicable reasons that prompted the conclusion.

Furthermore, age is a matter on which everyone has an opinion. Knowingly or unknowingly, we all form conclusions about people's ages every day. It is therefore particularly appropriate for a lay witness to express an opinion on the subject.

Here, the witnesses' opinions were especially appropriate for another reason. The issue was whether the defendant held an opinion and if so whether that opinion was reasonable. It is relevant that others having a similar opportunity to observe the minor formed an opinion as to her age that was similar to the opinion the defendant claimed to have formed. Their testimony goes both to Yazzie's credibility and to the reasonableness of his belief. The district court's decision deprived the jury of the most direct evidence available as to the age that the minor reasonably appeared to be on the night of the incident. Thus, the judge's ruling constituted a clear abuse of discretion.

III.

* * *

We * * * conclude that the error was not harmless and that Yazzie's conviction must be

Reversed.

NOTE

When can a lay witness properly draw an inference from the facts that she knows?

Lay witnesses are permitted to draw reasonable inferences from their personal perceptions. For example, a witness who sees a driver with an unruly look on his face shaking a middle finger and yelling out the window at another driver is permitted to draw the inference that the driver was angry. The witnesses in *Yazzie* properly drew an inference about a person's age on the basis of information known to them. However, where the lay witness draws a conclusion that is simply not reasonably supported by what they know, their opinion is unhelpful to the factfinder and should be excluded under Rule 701. Illustrative is *United States v. Santos*, 201 F.3d 953 (7th Cir. 2000). The defendant was a public official, the Treasurer for the City of Chicago, charged with extorting campaign contributions. Crucial to the case was evidence that certain contractors with the defendant's office were terminated for refusing to pay up. The actual terminations were ordered by an assistant in the office, John Henry, but employees in the office were permitted to testify that they had "no doubt" or a "personal feeling" that Santos, the head of the office, ordered Henry to order the terminations. These witnesses drew an inference from their knowledge of Santos' management style, which they described as dictatorial and intrusive. Judge Posner declared that the witnesses were properly permitted to testify to Santos' management style, but they should not have been permitted to draw the inference that Santos ordered Henry to terminate the contractors. He explained as follows:

> The way in which Santos managed the Treasurer's office — a small office — was a matter within the range of these witnesses' personal observation. Had they stopped with their testimony about Santos' management style, the prosecutor could have asked the jury to infer that it was likely that Henry would not have ordered the cutoffs himself, that he was just her messenger boy. But instead the witnesses were permitted to draw the inference themselves, and in doing so they stepped outside the boundaries of their personal knowledge and invaded the province of the jury.
>
> It is true that Rule 701 does not interdict all inference drawing by lay witnesses. That would be absurd, since almost all testimony, even testimony as to what one has seen, is inferential in the sense that a reasoning process, however rudimentary, is being applied to the raw sense data. But the inferences must be tethered to perception, to what the witness saw or heard. What the witnesses here saw and heard was how Santos managed the office, but it was an impermissible leap to infer the existence of an express order by Santos on a particular matter. Not because the witnesses were not expert witnesses, who are permitted to testify to matters of which they lack personal knowledge, but because the inferences that they tried to draw were too speculative to count as evidence.

Santos is arguably a closer case than Judge Posner would have it. If the witnesses knew that Santos was a dictator and a control freak, it would seem reasonable for them to infer that a major matter such as a public contract would be within her control. It would be another thing if the witnesses were to infer, for example, that the Mayor of Chicago must have ordered the terminations because, after all, the Mayor is the top public official. That inference would be unreasonable and speculative; the inference that the witnesses drew in *Santos* seems significantly more reasonable.

[b] State of Mind of Another

UNITED STATES v. REA
958 F.2d 1206 (2d Cir. 1992)

Kearse, Circuit Judge:

Defendants William Rea, Getty Terminals Corp. ("Getty"), and John Pabone appeal from judgments entered in the United States District Court for the Eastern District of New York, following a jury trial * * *, convicting each on one count of conspiracy to defraud the United States, * * * (count 1), and three counts of tax evasion, * * * (counts 2-4).

* * *

I. *Background*

The government's case at trial was presented through documentary evidence and the testimony of a variety of witnesses, including Charles Sarowitz, who had served as J & J's accountant and negotiated purchases of gasoline for J & J, and persons who during the pertinent period had worked as clerical employees of Getty in connection with the invoicing of gasoline sales. Taken in the light most favorable to the government, the evidence painted the following general picture.

A. *The Tax Evasion Scheme*

In May 1985, J & J was seeking a new supplier of gasoline. Sarowitz, who performed business functions for J & J on instructions from Pabone, saw Rea's name on a list of wholesalers he had been given, and he telephoned Rea to set up a meeting. Shortly thereafter, in late May or early June, Sarowitz and Pabone met with Rea at Getty's offices (the "May/June meeting"). Sarowitz told Rea that J & J wanted to purchase gasoline from Getty. He also informed Rea that J & J did not hold a 637 License. At some point during this meeting, which lasted some 30-40 minutes, Getty senior vice president Alvin Smith stopped in to introduce himself; he expressed the view that Sarowitz and Pabone were probably "a bunch of bootleggers," *i.e.*, persons who sell gasoline without paying the required excise taxes. Sarowitz and Pabone denied that they were bootleggers. At this meeting, Rea agreed that Getty would become a supplier of gasoline to J & J.

Shortly thereafter, on June 4, Sarowitz and Pabone met with John Quock, president and owner of Tun Yung Fuel Oil Corp. ("Tun Yung"). Tun Yung held a valid 637 License. At that meeting, Quock agreed to allow J & J to use Tun Yung's 637 License in order to avoid paying the nine-cent-per-gallon federal excise tax that Getty would ordinarily charge on J & J's purchases. It was agreed at that meeting that these federal taxes would not be paid. In return for allowing J & J to use Tun Yung's 637 License, Quock was to receive half of the tax money J & J saved; he was to receive his payment not in cash but in gasoline drawn from J & J's accounts at Getty's terminals. Pabone later told a J & J salesman that J & J was in a position to sell gasoline at very competitive prices because it was using Tun Yung's 637 License to buy gasoline from Getty tax-free.

On June 7, J & J began to make purchases from Getty, buying barges of gasoline. J & J paid Getty for the gasoline by means of a wire transfer in accordance with instructions Sarowitz received from Rea. On its invoices for the barges of gasoline, Getty listed Tun Yung as the purchaser. Sarowitz testified that he did not place the order for the June 7 barge purchase, and he was not sure who had done so. There was no testimony as to who instructed Rea that Tun Yung should be invoiced on this first sale to J & J.

Getty's billing procedure called for Rea to prepare for each sale a bulk transaction sheet called a "BT," which typically included the name of the purchaser, the quantity, type, and price of the gasoline being purchased, the method of payment, and an indication of whether federal excise tax was to be charged. The information shown on the BTs was then transferred to "deal sheets" prepared by Rea or employees working under him in the supply and distribution department. Copies of each deal sheet would then be sent to other Getty departments, *e.g.*, the tax, inventory, and billing departments. Using the deal sheets given them, employees in the billing department would charge tax only on those sales for which the BT, prepared by Rea, had indicated that taxes should be charged.

On the J & J sales, Rea's BTs indicated that Tun Yung should be invoiced and that no tax should be charged. Accordingly, Getty neither billed nor paid federal excise taxes on any of the barge sales to J & J.

* * *

II. *Discussion*

On appeal, Rea and Getty contend principally * * * that the trial court erred in allowing Sarowitz to testify that Rea must have known he was participating in a tax evasion scheme.* * * Though we conclude that Sarowitz's testimony with respect to Rea's knowledge was improperly admitted, we find in that error no basis for reversal, and we conclude that the other contentions are meritless.

A. *The Testimony that Rea "Had To" Know that the Reason for Invoicing Tun Yung Was To Permit the Evasion of Taxes*

* * *

At the trial of the present case, Sarowitz was allowed to testify that Rea "had to" know that the reason he was asked to list Tun Yung on the invoices as the purchaser of the gasoline on sales to J & J was to permit the evasion of the federal excise taxes on those sales. Rea and Getty contend that Sarowitz should not have been allowed to give his opinion as to Rea's state of mind, because * * * the opinion was not "helpful" to the jury, as that term is used in Fed. R. Evid. 701.

* * *

2. *The Rational-Basis and Helpfulness Preconditions to Admissibility Under Rule 701*

* * *

When the issue is a party's knowledge, which is perhaps a more easily fathomed state of mind than, for example, intent or motivation, we suspect that in most instances a proffered lay opinion will not meet the requirements of Rule 701. There are a number of objective factual bases from which it is possible to infer with some confidence that a person knows a given fact. These include what the person was told directly, what he was in a position to see or hear, what statements he himself made to others, conduct in which he engaged, and what his background and experience were. When a witness has not identified the objective bases for his opinion, the proffered opinion obviously fails completely to meet the requirements of Rule 701, first because there is no way for the court to assess whether it is rationally based on the witness's perceptions, and second because the opinion does not help the jury but only tells it in conclusory fashion what it should find. *See, e.g., United States v. Whitworth*, 856 F.2d 1268, 1284-85 (9th Cir. 1988) (opinion that defendant had requisite knowledge based simply on "[c]ommon sense" did not meet Rule 701 requirements). On the other hand, when a witness has fully described what a defendant was in a position to observe, what the defendant was told, and what the defendant said or did, the witness's opinion as to the defendant's knowledge will often not be "helpful" within the meaning of Rule 701 because the jury will be in as good a position as the witness to draw the inference as to whether or not the defendant knew. * * * Lay opinion testimony will probably be more helpful when the inference of knowledge is to be drawn not from observed events or communications that can be adequately described to the jury, but from such factors as the defendant's history or job experience. *See, e.g., United States v. Fowler*, 932 F.2d at 312 (Department of Defense officials properly allowed to give opinion that a person with defendant's experience in the department would know rules forbidding giving certain documents to contractors); *United States v. Smith*, 550 F.2d at 281 (witness properly allowed to testify to her belief that defendant who ran a federally funded program understood certain federal regulations).

In addition, even those lay opinions that pass Rule 701's dual test of admissibility may be excluded by the court under Fed. R. Evid. 403 if the court determines that the admission of the opinion will be cumulative or a waste of time, or that its helpfulness is substantially outweighed by the danger of unfair prejudice to the party opposing admission of the evidence.

The questions of whether the proffered opinion is rationally based on the witness's knowledge and whether it will be helpful are, like all preconditions to the admissibility of evidence, determinations to be made by the trial judge. Some preconditions to admissibility, of course, are principally factual and permit the court to admit proposed testimony "subject to * * * the introduction of evidence sufficient to support a finding of the fulfillment of the condition." Fed. R. Evid. 104(b). We view the first Rule 701 precondition, *i.e.*, the requirement that a witness's opinion have a rational basis in his own perceptions, as one that in theory would be amenable to this kind of treatment. On the other hand, we view the question of whether the witness's opinion will be "helpful" within the meaning of Rule 701 as a legal matter that must be determined by the court before it may allow the opinion to be heard by the jury. Given the fact that often the same evidence is pertinent to both determinations, we think it will be rare that the court can safely accept lay opinion testimony "subject to connection."

* * *

Nonetheless, other post-opinion evidence appears to have provided a rational basis for Sarowitz's opinion. That evidence included Sarowitz's testimony that he several times told Rea that J & J had no 637 License, and that despite having received that information Rea prepared BTs that ensured that J & J would not be charged excise taxes on sales to J & J even when it was invoiced as the purchaser. If all of this evidence had been presented before Rea was permitted to state his opinion, and the court at that point had found the rational basis precondition satisfied, we would not have viewed that finding as clearly erroneous. Thus, though it was inappropriate for the court to admit the Sarowitz opinion on the record as it stood when the opinion was offered, we conclude that the lack-of-foundation problem was ultimately cured.

The question of whether Sarowitz's testimony could properly be found helpful, however, is a different matter. The trial court gave no indication that it considered the question of whether this testimony would be helpful to the jury, and we cannot conclude that the opinion passed the helpfulness test since, given all the evidence, it would appear that the jury was perhaps even more capable than Sarowitz — on the basis of his own perceptions — of inferring whether or not Rea knew he was participating in a tax evasion scheme. For example, the government introduced into evidence records kept by Rea (which there was no evidence Sarowitz had seen), and evidence as to Rea's extensive experience in the petroleum industry (of which Sarowitz may or may not have been aware, having simply selected Rea's name from a list someone had given him). Further, there was eventually expert testimony that it was unusual to invoice one company when the gasoline was being ordered, picked up, and paid for by another. Thus, in summation, the government did not rely on Sarowitz's opinion but instead argued that the pertinent knowledge was disclosed by Rea's own records, which revealed that Rea knew J & J was the real purchaser of the gasoline, and by his common sense based on 25 years' experience in the industry. It argued that this evidence compelled the inference that Rea knew the taxes were due and were not being paid, stating that Sarowitz "didn't need to tell Mr. Rea that they were evading the taxes. You don't need to tell someone who has been in the gasoline business for 25 years how to invoice gasoline, how to use a 637. You don't have to tell somebody that has been in the gasoline business for 25 years that you could use somebody else's 637 to invoice when somebody else is paying for the gasoline. Bill Rea knew."

Thus, by the conclusion of the presentation of evidence, the jury knew what Sarowitz had told Rea and what Rea had done, and in addition it possessed more evidence as to Rea's industry experience and as to the contents of Rea's records than Sarowitz indicated he possessed by the time of the July 3 meeting. In all the circumstances, the Sarowitz testimony that Rea "had to" have known that he was to invoice Tun Yung in order to evade payment of excise taxes was not "helpful" within the meaning of Rule 701. It did no more than instruct the jury as to what result it should reach on the issue of knowledge. We conclude that the admission of this opinion was therefore an abuse of discretion. [The court found the error to be harmless, for the very reason it was unhelpful — the jury already had enough evidence to come to the conclusion drawn by the witness, and therefore the witness' opinion could not have had a harmful effect.]

AFFIRMED.

NOTE

Can a lay witness testify to the intent of another person?

See United States v. Bogan, 267 F.3d 614 (7th Cir. 2001): The defendants were charged with assault with intent to kill a prison guard. An inmate who witnessed the event was properly permitted to testify that the defendants were "trying to kill" the guard. *See also Government of Virgin Islands v. Knight,* 989 F.2d 691 (3d Cir. 1993) (error to exclude testimony from a lay witness that the defendant's firing of his gun was an accident).

[c] Ultimate Issue

KOSTELECKY v. NL ACME TOOL/NL INDUSTRIES, INC.
837 F.2d 828 (8th Cir. 1988)

HEANEY, CIRCUIT JUDGE:

Robert and Linda Kostelecky appeal from a jury verdict dismissing their claims against N.L. Acme Tool Company (N.L.). We affirm.

On May 6, 1987, Robert Kostelecky injured his hand and wrist in an accident while working for his employer, Noble Drilling Corporation (Noble), on an oil rig near Killdeer, North Dakota. Gulf Oil Corporation operated the oil venture and hired Noble as a drilling contractor. Gulf had also hired N.L. to perform specialized operations and field service work on the rig. Kostelecky alleges that his injury occurred while working on a Noble crew under the supervision and control of an N.L. representative.

On April 3, 1984, Kostelecky filed a complaint in federal district court alleging negligence by Gulf and N.L. and asserting various vicarious liability theories against Gulf. On November 10, 1986, the district court issued a pretrial Order and Memorandum in which it, among other things, granted motions by Gulf and N.L. requesting separate trials on the issues of liability and damages. On December 31, 1986, Gulf was dismissed pursuant to a stipulation. On April 8, 1987, the jury returned a verdict finding N.L. was not negligent. Judgment was entered in accordance with the jury verdict on April 9, 1987.

* * *

Report of Jester Beck

Kostelecky contends that the district court erred in admitting into evidence an accident report of Jester Beck, one of Kostelecky's co-workers and an eyewitness to the accident. In particular, Kostelecky objects to statements in the report that the accident was caused by "the injured's own conduct" and that the accident could have been avoided if Kostelecky had listened to warnings and instructions given to him just prior to the accident. He contends that the statements are inadmissible because they are nothing more than the legal conclusions of a lay witness and could not have assisted the trier of fact in determining a factual issue. N.L. argues that the report is admissible because it represents Beck's firsthand observations, recorded within hours of the accident, which were therefore helpful to the jury in its deliberations. Moreover, N.L. argues that under Fed. R. Evid. 704(a), testimony in the form of an opinion is not rendered inadmissible merely because it embraces an ultimate issue to be decided by the trier of fact.

The admissibility of opinion testimony is generally committed to the sound discretion of the trial court. Under the Federal Rules of Evidence, opinion testimony is not inadmissible solely because it embraces an ultimate issue to be decided by the trier of fact. This does not, however, mean that all opinion testimony as to ultimate issues is admissible.

* * *

[E]vidence that merely tells the jury what result to reach is not sufficiently helpful to the trier of fact to be admissible. Often such evidence is labeled a "legal conclusion." As the comment of the Advisory Committee on the federal rules states:

> [T]he question, "Did T have capacity to make a will?" would be excluded, while the question, "Did T have sufficient mental capacity to know the nature and extent of his property and the natural objects of his bounty and to formulate a rational scheme of distribution?" would be allowed.

Although it is not easy to distinguish permissible questions from those that are not permissible, we find that the trial court abused its discretion in admitting the accident report. The case was tried on a theory of negligence. Legal causation was very much in dispute. Therefore, in the context of this case, the opinion as to causation served to do nothing more than tell the jury what result it should reach. Using the example in the advisory committee comment, the question was more akin to "Did T have capacity to make a will?" than a request for the specific perceptions of the witness.

* * *

The error in admitting the report was, however, harmless in this instance because it did not substantially affect Kostelecky's rights.

* * *

Accordingly, we affirm the entry of judgment in favor of N.L. on the jury verdict.

NOTES

1. When are opinions on the ultimate issue not otherwise admissible?

In *Torres v. County of Oakland*, 758 F.2d 147 (6th Cir. 1985), the court noted that an objection based on testimony going to the ultimate issue is no longer valid under Fed. R. Evid. 704(a). Nonetheless, the court ruled that it was error to permit a lay witness to testify that the plaintiff had not been subjected to racial discrimination. That statement was a legal conclusion which is "otherwise inadmissible" under Rule 704 because it invades the role of the court to determine the applicable law and instruct the jury, and as such does not satisfy the helpfulness requirement of Rule 701. The court suggested that "a more carefully phrased question could have elicited similar information and avoided the problem of testimony containing a legal conclusion."

In *Slayton v. Ohio Dept. Of Youth Servs.*, 206 F.3d 669 (6th Cir. 2000), affirming a judgment for the plaintiff in her Title VII action for a hostile work environment, the Court found no error in admitting testimony by two agency officials who concluded that if the plaintiff's assertions of fact were true, then the plaintiff had been subjected to "sexual harassment" within the meaning of the internal policy of the employing agency. The Court notes that while lay testimony embracing an ultimate issue is specifically allowed by Rule 704(a), it will seldom be helpful to the trier of fact. In this case, however, the witnesses were not giving testimony on an ultimate issue, as they did not refer to Title VII liability, but expressly addressed only the internal agency policy. The Judge's instructions were sufficient to cure any confusion between statutory and agency standards of "sexual harassment."

2. How close can a lay witness's opinion come to an ultimate issue for the jury, and still remain admissible?

In *United States v. Koon,* 34 F.3d 1416 (9th Cir. 1994), the court affirmed the convictions of two police officers for the deprivation of the rights of an arrestee, Rodney King, who was severely beaten after a high speed chase. This federal conviction was obtained after a state trial on the same matter resulted in a mistrial on one state count and an acquittal on all other state counts. The court held that testimony in the state trial by an officer who was at the scene of the beating (and who was actually acquitted as a defendant in both trials), was properly admitted against the two convicted defendants in the federal trial. The defendants argued that the officer's testimony contained impermissible lay opinion. Specifically they objected to the officer's testimony that, after the beating, he went to the police station intending to report a use of excessive force. The defendants argued that this was another way of saying that the officer was of the opinion that excessive force had been used. But the court declined "to adopt a rule barring testimony about actions which are motivated by opinions." The court also held that the officer's testimony that one of the defendants was "out of control" during the beating was properly admitted. While the defendants argued that this statement was a conclusory assertion about an ultimate issue, the court observed that "the ultimate issue was not whether the defendants were out of control, but whether they willfully used unreasonable force." The court concluded that the officer's observation was helpful to the jury and was rationally based on the officer's personal perception of the beating.

United States v. Espino, 32 F.3d 253 (7th Cir. 1994), can be compared usefully with *Koon*. In a drug case, the court found error where the prosecution asked the defendant on cross-examination whether he was "admitting the conspiracy." The question was improper because it called for a "conclusion regarding the legal implications" of the defendant's conduct, which would have been inadmissible under Rule 701. The court noted that a more appropriately phrased question would have been to ask the defendant whether he had an "agreement" with others to supply cocaine.

[5] The Line between Lay and Expert Testimony

[a] Lay Witnesses Giving Expert Testimony

UNITED STATES v. FIGUEROA-LOPEZ
125 F.3d 1241 (9th Cir. 1997)

TROTT, CIRCUIT JUDGE:

OVERVIEW

Raul Figueroa-Lopez ("Lopez") appeals his jury conviction and sentence for possession of cocaine with intent to distribute * * *. Lopez contends that the district court erred by * * * admitting damaging opinion testimony from law-enforcement officers, who the Government did not qualify as experts, that Lopez's behavior was consistent with that of an experienced drug trafficker * * *. Although the district court erred by allowing in evidence as "lay opinion" testimony specialized opinion testimony by law-enforcement officers, we conclude that the error was harmless, and we affirm Lopez's conviction and sentence.

BACKGROUND

I. The Underlying Offense

At the end of May 1994, federal agents arrested Darryl Storm. Storm and others were charged with conspiracy to distribute cocaine and marijuana, and with money laundering. Storm agreed to cooperate with the government and provided agents with a list of names of narcotics traffickers known to him. This list included Lopez, although at that time Storm only knew him as "Raul." At the instruction of DEA Agent Sam Larsen, Storm contacted Lopez to explore whether Lopez would sell him some narcotics. Storm met with Lopez on February 1, 1995. * * * According to Storm, Storm told Lopez that he wanted to buy 5-10 kilograms of cocaine. On March 24, 1995, Storm taped a telephone conversation with Lopez, during which Lopez offered to sell Storm ten kilograms of cocaine for $170,000. Lopez and Storm used oblique terminology borrowed from the construction industry to refer to the type, quantity, and price of the drugs. On March 27, 1995, Storm again met with Lopez. * * * Lopez gave Storm a sample of cocaine.

During the next month, Storm and Lopez spoke by telephone several times about the impending cocaine deal. * * * On May 25, 1995, Storm called Lopez and arranged to meet later that day to complete the cocaine transaction. Before meeting with Storm, Lopez drove in circles around the parking lot in a Monte Carlo. Storm and Lopez then met in the parking lot. Lopez drove away from Storm and parked next to a silver Nissan Sentra. Lopez entered the Nissan, bent down for several minutes, and then returned to the Monte Carlo.

Lopez returned to Storm's location and showed Storm a kilogram package of cocaine. Storm gave the arrest signal, and agents arrested Lopez. In the Monte Carlo, the agents found the keys to the Nissan and one kilogram of cocaine on the floor below the front seat. In the Nissan, the agents found nine kilograms of cocaine concealed in the car's door panels.

II. The Trial

A. Opinion Testimony

Throughout the trial, the Government presented opinion testimony by law-enforcement witnesses as to how Lopez's conduct, as observed by the agents, conformed to the methods and techniques of experienced drug dealers. Lopez objected to this testimony, claiming that it was * * * improper expert testimony because the Government had not given prior notice as required by Federal Rule of Criminal Procedure 16(a)(1)(E). The district court * * * admitted the testimony as lay opinion testimony, presumably pursuant to Federal Rule of Evidence 701. The court ruled that the testimony regarding the way Lopez was driving — from which the agent inferred that Lopez was behaving as an "experienced narcotics trafficker"— was admissible notwithstanding Lopez's objections because the officer was a "percipient witness." The court also overruled without explanation Lopez's objections to Agent Larsen's testimony that: 1) Lopez's actions were "countersurveillance" and "a common practice for narcotics dealers"; and 2) the use of a rental car was "indicative of an experienced narcotics trafficker." In response to Lopez's objection to an agent's opinion as to the street value of the cocaine found in the Nissan, the district court stated that "[t]he Court has repeated over and over that the witness is giving testimony relating to matters in which he has participated and which he personally observed, and his testimony may incorporate his knowledge and his observations, so on that basis, it will be admitted." Agents repeatedly referred to Lopez's actions as consistent with an "experienced narcotics trafficker." The prosecution relied on this testimony in its closing arguments.

DISCUSSION

I. The Law-Enforcement Opinion Testimony

A. The Error

Lopez contends that the district court abused its discretion by admitting without a proper foundation opinion testimony of law-enforcement officers that Lopez's actions were consistent with those of an experienced drug trafficker. Specifically, Lopez contends that the testimony * * * was not the proper subject of lay opinion testimony.

* * *

If "specialized knowledge will assist the trier of fact to understand the evidence or to determine a fact in issue," a qualified expert witness may provide opinion testimony on the issue in question. Fed. R. Evid. 702. * * * In this light, we have held that "drug enforcement experts * * * may testify that a defendant's activities were consistent with a common criminal modus operandi." *United States v. Webb*, 115 F.3d 711, 713-14 (9th Cir. 1997). This testimony "helps the jury to understand complex criminal activities, and alerts it to the possibility that combinations of seemingly innocuous events may indicate criminal behavior." * * * The testimony in the instant case is similar to expert testimony properly admitted in other drug cases. *See, e.g., United States v. Espinosa*, 827 F.2d 604, 611-12 (9th Cir. 1987) (allowing expert testimony regarding the use of apartments as "stash pads" for drugs and money); *United States v. Maher*, 645 F.2d 780, 783 (9th Cir. 1981) (permitting expert testimony that defendant's actions were consistent with the modus operandi of persons transporting drugs and engaging in countersurveillance).

In the above cases, the testimony was necessary to inform the jury of the techniques employed by drug dealers in their illegal trade, techniques with which an ordinary juror would most probably be unfamiliar. Thus, the testimony in the instant case could have been admitted as expert opinion testimony to inform the jury about the methods and techniques used by experienced drug dealers, if the law-enforcement agents had been called as experts and properly qualified as such pursuant to Rule 104 of the Federal Rules of Evidence. In fact, Special Agent Larsen began his testimony with a recitation of his extensive training and experience with the DEA. It appears virtually certain that had the Government opted to do so, Larsen could have been formally qualified as an expert witness on the dispositive issue of whether Lopez's behavior suggested that he was an "experienced" — as contrasted with a fledgling-drug trafficker. However, this routine process did not occur. The testimony was neither offered nor admitted as expert testimony, but rather as lay opinion testimony.

* * *

The Government contends that "the same analysis applies whether the witness is testifying as an expert or as a lay witness." Here, the agents testified that the following behaviors were consistent with an experienced drug trafficker: 1) countersurveillance driving; 2) use of code words to refer to drug quantities and prices; 3) use of a third-person lookout when attending a narcotics meeting; 4) use of a rental car to make the drug delivery; 5) hiding the cocaine in the door panels of a car; and 6) dealing in large amounts of very pure cocaine. These "observations" require demonstrable expertise; in fact, several times, the Government instructed the witness to answer questions "based upon your training and experience." Additionally, one agent testified that his familiarity with the fact that narcotics traffickers sometimes speak in code is based upon the training that he had at the DEA Academy.

However, part of the testimony in this case does provide us with a clear example of when a witness may give his lay opinion as to the implications of his observations. INS Special Agent Rapp testified that the movements of the Monte Carlo were "suspicious." * * * [S]uch testimony related to matters "common enough" to qualify as lay opinion testimony.

The Government's argument simply blurs the distinction between Federal Rules of Evidence 701 and 702. Lay witness testimony is governed by Rule 701, which limits opinions to those "rationally based on the perception of the witness." Rule 702, on the other hand, governs admission of expert opinion testimony concerning "specialized knowledge." The testimony in this case is precisely the type of "specialized knowledge" governed by Rule 702. A holding to the contrary would encourage the Government to offer all kinds of specialized opinions without pausing first properly to establish the required qualifications of their witnesses. The mere percipience of a witness to the facts on which he wishes to tender an opinion does not trump Rule 702. Otherwise, a layperson witnessing the removal of a bullet from a heart during an autopsy could opine as to the cause of the decedent's death. Surely a civilian bystander, or for that matter a raw DEA recruit would not be allowed to interpret for the jury Lopez's behavior in the parking lot on May 25, 1995 as that of an "experienced" trafficker merely because that person was an eyewitness to the same.

In addition, the Government's argument subverts the requirements of Federal Rule of Criminal Procedure 16(a)(1)(E). Rule 16 requires the Government to "disclose to the defendant a written summary of [expert] testimony the government intends to use * * * during its case in chief." The Rule "is intended to minimize surprise that often results from unexpected testimony, reduce the need for continuances, and to provide the opponent with a fair opportunity to test the merit of the expert's testimony through focused cross-examination." Fed. R. Crim. Proc. 16(a)(1)(E) (advisory committee's note).

In sum, rather than testimony "based on the perceptions of the witness" — as the district court described it when overruling Lopez's objections — the bulk of the above opinion testimony is properly characterized as testimony based on the perceptions, education, training, and experience of the witness. It requires precisely the type of "specialized knowledge" of law enforcement governed by Rule 702. Trial courts must ensure that experts are qualified to render their opinions and that the opinions will assist the trier of fact. This careful analysis was absent in this case. * * * As judges who have heard such testimony many times, we must not forget that our familiarity with it does not bring it within Rule 701, especially given the purpose of Rule 16(a)(1)(E).

[The Court finds the error to be harmless, because the law enforcement agents could have been qualified as experts and could then have given the same testimony. While the government violated the discovery requirements of Fed. R. Crim. P. 16 by failing to disclose expert testimony in advance of trial, the Court held that this violation did not prejudice the defense].

AFFIRMED.

[b] Advisory Committee Note to 2000 Amendment to Rule 701

[In 2000, Rule 701 was amended to provide that a lay witness cannot give testimony "based on scientific, technical or other specialized knowledge within the scope of Rule 702."]

COMMITTEE NOTE

Rule 701 has been amended to eliminate the risk that the reliability requirements set forth in Rule 702 will be evaded through the simple expedient of proffering an expert in lay witness clothing. Under the amendment, a witness' testimony must be scrutinized under the rules regulating expert opinion to the extent that the witness is providing testimony based on scientific, technical, or other specialized knowledge within the scope of Rule 702. *See generally Asplundh Mfg. Div. v. Benton Harbor Eng'g*, 57 F.3d 1190 (3d Cir. 1995). By channeling testimony that is actually expert testimony to Rule 702, the amendment also ensures that a party will not evade the expert witness disclosure requirements set forth in Fed.R.Civ.P. 26 and Fed.R.Crim.P.16 by simply calling an expert witness in the guise of a layperson. *See* Joseph, *Emerging Expert Issues under the 1993 Disclosure Amendments to the Federal Rules of Civil Procedure,* 164 F.R.D. 97, 108 (1996) (noting that "there is no good reason to allow what is essentially surprise expert testimony," and that "the court should be vigilant to preclude manipulative conduct designed to thwart the expert disclosure and discovery process"). *See also United States v. Figueroa-Lopez*, 125 F.3d 1241, 1246 (9th Cir. 1997) (law enforcement agents testifying that the defendant's conduct was consistent with that of a drug trafficker could not testify as lay witnesses; to permit such testimony under Rule 701 "subverts the requirements of Federal Rule of Criminal Procedure 16(a)(1)(E)").

The amendment does not distinguish between expert and lay *witnesses*, but rather between expert and lay *testimony*. Certainly it is possible for the same witness to provide both lay and expert testimony in a single case. *See, e.g, United States v. Figueroa-Lopez*, 125 F.3d 1241, 1246 (9th Cir. 1997) (law enforcement agents could testify that the defendant was acting suspiciously, without being qualified as experts; however, the rules on experts were applicable where the agents testified on the basis of extensive experience that the defendant was using code words to refer to drug quantities and prices). The amendment makes clear that any part of a witness's testimony that is based upon scientific, technical, or other specialized knowledge within the scope of Rule 702 is governed by the standards of Rule 702 and the corresponding disclosure requirements of the Civil and Criminal Rules.

The amendment is not intended to affect the "prototypical example[s] of the type of evidence contemplated by the adoption of Rule 701 relat[ing] to the appearance of persons or things, identity, the manner of conduct, competency of a person, degrees of light or darkness, sound, size, weight, distance, and an endless number of items that cannot be described factually in words apart from inferences." *Asplundh Mfg. Div. v. Benton Harbor Eng'g*, 57 F.3d 1190, 1196 (3d Cir. 1995).

For example, most courts have permitted the owner or officer of a business to testify to the value or projected profits of the business, without the necessity of qualifying the witness as an accountant, appraiser, or similar expert. *See, e.g., Lightning Lube, Inc. v. Witco Corp.* 4 F.3d 1153 (3d Cir. 1993) (no abuse of discretion in permitting the plaintiff's owner to give lay opinion testimony as to damages, as it was based on his knowledge and participation in the day-to-day affairs of the business). Such opinion testimony is admitted not because of experience, training or specialized knowledge within the realm of an expert, but because of the particularized knowledge that the witness has by virtue of his or her position in the business. The amendment does not purport to change this analysis. Similarly, courts have permitted lay witnesses to testify that a substance appeared to be a narcotic, so long as a foundation of familiarity with the substance is established. *See, e.g., United States v. Westbrook,* 896 F.2d 330 (8th Cir. 1990) (two lay witnesses who were heavy amphetamine users were properly permitted to testify that a substance was amphetamine; but it was error to permit another witness to make such an identification where she had no experience with amphetamines). Such testimony is not based on specialized knowledge within the scope of Rule 702, but rather is based upon a layperson's personal knowledge. If, however, that witness were to describe how a narcotic was manufactured, or to describe the intricate workings of a narcotic distribution network, then the witness would have to qualify as an expert under Rule 702. *United States v. Figueroa-Lopez, supra.*

The amendment incorporates the distinctions set forth in *State v. Brown*, 836 S.W.2d 530, 549 (1992), a case involving former Tennessee Rule of Evidence 701, a rule that precluded lay witness testimony based on "special knowledge." In *Brown,* the court declared that the distinction between lay and expert witness testimony is that lay testimony "results from a process of reasoning familiar in everyday life," while expert testimony "results from a process of reasoning which can be mastered only by specialists in the field." The court in *Brown* noted that a lay witness with experience could testify that a substance appeared to be blood, but that a witness would have to qualify as an expert before he could testify that bruising around the eyes is indicative of skull trauma. That is the kind of distinction made by the amendment to this Rule."

[c] Comment by Reporter on Amendment to Rule 701

[One of the authors of this casebook is the Reporter to the Advisory Committee on Evidence Rules. He prepared the amendment to Rule 701 and the Committee Note. What follows are his comments on the amendment.]

The Department of Justice adamantly opposed the amendment to Rule 701. DOJ officials argued that the amendment would require the government to qualify many witnesses as experts who have traditionally been considered lay witnesses. As an example, DOJ postulated a case where a senior citizen who lived in a neighborhood for a long time would be called to testify that she saw the defendant engaged in drug activity on the street corner. DOJ argued that this would be testimony based on "specialized knowledge" and therefore the witness would have to be qualified as an expert under the amendment. Moreover, she would have to be disclosed as an expert in advance of trial under Fed. R. Crim. P. 16. And this could mean that her safety would be put in jeopardy.

The Advisory Committee took the position that DOJ's concerns were overstated. As to the senior citizen hypothetical, whether the testimony would be treated under amended Rule 701 or under Rule 702 would depend on the exact nature of the testimony. If the witness were to testify that the defendant was acting as a steerer in a drug transaction, or that the defendant was engaged in a coded conversation, this would indeed be expert testimony. And the Advisory Committee had no problem with requiring such a witness to be qualified as an expert, disclosed in advance, and subject to a reliability inquiry under Rule 702. If advance disclosure could risk the safety of the witness, then nothing would prevent the government from getting a protective order that would limit or excuse such disclosure. In contrast, if the witness were to testify that she saw the defendant drop a packet of drugs on the street, this would not be expert testimony. You don't need specialized knowledge to know that white powder in certain circumstances is drugs. That is common knowledge, not specialized knowledge.

Another example given by the DOJ was a game warden who would testify that an eagle flew over his head at a certain location. Is that expert testimony? The Advisory Committee took the position that drawing an inference that a bird is an eagle is within the common experience of most people, so the testimony would be that of a lay witness. However, if the witness were to testify that based on the eagle's height it must have come from a nesting grounds, or it had an irregular heartbeat, or it was a particular type of eagle outside its normal environment, then this would be testimony on the basis of specialized knowledge, and would have to be qualified under Rule 702. The Advisory Committee noted that if the witness were called to give such specialized testimony, counsel would clearly have to establish a foundation that the witness had substantial experience in the field of eagles. That kind of foundation looks a lot like — indeed it is exactly like — what counsel would have to do to qualify the witness as an expert. The Advisory Committee's position was essentially that if is looks like an expert and talks like an expert and a foundation is established in the manner required for an expert, then it's an expert and should be subject to the reliability requirements of Rule 702 and the disclosure requirements of the Civil and Criminal Rules.

The Advisory Committee recognized that the line between specialized knowledge and common knowledge would not always be easy to draw. But the Committee believed that the cost of such a delineation was worth it. Otherwise, parties could routinely evade the strictures of Rule 702, and the disclosure requirements of the Civil and Criminal rules, by presenting expert testimony and yet calling it lay testimony. The last paragraph of the Committee Note is an attempt to provide some guidance to Judges and practitioners in distinguishing specialized-knowledge testimony from common knowledge testimony. The Note observes that the distinction between lay and expert witness testimony is that lay testimony "results from a process of reasoning familiar in everyday life", while expert testimony "results from a process of reasoning which can be mastered only by specialists in the field." The example given is that a lay witness with experience could testify that a substance appeared to be blood, but a witness would have to qualify as an expert before he could testify that bruising around the eyes is indicative of skull trauma. The former opinion is based on fairly common if not necessarily universal experience, while the latter is based on fairly narrow experience that is not part of the everyday life of most persons.

It must be remembered that a single witness can be both an expert and a lay witness. As the Committee Note states, the Rule focuses on *testimony*, not *witnesses*. A typical example is a treating physician. When the physician testifies that the plaintiff was coughing and running a fever, this is lay witness testimony governed by Rule 701. However, if the physician also testifies that he diagnosed the patient as having Reactive Airways Dysfunction Syndrome caused by exposure to a toxic chemical, then this is testimony based on scientific, technical or other specialized knowledge and must be qualified under Rule 702.

[d] Post-amendment Case Law

UNITED STATES v. PERKINS
470 F.3d 150 (4th Cir. 2006)

WILLIAMS, CIRCUIT JUDGE:

Michael Perkins, a Petersburg, Virginia city police officer, was convicted by a jury of kicking and causing bodily injury under color of law to Lamont Koonce, a motorist stopped for a traffic violation who fled from the police, thus willfully depriving Koonce of his constitutional right to be free from unreasonable force, a felony under 18 U.S.C.A. § 242 (West 2000). Perkins challenges both the admission of opinion evidence at trial and the sufficiency of the evidence. Finding no reversible error, we affirm.

I.

Shortly before midnight on October 13, 2003, Petersburg police officers Michael Tweedy and David House observed a car traveling with no headlights on and damage to its front end. The officers, in separate vehicles, followed the car, pulled it over, and approached the driver to issue a warning or ticket for driving at night without lights. After the officers assisted the driver, Lamont Koonce, out of his car, Koonce broke loose from their hold and fled on foot. House and Tweedy gave chase.

During the chase, Koonce leaped over a fence "like a Superman" and fell on his right side. Koonce quickly gathered himself and kept running until finally, after a lengthy pursuit, Tweedy caught him and forced him face-down onto the ground, with both of his arms pinned beneath his body. At some point, Tweedy also used pepper spray on Koonce.

After Tweedy moved away from Koonce, House approached Koonce's left side to handcuff him. House attempted to remove Koonce's left arm from under his body, but Koonce resisted. When Koonce finally released his left arm, Koonce grabbed House's ankle. House responded by striking Koonce with a closed fist twice on the arm and once in the underarm to try to free his ankle, but Koonce maintained his hold. Tweedy then forcefully stomped on Koonce's head three times. When Koonce continued to resist, Tweedy stomped on his head three more times. After this second round of stomps, Koonce said, "[a]ll right, man, all right," and allowed House to pull his left arm out from under him and place a handcuff on his wrist.

Tweedy made a radio call stating that he had a subject in custody. Sergeant John Waldron responded by making a radio call for backup. At this point, House believed that he and Tweedy did not need assistance because Koonce's left wrist was in a handcuff. House radioed Sergeant Waldron and told him that the situation was under control. Waldron responded by telling all officers to disregard his earlier call for backup.

Despite this call, Officer Benjamin Fisher responded to Tweedy's earlier call and arrived at the scene soon thereafter. House asked Fisher to help him secure Koonce's right arm. Tweedy then walked over and kicked Koonce two or three times in the side and stomped on Koonce's head three more times.

A few moments later Perkins, an off-duty Petersburg police officer, arrived at the scene. By the time Perkins arrived, both House and Fisher believed that Koonce was under control, as the bloodied, motionless Koonce was lying face-down on the ground and was not "going anywhere." Without consulting or speaking with any of the officers standing nearby, Perkins immediately ran up to Koonce and delivered a running kick to Koonce's side. Perkins then kicked Koonce a second time, with slightly less force. Immediately after Perkins's second kick, Tweedy stomped on Koonce's head two more times before Perkins grabbed Tweedy and pulled him away from Koonce. Fisher then helped House place a handcuff on Koonce's right wrist.

Koonce sustained a number of life-threatening injuries, including multiple skull fractures, multiple facial fractures, a pneumothorax (puncture) to his right lung, bleeding in and contusions on the brain, and bruising on his left lung. At the time he was admitted to the Southside Regional Medical Center, Koonce was unconscious; he remained so for several hours.

At the hospital, Koonce was tested on the Glasgow coma scale, a clinical scale that assesses impaired consciousness. Koonce received a score of 1 for mental status, indicating that he did not open his eyes; a score of 1 for verbal response, indicating that he was not speaking; and a score of 3 for motor response, indicating that he moved away in response to pain. Due to the severity of his injuries, the still unconscious Koonce was transferred to the Medical College of Virginia (MCV) hospital later that night.

On November 16, 2004, a grand jury indicted Perkins. The indictment charged that Perkins, while acting under color of state law, kicked and caused bodily injury to Koonce, thus willfully depriving Koonce of his right to be free from unreasonable force, a felony under 18 U.S.C.A. § 242. The case proceeded to a jury trial.

At trial, Perkins argued that his kicks to Koonce were reasonable under the circumstances. In response to this argument, the Government offered opinion testimony from several officers regarding the reasonableness of Perkins's use of force against Koonce. Of the officers that testified, the Government offered only Inspector Carter Burnett as an expert under Federal Rule of Evidence 702.

Officers House and Fisher — both eyewitnesses to Perkins's kicks to Koonce — testified about their departmental training in defensive tactics and the use of force. Using a use-of-force dummy, they both demonstrated the kicks that they witnessed Perkins deliver to Koonce. The Government asked House whether, based on his experience and his assessment of the situation, he saw "any law enforcement reason for those kicks[.]" Perkins objected to this question on the ground of "ultimate issue." The district court overruled the objection, and House answered that he did not see any reason for the kicks. Likewise, in response to the Government's question whether, based on his experience and his assessment of the scene, Perkins's kicks to Koonce were "reasonable," Fisher answered, "No." Fisher also testified that, in his opinion, the kicks were not necessary and that there were other techniques he was trained to use that would have been appropriate. Perkins did not object to any of Fisher's testimony.

Other officers who had not witnessed Perkins's kicks to Koonce also testified about the reasonableness of the kicks. In response to the Government's question whether it would have been appropriate for an officer to "deliver a hard kick into the side of [a motionless] individual lying on the ground," Corporal Stan Allen, Perkins's defensive tactics instructor, replied, "[n]ot unless [the individual] was armed with a weapon and w[as] threatening the officer." Perkins only made a general objection to Allen's testimony that reasonable officers would not disagree with Allen's conclusion that Perkins's kicks were inappropriate. Similarly, Sergeant Philip Jones testified that kicks like those Perkins delivered to Koonce were "not appropriate." He also testified that reasonable officers would not disagree with his opinion. Sergeant Waldron testified that kicking a motionless person on the ground was not "reasonable" under the General Orders of the Petersburg Police Department. Perkins did not object to Jones's or Waldron's testimony.

Inspector Burnett, the Government's "force expert," testified regarding the classes he taught in defensive tactics and controlling suspects. Burnett stated that he saw no "legitimate" law enforcement reason for Perkins to kick Koonce. In response to a number of hypotheticals positing a suspect lying motionless on the ground with one arm in a handcuff, Burnett testified that it was inappropriate for an officer to kick a suspect in that posture. Burnett also testified that reasonable officers would not disagree with his conclusions. Perkins's sole objection was to the Government's use of the term "legitimate" in its question to Burnett.

The Government also introduced expert medical testimony about the cause of Koonce's injuries. Dr. Jamal Farran, Koonce's attending physician at MCV and one of the Government's medical experts, testified that the likely cause of Koonce's punctured right lung and bruised left lung was blunt force trauma. When asked about Koonce's Glasgow coma test, Dr. Farran testified that an individual can react to painful stimuli while unconscious.

* * *

On February 17, 2005, after a three-day trial, the jury convicted Perkins of a felony under 18 U.S.C.A. § 242, and he was sentenced to 51 months' imprisonment. Perkins timely noted an appeal.

* * *

II.

Perkins argues on appeal that the district court erred in admitting expert testimony without a proper foundation, in admitting lay and expert opinion testimony that improperly stated a legal conclusion, and that the evidence was insufficient to prove that Perkins caused "bodily injury" to Koonce. We address each of these arguments in turn.

* * * Perkins first contends that the district court erred in admitting without a proper foundation the opinion testimony of Officers House and Fisher, Sergeants Jones and Waldron, and Corporal Allen, none of whom were qualified as expert witnesses. Because Perkins did not object at trial to any of the testimony on this ground, we review for plain error.

Federal Rule of Evidence 701 permits a lay witness to give opinion testimony that is "(a) rationally based on the perception of the witness, (b) helpful to a clear understanding of the witness' testimony or the determination of a fact in issue, and (c) not based on scientific, technical, or other specialized knowledge within the scope of Rule 702."[1] Fed. R. Evid. 701. Because Rule 701 "does not distinguish between expert and lay *witnesses*, but rather between expert and lay *testimony*," Fed. R. Evid. 701 advisory committee's note, the line between lay opinion testimony under Rule 701 and expert testimony under Rule 702 "is a fine one," 3 Stephen A. Saltzburg, Michael M. Martin & Daniel J. Capra, *Federal Rules of Evidence Manual* 701-14 (9th ed. 2006). *See also United States v. Ayala-Pizarro*, 407 F. 3d, 25, 28 (1st Cir.

[1] Rule 701 was amended in 2000 to include subsection (c). The Advisory Commitee's position was that the amendment did not work a sea change to the rule. 3 Stephen A. Saltzburg, Michael M. Martin & Daniel J. Capra, Federal Rules of Evidence Manual 701-15 (9th ed. 2006). We agree. The amendment "serves more to prohibit the inappropriate admission of expert opinion under Rule 701 than to change the substantive requirements of the admissibility of lay opinion." *United States v. Garcia*, 291 F.3d 127, 139 n. 8 (2d Cir. 2002).

2005)(noting that "[t]he line between expert testimony under Fed. R. Evid. 702 * * * and lay opinion testimony under Fed. R. Evid. 701 * * * is not easy to draw")(internal quotation marks omitted). As an example of the kinds of distinctions that Rule 701 makes, the Committee instructs that the rule would permit a lay witness with personal experience to testify that a substance appeared to be blood, but that it would not allow a lay witness to testify that bruising around the eyes is indicative of skull trauma. Fed. R. Evid. 701 advisory committee's note.

As helpful as this example may be to our interpretive cause, the fine line remains. While we have noted that "[a] critical distinction between Rule 701 and Rule 702 testimony is that an expert witness must possess some specialized knowledge or skill or education that is not in possession of the jurors," *Certain Underwriters at Lloyd's, London v. Sinkovich*, 232 F.3d 200, 203 (4th Cir. 2000) (internal quotation marks omitted), we also have acknowledged that the "subject matter of Rule 702 testimony need not be arcane or even especially difficult to comprehend," *Kopf v. Skyrm*, 993 F.2d 374, 377 (4th Cir. 1993). The interpretive waters are muddier still: while lay opinion testimony *must* be based on personal knowledge, *see* Fed. R. Evid. 701, "expert opinions may [also] be based on firsthand observation and experience." 29 Charles Wright & Victor Gold, *Federal Practice and Procedure: Evidence* § 6253 (1997 & Supp. 2006). At bottom, then, Rule 701 forbids the admission of expert testimony dressed in lay witness clothing, but it "does not interdict all inference drawing by lay witnesses." *United States v. Santos*, 201 F.3d 953, 963 (7th Cir. 2000).

Where opinion testimony focuses on the standard of the objectively reasonable officer, "it is more likely that Rule 702's line between common and specialized knowledge has been crossed." *Kopf*, 993 F.2d at 378. In Perkins's case we conclude that the district court, although close to crossing that line, properly admitted the challenged testimony given by Officers House and Fisher. Both officers observed Perkins kick Koonce and thus testified based on their contemporaneous perceptions; as such, their testimony satisfies Rule 701's personal knowledge requirement. *See* Fed. R. Evid. 701. Moreover, their observations were "common enough and require[d] such a limited amount of expertise * * * that they can, indeed, be deemed lay witness opinion[s]." *United States v. Von Willie*, 59 F.3d 922, 929 (9th Cir. 1995). Because their testimony was framed in terms of their eyewitness observations and particularized experience as police officers, we have no trouble finding that their opinions were admissible under Rule 701.

On the other hand, the "reasonableness" testimony given by Sergeants Waldron and Jones and Corporal Allen crossed the line between Rules 701 and 702. None of those officers observed Perkins's use of force on Koonce. Their opinions that Perkins's use of force was inappropriate were elicited in response to hypothetical questions based on second-hand accounts, making their testimony similar, if not indistinguishable, from the properly qualified *expert* testimony admitted at Perkins's trial and admitted in other excessive force cases. *See, e.g., United States v. Mohr*, 318 F.3d 613, 623-24 (4th Cir. 2003)(admitting *expert* testimony on the reasonableness of the defendant's use of force when the expert did not observe the defendant's actions but instead gave his opinion in response to abstract questions). Such opinion testimony does not satisfy Rule 701's personal knowledge requirement. *See United States v. Glenn*, 312 F.3d 58, 67 (2d Cir. 2002)(drug dealer's testimony that the defendant must have been carrying a gun was erroneously admitted under Rule 701 because the witness lacked first-hand knowledge); *Washington v. Dep't of Transp.*, 8 F.3d 296, 300 (5th Cir. 1993) ("Under the Federal Rules of Evidence, speculative opinion testimony by lay witnesses — *i.e.*, testimony not based upon the witness's perception — is generally considered inadmissible."). Accordingly, the district court erred in admitting Jones's, Waldron's, and Allen's opinion testimony without a proper foundation.

Nevertheless, we are confident that this error did not affect the outcome of Perkins's trial. Sergeant Jones's brief "reasonableness" testimony came on the heels of his clearly admissible and extensive testimony about a conversation he had with Perkins during which Perkins admitted to kicking Koonce and demonstrated for Jones how he had kicked him. Furthermore, both Sergeant Waldron, who recounted that his fourteen years of experience included time as a training officer, corporal, and sergeant, and Corporal Allen, whose experience and training was enough to cause the district court to assume his expert status, could have been offered as expert police witnesses in the first instance.[2] *See Kopf*, 993 F.2d at 376 (a "witness' qualifications to render an expert opinion are * * * liberally judged by Rule 702"); *United States v. Figueroa-Lopez*, 125 F.3d 1241, 1246-47 (9th Cir. 1997)(holding that, although it was error for the district court to admit opinion testimony under 701, the error was harmless because the witnesses could have been qualified as experts under 702). Therefore, under plain error review, Perkins's challenge fails.

* * *

B. EXPERTS

[1] Federal Rule of Evidence 702

Rule 702. Testimony by Experts

If scientific, technical, or other specialized knowledge will assist the trier of fact to understand the evidence or to determine a fact in issue, a witness qualified as an expert by knowledge, skill, experience, training, or education, may testify thereto in the form of an opinion or otherwise, if (1) the testimony is based upon sufficient facts or data, (2) the testimony is the product of reliable principles and methods, and (3) the witness has applied the principles and methods reliably to the facts of the case.

---

[2] We note that we are not concerned that our holding will encourage parties to ignore the disclosure requirements of Federal Rule of Criminal Procedure 16 and the foundation requirements of Rule 702 when offering an expert witness. Unless parties are enlivened by the prospects of potential Rule 701/702 challenges to the opinion testimony that they elicited at trial, they will continue to "play by the rules" in offering experts. Moreover, district courts are not free to misapply federal rules simply because courts sitting in review may find these misapplications harmless.

[2] Qualification of Experts

BERRY v. CITY OF DETROIT

25 F.3d 1342 (6th Cir. 1994)

RALPH B. GUY, JR., CIRCUIT JUDGE:

A jury awarded Doris Berry (plaintiff), six million dollars for the death of her son, Lee Berry, Jr., who was shot by a Detroit police officer.

* * *

I.

On June 23, 1987, Lee Berry, Jr. (Lee), who was employed in a family moving business, was driving the company van in rush-hour traffic to the family residence in Detroit. According to the testimony of Lee's sixteen-year-old brother, Dwayne Berry, and his eight-year-old nephew, David Askew, both of whom were in the van, Lee committed several misdemeanor traffic violations during this journey. The infractions consisted of running a red light, driving on the wrong side of the road, and passing three cars that were stopped for a red light.

These traffic offenses attracted the attention of Officer Joseph Hall, a 17-year veteran of the Detroit Police Department. Exactly what happened immediately thereafter, however, is a matter of some dispute. On the witness stand, Hall testified — in contrast to the testimony of the surviving occupants of the van and in partial contradiction of his earlier deposition testimony — that the violations prompted a dangerous, high-speed chase involving the police. Dwayne and David, on the other hand, offered a markedly different account of what transpired. They testified that Lee had not been speeding, had not attempted to flee from arrest, and had not committed any traffic violations other than those described above.

Moments after the van arrived at the Berry family home, Hall arrived on the scene. Hall confronted Lee Berry and a struggle then ensued, during which Hall shot Lee in the back from a distance estimated as being between three and ten feet. Although no eyewitnesses observed the shooting, David, Dwayne, and several bystanders stated that Hall, upon his arrival at the Berry home, used profanity, threats, and physical force in attempting to effect an arrest. Hall, however, claimed that Lee attacked him; that the gun fired accidently when Lee, during their struggle, attempted to wrestle the pistol away from him; and that he continued to fire at Lee while Lee was fleeing because the firearm was set on "automatic" and because his (Hall's) vision had been impaired by blood. Plaintiff's expert witnesses opined that Lee had not touched Hall's revolver because Lee was several feet away from the gun when it fired, that Hall had not been blinded by blood, and that Hall's service revolver lacked any type of "automatic" firing mechanism.

Shortly after the incident, the police department conducted an investigation that exonerated Hall. No criminal charges were brought against him and no sanctions were imposed upon him. At the time of trial, Hall remained a member of the Detroit Police Department on disability retirement with full pension benefits.

Plaintiff initiated this suit against Hall and the City under 42 U.S.C. § 1983. Plaintiff's complaint also listed several state law causes of action. Plaintiff claimed that the City pursued a deliberate policy of failing to train or discipline adequately its police officers in the proper use of deadly force, which failures caused the violation of Lee's constitutional rights under the Fourth and Fourteenth Amendments. At the conclusion of the trial, the jury returned verdicts against both Hall and the City in the amount of six million dollars.

* * *

Nature of Expert Testimony

* * * [A] problem with the award of a money judgment in this instance stems from the nature of the "expert" testimony offered by plaintiff. There are two facets to this problem. First, we have grave concerns about the qualifications of plaintiff's witness, Frederick Postill, to opine as he did. As we have now defined the issue on appeal, Postill's testimony must have provided the basis for the jury to determine that the alleged failure of the Detroit Police Department to discipline properly officers other than Hall was the proximate cause of Hall shooting Lee Berry. As we view the record, Postill did not have the qualifications to testify as an expert on this question, and, if he did, no proper foundation was laid for his ultimate opinion.

In order not to be simply conclusory on this point, a detailed review of Postill's credentials must be undertaken. Postill received a degree in sociology in 1971, and a master's degree in education in 1976. He also took courses in criminal justice, but how many and what kind was never revealed. His law enforcement career started when he received an appointment as a deputy sheriff in 1966, a position for which, Postill admits, no qualifications were required. Equally important, however, is that he did not receive formal training. Postill simply started and worked with more experienced officers. The only information conveyed by the record as to what he did or learned as a deputy sheriff is the following:

> Q: All right. During your tenure as a deputy sheriff, could you tell us what types of duties you were involved in?
>
> A: Basically, general patrol, investigation work, riding a black and white, responding to calls.
>
> Q: Were you ever certified to instruct as a deputy sheriff other members of — of the Sheriff's Department?
>
> A: I was an instructor there in the Department. I taught defensive tactics, things of that nature.
>
> Q: What do you mean by "defensive tactics"?
>
> A: Physical control of subjects that you would be arresting.

Postill also admits that he was fired twice during his two-year stint as a deputy, apparently as a result of trying to organize the deputies into a labor union against the wishes of the incumbent sheriff. Postill's disagreement with the sheriff culminated in his decision to run against the sheriff in the 1972 election. Although his election bid was successful, the electorate decided to retire him four years later. Interestingly, not one question was asked during trial to elicit what Postill did or learned during his four years as sheriff, a job for which the only necessary qualification is the ability to get elected.

Postill's testimony as to what he did after being deposed as sheriff illustrates the problem that courts and juries have with expert testimony, particularly of the type offered here. If an expert has a degree in electrical engineering, there are some assumptions that safely can be made relative to his general training, since all electrical engineers receive similar training. In this same vein, if an electrical engineer says his first job was designing generator motors, there is some notion of what that job entails. But when a sociologist cum sheriff is allowed to testify as to all manners of police practices and procedures, the slopes become slippery indeed.

Postill's next job after being sheriff was to work for four years for the Justice Department where he "developed the training criteria to train sheriffs and managers of large sheriffs' departments * * * ." Since up to this point in time he had had little or no training himself, exactly why he got this assignment is difficult to understand.

From 1981 to the present, Postill appears to have conducted seminars in police management techniques; taught; formed a one-man corporation called "Criminal Justice Consultants"; testified in court; and purchased a hunting and fishing resort in Canada, where he spends five months a year. The fact that some of this would sound impressive to a jury is its vice, not its virtue. The fault lies not with Postill but, rather, with the system. The courts have had a difficult time in appropriately cabining the opinion testimony of "scientific" experts. At least with scientific testimony there is some objective criteria to look to and there is some basis for evaluating a given expert's testimony against the scientific norm on the subject about which an opinion is offered. The problem that "junk science" has caused in the courtrooms has not gone unnoticed. * * * It would appear obvious, however, that evidentiary problems are exacerbated when courts must deal with the even more elusive concept of non-scientific expert testimony, as is the case here.

The distinction between scientific and non-scientific expert testimony is a critical one. By way of illustration, if one wanted to explain to a jury how a bumblebee is able to fly, an aeronautical engineer might be a helpful witness. Since flight principles have some universality, the expert could apply general principles to the case of the bumblebee. Conceivably, even if he had never seen a bumblebee, he still would be qualified to testify, as long as he was familiar with its component parts.

On the other hand, if one wanted to prove that bumblebees always take off into the wind, a beekeeper with no scientific training at all would be an acceptable expert witness if a proper foundation were laid for his conclusions. The foundation would not relate to his formal training, but to his firsthand observations. In other words, the beekeeper does not know any more about flight principles than the jurors, but he has seen a lot more bumblebees than they have.

Carrying this example into the instant case, it is clear that Postill's testimony, if admissible at all, would have been from the viewpoint of the beekeeper, not the aeronautical engineer. If there is some formal training that would allow one to testify from a scientific standpoint on how failure to discipline officer "A" would impact on the conduct of his peer, officer "B," it is clear that Postill does not have such training. Thus, for this kind of testimony to be admissible, a foundation would have to have been laid based upon the witness's firsthand familiarity with disciplining police officers and the effect of lax discipline on the entire force. To the degree one might be tempted to argue that "everyone knows that if discipline is lax more infractions occur," this argument proves too much. If everyone knows this, then we do not need an expert because the testimony will not "assist the trier of fact to understand the evidence or to determine a fact in issue * * * ." Fed. R. Evid. 702.

If, for example, Postill had testified that when he became sheriff there were "*x*" number of incidents involving alleged excessive force, but two years after he instituted a training program, there were "*x-y*" incidents, we would have a starting point. If he then said that after the training program was in place, he increased the regularity and severity of discipline for infractions and incidents fell to "*x-y2*," then at least there would be some basis for his opinions. Here, however, the only discipline experience referenced was the discipline imposed *upon* Postill.

* * *

With all due respect to Mr. Postill, his credentials *as set forth in the record* do not qualify him to know any more about what effect claimed disciplinary shortcomings would have on the future conduct of 5,000 different police officers than does any member of the jury. Among other things, Postill's testimony assumes that all 5,000 police officers would know enough about the facts of each *claimed* event to evaluate the sufficiency of the discipline, and that the officers would formulate their future course of conduct accordingly. It also assumes, without any basis in fact or logic, that police officers will be extravagant in their use of deadly force if they know discipline will not be severe if a shooting occurs. We are not talking about cheating on overtime here, or some other minor peccadillo; we are talking about the taking of the life of another person.

* * *

The jury verdict against the City of Detroit is REVERSED, and the case is REMANDED for an entry of judgment as a matter of law in favor of the City of Detroit. Fed. R. Civ. P. 50(b).

NOTES

1. Is experience alone ever enough to qualify a witness as an expert?

Experience in the field can be sufficient. In *Satcher v. Honda Motor Co.*, 52 F.3d 1311 (5th Cir. 1995), the Court affirmed an award of actual damages in favor of a rider who lost his leg in a collision between his motorcycle and an automobile. The Court found no error in permitting a former Miami police chief to testify that motorcycle crash guards (which were lacking on the motorcycle used by the plaintiff) are effective in reducing injuries. While the witness had no scientific or engineering expertise in motorcycle design, he had been on the police motor squad for nine years and had investigated hundreds of motorcycle accidents. *See also Hamel v. General Motors Corp.*, 1990 WL 7490 (D. Kan.) (a small town assistant chief of police who owned a cabinet-making shop and worked part time in law enforcement was qualified to testify regarding a car accident based on experience in investigating thirty to thirty-five prior accidents, even though it was acknowledged he had very limited formal training).

2. Can an expert who is qualified on one scientific or technical subject nonetheless be precluded from testifying on other scientific or technical subjects?

In *McCullock v. H.B. Fuller Co.,* 981 F.2d 656 (2d Cir. 1992), the plaintiff challenged the exclusion of her expert in a tort case, in which she alleged that the defendant failed to warn her adequately of the dangers of an unventilated glue pot. Her expert was a mechanical and industrial engineer with substantial experience in the safety field. The court held that the trial court did not err in finding the expert unqualified to testify to the adequacy of the defendant's warnings: "Wooley's training * * * might qualify him to testify as to the need for a ventilation system, but that was not an issue in dispute. The adequacy of the warning labels was at issue, and Wooley is not an expert in that field because he lacks training or experience in chemical engineering, toxicology, environmental engineering, or the design of warning labels." *See also Osburn v. Anchor Labs.*, 825 F.2d 908 (5th Cir. 1987) (expert on toxicology and cancer is not qualified to testify that the defendant violated EPA reporting requirements);

United States v. Chang, 207 F.3d 1169 (9th Cir. 2000) (affirming convictions for uttering and possessing a counterfeit Japanese certificate, the Court held there was no abuse of discretion in excluding the testimony of a defense expert, an assistant professor of clinical marketing, who would have testified that the certificate was genuine; although the expert had knowledge of the history and purpose for the issuance of such certificates, he admitted that he had no formal training in the identification of foreign certificates and did not claim any special training in detecting counterfeit securities; the witness's "practical experience in international finance did not amount to practical experience in determining whether a particular security is counterfeit, the fact at issue in this case").

3. If the expert testimony is on a specialized subject matter, must the expert specialize in that area to be qualified?

See Saltzburg, Martin, and Capra, *Federal Rules of Evidence Manual* (9th ed. 2006):

> Courts have shown an increasing interest in keeping an expert's testimony within the witness' designated area of expertise. An example is *Ancho v. Pentek Corp.*, 157 F.3d 512 (7th Cir. 1998), where the plaintiff proffered a mechanical engineer to testify that an injury at a factory could have been avoided if the plant had been redesigned. The Court found no error in excluding the expert, reasoning as follows:
>
>> Just as a qualified and board certified heart surgeon does not possess sufficient knowledge of orthopaedic medicine to render an expert opinion on spine surgery, likewise we agree with the trial court's ruling that a mechanical engineer * * * lacks qualifications to give expert testimony about plant configuration. Ancho should have retained a qualified plant engineer to testify at trial and his failure to do so was a mistake in judgment for which he has no one to blame but himself.
>
> *See also Hardin v. Ski Venture, Inc.*, 50 F.3d 1291 (4th Cir. 1995) (expert on ski accidents was not qualified to testify about the principles of snowmaking). *See also Eagleston v. Guido*, 41 F.3d 865 (2d Cir. 1994) (testimony that a police department failed to provide sufficient training to officers concerning domestic violence cases was properly excluded; the witness's doctorate in sociology was "a credential that does not in itself describe any specific body of scientific or technical expertise pertinent to this case").
>
> While a Court must be attuned to a qualifications problem when an expert appears to be opining outside a "specialty," a Court should also be concerned about requiring "superspecialized" experts in all cases. There is a danger that a requirement of specialization can be applied so stringently as to exclude most objective experts. Such a danger is discussed in *Stagl v. Delta Air Lines, Inc.*, 117 F.3d 76 (2d Cir. 1997). Stagl was a senior citizen who was injured near a baggage carousel, during a typical mob scene in which passengers were retrieving their baggage. Stagl proffered a mechanical engineer to testify that the baggage delivery system was unsafe for older people, given the crowds around the baggage carousel and the heavy luggage flying about. The Trial Judge ruled that the witness was not qualified because he had no specialized expertise in airline terminal or baggage claim area design. But the Court of Appeals found this to be error. The Court observed:
>
>> In determining whether an expert is sufficiently knowledgeable to be admitted to testify, one of the factors that the district court ought to consider is whether other experts exist who are more specifically qualified and who are nonetheless not in the employ of the company or industry whose practices are being challenged. If the only experts permitted to testify inevitably represent the same side of a civil case,

> those who possess these experts can, for all practical purposes, set their own standards. And allowing an industry to do this is improper because it is very similar to what has been long since held inappropriate, namely, letting the custom of an industry or trade define what is reasonable in that trade.

Addressing the Trial Judge's concern over the witness's lack of expertise with respect to airports, the Court noted that "[i]t is hard to imagine an expert in airport terminal design or baggage claim systems who developed that expertise in any way other than by working for the airline industry," and that "to require the degree of specificity the court imposed came close to letting that industry indirectly set its own standards." The Court observed that the plaintiff's expert had a master's degree in mechanical engineering from Columbia University and had worked as a licensed engineer for twenty years. It concluded, therefore, that the witness was qualified to testify about the interaction of machines and people based on his education and experience even though he had no expertise in airline terminal or baggage claim design. *Stagl* provides the valuable insight that while a Court should not lightly permit testimony from an expert outside his or her "specialty," a Court must also guard against requiring an expertise so specialized as to disqualify anyone who is not a captive of the specialized industry.

4. Should an expert be prohibited from testifying if he switches sides in the litigation?

Peterson v. Willie, 81 F.3d 1033 (11th Cir. 1996), was an action brought by a pretrial detainee for deliberate indifference to his medical needs. The defendants called an expert who had been retained by the plaintiff and designated as an expert witness expected to testify, but who had subsequently been discharged by the plaintiff's counsel. The trial court permitted the expert to testify, and also to state that he had been previously retained by the plaintiff. The Court of Apeals noted that various approaches have been taken when an expert originally retained by one side is called by the other. Some courts have permitted such experts to be called, but prohibited reference to the fact that they were originally retained by the adversary; some have refused to permit such experts to testify absent a showing of need. The Court concluded that the issue of whether such experts should be permitted to testify is committed to the discretion of the trial court, but cautioned that leave should not ordinarily be granted if other experts are readily available. As to whether the expert can refer to the previous retention, the Court concluded that "the unfair prejudice resulting from disclosing this fact usually outweighs any probative value." It recognized, however, that a reference to the previous retention would be warranted if the adversary were to attack the qualifications of the expert. As the plaintiff made no such attack in this case, the Court found error in permitting evidence that the expert had been retained by the plaintiff. The error was harmless, however, and the judgment for the defendant was affirmed.

[3] Proper Subject Matter for Expert Testimony

SCOTT v. SEARS, ROEBUCK & CO.
789 F.2d 1052 (4th Cir. 1986)

HAYNSWORTH, SENIOR CIRCUIT JUDGE:

This is a slip and fall case in the diversity jurisdiction. The question before us is whether the district court abused its discretion when, over the defendant's objection, it admitted the testimony of an expert in "ergonomics", i.e., a "human factors" expert.

* * *

I.

Margaret Scott, with visiting friends, went to the Sears store in Roanoke, Virginia to pick up a rug she had ordered. They entered the store through a special parcel post entrance. After picking up the rug, carried by the two men in the group, they left by the same entrance. In order to reach their parked car, however, they inexplicably turned to their left, opposite the direction from which they had approached the parcel post entrance.

The parcel post entrance opens upon a sidewalk running to the right and to the left. The curb is painted yellow and, in the direction in which Ms. Scott walked, a series of metal grates is set in the concrete. The first and second of those grates end approximately four feet from the yellow curb, and the third ends approximately three feet from the curb. On the day of Ms. Scott's visit, the concrete in the vicinity of the third grate was deteriorated, and the surface was spalling [i.e., chipping off]. At the third expansion joint near the third grate, the curb had subsided some three inches below the surface of the walkway and the adjacent curbing. It had been in that condition fifteen years or more. When approached from the parcel post entrance, the subsided curb was more distant than the undisplaced curbing. Ms. Scott walked diagonally across the sidewalk, avoiding the grates, apparently intending to step off the sidewalk at the third expansion joint. It was broad daylight, and Ms. Scott was in good health and possessed of all her faculties. Nevertheless, one of her one-inch heels caught in the space left by the displaced curb at the third expansion joint. She fell and broke her leg.

II.

Virginia law places a significant duty of care upon persons using sidewalks open to the public. The pedestrian must be aware of the "irregularities in grade, unevenness in surface [and] sharp depressions" frequently present in public walkways. If the defect is open and obvious, an injured pedestrian may not recover unless he can prove that external conditions prevented his seeing the defect or would excuse his failure to see it. Failure to observe would be excused only by a distraction that was unexpected and substantially beyond the miscellany of activity normally found on public sidewalks.

III.

In an attempt to avoid the defense of contributory negligence, Ms. Scott offered the testimony of Dr. Snydor, a professor at Virginia Polytechnic Institute and an expert in "human factors." Through him she undertook to prove that the defect, though open, was not obvious. He expressed the opinion that the physical environment and the limitations of human perception were such that "a substantial proportion of people [would] not see the three inch drop of the curb when approaching the area from the direction of the parcel post entrance." He stated that as Ms. Scott approached the area, the undamaged curb would obscure the drop off, though we may observe that this would not necessarily be true as one approached the area closely. Moreover, he testified that the human eye has a tendency to "fill in any slight discontinuity or break," and that the yellow paint on the curb would trick the eye into seeing the curb "as the person would typically expect it to be." He testified that most people, particularly women wearing heels, do not like to walk on gratings and that the fact that the third grating was closer to the curb than the first two would cause most pedestrians to veer to the right near the curb. Finally, and of greater moment, he testified that the spalling on the sidewalk would draw and hold the attention of a pedestrian. Dr. Snydor concluded by expressing the opinion that, in light of Ms. Scott's unfamiliarity with the sidewalk, the conditions he had described created "an accident waiting to happen * * * waiting for a woman in particular with a heel to come along, to see [the sidewalk] for the first time from that direction and to simply be involved with looking at the other things in the immediate environment and unfortunately stepping at the wrong place at the wrong time."

The jury returned a verdict in plaintiff's favor of $125,000.

IV.

* * *

V.

Sears contends that the testimony of "human factors" experts should always be rejected because it deals with probable human reaction to environmental conditions. This is so, it is contended, because such testimony concerns matters within the "common knowledge" of jurors. However, there simply is no support for a rule of per se inadmissibility on that account. * * * Rule 702 provides that expert testimony may be admitted if it will "assist the trier of fact to understand the evidence or to determine a fact in issue." The question whether such assistance will be provided is within the sound discretion of the district judge.

Though we would normally defer to the exercise by the district court of its judgment, Rule 702 makes inadmissible expert testimony as to a matter which obviously is within the common knowledge of jurors because such testimony, almost by definition, can be of no assistance. At the same time, the admission of such testimony, though technical error, will almost invariably be harmless. * * * Trouble is encountered only when the evaluation of the commonplace by an expert witness might supplant a jury's independent exercise of common sense. This, however, does not seem to be an inquiry under Rule 702, but rather a necessary, independent inquiry under Rule 403 to exclude evidence which is prejudicial.

* * *

VI.

Dr. Snydor's testimony that the higher, nearer section of the curb hid the displaced, further section from the sight of one outside the parcel post door could have been of scant help to the jury. The jurors had an opportunity to observe that for themselves when taken to the scene, and they could see it in the photographs which were in evidence. The statistical evidence introduced through Dr. Snydor that persons wearing heels tend to avoid walking on grates was of no greater help. As to both matters, the witness was simply repeating what is common knowledge and common sense. That would lead to the conclusion that the admission of such testimony was erroneous under Rule 702, but the error was clearly harmless.

On the other hand, Dr. Snydor's testimony that the yellow color of the curb might prompt the human eye to fill in discontinuities is not a matter within the common knowledge of jurors. This would seem to be a paradigm of admissible human factors testimony. It professed to be a statement of scientific understanding of the effect of color upon human perception under some circumstances. There was no abuse of discretion in the admission of that testimony.

It was error, however, to have permitted Dr. Snydor's testimony that the spalling of the concrete was an effective distraction or to comment that the scene was an "accident waiting to happen." Under Virginia law, the spalling of the concrete would not excuse the plaintiff's failure to see the defect in the curbing. The jury, however, was not told that it could not use the spalling as a basis for finding Ms. Scott reasonably distracted and therefore innocent of contributory negligence. In the absence of instructions clearly requiring the jury to disregard Dr. Snydor's testimony about the spalling, its admission was prejudicial error.

Similarly, Dr. Snydor's comment that the defect was an "accident waiting to happen" was overly prejudicial and inflammatory. It should have been excluded. Since prejudicial testimony was admitted in violation of Rule 403, there must be a new trial.

REVERSED AND REMANDED.

NOTES

1. When will expert testimony assist the trier of fact?

Courts generally hold that expert testimony is on a proper subject matter if it deals with an issue that is not of common knowledge to a reasonable juror.

Thus, an expert may testify concerning trade usage and banking customs, *First Nat'l State Bank v. Reliance Elec. Co.*, 668 F.2d 725 (3d. Cir. 1981); concerning the cultural attitudes among Hmong refugees, *Dang Vang v. Vang Xiong X. Toyed*, 944 F.2d 476 (9th Cir. 1991); and concerning proper engineering design standards, *Frazier v. Continental Oil Co.*, 568 F.2d 378 (5th Cir. 1978). *See also United States v. Diallo*, 40 F.3d 32 (2d Cir. 1994), where the court reversed a defendant's convictions for importing and possessing heroin, finding that the trial court abused its discretion in refusing to allow a commodities analyst to testify as an expert regarding the market price of gold in the United States and the profit to be made by smuggling gold out of Africa. The testimony supported the defendant's claim that he thought he was smuggling gold, not drugs. And it was on a subject that jurors would not generally know about.

On the other hand, testimony that relates to matters within the common knowledge of the jurors has been held inadmissible, as by definition it will not "assist" the jurors within the meaning of Rule 702. Examples include testimony on the weight a plaintiff had to lift as part of his job duties being unreasonable, *Persinger v. Norfolk & W. Ry.*, 920 F.2d 1185 (4th Cir. 1990), and expert testimony that offloading a ship in bad weather was hazardous, *Peters v. Fire Star Marine Serv.*, 898 F.2d 448 (5th Cir. 1990). *See also United States v. Fuentes-Cariaga*, 209 F.3d 1140 (9th Cir. 2000) (no error to preclude expert testimony from a law enforcement officer that a driver's nervousness at a border crossing is not indicative of guilt; the nervousness of drivers stopped at the border is within the ordinary understanding of jurors); *United States v. Thomas*, 74 F.3d 676 (6th Cir. 1996) (no error in the trial judge's exclusion of a defense expert who would have testified about the incentive for a government witness to lie under oath in order to obtain a sentence reduction; there was no need for expert testimony, because the jury could understand the witness's incentive on the basis of cross-examination without expert help).

It has also been held that expert testimony will not assist the trier of fact when it is in the form of speculation (expert cannot testify on the value of living, *Mercado v. Ahmed*, 974 F.2d 863 (7th Cir. 1992)); or when it is a mere legal conclusion (a witness' testimony that a party is guilty or innocent, *United States v. Lockett*, 919 F.2d 585, 590 (9th Cir. 1990)).

2. Can the testimony of a law enforcement agent ever be admissible as expert testimony in a criminal case?

In *United States v. Cruz,* 981 F.2d 659 (2d Cir. 1992), a law enforcement agent, with considerable experience in policing drug activity, testified to the function of a "broker" in a drug transaction. This general testimony corroborated the testimony of the prosecution's star fact witness, who testified that the defendant had acted as an intermediary in the sale of drugs purchased by the witness. The defendant testified that he was not present at the drug transactions, and that his meetings with the prosecution's witness concerned car repairs. The court found that the expert's *modus operandi* testimony was improperly admitted because it was not helpful to the jury. It reasoned: "That drug traffickers may seek to conceal their identities by using intermediaries would seem evident to the average juror from movies, television crime dramas, and news stories." *See also United States v. Castillo,* 924 F.2d 1227 (2d Cir.

1991) (testimony that drug dealers force buyers to use drugs at gunpoint found not helpful since most New York jurors would figure this to be the case); *United States v. Cruz*, 363 F.3d 187 (2d Cir. 2004) (while government agents could assist in deciphering drug jargon, it was improper to permit them to testify about the meaning of a phrase like "to watch someone's back" that is neither "coded nor esoteric," and the dangers of admitting such testimony are particularly acute when, as in this case, the law enforcement agent is also testifying as a fact witness).

But this is not to say that law enforcement agents can never testify as experts in criminal cases. Quite the contrary. The line between permissible and impermissible expert testimony is illustrated by Judge Becker, in *United States v. Gibbs*, 190 F.3d 188 (3d Cir. 1999). In *Gibbs,* a law enforcement expert testified to the meaning of conversations between members of a drug conspiracy that had been intercepted by the government. The expert testified that "jawn" meant cocaine, that to "hit" someone meant to page them on their beeper, and that a "quarter" meant $2500. Judge Becker found this testimony permissible because these terms were not within the ordinary understanding of jurors, and the expert's translation was therefore helpful. However, the expert also testified that "tonight is the night" was a reference to the fact that two coconspirators were going to take part in a particular mission that night. Judge Becker found that this testimony was erroneously (though harmlessly) admitted, because " 'tonight is the night' contains no intrinsic code that a jury would be unable to understand."

[4] The Requirement that Expert Testimony be Reliable

[a] Scientific Expert Testimony — The General Acceptance Test

FRYE v. UNITED STATES
293 F. 1013 (D.C. Cir. 1923)

Van Orsdel, Associate Justice:

Appellant, defendant below, was convicted of the crime of murder in the second degree, and from the judgment prosecutes this appeal.

A single assignment of error is presented for our consideration. In the course of the trial counsel for defendant offered an expert witness to testify to the result of a deception test made upon defendant. The test is described as the systolic blood pressure deception test. It is asserted that blood pressure is influenced by change in the emotions of the witness, and that the systolic blood pressure rises are brought about by nervous impulses sent to the sympathetic branch of the autonomic nervous system. Scientific experiments, it is claimed, have demonstrated that fear, rage, and pain always produce a rise of systolic blood pressure, and that conscious deception or falsehood, concealment of facts, or guilt of crime, accompanied by fear of detection when the person is under examination, raises the systolic blood pressure in a curve, which corresponds exactly to the struggle going on in the subject's mind, between fear and attempted control of that fear, as the examination touches the vital points in respect of which he is attempting to deceive the examiner.

In other words, the theory seems to be that truth is spontaneous, and comes without conscious effort, while the utterance of a falsehood requires a conscious effort, which is reflected in the blood pressure. The rise thus produced is easily detected and distinguished from the rise produced by mere fear of the examination itself. In the former instance, the pressure rises higher than in the latter, and is more pronounced as the examination proceeds, while in the latter case, if the subject is telling the truth, the pressure registers highest at the beginning of the examination, and gradually diminishes as the examination proceeds.

Prior to the trial defendant was subjected to this deception test, and counsel offered the scientist who conducted the test as an expert to testify to the results obtained. The offer was objected to by counsel for the government, and the court sustained the objection.

* * *

* * * Numerous cases are cited in support of this rule. Just when a scientific principle or discovery crosses the line between the experimental and demonstrable stages is difficult to define. Somewhere in this twilight zone the evidential force of the principle must be recognized, and while courts will go a long way in admitting expert testimony deduced from a well-recognized scientific principle or discovery, the thing from which the deduction is made must be sufficiently established to have gained general acceptance in the particular field in which it belongs.

We think the systolic blood pressure deception test has not yet gained such standing and scientific recognition among physiological and psychological authorities as would justify the courts in admitting expert testimony deduced from the discovery, development, and experiments thus far made.

The judgment is affirmed.

[b] Scientific Expert Testimony — The Reliability Test and the Trial Court's Gatekeeping Function

DAUBERT v. MERRELL DOW PHARMACEUTICALS, INC.
509 U.S. 579 (1993)

JUSTICE BLACKMUN delivered the opinion of the Court.

In this case we are called upon to determine the standard for admitting expert scientific testimony in a federal trial.

I

Petitioners Jason Daubert and Eric Schuller are minor children born with serious birth defects. They and their parents sued respondent in California state court, alleging that the birth defects had been caused by the mothers' ingestion of Bendectin, a prescription anti-nausea drug marketed by respondent. Respondent removed the suits to federal court on diversity grounds.

After extensive discovery, respondent moved for summary judgment, contending that Bendectin does not cause birth defects in humans and that petitioners would be unable to come forward with any admissible evidence that it does. In support of its motion, respondent submitted an affidavit of Steven H. Lamm, physician and epidemiologist, who is a well-credentialed expert on the risks from exposure to various chemical substances. Doctor Lamm stated that he had reviewed all the literature on Bendectin and human birth defects — more than 30 published studies involving over 130,000 patients. No study had found Bendectin to be a human teratogen (i.e., a substance capable of causing malformations in fetuses). On the basis of this review, Doctor Lamm concluded that maternal use of Bendectin during the first trimester of pregnancy has not been shown to be a risk factor for human birth defects.

Petitioners did not (and do not) contest this characterization of the published record regarding Bendectin. Instead, they responded to respondent's motion with the testimony of eight experts of their own, each of whom also possessed impressive credentials. These experts had concluded that Bendectin can cause birth defects. Their conclusions were based upon "in vitro" (test tube) and "in vivo" (live) animal studies that found a link between Bendectin and malformations; pharmacological studies of the chemical structure of Bendectin that purported to show similarities between the structure of the drug and that of other substances known to cause birth defects; and the "reanalysis" of previously published epidemiological (human statistical) studies.

The District Court granted respondent's motion for summary judgment. The court stated that scientific evidence is admissible only if the principle upon which it is based is " 'sufficiently established to have general acceptance in the field to which it belongs.' " The court concluded that petitioners' evidence did not meet this standard. Given the vast body of epidemiological data concerning Bendectin, the court held, expert opinion which is not based on epidemiological evidence is not admissible to establish causation. Thus, the animal-cell studies, live-animal studies, and chemical-structure analyses on which petitioners had relied could not raise by themselves a reasonably disputable jury issue regarding causation. Petitioners' epidemiological analyses, based as they were on recalculations of data in previously published studies that had found no causal link between the drug and birth defects, were ruled to be inadmissible because they had not been published or subjected to peer review.

The United States Court of Appeals for the Ninth Circuit affirmed. *Citing Frye v. United States*, 293 F. 1013, 1014 (1923), the court stated that expert opinion based on a scientific technique is inadmissible unless the technique is "generally accepted" as reliable in the relevant scientific community. The court declared that expert opinion based on a methodology that diverges "significantly from the procedures accepted by recognized authorities in the field * * * cannot be shown to be 'generally accepted as a reliable technique' ".

The court emphasized that other Courts of Appeals considering the risks of Bendectin had refused to admit reanalyses of epidemiological studies that had been neither published nor subjected to peer review. Those courts had found unpublished reanalyses "particularly problematic in light of the massive weight of the original published studies supporting [respondent's] position, all of which had undergone full scrutiny from the scientific community." Contending that reanalysis is generally accepted by the scientific community only when it is subjected to verification and scrutiny by others in the field, the Court of Appeals rejected petitioners' reanalyses as "unpublished, not subjected to the normal peer review process and generated solely for use in litigation." The court concluded that petitioners' evidence provided an insufficient foundation to allow admission of expert testimony that Bendectin caused their injuries and, accordingly, that petitioners could not satisfy their burden of proving causation at trial.

We granted *certiorari* * * * in light of sharp divisions among the courts regarding the proper standard for the admission of expert testimony.

* * *

II

A

In the 70 years since its formulation in the *Frye* case, the "general acceptance" test has been the dominant standard for determining the admissibility of novel scientific evidence at trial.* * * Although under increasing attack of late, the rule continues to be followed by a majority of courts, including the Ninth Circuit.

* * *

The merits of the *Frye* test have been much debated, and scholarship on its proper scope and application is legion. Petitioners' primary attack, however, is not on the content but on the continuing authority of the rule. They contend that the *Frye* test was superseded by the adoption of the Federal Rules of Evidence. We agree.

We interpret the legislatively-enacted Federal Rules of Evidence as we would any statute.* * * Rule 402 provides the baseline:

> All relevant evidence is admissible, except as otherwise provided by the Constitution of the United States, by Act of Congress, by these rules, or by other rules prescribed by the Supreme Court pursuant to statutory authority. Evidence which is not relevant is not admissible.

"Relevant evidence" is defined as that which has "any tendency to make the existence of any fact that is of consequence to the determination of the action more probable or less probable than it would be without the evidence." Rule 401. The Rule's basic standard of relevance thus is a liberal one.

Frye, of course, predated the Rules by half a century. In *United States v. Abel*, 469 U.S. 45 (1984), we considered the pertinence of background common law in interpreting the Rules of Evidence. We noted that the Rules occupy the field, but, quoting Professor Cleary, the Reporter, explained that the common law nevertheless could serve as an aid to their application:

> In principle, under the Federal Rules no common law of evidence remains. 'All relevant evidence is admissible, except as otherwise provided * * *.' In reality, of course, the body of common law knowledge continues to exist, though in the somewhat altered form of a source of guidance in the exercise of delegated powers.

We found the common-law precept at issue in the *Abel* case entirely consistent with Rule 402's general requirement of admissibility, and considered it unlikely that the drafters had intended to change the rule. In *Bourjaily v. United States*, 483 U.S. 171 (1987), on the other hand, the Court was unable to find a particular common-law doctrine in the Rules, and so held it superseded.

Here there is a specific Rule that speaks to the contested issue. Rule 702, governing expert testimony, provides:

> If scientific, technical, or other specialized knowledge will assist the trier of fact to understand the evidence or to determine a fact in issue, a witness qualified as an expert by knowledge, skill, experience, training, or education, may testify thereto in the form of an opinion or otherwise.

Nothing in the text of this Rule establishes "general acceptance" as an absolute prerequisite to admissibility. Nor does respondent present any clear indication that Rule 702 or the Rules as a whole were intended to incorporate a "general acceptance" standard. The drafting history makes no mention of *Frye*, and a rigid "general acceptance" requirement would be at odds with the "liberal thrust" of the Federal Rules and their "general approach of relaxing the traditional barriers to 'opinion' testimony." *Beech Aircraft Corp. v. Rainey*, 488 U.S., at 169 (*citing* Rules 701 to 705).* * * Given the Rules' permissive backdrop and their inclusion of a specific rule on expert testimony that does not mention "general acceptance," the assertion that the Rules somehow assimilated *Frye* is unconvincing. *Frye* made "general acceptance" the exclusive test for admitting expert scientific testimony. That austere standard, absent from and incompatible with the Federal Rules of Evidence, should not be applied in federal trials.

B

That the *Frye* test was displaced by the Rules of Evidence does not mean, however, that the Rules themselves place no limits on the admissibility of purportedly scientific evidence. Nor is the trial judge disabled from screening such evidence. To the contrary, under the Rules the trial judge must ensure that any and all scientific testimony or evidence admitted is not only relevant, but reliable.

The primary locus of this obligation is Rule 702, which clearly contemplates some degree of regulation of the subjects and theories about which an expert may testify. "*If scientific*, technical, or other specialized *knowledge will assist the trier of fact* to understand the evidence or to determine a fact in issue" an expert "may testify *thereto*." The subject of an expert's testimony must be "scientific * * * knowledge." The adjective "scientific" implies a grounding in the methods and procedures of science. Similarly, the word "knowledge" connotes more than subjective belief or unsupported speculation. The term "applies to any body of known facts or to any body of ideas inferred from such facts or accepted as truths on good grounds." Webster's Third New International Dictionary 1252 (1986). Of course, it would be unreasonable to conclude that the subject of scientific testimony must be "known" to a certainty; arguably, there are no certainties in science. But, in order to qualify as "scientific knowledge," an inference or assertion must be derived by the scientific method. Proposed testimony must be supported by appropriate validation -*i.e.*, "good grounds," based on what is known. In short, the requirement that an expert's testimony pertain to "scientific knowledge" establishes a standard of evidentiary reliability.

Rule 702 further requires that the evidence or testimony "assist the trier of fact to understand the evidence or to determine a fact in issue." This condition goes primarily to relevance. "Expert testimony which does not relate to any issue in the case is not relevant and, *ergo*, non-helpful." The consideration has been aptly described by Judge Becker as one of "fit." *United States v. Downing*, 723 F.2d at 1242. "Fit" is not always obvious, and scientific validity for one purpose is not necessarily scientific validity for other, unrelated purposes. The study of the phases of the moon, for example, may provide valid scientific "knowledge" about whether a certain night was dark, and if darkness is a fact in issue, the knowledge will assist the trier of fact. However (absent creditable grounds supporting such a link), evidence that the moon was full on a certain night will not assist the trier of fact in determining whether an individual was unusually likely to have behaved irrationally on that night. Rule 702's "helpfulness" standard requires a valid scientific connection to the pertinent inquiry as a precondition to admissibility.

That these requirements are embodied in Rule 702 is not surprising. Unlike an ordinary witness, *see* Rule 701, an expert is permitted wide latitude to offer opinions, including those that are not based on first-hand knowledge or observation. *See* Rules 702 and 703. Presumably, this relaxation of the usual requirement of first-hand knowledge * * * is premised on an assumption that the expert's opinion will have a reliable basis in the knowledge and experience of his discipline.

C

Faced with a proffer of expert scientific testimony, then, the trial judge must determine at the outset, pursuant to Rule 104(a), whether the expert is proposing to testify to (1) scientific knowledge that (2) will assist the trier of fact to understand or determine a fact in issue. This entails a preliminary assessment of whether the reasoning or methodology underlying the testimony is scientifically valid and of whether that reasoning or methodology properly can be applied to the facts in issue. We are confident that federal judges possess the capacity to undertake this review. Many factors will bear on the inquiry, and we do not presume to set out a definitive checklist or test. But some general observations are appropriate.

Ordinarily, a key question to be answered in determining whether a theory or technique is scientific knowledge that will assist the trier of fact will be whether it can be (and has been) tested. "Scientific methodology today is based on generating hypotheses and testing them to see if they can be falsified; indeed, this methodology is what distinguishes science from other fields of human inquiry."

* * *

Another pertinent consideration is whether the theory or technique has been subjected to peer review and publication. Publication (which is but one element of peer review) is not a *sine qua non* of admissibility; it does not necessarily correlate with reliability, and in some instances well-grounded but innovative theories will not have been published. Some propositions, moreover, are too particular, too new, or of too limited interest to be published. But submission to the scrutiny of the scientific community is a component of "good science," in part because it increases the likelihood that substantive flaws in methodology will be detected. The fact of publication (or lack thereof) in a peer-reviewed journal thus will be a relevant, though not dispositive, consideration in assessing the scientific validity of a particular technique or methodology on which an opinion is premised.

Additionally, in the case of a particular scientific technique, the court ordinarily should consider the known or potential rate of error * * * and the existence and maintenance of standards controlling the technique's operation.

* * *

Finally, "general acceptance" can yet have a bearing on the inquiry. A "reliability assessment does not require, although it does permit, explicit identification of a relevant scientific community and an express determination of a particular degree of acceptance within that community." *United States v. Downing*, 753 F.2d, at 1238. Widespread acceptance can be an important factor in ruling particular evidence admissible, and "a known technique that has been able to attract only minimal support within the community," *Downing, supra*, at 1238, may properly be viewed with skepticism.

The inquiry envisioned by Rule 702 is, we emphasize, a flexible one. Its overarching subject is the scientific validity — and thus the evidentiary relevance and reliability — of the principles that underlie a proposed submission. The focus, of course, must be solely on principles and methodology, not on the conclusions that they generate.

Throughout, a judge assessing a proffer of expert scientific testimony under Rule 702 should also be mindful of other applicable rules. Rule 703 provides that expert opinions based on otherwise inadmissible hearsay are to be admitted only if the facts or data are "of a type reasonably relied upon by experts in the particular field in forming opinions or inferences upon the subject." Rule 706 allows the court at its discretion to procure the assistance of an expert of its own choosing. Finally, Rule 403 permits the exclusion of relevant evidence "if its probative value is substantially outweighed by the danger of unfair prejudice, confusion of the issues, or misleading the jury * * * ." Judge Weinstein has explained: "Expert evidence can be both powerful and quite misleading because of the difficulty in evaluating it. Because of this risk, the judge in weighing possible prejudice against probative force under Rule 403 of the present rules exercises more control over experts than over lay witnesses."

III

We conclude by briefly addressing what appear to be two underlying concerns of the parties and *amici* in this case. Respondent expresses apprehension that abandonment of "general acceptance" as the exclusive requirement for admission will result in a "free-for-all" in which befuddled juries are confounded by absurd and irrational pseudoscientific assertions. In this regard respondent seems to us to be overly pessimistic about the capabilities of the jury, and of the adversary system generally. Vigorous cross-examination, presentation of contrary evidence, and careful instruction on the burden of proof are the traditional and appropriate means of attacking shaky but admissible evidence. Additionally, in the event the trial court concludes that the scintilla of evidence presented supporting a position is insufficient to allow a reasonable juror to conclude that the position more likely than not is true, the court remains free to direct a judgment, Fed. Rule Civ. Proc. 50(a), and likewise to grant summary judgment, Fed. Rule Civ. Proc. 56. These conventional devices, rather than wholesale exclusion under an uncompromising "general acceptance" test, are the appropriate safeguards where the basis of scientific testimony meets the standards of Rule 702.

Petitioners and, to a greater extent, their *amici* exhibit a different concern. They suggest that recognition of a screening role for the judge that allows for the exclusion of "invalid" evidence will sanction a stifling and repressive scientific orthodoxy and will be inimical to the search for truth. It is true that open debate is an essential part of both legal and scientific analyses. Yet there are important differences between the quest for truth in the courtroom and the quest for truth in the laboratory. Scientific conclusions are subject to perpetual revision. Law, on the other hand, must resolve disputes finally and quickly. The scientific project is advanced by broad and wide-ranging consideration of a multitude of hypotheses, for those that are incorrect will eventually be shown to be so, and that in itself is an advance. Conjectures that are probably wrong are of little use, however, in the project of reaching a quick, final, and binding legal judgment — often of great consequence — about a particular set of events in the past. We recognize that in practice, a gatekeeping role for the judge, no matter how flexible, inevitably on occasion will prevent the jury from learning of authentic insights and innovations. That, nevertheless, is the balance that is struck by Rules of Evidence designed not for the exhaustive search for cosmic understanding but for the particularized resolution of legal disputes.

IV

To summarize: "General acceptance" is not a necessary precondition to the admissibility of scientific evidence under the Federal Rules of Evidence, but the Rules of Evidence — especially Rule 702 — do assign to the trial judge the task of ensuring that an expert's testimony both rests on a reliable foundation and is relevant to the task at hand. Pertinent evidence based on scientifically valid principles will satisfy those demands.

The inquiries of the District Court and the Court of Appeals focused almost exclusively on "general acceptance," as gauged by publication and the decisions of other courts. Accordingly, the judgment of the Court of Appeals is vacated and the case is remanded for further proceedings consistent with this opinion.

It is so ordered.

[Concurring opinion omitted.]

[c] Applications of the *Daubert* Gatekeeping Function to Scientific Expert Testimony

GENERAL ELECTRIC CO. v. JOINER
522 U.S. 136 (1997)

Chief Justice Rehnquist delivered the opinion of the Court.

We granted certiorari in this case to determine what standard an appellate court should apply in reviewing a trial court's decision to admit or exclude expert testimony under *Daubert v. Merrell Dow Pharmaceuticals, Inc.*, 509 U.S. 579 (1993). We hold that abuse of discretion is the appropriate standard. We apply this standard and conclude that the District Court in this case did not abuse its discretion when it excluded certain proffered expert testimony.

I

Respondent Robert Joiner began work as an electrician in the Water & Light Department of Thomasville, Georgia (City) in 1973. This job required him to work with and around the City's electrical transformers, which used a mineral-based dielectric fluid as a coolant. Joiner often had to stick his hands and arms into the fluid to make repairs. The fluid would sometimes splash onto him, occasionally getting into his eyes and mouth. In 1983 the City discovered that the fluid in some of the transformers was contaminated with polychlorinated biphenyls (PCBs). PCBs are widely considered to be hazardous to human health. Congress, with limited exceptions, banned the production and sale of PCBs in 1978.

Joiner was diagnosed with small cell lung cancer in 1991. He sued petitioners in Georgia state court the following year. Petitioner Monsanto manufactured PCBs from 1935 to 1977; petitioners General Electric and Westinghouse Electric manufactured transformers and dielectric fluid. In his complaint Joiner linked his development of cancer to his exposure to PCBs and their derivatives, polychlorinated dibenzofurans (furans) and polychlorinated dibenzodioxins (dioxins). Joiner had been a smoker for approximately eight years, his parents had both been smokers, and there was a history of lung cancer in his family. He was thus perhaps already at a heightened risk of developing lung cancer eventually. The suit alleged that his exposure to PCBs "promoted" his cancer; had it not been for his exposure to these substances, his cancer would not have developed for many years, if at all.

Petitioners removed the case to federal court. Once there, they moved for summary judgment. They contended that (1) there was no evidence that Joiner suffered significant exposure to PCBs, furans, or dioxins, and (2) there was no admissible scientific evidence that PCBs promoted Joiner's cancer. Joiner responded that there were numerous disputed factual issues that required resolution by a jury. He relied largely on the testimony of expert witnesses. In depositions, his experts had testified that PCBs alone can promote cancer and that furans and dioxins can also promote cancer. They opined that since Joiner had been exposed to PCBs, furans, and dioxins, such exposure was likely responsible for Joiner's cancer.

The District Court ruled that there was a genuine issue of material fact as to whether Joiner had been exposed to PCBs. But it nevertheless granted summary judgment for petitioners because (1) there was no genuine issue as to whether Joiner had been exposed to furans and dioxins, and (2) the testimony of Joiner's experts had failed to show that there was a link between exposure to PCBs and small cell lung cancer. The court believed that the testimony of respondent's experts to the contrary did not rise above "subjective belief or unsupported speculation." Their testimony was therefore inadmissible.

The Court of Appeals for the Eleventh Circuit reversed. It held that "[b]ecause the Federal Rules of Evidence governing expert testimony display a preference for admissibility, we apply a particularly stringent standard of review to the trial judge's exclusion of expert testimony." Applying that standard, the Court of Appeals held that the District Court had erred in excluding the testimony of Joiner's expert witnesses. The District Court had made two fundamental errors. First, it excluded the experts' testimony because it "drew different conclusions from the research than did each of the experts." The Court of Appeals opined that a district court should limit its role to determining the "legal reliability of proffered expert testimony, leaving the jury to decide the correctness of competing expert opinions." Second, the District Court had held that there was no genuine issue of material fact as to whether Joiner had been exposed to furans and dioxins. This was also incorrect, said the Court of Appeals, because testimony in the record supported the proposition that there had been such exposure.

We granted petitioners' petition for a writ of certiorari, and we now reverse.

II

Petitioners challenge the standard applied by the Court of Appeals in reviewing the District Court's decision to exclude respondent's experts' proffered testimony. They argue that that court should have applied traditional "abuse of discretion" review.

* * *

We have held that abuse of discretion is the proper standard of review of a district court's evidentiary rulings. * * * The Court of Appeals suggested that *Daubert* somehow altered this general rule in the context of a district court's decision to exclude scientific evidence. But *Daubert* did not address the standard of appellate review for evidentiary rulings at all. It did hold that the "austere" *Frye* standard of "general acceptance" had not been carried over into the Federal Rules of Evidence. But the opinion also said:

> That the *Frye* test was displaced by the Rules of Evidence does not mean, however, that the Rules themselves place no limits on the admissibility of purportedly scientific evidence. Nor is the trial judge disabled from screening such evidence. To the contrary, under the Rules the trial judge must ensure that any and all scientific testimony or evidence admitted is not only relevant, but reliable.

Thus, while the Federal Rules of Evidence allow district courts to admit a somewhat broader range of scientific testimony than would have been admissible under *Frye*, they leave in place the "gatekeeper" role of the trial judge in screening such evidence. A court of appeals applying "abuse of discretion" review to such rulings may not categorically distinguish between rulings allowing expert testimony and rulings which disallow it. We likewise reject respondent's argument that because the granting of summary judgment in this case was "outcome determinative," it should have been subjected to a more searching standard of review. On a motion for summary judgment, disputed issues of fact are resolved against the moving party — here, petitioners. But the question of admissibility of expert testimony is not such an issue of fact, and is reviewable under the abuse of discretion standard.

We hold that the Court of Appeals erred in its review of the exclusion of Joiner's experts' testimony. In applying an overly "stringent" review to that ruling, it failed to give the trial court the deference that is the hallmark of abuse of discretion review.

III

We believe that a proper application of the correct standard of review here indicates that the District Court did not abuse its discretion. Joiner's theory of liability was that his exposure to PCBs and their derivatives "promoted" his development of small cell lung cancer. In support of that theory he proffered the deposition testimony of expert witnesses. Dr. Arnold Schecter testified that he believed it "more likely than not that Mr. Joiner's lung cancer was causally linked to cigarette smoking and PCB exposure." Dr. Daniel Teitelbaum testified that Joiner's "lung cancer was caused by or contributed to in a significant degree by the materials with which he worked."

Petitioners contended that the statements of Joiner's experts regarding causation were nothing more than speculation. Petitioners criticized the testimony of the experts in that it was "not supported by epidemiological studies * * * [and was] based exclusively on isolated studies of laboratory animals." Joiner responded by claiming that his experts had identified "relevant animal studies which support their opinions." He also directed the court's attention to four epidemiological studies on which his experts had relied. [Editor's Note:

Epidemiological studies examine the pattern of disease in human populations.]

The District Court agreed with petitioners that the animal studies on which respondent's experts relied did not support his contention that exposure to PCBs had contributed to his cancer. The studies involved infant mice that had developed cancer after being exposed to PCBs. The infant mice in the studies had had massive doses of PCBs injected directly into their peritoneums or stomachs. Joiner was an adult human being whose alleged exposure to PCBs was far less than the exposure in the animal studies. The PCBs were injected into the mice in a highly concentrated form. The fluid with which Joiner had come into contact generally had a much smaller PCB concentration of between 0-500 parts per million. The cancer that these mice developed was alveologenic adenomas; Joiner had developed small-cell carcinomas. No study demonstrated that adult mice developed cancer after being exposed to PCBs. One of the experts admitted that no study had demonstrated that PCBs lead to cancer in any other species.

Respondent failed to reply to this criticism. Rather than explaining how and why the experts could have extrapolated their opinions from these seemingly far-removed animal studies, respondent chose "to proceed as if the only issue [was] whether animal studies can ever be a proper foundation for an expert's opinion." *Joiner*, 864 F.Supp., at 1324. Of course, whether animal studies can ever be a proper foundation for an expert's opinion was not the issue. The issue was whether these experts' opinions were sufficiently supported by the animal studies on which they purported to rely. The studies were so dissimilar to the facts presented in this litigation that it was not an abuse of discretion for the District Court to have rejected the experts' reliance on them.

The District Court also concluded that the four epidemiological studies on which respondent relied were not a sufficient basis for the experts' opinions. The first such study involved workers at an Italian capacitor plant who had been exposed to PCBs. Bertazzi, Riboldi, Pesatori, Radice, & Zocchetti, *Cancer Mortality of Capacitor Manufacturing Workers*, 11 American Journal of Industrial Medicine 165 (1987). The authors noted that lung cancer deaths among ex-employees at the plant were higher than might have been expected, but concluded that "there were apparently no grounds for associating lung cancer deaths (although increased above expectations) and exposure in the plant." Given that Bertazzi et al. were unwilling to say that PCB exposure had caused cancer among the workers they examined, their study did not support the experts' conclusion that Joiner's exposure to PCBs caused his cancer.

The second study followed employees who had worked at Monsanto's PCB production plant. J. Zack & D. Munsch, *Mortality of PCB Workers at the Monsanto Plant in Sauget, Illinois* (Dec. 14, 1979) (unpublished report), 3 Rec., Doc. No. 11. The authors of this study found that the incidence of lung cancer deaths among these workers was somewhat higher than would ordinarily be expected. The increase, however, was not statistically significant and the authors of the study did not suggest a link between the increase in lung cancer deaths and the exposure to PCBs.

The third and fourth studies were likewise of no help. The third involved workers at a Norwegian cable manufacturing company who had been exposed to mineral oil. Ronneberg, Andersen, Skyberg, *Mortality and Incidence of Cancer Among Oil-Exposed Workers in a Norwegian Cable Manufacturing Company*, 45 British Journal of Industrial Medicine 595 (1988). A statistically significant increase in lung cancer deaths had been observed in these workers. The study, however, (1) made no mention of PCBs and (2) was expressly limited to the type of mineral oil involved in that study, and thus did not support these experts' opinions. The fourth and final study involved a PCB-exposed group in Japan that had seen a statistically significant increase in lung cancer deaths. Kuratsune, Nakamura, Ikeda, & Hirohata, *Analysis of Deaths Seen Among Patients with Yusho-A Preliminary Report*, 16 Chemosphere, Nos. 8/9, 2085 (1987). The subjects of this study, however, had been exposed to numerous potential carcinogens, including toxic rice oil that they had ingested.

Respondent points to *Daubert's* language that the "focus, of course, must be solely on principles and methodology, not on the conclusions that they generate." He claims that because the District Court's disagreement was with the conclusion that the experts drew from the studies, the District Court committed legal error and was properly reversed by the Court of Appeals. But conclusions and methodology are not entirely distinct from one another. Trained experts commonly extrapolate from existing data. But nothing in either Daubert or the Federal Rules of Evidence requires a district court to admit opinion evidence which is connected to existing data only by the ipse dixit of the expert. A court may conclude that there is simply too great an analytical gap between the data and the opinion proffered. That is what the District Court did here, and we hold that it did not abuse its discretion in so doing.

We hold, therefore, that abuse of discretion is the proper standard by which to review a district court's decision to admit or exclude scientific evidence. We further hold that, because it was within the District Court's discretion to conclude that the studies upon which the experts relied were not sufficient, whether individually or in combination, to support their conclusions that Joiner's exposure to PCBs contributed to his cancer, the District Court did not abuse its discretion in excluding their testimony. These conclusions, however, do not dispose of this entire case.

Respondent's original contention was that his exposure to PCBs, furans, and dioxins contributed to his cancer. The District Court ruled that there was a genuine issue of material fact as to whether Joiner had been exposed to PCBs, but concluded that there was no genuine issue as to whether he had been exposed to furans and dioxins. The District Court accordingly never explicitly considered if there was admissible evidence on the question whether Joiner's alleged exposure to furans and dioxins contributed to his cancer. The Court of Appeals reversed the District Court's conclusion that there had been no exposure to furans and dioxins. Petitioners did not challenge this determination in their petition to this Court. Whether Joiner was exposed to furans and dioxins, and whether if there was such exposure, the opinions of Joiner's experts would then be admissible, remain open questions. We accordingly reverse the judgment of the Court of Appeals and remand this case for proceedings consistent with this opinion.

It is so ordered.

JUSTICE BREYER, concurring.

The Court's opinion, which I join, emphasizes *Daubert's* statement that a trial judge, acting as "gatekeeper," must " 'ensure that any and all scientific testimony or evidence admitted is not only relevant, but reliable.' " This requirement will sometimes ask judges to make subtle and sophisticated determinations about scientific methodology and its relation to the conclusions an expert witness seeks to offer — particularly when a case arises in an area where the science itself is tentative or uncertain, or where testimony about general risk levels in human beings or animals is offered to prove individual causation. Yet, as amici have pointed out, judges are not scientists and do not have the scientific training that can facilitate the making of such decisions. *See, e.g.*, Brief for Trial Lawyers for Public Justice as Amicus Curiae 15; Brief for The New England Journal of Medicine et al. as Amici Curiae 2 ("Judges * * * are generally not trained scientists").

Of course, neither the difficulty of the task nor any comparative lack of expertise can excuse the judge from exercising the "gatekeeper" duties that the Federal Rules impose — determining, for example, whether particular expert testimony is reliable and "will assist the trier of fact," Fed. Rule Evid. 702, or whether the "probative value" of testimony is substantially outweighed by risks of prejudice, confusion or waste of time. Fed. Rule Evid. 403. To the contrary, when law and science intersect, those duties often must be exercised with special care.

Today's toxic tort case provides an example. The plaintiff in today's case says that a chemical substance caused, or promoted, his lung cancer. His concern, and that of others, about the causes of cancer is understandable, for cancer kills over one in five Americans. Moreover, scientific evidence implicates some chemicals as potential causes of some cancers. Yet modern life, including good health as well as economic well-being, depends upon the use of artificial or manufactured substances, such as chemicals. And it may, therefore, prove particularly important to see that judges fulfill their *Daubert* gatekeeping function, so that they help assure that the powerful engine of tort liability, which can generate strong financial incentives to reduce, or to eliminate, production, points towards the right substances and does not destroy the wrong ones. It is, thus, essential in this science-related area that the courts administer the Federal Rules of Evidence in order to achieve the "end[s]" that the Rules themselves set forth, not only so that proceedings may be "justly determined," but also so "that the truth may be ascertained." Fed. Rule Evid. 102.

I therefore want specially to note that, as cases presenting significant science-related issues have increased in number, see Judicial Conference of the United States, *Report of the Federal Courts Study Committee* 97 (Apr. 2, 1990) ("Economic, statistical, technological, and natural and social scientific data are becoming increasingly important in both routine and complex litigation"), judges have increasingly found in the Rules of Evidence and Civil

Procedure ways to help them overcome the inherent difficulty of making determinations about complicated scientific or otherwise technical evidence. Among these techniques are an increased use of Rule 16's pretrial conference authority to narrow the scientific issues in dispute, pretrial hearings where potential experts are subject to examination by the court, and the appointment of special masters and specially trained law clerks. *See* J. Cecil & T. Willging, *Court-Appointed Experts: Defining the Role of Experts Appointed Under Federal Rule of Evidence 706*, pp. 83-88 (1993).

In the present case, the New England Journal of Medicine has filed an amici brief "in support of neither petitioners nor respondents" in which the Journal writes:

> "[A] judge could better fulfill this gatekeeper function if he or she had help from scientists. Judges should be strongly encouraged to make greater use of their inherent authority * * * to appoint experts * * *. Reputable experts could be recommended to courts by established scientific organizations, such as the National Academy of Sciences or the American Association for the Advancement of Science."

Brief for The New England Journal of Medicine 18-19; cf. Fed. Rule Evid. 706 (court may "on its own motion or on the motion of any party" appoint an expert to serve on behalf of the court, and this expert may be selected as "agreed upon by the parties" or chosen by the court). Given this kind of offer of cooperative effort, from the scientific to the legal community, and given the various Rules-authorized methods for facilitating the courts' task, it seems to me that *Daubert's* gatekeeping requirement will not prove inordinately difficult to implement; and that it will help secure the basic objectives of the Federal Rules of Evidence; which are, to repeat, the ascertainment of truth and the just determination of proceedings.

JUSTICE STEVENS, concurring in part and dissenting in part.

The question that we granted certiorari to decide is whether the Court of Appeals applied the correct standard of review. That question is fully answered in Parts I and II of the Court's opinion. Part III answers the quite different question whether the District Court properly held that the testimony of plaintiff's expert witnesses was inadmissible. Because I am not sure that the parties have adequately briefed that question, or that the Court has adequately explained why the Court of Appeals' disposition was erroneous, I do not join Part III. Moreover, because a proper answer to that question requires a study of the record that can be performed more efficiently by the Court of Appeals than by the nine members of this Court, I would remand the case to that court for application of the proper standard of review.

* * * In general, scientific testimony that is both relevant and reliable must be admitted and testimony that is irrelevant or unreliable must be excluded. In this case, the District Court relied on both grounds for exclusion.

The relevance ruling was straightforward. The District Court correctly reasoned that an expert opinion that exposure to PCBs, "furans" and "dioxins" together may cause lung cancer would be irrelevant unless the plaintiff had been exposed to those substances. Having already found that there was no evidence of exposure to furans and dioxins, it necessarily followed that this expert opinion testimony was inadmissible. Correctly applying *Daubert*, the District Court explained that the experts' testimony "manifestly does not fit the facts of this case, and is therefore inadmissible." Of course, if the evidence raised a genuine issue of fact on the question of Joiner's exposure to furans and dioxins — as the Court of Appeals held that it did — then this basis for the ruling on admissibility was erroneous, but not because the district judge either abused her discretion or misapplied the law.

The reliability ruling was more complex and arguably is not faithful to the statement in *Daubert* that "[t]he focus, of course, must be solely on principles and methodology, not on the conclusions that they generate." Joiner's experts used a "weight of the evidence" methodology to assess whether Joiner's exposure to transformer fluids promoted his lung cancer. They did not suggest that any one study provided adequate support for their conclusions, but instead relied on all the studies taken together (along with their interviews of Joiner and their review of his medical records). The District Court, however, examined the studies one by one and concluded that none was sufficient to show a link between PCBs and lung cancer. The focus of the opinion was on the separate studies and the conclusions of the experts, not on the experts' methodology.

Unlike the District Court, the Court of Appeals expressly decided that a "weight of the evidence" methodology was scientifically acceptable. The court explained: "Opinions of any kind are derived from individual pieces of evidence, each of which by itself might not be conclusive, but when viewed in their entirety are the building blocks of a perfectly reasonable conclusion, one reliable enough to be submitted to a jury along with the tests and criticisms cross-examination and contrary evidence would supply."

To this extent, the Court of Appeals' opinion is persuasive. It is not intrinsically "unscientific" for experienced professionals to arrive at a conclusion by weighing all available scientific evidence — this is not the sort of "junk science" with which *Daubert* was concerned. After all, as Joiner points out, the Environmental Protection Agency (EPA) uses the same methodology to assess risks, albeit using a somewhat different threshold than that required in a trial. Petitioners' own experts used the same scientific approach as well. And using this methodology, it would seem that an expert could reasonably have concluded that the study of workers at an Italian capacitor plant, coupled with data from Monsanto's study and other studies, raises an inference that PCBs promote lung cancer.

The Court of Appeals' discussion of admissibility is faithful to the dictum in *Daubert* that the reliability inquiry must focus on methodology, not conclusions. Thus, even though I fully agree with both the District Court's and this Court's explanation of why each of the studies on which the experts relied was by itself unpersuasive, a critical question remains unanswered: when qualified experts have reached relevant conclusions on the basis of an acceptable methodology, why are their opinions inadmissible?

Daubert quite clearly forbids trial judges from assessing the validity or strength of an expert's scientific conclusions, which is a matter for the jury.

Because I am persuaded that the difference between methodology and conclusions is just as categorical as the distinction between means and ends, I do not think the statement that "conclusions and methodology are not entirely distinct from one another," is either accurate or helps us answer the difficult admissibility question presented by this record.

In any event, it bears emphasis that the Court has not held that it would have been an abuse of discretion to admit the expert testimony. The very point of today's holding is that the abuse of discretion standard of review applies whether the district judge has excluded or admitted evidence. And nothing in either *Daubert* or the Federal Rules of Evidence requires a district judge to reject an expert's conclusions and keep them from the jury when they fit the facts of the case and are based on reliable scientific methodology.

Accordingly, while I join Parts I and II of the Court's opinion, I do not concur in the judgment or in Part III of its opinion.

WESTBERRY v. GISLAVED BUMMI AB

178 F.3d 257, 262 (4th Cir. 1999)

Wilkins, Circuit Judge:

James Curtis and Connie Rena Westberry brought this action against Gislaved Gummi AB (GGAB), claiming that GGAB was liable under South Carolina law for damages the Westberrys suffered as a result of the company's failure to warn of the danger of the talcum powder (talc) lubricant GGAB placed on rubber gaskets it manufactured. GGAB presently appeals the judgment against it following a jury verdict in favor of the Westberrys * * *. We affirm.

I.

GGAB manufactured rubber products, including rubber gaskets used in window frames. Westberry's employer purchased gaskets produced by GGAB for use in manufacturing skylights and windows in the Greenwood, South Carolina plant where Westberry was employed. Because the rubber gaskets were difficult to handle without a protective lubricant, GGAB applied a coating of talc to the gaskets prior to shipping.

Westberry's first duties in the plant involved working on a production line adjacent to the area where the GGAB gaskets were cut. In January 1994, he changed to the position of gasket cutter, which required him to remove the gaskets from their boxes and to place them in the cutting machine. Although the evidence was conflicting, Westberry testified that these duties brought him into contact with high concentrations of airborne talc. Westberry received no warning that talc could be dangerous, and he wore no protective gear when performing his duties as a gasket cutter.

Following his change to the position of gasket cutter, Westberry began to experience unrelenting sinus problems. He was hospitalized for four days in

July 1994 with a severe sinus infection and was treated with antibiotics by his physician, Dr. W. David Isenhower, Jr. Beginning in September 1994, Westberry underwent several sinus surgeries in an attempt to alleviate his sinus pain, including a procedure in which his frontal sinuses were obliterated. Westberry brought the present action against GGAB, claiming that its failure to warn him of the dangers of breathing airborne talc proximately caused the aggravation of his pre-existing sinus condition. He alleged causes of action sounding in strict liability, breach of warranty, and negligence. Following a trial at which Westberry's treating physician, Dr. Isenhower, provided the principal evidence of causation, the jury returned a verdict in favor of Westberry. Although GGAB challenges the judgment on a number of grounds, the only one warranting extended discussion is its contention that the district court abused its discretion in admitting the opinion testimony of Dr. Isenhower concerning the cause of Westberry's sinus problems.

II.

* * * Expert testimony is admissible under Rule 702 * * * if it concerns (1) scientific, technical, or other specialized knowledge that (2) will aid the jury or other trier of fact to understand or resolve a fact at issue. *See Daubert v. Merrell Dow Pharms., Inc.,* 509 U.S. 579 (1993). The first prong of this inquiry necessitates an examination of whether the reasoning or methodology underlying the expert's proffered opinion is reliable — that is, whether it is supported by adequate validation to render it trustworthy. The second prong of the inquiry requires an analysis of whether the opinion is relevant to the facts at issue. * * * A district court considering the admissibility of expert testimony exercises a gate keeping function to assess whether the proffered evidence is sufficiently reliable and relevant. The inquiry to be undertaken by the district court is "a flexible one" focusing on the "principles and methodology" employed by the expert, not on the conclusions reached. *Daubert*, 509 U.S. at 594-95. * * * The court, however, should be conscious of two guiding, and sometimes competing, principles. On the one hand, the court should be mindful that Rule 702 was intended to liberalize the introduction of relevant expert evidence. And, the court need not determine that the expert testimony a litigant seeks to offer into evidence is irrefutable or certainly correct. As with all other admissible evidence, expert testimony is subject to being tested by "[v]igorous cross-examination, presentation of contrary evidence, and careful instruction on the burden of proof." *Daubert*, 509 U.S. at 596. On the other hand, the court must recognize that due to the difficulty of evaluating their testimony, expert witnesses have the potential to "be both powerful and quite misleading." *Id.* at 595. And, given the potential persuasiveness of expert testimony, proffered evidence that has a greater potential to mislead than to enlighten should be excluded.

* * *

* * * With these principles in mind, we turn to a consideration of the decision of the district court to permit Dr. Isenhower to testify that in his opinion the sinus problems experienced by Westberry were caused by the inhalation of airborne talc in the workplace.

A.

* * *

B.

GGAB contends that Dr. Isenhower's testimony was inadmissible because it was not based on reliable scientific methodology. This is so, it argues, because Dr. Isenhower had no epidemiological studies, no peer-reviewed published studies, no animal studies, and no laboratory data to support a conclusion that the inhalation of talc caused Westberry's sinus disease. Further, GGAB continues, Dr. Isenhower did not have any tissue samples indicating that talc was found in Westberry's sinuses, nor did he have studies showing that talc, at any threshold level, causes sinus disease. Instead, Dr. Isenhower merely relied on a differential diagnosis-supported in part by the temporal relationship between Westberry's exposure to talc and the problems he experienced with his sinuses-in reaching the conclusion that Westberry's sinus problems were caused by his exposure to talc from GGAB's gaskets. GGAB maintains that neither a differential diagnosis nor a temporal relationship between exposure and onset or worsening of symptoms is sufficient to establish the reliability of Dr. Isenhower's opinion. We disagree.

Differential diagnosis, or differential etiology, is a standard scientific technique of identifying the cause of a medical problem by eliminating the likely causes until the most probable one is isolated. A reliable differential diagnosis typically, though not invariably, is performed after "physical examinations, the taking of medical histories, and the review of clinical tests, including laboratory tests," and generally is accomplished by determining the possible causes for the patient's symptoms and then eliminating each of these potential causes until reaching one that cannot be ruled out or determining which of those that cannot be excluded is the most likely. *Kannankeril v. Terminix Int'l,* Inc., 128 F.3d 802, 807 (3d Cir. 1997) (explaining that "[d]ifferential diagnosis is defined for physicians as 'the determination of which of two or more diseases with similar symptoms is the one from which the patient is suffering, by a systematic comparison and contrasting of the clinical findings' "); see *McCullock v. H.B. Fuller Co.,* 61 F.3d 1038, 1044 (2d Cir. 1995) (describing differential etiology as an analysis "which requires listing possible causes, then eliminating all causes but one"); *Glaser v. Thompson Med. Co.,* 32 F.3d 969, 978 (6th Cir. 1994) (recognizing that differential diagnosis is "a standard diagnostic tool used by medical professionals to diagnose the most likely cause or causes of illness, injury and disease"). This technique "has widespread acceptance in the medical community, has been subject to peer review, and does not frequently lead to incorrect results." *See Heller v. Shaw Indus., Inc.*, 167 F.3d 146, 154-55 (3d Cir. 1999) (noting "that differential diagnosis consists of a testable hypothesis, has been peer reviewed, contains standards for controlling its operation, is generally accepted, and is used outside of the judicial context"). We previously have upheld the admission of an expert opinion on causation based upon a differential diagnosis. *See Benedi v. McNeil-P.P.C., Inc.*, 66 F.3d 1378 (4th Cir. 1995) (holding that expert testimony by treating physician concerning cause of plaintiff's liver failure — acetaminophen combined with alcohol — was admissible despite the lack of epidemiological data). And, the overwhelming majority of the courts of appeals that have addressed the issue have held that a medical opinion on causation based upon a reliable differential diagnosis is sufficiently valid to satisfy the first prong of the Rule 702 inquiry. Thus, we hold that a reliable differential diagnosis provides a valid foundation for an expert opinion.

C.

GGAB next maintains that, assuming a differential diagnosis may provide a trustworthy foundation for an opinion on causation, Dr. Isenhower's differential diagnosis did not. According to GGAB, Dr. Isenhower's differential diagnosis was unreliable because he could not "rule in" talc as a possible cause of sinus disease. *See Raynor v. Merrell Pharms., Inc.*, 104 F.3d 1371, 1374-76 (D.C. Cir. 1997) (holding that expert opinion that exposure to Bendectin caused birth defects based in part on differential diagnosis was not admissible in light of "overwhelming body of contradictory epidemiological evidence"). Further, GGAB contends that Dr. Isenhower's differential diagnosis was not reliable because he failed to "rule out" all other possible causes.

GGAB asserts that Dr. Isenhower could not "rule in" talc because he had no means of accurately assessing what level of exposure was adequate to produce the sinus irritation Westberry experienced. In order to carry the burden of proving a plaintiff's injury was caused by exposure to a specified substance, the "plaintiff must demonstrate the levels of exposure that are hazardous to human beings generally as well as the plaintiff's actual level of exposure." *See Allen v. Pennsylvania Eng'g Corp.*, 102 F.3d 194, 199 (5th Cir. 1996) (concluding that "[s]cientific knowledge of the harmful level of exposure to a chemical, plus knowledge that the plaintiff was exposed to such quantities, are minimal facts necessary to sustain the plaintiffs' burden in a toxic tort case"); cf. *Black v. Food Lion, Inc.*, 171 F.3d 308, 314 (5th Cir. 1999) (explaining that "[t]he underlying predicates of any cause-and-effect medical testimony are that medical science understands the physiological process by which a particular disease or syndrome develops and knows what factors cause the process to occur"). But, it must also be recognized that "[o]nly rarely are humans exposed to chemicals in a manner that permits a quantitative determination of adverse outcomes * * *. Human exposure occurs most frequently in occupational settings where workers are exposed to industrial chemicals like lead or asbestos; however, even under these circumstances, it is usually difficult, if not impossible, to quantify the amount of exposure." Federal Judicial Center, Reference Manual on Scientific Evidence 187 (1994).

Consequently, while precise information concerning the exposure necessary to cause specific harm to humans and exact details pertaining to the plaintiff's exposure are beneficial, such evidence is not always available, or necessary, to demonstrate that a substance is toxic to humans given substantial exposure and need not invariably provide the basis for an expert's opinion on causation. *See Heller*, 167 F.3d at 157 (noting "that even absent hard evidence of the level of exposure to the chemical in question, a medical expert could offer an opinion that the chemical caused plaintiff's illness"). Although GGAB is correct that Dr. Isenhower had no scientific literature on which to rely to "rule in" talc as a possible basis for Westberry's sinus condition, it was undisputed that inhalation of high levels of talc irritates mucous membranes. The Material Safety Data Sheet (MSDS) for talc provided by GGAB for Dr. Isenhower's examination provided that "[i]nhalation of dust in high concentrations irritates mucous membranes," and it is undisputed that sinuses are mucous membranes. Further, although Dr. Isenhower did not point to Westberry's exposure to a specific level of airborne talc, there was evidence of a substantial exposure. Westberry testified that he was exposed to very high levels of airborne talc throughout his workday. According to his testimony, when he removed the gaskets from the box in which they had been shipped, the gaskets, which were black, had so much talc on them that they appeared to be white or gray. And, talc was released into the air as the gaskets went through the cutting machines. Westberry testified that the talc that settled from the air around his work area was so thick that one could see footprints in it on the floor. He further stated that he worked in clouds of talc and that it covered him and his clothes. Moreover, at the close of his workday Westberry was required to blow off his work area and machinery with a blower, stirring up all of the talc that had fallen. This testimony concerning the level of airborne talc was adequate to permit a factfinder to conclude that Westberry was exposed to high concentrations of airborne talc, and there was no dispute that exposure to high concentrations of airborne talc could cause irritation to mucous membranes. Indeed, GGAB's expert conceded on cross-examination that if the levels of airborne talc were those testified to by Westberry (and relied upon by Dr. Isenhower), his own opinion that talc did not cause Westberry's sinus problems would change. Thus, this clearly is not a case in which the plaintiff was unable to establish any substantial exposure to the allegedly defective product. Cf. *Wintz v. Northrop Corp.*, 110 F.3d 508, 512-14 (7th Cir. 1997) (holding that expert opinion was not reliable when expert formed opinion that in utero exposure to bromide caused birth defects, but expert had no information concerning the mother's work environment or her exposure to bromide).

Additionally, Dr. Isenhower testified that he relied in part on the temporal proximity of Westberry's exposure to talc in his workplace to the onset and worsening of Westberry's sinus problems to conclude that talc was the cause. GGAB makes no serious argument that a strong temporal relationship between Westberry's exposure to talc and his sinus disease did not exist, but contends that the temporal relationship between Westberry's exposure to talc and his sinus problems was not a proper basis for an expert opinion on causation. Again, we disagree.

Of course, the mere fact that two events correspond in time does not mean that the two necessarily are related in any causative fashion. But, depending on the circumstances, a temporal relationship between exposure to a substance and the onset of a disease or a worsening of symptoms can provide compelling evidence of causation. *See Cavallo v. Star Enter.*, 892 F.Supp. 756, 774 (E.D. Va.1995) (explaining that "there may be instances where the temporal connection between exposure to a given chemical and subsequent injury is so compelling as to dispense with the need for reliance on standard methods of toxicology," for example, if one were exposed to a substantial amount of "chemical X and immediately thereafter developed symptom Y");

see also 2 Saltzburg, Martin, and Capra, *Federal Rules of Evidence Manual* 1233-34 (7th ed.1998). *But see Moore v. Ashland Corp.*, 151 F.3d at 278 (holding that "[i]n the absence of an established scientific connection between exposure and illness, or compelling circumstances such as those discussed in *Cavallo*, the temporal connection between exposure to chemicals and an onset of symptoms, standing alone, is entitled to little weight").

Here, Dr. Isenhower testified that Westberry's sinus disease began shortly after Westberry began working as a gasket cutter. Furthermore, during the time he was treating Westberry, Dr. Isenhower experimented with keeping Westberry out of work and noticed that his sinus condition improved when he was not working but worsened when he returned. Under these circumstances, we conclude that the temporal relationship between Westberry's exposure and the onset and worsening of his sinus disease provided support for Dr. Isenhower's opinion that talc was the source of the problem.

GGAB also argues that Dr. Isenhower's differential diagnosis was unreliable because he failed to "rule out" all potential causes other than talc because he did not explain why a cold Westberry developed in May 1994 and water skiing he did over the summer of 1994 could not have accounted for his sinus problems. A differential diagnosis that fails to take serious account of other potential causes may be so lacking that it cannot provide a reliable basis for an opinion on causation. However, "[a] medical expert's causation conclusion should not be excluded because he or she has failed to rule out every possible alternative cause of a plaintiff's illness." *Heller*, 167 F.3d at 156. The alternative causes suggested by a defendant "affect the weight that the jury should give the expert's testimony and not the admissibility of that testimony," *id.* at 157, unless the expert can offer "no explanation for why she has concluded [an alternative cause offered by the opposing party] was not the sole cause." *See also Kannankeril*, 128 F.3d at 808 (explaining that "[i]n attacking the differential diagnosis performed by the plaintiff's expert, the defendant may point to a plausible cause of the plaintiff's illness other than the defendant's actions" and "[i]t then becomes necessary for the plaintiff's experts to offer a good explanation as to why his or her conclusion remains reliable"); *In re Paoli R.R. Yard PCB Litig.,* 35 F.3d at 764-65 (recognizing that failure to account for all possible causes does not render expert opinion based on differential diagnosis inadmissible; only if expert utterly fails to consider alternative causes or fails to explain why the opinion remains sound in light of alternative causes suggested by the opposing party is expert's opinion unreliable for failure to account for all potential causes).

Dr. Isenhower's testimony made clear that he considered and excluded other potential causes for Westberry's sinus disease. Furthermore, on cross-examination Dr. Isenhower explained why he did not believe that the cold Westberry developed in 1994 or the waterskiing he did over that summer accounted for his sinus problems. Accordingly, Dr. Isenhower's alleged failure to account for all possible alternative causes for Westberry's sinus problems did not prohibit the admissibility of his opinion as to causation.

III.

In sum, we reject GGAB's contention that Dr. Isenhower's testimony was invalid and untrustworthy. A reliable differential diagnosis provides a valid basis for an expert opinion on causation. And, Dr. Isenhower's differential diagnosis was sufficiently reliable. Because Dr. Isenhower's testimony satisfied the reliability and relevance standards of Rule 702, the district court properly admitted this testimony.

AFFIRMED.

[d] Applications of the *Daubert* Gatekeeping Function to Non-Scientific Expert Testimony

KUMHO TIRE COMPANY, LTD. v. CARMICHAEL
526 U.S. 137 (1999)

JUSTICE BREYER delivered the opinion of the Court.

In *Daubert v. Merrell Dow Pharmaceuticals, Inc.*, 509 U. S. 579 (1993), this Court focused upon the admissibility of scientific expert testimony. It pointed out that such testimony is admissible only if it is both relevant and reliable. And it held that the Federal Rules of Evidence "assign to the trial judge the task of ensuring that an expert's testimony both rests on a reliable foundation and is relevant to the task at hand." The Court also discussed certain more specific factors, such as testing, peer review, error rates, and "acceptability" in the relevant scientific community, some or all of which might prove helpful in determining the reliability of a particular scientific "theory or technique."

This case requires us to decide how *Daubert* applies to the testimony of engineers and other experts who are not scientists. We conclude that *Daubert's* general holding-setting forth the trial judge's general "gatekeeping" obligation-applies not only to testimony based on "scientific" knowledge, but also to testimony based on "technical" and "other specialized" knowledge. *See* Fed. Rule Evid. 702. We also conclude that a trial court may consider one or more of the more specific factors that *Daubert* mentioned when doing so will help determine that testimony's reliability. But, as the Court stated in *Daubert*, the test of reliability is "flexible," and *Daubert's* list of specific factors neither necessarily nor exclusively applies to all experts or in every case. Rather, the law grants a district court the same broad latitude when it decides how to determine reliability as it enjoys in respect to its ultimate reliability determination. *See General Electric Co. v. Joiner*, 522 U. S. 136, 143 (1997) (courts of appeals are to apply 'abuse of discretion' standard when reviewing district court's reliability determination). Applying these standards, we determine that the District Court's decision in this case — not to admit certain expert testimony — was within its discretion and therefore lawful.

I

On July 6, 1993, the right rear tire of a minivan driven by Patrick Carmichael blew out. In the accident that followed, one of the passengers died, and others were severely injured. In October 1993, the Carmichaels brought this diversity suit against the tire's maker and its distributor, whom we refer to collectively as Kumho Tire, claiming that the tire was defective. The plaintiffs rested their case in significant part upon deposition testimony provided by an expert in tire failure analysis, Dennis Carlson, Jr., who intended to testify in support of their conclusion.

Carlson's depositions relied upon certain features of tire technology that are not in dispute. A steel-belted radial tire like the Carmichaels' is made up of a "carcass" containing many layers of flexible cords, called "plies," along which (between the cords and the outer tread) are laid steel strips called "belts." Steel wire loops, called "beads," hold the cords together at the plies' bottom edges. An outer layer, called the "tread," encases the carcass, and the entire tire is bound together in rubber, through the application of heat and various chemicals. The bead of the tire sits upon a "bead seat," which is part of the wheel assembly. That assembly contains a "rim flange," which extends over the bead and rests against the side of the tire.

Carlson's testimony also accepted certain background facts about the tire in question. He assumed that before the blowout the tire had traveled far. (The tire was made in 1988 and had been installed some time before the Carmichaels bought the used minivan in March 1993; the Carmichaels had driven the van approximately 7,000 additional miles in the two months they had owned it.) Carlson noted that the tire's tread depth, which was 11/32 of an inch when new, had been worn down to depths that ranged from 3/32 of an inch along some parts of the tire, to nothing at all along others. He conceded that the tire tread had at least two punctures which had been inadequately repaired.

Despite the tire's age and history, Carlson concluded that a defect in its manufacture or design caused the blow-out. He rested this conclusion in part upon three premises which, for present purposes, we must assume are not in dispute: First, a tire's carcass should stay bound to the inner side of the tread for a significant period of time after its tread depth has worn away. Second, the tread of the tire at issue had separated from its inner steel-belted carcass prior to the accident. Third, this "separation" caused the blowout.

Carlson's conclusion that a defect caused the separation, however, rested upon certain other propositions, several of which the defendants strongly dispute. First, Carlson said that if a separation is not caused by a certain kind of tire misuse called "overdeflection" (which consists of underinflating the tire or causing it to carry too much weight, thereby generating heat that can undo the chemical tread/carcass bond), then, ordinarily, its cause is a tire defect. Second, he said that if a tire has been subject to sufficient overdeflection to cause a separation, it should reveal certain physical symptoms. These symptoms include (a) tread wear on the tire's shoulder that is greater than the tread wear along the tire's center; (b) signs of a "bead groove," where the beads have been pushed too hard against the bead seat on the inside of the tire's rim; (c) sidewalls of the tire with physical signs of deterioration, such as discoloration; and/or (d) marks on the tire's rim flange. Third, Carlson said that where he does not find at least two of the four physical signs just mentioned (and presumably where there is no reason to suspect a less common cause of separation), he concludes that a manufacturing or design defect caused the separation.

Carlson added that he had inspected the tire in question. He conceded that the tire to a limited degree showed greater wear on the shoulder than in the center, some signs of "bead groove," some discoloration, a few marks on the rim flange, and inadequately filled puncture holes (which can also cause heat that might lead to separation). But, in each instance, he testified that the symptoms were not significant, and he explained why he believed that they did not reveal overdeflection. For example, the extra shoulder wear, he said, appeared primarily on one shoulder, whereas an overdeflected tire would reveal equally abnormal wear on both shoulders. Carlson concluded that the tire did not bear at least two of the four overdeflection symptoms, nor was there any less obvious cause of separation; and since neither overdeflection nor the punctures caused the blowout, a defect must have done so.

Kumho Tire moved the District Court to exclude Carlson's testimony on the ground that his methodology failed Rule 702's reliability requirement. The court agreed with Kumho that it should act as a *Daubert*-type reliability "gatekeeper," even though one might consider Carlson's testimony as "technical,"rather than "scientific." The court then examined Carlson's methodology in light of the reliability-related factors that *Daubert* mentioned, such as a theory's testability, whether it "has been a subject of peer review or publication," the "known or potential rate of error," and the "degree of acceptance * * * within the relevant scientific community." The District Court found that all those factors argued against the reliability of Carlson's methods, and it granted the motion to exclude the testimony (as well as the defendants' accompanying motion for summary judgment).

The plaintiffs, arguing that the court's application of the *Daubert* factors was too "inflexible," asked for reconsideration. And the Court granted that motion. After reconsidering the matter, the court agreed with the plaintiffs that *Daubert* should be applied flexibly, that its four factors were simply illustrative, and that other factors could argue in favor of admissibility. It conceded that there may be widespread acceptance of a "visual-inspection method" for some relevant purposes. But the court found insufficient indications of the reliability of "the component of Carlson's tire failure analysis which most concerned the Court, namely, the methodology employed by the expert in analyzing the data obtained in the visual inspection, and the scientific basis, if any, for such an analysis." It consequently affirmed its earlier order declaring Carlson's testimony inadmissable and granting the defendants' motion for summary judgment.

The Eleventh Circuit reversed. It "review[ed] * * * de novo" the "district court's legal decision to apply *Daubert*." It noted that "the Supreme Court in *Daubert* explicitly limited its holding to cover only the 'scientific context,'" adding that "a *Daubert* analysis" applies only where an expert relies "on the application of scientific principles," rather than "on skill — or experience — based observation." It concluded that Carlson's testimony, which it viewed as relying on experience, "falls outside the scope of *Daubert*," that "the district court erred as a matter of law by applying *Daubert* in this case," and that the case must be remanded for further (non-*Daubert*-type) consideration under Rule 702.

* * *

II

A

In *Daubert*, this Court held that Federal Rule of Evidence 702 imposes a special obligation upon a trial judge to "ensure that any and all scientific testimony * * * is not only relevant, but reliable." ' The initial question before us is whether this basic gatekeeping obligation applies only to 'scientific' testimony or to all expert testimony. We, like the parties, believe that it applies to all expert testimony.

For one thing, Rule 702 itself says: "If scientific, technical, or other specialized knowledge will assist the trier of fact to understand the evidence or to determine a fact in issue, a witness qualified as an expert by knowledge, skill, experience, training, or education, may testify thereto in the form of an opinion or otherwise."

This language makes no relevant distinction between "scientific" knowledge and "technical" or "other specialized" knowledge. It makes clear that any such knowledge might become the subject of expert testimony. In *Daubert*, the Court specified that it is the Rule's word "knowledge," not the words (like "scientific") that modify that word, that "establishes a standard of evidentiary reliability." Hence, as a matter of language, the Rule applies its reliability standard to all "scientific," "technical," or "other specialized" matters within its scope. We concede that the Court in *Daubert* referred only to "scientific" knowledge. But as the Court there said, it referred to "scientific" testimony "because that [wa]s the nature of the expertise" at issue.

Neither is the evidentiary rationale that underlay the Court's basic *Daubert* "gatekeeping" determination limited to "scientific" knowledge. *Daubert* pointed out that Federal Rules 702 and 703 grant expert witnesses testimonial latitude unavailable to other witnesses on the "assumption that the expert's opinion will have a reliable basis in the knowledge and experience of his discipline." * * * The Rules grant that latitude to all experts, not just to "scientific" ones.

Finally, it would prove difficult, if not impossible, for judges to administer evidentiary rules under which a gatekeeping obligation depended upon a distinction between "scientific" knowledge and "technical" or "other specialized" knowledge. There is no clear line that divides the one from the others. Disciplines such as engineering rest upon scientific knowledge. Pure scientific theory itself may depend for its development upon observation and properly engineered machinery. And conceptual efforts to distinguish the two are unlikely to produce clear legal lines capable of application in particular cases.

Neither is there a convincing need to make such distinctions. Experts of all kinds tie observations to conclusions through the use of what Judge Learned Hand called "general truths derived from * * * specialized experience." Hand, *Historical and Practical Considerations Regarding Expert Testimony*, 15 Harv. L. Rev. 40, 54 (1901). And whether the specific expert testimony focuses upon specialized observations, the specialized translation of those observations into theory, a specialized theory itself, or the application of such a theory in a particular case, the expert's testimony often will rest "upon an experience confessedly foreign in kind to [the jury's] own." The trial judge's effort to assure that the specialized testimony is reliable and relevant can help the jury evaluate that foreign experience, whether the testimony reflects scientific, technical, or other specialized knowledge.

We conclude that *Daubert's* general principles apply to the expert matters described in Rule 702. The Rule, in respect to all such matters, "establishes a standard of evidentiary reliability." It "requires a valid * * * connection to the pertinent inquiry as a precondition to admissibility." And where such testimony's factual basis, data, principles, methods, or their application are called sufficiently into question, see Part III, infra, the trial judge must determine whether the testimony has "a reliable basis in the knowledge and experience of [the relevant] discipline."

B

The petitioners ask more specifically whether a trial judge determining the "admissibility of an engineering expert's testimony" may consider several more specific factors that *Daubert* said might "bear on" a judge's gate-keeping determination. These factors include:

— Whether a "theory or technique * * * can be (and has been) tested;

— Whether it "has been subjected to peer review and publication;

— Whether, in respect to a particular technique, there is a high known or potential rate of error and whether there are standards controlling the technique's operation; and

— Whether the theory or technique enjoys "general acceptance" within a "relevant scientific community." 509 U. S., at 592-594.

Emphasizing the word "may" in the question, we answer that question yes.

Engineering testimony rests upon scientific foundations, the reliability of which will be at issue in some cases. In other cases, the relevant reliability concerns may focus upon personal knowledge or experience. As the Solicitor General points out, there are many different kinds of experts, and many different kinds of expertise. *See* Brief for United States as Amicus Curiae 18-19, and n. 5 (citing cases involving experts in drug terms, handwriting analysis, criminal modus operandi, land valuation, agricultural practices, railroad procedures, attorney's fee valuation, and others). Our emphasis on the word "may" thus reflects *Daubert's* description of the Rule 702 inquiry as "a flexible one." *Daubert* makes clear that the factors it mentions do not constitute a "definitive checklist or test." And *Daubert* adds that the gatekeeping inquiry must be " 'tied to the facts' " of a particular "case." We agree with the Solicitor General that "[t]he factors identified in *Daubert* may or may not be pertinent in assessing reliability, depending on the nature of the issue, the expert's particular expertise, and the subject of his testimony." Brief for United States as Amicus Curiae 19. The conclusion, in our view, is that we can neither rule out, nor rule in, for all cases and for all time the applicability of the factors mentioned in *Daubert*, nor can we now do so for subsets of cases categorized by category of expert or by kind of evidence. Too much depends upon the particular circumstances of the particular case at issue.

Daubert itself is not to the contrary. It made clear that its list of factors was meant to be helpful, not definitive. Indeed, those factors do not all necessarily apply even in every instance in which the reliability of scientific testimony is challenged. It might not be surprising in a particular case, for example, that a claim made by a scientific witness has never been the subject of peer review, for the particular application at issue may never previously have interested any scientist. Nor, on the other hand, does the presence of *Daubert's* general acceptance factor help show that an expert's testimony is reliable where the discipline itself lacks reliability, as, for example, do theories grounded in any so-called generally accepted principles of astrology or necromancy.

At the same time, and contrary to the Court of Appeals' view, some of *Daubert's* questions can help to evaluate the reliability even of experience-based testimony. In certain cases, it will be appropriate for the trial judge to ask, for example, how often an engineering expert's experience-based methodology has produced erroneous results, or whether such a method is generally accepted in the relevant engineering community. Likewise, it will at times be useful to ask even of a witness whose expertise is based purely on experience, say, a perfume tester able to distinguish among 140 odors at a sniff, whether his preparation is of a kind that others in the field would recognize as acceptable.

We must therefore disagree with the Eleventh Circuit's holding that a trial judge may ask questions of the sort *Daubert* mentioned only where an expert "relies on the application of scientific principles," but not where an expert relies "on skill — or experience-based observation." We do not believe that Rule 702 creates a schematism that segregates expertise by type while mapping certain kinds of questions to certain kinds of experts. Life and the legal cases that it generates are too complex to warrant so definitive a match.

To say this is not to deny the importance of *Daubert's* gatekeeping requirement. The objective of that requirement is to ensure the reliability and relevancy of expert testimony. It is to make certain that an expert, whether basing testimony upon professional studies or personal experience, employs in the courtroom the same level of intellectual rigor that characterizes the practice of an expert in the relevant field. Nor do we deny that, as stated in *Daubert*, the particular questions that it mentioned will often be appropriate for use in determining the reliability of challenged expert testimony. Rather, we conclude that the trial judge must have considerable leeway in deciding in a particular case how to go about determining whether particular expert testimony is reliable. That is to say, a trial court should consider the specific factors identified in *Daubert* where they are reasonable measures of the reliability of expert testimony.

C

The trial court must have the same kind of latitude in deciding how to test an expert's reliability, and to decide whether or when special briefing or other proceedings are needed to investigate reliability, as it enjoys when it decides whether that expert's relevant testimony is reliable. Our opinion in *Joiner* makes clear that a court of appeals is to apply an abuse-of-discretion standard when it 'review[s] a trial court's decision to admit or exclude expert testimony.' 522 U. S., at 138-139. That standard applies as much to the trial court's decisions about how to determine reliability as to its ultimate conclusion. Otherwise, the trial judge would lack the discretionary authority needed both to avoid unnecessary "reliability" proceedings in ordinary cases where the reliability of an expert's methods is properly taken for granted, and to require appropriate proceedings in the less usual or more complex cases where cause for questioning the expert's reliability arises. * * * Thus, whether *Daubert's* specific factors are, or are not, reasonable measures of reliability in a particular case is a matter that the law grants the trial judge broad latitude to determine. And the Eleventh Circuit erred insofar as it held to the contrary.

III

We further explain the way in which a trial judge "may" consider *Daubert's* factors by applying these considerations to the case at hand, a matter that has been briefed exhaustively by the parties and their 19 amici. The District Court did not doubt Carlson's qualifications, which included a masters degree in mechanical engineering, 10 years' work at Michelin America, Inc., and testimony as a tire failure consultant in other tort cases. Rather, it excluded the testimony because, despite those qualifications, it initially doubted, and then found unreliable, "the methodology employed by the expert in analyzing the data obtained in the visual inspection, and the scientific basis, if any, for such an analysis." After examining the transcript in "some detail," and after considering respondents' defense of Carlson's methodology, the District Court determined that Carlson's testimony was not reliable. It fell outside the range where experts might reasonably differ, and where the jury must decide among the conflicting views of different experts, even though the evidence is "shaky." In our view, the doubts that triggered the District Court's initial inquiry here were reasonable, as was the court's ultimate conclusion.

For one thing, and contrary to respondents' suggestion, the specific issue before the court was not the reasonableness in general of a tire expert's use of a visual and tactile inspection to determine whether overdeflection had caused the tire's tread to separate from its steel-belted carcass. Rather, it was the reasonableness of using such an approach, along with Carlson's particular method of analyzing the data thereby obtained, to draw a conclusion regarding the particular matter to which the expert testimony was directly relevant. That matter concerned the likelihood that a defect in the tire at issue caused its tread to separate from its carcass. The tire in question, the expert conceded, had traveled far enough so that some of the tread had been worn bald; it should have been taken out of service; it had been repaired (inadequately) for punctures; and it bore some of the very marks that the expert said indicated, not a defect, but abuse through overdeflection. The relevant issue was whether the expert could reliably determine the cause of this tire's separation. Nor was the basis for Carlson's conclusion simply the general theory that, in the absence of evidence of abuse, a defect will normally have caused a tire's separation. Rather, the expert employed a more specific theory to establish the existence (or absence) of such abuse. Carlson testified precisely that in the absence of at least two of four signs of abuse (proportionately greater tread wear on the shoulder; signs of grooves caused by the beads; discolored sidewalls; marks on the rim flange) he concludes that a defect caused the separation. And his analysis depended upon acceptance of a further implicit proposition, namely, that his visual and tactile inspection could determine that the tire before him had not been abused despite some evidence of the presence of the very signs for which he looked (and two punctures).

For another thing, the transcripts of Carlson's depositions support both the trial court's initial uncertainty and its final conclusion. Those transcripts cast considerable doubt upon the reliability of both the explicit theory (about the need for two signs of abuse) and the implicit proposition (about the significance of visual inspection in this case). Among other things, the expert could not say whether the tire had traveled more than 10, or 20, or 30, or 40, or 50 thousand miles, adding that 6,000 miles was "about how far" he could "say with any certainty." The court could reasonably have wondered about the reliability of a method of visual and tactile inspection sufficiently precise to ascertain with some certainty the abuse-related significance of minute shoulder/center relative tread wear differences, but insufficiently precise to tell "with any certainty" from the tread wear whether a tire had traveled less than 10,000 or more than 50,000 miles. And these concerns might have been augmented by Carlson's repeated reliance on the "subjective[ness]" of his mode of analysis in response to questions seeking specific information regarding how he could differentiate between a tire that actually had been overdeflected and a tire that merely looked as though it had been. They would have been further augmented by the fact that Carlson said he had inspected the tire itself for the first time the morning of his first deposition, and then only for a few hours. (His initial conclusions were based on photographs.)

Moreover, prior to his first deposition, Carlson had issued a signed report in which he concluded that the tire had "not been * * * overloaded or underinflated," not because of the absence of "two of four" signs of abuse, but simply because "the rim flange impressions * * * were normal." That report also said that the "tread depth remaining was 3/32 inch," though the opposing expert's (apparently undisputed) measurements indicate that the tread depth taken at various positions around the tire actually ranged from .5/32 of an inch to 4/32 of an inch, with the tire apparently showing greater wear along both shoulders than along the center.

Further, in respect to one sign of abuse, bead grooving, the expert seemed to deny the sufficiency of his own simple visual-inspection methodology. He testified that most tires have some bead groove pattern, that where there is reason to suspect an abnormal bead groove he would ideally "look at a lot of [similar] tires" to know the grooving's significance, and that he had not looked at many tires similar to the one at issue.

Finally, the court, after looking for a defense of Carlson's methodology as applied in these circumstances, found no convincing defense. Rather, it found (1) that "none" of the *Daubert* factors, including that of "general acceptance" in the relevant expert community, indicated that Carlson's testimony was reliable; (2) that its own analysis "revealed no countervailing factors operating in favor of admissibility which could outweigh those identified in *Daubert*; and (3) that the "parties identified no such factors in their briefs." For these three reasons taken together, it concluded that Carlson's testimony was unreliable.

Respondents now argue to us, as they did to the District Court, that a method of tire failure analysis that employs a visual/tactile inspection is a reliable method, and they point both to its use by other experts and to Carlson's long experience working for Michelin as sufficient indication that that is so. But no one denies that an expert might draw a conclusion from a set of observations based on extensive and specialized experience. Nor does anyone deny that, as a general matter, tire abuse may often be identified by qualified experts through visual or tactile inspection of the tire. As we said before, the question before the trial court was specific, not general. The trial court had to decide whether this particular expert had sufficient specialized knowledge to assist the jurors "in deciding the particular issues in the case." 4 J. McLaughlin, Weinstein's Federal Evidence & 702.05[1], p. 702-33 (2d ed. 1998); *see also* Advisory Committee's Note on Proposed Fed. Rule Evid. 702, Preliminary Draft of Proposed Amendments to the Federal Rules of Civil Procedure and Evidence: Request for Comment 126 (1998) (stressing that district courts must "scrutinize" whether the "principles and methods" employed by an expert "have been properly applied to the facts of the case").

The particular issue in this case concerned the use of Carlson's two-factor test and his related use of visual/tactile inspection to draw conclusions on the basis of what seemed small observational differences. We have found no indication in the record that other experts in the industry use Carlson's two-factor test or that tire experts such as Carlson normally make the very fine distinctions about, say, the symmetry of comparatively greater shoulder tread wear that were necessary, on Carlson's own theory, to support his conclusions. Nor, despite the prevalence of tire testing, does anyone refer to any articles or papers that validate Carlson's approach. Indeed, no one has argued that Carlson himself, were he still working for Michelin, would have concluded in a report to his employer that a similar tire was similarly defective on grounds identical to those upon which he rested his conclusion here. Of course, Carlson himself claimed that his method was accurate, but, as we pointed out in Joiner, "nothing in either *Daubert* or the Federal Rules of Evidence requires a district court to admit opinion evidence that is connected to existing data only by the ipse dixit of the expert."

Respondents additionally argue that the District Court too rigidly applied *Daubert's* criteria. They read its opinion to hold that a failure to satisfy any one of those criteria automatically renders expert testimony inadmissible. The District Court's initial opinion might have been vulnerable to a form of this argument. There, the court, after rejecting respondents' claim that Carlson's testimony was "exempted from *Daubert*-style scrutiny" because it was "technical analysis" rather than "scientific evidence," simply added that "none of the four admissibility criteria outlined by the *Daubert* court are satisfied." Subsequently, however, the court granted respondents' motion for reconsideration. * * * And the court ultimately based its decision upon Carlson's failure to satisfy either *Daubert's* factors or any other set of reasonable reliability criteria. In light of the record as developed by the parties, that conclusion was within the District Court's lawful discretion.

In sum, Rule 702 grants the district judge the discretionary authority, reviewable for its abuse, to determine reliability in light of the particular facts and circumstances of the particular case. The District Court did not abuse its discretionary authority in this case. Hence, the judgment of the Court of Appeals is

Reversed.

JUSTICE SCALIA, with whom JUSTICE O'CONNOR AND JUSTICE THOMAS join, concurring.

I join the opinion of the Court, which makes clear that the discretion it endorses — trial-court discretion in choosing the manner of testing expert reliability — is not discretion to abandon the gatekeeping function. I think it worth adding that it is not discretion to perform the function inadequately. Rather, it is discretion to choose among reasonable means of excluding expertise that is false and science that is junky. Though, as the Court makes clear today, the *Daubert* factors are not holy writ, in a particular case the failure to apply one or another of them may be unreasonable, and hence an abuse of discretion.

[e] The 2000 Amendment to Federal Rule 702

Effective December 1, 2000, Rule 702 was amended to add the following underlined language:

> If scientific, technical, or other specialized knowledge will assist the trier of fact to understand the evidence or to determine a fact in issue, a witness qualified as an expert by knowledge, skill, experience, training, or education, may testify thereto in the form of an opinion or otherwise, <u>if (1) the testimony is based upon sufficient facts or data, (2) the testimony is the product of reliable principles and methods, and (3) the witness has applied the principles and methods reliably to the facts of the case.</u>

The Committee Note to the amendment explains the intent behind the change, and is also intended to assist courts and litigants in applying the *Daubert* standards to expert testimony. The Note states as follows:

2000 Amendment Advisory Committee Note

Rule 702 has been amended in response to *Daubert v. Merrell Dow Pharmaceuticals, Inc.,* 509 U.S. 579 (1993), and to the many cases applying *Daubert,* including *Kumho Tire Co. v. Carmichael,* 119 S. Ct. 1167 (1999). In *Daubert* the Court charged trial judges with the responsibility of acting as gatekeepers to exclude unreliable expert testimony, and the Court in *Kumho* clarified that this gatekeeper function applies to all expert testimony, not just testimony based in science. *See also Kumho,* 119 S. Ct. at 1178 (citing the Committee Note to the proposed amendment to Rule 702, which had been released for public comment before the date of the *Kumho* decision). The amendment affirms the trial court's role as gatekeeper and provides some general standards that the trial court must use to assess the reliability and helpfulness of proffered expert testimony. Consistently with *Kumho,* the Rule as amended provides that all types of expert testimony present questions of admissibility for the trial court in deciding whether the evidence is reliable and helpful. Consequently, the admissibility of all expert testimony is governed by the principles of Rule 104(a). Under that Rule, the proponent has the burden of establishing that the pertinent admissibility requirements are met by a preponderance of the evidence. *See Bourjaily v. United States,* 483 U.S. 171 (1987).

Daubert set forth a non-exclusive checklist for trial courts to use in assessing the reliability of scientific expert testimony. The specific factors explicated by the *Daubert* Court are (1) whether the expert's technique or theory can be or has been tested — that is, whether the expert's theory can be challenged in some objective sense, or whether it is instead simply a subjective, conclusory approach that cannot reasonably be assessed for reliability; (2) whether the technique or theory has been subject to peer review and publication; (3) the known or potential rate of error of the technique or theory when applied; (4) the existence and maintenance of standards and controls; and (5) whether the technique or theory has been generally accepted in the scientific community. The Court in *Kumho* held that these factors might also be applicable in assessing the reliability of non-scientific expert testimony, depending upon "the particular circumstances of the particular case at issue." 119 S. Ct. at 1175.

No attempt has been made to "codify" these specific factors. *Daubert* itself emphasized that the factors were neither exclusive nor dispositive. Other cases have recognized that not all of the specific *Daubert* factors can apply to every type of expert testimony. In addition to *Kumho,* 119 S. Ct. at 1175, *see Tyus v. Urban Search Management,* 102 F.3d 256 (7th Cir. 1996) (noting that the factors mentioned by the Court in *Daubert* do not neatly apply to expert testimony from a sociologist). *See also Kannankeril v. Terminix Int'l, Inc.,* 128 F.3d 802, 809 (3d Cir. 1997) (holding that lack of peer review or publication was not dispositive where the expert's opinion was supported by "widely accepted scientific knowledge"). The standards set forth in the amendment are broad enough to require consideration of any or all of the specific *Daubert* factors where appropriate.

Courts both before and after *Daubert* have found other factors relevant in determining whether expert testimony is sufficiently reliable to be considered by the trier of fact. These factors include:

(1) Whether experts are "proposing to testify about matters growing naturally and directly out of research they have conducted independent of the litigation, or whether they have developed their opinions expressly for purposes of testifying." *Daubert v. Merrell Dow Pharmaceuticals, Inc.,* 43 F.3d 1311, 1317 (9th Cir. 1995).

(2) Whether the expert has unjustifiably extrapolated from an accepted premise to an unfounded conclusion. *See General Elec. Co. v. Joiner,* 522 U.S. 136, 146 (1997) (noting that in some cases a trial court

"may conclude that there is simply too great an analytical gap between the data and the opinion proffered").

(3) Whether the expert has adequately accounted for obvious alternative explanations. *See Claar v. Burlington N.R.R.*, 29 F.3d 499 (9th Cir. 1994) (testimony excluded where the expert failed to consider other obvious causes for the plaintiff's condition). *Compare Ambrosini v. Labarraque*, 101 F.3d 129 (D.C. Cir. 1996) (the possibility of some uneliminated causes presents a question of weight, so long as the most obvious causes have been considered and reasonably ruled out by the expert).

(4) Whether the expert "is being as careful as he would be in his regular professional work outside his paid litigation consulting." *Sheehan v. Daily Racing Form, Inc.*, 104 F.3d 940, 942 (7th Cir. 1997). *See Kumho Tire Co. v. Carmichael,* 119 S. Ct. 1167, 1176 (1999) (*Daubert* requires the trial court to assure itself that the expert "employs in the courtroom the same level of intellectual rigor that characterizes the practice of an expert in the relevant field").

(5) Whether the field of expertise claimed by the expert is known to reach reliable results for the type of opinion the expert would give. *See Kumho Tire Co. v. Carmichael,* 119 S. Ct.1167, 1175 (1999) (*Daubert's* general acceptance factor does not "help show that an expert's testimony is reliable where the discipline itself lacks reliability, as, for example, do theories grounded in any so-called generally accepted principles of astrology or necromancy."); *Moore v. Ashland Chemical, Inc.*, 151 F.3d 269 (5th Cir. 1998) (en banc) (clinical doctor was properly precluded from testifying to the toxicological cause of the plaintiff's respiratory problem, where the opinion was not sufficiently grounded in scientific methodology); *Sterling v. Velsicol Chem. Corp.*, 855 F.2d 1188 (6th Cir. 1988) (rejecting testimony based on "clinical ecology" as unfounded and unreliable).

All of these factors remain relevant to the determination of the reliability of expert testimony under the Rule as amended. Other factors may also be relevant. *See Kumho,* 119 S. Ct. 1167, 1176 ("[W]e conclude that the trial judge must have considerable leeway in deciding in a particular case how to go about determining whether particular expert testimony is reliable."). Yet no single factor is necessarily dispositive of the reliability of a particular expert's testimony. *See, e.g., Heller v. Shaw Industries, Inc.,* 167 F.3d 146, 155 (3d Cir. 1999) ("not only must each stage of the expert's testimony be reliable, but each stage must be evaluated practically and flexibly without bright-line exclusionary (or inclusionary) rules"); *Daubert v. Merrell Dow Pharmaceuticals, Inc.,* 43 F.3d 1311, 1317, n.5 (9th Cir. 1995) (noting that some expert disciplines "have the courtroom as a principal theatre of operations" and as to these disciplines "the fact that the expert has developed an expertise principally for purposes of litigation will obviously not be a substantial consideration").

A review of the caselaw after *Daubert* shows that the rejection of expert testimony is the exception rather than the rule. *Daubert* did not work a "seachange over federal evidence law," and "the trial court's role as gatekeeper is not intended to serve as a replacement for the adversary system." *United States v. 14.38 Acres of Land Situated in Leflore County, Mississippi,* 80 F.3d 1074, 1078 (5th Cir. 1996). As the Court in *Daubert* stated: "Vigorous cross-examination, presentation of contrary evidence, and careful instruction on the burden of proof are the traditional and appropriate means of attacking shaky but admissible evidence." 509 U.S. at 595. Likewise, this amendment is not intended to provide an excuse for an automatic challenge to the testimony of every expert. *See Kumho Tire Co. v. Carmichael,* 119 S. Ct.1167, 1176 (1999) (noting that the trial judge has the discretion "both to avoid unnecessary 'reliability' proceedings in ordinary cases where the reliability of an expert's methods is properly taken for granted, and to require appropriate proceedings in the less usual or more complex cases where cause for questioning the expert's reliability arises").

When a trial court, applying this amendment, rules that an expert's testimony is reliable, this does not necessarily mean that contradictory expert testimony is unreliable. The amendment is broad enough to permit testimony that is the product of competing principles or methods in the same field of expertise. *See, e.g., Heller v. Shaw Industries, Inc.,* 167 F.3d 146, 160 (3d Cir. 1999) (expert testimony cannot be excluded simply because the expert uses one test rather than another, when both tests are accepted in the field and both reach reliable results). As the court stated in *In re Paoli R.R. Yard PCB Litigation*, 35 F.3d 717, 744 (3d Cir. 1994), proponents "do not have to demonstrate to the judge by a preponderance of the evidence that the assessments of their experts are correct, they only have to demonstrate by a preponderance of evidence that their opinions are reliable * * * . The evidentiary requirement of reliability is lower than the merits standard of correctness." *See also Daubert v. Merrell Dow Pharmaceuticals, Inc.*, 43 F.3d 1311, 1318 (9th Cir. 1995) (scientific experts might be permitted to testify if they could show that the methods they used were also employed by "a recognized minority of scientists in their field"); *Ruiz-Troche v. Pepsi Cola,* 161 F.3d 77, 85 (1st Cir. 1998) ("*Daubert* neither requires nor empowers trial courts to determine which of several competing scientific theories has the best provenance.").

The Court in *Daubert* declared that the "focus, of course, must be solely on principles and methodology, not on the conclusions they generate." 509 U.S. at 595. Yet as the Court later recognized, "conclusions and methodology are not entirely distinct from one another." *General Elec. Co. v. Joiner,* 522 U.S. 136, 146 (1997). Under the amendment, as under *Daubert,* when an expert purports to apply principles and methods in accordance with professional standards, and yet reaches a conclusion that other experts in the field would not reach, the trial court may fairly suspect that the principles and methods have not been faithfully applied. *See Lust v. Merrell Dow Pharmaceuticals, Inc.,* 89 F.3d 594, 598 (9th Cir. 1996). The amendment specifically provides that the trial court must scrutinize not only the principles and methods used by the expert, but also whether those principles and methods have been properly applied to the facts of the case. As the court noted in *In re Paoli R.R. Yard PCB Litig.*, 35 F.3d 717, 745 (3d Cir. 1994), "*any* step that renders the analysis unreliable * * * renders the expert's testimony inadmissible. *This is true whether the step completely changes a reliable methodology or merely misapplies that methodology.*"

If the expert purports to apply principles and methods to the facts of the case, it is important that this application be conducted reliably. Yet it might also be important in some cases for an expert to educate the factfinder about general principles, without ever attempting to apply these principles to the specific facts of the case. For example, experts might instruct the factfinder on the principles of thermodynamics, or bloodclotting, or on how financial markets respond to corporate reports, without ever knowing about or trying to tic their testimony into the facts of the case. The amendment does not alter the venerable practice of using expert testimony to educate the factfinder on general principles. For this kind of generalized testimony, Rule 702 simply requires that: (1) the expert be qualified; (2) the testimony address a subject matter on which the factfinder can be assisted by an expert; (3) the testimony be reliable; and (4) the testimony "fit" the facts of the case.

As stated earlier, the amendment does not distinguish between scientific and other forms of expert testimony. The trial court's gatekeeping function applies to testimony by any expert. *See Kumho Tire Co. v. Carmichael,* 119 S. Ct. 1167, 1171 (1999) ("We conclude that *Daubert's* general holding — setting forth the trial judge's general 'gatekeeping' obligation — applies not only to testimony based on 'scientific' knowledge, but also to testimony based on 'technical' and 'other specialized' knowledge."). While the relevant factors for determining reliability will vary from expertise to expertise, the amendment rejects the premise that an expert's testimony should be treated more permissively simply because it is outside the realm of science. An opinion from an expert who is not a scientist should receive the same degree of scrutiny for reliability as an opinion from an expert who purports to be a scientist. *See Watkins v. Telsmith, Inc.*, 121 F.3d 984, 991 (5th Cir. 1997) ("[I]t seems exactly backwards that experts who purport to rely on general engineering principles and practical experience might escape screening by the district court simply by stating that their conclusions were not reached by any particular method or technique."). Some types of expert testimony will be more objectively verifiable, and subject to the expectations of falsifiability, peer review, and publication, than others. Some types of expert testimony will not rely on anything like a scientific method, and so will have to be evaluated by reference to other standard principles attendant to the particular area of expertise. The trial judge in all cases of proffered expert testimony must find that it is properly grounded, well-reasoned, and not speculative before it can be admitted. The expert's testimony must be grounded in an accepted body of learning or experience in the expert's field, and the expert must explain how the conclusion is so grounded. *See, e.g.*, American College of Trial Lawyers, *Standards and Procedures for Determining the Admissibility of Expert Testimony after* Daubert, 157 F.R.D. 571, 579 (1994) ("[W]hether the testimony concerns economic principles, accounting standards, property valuation or other non-scientific subjects, it should be evaluated by reference to the 'knowledge and experience' of that particular field.").

The amendment requires that the testimony must be the product of reliable principles and methods that are reliably applied to the facts of the case. While the terms "principles" and "methods" may convey a certain impression when applied to scientific knowledge, they remain relevant when applied to testimony based on technical or other specialized knowledge. For example, when a law enforcement agent testifies regarding the use of code words in a drug transaction, the principle used by the agent is that participants in such transactions regularly use code words to conceal the nature of their activities. The method used by the agent is the application of extensive experience to analyze the meaning of the conversations. So long as the principles and methods are reliable and applied reliably to the facts of the case, this type of testimony should be admitted.

Nothing in this amendment is intended to suggest that experience alone — or experience in conjunction with other knowledge, skill, training or education — may not provide a sufficient foundation for expert testimony. To the contrary, the text of Rule 702 expressly contemplates that an expert may be qualified on the basis of experience. In certain fields, experience is the predominant, if not sole, basis for a great deal of reliable expert testimony. *See, e.g., United States v. Jones,* 107 F.3d 1147 (6th Cir. 1997) (no abuse of discretion in admitting the testimony of a handwriting examiner who had years of practical experience and extensive training, and who explained his methodology in detail); *Tassin v. Sears Roebuck,* 946 F. Supp. 1241, 1248 (M.D. La. 1996) (design engineer's testimony can be admissible when the expert's opinions "are based on facts, a reasonable investigation, and traditional technical/mechanical expertise, and he provides a reasonable link between the information and procedures he uses and the conclusions he reaches"). *See also Kumho Tire Co. v. Carmichael*, 119 S. Ct. 1167, 1178 (1999) (stating that "no one denies that an expert might draw a conclusion from a set of observations based on extensive and specialized experience").

If the witness is relying solely or primarily on experience, then the witness must explain how that experience leads to the conclusion reached, why that experience is a sufficient basis for the opinion, and how that experience is reliably applied to the facts.. The trial court's gatekeeping function requires more than simply "taking the expert's word for it." *See Daubert v. Merrell Dow Pharmaceuticals, Inc.,* 43 F.3d 1311, 1319 (9th Cir. 1995) ("We've been presented with only the experts' qualifications, their conclusions and their assurances of reliability. Under *Daubert*, that's not enough."). The more subjective and controversial the expert's inquiry, the more likely the testimony should be excluded as unreliable. *See O'Conner v. Commonwealth Edison Co.*, 13 F.3d 1090 (7th Cir. 1994) (expert testimony based on a completely subjective methodology held properly excluded). *See also Kumho Tire Co. v. Carmichael*, 119 S. Ct. 1167, 1176 (1999) ("[I]t will at times be useful to ask even of a witness whose expertise is based purely on experience, say, a perfume tester able to distinguish among 140 odors at a sniff, whether his preparation is of a kind that others in the field would recognize as acceptable.").

Subpart (1) of Rule 702 calls for a quantitative rather than qualitative analysis. The amendment requires that expert testimony be based on sufficient underlying "facts or data." The term "data" is intended to encompass the reliable opinions of other experts. See the original Advisory Committee Note to Rule 703. The language "facts or data" is broad enough to allow an expert to rely on hypothetical facts that are supported by the evidence. *Id.*

When facts are in dispute, experts sometimes reach different conclusions based on competing versions of the facts. The emphasis in the amendment on "sufficient facts or data" is not intended to authorize a trial court to exclude an expert's testimony on the ground that the court believes one version of the facts and not the other.

There has been some confusion over the relationship between Rules 702 and 703. The amendment makes clear that the sufficiency of the basis of an expert's testimony is to be decided under Rule 702. Rule 702 sets forth the overarching requirement of reliability, and an analysis of the sufficiency of the expert's basis cannot be divorced from the ultimate reliability of the expert's opinion. In contrast, the "reasonable reliance" requirement of Rule 703 is a relatively narrow inquiry. When an expert relies on inadmissible information, Rule 703 requires the trial court to determine whether that information is of a type reasonably relied on by other experts in the field. If so, the expert can rely on the information in reaching an opinion. However, the question whether the expert is relying on a *sufficient* basis of information — whether admissible information or not — is governed by the requirements of Rule 702.

The amendment makes no attempt to set forth procedural requirements for exercising the trial court's gatekeeping function over expert testimony. *See* Daniel J. Capra, *The Daubert Puzzle*, 38 Ga. L. Rev. 699, 766 (1998) ("Trial courts should be allowed substantial discretion in dealing with *Daubert* questions; any attempt to codify procedures will likely give rise to unnecessary changes in practice and create difficult questions for appellate review."). Courts have shown considerable ingenuity and flexibility in considering challenges to expert testimony under *Daubert*, and it is contemplated that this will continue under the amended Rule. *See, e.g., Cortes-Irizarry v. Corporacion Insular*, 111 F.3d 184 (1st Cir. 1997) (discussing the application of *Daubert* in ruling on a motion for summary judgment); *In re Paoli R.R. Yard PCB Litig.,* 35 F.3d 717, 736, 739 (3d Cir. 1994) (discussing the use of *in limine* hearings); *Claar v. Burlington N.R.R.,* 29 F.3d 499, 502-05 (9th Cir. 1994) (discussing the trial court's technique of ordering experts to submit serial affidavits explaining the reasoning and methods underlying their conclusions).

The amendment continues the practice of the original Rule in referring to a qualified witness as an "expert." This was done to provide continuity and to minimize change. The use of the term "expert" in the Rule does not, however, mean that a jury should actually be informed that a qualified witness is testifying as an "expert." Indeed, there is much to be said for a practice that prohibits the use of the term "expert" by both the parties and the court at trial. Such a practice "ensures that trial courts do not inadvertently put their stamp of authority" on a witness' opinion, and protects against the jury's being "overwhelmed by the so-called 'experts.' " Hon. Charles Richey, *Proposals to Eliminate the Prejudicial Effect of the Use of the Word "Expert" Under the Federal Rules of Evidence in Criminal and Civil Jury Trials,* 154 F.R.D. 537, 559 (1994) (setting forth limiting instructions and a standing order employed to prohibit the use of the term "expert" in jury trials).

[f] Cases Decided Under the 2000 Amendment to Rule 702

An evaluation of the effect of the 2000 amendment to Rule 702 is provided by Saltzburg, Martin, and Capra in the *Federal Rules of Evidence Manual* (9th ed. 2006):

> Some commentators have contended that the amendment to Rule 702 does much more than codify *Daubert* and its progeny. They assert that the intent of the amendment is to cast the Trial Judge in the role of a super-expert, excluding all expert testimony that he or she does not personally find credible. They contend that the amendment instructs trial judges to exclude all proffered expert testimony unless they find it so sound as to be immune from attack. In the elegant words of one critical lawyer, Bert Black, anyone who thinks that the amendment merely codifies *Daubert* "is smoking something funny."
>
> However, the amendment does nothing more than apply the *Daubert* gatekeeping function to all expert testimony, as the Supreme Court emphasized in *Kumho*. The three general standards set forth in the amended Rule can clearly be found in *Daubert* and its progeny, though those cases do not set forth these standards as clearly or as helpfully as does the amendment. The amended Rule crystallizes the central tenets of *Daubert* and provides the courts with a straightforward checklist that can be applied, with considerable flexibility, to all kinds of expert testimony. *See generally* Brixen and Meis, *Codifying the "Daubert Trilogy": The Amendment to Federal Rule of Evidence 702*, 40 Jurimetrics 527 (2000) ("The amendment to Rule 702 codifies existing case law interpreting the existing rule.").

The cases decided under the amended Rule 702 belie the paranoid contention that the amendment works a sea change in the regulation of expert testimony. The courts have so far held that the amendment simply codifies *Daubert* by extracting the three general requirements from the Court's basic premises about the trial court's gatekeeping function. *See, e.g., Nelson v. Tennessee Gas Pipeline Co.*, 243 F.3d 244 (6th Cir. 2001) (the language added by the amendment "is consistent with the gatekeeping function articulated in *Daubert*. The Advisory Committee Notes explain that no specific factors were articulated in the new rule because the factors mentioned in *Daubert* are neither exclusive, nor dispositive, and do not apply to every type of expert testimony. We are satisfied that the amendment to Fed. R. Evid. 702 does not alter the standard for evaluating the admissibility of expert opinions in this case."); *Pappas v. Sony Electronics, Inc.*, 136 F. Supp. 2d 413 (W.D. Pa. 2000) ("amended Rule 702 does not effect a change in the application of *Daubert* in the Third Circuit").

Three exemplary cases illustrate the proper approach to expert testimony under *Daubert* and the amendment to Rule 702. In *Blevins v. New Holland North America*, 128 F. Supp. 2d 952 (W.D. Va. 2001), the plaintiff was injured by a hay baler. The plaintiff disembarked from the hay baler to lift up the tail gate and dislodge some hay that was stuck in the baler. He did not turn the baler off. His arm got caught in the machinery. The plaintiff proffered an expert to testify that the baler could have been designed with an emergency stop system that would enable somebody caught in the machinery to turn it off and avoid further injury. The defendant argued that this testimony should be excluded under Rule 702 for three reasons: (1) the expert failed to perform any "scientific testing"; (2) his views had not been "peer reviewed"; and (3) an emergency stop system has not been installed on any hay balers manufactured in the United States.

The *Blevins* Court turned to the amended Rule 702. It stated that the Rule as amended "has adopted the *Daubert* principles." It referred to the Advisory Committee Note to the amendment, which sets forth the specific *Daubert* standards (testing, peer review, general acceptance, etc.) and noted that the amendment does not codify these specific standards, because *Daubert* itself says that these specific requirements are not exclusive or dispositive. The Court then applied the flexible three-step test of the amendment and determined that the expert's testimony was sufficiently reliable to be admissible. The Court concluded as follows:

> Sevart [the expert] is an experienced professional engineer, with academic as well as practical credentials. He has carefully studied the issue and written about it under the official auspices of a recognized professional organization. He himself has designed and built at least ten emergency stop systems for various types of hay balers and corn pickers and after examining the hay baler in question is of the opinion that it would be feasible to install such a system on that model. While he may be wrong, the value and weight of this opinion are proper matters for the jury to determine.

The Court's analysis of the expert testimony in *Blevins* is an excellent application of the amended Rule and of *Daubert* itself. The expert had a sufficient basis — designing emergency stop systems on other hay balers and personally investigating the model in question. The expert used a reliable method — extensive experience, training, and reasoning consistent with other professionals in his field. And he properly applied this experience to the facts of the case by determining whether there was any material difference between the machine at issue and those machines on which the expert had successfully installed emergency stop systems. The Court properly noted that an expert's testimony need not be perfect to be admissible; minimal inconsistencies and gaps in the expert's analysis can be addressed on cross-examination.

The second exemplary case under the amended Rule 702 is *Lennon v. Norfolk and Western Ry. Co.*, 123 F. Supp. 2d 1143 (N.D. Ind. 2000). The plaintiff proffered an expert to testify that his multiple sclerosis resulted from the plaintiff's having taken a nasty fall while on the job. The Court observed that Rule 702 had been amended "in response to *Daubert*" and held that under the amended Rule, as under *Daubert*, the expert's testimony was not reliable enough to be admissible. The expert's proposition, that MS could be caused by a fall, was unsupported by most of the medical literature. The expert's reliance on a few case studies was an insufficient basis for his conclusion. The expert responded that he had performed a differential diagnosis on the plaintiff — ruling out all causes for his MS other than trauma, and therefore concluding that trauma must have caused the MS. But the Court noted that a differential diagnosis is only reliable if it rules out all *known causes* of an injury but one, and only if the one cause left is in fact a *known cause* of the injury. In this case, the expert's assumption that trauma causes MS was just that — an unsupported assumption. The analysis under *Lennon* is perfectly correct under *Daubert* and the amended Rule 702. It is also consistent with the pre-amendment cases decided under *Daubert*. *See, e.g.*, *Black v. Food Lion*, 171 F.3d 308 (5th Cir. 1999) (doctor's testimony that fibromyalgia syndrome was caused by a fall was inadmissible under *Daubert* and *Kumho*; the exact process that results in fibromyalgia or the factors that trigger the process remain unknown, so "no scientifically reliable conclusion on causation can be drawn" and no differential diagnosis can be conducted).

The gatekeeper function means that the Trial Court must exclude expert testimony that is nothing but hypothesis and speculation. If the expert in *Lennon* had been the plaintiff's doctor, it is extremely unlikely that he would have relied on a theory of "trauma causes MS" if that theory were material to treating the patient. And yet he was willing to testify to that theory at trial. As the Committee Note to the amended Rule 702 states, the court's gatekeeping duty under the amendment, as under *Daubert*, is to make certain that an expert "employs in the courtroom the same level of intellectual rigor that characterizes the practice of an expert in the relevant field." If the method is good enough for an expert in his professional life, it is good enough for a courtroom; but if an expert is willing to testify in court to a theory he would not use in his professional life, then that testimony should be excluded. It is to be hoped that the Courts will continue to apply the amended Rule 702 with this helpful rule of thumb in mind. *Daubert* and *Kumho* are very much alive in the amended Rule 702.

The final exemplary case illustrates the proper treatment of experience-based experts under *Daubert* and the amended Rule 702. The defendant in *United States v. Frazier,* 387 F.3d 1244 (11th Cir. 2004) (en banc) was charged with kidnaping. The victim was sexually assaulted. Forensic evidence failed to show any traces of the defendant's hair or bodily fluids on the victim. The defendant proffered a forensic expert who would have testified, on the basis of his experience in the field, that he would have expected to find some transfer of hairs or seminal fluid if a sexual assault had occurred. The Trial Court excluded the expert on the ground that he gave no explanation for his expectation, other than a reference to his extensive experience in the field of forensic testing. The Court found no error in excluding the expert. It relied heavily on the Committee Note to the 2000 amendment to Rule 702, which indicates that the gatekeeping function requires scrutiny of experience-based experts. The Court noted first that experts can give helpful testimony on the basis of their experience — a point recognized in the Committee Note to the 2000 amendment. The Court then proceeded as follows:

> Of course, the unremarkable observation that an expert may be qualified by experience does not mean that experience, standing alone, is a sufficient foundation rendering reliable any conceivable opinion the expert may express. * * * Indeed, the Committee Note to the 2000 Amendments of Rule 702 expressly says that, "[i]f the witness is relying solely or primarily on experience, then the witness must

> explain how that experience leads to the conclusion reached, why that experience is a sufficient basis for the opinion, and how that experience is reliably applied to the facts. The trial court's gatekeeping function requires more than simply 'taking the expert's word for it.'" If admissibility could be established merely by the ipse dixit of an admittedly qualified expert, the reliability prong would be, for all practical purposes, subsumed by the qualification prong. * * * Exactly how reliability is evaluated may vary from case to case, but what remains constant is the requirement that the trial judge evaluate the reliability of the testimony before allowing its admission at trial. *See* Fed. R. Evid. 702 advisory committee's note (2000 amends.) ("The trial judge in all cases of proffered expert testimony must find that it is properly grounded, well-reasoned, and not speculative before it can be admitted.").

In this case, the expert provided nothing other than an assertion based on his experience. Thus the testimony could not be admitted under *Daubert* and the amended Rule 702. The *Frazier* Court explained as follows:

> Tressel offered precious little in the way of a reliable foundation or basis for his opinion. After the government moved to exclude Tressel's expert testimony, the district court was obliged to exercise its gatekeeping role by determining whether Tressel provided a reliable foundation or basis for his opinion. When questioned specifically about the basis for his opinion, Tressel said his opinion was based on his experience, and on various texts in forensic investigation. However, even after repeated prompting, Tressel never explained just how his own experience, or the texts he mentioned, supported his "expectancy" opinion. Indeed, Tressel identified only a single investigation he had worked on in which hair evidence was recovered during the investigation of a serial rapist, and could suggest no study that had ever examined the rate of transfer of hair in sexual assault cases. * * * Without knowing how frequently hair or seminal fluid is transferred during sexual conduct in similar cases — whether derived from reliable studies or based on some quantification derived from his own experience — it would be very difficult indeed for the district court (or for that matter the jury) to make even an informed assessment, let alone to verify that the recovery of hair or fluid evidence in this case "would be expected." Nor could the district court tell from Tressel's testimony whether his opinions had been subjected to peer review or, even, the percentage of cases in which his opinion had been erroneous. Simply put, Tressel did not offer any hard information concerning the rates of transfer of hair or fluids during sexual conduct.
>
> Since Tressel was relying solely or primarily on his experience, it remained the burden of the proponent of this testimony to explain how that experience led to the conclusion he reached, why that experience was a sufficient basis for the opinion, and just how that experience was reliably applied to the facts of the case. Again, "[t]he court's gatekeeping function requires more than simply 'taking the expert's

> word for it.'" Fed. R. Evid. 702 advisory committee's note (2000 amends.). Our review of this record leads us to the conclusion that the district court did not abuse its discretion in finding the absence of a sufficiently verifiable, quantitative basis for Tressel's opinion. As we have noted, the application of an abuse-of-discretion standard recognizes a range of possible conclusions that the trial judge may reach. In this case, we are satisfied that the district judge acted well within that range in finding an insufficient nexus between the experience proffered by the expert and the essential opinion propounded.

The three illustrative cases above can be used as a blueprint for assessing most if not all of the challenged expert testimony under the amended Rule 702.

[g] A Specialized Application of Reliability Standards: Proof of Probability

PEOPLE v. COLLINS
438 P.2d 33 (Cal. 1968)

SULLIVAN, JUSTICE:

We deal here with the novel question whether evidence of mathematical probability has been properly introduced and used by the prosecution in a criminal case. While we discern no inherent incompatibility between the disciplines of law and mathematics and intend no general disapproval or disparagement of the latter as an auxiliary in the fact-finding processes of the former, we cannot uphold the technique employed in the instant case. As we explain in detail *infra*, the testimony as to mathematical probability infected the case with fatal error and distorted the jury's traditional role of determining guilt or innocence according to long-settled rules. Mathematics, a veritable sorcerer in our computerized society, while assisting the trier of fact in the search for truth, must not cast a spell over him. We conclude that on the record before us defendant should not have had his guilt determined by the odds and that he is entitled to a new trial. We reverse the judgment.

A jury found defendant Malcolm Ricardo Collins and his wife defendant Janet Louise Collins guilty of second degree robbery. Malcolm appeals from the judgment of conviction. Janet has not appealed.

On June 18, 1964, about 11:30 a.m. Mrs. Juanita Brooks, who had been shopping, was walking home along an alley in the San Pedro area of the City of Los Angeles. She was pulling behind her a wicker basket carryall containing groceries and had her purse on top of the packages. She was using a cane. As she stooped down to pick up an empty carton, she was suddenly pushed to the ground by a person whom she neither saw nor heard approach. She was stunned by the fall and felt some pain. She managed to look up and saw a young woman running from the scene. According to Mrs. Brooks the latter appeared to weigh about 145 pounds, was wearing "something dark," and had hair "between a dark blond and a light blond," but lighter than the color of defendant Janet Collins' hair as it appeared at trial. Immediately after the incident, Mrs. Brooks discovered that her purse, containing between $35 and $40, was missing.

About the same time as the robbery, John Bass, who lived on the street at the end of the alley, was in front of his house watering his lawn. His attention was attracted by "a lot of crying and screaming" coming from the alley. As he looked in that direction, he saw a woman run out of the alley and enter a yellow automobile parked across the street from him. He was unable to give the make of the car. The car started off immediately and pulled wide around another parked vehicle so that in the narrow street it passed within six feet of Bass. The latter then saw that it was being driven by a male Negro, wearing a mustache and beard. At the trial Bass identified defendant as the driver of the yellow automobile. However, an attempt was made to impeach his identification by his admission that at the preliminary hearing he testified to an uncertain identification at the police lineup shortly after the attack on Mrs. Brooks, when defendant was beardless.

In his testimony Bass described the woman who ran from the alley as a Caucasian, slightly over five feet tall, of ordinary build, with her hair in a dark blond ponytail, and wearing dark clothing. He further testified that her ponytail was "just like" one which Janet had in a police photograph taken on June 22, 1964.

On the day of the robbery, Janet was employed as a housemaid in San Pedro. Her employer testified that she had arrived for work at 8:50 a.m. and that defendant had picked her up in a light yellow car about 11:30 a.m. On that day, according to the witness, Janet was wearing her hair in a blonde ponytail but lighter in color than it appeared at trial.

There was evidence from which it could be inferred that defendants had ample time to drive from Janet's place of employment and participate in the robbery. Defendants testified, however, that they went directly from her employer's house to the home of friends, where they remained for several hours.

* * *

At the seven-day trial the prosecution experienced some difficulty in establishing the identities of the perpetrators of the crime. The victim could not identify Janet and had never seen defendant. The identification by the witness Bass, who observed the girl run out of the alley and get into the automobile, was incomplete as to Janet and may have been weakened as to defendant. There was also evidence, introduced by the defense, that Janet had worn light-colored clothing on the day in question, but both the victim and Bass testified that the girl they observed had worn dark clothing.

In an apparent attempt to bolster the identifications, the prosecutor called an instructor of mathematics at a state college. Through this witness he sought to establish that, assuming the robbery was committed by a Caucasian woman with a blond ponytail who left the scene accompanied by a Negro with a beard and mustache, there was an overwhelming probability that the crime was committed by any couple answering such distinctive characteristics. The witness testified, in substance, to the "product rule," which states that the probability of the joint occurrence of a number of *mutually independent* events is equal to the product of the individual probabilities that each of the events will occur.[3]

Without presenting any statistical evidence whatsoever in support of the probabilities for the factors selected, the prosecutor then proceeded to have the witness * * * assume probability factors for the various characteristics which he deemed to be shared by the guilty couple and all other couples answering to such distinctive characteristics.[4]

Applying the product rule to his own factors the prosecutor arrived at a probability that there was but one chance in 12 million that any couple possessed the distinctive characteristics of the defendants. Accordingly, under this theory, it was to be inferred that there could be but one chance in 12 million that defendants were innocent and that another equally distinctive couple actually committed the robbery. Expanding on what he had thus purported to suggest as a hypothesis, the prosecutor offered the completely unfounded and improper testimonial assertion that, in his opinion, the factors he had assigned were "conservative estimates" and that, in reality "the chances of anyone else besides these defendants being there, * * * having every similarity, * * * is somewhat like one in a billion."

Objections were timely made to the mathematician's testimony on the grounds that it was immaterial, that it invaded the province of the jury, and that it was based on unfounded assumptions. The objections were "temporarily overruled" and the evidence admitted subject to a motion to strike. When that motion was made at the conclusion of the direct examination, the court denied it, stating that the testimony had been received only for the "purpose of illustrating the mathematical probabilities of various matters, the possibilities for them occurring or re-occurring."

---

[3] [8] In the example employed for illustrative purposes at the trial, the probability of rolling one die and coming up with a A2 is 1/6, that is, any one of the six faces of a die has one chance in six of landing face up on any particular roll. The probability of rolling two A2's in succession is 1/6 × 1/6, or 1/36, that is, on only one occasion out of 36 double rolls (or the roll of two dice), will the selected number land face up on each roll or die.

[4] [10] Although the prosecutor insisted that the factors he used were only for illustrative purposes — to demonstrate how the probability of the occurrence of mutually independent factors affected the probability that they would occur together — he nevertheless attempted to use factors which he personally related to the distinctive characteristics of defendants. In his argument to the jury he invited the jurors to apply their own factors, and asked defense counsel to suggest what the latter would deem as reasonable. The prosecutor himself proposed the individual probabilities set out in the table below. Although the transcript of the examination of the mathematics instructor and the information volunteered by the prosecutor at that time create some uncertainty as to precisely which of the characteristics the prosecutor assigned to the individual probabilities, he restated in his argument to the jury that they should be as follows:

Characteristic Individual Probability

A. Partly yellow automobile 1/10

B. Man with mustache 1/4

C. Girl with ponytail 1/10

D. Girl with blond hair 1/3

E. Negro man with beard 1/10

F. Interracial couple in car 1/1000

In his brief on appeal defendant agrees that the foregoing appeared on a table presented in the trial court.

* * *

Defendant [contends] * * * that the introduction of evidence pertaining to the mathematical theory of probability and the use of the same by the prosecution during the trial was error prejudicial to defendant.

* * *

As we shall explain, the prosecution's introduction and use of mathematical probability statistics injected two fundamental prejudicial errors into the case: (1) The testimony itself lacked an adequate foundation both in evidence and in statistical theory; and (2) the testimony and the manner in which the prosecution used it distracted the jury from its proper and requisite function of weighing the evidence on the issue of guilt, encouraged the jurors to rely upon an engaging but logically irrelevant expert demonstration, foreclosed the possibility of an effective defense by an attorney apparently unschooled in mathematical refinements, and placed the jurors and defense counsel at a disadvantage in sifting relevant fact from inapplicable theory.

We initially consider the defects in the testimony itself. As we have indicated, the specific technique presented through the mathematician's testimony and advanced by the prosecutor to measure the probabilities in question suffered from two basic and pervasive defects — an inadequate evidentiary foundation and an inadequate proof of statistical independence. First, as to the foundation requirement, we find the record devoid of any evidence relating to any of the six individual probability factors used by the prosecutor * * *. To put it another way, the prosecution produced no evidence whatsoever showing, or from which it could be in any way inferred, that only one out of every ten cars which might have been at the scene of the robbery was partly yellow, that only one out of every four men who might have been there wore a mustache, that only one out of every ten girls who might have been there wore a ponytail, or that any of the other individual probability factors listed were even roughly accurate.

The bare, inescapable fact is that the prosecution made no attempt to offer any such evidence. Instead, through leading questions having perfunctorily elicited from the witness the response that the latter could not assign a probability factor for the characteristics involved, the prosecutor himself suggested what the various probabilities should be and these became the basis of the witness' testimony. It is a curious circumstance of this adventure in proof that the prosecutor not only made his own assertions of these factors in the hope that they were "conservative" but also in later argument to the jury invited the jurors to substitute their "estimates" should they wish to do so. We can hardly conceive of a more fatal gap in the prosecution's scheme of proof. A foundation for the admissibility of the witness' testimony was never even attempted to be laid, let alone established. His testimony was neither made to rest on his own testimonial knowledge nor presented by proper hypothetical questions based upon valid data in the record.

* * *

But, as we have indicated, there was another glaring defect in the prosecution's technique, namely an inadequate proof of the statistical independence of the six factors. No proof was presented that the characteristics selected were mutually independent, even though the witness himself acknowledged that such condition was essential to the proper application of the "product rule" or "multiplication rule." * * * To the extent that the traits or characteristics were not mutually independent (*e.g.*, Negroes with beards and men with mustaches obviously represent overlapping categories), the "product rule" would inevitably yield a wholly erroneous and exaggerated result even if all of the individual components had been determined with precision.

* * *

In the instant case, therefore, because of the aforementioned two defects — the inadequate evidentiary foundation and the inadequate proof of statistical independence — the technique employed by the prosecutor could only lead to wild conjecture without demonstrated relevancy to the issues presented. It acquired no redeeming quality from the prosecutor's statement that it was being used only "for illustrative purposes" since, as we shall point out, the prosecutor's subsequent utilization of the mathematical testimony was not confined within such limits.

We now turn to the second fundamental error caused by the probability testimony. Quite apart from our foregoing objections to the specific technique employed by the prosecution to estimate the probability in question, we think that the entire enterprise upon which the prosecution embarked, and which was directed to the objective of measuring the likelihood of a random couple possessing the characteristics allegedly distinguishing the robbers, was gravely misguided. At best, it might yield an estimate as to how infrequently bearded Negroes drive yellow cars in the company of blonde females with ponytails.

The prosecution's approach, however, could furnish the jury with absolutely no guidance on the crucial issue: *Of the admittedly few such couples, which one, if any, was guilty of committing this robbery?* Probability theory necessarily remains silent on that question, since no mathematical equation can prove beyond a reasonable doubt (1) that the guilty couple *in fact* possessed the characteristics described by the People's witnesses, or even (2) that only *one* couple possessing those distinctive characteristics could be found in the entire Los Angeles area.

As to the first inherent failing we observe that the prosecution's theory of probability rested on the assumption that the witnesses called by the People had conclusively established that the guilty couple possessed the precise characteristics relied upon by the prosecution. But no mathematical formula could ever establish beyond a reasonable doubt that the prosecution's witnesses correctly observed and accurately described the distinctive features which were employed to link defendants to the crime.* * * Conceivably, for example, the guilty couple might have included a light-skinned Negress with bleached hair rather than a Caucasian blonde; or the driver of the car might have been wearing a false beard as a disguise; or the prosecution's witnesses might simply have been unreliable.

The foregoing risks of error permeate the prosecution's circumstantial case. Traditionally, the jury weighs such risks in evaluating the credibility and probative value of trial testimony, but the likelihood of human error or of falsification obviously cannot be quantified; that likelihood must therefore be excluded from any effort to assign a *number* to the probability of guilt or innocence. Confronted with an equation which purports to yield a numerical index of probable guilt, few juries could resist the temptation to accord disproportionate weight to that index; only an exceptional juror, and indeed only a defense attorney schooled in mathematics, could successfully keep in mind the fact that the probability computed by the prosecution can represent, *at best*, the likelihood that a random couple would share the characteristics testified to by the People's witnesses — *not necessarily the characteristics of the actually guilty couple.*

As to the second inherent failing in the prosecution's approach, even assuming that the first failing could be discounted, the most a mathematical computation could *ever* yield would be a measure of the probability that a random couple would possess the distinctive features in question. In the present case, for example, the prosecution attempted to compute the probability that a random couple would include a bearded Negro, a blonde girl with a ponytail, and a partly yellow car; the prosecution urged that this probability was no more than one in 12 million. Even accepting this conclusion as arithmetically accurate, however, one still could not conclude that the Collinses were probably *the* guilty couple. On the contrary, * * * the prosecution's figures actually imply a likelihood of over 40 percent that the Collinses could be "duplicated" by at least *one other couple who might equally have committed the San Pedro robbery*. Urging that the Collinses be convicted on the basis of evidence which logically establishes no more than this seems as indefensible as arguing for the conviction of X on the ground that a witness saw either X or X's twin commit the crime.

Again, few defense attorneys, and certainly few jurors, could be expected to comprehend this basic flaw in the prosecution's analysis. Conceivably even the prosecutor erroneously believed that his equation established a high probability that no other bearded Negro in the Los Angeles area drove a yellow car accompanied by a ponytailed blonde. In any event, although his technique could demonstrate no such thing, he solemnly told the jury that he had supplied mathematical proof of guilt.

Sensing the novelty of that notion, the prosecutor told the jurors that the traditional idea of proof beyond a reasonable doubt represented "the most hackneyed, stereotyped, trite, misunderstood concept in criminal law." He sought to reconcile the jury to the risk that, under his "new math" approach to criminal jurisprudence, "on some rare occasion * * * an innocent person may be convicted." "Without taking that risk," the prosecution continued, "life would be intolerable * * * because * * * there would be immunity for the Collinses, for people who chose not to be employed to go down and push old ladies down and take their money and be immune because how could we ever be sure they are the ones who did it?"

In essence this argument of the prosecutor was calculated to persuade the jury to convict defendants whether or not they were convinced of their guilt to a moral certainty and beyond a reasonable doubt.* * * Undoubtedly the jurors were unduly impressed by the mystique of the mathematical demonstration but were unable to assess its relevancy or value. Although we make no appraisal of the proper applications of mathematical techniques in the proof of facts * * * we have strong feelings that such applications, particularly in a criminal case, must be critically examined in view of the substantial unfairness to a defendant which may result from ill conceived techniques with which the trier of fact is not technically equipped to cope.* * * We feel that the technique employed in the case before us falls into the latter category.

* * *

The judgment is reversed.

NOTES

1. Is probabilistic evidence alone sufficient to support a verdict?

The most cited case on this issue is *Smith v. Rapid Transit, Inc.*, 58 N.E.2d 754 (Mass. 1945), which held that evidence showing only that the defendant's bus was licensed to operate in a given street and the accident occurred near the scheduled time for the defendant's bus to be at the accident scene was insufficient proof to get to the jury the question of whether the defendant's bus caused the plaintiff's injuries. The statistical probability was insufficient to prove that the defendant had done anything wrong. Similarly, in *Guenther v. Armstrong Rubber Co.*, 406 F.2d 1315 (3d Cir. 1969), the court held it proper to direct a verdict for defendant although plaintiff, who was injured by a defective tire sold by a department store, introduced evidence that the defendant manufactured 75 to 80 percent of the tires sold by that store. For an interesting discussion on this issue, *see United States v. Hannigan*, 27 F.3d 890 (3d Cir. 1994).

2. How is statistical evidence analyzed under the *Daubert* reliability test?

Under *Daubert* and the amended Rule 702, statistical evidence is analyzed under the same standards applicable to all expert testimony: the statistics must be supported by a sufficient factual basis, the statistician must be using reliable methods, and those methods must be reliably applied to the facts of the case. What is particularly important is that the statistician has ruled out what are called "confounding factors," *i.e.*, alternate explanations for an apparent statistical disparity.

Some examples of statistical evidence evaluated under *Daubert* include:

Raskin v. Wyatt Co., 125 F.3d 55 (2d Cir. 1997): In an action charging an employer with age discrimination, the trial court granted summary judgment for the defendant, excluding testimony from the plaintiff's expert statistician. The expert found that the defendant's employees retired earlier than comparable employees in the workforce generally, and concluded that this was attributable to the defendant's discrimination against older workers. "Affirming, the court found that this testimony was properly excluded as unreliable under *Daubert*. The statistical conclusion was defective in at least two respects. First, the expert did not account for the presence in the comparison group of those without pension plans and those who were self-employed — "categories of people who tend to work longer and to an older age than people who work for companies that have pension plans." Thus, the expert artificially inflated the retirement age in the comparison group. Second, the expert failed to account for other possible causes of differentiation between the defendant's employees and the population at large.

Muñoz v. Orr, 200 F.3d 291 (5th Cir. 2000), the Court affirmed summary judgment for the defendants in a Title VII class action by Hispanic males challenging promotion practices at an Air Force base. It found no abuse of discretion in exclusion of testimony from the plaintiffs' statistical expert. The expert's analysis began with an assumption that there was discrimination, an indicator of lack of objectivity; his report stated that discrimination was the "cause" of disparities, when statistics can show only correlation, not causation; the analysis failed to consider other variables, such as education and experience, as explanations for observed discrepancies, and it did not include a multiple regression analysis; and the expert relied only on the plaintiffs' compilations of data, giving rise to "common-sense skepticism" regarding the evaluation.

Sheehan v. Daily Racing Form, Inc., 104 F.3d 940 (7th Cir. 1997): The plaintiff brought an age discrimination action when he was terminated from employment after his job was computerized and the offices of the employer were consolidated. The district court's grant of summary judgment in favor of the employer was upheld. The plaintiff had relied on the analysis of a statistician, who compared the age of those who were dismissed with those who were retained. The statistician concluded that the probability that retention of office personnel was uncorrelated with age was less than five percent. The court held that the expert's affidavit failed to meet the *Daubert* standard, "which requires the district judge to satisfy himself that the expert is being as careful as he would be in his regular professional work outside his paid litigation consulting." The statistician's methodology was defective because: 1) He arbitrarily excluded certain personnel from the sample tested; and 2) He failed to correct for any potential explanatory variations other than age (e.g., that those who were retained might have had better computer skills than those who were let go, and that the employees in the office held a variety of jobs). The court concluded as follows:

> The expert's failure to make any adjustment for variables bearing on the decision whether to discharge or retain a person on the list other than age — his equating a simple statistical correlation to a causal relation * * * — true only if no other factor relevant to termination is correlated with age) — indicates a failure to exercise the degree of care that a statistician would use in his scientific work, outside the context of litigation. In litigation an expert may consider (he may have a financial incentive to consider) looser standards to apply.

United States v. Artero, 121 F.3d 1256 (9th Cir. 1997): The court rejected the defendant's challenge to the ethnic composition of the grand jury. The defendant presented testimony from a statistician that the percentage of Hispanics on the jury wheel was substantially less than the percentage of

Hispanics in the local population. This conclusion of underrepresentation was unreliable, however, because "the defense expert used the wrong numerator for the ratio of Hispanics to the general population." The expert used the number of Hispanics in the general population, whereas "[t]he right question is whether Hispanics *eligible to serve on federal juries* were unreasonably represented because of systematic exclusion." The court declared:

> But Dr. Weeks did not provide any data responsive to that question. He provided an answer to a different question, whether Hispanics, whether eligible to serve on federal juries or not, were represented in jury wheels at a lower rate than their proportion of the population as a whole. Irrelevant question, irrelevant answer. * * * An expert witness's post-graduate degree does not protect the court against the tendentiousness of advocacy research. A judge must exercise independent judgment to ensure that any and all scientific testimony or evidence is not only relevant, but reliable.

City of Tuscaloosa v. Harcross Chemicals, Inc., 158 F.3d 548 (11th Cir. 1998): Alabama municipalities brought an antitrust action against five chemical companies alleging that the defendants engaged in a conspiracy to fix prices for repackaged chlorine. The court held that the trial court abused its discretion in excluding the testimony of the statistician proffered by the plaintiffs. The trial court excluded the testimony because it failed to show a successful conspiracy, but the court stated that this ruling presented "a conflation of admissibility issues with issues regarding the sufficiency of the plaintiffs' evidence." The expert was not required to prove the plaintiffs' case by himself. The court found that the expert utilized well-established and reliable methodologies in the preparation of most of his statistics; he generated the statistics underlying his testimony from simple compilation of data from purchase records, documents obtained from the defendants through discovery, and from public sources. The court also found that the expert's compilation of that data into utile measurements of bid prices, costs, tie bid frequencies, etc., "are the products of simple arithmetic and algebra and of multiple regression analysis, a methodology that is well-established as reliable." However, the trial court was found correct in excluding the statistician's testimony insofar as he characterized certain bids as "signals" to coconspirators; that testimony was outside the witness's expertise, as was his testimony about applicable legal standards.

[5] Basis of Opinion and Underlying Data

[a] Federal Rules of Evidence 703 and 705

Rule 703. Bases of Opinion Testimony by Experts

The facts or data in the particular case upon which an expert bases an opinion or inference may be those perceived by or made known to the expert at or before the hearing. If of a type reasonably relied upon by experts in the particular field in forming opinions or inferences upon the subject, the facts or data need not be admissible in evidence in order for the opinion or inference to be admitted. Facts or data that are otherwise inadmissible shall not be disclosed to the jury by the proponent of the opinion or inference unless the court determines that their probative value in assisting the jury to evaluate the expert's opinion substantially outweighs their prejudicial effect.

Rule 705. Disclosure of Facts or Data Underlying Expert Opinion

The expert may testify in terms of opinion or inferences and give reasons therefor without first testifying to the underlying facts or data, unless the court requires otherwise. The expert may in any event be required to disclose the underlying facts or data on cross-examination.

[b] The 2000 Amendment to Rule 703 — Committee Note and Reporter's Observations

[Rule 703 was amended, effective December 1, 2000 and as indicated above, to provide that where inadmissible evidence, such as hearsay, is offered to explain the basis of an expert's opinion, this information cannot be disclosed to the jury unless its probative value in explaining the expert's opinion substantially outweighs the risk of prejudice to the opponent.]

COMMITTEE NOTE

Rule 703 has been amended to emphasize that when an expert reasonably relies on inadmissible information to form an opinion or inference, the underlying information is not admissible simply because the opinion or inference is admitted. Courts have reached different results on how to treat inadmissible information when it is reasonably relied upon by an expert in forming an opinion or drawing an inference. *Compare United States v. Rollins,* 862 F.2d 1282 (7th Cir. 1988) (admitting, as part of the basis of an FBI agent's expert opinion on the meaning of code language, the hearsay statements of an informant), with *United States v. 0.59 Acres of Land,* 109 F.3d 1493 (9th Cir. 1997) (error to admit hearsay offered as the basis of an expert opinion, without a limiting instruction). Commentators have also taken differing views. *See, e.g.,* Ronald Carlson, *Policing the Bases of Modern Expert Testimony,* 39 Vand. L. Rev. 577 (1986) (advocating limits on the jury's consideration of otherwise inadmissible evidence used as the basis for an expert opinion); Paul Rice, *Inadmissible Evidence as a Basis for Expert Testimony: A Response to Professor Carlson,* 40 Vand. L. Rev. 583 (1987) (advocating unrestricted use of information reasonably relied upon by an expert).

When information is reasonably relied upon by an expert and yet is admissible only for the purpose of assisting the jury in evaluating an expert's opinion, a trial court applying this Rule must consider the information's probative value in assisting the jury to weigh the expert's opinion on the one hand, and the risk of prejudice resulting from the jury's potential misuse of the information for substantive purposes on the other. The information may be disclosed to the jury, upon objection, only if the trial court finds that the probative value of the information in assisting the jury to evaluate the expert's opinion substantially outweighs its prejudicial effect. If the otherwise inadmissible information is admitted under this balancing test, the trial judge must give a limiting instruction upon request, informing the jury that the underlying information must not be used for substantive purposes. *See* Rule 105. In determining the appropriate course, the trial court should consider the probable effectiveness or lack of effectiveness of a limiting instruction under the particular circumstances.

The amendment governs only the disclosure to the jury of information that is reasonably relied on by an expert, when that information is not admissible for substantive purposes. It is not intended to affect the admissibility of an expert's testimony. Nor does the amendment prevent an expert from relying on information that is inadmissible for substantive purposes.

Nothing in this Rule restricts the presentation of underlying expert facts or data when offered by an adverse party. *See* Rule 705. Of course, an adversary's attack on an expert's basis will often open the door to a proponent's rebuttal with information that was reasonably relied upon by the expert, even if that information would not have been discloseable initially under the balancing test provided by this amendment. Moreover, in some circumstances the proponent might wish to disclose information that is relied upon by the expert in order to "remove the sting" from the opponent's anticipated attack, and thereby prevent the jury from drawing an unfair negative inference. The trial court should take this consideration into account in applying the balancing test provided by this amendment.

This amendment covers facts or data that cannot be admitted for any purpose other than to assist the jury to evaluate the expert's opinion. The balancing test provided in this amendment is not applicable to facts or data that are admissible for any other purpose but have not yet been offered for such a purpose at the time the expert testifies.

The amendment provides a presumption against disclosure to the jury of information used as the basis of an expert's opinion and not admissible for any substantive purpose, when that information is offered by the proponent of the expert. In a multi-party case, where one party proffers an expert whose testimony is also beneficial to other parties, each such party should be deemed a "proponent" within the meaning of the amendment.

Comment on the Amendment to Rule 703 by Professor Daniel Capra, Reporter to the Advisory Committee on Evidence Rules

Rule 703 permits an expert to rely on inadmissible information, such as hearsay, if it is the type of information on which other experts in the field would reasonably rely. Rule 703 is not a hearsay exception, however. Simply because an expert reasonably relies on hearsay does not make it admissible for its truth. Yet if an expert reasonably relies on the hearsay, the information is admissible in a certain sense — it is admissible to assist the factfinder in weighing the expert's testimony. That is, the hearsay is admissible for credibility purposes.

A danger arises when a proponent calls an expert who relies on hearsay, and introduces the hearsay "solely for the purpose of assisting the jury in evaluating the expert's testimony." The danger is obviously that the credibility tail will wag the hearsay dog. A proponent might even call an expert solely to admit the hearsay information on which the expert "relied." Thus, there is a danger that Rule 703 could be used as a backdoor hearsay exception.

The 2000 amendment to Rule 703 is intended to prevent a party from abusing the hearsay rule and other exclusionary rules by using an expert as a conduit for inadmissible evidence. (One member of the Standing Committee on Rules of Practice and Procedure lamented that the Advisory Committee was "trying to take all the fun out of practicing law.") The Rule provides that if the information is admissible only to illustrate the basis for an expert's opinion, then the jury can hear it only if its probative value substantially outweighs the risk of prejudice. This is an exclusionary balancing test that is the reverse of the standard Rule 403 balancing test. The probative value to be assessed is the degree to which the otherwise inadmissible information will assist the jury in assessing the weight of the expert's opinion; of course, this probative value will rise or fall depending on how important the expert's opinion is in the case. The prejudicial effect to be considered is the risk that the jury will consider the otherwise inadmissible information for its truth, even though instructed not to do so.

The amendment comes with a cost, because in certain cases the jury might have some difficulty assessing the weight of the expert's testimony because the expert will not be permitted to mention with specificity all of the information he relied upon. The Advisory Committee determined that such a hindrance of the jury's function will be rare. If the information is critical to assessing the expert's opinion, and if the expert's opinion is sufficiently important to the case, the information will ordinarily survive even the strict balancing test set forth in the amendment. Moreover, the trial court has discretion under the balancing test to employ compromise measures. For example, the trial court might permit the expert to make a general reference to the underlying information relied upon, while prohibiting a detailed disclosure. An illustration is a medical report that is not admissible; a medical expert might be permitted to state that he relied on a medical report, without being permitted to state in detail all of the assertions in that report. In this way, the jury can fairly assess the expert's opinion without the risk that the medical report will be considered for its truth.

What happens if the witness is not permitted to refer to the inadmissible information on direct examination, and then the adversary attacks the expert's basis as insufficient on cross-examination? (E.g., "Mr. Medical Expert, why did you not consult the pertinent medical reports?") Can the expert then disclose his reliance on the inadmissible information if he could not have done so on direct? The answer depends on the circumstances. The balancing test set forth in the amendment is certainly flexible enough to accommodate this situation. And clearly the balancing test would be tilted more toward allowing disclosure of the inadmissible information if it was necessary to respond to an attack on the expert's basis. Similarly, if the adversary makes a closing argument about the insufficiency of the expert's basis, the proponent should ordinarily be permitted to respond by disclosing the inadmissible information relied upon by the expert.

It is critical to note that the amendment does not in any way affect the admissibility of the expert opinion itself. It does not provide new limits on the kind of information that the expert may rely upon. It simply regulates whether the information (assuming it is admissible only to illustrate the expert's opinion) can be disclosed to the jury. It is also important to emphasize that the amendment does not impose a balancing requirement on information relied upon by an expert that is *admissible at trial but not yet admitted.* For example, a summary expert could testify in an early part of the case and disclose the information relied upon that will be admitted later at trial. Such a practice is not an abuse — the expert is not being called as a conduit to admit evidence that would otherwise be inadmissible. Thus, the balancing test of Rule 703 applies only to information that will never be admitted for its truth at the trial.

A number of public commentators saw negative consequences from the application of the balancing test set forth in the amendment to Evidence Rule 703. The scenario of asserted negative consequences proceeds as follows: 1. The expert will be unable to disclose his basis and will thus be forced to limit his testimony to a bare conclusion, an *ipse dixit*, as the comments put it. 2. The opponent will be permitted to attack the expert's basis as inadequate, creating an unfair presentation of the evidence. 3. The proponent will then be permitted, in rebuttal, to disclose the basis that was not allowed to be disclosed on direct. The complaint is that this procedure gets you right back where you started from — the jury hearing about inadmissible evidence — but with the proponent having suffered a negative inference from not having disclosed the information on direct (i.e., the jury could think that the proponent was hiding something).

The Advisory Committee believed that these criticisms overstated the impact of the amendment. The amendment does not *preclude* the proponent from disclosing, on direct examination, inadmissible information relied upon by the expert. It simply sets forth a balancing test. Sometimes the probative value of the inadmissible information, in helping the jury to weigh the expert's opinion, will substantially outweigh the prejudice resulting from disclosure, especially when a limiting instruction is given to reduce the risk of prejudice. Sometimes the expert may be permitted to disclose some pieces of inadmissible information and not others. Sometimes, as recognized in the Committee Note, the expert will be permitted to refer generally to inadmissible information, but will not be able to disclose it in detail. Thus, the chance that an expert will be left with an *ipse dixit* — no basis disclosed at all — is remote. Indeed, if an expert is left with a bare conclusion, that would be a good indication that the expert should not be testifying in the first place. Such an expert would have to be relying exclusively on inadmissible information, not reliable enough to be admitted under a hearsay exception. It is hard to see how any expert in those circumstances could expect to satisfy the reliability test imposed by *Daubert*.

A trial judge could rule in some cases that inadmissible information relied upon by an expert could be disclosed on direct when it is apparent that the opponent will attack the witness' basis on cross-examination; under these circumstances, the probative value of disclosure could substantially outweigh the prejudicial effect remaining after a limiting instruction. It would depend on the circumstances. But even if the trial judge does not permit the mention of the inadmissible information on direct, the opponent will have to be careful in attacking the expert's basis on cross-examination, because of the possibility of rebuttal. Often, the opponent may consider that the risks of an attack are too great (i.e., the inadmissible information will be disclosed in detail in rebuttal), and in these cases the risk of a skewed presentation of the evidence is accordingly diminished-that risk is diminished by the opponent's concern that the rebuttal will lose the proponent more points than the attack will gain.

It is true that the balancing test in the amendment is tilted toward prevention of disclosure of inadmissible information. But that was considered justified by the real risk that the proponent might simply be using the expert as a vehicle for obtaining backdoor admission of inadmissible evidence. Where that risk is high in the particular circumstances, the amendment essentially shifts some of the control over the disclosure from the proponent to the opponent — the opponent can keep it out by not raising a basis question when cross-examining the expert. That shift was considered fair because it is the proponent who is creating the risk of using Rule 703 as a backdoor.

[c] Facts Reasonably Relied Upon

THOMAS v. METZ
714 P.2d 1205 (Wyo. 1986)

BROWN, JUSTICE:

* * *

The facts show that on April 17, 1982, appellant rolled over in bed and experienced pain in her back between her shoulder blades. She was admitted to the hospital that same day, complaining of pain between her shoulder blades, pain in her left arm, and numbness in the left thumb, index finger and middle finger. After consultation and testing by Dr. James Maddy and Dr. Malvin Cole, it was concluded that appellant was suffering a disc herniation at the Cervical 6/Cervical 7 (C-6/C-7) level, primarily on the left side. Neurosurgical consultation was then sought from appellee, who, after evaluation, confirmed the findings of Drs. Maddy and Cole, and recommended that surgery be performed to remove disc fragments that were pressing on the spinal cord and the left C-7 nerve root.

After obtaining appellant's consent, appellee performed surgery to remove the disc fragments. A bone plug was then removed from appellant's hip and placed in the spine to fuse the two vertebral bodies. After surgery, appellant experienced pain on her right side, similar to that previously experienced on the left side. Further testing revealed the bone plug was encroaching upon the C-7 nerve root on the right side. Additional surgery was performed to alleviate the condition on April 27, 1982.

When appellant continued to experience pain, she consulted several physicians in Denver during the months of May and June, 1982. In June of 1982, appellant underwent further surgery in Denver. This surgery was performed by another physician, and consisted of removal of the first right thoracic rib.

The pain persisted. An expert witness for appellant, Dr. John Williams, testified appellant now suffers from a condition known as "hysterical conversion" — where pain is a stress reaction and has no medical, anatomical or physiological basis. Dr. Robert Kelso, a clinical psychologist, examined and evaluated appellant and concluded that he believed "this disorder should show significant improvement within a 12-month period."

Appellant filed the present action on January 25, 1983. * * * Trial to the jury resulted in a verdict for appellee.

* * *

The two expert witnesses who testified on behalf of appellee were Drs. Federico Mora and Philip Gordy. Dr. Mora is a graduate of Harvard Medical school and is a neurosurgeon practicing in New Mexico. He testified he knew appellee and had performed surgery with him on occasion. Dr. Mora further testified he thought the operation performed by appellee was appropriate, followed the proper procedure, and that the bone plug inserted was not too long. To demonstrate, he measured the bone plug in the presence of the jury using a caliper and the CAT scan film of the bone plug. Dr. Mora also explained the complicated nature of the surgery and the various causes of a bone plug protrusion other than the plug being too long.

Dr. Philip Gordy also testified as an expert witness for appellee. Dr. Gordy is a graduate of the University of Michigan Medical School and is presently a consultant in neurosurgery and neurology. He testified he has performed this surgical procedure approximately 1,000 times, and that in his opinion, the bone plug placed by appellee was neither too long nor too far to the right. Dr. Gordy further testified as to the possible cause of a bone plug protrusion other than the same being too long.

* * * Appellant's main objection to the testimony of both expert witnesses is that such testimony was improperly based on material not reasonably relied upon by experts. Specifically, appellant claims it was improper for Dr. Mora to rely upon appellee's discovery deposition in giving his opinion at trial. Appellant further claims it was also error for Dr. Gordy to base his opinion upon appellee's discovery deposition, as well as Dr. Mora's deposition.

* * *

It is significant to note that appellee's deposition was only one of several sources of information Dr. Mora relied upon to base his opinion. When asked what materials he had reviewed to form his opinion, Dr. Mora testified: "Basically what I examined is I looked over the hospital records of Ms. Thomas here when she was treated in Casper. I have also looked at hospital records and personal notes of physicians who treated her when she went to Denver later on. Furthermore, I have read the depositions that were given by Dr. Metz, by Ms. Thomas, and by Dr. Williams, two that come to mind."

And when asked if he felt the surgery performed by appellee was appropriate, Dr. Mora answered: "Well, basing myself on the hospital record and the review of the X rays, the operation was appropriate."

Dr. Gordy based his opinion upon a review of hospital records, as well as appellee's deposition and depositions from the other physicians. * * *

We are not able to find prejudicial error inasmuch as appellee's two expert witnesses based their opinions *in part* upon the deposition of appellee. Appellant has failed to show how such prejudiced her or how such affected the jury's verdict. Both of the witnesses were qualified as experts and possessed a great deal of expertise in the area of neurosurgery.

> It is common practice for a prospective witness, in preparing himself to express an expert opinion, to pursue pretrial studies and investigations of one kind or another. Frequently, the information so gained is hearsay or double hearsay, insofar as the trier of the facts is concerned. This, however, does not necessarily stand in the way of receiving such expert opinion in evidence. It is for the trial court to determine, in the exercise of its discretion, whether the expert's sources of information are sufficiently reliable to warrant reception of the opinion. If the court so finds, the opinion may be expressed.

* * * *Standard Oil Co. of California v. Moore*, 251 F.2d 188, 222 (9th Cir. 1957).

* * *

We have carefully reviewed the issues raised by appellant and are unable to find the trial court committed reversible error in allowing the testimony of appellee's expert witnesses.

Affirmed.

UNITED STATES v. LEESON
453 F.3d 631 (4th Cir. 2006)

HAMILTON, SENIOR CIRCUIT JUDGE:

Larry Leeson (Leeson) appeals his conviction and sentence on one count of being a felon in possession of a firearm, U.S.C. §§ 922(g)(1), 924(a)(2). For reasons that follow, we affirm.

I.

On August 6, 2003, Leeson, of Nutter Fort, West Virginia, presented himself at the Veteran's Administration (V.A.) hospital in Pittsburgh, Pennsylvania. Following interaction with Leeson, the admissions desk clerk at the hospital reported to hospital security that a man, later identified as Leeson, was acting strangely in that he had used three different surnames in an attempt to obtain medical treatment or medication. The admissions desk clerk also reported that the man had a bulge in his coat which might be a gun.

Two uniformed police officers of the V.A. arrived on the scene to investigate. The first officer approached Leeson while the other hung back as back-up.

After observing some sort of badge on Leeson's belt, the first officer asked Leeson if he was a police officer. Leeson falsely identified himself as Larry McDonald and falsely claimed to be an agent of the Federal Bureau of Investigation (FBI). The first officer then asked Leeson whether he had a weapon, to which question Leeson replied: "of course I have a weapon."

The two officers then requested Leeson to accompany them to the police station at the V.A. hospital in order to secure Leeson's weapon in accordance with V.A. policy. Once at the police station, Leeson surrendered his weapon, which was a .357 caliber revolver. * * * On September 4, 2003, a federal grand jury sitting in the Northern District of West Virginia indicted Leeson on one count of being a convicted felon in possession of a firearm. 18 U.S.C. §§ 922(g)(1), 924(a)(2). Following Leeson's arraignment, he was remanded to custody to await his trial. Leeson then filed a notice of insanity defense and moved for a psychiatric examination. Leeson's motion for a psychiatric examination was granted by a United States Magistrate Judge and, as a consequence, Leeson was transported to the Metropolitan Correctional Center (MCC Chicago), Federal Bureau of Prisons, Chicago, Illinois, for psychiatric examination.

Once at MCC Chicago, Dr. Jason Dana (Dr. Dana), holder of a doctorate in clinical psychology, examined and evaluated Leeson's mental health. On April 6, 2004, Dr. Dana prepared a forensic psychological report detailing his findings and diagnosis regarding Leeson. With regard to Leeson's sanity at the time of the instant offense, Dr. Dana's report opined: "there is no indication that he was suffering from any form of cognitive impairment or mental illness impacting his ability to understand the nature and quality, or wrongfulness of his actions at the time of the instant offense." (J.A. 867). Rather, Dr. Dana's report diagnosed Leeson as being a malingerer and of having opiate dependence by history. At trial, Dr. Dana testified that "malingering is specifically the reporting of symptoms of mental illness for the purposes of obtaining a secondary gain."

Leeson's trial commenced on September 16, 2004, wherein he continued to assert an insanity defense. Leeson called Dr. Jonathan Himmelhoch (Dr. Himmelhoch), a psychiatrist, to render an expert opinion in support of his insanity defense. The district court ruled that Dr. Himmelhoch was qualified to render such an expert opinion. At trial, Dr. Himmelhoch testified that he diagnosed Leeson with Post Traumatic Stress Disorder, partial lobe epilepsy, depression, and migraine headaches. He then testified that, on the day of Leeson's charged offense, August 6, 2003, these illnesses worked together to make Leeson severely mentally ill such that Leeson did not understand the nature and quality or the wrongfulness of his conduct.

The government called Dr. Dana in rebuttal. The district court ruled that Dr. Dana was qualified to render an expert opinion regarding the presence or absence of severe mental illness or defect in connection with Leeson's insanity defense. Consistent with his expert witness report, Dr. Dana testified at trial that, in his opinion, Leeson was not suffering from any form of cognitive impairment or mental illness which impacted his ability to understand the nature and quality of or the wrongfulness of his actions on August 6, 2003. Also consistent with his expert witness report, Dr. Dana testified that his diagnostic workup of Leeson indicated malingering and opiate dependence. At issue on appeal is the following portion of Dr. Dana's direct testimony at trial in rebuttal to Leeson's offered testimony of Dr. Himmelhoch:

Q: Now regarding your — your diagnosis of malingering, what specific action or criteria did you utilize in reaching that conclusion?

A: Going through the different information that he provided to me, cross-referencing it with records and other information that was available to me in order to identify the validity of the claims, the assessment of malingering, it was done with the services that we mentioned before and behavioral observations, providing him with opportunities to speak to other members of the psychology services department. Generally the more times a person is asked to explain their problems and concerns, the more opportunity they have to be inconsistent, so it gets into all of those things.

Q: And you said, of course, he was observed in the — in the department?

A: Yes.

Q: And so you relied upon information from other members, of course?

A: Not only other members of the department but information regarding observed behaviors from people who were not in our department as well.

Q: Give us some examples of information that you utilized that came from people not within the department but still up there at the BOP Institution in Chicago.

A: The Correctional Officers that are responsible for supervising the units, often times when they see information that is not in the realm of mainstream, not what is usually identified, they will leave messages for us, contact us of course personally about information.

Q: What about other inmates, do you ever receive information from other inmates or people incarcerated at the BOP?

A: Yeah. Occasionally. Though you have to be careful about that information but in this case there were two separate inmates during the time that Mr. Leeson was there that approached the other forensic psychologist. They did not talk to me directly.

Q: MR. WALKER [(counsel for Leeson)]: Your Honor, I object to this. I think this is inappropriate and it is not something that is considered a basis for his medical or psychological evaluation and it's hearsay.

A: THE COURT: Overruled.

Q: MR. WALKER: I'd like to cross-examine those individuals.

A: THE COURT: I said overruled.

A: It is actually a standard in order to gather information about a person from sources and information. Again, you have to weigh the validity of all circumstances. In a situation where this was the only piece of information that I had, [I] would not generally rely on it. In situations where it's one of several pieces of information, it then becomes more reliable.

Q: And, of course, you're speaking of the information provided by the inmates at the institution?

A: Yes.

Q: And — and what information did they provide? You said there were two separate ones.

A: Yeah. They — they essentially indicated that Mr. Leeson had approached them to recruit them in assisting him in looking crazy while he was on the unit.

Q: I — I'm sorry?

A: And, that — that — that he had approached them and asked them to assist him in looking crazy on the unit. And one-one of the inmates said that he was asked by Mr. Leeson to go to the officer and tell him that an inmate in the back was acting crazy.

On appeal, Leeson contends the district court abused its discretion in allowing Dr. Dana to testify regarding the statements of Leeson's fellow inmates at MCC Chicago.

On September 22, 2004, the jury rejected Leeson's insanity defense and convicted him on the single count of being a felon in possession of a firearm.

* * *

III.

Leeson's second assignment of error pertains to Dr. Dana's testimony to the effect that, in forming his expert opinion that Leeson did not suffer from a severe mental illness which prevented him from appreciating the nature and quality or the wrongfulness of possessing a firearm as a convicted felon on August 6, 2003, he (Dr. Dana) relied, *inter alia,* upon statements by two different prison inmates that Leeson "had approached them to recruit them in assisting him in looking crazy while he was on the unit," and upon a statement by one of those inmates that "he was asked by Mr. Leeson to go to the officer and tell him that an inmate in the back was acting crazy." (J.A. 547). According to Leeson, the district court abused its discretion in admitting this testimony because it was hearsay, *see* Fed. R. Evid. 801, which did not otherwise qualify for admission under Federal Rule of Evidence 703 (Rule 703).

* * *

Leeson argues that the challenged testimony did not qualify for admission under Rule 703 for three reasons. First, he claims that Dr. Dana did not sufficiently establish that inmates in a federal mental health facility, in general, are reasonably relied upon by experts in his field. Second, he claims that Dr. Dana was not in a position to determine whether the two fellow inmates were trustworthy sources of information, and therefore, Dr. Dana could not have reasonably relied upon their statements. Finally, he claims the district court failed to make a finding that the probative value of the inmates' statements substantially outweighed their prejudicial effect.

* * * [W]e hold the challenged testimony otherwise qualifies for admission under Rule 703. First, contrary to Leeson's position, during Dr. Dana's testimony, Dr. Dana sufficiently established that inmates in a federal mental health facility, in general, are reasonably relied upon by experts in his field. Critically, we read the following portion of Dr. Dana's trial testimony to state that the inmates' statements were of a type reasonably, but admittedly cautiously, relied upon by experts in the mental health field in forming opinions regarding whether a particular inmate is a malingerer:

Q: And so you relied upon information from other members, of course?

A: Not only other members of the department but information regarding observed behaviors from people who were not in our department as well.

Q: What about other inmates, do you ever receive information from other inmates or people incarcerated at the BOP?

A: Yeah. Occasionally. Though you have to be careful about that information but in this case there were two separate inmates during the time that Mr. Leeson was there that approached the other forensic psychologist. They did not talk to me directly.

A: It is actually a standard in order to gather information about a person from sources and information. Again, you have to weigh the validity of all circumstances. In a situation where this was the only piece of information that I had, [I] would not generally rely on it * * *

Q: And, of course, you're speaking of the information provided by the inmates at the institution?

A: Yes.

"(Emphasis added)." Get emphasis from text of case 453 F.3d 631. As for Leeson's argument that Dr. Dana was not in a position to determine whether the two fellow inmates were trustworthy sources of information, and therefore Dr. Dana could not have reasonably relied upon their statements in forming his expert opinion, Leeson's argument is a nonstarter given that Leeson had full opportunity at trial to cross-examine Dr. Dana on this point and to make such an argument to the jury in closing argument. Finally, on the issue of whether the district court made a determination that the probative value of the inmates' out-of-court statements substantially outweighed their prejudicial effect, we conclude from our reading of the trial transcript that the district court implicitly made such a finding.

We also conclude the district court properly determined that the probative value of the inmates' out-of-court statements outweighed their prejudicial effect. The information that Dr. Dana relied upon in formulating his expert opinion was highly and directly relevant to the jury's task of evaluating that opinion. The district court did not abuse its discretion in finding that such probative value substantially outweighed any prejudicial effect of the statements, especially given that Leeson had the opportunity to cross-examine Dr. Dana regarding the reasonableness of his reliance on the statements and the opportunity during closing argument to downgrade the credibility of such out-of-court statements in the eyes of the jury.

In conclusion, we uphold the district court's admission of Dr. Dana's testimony regarding the challenged out-of-court statements by two of Leeson's fellow inmates at MCC Chicago.

* * *

AFFIRMED.

NOTES

1. When inadmissible evidence is disclosed by the expert, should a limiting instruction be given to the jury?

In *Engebetsen v. Fairchild Aircraft Corp.*, 21 F.3d 721 (6th Cir. 1994), the Court held that a limiting instruction should be given, upon request, that the inadmissible evidence is not being received for its truth. The Committee Note to the 2000 amendment to Rule 703 states that if inadmissible information is disclosed to the jury for the purposes of explaining the basis of the expert's opinion, then the court should instruct the jury that it is not to use the information as substantive evidence.

2. How are facts or data made known to an expert at trial?

There are two methods. The witness may listen to the testimony, *United States v. Crabtree*, 979 F.2d 1261 (7th Cir. 1992), or a hypothetical question may be posed based on all relevant facts admitted in evidence, *Ramey v. Shalala*, 26 F.3d 58 (8th Cir. 1994).

3. Does *Daubert*, which construed Rule 702, have any effect on the type of information upon which an expert can rely under Rule 703?

See Saltzburg, Martin, and Capra, *Federal Rules of Evidence Manual* (9th ed. 2006):

> The reasonable reliance requirement of Rule 703 is a relatively narrow inquiry — much narrower, for example, than is the inquiry into whether the expert's opinion is helpful and reliable under Rule 702. While an opinion unreasonably based on inadmissible information is also unhelpful, we believe that it avoids confusion to consider the two Rules separately. Rule 703 regulates the expert's use of inadmissible information, while Rule 702 regulates the methodology, reliability, adequacy of basis, and helpfulness of the opinion, as well as the qualification of the expert witness. In our view, the proper delineation between the two Rules was set forth in *DeLuca v. Merrell Dow Pharmaceuticals, Inc.*, 911 F.2d 941 (3d Cir. 1990). *DeLuca* was a Bendectin case in which the plaintiff proffered expert testimony that Bendectin caused limb reduction in fetuses. The Trial Judge rejected the proffered testimony of the plaintiff's expert on the ground that the expert's recalculation of epidemiological studies was not accepted as reliable by experts in the field. The Court relied on Rule 703. But the Third Circuit reversed and remanded, noting that Rule 703 has a

narrow function; it seeks to delimit the type of information that an expert can rely upon. The Court concluded that Rule 703 would be satisfied if the epidemiological studies used as a basis for the expert's opinions were the same as those used by all other experts in the field, including the defendant's experts. The defendant's objection that the expert's reanalysis of those studies was unreliable could not be considered under Rule 703:

> Rule 703 is satisfied once there is a showing that an expert's testimony is based on the type of data a reasonable expert in the field would use. * * * It does not address the reliability or general acceptance of an expert's methodology. When a statistician refers to a study as not statistically significant, he is not making a statement about the reliability of the data used, rather he is making a statement about the propriety of drawing a particular inference from that data.

This did not necessarily mean that the plaintiff's expert's reanalysis of epidemiological data was admissible. The *DeLuca* Court noted that if an expert's methodology is itself unreliable, the testimony can be excluded under Rule 702, even if the basis of the expert's opinion satisfied the reasonable reliance standard of Rule 703. The Court explained that the helpfulness standard of Rule 702 prevents an expert from using accepted data in an unreliable manner. The distinction between Rule 703, which regulates the expert's use of inadmissible information, and Rule 702, which more broadly regulates the helpfulness, adequacy of basis, and reliability of the expert opinion, was also made by the Supreme Court in *Daubert v. Merrell Dow Pharmaceuticals, Inc.*, 509 U.S. 579 (1993). The Court held that the reliability of scientific expert testimony was governed by a flexible test under Rule 702. The Court further stated that a judge assessing a proffer of expert scientific testimony under Rule 702 should also be mindful of other applicable rules. Rule 703 provides that expert opinions based on otherwise inadmissible hearsay are to be admitted only if the facts or data are of a type reasonably relied upon by experts in the particular field in forming opinions or inferences upon the subject.

The distinction between Rule 703's regulation of inadmissible information and Rule 702's regulation of adequacy of basis and reliability is further clarified in the 2000 amendment to Rule 702. The amendment specifically states that under Rule 702, the Trial Court must find that the expert is relying on "sufficient facts or data." Thus, the question of adequacy of basis — what lawyers and Courts call the "foundation requirement" — is now specifically located in Rule 702. Rule 703 is left to regulate the *quality* of information relied upon by the expert.

The Advisory Committee Note to Rule 702 drives this point home. It states as follows:

> There has been some confusion over the relationship between Rules 702 and 703. The amendment makes clear that the sufficiency of the basis of an expert's testimony is to be decided under Rule 702.

Rule 702 sets forth the overarching requirement of reliability, and an analysis of the sufficiency of the expert's basis cannot be divorced from the ultimate reliability of the expert's opinion. In contrast, the "reasonable reliance" requirement of Rule 703 is a relatively narrow inquiry. When an expert relies on inadmissible information, Rule 703 requires the trial court to determine whether that information is of a type reasonably relied on by other experts in the field. If so, the expert can rely on the information in reaching an opinion. However, the question whether the expert is relying on a *sufficient* basis of information — whether admissible information or not — is governed by the requirements of Rule 702.

[6] Ultimate Issue

[a] Federal Rule of Evidence 704

Rule 704. Opinion on Ultimate Issue

(a) Except as provided in subdivision (b), testimony in the form of an opinion or inference otherwise admissible is not objectionable because it embraces an ultimate issue to be decided by the trier of fact.

(b) No expert witness testifying with respect to the mental state or condition of a defendant in a criminal case may state an opinion or inference as to whether the defendant did or did not have the mental state or condition constituting an element of the crime charged or of a defense thereto. Such ultimate issues are matters for the trier of fact alone.

[b] Use of Terminology with Both Legal and Colloquial Connotations

UNITED STATES v. PERKINS
470 F.3d 150 (4th Cir. 2006)

Williams, Circuit Judge:

[The earlier part of the opinion is set forth supra at page 456. Recall that the defendant is a police officer charged with using excessive force. The trial judge permitted Officer House to give an opinion as to whether there was a legitimate law enforcement reason for the defendant's use of force, and Inspector Burnett to testify that he saw no legitimate reason for the defendant to kick the victim.]

III.

Perkins also argues that the district court erred in admitting both expert and non-expert testimony regarding the reasonableness of Perkins's use of force because such testimony impermissibly stated a legal conclusion. During

House's testimony, Perkins objected on the ground that the testimony went to the "ultimate issue" of the reasonableness of Perkins's use of force. Likewise, during Inspector Burnett's testimony, Perkins objected to the Government's question asking whether Burnett saw any "legitimate" reason for Perkins's kicks. Therefore, we review the admission of the challenged portions of House's and Burnett's testimony for abuse of discretion. We review the admission of all other opinion testimony about the reasonableness of Perkins's kicks for plain error.

Federal Rule of Evidence 704(a) provides that, with exceptions not relevant here, "testimony in the form of an opinion or inference otherwise admissible is not objectionable because it embraces an ultimate issue to be decided by the trier of fact." Although this rule officially abolished the so-called "ultimate issue" rule, *see* Fed. R. Evid. 704 advisory committee's notes, it did not lower the bar "so as to admit all opinions." *Id.* Testimony on ultimate issues still "must be otherwise admissible under the Rules of Evidence." *Weinstein's Federal Evidence* § 704.03[1] (2d ed. 2002). This means that the testimony must be helpful to the trier of fact, in accordance with Rules 701 and 702, and must not waste time, in accordance with Rule 403. "These provisions afford ample assurances against the admission of opinions which would merely tell the jury what result to reach, somewhat in the manner of the oath-helpers of an earlier day." *United States v. Barile*, 286 F.3d 749, 759-60 (4th Cir. 2002)(quoting Fed. R. Evid. 704 advisory committee's notes). * * * Thus, the district court's task "is to distinguish [helpful] opinion testimony that embraces an ultimate fact from [unhelpful] opinion testimony that states a legal conclusion," a task that we have acknowledged "is not an easy one." *Barile*, 286 F.3d at 760.

We have stated that "[t]he best way to determine whether opinion testimony [is unhelpful because it merely states] legal conclusions, 'is to determine whether the terms used by the witness have a separate, distinct and specialized meaning in the law different from that present in the vernacular.'" *Id.* (quoting *Torres v. County of Oakland*, 758 F.2d 147, 150 (6th Cir. 1985)). The district court should first consider whether the question tracks the language of the legal principle at issue or of the applicable statute; then, the court should consider whether any terms employed have a specialized legal meaning. *Barile*, 286 F.3d at 760.

To state the general rule, however, "is not to decide the far more complicated and measured question of when there is a transgression of the rule." *Nieves-Villanueva v. Soto-Rivera*, 133 F.3d 92, 99 (1st Cir. 1997). The rule makes ultra-fine distinctions, with admissibility often turning on word choice: the question "Did T have capacity to make a will?" impermissibly asks for a legal conclusion, while the question "Did T have sufficient mental capacity to know the nature and extent of his property?" does not. Fed. R. Evid. 704 advisory committee's notes.

On the one hand, conclusory testimony that a company engaged in "discrimination," that a landlord was "negligent," or that an investment house engaged in a "fraudulent and manipulative scheme" involves the use of terms with considerable legal baggage; such testimony nearly always invades the province of the jury. *See, e.g., Andrews v. Metro N. Commuter R.R. Co.*, 882 F.2d 705,

709-10 (2d Cir. 1989)(testimony that defendant was "negligent" stated a legal conclusion); *United States v. Scop*, 846 F.2d 135, 140 (2d Cir. 1988)(testimony that defendants had engaged in a "fraudulent and manipulative scheme" stated a legal conclusion); *Torres*, 758 F.2d at 151 (testimony that county engaged in "discrimination" violated Rule 704). On the other hand, the legal meaning of some terms is not so distinctive from the colloquial meaning, if a distinction exists at all, making it difficult to gauge the helpfulness, and thus admissibility, of the testimony under Rule 704. *See, e.g., United States v. Sheffey*, 57 F.3d 1419, 1426 (6th Cir. 1996)(testimony that the defendant had driven "recklessly, in extreme disregard for human life," did not state a legal conclusion because the terms "recklessly" and "extreme disregard for human life" do not have a legal meaning distinct from everyday usage).

At Perkins's trial, the Government asked House whether, based on his assessment of the situation, he saw "any law enforcement reason for [Perkins's] kicks[.]" Similarly, the Government asked Burnett whether there was "any legitimate reason for [Perkins to kick] Mr. Koonce[.]" Under 18 U.S.C.A. § 242, courts employ an "objective reasonableness" standard to assess an officer's use of force. *See [United States v.] Mohr*, 318 F.3d 613, 623 (4th Cir. 2003). This standard requires the jury to determine "whether a reasonable officer in the same circumstances would have concluded that a threat existed justifying the particular use of force." *Elliott v. Leavitt*, 99 F.3d 640, 642 (4th Cir. 1996). Clearly, then, the word "reasonable" in the § 242 context has a specific legal meaning, but the distinction between its legal and common meaning is not as clear as with other more technical terms like "negligence" or "fraud," i.e., terms that had their common vernacular stem from their legalistic roots.

In *Kopf* [*v. Skyrm,* 993 F.2d 374, 377 (4th Cir. 1993)], a § 1983 excessive force case involving the use of slapjacks and a police dog, we stated that the facts of every case should determine whether testimony would be helpful to the jury and suggested that "[w]here force is reduced to its most primitive form — the bare hands — expert testimony might not be helpful." *Kopf*, 993 F.2d at 378. We declined to decide whether the experts in that case could have given their opinion on the "ultimate issue" of whether the force used was "reasonable"; indeed, we acknowledged that such testimony might have been inadmissible. *Id.* n.3.

Later in *Mohr*, a § 242 case also involving a police dog, we held that an expert's rebuttal testimony that an officer "violated 'prevailing police practices nationwide in 1995,'" that the officer's use of the dog was "inappropriate," and that there was "no reason" for the officer's failure to give a canine warning was admissible under Rule 704(a). *Mohr*, 318 F.3d at 624. We attached particular importance to the fact that the testimony was delivered during rebuttal, after the defendant's experts had testified to the reasonableness of the defendant's use of the police dog. *Id.*

Mohr suggests that the challenged testimony in this case did not transgress Rule 704(a). Like in *Mohr*, the officers here testified that they saw "no reason" for Perkins's use of force. Taking helpfulness to the jury as our guiding principle, we conclude that the district court did not err in admitting the challenged portions of Officer House's and Inspector Burnett's testimony.

While a very close question, we conclude that the Government's questions were phrased in such a manner so as to avoid the baseline legal conclusion of reasonableness. The officers' responses that they personally saw no reason for Perkins's kicks provided the jury with concrete examples against which to consider the more abstract question of whether an "objectively reasonable officer" would have employed the same force. The Government's questions were not couched in terms of objective reasonableness; instead, they honed in on Officer House's and Inspector Burnett's *personal* assessments of Perkins's use of force. We recognize that this distinction is a fine one. When the common and legal meanings of a term are not easily unfurled from each other, however, as is certainly the case with "reasonable," it is difficult for us to conclude that testimony was unhelpful to the jury unless the testimony actually framed the term in its traditional legal context. In this case, then, Rule 704 justifies differentiating between the officers' testimony that they saw no "law enforcement" or "legitimate" reason for Perkins's kicks and testimony that Perkins's actions were "objectively unreasonable." To be sure, this distinction must be measured in inches, not feet. Nevertheless, we cannot hold that the officers' testimony was necessarily unhelpful, nor can we say that it merely told the jury what verdict to reach or "supplant[ed] [the] jury's independent exercise of common sense." *Kopf*, 993 F.2d at 377.

* * *

NOTE

When has an expert been allowed to give an opinion on an ultimate issue?

In *Werth v. Makita Electric Works, Ltd.*, 950 F.2d 643 (10th Cir. 1991), the court found no error when an expert was permitted to testify that the defendant's product was unreasonably dangerous under the consumer expectations test. In *Hanson v. Waller*, 888 F.2d 806 (11th Cir. 1989), an expert was allowed to testify whether behavior of the parties contributed to the automobile-pedestrian accident. For a different view, *see Shahid v. City of Detroit*, 889 F.2d 1543 (6th Cir. 1989), where the court held that an expert could not give an opinion that the defendant police officers had been negligent. *See also Peterson v. City of Plymouth*, 60 F.3d 469 (8th Cir. 1995), where the court reversed and remanded a judgment for police officers in an action brought by the plaintiff arising from an arrest allegedly without probable cause. At trial, the defendants were permitted to call an expert in police practices, who testified that the officers' conduct comported with the "standards under the Fourth Amendment." The court held that admission of this testimony was an abuse of discretion, because it was simply a legal conclusion and as such it could not assist the jury in its factfinding role.

[c] Mental State of a Criminal Defendant

UNITED STATES v. THIGPEN

4 F.3d 1573 (11th Cir. 1993)

BIRCH, CIRCUIT JUDGE:

* * *

I. *Background*

* * *

B. *Thigpen*

William James Thigpen, a felon, illegally obtained three semi-automatic pistols. At times prior to trial, he resided in an adult congregate living facility for the mentally disturbed and at another medical facility. He complained of voices informing him that others were trying to kill him. Thigpen was charged with making false statements concerning his criminal background when purchasing the pistols and with illegally possessing those weapons after a felony conviction. His sole defense was insanity. At trial, two psychiatrists testified that Thigpen suffered from a schizophrenic disorder. The jury also heard testimony that Thigpen had been diagnosed by no less than eleven psychiatrists as schizophrenic. During the prosecutor's cross-examination of the psychiatric expert called by the defense, the following transpired:

> Q: [Mr. Devereaux, Assistant United States Attorney] If Mr. Thigpen stays on his medications, he's okay to go out in the world amongst society; correct? Is that your opinion?
>
> A: He's not okay. He's stable and can function.
>
> Q: Well, he's released from the hospital, he's on society?

Defense counsel did not object following this exchange. The prosecutor also asked a series of questions aimed at eliciting an opinion as to whether a person suffering from schizophrenia would necessarily be unable to appreciate the nature of wrongfulness of his actions. The court overruled Thigpen's objections to these questions. The prosecutor was permitted to ask the government's expert a similar question on direct examination, again over Thigpen's objection.

* * *

III. *Expert Testimony*

Thigpen contends that, in violation of Federal Rule of Evidence 704(b), the district court allowed the government to elicit expert testimony as to his ability to appreciate the nature or wrongfulness of his actions. * * * At trial, Thigpen sought to prove as an affirmative defense that "at the time of the commission of the acts constituting the offense, the defendant, as a result of severe mental disease or defect, was unable to appreciate the nature and quality or the wrongfulness of his acts." 18 U.S.C. § 17. The psychiatric experts offered by the government and the defense both testified that Thigpen suffered from schizophrenia. When cross-examining the defense's expert, the prosecutor asked a series of questions to elicit an opinion as to whether such a condition by necessity implies that a person would be unable to appreciate the nature and quality of his acts. The prosecutor asked a similar question of its psychiatric expert on direct examination. No question by the prosecutor asked the witness to opine whether Thigpen was able to appreciate his actions.

Expert testimony concerning the nature of a defendant's mental disease or defect, including its typical effect on a person's mental state is admissible. *United States v. Davis*, 835 F.2d 274, 276 (11th Cir. 1988). In *Davis*, the defendant, who attempted to establish an insanity defense based on a multiple personality disorder, objected to the testimony of a government expert that such a disorder does not in itself indicate that a person does not understand what he is doing. We upheld the admission of this testimony since it "did not include an opinion as to *Davis'* capacity to conform his conduct to the law at the time of the robbery." Similarly, the testimony elicited by the government in Thigpen's case concerned the general effect of a schizophrenic disorder on a person's ability to appreciate the nature or wrongfulness of his actions.

In *United States v. Manley*, 893 F.2d 1221, 1224 (11th Cir. 1990) (*per curiam*), we upheld the exclusion of opinion testimony by a defense expert where counsel inquired as to the mental capacity of a hypothetical person with each of the pertinent characteristics of the defendant. While "a thinly veiled hypothetical" may not be used to circumvent Rule 704(b), the rule does not bar "an explanation of the disease and its typical effect on a person's mental state." *Manley*, 893 F.2d at 1224. The government's questions in Thigpen's case sought the latter and were therefore allowed without error.

* * *

AFFIRMED

NOTES

1. In a criminal case, what kind of expert testimony concerning the defendant's mental state will be admissible?

In *United States v. Williams*, 980 F.2d 1463 (D.C. Cir. 1992), the defendant was charged with drug distribution. The prosecution's expert testified that the more than 100 zip-lock bags containing small amounts of drugs, which were found in a police raid on a premises, "were meant to be distributed at street level." The Court held that admitting the opinion did not violate Rule 704(b)'s prohibition of testimony on the defendant's mental state. Rather, this testimony addressed "the intentions of a hypothetical individual, not Williams in particular."

United States v. Brown, 32 F.3d 236 (7th Cir. 1994), involved a prosecution for bank robbery, in which the defendant interposed a defense of insanity. The government's psychiatric expert testified that the defendant suffered from, among other things, a major depressive disorder. The trial court permitted the prosecution to ask both the prosecution and defense psychiatric experts whether such a major depressive disorder indicates "that a person is unable to understand the wrongfulness of his acts?" The experts answered in the negative. The court of appeals held that the defendant's objection under Rule 704(b) was properly rejected. It reasoned that the expert never testified "as to Brown's peculiar mental state; he merely described Brown's mental disorder and that such an affliction does not preclude one from appreciating the nature or quality of his acts." While finding that the rule was not violated, the court criticized the rule as denying juries "the specialized knowledge of experts in just the type of complex case in which it is most useful."

2. Does Rule 704(b) impose any limitations on evidence proffered by the defense?

Defense experts are subject to Rule 704(b). For example, in *United States v. Bennett,* 161 F.3d 171 (3d Cir. 1998), the defendant was charged with fraud, check-kiting, money-laundering, and filing false statements and tax returns. In a pretrial ruling, the court precluded the defendant's psychiatric expert from testifying that the defendant's mental disorders made it "unlikely that he could form the intent to defraud" and "affected his ability to knowingly and wilfully submit false statements to the I.R.S." This ruling was upheld by the Court of Appeals, even though the end result was that the jury was left with general testimony about the defendant's mental disorders without a sufficient explanation of how these disorders might have affected his culpability for the charged crimes. Rule 704(b) has also been invoked to preclude defendants from introducing exculpatory polygraph evidence, on the ground that the expert's opinion that the defendant was truthful constitutes testimony as to the defendant's mental state. *United States v. Morales*, 108 F.3d 1031 (9th Cir. 1997). Rule 704(b) has further been applied to preclude testimony even as to the defendant's physiological responses to a polygraph; courts have found "no principled distinction" between evaluations of physiological reactions and an opinion that the defendant was telling the truth. *United States v. Campos*, 217 F.3d 707 (9th Cir. 2000).

PROBLEM 9-1

Plaintiff, Farmer Brown, sued Chemical Co., Inc. for the loss of his entire corn crop, alleging that the defendant's herbicide killed the crop. Plaintiff calls the farmer next door to the stand to testify in part that defendant's herbicide caused the crop failure.

Plaintiff: State your name.

Witness: Good Old Boy.

Plaintiff: Do you know Farmer Brown?

Witness: Yes, I've known him for thirty years. He lives on the farm next to mine.

Plaintiff: Are you a crop farmer?

Witness: Yes, I've been a farmer for thirty years.
Plaintiff: During that time have you ever used herbicides?
Witness: Yes, a total of eighteen different kinds.
Plaintiff: Have any of them destroyed an entire crop?
Witness: No. I've had varying results. Some work good, some not so good. But I've never had one that done what happened to Farmer Brown.
Plaintiff: Do you test herbicides?
Witness: Yes, I always plant test rows to compare the effect of each kind of herbicide.
Plaintiff: Do you keep records of the outcome of your tests?
Witness: Yes, since day one.
Plaintiff: Did you go over and look at Farmer Brown's destroyed crops?
Witness: You bet.
Plaintiff: Did you plant corn the year that Farmer Brown's crop was destroyed?
Witness: Yep, right next to Farmer Brown's crop.
Plaintiff: Is there any difference between your land and Farmer Brown's land?
Witness: Nope. Same soil, same drainage, same rain.
Plaintiff: Was your crop successful?
Witness: Best ever.
Plaintiff: Did you do anything different than Farmer Brown other than using a different herbicide?
Witness: Nope.
Plaintiff: Do you have an opinion as to what caused Farmer Brown's crop failure?
Witness: Yep.
Plaintiff: What is your opinion?
Defendant: (1) Objection __________.
Plaintiff: (2) __________.
The court: (3) __________.

PROBLEM 9-2

On August 12, 2000, Paula Perry and her husband went to the brand new mall store "D-Mart" to purchase mints. While shopping, Perry slipped and fell on a waxy substance that had built up on the floor. Perry reported her fall to customer service, and a D-Mart employee placed her in a wheelchair. Perry told D-Mart representatives that she had injured her back and right leg and was in excruciating pain. D-Mart offered her the opportunity to visit a physician of her choice at its expense, but informed her that it would pay for only one visit.

Perry declined the offer and visited her own doctor, Dr. Arvy B. Dixon. Dixon diagnosed her as suffering from a lumbar sprain. Because Perry complained of low back pain and cramps in her right leg, Dixon prescribed painkillers for her. Perry, however, never used the prescription. Dixon stated that Perry's back and leg injuries would interfere with her flexibility and cause her pain, and that her injury was "an ongoing thing. It may be forever."

Perry sought a second opinion from an orthopedist, Dr. Rip Henry. During her initial visit, four days after the slip and fall, Henry also diagnosed Perry with a low back sprain. He found limitation in Perry's range of motion, as well as tenderness and irritation in her right leg and back "in the right LV-3 which is lumbar third to LV-1 which is the paraspinal along the spine on the right side." He considered both symptoms to be indicative of nerve root irritation arising out of an injury to muscles, ligaments, and the outer portion of the disc area in Perry's back. Henry prescribed physical therapy, x-rays, and an anti-inflammatory drug, and recommended that Perry limit her physical activity. The x-rays revealed that she had "minimal spurring [i.e., the accretion of calcium deposits in] the anterior portion of the vertebral bodies of the lower back." In Henry's opinion, this preexisting condition made her more susceptible to suffering a low-back sprain when she slipped and fell.

During a second visit, Henry diagnosed Perry with resolving post-traumatic radiculopathy. Radiculopathy is often caused by a herniated intervertebral disc. Henry noted that Perry suffered pain and nerve irritation, and complained of a limited range of motion in her back and right leg. He described these injuries as "chronic," meaning that they could "exist off and on for an indefinite period," possibly for the rest of Perry's life. The two visits with Henry took place over a span of seven months. During this time and in the months thereafter, Perry also saw a Dr. Ali once a month; Ali had been treating her for an unrelated diabetes condition. Perry never made any mention of her back and leg pain to Dr. Ali, a fact that is reflected in his notes.

Perry brought a lawsuit in federal district court, which had diversity jurisdiction over D-Mart. Perry claimed that the injuries she received as a result of the fall profoundly impacted her life. At the time of the accident, Perry was fifty-one years old and self-employed as a salesperson for Mary Kay Cosmetics. Perry contended that she suffered extreme and uninterrupted physical pain, as well as depression that often caused her to cry until her eyes became swollen. She reasoned that this depression arose in large part from the fact that her debilitating injuries affected other aspects of her life.

Seventeen months after the slip and fall, Perry visited Dr. Sylvia Payne, a specialist in physical medicine and rehabilitation, so that Payne might give an opinion as to Perry's medical condition in relation to the fall for purposes of this litigation. Payne found that Perry suffered from lumbar myositis (inflammation of the lower back muscles, characterized by pain, tenderness, and sometimes spasms in the affected area) and from two "trigger points" in the gluteus maximus muscle. Trigger points, according to Payne, are "very tiny point[s] in the muscle believed to be part of a muscle spindle that is firing constantly and causing pain at the sight [sic] and causing pain in another area not anatomically related." Payne testified that the trigger points were responsible for the pain Perry felt radiating down her right leg to her knee. Payne also concluded that Perry's "pain was severe and it interfered with several of her activities," that Perry would be in pain for the rest of her life because of her fall, and that the injuries resulting from the fall were permanently disabling. Dr. Perry also noted that Perry suffered from poorly controlled diabetes that could cut her life span — and perhaps her working life — short.

Perry was also referred to Dr. Chester Davis, a psychologist and purported expert in vocational rehabilitation. A vocational rehabilitationist assesses the extent of an individual's disability, evaluates how the disability affects the individual's employment opportunities, and assists the individual's re-entry into the labor market. Davis examined Perry for the purposes of this litigation, but also treated her for her chronic pain. As part of his examination, he diagnosed Perry's psychological condition and evaluated her lost earning capacity in light of her physical and psychological disabilities. Davis concluded that Perry suffered from depression, pain disorder, and adjustment disorder with anxiety, and opined that these symptoms were caused by her slip and fall and the physical injuries that arose therefrom. Davis also concluded that Perry's psychological condition was improving and was not permanent. Based on his assessment of Perry's psychological condition, the extent of her physical injuries, relevant employment factors, and the results of diagnostic tests he had performed, Davis opined that Perry was between 50 and 60 percent vocationally disabled and that this disability was permanent.

Perry indicated that she planned to call all of these medical experts except Dr. Ali plus an economist to testify.

D-Mart has moved in advance of trial to exclude Dr. Davis under Rule 702. D-Mart's objection is that Dr. Davis is not qualified to give an opinion. The plaintiff relies upon these facts to support Davi's qualifications:

(1) Davis received general training in "assessing" individuals while earning his Ph.D. in psychology.

(2) Davis has twenty years previous experience in helping drug addicts reenter the workforce.

(3) Davis's experience in the last two years has been primarily dealing with the State's Division of Workers' Compensation, which he had advised regarding the ability of approximately fifty to sixty-five disabled employees to return to their previous jobs. This experience consisted primarily of diagnosing whether patients were so disabled that they could not return to a particular job; this experience did not include assessing what range of jobs those injured individuals were capable of performing.

(4) He has previously testified as an expert witness making lost earning capacity assessments.

(5) He attended two seminars regarding vocational rehabilitation, claims familiarity with the literature in the area.

(6) He is a member in two vocational rehabilitation organizations, both of which place no restrictions on membership.

(7) When Davis was in school, a degree in vocational rehabilitation therapy was not available, but he received similar training nonetheless.

(8) Davis maintains that there is no difference between a psychologist and a vocational rehabilitationist.

D-Mart claims that these are insufficient qualifications and adds three points:

(1) Davis's experience as a counselor for drug addicts did not include performing assessments of which jobs the recovered addicts would be able to perform.

(2) Davis did not seek or obtain advanced degrees after graduation.

(3) D-Mart's vocational rehabilitation therapist testified that despite a common psychological diagnostic component in both jobs, the vocational rehabilitationist's expertise entails a distinct speciality: the capacity to "translate" psychological *and* physical impairments into the "ability to work, earn income, [and] get a job * * * ."

The Court's ruling:

D-Mart has also challenged Davis' opinion under *Daubert*. In his deposition, Davis described his method for arriving at the 50 to 60 percent disability opinion he rendered. D-Mart relies upon the following testimony, summary of testimony and argument to make the case that Davis' opinion fails to satisfy *Daubert*:

> My vocational assessment consisted of testing Mrs. Elcock for intelligence level achievement, that is school level, getting a work history on her and then doing an analysis of the *Dictionary of Occupational Titles* aptitude testing on her, and then doing a search of the *Dictionary of Occupational Titles*.
>
> [In addition to a clinical interview,] I performed the [Wechsler] Adult Intelligence Scale revised and she had an IQ of 98 which is in the normal or average range. And I also performed the wide range achievement test revised which indicated that she had a reading level of above 12th grade level, spelling level of beginning 10th grade, and an arithmetic level of ending 6th grade.
>
> Then I performed the aptitude testing on her, and I think we need to, I need to explain the aptitude test. Each job in the United States is categorized in this *Dictionary of Occupational Titles* put out by the U.S. Department of Labor and the characteristics of those jobs. Those jobs are listed, characterized and listed for each job, and every job has a set of aptitudes that tells you what is needed or what are needed in order to be able to do those jobs. And there are tests that you can give to determine what a person's aptitude are for doing a particular job.

Davis further testified that he also assessed which jobs were available in the local job market by reviewing the job listings his office receives weekly from the State's labor department, and by searching a database his office creates of jobs listed in the local newspapers within the prior two months. He then stated that he "took into consideration Perry's physical injuries and * * * her psychological impairments," and, in sum, concluded that he "rated

Perry's capacity after [he] had done all the analysis as somewhere between 50 and 60 percent."

When asked by Perry's counsel to describe his methodology, Davis testified as follows:

> You take into comparison her education, her intelligence, her aptitude, her previous work experience and her medical injuries, what she says, she would like to do, what her desires are as a person, her temperaments, whether she likes working by herself or she likes working with groups of people, whether she likes working on detailed stuff or she doesn't like working on detailed things because those are important, and her limitations as she states them, not only the medical findings but her limitations as she states them. So when you take all of those things together the closest I could come to it as a 50 to 60 percent disability.
>
> [What that disability means] is that she is at a disadvantage when she goes out into the labor market because she's going to be competing with healthier individuals and she's going to be competing with [non]impaired individuals.
>
> I use a combination of the procedure recommended by Fields which is to look at level of preinjury access to the labor market and post injury access and the percentage and the difference between those percentages Fields says is the loss of jobs or the lost percentage.
>
> I also looked at which is what I normally do at the procedure recommended by Anthony Gamboa and he suggests that you look at all the factors involved in the client's analysis, injury, test results, psychological results, the client's statements, and so on, and then you as the clinician must make a, you as a vocational expert must make an estimate. And so what I do is I use Fields analysis as a starting point and then I revert to Gamboa to depart from Fields to come up with an estimate.

D-Mart made several attempts to have Davis explain how he arrived at the 50 to 60 percent figure other than his *ipse dixit* statement that the consideration of these factors produced these numbers. D-Mart pointed out that, in his report, Davis had diagnosed Perry's disability at 50 to 75 percent, and asked him to explain the discrepancy. Other than to state that his initial "estimate was too broad," Davis did not explain why the range changed by 15 percent.

D-Mart conceded that the Fields and Gamboa methodologies were sound, but attacked the combination of the two by Davis. D-Mart continued to attack Davis's qualifications. And D-Mart emphasized that Davis and the corporation for which he served as chief executive officer, Caribbean Behavioral Institute, Inc. (CBI), had pled guilty to violating 18 U.S.C. § 641, which prohibits "embezzl[ing] * * * or knowingly converting to [one's] use * * * any property made or being made under contract for the United States * * * ." D-Mart offered to prove that Davis and CBI had misappropriated $331,000 from the federal government.

The Court's ruling: __________

D-Mart has also moved to exclude under *Daubert* the opinion of Perry's economist regarding lost wages. D-Mart claims that the economist's testimony does not "fit" the case.

Karen Petty, an economist, testified regarding Perry's economic losses. She prepared an economic damages model that relied on several empirical assumptions about the extent of Perry's injuries, her earning capacity before and after the accident, and her life expectancy.

Petty testified that, in preparing her economic damages model on Perry's behalf, she had received a copy of Davis's report, which presumably described Perry as either 50 to 60 or 50 to 75 percent disabled. Nonetheless, Petty assumed that Elcock was 100 percent disabled when arriving at his opinion.

Petty also testified that she was familiar with Elcock's past earnings, which were relatively meager. Perry's husband had testified that she worked fourteen hours a day as a Mary Kay representative, and the record shows that she earned $5,774 in 1995 (before the injury) and $1,070 in 1996 (after the injury). Petty nevertheless assumed, in rendering his opinion, that Perry would have made $6 an hour, working 40 hours a week. Those figures indicate that Petty presumed that Elcock would have made a $12,480 a year but for her 100 percent disability.

In constructing his damages model, Petty assumed that Elcock would live and work to the average retirement age expected of African American females.

The Court's ruling: __________

Chapter 10

HEARSAY DEFINED

A. FEDERAL RULES OF EVIDENCE 801 AND 802

Rule 801. Definitions

The following definitions apply under this article:

(a) Statement. A "statement" is (1) an oral or written assertion or (2) nonverbal conduct of a person, if it is intended by the person as an assertion.

(b) Declarant. A "declarant" is a person who makes a statement.

(c) Hearsay. "Hearsay" is a statement, other than one made by the declarant while testifying at the trial or hearing, offered in evidence to prove the truth of the matter asserted.

Rule 802. Hearsay Rule

Hearsay is not admissible except as provided by these rules or by other rules prescribed by the Supreme Court pursuant to statutory authority or by Act of Congress.

B. TRUTH OF THE MATTER ASSERTED

[1] Illustrations

The Sheriff of Metropolis believes that Robin Rich slandered him by calling him "a liar and bribe taker" in front of Marty Manners. Robin Rich denies making the statement and alternatively contends that the statements are true.

The Sheriff of Metropolis calls Marty Manners to the stand.

Plaintiff:	State your name.
Marty Manners:	Marty Manners.
Plaintiff:	Were you with the Sheriff and Robin Rich on the date of the alleged slander?
Marty Manners:	Yes.
Plaintiff:	What did Robin Rich call the Sheriff?
Defendant:	Objection! That's an out of court statement. It's hearsay.
Court:	________ .

Barry Buyer entered into an oral contract with Sandy Seller to buy Sandy Seller's car. Barry Buyer paid Sandy Seller, but Sandy Seller refuses to deliver the car, defending on the theory that he had no such agreement with Barry Buyer and any money received was payment on an old gambling debt.

Barry Buyer takes the stand.

Plaintiff:	State your name.
Barry Buyer:	Barry Buyer.
Plaintiff:	Did you enter into an oral agreement with Sandy Seller?
Barry Buyer:	Yes.
Plaintiff:	What did you say?
Defendant:	Objection! That's an out of court statement. It's hearsay.
Court:	________ .

If the defendant is correct, can a slander or oral contract ever be proven in court? How about proving a threat or fear of a threat? Could you ever show that someone had notice of a defect in property if the notice was given orally? How would you prove someone's reputation?

[2] Independent Legal Significance

[a] Oral Contracts

CREAGHE v. IOWA HOME MUTUAL CASUALTY CO.
323 F.2d 981 (10th Cir. 1963)

SETH, CIRCUIT JUDGE:

The plaintiff-appellant has an unsatisfied judgment against Muril J. Osborn obtained in a damage action which arose from a collision between the plaintiff's car and Osborn's truck. In the case at bar, appellant alleges that the appellee insurance company was the insurer of Osborn's truck at the time of the accident, and seeks to collect this judgment from it. The appellee admits that at one time it issued a liability policy to Osborn, but asserts that he cancelled it shortly before the accident. Osborn was not a party to this suit and did not appear as a witness. Motions for directed verdict were made by both parties. The judge reserved his ruling and submitted interrogatories to the jury. These were answered favorably for appellant, but the court found that there was no material fact for the jury and gave appellee a directed verdict. The plaintiff-appellant has taken this appeal.

The appellant * * * argues that the trial court committed error in admitting certain testimony relating to statements made by the insured on the occasion when the cancellation purportedly took place.

The record shows that the policy in question was one which Osborn was required to have as an operator of a commercial vehicle. A copy of such policy had to be filed with the Colorado Public Utilities Commission and the policy could not be cancelled without first giving the Commission a ten-day notice. The policy states that the insured may cancel it by a surrender of the policy or by mailing notice of cancellation. The policy also provides that the premium adjustment be made as soon as practicable after cancellation becomes effective.

When one of appellee's agents wrote the policy in appellee's company, only one-half of the premium was paid to the agent. The unpaid balances were on account between the agent and the insured, and did not involve appellee. The policy was thereafter changed from time to time as the coverage expanded, and the agent retained the policy in order to make the changes. As the coverage increased, so did the premium due. Osborn sent the agent a check for a part of the balance due after the initial payment, but it was returned by the bank marked insufficient funds. The agent testified that he called Osborn about the check, and was told by Osborn that he was going to cancel the insurance and would come by to pick up the returned check. Osborn did come to the agent's office on October 19 and, in the presence of the agent and a secretary, stated he wanted the insurance cancelled immediately. The check was returned to Osborn and the agent told him he did not know whether there would be a refund or not. The policy was then in the possession of the agent because of changes in coverage mentioned above, and thus there was no change in the possession of the policy as Osborn did not have it to physically surrender it. The agent then sent the policy to the appellee insurance company and advised it of the cancellation. Appellee notified the Colorado Public Utilities Commission of the cancellation. The date of receipt of this notice was not determined, but on October 29 the Commission responded to the notice. The collision between Osborn's truck and appellant's car occurred on November 25.

* * *

The trial judge found that there was no question of fact for the jury, and with this we agree.

* * *

Appellant challenges the action of the trial court in admitting the testimony of the agent of appellee and his employee as to what took place, and what was said by the insured, on the occasion when he came to the agent's office to receive back the check. The agent's testimony and that of his employee was, as mentioned, that the insured stated he wanted the policy cancelled, also that his check for some of the premiums in addition to those initially made was then returned. Appellant asserts that this testimony was hearsay.

The hearsay rule does not exclude *relevant* testimony as to what the contracting parties said with respect to the making or the terms of an oral agreement. The presence or absence of such words and statements of themselves are part of the issues in the case. This use of such testimony does not require a reliance by the jury or the judge upon the competency of the person who originally made the statements for the truth of their content. Neither the truth of the statements nor their accuracy are then involved. In the case at bar we are not concerned with whether the insured was truthful or not when he told the agent he wanted the policy cancelled and that he did not need it any more. It is enough for the issues here presented to determine only whether or not he made such statements to the agent. The fact that these statements were made was testified to by the agent, and his competency and truthfulness as to this testimony was subject to testing through cross-examination by counsel for appellant, and this was done at considerable length. The fact that the statements with which we are here concerned related to an oral termination of a written contract does not lead to a rule different from that prevailing for the formation of an oral agreement. The reasons for the rule permitting such testimony are the same in both instances.

* * *

[T]he testimony with which we are here concerned is admissible since it is part of, or is the oral agreement to cancel the insurance policy. Oral agreements can only be established by testimony as to the conversation which was had between the parties. This testimony may be given by a witness to such conversation, as was the agent of the appellee in this instance.

* * *

Affirmed.

NOTES

1. In the formation of a contract, does it matter whether the words of offer and acceptance are true?

See *Kepner-Tregoe v. Leadership Software, Inc.*, 12 F.3d 527, 540 (5th Cir. 1994), where the court noted that under the objective theory of contracting, it does not matter what the parties are thinking when they enter into a contract. Instead, it is the words spoken or written that determine the rights and responsibilities of the parties. Accordingly, testimony concerning the words spoken is not prohibited by the hearsay rule.

2. Under what other circumstances are words, spoken to create or terminate a legal relationship, not hearsay?

Words spoken to create agency relationships, promissory notes, wills, leases, and assignments are all nonhearsay when offered to show the existence of the legal relationship.

United States v. Bellucci, 995 F.2d 157 (9th Cir. 1993), was a bank fraud case, in which the government proved the federally insured status of the bank by introducing the bank's FDIC certificate of insurance. The defendant argued that proof of the bank's status through the certificate violated the hearsay rule. But the Court rejected this argument, reasoning that the FDIC certificate "affects the legal rights of the parties" independent of the truth of any assertion in the certificate. In this respect, the certificate is like a written contract that memorializes the fact of an agreement. Statements that create substantive rights and liabilities are not hearsay.

In *Stuart v. Unum Life Ins. Co. Of Am.*, 217 F.3d 1145 (9th Cir. 2000), the Trial Judge remanded an insurance dispute removed from State Court on the ground that the defendants had not carried their burden of showing that the plan was an ERISA plan, which would have subjected the case to federal jurisdiction. Reversing an order granting the plaintiff's costs and expenses for improper removal, the Court held that it was error to treat the group insurance policy as inadmissible hearsay, since it was a legally operative document that defined the rights and liabilities of the parties in the case, including the rights and liabilities bearing on whether it was an ERISA plan.

[b] Slander and Perjury

UNITED STATES v. ANFIELD
539 F.2d 674 (9th Cir. 1976)

Sneed, Circuit Judge:

Appellant was convicted on five counts of perjury * * *. The trial court allowed a motion for judgment of acquittal as to Count One and imposed sentence on the remaining counts. We affirm.

Statement of Facts

Appellant's indictment on five counts of perjury stemmed from his testimony before the grand jury and during the trial in the case of *United States v. Leslie Jackson*, CR 74-250. His involvement in the *Jackson* case arose when he reported a burglary of his mother's house to the police and indicated that he suspected Leslie Jackson, the brother of a friend. The FBI, also suspecting Jackson of bank robbery, contacted appellant and sought to elicit information from him about his knowledge of Jackson's involvement in the bank robbery. Appellant on several occasions exhibited reluctance to become involved, but upon issuance of a subpoena did appear and testify before the grand jury and gave evidence which linked Jackson to the robbery.

* * *

At the *Jackson* trial appellant testified concerning the same matter with respect to which he testified before the grand jury, but his testimony differed in certain pertinent respects from that given before the grand jury. * * *

Subsequent to the final disposition of the *Jackson* case, appellant was indicted and charged with five counts of perjury. * * *

Appellant has let fly a quiver full of arrows directed at his perjury convictions. All have missed their mark.

* * *

Motion To Strike As Hearsay Evidence the Testimony of Prosecutor in Jackson Trial

Appellant * * * complains that the testimony in his perjury trial of the prosecutor in the *Jackson* trial, was hearsay and, as such, should have been excluded. We do not agree.

The hearsay rule does not operate to render inadmissible every statement repeated by a witness as made by another person. It does not exclude evidence offered to prove the fact that a statement was made, rather than the truth. * * * The prosecutor's testimony at appellant's trial that appellant had testified before the grand jury that Jackson told him that there was a camera and a single girl in the bank which was robbed and then denied this at Jackson's trial was not hearsay for the purposes of the present case. The prosecutor was not attempting to prove that there was in fact a camera and single girl in the bank; those facts were not in issue at appellant's trial. Rather, the prosecutor's statements indicate only that the appellant made inconsistent statements under oath. His testimony was independently relevant.

Affirmed.

NOTE

Is a slanderous statement hearsay when offered by the plaintiff in a suit for defamation? To prevail, doesn't the plaintiff have to prove the slanderous statement was untrue?

In *M.F. Patterson Dental Supply Co., Inc. v. Wadley*, 401 F.2d 167 (10th Cir. 1968), the court held that slanderous statements were not hearsay since they were not offered for the truth of the statements, but instead to show the statements were made and therefore had independent legal significance.

[c] Threats and Fraud

UNITED STATES v. JONES
663 F.2d 567 (5th Cir. 1981)

JAMES C. HILL, CIRCUIT JUDGE:

On May 4, 1979, appellant Lloyd Jones stood before the United States District Court, Northern District of Georgia, for sentencing in connection with his conviction for murder committed at the Atlanta Federal Penitentiary. Judge William C. O'Kelley addressed Jones, who appeared with counsel, to determine whether Jones wished to be heard on matters bearing upon his sentence. Jones responded:

> Yes, sir. I'd like to say that, I'd like to say that I don't think you passed sentence on me, you know, like, I think, during the process of the trial that I was totally insane, you know, which I also think that you should have looked over into the matter when I told you that them people out there was threatening me and stuff, which you said you would but you never have. But now today you bring me down here to pass sentence on me. It's nothing really too much I could do about it. When you can't beat them you join them. *So, Judge O'Kelley, U.S. Attorney, Mr. Bostic, I pass sentence on you, the sentence would be death, you and all your relatives. Now you can pass your sentence. It is death to*

you, you, and you, and all your relatives by gunshot wound. Now do as you please. I don't give a fuck if you throw the whole Empire State building at me, the whole State of Georgia.

For threatening the lives of Judge O'Kelley and the prosecutor, Jones was indicted and convicted under 18 U.S.C. § 1503 (1976), and sentenced to five years in prison. * * * We affirm the conviction.

* * *

The district court permitted the transcript of the hearing, save certain prejudicial portions and a short final section, to be read to the jury. Only the language containing the actual threats * * * was admitted into evidence as an exhibit for the jury during its deliberation. * * * The statement at issue is paradigmatic nonhearsay; it was offered because it contains threats made against officers of the federal courts, *i.e.*, it contains the operative words of this criminal action. It was not "offered in evidence to prove the truth of the matter asserted" * * *.

* * *

This conviction is AFFIRMED.

NOTE

Is a fraudulent statement hearsay when offered against the declarant of the statement as proof of the fraud?

In *United States v. Adkins*, 741 F.2d 744 (5th Cir. 1984), the prosecution offered the defendant's Dun and Bradstreet report in a fraud case against the defendant. The Court held that the report was not hearsay because it was not offered to prove the truth of the contents of the report. Rather, the report was offered to establish a foundation for a later showing, through other evidence, that the information in the report was false. *See also United States v. Perholtz,* 842 F.2d 343 (D.C. Cir. 1988) (in a racketeering case involving procurement of Postal Service contracts, the Court held that a "script" prepared by one defendant for another person, in an effort to influence what he would say about the scheme, was nonhearsay; the government offered the script to prove that the information therein was false, rather than true); *United States v. Costa,* 31 F.3d 1073 (11th Cir. 1994) (custodial statement in which the declarant sought to exculpate himself was not hearsay, where the government sought to create an inference of the declarant's guilt by showing, through the introduction of other evidence, that the declarant had lied to his interrogators).

[3] Notice — Statement Offered for Its Effect on the Listener

VINYARD v. VINYARD FUNERAL HOME, INC.

435 S.W.2d 392 (Mo. Ct. App. 1968)

CLEMENS, COMMISSIONER:

Plaintiff got a verdict and $13,000 judgment for injuries from a fall on defendant's parking lot. (Plaintiff was the daughter-in-law of the corporate defendant's president.) Defendant appeals, challenging * * * the admission of evidence about other patrons slipping on the parking lot.

Defendant contends the evidence failed to show that its premises were unsafe and, even so, that the condition was undiscoverable by plaintiff. We recite the verdict-consistent evidence.

In short, one rainy night plaintiff slipped and fell when she stepped from a roughly paved surface onto a smoothly paved surface of a ramp in defendant's dimly lighted parking lot. The defendant knew the smoothly paved area was slippery when wet. * * * In September, 1961 — fourteen months before plaintiff's fall — the defendant spread a clear liquid sealer on the upper level of the parking lot. This sealed area extended half way down the ramps; it was smoother than the unsealed area and slick when wet. Thus a person walking up the ramp would start out on a rough surface and cross over onto a smooth surface. Daylight photographs show the two surfaces differ only slightly in color.

* * *

Defendant's prior knowledge that the sealed surface was dangerously slick when wet was shown in three ways: observations by defendant's officers and employees, remedial actions taken by them, and notice received through other patrons' complaints of slickness.

As soon as the clear sealer was applied on the lot's upper level, the defendant's officers and employees noticed the surface was slick when it rained. They discussed the condition numerous times; they spoke to paving contractors about "roughing it up" but did nothing except spread sand on the smooth paving when it rained. (This, however, was not done on the night plaintiff fell.) This sanding followed complaints by patrons about the slickness. These complaints began right after the sealer was applied and came from several persons.

* * *

Defendant * * * [claims error in] the admission of evidence that people complained to its officers and employees that the sealed surface was slippery when wet. Plaintiff offered this evidence to show that defendant knew its parking lot was slippery when wet. Witness Keith Vinyard was defendant's vice-president and plaintiff's husband. Testifying for plaintiff he was asked: "Now, Keith, after this sealer was put on did you receive any complaints from anyone visiting the funeral home?" Over defense objection that the question was hearsay unless limited to the same conditions as plaintiff's fall, the witness answered: "Yes, several people said it was slick." Later, witness Leroy Lucas, one of defendant's regular employees, was asked: "Did you yourself hear complaints of people that would come in and complain about it being slick when it was wet?" Over the defendant's hearsay objection Mr. Lucas answered: "I had heard different people comment on it that it was slick when it was wet."

These questions and answers were improper as hearsay if offered only to prove the fact that the sealed area was slick. But aside from the *fact* of slickness there was the issue of defendant's *knowledge* of slickness. Evidence of *complaints* of slickness made to defendant was relevant to the material issue of defendant's knowledge.* * *

* * * [T]o make her case the plaintiff was obliged to show that defendant's officers knew about the slickness. Under the circumstances of this case the trial court properly admitted evidence that this knowledge had come to them through complaints of patrons that the parking lot's sealed area was slick when wet.

* * *

NOTE

Is there a foundation requirement for introducing an out-of-court statement to prove notice?

To be probative of notice and thus admissible as nonhearsay, the statement must be one that either was or should have been known about by the party whose state of mind is in dispute. Thus, in *George v. Celotex Corp.,* 914 F.2d 26 (2d Cir. 1990), the court held that an unpublished 1947 report regarding the dangers of asbestos could not be admitted for the nonhearsay purpose of showing notice. There was no proof presented by the plaintiff that the defendant ever saw the report or should have seen it as part of the published literature in the industry.

McCLURE v. STATE

575 S.W.2d 564 (Tex. Crim. App. 1979)

Onion, Presiding Judge:

This is an appeal from a conviction for the offense of murder; punishment is imprisonment for ninety-nine years.

* * *

Appellant's testimony raised the issue of voluntary manslaughter, and the court instructed the jury thereon. In support of the defensive theory that he was guilty of only this lesser included offense, appellant offered the testimony of Keith Crowder, Harvey Gordon and Ronnie Davis. Each of these witnesses testified outside of the presence of the jury that he had had sexual intercourse with the deceased while she was married to appellant. Crowder also testified to seeing appellant in a restaurant while Crowder and the deceased were eating breakfast together, and that appellant appeared "real nervous, shaky, upset." Appellant also offered the testimony of Larry Subia. Subia was allowed to testify outside the presence of the jury that the deceased, clad in a bath robe, had answered the door of Davis' apartment at approximately 2 a.m. at a time when she was married to appellant. Appellant also offered to testify — and was allowed to do so only outside the presence of the jury — that one Cindy Haynes had told him that the deceased had had sexual relations with Crowder and Davis. Appellant testified before the jury that he had seen the deceased leave on a "date" with Gordon, and that she had not returned home until 10 a.m. the next day.

* * *

* * * It long has been the rule in this state that evidence such as that offered by appellant to prove his wife's infidelity is admissible as bearing on the accused's state of mind.

* * *

In order for the evidence of the deceased's infidelity to be admissible, appellant was required to show that he had knowledge thereof. * * * To prove that he had knowledge of the deceased having had sexual relations with Crowder and Davis, appellant offered to testify that Cindy Haynes had so informed him. The court erred in refusing to allow appellant to testify as to what Haynes had told him on the ground that such testimony would have been hearsay.

> When it is proved that D made a statement to X, with the purpose of showing the probable state of mind thereby induced in X, such as being put on notice or having knowledge, or motive, or to show the information which X had as bearing on the reasonableness or good faith of the subsequent conduct of X, or anxiety, the evidence is not subject to attack as hearsay.

McCormick, Evidence § 249, pp. 589-90 (2d ed. 1972).

> Whenever an utterance is offered to evidence the *state of mind* which ensued *in another person* in consequence of the utterance, it is obvious that no assertive or testimonial use is to be made of it, and the utterance is therefore admissible, so far as the hearsay rule is concerned.

6 Wigmore, Evidence § 1789, p. 314 (Chadbourn rev. 1976).

* * *

The judgment is reversed and the cause remanded.

NOTE

In what other circumstances would the state of mind of the listener apply to render a statement non-hearsay?

In *United States v. Norwood*, 798 F.2d 1094 (7th Cir. 1986), the defendant was allowed to testify that the person who gave him a stolen credit card told him it was a friend's card and that it was okay to use it. Because the statement was offered to show the listener's state of mind (i.e., the belief that his use of the card was legal), the statement was not hearsay.

United States v. Cantu, 876 F.2d 1134 (5th Cir. 1989), provides a good example of the nonhearsay use of an out-of-court statement for its effect on the listener. Cantu was charged with a drug crime and offered a defense of entrapment. At trial he was not permitted to testify to the statements that were made to him by Santander, an undercover government agent, that reflected a persistent effort on Santander's part to get Cantu to secure drug customers. Santander's statements were excluded as hearsay, but the court found that this was error. The court reasoned that the statements "were offered as evidence of Cantu's state of mind, bearing directly on his entrapment defense," and that the actual truth of the statements was therefore irrelevant. The trial court in *Cantu* had expressed concern that Cantu might have been lying on the witness stand about whether Santander actually made these statements. But the Court of Appeals rightly rejected this concern as misplaced. As the court explained: "Cantu's credibility, like the testimony of any witness, was subject to the crucible of cross-examination and was within the exclusive province of the jury. The veracity of a claim that certain statements were made was subject to evaluation like any other testimony presented at trial." The hearsay rule is concerned about the credibility of out-of-court declarants; the credibility of in-court witnesses is left to the jury.

In criminal cases, police officers are often called to testify to information they heard about the defendant, e.g., the defendant was selling drugs from a third-floor apartment. These statements are purportedly offered not for their truth (that the defendant was actually selling drugs), but rather for the effect on the listener, i.e., the police officer. While use of the out of court statement for these purposes does not offend the hearsay rule, the relevance of the statements for the nonhearsay purpose is often questionable. Some courts have admitted such statements in order to explain why the *officer* acted as he did, e.g., why he got a search warrant, why he arrested the defendant, etc. where there is probative value for the non-hearsay purpose, and the prejudicial effect — i.e., the risk that the jury will use the statement for its truth — does not substantially outweigh that probative value under Rule 403. *See, e.g.*, *United States v. Slaughter*, 386 F.3d 401 (2d Cir. 2004) (the court affirmed a conviction for felon firearm possession, finding no abuse of discretion in the admission of testimony that a civilian had pointed out the discarded weapon, allowing a policeman to recover it. The testimony was proffered for the legitimate purpose of explaining how the officer came to find the weapon and its probative value was not substantially outweighed by any danger of prejudice). Some courts have not troubled themselves much, however, in applying that Rule 403 balance where the statement is offered for its effect on the listener. *See, e.g.*, *United States v. Norquay*, 987 F.2d 475 (8th Cir. 1993) (in a rape case, witnesses testified concerning statements made by the victim to the effect that she had been raped; the court held that the statements were not hearsay, because they were offered not for the truth of their content but rather "to explain why the witnesses stopped on the highway late at night, took her to the police station, and sent her to be interviewed by the investigator").

Other courts note that in a criminal case, where the disputed issue is the guilt of the defendant, it is often unimportant to explain why an officer acted as he did in response to an accusation about the defendant; and they further recognize that accusations of guilt may be misused by the jury for their truth. Accordingly, these courts have excluded accusatory statements about the defendant when offered for their effect on the listener. *See United States v. Dean,* 980 F.2d 1286 (9th Cir. 1992) (statements accusing the defendant of criminal activity, made to a police officer, were improperly admitted for the nonhearsay purpose of explaining why the officer went to the defendant's home to arrest him: the officer's reasons for going to the defendant's home "are not of consequence to the determination of the action, i.e., they do not bear on any issue involving the elements of the charged offense"); *United States v. Fountain*, 2 F.3d 656 (6th Cir. 1993) (information on defendant's criminal activity, offered not for its truth but rather to explain why the agents searched where they did, held improperly admitted because the "reason Agent Primak searched the back bedroom simply was not a matter of dispute and was not in issue in this case": "Because the agents' action needed no explanation, we can conclude only that Primak's information was offered to prove the truth of the matter asserted — that guns and narcotics were in the bedroom.").

[4] Other Not-for-Truth Purposes

UNITED STATES v. WICKS

995 F.2d 964 (10th Cir. 1993)

STEPHEN H. ANDERSON, CIRCUIT JUDGE. Defendant James T. Wicks appeals his conviction, after a jury trial, on eight counts relating to drug trafficking, resulting in a total sentence of 387 months imprisonment. * * * [Officers discovered evidence in a motel room tending to indicate that Wicks was involved in drug activity. The evidence was admitted at trial over the defendant's hearsay objection].

* * *

II. *Evidentiary Rulings.*

We turn now to Wicks' argument that the district court erred in overruling his objections to the admission of the papers containing a formula for making methamphetamine, a list of precursor chemicals, and a recipe to "cook" crack cocaine, all of which were found in one of the briefcases seized from Wicks' motel rooms. Wicks objected to their admission at trial on the grounds that they were hearsay, and did not fall within any of the exceptions to the hearsay rule. We disagree. * * * Fed. R. Evid. 801(c) defines hearsay as "a statement, other than one made by the declarant while testifying at the trial or hearing, offered in evidence to prove the truth of the matter asserted." A "statement" can include a written assertion. The district court overruled Wicks' objection to these papers "because of the inference that the Jury can draw that the possession of these matters connotes or implies knowledge of the preparation and possession of drugs." The government subsequently presented expert testimony identifying the papers as containing a methamphetamine recipe and a list of chemical ingredients.

We hold that the papers were not hearsay, because they were not admitted for the purpose of proving the truth of any matter asserted therein. They were admitted solely to permit the inference to be drawn that Wicks' was involved in drug trafficking. While some amount of "reading" or comprehending of the nature of the written material was required in order to identify them as drug-related, no further use was made of the contents of those materials. *See United States v. Peveto,* 881 F.2d 844, 853-54 (10th Cir. 1989) (traffic ticket admitted to tie defendant to van, not to prove truth of any matters asserted in the ticket; "[t]he existence of the ticket, not its assertions, was the point of its admission"); *United States v. Ashby,* 864 F.2d 690, 693 (10th Cir. 1988) (car title used to tie defendant to car, not to prove she was owner; work order documents admitted to inferentially tie defendant and co-defendant to drug running, not to prove truth of matters asserted therein; "[s]ince these documents were used to tie appellant to the car, they were not hearsay"); *United States v. Markopoulos,* 848 F.2d 1036, 1039 (10th Cir. 1988) (spiral notebook which was used to log travel expenses not hearsay when admitted only to link defendant circumstantially to conspiracy, whereas rental car contract, credit card voucher and receipts were hearsay when admitted to show identity of renter or fact of payment); *see also United States v. Jaramillo-Suarez,* 950 F.2d 1378, 1383 (9th Cir. 1991) ("pay/owe sheet * * * was admitted for the specific and limited purpose of showing the character and use of the * * * apartment" and was therefore not hearsay).

AFFIRMED

[The concurring opinion of Judge Ebel is omitted.].

NOTES

1. In what other circumstances can out-of-court statements be admitted for a purpose other than proving that the contents are true?

See United States v. Enriquez-Estrada, 999 F.2d 1355 (9th Cir. 1993) (drug ledgers admissible as not hearsay, where the court "admitted the ledgers for the limited purpose of showing the nature and use" of the residence where the ledgers were found); *United States v. Thorne,* 997 F.2d 1504 (D.C. Cir. 1993) (no error to admit drug records to show that the names listed were connected with each other and were also connected with amounts of money and beeper extensions; testimony did not indicate the amounts of money or the actual numbers listed); *United States v. McIntyre,* 997 F.2d 687 (10th Cir. 1993) (receipts admissible not for truth but "only to link various of the defendants together by the circumstance that documents bearing the names of certain defendants and the location of certain drug transactions" were found in the possession of one of the conspirators).

2. Can a witness's testimony be hearsay when the witness does not specifically testify to any out-of-court statement having been made?

See Pelster v. Ray, 987 F.2d 514 (8th Cir. 1993): Plaintiffs sued for fraud when they discovered that the car they bought had a turned-back odometer. They called an investigator who testified that, based on his review of relevant documents, the odometer on the purchased car had been turned back when it was in the possession of the defendants. He also testified that his review of other documents indicated that the defendants had rolled back the odometers on many other cars. The Court held that the trial court erroneously admitted the testimony in violation of the hearsay rule. The witness based his conclusion on an assumption that the documents he had referred to were true, with respect to mileages, dates, etc. While those records were never introduced at trial, the hearsay rule applies where the probative value of a witness's in-court testimony is dependent on the truth of an out of court statement upon which the witness relies.

3. Is a statement offered to prove the state of mind of the declarant offered for its truth?

One problem type of case has spurred much commentary, but it is a problem in theory more than in practice. An example is when one spouse makes a statement such as "I hate you" to the other spouse in the presence of third parties. If this statement were offered in a case to prove that the declarant was no longer in love with the other spouse, it would appear to be hearsay. It could be argued, however, that the fact that such a statement was made in the presence of other people itself is evidence of an absence of love so that the making of the statement in these circumstances is circumstantial evidence of state of mind, not hearsay. This kind of case may produce differences of opinion as to the proper classification, but the existence of a state of mind exception to the hearsay rule in Rule 803(3) indicates that such statements will be admissible in any case, and that the theoretical debate has little practical significance. *See, e.g.*, *Fun-damental Too, Ltd. v. Gemmy Indus. Corp.*, 111 F.3d 993 (2d Cir. 1997) (evidence that retail customers complained about product confusion was admissible, either as non-hearsay under Rule 801, or under the Rule 803(3) exception for statements of the declarants' state of mind).

4. In determining whether a statement is offered for the truth of its content, do courts ever get it wrong?

See Saltzburg, Martin, and Capra, *Federal Rules of Evidence Manual* (9th ed. 2006):

> It is not always easy to delineate the line between statements offered for their truth and those that are not. Indeed, Courts have sometimes erred in this task. An example is *United States v. Sadler*, 234 F.3d 368 (8th Cir. 2000). Sadler was charged with bank robbery. An officer testified that Sadler confessed his guilt to him without even being asked to do so. Sadler contended that the officer was lying. Sadler

proffered the testimony of the attorney who was representing him at the time of the alleged confession. The attorney would have testified that moments before allegedly confessing to the deputy, Sadler spoke to the attorney and unequivocally asserted his innocence. In response to a hearsay objection, the defendant argued that his statement to his former attorney was admissible for the nonhearsay purpose of impeaching the credibility of the officer who testified that the defendant confessed to him. The Trial Court excluded Sadler's statement as hearsay and the Court found no error. The Court stated that "the proffered testimony would only have its desired effect if in fact the statements [to the attorney] were true." In our view, this analysis is misguided. Sadler's protestation of innocence was relevant regardless of its truth. The police officer testified that Sadler went out of his way to volunteer a confession. Even if Sadler was not telling his attorney the truth, his declaration of innocence impeaches the police officer's testimony because it makes the officer's account less plausible. It seems unlikely that Sadler would be protesting innocence to his lawyer and then, a short time later, loudly volunteering his guilt to a police officer. *See also Ostad v. Oregon Health Sciences Univ.*, 327 F.3d 876 (9th Cir. 2003) (prior inconsistent statement was not hearsay because it was offered to impeach the witness's credibility and not for its truth).

PROBLEM 10-1

Slippery Sammy sues a grocery store on the theory that he slipped and fell on a banana peel in Aisle Two. The grocery store denies that it had sufficient notice of the peel's presence to remedy the situation; therefore, the store is not liable. It also claims contributory negligence and assumption of the risk.

Slippery Sammy also sues the grocery store for civil assault on the theory of respondent superior, alleging that an employee of the store said, "I'll lose my job if you tell anyone about the accident. I'll kill you if you tell."

The grocery store presents two affirmative defenses, alleging that Sammy assumed the risk and that the case was settled because the plaintiff said, "I agree to accept your offer of $5,000." The grocery store brings a counterclaim against Slippery Sammy, alleging defamation when Slippery Sammy told his bartender, "Everyone at that grocery store is a lying cheat who would steal from your grandmother."

Slippery Sammy takes the stand:

Plaintiff: State your name.
Slippery: Slippery Sammy.
Plaintiff: Were you at the grocery store?
Slippery: Yes.
Plaintiff: Did you slip and fall on a banana peel in Aisle Two?
Slippery: I certainly did.

Plaintiff: How long had it been there?
Slippery: I overheard a store employee say to the manager, "I told you half an hour ago about that banana peel on the floor in Aisle Two."
Defendant: (1) Objection! ________.
Plaintiff: (2) ________.
The court: (3) ________.
Plaintiff: Did you talk to another employee after the accident?
Slippery: Yes, I did.
Plaintiff: What did he say?
Slippery: "I'll lose my job if you tell anyone about this accident. I'll kill you if you tell."
Defendant: (4) Objection! ________.
Plaintiff: (5) ________.
The court: (6) ________.
Plaintiff: Were you afraid after he said that?
Slippery: You bet, I haven't slept since.
Plaintiff: Why were you afraid?
Slippery: I sort of knew about the employee. My friend Bob had told me before all this happened that the employee had beat up some guys at the bar.
Defendant: (7) Objection! ________.
Plaintiff: (8) ________.
The court: (9) ________.

Slippery Sammy rests, and the grocery store calls the store manager to the stand:

Defendant: State your name.
Manager: Miss Management.
Defendant: Are you the grocery store manager?
Manager: Yes.
Defendant: Did you talk to Slippery about settling this case?
Manager: Yes.
Defendant: What did he say?
Plaintiff: (10) Objection! ________.
Defendant: (11) ________.
The court: (12) ________.
Defendant: I'll ask again. What did he say?
Manager: He said, "I'll agree to accept your offer of $5,000."

The grocery store calls a customer to the stand:

Defendant: Do you know the plaintiff?
Customer: Yes.
Defendant: Were you in the grocery store on the day of his accident?
Customer: Yes.

Defendant:	Did you speak with the plaintiff?
Customer:	Yes.
Defendant:	What was said between you?
Customer:	A half hour before the accident I told him to watch out for a banana peel in Aisle Two. He said he would.
Plaintiff:	(13) Objection. ________.
The court:	(14) ________.

The grocery store calls the bartender to the stand:

Defendant:	Do you know the plaintiff?
Bartender:	Yes.
Defendant:	Did you talk to him the next day after his alleged accident?
Bartender:	Yes, I did.
Defendant:	What did he say?
Bartender:	He said, "Everyone at that grocery store is a lying, no-good S.O.B."
Plaintiff:	(15) Objection! ________.
Defendant:	(16) ________.
The court:	(17) ________.

C. STATEMENT

[1] Assertive Conduct

[a] Illustration

The defendant is charged with armed robbery. He was arrested two blocks from the crime scene and the store manager was brought to the arrest scene to identify the suspect. The police officer who accompanied the store manager to the scene is on the stand.

Prosecutor:	Did you take the store manager to identify the perpetrator of the crime?
Officer:	Yes, I did.
Prosecutor:	What happened?
Officer:	Well, I told the store manager to point out the criminal and he pointed at the defendant.
Defense:	Objection! That's hearsay.
Prosecutor:	But your honor, no statement was made.
Defense:	________.

[b] Response to Question with Action

STEVENSON v. COMMONWEALTH
237 S.E.2d 779 (Va. 1977)

IVANSON, CHIEF JUSTICE:

On July 16, 1976, a jury found the defendant, John Paul Stevenson, guilty of murder of the second degree and fixed his punishment at confinement in the state penitentiary for a period of 10 years. He was sentenced accordingly.

We granted defendant a writ of error limited to the question whether the trial court erred in admitting into evidence a bloodstained shirt allegedly worn by the defendant on the day of the homicide and in allowing testimony concerning scientific tests run on the shirt.

The evidence, briefly stated, shows that at approximately six o'clock in the afternoon of December 2, 1975, the partially clothed body of Lillian M. Keller was found on the bed in her apartment at the Holly Court Motel in Ashland. Her death resulted from multiple stab wounds. Mrs. Keller was manager of the motel, and she occupied an apartment adjoining the front office. Her apartment also adjoined another unit which was the residence of Howard Franklin Bittorf. There was a connecting door between the Keller apartment and the living quarters of Bittorf.

In the early morning hours of December 2, 1975, the defendant, who is Bittorf's brother-in-law and a resident of Baltimore, Maryland, entered Bittorf's apartment through an unlocked door and spent the rest of the night there. That day Stevenson, Bittorf, and Jeffrey A. Taylor, an occupant of another unit in the motel, spent the morning and early afternoon drinking and "riding around" in defendant's automobile.

Taylor testified that when they returned to Bittorf's apartment in the early afternoon, Mrs. Keller was engaged in cleaning the apartment. He left shortly thereafter and went to his room to rest. He said that he did not see the defendant and Bittorf anymore that day, but when he last saw the defendant he was wearing a long-sleeve buttoned shirt with the sleeves rolled up.

* * *

On December 5, 1975, Police Officer Schultze went to the address in Baltimore which was shown on Stevenson's operator's license. There he met two women who identified themselves as the wives of Bittorf and Stevenson. After identifying himself, he told the ladies the purpose of his visit. He asked them if John Stevenson had changed clothes when he arrived home on either the night of the second or the early morning of the third of December. As a result of the answer given by Mrs. Stevenson, Schultze requested her to give him the clothes worn by Stevenson when he returned home from Ashland. Mrs. Stevenson then took Officer Schultze to another Baltimore address and presented him with a knit-type pullover shirt. On December 8, 1975, Schultze took the shirt to the Consolidated Laboratory in Richmond and turned it over to Mary Jane Burton. Over the objection of the defendant, the shirt was admitted into evidence.

Mary Jane Burton testified that she examined the shirt and found a small stain which she chemically identified as human blood. * * * She said the blood on the shirt was the same type as the blood of the victim in the two systems she was able to type. She further said that 4.7 percent of the population have the same blood type as the victim.

Defendant argues that the trial court erred in admitting the shirt into evidence on the ground that the nonverbal conduct of Mrs. Stevenson was equivalent to a verbal assertion of the truth of the matter asserted and was thus inadmissible under the rule against hearsay.

* * *

Nonverbal conduct of a person intended by him as an assertion and offered in evidence to prove the truth of the matter asserted falls within the ban on hearsay evidence. * * * This type of conduct has the same infirmities of the more familiar oral form of hearsay and should likewise be excluded.

In the present case, the act by Mrs. Stevenson came in response to the question of the officer as to what the defendant was wearing when he returned home from Ashland as well as the officer's request to obtain that clothing. Thus, the conduct of Mrs. Stevenson was intended as a nonverbal assertion for the purpose of showing that the shirt not only belonged to Stevenson but was in fact worn by him on the day of the crime. Moreover, it formed the basis of the Commonwealth's argument that he was wearing the shirt at the time the crime was committed. Accordingly, the officer's testimony relating to the shirt was inadmissible as violative of the hearsay rule, and the introduction into evidence of the shirt and the result of the scientific tests conducted thereon was without proper foundation.

For the reasons stated, the judgment of the court below is reversed and the case remanded for a new trial.

Reversed and remanded.

NOTES

1. When a person points at something, is that person making a statement?

In *United States v. Caro*, 569 F.2d 411 (5th Cir. 1978), a heroin dealer pointed out the location of his drug source to DEA agents. The Court recognized "that assertive conduct, like an oral declaration, is subject to the hearsay rule" under Fed. R. Evid. 801(a)(2). The Court held that the heroin dealer's "pointing out" constitutes such assertive conduct.

2. When a person nods his head, is that person making a statement?

In *United States v. Katsougrakis,* 715 F.2d 769 (2d Cir. 1983), the Court affirmed convictions resulting from the arson of a diner. The government witness had visited his friend, who had been burned in the arson. The friend was heavily bandaged and unable to speak. The friend nodded affirmatively when asked whether he had been paid by the defendant to burn the diner. The Court held that this testimony was hearsay, because the government plainly used the nod for the truth of an assertion. However, the affirmative nod was admissible under the hearsay exception for declarations against penal interest.

[2] Non-Assertive Conduct and Words

[a] Illustrations

In a will contest case, the plaintiff is trying to show that the testator was competent at the time the will was executed. After laying the proper foundation, the plaintiff offers into evidence a letter written to the testator the same day the will was executed.

Defendant:	Objection! Your honor, the letter is blatantly hearsay and should not be admitted.
Plaintiff:	Your honor, the letter is not being offered to prove anything in the letter is true. It is being offered only to show that it involved a complicated business transaction and was directed at the testator. From this, one can infer that the author of the letter believed that the testator was competent, but the truth of the letter itself is meaningless. It's not hearsay at all.
The court:	________.

Plaintiff sues defendant because cargo sent on defendant's ship did not arrive safely at its destination. To prevail, the plaintiff must show that the ship was not seaworthy. Defendant defends on the theory that the ship was seaworthy. The defendant calls a longshoreman to the stand.

Defendant:	State your name.
Longshoreman:	Dock Loader.
Defendant:	Were you on the dock the day that *Lost Souls* sailed?
Longshoreman:	Yes, I was.
Defendant:	Did you see the captain?
Longshoreman:	Yes.
Defendant:	What did he do?
Longshoreman:	He inspected the ship, took his entire family aboard, and then prepared to depart on the trip.
Plaintiff:	Objection! That's hearsay.
Defendant:	But your honor, the captain didn't say anything and didn't intend to convey any meaning by his actions.
The court:	________.

[b] Implied Assertions

UNITED STATES v. ZENNI

492 F. Supp. 464 (E.D. Ky. 1980)

BERTELSMAN, DISTRICT JUDGE:

This prosecution for illegal bookmaking activities presents a classic problem in the law of evidence, namely, whether implied assertions are hearsay. The problem was a controversial one at common law, the discussion of which has filled many pages in the treatises and learned journals. Although the answer to the problem is clear under the Federal Rules of Evidence, there has been little judicial treatment of the matter, and many members of the bar are unfamiliar with the marked departure from the common law the Federal Rules have effected on this issue.

Facts

The relevant facts are simply stated. While conducting a search of the premises of the defendant, Ruby Humphrey, pursuant to a lawful search warrant which authorized a search for evidence of bookmaking activity, government agents answered the telephone several times. The unknown callers stated directions for the placing of bets on various sporting events. The government proposes to introduce this evidence to show that the callers believed that the premises were used in betting operations. The existence of such belief tends to prove that they were so used. The defendants object on the ground of hearsay.

Common Law Background

* * *

In the instant case, the utterances of the absent declarants are not offered for the truth of the words, and the mere fact that the words were uttered has no relevance of itself. Rather they are offered to show the declarants' belief in a fact sought to be proved. At common law this situation occupied a controversial no-man's land. It was argued on the one hand that the out-of-court utterance was not hearsay, because the evidence was not offered for any truth stated in it, but for the truth of some other proposition inferred from it. On the other hand, it was also argued that the reasons for excluding hearsay applied, in that the evidence was being offered to show declarant's belief in the implied proposition, and he was not available to be cross-examined. Thus, the latter argument was that there existed strong policy reasons for ruling that such utterances were hearsay.

The classic case, which is discussed in virtually every textbook on evidence, is *Wright v. Tatham*, 7 Adolph. & E. 313, 386, 112 Eng. Rep. 488 (Exch. Ch. 1837), and 5 Cl. & F. 670, 739, 47 Rev. Rep. 136 (H.L. 1838). Described as a "celebrated and hard-fought cause," *Wright v. Tatham* was a will contest, in which the will was sought to be set aside on the grounds of the incompetency of the testator at the time of its execution. The proponents of the will offered to introduce into evidence letters to the testator from certain absent individuals on various business and social matters. The purpose of the offer was to show that the writers of the letters believed the testator was able to make intelligent decisions concerning such matters, and thus was competent.

One of the illustrations advanced in the judicial opinions in *Wright v. Tatham* is perhaps even more famous than the case itself. This is Baron Parke's famous sea captain example. Is it hearsay to offer as proof of the seaworthiness of a vessel that its captain, after thoroughly inspecting it, embarked on an ocean voyage upon it with his family?

The court in *Wright v. Tatham* held that implied assertions of this kind were hearsay. The rationale, as stated by Baron Parke, was as follows:

> The conclusion at which I have arrived is, that proof of a particular fact which is not of itself a matter in issue, but which is relevant only as implying a statement or opinion of a third person on the matter in issue, is inadmissible in all cases where such a statement or opinion not on oath would be of itself inadmissible; and, therefore, in this case the letters which are offered only to prove the competence of the testator, that is the truth of the implied statements therein contained, were properly rejected, as the mere statement or opinion of the writer would certainly have been inadmissible.

This was the prevailing common law view, where the hearsay issue was recognized. But frequently, it was not recognized. Thus, two federal appellate cases involving facts virtually identical to those in the case at bar did not even discuss the hearsay issue, although the evidence admitted in them would have been objectionable hearsay under the common law view.

The Federal Rules of Evidence

The common law rule that implied assertions were subject to hearsay treatment was criticized by respected commentators for several reasons.* * *

In a frequently cited article the following analysis appears:

> But ought the hearsay rule be deemed applicable to evidence of conduct? As McCormick has observed, the problem 'has only once received any adequate discussion in any decided case,' *i.e.*, in *Wright v. Tatham*, already referred to. And even in that case the court did not pursue its inquiry beyond the point of concluding that evidence of an 'implied' assertion must necessarily be excluded wherever evidence of an 'express' assertion would be inadmissible. But as has been pointed out more than once (although I find no *judicial* recognition of the difference), the "implied" assertion is, from the hearsay standpoint, not nearly as vulnerable as an express assertion of the fact which the evidence is offered to establish.
>
> This is on the assumption that the conduct was "nonassertive;" that the passers-by had their umbrellas up for the sake of keeping dry, not for the purpose of telling anyone it was raining; that the truck driver started up for the sake of resuming his journey, not for the purpose

> of telling anyone that the light had changed; that the vicar wrote the letter to the testator for the purpose of settling the dispute with the latter, rather than with any idea of expressing his opinion of the testator's sanity. And in the typical 'conduct as hearsay' case this assumption will be quite justifiable.
>
> On this assumption, it is clear that evidence of conduct must be taken as freed from at least one of the hearsay dangers, *i.e.*, mendacity. A man does not lie to himself. Put otherwise, if in doing what he does a man has no intention of asserting the existence or non-existence of a fact, it would appear that the trustworthiness of evidence of this conduct is the same whether he is an egregious liar or a paragon of veracity. Accordingly, the lack of opportunity for cross-examination in relation to his veracity or lack of it, would seem to be of no substantial importance. Accordingly, the usual judicial disposition to equate the "implied" to the "express" assertion is very questionable.

The drafters of the Federal Rules agreed with the criticisms of the common law rule that implied assertions should be treated as hearsay and expressly abolished it. They did this by providing that no oral or written expression was to be considered as hearsay, unless it was an "assertion" concerning the matter sought to be proved and that no nonverbal conduct should be considered as hearsay, unless it was intended to be an "assertion" concerning said matter.* * *

"Assertion" is not defined in the rules, but has the connotation of a forceful or positive declaration.

The Advisory Committee note concerning this problem states:

> The definition of "statement" assumes importance because the term is used in the definition of hearsay in subdivision (c). *The effect of the definition of "statement" is to exclude from the operation of the hearsay rule all evidence of conduct, verbal or nonverbal, not intended as an assertion. The key to the definition is that nothing is an assertion unless intended to be one.*
>
> It can scarcely be doubted that an assertion made in words is intended by the declarant to be an assertion. Hence verbal assertions readily fall into the category of "statement." Whether nonverbal conduct should be regarded as a statement for purposes of defining hearsay requires further consideration. Some nonverbal conduct, such as the act of pointing to identify a suspect in a lineup, is clearly the equivalent of words, assertive in nature, and to be regarded as a statement. Other nonverbal conduct, however, may be offered as evidence that the person acted as he did because of his belief in the existence of the condition sought to be proved, from which belief the existence of the condition may be inferred. This sequence is, arguably, in effect an assertion of the existence of the condition and hence properly includable within the hearsay concept. * * * Admittedly evidence of this character is untested with respect to the perception, memory, and narration (or their equivalents) of the actor, *but the*

Advisory Committee is of the view that these dangers are minimal in the absence of an intent to assert and do not justify the loss of the evidence on hearsay grounds. No class of evidence is free of the possibility of fabrication, but the likelihood is less with nonverbal than with assertive verbal conduct. The situations giving rise to the nonverbal conduct are such as virtually to eliminate questions of sincerity. Motivation, the nature of the conduct, and the presence or absence of reliance will bear heavily upon the weight to be given the evidence.* * * *Similar considerations govern nonassertive verbal conduct and verbal conduct which is assertive but offered as a basis for inferring something other than the matter asserted*, also excluded from the definition of hearsay by the language of subdivision (c). (Emphasis added).

* * *

Applying the principles discussed above to the case at bar, this court holds that the utterances of the betters telephoning in their bets were nonassertive verbal conduct, offered as relevant for an implied assertion to be inferred from them, namely that bets could be placed at the premises being telephoned. The language is not an assertion on its face, and it is obvious these persons did not intend to make an assertion about the fact sought to be proved or anything else.

As an implied assertion, the proffered evidence is expressly excluded from the operation of the hearsay rule by Rule 801 of the Federal Rules of Evidence, and the objection thereto must be overruled. An order to that effect has previously been entered.

NOTE

When should an implied assertion be considered hearsay?

Professors Saltzburg, Martin, and Capra address the problem of implied assertions in the following passage from the *Federal Rules of Evidence Manual* (9th ed. 2006):

> An out-of-court statement is hearsay only if the statement is offered to prove the truth of the "matter asserted." Does this mean that the hearsay rule excludes only statements offered for the truth of matters *expressly* asserted? If a statement is offered for the truth of a matter that is implied rather than expressed, does the utterance escape the hearsay prohibition? Professor Milich, in *Re-examining Hearsay Under the Federal Rules: Some Method for the Madness*, 39 Kan. L. Rev. 893 (1991), considers the following hypothetical illustration of the problem of implied assertions:
>
> > Assume, in a murder case, that the prosecution wants to prove that Joe is a sharpshooter. If a declarant makes a statement that

"Joe is a sharpshooter," this is an express assertion of fact and is excluded as hearsay. But there are a number of equivalent statements that make the same point without making an express assertion. Among them: (1) "Joe can shoot a tick off a running jaguar at 200 yards"; (2) "You ought to go hunting with Joe"; and (3) "Have you ever seen anyone shoot a rifle like Joe?"

If the hearsay rule excludes only out-of-court statements offered for the truth of matters *expressly* asserted, then none of these three statements are hearsay. The government is not offering the statement to show that Joe can actually shoot a tick off a jaguar at 200 yards; nor that anyone ought to go hunting with Joe; nor that anyone has seen anyone else shoot a rifle like Joe. A strong argument can be made, however, that there should be no difference between express and implied assertions, at least where the declarant is trying to make the same point by implication that he could otherwise make expressly. Given the subtlety of language, there is no reason to rest the hearsay rule on purely semantic distinctions. Certainly the hearsay dangers of an implied assertion are on a par with those attendant to an express assertion: The factfinder will be relying on the credibility of an uncross-examined declarant who may be lying or mistaken.

As Professor Milich states, a literalist approach to hearsay "guts the hearsay rule." *See also* Seidelson, *Implied Assertions and Federal Rule of Evidence 801: A Quandary for Federal Courts*, 24 Duq. L. Rev. 741 (1986) (arguing that hearsay rule should not rest on a semantic distinction between express and implied assertions). In the above hypothetical, it would lead to the bizarre result that a wild exaggeration (shooting the tick off a jaguar) could be heard by the jury, whereas a more careful attempt to approximate the truth (he is a good shot) could not. A literalist approach would also mean that the use of irony, aphorism, or metaphor could never be excluded as hearsay, even though everyone would know what the declarant intended to assert. Finally, Professor Milich makes the important point that "making the hearsay issue turn on the mere form of the out-of-court statement may tempt witnesses to 'recall' the statements in a nondeclarative form to circumvent the rule." *See also Park v. Huff*, 493 F.2d 923 (5th Cir. 1974) (noting that if the hearsay rule covered only express assertions of fact, the rule "could easily be circumvented through clever questioning and coaching of witnesses, so that answers were framed as implied rather than as direct assertions").

The Advisory Committee Note to Rule 801 states that "verbal conduct which is assertive but offered as a basis for inferring something other than the matter asserted" is "excluded from the definition of hearsay by the language of subdivision (c)." We think that the Advisory Committee's reading is not self-evident. The language "truth of the matter asserted" is flexible enough to cover "matters" that are implied as well as express.

Most Courts have been reluctant to adopt the implication of the Advisory Committee that the hearsay rule is completely inapplicable to implied verbal assertions. One well-known example is *United States v. Reynolds*, 715 F.2d 99 (3d Cir. 1983). Parran and a codefendant, Reynolds, were charged with conspiring to possess and cash a social security check belonging to someone else. Reynolds was arrested after he attempted to cash the check. Parran was across the street observing the proceedings. Parran crossed the street and casually walked by Parran and the officers. As Parran walked by, Reynolds called out to Parran, "I didn't tell them anything about you." The Court analyzed the admissibility of that statement as follows:

> As the government uses it, the statement's probative value depends on the truth of an assumed fact it implies. Unless the trier assumes that the statement implies that Reynolds did not tell the postal inspectors that Parran was involved in the conspiracy to defraud, even though Parran was in fact involved, the statement carries no probative weight for the government's case. * * * Consequently, we believe that, as the government uses it, the statement's relevance goes well beyond the fact that it was uttered. * * * [T]he government offers it to prove the truth of the assumed fact of defendant's guilt implied by its conduct. Accordingly, we reject the government's suggestion in this case that only a statement's express assertion should be considered in deciding whether it constitutes hearsay.

The problems of a literalist approach to the hearsay rule, excluding only express assertions, are well illustrated by the case of *United States v. Ybarra*, 70 F.3d 362 (5th Cir. 1995). To prove that the defendant lived in a house where a firearm was found, the government offered this statement from the defendant's wife to police officers: "[T]here is no way [Ybarra] is coming home as long as you police are here." The Court held that the statement was not hearsay because it was offered to prove something other than the fact that Ybarra would not come home. Rather, it was offered to prove that Ybarra lived in the house. This ignores the fact that the government did offer the statement for the truth of the assertion that was *implied* by the wife's statement — i.e., that Ybarra lived there. The Court's decision that the statement was not offered for the truth of the matter asserted rests on a constricted and highly semantic view of "the matter asserted," and creates problems if the statement is changed in any slight degree. If the wife had said, "Yeah, he lives here and he won't be coming back while police are here," the statement would undeniably be hearsay. There is no substantial distinction between that hypothetical statement and the statement actually made by the wife in *Ybarra*. Moreover, what would the Court have done if the wife had said, "This is Ybarra's castle," or more obliquely, "Don't you cops have any respect? A man's home is his castle." Would these statements not be hearsay because the government would not be offering them to prove that the place was Ybarra's castle? The "express assertion" view of the hearsay rule leads to absurd results. We believe that a statement should be treated as hearsay whenever it is offered to prove the truth of either an express or implied assertion, so long as the Trial Judge finds that the declarant intended to communicate that assertion when he made the statement.

We note that most Federal Courts are in agreement agree with the view that implied assertions are hearsay if they are intentionally communicated by the speaker — and not hearsay if there is no intent to communicate the implication. An example is *United States v. Summers*, 414 F.3d 1287 (10th Cir. 2005), where the defendant's accomplice in a bank robbery was arrested and said to the officer, "How did you guys find us so fast?" The Court held that an implied assertion is hearsay if the speaker intended to communicate the implication that is sought to be used at trial. It also noted that the burden is on the opponent to show that the speaker had the intent to assert the implication in the statement. Applying this intent-based test to the facts, the Court held that the defendant satisfied his burden of demonstrating that by positing the question, "How did you guys find us so fast?", the declarant intended to make an assertion. It explained as follows:

> It begs credulity to assume that in positing the question Mohammed was exclusively interested in modern methods of law enforcement, including surveillance, communication, and coordination. Rather, fairly construed the statement intimated both guilt and wonderment at the ability of the police to apprehend the perpetrators of the crime so quickly.

An intent-based approach to implied assertions has several virtues. First, at least where statements intentionally asserting one thing are being used to prove something else that the declarant was not trying to say, the hearsay risks are reduced. This is because the declarant is unlikely to have intended to mislead on matters that he had no intent to communicate in the first place. One of the major dangers of hearsay — the risk of insincerity — is thus minimized, and an intent-based test would allow such unintentional statements to be admitted.

Second, an intent-based approach provides a unitary test for non-assertive conduct and verbal communications. As discussed above, conduct is hearsay only if the actor intends to communicate by his action and the conduct is offered for the truth of that communication. An intent-based approach applies the same rule for verbal communications.

Third, an intent-based approach toward implied assertions is favored by most modern commentators. *See, e.g.*, Milich, *supra*, at 907 ("[I]ntent to communicate is the key to distinguishing between hearsay and non-hearsay under the federal definition."); Callen, *Hearsay and Informal Reasoning*, 47 Vand. L. Rev. 43, 113 (1994) ("When deciding whether a statement is hearsay for a particular purpose, courts should recognize that propositions the speaker generally intends the hearer to understand from the communication should be part of an assertion for purposes of the hearsay rule. Classifying assertions implied from communicative conduct as hearsay facilitates factfinders' use of their experience in informal reasoning at trial.").

Fourth, an intent-based test allows the hearsay rule to apply and exclude statements that are exaggerations (such as "Joe can shoot a tick off a jaguar"), or metaphor or sarcasm. All such statements are basically the equivalent of an express assertion. If offered to prove the truth of the implied *and intended* meaning, the evidence is hearsay under an intent-based approach. This is clearly the appropriate result, even though the statement is not being offered to prove the literal truth of the matter *expressly* asserted; reserving the hearsay rule to express assertions only will deprive the rule of almost all practical effect. There are many examples of implied but intentional assertions that should be treated as hearsay. A declarant's statement that "the sky is on fire" is hearsay when offered to show that the speaker witnessed a sunset. A declarant's statement, "Well, at least I never forged a will!" is hearsay when offered to prove the implication that the person to whom the statement was made is a forger. A declarant's statement, "The automobile was going faster than a speeding bullet," is hearsay when offered to prove that the car was exceeding the speed limit. These statements are hearsay because the "matter asserted" includes what the declarant reasonably intended to assert. Given the subtlety of language, there is no reason to rest the hearsay rule on purely semantic distinctions between express and implied assertions.

This is not to say that an intent-based approach to implied assertions is free from difficulty. There is some indeterminacy in the application of any intent-based test. As Professor Milich puts it, "the quest for the declarant's intent in cases of verbal conduct involves a search for what the declarant truly had in mind." But any problem, we think, can be adequately handled by an objective, rather than subjective, test of intent. The question should be whether a reasonable person making a statement such as the declarant made would have intended to communicate the implied assertion that the proponent is offering for its truth. As with conduct, the burden should be placed on the nonoffering party to show that the declarant had the intent to communicate the implied assertion.

A good example of the intent-based approach to implied assertions is *United States v. Weeks*, 919 F.2d 248 (5th Cir. 1990). Weeks was charged with kidnapping. The victims testified that their abductors used the names "Jimmy" and "Gato" in addressing each other. To establish that Weeks was "Gato," the government called a witness who testified that he had heard others refer to Weeks as "Gato" when they addressed him, e.g., "How ya doin' Gato?" The Court held that the out-of-court statements addressed to "Gato" were properly admitted. It found that Weeks had not satisfied his burden of showing that declarants who referred to him as "Gato" were intending to communicate an implied assertion, i.e., "Weeks is nicknamed 'Gato.'" Rather, it was more likely that they were trying to communicate other ideas, and were simply using the term "Gato" as they would any other name: as a means of introduction or reference. As the declarants probably had other things in mind than simply to advertise their belief about Weeks' nickname, the statements were not hearsay. *See also United*

States v. Jackson, 88 F.3d 845 (10th Cir. 1996): The defendant, whose name was Kenny, was charged with narcotics violations. The police officer who arrested him testified that he seized the defendant's pager and called the telephone number displayed on the pager; the person who answered said "Is this Kenny?" This testimony was held properly admitted as non-hearsay. The Court stated that "the important question is whether the assertion is intended" and found it "hard to believe that the declarant intended to assert that Mr. Jackson was in possession of the pager and that he was responding to her call."

In contrast, in *United States v. Berrios*, 132 F.3d 834 (1st Cir. 1998), the government had proof that a man named "Pablo" was a drug dealer, and sought to prove that the defendant went by the nickname "Pablo." The defendant called a witness who would have testified that she was present at a drug deal with her husband, and her husband introduced her to the seller, saying "This is Pablo." The witness would have testified that the person introduced as "Pablo" was not the defendant. The Court held that the out-of-court statement of the witness's husband, "This is Pablo", was properly excluded as hearsay. That is the correct result under an intent-based test. The intent of the husband was to assert to his wife that the person before her went by the name "Pablo." If the husband had said to his wife privately, "watch out for Pablo, he is dangerous", this would not be an intentional assertion that the person identified went by the name Pablo. Rather, the intent of the speaker would be to warn his wife to stay away from the identified person.

D. OUT-OF-COURT STATEMENTS OF DECLARANTS WHO TESTIFY AT TRIAL

UNITED STATES v. CHECK
582 F.2d 668 (2d Cir. 1978)

WATERMAN, CIRCUIT JUDGE:

[Check was convicted on charges of drug distribution.] In contending that his convictions should be overturned, Check raises troublesome arguments concerning the introduction into evidence of certain portions of the testimony of the undercover police officer who was the government's principal witness against Check. * * *

The government's evidence at trial was primarily presented through the testimony of Stephen Spinelli, a detective in the New York City Police Department who had been assigned to investigate allegations that a fellow New York City police officer, Patrolman Sandy Check, was engaging in illegal narcotics trafficking. Operating in an undercover capacity and using the pseudonym "Danny Gennaro," Spinelli was initially introduced to one William Joseph Cali, a confidential informant who knew Check and who agreed to introduce Spinelli to Check so that Spinelli, in his assumed role of a prospective purchaser of narcotics, could either substantiate or disprove the serious allegations of criminal conduct which had been made against Check.

Spinelli testified that, as anticipated, Cali arranged for a meeting with Check which was to take place on August 8, 1974 at Dave's Corner Restaurant, located at the corner of Canal Street and Broadway in lower Manhattan. Shortly after Spinelli and Cali had entered the restaurant Check appeared outside the front window of the building and motioned to have Cali meet with him outside. This Cali did and, after a conversation with Check, Cali rejoined Spinelli who was still seated in the restaurant. Cali refused to testify at the trial. So, in view of the potential hearsay problems connected with any attempt to elicit the content of Spinelli's conversations with him, and after an objection on hearsay grounds had already been voiced, the prosecutor employed a method of questioning which he argued circumvented any hearsay problems. The prosecutor, after establishing that Check and Cali had conversed and that Cali had thereafter returned to speak to Spinelli, inquired of Spinelli (as he would ultimately inquire of him at least twelve additional times): "Without telling us what Mr. Cali said to you, what did you say to him?" In response, Spinelli told the prosecutor, and also, of course, the jury, what he had purportedly said to Cali:

> I — after we had the conversation, I instructed William Cali that by no means did I intend to front any sum of money to Sandy Check, I didn't particularly care for the fact that — initially he was supposed to come with an ounce of cocaine, and the taste which he had, which I was supposed to get prior to making the ounce buy of cocaine, was at his house, and due to the fact that it wasn't of good quality, I wasn't particularly concerned, as good faith wasn't being shown to me, especially for the fact I also told William Cali I had no intentions of giving Sandy Check $300 which William Cali owed to him from a previous narcotics deal.

Spinelli next testified that, following the conversation he had with Cali, Cali again departed the restaurant and spoke with Check. Cali then reentered the restaurant and "again (Spinelli and Cali) had a conversation." As before, Spinelli now related what he had supposedly "told William Cali":

> At that time I told William Cali I didn't particularly care whether or not Check was concerned about rats and not wanting to meet anyone new or about being busted by the man, and I had again still no intention of fronting any money or the $300 which Cali owed him.

Leaving the restaurant for a third time and having his third powwow with Check, Cali, as before, returned, talked to Spinelli and, again, Spinelli now testified as to what this third time he had "told William Cali":

> I told William Cali at the time I didn't particularly care whether or not the cocaine which I was supposed to get was 70 percent pure, nor the fact that it was supposed to come from a captain of detectives; I had again still no intention of fronting any money to him, the $1,200 for the ounce of cocaine or the $300 which William Cali owed to him.

[Eventually, Spinelli received a "taste" of drugs from Cali for a payment of $50. Subsequently, Spinelli testified that received a half ounce of heroin from Cali for a payment of $1,350. During some later negotiations, Check purportedly stated directly to Spinelli that he could provide Spinelli with drugs.]

Testifying in his own defense at his trial, Check did not deny that he had met with Cali on August 8, 1974, at Dave's Corner Restaurant. According to Check, however, he had agreed to meet with Cali on that occasion only because Cali had previously proposed helping Check make "a good drug arrest" and shortly before their rendezvous Cali had called Check to tell him that he might "have something for" him and that "it was important that [Check] meet him." He testified that when he learned from Cali that Spinelli was interested in purchasing narcotics rather than in selling them, he was no longer interested in pursuing the matter. He denied meeting with Spinelli on August 9, 1974, and, accordingly, denied that he had agreed at that time to sell narcotics to Spinelli or that he had received $1,350 from Spinelli on that occasion. While admitting that he had met and talked with Spinelli at the ROK Bar on August 22, 1974, Check testified that he had not filed a report of the incident, as departmental regulations required, because he had regarded Spinelli as a "crackpot" inasmuch as Spinelli "was talking quite openly at the bar about drugs, and he didn't impress [Check] at all as being anything, being a smart person, because a person that deals in drugs doesn't let everybody know their business."

* * *

At trial the government took the position * * * that Spinelli's testimony regarding his conversations with Cali could not constitute hearsay because Spinelli carefully limited that testimony to what he said to Cali and he scrupulously avoided relating any statements which Cali had made to him. Check argues, however, that, notwithstanding the artful phrasing of the prosecutor's questions and Spinelli's equally adroit responses to them, Spinelli actually was on numerous occasions throughout his testimony in essence conveying to the jury the precise substance of the out-of-court statements Cali made to him. Check further contends that, even if Spinelli's testimony were not excludable on the ground that he was merely serving as an improper conduit for Cali's hearsay statements, there is an additional reason why Spinelli's testimony of what he told Cali would nonetheless still be inadmissible hearsay. Specifically, Check contends that, notwithstanding the government's position at trial and the district court's holding, the federal courts do not recognize any exception to the hearsay rule, or, except in the limited circumstances set forth in Fed. R. Evid. 801(d), any exclusion from the definition of hearsay, which would permit testimony in court relating to the prior out-of-court statements of a witness merely because the witness is available at trial for cross-examination and subject to cross-examination concerning those statements. On either of the grounds he advances, Check is clearly correct.

* * *

* * * [W]e agree with Check that for much of his testimony Spinelli was serving as a transparent conduit for the introduction of inadmissible hearsay information obviously supplied by and emanating from the informant Cali. * * * There is * * * no doubt that the out-of-court statements uttered by Cali, audaciously introduced through the artifice of having Spinelli supposedly restrict his testimony to his half of his conversations with Cali, were being offered to prove the truth of the matters asserted in them. * * * We thus conclude that, in substance, significant portions of Spinelli's testimony regarding his conversations with Cali were indeed hearsay, for that testimony was a transparent attempt to incorporate into the officer's testimony information supplied by the informant who did not testify at trial. Such a device is improper and cannot miraculously transform inadmissible hearsay into admissible evidence. * * *

Even if we were inclined to accept the government's contention that Spinelli's testimony at trial was an honest narration of various out-of-court statements he himself had made, and we were thereby to exalt form over substance to the extent of blinding ourselves to the true character of Spinelli's answers, we would nonetheless continue to hold that substantial portions of Spinelli's testimony were inadmissible hearsay. Throughout the trial the government adamantly maintained, and Judge Motley unfortunately agreed, that, if the out-of-court statements which Spinelli was relating during his in-court testimony could properly be regarded as his very own statements, and not merely as a subterfuge for the indirect introduction of Cali's hearsay, those statements were admissible under some exclusion from the definition of hearsay or under some exception to the hearsay rule which would permit them to be admitted as the out-of-court statements of a person who testifies at trial and who can therefore be subjected to the rigors of cross-examination as to them. * * * In response, Check argues that under the law of evidence presently in force in the federal courts there is no such exception to the hearsay rule. We agree. * * * To be sure, Fed. R. Evid. 801(d)(1)(B), by excluding from the definition of hearsay, see Fed. R. Evid. 801(c), certain prior consistent statements which otherwise would be so included, does potentially permit some of a witness's prior consistent statements to be used as substantive evidence to prove the truth of the matters asserted. But the class of such prior statements which can potentially be so utilized as substantive evidence because of their exclusion from the definition of hearsay is carefully confined to those "[p]rior consistent statements [which] traditionally have been admissible [but only for the rehabilitative purpose of] rebut[ting] charges of recent fabrication or improper influence or motive." Note to Rule 801, Notes of the Advisory Committee on Proposed Rules of Evidence, 56 F.R.D. at 296. Such prior statements are, of course, those which are "offered to rebut an express or implied charge against [the witness] of recent fabrication or improper influence or motive," Fed. R. Evid. 801(d)(1)(B), and which were made prior to the time the supposed motive to falsify arose. To repeat, aside from the relatively small number of prior statements that are admissible as being within the dispensation conferred by Fed. R. Evid. 801(d)(1)(B), a witness's prior statements offered to prove the truth of the matters asserted therein are not immunized from the proscriptive effect of the hearsay rule. We therefore conclude that the challenged portions of Spinelli's testimony were inadmissible hearsay even if they could be regarded as being a literal recitation of Spinelli's own prior out-of-court statements.

[The Court rejected the government's argument that the erroneous admission of hearsay was harmless error.]

Judgment of conviction reversed and case remanded for a new trial on all counts of the indictment.

Chapter 11

HEARSAY EXCLUSIONS

A. STATEMENTS THAT ARE "NOT HEARSAY" UNDER FEDERAL RULE 801(d)

Rule 801(d) technically provides an exemption from, rather than an exception to, the hearsay rule. The statements covered by subdivision (d) are categorized as "not hearsay" rather than as "hearsay subject to an exception" because the basis for admitting these statements is different from that supporting the other standard hearsay exceptions (such as excited utterances and dying declarations) which are found in Rules 803, 804, and 807. Statements falling within these latter exceptions are admitted because they are made pursuant to circumstantial guarantees of reliability that substitute for the in-court guarantees of oath, cross-examination, etc. For example, excited utterances are made while the declarant is under the influence of a startling event and for that reason is less likely to be able to lie.

In contrast, prior statements of testifying witnesses (subdivision (d)(1)) are admitted not because they were reliable when made, but because the person who made them is testifying at the trial or hearing under oath and subject to cross-examination. And admissions (subdivision (d)(2)) are permitted not because they are reliable, but because the adversary or his agents made them — if a party happens to make an unreliable statement, it is not up to the judge to protect him from use of the statement by the adversary; it is up to the party to try to explain the statement or to diminish its importance.

The drafters of the Federal Rules thought that it would be confusing to lump prior statements of testifying witnesses and admissions together with reliability-based exceptions under a single label of "hearsay exceptions." In fact, however, the Federal Rules regime is more confusing in the end because statements that clearly fit the definition of hearsay are labeled, *ipse dixit*, "not hearsay."

There is no practical difference between an exception to the hearsay rule and an exclusion or exemption from that rule. (We use the terms "exclusion" and "exemption" interchangeably throughout this chapter.) If a statement fits either exemption or an exception, it is not excluded by the hearsay rule, and it can be considered as substantive evidence if it is not excluded by any other Rule (e.g., Rule 403).

B. PRIOR STATEMENTS BY A WITNESS

[1] Inconsistent Statements Under Oath

[a] Common Law

At common law, prior inconsistent statements were considered hearsay and could be used to impeach a witness' truthfulness, but could not be used to prove the prior inconsistent statement was true.

A classic example of the effect of this rule is the criminal case where the prosecution's star witness told the police that the defendant committed the crime, but then at trial testifies: "I don't think I've ever seen that guy before." At common law, the prosecution could use the prior inconsistent statement only to show that the witness is lying at trial. The prosecution could not use the statement as substantive proof that the defendant actually committed the crime. Result? If the government presents no evidence other than the prior inconsistent statement, there is no substantive proof that the defendant committed the crime, and a directed verdict must be granted in the defendant's favor. If, however, the prior statement were admissible under a hearsay exception, the statement could be counted in the substantive evidence necessary to create a jury question.

[b] Federal Rule of Evidence 801(d)(1)(A)

Rule 801. Definitions

* * *

(d) Statements which are not hearsay. A statement is not hearsay if —

(1) Prior statement by witness. The declarant testifies at the trial or hearing and is subject to cross-examination concerning the statement, and the statement is (A) inconsistent with the declarant's testimony, and was given under oath subject to the penalty of perjury at a trial, hearing, or other proceeding, or in a deposition.

* * *

[c] Illustrations

The Sheriff of Metropolis sues Robin Rich for slander, alleging that Robin Rich told Marty Manners that "the Sheriff of Metropolis took a bribe." Marty Manners was the only witness and relayed the conversation to the Sheriff the next day. The Sheriff calls Marty Manners to the stand.

Example 1

Plaintiff: State your name.
Marty Manners: Marty Manners.
Plaintiff: Do you know the defendant, Robin Rich?
Marty Manners: Yes.

Plaintiff:	Did you have a conversation with the defendant on the date in question about the plaintiff, the Sheriff of Metropolis?
Marty Manners:	Yes, I did.
Plaintiff:	Was anyone else there?
Marty Manners:	No, just the two of us.
Plaintiff:	(Dramatically) And what did Robin Rich say about the Sheriff?
Marty Manners:	Ah, well, nothing much. Just that "the Sheriff has a new bride."
Plaintiff:	(Extensive coughing) Well, didn't you tell the Sheriff the next day that Robin Rich said "the Sheriff took a bribe?"
Defendant:	Objection! That's not substantive proof. I move for a directed verdict.
Court:	__________.

Example 2

Plaintiff:	State your name.
Marty Manners:	Marty Manners.
Plaintiff:	Do you know the defendant, Robin Rich?
Marty Manners:	Yes.
Plaintiff:	Did you have a conversation with the defendant on the date in question about the plaintiff, the Sheriff of Metropolis?
Marty Manners:	Yes, I did.
Plaintiff:	Was anyone else there?
Marty Manners:	No, just the two of us.
Plaintiff:	(Dramatically) And what did Robin Rich say about the Sheriff?
Marty Manners:	Ah, well, nothing much. Just that "the Sheriff has a new bride."
Plaintiff:	Isn't it true that you gave a deposition in my office?
Marty Manners:	Yes.
Plaintiff:	I'd like you to look at a copy of that deposition (handing a document to the witness). Didn't you say at the deposition that the defendant said "the Sheriff took a bribe?"
Defendant:	Objection! That's not substantive proof. I move for a directed verdict.
Court:	__________.

[d] Other Proceeding

UNITED STATES v. LIVINGSTON
661 F.2d 239 (D.C. Cir. 1981)

J. SKELLY WRIGHT, CIRCUIT JUDGE:

Appellants, who were tried jointly for armed robbery of a post office, challenge their convictions on several evidentiary and procedural grounds. Because we agree that the trial court improperly instructed the jury regarding the use of prior inconsistent statements, we reverse the convictions and remand for a new trial. We do not reach any of the other issues raised by appellants.

I. *Background*

On March 5, 1980 two men robbed the Brookland Station Post Office in Washington, D.C. The pair had approached the last employee leaving the office and forced him at gunpoint to let them into the post office and open the safes. The men took about $550 in cash, a money order writing machine, a validating plate, and 97 money orders.

On June 3, 1980 appellants John T. Livingston and David Coyle were indicted on two counts: armed robbery of a post office and possession of stolen United States money orders. At trial the Government introduced several witnesses to testify about the events on the day of the robbery and about property stolen from the post office. Several witnesses also testified about the cashing and attempted cashing of a number of stolen money orders in Philadelphia and Trenton. These two lines of evidence were linked by testimony of three women, acquaintances of Livingston and Coyle, who accompanied them on a trip to Philadelphia and Trenton one week after the robbery. The defense presented no evidence. The jury returned verdicts of guilty as to both appellants on the armed robbery count. Appellants were sentenced to 25 years' incarceration, and they subsequently brought this appeal.

II. *Use of Prior Inconsistent Statements*

Prior to trial each of the women accompanying appellants to Philadelphia and Trenton was questioned by, and gave at least one sworn statement to, postal inspectors. In particular, the statement of Yvonne Hester indicated that the appellants had discussed and joked about several aspects of the robbery. At trial Ms. Hester appeared as a Government witness. When she denied or failed to recall conversations mentioned in the statement to the postal inspector, the prosecutor read damaging excerpts from it. On cross-examination Ms. Hester stated that when she signed the statement she did not know what she was signing and that she did not remember the conversations mentioned in the statement.

In his instructions to the jury the trial judge noted the confrontation with prior statements. He then gave guidance as to how the prior inconsistent statements could be used. The pertinent instruction, based in part on language in Rule 801(d)(1)(A) of the Federal Rules of Evidence, read as follows:

> However, if the prior statement was given by the witness while under oath, subject to the penalty of perjury, at a prior trial, hearing, or other proceeding, or in a deposition, and if you find that such prior statement under oath is inconsistent with the present statement in court, you may accept either the prior statement or the present testimony in court as reflecting the truth of any matter contained therein.

Defense counsel objected to this instruction, and appellants contend that the trial court erred in giving it. They argue that Hester's prior statements did not meet the requirements of Rule 801(d)(1)(A) and that they therefore should never have been considered as substantive evidence.

A. *Prior Statements as Substantive Evidence*

Under the Federal Rules a prior inconsistent statement by a witness is not hearsay if "given under oath subject to the penalty of perjury at a *trial, hearing, or other proceeding, or in a deposition* * * * ." Fed. R. Evid. 801(d)(1)(A) (emphasis added). Here, a postal inspector went to Ms. Hester's residence, asked her questions, took notes, wrote a statement based on her responses, asked her to read a typewritten copy and to make any necessary changes, and then obtained her signature swearing to the accuracy of the statement [i.e., under oath and subject to the penalty of perjury]. We do not think that these circumstances satisfy the Rule's requirement of "a trial, hearing, or other proceeding."

In order to assure authenticity and reliability, "the Rule seems to contemplate situations in which an official verbatim record is routinely kept, whether stenographically or by electronic means, under legal authority." The Rule's requirements were designed "to limit substantive use of prior inconsistent statements to those situations in which there is likely to be *overwhelming* proof that the witness did in fact make the prior inconsistent statement." Blakey, *Substantive Use of Prior Inconsistent Statements Under the Federal Rules of Evidence*, 64 Ky. L.J. 3, 10 (1975) (emphasis added). In this case no official verbatim record was routinely kept by postal inspectors. The formalities used "provide less assurance that a statement was in fact made and sworn to than the formalities which surround a firsthand appearance at an on-the-record proceeding."

Courts of Appeals have generally found that statements made to investigating officials fail to qualify as made at a proceeding under Rule 801(d)(1)(A). *United States v. Ragghianti*, 560 F.2d 1376, 1381 (9th Cir. 1977) (prior statement obtained by Federal Bureau of Investigation in the course of a criminal investigation not admissible for substantive purposes); *Martin v. United States*, 528 F.2d 1157, 1161 (4th Cir. 1975) (statement before two investigating officers was not made at a proceeding and therefore does not qualify as substantive evidence). These cases provide the clearest analogy to the present case; they suggest that Hester's statement was hearsay inadmissible to prove the truth of matters contained within it.

The one exception to the line of cases in this area is *United States v. Castro-Ayon*, 537 F.2d 1055 (9th Cir. 1976). There the court found that statements made to a federal agent during an interrogation at a Border Patrol station fell within the Rule's requirements. However, the court noted that "the immigration proceeding before Agent Pearce bears many similarities to a grand-jury proceeding: both are investigatory, *ex parte*, inquisitive, sworn, basically prosecutorial, held before an officer other than the arresting officer, recorded, and held in circumstances of some legal formality. Indeed, this immigration proceeding provides more legal rights for the witnesses than does a grand jury: the right to remain totally silent, the right to counsel, and the right to have the interrogator inform the witness of these rights."

Hester's statement to the postal inspector lacks many of the circumstantial guarantees of reliability identified in *Castro-Ayon*. The questioning was not held before an independent officer; no recordings were made; the interrogation occurred at Hester's home; and no rights were afforded to her. Indeed, the circumstances fall far short of those in a grand jury proceeding, the paradigmatic "other proceeding" under the Rule.

Accordingly, Hester's statement should have been admitted only for the purpose of impeaching her credibility. It should not have been treated as having any potential substantive or independent testimonial value. While some commentators doubt that juries can distinguish between the use of prior statements for impeachment as opposed to substantive purposes, the distinction remains an important one if the Rules as drafted are to retain their vitality.

B. *Reversible Error*

The prior inconsistent statements were important to the Government's case and might well have influenced the jury's verdict. The Government itself recognized that Hester's statement "was clearly probative of the identity of the robbers." Hester's statement to the postal inspector included a comment allegedly made by one defendant about the division of the proceeds from the robbery and a detailed exchange between both appellants about several aspects of the robbery. These statements provided the most direct evidence linking the defendants to the thefts and the stolen money orders. Not only were they read into the record on direct examination, but the prosecutor also read the statements twice in his closing argument and then summarized them at the end of his argument. The repeated emphasis on Hester's prior statement surely must have made an impression on the jurors. Moreover, the prosecutor's reliance on the statement suggests its importance to the Government's entire case.

Under these circumstances we can hardly say that the judge's error in allowing the prior statement to be considered for its substantive value "did not influence the jury, or had but very slight effect * * * ." *Kotteakos v. United States*, 328 U.S. 750, 764 (1946) (discussing harmless error standard). Thus the error in this case was sufficiently grave to warrant reversal.

REVERSED

NOTES

1. How should the term "other proceedings" in Federal Rule 801(d)(1)(A) be interpreted?

See United States v. Day, 789 F.2d 1217 (6th Cir. 1986), where the Court held that statements made to investigative agents did not qualify as statements from an "other proceeding" even though they had been made under oath; *United States v. Perez*, 870 F.2d 1222 (7th Cir. 1989) (pretrial interview with an adverse witness, even though transcribed by a court reporter, was not admissible under Rule 801(d)(1)(A) since it was not a trial-like proceeding); Saltzburg, Martin, and Capra, *Federal Rules of Evidence Manual* (9th ed. 2006) ("In our view, 'other proceedings' must be routine and formal proceedings conducted by a legal officer or under her supervision, and of a type that would lead a declarant to believe that the duty to tell the truth was the same, or nearly the same, as at a trial.").

2. Must the prior statement be diametrically opposed to the trial testimony to be "inconsistent"?

In *United States v. Dennis*, 625 F.2d 782, 795 (8th Cir. 1980), the Court stated that an inconsistency "may be found in evasive answers, inability to recall, silence, or changes of position." *See also United States v. Williams*, 737 F.2d 594 (7th Cir. 1984) (no error in admitting grand jury testimony of witness whose testimony at trial was "limited, vague and not inculpatory"; a statement, to be inconsistent, need not be diametrically opposed or logically incompatible).

3. Is a witness's inability to recall the event or the prior statement at trial inconsistent with the prior statement?

The case results, at first glance, appear conflicting. In *United States v. Bigham*, 812 F.2d 943 (5th Cir. 1987), the court held that the inconsistency requirement of Rule 801(d)(1)(A) was met when the witness claimed no memory of the events that were the subject of the trial. In *United States v. Palumbo*, 639 F.2d 123 (3d Cir. 1981), the court indicated that a prior statement of a government witness who suffered a memory lapse at trial was not admissible under Rule 801(d)(1)(A). The *Palumbo* Court reasoned that the witness's current lack of memory was not necessarily inconsistent with her positive declaration to police as to the source of her drugs. Upon closer inspection, the cases are reconcilable on the following ground: if the witness really does lack memory of the underlying facts, then the trial testimony as to lack of memory is not inconsistent with the witness' prior positive statement. However, if the witness is feigning lack of memory, an inconsistency can be found, because the witness is trying to use lack of memory as a lame excuse to distance himself from his previous statement. This is sufficient repudiation of the prior statement to be considered inconsistent. As noted in *United States v. Thompson*, 708 F.2d 1294 (8th Cir. 1983), the trial court has considerable discretion in determining whether the witness' memory loss is sincere or feigned and thus inconsistent with an earlier statement.

4. If a prior inconsistent statement is admissible as substantive proof under Federal Rule 801(d)(1)(A), is the statement alone sufficient to support a verdict in favor of the one who offered the inconsistent statement?

It is important to recognize the difference between admissibility of evidence and sufficiency. In *United States v. Orrico*, 599 F.2d 113 (6th Cir. 1979), the Court noted that prior inconsistent statements admissible as substantive proof under 801(d)(1)(A) may not be sufficient as the sole proof of an allegation central to the litigation.

5. May a prior inconsistent statement that is not admissible as substantive proof under Federal Rule 801(d)(1)(A) nonetheless be used to impeach the witness?

With some limitations it is generally settled that a prior inconsistent statement may be used to impeach even though it is not admissible as substantive proof. The major limitation is that a party may not call a witness solely to impeach them with a prior inconsistent statement that would not be admissible under Rule 801(d)(1)(A) or any other hearsay exception — to permit such an action would allow a party to end-run the strictures of the hearsay rule.

When a prior inconsistent statement is admissible only for impeachment purposes and not for its truth, a judge should, upon request, instruct the jury accordingly.

[2] Consistent Statements

[a] Federal Rule of Evidence 801(d)(1)(B)

Rule 801. Definitions

* * *

(d) Statements which are not hearsay. A statement is not hearsay if —

(1) Prior statement by witness. The declarant testifies at the trial or hearing and is subject to cross-examination concerning the statement, and the statement is * * * (B) consistent with the declarant's testimony and is offered to rebut an express or implied charge against the declarant of recent fabrication or improper influence or motive.

* * *

[b] Illustration

The defendant is charged with armed robbery. The only witness that can identify the defendant is Dirty Rat, who allegedly drove the get-away car. Dirty Rat has testified on direct that the defendant walked into the store with a gun and came out with a bag of cash. The defendant cross-examines.

Defendant:	Now, Mr. Rat, you just testified that the defendant went into the store, isn't that true?

Dirty Rat:	Yes.
Defendant:	But you didn't tell that to the police the day you were arrested, did you? In fact, didn't you deny that you were even in town?
Dirty Rat:	Yes, I said I was in New Jersey.
Defendant:	But now you've been granted immunity from these charges, haven't you?
Dirty Rat:	Yes.
Defendant:	And the D.A. has cut a deal on some other charges pending against you, hasn't he?
Dirty Rat:	Yes.
Defendant:	No further questions.

The State calls Top Cop.

Prosecution:	State your name.
Top Cop:	Top Cop.
Prosecution:	Did you interview Dirty Rat about this case?
Top Cop:	Yes.
Prosecution:	Was that before he was arrested on the new charges and before immunity was granted on the other charges?
Top Cop:	Yes.
Prosecution:	What did he tell you then?
Defendant:	Objection! Prior consistent statements are inadmissible.
Prosecution:	___________.

[c] Allegations of Recent Fabrication

TOME v. UNITED STATES
513 U.S. 150 (1995)

JUSTICE KENNEDY delivered the opinion of the Court, except as to Part IIB.

Various federal Courts of Appeals are divided over the evidence question presented by this case. At issue is the interpretation of a provision in the Federal Rules of Evidence bearing upon the admissibility of statements, made by a declarant who testifies as a witness, that are consistent with the testimony and are offered to rebut a charge of a "recent fabrication or improper influence or motive." Fed. Rule Evid. 801(d)(1)(B). The question is whether out-of-court consistent statements made after the alleged fabrication, or after the alleged improper influence or motive arose, are admissible under the Rule.

I

Petitioner Tome was charged in a one-count indictment with the felony of sexual abuse of a child, his own daughter, aged four at the time of the alleged crime. The case having arisen on the Navajo Indian Reservation, Tome was tried by a jury in the United States District Court for the District of New Mexico, where he was found guilty of violating 18 U.S.C. §§ 1153, 2241(c), and 2245(2)(A) and (B).

Tome and the child's mother had been divorced in 1988. A tribal court awarded joint custody of the daughter, A.T., to both parents, but Tome had primary physical custody. * * * On August 27, 1990, the mother contacted Colorado authorities with allegations that Tome had committed sexual abuse against A.T.

The prosecution's theory was that Tome committed sexual assaults upon the child while she was in his custody and that the crime was disclosed when the child was spending vacation time with her mother. The defense argued that the allegations were concocted so the child would not be returned to her father. At trial A.T., then six and one half years old, was the Government's first witness. For the most part, her direct testimony consisted of one-and two-word answers to a series of leading questions. * * * Defense counsel then began questioning her about the allegations of abuse, and it appears she was reluctant at many points to answer. * * *

After A.T. testified, the Government produced six witnesses who testified about a total of seven statements made by A.T. describing the alleged sexual assaults: A.T.'s babysitter recited A.T.'s statement to her on August 22, 1990, that she did not want to return to her father because he "gets drunk and he thinks I'm his wife"; the babysitter related further details given by A.T. on August 27, 1990, while A.T.'s mother stood outside the room and listened after the mother had been unsuccessful in questioning A.T. herself; the mother recounted what she had heard A.T. tell the babysitter; a social worker recounted details A.T. told her on August 29, 1990 about the assaults; and three pediatricians, Drs. Kuper, Reich and Spiegel, related A.T.'s statements to them describing how and where she had been touched by Tome. All but A.T.'s statement to Dr. Spiegel implicated Tome. (The physicians also testified that their clinical examinations of the child indicated that she had been subjected to vaginal penetrations. That part of the testimony is not at issue here.)

A.T.'s out-of-court statements, recounted by the six witnesses, were offered by the Government under Rule 801(d)(1)(B). The trial court admitted all of the statements over defense counsel's objection, accepting the Government's argument that they rebutted the implicit charge that A.T.'s testimony was motivated by a desire to live with her mother. * * *

On appeal, the Court of Appeals for the Tenth Circuit affirmed, adopting the Government's argument that all of A.T.'s out-of-court statements were admissible under Rule 801(d)(1)(B) even though they had been made after A.T.'s alleged motive to fabricate arose. The court reasoned that "the pre-motive requirement is a function of the relevancy rules, not the hearsay rules" and that as a "function of relevance, the pre-motive rule is clearly too broad * * * because it is simply not true that an individual with a motive to lie always will do so." "Rather, the relevance of the prior consistent statement is more accurately determined by evaluating the strength of the motive to lie, the circumstances in which the statement is made, and the declarant's demonstrated propensity to lie." * * *

We granted certiorari, and now reverse.

II

The prevailing common-law rule for more than a century before adoption of the Federal Rules of Evidence was that a prior consistent statement introduced to rebut a charge of recent fabrication or improper influence or motive was admissible if the statement had been made before the alleged fabrication, influence, or motive came into being, but it was inadmissible if made afterwards. As Justice Story explained: "[W]here the testimony is assailed as a fabrication of a recent date * * * in order to repel such imputation, proof of the *antecedent* declaration of the party may be admitted." *Ellicott v. Pearl*, 35 U.S. (10 Pet.) 412, 439 (1836) (emphasis supplied).

McCormick and Wigmore stated the rule in a more categorical manner: "[T]he applicable principle is that the prior consistent statement has no relevancy to refute the charge unless the consistent statement was made before the source of the bias, interest, influence or incapacity originated." E. Cleary, McCormick on Evidence § 49, p. 105 (2d ed. 1972) (hereafter McCormick). *See also* 4 J. Wigmore, Evidence § 1128, p. 268 (J. Chadbourn rev. 1972) (hereafter Wigmore) ("A consistent statement, at a *time prior* to the existence of a fact said to indicate bias * * * will effectively explain away the force of the impeaching evidence" (emphasis in original)). The question is whether Rule 801(d)(1)(B) embodies this temporal requirement. We hold that it does.

A

* * *

Rule 801 defines prior consistent statements as nonhearsay only if they are offered to rebut a charge of "recent fabrication or improper influence or motive." Fed. Rule Evid. 801(d)(1)(B). Noting the "troublesome" logic of treating a witness' prior consistent statements as hearsay at all (because the declarant is present in court and subject to cross-examination), the Advisory Committee decided to treat those consistent statements, once the preconditions of the Rule were satisfied, as nonhearsay and admissible as substantive evidence, not just to rebut an attack on the witness' credibility. A consistent statement meeting the requirements of the Rule is thus placed in the same category as a declarant's inconsistent statement made under oath in another proceeding, or prior identification testimony, or admissions by a party opponent. *See* Fed. Rule Evid. 801.

The Rules do not accord this weighty, nonhearsay status to all prior consistent statements. To the contrary, admissibility under the Rules is confined to those statements offered to rebut a charge of "recent fabrication or improper influence or motive," the same phrase used by the Advisory Committee in its description of the "traditiona[l]" common law of evidence, which was the background against which the Rules were drafted. Prior consistent statements may not be admitted to counter all forms of impeachment or to bolster the witness merely because she has been discredited. In the present context, the question is whether A.T.'s out-of-court statements rebutted the alleged link between her desire to be with her mother and her testimony, not whether they suggested that A.T.'s in-court testimony was true. The Rule speaks of a party rebutting an alleged motive, not bolstering the veracity of the story told.

This limitation is instructive, not only to establish the preconditions of admissibility but also to reinforce the significance of the requirement that the consistent statements must have been made before the alleged influence, or motive to fabricate arose. That is to say, the forms of impeachment within the Rule's coverage are the ones in which the temporal requirement makes the most sense. Impeachment by charging that the testimony is a recent fabrication or results from an improper influence or motive is, as a general matter, capable of direct and forceful refutation through introduction of out-of-court consistent statements that predate the alleged fabrication, influence or motive. A consistent statement that predates the motive is a square rebuttal of the charge that the testimony was contrived as a consequence of that motive. By contrast, prior consistent statements carry little rebuttal force when most other types of impeachment are involved. McCormick § 49, p. 105 ("When the attack takes the form of impeachment of character, by showing misconduct, convictions or bad reputation, it is generally agreed that there is no color for sustaining by consistent statements. The defense does not meet the assault.") * * *

There may arise instances when out-of-court statements that postdate the alleged fabrication have some probative force in rebutting a charge of fabrication or improper influence or motive, but those statements refute the charged fabrication in a less direct and forceful way. Evidence that a witness made consistent statements after the alleged motive to fabricate arose may suggest in some degree that the in-court testimony is truthful, and thus suggest in some degree that that testimony did not result from some improper influence; but if the drafters of Rule 801(d)(1)(B) intended to countenance rebuttal along that indirect inferential chain, the purpose of confining the types of impeachment that open the door to rebuttal by introducing consistent statements becomes unclear. If consistent statements are admissible without reference to the time frame we find imbedded in the Rule, there appears no sound reason not to admit consistent statements to rebut other forms of impeachment as well. Whatever objections can be leveled against limiting the Rule to this designated form of impeachment and confining the rebuttal to those statements made before the fabrication or improper influence or motive arose, it is clear to us that the drafters of Rule 801(d)(1)(B) were relying upon the common-law temporal requirement.

The underlying theory of the Government's position is that an out-of-court consistent statement, whenever it was made, tends to bolster the testimony of a witness and so tends also to rebut an express or implied charge that the testimony has been the product of an improper influence. Congress could have adopted that rule with ease, providing, for instance, that "a witness' prior consistent statements are admissible whenever relevant to assess the witness's truthfulness or accuracy." The theory would be that, in a broad sense, any prior statement by a witness concerning the disputed issues at trial would have some relevance in assessing the accuracy or truthfulness of the witness's in-court testimony on the same subject. The narrow Rule enacted by Congress, however, cannot be understood to incorporate the Government's theory. * * *

The language of the Rule, in its concentration on rebutting charges of recent fabrication, improper influence and motive to the exclusion of other forms of impeachment, as well as in its use of wording which follows the language of the common-law cases, suggests that it was intended to carry over the common-law pre-motive rule.

B

Our conclusion that Rule 801(d)(1)(B) embodies the common-law premotive requirement is confirmed by an examination of the Advisory Committee Notes to the Federal Rules of Evidence. We have relied on those well-considered Notes as a useful guide in ascertaining the meaning of the Rules. Where, as with Rule 801(d)(1)(B), "Congress did not amend the Advisory Committee's draft in any way * * * the Committee's commentary is particularly relevant in determining the meaning of the document Congress enacted." *Beech Aircraft Corp. v. Rainey*, 488 U.S. 153, at 165-166, n. 9 (1988). The Notes are also a respected source of scholarly commentary. Professor Cleary was a distinguished commentator on the law of evidence, and he and members of the Committee consulted and considered the views, criticisms, and suggestions of the academic community in preparing the Notes.

The Notes disclose a purpose to adhere to the common law in the application of evidentiary principles, absent express provisions to the contrary. Where the Rules did depart from their common-law antecedents, in general the Committee said so. * * * The Notes give no indication, however, that Rule 801(d)(1)(B) abandoned the premotive requirement.* * *

Throughout their discussion of the Rules, the Advisory Committee Notes rely on Wigmore and McCormick as authority for the common-law approach. In light of the categorical manner in which those authors state the premotive requirement, it is difficult to imagine that the drafters, who noted the new substantive use of prior consistent statements, would have remained silent if they intended to modify the premotive requirement. As we observed with respect to another provision of the Rules, "[w]ith this state of unanimity confronting the drafters of the Federal Rules of Evidence, we think it unlikely that they intended to scuttle entirely [the common-law requirement]." *United States v. Abel*, 469 U.S. 45, 50 (1984). Here, we do not think the drafters of the Rule intended to scuttle the whole premotive requirement and rationale without so much as a whisper of explanation.

* * *

Our conclusion is bolstered by the Advisory Committee's stated "unwillingness to countenance the general use of prior prepared statements as substantive evidence." Rule 801(d), which "enumerates three situations in which the statement is excepted from the category of hearsay," was expressly contrasted by the Committee with Uniform Rule of Evidence 63(1) (1953), "which allows *any* out-of-court statement of a declarant who is present at the trial and available for cross-examination." When a witness presents important testimony damaging to a party, the party will often counter with at least an implicit charge that the witness has been under some influence or motive to fabricate. If Rule 801 were read so that the charge opened the floodgates to any prior consistent statement that satisfied Rule 403, as the Tenth Circuit concluded, the distinction between rejected Uniform Rule 63(1) and Rule 801(d)(1)(B) would all but disappear. * * * Nothing in the Advisory Committee's Notes suggests that it intended to alter the common-law premotive requirement.

C

The Government's final argument in favor of affirmance is that the common-law premotive rule advocated by petitioner is inconsistent with the Federal Rules' liberal approach to relevancy and with strong academic criticism, beginning in the 1940's, directed at the exclusion of out-of-court statements made by a declarant who is present in court and subject to cross-examination. This argument misconceives the design of the Rules' hearsay provisions.

Hearsay evidence is often relevant. "The only way in which the probative force of hearsay differs from the probative force of other testimony is in the absence of oath, demeanor, and cross-examination as aids in determining credibility." Advisory Committee's Introduction to Article VIII, 28 U.S.C. App., p. 771. That does not resolve the matter, however. Relevance is not the sole criterion of admissibility. Otherwise, it would be difficult to account for the Rules' general proscription of hearsay testimony (absent a specific exception), *see* Fed. Rule Evid. 802, let alone the traditional analysis of hearsay that the Rules, for the most part, reflect. * * *

The Government's reliance on academic commentators critical of excluding out-of-court statements by a witness * * * is subject to like criticism. To be sure, certain commentators in the years preceding the adoption of the Rules had been critical of the common-law approach to hearsay, particularly its categorical exclusion of out-of-court statements offered for substantive purposes. *See, e.g.*, Weinstein, *The Probative Force of Hearsay*, 46 Iowa L. Rev. 331, 344-345 (1961) (gathering sources). General criticism was directed to the exclusion of a declarant's out-of-court statements where the declarant testified at trial. *See, e.g.*, Weinstein, *supra*, at 333 ("treating the out of court statement of the witness himself as hearsay" is a "practical absurdity in many instances"); Morgan, *Hearsay Dangers and the Application of the Hearsay Concept*, 62 Harv. L. Rev. 177, 192-196 (1948). As an alternative, they suggested moving away from the categorical exclusion of hearsay and toward a case-by-case balancing of the probative value of particular statements against their likely prejudicial effect. The Advisory Committee, however, was explicit in rejecting this balancing approach to hearsay: "The Advisory Committee has rejected this approach to hearsay as involving too great a measure of judicial discretion, minimizing the predictability of rulings, [and] enhancing the difficulties of preparation for trial."

The statement-by-statement balancing approach advocated by the Government and adopted by the Tenth Circuit creates the precise dangers the Advisory Committee noted and sought to avoid: It involves considerable judicial discretion; it reduces predictability; and it enhances the difficulties of trial preparation because parties will have difficulty knowing in advance whether or not particular out-of-court statements will be admitted.

D

The case before us illustrates some of the important considerations supporting the Rule as we interpret it, especially in criminal cases. If the Rule were to permit the introduction of prior statements as substantive evidence to rebut every implicit charge that a witness' in-court testimony results from recent fabrication or improper influence or motive, the whole emphasis of the trial could shift to the out-of-court statements, not the in-court ones. The present case illustrates the point. In response to a rather weak charge that A.T.'s testimony was a fabrication created so the child could remain with her mother, the Government was permitted to present a parade of sympathetic and credible witnesses who did no more than recount A.T.'s detailed out-of-court statements to them. Although those statements might have been probative on the question whether the alleged conduct had occurred, they shed but minimal light on whether A.T. had the charged motive to fabricate. At closing argument before the jury, the Government placed great reliance on the prior statements for substantive purposes but did not once seek to use them to rebut the impact of the alleged motive.

We are aware that in some cases it may be difficult to ascertain when a particular fabrication, influence, or motive arose. Yet, as the Government concedes, a majority of common-law courts were performing this task for well over a century * * * and the Government has presented us with no evidence that those courts, or the judicial circuits that adhere to the rule today, have been unable to make the determination. Even under the Government's hypothesis, moreover, the thing to be rebutted must be identified, so the date of its origin cannot be that much more difficult to ascertain. By contrast, the Government's approach, which would require the trial court to weigh all of the circumstances surrounding a statement that suggest its probativeness against the court's assessment of the strength of the alleged motive, would entail more of a burden, with no guidance to attorneys in preparing a case or to appellate courts in reviewing a judgment.

III

Courts must be sensitive to the difficulties attendant upon the prosecution of alleged child abusers. In almost all cases a youth is the prosecution's only eye witness. But "[t]his Court cannot alter evidentiary rules merely because litigants might prefer different rules in a particular class of cases." When a party seeks to introduce out-of-court statements that contain strong circumstantial indicia of reliability, that are highly probative on the material questions at trial, and that are better than other evidence otherwise available, there is no need to distort the requirements of Rule 801(d)(1)(B). If its requirements are met, Rule 803(24) [now Rule 807] exists for that eventuality. We intimate no view, however, concerning the admissibility of any of A.T.'s out-of-court statements under that section, or any other evidentiary principle. These matters, and others, are for the Court of Appeals to decide in the first instance.

Our holding is confined to the requirements for admission under Rule 801(d)(1)(B). The Rule permits the introduction of a declarant's consistent out-of-court statements to rebut a charge of recent fabrication or improper influence or motive only when those statements were made before the charged recent fabrication or improper influence or motive. These conditions of admissibility were not established here.

The judgment of the Court of Appeals for the Tenth Circuit is reversed, and the case is remanded for further proceedings consistent with this opinion.

It is so ordered.

[Concurring opinion of JUSTICE SCALIA omitted.]

JUSTICE BREYER, with whom the CHIEF JUSTICE, JUSTICE O'CONNOR and JUSTICE THOMAS join, dissenting.

The basic issue in this case concerns, not hearsay, but relevance. As the majority points out, the common law permitted a lawyer to rehabilitate a witness (after a charge of improper motive) by pointing to the fact that the witness had said the same thing earlier — but only if the witness made the earlier statement *before* the motive to lie arose. The reason for the time limitation was that, otherwise, the prior consistent statement had no *relevance* to rebut the charge that the in-court testimony was the product of the motive to lie. * * *

The majority believes that a hearsay-related rule, Federal Rule of Evidence 801(d)(1)(B), codifies this absolute timing requirement. I do not. Rule 801(d)(1)(B) has nothing to do with relevance. Rather, that Rule carves out a subset of prior consistent statements that were formerly admissible only to rehabilitate a witness (a nonhearsay use that relies upon the fact that the statement was made). It then says that members of that subset are "not hearsay." This means that, *if* such a statement is admissible for a particular rehabilitative purpose (to rebut a charge of recent fabrication, improper influence or motive), its proponent now may use it substantively, for a hearsay purpose (*i.e.*, as evidence of its truth), as well.

* * *

Assuming Rule 801(d)(1)(B) does not codify the absolute timing requirement, I must still answer the question whether, as a *relevance* matter, the common-law statement of the premotive rule stands as an absolute bar to a trial court's admission of a postmotive prior consistent statement for the purpose of rebutting a charge of recent fabrication or improper influence or motive. The majority points to statements of the timing rule that do suggest that, for reasons of relevance, the law of evidence *never* permits their admission. Yet, absolute-sounding rules often allow exceptions. And, there are sound reasons here for permitting an exception to the timing rule where circumstances warrant.

For one thing, one can find examples where the timing rule's claim of "no relevancy" is simply untrue. A postmotive statement *is* relevant to rebut, for example, a charge of recent fabrication based on improper motive, say, when the speaker made the prior statement while affected by a far more powerful motive to tell the truth. A speaker might be moved to lie to help an acquaintance. But, suppose the circumstances *also* make clear to the speaker that only the truth will save his child's life. Or, suppose the postmotive statement was made spontaneously, or when the speaker's motive to lie was much weaker than it was at trial. In these and similar situations, special circumstances may indicate that the prior statement was made for some reason other than the alleged improper motivation; it may have been made not *because of*, but *despite*, the improper motivation. Hence, postmotive statements can, *in appropriate circumstances*, directly refute the charge of fabrication based on improper motive, not because they bolster in a general way the witness' trial testimony, but because the circumstances indicate that the statements are not causally connected to the alleged motive to lie.

* * *

Accordingly, I would hold that the Federal Rules authorize a district court to allow (where probative in respect to rehabilitation) the use of postmotive prior consistent statements to rebut a charge of recent fabrication, improper influence or motive (subject of course to, for example, Rule 403). Where such statements are admissible for this rehabilitative purpose, Rule 801(d)(1)(B), as stated above, makes them admissible as substantive evidence as well (provided, of course, that the Rule's other requirements, such as the witness' availability for cross-examination, are satisfied). In most cases, this approach will not yield a different result from a strict adherence to the premotive rule for, in most cases, postmotive statements will not be significantly probative. And, even in cases where the statement is admitted as significantly probative (in respect to rehabilitation), the effect of admission on the trial will be minimal because the prior consistent statements will (by their nature) do no more than repeat in-court testimony.

In this case, the Court of Appeals, applying an approach consistent with what I have described above, decided that A.T.'s prior consistent statements were probative on the question of whether her story as a witness reflected a motive to lie. There is no reason to reevaluate this factbound conclusion. Accordingly, I would affirm the judgment of the Court of Appeals.

NOTES

1. Under what circumstances may a charge of recent fabrication or improper motive be implied?

A typical example of such an implied attack occurred in *United States v. Montague*, 958 F.2d 1094 (D.C. Cir. 1992), where, on cross-examination, the defendant inquired of a government witness whether the witness hoped to secure clemency by testifying against the defendant. The Court held the question constituted an implied charge of improper motive, making prior consistent statements admissible. Extensive and intense cross-examination can sometimes cross the line from simply challenging the witness's account to a charge of fabrication. *See also United States v. Cherry*, 938 F.2d 748 (7th Cir. 1991) (extensive cross-examination challenging the core of the victim's testimony in a sex abuse case constituted an implied charge of fabrication justifying admissibility of prior consistent statements).

2. Can a prior consistent statement be introduced through a witness other than the person who made the statement?

In *United States v. Hebeka*, 25 F.3d 287 (6th Cir. 1994), a food stamp fraud prosecution, defense counsel attacked the credibility of the government's star witness, Dennis Alfred, implying that Alfred fabricated his testimony to avoid prosecution. The Government sought to rehabilitate Alfred by introducing his prior consistent statement; but instead of introducing the statement through Alfred himself, the Government called another witness who testified to what Alfred told him. The Court held that the "literal requirements of Rule 801 can be met even when a third party testifies as to someone else's prior statement." The Court noted that Alfred was in court, subject to cross-examination, and could easily have been recalled after the third party's testimony. While recognizing that the Seventh Circuit has ruled that prior statements may be admitted through the declarant only — *see United States v. West*, 670 F.2d 675 (7th Cir. 1982) — the *Hebeka* Court stated that "the Seventh Circuit appears to be a minority of one" on this question. Note that the result in *Hebeka* was contingent upon Alfred being present at trial and subject to cross-examination; this is a predicate for all statements offered under Rule 801(d)(1).

3. Can a criminal defendant's prior consistent statement ever be admissible under Rule 801(d)(1)(B)?

In *United States v. Lewis*, 987 F.2d 1349 (8th Cir. 1993), the defendant's defense to a drug charge was that he was luring drug dealers to Florida in order to turn them in to the authorities. At trial, the Government argued that the defense was an afterthought. The defendant had made a statement prior to his arrest that was consistent with his defense. The trial court excluded the statement, but the Court of Appeals found this to be error; the statement was admissible as a prior consistent statement to rebut a charge of recent fabrication. But the Court found the error to be harmless, because the jury had already heard the defendant testify concerning his defense.

4. Can prior consistent statements be used to rehabilitate the credibility of a witness, even if they are not admissible under Rule 801(d)(1)(B)?

Professor Capra, in *Prior Consistent Statements and the Supreme Court*, N.Y.L.J., July 9, 1995, p.3, had this to say about the law concerning prior consistent statements after *Tome:*

> It is important to remember that the Court in *Tome* did not hold that the pre-motive requirement must always be satisfied before prior consistent statements may even be heard by the factfinder. Prior consistent statements can be introduced for *credibility* purposes, to rehabilitate a witness, whenever they are responsive to an attack on credibility. One such situation is where the consistent statement is offered to explain or to clarify an inconsistent statement introduced by the adversary. If the witness claims for example that the apparently inconsistent statement was taken out of context, he can explain the context, which may include statements consistent with his testimony. Rule 801 is not needed to justify such an explanation. The evidence

is relevant under Rule 401 and admissible under Rule 402. As the Court stated in *United States v. Harris*, 761 F.2d 394 (7th Cir. 1985), the general principle set forth in Rule 801(d)(1)(B) — *i.e.*, "the motive to fabricate must not have existed at the time the statements were made or they are inadmissible" — "need not be met to admit into evidence prior consistent statements which are offered solely to rehabilitate a witness rather than as evidence of the matters asserted in those statements."

However, to be admitted *substantively*, in the absence of some other hearsay exception, a prior consistent statement must be relevant to rebut (and therefore must pre-date) a charge of recent fabrication or improper influence or motive. Where a consistent statement is admissible for other, rehabilitation purposes such as to explain an inconsistency or to rebut a charge of bad memory, and yet is not admissible as substantive evidence under Rule 801(d)(1)(B), the adversary is entitled to a limiting instruction as to the appropriate use of the evidence.

Perhaps the distinction just made — between consistent statements offered solely for rehabilitation and those offered under the Rule as substantive evidence to rebut a charge of recent fabrication or improper influence or motive — is an insubstantial one. Since consistent statements are identical to trial testimony, an instruction that some of them should not be considered for their truth is unlikely to be understood by a jury. A line between substantive and rehabilitative use of these statements may well be of little use. Yet this is the line drawn by the Rule, which carves out only certain prior consistent statements for substantive use: those that rebut a charge of recent fabrication or improper influence or motive. And most importantly, the *Tome* pre-motive requirement assures that many prior consistent statements — those offered to rebut a charge of fabrication or motive and yet which post-date the motive — will not be admissible at all, neither substantively nor for impeachment purposes. This will help to ensure that the jury decides the case on the basis of testimony at the trial rather than on prior statements of witnesses.

[3] Prior Identifications

[a] Federal Rule of Evidence 801(d)(1)(C)

Rule 801. Definitions

* * *

(d) Statements which are not hearsay. A statement is not hearsay if—

(1) Prior statement by witness. The declarant testifies at the trial or hearing and is subject to cross-examination concerning the statement, and the statement is * * * (C) one of identification of a person made after perceiving the person.

* * *

[b] Illustration

Defendant is charged with murder. The only evidence that the defendant is guilty is highly circumstantial evidence and the testimony from one eye-witness, Scared Witless. The prosecution calls Witless to the stand.

Prosecution:	State your name.
Witless:	Scared Witless.
Prosecution:	Where were you at 3:00 p.m. on June 8?
Witless:	At the victim's house.
Prosecution:	What did you see?
Witless:	A man came in the door with a shotgun, laughed, then blew my friend's brains out.
Prosecution:	Can you identify the killer in the courtroom today (said with great confidence)?
Witless:	No, I don't think so.
Prosecution:	What!?
Witless:	No, I can't identify the killer.
Prosecution:	No further questions.
Defendant:	No cross, your honor.

The prosecution calls Top Cop to the stand.

Prosecution:	State your name.
Top Cop:	Top Cop.
Prosecution:	Did you interview Scared Witless the day of the murder?
Top Cop:	Yes.
Prosecution:	Did you take him to a line-up that day?
Top Cop:	Yes.
Prosecution:	Was the defendant in the line-up?
Top Cop:	Yes.
Prosecution:	Did Scared Witless identify the defendant as the murderer?
Top Cop:	Yes, he said * * *
Defendant:	Objection! Prior statements aren't admissible. That's hearsay.
Prosecution:	__________. (What additional steps must the prosecutor take?)

[c] Subject to Cross-Examination

UNITED STATES v. OWENS
484 U.S. 554 (1988)

JUSTICE SCALIA delivered the opinion of the Court.

This case requires us to determine whether either the Confrontation Clause of the Sixth Amendment or Rule 802 of the Federal Rules of Evidence bars testimony concerning a prior, out-of-court identification when the identifying witness is unable, because of memory loss, to explain the basis for the identification.

I

On April 12, 1982, John Foster, a correctional counselor at the federal prison in Lompoc, California, was attacked and brutally beaten with a metal pipe. His skull was fractured, and he remained hospitalized for almost a month. As a result of his injuries, Foster's memory was severely impaired. When Thomas Mansfield, an FBI agent investigating the assault, first attempted to interview Foster, on April 19, he found Foster lethargic and unable to remember his attacker's name. On May 5, Mansfield again spoke to Foster, who was much improved and able to describe the attack. Foster named respondent as his attacker and identified respondent from an array of photographs.

Respondent was tried in Federal District Court for assault with intent to commit murder under 18 U.S.C. § 113(a). At trial, Foster recounted his activities just before the attack, and described feeling the blows to his head and seeing blood on the floor. He testified that he clearly remembered identifying respondent as his assailant during his May 5th interview with Mansfield. On cross-examination, he admitted that he could not remember seeing his assailant. He also admitted that, although there was evidence that he had received numerous visitors in the hospital, he was unable to remember any of them except Mansfield, and could not remember whether any of these visitors had suggested that respondent was the assailant. Defense counsel unsuccessfully sought to refresh his recollection with hospital records, including one indicating that Foster had attributed the assault to someone other than respondent. Respondent was convicted and sentenced to 20 years' imprisonment to be served consecutively to a previous sentence.

On appeal, the United States Court of Appeals for the Ninth Circuit considered challenges based on the Confrontation Clause and Rule 802 of the Federal Rules of Evidence.[1]

By divided vote it upheld both challenges (though finding the Rule 802 violation harmless error), and reversed the judgment of the District Court. We granted certiorari * * * to resolve the conflict with other Circuits on the significance of a hearsay declarant's memory loss both with respect to the Confrontation Clause.

II

The Confrontation Clause of the Sixth Amendment gives the accused the right "to be confronted with the witnesses against him." This has long been read as securing an adequate opportunity to cross-examine adverse witnesses.

[1] This case has been argued, both here and below, as though Federal Rule of Evidence 801(d)(1)(C) were the basis of the challenge. That is substantially but not technically correct. If respondent's arguments are accepted, it is Rule 802 that would render the out-of-court statement inadmissible as hearsay; but as explained in Part III, it is ultimately Rule 801(d)(1)(C) that determines whether Rule 802 is applicable.

See, e.g., Mattox v. United States, 156 U.S. 237, 242-243 (1895); *Douglas v. Alabama*, 380 U.S. 415, 418 (1965).

* * *

In *Delaware v. Fensterer*, 474 U.S. 15 (1985) (*per curiam*), we determined that there was no Confrontation Clause violation when an expert witness testified as to what opinion he had formed, but could not recollect the basis on which he had formed it. We said:

> The Confrontation Clause includes no guarantee that every witness called by the prosecution will refrain from giving testimony that is marred by forgetfulness, confusion, or evasion. To the contrary, the Confrontation Clause is generally satisfied when the defense is given a full and fair opportunity to probe and expose these infirmities through cross-examination, thereby calling to the attention of the factfinder the reasons for giving scant weight to the witness' testimony.

Our opinion noted that a defendant seeking to discredit a forgetful expert witness is not without ammunition, since the jury may be persuaded that "his opinion is as unreliable as his memory." * * *

* * * [T]he Confrontation Clause guarantees only "an *opportunity* for effective cross-examination, not cross-examination that is effective in whatever way, and to whatever extent, the defense might wish." *Kentucky v. Stincer*, 482 U.S. 730, 739 (1987); as *Fensterer* demonstrates, that opportunity is not denied when a witness testifies as to his current belief but is unable to recollect the reason for that belief. It is sufficient that the defendant has the opportunity to bring out such matters as the witness' bias, his lack of care and attentiveness, his poor eyesight, and even (what is often a prime objective of cross-examination) the very fact that he has a bad memory. If the ability to inquire into these matters suffices to establish the constitutionally requisite opportunity for cross-examination when a witness testifies as to his current belief, the basis for which he cannot recall, we see no reason why it should not suffice when the witness' past belief is introduced and he is unable to recollect the reason for that past belief. In both cases the foundation for the belief (current or past) cannot effectively be elicited, but other means of impugning the belief are available. Indeed, if there is any difference in persuasive impact between the statement "I believe this to be the man who assaulted me, but can't remember why" and the statement "I don't know whether this is the man who assaulted me, but I told the police I believed so earlier," the former would seem, if anything, more damaging and hence give rise to a greater need for memory-testing, if that is to be considered essential to an opportunity for effective cross-examination. We conclude with respect to this latter example, as we did in *Fensterer* with respect to the former, that it is not. The weapons available to impugn the witness' statement when memory loss is asserted will of course not always achieve success, but successful cross-examination is not the constitutional guarantee. They are, however, realistic weapons, as is demonstrated by defense counsel's summation in this very case, which emphasized Foster's memory loss and argued that

his identification of respondent was the result of the suggestions of people who visited him in the hospital.

* * *

III

Respondent urges as an alternative basis for affirmance a violation of Federal Rule of Evidence 802, which generally excludes hearsay. Rule 801(d)(1)(C) defines as not hearsay a prior statement "of identification of a person made after perceiving the person," if the declarant "testifies at the trial or hearing and is subject to cross-examination concerning the statement." The Court of Appeals found that Foster's identification statement did not come within this exclusion because his memory loss prevented his being "subject to cross-examination concerning the statement." * * *

It seems to us that the more natural reading of "subject to cross-examination concerning the statement" includes what was available here. Ordinarily a witness is regarded as "subject to cross-examination" when he is placed on the stand, under oath, and responds willingly to questions. Just as with the constitutional prohibition, limitations on the scope of examination by the trial court or assertions of privilege by the witness may undermine the process to such a degree that meaningful cross-examination within the intent of the Rule no longer exists. But that effect is not produced by the witness' assertion of memory loss — which, as discussed earlier, is often the very result sought to be produced by cross-examination, and can be effective in destroying the force of the prior statement. Rule 801(d)(1)(C), which specifies that the cross-examination need only "concer[n] the statement," does not on its face require more.

This reading seems even more compelling when the Rule is compared with Rule 804(a)(3), which defines "[u]navailability as a witness" to include situations in which a declarant "testifies to a lack of memory of the subject matter of the declarant's statement." Congress plainly was aware of the recurrent evidentiary problem at issue here — witness forgetfulness of an underlying event — but chose not to make it an exception to Rule 801(d)(1)(C).

The reasons for that choice are apparent from the Advisory Committee's Notes on Rule 801 and its legislative history. The premise for Rule 801(d)(1)(C) was that, given adequate safeguards against suggestiveness, out-of-court identifications were generally preferable to courtroom identifications. Thus, despite the traditional view that such statements were hearsay, the Advisory Committee believed that their use was to be fostered rather than discouraged. Similarly, the House Report on the Rule noted that since, "[a]s time goes by, a witness' memory will fade and his identification will become less reliable," minimizing the barriers to admission of more contemporaneous identification is fairer to defendants and prevents "cases falling through because the witness can no longer recall the identity of the person he saw commit the crime." H.R. Rep. No. 94-355, p. 3 (1975). To judge from the House and Senate Reports, Rule 801(d)(1)(C) was in part directed to the very problem here at issue: a memory loss that makes it impossible for the witness to provide an in-court identification or testify about details of the events underlying an earlier identification.

Respondent argues that this reading is impermissible because it creates an internal inconsistency in the Rules, since the forgetful witness who is deemed "subject to cross-examination" under 801(d)(1)(C) is simultaneously deemed "unavailable" under 804(a)(3). * * * It seems to us, however, that this is not a substantive inconsistency, but only a semantic oddity resulting from the fact that Rule 804(a) has for convenience of reference in Rule 804(b) chosen to describe the circumstances necessary in order to admit certain categories of hearsay testimony under the rubric "Unavailability as a witness." These circumstances include not only absence from the hearing, but also claims of privilege, refusals to obey a court's order to testify, and inability to testify based on physical or mental illness or memory loss. Had the rubric instead been "unavailability as a witness, memory loss, and other special circumstances" there would be no apparent inconsistency with Rule 801, which is a definition section excluding certain statements entirely from the category of "hearsay." The semantic inconsistency exists not only with respect to Rule 801(d)(1)(C), but also with respect to the other subparagraphs of Rule 801(d)(1). It would seem strange, for example, to assert that a witness can avoid introduction of testimony from a prior proceeding that is inconsistent with his trial testimony, *see* Rule 801(d)(1)(A), by simply asserting lack of memory of the facts to which the prior testimony related. But that situation, like this one, presents the verbal curiosity that the witness is "subject to cross-examination" under Rule 801 while at the same time "unavailable" under Rule 804(a)(3). Quite obviously, the two characterizations are made for two entirely different purposes and there is no requirement or expectation that they should coincide.

For the reasons stated, we hold that neither the Confrontation Clause nor Federal Rule of Evidence 802 is violated by admission of an identification statement of a witness who is unable, because of a memory loss, to testify concerning the basis for the identification. The decision of the Court of Appeals is reversed, and the case is remanded for proceedings consistent with this opinion.

So ordered.

[Dissenting opinion of JUSTICE BRENNAN omitted.]

NOTES

1. Is an identification based on a police artist's sketch admissible as a statement of prior identification?

In *United States v. Moskowitz*, 581 F.2d 14 (2d Cir. 1978), the Court gave a sketch the same treatment as it would have given a photograph and ruled that the statements of a witness making an identification based on a police artist's sketch and the sketch itself were both admissible.

2. Is a pre-trial identification admissible if the witness who made the identification cannot identify the defendant at trial?

In *United States v. Blackman,* 66 F.3d 1572 (11th Cir. 1995), a bank teller was unable to identify the defendant at trial as the robber. An FBI agent then took the stand and testified that the teller had previously identified the defendant from a photospread. The Court found this testimony properly admitted. The teller was available for cross-examination, even though she could not identify the defendant at trial. Indeed, the fact that she could not make an identification at trial was fertile ground for cross-examination.

3. Is the witness "subject to cross-examination" if she makes an identification but later refuses to testify?

Professors Saltzburg, Martin, and Capra, in *Federal Rules of Evidence Manual* (9th ed. 2006), advise:

> A witness who refuses to testify cannot be found "subject to cross-examination" within the meaning of Rule 801(d)(1). Thus, in *United States v. Torres-Ortega*, 148 F.3d 1128 (10th Cir. 1999), the Court found reversible error when a prosecution witness refused to testify and the government introduced his prior grand jury statement under Rule 801(d)(1)(A). The Court distinguished *Owens* as a case in which the witness who made the prior statement answered all questions on cross-examination; obtaining a concession of lack of memory might well be effective cross-examination, whereas no cross-examination is possible if the witness simply refuses to answer all questions.

C. ADMISSIONS BY A PARTY

[1] Federal Rule of Evidence 801(d)(2)

Rule 801. Definitions

* * *

(d) Statements which are not hearsay. A statement is not hearsay if—

* * *

(2) Admission by party-opponent. — The statement is offered against a party and is (A) the party's own statement, in either an individual or a representative capacity or (B) a statement of which the party has manifested an adoption or belief in its truth, or (C) a statement by a person authorized by the party to make a statement concerning the subject, or (D) a statement by the party's agent or servant concerning a matter within the scope of the agency or employment, made during the existence of the relationship, or (E) a statement by a coconspirator of a party during the course and in furtherance of the conspiracy. The contents of the statement shall be considered but are not alone sufficient to establish the declarant's authority under subdivision (C), the agency or employment relationship and scope thereof under subdivision (D), or the existence of the conspiracy and the participation therein of the declarant and the party against whom the statement is offered under subdivision (E).

[2] Own Statement

Illustration

The defendant is charged with failing to pay withholding taxes. The defendant is an employee of XYZ, Inc. and defends on the theory that he did not control the corporate fund that should have paid the withholdings. The prosecution calls the defendant's barber to the stand.

Prosecution:	Did you have a conversation with the defendant on April 14, 2000?
Barber:	Yes.
Prosecution:	Did you talk about the withholding of taxes by XYZ, Inc.?
Barber:	Yes.
Prosecution:	What did he say? (seeking: the defendant told me he didn't pay withholding taxes)
Defense:	(1) Objection ________.
The Court:	(2) ________.
Barber:	The defendant said he didn't pay the withholding taxes.

The state has no further questions and the defense cross-examines.

Defense:	Did you have a conversation with the defendant two days later?
Barber:	Yes.
Defense:	What did the defendant say?
Prosecution:	Objection. Calls for hearsay.
Defense:	Your honor, if the prosecutor is allowed to introduce my client's statements to incriminate him, I should be allowed to admit my client's statements to exculpate him.
Court:	(3) ________.

STATE v. JOHNSON
245 N.W.2d 687 (Wisc. 1976)

CONNOR T. HANSEN, JUSTICE.

Johnson was the incorporator of Midwestern Pacific Corporation, with offices in Appleton, Wisconsin. He served as president and director of the company from July of 1970, through September of 1972. He was charged with eleven counts of willfully failing to deposit with the State, certain withholding taxes * * *.

Midwestern was engaged in the business of subcontracting right-of-way clearance work. The corporation operated mainly in the State of Wisconsin, with occasional jobs out of state, and "altogether" had approximately 40-45 employees. The corporation was financed through an arrangement with the First National Bank of Menasha and a guarantee of George Banta of the George Banta Company. * * * Testimony was in conflict as to the actual amount of control over funds possessed by Johnson, First National and George Banta, and thus, the responsibility of Johnson for failure to make the required withholding tax deposits was in issue.

The parties stipulated that the amounts alleged in the complaint were withheld from the employees during the periods alleged and that such sums were not deposited with the State of Wisconsin. The defendant did not stipulate that the failure to deposit such sums was a willful act on his part; therefore, at trial, the principal issue became the willfulness of Johnson in failing to deposit the sums required.

* * *

Exclusion of Testimony as Hearsay

The prosecution called accountant, John Myron, as a witness. On direct examination, Myron testified extensively concerning accounting work which he had done for Johnson and Midwestern in 1971 and 1972. He stated that late in October, 1971, John Weber (of the Wisconsin Department of Revenue) assisted Johnson in filling out and filing new WT-6 forms (forms which reflected the total amount of income tax withheld from employees and due to the state) because the original WT-6 forms filled out by Myron had never been filed. In response to the question, "Did Mr. Johnson pay any amount at that time?" Myron answered, "Well, I know he didn't because later on he told me he hadn't." Defense counsel did not object to Myron's testimony.

On cross-examination, defense counsel asked Myron if he specifically remembered any conversations with Mr. Johnson about his financial condition. The prosecution objected that to the extent that Myron's answers would involve statements of the defendant, they would be hearsay. The trial court sustained the objection. Defense counsel acknowledged that the statements, if made by the defendant, would be self-serving and stated in his offer of proof:

> Well, Your Honor, we would show that this man — that the statements were that he did instruct Mr. Johnson to pay these taxes and that Mr. Johnson indicated that he did not * * *. But he indicated and expressed he did not control the funds. And he could not pay them and he was very disturbed about it.

The trial court subsequently ruled that there would be no valid objection if Myron testified that based on his observations of the defendant during discussions of the question of the tax liability, and in his opinion, the defendant was concerned about making payments; but that Myron could not testify as to what was said by the defendant in that such statements that were self-serving would be inadmissible.

* * *

Johnson argues that since admissions * * * were admitted [against him], there should be a correlative right to introduce beneficial admissions on cross-examination. The Rules of Evidence do not allow for such symmetry in this case.

* * *

The testimony of Myron on direct examination constituted evidence of an "admission" of the defendant, a party to this action, which was offered against the defendant, and it was admissible on this basis * * * .

It appears that both the prosecution and the defense have confused "admission[s]" * * * , with "STATEMENTS AGAINST INTEREST" * * * .

In Wisconsin Rules of Evidence, * * * the judicial council committee's notes, * * * point out the problems of confusing the two:

> A type of evidence with which admissions may be confused is evidence of Declarations against Interest. Such declarations, coming in under a separate exception to the hearsay rule, to be admissible must have been against the declarant's interest when made. No such requirement applies to admissions * * * . Of course, most admissions are actually against interest when made, but there is no such requirement. Hence the common phrase in judicial opinions, "admissions against interest" is an invitation to confuse two separate exceptions to the hearsay rule. Other apparent distinctions are that admissions must be statements of a party to a lawsuit (or his predecessor or representative) and must be offered, not for, but against him, whereas the Declaration against Interest need not be and usually is not made by a party or his predecessor or representative, but by some third person. Finally the Declaration against Interest exception admits the declaration only when the declarant, by death or otherwise, has become unavailable as a witness, whereas obviously no such requirement is applied to admissions of a party.

* * *

The testimony sought to be elicited from the witness-Myron on cross-examination concerning self-serving statements made by the defendant was clearly hearsay and was properly excluded by the trial court.

* * *

Order affirmed.

NOTES

1. Does the admission exclusion to the hearsay rule require that the defendant have personal knowledge of the truth of the statement made?

As a general rule, the constraints of Federal Rule 602, which require personal knowledge, do not apply to admissions. Thus, a statement by the keeper of a wolf that the wolf bit a child was admissible against the keeper even though he had not witnessed the event. *Mahlandt v. Wild Canid Survival & Research Ctr., Inc.*, 588 F.2d 626 (8th Cir. 1978).

2. Must an admission be incriminatory when made?

It is well-established that a statement need not have been incriminatory at the time it was made for the statement to qualify as an admission. Thus, in *United States v. Turner*, 995 F.2d 1357 (6th Cir. 1993), the defendant made statements to government agents in a misguided attempt to exculpate himself. These statements proved false, and the government admitted them at trial as evidence of the defendant's consciousness of guilt. The Court found that these statements were properly admitted under Rule 801(d)(2)(A). On its face, the rule is not limited to statements against interest when made. All that is required under this rule is that the statement was made by the party-opponent and offered against him at trial.

3. If a statement is admissible as an admission, is further analysis required?

Further analysis may be required under other evidence rules, because qualifying a statement under an exemption or exception to the hearsay rule simply means that it will not be excluded as hearsay. For example, a statement otherwise admissible as a party-admission might be excluded under Rule 404(b) or Rule 403 if it is an admission of uncharged misconduct. *See, e.g., United States v. Manafzadeh*, 592 F.2d 81 (2d Cir. 1979).

4. In a multiple-defendant trial, can one defendant offer a statement made by the other as an admission?

In *United States v. Harwood*, 998 F.2d 91 (2d Cir. 1993), the Court held that a statement made by a co-defendant, in which the co-defendant admitted sole responsibility for the crime, could not be admitted in favor of the other defendant under Rule 801(d)(2)(A). This exemption covers only admissions by a party-opponent. A co-defendant is not a party-opponent. The government is the opponent of both co-defendants. Thus, the government could have offered the statement against the defendant who made it, but it chose not to.

[3] Adoptive Admissions

[a] Federal Rule of Evidence 801(d)(2)(B)

Rule 801. Definitions

* * *

(d) Statements which are not hearsay. A statement is not hearsay if—

* * *

(2) Admission by party-opponent. The statement is offered against a party and is * * *. (B) a statement of which the party has manifested an adoption or belief in its truth.

[b] By Conduct or Silence

CARR v. DEEDS
453 F.3d 593 (4th Cir. 2006)

TRAXLER, CIRCUIT JUDGE:

Plaintiff Sharon Carr, individually and as administratrix of the estate of her son Joshua Morgan, brought this action under 42 U.S.C.A. § 1983 (West 2003), and various state law provisions, against the State of West Virginia, the Superintendent of the West Virginia State Police, and two of its troopers. Plaintiff's § 1983 claims allege that Trooper V.S. Deeds unconstitutionally employed excessive force against Morgan following Morgan's arrest on June 20, 2001, and that Trooper Deeds and Trooper T.D. Bradley unconstitutionally employed deadly force during an attempted arrest of Morgan on July 10, 2001. On appeal, plaintiff challenges the district court's orders excluding her independent expert, and granting summary judgment to defendants on the § 1983 claims. We affirm both orders.

I.

Because this is an appeal from the grant of summary judgment to the defendants, we review the facts in the light most favorable to the plaintiff.

On June 20, 2001, Trooper Deeds and at least two other law enforcement officers arrested Morgan at the home of Dale Arbaugh pursuant to an outstanding arrest warrant for suspected arson of Arbaugh's home. Morgan was transported to the State Police Barracks in Lewisburg, and then to the Southern Regional Jail in Beckley, by one or more of these officers. Upon his arrival at the Regional Jail, Morgan was medically evaluated and found to have a cut on his lip, also described as a "busted lip," and an abrasion on his right flank or abdomen. No other injuries were noted, and there was no report or complaint of a physical altercation.

Morgan's mother, stepfather, and brother visited Morgan at the police station later that day. Morgan's mother testified that Morgan was bleeding from his mouth and had abrasions to his shoulder and rib area. Morgan's stepfather testified that Morgan had a swollen lip, "blood coming out of his mouth when he would spit," and abrasions to his shoulders and abdomen area. Morgan's brother testified that Morgan had a swollen eye and "a couple [of] cuts and bruises." None of the witnesses observed any use of force by any officer. However, they testified that, when Morgan was asked about the injuries, he either pointed to or verbally indicated that Deeds had inflicted them.

Two days later, after Morgan had been released from custody, he saw Dr. Craig Bookout at the Greenbrier Valley Medical Center emergency room. According to Dr. Bookout, Morgan had a small cut on his lip and abrasions to his right shoulder and elbows, which Morgan reported to be from "an altercation with a state police officer" on June 20. Morgan also complained of pain in his ribs and a bruised temple, but indicated these were not the result of the altercation. No other injuries were noted. Dr. Bookout was given no information regarding the circumstances of the alleged altercation, nor was the identity of the officer revealed to him. Arbaugh, who had been present when Morgan was arrested, testified that he also saw Morgan after he was released from custody. He testified that Morgan had a black eye, a couple of "places" on the side of his face, and bruises on his arms and legs. Morgan filed no complaint with the West Virginia State Police for any alleged wrongful conduct by its officers.

* * *

On July 1, 2004, defendants also filed a motion for summary judgment. with regard to the June 20 arrest, defendants asserted that plaintiff had failed to produce sufficient evidence that Morgan was injured in an altercation with Deeds and, in the alternative, that the claim should be dismissed because Morgan's injuries were *de minimis*. * * *

* * * The district court found that Deeds was entitled to qualified immunity from the assault claim because Morgan's injuries were *de minimis* * * *.

III.

We now turn to plaintiff's appeal from the district court's order granting summary judgment on her claim that Deeds employed excessive force against Morgan following the June 20 arrest. * * *

* * *

[I]n order to avoid summary judgment * * * it was incumbent upon plaintiff to produce sufficient admissible evidence from which a jury could conclude that Deeds employed at least some force against Morgan in a malicious or sadistic manner, and that the injuries resulting from such force were more than *de minimis*. Deeds is entitled to qualified immunity because, regardless of the severity of Morgan's alleged injuries, the record is devoid of any facts to prove that Deeds employed the force that inflicted those injuries.

* * *

No witness observed any altercation between Morgan and any state police officer. Although Dr. Bookout testified that Morgan told him that some of the injuries were the result of an altercation with a state police officer, Morgan did not identify Deeds as the officer involved or provide any facts as to the circumstances of the alleged altercation. Thus, the only evidence that plaintiff can point to in an effort to implicate Deeds is the testimony of the three family members and Arbaugh to the effect that Morgan either told them or indicated by pointing that Deeds had inflicted the injuries. These statements by Morgan are hearsay and not admissible to create a genuine issue of material fact on the question of whether Deeds inflicted those injuries.

Plaintiff's attempt to demonstrate that Deeds made an "adoptive admission" to assaulting Morgan because he was present in the room when Morgan made the statements to his family members also fails. Under the Federal Rules of Evidence, "[a] statement is not hearsay if * * * [t]he statement is offered against a party and is * * * a statement of which the party has manifested an adoption or belief in its truth." Fed. R. Evid. 801(d)(2)(B). "A party may manifest adoption of a statement in any number of ways, including through words, conduct, or silence." *United States v. Robinson*, 275 F.3d 371, 383 (4th Cir. 2001). However, "[w]hen a statement is offered as an adoptive admission, the primary inquiry is whether the statement was such that, under the circumstances, an innocent defendant would normally be induced to respond, and whether there are sufficient foundational facts from which the jury could infer that the defendant heard, understood, and acquiesced in the statement." *United States v. Williams*, 445 F.3d 724, 735 (4th Cir. 2006) (internal quotation marks omitted).

In this case, there is testimony that Deeds was in the room when the family was visiting, but plaintiff has not demonstrated sufficient foundational facts from which the jury could infer that the defendant heard, understood, and acquiesced in the statement. Nor has plaintiff offered an argument that a police officer, conducting his official duties in the presence of a detainee and his family, "would normally be induced to respond" to the detainee's claim, made solely to his family, that the officer had assaulted him. Indeed, we think it more likely that the officer would ignore the statement rather than risk antagonizing or inciting the detainee or his family by disputing it.

* * *

UNITED STATES v. HOOSIER

661 F.2d 239 (6th Cir. 1976)

PER CURIAM:

Appellant seeks to overturn his jury conviction on one count of armed robbery of a federally insured bank. Four witnesses identified him, three of them positively, as the person who robbed the bank in Clarksville, Tennessee. Another witness, Robert E. Rogers, testified that he had been with the robbery defendant before and after the bank robbery, that before the bank robbery defendant told him that he was going to rob a bank, and that three weeks after the bank robbery, he saw defendant with money and wearing what he thought were diamond rings, and that in the presence of defendant, the defendant's girl friend said concerning defendant's affluence at that point, "That ain't nothing, you should have seen the money we had in the hotel room," and that she spoke of "sacks of money." Although both defendant and his girl friend disputed these facts in their testimony, obviously the resolution of that fact dispute was for the jury, and we must assume the jury resolved it in favor of the government by its verdict of "guilty."

Appellant's sole appellate argument to this court * * * is that the testimony * * * concerning appellant's girl friend's statement was inadmissible hearsay, and that it was reversible error for the District Judge to fail to grant the objection to its admission. Relevant to this issue is Rule 801(d)(2)(B) of the Federal Rules of Evidence * * * . The Advisory Committee's note concerning this rule is as follows:

> (B) Under established principles an admission may be made by adopting or acquiescing in the statement of another. While knowledge of contents would ordinarily be essential, this is not inevitably so: "X is a reliable person and knows what he is talking about." *See* McCormick § 246, p. 527, n. 15. Adoption or acquiescence may be manifested in any appropriate manner. When silence is relied upon, the theory is that the person would, under the circumstances, protest the statement made in his presence, if untrue. The decision in each case calls for an evaluation in terms of probable human behavior. In civil cases, the results have generally been satisfactory. In criminal cases, however, troublesome questions have been raised by decisions holding that failure to deny is an admission: the inference is a fairly weak one, to begin with; silence may be motivated by advice of counsel or realization that "anything you say may be used against you"; unusual opportunity is afforded to manufacture evidence; and encroachment upon the privilege against self-incrimination seems inescapably to be involved. However, recent decisions of the Supreme Court relating to custodial interrogation and the right to counsel appear to resolve these difficulties. Hence the rule contains no special provisions concerning failure to deny in criminal cases.

Our analysis of our present problem is made in the context of the Advisory Committee note which is an appropriately guarded one. First, we note that the statement was made in appellant's presence, with only his girl friend and Rogers present. Since appellant had previously trusted Rogers sufficiently to tell him his plan to rob a bank, we see little likelihood that his silence in the face of these statements was due to "advice of counsel" or fear that anything he said might "be used against him." Under the total circumstances, we believe that probable human behavior would have been for appellant promptly to deny his girl friend's statement if it had not been true — particularly when it was said to a person to whom he had previously related a plan to rob a bank. While we agree with appellant's counsel that more is needed to justify admission of this statement than the mere presence and silence of the appellant, we observe that there was more in this record. Finding no reversible error, the judgment of conviction is affirmed.

NOTES

1. What kinds of actions will constitute an adoption?

In *United States v. Ordonez*, 737 F.2d 793 (9th Cir. 1983), the Court ruled that the defendant had not adopted the contents of ledgers seized during a search warrant executed at the defendant's residence. The Court rejected the state's argument that mere possession of the document was enough to establish that the defendant had adopted the statements, which would make them admissible under Rule 801(d)(2)(B). In contrast, in *United States v. Gil*, 58 F.3d 1414 (9th Cir. 1995), the Court held that a drug ledger was properly admitted for its truth as an adoptive admission. The government established an adequate foundation under Rule 104(b) to support a finding that the defendant adopted the ledger. The ledger was found on the defendant's coffee table; the transactions described in the ledger corresponded with the defendant's activities that were observed by police; and the entries corresponded with a separate ledger that had been prepared by the defendant. In *Southern Stone Co. v. Singer*, 665 F.2d 698 (5th Cir. 1982), the Court stated that "the mere failure to respond to a letter does not indicate an adoption unless it was reasonable under the circumstances for the sender to expect the recipient to respond to and to correct erroneous assertions." In *United States v. Hove*, 52 F.3d 233 (9th Cir. 1995), the Court held that "declining an invitation to testify in front of the grand jury simply does not constitute" an adoptive admission of the prosecutor's accusations.

2. Are there any foundation requirements that must be satisfied before a statement can be admitted as an adoptive admission?

As shown in *Carr*, admitting a statement as a party's adoptive admission is dependent upon a showing that the party heard the statement and understood it. This is a question of conditional relevance governed by Rule 104(b). Thus, "before admitting a statement as an adoptive admission, the trial court must determine whether a jury could find that the defendant comprehended and acquiesced in the statement." *United States v. Joshi,* 896 F.2d 1303, 1312 (11th Cir. 1990) (sufficient foundation was laid where the defendant responded with comprehension to other inquiries at the same time).

[4] Authorized Admissions and Admissions by Agent

[a] Federal Rule of Evidence 801(d)(2)(C), (D)

Rule 801. Definitions

* * *

(d) Statements which are not hearsay. A statement is not hearsay if—

* * *

(2) Admission by party-opponent. The statement is offered against a party and is * * * (C) a statement by a person authorized by the party to make a statement concerning the subject, or (D) a statement by the party's agent or servant concerning a matter within the scope of the agency or employment, made during the existence of the relationship * * * The contents of the statement shall be considered but are not alone sufficient to establish the declarant's authority under subdivision (C), the agency or employment relationship and scope thereof under subdivision (D) * * *.

[b] Applying the Rules on Personal Admissions, Admissions by Speaking Agents, and Admissions by Agents Acting within the Scope of Their Authority

MAHLANDT v. WILD CANID SURVIVAL & RESEARCH CENTER, INC.

588 F.2d 626 (8th Cir. 1978)

VAN SICKLE, DISTRICT JUDGE:

This is a civil action for damages arising out of an alleged attack by a wolf on a child. The sole issues on appeal are as to the correctness of three rulings which excluded conclusionary statements against interest. Two of them were made by a defendant, who was also an employee of the corporate defendant; and the third was in the form of a statement appearing in the records of a board meeting of the corporate defendant.

On March 23, 1973, Daniel Mahlandt, then 3 years, 10 months, and 8 days old, was sent by his mother to a neighbor' s home on an adjoining street to get his older brother, Donald. Daniel's mother watched him cross the street, and then turned into the house to get her car keys. Daniel's path took him along a walkway adjacent to the Poos' residence. Next to the walkway was a five foot chain link fence to which Sophie had been chained with a six foot chain. In other words, Sophie was free to move in a half circle having a six foot radius on the side of the fence opposite from Daniel.

Sophie was a bitch wolf, 11 months and 28 days old, who had been born at the St. Louis Zoo, and kept there until she reached 6 months of age, at which time she was given to the Wild Canid Survival and Research Center, Inc. It was the policy of the Zoo to remove wolves from the Children's Zoo after they reached the age of 5 or 6 months. Sophie was supposed to be kept at the Tyson Research Center, but Kenneth Poos, as Director of Education for the Wild Canid Survival and Research Center, Inc., had been keeping her at his home because he was taking Sophie to schools and institutions where he showed films and gave programs with respect to the nature of wolves. Sophie was known as a very gentle wolf who had proved herself to be good natured and stable during her contacts with thousands of children, while she was in the St. Louis Children's Zoo.

Sophie was chained because the evening before she had jumped the fence and attacked a beagle who was running along the fence and yapping at her.

A neighbor who was ill in bed in the second floor of his home heard a child's screams and went to his window, where he saw a boy lying on his back within the enclosure, with a wolf straddling him. The wolf's face was near Daniel's face, but the distance was so great that he could not see what the wolf was doing, and did not see any biting. Within about 15 seconds the neighbor saw Clarke Poos, about seventeen, run around the house, get the wolf off of the boy, and disappear with the child in his arms to the back of the house. Clarke took the boy in and laid him on the kitchen floor.

Clarke had been returning from his friend's home immediately west when he heard a child's cries and ran around to the enclosure. He found Daniel lying within the enclosure, about three feet from the fence, and Sophie standing back from the boy the length of her chain, and wailing. An expert in the behavior of wolves stated that when a wolf licks a child's face that it is a sign of care, and not a sign of attack; that a wolf's wail is a sign of compassion, and an effort to get attention, not a sign of attack. No witness saw or knew how Daniel was injured. Clarke and his sister ran over to get Daniel's mother. She says that Clarke told her, "a wolf got Danny and he is dying." Clarke denies that statement. The defendant, Mr. Poos, arrived home while Daniel and his mother were in the kitchen. After Daniel was taken in an ambulance, Mr. Poos talked to everyone present, including a neighbor who came in. Within an hour after he arrived home, Mr. Poos went to Washington University to inform Owen Sexton, President of Wild Canid Survival and Research Center, Inc., of the incident. Mr. Sexton was not in his office so Mr. Poos left the following note on his door: "Owen, would you call me at home, 727-5080? Sophie bit a child that came in our back yard. All has been taken care of. I need to convey what happened to you."

Denial of admission of this note is one of the issues on appeal.

Later that day, Mr. Poos found Mr. Sexton at the Tyson Research Center and told him what had happened. Denial of plaintiff's offer to prove that Mr. Poos told Mr. Sexton that, "Sophie had bit a child that day," is the second issue on appeal.

A meeting of the Directors of the Wild Canid Survival and Research Center, Inc., was held on April 4, 1973. Mr. Poos was not present at that meeting. The minutes of that meeting reflect that there was a "great deal of discussion * * * about the legal aspects of the incident of Sophie biting the child." Plaintiff offered an abstract of the minutes containing that reference. Denial of the offer of that abstract is the third issue on appeal.

Daniel had lacerations of the face, left thigh, left calf, and right thigh, and abrasions and bruises of the abdomen and chest. Mr. Mahlandt was permitted to state that Daniel had indicated that he had gone under the fence. Mr. Mahlandt and Mr. Poos, about a month after the incident, examined the fence to determine what caused Daniel's lacerations. Mr. Mahlandt felt that they did not look like animal bites. The parallel scars on Daniel's thigh appeared to match the configuration of the barbs or tines on the fence. The expert as to the behavior of wolves opined that the lacerations were not wolf bites or wounds caused by wolf claws. Wolves have powerful jaws and a wolf bite will result in massive crushing or severing of a limb. He stated that if Sophie had bitten Daniel there would have been clear apposition of teeth and massive crushing of Daniel's hands and arms which were not injured. Also, if Sophie had pulled Daniel under the fence, tooth marks on the foot or leg would have been present, although Sophie possessed enough strength to pull the boy under the fence.

The jury brought in a verdict for the defense.

The trial judge's rationale for excluding the note, the statement, and the corporate minutes, was the same in each case. He reasoned that Mr. Poos did not have any personal knowledge of the facts, and accordingly, the first two admissions were based on hearsay; and the third admission contained in the minutes of the board meeting was subject to the same objection of hearsay, and unreliability because of lack of personal knowledge.

* * *

The statement in the note pinned on the door is * * * admissible against Mr. Poos. It was his own statement, and as such was clearly different from the reported statement of another. Example, "I was told that * * * ." * * * It was also a statement of which he had manifested his adoption or belief in its truth. And the same observations may be made of the statement made later in the day to Mr. Sexton that, "Sophie had bit a child."

Are these statements admissible against Wild Canid Survival and Research Center, Inc.? They were made by Mr. Poos when he was an agent or servant of the Wild Canid Survival and Research Center, Inc., and they concerned a matter within the scope of his agency, or employment, *i.e.*, his custody of Sophie, and were made during the existence of that relationship.

* * *

[W]e conclude that the two statements made by Mr. Poos were admissible under 801(d)(2)(D) against Wild Canid Survival and Research Center, Inc.

As to the entry in the records of a corporate meeting, the directors as primary officers of the corporation had the authority to include their conclusions in the record of the meeting. So the evidence would fall within 801(d)(2)(C) as to Wild Canid Survival and Research Center, Inc., and be admissible. * * *

But there was no servant, or agency, relationship which justified admitting the evidence of the board minutes as against Mr. Poos.

None of the conditions of 801(d)(2) cover the claim that minutes of a corporate board meeting can be used against a non-attending, non-participating employee of that corporation. The evidence was not admissible as against Mr. Poos.

* * *

The judgment of the District Court is reversed and the matter remanded to the District Court for a new trial consistent with this opinion.

NOTES

1. The court in *Mahlandt* held that some of the agent's statements could be admitted under Rule 801(d)(2)(C) and others under 801(d)(2)(D). What is the distinction between the two provisions?

The Fourth Circuit Court of Appeals in *United States v. Portsmouth Paving Corp.*, 694 F.2d 312, 321 (4th Cir. 1982), addressed the issue as follows:

> Clause (C) provides that a statement offered against a party is not hearsay if it is "a statement by a person authorized by him to make a statement concerning the subject." This provision states the "orthodox" rule, and demands as a prerequisite to admissibility a showing based on evidence independent of the alleged hearsay that the declarant is an agent of the party with authority to speak on the subject. Ordinarily, under this rule, an employee's admissions damaging to his employer would be inadmissible on the grounds that the employee was not authorized to make damaging admissions. * * *
>
> Clause (D) broadens the narrower "orthodox" rule embodied in Clause (C). Clause (D) excludes from the definition of hearsay when offered against a party a statement "by his agent or servant concerning a matter within the scope of his agency or employment, made during the existence of the relationship." Here, too, independent evidence establishing the existence of the agency must be adduced, but specific authorization to speak need not be shown. That the statement is made about a matter within the scope of the agency is sufficient.

2. Must an agent make a statement to a third party before there is an admission?

In *Reid Bros. Logging Co. v. Ketchikan Pulp Co.*, 699 F.2d 1292, 1307 n. 25 (9th Cir. 1983), the Court ruled that the common law requirement that an agent make a statement to a third party had been overruled by Rule 801. Therefore, the Court admitted a report on the defendant's business that had been prepared by an agent at the request of the defendant, despite the fact that the report had not been delivered to anyone other than executives in the defendant's business or the business's shareholders.

3. Can the statement of an expert witness retained by a party be admissible against that party as an agency-admission?

In *Kirk v. Raymark Indus., Inc.*, 61 F.3d 147 (3rd Cir. 1995), an asbestos case, the court held that the testimony of an expert called by the defendant in an unrelated asbestos case could not be used in the instant case against the defendant as an admission by an authorized agent. The court noted that the expert witness was not one of the defendant's employees, and that an agency could not be found simply because the expert testified at the previous trial on the defendant's behalf. The court stated: "Because an expert witness is charged with the duty of giving his or her expert opinion regarding the matter before the court, we fail to comprehend how an expert witness, who is not an agent of the party who called him, can be authorized to make an admission for that party."

[c] Within the Scope of the Agency or Employment

HILL v. SPIEGEL, INC.

708 F.2d 233 (6th Cir. 1983)

Bailey Brown, Senior Circuit Judge:

* * * Plaintiff-appellee Emery J. Hill brought this action against defendant-appellant Spiegel, Inc., a Delaware corporation, alleging that Spiegel terminated his employment on the basis of age. The case was tried before a jury which returned a verdict in favor of Hill. The jury awarded Hill $230,000.00 actual and compensatory damages for the loss of wages and income, $80,000.00 damages for pain and suffering, moving and related expenses, and found Spiegel's conduct to be "willful." The district court thereafter ordered a remittitur reducing the amount of actual and compensatory damages to $115,000.00, awarding liquidated damages in an equal amount, and awarding $80,000.00 for pain and suffering and moving costs. The court further awarded Hill attorneys' fees, costs and expenses. Spiegel brings this appeal claiming numerous errors below, including the award of damages for pain and suffering. We find merit in some of Spiegel's claims, and thus vacate the judgment of the district court and remand for further proceedings consistent with this opinion.

Background

On February 26, 1976, Emery Hill was terminated from his job as an executive with Spiegel, Inc., a well known mail-order business. Hill was 57 years old at the time and had been in the employ of Spiegel for more than 26 years, most recently as a regional manager in the company's catalog order store (COS) division. Hill's termination came at a time when Spiegel was suffering from a serious decline both in revenues and sales.

Faced with Spiegel's declining profitability, the Beneficial Corporation, Spiegel's parent company, retained a management consulting firm, Booz, Allen & Hamilton, to study the Spiegel organization. The consulting firm concluded that Spiegel's management was "old, inbred, [and] overpaid," and recommended that the entire COS division be liquidated. Beginning sometime in 1975, Spiegel effected a reorganization of the COS division. At that time there were four regional managers in the COS division, one of whom was Hill. In 1976, Hill's employment was terminated and shortly thereafter his position was eliminated. In March 1978, Spiegel abolished the entire COS division.

* * *

III

We now address the district court's admission of testimony pursuant to Rule 801(d)(2)(D) of the Federal Rules of Evidence. This Rule provides that a statement is not hearsay if it is offered against a party and is "a statement by his agent or servant concerning a matter within the scope of his agency or employment, made during the existence of the relationship * * * ."

Spiegel argues on appeal, as it did at trial, that the testimony of Matthew Baker constituted hearsay in that it fell outside the coverage of Rule 801(d)(2)(D). We agree. Baker, a former Spiegel district manager employed under Hill's supervision, testified in behalf of Hill to conversations he had with several other Spiegel employees concerning Hill's discharge. The essence of Baker's testimony was that he was told by Spiegel employees Ed Williams, Danny Seligman, and George Phillips, that Hill had been discharged because of his age and income. Baker further testified as to how these men relayed to him the terrible and traumatic experience of Hill's discharge, and its effect on incumbent management.

Spiegel submits that there was no evidence that these declarants, as to whose comments Baker testified, were involved in the decision to discharge Emery Hill. Spiegel argues, and we agree, that since there was no evidence that either Williams, Seligman, or Phillips had any involvement in the decision to discharge Hill, there was no basis for finding that the statements of these declarants concerned "a matter within the scope of [their] agency." Rule 801(d)(2)(D). We recognize that under this Rule, as is pointed out in the Notes of the Advisory Committee, it is not necessary to show that the declarant had authority to make the statement. But it is necessary, we repeat, to show, to support admissibility, that the content of the declarant's statement concerned a matter within the scope of his agency. The evidence of record tends to establish that Williams was an "operations manager" at Spiegel, about whose duties and responsibilities Baker testified he was uncertain. Baker further testified that Seligman was employed as a "catalog distribution manager," involved in the requisition and circulation of catalogs. Finally, Baker testified that George Phillips became a regional manager of the COS division upon Hill's discharge. The mere fact that each of these men was a "manager" within the expansive Spiegel organization is clearly insufficient to establish that matters bearing upon Hill's discharge were within the scope of their employment. Their statements to Baker concerning Hill's discharge cannot, on this record, be considered as vicarious admissions by Spiegel * * * We conclude that the admission of this evidence on this record was reversible error.

* * *

Accordingly, for the reasons stated herein, we vacate the judgment of the district court and remand for a new trial and such other proceedings as may be required.

NOTES

1. Must there be proof independent of the statement to establish the agency relationship?

In *United States v. Bensinger Co.*, 430 F.2d 584 (8th Cir. 1970), the court ruled that for purposes of the party admission exception to the hearsay rule the existence or extent of an agency relationship cannot be established solely by the content of the out-of-court statement. There must be at least some other evidence of agency that can be considered with the hearsay statement itself, before a statement can be admitted as an exception based on the agency relationship. A 1997 amendment to the Federal Rules of Evidence codified the result in *Bensinger*. Rule 801(d)(2) now provides: "The contents of the statement shall be considered but are not alone sufficient to establish the declarant's authority under subdivision (C), the agency or employment relationship and scope thereof under subdivision (D), or the existence of the conspiracy and the participation therein of the declarant and the party against whom the statement is offered under subdivision (E)."

2. Can the agency relationship be established through circumstantial evidence?

In *Pappas v. Middle Earth Condominium Ass'n,* 963 F.2d 534 (2d Cir. 1992), the plaintiff brought suit for injuries he suffered when he slipped and fell on an icy walkway leading to his condominium. When the plaintiff fell, he called the condominium office to complain. Shortly thereafter, a person came to fix the walkway, and remarked that the walkway was frequently icy and poorly maintained. The trial court held that the plaintiff had not established a sufficient foundation of agency to admit the statement against the condominium association. But the Court of Appeals held that adequate foundation was shown and that the declarant's statements were erroneously excluded. To provide a sufficient foundation to admit vicarious admissions, a party need only establish: "(1) the existence of the agency relationship, (2) that the statement was made during the course of the relationship, and (3) that it relates to a matter within the scope of the agency. The authority granted in the agency relationship need not include authority to make damaging statements, but simply the authority to take action about which the statements relate."

The Court accepted the generally held notion that the proffered hearsay statement does not itself suffice to establish the agency relationship — a notion that was subsequently codified by the 1997 amendment to Rule 801(d)(2). That is, it would not have been enough for the man with the shovel to simply say, "the condominium management sent me to clean up the ice." But the plaintiff did not simply rely on the declarant's own statement of his agency. Here, circumstantial evidence existed to demonstrate that the declarant was an agent and that the agency relationship extended to maintaining the walkway. The declarant responded immediately to the plaintiff's complaint to the defendant, and came prepared with materials to repair the icy conditions. It was unlikely under the circumstances that he was a passing bystander, or that he was an employee acting beyond the scope of the employment relationship. Considering the circumstantial evidence together with the declarant's own statements indicating knowledge of the continuing icy condition, the Court held that the plaintiff had established the existence and scope of the agency.

3. Can the statement of one employee be admitted against another as an agency admission?

In *Zaken v. Boerer*, 964 F.2d 1319 (2d Cir. 1992), the Court held that a statement of one employee could be offered against another as an agency admission, if the relationship between the two was tantamount to a principal/agent relationship. When a *de facto* agency relationship is present, the testimony should not be excluded merely because it is offered against a corporate employee rather than the company itself. In this case, the declarant was answerable to the defendant; the defendant was the company's principal owner, who directed its operations and made all final decisions. Therefore the statement, which concerned a matter within the scope of the declarant's employment and which was made while he was still an employee, was admissible against the defendant. *See also United States v. Agne*, 214 F.3d 47 (1st Cir. 2000) (the statements of a corporate employee may be admitted against an officer when "the factors which normally make up an agency relationship are present"; in this case, the employee was specifically designated by the defendant to handle and report on the business matter at issue in the case, and was directly responsible to the defendant on those matters). *Lippay v. Christos*, 996 F.2d 1490 (3d Cir. 1993) (agency is determined by whether the declarant is continually supervised by the party-opponent; the statements of a government informant were not admissible as vicarious admissions against a law enforcement official, where the informant operated more as a "partner" than as a subordinate).

4. Can a lawyer's statements be admissible against the client as agency admissions?

Professors Saltzburg, Martin, and Capra, in *Federal Rules of Evidence Manual* (9th ed. 2006), have this to say about the use of counsel's statements as agency-admissions:

> A statement of an attorney is, subject to certain conditions, admissible against the client under either Federal Rule 801(d)(2)(C) or (D). The leading case on this subject is *United States v. McKeon*, 738 F.2d 26 (2d Cir. 1984), where the defendant was charged with conspiracy to export firearms. A crucial piece of evidence against him was a copy of a document that the government argued was made from a copier in McKeon's wife's office. In his opening argument, defense counsel stated that a defense expert would show that the copy was not, in fact, made on the copier in Mrs. McKeon's office. The case was subsequently terminated by mistrial. Before the retrial, defense counsel was informed that the prosecution would call an expert to testify that the copy was made on the copier in Mrs. McKeon's office, and that the expert to be called was the teacher of the expert retained by the defense. Given his now-dim prospects in a battle of the experts, defense counsel at the new trial argued that McKeon had been duped into having the crucial documents copied on the copying machine at his wife's office. The government moved to introduce defense counsel's opening statement at the prior trial as an admission by an agent, to prove McKeon's consciousness of guilt.
>
> The Court in *McKeon* recognized that statements by an attorney are generally admissible as agency admissions against the client. It observed, however, that caution should be exercised before admitting statement made by counsel in prior criminal cases. The Court noted

five concerns, some of them in the nature of those considered under Rule 403:

(1) Free use of prior jury argument might consume substantial time to explore marginal matters, because the probative value of a change in strategy may only be evident after an in-depth consideration of such matters as whether new evidence has been found.

(2) The jury might draw unfair inferences from a prior jury argument. The defendant has the right to choose the weak spots in the government's case, and choosing a different weak spot in the second trial does not necessarily mean that the defendant admits the strength of other aspects of the prosecution's case.

(3) The free admissibility of prior jury argument may deter counsel from vigorous advocacy. Unless the truth-seeking process demands it, counsel should not have to pull her punches at one trial due to apprehension about arguments to be made at a second trial.

(4) In order to explain the inconsistency between the two arguments of counsel, the defendant may have to testify, thus risking impeachment and the waiver of the attorney-client privilege.

(5) Introduction of the attorney's statement may mean that the attorney would become one who "ought to be called as a witness" by the defendant. Where that is the case, admission of the prior jury argument will result in disqualification of the defense counsel.

For all these reasons, the *McKeon* Court imposed three limitations before an argument of counsel in a prior trial could be offered against a criminal defendant.

First, there must be a true inconsistency between the arguments. Speculations of counsel, arguments about the credibility of witnesses, and general attacks on the prosecution's case should not be admitted against the defendant at a different trial, because these arguments are too ambiguous to be inconsistent with a later factual assertion.

Second, the Court must determine that the statements of counsel "were such as to be the equivalent of testimonial statements by the defendant"; in other words, the Trial Court must find that the defendant authorized the attorney to make the statements. The mere fact of an attorney-client relationship is insufficient proof on this point, because "considerable delegation is normally involved and such delegation tends to drain the evidentiary value" from the attorney's statement. Therefore, there must be evidence of the client's participatory role, either directly or inferentially. An example of a sufficient showing is where the attorney's statement must have been derived from factual input supplied by the client.

Third, the Court should, after a hearing, determine by a preponderance of the evidence that the prosecution seeks to draw a fair inference from the inconsistency and that an innocent explanation does not exist.

On the facts, the *McKeon* Court found that the attorney's prior opening statement was admissible. The Court reasoned that the opening argument in the later trial was facially inconsistent with the previous one: the copy was either made on the copier at Mrs. McKeon's office or it was not. Also, there was every reason to believe, given the points argued by counsel, that McKeon participated in forming the strategy at both trials. Moreover, McKeon "did not stand mute and put the government to its proof at the last trial." Rather, he took a completely inconsistent stance. Finally, McKeon could give no innocent explanation for the inconsistency, even though the Trial Judge offered to consider such an explanation *in camera* to prevent disclosure of privileged communications or work product. *See also United States v. Harris,* 914 F.2d 927 (7th Cir. 1990) (statements made by defense counsel to an eyewitness concerning the possibility of mistaken identification, were held admissible as agency admissions where the mistaken identity defense was abandoned at trial); *Purgess v. Sharrock*, 33 F.3d 134 (2d Cir. 1994) (a footnote in a brief filed on the defendant's behalf by counsel in a related case was admissible as an agency admission).

It therefore appears, on the basis of *McKeon* and like cases, that statements by counsel will be admitted as agency admissions, so long as there is some evidence to indicate that the attorney was authorized to make the statements. This means that it behooves counsel to get his or her story straight at the outset. While some may argue that the free use of attorney's statements as admissions will chill counsel from vigorous advocacy, it can be argued with equal force that such free admissibility will encourage counsel "to be more careful in verifying the accuracy of information offered by the client." *United States v. Valencia*, 826 F.2d 169, 175 (2d Cir. 1987) (Meskill, J., dissenting). The Court in *Valencia* refused to find an agency admission where defense counsel allegedly made a statement to the prosecutor at an informal bail conference. The Court was concerned that proving that the attorney even made the statement would result in mutual disqualification of prosecutor and defense counsel, a process that would not be worth the benefit of admitting the evidence. There was no such concern in *McKeon*, where the defense attorney made the statement in open court.

While *McKeon* concerns statements made by criminal defense counsel, the principles of agency-admission are applicable to statements by other counsel as well. For example, in *United States v. Salerno*, 937 F.2d 797 (2d Cir. 1991), *rev'd on other grounds*, 505 U.S. 317 (1992), the government in one megatrial sought to show that Auletta was an extortion victim — a "puppet on a string" as the government put it. In a different megatrial involving similar as well as overlapping facts, the government indicted Auletta and sought to prove at trial that he was a voluntary bid-rigger, a major player. Auletta sought to introduce the indictment from the previous megatrial that referred to him as a victim of extortion. The Court held that statements made by government counsel at the prior megatrial concerning Auletta's minimal role, were admissible under Rules 801(d)(2)(C) and (D). As the Court put it, "the government has taken the same evidentiary clay that they used in the [first] case and, for purposes of this trial, resculpted Auletta from a puppet on a string to a bid-rigger." The Court recognized that the government was free to characterize the actors in the prior trial as it wished, but concluded that the jury "is at least entitled to know that the government at one time believed, and stated, that its proof established something different from what it currently claims."

Similarly, attorney-as-agent admissions are often found in civil cases where pleadings are superseded, or inconsistent positions are taken in separate litigations. A typical case is *Andrews v. Metro North Commuter R. Co.*, 882 F.2d 705 (2d Cir. 1989), where the plaintiff's initial complaint alleged that he was struck by a train while walking along the tracks in a train yard. There was substantial evidence that the plaintiff was highly intoxicated at the time. The plaintiff's counsel filed an amended pleading that purported to explain how the plaintiff found himself walking in a train yard: He was waiting on a commuter platform and slipped and fell because of a defective condition consisting of ice and snow; unable to get back on the platform, he wandered along the track bed in a daze until he was struck by the train. The Court of Appeals held that the Trial Court had abused its discretion in refusing to allow the jury to consider the superseded complaint as an admission. The Court relied on *McKeon* for the proposition that "a party cannot advance one version of the facts in his pleadings, conclude that his interests would be better served by a different version, and amend his pleadings to incorporate that version, safe in the belief that the trier of fact will never learn of the change in stories."

5. Must an agent have personal knowledge of the events in order to make a statement that qualifies as an admission?

In *Brookover v. Mary Hitchcock Mem. Hosp.*, 893 F.2d 411 (1st Cir. 1990), some nurses' statements that it would have been advisable to use bed restraints on the plaintiff because of his epilepsy were admitted to show that the hospital's negligence caused the plaintiff's fall from his bed. The Court held that the nurses' statements were admissible as agency-admissions, even though they did not have personal knowledge of the plaintiff's case. *See also Mahlandt v. Wild Canid Survival & Research Ctr., Inc.*, 588 F.2d 626 (8th Cir. 1978) (statement that a wolf bit a child, made by corporate agent, held admissible against the corporation even though the agent had no personal knowledge).

[5] Coconspirators

[a] Federal Rule of Evidence 801(d)(2)(E)

Rule 801. Definitions

* * *

(d) Statements which are not hearsay. A statement is not hearsay if—

* * *

(2) Admission by party-opponent. The statement is offered against a party and is * * * (E) a statement by a coconspirator of a party during the course and in furtherance of the conspiracy. The contents of the statement shall be considered but are not alone sufficient to establish the declarant's authority under subdivision (C), the agency or employment relationship and scope thereof under subdivision (D), or the existence of the conspiracy and the participation therein of the declarant and the party against whom the statement is offered under subdivision (E).

[b] Existence of Conspiracy

BOURJAILY v. UNITED STATES
483 U.S. 171 (1987)

CHIEF JUSTICE REHNQUIST delivered the opinion of the Court.

Federal Rule of Evidence 801(d)(2)(E) provides: "A statement is not hearsay if * * * [t]he statement is offered against a party and is * * * a statement by a coconspirator of a party during the course and in furtherance of the conspiracy." We granted *certiorari* to answer three questions regarding the admission of statements under Rule 801(d)(2)(E): (1) whether the court must determine by independent evidence that the conspiracy existed and that the defendant and the declarant were members of this conspiracy; (2) the quantum of proof on which such determinations must be based; and (3) whether a court must in each case examine the circumstances of such a statement to determine its reliability.* * *

In May 1984, Clarence Greathouse, an informant working for the Federal Bureau of Investigation (FBI), arranged to sell a kilogram of cocaine to Angelo Lonardo. Lonardo agreed that he would find individuals to distribute the drug. When the sale became imminent, Lonardo stated in a tape-recorded telephone conversation that he had a "gentleman friend" who had some questions to ask about the cocaine. In a subsequent telephone call, Greathouse spoke to the "friend" about the quality of the drug and the price. Greathouse then spoke again with Lonardo, and the two arranged the details of the purchase. They agreed that the sale would take place in a designated hotel parking lot, and Lonardo would transfer the drug from Greathouse's car to the "friend," who would be waiting in the parking lot in his own car. Greathouse proceeded with the transaction as planned, and FBI agents arrested Lonardo and petitioner immediately after Lonardo placed a kilogram of cocaine into petitioner's car in the hotel parking lot. In petitioner's car, the agents found over $20,000 in cash.

Petitioner was charged with conspiring to distribute cocaine, in violation of 21 U.S.C. § 846, and possession of cocaine with intent to distribute, a violation of 21 U.S.C. § 841(a)(1). The Government introduced, over petitioner's objection, Angelo Lonardo's telephone statements regarding the participation of the "friend" in the transaction. The District Court found that, considering the events in the parking lot and Lonardo's statements over the telephone, the Government had established by a preponderance of the evidence that a conspiracy involving Lonardo and petitioner existed, and that Lonardo's statements over the telephone had been made in the course of and in furtherance of the conspiracy. Accordingly, the trial court held that Lonardo's out-of-court statements satisfied Rule 801(d)(2)(E) and were not hearsay. Petitioner was convicted on both counts and sentenced to 15 years. The United States Court of Appeals for the Sixth Circuit affirmed. The Court of Appeals agreed with the District Court's analysis and conclusion that Lonardo's out-of-court statements were admissible under the Federal Rules of Evidence. The court also rejected petitioner's contention that because he could not cross-examine Lonardo, the admission of these statements violated his constitutional right to confront the witnesses against him. We affirm.

Before admitting a co-conspirator's statement over an objection that it does not qualify under Rule 801(d)(2)(E), a court must be satisfied that the statement actually falls within the definition of the Rule. There must be evidence that there was a conspiracy involving the declarant and the nonoffering party, and that the statement was made "during the course and in furtherance of the conspiracy." Federal Rule of Evidence 104(a) provides: "Preliminary questions concerning * * * the admissibility of evidence shall be determined by the court." Petitioner and the Government agree that the existence of a conspiracy and petitioner's involvement in it are preliminary questions of fact that, under Rule 104, must be resolved by the court. The Federal Rules, however, nowhere define the standard of proof the court must observe in resolving these questions.

We are therefore guided by our prior decisions regarding admissibility determinations that hinge on preliminary factual questions. We have traditionally required that these matters be established by a preponderance of proof. Evidence is placed before the jury when it satisfies the technical requirements of the evidentiary Rules, which embody certain legal and policy determinations. The inquiry made by a court concerned with these matters is not whether the proponent of the evidence wins or loses his case on the merits, but whether the evidentiary Rules have been satisfied. Thus, the evidentiary standard is unrelated to the burden of proof on the substantive issues, be it a criminal case or a civil case. The preponderance standard ensures that before admitting evidence, the court will have found it more likely than not that the technical issues and policy concerns addressed by the Federal Rules of Evidence have been afforded due consideration. As in *Lego v. Twomey*, 404 U.S. 477, 488 (1972), we find "nothing to suggest that admissibility rulings have been unreliable or otherwise wanting in quality because not based on some higher standard." We think that our previous decisions in this area resolve the matter. Therefore, we hold that when the preliminary facts relevant to Rule 801(d)(2)(E) are disputed, the offering party must prove them by a preponderance of the evidence.

Even though petitioner agrees that the courts below applied the proper standard of proof with regard to the preliminary facts relevant to Rule 801(d)(2)(E), he nevertheless challenges the admission of Lonardo's statements. Petitioner argues that in determining whether a conspiracy exists and whether the defendant was a member of it, the court must look only to independent evidence — that is, evidence other than the statements sought to be admitted. Petitioner relies on *Glasser v. United States*, 315 U.S. 60 (1942), in which this Court first mentioned the so-called "bootstrapping rule." The relevant issue in *Glasser* was whether Glasser's counsel, who also represented another defendant, faced such a conflict of interest that Glasser received ineffective assistance. Glasser contended that conflicting loyalties led his lawyer not to object to statements made by one of Glasser's co-conspirators. The Government argued that any objection would have been fruitless because the statements were admissible. The Court rejected this proposition:

> "[S]uch declarations are admissible over the objection of an alleged co-conspirator, who was not present when they were made, only if there is proof *aliunde* that he is connected with the conspiracy. Otherwise, hearsay would lift itself by its own bootstraps to the level of competent evidence."

* * * Read in the light most favorable to petitioner, *Glasser* could mean that a court should not consider hearsay statements at all in determining preliminary facts under Rule 801(d)(2)(E). Petitioner, of course, adopts this view of the bootstrapping rule. *Glasser*, however, could also mean that a court must have *some* proof *aliunde*, but may look at the hearsay statements themselves in light of this independent evidence to determine whether a conspiracy has been shown by a preponderance of the evidence. The Courts of Appeals have widely adopted the former view and held that in determining the preliminary facts relevant to co-conspirators' out-of-court statements, a court may not look at the hearsay statements themselves for their evidentiary value.

[*Glasser* was] decided before Congress enacted the Federal Rules of Evidence in 1975. These Rules now govern the treatment of evidentiary questions in federal courts. Rule 104(a) provides: "Preliminary questions concerning * * * the admissibility of evidence shall be determined by the court * * * . In making its determination it is not bound by the rules of evidence except those with respect to privileges." Similarly, Rule 1101(d)(1) states that the Rules of Evidence (other than with respect to privileges) shall not apply to "[t]he determination of questions of fact preliminary to admissibility of evidence when the issue is to be determined by the court under rule 104." The question thus presented is whether any aspect of *Glasser*'s bootstrapping rule remains viable after the enactment of the Federal Rules of Evidence.

Petitioner concedes that Rule 104, on its face, appears to allow the court to make the preliminary factual determinations relevant to Rule 801(d)(2)(E) by considering any evidence it wishes, unhindered by considerations of admissibility. * * * That would seem to many to be the end of the matter. Congress has decided that courts may consider hearsay in making these factual determinations. Out-of-court statements made by anyone, including putative co-conspirators, are often hearsay. Even if they are, they may be considered, *Glasser* and the bootstrapping rule notwithstanding. But petitioner nevertheless argues that the bootstrapping rule, as most Courts of Appeals have construed it, survived this apparently unequivocal change in the law unscathed and that Rule 104, as applied to the admission of co-conspirator's statements, does not mean what it says. We disagree.

Petitioner claims that Congress evidenced no intent to disturb the bootstrapping rule, which was embedded in the previous approach, and we should not find that Congress altered the rule without affirmative evidence so indicating. It would be extraordinary to require legislative history to *confirm* the plain meaning of Rule 104. The Rule on its face allows the trial judge to consider any evidence whatsoever, bound only by the rules of privilege. We think that the Rule is sufficiently clear that to the extent that it is inconsistent with petitioner's interpretation of *Glasser* * * *, the Rule prevails.

Nor do we agree with petitioner that this construction of Rule 104(a) will allow courts to admit hearsay statements without any credible proof of the conspiracy, thus fundamentally changing the nature of the co-conspirator exception. Petitioner starts with thc proposition that co-conspirators' out-of-court statements are deemed unreliable and are inadmissible, at least until a conspiracy is shown. Since these statements are unreliable, petitioner contends that they should not form any part of the basis for establishing a conspiracy, the very antecedent that renders them admissible.

Petitioner's theory ignores two simple facts of evidentiary life. First, out-of-court statements are only *presumed* unreliable. The presumption may be rebutted by appropriate proof. *See* Fed. Rule Evid. 803(24) [now Rule 807] (otherwise inadmissible hearsay may be admitted if circumstantial guarantees of trustworthiness demonstrated). Second, individual pieces of evidence, insufficient in themselves to prove a point, may in cumulation prove it. The sum of an evidentiary presentation may well be greater than its constituent parts. Taken together, these two propositions demonstrate that a piece of evidence, unreliable in isolation, may become quite probative when corroborated by other evidence. A *per se* rule barring consideration of these hearsay statements during preliminary factfinding is not therefore required. Even if out-of-court declarations by co-conspirators are presumptively unreliable, trial courts must be permitted to evaluate these statements for their evidentiary worth as revealed by the particular circumstances of the case. Courts often act as factfinders, and there is no reason to believe that courts are any less able to properly recognize the probative value of evidence in this particular area. The party opposing admission has an adequate incentive to point out the shortcomings in such evidence before the trial court finds the preliminary facts. If the opposing party is unsuccessful in keeping the evidence from the factfinder, he still has the opportunity to attack the probative value of the evidence as it relates to the substantive issue in the case. * * *

We think that there is little doubt that a co-conspirator's statements could themselves be probative of the existence of a conspiracy and the participation of both the defendant and the declarant in the conspiracy. Petitioner's case presents a paradigm. The out-of-court statements of Lonardo indicated that Lonardo was involved in a conspiracy with a "friend." The statements indicated that the friend had agreed with Lonardo to buy a kilogram of cocaine and to distribute it. The statements also revealed that the friend would be at the hotel parking lot, in his car, and would accept the cocaine from Greathouse's car after Greathouse gave Lonardo the keys. Each one of Lonardo's statements may itself be unreliable, but taken as a whole, the entire conversation between Lonardo and Greathouse was corroborated by independent evidence. The friend, who turned out to be petitioner, showed up at the prearranged spot at the prearranged time. He picked up the cocaine, and a significant sum of money was found in his car. On these facts, the trial court concluded, in our view correctly, that the Government had established the existence of a conspiracy and petitioner's participation in it.

We need not decide in this case whether the courts below could have relied solely upon Lonardo's hearsay statements to determine that a conspiracy had been established by a preponderance of the evidence. To the extent that *Glasser* meant that courts could not look to the hearsay statements themselves for any purpose, it has clearly been superseded by Rule 104(a). It is sufficient for today to hold that a court, in making a preliminary factual determination under Rule 801(d)(2)(E), may examine the hearsay statements sought to be admitted. As we have held in other cases concerning admissibility determinations, "the judge should receive the evidence and give it such weight as his judgment and experience counsel." The courts below properly considered the statements of Lonardo and the subsequent events in finding that the Government had established by a preponderance of the evidence that Lonardo was involved in a conspiracy with petitioner. We have no reason to believe that the District Court's factfinding of this point was clearly erroneous. We hold that Lonardo's out-of-court statements were properly admitted against petitioner.

* * *

The judgment of the Court of Appeals is *Affirmed.*

[Concurring and dissenting opinions omitted.]

NOTES

1. In making a Rule 801(d)(2)(E) determination, can a court find conspiracy by a preponderance of the evidence solely on the basis of the hearsay statement itself?

Courts making the admissibility determination do require some independent evidence of the existence of the conspiracy, apart from the hearsay statement. *See United States v. Tellier*, 83 F.3d 578 (2d Cir. 1996) (RICO conviction reversed because the sole evidence for one of the predicate acts — conspiracy to distribute marijuana — was a hearsay statement from the defendant's alleged coconspirator; coconspirator hearsay is "presumptively unreliable, and, for such statements to be admissible, there must be some independent corroborating evidence of the defendant's participation in the conspiracy."). The 1997 amendment to Rule 801(d)(2) requires some evidence of conspiracy independent of the statement itself. Note that the amendment also provides that the trial court *must* consider the hearsay statement itself as part of the proof of conspiracy — the court does not have the discretion to reject the statement as proof.

2. Must a conspiracy be charged in the case before a hearsay statement can be admitted under Rule 801(d)(2)(E)?

"[I]t is not necessary that the Government charge a conspiracy to take advantage of Fed. R. Evid. 801(d)(2)(E). The Government merely needs to demonstrate that the declarant and the defendants against whom the statements are offered are members of a conspiracy in furtherance of which the statements are made." *United States v. Stratton*, 779 F.2d 820, 829 (2d Cir. 1985).

3. Can a declarant's statement be admissible even if the declarant has been acquitted of conspiracy?

The mere fact that the declarant has been acquitted of criminal conspiracy charges does not render statements by that declarant inadmissible under the coconspirator exemption of Rule 801(d)(2)(E). The fact that the Government failed to prove the conspiracy beyond a reasonable doubt does not mean that it cannot prove a conspiracy under the *Bourjaily* preponderance standard. *United States v. Peralta*, 941 F.2d 1003 (9th Cir. 1991).

4. How much independent evidence is needed to satisfy the preponderance of the evidence requirement set forth in *Bourjaily*?

See Saltzburg, Martin, and Capra, *Federal Rules of Evidence Manual* (9th ed. 2006):

> Courts after *Bourjaily* have held that the independent evidence must be at least "fairly incriminating" on its own before that evidence together with the hearsay statement can satisfy the *Bourjaily* preponderance requirement. As the Ninth Circuit put it in *United States v. Silverman*, 861 F.2d 571, 578 (9th Cir. 1988):
>
> > Evidence of wholly innocuous conduct or statements by the defendant will rarely be sufficiently corroborative of the co-conspirator's statement to constitute proof, by a preponderance of the evidence, that the defendant knew of and participated in the conspiracy. Evidence of innocent conduct does little, if anything, to enhance the reliability of the co-conspirator's statement. A co-conspirator's statement, which is presumptively unreliable hence inadmissible standing alone, is no more reliable when coupled with evidence of conduct that is completely consistent with defendant's unawareness of the conspiracy.
>
> In *Silverman*, the Court held that statements of the defendant's sister identifying the defendant as her drug supplier were

> inadmissible under the coconspirator exception. The only independent evidence of a conspiratorial connection put forth by the government was that the sister would travel to the town where the defendant lived; that the defendant would pick her up at the airport; that when the sister returned to her home, she would have drugs; and that the defendant subsequently concealed his identity from a DEA agent. The Court held that the brother-sister association was "too innocent" to connect the defendant to any conspiracy, and that the subsequent concealment of identity was not sufficiently related to the brother-sister connection to render it sufficiently probative of a conspiracy between them. The Court concluded that the independent evidence proffered by the government "was so marginally corroborative that it failed to overcome the presumptive unreliability" of the sister's hearsay statements.
>
> We agree with the *Silverman* Court that the independent evidence must at least establish a reasonable suspicion of conspiracy before the jury can be permitted to consider the declarant's statement. Otherwise there is an unacceptable risk that the defendant will be convicted solely from the mouths of self-appointed coconspirators who are not produced for trial.

We suggest that the Courts, in evaluating the independent evidence presented, use a standard analogous to the reasonable suspicion test that is used to determine the legality of a *Terry* stop under the Fourth Amendment. That test, as applied to coconspirator hearsay, would be: whether the independent evidence, standing alone, presents a fair possibility that the defendant and the declarant are coconspirators. (For a discussion of the reasonable suspicion standard, with examples, see S. Saltzburg & D. Capra, American Criminal Procedure ch. 2 (8th ed. 2007)). The government need not overcome every possible innocent explanation of the facts presented. But, on the other hand, independent evidence that is not at all suggestive of criminal association (such as the brother-sister evidence in *Silverman*) should not suffice. We believe that if the independent evidence is reasonably suspicious, and if that evidence combined with the hearsay statement itself establishes a conspiracy by a preponderance of the evidence, then the defendant will be sufficiently protected from unfair conviction out of the mouths of self-appointed coconspirators.

4. At what point must the trial court make a determination as to whether the government has shown a conspiracy by a preponderance of the evidence, so as to meet the foundation requirement for Rule 801(d)(2)(E)?

Trial judges have several procedural options when deciding whether the prosecution has satisfied the foundation requirements of Rule 801(d)(2)(E). One option is to hold a pretrial hearing and make a ruling on admissibility following the hearing, as the judge does with an ordinary evidence problem. Appellate courts have expressed a preference for this procedure, but they also recognize that in many complex conspiracy cases, this would be tantamount to trying a case twice: the prosecution would introduce evidence of conspiracy to establish the foundation requirements for the admissibility of the hearsay, and then proffer the same evidence again at trial. So trial judges also have the option to allow coconspirator hearsay to be admitted at trial, subject to a condition — i.e., the government must satisfy the preponderance of the evidence standard as the case progresses. *See, e.g., United States v. McCarthy,* 961 F.2d 972 (1st Cir. 1992) (there was no error in admitting coconspirator statements conditionally, where previous trials of other alleged coconspirators indicated it was likely that the foundation would be established; at the close of evidence, the trial judge reviewed only the evidence adduced at the defendant's trial and found that the prosecution had met its burden of showing the existence of the conspiracy and the participation of the declarant and the defendant therein); *United States v. Ferra,* 900 F.2d 1057 (7th Cir. 1990) (admitting coconspirator hearsay statements subject to connection is not a routine but, rather, an exceptional procedure, appropriate only when the evidence on the question of conspiracy is extensive; most of the time it is better, especially because of double jeopardy problems, to make a preliminary determination rather than to decide the admissibility question on a mistrial motion).

If the judge defers the admissibility question and subsequently finds that the government has not met its burden of establishing the Rule 801(d)(2)(E) requirements, then a mistrial should be declared unless it is clear that a limiting instruction will suffice to protect the defendant from the obvious prejudice arising from the jury's having already heard the inadmissible hearsay. *See, e.g., United States v. Wood,* 851 F.2d 185 (8th Cir. 1988) (the judge may admit coconspirator hearsay subject to connection, but the government is on notice that at the conclusion of all the evidence, the judge will make an explicit determination on the record of whether, in its view, the government has proved a conspiracy by a preponderance of the evidence; if the judge determines that the government has failed to carry its burden, a mistrial should be declared unless an instruction to the jury to disregard the evidence would suffice to cure any prejudice). Compare *United States v. Freeman,* 208 F.3d 332 (1st Cir. 2000) (coconspirator hearsay was admitted subject to establishing a conspiratorial connection between the defendant and the declarant; when the government failed to make that connection at trial, the judge struck the statement and issued a curative instruction; this was held a sufficient remedy, the court noting that the hearsay statement was only a small part of the evidence in a seven-day trial and had little relevance to the only charge on which the defendant was convicted).

If the judge is thinking about deferring the question of admissibility of coconspirator hearsay until trial, it is prudent practice to require the government to provide a summary of its foundation evidence. If the summary indicates that the government will have trouble providing a foundation, then the judge should either require a hearing on the admissibility of the hearsay, or else structure the order of proof at trial so that a ruling can be made before the hearsay is admitted. By these methods, a subsequent mistrial can perhaps be avoided. *See, e.g., United States v. Shoffner,* 826 F.2d 619 (7th Cir. 1987) (the court upheld the trial judge's finding that statements were in furtherance of conspiracy, but it observed that it might have been preferable for the judge to preview the government's evidence that would support its Rule 801(d)(2)(E) ruling rather than admit statements upon a representation that the government would prove at trial they were made in furtherance of conspiracy).

[c] In Furtherance of the Conspiracy

UNITED STATES v. HARRIS
546 F.2d 234 (8th Cir. 1976)

STEPHENSON, CIRCUIT JUDGE:

Walter B. Harris appeals his conviction by jury on one count of conspiracy to commit mail fraud in violation of 18 U.S.C. § 371. Appellant Harris alleges that the district court * * * erred in admitting hearsay statements of the alleged coconspirator which were not "in furtherance of" the conspiracy.* * * We affirm the conviction.

The indictment charged that appellant Harris, Edward Williams and Vernon French conspired to defraud insurance companies and to use the United States mails for the purpose of executing the scheme. More specifically the indictment alleged that the three coconspirators staged and contrived an accident in which a vehicle driven by Vernon French collided with the rear of a car owned by Harris and supposedly occupied by Harris and Williams. It was further alleged that Harris and Williams had multiple insurance policies on the date of the staged accident and submitted fraudulent claims as a result of the accident.

* * *

The government called as a witness A. J. Rupe, who was in the hospital during the same period as Harris and Williams. Rupe was in the hospital after staging an accident as part of his own scheme to defraud insurance companies. While in the hospital Rupe had conversations with both Harris and Williams. At trial he was allowed to testify over Harris' objection that coconspirator Williams made statements to him to the effect that the collision involving Harris, Williams and French was staged. Although Harris readily admits that the statements made by Williams were during the course of the conspiracy, Harris contends the statements were not "in furtherance of" the conspiracy and therefore were erroneously admitted.

The "in furtherance of" requirement arises from Rule 801(d)(2)(E) which makes admissible against a party a statement by a coconspirator during the course of and in furtherance of the conspiracy. Fed. R. Evid. 801(d)(2)(E). The inclusion of the "in furtherance of" requirement appears to have been a considered decision by Congress. Before the present Rule 801(d)(2)(E) was promulgated, Senator John L. McClellan of Arkansas strenuously advocated the abolishment of the "in furtherance of" requirement, substituting in its place a more relaxed standard and thereby enlarging the existing hearsay exception. This suggestion was rejected, however, by Congress.

The Fifth Circuit has stated that although the phrase "in furtherance of the conspiracy" has a talismanic ring to it, the standard should not be applied too strictly, lest the purpose of the exception be defeated. *United States v.*

James, 510 F.2d 546, 549 (5th Cir. 1975). We are also mindful that several commentators have noted that the courts have tended to construe broadly the requirement that the coconspirator's statement be made in furtherance of the conspiracy. *See* discussion *United States v. Overshon*, 494 F.2d 894, 899 (8th Cir. 1974). Nevertheless, Congress has expressly retained the "in furtherance of" requirement. Furthermore, the Supreme Court continues to include this requirement in its statement of the coconspirator's rule. Therefore we conclude that the "in furtherance of" requirement remains viable in the federal courts.

In the instant case, whether Williams' statements to Rupe were in the furtherance of the conspiracy is a close question. Both Rupe and Williams were actively engaged in parallel schemes to defraud insurance companies. In this light their conversations can be viewed as mutual attempts to gather useful information to further each other's conspiracy. On the other hand appellant argues that the statements were nothing more than casual admissions of culpability by Williams to someone he had individually decided to trust. [The court finds that the statement was probably in furtherance, but that even if not, any error in admitting the hearsay was harmless.]

* * *

AFFIRMED.

NOTES

1. What types of statements will be considered in furtherance of a conspiracy?

The statement must be made with the intent to further the conspiracy. If the statement was simply idle chatter by a conspirator, or simply serves to blame or "finger" people as conspirators, it will not be admissible under this exemption. *See, e.g., United States v. LiCausi*, 167 F.3d 36 (1st Cir. 1999) (statements made by one conspirator to his girlfriend should not have been admitted under the coconspirator hearsay exemption; the declarant was simply venting his anxiety and blowing off steam in reaction to developments in the conspiracy); *United States v. Cornett*, 195 F.3d 776 (5th Cir. 1999) (statements by coconspirator did not further the conspiracy, when they were made by the declarant to her former boyfriend as a "casual aside"). However, statements that on their face seem only to inculpate members of the conspiracy may in fact further the conspiracy by keeping other members apprised of conspiratorial developments, or by encouraging others to join, assist or deal with the conspiracy. *See, e.g., United States v. Jefferson,* 215 F.3d 820 (8th Cir. 2000) (statements made by one conspirator to another were in furtherance of the conspiracy where the declarant was reporting a botched murder attempt to keep the other conspirators apprised of developments: "Statements that describe past events are in furtherance of the conspiracy if they are made simply to keep coconspirators abreast of current developments and problems facing the group."); *United States v. Bowman,* 215 F.3d 951 (9th Cir. 2000) (narrations of past events are sometimes inadmissible as coconspirator statements, but in this case the coconspirator's statements to his girlfriend were in furtherance of the conspiracy because the declarant was seeking his girlfriend's assistance in criminal acts). *United States v. Tom*, 330 F.3d 83 (1st Cir. 2003) (coconspirator's statement to a drug buyer that he had dealt with the defendant for a year was a statement of reassurance and so in furtherance of the conspiracy). In *United States v. Arambula-Ruiz,* 987 F.2d 599 (9th Cir. 1993), the defendant's coconspirator, in preparation for a drug transaction, told a putative buyer that the defendant owned the drugs and would follow the buyer to the delivery site and would be present when the sale was made. The buyer turned out to be an undercover agent. The Court held that the statements to the undercover agent were admissible under Rule 801(d)(2)(E). The statement furthered the objectives of the conspiracy because it gave necessary information to the putative buyer on the details of the forthcoming drug transaction.

2. When does a conspiracy end so that statements made thereafter are not made within the course of the conspiracy?

The conspiracy must be in operation at the time the statement was made. Generally speaking, a conspiracy is terminated when its central criminal goal has been achieved or abandoned. *See, e.g.*, *United States v. Tse*, 135 F.3d 200 (1st Cir. 1998) (gang members' statements made eight months after attempted murders were not made in the course of the conspiracy, because at that time it was clear that the murder plans had been abandoned). For monetary crimes, the central criminal goal is achieved when the money is divided up among the coconspirators. Courts have held that actions designed to evade detection, after money has been divided up, are not in the course of the original conspiracy. *See, e.g.*, *United States v. Mojica-Baez*, 229 F.3d 292 (1st Cir. 2000) (no error to admit hearsay statement made by a conspirator shortly after a bank robbery occurred: "there is a distinction, for purposes of the conspirator statement exception to the hearsay rule, between an initial conspiracy to commit a crime and later actions to conceal a crime"; however, in this case the statement was made during the course of the bank robbery conspiracy because the proceeds had not yet been divided). Statements made to evade detection might well be part of a subsequent conspiracy, however.

In *United States v. Ibern-Maldonado,* 823 F.2d 698 (1st Cir. 1987), the court held that a statement made at the time a pilot was being paid for transporting marijuana was admissible under Rule 801(d)(2)(E), since the conspiracy continues until the proceeds are divided. In *United States v. Perez-Garcia,* 904 F.2d 1534 (11th Cir. 1990), the court held that it was error to admit a statement made after the defendant and all of his coconspirators had been arrested, as by that time the conspiracy had terminated. In *United States v. Serrano,* 870 F.2d 1 (1st Cir. 1989), the court declared that "when the acts of concealment are done after the central objectives have been attained, for the purpose only of covering up after the crime, they are inadmissible." Any other rule "would, for all practical purposes, wipe out the statute of limitations in conspiracy cases, as well as extend indefinitely the time within which hearsay declarations will bind coconspirators." *Grunewald v. United States,* 353 U.S. 391 (1957).

3. Can the statement of an unidentified conspirator be admitted under Rule 801(d)(2)(E)?

In *United States v. Squillacote*, 221 F.3d 542 (4th Cir. 2000), the Court upheld the admission of written statements under Rule 801(d)(2)(E) despite the government's failure to identify the author of the statements. The defendants in *Squillacote* were accused of performing acts of espionage for the former German Democratic Republic during the Cold War. The court held that "while the identity of the declarant of the unsigned documents may not be known, the only conclusion that can be drawn from the information included in the documents — information that was corroborated in many respects by [witness] testimony and by Squillacote's own statements to the undercover agent — is that the documents were created by or at the direction of East German agents who had knowledge of and were involved in the conspiracy with the Appellants."

[6] Relationship between Agency Admissions and Coconspirator Admissions

CITY OF TUSCALOOSA v. HARCROS CHEMICALS, INC.

158 F.3d 548 (11th Cir. 1998)

TJOFLAT, CIRCUIT JUDGE:

In the instant case, thirty-nine Alabama municipal entities brought suit in the United States District Court for the Northern District of Alabama, alleging that five defendant chemical companies engaged in a conspiracy to fix prices for repackaged chlorine in Alabama in violation of both federal and state antitrust law. The plaintiffs also asserted claims for fraud under Alabama law. In a memorandum opinion, the district court ruled much of the plaintiffs' evidence inadmissible and granted summary judgment to all five defendants on the antitrust claims and the fraud claims. * * *

I.

A.

The plaintiffs and plaintiffs-intervenors in this case are thirty-nine Alabama municipal entities that purchase repackaged chlorine for the treatment of drinking water, sewage, and swimming pools. Repackaged chlorine is liquid chlorine that has been pressurized and stored in containers for delivery to, and use by, chlorine consumers. The five defendant corporations are chemical companies that repackage or distribute chlorine in Alabama.

At the core of the plaintiffs' claims are their allegations that the defendants colluded with each other to set prices for repackaged chlorine distribution contracts. During the period of the alleged collusion, many Alabama municipal entities purchased chlorine by auction. An entity seeking to purchase chlorine would solicit sealed bids from companies that had submitted bids in the past. Once the bids were received, the buyer would publicly open the bids and announce what each competitor had bid. The buyer would then award its contract to the lowest bidder. The plaintiffs allege that the defendants submitted sealed bids based on "list prices" previously determined amongst themselves, and in this way allocated the repackaged chlorine contracts as they wished.

* * * After discovery, the defendants moved to exclude * * * several pieces of evidence that they asserted were inadmissible hearsay. The district court * * * excluded the purported hearsay testimony, and * * * granted summary judgment for the defendants on all claims. The plaintiffs now appeal, asserting that the district court improperly excluded their proffered evidence and that summary judgment was erroneously entered.

* * *

B.

* * *

1.

The plaintiffs proffered testimony regarding an alleged admission by the late Robert Jones ("Jones"), the former chairman, chief executive officer, and president of defendant Jones Chemicals. Loraine and Peter Cassassa, friends of Jones during the period of the alleged conspiracy, testified in depositions that on several occasions in the mid-1980s, Jones admitted to them that he was at that time involved in fixing chlorine prices in the Southeast. Loraine Cassassa testified that Jones told her that he "got together with the people [who were] submitting the bids and they knew what each other were going to bid before that bid was ever submitted." She also testified that Jones told her that he knew such conduct was illegal, but that "[t]hat's how big business goes." Peter Cassassa gave substantially identical testimony.

The district court excluded the testimony of the Cassassas as "hearsay." We conclude that the court erred as a matter of law by making this determination and therefore abused its discretion. Accordingly, we reverse the ruling excluding that testimony.

Under the Federal Rules of Evidence, " '[h]earsay' is a statement, other than one made by the declarant while testifying at the trial or hearing, offered in evidence to prove the truth of the matter asserted." Fed. R. Evid. 801(c). In general, "[h]earsay is not admissible except as provided by [the federal] rules * * * ." Fed. R. Evid. 802. A "statement by [a] party's agent or servant concerning a matter within the scope of the agency or employment, made during the existence of the relationship," however, is deemed an admission by a party opponent and is excluded from the definition of hearsay. Fed. R. Evid. 801(d)(2)(D); *see Zaben v. Air Prods. & Chems., Inc.*, 129 F.3d 1453, 1456 (11th Cir.1997).

Robert Jones, as president of Jones Chemicals from 1986 to 1989, and as the chairman and CEO of the company from 1986 to 1993, clearly was an "agent or servant" of the company. Moreover, the record on appeal establishes that Jones set chlorine prices for Jones Chemicals throughout the period of the alleged conspiracy. His purported statements regarding Jones Chemical's chlorine pricing practices thus "concern[ed] a matter within the scope of [his] agency or employment, made during the existence of the relationship." Jones' purported statements to the Cassassas are therefore admissible as non-hearsay party admissions under Fed. R. Evid. 801(d)(2)(D).

The appellants argue that the Cassassas' testimony ought also to be admitted against the other defendants, on the ground that Jones' purported statements were made "during the course and in furtherance of the conspiracy" and therefore fall within the exemption contained in Rule 801(d)(2)(E). Declarations by one defendant in a conspiracy case may be admissible against other defendants as non-hearsay upon sufficient showing that the statement was made by a co-conspirator during the course and in furtherance of the conspiracy. * * * This circuit applies "a liberal standard in determining whether a statement is made in furtherance of a conspiracy." *United States v. Santiago*, 837 F.2d 1545, 1549 (11th Cir.1988). The statement need not be necessary to the conspiracy, but must only further the interests of the conspiracy in some way. Statements made to solicit membership or participation in the conspiracy, for example, or statements explaining the conspiracy to a new member, are made in furtherance of the conspiracy.

Jones' purported statements do not satisfy even this liberal standard. The purported statements were made to friends, who were neither involved in the alleged conspiracy nor invited to participate therein, over drinks or on the golf course. The statements could not have furthered the interests of the alleged conspiracy in any way. A statement that merely discloses the existence of a conspiracy to a non-conspirator, that merely "spills the beans," with no intention of recruiting the auditor into the conspiracy does not further the conspiracy. * * * We conclude that the district court did not err in finding that Jones' purported statements were not made in furtherance of the alleged conspiracy, and that the Cassassas' testimony is therefore not admissible against the alleged co-conspirators. Because Jones' purported statements were non-hearsay party admissions, however, we conclude that the statements do fall within the exception contained in Rule 801(d)(2)(D), and that the Cassassas' testimony is therefore admissible against Jones Chemicals.

2.

* * *

3.

The district court also excluded the testimony of Barbara Krysti, who offered testimony against Harcros. Barbara Krysti is the widow of Lloyd Krysti, who was a sales manager at Harcros. Barbara Krysti stated in an affidavit that

> [i]n 1987 or 1988, Lloyd found out that Joe Ragusa [(Harcros' vice-president for the Southeast)] was getting together with his competitors and fixing the price of chlorine before bids were submitted. Lloyd's reaction to me was that Joe was crazy for doing this and that it was illegal and that he could go to jail * * * . Lloyd first told me about the price fixing in 1988. We talked about it several times after that.

The proffered testimony is double hearsay; Barbara Krysti relates Lloyd Krysti's account of what Joe Ragusa said. Such "hearsay included within hearsay is not excluded under the hearsay rule if each part of the combined statements conforms with an exception to the hearsay rule provided in these rules." Fed. R. Evid. 805; *see, e.g.*, Mahlandt v. Wild Canid Survival and Research Ctr., Inc., 588 F.2d 626, 630 (8th Cir.1978). Because chlorine pricing and sales were within the scope of Joe Ragusa's employment with Harcros, Ragusa's statements to Lloyd Krysti clearly fall within the party admission exception to the hearsay rule.

Lloyd Krysti's statements to Barbara Krysti, however, do not fall within any exception to the hearsay rule. The record establishes that chlorine pricing was not substantially within the scope of Lloyd Krysti's employment. Lloyd Krysti was involved in the pricing and sales of other chemicals and was rarely and only ministerially involved in chlorine sales. Lloyd Krysti did not set prices for chlorine. Indeed, the plaintiffs themselves assert that Joe Ragusa was solely responsible for setting chlorine prices in Alabama, and none of the many Harcros documents in the record indicate otherwise. On the contrary, in a 1984 memorandum, Ragusa severely upbraided several Harcros sales managers who set chlorine prices without his approval.

Because the content of Lloyd Krysti's statements did not concern a matter within the scope of his employment or agency, they do not fall within the party admission exception in Rule 801(d)(2)(D). In addition, Lloyd Krysti's statements were not made in furtherance of the alleged conspiracy, but "merely informed" Barbara Krysti — a non-conspirator — of the existence of the alleged conspiracy. Because Lloyd Krysti's statements to Barbara Krysti do not fall within any exception to the hearsay rule, we affirm the district court's ruling excluding the testimony of Barbara Krysti.

* * *

REVERSED in part and AFFIRMED in part.

PROBLEM 11-1

In response to increased drug availability at the high school, the local F.B.I. agent, Clean Cut, goes undercover in a drug sting operation. A shabbily dressed Clean Cut meets Middle Man at a local bar who agrees to arrange a sale of drugs from Clean Cut to Middle Man's friend, Drug Dealer. The deal is set for 1:00 a.m. at a local park. Drug Dealer shows up at the appointed hour wearing a top hat and pays for the drugs with $5000 in one-hundred dollar bills. Middle Man and Drug Dealer are arrested on the spot and later charged with conspiracy to distribute illegal drugs. Drug Dealer intends to defend the case on the theory that his purchase was simply for his own use.

Drug Dealer files a motion in limine asking for suppression at trial of certain statements made by Middle Man. Clean Cut is on the stand at the pre-trial hearing.

Prosecution: State your name.
Clean Cut: Clean Cut.
Prosecution: Did you arrest the defendant?
Clean Cut: Yes, I did.
Prosecution: When did you first hear anything about the defendant?
Clean Cut: Well, I was sitting at the bar with Middle Man. We were talking about the sale of some drugs. We agreed that $5000 was the right price for the quantity that I was selling. I also let him know that I wanted the money in $100 bills.
Prosecution: Did Middle Man say anything then?
Clean Cut: No, he got up and went over to the telephone.
Prosecution: Then what happened?
Clean Cut: He came back and said, "I've got this buddy named Drug Dealer. He can really move the product. He said to meet him at the park at 1:00 a.m." Then I asked Middle Man how I would know it was Drug Dealer and he said that Drug Dealer always wears a top hat.
Prosecution: Did Middle Man say anything else to you before you left the bar?
Clean Cut: Yeah, he said "If this goes down clean I know another dealer who can double the score."
Prosecution: When you arrested the defendant, did Middle Man say anything?
Clean Cut: Yes, even before I could give him his rights he blurted out, "I guess Drug Dealer won't be able to peddle that stuff at the high school after all."

You be the judge.

PROBLEM 11-2

Karyl Keaty has filed an action against his former employer, the Ace Equipment Company, alleging that he was terminated at age 52 as a result of age discrimination. Karyl was fired a year ago after working for the company for 22 years. At trial Karyl calls several witnesses, including Shannon Sman.

Direct Examination of Shannon Sman

Plaintiff: Where do you work?
Witness: Ace Equipment Company.
Plaintiff: How long have you worked there?
Witness: Fourteen years.
Plaintiff: Were you working there a year ago?
Witness: Yes.

Plaintiff: In what capacity?
Witness: Assistant Director of Personnel.
Plaintiff: Who was the Director of Personnel?
Witness: Nat Nopes. She was in charge.
Plaintiff: What role did Ms. Naps have in termination decisions?
Witness: She was part of the team that decided whether to let someone go, but I wasn't involved in termination decisions.
Plaintiff: When did you learn that the plaintiff was terminated?
Witness: When I heard Ms. Naps say that "we had to let the old guy go."
Defendant: (1) Objection. __________.
Plaintiff: (2) __________.
Court: (3) __________.
Plaintiff: Did you say anything when Ms. Nopes told you "we had to let the old guy go"?
Witness: I said to her, "you didn't fire Mr. Keaty because he's 50 years old, I hope. That would be wrong."
Plaintiff: What response did Ms. Nopes make?
Witness: She looked at me with an angry look on her face, and said nothing.
Defendant: Objection and move to strike the witness' out-of-court statement. It's hearsay.
Plaintiff: (4) __________.
Court: (5) __________.
Plaintiff: Did you hear Ms. Nopes say anything else about the plaintiff?
Witness: Yes, I did. Ms. Nopes had a friend who worked for a competitor but who often stopped by to give her a ride home from work. On the day the plaintiff was fired, the friend stopped by, and when she asked Ms. Nopes why she appeared in a bad mood, Ms. Nopes said "we just canned a guy because he was too old."
Defendant: Objection. Hearsay.
Plaintiff: (6) __________.
Defendant: It cannot be an admission. It's a statement to a friend who works for a competitor.
Court: (7) __________.
Plaintiff: Did you have any conversation with the president of the company about the plaintiff after he was fired?
Witness: Yes, at the water cooler the president of the company, Larry Lester, said "I don't want old guys here."
Defendant: (8) Objection. __________.
Plaintiff: (9) __________.

Court: (10)__________.

Plaintiff: Did you tell anyone else what Ms. Nopes told you?

Witness: Sure, the day he got fired I went home and told my roommate that the Director of Personnel told me that the plaintiff got fired because "we had to let the old guy go."

Defendant: (11) Objection. __________.

Plaintiff: It's an admission.

Court: (12) __________.

Cross-Examination by the Defendant

Defendant: Six months ago you actually received a reduction in pay, right?

Witness: Yes.

Defendant: It was after that reduction that you contacted the plaintiff's attorney for the first time?

Witness: Yes, that's true.

Defendant: You had your deposition taken in this case before your reduction in pay?

Witness: Yes.

Defendant: The reduction in pay made you angry?

Witness: I suppose so.

Defendant: Do you recall being asked on page 10, lines 3-4, "Did you hear anything about the plaintiff's termination on the day it occurred, and giving the answer, 'no'?" Do you recall that question and that answer?

Plaintiff: Objection. Hearsay. The witness is present. If this is admissible at all, it should only be for impeachment, not for its truth.

Defendant: (13) __________.

Court: (14) __________.

Re-Direct Examination

Plaintiff: When you first contacted me, what did you tell me about your deposition testimony?

Witness: I told you that I had not been truthful.

Plaintiff: What exactly did you say that you had not been truthful about?

Witness: I told you that when I said I did not hear anything about the plaintiff's termination on the day it occurred, I was not truthful because I did hear the Director of Personnel say * * *

Defendant: (15) Objection. __________.

Plaintiff: (16) __________.

Court: (17) __________.

Chapter 12

HEARSAY EXCEPTIONS DEPENDENT ON THE UNAVAILABILITY OF THE DECLARANT

A. INTRODUCTION

The exceptions to the hearsay rule covered in this Chapter require that the declarant be unavailable to testify at trial. The rationale of these exceptions is that the hearsay they cover is reliable, but it would be better to have testimony from the declarant at trial. Unavailability may arise because the witness is not physically present because of illness, death, or absence from the jurisdiction. Unavailability may also occur when, although physically present, the declarant refuses or is unable to testify. For example, the witness may assert a privilege, may refuse to testify, or may have a lack of memory.

The next Chapter will deal with the exceptions to the hearsay rule that do not require declarant unavailability.

B. UNAVAILABILITY DEFINED

[1] Federal Rule of Evidence 804(a)

Rule 804. Hearsay Exceptions; Declarant Unavailable

(a) Definition of unavailability. "Unavailability as a witness" includes situations in which the declarant —

(1) is exempted by ruling of the court on the ground of privilege from testifying concerning the subject matter of the declarant's statement; or

(2) persists in refusing to testify concerning the subject matter of the declarant's statement despite an order of the court to do so; or

(3) testifies to a lack of memory of the subject matter of the declarant's statement; or

(4) is unable to be present or to testify at the hearing because of death or then existing physical or mental illness or infirmity; or

(5) is absent from the hearing and the proponent of the statement has been unable to procure the declarant's attendance (or in the case of a hearsay exception under subdivision (b)(2), (3), or (4), the declarant's attendance or testimony) by process or other reasonable means. A declarant is not unavailable as a witness if exemption, refusal, claim of lack of memory, inability, or absence is due to the procurement of wrongdoing of the proponent of a statement for the purpose of preventing the witness from attending or testifying.

[2] Privilege

[a] Federal Rule of Evidence 804(a)(1)

Rule 804. Hearsay Exceptions; Declarant Unavailable

(a) Definition of unavailability. "Unavailability as a witness" includes situations in which the declarant —

(1) is exempted by ruling of the court on the ground of privilege from testifying concerning the subject matter of the declarant's statement; * * *

* * *

[b] Illustration

The prosecutor desperately needs the testimony of a certain witness to ensure a conviction of the defendant. The witness testified at the preliminary hearing in the same case. The prosecutor would be happy with either the introduction of the transcript from the preliminary hearing or the live testimony of the witness. It is time to call the witness to the stand. The prosecutor addresses the court:

Prosecutor:	Your Honor, I understand that Mr. I. Refuse has decided not to testify in this case and that he will take the 5th if called to the stand. I therefore request that I be allowed to introduce the transcript of Refuse's preliminary hearing testimony.
Defendant:	_________.

[c] Burden of Proof

UNITED STATES v. PELTON & RICH
578 F.2d 701 (8th Cir. 1978)

GIBSON, CHIEF JUDGE.

This case involves charged violations of the Mann Act arising out of certain interstate activities undertaken by a prostitution operation based in St. Louis, Missouri. In July 1977, the Government returned an eight-count indictment against Jacqueline "Pat" Rich, Lloyd Pelton and Ann Frazier. The first four counts of the indictment related to travel by prostitutes between St. Louis, Missouri, and Chicago, Illinois * * *.

Grand jury testimony of Kathleen Waggoner

Count II of the indictment underlying the instant case charged Rich * * * with regard to the transportation of Kathleen Waggoner to Chicago. Waggoner's trip to Chicago was also one of the overt acts alleged in support of the conspiracy charged in Count I. On June 1, 1977, pursuant to a grant of use immunity, Waggoner testified before a grand jury * * *. During her appearance before the grand jury, Waggoner denied that Rich had sent her to Chicago in 1976 to work as a prostitute at the boat show and also denied that Rich had ever set her up on prostitution dates. As a consequence of this testimony, Waggoner was indicted on two counts of perjury before the grand jury in violation of 18 U.S.C. § 1623. This indictment, which was handed down on June 25, 1977, set forth verbatim those portions of the grand jury transcript in which Waggoner denied that Rich had sent her to Chicago or set her up on prostitution dates. Waggoner was convicted on both counts of perjury at a trial which took place after the trial of Rich and Pelton.

* * *

Waggoner was not called as a witness at Rich's trial. Rich herself did not attempt to call Waggoner as a witness. Rather, she assumed that Waggoner would refuse to testify and sought, on that basis, to introduce a transcript of Waggoner's grand jury testimony into evidence.

On the morning of the third day of trial, counsel for Rich made the following in-chambers presentation to the trial court:

> I have caused a subpoena to be served upon Kathleen Waggoner to testify. It is my understanding that she is under charges at the present time in this Court or in another Division and her attorney has indicated that he will advise her to invoke her privilege under the Fifth Amendment and refuse to testify. On that basis, Your Honor, I would request an opportunity to utilize her Grand Jury testimony and introduce portions of the Grand Jury testimony which would be relevant and request that the Government furnish me with a copy of her Grand Jury testimony. I believe that it would be admissible pursuant to Rule 804 of the Federal Rules of Evidence.

The Government objected to the use of Waggoner's grand jury testimony. The court and both parties then discussed the general nature of Waggoner's testimony before the grand jury, the use immunity under which she had testified and the perjury indictment then pending against her. The district judge ultimately refused to allow Rich to introduce the transcript of Waggoner's grand jury testimony into evidence. Contemporaneously, however, he ruled that Rich could read Waggoner's indictment to the jury. Although this indictment contained testimony in which Waggoner denied that Rich had sent her to Chicago or had set her up on prostitution dates, counsel for Rich chose not to introduce it into evidence.

Rich now contends that Waggoner's grand jury testimony was admissible under Fed. R. Evid. 804(a)(1) [the hearsay exception for prior testimony] and that the trial court erred in refusing to allow her to introduce the relevant portions of this transcript at trial. Rule 804 sets forth those instances in which the hearsay statements of unavailable declarants may be admitted into evidence at trial. Rich relies upon § (a)(1) of Rule 804, which provides that a declarant is "unavailable" if he or she "is exempted by ruling of the court on the ground of privilege from testifying concerning the subject matter of his statement."

The unavailability requirement of Rule 804 places the burden of producing an unavailable declarant upon the proponent of the evidence. * * * Rich, the proponent here, accordingly had the burden of establishing that Waggoner would invoke her fifth amendment privilege and thus be unavailable to testify. Our review of the record convinces us that Rich utterly failed to carry this burden. Counsel for Rich made no effort to produce Waggoner, whom he had subpoenaed, and to demonstrate firsthand and in the court's presence that she did intend to refuse to testify in reliance on her fifth amendment privilege against self-incrimination. Rather, he chose to raise the issue of her privilege in an extenuated and circuitous manner which gave the court nothing more than a speculative basis for determining whether she was available. Rich's proof that Waggoner was unavailable under Rule 804(a)(1) was that Waggoner's attorney had said that he was going to advise Waggoner not to testify. There was no indication that Waggoner had in fact been so advised or that, if she had been, she had decided to exercise her privilege. We consider Rich's suggestion, that Waggoner might in the future be advised of and then choose to exercise her fifth amendment privilege, to be a wholly inadequate showing of unavailability under Rule 804(a)(1). The trial court did not err in refusing, on this speculative basis, to allow Rich to introduce into evidence the transcript of Waggoner's testimony before the grand jury.

* * *

Affirmed.

NOTES

1. Is a declarant unavailable under Federal Rule 804(a)(1) by merely asserting the privilege in open court?

More is required. In *United States v. MacCloskey*, 682 F.2d 468 (4th Cir. 1982), the Court noted that the rule also requires a judicial ruling that the witness is exempt from testifying.

2. If a criminal defendant invokes his privilege to refuse to testify at trial, is he considered unavailable so that his hearsay statement, otherwise admissible under one of the Rule 804 exceptions, can be admitted?

In *United States v. Kimball*, 15 F.3d 54 (5th Cir. 1994), Kimball's first trial ended in a mistrial. At his second trial, he proffered a transcript of his own testimony given at his first trial. He argued that his testimony was admissible as prior testimony under Rule 804(b)(1), and that he was unavailable to testify at his second trial due to his invocation of his Fifth Amendment privilege. The Court held that the prior testimony was inadmissible because "the sponsor of a declarant's former testimony may not create the condition of unavailability and then benefit therefrom." It reasoned that Kimball had created his own unavailability by declaring the Fifth Amendment privilege. Was Kimball essentially penalized for exercising a constitutional right? The court, in support of its conclusion, stated that "a defendant seeking to testify and make exculpatory statements must face cross-examination." But hadn't Kimball already faced cross-examination at his prior trial?

[3] Refusal

[a] Federal Rule of Evidence 804(a)(2)

Rule 804. Hearsay Exceptions; Declarant Unavailable

(a) Definition of unavailability. "Unavailability as a witness" includes situations in which the declarant —

* * *

(2) persists in refusing to testify concerning the subject matter of the declarant's statement despite an order of the court to do so; * * *

[b] Illustration

Again, the prosecutor needs the testimony of I. Refuse, either live or from the transcript of the preliminary hearing. I. Refuse is on the stand.

Prosecutor:	State your name.
Witness:	I. Refuse.
Prosecutor:	Were you at the scene of the hold-up?
Witness:	Why do you ask?
Prosecutor:	Just answer my question. Were you at the scene of the hold-up?
Witness:	What I do is my own business.
Prosecutor:	Will you answer my question?
Witness:	No.
Prosecutor:	Your Honor, __________.

NOTE

How should the court determine that the witness refuses to testify even though ordered to do so?

See United States v. MacCloskey, 682 F.2d 468 (4th Cir. 1982), where the court indicated that the correct procedure is to require the witness to testify outside of the jury's presence and the judge should order the witness to testify subject to the threat of contempt. If the witness still refuses, then the witness is unavailable under Rule 804(a)(2).

[4] Lack of Memory

[a] Federal Rule of Evidence 804(a)(3)

Rule 804. Hearsay Exceptions; Declarant Unavailable

(a) Definition of unavailability. "Unavailability as a witness" includes situations in which the declarant —

* * *

(3) testifies to a lack of memory of the subject matter of the declarant's statement; * * *

[b] Illustration

The prosecutor needs the testimony of I. Forget, either live or through the transcript of the preliminary hearing. I. Forget takes the stand.

Prosecutor:	State your name.
Witness:	They tell me it's I. Forget.
Prosecutor:	Excuse me?
Witness:	They tell me it's I. Forget.
Prosecutor:	Don't you know your own name?
Witness:	No.
Prosecutor:	Were you at the scene of the hold-up?
Witness:	I don't know.
Prosecutor:	What do you mean, you don't know?
Witness:	Like I said, I don't know.
Prosecutor:	Why don't you know?
Witness:	I don't remember anything.
Prosecutor:	And why not?
Witness:	Total amnesia from a car wreck.
Prosecutor:	__________.

[c] Permanent Loss

UNITED STATES v. AMAYA
533 F.2d 188 (5th Cir. 1976)

Roney, Circuit Judge:

* * * The case involves the alleged activity of defendant, a practicing attorney, to organize and arrange contact between an alleged seller and buyer in a particular transaction for an unnamed quantity of heroin. Defendant's challenge to his conviction concerns the use of transcribed testimony of a Government witness from a prior trial because of the witness's subsequent loss of memory.* * * We affirm.

Facts

A one count indictment charged a conspiracy between the defendant, a San Antonio attorney, and two of his clients to distribute heroin. The Drug Enforcement Agency was apprised of the formation of the alleged conspiracy by Gregory Sprouse, a former client of the defendant. Sprouse reported to the D.E.A. that during a conversation on or about the middle of February 1973, defendant solicited his help in finding buyers for heroin that the defendant could procure from another individual. Special Agent Jeffrey Wood was dispatched by the D.E.A. to act as an undercover agent with the task of posing as a buyer of heroin to gather evidence of the alleged conspiracy. The central controversy in the case revolves around a meeting at a restaurant on March 1, 1973, attended by defendant Amaya, Sprouse, Agent Wood and another individual who is at present a fugitive. This meeting was for the purpose of establishing the procedures of exchange, price and quantity of heroin that Agent Wood would purchase. Most of the conversation was secretly recorded by Agent Wood and the transcript of that recording contained the bulk of the Government's case against Amaya.

At the first trial Sprouse testified at length against the defendant. The case was tried before a jury and defendant Amaya was convicted. On appeal, we reversed the conviction and granted a new trial because of an impermissible *Allen* charge. Prior to the commencement of the second trial Sprouse suffered injury in an automobile accident resulting in a loss of memory regarding his prior testimony. The district judge, who presided at both trials, determined that Sprouse was unavailable within the meaning of Rule 804(a)(3), Federal Rules of Evidence, and permitted his prior testimony to be read into the record *in toto*.

* * *

Amaya * * * argues that Sprouse was never conclusively shown to be unavailable because it was never established by expert testimony that his lack of memory was permanent. The party offering the prior testimony has the burden of proving the unavailability of the witness.* * * Determination of unavailability is a judicial exercise reviewable by this Court only for abuse of discretion.* * * Defendant alleges that a continuance should have been given to allow expert testimony bearing on the permanence of the loss of memory before establishing unavailability for trial. Although the duration of an illness is a proper element of unavailability, the establishment of permanence as to the particular illness is not an absolute requirement. The duration of the illness need only be in probability long enough so that, with proper regard to the importance of the testimony, the trial cannot be postponed. * * * There was no guarantee that Sprouse's memory would ever return. The trial judge did not abuse his discretion in deciding on the evidence in the record that Sprouse was unavailable for trial.

The Eighth Circuit reached a similar result in *McDonnell v. United States*, 472 F.2d 1153 (8th Cir. 1973). In that case the witness was present at the second trial and testified. Testimony at a prior trial was admitted, however, because of the witness's faulty memory. The court said: "Since [the witness] testified to a lack of memory as to a material portion of the subject matter of his prior testimony, he would be unavailable under Rule 804 and his former testimony on the subject would be admissible. Such a rule of evidence is supported by textwriters and case law * * * ."

* * *

Upon full examination of the record and consideration of all of the arguments of counsel, we are satisfied that the conviction should stand.

Affirmed.

NOTE

How extensive must the memory loss be for the witness to be found unavailable?

In *North Miss. Commun., Inc. v. Jones,* 792 F.2d 1330 (5th Cir. 1986), the Court held that a witness was not unavailable where he remembered the general subject matter of a conversation but could not remember certain details.

[5] Death or Disability

[a] Federal Rule of Evidence 804(a)(4)

Rule 804. Hearsay Exceptions; Declarant Unavailable

(a) Definition of unavailability. "Unavailability as a witness" includes situations in which the declarant —

* * *

(4) is unable to be present or to testify at the hearing because of death or then existing physical or mental illness or infirmity; * * *

[b] Illustration

The prosecutor needs the testimony of I. M. Sick, either live or through the transcript of the preliminary hearing. I. M. Sick is in the hospital, having just undergone surgery for a brain tumor.

Prosecutor:	Your Honor, I have here a letter from I. M. Sick's physician which indicates that he is incapable of attending the trial or being a witness.
Defendant:	__________.

[c] Temporary Disability

UNITED STATES v. FAISON
679 F.2d 292 (3d Cir. 1982)

GIBBONS, CIRCUIT JUDGE:

James Raymond Faison, convicted of violating the "wire fraud" statute, 18 U.S.C. § 1343 *et seq*. (1976), and of transporting stolen securities in interstate commerce, 18 U.S.C. § 2314 (1976), contends that the court erred * * * in denying his motion for a new trial. We vacate the judgment and remand for further proceedings.

I.

* * *

The evidence suggests that Faison, a New Jersey resident, operated an autobody shop in New York City. In August 1980, he decided to move his business to New Jersey, whereupon he started negotiating with one Cal Mancuso to lease Mancuso's New Jersey trucking terminal. Meanwhile, defendant had obtained blank checks stolen from the American Foundation for the Blind whose offices are also in New York City. In due time, defendant asked Mancuso to help him cash these illegal checks in a scheme to raise money for both men. * * * Mancuso then made contact in New Jersey with Michael Selvanto, who was thought to have the necessary connections to cash the illicit checks. Selvanto, in turn, notified the FBI with whom he thereafter cooperated by recording his conversations with the conspirators and by keeping the FBI informed of Faison's and Mancuso's activities. * * * Faison personally delivered the stolen checks to Mancuso in New Jersey. Mancuso, copying from a cancelled check provided by Faison, forged the Foundation's signature on the blanks and turned the checks over to Selvanto.

* * *

II.

* * *

Faison's first trial started on January 21, 1981. Mancuso, who had entered a guilty plea * * *, testified as a government witness. The jury was unable to reach a verdict, and the District Court declared a mistrial. A second trial began on March 17, 1981. By this time Mancuso was in the hospital for treatment of his heart problem. Defense counsel requested an adjournment of the trial so that the jury would have the benefit of Mancuso's live testimony and live cross-examination. This request was repeated throughout the trial. The District Court, however, refused to adjourn the trial and instead permitted the introduction of the testimony which Mancuso gave at the first trial. On March 25, the jury found Faison guilty of all counts.

Faison argues that the admission of Mancuso's testimony violated his Sixth Amendment confrontation rights. Alternatively he urges that the court improperly applied Fed. R. Evid. 804(a)(4), or abused its discretion in failing to grant a continuance to determine whether Mancuso would be available in the near future.

* * *

In this instance, the trial court decided that Mancuso, who was in the hospital suffering from a heart attack, was unavailable. * * * There is no question Mancuso was too sick to testify at the time of trial. That is not, however, dispositive. Our inquiry, instead, is whether the District Court properly exercised discretion in not adjourning the trial for a reasonable period to afford the witness enough time to recover from an illness which might be temporary, and thus to be available once more for live testimony.

There is evidence in this record that a decision not to adjourn might well have been within the parameters which we must accord to trial judges in their exercises of discretion in matters such as this. On the date that the trial court made its determination not to adjourn, the court had before it information that Mancuso was about to undergo coronary bypass surgery and would not be available to testify for at least four to five weeks after the surgery.* * * Although the United States Attorney expressed his expectation that Mancuso would be available to testify in four to five weeks, the trial court had no assurance that even if Mancuso successfully underwent surgery, his physician would accede to his appearance at trial in four or five weeks in light of his heart condition. Appearance at a major criminal trial, particularly when a witness, such as Mancuso, was personally implicated in the events, must be an emotional and traumatic experience. The trial court may have been aware of the frequency with which requests to excuse appearance of a witness are made and granted on medical evidence less compelling than that which seemed likely to have been presented on behalf of Mancuso were the trial adjourned. Thus, the trial court's refusal to adjourn may have been warranted, particularly when the Federal Rules of Evidence explicitly provide that in such a situation prior reliable testimony is admissible in lieu of live testimony.

* * *

The trial judge's discretion in granting an adjournment for witnesses unavailable due to illness must be guided on the one hand by the policy of favoring live testimony and confrontation in the presence of the factfinder and, on the other, by the policy, manifested in the Speedy Trial Act, 18 U.S.C. § 3161 (1976), of prompt disposition of criminal trials. Moreover, since witness availability affects the court's ability to manage its cases, the trial court's decision to refuse an adjournment and to admit prior testimony must be treated with respectful deference. In exercising discretion a trial judge must consider all relevant circumstances, including: the importance of the absent witness for the case; the nature and extent of cross-examination in the earlier testimony; the nature of the illness; the expected time of recovery; the reliability of the evidence of the probable duration of the illness; and any special circumstances counseling against delay. * * *

Applying the above standards to this record, we hold that the District Court abused his discretion by not adjourning Faison's trial for a reasonable period. Here Mancuso was an important witness against defendant. The live cross-examination of such a witness before a jury, even if not constitutionally mandated, ought not to be lightly dispensed with. The fact that the first trial yielded a hung jury suggests that the evidence against defendant had weaknesses. The District Court should have been especially careful that the omission of live cross-examination of Mancuso before the new jury not tip the balance in a close case against defendant.

Since the court's error — one of nonconstitutional dimensions, deprived Faison, at most, of the opportunity to present Mancuso's testimony live, an outright reversal for a new trial is inappropriate without further inquiry. By now Mancuso has undergone surgery. Whether he has recovered sufficiently to testify is not known. If his health is such that he would be unavailable at a new trial, granting a new trial would serve no purpose. Faison already had a trial at which Mancuso's prior testimony was read to the jury. If he could testify at a new trial, however, Faison should be afforded the opportunity to have him do so. Thus the case will be remanded to the trial court for appropriate proceedings to determine whether Mancuso would now be available to testify. If he would be, the trial court is directed to grant a new trial.

III.

The judgment appealed from is vacated and the case remanded for further proceedings consistent with this opinion.

[Concurring opinion omitted.]

NOTE

On remand in *Faison*, the District Court found that the government witness was unavailable because of a serious heart condition from which he was unlikely ever to recover. Thus, no purpose would be served in granting the defendant a new trial. 564 F. Supp. 514 (D. N.J. 1983). *See also Mutuelles Unies v. Kroll & Linstrom,* 957 F.2d 707 (9th Cir. 1992) (witness was sufficiently shown to be unavailable where he required surgery that would leave him indisposed for one to two weeks). *Compare United States v. Acosta,* 769 F.2d 721 (11th Cir. 1985) (uncorroborated statement of defense counsel that witness was unavailable to testify because of her child's illness was insufficient to permit the introduction of her prior testimony).

[6] Absence

[a] Federal Rule of Evidence 804(a)(5)

Rule 804. Hearsay Exceptions; Declarant Unavailable

(a) Definition of unavailability. "Unavailability as a witness" includes situations in which the declarant —

* * *

(5) is absent from the hearing and the proponent of the statement has been unable to procure the declarant's attendance (or in the case of a hearsay exception under subdivision (b)(2), (3), or (4), the declarant's attendance or testimony) by process or other reasonable means.

NOTE

Is Rule 804(a)(5) concerned with the physical absence of the declarant, or with the absence of testimony from the declarant?

Professors Saltzburg, Martin, and Capra, *Federal Rules of Evidence Manual* (9th ed. 2006), point out that absence for purposes of the Rule means absence of *testimony*, not physical absence of the declarant:

> A declarant is not absent under the terms of Rule 804(a)(5) simply because he is out of the jurisdiction or cannot be located. The party relying on absence to support an offer of hearsay evidence, in the case of any of the basic exceptions covered by subdivision (b) of Rule 804 aside from former testimony, must demonstrate that it has not been possible to take a deposition. The Senate objected to the requirement that an attempt to depose be required. However, the Rule follows the House provision in requiring a showing of inability to obtain *testimony* of a declarant before a dying declaration, statement against interest, or statement of pedigree can be admitted on the ground that the declarant is absent. As a practical matter, the issue does not arise for statements offered as dying declarations or statements of pedigree. The ground of unavailability for dying declarations is ordinarily death, not absence; and statements of pedigree are rarely offered. So the deposition requirement with respect to the absence ground of unavailability is really limited to situations in which the proponent has a statement that would otherwise be admissible as a declaration against interest, and the asserted ground of unavailability is absence.
>
> (The deposition preference issue will probably not arise under Rule 804(b)(6), the hearsay exception based on forfeiture by misconduct. That exception applies only if the party against whom the hearsay is offered intentionally created the witness's unavailability. If the party has engaged in such conduct, the declarant is quite unlikely to be available for a deposition. At any rate, the deposition preference by its terms applies only to statements offered under Rules 804(b)(2)-(4)).
>
> Rule 804(a)(5) requires an attempt to depose. The rationale is that if a deposition can be taken, the deposition testimony will be admissible as prior testimony; and prior testimony is preferred to the declaration against interest, because prior testimony has been subject to cross-examination. Consequently, if the attempt to depose is successful, the hearsay declarant is no longer considered unavailable and statements falling within 804(b)(3), (or technically (2) or (4)) are no longer admissible for their truth. Note, however, that if the deposition is offered, the deponent may be *impeached* under Rule 806 with the statements that are inadmissible for their truth.
>
> If the hearsay statement is offered under Rule 804(b)(1), the proponent need not prove an attempt to depose, for the obvious reason that a deposition or its equivalent has already been taken. When the statement is admissible under Rule 804(b)(1), the declarant has *already* testified under oath and subject to cross-examination; there is thus no need to obtain what would amount to duplicative evidence.

The problems created by the deposition preference in Rule 804(a)(5) are well-illustrated by *Campbell v. Coleman Co.*, 786 F.2d 892 (8th Cir. 1986). The minor plaintiffs alleged that they were severely burned by a defective gasoline lantern that exploded. Coleman had a different theory: that Johnnie Hayes, who was babysitting the children, overfilled the lighted lantern with gasoline, then panicked and threw the burning lantern out of the house where it accidentally hit the children. Coleman had deposed Hayes, but at the deposition, Hayes flatly denied having anything to do with the accident. The deposition was not introduced at trial. However, Hayes had made several statements to various people implicating himself in the accident, and these were introduced at trial as declarations against interest. Coleman contended that Hayes was unavailable on the ground of absence because it had made good faith attempts to locate him before trial, and he could not be found. The trial court admitted the statements, but the Court of Appeals found that this was reversible error, because Hayes was not absent within the meaning of Rule 804(a)(5). As the Court put it, the "subsection is concerned with the absence of testimony, rather than the physical absence of the declarant." Thus, while Hayes was absent from the trial, his testimony was available (i.e., the deposition), and his hearsay statements were therefore not admissible under Rule 804(b)(3).

The result in *Coleman* shows that the deposition preference can create anomalous results. Hayes's deposition was undoubtedly a *less* reliable indicator of what happened than were his informal statements against interest. The congressional assumption that a declaration against interest is not necessary where a deposition can be or has been taken assumes that the proponent will get the same information, only better, from the deposition as from the declaration against interest. But, *Coleman* shows that this is not always the case. The anomaly of the Rule is even more striking when it is considered that if Hayes were dead or declaring the privilege at the time of trial, the declarations against interest would have been admissible. The deposition preference is applied only when absence is the asserted ground of unavailability. Clearly, this makes no sense. If nothing else it is inconsistent with the general goal of Rule 804(a), which was to provide a unitary test of unavailability for all hearsay exceptions. Finally, the deposition preference is problematic because it ends up penalizing parties who depose witnesses in a timely fashion. If Coleman had not bothered to depose Hayes before he disappeared, the declarations against interest would have been admissible. It seems odd to penalize Coleman for engaging in diligent efforts to prepare for litigation.

Of course, as discussed above, the declarations against interest in *Coleman* would still have been admissible to impeach Hayes under Rule 806. But this assumes that the Hayes deposition would be proffered at the trial. The plaintiffs in *Coleman* were unlikely to do so, and in fact did not do so, because introducing the deposition would have accomplished little more than to open the door to the damaging "impeachment" evidence that the jury would misuse for its truth. The plaintiffs did not need the Hayes deposition as substantive evidence, given the availability of expert testimony and the sympathetic nature of their case. Moreover, even if the plaintiffs had introduced the deposition, the declarations against interest could not have been used as substantive evidence on Coleman's behalf. This point was made by the Court in *Coleman* when it rejected Coleman's argument that the introduction of the declarations against interest at trial was harmless error:

> At the close of plaintiffs' case-in-chief, no evidence had been introduced from which Coleman could have argued that plaintiffs' injuries were caused by the negligent actions of a nonparty. Introduction of the inadmissible hearsay created a substantive defense for Coleman.* * * Plaintiffs were thereby prejudiced.

Because there is a deposition preference in Rule 804(a)(5), however misguided it might be, it follows that a declarant will not be considered absent for purposes of Rules 804(b)(2)-(4) simply because he is outside the jurisdiction and beyond the subpoena power. The Federal Rules of Civil and Criminal Procedure make provision for deposing witnesses who are beyond the territorial jurisdiction of the court. If the witness is deposeable, he is not absent under Rule 804(a)(5). *See, e.g.*, *United States v. Curbello*, 940 F.2d 1503 (11th Cir. 1991) (a declaration against interest was not admissible where the declarant was incarcerated in the Bahamas and could have been deposed under Fed. R. Crim. P. 15).

[7] Procurement or Wrongdoing

[a] Federal Rule of Evidence 804(a)

Rule 804. Hearsay Exceptions; Declarant Unavailable

(a) Definition of unavailability. * * *

A declarant is not unavailable as a witness if exemption, refusal, claim of lack of memory, inability, or absence is due to the procurement or wrongdoing of the proponent of a statement for the purpose of preventing the witness from attending or testifying.

[b] Negligence

UNITED STATES v. MATHIS

550 F.2d 180 (4th Cir. 1976)

PER CURIAM:

David Mathis and Samuel Moore both appeal their convictions for armed bank robbery. They assert numerous grounds for reversal, but we find none meritorious. We affirm.

I.

Defendants' principal argument is that the district court committed reversible error in permitting the testimony of Karen Jones, given at a previous trial in which a mistrial was granted, to be read to the jury. Karen Jones was not available to testify in person because she could not be located; inadvertently she had been released from a District of Columbia penal institution pursuant to a court order requiring the release of another prisoner bearing the same name.

Jones' prior testimony was admissible under Rule 804 of the Federal Rules of Evidence if her attendance at the trial could not be procured by process or other reasonable means. Rule 804(a)(5). The record shows that reasonable efforts were made to find her, but to no avail. * * * In the instant case * * * the disappearance of Jones was due to inadvertence, not reckless disregard of an obligation to produce her, and there is no evidence that the prison official who released her knew that she would be needed as a witness.

* * *

Affirmed.

[Dissenting opinion omitted.]

C. UNAVAILABILITY EXCEPTIONS

[1] Federal Rule of Evidence 804(b)

Rule 804. Hearsay Exceptions; Declarant Unavailable

* * *

(b) Hearsay exceptions. The following are not excluded by the hearsay rule if the declarant is unavailable as a witness.

(1) Former testimony. Testimony given as a witness at another hearing of the same or a different proceeding, or in a deposition taken in compliance with law in the course of the same or another proceeding, if the party against whom the testimony is now offered, or, in a civil action or proceeding, a predecessor in interest, had an opportunity and similar motive to develop the testimony by direct, cross, or redirect examination.

(2) Statement under belief of impending death. In a prosecution for homicide or in a civil action or proceeding, a statement made by a declarant while believing that the declarant's death was imminent, concerning the cause or circumstances of what the declarant believed to be impending death.

(3) Statement against interest. A statement which was at the time of its making so far contrary to the declarant's pecuniary or proprietary interest, or so far tended to subject the declarant to civil or criminal liability, or to render invalid a claim by the declarant against another, that a reasonable person in the declarant's position would not have made the statement unless believing it to be true. A statement tending to expose the declarant to criminal liability and offered to exculpate the accused is not admissible unless corroborating circumstances clearly indicate the trustworthiness of the statement.

(4) Statement of personal or family history. (A) A statement concerning the declarant's own birth, adoption, marriage, divorce, legitimacy, relationship by blood, adoption, or marriage, ancestry, or other similar fact of personal or family history, even though declarant had no means of acquiring personal knowledge of the matter stated; or (B) a statement concerning the foregoing matters, and death also, of another person, if the declarant was related to the other by blood, adoption, or marriage or was so intimately associated with the other's family as to be likely to have accurate information concerning the matter declared.

(5) [Transferred to Rule 807].

(6) Forfeiture by wrongdoing. A statement offered against a party that has engaged or acquiesced in wrongdoing that was intended to, and did, procure the unavailability of the declarant as a witness.

[2] Former Testimony

[a] Federal Rule of Evidence 804(b)(1)

Rule 804. Hearsay Exceptions; Declarant Unavailable

* * *

(b) Hearsay exceptions. The following are not excluded by the hearsay rule if the declarant is unavailable as a witness.

(1) Former testimony. Testimony given as a witness at another hearing of the same or a different proceeding, or in a deposition taken in compliance with law in the course of the same or another proceeding, if the party against whom the testimony is now offered, or, in a civil action or proceeding, a predecessor in interest, had an opportunity and similar motive to develop the testimony by direct, cross, or redirect examination.

* * *

[b] Predecessor in Interest and Similarity of Motive

IN THE MATTER OF JOHNS-MANVILLE/ASBESTOSIS CASES

93 F.R.D. 853 (N.D. Ill. 1981)

SHADUR, DISTRICT JUDGE:

Dr. Kenneth W. Smith ("Dr. Smith") was hired in 1944 as a Canadian Johns-Manville Company, Ltd. ("Canadian J-M") plant physician and eventually served as Medical Director for Johns-Manville Corporation ("J-M") from 1952 to 1966. Dr. Smith died in July 1977.

Dr. Smith was deposed in two earlier asbestos-related cases: *Louisville Trust Co. v. Johns-Manville Corp.*, No. 164922 (Jefferson Cty., Ky. Cir. Ct. 1972) (the "*Louisville Trust* deposition," taken April 21, 1976 * * *) and *DeRocco v. Forty-Eight Insulations, Inc.*, Nos. 2880, 2881 (Allegheny Cty., Pa. Ct. of Common Pleas 1974) (the "*DeRocco* deposition," taken January 13, 1976 * * *). Plaintiffs have moved to permit use of the *Louisville Trust* deposition at trial in these consolidated actions. J-M, Johns-Manville Sales Corporation ("J-M Sales") and Canadian J-M have filed a cross-motion *in limine* seeking to exclude use of both the *Louisville Trust* and *DeRocco* depositions. * * * Because of Dr. Smith's death his testimony is admissible if it satisfies the requirements of Rule 804(b)(1).

* * *

Relationship of the Parties

Rule 804(b)(1) * * * requires that the party against whom a deposition is offered, or that party's "predecessor in interest," have been a party in the earlier proceeding. Johns-Manville Products Corporation ("J-M Products") was a defendant in both *Louisville Trust* and *DeRocco*, while none of J-M Defendants was. Nonetheless this Court finds the "predecessor in interest" condition satisfied.

First, as to J-M Sales plaintiffs' R. Mem. 7 asserts:

The Johns-Manville Waukegan Plant at which plaintiffs were employed was previously under the name of Johns-Manville Products Corporation and is now under the name of Johns-Manville Sales Corporation.

It is unclear whether that statement denotes the same corporate entity with a name change or a transfer of assets between two J-M subsidiaries. In either event even the strictest reading of the "predecessor" language is met.

Even were that not the case, the relationships among the J-M Defendants compel the same result as to each. As the December 2, 1977 affidavit of J-M's Vice President, Secretary and General Counsel in these actions explains:

> (1) J-M is the publicly-owned parent corporation.
>
> (2) All the other entities (other J-M Defendants and J-M Products) are its wholly-owned subsidiaries.
>
> (3) There are interlocking officers, uniformity of employee benefit programs, centralization of all major staff functions, common "Johns-Manville" advertising and a total general integration among all the corporations.
>
> (4) Ultimate responsibility for all management decisions rests with J-M and its corporate officers.

In summary the affidavit puts it: "That in a defacto and operations sense there is but one integrated entity, to wit: 'Johns-Manville.'"

That centralization and integration extended to Dr. Smith himself as the only full-time physician in the whole J-M corporate structure. Dr. Smith said * * * he acted "as sort of an *ad hoc* consultant to the total corporation * * * ."

How does such a close-knit corporate family fare in "predecessor in interest" terms? As originally proposed by the Supreme Court Rule 804(b)(1) would have permitted use of prior testimony whenever any party with a similar motive or interest had an opportunity to examine the witness in the earlier proceeding. However the House Judiciary Committee rejected that innovation and proposed the language eventually adopted because: "it is generally unfair to impose upon the party against whom the hearsay evidence is being offered responsibility for the manner in which the witness was previously handled by another party * * * ." In accepting the House amendment, the Senate noted "that the difference between the two versions is not great." * * *

Based on that legislative history the Third Circuit has given an expansive reading to "predecessor in interest." In *Lloyd v. American Export Lines, Inc.*, 580 F.2d 1179, 1185-87 (3d Cir. 1978) that Court required only that the parties to the earlier and later actions have a "sufficient community of interest" or a "like motive" for cross-examination. That approach would clearly permit use of the Smith depositions against all J-M Defendants. * * *

* * * Congress certainly did not intend to use "predecessor in interest" in the strict sense of corporate privity. Given the policies underlying the hearsay concept, it is eminently fair to admit testimony, cross-examined by J-M's lawyers on behalf of one J-M subsidiary, against all J-M Defendants.

It is true that this Court has held the J-M corporations separate legal entities in a worker's compensation context. *In re Johns-Manville/Asbestosis Cases*, 511 F. Supp. 1229, 1234 (N.D. Ill. 1981). But the considerations there were very different from those now at issue, those with which the Supreme Court and Congress were concerned in drafting the Rule 804(b) (1) hearsay exception. All Johns-Manville entities, though not a single party, are successors in interest to J-M Products for purposes of the Dr. Smith depositions.

"Similar Motive"

J-M Defendants urge that J-M Products lacked motive in *Louisville Trust* and *DeRocco* to develop testimony on issues relevant to these consolidated actions. Specifically they point out that those cases were brought by end users of asbestos, while these involve employees. Both the depositions, they argue, involved the issue whether a warning label was appropriate on asbestos products. J-M Defendants thus assertedly lacked the motive to explore issues such as warnings given to employees.

But the depositions were much broader than J-M Defendants would have it. * * * To a substantial extent plaintiffs' focus in the depositions was the same as that of the current plaintiffs. They were exploring the degree of J-M's awareness of various aspects of asbestos-related diseases from the 1940s through the 1960s. Warnings of the hazards (including warning labels) were only part of the many issues touched on during the depositions.

As to at least two currently critical issues — knowledge of J-M's corporate officers and knowledge of J-M's only medical officer Dr. Smith — J-M Products had full motive and opportunity to cross-examine Dr. Smith. *Louisville Trust* and *DeRocco* were personal injury actions based on asbestos-related claims. Like the current consolidated actions, they asserted J-M's culpability. Suits by end users of asbestos and suits by J-M employees implicate J-M's corporate knowledge equally.

J-M Defendants point out that the *Louisville Trust* and *DeRocco* plaintiffs sought recovery on theories of negligence, breach of warranty and misrepresentation, while the current actions involve allegations of intentional and fraudulent activity. That distinction is irrelevant. Under whatever label, the cases pose the question of J-M's awareness of asbestos-related problems. On that score the "similar motive" test is plainly met.

Several other arguments by J-M Defendants appear to suffer from the simplistic notion that a witness' testimony is not admissible unless it deals with all the issues relevant to the litigation. Of course that is not so. To the extent J-M Defendants do not view Dr. Smith's testimony as fully representative of J-M's knowledge of the art, efforts to protect its employees against asbestos-related risks or any other matter, they are free to adduce any other evidence they choose.

This opinion does not treat with the possibility that some portions of Dr. Smith's deposition testimony (as distinct from the depositions as a whole) may be excludable because of the absence of "similar motive." That prospect has not been posed adequately by the parties' memoranda.

* * *

Conclusion

Plaintiffs' motion to permit use of the *Louisville Trust* deposition at trial is granted. J-M Defendants' motion *in limine* to exclude the Dr. Smith depositions is denied. Any decision as to exclusion of designated portions of Dr. Smith's testimony must await more specific submissions by the parties.

NOTES

1. Does the "predecessor in interest" requirement prohibit prior testimony even if the testimony was developed by someone who had a motive similar to that of the party against whom the testimony is now offered?

Professors Saltzburg, Martin, and Capra, *Federal Rules of Evidence Manual* (9th ed. 2006), have this to say about the "predecessor in interest" and "similar motive" requirements of Rule 804(b)(1):

> The touchstone of admissibility is a similar motive to develop the testimony on the part of the nonoffering party (or a predecessor in

interest in a civil case). The way to determine whether or not motives are similar is to look at the issues and the context in which the opportunity for examination previously arose, and compare that to the issues and context in which the testimony is currently proffered. The similar motive inquiry is essentially a hypothetical one: is the motive to develop the testimony at the prior time similar to the motive that would exist if the declarant were produced (which of course he is not) at the current trial or hearing? *See, e.g., United States v. Tannehill*, 49 F.3d 1049 (5th Cir. 1995) (testimony from a prior multi-defendant trial on the same charges was admissible under Rule 804(b)(1); the defendant argued that at the first trial, his strategy was to "disappear into the woodwork and hope for the best," but the defendant's motive for cross-examination at both trials was similar: "to discredit the witness and separate himself from the other members of the conspiracy"). *See also Battle v. Memorial Hosp.*, 228 F.3d 544 (5th Cir. 2001) (deposition testimony should have been admitted against the defendants under Rule 804(b)(1); the defendants were on the same side of the same issues at the deposition and at trial and they had the same interest in asserting and prevailing on those issues; the defendants claimed that they did not aggressively test the witness's deposition answers with cross-examination-type questions because they were motivated only by the desire to understand the plaintiffs' case; but the defendants could not suggest a single question or line of questions that would have added reliability to the deposition). Compare *New England Mut. Life Ins. Co. v. Anderson*, 888 F.2d 646 (10th Cir. 1989) (an insurance company brought an action to set aside a life insurance policy as fraudulently procured by a beneficiary, who allegedly conspired to murder the insured, her first husband; testimony given by an unavailable witness at the trial of another conspirator was properly excluded, as the defendant in that case was not disposed to protect the interests of the defendant in the instant case, but rather would be likely to shift the blame to her, so he had no "like motive" to develop the same facts).

Under Rule 804(b)(1), it does not matter whether the opportunity for examination came in the form of direct or cross-examination, as long as there was a similar motive and adequate opportunity to develop the testimony of the witness.

In civil cases only, it will suffice that a predecessor in interest had an opportunity and a motive to examine the testimony similar to that of the party against whom the testimony is offered. The Advisory Committee attempted to expand this exception in civil cases to cover situations in which some unrelated party had a similar motive and opportunity for examination. But Congress rejected this innovation. There was a general feeling that it was unfair to bind one party to the examination of another, and so the term "predecessor in interest" was included, to provide for binding effect against nonparties only if they had some juridical relationship with a party to the prior litigation. Yet many of the court decisions under the Rule are closer to the Advisory Committee's view than to that of Congress. Most courts apply the term "predecessor in interest" broadly. *See, e.g.*, *Supermarket of Marlinton, Inc. v. Meadow Gold Dairies, Inc.*, 71 F.3d 119 (4th Cir. 1995) (in an antitrust action, testimony by a dairy official testifying as a government witness in a prior criminal conspiracy trial was admissible as former testimony, even though the dairies were not the defendants in the criminal case; privity is not the gravamen of a Rule 804(b)(1) analysis; rather, the issue is whether the party who cross-examined the witness had a motive similar to that of the party against whom the testimony is offered).

The difference in views is set forth by Judge Becker and Professor Orenstein in *The Federal Rules of Evidence After Sixteen Years — The Effect of "Plain Meaning" Jurisprudence, the Need for an Advisory Committee on the Rules of Evidence, and Suggestions for Selective Revision of the Rules*, 60 Geo. Wash. L. Rev. 857, 898 (1992):

> Another circuit split revolves around the definition of the "predecessor-in-interest" requirement of the former testimony exception to hearsay. Rule 804(b)(1) admits testimony of an unavailable witness in a civil case if the party against whom the testimony is offered, or his predecessor in interest, possessed a similar motive and opportunity to cross examine the witness. The definition is complicated by a tortured legislative history. The predecessor-in-interest requirement was added to the Rule to restrict its scope. * * * In *Lloyd v. American Export Lines, Inc.*, 580 F.2d 1179 (3d Cir. 1978), the Third Circuit construed the predecessor-in-interest language as mandating only a "sufficient community of interest" between the prior litigant and party against whom the hearsay is offered. This construction arguably reads the predecessor-in-interest standard out of the Rule. * * * Many courts have followed *Lloyd's* interpretation. *See, e.g.*, *Horne v. Owens-Corning Fiberglas Corp.*, 4 F.3d 276 (4th Cir. 1993) (in a product liability case resulting from asbestos exposure, the Court held that a deposition from another asbestos case was properly admitted against the plaintiff as prior testimony, even though she had no relationship to the plaintiff in that prior litigation; the party against whom the deposition is offered "must point up distinctions in her case not evident in the earlier litigation that would preclude similar motives of witness examination"; the plaintiff in this case was in the same situation with respect to asbestos exposure as the plaintiff in the case in which the deposition was taken); *Clay v. Johns-Manville Sales Corp.*, 722 F.2d 1289 (6th Cir. 1983) (deposition from a prior litigation is admissible against a nonparty to that litigation, where the party who cross-examined the deponent had the same goal in cross-examination as the party against whom the deposition is now offered). But others have adhered to a more narrow interpretation. *See, e.g.*, *In re Screws Antitrust Litig.*, 526 F. Supp. 1316 (D. Mass. 1981) (testimony was not admissible against a nonparty to the prior litigation who had no legal relationship with the party against whom the testimony was originally offered).

In our view, the "predecessor-in-interest" language of the Rule should be revised. Congress was concerned about one party being bound by the inadequate cross-examination of a previous litigant with whom the party had no legal relationship. But this assumes that the previous litigant in fact engaged in inadequate cross-examination. As most Courts recognize, if the prior cross-examination was as effective and thorough as the subsequent party could expect to have done, it is not unfair to admit the testimony against that later party. We note that those Courts that adhere to a strict construction of the "predecessor-in-interest" requirement of Rule 804(b)(1) have nonetheless admitted prior testimony under the residual exception [Rule 807, infra] as a "near miss" — so long as the prior cross-examination was effective enough to bind the party against whom the testimony is offered. *See, e.g., Dartez v. Fibreboard Corp.*, 765 F.2d 456 (5th Cir. 1985) (a deposition was offered against a defendant who was not a party to the litigation in which the deposition was taken; the party who cross-examined the deponent was not a predecessor in interest because there was no legal relationship between them; however, because the defendant could have added nothing to the cross-examination that did take place, the deposition was admissible against the defendant under the residual exception, as a "near miss" of the prior testimony exception). These Courts are simply evading the "predecessor-in-interest" requirement by invoking the residual exception rather than reading it out of Rule 804(b)(1) — but the end result is the same. Obviously the courts are showing discontent with the "predecessor-in-interest" requirement; Congress may have intended to protect against unfairness, but in fact, unfairness is created if probative and reliable evidence is unnecessarily excluded.

2. Can grand jury testimony that exculpates the defendant be offered against the government at trial under the prior testimony exception?

Professors Saltzburg, Martin, and Capra, *Federal Rules of Evidence Manual* (9th ed. 2006), provide this comment on the admissibility of grand jury testimony against the government under Federal Rule 804(b)(1):

Grand jury testimony is not admissible under Rule 804(b)(1) against a criminal defendant, because the defendant has no opportunity to cross-examine a witness at a grand jury proceeding. But, can grand jury testimony be admitted against the government under Rule 804(b)(1) when it exculpates the defendant? This question arose in *United States v. Salerno*, 505 U.S. 317 (1992).

The prosecutor in *Salerno* granted use immunity to two witnesses who then testified before the grand jury. Contrary to the prosecutor's expectations, the testimony was exculpatory to the defendants. At trial the defendants called the two witnesses, hoping either to obtain favorable trial testimony, or to use the grand jury testimony as prior inconsistent statements admissible under Rule 801(d)(1)(A), should the witnesses change their testimony on the stand. But the witnesses invoked their Fifth Amendment privileges and refused to testify. So the defendants argued that the grand jury testimony was admissible against the government as prior testimony. The government contended that the grand jury testimony could not be admitted under that Rule because the "similar motive" requirement had not been met. The Trial Court agreed with the government, stating that the "motive of a prosecutor in questioning a witness before the grand jury in the investigatory stages of a case is far different from the motive of a prosecutor in conducting a trial."

The Second Circuit held that it was reversible error to exclude the exculpatory grand jury testimony. It found it unnecessary to decide whether a similar motive existed, because it held that "adversarial fairness" prohibited the Government from relying on the similar motive requirement to exclude the exculpatory testimony. The Court of Appeals found it unfair for the government to develop evidence in a one-sided manner, by immunizing some witnesses and not others, depending on whether their testimony was favorable to the Government.

However, the "adversarial fairness" rationale of the Court of Appeals was rejected by the Supreme Court in *Salerno.* The Court declared that the plain language of Rule 804(b)(1) requires proof of a similar motive in all cases in which hearsay is proffered as prior testimony. The Court contended that it had no authority to override the plain meaning of the Rule by applying notions of adversarial fairness, because Congress "presumably made a careful judgment as to what hearsay may come into evidence and what may not," and that to respect Congress's determination, "we must enforce the words that it enacted." In essence, the Court held that it didn't matter if the government had acted unfairly and had developed the evidence in a one-sided manner: the plain meaning rule prohibited the Court from considering this unfairness.

The question remained whether the prosecution indeed *had* a similar motive to develop the witnesses' testimony at the grand jury as it would have had at the trial. The Supreme Court remanded this question to the Second Circuit, which ultimately decided it in an *en banc* opinion. *United States v. DiNapoli*, 8 F.3d 909 (2d Cir. 1993) (Salerno having died in the interim). The *DiNapoli* Court rejected the extreme views of both the government and the defendant — the government arguing that the prosecution *never* has a similar motive to develop testimony at the grand jury as it would have at trial, and the defendant arguing that the prosecution *always* has a similar motive to develop grand jury testimony as it would have at trial. The Court analyzed the question of similar motive as follows:

> The proper approach * * * in assessing similarity of motive under rule 804(b)(1) must consider whether the party resisting the offered testimony at a pending proceeding has at a prior proceeding an interest of substantially similar intensity to prove (or disprove) the

> same side of a substantially similar issue. The nature of the two proceedings — both what is at stake and the applicable burden of proof — and, to a lesser extent, the cross-examination at the prior proceeding — both what was undertaken and what was foregone — will be relevant though not conclusive on the ultimate issue of similarity of motive.

Applying these principles to the facts, the *DiNapoli* Court found that the government did not, in the instant case, have a similar motive to develop the testimony of the witnesses at the grand jury as it would have had at the trial. The Court noted that at the time the witnesses gave exculpatory testimony at the grand jury, there was no question of probable cause as to any of the defendants in the case, because they had already been indicted, and the grand jury was simply investigating whether other defendants should be indicted. The witnesses had essentially denied that there was any conspiracy among the defendants, and at that point, the prosecution could not have been concerned that the grand jury proceeding would have been altered in any way as to the defendants by the testimony. As the Court put it, "the grand jury had already been persuaded, at least by the low standard of probable cause, to believe that the [conspiracy] existed and that the defendants had participated in it to commit crimes." In contrast, at trial, where the government has the burden to prove the defendants guilty beyond a reasonable doubt, the prosecutor would have had a substantial incentive to attack the testimony of exculpatory witnesses.

The *DiNapoli* Court also relied on the fact that the record showed that the grand jurors had indicated to the prosecutor that they did not believe the testimony of the exculpatory witnesses. The Court concluded that "a prosecutor has no interest in showing the falsity of testimony that a grand jury already disbelieves."

The defendants in *DiNapoli* argued that the prosecutor himself showed a similar motive to attack the testimony at the grand jury proceeding when he challenged the witnesses, accused them of lying, and confronted them with contradictory evidence. However, the Court did not find this enough for the grand jury proceeding to be considered a trial-like situation:

> A prosecutor may have varied motives for asking a few challenging questions of a grand jury witness who the prosecutor thinks is lying. The prosecutor might want to afford the witness a chance to embellish the lie, thereby strengthening the case for a subsequent perjury prosecution. Or the prosecutor might want to provoke the witness into volunteering some critical new fact in the heat of an emphatic protestation of innocence.

Thus, a prosecutor can challenge an exculpatory witness at a grand jury, to some extent, without crossing the line into a trial-like cross-examination that would result in a finding of a similar motive under Rule 804(b)(1). The *DiNapoli* Court particularly noted the prosecutor's "careful limitation of questioning to matters already publicly disclosed." That is, the prosecutor was not pulling out all the stops at the grand jury by attacking the witness with secret information, as he might well have done at trial.

While the *DiNapoli* Court refused to establish a bright-line rule, it is clear that, under the Court's decision, exculpatory grand jury testimony will only rarely be admissible against the government under Rule 804(b)(1). A similarity of motive is likely to be found only where some kind of combination of three factors exists: (1) the issuance of an indictment is in doubt because the case as to probable cause is close; (2) it appears as if the grand jury could have believed the witness; and (3) the witness is in fact attacked in much the same way as he would have been at trial. *See, e.g., United States v. Peterson*, 100 F.3d 7 (2d Cir. 1996) (exculpatory grand jury testimony in a prior state criminal proceeding was not admissible as prior testimony in a federal trial on firearm charges; even assuming that the state government could be considered a predecessor in interest of the federal government, the similar motive requirement of Rule 804(b)(1) was not met; the evidence before the state grand jury "provided ample probable cause to indict Peterson for possession" and therefore there was no reason for the government to attack Peterson's exculpatory testimony in the same manner as it would have done at trial). Compare *United States v. Foster*, 128 F.3d 949 (6th Cir. 1997) (exculpatory grand jury testimony should have been admitted against the government under Rule 804(b)(1); at the time the witness testified, the outcome of the grand jury proceeding was in doubt, and there was no indication that the grand jury did not believe the witness).

[3] Dying Declarations

[a] Federal Rule of Evidence 804(b)(2)

Rule 804. Hearsay Exceptions; Declarant Unavailable

* * *

(b) Hearsay exceptions. The following are not excluded by the hearsay rule if the declarant is unavailable as a witness.

* * *

(2) Statement under belief of impending death. In a prosecution for homicide or in a civil action or proceeding, a statement made by a declarant while believing that the declarant's death was imminent, concerning the cause or circumstances of what the declarant believed to be impending death.

[b] Declarant's Belief in Impending Death

STATE v. QUINTANA
644 P.2d 531 (N.M. 1982)

RIORDAN, JUSTICE.

Rosinaldo Quintana (Quintana) was convicted of voluntary manslaughter. Quintana alleged on appeal that the deathbed statement of Telesfor Lopez (Lopez), the decedent, was erroneously admitted into evidence. The Court of Appeals held that the admission of the statement was reversible error. We granted *certiorari*; and we reverse the Court of Appeals.

The issue on appeal is:

Whether Lopez' deathbed statement was a dying declaration that was properly admitted into evidence.

In the early evening of May 21, 1980, there was an altercation between two groups of men at the bridge that separates East and West Pecos, New Mexico. One of the men from Lopez' group smashed the windshields of three trucks belonging to men of the other group. After this incident, Lopez' group went to the Valencia residence in East Pecos. The residence was on top of a wooded hill off the main roadway. A bonfire was built, and the group sat outside by the fire and drank beer.

The other group drove their damaged trucks to Quintana's trailer. Quintana, for approximately seven months, had been the deputy marshal for the Village of West Pecos and a special deputy sheriff for San Miguel County. The men reported the incident to Quintana and he inspected the damage to their windshields. Quintana then got dressed in his official shirt and badge. He borrowed a truck belonging to his nephew, a member of the group whose vehicles were damaged, because the tires on his police car were low and the car would not start. Quintana intended to investigate the incident.

First, Quintana drove to the bridge and observed the glass. The other men followed in their trucks. Then he drove to the Valencia residence in East Pecos. He parked the borrowed truck in the driveway where he could see the bonfire. He testified that when he got out of the truck, he identified himself twice as the deputy marshal and said he wanted to talk. He then heard several "pop shots" like the discharge of a small automatic weapon. He assumed that someone was shooting at him. He testified that he then shot his rifle into the air three or four times. Someone then grabbed Quintana and said "let's go"; the group left and returned to Quintana's trailer. Quintana denied ever shooting towards the group of men.

Members from the Lopez group testified that they were sitting by the bonfire. They saw a truck drive part way up the driveway, followed by other vehicles. They heard what they thought was a gun being fired. They ran for cover and heard more shots fired. After Quintana and the group of men left, Lopez was found hiding near a car. It was discovered that he had been shot, and he was taken to the hospital. All members of the Lopez group testified that none of them had any firearms. Also, they did not see who shot at them.

Lopez died May 26, 1980 from infection caused by a single gunshot wound. The bullet removed during the autopsy on Lopez was tested and found to have come from Quintana's rifle. Quintana was then charged with Lopez' death.

At trial, the State sought admission of a hearsay statement made by Lopez just before his death. The statement had been elicited at the hospital by the attorney retained by Lopez' family to investigate the civil liability aspect of the shooting. The statement was admitted over Quintana's objection.

The family attorney testified that he went to the hospital on May 26th for the express purpose of obtaining a dying declaration from Lopez. He spoke to Lopez for two to six minutes. The attorney testified that when he went to the intensive care unit, he saw Lopez: "wired to any number of machines. They were monitoring his heartbeat. They were monitoring his blood pressure. He had oxygen — he was breathing oxygen. They had his feet elevated. It was my understanding — and I saw that myself — it was my understanding that the reason they had his feet slightly elevated was because the kid was choking on his own blood. When I saw him and during the time that I spoke to him, his breathing was labored; his speech was somewhat difficult. During the entire time that I talked to him, the blood continued to ooze out of his nose and mouth and he was in great pain."

The attorney testified that during the conversation Lopez was conversant, conscious and lucid. Lopez was *never* told by his doctors that he was going to die; however, Lopez told the attorney that he knew he was very seriously injured; he knew that his back was broken, and he was paralyzed; and he knew that there was a strong possibility of dying. During the interview, the attorney elicited answers from Lopez as to circumstances surrounding the shooting; however, Lopez was not able to identify the person who shot him.

* * *

The admissibility of evidence is within the sound discretion of the trial court, and its ruling will be upheld unless there is a showing of an abuse of that discretion. We find there was no abuse of the trial judge's discretion.

A dying declaration is admissible when there is a showing that the statement was made under a sense of "impending death". When such a declaration is made, the declarant must be conscious and the realization of approaching death must exist. The determination as to whether the particular testimony is admissible must depend upon the particular circumstances of each case.

In determining "impending death", one is to look to the state of mind of the victim. * * * Fear or even the belief that the illness will end in death is not enough for a dying declaration. There must be a settled hopeless expectation that death is near, and what is said must have been spoken in the hush of impending death.* * * The state of mind must be exhibited in the evidence and not left to conjecture.* * * Therefore, a dying person can declare that he believes he is dying; however, there are no specific words that have to be spoken by the declarant.* * * Alternatively, if it can reasonably be inferred from the state of the wound or the state of the illness that the dying person was aware of his danger, then the requirement of impending death is met.* * * Therefore, a decedent does not have to be told he is dying; it can be obvious from the circumstances that death is impending.* * *

* * *

Lopez' statements and circumstances surrounding his statements are sufficient to show that he believed his death was imminent. He stated that he knew that he was seriously injured; he knew his back was broken, and he was paralyzed; he also stated that there was a strong possibility of dying. The attorney also testified as to what he witnessed about Lopez' condition. He stated that he was hooked up to several machines and was oozing blood from his nose and mouth. Lopez died about three hours after giving the statement. Therefore, we hold that the dying declaration was properly admitted into evidence.

However, a dying declaration by no means implies absolute verity. It can be impeached.* * * After the declaration has been found to be admissible, the defendant can impeach the statement in the same manner as the defendant could impeach a witness. He can discredit the statement by showing that the deceased bore a bad reputation or that he did not believe in a future state of rewards or punishment.* * *

Therefore, we find that the trial court did not abuse its discretion in admitting the dying declaration. The Court of Appeals is reversed and the trial court's verdict is affirmed.

NOTES

1. Are statements by a homicide victim that tend to exculpate the accused admissible into evidence?

Federal Rule 804(b)(2) does not by its language limit the exception to use by the prosecution against the defendant. Thus, it would seem that a dying statement that someone other than the defendant committed the homicide could be admitted on behalf of the defendant.

2. Must the declarant have personal knowledge of the facts alleged in the statement?

According to the court in *Shepard v. United States*, 290 U.S. 96 (1933), the statement should not be admitted absent a showing of some knowledge by the declarant. Suspicion or conjecture is insufficient. The reason for a personal knowledge requirement is that hearsay testimony is the equivalent of the declarant testifying at trial. Because the declarant could not testify without personal knowledge, it follows that the declarant's hearsay statement made without personal knowledge is equally inadmissible. The only exception to the personal knowledge requirement for hearsay statements is admissions — see the discussion of Rule 801(d)(2), supra. If a party's own statement (or that of an agent) is offered against the party, that party has no right to complain that there was no basis for making the statement.

3. What factors are relevant to the determination of whether the declarant was aware of impending death?

The nature of this inquiry was discussed in detail in *People v. Nieves*, 67 N.Y.2d 125, 501 N.Y.S.2d 1 (1986). In *Nieves*, a stabbing victim was brought into a hospital emergency room by the defendant and another person. She was in shock and unable to speak. The initial medical examination showed a small incision which indicated a possible heart wound. After some treatment, the victim improved and became lucid. Pursuant to questioning from medical personnel, the victim identified the defendant as the person who stabbed her. The victim began complaining of strong chest pains, and stated several times that she did not want to die. She was never told that her condition was critical. Her condition worsened and she died within 90 minutes of making her statements.

The *Nieves* Court set forth the following guidelines for assessing the dying declarant's mental state:

> Under any justification for permitting the use of dying declarations, the crucial inquiry is directed toward the state of mind of the declarant. Thus, by the early part of this century it was established that for a statement to constitute a dying declaration, the declarant must not only have been in extremist, but must also have spoken under a sense of impending death, with no hope of recovery. Belief by the declarant that death is possible, or even probable, is not sufficient. Rather, "[there] must be 'a settled hopeless expectation' * * * that death is near at hand" (*Shepard v United States*, 290 U.S. 96, 100 [Cardozo, J.]).
>
> * * *
>
> * * * The People correctly point out that a statement's qualification as a dying declaration does not hinge upon the declarant having actually expressed a certainty of impending death. * * * [T]here is no standardized ritual spoken by all dying persons. There is also no unvarying requirement that the declarant had been told by a doctor that an imminent death was certain.
>
> Rather, the requisite state of mind of declarant may be found from all of the circumstances surrounding the statement sought to be admitted. Any statements made by the declarant as to his condition or his expectations, as well as any statements made by medical personnel to the declarant as to the severity of his injury, are, of course, highly relevant. Among the other factors to be considered by the trial court are the nature and severity of the wound, as apparent to the declarant; whether the person's condition appeared to be improving or declining when the declaration was made; and, whether any actions normally associated with an expectation of imminent death, such as asking for last rites, disposing of property, or attempting to make arrangements for the care of family members were taken.

Applying this totality of the circumstances test to the facts, the *Nieves* Court held that the victim's identification of the defendant was not made while under a certainty of imminent death. The Court noted that the proponent, in this case the prosecution, had the burden of proving that the admissibility requirements of the hearsay exception were met. The government pointed out that the declarant stated that she did not want to die, but the court reasoned that this did not necessarily mean that she had given up all hope of recovery; it might well have meant the opposite. The fact that the victim had never been informed of her critical condition, while not dispositive, certainly cut against her having a certainty of impending death. While the wound turned out to be fatal, the victim was never bleeding profusely and thus the wound "was not of such nature that its severity would have been obvious" to the victim. Furthermore, the emergency room doctor testified at the admissibility hearing that at the time the declarant spoke, he did not think that she would die, and that when she spoke her condition was improving, or at least stabilizing. Finally, the victim took no steps which would reveal an expectation of death (such as ordering her affairs) despite having had ample opportunity to do so.

[4] Statement Against Interest

[a] Federal Rule of Evidence 804(b)(3)

Rule 804. Hearsay Exceptions; Declarant Unavailable

* * *

(b) Hearsay exceptions. The following are not excluded by the hearsay rule if the declarant is unavailable as a witness.

* * *

(3) Statement against interest. A statement which was at the time of its making so far contrary to the declarant's pecuniary or proprietary interest, or so far tended to subject the declarant to civil or criminal liability, or to render invalid a claim by the declarant against another, that a reasonable person in the declarant's position would not have made the statement unless believing it to be true. A statement tending to expose the declarant to criminal liability and offered to exculpate the accused is not admissible unless corroborating circumstances clearly indicate the trustworthiness of the statement.

* * *

[b] Pecuniary Interest

GHELIN v. JOHNSON
243 N.W. 443 (Minn. 1932)

OLSEN, J.

Marie Chapman, or Marie Chapman Ghelin, appeals from an order denying her alternative motion for judgment or a new trial. For convenience, we refer to her as claimant.

Franz Frithiof Lust, known also as Frank Ghelin, a resident of Hennepin county, died on March 28, 1929, leaving an estate in said county. He died while abroad, leaving no legally executed will. Clara Johnson, a sister of the deceased, petitioned the probate court of said county for the appointment of the Minnesota Loan & Trust Company as administrator of the estate. Two other sisters and a brother of deceased thereafter joined with the petitioner in asking for the appointment of that company as administrator. The claimant appeared and opposed the appointment of the Minnesota Loan & Trust Company as administrator, and asked that she be appointed as sole administratrix of the estate, on the ground that she was the surviving spouse, the widow, of said deceased. The question of whether Marie Chapman was the wife of the deceased at the time of his death, and hence his surviving spouse, was tried in the probate court, and that court found that she was not the wife or surviving spouse of the decedent. That court then granted the petition for the appointment of the Minnesota Loan & Trust Company as administrator of the estate. Appeal was taken by Marie Chapman to the district court. In the district court the same question was tried to a jury, and the jury, by its verdict, found that she was not the wife or surviving spouse of decedent. The trial court has approved the verdict.

* * * A preliminary consideration of the nature and kind of proof required to prove the marriage may be of assistance in passing upon the claimed errors. There was no written contract of marriage.* * * There was no civil or religious ceremony of marriage and no license to marry. The other party being dead, claimant could not and did not testify to any verbal contract of marriage, and no other witness testified to the making of any such contract by the parties. In that situation, the claimant necessarily had to rely on circumstantial evidence to prove the contract of marriage. * * * The inquiry then is: What is proper evidence for that purpose? * * *

Income tax statements made by the deceased regularly during the time the marriage is claimed to have existed were received in evidence. In these statements decedent declared that he was not married. We think these statements may be admissible as declarations against interest. A declaration by him in these statements that he was a married man might have resulted in the immediate saving of a substantial amount of tax money. A declaration therein that he was not married, if he in fact was a married man, resulted in the payment by him of substantial amounts of tax money in excess of what he would have been required to pay if he had been and had declared that he was married.

* * *

NOTE

What is the difference between a statement against interest and a party admission?

See Martin, Capra, and Rossi, *New York Evidence* (2d ed. 2002):

> The exception for party admissions is sometimes unfortunately confused with the separate hearsay exception for declarations against interest. These two exceptions in fact have little in common. The admissions exception covers statements by the party or his agents. In contrast, a declaration against interest is made by a non-party to the action, and the declarant must be unavailable for trial. Moreover, declarations against interest are admitted because they are thought to be reliable — the declarant would not say something disserving to his interest unless it were true. In contrast, admissions need not be disserving when made, and in fact many statements admitted under the exception are misguided attempts by the party to exculpate himself by telling a story that turns out to be inconsistent from the later story told at trial. An admission need not be reliable to be admitted, because the basis for admissibility lies in the adversarial theory of litigation.

[c] Penal Interest

WILLIAMSON v. UNITED STATES
512 U.S. 594 (1994)

JUSTICE O'CONNOR delivered the opinion of the Court.

In this case we clarify the scope of the hearsay exception for statements against penal interest. Fed. Rule Evid. 804(b)(3).

I

A deputy sheriff stopped the rental car driven by Reginald Harris for weaving on the highway. Harris consented to a search of the car, which revealed 19 kilograms of cocaine in two suitcases in the trunk. Harris was promptly arrested.

Shortly after Harris' arrest, Special Agent Donald Walton of the Drug Enforcement Administration (DEA) interviewed him by telephone. During that conversation, Harris said that he got the cocaine from an unidentified Cuban in Fort Lauderdale; that the cocaine belonged to petitioner Williamson; and that it was to be delivered that night to a particular dumpster. Williamson was also connected to Harris by physical evidence: The luggage bore the initials of Williamson's sister, Williamson was listed as an additional driver on the car rental agreement, and an envelope addressed to Williamson and a receipt with Williamson's girlfriend's address were found in the glove compartment.

Several hours later, Agent Walton spoke to Harris in person. During that interview, Harris said he had rented the car a few days earlier and had driven it to Fort Lauderdale to meet Williamson. According to Harris, he had gotten the cocaine from a Cuban who was Williamson's acquaintance, and the Cuban had put the cocaine in the car with a note telling Harris how to deliver the drugs. Harris repeated that he had been instructed to leave the drugs in a certain dumpster, to return to his car, and to leave without waiting for anyone to pick up the drugs.

Agent Walton then took steps to arrange a controlled delivery of the cocaine. But as Walton was preparing to leave the interview room, Harris * * * told Walton he had lied about the Cuban, the note, and the dumpster. The real story, Harris said, was that he was transporting the cocaine to Atlanta for Williamson, and that Williamson was traveling in front of him in another rental car. Harris added that after his car was stopped, Williamson turned around and drove past the location of the stop, where he could see Harris' car with its trunk open. * * * Because Williamson had apparently seen the police searching the car, Harris explained that it would be impossible to make a controlled delivery.* * *

Harris told Walton that he had lied about the source of the drugs because he was afraid of Williamson.* * * Though Harris freely implicated himself, he did not want his story to be recorded, and he refused to sign a written version of the statement.* * * Walton testified that he had promised to report any cooperation by Harris to the Assistant United States Attorney. Walton said Harris was not promised any reward or other benefit for cooperating.* * *

Williamson was eventually convicted of possessing cocaine with intent to distribute, conspiring to possess cocaine with intent to distribute, and traveling interstate to promote the distribution of cocaine * * *. When called to testify at Williamson's trial, Harris refused, even though the prosecution gave him use immunity and the court ordered him to testify and eventually held him in contempt. The District Court then ruled that, under Rule 804(b)(3), Agent Walton could relate what Harris had said to him. * * * Williamson appealed his conviction, claiming that the admission of Harris' statements violated Rule 804(b)(3) and the Confrontation Clause of the Sixth Amendment. The Court of Appeals for the Eleventh Circuit affirmed without opinion, and we granted *certiorari*.

II

A

The hearsay rule, Fed. Rule Evid. 802, is premised on the theory that out-of-court statements are subject to particular hazards. The declarant might be lying; he might have misperceived the events which he relates; he might have faulty memory; his words might be misunderstood or taken out of context by the listener. And the ways in which these dangers are minimized for in-court statements — the oath, the witness' awareness of the gravity of the proceedings, the jury's ability to observe the witness' demeanor, and, most importantly, the right of the opponent to cross-examine — are generally absent for things said out of court.

Nonetheless, the Federal Rules of Evidence also recognize that some kinds of out-of-court statements are less subject to these hearsay dangers, and therefore except them from the general rule that hearsay is inadmissible. One such category covers statements that are against the declarant's interest: "statement[s] which * * * at the time of [their] making * * * so far tended to subject the declarant to * * * criminal liability * * * that a reasonable person in the declarant's position would not have made the statement[s] unless believing [them] to be true." Fed. Rule Evid. 804(b)(3).

To decide whether Harris' confession is made admissible by Rule 804(b)(3), we must first determine what the Rule means by "statement," which Federal Rule of Evidence 801(a)(1) defines as "an oral or written assertion." One possible meaning, "a report or narrative," *Webster's Third New International Dictionary* 2229, defn. 2(a) (1961), connotes an extended declaration. Under this reading, Harris' entire confession — even if it contains both self-inculpatory and non-self-inculpatory parts — would be admissible so long as in the aggregate the confession sufficiently inculpates him. Another meaning of "statement," "a single declaration or remark," *ibid.*, defn. 2(b), would make Rule 804(b)(3) cover only those declarations or remarks within the confession that are individually self-inculpatory.

Although the text of the Rule does not directly resolve the matter, the principle behind the Rule, so far as it is discernible from the text, points clearly to the narrower reading. Rule 804(b)(3) is founded on the commonsense notion that reasonable people, even reasonable people who are not especially honest, tend not to make self-inculpatory statements unless they believe them to be true. This notion simply does not extend to the broader definition of "statement." The fact that a person is making a broadly self-inculpatory confession does not make more credible the confession's non-self-inculpatory parts. One of the most effective ways to lie is to mix falsehood with truth, especially truth that seems particularly persuasive because of its self-inculpatory nature.

In this respect, it is telling that the non-self-inculpatory things Harris said in his first statement actually proved to be false, as Harris himself admitted during the second interrogation. And when part of the confession is actually self-exculpatory, the generalization on which Rule 804(b)(3) is founded becomes even less applicable. Self-exculpatory statements are exactly the ones which people are most likely to make even when they are false; and mere proximity to other, self-inculpatory, statements does not increase the plausibility of the self-exculpatory statements.

We therefore cannot agree with JUSTICE KENNEDY's suggestion that the Rule can be read as expressing a policy that collateral statements — even ones that are not in any way against the declarant's interest — are admissible. * * * Nothing in the text of Rule 804(b)(3) or the general theory of the hearsay Rules suggests that admissibility should turn on whether a statement is collateral to a self-inculpatory statement. The fact that a statement is self-inculpatory does make it more reliable; but the fact that a statement is collateral to a self-inculpatory statement says nothing at all about the collateral statement's reliability. We see no reason why collateral statements, even ones that are neutral as to interest * * * should be treated any differently from other hearsay statements that are generally excluded.

Congress certainly could, subject to the constraints of the Confrontation Clause, make statements admissible based on their proximity to self-inculpatory statements. But we will not lightly assume that the ambiguous language means anything so inconsistent with the Rule's underlying theory. * * * In our view, the most faithful reading of Rule 804(b)(3) is that it does not allow admission of non-self-inculpatory statements, even if they are made within a broader narrative that is generally self-inculpatory. The district court may not just assume for purposes of Rule 804(b)(3) that a statement is self-inculpatory because it is part of a fuller confession, and this is especially true when the statement implicates someone else. "[T]he arrest statements of a codefendant have traditionally been viewed with special suspicion. Due to his strong motivation to implicate the defendant and to exonerate himself, a codefendant's statements about what the defendant said or did are less credible than ordinary hearsay evidence."* * *

B

* * *

C

In this case * * * we cannot conclude that all that Harris said was properly admitted. * * * [P]arts of his confession, especially the parts that implicated Williamson, did little to subject Harris himself to criminal liability. A reasonable person in Harris' position might even think that implicating someone else would decrease his practical exposure to criminal liability, at least so far as sentencing goes. Small fish in a big conspiracy often get shorter sentences than people who are running the whole show, *see, e.g.*, United States Sentencing Commission, Guidelines Manual § 3B1.2 (Nov. 1993), especially if the small fish are willing to help the authorities catch the big ones, *see, e.g.*, *id.*, at § 5K1.1.

Nothing in the record shows that the District Court or the Court of Appeals inquired whether each of the statements in Harris' confession was truly self-inculpatory. As we explained above, this can be a fact-intensive inquiry, which would require careful examination of all the circumstances surrounding the criminal activity involved; we therefore remand to the Court of Appeals to conduct this inquiry in the first instance.

In light of this disposition, we need not address Williamson's claim that the statements were also made inadmissible by the Confrontation Clause * * *. We also need not decide whether, as some Courts of Appeals have held, the second sentence of Rule 804(b)(3) — "A statement tending to expose the declarant to criminal liability *and offered to exculpate the accused* is not admissible unless corroborating circumstances clearly indicate the trustworthiness of the statement" (emphasis added) — also requires that statements inculpating the accused be supported by corroborating circumstances. The judgment of the Court of Appeals is vacated, and the case is remanded for further proceedings consistent with this opinion.

So ordered.

[The concurring opinion of JUSTICE SCALIA is omitted.]

JUSTICE GINSBURG, with whom JUSTICE BLACKMUN, JUSTICE STEVENS, and JUSTICE SOUTER join, concurring in part and concurring in the judgment.

* * * I agree with the Court that Federal Rule of Evidence 804(b)(3) excepts from the general rule that hearsay statements are inadmissible only "those declarations or remarks within [a narrative] that are individually self-inculpatory." As the Court explains, the exception for statements against penal interest "does not allow admission of non-self-inculpatory statements, even if they are made within a broader narrative that is generally self-inculpatory,"* * * the exception applies only to statements that are "sufficiently against the declarant's penal interest 'that a reasonable person in the declarant's position would not have made the statement unless believing it to be true.' "* * *

Further, the Court recognizes the untrustworthiness of statements implicating another person.* * * A person arrested in incriminating circumstances has a strong incentive to shift blame or downplay his own role in comparison with that of others, in hopes of receiving a shorter sentence and leniency in exchange for cooperation. * * *

* * * I conclude that Reginald Harris' statements, as recounted by DEA Special Agent Donald E. Walton, do not fit, even in part, within the exception described in Rule 804(b)(3), for Harris' arguably inculpatory statements are too closely intertwined with his self-serving declarations to be ranked as trustworthy. Harris was caught red-handed with 19 kilos of cocaine — enough to subject even a first-time offender to a minimum of 12 1/2 years' imprisonment. He could have denied knowing the drugs were in the car's trunk, but that strategy would have brought little prospect of thwarting a criminal prosecution. He therefore admitted involvement, but did so in a way that minimized his own role and shifted blame to petitioner Fredel Williamson (and a Cuban man named Shawn).

Most of Harris' statements to DEA Agent Walton focused on Williamson's, rather than Harris', conduct.

* * * To the extent some of these statements tended to incriminate Harris, they provided only marginal or cumulative evidence of his guilt. They project an image of a person acting not against his penal interest, but striving mightily to shift principal responsibility to someone else. *See United States v. Sarmiento-Perez*, 633 F.2d 1092, 1102 (CA5 1981) ("[The declarant] might well have been motivated to misrepresent the role of others in the criminal enterprise, and might well have viewed the statement[s] as a whole — including the ostensibly disserving portions — to be *in* his interest rather than against it.").

For these reasons, I would hold that none of Harris' hearsay statements were admissible under Rule 804(b)(3). * * * I concur in the Court's decision to vacate the Court of Appeals' judgment, however, because I have not examined the entire trial court record; I therefore cannot say the Government should be denied an opportunity to argue that the erroneous admission of the hearsay statements, in light of the other evidence introduced at trial, constituted harmless error.

JUSTICE KENNEDY, with whom THE CHIEF JUSTICE and JUSTICE THOMAS join, concurring in the judgment.

* * *

I would adhere to the following approach with respect to statements against penal interest that inculpate the accused. A court first should determine whether the declarant made a statement that contained a fact against penal interest. * * * If so, the court should admit all statements related to the precise statement against penal interest, subject to two limits. Consistent with the Advisory Committee's Note, the court should exclude a collateral statement that is so self-serving as to render it unreliable (if, for example, it shifts blame to someone else for a crime the defendant could have committed). In addition, in cases where the statement was made under circumstances where it is likely that the declarant had a significant motivation to obtain favorable treatment, as when the government made an explicit offer of leniency in exchange for the declarant's admission of guilt, the entire statement should be inadmissible.

* * *

UNITED STATES v. PAGUIO
114 F.3d 928 (9th Cir. 1997)

KLEINFELD, CIRCUIT JUDGE:

This case turns on Federal Rule of Evidence 804(b)(3), the hearsay exception for inculpatory statements by unavailable witnesses.

I. Facts

Appellants Gil Manuel Paguio, Jr. and Angelica D. Acosta, husband and wife, were convicted of false statements to a bank to influence action on a loan application * * *. Paguio Jr.'s father, Gil Paguio, Sr., initiated the loan process. The father approached the institution's loan officer about a $204,000 loan so that his son, Paguio Jr., and Acosta, could buy property next to his house. The loan officer gave the father the application, and the father returned the handwritten loan application with what purported to be the son's and the fiancee's signatures.

The application was fraudulent. It showed that Paguio Jr. and Acosta made $1,900 and $1,300 a month in self-employment income from the father's insurance company. That was not true. As part of its routine for loan processing, the bank had to verify employment and income by examining W-2 Forms, or for self-employed people, copies of tax returns. As "verification" the father showed the bank fictitious 1988 and 1989 tax returns and 1099 forms for Paguio Jr. and Acosta. None of these forms had actually been filed with the IRS.

In truth, Paguio Jr. and Acosta were in no position to finance anything for $200,000 dollars. Acosta had been turned down for an $18,000 car loan. The bank manager had noted on the denial: "excessive obligations for amount requested. Good credit history. Will reconsider in lesser amount * * * ." Paguio Jr. had asked for forbearance on his $10,000 dollar student loan because of inability to make the payments. Nevertheless, both Paguio Jr. and Acosta signed the final loan application. Paguio Jr. worked in the computer room of another bank. He was under investigation by the FBI, because the bank had processed a counterfeit computer tape, which caused a $70 million dollar funds transfer to a Swiss bank. Paguio Jr. was the last person to handle the tape, so the FBI suspected he probably knew something about the computer theft, but he did not provide any useful information. The FBI investigated Paguio Jr.'s financial situation. They discovered the $204,000 loan and other evidence that Paguio Jr. and his fiancee were not as financially secure as the loan application suggested. The United States Attorney ultimately indicted appellants Paguio Jr. and Acosta in order to pressure Paguio Jr. to tell what the government suspected he knew about the computer theft.

Paguio Jr. and Acosta went to trial on their indictment. The defense was in substance that the house loan was the father's deal, and the son and fiancee lacked mens rea. The jury hung, but the government got convictions when the case was retried.

II. Analysis

* * *

C. The Absent Witness Statement.

Paguio Jr.'s lawyer had obtained a statement from Paguio Sr. that his son had "nothing to do with it." When the case was retried, Paguio Sr. was a fugitive, so the defense tried to get the statement into evidence by means of the absent witness hearsay exception for statements against penal interest, Federal Rule of Evidence 804(b)(3). The district court excluded it, and Paguio Jr. and Acosta appeal this evidentiary ruling.

Paguio Jr.'s lawyer and paralegal assistant interviewed Paguio Sr. Defense counsel advised Paguio Sr. that she was not his attorney, she represented his son, and what he told her was not privileged. He told her that the whole scheme was his, and his son (and by implication, his son's fiancee) had nothing to do with it. The father had refused to testify about this, claiming his Fifth Amendment privilege at the first trial, and he became a fugitive prior to the retrial. The district court ruled that the portions of the evidence in which the father admitted his own criminal responsibility, but not those exonerating the son, could come into evidence.

Certain statements against penal interest have long been admissible as an exception to the hearsay rule, and the common law exception has been codified in the Federal Rules of Evidence * * *. To get a statement against penal interest into evidence under 804(b)(3), the proponent must show that: (1) the declarant is unavailable as a witness; (2) the statement so far tended to subject the declarant to criminal liability that a reasonable person in the declarant's position would not have made the statement unless he believed it to be true; and (3) corroborating circumstances clearly indicate the trustworthiness of the statement.

The government concedes the first requirement, that Paguio Sr. was unavailable. As to the third element, corroboration of trustworthiness, the district court found in favor of appellants. The government challenges this determination. There were factors which cut both ways, and plenty to support the district court decision. The evidence showed that the father initiated the transaction and walked the papers through all the relevant offices. The father's role was so dominant that the escrow officer had some confusion about which Paguio she was dealing with, father or son. She eventually received documentation through the mail confirming that Paguio, Jr. and Acosta were the ultimate buyers, but was suspicious that Paguio Sr. had in fact signed the documents. The loan officer, escrow agent and the tax preparer all testified that their dealings were with the father, not the son. The father had prior business relations with the loan officer and the tax preparer, and the son had none. The father's business generated the false 1099 forms which were used to support the false statement of income. The father distributed the papers to the various parties. And of course the whole point of the transaction was for the father to get his son and the son's prospective wife into the house next door. There is one factor that cuts against the trustworthiness of the father's statement, and that is that the appellant is his son. * * * A motive of love might * * * induce a reasonable father to make a false self-inculpatory statement in order to save his son. The possibility that this noble motive would induce a false statement against penal interest cuts in favor of exclusion. But the district judge reasonably concluded that the loan officer, escrow agent, and accountant all corroborated the proposition that the father and not the son managed the entire transaction, and the circumstances were consistent with that, so the corroboration of trustworthiness requirement was satisfied. While a jury could still conclude that the father was lying to save his son, the corroboration sufficed for admissibility of the evidence. As the district judge correctly decided, it was up to the jury to decide whether the father's statement against penal interest was motivated by truthfulness or a noble motive to lie.

The district court ruled that the father's statement should be parsed, and only the self-inculpatory portions admitted. Thus the jury was permitted to hear that the father had falsified the W-2 forms (really 1099s) and provided the information to the accountant. The jury was not permitted to hear that the father said his son had nothing to do with the negotiations, nothing to do with preparation of the false 1099s, and no involvement with preparing the false tax returns.

* * *

A reasonable person in the father's position would have believed that admitting to preparing false tax returns and engineering an admittedly fraudulent loan application would subject him to criminal liability. The issue arises from the father's statements that his son had "nothing to do with it."

The government argues that the statement should be seen merely as exculpatory of the son, not inculpatory of the father. We disagree, and conclude that the father's statement should have been admitted in its entirety, not parsed and admitted only in part.

"Whether a statement is in fact against interest must be determined from the circumstances of each case," *Williamson,* 512 U.S. at 601, and "can only be determined by viewing it in context." *Id.* at 603. In context, the father's statement that his son had nothing to do with it was inculpatory of the father as well as exculpatory of the son. The father admitted not only participation but leadership, leading his son and daughter-in-law into the abyss. Because leading others into wrongdoing has always been seen as especially bad, there is a sentencing enhancement for it. U.S.S.G. §§ 3B1.1(c) (1993). Also, in context, the inculpating and exculpating statements were not practically separable. The government argues that *Williamson* required the district judge to parse the statement and exclude the non-inculpatory parts. That reading is incorrect. * * *

Williamson does not mean that the trial judge must always parse the statement and let in only the inculpatory part. It means that the statement must be examined in context, to see whether as a matter of common sense the portion at issue was against interest and would not have been made by a reasonable person unless he believed it to be true. Sometimes that requires exclusion of part of the statement, sometimes not. A reasonable man caught with a trunk full of cocaine, like the unavailable declarant in *Williamson,* might well imagine that he could advance his own penal interest by fingering someone else. But Paguio Sr.'s statement that "my son had nothing to do with it" was not an attempt to "shift blame or curry favor." *Williamson,* 512 U.S. at 603. * * *

When the prosecution attempts to take advantage of the rule, as in *Williamson,* the statement is typically in the form, "I did it, but X is guiltier than I am." As a matter of common sense, that is less likely to be true of X than "I did it alone, not with X." That is because the part of the statement touching on X's participation is an attempt to avoid responsibility or curry favor in the former, but to accept undiluted responsibility in the latter.

Prosecution use of an unavailable declarant's accusation of the defendant, as in *Williamson,* raises different concerns from a defendant's use of an unavailable declarant's confession which exonerates him. Were it not for the fence around the Confrontation Clause provided by the hearsay rule, prosecution use would implicate the accused's right to be "confronted with the witnesses against him." U.S. Const. amend. VI. The Constitution gives the "accused," not the government, the right of confrontation. When the defendant seeks to introduce the evidence, but is unable to procure the attendance of the witness, the relevant Constitutional right is the accused's right "to have compulsory process for obtaining witnesses in his favor." U.S. Const. amend. VI. The accused's right to present witnesses in his own defense may be implicated where an absent declarant's testimony is improperly excluded from evidence. We do not intimate that the exclusion of part of the statement violated appellants' constitutional rights in this case, and we do not need to reach the question. We raise the constitutional asymmetry because it helps explain why application of the rule of evidence is to some extent asymmetrical between defense and prosecution.

We conclude that the unavailable witness exception for statements against penal interest, Federal Rule of Evidence 804(b)(3) applied, so the parts of Paguio Sr.'s statement exonerating his son should have been admitted. We cannot characterize the error as harmless, because the hung jury at the first trial persuades us that the case was close and might have turned on this evidence. Though Paguio Sr.'s statement that his son had "nothing to do with it" expressly exonerated only Paguio Jr. and not Acosta, the context makes it clear that if the son had nothing to do with it, then the son's fiancee was even more marginal, so the error was prejudicial as to her too.

REVERSED.

NOTES

1. When are statements sufficiently disserving to a declarant's penal interest to qualify for admissibility under Rule 804(b)(3)?

In *United States v. Butler*, 71 F.3d 243 (7th Cir. 1995), a case involving firearms charges, the Court held that the trial court properly excluded a hearsay statement offered by the defendant, made by a person on the premises during a police raid. The hearsay declarant accused the police of planting, on the defendant, guns found in the house, because they knew that the defendant was a felon. The defendant argued that the hearsay statement was disserving to the declarant, because the declarant admitted that he was in the room where the weapons were found, and was thus opening himself up to possible weapons charges. But the Court held that the declarant had not admitted anything remotely criminal; he did not admit that he had possession of or owned any gun. At most, the statement put the declarant at risk of being in some type of constructive possession of a gun, which "is not a risk sufficient to provide the guarantee of reliability or truthfulness the 804(b)(3) exception is based on."

Professors Professors Saltzburg, Martin, and Capra, *Federal Rules of Evidence Manual* (9th ed. 2006), analyze the "against penal interest" requirement as follows:

> The Courts are in some disagreement about the degree to which a statement must be disserving to the declarant in order to qualify as a declaration against interest under Rule 804(b)(3). An example of the problem is *United States v. Harwood*, 998 F.2d 91 (2d Cir. 1993). Harwood and McKee were both charged with drug offenses arising from a search of a van in which drugs were found. Both defendants employed blame-shifting defenses, each claiming that he was an unwitting rider and the other defendant was the drug dealer. Harwood offered a statement made by McKee to a newspaper reporter after they were arrested. McKee had stated that Harwood had simply been "at the wrong place at the wrong time," and that the same thing would

have happened to anyone who was driving with McKee at that time. The Trial Court excluded the statement, and the Court of Appeals found no error. Judge McLaughlin concluded that McKee's statement was not sufficiently disserving to qualify under Rule 804(b)(3). He argued that the statement did not "expose McKee to criminal liability" and that it seemed "only to suggest that Harwood was arrested at an inopportune time."

According to the *Harwood* Court, a statement will not be sufficiently disserving to qualify under the Rule unless it squarely and unequivocally implicates the declarant in criminal activity or exposes the declarant to civil liability. *See also United States v. Wilkinson*, 754 F.2d 1427 (2d Cir. 1985) (a statement made by the declarant that the defendant did not know that the declarant was selling drugs was held insufficiently disserving to qualify under Rule 804(b)(3)).

Yet this is not the only possible reading of the Rule; that strict reading conflicts with the Rule's permissive language that a statement need only "tend" to subject the declarant to criminal liability. As the Ninth Circuit has stated: "If Congress had wanted courts to take a restrictive approach to whether a statement is against penal interest, it would not have chosen the broadly worded phrase 'tended to subject' in Rule 804(b)(3)." *United States v. Satterfield*, 572 F.2d 687 (9th Cir. 1978). *See also United States v. Thomas*, 571 F.2d 285 (5th Cir. 1978) (rejecting a government argument that the statement did not qualify as a declaration against interest because the declarant did not expressly confess guilt: "by referring to statements that 'tend' to subject the declarant to criminal liability, the Rule encompasses disserving statements by a declarant that would have probative value in a trial against the declarant").

In fact situations similar to *Harwood*, other courts have found statements exculpating a defendant to be sufficiently disserving to the declarant. *See, e.g.*, *United States v. Barrett*, 539 F.2d 244 (1st Cir. 1976) (statement that Buzzy was not at the robbery inculpates the declarant due to the implication that the declarant was at the robbery). These courts reason that when the declarant says that the defendant was not involved, he is implicitly stating that he, the declarant, *was* involved. This reasoning is, we think in harmony with the permissive language of the Rule.

It is true that McKee did not explicitly state that Harwood was never involved in the drug transaction. He said, more colloquially, that Harwood was in the wrong place at the wrong time. But certainly, a reasonable person in the declarant's position would know what could be taken from that statement. Given the oblique and coded manner in which most people talk in real life, it is unreasonable to limit Rule 804(b)(3) to explicit statements admitting guilt. We think that the Rule was designed for real life, and was not intended to be limited to the statements of masters of locution or students of English composition.

All this is not to say that the context in which a statement is made is irrelevant. A statement that appears to be highly incriminating on its face may in fact be either neutral or self-serving depending on the context in which it was made. For example, in *United States v. Silverstein*, 732 F.2d 1338 (7th Cir. 1984), the defendant was charged with murdering a prison guard. He proffered a statement from another prisoner who confessed to the murder. However, the Court found that the statement was not sufficiently disserving because the declarant was already serving three consecutive life sentences — "and what would a fourth consecutive life sentence add to the three previous ones?" In addition, there was evidence that the declarant was a sympathizer with the prison gang to which the defendant belonged. Accordingly, the Court, correctly we think, held that the statement was only facially and not contextually disserving, and thus was inadmissible even under the liberal "tendency" test set forth in the Rule. *See also United States v. Albert*, 773 F.2d 386 (1st Cir. 1985) (codefendant's statement accepting total responsibility for a crime was not admissible to exculpate the defendant; the statement was taken at the time of the codefendant's sentencing, at which point the codefendant had a self-interest in accepting responsibility).

2. How is the "corroborating circumstances" requirement of the rule to be applied?

Professors Saltzburg, Martin, and Capra, *Federal Rules of Evidence Manual* (9th ed. 2006), analyze the corroborating circumstances requirement of Rule 804(b)(3) as follows:

> If the defendant in a criminal case offers evidence of a declaration against penal interest to exculpate himself, he must make a showing that corroborating circumstances exist that "clearly indicate the trustworthiness of the statements." By the terms of the Rule, there is no corroborating circumstances requirement for statements against the declarant's pecuniary interest. Such a statement is admissible upon a showing that it so tends to disserve the declarant's pecuniary interest that a reasonable person would not have made the statement unless it were true.
>
> The mere fact that the statement could tend to subject the declarant to criminal liability is not enough if the accused offers it in his favor; the accused must also show other factors supporting the truthfulness of the statement. *See, e.g., United States v. Dean*, 59 F.3d 1479 (5th Cir. 1995) (finding no error in the Trial Court's exclusion of a hearsay statement by the defendants' accomplice, made during the accomplice's plea negotiations, and which exculpated the defendants; the statement was not sufficiently corroborated; the fact that the accomplice admitted guilt did not preclude others' guilt; the statement contained many questionable claims; and the evidence of the defendants' involvement in the crime was strong). This is apparently an attempt to respond to the problem of one criminal of dubious credibility trying to exculpate another. *See, e.g., United States v. Mackey*, 117 F.3d 24 (1st Cir. 1997)

(justifying the corroborating circumstances requirement in light of the possibility that "one criminal can make out-of-court statements exculpating another and then rather easily claim the privilege when the government seeks to cross-examine him to discredit the statement").

Rule 804(b)(3) does not purport to define "corroborating circumstances." The Advisory Committee on Evidence Rules once considered an amendment to Rule 804(b)(3), and the Advisory Committee Note to the proposed amendment provides a helpful discussion of the corroborating circumstances requirement. That discussion proceeds as follows:

> The Committee notes that there has been some confusion over the meaning of the "corroborating circumstances" requirement. *See United States v. Garcia*, 897 F.2d 1413, 1420 (7th Cir. 1990) ("the precise meaning of the corroboration requirement in rule 804(b)(3) is uncertain"). For example, some courts look to whether independent evidence supports or contradicts the declarant's statement. *See, e.g., United State v. Mines*, 894 F.2d 403 (4th Cir. 1990) (corroborating circumstances requirement not met because other evidence contradicts the declarant's account). Other courts hold that independent evidence is irrelevant and the court must focus only on the circumstances under which the statement was made. *See, e.g., United States v. Barone*, 114 F.3d 1284, 1300 (1st Cir. 1997) ("The corroboration that is required by Rule 804(b)(3) is not independent evidence supporting the truth of the matters asserted by the hearsay statements, but evidence that clearly indicates that the statements are worthy of belief, based upon the circumstances in which the statements were made."). The case law identifies some factors that may be useful to consider in determining whether corroborating circumstances clearly indicate the trustworthiness of the statement. Those factors include (*see, e.g., United States v. Bumpass*, 60 F.3d 1099, 1102 (4th Cir. 1995)):
>
> (1) the timing and circumstances under which the statement was made;
>
> (2) the declarant's motive in making the statement and whether there was a reason for the declarant to lie;
>
> (3) whether the declarant repeated the statement and did so consistently, even under different circumstances;
>
> (4) the party or parties to whom the statement was made;
>
> (5) the relationship between the declarant and the opponent of the evidence; and
>
> (6) the nature and strength of independent evidence relevant to the conduct in question.
>
> Other factors may be pertinent under the circumstances. The credibility of the witness who relates the statement in court is not, however, a proper factor for the court to consider in assessing corroborating circumstances. To base admission or exclusion of a hearsay statement on the credibility of the witness would usurp the

jury's role in assessing the credibility of testifying witnesses. *United States v. Katsougrakis*, 715 F.2d 769 (2d Cir. 1985).

The corroborating circumstances requirement assumes that the court has already found that the hearsay statement is genuinely disserving of the declarant's penal interest. *See Williamson v. United States*, 512 U.S. 594, 603 (1994) (statement must be "squarely self-inculpatory" to be admissible under Rule 804(b)(3)). "Corroborating circumstances" therefore must be independent from the fact that the statement tends to subject the declarant to criminal liability. The "against penal interest" factor should not be double-counted as a corroborating circumstance.

Neither the text of Rule 804(b)(3) nor the legislative history is precise on the *degree* of corroboration required. Some courts have construed the "clearly indicating trustworthiness" requirement very strictly, demanding that "the inference of trustworthiness from the proffered corroborating circumstances must be strong, not merely allowable." *United States v. Salvador*, 820 F.2d 558 (2d Cir. 1987) (independent evidence must corroborate both the declarant's trustworthiness and the truth of the statement). *See also United States v. Silverstein*, 732 F.2d 1338 (7th Cir. 1984) (the fact that the declarant had the opportunity to commit the crime with which the defendant was charged "was not *clearly* corroborative of his confession, but merely consistent with it"); *United States v. McDonald*, 688 F.2d 224 (4th Cir. 1982) (statement by a declarant that she was involved in the murder of the defendant doctor's family was not sufficiently corroborated, in part because the declarant was a drug addict, even though the defendant's claim was that his family was killed by drug addicts looking for drugs in his home).

Other courts, in consideration of the defendant's constitutional right to due process and an effective defense, have refused to apply the corroboration requirement in so strict a manner. *See, e.g.*, *United States v. Barrett*, 539 F.2d 244 (1st Cir. 1976) (noting that because of constitutional concerns, the standard for corroboration cannot be so strict "as to be utterly unrealistic").

We believe that the burden placed on the accused has in many cases been too high — so high that the exception itself often has little utility. It makes no sense to apply the corroboration standard so strictly that, if the defendant can meet it, he will probably never have been charged or tried in the first place.

On the other hand, the defendant's own protestations of innocence cannot be deemed sufficient corroboration; if that were enough, the corroboration requirement would be read out of the Rule as a practical matter. *See, e.g.*, *United States v. Rodriguez*, 706 F.2d 31 (2d Cir. 1983) (a statement is not admissible where the only corroboration is the defendant's own statements).

3. Does the corroborating circumstances requirement apply to declarations against penal interest offered by the government?

See Saltzburg, Martin, and Capra, *Federal Rules of Evidence Manual* (9th ed. 2006):

> Rule 804(b)(3) is striking in its asymmetry. Assume that three people are allegedly involved in a drug conspiracy — Declarant, who is now dead, and Bill and Mike, who are being tried separately. Assume further that Declarant told a friend that he and Bill were selling the drugs as a two-person team. Under the plain meaning of the Rule, assuming this entire statement in context is disserving to Declarant's penal interest, it would be admissible against Bill without more. However, Mike would have to provide corroborating circumstances supporting the trustworthiness of the statement before it could be admitted in his favor. Thus, the Rule on its face imposes an evidentiary burden on the accused, to which the prosecution is not subject for the same statement.
>
> Congress gave no explanation for its discriminatory application of the corroborating circumstances requirement of Rule 804(b)(3). * * * Commentators have argued that it violates due process and equal protection to impose an evidentiary burden on the defendant, but not on the state, for the same statement. *See, e.g.*, Tague, *Perils of the Rulemaking Process: The Development, Application, and Unconstitutionality of Rule 804(b)(3)'s Penal Interest Exception*, 69 Geo. L.J. 851, 990 (1981) (arguing that due process and equal protection are violated by an asymmetrical corroborating circumstances requirement). If anything, the admissibility requirements for a declaration against penal interest should be applied more strictly against the prosecution than against the defendant. The defendant has both a right to confront adverse witnesses, and a right to compulsory process for favorable witnesses. This should mean that as a general matter the defendant should receive at least some slight benefit of the doubt in excluding hearsay offered by the prosecution and in admitting hearsay offered by the defense.
>
> These arguments have led some courts to impose a corroborating circumstances requirement for *all* declarations against penal interest, whether they are offered by the prosecution or the defense. *See, e.g.*, *United States v. Barone*, 114 F.3d 1284 (1st Cir. 1997) (applying a corroborating circumstances requirement for statements offered by the prosecution under Rule 804(b)(3), while noting that the Rule "does not explicitly require" corroboration for such statements); *United States v. Garcia*, 897 F.2d 1413 (7th Cir. 1990) (requiring corroborating circumstances for inculpatory declarations against penal interest); *United States v. Alvarez*, 584 F.2d 694 (5th Cir. 1978) (noting that "by transplanting the language governing exculpatory statements onto the analysis for admitting inculpatory hearsay, a unitary standard is derived which offers the most workable basis for applying Rule 804(b)(3)").

The problem is that a symmetrical application of the Rule, though reasonable, is contrary to the plain meaning of the Rule; and as indicated in *Salerno*, the Court construes the Rules by their plain meaning without regard to whether they are fair in application — at least so long as the unfairness does not approach absurdity or unconstitutionality. In light of the plain meaning mandate of the Supreme Court cases, some Courts have felt constrained to hold that declarations against penal interest need not be corroborated when offered by the prosecution. *See, e.g., United States v. Bakhtiar*, 994 F.2d 970 (2d Cir. 1993) (an inculpatory declaration against interest was properly admitted even without a showing of corroboration).

The Advisory Committee considered an amendment to Rule 804(b)(3) that would have applied a corroborating circumstances requirement to government-offered statements. But this proposal was ultimately rejected due to strong opposition from the Justice Department. The Department argued that it already had an evidentiary burden beyond that set forth in the Rule — specifically the requirement that the hearsay statement satisfy not only the text of the Rule but also the accused's right to confrontation. The argument was that it would be unduly burdensome to saddle the government with a third evidentiary requirement of corroborating circumstances. This argument no longer has relevance, however, because the Supreme Court has changed the meaning of the Confrontation Clause in *Crawford v. Washington*. As applied to Rule 804(b)(3), *Crawford* means that if a declaration against interest is "non-testimonial" there is no extra requirement of reliability beyond that required by the hearsay exception. So perhaps the proposal to add a corroborating circumstances requirement for against-interest statements offered by the prosecution will be revived.

Another question is whether corroborating circumstances should be required when a declaration against penal interest is offered in civil cases. The Rule does not by its terms require such a showing. Yet at least one Court has held that the requirement must be met. In *American Automotive Accessories, Inc. v. Fishman*, 175 F.3d 534 (7th Cir. 1999), the Court found it important to have a "unitary standard" for declarations against penal interest, no matter in what case and no matter by whom they are offered.

4. Can statements implicating the accused ever be admitted under Rule 804(b)(3) after *Williamson*?

When considering the admissibility of statements of accomplices offered against the accused, lower courts after *Williamson* have tended to distinguish between statements made to police officers in custody (*i.e.*, those found inadmissible in *Williamson*) and statements made to others before the declarant has been arrested. Statements implicating others made to police officers have been found neutral or self-serving, given their context and the likelihood that the declarant may be simply shifting blame or currying favor with law enforcement. Indeed, the very facts and result in *Williamson* indicate that it is not disserving to the declarant to implicate others by name in a post-arrest confession. *See, e.g., United States v. McCleskey*, 228 F.3d 640 (6th Cir. 2000) (statement by declarant implicating the defendant, made to police officers after arrest, was erroneously admitted; the statement was not admissible under Rule 804(b)(3) because of "the incentive brought to bear upon such an accomplice to shift and spread blame to other persons").

On the other hand, if the statement is made outside the context of a post-custodial confession, courts are more likely to assume that a statement identifying another as taking part in a crime tends to implicate the declarant as well. A good example is *United States v. Moses*, 148 F.3d 277 (3d Cir. 1998). Moses was a County official who allegedly accepted kickbacks from Gaudelli, a commercial vendor who did business with the County. Moses challenged the admissibility of Gaudelli's statements implicating Moses in the kickback scheme. At the trial, Gaudelli was unavailable, and Gaudelli's friend and colleague testified that Gaudelli said on several occasions that he was "taking care" of Moses "moneywise." The court held that those statements directly implicating Moses were also self-inculpatory of Gaudelli, and therefore were properly admitted under Rule 804(b)(3). The court analyzed the impact of *Williamson* as follows:

> Under *Williamson,* the proper approach in cases involving out-of-court statements implicating other people is to examine the circumstances in which the statements are made in order to determine whether they are self-inculpatory or self-serving. In *Williamson*, where the declarant implicated another person while in police custody and after already having confessed to the crime, the Court concluded that the naming of the defendant did little to further implicate the declarant and may have been an effort to secure a lesser punishment through cooperation. *See also United States v. Boyce,* 849 F.2d 833, 836 (3d Cir. 1988) (statement given in custody not reliable because circumstances indicated that it may have been "motivated by a desire to curry favor"). In the instant case, by contrast, Gaudelli made his statements to a friend during lunch conversations that took place long before Gaudelli was arrested. Under these circumstances, there is no reason to believe that Gaudelli was trying to avoid criminal consequences by passing blame to Moses. Moreover, by naming Moses, as well as the place where he was meeting Moses to make payments, Gaudelli provided self-inculpatory information that might have enabled the authorities to better investigate his wrongdoing. *See Williamson* (explaining that a declarant's statement as to where he hid a gun would be self-inculpatory "if it is likely to help the police find the murder weapon").

Thus, Gaudelli's statement "I am paying off Moses" tends to inculpate Gaudelli more than a statement like "I am paying kickbacks." The specific identification of Moses, as opposed to anyone else, would make it easier for the police to investigate the crime and prosecute Gaudelli if they ever received the information. Moreover, by identifying Moses, who was a government official, Gaudelli implicated himself in a more serious crime of bribery than if he simply admitted making kickbacks to an unidentified person.

See also United States v. Tocco, 200 F.3d 401 (6th Cir. 2000) (in a RICO prosecution of a Mafia leader, it was not error to admit statements made by another Mafia leader to his son that described the roles of the declarant, the defendant and others in the organization; the statements were not inadmissible simply because they identified someone other than the declarant; the declarant's statements linked him to specific coconspirators and thus were against his own penal interest, especially since the statements were not made with the hope of implicating others to gain favor with the police).

In contrast, if the specific identification of Moses occurred in Gaudelli's post-arrest interview, it could not be deemed inculpatory of Gaudelli. Once Gaudelli has been arrested, the incentive to curry favor with authorities would outweigh any self-inculpatory possibility of any statement that could be offered against Moses.

[5] Family History

[a] Federal Rule of Evidence 804(b)(4)

Rule 804. Hearsay Exceptions; Declarant Unavailable

* * *

(b) Hearsay exceptions. The following are not excluded by the hearsay rule if the declarant is unavailable as a witness.

* * *

(4) Statement of personal or family history. (A) A statement concerning the declarant's own birth, adoption, marriage, divorce, legitimacy, relationship by blood, adoption, or marriage, ancestry, or other similar fact of personal or family history, even though declarant had no means of acquiring personal knowledge of the matter stated; or (B) a statement concerning the foregoing matters, and death also, of another person, if the declarant was related to the other by blood, adoption, or marriage or was so intimately associated with the other's family as to be likely to have accurate information concerning the matter declared.

[6] Forfeiture by Wrongdoing

[a] Federal Rule of Evidence 804(b)(6)

Rule 804. Hearsay Exceptions; Declarant Unavailable

* * *

(b) Hearsay exceptions. The following are not excluded by the hearsay rule if the declarant is unavailable as a witness.

* * *

(6) Forfeiture by wrongdoing. A statement offered against a party that has engaged or acquiesced in wrongdoing that was intended to, and did, procure the unavailability of the declarant as a witness.

[b] Standards for Finding Forfeiture by Wrongdoing

UNITED STATES v. CHERRY
217 F.3d 811 (10th Cir. 2000)

LUCERO, CIRCUIT JUDGE:

This interlocutory appeal from the district court's grant of a motion to suppress out-of-court statements made by a murdered witness requires us to address the difficult question of how the doctrine of waiver by misconduct and Fed. R. Evid. 804(b)(6) apply to defendants who did not themselves directly procure the unavailability of a witness, but allegedly participated in a conspiracy, one of the members of which murdered the witness. [W]e conclude that co-conspirators can be deemed to have waived confrontation and hearsay objections as a result of certain actions that are in furtherance, within the scope, and reasonably foreseeable as a necessary or natural consequence of an ongoing conspiracy. We therefore remand to the district court for findings under our newly-enunciated standard.

I

The government charged five defendants with involvement in a drug conspiracy: Joshua Price ("Joshua"), Michelle Cherry, LaDonna Gibbs, Teresa Price ("Price"), and Sonya Parker. Much of the evidence in their case came from a cooperating witness, Ebon Sekou Lurks. Prior to trial, however, Lurks was murdered. The government moved to admit out-of-court statements by Lurks, pursuant to Fed. R. Evid. 804(b)(6), on the grounds that the defendants wrongfully procured Lurks's unavailability.

In support of their motion, the government offered the following evidence. Lurks's ex-wife told Joshua of Lurks's cooperation with the government in retaliation for his obtaining custody of the Lurks' children. After this, Lurks reported being followed by Joshua and by Price. Approximately one week later, Price arranged to borrow a car from a friend, Beatrice Deffebaugh * * *. Joshua picked up Deffebaugh's car, which a witness noticed near Lurks' home at around 10 p.m on January 28, 1998. One of Joshua's girlfriends, Kenesha Colbert, testified to receiving a call from him around 10:40 p.m. and hearing Price's voice singing in the background.

Around 11 p.m., several shots were fired in the vicinity of Lurks's home. Two witnesses saw a tall, thin black man (a description consistent with Joshua Price's appearance) chasing a short, stout black man (a description consistent with Lurks's appearance). Another witness stated she saw a car in the vicinity of Lurks's home, resembling the one borrowed by Joshua and Price, immediately after hearing shots fired. Additionally, one witness reported a license plate for the vehicle identical to that of the vehicle borrowed from Deffebaugh, save for the inversion of two digits. Police found Lurks's body not long after midnight. Price returned the borrowed car to her friend between midnight and 12:30 a.m. on January 29, 1998. Further investigation discovered physical evidence linking Joshua to the murder: "debris" on Joshua's tennis shoes matching Lurks's DNA.

The district court held that Joshua procured the absence of Lurks and hence Lurks's statements were admissible against him. It held, however, that there was insufficient evidence that Price procured Lurks's absence and "absolutely no evidence [that Cherry, Gibbs, and Parker] had actual knowledge of, agreed to or participated in the murder of * * * Lurks." The district court therefore refused to find that those defendants had waived their Confrontation Clause and hearsay objections to the admission of Lurks's statements.

II

* * *

A. Rule 804(b)(6) and the Waiver by Misconduct Doctrine

The Confrontation Clause of the Sixth Amendment protects a criminal defendant's "fundamental right" to confront the witnesses against him or her, including the right to cross-examine such witnesses. "There is a presumption against the waiver of constitutional rights, and for a waiver to be effective it must be clearly established that there was an intentional relinquishment or abandonment of a known right or privilege."

The Supreme Court has held repeatedly that a defendant's intentional misconduct can constitute waiver of Confrontation Clause rights. We have applied this principle to conclude that a defendant can waive confrontation rights by threatening a witness's life. "To permit the defendant to profit from such conduct would be contrary to public policy, common sense and the underlying purpose of the confrontation clause."

The recently-promulgated Rule 804(b)(6) of the Federal Rules of Evidence represents the codification, in the context of the federal hearsay rules, of this long-standing doctrine of waiver by misconduct. Although prior to Rule 804(b)(6), there was disagreement as to the proper burden of proof in making a showing of waiver by misconduct, it was established in this Circuit that, "before permitting the admission of grand jury testimony of witnesses who will not appear at trial because of the defendant's alleged coercion, the judge must hold an evidentiary hearing in the absence of the jury and find by a preponderance of the evidence that the defendant's coercion made the witness unavailable." The district court was correct in applying the same burden — preponderance of the evidence — and procedure in a case under the similar terms of Rule 804(b)(6). *See* Fed. R. Evid. 804(b)(6) advisory committee's note ("The usual Rule 104(a) preponderance of the evidence standard has been adopted in light of the behavior new Rule 804(b)(6) seeks to discourage.").

At issue in the instant case is whether Rule 804(b)(6) and the Confrontation Clause permit a finding of waiver based not on direct procurement but rather on involvement in a conspiracy, one of the members of which wrongfully procured a witness's unavailability. The government argues that under the principle of conspiratorial liability articulated in *Pinkerton v. United States*, 328 U.S. 640 (1946), defendants-appellees are responsible for the murder of Lurks as a foreseeable result of the drug conspiracy in which they were allegedly involved, and they thereby waive their Confrontation Clause and hearsay objections to his out-of-court statements.

* * *

[We] read the plain language of Rule 804(b)(6) to permit the admission of those hearsay statements that would be admissible under the constitutional doctrine of waiver by misconduct, and hold that, in the context of criminal proceedings, the Rule permits the admission of hearsay statements by unavailable witnesses against defendants if those statements are otherwise admissible under the doctrine of waiver by misconduct. Our analysis of whether and under what circumstances waiver can be imputed under that doctrine and the acquiescence prong of the Rule is guided by two important but sometimes conflicting principles: the right to confrontation is "a fundamental right essential to a fair trial in a criminal prosecution"; and "courts will not suffer a party to profit by his own wrongdoing."

B. *Pinkerton* Conspiratorial Liability

The government urges us to adopt the principles of conspiratorial liability enunciated in *Pinkerton v. United States*, 328 U.S. 640 (1946), in the context of Rule 804(b)(6) and the Confrontation Clause waiver-by-misconduct doctrine. The *Pinkerton* Court held that evidence of direct participation in a substantive offense is not necessary for criminal liability under the principles holding conspirators liable for the substantive crimes of the conspiracy: "The overt act of one partner in crime is attributable to all * * * . If that can be supplied by the act of one conspirator, we fail to see why the same or other acts in furtherance of the conspiracy are likewise not attributable to the others for the purpose of holding them responsible for the substantive offense."

> This Circuit has * * * described *Pinkerton* liability as follows:
>
> During the existence of a conspiracy, each member of the conspiracy is legally responsible for the crimes of fellow conspirators. Of course, a conspirator is only responsible for the crimes of the conspirators that are committed in furtherance of the conspiracy. As stated by the Supreme Court, conspirators are responsible for crimes committed "within the scope of the unlawful project" and thus "reasonably foreseen as a necessary or natural consequence of the unlawful agreement."

* * * *Pinkerton's* formulation of conspiratorial liability is an appropriate mechanism for assessing whether the actions of another can be imputed to a defendant for purposes of determining whether that defendant has waived confrontation and hearsay objections. It would make little sense to limit forfeiture of a defendant's trial rights to a narrower set of facts than would

be sufficient to sustain a conviction and corresponding loss of liberty. Therefore, we conclude that the acquiescence prong of Fed. R. Evid. 804(b)(6), consistent with the Confrontation Clause, permits consideration of a *Pinkerton* theory of conspiratorial responsibility in determining wrongful procurement of witness unavailability, and we turn to waiver-by-misconduct case law to define the precise contours of such responsibility.

C. Conspiratorial Responsibility and "Acquiescence" Under Rule 804(b)(6)

* * *

Based on our balancing of the aims of the Confrontation Clause with the grave evil the well-established waiver-by-misconduct rule aims to prevent, we hold that the following interpretation of the "acquiescence" prong of Rule 804(b)(6) is consistent with the Confrontation Clause:

A defendant may be deemed to have waived his or her Confrontation Clause rights (and, a fortiori, hearsay objections) if a preponderance of the evidence establishes one of the following circumstances: (1) he or she participated directly in planning or procuring the declarant's unavailability through wrongdoing; or (2) the wrongful procurement was in furtherance, within the scope, and reasonably foreseeable as a necessary or natural consequence of an ongoing conspiracy.

D. Application of Rule 804(b)(6)

We therefore examine the district court's order in light of our newly-elucidated standard. We conclude the district court did not abuse its discretion in holding that the government failed to show by a preponderance of the evidence that any of the defendants directly participated in the execution of the murder, but remand for application of the planning and *Pinkerton* tests. We take this opportunity to note that, even if the district court finds the standard for waiver by acquiescence to be met for some or all appellees, and thereby their Confrontation Clause and hearsay objections to be forfeited, the district court is still free to consider concerns of weighing prejudice against probative value under Fed. R. Evid. 403.

1. Scope of Conspiracy, Furtherance, and Reasonable Foreseeability as a Necessary and Natural Consequence

* * * [T]he district court concluded that "the mere fact [that defendants] may have participated in the drug conspiracy did not constitute a waiver of [their] constitutional confrontation rights." This statement is correct, as far as it goes. However, today we hold that participation in an ongoing drug conspiracy may constitute a waiver of constitutional confrontation rights if the following additional circumstances are present: the wrongdoing leading to the unavailability of the witness was in furtherance of and within the scope of the drug conspiracy, and such wrongdoing was reasonably foreseeable as a "necessary or natural" consequence of the conspiracy. We therefore remand

to the district court for findings on the *Pinkerton* factors as to Lurks's murder: whether it was in furtherance and within the scope of the conspiracy, and whether it was reasonably foreseeable as a necessary or natural consequence of that conspiracy. We note that the scope of the conspiracy is not necessarily limited to a primary goal — such as bank robbery — but can also include secondary goals relevant to the evasion of apprehension and prosecution for that goal — such as escape, or, by analogy, obstruction of justice. We further reiterate that, under *Pinkerton*, a defendant is not responsible for the acts of co-conspirators if that defendant meets the burden of proving he or she took affirmative steps to withdraw from the conspiracy before those acts were committed.

We note that the district court found "there is absolutely no evidence" that defendants Cherry, Gibbs, and Parker (although not Teresa Price) "had actual knowledge of, agreed to or participated in the murder of Ebon Sekou Lurks." After complete review of the record, we conclude that this finding of fact is not clearly erroneous. It does not, however, foreclose the possibility of waiver under a *Pinkerton* theory. Actual knowledge is not required for conspiratorial waiver by misconduct if the elements of *Pinkerton* — scope, furtherance, and reasonable foreseeability as a necessary or natural consequence — are satisfied. A defendant's actual knowledge of a co-conspirator's intent to murder a witness in order to prevent discovery or prosecution of the conspiracy may prove relevant to those elements.

2. Planning

Although the district court found the evidence was "insufficient to show that by a preponderance of the evidence the Defendant Teresa Price procured the absence of Ebon Sekou Lurks," it did not discuss whether the evidence that she obtained the car used in Lurks's murder under false pretenses, combined with her apparent proximity to Joshua around the time of the murder, would be sufficient circumstantial evidence to support a finding that she participated in the planning of the murder. We therefore remand for specific findings on whether the government can meet its burden of showing that Price participated in the planning of Lurks's murder so as to permit a finding of waiver by misconduct. * * *

III

To summarize, we remand to the district court for findings on the following issues: (1) did Teresa Price participate in the planning or carrying out of Lurks's murder by Joshua Price; (2) was Joshua Price's murder of Lurks within the scope, in furtherance, and reasonably foreseeable as a necessary or natural consequence, of an ongoing drug distribution conspiracy involving the defendants? The district court's order is REVERSED and REMANDED for proceedings consistent with this opinion.

[The dissenting opinion of JUDGE HOLLOWAY is omitted.]

NOTE

Can forfeiture by misconduct be applied to anyone other than a criminal defendant?

Any party who causes or acquiesces in wrongdoing with the intent to render a declarant unavailable forfeits the right to object to the unavailable declarant's hearsay statement. So, for example, if a prosecutor intentionally intimidates a defense witness so that the witness refuses to testify, the prosecution loses the right to interpose a hearsay objection with respect to any statement that the witness may have made. The same goes for parties in civil cases.

PROBLEM 12-1

The plaintiff, Real Estate Agent I, sues the defendant, Home Owner, to collect a real estate commission. Home Owner defends on the theory that he had a real estate sales contract with Real Estate Agent II, not Real Estate Agent I, and owes the commission to Real Estate Agent II, if anyone.

Plaintiff calls a bartender to the stand.

Plaintiff:	Do you know Real Estate Agent II?
Bartender:	Yes, very well.
Plaintiff:	Did you ever have a discussion with him about a real estate contract between Home Owner and Real Estate Agent II?
Bartender:	Yes. Right there at my bar.
Plaintiff:	What did he say?
Defendant:	(1) Objection! ________.
The court:	Well, let me hear the statement first. Then I'll rule.
Bartender:	He said, "Homeowner and I almost had an agreement signed, but then he backed out. All that work I did was for nothing. Somebody is going to get a big commission off that sale."
The court:	How do you respond to the defendant's objection?
Plaintiff:	(2) ________.
Defendant:	(3) I also object because ________.
The court:	(4) ________.
Plaintiff:	Your Honor, I have here a certified copy from the Bureau of Vital Statistics of the death certificate of Real Estate Agent II. It shows that he died last week.
The court:	(5) ________.

PROBLEM 12-2

The plaintiff, Dog Owner, sues the defendant, Next Door Neighbor, for the value of his dog, which he alleges the defendant poisoned. Neighbor defends on the theory that a third party, Dog Hater, poisoned the dog.

Defendant calls Dog Hater to the stand.

Defendant:	State your name.
Witness:	Dog Hater.
Defendant:	Do you know Dog Owner?
Witness:	I refuse to answer.
Defendant:	Let me ask you again. Do you know Dog Owner?
Witness:	Are you deaf? I said I refuse to answer.
Defendant:	Your Honor, would you instruct the witness to answer the question?
The court:	Mr. Hater, you are ordered to answer the question or I'll find you in contempt of court.
Witness:	Go for it, Judge; I've got my rights.
The court:	Are you asserting your privilege under the 5th Amendment?
Witness:	You bet.
Defendant:	Your Honor, this witness obviously is not going to answer questions. So we ask that he be deemed unavailable.
Plaintiff:	I object. He's obviously available or he wouldn't be here. The Supreme Court said in the Owens case that a witness is available if he is present in court and can be asked questions.
The court:	(1) _________.

Defendant calls a bartender.

Defendant:	Do you know Dog Hater?
Witness:	Yes.
Defendant:	Did he talk to you about Dog Owner's dog?
Witness:	He sure did.
Defendant:	What did he say?
Plaintiff:	(2) Objection! _________.
The court:	Let me hear the statement.
Witness:	He said, "That damn dog barked its head off so I poisoned the son of a bitch." Then he laughed real loud.
The court:	What is the basis for your objection?
Plaintiff:	As I said, it's a hearsay statement, obviously offered for its truth, and we have no opportunity to cross-examine the declarant.
Defendant:	(3) _________.
The court:	(4) _________.

Assume the same facts as in the last problem, except that this time Neighbor has been charged with the crime of cruelty to animals.

Assume that the colloquy is the same, except for the substitution of Prosecutor for Plaintiff, as in the civil suit until the end, when the following exchange occurs:

The court:	What is the basis for your objection?
Prosecutor:	As I said, it's a hearsay statement, obviously offered for its truth, and we have no opportunity to cross-examine the declarant.
Defendant:	It's a declaration against interest.
Prosecutor:	(5) ________.
The court:	(6) ________.

PROBLEM 12-3

In the following example, has the defendant established that the declarant is unavailable in either the civil or criminal case arising from the dog poisoning?

Defendant:	Your Honor, we tried to subpoena the witness Mr. Hater at the address listed in the telephone book, but it was returned by the Marshal with a notation that the witness no longer lived at that address. Here is the Marshal's return.
Plaintiff:	When was the attempt to serve the subpoena made?
Defendant:	Three days ago.
Plaintiff:	It should have been served long before that. This is not an adequate effort.
The court:	Does either party have an address for the witness?
Defendant:	No.
Plaintiff:	No.
The court:	________.

PROBLEM 12-4

Plaintiff sues defendant Hot Foot, Inc. in a civil action for severe injuries sustained when the inflatable tennis shoes he bought from Hot Foot exploded during a 360-degree dunk. The inflatable style shoe was originally developed by High Dunk, Inc. High Dunk has a patent on the design, and Hot Foot produces its shoes pursuant to a license from High Dunk. There is no other corporate connection between the two corporations. High Dunk was sued in a similar incident. At that trial, the chief engineer testified, "We should have warned people about blow-out during 360-degree slam dunks." The parties stipulate that the chief engineer has retired on the island of Bonaire.

Plaintiff: Your Honor, at this time we would like to introduce the trial testimony of the chief engineer of High Dunk, Inc. that was given in a trial in this district two years ago.

Defendant: Objection! Hearsay.

Plaintiff: (1) ________.

Defendant: There's no showing this witness is unavailable. He could have been deposed.

The court: Could you have taken his deposition?

Plaintiff: We could have, but we chose not to.

The court: (2) ________.

Defendant: I further object that Hot Foot was not a party to the earlier litigation and had no opportunity to examine the chief engineer.

Plaintiff: High Dunk was a predecessor in interest, since it had the same motive and opportunity to examine the engineer in the earlier trial.

Defendant: Hot Foot and High Dunk are separate entities. They have no legal relationship to each other.

The court: How much was at stake in the litigation against High Dunk?

Plaintiff: The plaintiff in that case sought a million dollars in damages. And, I might add that there is a relationship between High Dunk and Hot Foot, since Hot Foot is a licensee of High Dunk and produces shoes pursuant to the licensing agreement.

The court: (3) ________.

PROBLEM 12-5

Mad Dog Ryan is charged with murdering his ex-partner, Findel Maskov. Maskov was found in the parking lot of an apartment building shot in the chest and head. Several days after the body was found, Detective Webb located an eyewitness, Ryan's ex-roommate, who told Webb that he saw Ryan shoot Maskov after an argument in the parking lot. A week before Ryan"s trial is to start, Webb receives an emergency call at 1 a.m. from the ex-roommate who says, "I've just been shot. Ryan was here, out on bail, and I'm not sure I'm going to make it." Webb calls an ambulance to the ex-roommate's apartment and goes there himself. When Webb and the ambulance arrive, the ex-roommate is dead. At Ryan's trial, the police call Webb to testify.

Prosecutor: What did you do to investigate the death of Maskov?

Webb: I tried to contact people who knew Maskov, and I came upon the defendant"s ex-roommate a couple of days after the body was found.

Prosecutor: Did the ex-roommate have any information about the death?

Webb: Yes, he said that he saw Maskov being shot.
Defense Counsel: Objection! Hearsay. Move to strike.
Prosecutor: We're showing the scope of the investigation and what Detective Webb learned. It's not hearsay.
Defense Counsel: It's not relevant unless it's offered for its truth.
Court: (1) _________.
Prosecutor: Do you know who shot Maskov?
Webb: The ex-roommate told me that the defendant shot Maskov after an argument in the parking lot.
Defense Counsel: Objection! Hearsay. Move to strike.
Prosecutor: This is clearly admissible under Rule 804(b)(6).
Defense Counsel: There is nothing in the testimony of this witness that satisfies the rule.
Prosecutor: Maskov is dead and is unavailable. Therefore the statement should be admitted.
Court: (2) _________.
Prosecutor: Let me lay the foundation, your Honor. Detective Webb, after your conversation with the ex-roommate a couple of days after the body was found, did you have occasion to speak with him again?
Defense Counsel: Objection! Hearsay.
Prosecution: That question cannot call for a hearsay answer.
Court: (3) _________.
Webb: Yes, he called me approximately a week ago.
Prosecutor: What were the circumstances?
Webb: I received an emergency call at 1 a.m. from the ex-roommate who said, "I've just been shot. Ryan was here, out on bail, and I'm not sure I'm going to make it."
Defense Counsel: Objection! Hearsay. Move to strike.
Prosecutor: It's a dying declaration. We proffer to the court that Detective Webb will testify that he called an ambulance to the ex-roommate's apartment and went there himself. When Webb and the ambulance arrived, the ex-roommate was dead.
Defense Counsel: It's blatant hearsay.
Court: (4) _________.
Defense Counsel: Objection! Moreover, it is irrelevant and extremely prejudicial. The crime charged is the murder of Maskov not the ex-roommate.
Prosecutor: It is highly probative and not unduly prejudicial.
Court: (5) _________.
Prosecutor: Now, I ask you again, Detective Webb, what did the ex-roommate tell you two days after Maskov's body was found.
Defense Counsel: Objection! Hearsay. This is still hearsay.

Prosecutor: Now it should be clear that this is admissible under Rule 804(b)(6).

Defense Counsel: We have a hearsay statement being used to bootstrap another hearsay statement. That is not permissible.

Court: (6) _________.

The prosecution calls Andi Malis to testify.

Prosecution: Did you know the deceased, Findel Maskov?

Malis: Yes, I knew him well. We served time together in a federal penitentiary and were housed in the same unit.

Prosecution: Do you know of any reason why the defendant would have wanted to kill Maskov?

Malis: Maskov was the defendant's illegitimate son, and Maskov wanted the defendant to bear some financial responsibility for Maskov.

Defense Counsel: Objection! This witness cannot know whether or not Maskov was the defendant's son.

Court: How do you know that Maskov was the defendant's son?

Malis: Maskov told me that several times when we were incarcerated together.

Defense Counsel: My objection stands, and I add that this is inadmissible hearsay. May I ask the witness two questions in support of my objection?

Court: Certainly.

Defense Counsel: Have you ever met the defendant or any member of Maskov's family?

Malis: No.

Defense Counsel: Do you have any way of knowing whether Maskov was telling you the truth?

Malis: No.

Defense Counsel: This is pure hearsay and unreliable.

Prosecution: It is admissible under Rule 804(b)(4).

Court: (7) _________.

Prosecutor: How do you know that Maskov intended to seek support from the defendant?

Malis: He told me several times in prison that he intended to do so as soon as he was released.

Defense Counsel: Objection! Hearsay. This is not part of family history.

Prosecutor: It's admissible.

Court: (8) _________.

As part of the defense case, Ryan calls a bookmaker friend to testify.

Defense Counsel: Did you know Maskov?

Bookmaker: Very well. He placed bets with me all the time.

Defense Counsel: Did you and he ever speak of the defendant?

Bookmaker:	Yes, I told him that there was a rumor that he was the defendant's son, and he told me that it was a lie and that the defendant was not his father.
Prosecutor:	Objection! Hearsay. Move to strike.
Defense Counsel:	It's a declaration against interest.
Prosecutor:	It's not clearly against interest.
Court:	(9) ________.
Defense Counsel:	Additionally, it's admissible under Rule 804 (b)(4).
Court:	(10) ________.
Defense Counsel:	Did you ever ask the defendant about Maskov?
Bookmaker:	I told him there was a rumor that he was Maskov's father, and he told me that it was a lie and that he had no relationship with Maskov.
Prosecutor:	Objection! Hearsay. Self-serving. Move to strike.
Defense Counsel:	We're back to Rule 804 (b)(4).
Court:	(11) ________.

PROBLEM 12-6

Plaintiff sues her brother to stop probate of a will in which their grandmother left everything to the brother. Plaintiff alleges that the will was procured by duress one month before the grandmother died.

Plaintiff calls the grandmother's private nurse to the stand.

Plaintiff:	Did you know the grandmother?
Nurse:	Yes, I cared for her at the hospice, and she passed away in my arms.
Plaintiff:	What was she suffering from?
Nurse:	Bad heart. She had been in critical condition for several days. The day she died her doctor came in and told her that she might not see the morning. When he left, the grandmother told me she knew she was dying.
Plaintiff:	Did she say anything to you just before she passed away?
Defendant:	Objection! Hearsay.
The court:	Let me hear it so I can rule.
Nurse:	She said, "Brother held a pillow over my head about a month ago to make me sign that will."
The court:	Counsel, what is the basis for your objection?
Defendant:	The statement is obviously hearsay; it is offered for its truth.
Plaintiff:	Sure sounds like a dying declaration to me. She knew she was dying.

Defendant:	This is a civil case, not a criminal case.
Plaintiff:	It doesn't matter.
The court:	(1) __________.
Defendant:	(2) I still object.__________.
The court:	(3) __________.
Plaintiff:	Did the grandmother say anything else to you before she died?
Defendant:	Objection! Hearsay.
The court:	I need to know the contents of the statement in order to rule.
Nurse:	She said, "I've had this heart problem for a long time. But, it was Brother's forcing me to make a will leaving Sister out that is killing me."
The court:	Defendant, do you still object?
Defendant:	Sure do, the testimony once again is hearsay; it is offered for its truth.
The court:	(4) __________.

Chapter 13

HEARSAY EXCEPTIONS NOT REQUIRING DECLARANT UNAVAILABILITY

A. PRESENT SENSE IMPRESSION

[1] Federal Rule of Evidence 803(1)

Rule 803. Hearsay Exceptions; Availability of Declarant Immaterial

The following are not excluded by the hearsay rule, even though the declarant is available as a witness:

(1) Present Sense Impression. A statement describing or explaining an event or condition made while the declarant was perceiving the event or condition, or immediately thereafter.

* * *

[2] Illustration

The defendant is charged with killing his wife. He defends on the theory that someone else did it and that he was not even home with her at the time of the killing. The defendant calls a good friend to the stand.

Defendant:	State your name.
Witness:	Good Buddy.
Defendant:	Do you know the victim in this case?
Witness:	Yes, for many years.
Defendant:	Do you recognize her voice?
Witness:	Yes, I've spoken to her many times in person and over the phone.
Defendant:	Did you have a phone conversation with her on the date of her death?
Witness:	Yes, at the exact time of her death.
Defendant:	What did she say?
Plaintiff:	Objection! That's hearsay.
The court:	Let me hear the answer, so that I can rule.
Witness:	Well, we talked for a little bit about who was going to pick the kids up at the park, and then she said, "Hang on just a minute, there's some stranger knocking on the door." I'm sure she could see from the phone that it was a stranger because there's a window by the phone. Anyway, she said, "Hang on a minute," but then she never came back to the phone.

The court:	Counsel, what is your response to the Plaintiff's objection?
Defendant:	________.

[3] Event, Perception, and Time Requirements

UNITED STATES v. BREWER
36 F.3d 266 (2d Cir. 1994)

MAHONEY, CIRCUIT JUDGE:

* * * Brewer was convicted for robbing a branch of Chemical Bank located at 1500 Forest Avenue, Staten Island, New York (the "Bank"), on January 30, 1992. The primary evidence against Brewer consisted of eyewitness identification testimony and evidence recovered from a gray 1987 Chevrolet Celebrity bearing New York license plate "G2J 801" (the "Car"). On this appeal, Brewer contends that * * * the district court erred in refusing to allow Brewer to elicit testimony from a government witness concerning five witnesses to the bank robbery who did not select Brewer's photograph from photo arrays that were presented to them.

Background

On January 30, 1992, three men robbed the Bank during the middle of the day and made off with approximately $ 95,000. During the robbery, one of the malefactors stood by the front door of the Bank displaying a large gun. Acting on information provided by Joseph Calvanese, a bank customer waiting at the bank's drive-through window during the robbery who followed the robbers as they fled in the car and then abandoned it for another vehicle, Special Agent Edward M. McCabe of the Federal Bureau of Investigation found and searched the Car. The search recovered numerous rounds of live ammunition, an empty ammunition box, an owner's manual for an AP-9 firearm, a hand-held radio, a police scanner, an economics textbook, a piece of cardboard, two pullover ski masks, and a copy of a book, the Holy Koran. An envelope was inserted between the book's pages, addressed to Anthony J. Brewer and containing a letter, a card, and a photograph, all signed by "Sherry Ann." Brewer's fingerprints were found on the Holy Koran, the envelope and the photograph inside it, the economics textbook, and the piece of cardboard. The car was registered to an individual named Abdul Mohammed, 190 Wilson Avenue, Brooklyn, New York, whose date of birth was listed as November 3, 1967. It was stipulated that Brewer's birth date was November 3, 1967, and that he had stated on a previous occasion that he resided at the Wilson Avenue address.

This evidence focused suspicion on Brewer, and led McCabe to include Brewer's photograph in one of four six-photograph arrays shown to several witnesses to the Bank robbery. On February 14, 1992, McCabe interviewed the various witnesses and had each of them view the arrays. Each array contained a photograph of a man whom McCabe suspected of participating in the bank robbery, and individual photographs of five other men of like appearance. One of these arrays included Brewer's photograph. Three Bank employees who had been present during the robbery, Kathleen Cassiliano, Marta Marrano, and Agnes Charzewski (collectively the "Identifying Witnesses"), selected the photograph of Brewer as "resembling" the robber who had been stationed at the front door of the Bank, holding the large gun. Five other eyewitnesses viewed the photo arrays and did not select Brewer's photograph (the "Nonidentifying Witnesses").

Brewer was indicted and charged with the three counts that led to his conviction and this appeal. On September 15, 1993, the Identifying Witnesses viewed a lineup of Brewer and five other men of the same general physical appearance, conducted at Brewer's request, but none of them identified anyone in the lineup as being one of the Bank robbers.

* * *

Brewer argues on appeal that he was improperly denied the opportunity to cross-examine McCabe concerning the failure of five eyewitnesses to the bank robbery to identify Brewer when shown the photo arrays. Brewer relies upon Fed. R. Evid. 803(1), the present sense impression exception to the hearsay rule, in support of his argument that he could elicit this testimony through McCabe, rather than through the witnesses themselves. The district court believed the situation to be controlled by Rule 801(d)(1)(C), and ruled that Brewer could only elicit this testimony by calling the witnesses themselves, which Brewer declined to do.

Under Rule 801(d)(1)(C), a statement of prior identification may be received in evidence only if "the declarant testifies at * * * trial * * * and is subject to cross-examination" concerning the prior identification. Although the rule is not precisely directed to testimony concerning a prior failure to identify, we believe that the purpose and policy of the rule fairly encompasses such situations, as well. Whether or not a prior out-of-court identification is successful, the reliability of, and weight to be accorded to, the evidence can best be assessed by having the declarant available for cross-examination.

Brewer contends, however, that the nonidentifications should have been admitted as a present sense impression through cross-examination of McCabe pursuant to Rule 803(1). Statements may be admitted pursuant to Rule 803(1) without examination of the declarant, "even though the declarant is available as a witness."

Brewer's own description of Rule 803(1) shows why his contention must fail. Quoting 4 Louisell, Federal Evidence § 438 (1980), Brewer describes the rationale of Rule 803(1) as follows: "Statements of present sense impression are considered reliable because the immediacy eliminates the concern for lack of memory and precludes time for intentional deception." The essence of an identification such as at a photo array or a lineup, however, is a comparison between what the witness is contemporaneously viewing and the witness's recollection of a prior event, in this case the bank robbery. As the district court aptly noted: "The heart of a photographic identification [is that] you are asking someone about their perception of a past event * * * . You are asking them to recall[,] by definition[,] what happened in the past." Brewer's characterization of observations made during the viewing of a photo array as "highly trustworthy because they were made simultaneously with the event being perceived, namely, the photo array," ignores the vital element of memory.

The two cases relied on by Brewer to support his contention that the nonidentifications come within Rule 803(1) are inapposite. In *United States v. Hinton*, 719 F.2d 711 (4th Cir. 1983), the court concluded that a police officer's "contemporaneous response" to a defendant's offer to "cop" to a particular charge came within Rule 803(1), and alternatively, that any error in admitting this statement was harmless. In *MCA, Inc. v. Wilson*, 425 F. Supp. 443, 450-51 (S.D.N.Y. 1976), modified, 677 F.2d 180 (2d Cir. 1981), a copyright infringement case in which the issue was "whether the allegedly infringing work is recognizable by ordinary observation as having been pirated from the copyrighted source," the court concluded that out-of-court declarants' immediate reactions to a musical work were admissible pursuant to Rule 803(1). The statements admitted in both cases were obviously contemporaneous with the events to which they related.

In this case, by contrast, the Nonidentifying Witnesses' memory was at issue, and that is precisely why the statements of nonidentification do not come within Rule 803(1). *See United States v. Parker*, 936 F.2d 950, 954 (7th Cir. 1991) ("The underlying rationale of the present sense impression exception is that substantial contemporaneity of event and statement minimizes unreliability due to defective recognition or conscious fabrication."); see also *In re Japanese Elec. Prods. Antitrust Litig.*, 723 F.2d 238, 303 (3d Cir. 1983) (exception for present sense impressions founded on notion that contemporaneity of observation and impression protect against defective memory), *rev'd on other grounds sub nom. Matsushita Elec. Indus. Co. v. Zenith Radio Corp.*, 475 U.S. 574 (1986).

Accordingly, once Brewer had made it clear that he would not be calling the Nonidentifying Witnesses to testify, the district court correctly concluded that Rule 803(1) did not permit Brewer to cross-examine McCabe about the Nonidentifying Witnesses' failure to identify Brewer.

Conclusion

The judgment of the district court is affirmed.

NOTES

1. How long is "immediately thereafter"?

While contemporaneity is critical to admissibility, there is in fact no talismanic time period for admission as a present sense impression. Admissibility is determined on a case by case basis, in which the court investigates the circumstances of the statement to determine whether the declarant had significant time for reflection. *See Hilyer v. Howat Concrete Co.*, 578 F.2d 422 (D.C. Cir. 1978) (statement made fifteen to forty-five minutes after event held not contemporaneous and thus inadmissible under Rule 803(1); but statement was admissible under Rule 803(2) because made under the stress of excitement). If there is no evidence, circumstantial or otherwise, as to the time lapse, there is no foundation to admit the statement. *See, e.g.*, *United States v. Cruz*, 765 F.2d 1020 (11th Cir. 1985) (statement by a deceased officer to his superiors concerning the source of a cocaine sample was inadmissible where it was unclear how much time passed between the receipt and the statement).

2. Must the offeror of evidence pursuant to this exception establish a foundation that the declarant perceived the event?

In *Meder v. Everest & Jennings, Inc.*, 637 F.2d 1182 (8th Cir. 1981), the Court held that the trial court properly refused testimony by a police officer about what he was told by a witness, because there was insufficient evidence that the witness had actually perceived the event. *See also Bemis v. Edwards*, 45 F.3d 1369 (9th Cir. 1995): Affirming a judgment for police officers alleged to have used excessive force, the court held that a 911 tape recounting the event was properly excluded because the citizen caller apparently lacked personal knowledge of the events which he was reporting. The court stated that "this requirement that a declarant have personal knowledge of the events described applies to the present sense impression exception," and observed that the proponent of a hearsay declaration has "the burden of establishing personal perception by a preponderance of the evidence."

3. Must the proponent of the hearsay statement provide corroborating evidence that the event occurred the way the declarant said it did?

Professors Saltzburg, Martin, and Capra, *Federal Rules of Evidence Manual* (9th ed. 2006), analyze the relationship between the present sense impression and corroboration as follows:

> Professor Waltz, in *The Present Sense Impression Exception to the Rule Against Hearsay: Origins and Attributes*, 66 Iowa L. Rev. 869 (1981), carefully traces the present sense impression from early American cases through the early Federal Rules decisions. He indicates that the history supports some sort of corroboration requirement for a present sense impression — that is, a requirement that before the statement is admitted, there must be evidence independent of the statement itself to prove that the event described actually occurred.
>
> Most federal courts are reading a corroboration requirement into Rule 803(1). The corroboration can be found in the in-court testimony of the declarant, or testimony of another person who also saw some of what the declarant saw, or simply circumstantial evidence that the event occurred. Imposing a corroboration requirement is a sensible approach. Under the plain language of the Rule, the proponent must show that the declaration was made at the time of, or immediately after, *an event*, and that the statements explained or described that event. To satisfy the timing, relationship, and event requirements, the witness in court is probably going to have to be able to corroborate to some extent that the event actually occurred, unless the declarant is present to so testify or there is some other source of corroboration. In the absence of some proof other than the hearsay statement itself,

a trial judge should conclude that the proponent has failed to prove by a preponderance of the evidence that the event occurred the way the declarant described it. Otherwise, the admissibility requirement is proved *solely* through the hearsay statement itself — something that is not allowed, for example, with coconspirator hearsay statements. *See* Rule 801(d)(2)(E). While the hearsay statement itself may certainly be considered as proof of the admissibility requirement that an event occurred (see Rule 104(a)), some corroboration must be provided for the statement to be admissible under Rule 803(1).

The Advisory Committee Note to Federal Rule 803(1) stresses that present sense impressions are reliable in large part because the witness who testifies to the declarant's statement "may be examined as to the circumstances" described by the declarant. This indicates that the drafters intended a corroboration requirement for this exception, i.e., that the person who heard the declarant's statement was also at the event and could give his own account of it at trial. But this statement should not be taken to mean that a present sense impression is only admissible if an in-court witness can testify that the event occurred exactly as the declarant described it. While a witness who was in the same position to view the event as the declarant would certainly be able to provide sufficient corroboration, a requirement of equal percipience would rob the Rule of much of its practical effect; the declarant's hearsay statement would to some extent be cumulative if the witness could provide the same statement in court. The Rule should be and has been construed to permit corroboration short of equally percipient testimony.

A case that illustrates the correct approach to the corroboration requirement is *United States v. Blakey*, 607 F.2d 779 (7th Cir. 1979). The defendants in *Blakey* were charged with extortion. The government offered the victim's hearsay statement that "stuff like tonight cost me a thousand dollars." The statement was made immediately after the victim and the three defendants came out from a short meeting in the back of the victim's shop. The defendants argued that the statement could not be admitted under Federal Rule 803(1) because there were no witnesses, other than the declarant and the defendants, to the relevant event — the purported exchange of $1000 in the back of the declarant's shop — and the declarant was no longer available to testify. The Court held, however, that the statement was properly admitted because "there were several witnesses who could testify to the events leading up to and following the meeting" in the back of the shop. These witnesses would testify that the defendants acted in a very intimidating manner before going to the back of the shop with the declarant, and that after the defendants and the declarant briefly met in the back of the shop, the defendants came out looking "satisfied." The Court concluded that "it is not necessary that the witnesses be in the same position to observe as the declarant; it is only necessary that the witnesses be able to corroborate the declarant's statement." In other words, the government, through corroborative witnesses together with the hearsay statement itself, proved by a preponderance of the evidence that an "event" occurred as the declarant described it, and therefore satisfied that admissibility requirement of Rule 803(1).

B. EXCITED UTTERANCES

[1] Federal Rule of Evidence 803(2)

Rule 803. Hearsay Exceptions; Availability of Declarant Immaterial

The following are not excluded by the hearsay rule, even though the declarant is available as a witness:

* * *

(2) Excited Utterance. A statement relating to a startling event or condition made while the declarant was under the stress of excitement caused by the event or condition.

* * *

[2] Illustration

Plaintiff sues an automobile manufacturer because her husband died in a rear-end collision when the gas tank exploded. The primary issue at trial is whether the tank exploded on impact, as plaintiff alleges, or when the plaintiff's husband got out of the car and flipped a cigarette into a puddle of gasoline that had leaked out from the engine block of the other car. Plaintiff calls a police officer to the stand.

Plaintiff:	State your name.
Witness:	Top Cop.
Plaintiff:	Did you investigate this accident?
Witness:	Yes, I did.
Plaintiff:	Did you see it happen?
Witness:	No, I arrived about 15 minutes after the explosion.
Plaintiff:	Did you talk to a person named Freaked Out?
Witness:	Yes, I did, immediately upon arriving at the scene.
Plaintiff:	Could you describe his condition?
Witness:	He was extremely excited, there were tears in his eyes, and his voice was shaking.
Plaintiff:	What did he tell you?
Defendant:	Objection! That's hearsay.
The court:	Let's hear it so I can decide.

Witness:	He said, "Oh my God, that car back there rear-ended the other one and then there was this immediate gigantic explosion, and people were burning to death and we couldn't get to them to save them."
Plaintiff:	Did he say anything else?
Witness:	No, then he fainted.
Defendant:	Your Honor, it's clearly hearsay and due to the excited state of the declarant, it's not reliable anyway.
The court:	Counsel, how do you respond to the Defendant's argument?
Plaintiff:	__________.

[3] Under the Influence of the Startling Event

UNITED STATES v. MARROWBONE

211 F.3d 452 (8th Cir. 2000)

BEAM, CIRCUIT JUDGE:

Orville Marrowbone appeals his conviction for having sex with a person who was incapable of declining participation in or communicating an unwillingness to engage in sex. *See* 18 U.S.C. §§ 1153, 2242(2)(B), 2246(2)(A). * * *

Orville Marrowbone had sex with L.D., a sixteen-year-old, on the Cheyenne River Indian Reservation. At trial, L.D. testified that he got drunk on alcohol supplied by Marrowbone, passed out, and awoke to Marrowbone engaging in anal sex with him. Soon after this encounter, L.D. ran home and told his mother what happened. His mother called the tribal police to have L.D. arrested for unlawful intoxication. The police did not respond. About two hours later, L.D.'s mother again called the police to have him arrested for unlawful intoxication. Officer Donel Henry Takes the Gun then arrived and arrested L.D. Officer Takes the Gun later transferred L.D. to the custody of Officer Harlen E. Gunville, Jr.

While in the police officers' custody, L.D. made statements about his encounter with Marrowbone. Officer Takes the Gun testified that L.D. said Marrowbone had molested him. * * *

Marrowbone objected on hearsay grounds to the police officers' testimony about L.D.'s statements. The district court overruled the objections, and allowed the testimony without any limiting instructions. On appeal, Marrowbone renews his hearsay objection to the admission of this testimony from the officers. The government asserts the excited utterance exception to the hearsay rule allows for admission of this evidence.

Hearsay is an out of court statement offered in evidence to prove the truth of the matter asserted. *See* Fed. R. Evid. 801. Hearsay is generally not admissible, but there is an exception for excited utterances. *See* Fed. R. Evid. 802 and 803(2). Excited utterances are statements relating to a startling event made while under the stress of excitement caused by the event. *See* Fed. R.

Evid. 803(2). The rationale for this exception is that excited utterances are likely to be truthful because the stress from the event caused a spontaneous statement that was not the product of reflection and deliberation. *See Reed v. Thalacker*, 198 F.3d 1058, 1061 (8th Cir. 1999).

To determine whether L.D. was under the stress of excitement when he made these statements, we consider the lapse of time between the startling event and the statements, whether the statements were made in response to an inquiry, his age, the characteristics of the event, his physical and mental condition, and the subject matter of the statements. *See United States v. Moses*, 15 F.3d 774, 777-78 (8th Cir. 1994). The government has the burden of demonstrating that the excited utterance exception is applicable. *See Reed*, 198 F.3d at 1061. * * *

These statements do not qualify as excited utterances. The allegations of sexual abuse were made about three hours after the event occurred. In addition, these statements were made by a teenager, not by a small child. *See Reed*, 198 F.3d at 1061-62 (recognizing that some courts allow a longer time period between the event and the statement when a young child alleges sexual abuse). While small children may be less likely to fabricate a story, teenagers have an acute ability to deliberate and fabricate. This particular teenager also had reason to fabricate because making a charge of molestation might enable him to avoid a night in jail for being intoxicated. *See Stidum v. Trickey*, 881 F.2d 582, 585 (8th Cir. 1989) (finding an excited utterance because declarant had no reason to fabricate).

L.D.'s actions also do not show continuous excitement or stress from the time of the event until the time of the statements. *See United States v. Moss*, 544 F.2d 954, 958 (8th Cir. 1976) (showing of continuous unrelieved excitement after event provides evidence that statement was excited utterance). Officer Takes the Gun testified that when he arrived at the house, L.D. was standing with a group of people and, when handcuffed, said nothing about the incident with Marrowbone. It was only when L.D. was about to be placed in the patrol car for transport to jail that he raised a ruckus and began making these statements. Six other witnesses also testified that L.D. did not appear frightened or scared during the time after the encounter with Marrowbone. Based on the lapse of time, age, motive to lie, and known actions of L.D., we are wholly unconvinced these statements were excited utterances. Thus, the district court abused its discretion when it admitted this hearsay evidence.

* * *

[The Court found the error in admitting the hearsay statements to be harmless and affirmed the conviction.]

NOTES

1. What is the relationship between the excited utterance exception and the present sense impression exception?

Rules 803(1) and 803(2) are both derivatives of the common law *res gestae* exception. So it is unsurprising that admissibility of any statement which appears to be spontaneous is often analyzed under both Rules. A critical inquiry under each involves the timing of the event or condition and the declaration. However, the central requirement of Rule 803(2) is that the declarant must be excited; while the central requirement of Rule 803(1) is that the declarant must be speaking so close in time to the event that he has no opportunity for reflection. The respective Rules each prohibit an opportunity to fabricate, but in different ways. Thus, a statement may well be held admissible under both Rules or under only one but not the other. The most significant differences between the two exceptions are that: (1) an excited utterance must relate to a "startling" event or condition while a statement of present sense impression may describe any event or condition; (2) the present sense impression must "describe" the event, while the excited utterance need only "relate" to the event — the excited utterance exception thus allows a broader scope of subject matter coverage than does the present sense impression exception; and (3) the excited utterance exception of Rule 803(2) does not contain an express contemporaneity requirement, as does Rule 803(1). *See, e.g.*, *United States v. Moore*, 791 F.2d 566 (7th Cir. 1986) (statement referring to something which preceded the startling event does not describe the event, but is related to the event and hence admissible under Rule 803(2)); *David v. Pueblo Supermarket,* 740 F.2d 230 (3d Cir. 1984) (statement in slip and fall case that "I told them to clean it up two hours ago" does not describe the slip and fall for purposes of Rule 803(1) but does relate to the event for purposes of Rule 803(2)).

2. When is a statement too far removed in time from the event to qualify as an excited utterance?

Professors Saltzburg, Martin, and Capra analyze the effect of time on an excited utterance in the following excerpt from the *Federal Rules of Evidence Manual* (9th ed. 2006):

> There is no hard and fast rule prescribing the amount of time that may elapse between a startling event and an excited utterance. The closer in time the statement is to the startling event, the more likely the declarant is still to be under the influence of the event. Ordinary experience teaches that the stress of excitement tends to dissipate with time. *See, e.g.*, *United States v. Wesela*, 223 F.3d 656 (7th Cir. 2000) (wife made statement to police officers two days after her husband threatened her with a knife; it was error to admit this statement as an excited utterance because of the lengthy time period between the startling event and the statement; the declarant had regained her composure and made the statement while at work); *United States v. Winters*, 33 F.3d 720 (6th Cir. 1994) (statement made by a shooting victim to police officers, two days after the victim was shot, was held not admissible as an excited utterance; the statement was made so far after the shooting that it was "the product of conscious reflection").

The issue, however, is not the passage of time as such but the state of mind of the declarant — specifically whether the declarant has been excited during the entire time between the event and the statement. Even statements made an hour or so after the event can qualify for the exception if the proponent can establish by a preponderance that the declarant was under a continuous state of excitement during the entire period between the startling event and the making of the statement. *See, e.g., United States v. Hefferon*, 314 F.3d 211 (5th Cir. 2002) (statements by child-victim of sexual abuse, made within two hours of the abuse, were properly admitted as excited utterances); *United States v. Scarpa*, 913 F.2d 993 (2d Cir. 1990) (statement of a beating victim was admissible under Rule 803(2); the victim named the defendants as his assailants five or six hours after the beating, while he was being treated in a hospital emergency room and his sister screamed that one of the defendants had come into the emergency room; there was little doubt that the declarant was still under the stress of excitement caused by his beating and by his sister's screams).

There are several circumstances that are relevant to admissibility even though a significant amount of time has passed between the event and the statement. These include:

(1) The nature of the startling event. Some events are more startling than others; a declarant could be expected to be under the influence of a high impact event for a longer period of time. *See, e.g., United States v. Rivera*, 43 F.3d 1291 (9th Cir. 1995) (victim's statement, accusing the defendant of raping her, was properly admitted as an excited utterance; while the statement was made more than 30 minutes after intercourse, the victim was still under the influence of the startling event; the victim was only 15 years old, she reported the rape to her mother at the first opportunity to do so, and she was in a "semi-hysterical" state at the time she made the statement).

(2) Whether the declarant in fact appeared to be excited during the time between the event and the statement. *See, e.g., United States v. Moore*, 791 F.2d 566 (7th Cir. 1986) (statement made 20 minutes after an event was held admissible under Rule 803(2) where the declarant was "running around like a chicken with her head cut off" for the entire time).

(3) The nature of the declarant. Some declarants, especially children, can be expected to be under the influence of a startling event for a longer period than others. *See, e.g., United States v. Sowa*, 34 F.3d 447 (7th Cir. 1994) (statement made by a child-declarant 20 minutes after he was beaten, identifying the defendant as the perpetrator, was properly admitted as an excited utterance; the Court noted that the child had cried for the entire period between the beating and the statement); *Morgan v. Foretich*, 846 F.2d 941, 947 (4th Cir. 1988) (child's statements were held admissible under 803(2) when they were made within three hours of the child's first opportunity to speak with the mother, even though the alleged abuse had occurred more than a day earlier); *United States v. Iron Shell*, 633 F.2d 77 (8th Cir. 1980)

(child's statements concerning sexual assault were admissible when they were made to a police officer between 45 and 75 minutes after the assault; the Court emphasized "the surprise of the assault, its shocking nature and the age of the declarant" to find a continuous state of excitement).

(4) The fact that the statement is self-serving to the declarant, while not dispositive, certainly raises the possibility that the declarant had time to reflect. *See, e.g.*, *United States v. Sewell*, 90 F.3d 326 (8th Cir. 1996) (the defendant was stopped for a traffic violation; when a search of his car uncovered a gun, the defendant said the gun was not his; this statement was not admissible as an excited utterance; where "incriminating evidence is discovered in one's possession, it requires only the briefest reflection to conclude that a denial and a plea of ignorance is the best strategy. This hardly comports with the spirit of disinterested witness which pervades the rule.").

(5) If the statement describing a previous event also predicts a future event (e.g., "something bad is going to happen"), such a prediction generally shows deliberative thought, not excitedness.

3. For excited utterances, what proof is required that the event actually happened?

The hearsay declaration itself may be sufficient to establish that the event occurred. Federal Rule 104(a) permits the judge, in deciding on admissibility issues, to rely on inadmissible evidence, including the proffered evidence itself. *United States v. Moore*, 791 F.2d 566, 570 (7th Cir. 1986). However, courts are understandably reluctant to find that the admissibility requirements for a hearsay exception are met when the only evidence provided is the hearsay statement itself. Ordinarily, more will be required. For example, in addition to the statement itself, the "appearance, behavior, and condition of the declarant may establish that a startling event occurred." *Id.* Also, the proponent may provide independent evidence that the startling event occurred, e.g., eyewitness testimony.

4. Must the event be unexpected?

Some courts have held that an event cannot be startling if the declarant has planned for the event to occur, and the event occurs as planned. *See, e.g.*, *United States v. Knife*, 592 F.2d 472 (8th Cir. 1979) (pre-planned shooting of a police officer cannot be startling when it occurs). This presumes, however, that all the factors leading up to the event are within the declarant's control; if not, the element of surprise may create excitement when the event occurs, since the event may be hoped for, but cannot be planned in advance. *See, e.g.*, *United States v. Moore,* 791 F.2d 566 (7th Cir. 1986) (secretary planned to expose her boss as a bribe taker if and when she found evidence; actually finding the evidence was a startling event because the event was not within the declarant's control; even though hoped for, it was nonetheless a surprise when the event occurred). For example, a person has to plan to win the lottery in order to win, but actually winning the lottery is certainly a startling event.

[4] Unknown Declarant

MILLER v. KEATING

754 F.2d 507 (3d Cir. 1985)

Stern, District Judge:

* * *

I.

On January 18, 1982, Carol Miller was driving her white Ford LTD east on U.S. Route 22, a limited access highway, near Easton, Pennsylvania. She carried a passenger named Annette Vay. It is undisputed that Miller and Vay were traveling behind a UPS truck and that both vehicles switched into the lefthand lane to avoid a stalled vehicle in the righthand lane near the 25th Street exit ramp. It is also undisputed that, soon thereafter, the Miller car was struck from behind by defendant Texaco's tractor-trailer driven by co-defendant Lawrence Keating. The force of the collision propelled the Miller car first into the side of a car stopped in the righthand lane and then into the rear of the UPS truck. Mrs. Miller sustained serious injuries in the collision. The driver of the car stopped in the righthand lane was Kenneth Parris. His wife, Elfriede Parris, was a passenger.

One dispute at trial was over the amount of time that elapsed between the moment when Mrs. Miller pulled into the lefthand lane and the moment when her car was struck from the rear. Another conflict focused on whether the Miller car was stopped behind the UPS truck or was still moving when it was hit by the Texaco tractor-trailer.

Both Mrs. Miller and her passenger, Annette Vay, testified at trial that Miller had completely stopped her car before being rammed by the Texaco truck. According to Vay, the Miller car was stopped in the lefthand lane for "a few seconds" before the accident. Later, she testified that the time period could have been longer than "a second or two." Lawrence Keating testified, however, that he was driving his Texaco tractor-trailer in the lefthand lane, slowing down in order to stop, and there was no vehicle between him and the UPS truck. He testified that he never saw the Miller car pull in front of him, and the first time he saw it was when it was in his lane. He said he saw only a "white blur" half or three-quarters of the way into his lane. He claimed that by the time he saw the Miller car in his lane, he was too close to it to avoid the collision.

There were other inconsistencies at trial of less relevance to the issue here, but several deserve mention because they illustrate the profusion of accounts before the jury.* * * The Parrises, who were stopped in the right lane, both testified that the Texaco truck had come to a full stop in the left lane behind the Parris car (and two car lengths behind the UPS truck, according to Mr. Parris), before the Miller car pulled in front of it. However, both Keating and the UPS driver, Neil Rasmussen, Jr., who was watching out of his side view mirror, depicted the Texaco truck as moving continuously toward the rear of the UPS truck. * * * And Keating said he was making "a gradual rolling stop."

There is also a dispute as to when the Parris car arrived alongside the Miller car. Vay and Miller both testified that the Parris car pulled up next to the Miller car during the few seconds it was stopped before being rammed by the Texaco truck. But the Parrises testified that they were stopped in the right lane for "several minutes" or "two minutes" before the accident.

It is the testimony of the Parrises about an incident occurring after the accident that gives rise to this appeal. After being hit in the left side, Mr. Parris pulled his car over. He testified that he left his car, comforted one of the victims in the Miller car, then walked to the rear of the Miller car where his wife was writing down the license plate number of the Miller car. At that point, a man approached and said, "the bastard tried to cut in." In somewhat inconsistent testimony, Mrs. Parris stated that she and her husband "were running towards the car, and I heard this person that was driving — running towards us — * * * [a]nd said the s.o.b. or some words like that, tried to cut in." Mr. Parris could not identify the declarant beyond saying that he was a white male. Mrs. Parris could do no better. There is no indication in the record why she thought the declarant was a driver or which vehicle he drove. Mr. Parris testified that he did not know what vehicle the declarant was driving.

Over objections, the trial judge allowed the Parrises to relate their versions of the declaration to the jury. He admitted the statements as "*res gestae*." Parenthetically, we note that this terminology is inappropriate. As the trial judge implicitly recognized in his opinion denying post-trial relief, there is no such exception to the prohibition against hearsay. If admissible, the declaration must qualify under one of the genuine exceptions to the hearsay rule. The old catchall, "*res gestae*," is no longer part of the law of evidence.

As the trial judge also recognized, the excited utterance exception of Fed. R. Evid. 803(2) provides the most likely basis for admitting the statement. The question before us, therefore, is whether that statement by the unknown declarant should have been admitted under Fed. R. Evid. 803(2), which defines "excited utterance" as "[a] statement relating to a startling event or condition made while the declarant was under the stress of excitement caused by the event or condition."

II.

* * *

[One] question is whether the excited utterance exception may ever authorize the admission of a statement by an anonymous declarant. Fed. R. Evid. 806 provides that whenever a hearsay statement is admitted, the declarant's credibility may be attacked through cross-examination and the introduction of evidence of inconsistent statements. The rule confers no absolute right to cross-examination, because hearsay statements may often be admitted despite the unavailability of the declarant. For example, Fed. R. Evid. 804 defines various situations where hearsay testimony comes in even though the declarant is unavailable. Among these are dying declarations, former testimony, and declarations against interest. The unifying trait of all the Rule 803 exceptions is a circumstantial guarantee of trustworthiness sufficient to justify nonproduction of the declarant, whether available or not. Although Rule 806 cannot be read to confer a right to any particular form of attack on the credibility of a hearsay declarant, it does confer a generalized right that is significantly diminished when the hearsay declarant is not only unavailable, but is also unidentified, and the party against whom the hearsay declarant's statement is introduced is thus deprived not only of the right to cross-examine, but of any meaningful prospect of finding evidence of inconsistency or bias.

* * *

At minimum, when the declarant of an excited utterance is unidentified, it becomes more difficult to satisfy the established case law requirements for admission of a statement under Fed. R. Evid. 803(2). Wigmore defines these requirements as: (1) a startling occasion, (2) a statement relating to the circumstances of the startling occasion, (3) a declarant who appears to have had opportunity to observe personally the events, and (4) a statement made before there has been time to reflect and fabricate. There is no doubt that the present case presents a startling occasion and little doubt that the declarant's statement relates to the circumstances of the occurrence. Partly because the declarant is unidentified, however, problems arise with the last two requirements: personal knowledge and spontaneity.

The first of these expresses the familiar principle that a witness may not testify about a subject without personal knowledge. Fed. R. Evid. 602. This rule applies with equal force to hearsay statements.* * * To be admissible, the declarant of an excited utterance must personally observe the startling event. *McLaughlin v. Vinzant*, 522 F.2d 448, 451 (1st Cir. 1975). The burden of establishing perception rests with the proponent of the evidence. *David v. Pueblo Supermarkets of St. Thomas, Inc.*, 740 F.2d 230, 235 (3d Cir. 1984). As in all questions of admissibility, the resolution of any dispute of fact necessary to the question is confided to the trial judge to be decided by a preponderance of the evidence. And while the trial judge is not confined to legally admissible evidence in making the determination, Fed. R. Evid. 104(a), still he must make the findings necessary to support admissibility.

Direct proof of perception, or proof that forecloses all speculation is not required. On the other hand, circumstantial evidence of the declarant's personal perception must not be so scanty as to forfeit the "guarantees of trustworthiness" which form the hallmark of all exceptions to the hearsay rule. Fed. R. Evid. 803 advisory committee note. When there is no evidence of personal perception, apart from the declaration itself, courts have hesitated to allow the excited utterance to stand alone as evidence of the declarant's opportunity to observe.* * * In some cases, however, the substance of the statement itself does contain words revealing perception. A statement such as, "I saw that blue truck run down the lady on the corner," might stand alone to show perception if the trial judge finds, from the particular circumstances, that he is satisfied by a preponderance that the declarant spoke from personal perception.

* * *

In the present case, however, the record is empty of any circumstances from which the trial court could have inferred * * * that the declarant saw Miller "cut in." The disputed declaration itself does not proclaim it. Indeed, the district judge acknowledged as much in his opinion denying plaintiffs' motion for a new trial. Nevertheless, he drew an inference of perception, reasoning that "the declarant would have made the declaration only if he was in a position to observe the collision." Yet the statements reported by the Parrises — "the bastard tried to cut in" and "the s.o.b., or some words like that, tried to cut in" — alone, do not show more likely than not that the declarant saw the event. The declarant might have been drawing a conclusion on the basis of what he saw as he approached the scene of the accident. He might have been hypothesizing or repeating what someone else had said. It is even possible that the declarant was talking about some other driver who had just cut in front of him. It is far from unlikely that the declarant was a participant in the accident, for the Parrises could never identify or exclude anyone as the speaker. And the tenor of the declaration, *i.e.*, "the bastard tried to cut in," suggests at least the possibility that the declarant was a participant with a natural degree of bias. The self-serving exclamation by a participant in an auto accident "it was the other guy's fault," is hardly likely to qualify as trustworthy.

The circumstances external to the statement itself not only fail to demonstrate that the declarant was in a position to have seen what happened, they also fail to show that the declarant was excited when he spoke. No one so testified, and the trial judge made no finding of excitement. Thus, this last prong of the test for admissibility is also unsatisfied. The assumption underlying the hearsay exception of Rule 803(2) is that a person under the sway of excitement temporarily loses the capacity of reflection and thus produces statements free of fabrication.* * * Since lack of capacity to fabricate is the justification for excited utterances, courts have recognized that the length of time separating the event from the statement may be considerably longer than for statements qualifying under the present sense impression exception of Rule 803(1), which is based on the lack of time to fabricate.* * * In *McCurdy v. Greyhound Corporation*, 346 F.2d 224, 226 (3d Cir. 1965), for example, this Court approved admission of a statement made ten or fifteen minutes after an accident, recognizing that there can be no arbitrary time limits on the operation of Rule 803(2). Thus, even if several minutes elapsed between the exciting event and the utterance, it is not necessarily an abuse of discretion to admit the statement so long as the trial court explicitly finds it was not the product of conscious reflection. There is no such finding in this case.

We have considered appellants' other contentions and find them to be without merit. The judgment of the district court will be reversed and the case remanded for a new trial.

NOTE

Can the statement of an unidentified declarant ever be admitted?

See Saltzburg, Martin, and Capra, *Federal Rules of Evidence Manual* (9th ed. 2006):

> One question that has arisen concerning admissibility of present sense impressions and excited utterances is whether the declarant must be an identifiable person. The Advisory Committee's Note on Federal Rules 803(1) and 803(2) mentions cases in which Courts had refused to admit the hearsay statement of an unidentified bystander.
>
> There are two possible concerns that a court might have when a witness testifies that a present sense impression or excited utterance was made by an unidentified declarant. One is that if the declarant cannot be identified as a real person, there is a possibility that the declarant never even existed; the witness may be creating a "phantom declarant" in order to manufacture a hearsay statement ready-made to fit the present sense impression or excited utterance exception. For example, a plaintiff in a personal injury action might testify to an unidentified bystander's contemporaneous description of an accident, which just happens to track the plaintiff's version of the events, and the defendant may do likewise.
>
> We submit, however, that any concern over fabricated hearsay statements does not present a hearsay problem, and therefore it should not result in exclusion of present sense impressions or excited utterances made by unidentified declarants. The concern over phantom declarants is that the *in-court witness* may be lying, i.e., testifying about hearsay statements that were never really made. This raises a question concerning the credibility of the in-court witness. Credibility of trial witnesses can be assessed by the traditional methods of oath, cross-examination and the jury's opportunity to view the demeanor of the witness. Consequently, a statement proffered under Rules 803(1) or 803(2) should not be excluded simply because of the possibility that an unidentified declarant has been fabricated. The hearsay rule does not prohibit all lying; it simply provides that if a person is going to lie, it must be done on the witness stand so that he or she can be tested by the in-court guarantees of trustworthiness.
>
> A more legitimate concern with respect to unidentified declarants is that it may be difficult to determine whether the declarant had personal knowledge of the event described. *See, e.g., Meder v. Everest & Jennings*, 637 F.2d 1182 (8th Cir. 1981) (a portion of a police officer's report concerning the cause of an accident was not admissible under Rule 803(1), where the officer was unable to identify the source of the information, making it impossible to determine whether the declarant was an eyewitness to what occurred at the scene). If the declarant does not have personal knowledge of the event, then the statement describing the event is inadmissible under Rules 803(1) and 803(2). *See, e.g., Bemis v. Edwards*, 45 F.3d 1369 (9th Cir. 1995) (911 tape was not admissible either as an excited utterance or as a present sense

impression, because the citizen-caller apparently lacked personal knowledge of the events that he was reporting; the Court noted that the proponent of a hearsay declaration has "the burden of establishing personal perception by a preponderance of the evidence"). This is because Rule 803(1) requires that the statement must be made "while the declarant was perceiving the event or condition, or immediately thereafter," and Rule 803(2) requires that the declarant must be "under the influence" of the startling event. These requirements cannot be met in the absence of the declarant's personal knowledge of the event. More fundamentally, hearsay declarants in general must have personal knowledge of the facts related in their statements (with the exception of admissions).

Identification of the declarant will often be helpful in establishing that he or she had personal knowledge of the event described. But this does not mean that identification of the declarant is a precondition to admissibility. The statement itself, or circumstantial evidence, may create an inference that the declarant perceived the event. Illustrative is *United States v. Medico*, 557 F.2d 309 (2d Cir. 1977), where a bystander relayed the license plate number of a getaway car to a security guard who was locked inside a bank that had just been robbed. The bystander was never identified, but his personal knowledge was established by the fact that the guard saw him look in the direction of the getaway car as he relayed the license number. The Court held that the bystander's statement was admissible as a present sense impression.

In sum, if the declarant's personal knowledge can be established, the declarant need not be an identifiable person for purposes of Rules 803(1) and 803(2).

C. STATEMENT OF EXISTING MENTAL, EMOTIONAL, OR PHYSICAL CONDITION

[1] Federal Rule of Evidence 803(3)

Rule 803. Hearsay Exceptions; Availability of Declarant Immaterial

The following are not excluded by the hearsay rule, even though the declarant is available as a witness:

* * *

(3) Then existing mental, emotional, or physical condition. A statement of the declarant's then existing state of mind, emotion, sensation, or physical condition (such as intent, plan, motive, design, mental feeling, pain, and bodily health), but not including a statement of memory or belief to prove the fact remember or believed unless it relates to the execution, revocation, identification, or terms of the declarant's will.

[2] Illustration

In a custody battle, the mother wishes to show that her toddler becomes sick after every visit with the father. The mother is on the stand.

Plaintiff:	Now Ma'am, does the child say anything to you after each and every visit with the father?
Mother:	Yes, she does.
Plaintiff:	What does she say?
Defendant:	Objection! Hearsay.
The court:	Let me hear what she said so I can rule.
Mother:	"I feel sick at my stomach and the bruises hurt."
The court:	That's pretty powerful hearsay, counselor. How can it be admissible?
Plaintiff:	________.

[3] Statements Offered to Prove Conduct

MUTUAL LIFE INSURANCE CO. OF NEW YORK v. HILLMON

145 U.S. 285 (1892)

On July 13, 1880, Sallie E. Hillmon, a citizen of Kansas, brought an action against the Mutual Life Insurance Company, a corporation of New York, on a policy of insurance, dated December 10, 1878, on the life of her husband, John W. Hillmon, in the sum of $10,000, payable to her within sixty days after notice and proof of his death. On the same day the plaintiff brought two other actions, the one against the New York Life Insurance Company, a corporation of New York, on two similar policies of life insurance, dated respectively November 30, 1878, and December 10, 1878, for the sum of $5,000 each; and the other against the Connecticut Mutual Life Insurance Company, a corporation of Connecticut, on a similar policy, dated March 4, 1879, for the sum of $5,000.

In each case the declaration alleged that Hillmon died on March 17, 1879, during the continuance of the policy, but that the defendant, though duly notified of the fact, had refused to pay the amount of the policy, or any part thereof; and the answer denied the death of Hillmon, and alleged that he, together with John H. Brown and divers other persons, on or before November 30, 1878, conspiring to defraud the defendant, procured the issue of all the policies, and afterwards, in March and April, 1879, falsely pretended and represented that Hillmon was dead, and that a dead body which they had procured was his, whereas in reality he was alive and in hiding.

* * *

At the trial plaintiff introduced evidence tending to show that on or about March 5, 1879, Hillmon and Brown left Wichita, in the state of Kansas, and traveled together through southern Kansas in search of a site for a cattle ranch; that on the night of March 18th, while they were in camp at a place called Crooked Creek, Hillmon was killed by the accidental discharge of a gun; that Brown at once notified persons living in the neighborhood; and that the body was thereupon taken to a neighboring town, where, after an inquest, it was buried. The defendants introduced evidence tending to show that the body found in the camp at Crooked Creek on the night of March 18th was not the body of Hillmon, but was the body of one Frederick Adolph Walters. Upon the question whose body this was there was much conflicting evidence, including photographs and descriptions of the corpse, and of the marks and scars upon it, and testimony to its likeness to Hillmon and to Walters.

The defendants introduced testimony that Walters left his home at Ft. Madison, in the state of Iowa, in March, 1878, and was afterwards in Kansas in 1878, and in January and February, 1879; that during that time his family frequently received letters from him, the last of which was written from Wichita; and that he had not been heard from since March, 1879. The defendants also offered the following evidence:

Elizabeth Rieffenach testified that she was a sister of Frederick Adolph Walters, and lived at Ft. Madison; and thereupon, as shown by the bill of exceptions, the following proceedings took place:

> Witness further testified that she had received a letter written from Wichita, Kansas, about the 4th or 5th day of March, 1879, by her brother Frederick Adolph; that the letter was dated at Wichita, and was in the handwriting of her brother; that she had searched for the letter, but could not find the same, it being lost; that she remembered and could state the contents of the letter.
>
> Thereupon the defendants' counsel asked the question: "State the contents of that letter." To which the plaintiff objected, on the ground that the same is incompetent, irrelevant, and hearsay. The objection was sustained, and the defendants duly excepted. The following is the letter as stated by witness:
>
> Wichita, Kansas,
>
> March 4th or 5th or 3d or 4th, — I don't know, — 1879.
>
> Dear sister and all: I now in my usual style drop you a few lines to let you know that I expect to leave Wichita on or about March the 5th, with a certain Mr. Hillmon, a sheep trader, for Colorado or parts unknown to me. I expect to see the country now. News are of no interest to you, as you are not acquainted here. I will close with compliments to all inquiring friends. Love to all.
>
> I am truly your brother,
>
> FRED. ADOLPH WALTERS.

Alvina D. Kasten testified that she was 21 years of age, and resided in Ft. Madison; that she was engaged to be married to Frederick Adolph Walters; that she last saw him on March 24, 1878, at Ft. Madison; that he left there at that time, and had not returned; that she corresponded regularly with him, and received a letter about every two weeks until March 3, 1879, which was the last time she received a letter from him; that this letter was dated at

Wichita, March 1, 1879, and was addressed to her at Ft. Madison, and the envelope was postmarked "Wichita, Kansas, March 2, 1879;" and that she had never heard from or seen him since that time.

The defendants put in evidence the envelope with the postmark and address, and thereupon offered to read the letter in evidence. The plaintiff objected to the reading of the letter. The court sustained the objection, and the defendants excepted.

This letter was dated "Wichita, March 1, 1879," was signed by Walters, and began as follows:

> Dearest Alvina: Your kind and ever welcome letter was received yesterday afternoon about an hour before I left Emporia. I will stay here until the fore part of next week, and then will leave here to see a part of the country that I never expected to see when I left home, as I am going with a man by the name of Hillmon, who intends, to start a sheep ranch, and, as he promised me more wages than I could make at anything else, I concluded to take it, for a while at least, until I strike something better. There is so many folks in this country that have got the Leadville fever, and if I could not of got the situation that I have now I would have went there myself; but as it is at present I get to see the best portion of Kansas, Indian Territory, Colorado, and Mexico. The route that we intend to take would cost a man to travel from $150 to $200, but it will not cost me a cent; besides, I get good wages. I will drop you a letter occasionally until I get settled down. Then I want you to answer it.

* * *

The jury, being instructed by the court to return a separate verdict in each case, returned verdicts for the plaintiff against the three defendants respectively for the amounts of their policies and interest, upon which separate judgments were rendered.

* * *

MR. JUSTICE GRAY, after stating the case as above, delivered the opinion of the court.

* * *

There is, however, one question of evidence so important, so fully argued at the bar, and so likely to arise upon another trial, that it is proper to express an opinion upon it.

This question is of the admissibility of the letters written by Walters on the first days of March, 1879, which were offered in evidence by the defendants, and excluded by the court. * * *

The position taken at the bar that the letters were * * * memoranda made in the ordinary course of business, cannot be maintained, for they were clearly not such.

But upon another ground suggested they should have been admitted. A man's state of mind or feeling can only be manifested to others by countenance, attitude, or gesture, or by sounds or words, spoken or written. The nature of the fact to be proved is the same, and evidence of its proper tokens is equally competent to prove it, whether expressed by aspect or conduct, by voice or pen. When the intention to be proved is important only as qualifying an act, its connection with that act must be shown, in order to warrant the admission of declarations of the intention. But whenever the intention is of itself a distinct and material fact in a chain of circumstances, it may be proved by contemporaneous oral or written declarations of the party.

The existence of a particular intention in a certain person at a certain time being a material fact to be proved, evidence that he expressed that intention at that time is as direct evidence of the fact as his own testimony that he then had that intention would be. After his death there can hardly be any other way of proving it; and while he is still alive his own memory of his state of mind at a former time is no more likely to be clear and true than a bystander's recollection of what he then said, and is less trustworthy than letters written by him at the very time and under circumstances precluding a suspicion of misrepresentation.

The letters in question were competent not as narratives of facts communicated to the writer by others, nor yet as proof that he actually went away from Wichita, but as evidence that, shortly before the time when other evidence tended to show that he went away, he had the intention of going, and of going with Hillmon, which made it more probable both that he did go and that he went with Hillmon than if there had been no proof of such intention. In view of the mass of conflicting testimony introduced upon the question whether it was the body of Walters that was found in Hillmon's camp, this evidence might properly influence the jury in determining that question.

* * *

Upon an indictment of one Hunter for the murder of one Armstrong at Camden, the court of errors and appeals of New Jersey unanimously held that Armstrong's oral declarations to his son at Philadelphia, on the afternoon before the night of the murder, as well as a letter written by him at the same time and place to his wife, each stating that he was going with Hunter to Camden on business, were rightly admitted in evidence. CHIEF JUSTICE BEASLEY said: "In the ordinary course of things, it was the usual information that a man about leaving home would communicate, for the convenience of his family, the information of his friends, or the regulation of his business. At the time it was given, such declarations could, in the nature of things, mean harm to no one; he who uttered them was bent on no expedition of mischief or wrong, and the attitude of affairs at the time entirely explodes the idea that such utterances were intended to serve any purpose but that for which they were obviously designed. If it be said that such notice of an intention of leaving home could have been given without introducing in it the name of Mr. Hunter, the obvious answer to the suggestion, I think, is that a reference to the companion who is to accompany the person leaving is as natural a part of the transaction as is any other incident or quality of it. If it is legitimate to show by a man's own declarations that he left his home to be gone a week, or for a certain destination, which seems incontestable, why may it not be proved in the same way that a designated person was to bear him company?" * * *

Upon principle and authority, therefore, we are of [the] opinion that the two letters were competent evidence of the intention of Walters at the time of writing them, which was a material fact bearing upon the question in controversy; and that for the exclusion of these letters, as well as for the undue restriction of the defendants' challenges, the verdicts must be set aside, and a new trial had.

* * *

Judgment reversed, and case remanded to the circuit court, with directions to set aside the verdict and to order a new trial.

NOTES

1. What is the justification for the state of mind exception?

Rule 803(3) provides an exception for statements of present state of mind, emotion, or physical condition. The theory of trustworthiness supporting the admissibility of these statements is that they are based on unique perception; that is, the declarant has a unique perspective into his own feelings and emotions. There is also an argument that state of mind statements are spontaneous, because in order to be admissible under the exception they must be reflective of a "then existing state of mind." However, as applied to statements of a declarant's state of mind, the spontaneity requirement does not really guarantee sincerity. It is impossible to tell how spontaneous a state of mind statement really is, because it describes an internal event; a declarant's "then existing" state of mind could well be the product of days of contemplation and fabrication. *See, e.g., United States v. Lawal*, 736 F.2d 5 (2d Cir. 1984) (the defendant's statement of anger at being "set up," made at the time drugs were found in his suitcase in a Customs search, was admissible under Rule 803(3) as a statement of a then existing state of mind even though there was a likelihood of fabrication; the defendant had time during a long airplane trip to think up a story should he be caught). This is unlike, for instance, the present sense impression, where it can be determined through reference to an external event that the declarant did or did not have time to fabricate.

2. Can a statement of the declarant's state of mind be admitted to prove the subsequent conduct of a person other than the declarant?

See Saltzburg, Martin, and Capra, *Federal Rules of Evidence Manual* (9th ed. 2006):

> The legislative history of Rule 803(3) fails to resolve whether, as in the famous *Hillmon* dictum, a declarant's statement of state of mind

can be used to prove the subsequent conduct of someone other than the declarant. For example, if the declarant says, "I am going to meet Joe to buy some drugs from him," can the statement be used to prove the subsequent conduct of both the declarant *and* Joe?

The answer should be "no." The rationale for extending the state of mind exception to prove the subsequent conduct of a nondeclarant is dubious. Recall that the basis for admitting state of mind statements is that the declarant has a unique perspective into his own state of mind. This rationale obviously does not apply to the declarant's conclusion about the state of mind of someone else. A declarant might have unique perception of his own state of mind, but he has no special perspective into the thoughts and feelings of another person.

It is true that the Court in *Hillmon* stated that the letters were competent evidence to prove that Walters went to Colorado with Hillmon. However, the actual precedential import of that extension of the state of mind exception is subject to doubt. All of the cases relied upon by the *Hillmon* Court, except one, were cases in which the state of mind exception was used to prove only the conduct of the declarant (*e.g.*, to prove that the declarant took a certain train at a certain time). Almost all of the analysis in the *Hillmon* opinion considers the use of the state of mind exception to prove the declarant's conduct. Discussion of using this exception to prove the conduct of someone other than the declarant is clearly an afterthought. Finally, the entire evidentiary discussion in *Hillmon* is, at least technically, dictum, because the Court reversed judgments for the plaintiff not on the ground that evidence was improperly excluded, but rather on the ground that the insurer-defendants were entitled to separate verdicts.

The Court in *Hillmon* cited the old New Jersey case of *Hunter v. State*, 40 N.J.L. 495 (1878), where that Court allowed the state of mind exception to prove that a meeting between two people took place. But the reasoning in that case was peculiar, to say the least. The *Hunter* court stated that "a reference to the companion who is to accompany the person leaving is as natural a part of the transaction as is any other incident or quality of it. If it is legitimate to show by a man's own declarations that he left his home to be gone a week, or for a certain destination, which seems incontestable, why may it not be proved in the same way that a designated person was to bear him company?" This "analysis" amounts to an assertion that if one part of a statement is reliable, all parts of a statement must be admitted, no matter how unreliable those parts may be. Such a proposition has been rejected time and again by the United States Supreme Court, and would amount to an exception to the hearsay rule for "partly reliable narratives." *See Williamson v. United States*, 512 U.S. 594 (1994) (rejecting the notion that an entire narrative can be admissible simply because part of the narrative is reliable, and noting that "one of the most effective ways to lie is to mix falsehood with truth").

Finally, even if *Hillmon* were a holding that state of mind statements can be used to prove the conduct of a nondeclarant, this is a holding based on the common law. It is not a controlling discussion of the Federal Rules of Evidence, enacted almost 100 years later.

The report of the House Judiciary Committee stated that the Committee intended that Rule 803(3) be construed to limit the *Hillmon* doctrine "so as to render statements of intent by a declarant admissible only to prove his future conduct, not the future conduct of another person." The Senate Report made no mention of this limitation.

The Federal Courts have interpreted this ambiguous legislative history in differing ways. Some Courts have adopted the House limitation and refused to admit a statement that the declarant intended to meet with a third party as proof that the declarant and the third party did indeed meet. *See, e.g., Gual Morales v. Hernandez Vega*, 579 F.2d 677 (1st Cir. 1978) (excluding a witness' statement that "I intend to see [the defendant]" when offered to prove that the witness met with the defendant).

One Court has permitted the declarant's statement to be used to show another's conduct, at least where the trial court gives a limiting instruction that the statement cannot be used to prove the intent or conduct of another but can only be used for the inference that the declarant carried out his intended action (though that instruction seems to work at cross-purposes with the holding that the state of mind statement can be used to prove the conduct of a nondeclarant). *See, e.g., United States v. Astorga-Torres*, 682 F.2d 1331 (9th Cir. 1982).

The Second Circuit has taken a compromise approach, allowing a declarant's statement of intent to be admitted to prove the conduct of a nondeclarant only "when there is independent evidence which connects the declarant's statement with the non-declarant's activities." *See, e.g., United States v. Delvecchio*, 816 F.2d 859 (2d Cir. 1987) (an informant's statement that he was going to meet Delvecchio to complete a drug transaction was inadmissible where there was no independent evidence of Delvecchio's presence at the meeting). Compare *United States v. Sperling*, 726 F.2d 69 (2d Cir. 1984) (an informant's statement that he planned to meet Sperling to complete a drug transaction was admissible where the declarant's statement of intent to meet with the defendant was confirmed by later eyewitness testimony that the meeting actually took place).

It will often occur that the declarant's statement will refer to another person, directly or indirectly, but the statement is not in fact offered to show that the nondeclarant had a certain state of mind or acted in accordance with a particular mental state. For instance, a statement of the victim that he planned to go to the defendant's *house* to deliver a package contains a *reference* to a third party, but it does not refer directly or indirectly to that third party's *state of mind or action*. In such cases, the statement is admissible under any view of Rule 803(3) to prove that the declarant went to the defendant's house, because the statement is offered only to show that the declarant acted in accordance with his or her own mental state. As a result, there is no reliability problem of determining the state of mind of a nondeclarant, as to which the declarant has no unique perception. *See, e.g.*, *United States v. Donley*, 878 F.2d 735 (3d Cir. 1989) (in a first-degree murder prosecution a government witness testified that the victim said, in the presence of her husband the defendant, that she was moving out of thc marital home and separating from him; shortly thereafter, the victim was found dead; the testimony was properly admitted to show the existence of her intention and plan and the defendant's awareness of it, from which could be inferred a motive for the killing; the statement did not purport to express an opinion about the defendant's state of mind).

3. What is the relationship between the *Hillmon* doctrine and Rule 403?

Evidence of a declarant's state of mind is admissible only when it creates some inference with respect to a disputed issue, and then only if the probative value of the statement in proving the declarant's state of mind is not substantially outweighed by unfair prejudice suffered by the non-offering party. The most likely form of prejudice from a statement reflecting a state of mind is that created when the statement offered is one which can be used for the truth of an event other than the declarant's state of mind. For example, in a murder case, a victim's statement that she fears the defendant may properly be offered to show that the victim would not have acted the way the defendant contends (e.g., the defendant alleges that he and the victim were playing with guns and one accidentally misfired). However, such a statement is also subject to misuse — *e.g.*, for the impermissible purpose of showing that the victim's fear of the defendant was justified. This is not a problem in terms of Rule 803(3), under which the statement is being offered and admitted only to prove the declarant's state of mind. Rather, exclusion, if it is to occur, must be under Rule 403: the statement would be excluded when the probative value of the evidence as to the declarant's state of mind is substantially outweighed by the impermissible uses to which the evidence could be put. Thus, if the defendant claims that he and the victim were cleaning guns together when a gun accidentally went off and killed the victim, the victim's prior statement of fear would be admissible. The statement creates a strong inference that the victim would not have put himself in the position of cleaning guns with the defendant in a friendly manner if he was in fear of the defendant. *United States v. Green*, 680 F.2d 520 (7th Cir. 1982) (prosecution for kidnaping with intent to commit murder; statements by the victim concerning her attitude toward the defendant were properly admitted because they tended to negate the defendant's contention that she accompanied the defendant voluntarily). On the other hand, if the defendant claims that he was out of town when the murder occurred, then the victim's statement of fear of the defendant should be excluded under Rule 403, because there is no dispute about the declarant's conduct as to which his state of mind of fear would be relevant.

The D.C. Circuit has set forth the analysis that must be undertaken when a victim's expression of fear of the defendant is offered under *Hillmon:*

> The threshold requirement of admissibility of such hearsay statements of fear of defendant in homicide cases is some substantial degree of relevance to a material issue in the case. While there are undoubtedly a number of possible situations in which such statements may be relevant, the courts have developed three rather well-defined categories in which the need for such statements overcomes almost any possible prejudice. The most common of these involves the defendant's claim of self-defense as justification for the killing. When such a defense is asserted, a defendant's assertion that the deceased first attacked him may be rebutted by the extrajudicial declarations of the victim that he feared the defendant, thus rendering it unlikely that the deceased was in fact the aggressor in the first instance. Second, where defendant seeks to defend on the ground that the deceased committed suicide, evidence that the victim had made statements inconsistent with a suicidal bent are highly relevant. A third situation involves a claim of accidental death, where, for example, defendant's version of the facts is that the victim picked up defendant's gun and was accidentally killed while toying with it. In such cases, the deceased's statements of fear as to guns or of defendant himself (showing he would never go near defendant under any circumstances) are relevant in that they tend to rebut his defense. Of course, even in these cases, where the evidence is of a highly prejudicial nature, it has been held that it must be excluded in spite of a significant degree of relevance.

United States v. Brown, 490 F.2d 758 (D.C. Cir. 1973).

[4] Past Acts

SHEPARD v. UNITED STATES

290 U.S. 96 (1933)

MR. JUSTICE CARDOZO delivered the opinion of the Court.

The petitioner, Charles A. Shepard, a major in the medical corps of the United States Army, has been convicted of the murder of his wife, Zenana Shepard, at Fort Riley, Kan., a United States military reservation. The jury having qualified their verdict by adding thereto the words "without capital punishment" (18 U.S.C. § 567), the defendant was sentenced to imprisonment for life. * * *

The crime is charged to have been committed by poisoning the victim with bichloride of mercury. The defendant was in love with another woman, and wished to make her his wife. There is circumstantial evidence to sustain a finding by the jury that to win himself his freedom he turned to poison and murder. Even so, guilt was contested, and conflicting inferences are possible. The defendant asks us to hold that by the acceptance of incompetent evidence the scales were weighted to his prejudice and in the end to his undoing.

The evidence complained of was offered by the government in rebuttal when the trial was nearly over. On May 22, 1929, there was a conversation in the absence of the defendant between Mrs. Shepard, then ill in bed, and Clara Brown, her nurse. The patient asked the nurse to go to the closet in the defendant's room and bring a bottle of whisky that would be found upon a shelf. When the bottle was produced, she said that this was the liquor she had taken just before collapsing. She asked whether enough was left to make a test for the presence of poison, insisting that the smell and taste were strange. And then she added the words, "Dr. Shepard has poisoned me."

The conversation was proved twice. After the first proof of it, the government asked to strike it out, being doubtful of its competence, and this request was granted. A little later, however, the offer was renewed; the nurse having then testified to statements by Mrs. Shepard as to the prospect of recovery. "She said she was not going to get well; she was going to die." With the aid of this new evidence, the conversation already summarized was proved a second time. There was a timely challenge of the ruling.

She said, "Dr. Shepard has poisoned me." The admission of this declaration, if erroneous, was more than unsubstantial error. As to that the parties are agreed. The voice of the dead wife was heard in accusation of her husband, and the accusation was accepted as evidence of guilt. If the evidence was incompetent, the verdict may not stand.

1. Upon the hearing in this court the Government finds its main prop in the position that what was said by Mrs. Shepard was admissible as a dying declaration. This is manifestly the theory upon which it was offered and received. The prop, however, is a broken reed. To make out a dying declaration, the declarant must have spoken without hope of recovery and in the shadow of impending death. The record furnishes no proof of that indispensable condition. So, indeed, it was ruled by all the judges of the court below, though the majority held the view that the testimony was competent for quite another purpose, which will be considered later on.

* * *

2. We pass to the question whether the statements to the nurse, though incompetent as dying declarations, were admissible on other grounds.

The Circuit Court of Appeals determined that they were. Witnesses for the defendant had testified to declarations by Mrs. Shepard which suggested a mind bent upon suicide, or at any rate were thought by the defendant to carry that suggestion. More than once before her illness she had stated in the hearing of these witnesses that she had no wish to live, and had nothing to live for, and on one occasion she added that she expected some day to make an end to her life. This testimony opened the door, so it is argued, to declarations in rebuttal that she had been poisoned by her husband. They were admissible, in that view, not as evidence of the truth of what was said, but as betokening a state of mind inconsistent with the presence of suicidal intent.

(a) The testimony was neither offered nor received for the strained and narrow purpose now suggested as legitimate. It was offered and received as proof of a dying declaration. What was said by Mrs. Shepard lying ill upon her death bed was to be weighed as if a like statement had been made upon the stand. The course of the trial makes this an inescapable conclusion. The

Government withdrew the testimony when it was unaccompanied by proof that the declarant expected to die. Only when proof of her expectation had been supplied was the offer renewed and the testimony received again. For the reasons already considered, the proof was inadequate to show a consciousness of impending death and the abandonment of hope; but inadequate though it was, there can be no doubt of the purpose that it was understood to serve. There is no disguise of that purpose by counsel for the Government. They concede in all candor that Mrs. Shepard's accusation of her husband, when it was finally let in, was received upon the footing of a dying declaration, and not merely as indicative of the persistence of a will to live. Beyond question the jury considered it for the broader purpose, as the court intended that they should. A different situation would be here if we could fairly say in the light of the whole record that the purpose had been left at large, without identifying token. There would then be room for argument that demand should have been made for an explanatory ruling. Here the course of the trial put the defendant off his guard. The testimony was received by the trial judge and offered by the Government with the plain understanding that it was to be used for an illegitimate purpose, gravely prejudicial. A trial becomes unfair if testimony thus accepted may be used in an appellate court as though admitted for a different purpose, unavowed and unsuspected. * * * Such at all events is the result when the purpose in reserve is so obscure and artificial that it would be unlikely to occur to the minds of uninstructed jurors, and even if it did, would be swallowed up and lost in the one that was disclosed.

(b) Aside, however, from this objection, the accusatory declaration must have been rejected as evidence of a state of mind, though the purpose thus to limit it had been brought to light upon the trial. The defendant had tried to show by Mrs. Shepard's declarations to her friends that she had exhibited a weariness of life and a readiness to end it, the testimony giving plausibility to the hypothesis of suicide. By the proof of these declarations evincing an unhappy state of mind, the defendant opened the door to the offer by the government of declarations evincing a different state of mind, declarations consistent with the persistence of a will to live. The defendant would have no grievance if the testimony in rebuttal had been narrowed to that point. What the Government put in evidence, however, was something very different. It did not use the declarations by Mrs. Shepard to prove her present thoughts and feelings, or even her thoughts and feelings in times past. It used the declarations as proof of an act committed by some one else, as evidence that she was dying of poison given by her husband. This fact, if fact it was, the Government was free to prove, but not by hearsay declarations. It will not do to say that the jury might accept the declarations for any light that they cast upon the existence of a vital urge, and reject them to the extent that they charged the death to some one else. Discrimination so subtle is a feat beyond the compass of ordinary minds. The reverberating clang of those accusatory words would drown all weaker sounds. It is for ordinary minds, and not for psychoanalysts, that our rules of evidence are framed. They have their source very often in considerations of administrative convenience, of practical expediency, and not in rules of logic. When the risk of confusion is so great as to upset the balance of advantage, the evidence goes out.* * *

These precepts of caution are a guide to judgment here. There are times when a state of mind, if relevant, may be proved by contemporaneous declarations of feeling or intent. *Mutual Life Ins. Co. v. Hillmon*, 145 U.S. 285, 295. Thus, in proceedings for the probate of a will, where the issue is undue influence, the declarations of a testator are competent to prove his feelings for his relatives, but are incompetent as evidence of his conduct or of theirs. In suits for the alienation of affections, letters passing between the spouses are admissible in aid of a like purpose. In damage suits for personal injuries, declarations by the patient to bystanders or physicians are evidence of sufferings or symptoms, but are not received to prove the acts, the external circumstances, through which the injuries came about. Even statements of past sufferings or symptoms are generally excluded, though an exception is at times allowed when they are made to a physician. So also in suits upon insurance policies, declarations by an insured that he intends to go upon a journey with another may be evidence of a state of mind lending probability to the conclusion that the purpose was fulfilled. *Mutual Life Ins. Co. v. Hillmon, supra*. The ruling in that case marks the high-water line beyond which courts have been unwilling to go. It has developed a substantial body of criticism and commentary. Declarations of intention, casting light upon the future, have been sharply distinguished from declarations of memory, pointing backwards to the past. There would be an end, or nearly that, to the rule against hearsay if the distinction were ignored.

The testimony now questioned faced backward and not forward. This at least it did in its most obvious implications. What is even more important, it spoke to a past act, and, more than that, to an act by some one not the speaker. Other tendency, if it had any, was a filament too fine to be disentangled by a jury.

The judgment should be reversed and the cause remanded to the District Court for further proceedings in accordance with this opinion.

Reversed.

NOTE

What is the relationship between *Hillmon*, which permits state of mind statements offered to prove the subsequent conduct of the declarant, and *Shepard*, which prohibits state of mind statements offered to prove the prior conduct of anyone?

See Saltzburg, Martin, and Capra, *Federal Rules of Evidence Manual* (9th ed. 2006):

> Rule 803(3) does not permit a statement of memory or belief to prove the fact remembered or believed. The "statement of memory or belief" exclusion is a codification of the holding in *Shepard v. United States*, 290 U.S. 96 (1933), where the Court held that a statement of the defendant's wife, accusing him of poisoning her, could not be admitted under the state of mind exception when offered to prove that the

defendant had actually poisoned her. The *Shepard* exclusion is considered necessary "to avoid the virtual destruction of the hearsay rule which would otherwise result from allowing state of mind, provable by a hearsay statement, to serve as the basis for an inference of the happening of the event which produced the state of mind." Advisory Committee Note to Fed. R. Evid. 803(3). *See also United States v. Cardascia*, 951 F.2d 474 (2d Cir. 1991) (Rule 803(3) could not be applied to admit statements of the declarant's state of mind with regard to conduct that occurred eight months earlier; a contrary rule would significantly erode the hearsay rule, beyond the intended breadth of the hearsay exception).

Under the Rule, a statement of memory can be offered to prove a fact relating to the execution, revocation, identification, or term of the declarant's will. There are no particular assurances of trustworthiness that justify creating an exception for will cases. But as the Advisory Committee Note states, this provision represents an *ad hoc* judgment that finds ample support in the decisions, and rests on practical grounds of necessity and expediency. Not surprisingly, the "will exception" receives minimal application in the Federal Courts.

While a state of mind statement cannot be offered to prove that a past event occurred, it can be offered in some cases to prove the occurrence of an event *subsequent* to the statement. *See, e.g., United States v. Tokars*, 95 F.3d 1520 (11th Cir. 1996) (statements of one defendant's wife that she intended to divorce the defendant were admissible to show a motive for the defendant to murder her). The Advisory Committee states that Rule 803(3) preserves the rule of *Mutual Life Insurance Co. v. Hillmon*, 145 U.S. 285 (1892), allowing a hearsay statement by a declarant to prove the declarant's state of mind, when probative that the declarant subsequently acted in accordance with that state of mind. In *Hillman*, evidence a declarant's hearsay statement about his intent to go to a certain place was held admissible to prove that the declarant actually went there.

An example may help to illustrate what is included within the exception and what is not. If a declarant (*D*) states, "I am going to New York tomorrow," and subsequently disappears, the statement may be introduced as probative that *D* went to New York; intent to do an act in the future is probative that the act occurred. If, on the other hand, *D* states "Two years ago I went to New York," the statement may be said to reflect the state of mind called "memory," but the statement is not admissible under the state of mind exception, because that exception precludes a statement of memory when offered to prove that the fact remembered is actually true. If *D* says, "I am going to New York tomorrow because Joe stole my money and I have to get it back from him," the statement cannot be used to prove that Joe stole money from *D*, because that would be using the state of mind statement to prove the truth of a past fact, which is prohibited by Shepard. But it could be used to prove that *D* went to New York, because that is permitted by *Hillmon*.

Where the state of mind statement is offered to prove future conduct of the declarant, the hearsay rule poses no bar, but the declarant's statement must be scrutinized under Rule 403 (and of course a specific objection must be made under that Rule to preserve a claim of error on appeal). Exclusion under Rule 403 could occur if the inference from state of mind to subsequent action by the declarant is weak (see, e.g., *United States v. Williams*, 704 F.2d 315 (6th Cir. 1983) (statement of the defendant that he intended to satisfy a tax indebtedness when his mother sold her house, offered to explain his possession of a large amount of cash upon arrest, was admissible under Rule 803(3) as a statement of intent to prove subsequent conduct; however, the statement was properly excluded on relevance grounds because the intent to perform the future act was conditioned on the sale of the house, and this condition had not been met); or if there is no dispute about the declarant's subsequent conduct; or if prejudice, confusion, or delay is created that substantially outweighs the statement's probative value as to the declarant's future course of action. See generally the discussion in *United States v. Brown*, 490 F.2d 758 (D.C. Cir. 1973) (principal danger is that the jury will consider the declarant's statement for the truth of an out-of-court event, such as a prior threat by the defendant; such inferences are improper, and must be weighed against the probative value of the declarant's statement as tending to prove the declarant's subsequent course of action).

The most obvious risk of prejudice is that the jury will consider the hearsay statement not as proof of state of mind and the subsequent conduct of the declarant, but rather for the truth of the facts that are related in the statement. For instance, in *State v. Charo*, 156 Ariz. 561, 754 P.2d 288 (1988), a state case decided under a rule identical to Federal Rule 803(3), the defendant was accused of murder. The defendant denied the murder and presented evidence of an alibi. The prosecution offered the victim's out-of-court statement to the effect that she feared the defendant as the result of the defendant's prior sexual attack upon her. The Arizona Supreme Court held that if the statement was offered under Rule 803(3) to prove that the prior sexual attack occurred, it was clearly inadmissible under the "memory or belief" limitation of the Rule. To the extent the statement was offered to show the declarant's fearful state of mind, the Court held that the statement was inadmissible under Rule 403. The victim's state of mind was not at issue in the case; nor was the statement probative for any inference that could be drawn about the victim's subsequent course of conduct. There was no dispute about the victim's conduct in the case. The Court stated: "While there may be times when fear of the defendant is both admissible hearsay and relevant, the victim's statement in the present case is irrelevant unless the defendant asserts a defense which makes her feeling relevant."

In contrast to the facts of *Charo*, it is possible that a statement by the victim putting blame on the defendant might be admissible to prove the declarant's subsequent conduct if that conduct is in dispute and if the statement is relevant to prove that conduct. For example, assume a murder case in which the defendant claims that he killed the victim by accident. The defense is that the defendant and the victim were rabbit hunting together; the victim was walking ahead of the defendant to scare up rabbits; and the defendant tripped on a log and his gun accidentally discharged, killing the victim. The prosecution proffers a hearsay statement from the victim, made three days before his death, in which the victim told his mother that he was afraid the defendant was going to kill him because the victim still owed the defendant a large sum of money from a drug deal. This statement should be admitted under Rules 803(3) and 403, with an instruction that the jury is not to use the statement for the fact that the victim owed the defendant money from a drug deal or that the victim had reason to fear the defendant. Rather, it is admissible to show that the victim feared the defendant, whether that fear was reasonable or not. This fearful state of mind is probative of the victim's subsequent conduct; it makes it much less likely that the victim would be walking voluntarily ahead of a person he feared while that person was carrying a loaded gun. The hearsay statement is prejudicial because the jury may use it for the truth of the facts related even though instructed not to do so. But, a trial court would certainly be within its discretion in finding that the prejudicial effect does not substantially outweigh the probative value of the statement in proving the victim's disputed actions. *See, e.g.*, *United States v. Hartmann*, 958 F.2d 774 (7th Cir. 1992) (a homicide victim's wife and others were charged with defrauding life insurance companies by, *inter alia*, fraudulently listing the wife as the husband's beneficiary on life insurance policies, and subsequently killing the husband; the husband's statements describing the dismal state of his marriage, his desire to replace his wife as beneficiary on his insurance policies, and his fear of being murdered by his wife and her lover were admissible as evidence of his state of mind and were relevant to prove that the declarant would not have listed his wife as beneficiary); *United States v. Green*, 680 F.2d 520 (7th Cir. 1982) (in a prosecution for kidnaping with intent to commit murder, statements by the victim concerning her attitude toward the defendant were properly admitted because they tended to negate the defendant's contention that she accompanied the defendant voluntarily).

PROBLEM 13-1

(a) Billy Bob tells Tattle Tale, "I'm going to the bank tomorrow to meet with the bank manager." Billy Bob disappears. Tattle Tale takes the stand. Assuming relevance in the pending litigation, is the statement admissible under the state of mind exception:

(1) to show Billy Bob intended to go to the bank?

(2) to show Billy Bob went to the bank?

(3) to show the office manager was at the bank the next day?

(b) Billy Bob tells Tattle Tale, "I was at the bank yesterday and talked to the office manager." Billy Bob disappears. Tattle Tale takes the stand. Assuming relevance in the pending litigation, is the statement admissible under the state of mind exception:

(1) to show Billy Bob made an appointment with the office manager before seeing him?

(2) to show Billy Bob was at the bank?

(3) to show that the office manager was at the bank?

(c) Billy Bob tells Tattle Tale, "You remember when I wrote my will, the witnesses weren't really there when I signed it." Billy Bob dies. Tattle Tale takes the stand in a probate contest. Is the statement admissible under Rule 803(3) to show the witnesses weren't there when the will was signed?

D. STATEMENT FOR TREATMENT OR DIAGNOSIS

[1] Federal Rule of Evidence 803(4)

Rule 803. Hearsay Exceptions; Availability of Declarant Immaterial

The following are not excluded by the hearsay rule, even though the declarant is available as a witness:

* * *

(4) Statements for purposes of medical diagnosis or treatment. Statements made for purposes of medical diagnosis or treatment and describing medical history, or past or present symptoms, pain, or sensations, or the inception or general character of the cause or external source thereof insofar as reasonably pertinent to diagnosis or treatment.

* * *

[2] Illustration

Dead Guy passed away four weeks after surgery for an ulcer. His estate sues the treating physician and the hospital, alleging malpractice. One of the issues at trial is whether the decedent suffered any excruciating abdominal pain after surgery. To prevail, the estate must show that he did. The only evidence on this issue comes from the decedent's widow. She takes the stand.

Plaintiff: State your name.
Widow: Mrs. Dead Guy.
Plaintiff: Did you have a conversation with your husband just before he passed away?
Widow: Yes, he looked like he was feeling really awful, so I suggested he get a second opinion.

Plaintiff:	What did you do?
Widow:	I called a doctor I've known for years, but my husband couldn't even come to the phone, so I acted as a go between for the phone call.
Plaintiff:	What did your husband tell you to tell the doctor?
Defendant:	Objection! That's hearsay.
The court:	Let me hear it so I can rule.
Widow:	He told me to tell the doctor that he had been suffering excruciating pain in his abdomen for the last four weeks and that there must have been something wrong with the surgery.
Defendant:	Your Honor, this statement is clearly being offered to prove the truth of the matter asserted and there is no exception that could apply. The statement wasn't made to a doctor; the statement deals with past history, not a current condition. Further, it wasn't conveyed to a treating physician and it deals with causation.
Plaintiff:	________.
The court:	________.

[3] Causation

ROCK v. HUFFCO GAS & OIL CO.

922 F.2d 272 (5th Cir. 1991)

THORNBERRY, CIRCUIT JUDGE:

An employee for an offshore catering business brought this negligence suit for injuries allegedly suffered during his employment. The employee has died since the instigation of this litigation, and his family members have been substituted as plaintiffs for the purposes of continuing the action. Two of the defendants, Huffco Petroleum Corporation and Dual Drilling Company, filed a motion for summary judgment, which the district court granted. The court ruled that the evidence tendered by the plaintiffs constituted hearsay, which was not admissible under any of the exceptions to the hearsay rule. The plaintiffs appeal the district court's determination that none of the proffered evidence is admissible and its decision to grant the summary judgment.

Finding no error, we AFFIRM.

I. *Facts and Procedural History*

This litigation stems from two accidents allegedly suffered by Richard D. Rock while employed as a steward/cook for Offshore Food Service, Inc. of Houma, Louisiana. Offshore Food Service provides food catering services to offshore drilling platforms and vessels in the Gulf of Mexico.

On July 13, 1987, Rock was assigned to work on the Huffco Fixed Platform 206A, which was located in the High Island Region off the coast of Galveston,

Texas. On the morning following his arrival, as he was leaving his sleeping quarters, Rock claimed that his foot fell through a rusted part of a step located just outside of his doorway causing him to sprain his ankle. There were no witnesses to the accident, which occurred between 5:00 and 6:00 a.m. as Rock was making his way to the galley to prepare breakfast. Rock reported the incident to the chief supervisor on the platform at the time, Joe Lee Satsky. Satsky asked Rock if he wanted a doctor to examine the ankle, but Rock responded that he did not think the sprain was that bad and that he wanted to stay and work. Satsky did not prepare an accident report form.

The ankle continued to bother Rock over the next two days, and when shifts changed and a new chief supervisor came on board the platform, Rock again reported the incident. At this time, the new supervisor, Donald Earl Christian, decided to complete an accident report form. The form was completed in both Rock's handwriting and Christian's handwriting. Among the statements written by Christian was a description of the accident. Christian wrote that Rock's "foot slipped to bad part of porch." Christian also investigated the site of the accident and confirmed the rusted condition of the step and the existence of a hole and noted that he had not seen the hole during previous inspections.

Christian then decided that Rock should consult a physician about the sprain and arranged to have Rock transported by helicopter to St. Mary's hospital in Galveston, Texas. Doctors reported that Rock had a tender and swollen right ankle and described the injury as a moderate sprain. The ankle was placed in a six inch plaster splint, and Rock was instructed not to put any weight on the ankle, to walk with crutches, and to elevate the ankle when possible.

On July 21, 1987, after a few days of rest, Rock returned to work. Rock worked on three different assignments before arriving on a jack-up rig owned by the Dual Drilling Company (Dual Rig No. 41) on August 26, 1987. Within hours of arriving on the drilling rig, Rock claimed to have re-injured his ankle by slipping in some grease on the floor of the rig's galley. The only potential witness to the accident was Barry Breaux, another Offshore Food's employee assigned to work with Rock. During his deposition, Breaux reported that he was in the galley at the time of the accident but did not see Rock fall. In fact, Breaux claims that Rock had previously advised him of a plan to fake such an accident. For his cooperation in remaining silent, Rock promised Breaux that he would report back to Offshore Food that Breaux was a "good worker."

Another Offshore Food's employee, Carl Trahan, was friendly with Rock and corroborated Breaux's story. Trahan was not on board the Dual 41 when the accident happened, but Trahan claims that Rock later told him that he had a bad ankle and had staged a slip-and-fall accident: "he told me that he was going to keep on walking on it and make sure it stayed swollen so he could get some money out of it."

Following the alleged re-injury on the Dual 41, the foreman on board, John Gardner, filed an accident report with information provided to him by Rock. In the space provided for a description of the accident, Gardner wrote that Rock had "stepped in greasy [*sic*] spot on floor and slipped and twisted right ankle." Gardner also questioned Breaux about the accident, but Breaux said nothing about the accident being staged.

Rock was treated for a sprained ankle on the day following the alleged accident on the Dual 41. Rock continued working on various offshore vessels in the Gulf of Mexico after the alleged incident and eventually obtained a light-duty job in the Offshore Food's office in Houma, Louisiana. Rock finally quit working for Offshore Food altogether on April 18, 1988.

Because of his ankle's worsening condition, Rock consulted Dr. A. Delmar Walker on September 17th and 27th of 1987. As part of those examinations, Rock provided the doctor with a history of the injury to his ankle including a description of the two incidents discussed above. On October 1, 1987, Dr. Walker referred Rock to a vascular surgeon, Dr. Fritz J. Rau, who again asked Rock for a history of the injury to his ankle. These medical histories are contained in office notes and medical reports.

Apparently, as a result of the injury to his ankle, Rock was suffering from a condition known as venous insufficiency. This occurs when the veins in the lower legs fail to return blood to the torso. Several surgeries were performed on Rock in an attempt to restore normal blood flow, but his condition deteriorated. In addition to his vascular condition, Rock developed infections, possibly resulting from the surgical procedures themselves. Rock died from a heart attack on December 12, 1988.

* * * On October 5, 1989, the court entered judgment in favor of the defendants, and dismissed Rock's complaint. Specifically, the court concluded that the evidence offered by plaintiffs constituted hearsay, which did not fall within any of the recognized exceptions to the hearsay rule.

* * *

II. *Discussion*

A. *Inadmissibility of Hearsay*

* * *

1. *Statements to Physicians*

Appellants first suggest that written and testimonial evidence concerning the history of Rock's alleged accidents, which were given by Rock to the doctors treating his ankle, should be admissible under Federal Rule of Evidence 803(4). This rule provides that otherwise inadmissible hearsay should not be excluded if the statement was initially "made for purposes of medical diagnosis or treatment and describ[es] medical history, or past or present symptoms, pain, or sensations, or the inception or general character of the cause or external source thereof insofar as *reasonably pertinent to diagnosis or treatment*." Fed. R. Evid. 803(4) (emphasis added).

Admissibility of a statement made to one's physician turns on the guarantee of the * * * declarant's trustworthiness. *See* Fed. R. Evid. 803(4) advisory committee's note. Therefore, before admitting such hearsay statements, the court should determine whether the statements were reasonably considered by the declarant as being pertinent to the diagnosis or treatment sought.

Details of the injury not necessary for treatment but serving only to suggest fault "would not ordinarily qualify" as an exception to the hearsay rule under Rule 803(4). A case cited by plaintiffs, *Ramrattan v. Burger King Corp.*, 656 F. Supp. 522 (D. Md. 1987), illustrates the application of this rule. In *Ramrattan*, the district court held that a statement made to a physician that the defendant's car struck his vehicle was admissible under Rule 803(4), but that "statements concerning who ran the red light or the fault of the parties are not pertinent to diagnosis or treatment."

The plaintiffs argue that Drs. Walker and Rau considered the cause of Rock's injury pertinent to their diagnosis, however, deposition transcripts do not bear this out. For instance, Dr. Walker explained that "what caused [Rock] to fall is important from [a legal] standpoint but certainly not from a medical treatment standpoint." Although Dr. Rau was not as explicit, his comments suggest that the history of Rock's injury was pertinent only to the extent that he was aware that Rock's foot had, at some point, sustained an injury caused by a trauma to his ankle:

> Q: [I]s it significant that he fell through a steel plate as opposed to a wooden porch, as opposed to a hole in the log or anything like that?
>
> A: [Rau]: No. I'd have to say no to that.
>
> * * *
>
> Q: So what you were looking for is that something happened that could explain the condition that he had?
>
> A: [Rau]: That's correct.
>
> Q: And the fact that he fell — he stated he fell through a steel plate really was not — those words and that description was not significant as far as your treatment and diagnosis was concerned?
>
> A: [Rau]: That's correct, other than it does sort of give you a general idea of what the injury was.

The doctors stated that they only needed to know that Rock had twisted his ankle; they did not need to know the additional detail that Rock may have twisted the ankle while stepping through a rusted-out or defective step or by slipping in some grease in order to diagnose or treat Rock's injury.

The plaintiffs cite two additional cases that they claim support the admissibility of Rock's statements to his physicians. *See United States v. Renville*, 779 F.2d 430 (8th Cir. 1985) and *United States v. Iron Shell*, 633 F.2d 77 (8th Cir. 1980). In both cases the Eighth Circuit applied a more liberal interpretation of the Rule 803(4) exception to the hearsay rule; however, both cases dealt with statements made by victims of child abuse to their treating physicians. In *Renville*, the court explained why statements, which ordinarily may not be admitted under Rule 803(4), may be admitted in a child abuse case: physicians must consider not only the physical harm involved but also the psychological and emotional injuries that accompany the crime of child abuse. Statements of fault may dictate the extent of the psychological injury and suggest the appropriate treatment. Rock's statements would not qualify under this broader application of the Rule 803(4) exception.

For the foregoing reasons, the district court was correct in ruling Rock's statements to his doctors as inadmissible under Federal Rule of Evidence 803(4).

* * *

Affirmed.

NOTES

1. Must the statement be made to a physician?

Statements to family members and social workers have been held admissible under the medical diagnosis or treatment exception, so long as the statements were made for the purposes of obtaining medical treatment or diagnosis. *Davignon v. Clemmey*, 322 F.3d 1 (1st Cir. 2003).

2. Is the exception broad enough to cover statements of medical history, or statements attributing causation or fault?

Professors Saltzburg, Martin, and Capra describe the applicability of Rule 803(4) to such statements in *Federal Rules of Evidence Manual* (9th ed. 2006):

> Rule 803(4) breaks with prior practice by admitting statements regarding past symptoms, medical history, and those that relate to the cause of the injury, whenever these statements are pertinent to treatment or diagnosis. Traditionally, statements of past symptoms and medical history were admissible only as part of the factual basis of expert testimony. Statements of cause (e.g., "my back hurts because I slipped on some ice") were excluded as inherently unreliable. The Advisory Committee took the position that statements of medical history and causation are likely to be reliable at least insofar as reasonably pertinent to treatment or diagnosis, given the motive for making the statements, and the reliance thereon by medical personnel. *See, e.g., United States v. Pollard*, 790 F.2d 1309 (7th Cir. 1986) (a statement of a patient describing how his arm was twisted was admissible because the cause of arm pain was reasonably pertinent to treatment, and the declarant made the statement with a motive to obtain treatment). Compare *Cook v. Hoppin*, 783 F.2d 684 (7th Cir. 1986) (a statement that a patient fell from a third-story stairway while wrestling was not admissible under Rule 803(4) to prove that the patient was wrestling; the cause of the accident was not pertinent to treatment because the doctor would treat a patient who fell from three stories the same way no matter what the cause of the fall).
>
> On the other hand, statements attributing fault (e.g., "my back hurts because I slipped on some ice at a poorly maintained bus stop") are ordinarily excluded under the Rule, because they do not further and are not pertinent to the patient's treatment or diagnosis. The Advisory Committee provided a pertinent hypothetical: "A patient's statement

that he was struck by an automobile would qualify, but not his statement that a car was driven through a red light." Adding the reference to the red light will not affect the treatment, nor would the patient expect it to have any effect on treatment.

A major exception has developed to the principle that statements attributing fault are not within the exception: cases involving child abuse. A statement from the child-declarant to medical personnel concerning abuse is ordinarily held admissible under the Rule even when the declarant identifies the abuser. The rationale is that the "pertinence" prong of the Rule is satisfied because a statement of identification is pertinent to treatment of the child-victim; the doctor must be concerned not only with the child's current physical condition, but also with the child's future welfare and safety and psychological well-being. *See, e.g.*, *United States v. Yazzie*, 59 F.3d 807, 812 (9th Cir. 1995):

> Generally, statements of fault are not admissible under this exception. However, this Circuit has adopted a special rule for sexual abuse cases because sexual abuse involves more than physical injury; the physician must be attentive to treating the victim's emotional and psychological injuries, the exact nature and extent of which often depend on the identity of the abuser. Thus, a child victim's statements about the identity of the perpetrator are admissible under the medical treatment exception when they are made for the purposes of medical diagnosis and treatment.

See also United States v. Provost, 875 F.2d 172 (8th Cir. 1989) (a statement identifying the defendant as the perpetrator was pertinent to treatment where the defendant occasionally lived in the victim's home).

As to the "treatment motive" prong of the Rule, many courts require a showing that the child understood that she was speaking to medical personnel and needed to tell the truth in order to get properly treated. *See, e.g.*, *United States v. Renville*, 779 F.2d 430 (8th Cir. 1985) (child's statement attributing fault is admissible under Rule 803(4) only "where the physician makes clear to the victim that the inquiry into the identity of the abuser is important to diagnosis and treatment, and the victim manifests such an understanding."). *See also United States v. Sumner*, 204 F.3d 1182 (8th Cir. 2000) (child's statement to doctor accusing the defendant of sexual abuse was erroneously admitted under Rule 803(4): "Although Dr. Zitzlow explained that he was a doctor, he did not discuss with [the victim] the need for truthful revelations or emphasize that the identification of the abuser was important to Dr. Zitzlow's attempts to help her overcome any emotional trauma resulting from the abuse to which she had been subjected."). Compare *United States v. Pacheco*, 154 F.3d 1236 (10th Cir. 1998) (placing the burden on the defendant to provide evidence that the child-declarant did not understand she was being treated by doctors and needed to be truthful). Other courts are more flexible and look to the circumstances to determine whether the child was seeking treatment or diagnosis. *See, e.g.*, *Danaipour v. McLarey*, 386 F.3d 289 (1st Cir. 2004) (rejecting as "unnecessary inflexible" the rule that statements by children are admissible only where the physician makes clear to the child that truthfully identifying the abuser is necessary to diagnosis and treatment: "there are many ways in which a party wishing to enter into evidence as statement under Rule 803(4) can demonstrate that the statement was made for the purpose of diagnosis and treatment.").

Courts have occasionally extended the principles established in child abuse cases to other cases involving domestic abuse, allowing statements from an adult-declarant identifying the perpetrator to be admitted under Rule 803(4). As the Court put it in *United States v. Joe*, 8 F.3d 1488, 1494 (10th Cir. 1993):

> [T]he identity of the abuser is reasonably pertinent to treatment in virtually every domestic sexual assault case, even those not involving children. All victims of domestic sexual abuse suffer emotional and psychological injuries, the exact nature and extent of which depend on the identity of the abuser. The physician generally must know who the abuser was in order to render proper treatment because the physician's treatment will necessarily differ when the abuser is a member of the victim's family or household. * * * [T]he domestic sexual abuser's identity is admissible under Rule 803(4) where the abuser has such an intimate relationship with the victim that the abuser's identity becomes reasonably pertinent to the victim's proper treatment.

Similarly, the principle from the child sex abuse cases can be applied to cases involving sexual abuse of adult-victims. Because of the possibility of sexually communicated diseases, the victim's identification of the perpetrator is pertinent to the victim's treatment.

3. Are statements made to medical experts for purposes of litigation admissible under the exception?

Federal Rule 803(4) marks a departure from the analogous common law exception in its treatment of statements made to nontreating physicians. Under common law, statements made to a doctor consulted solely for diagnostic purposes (such as in anticipation of litigation) were not considered sufficiently trustworthy to escape hearsay proscription. Rule 803(4), however, permits testimony of a nontreating physician as substantive evidence. The reasoning is that the doctor consulted for litigation purposes would at any rate testify to the nature of statements given to him by the patient as a basis for forming his or her opinion, as is permitted by Rule 703. While the jury would be instructed that those facts are to be used only to determine the weight accorded the opinion, the Advisory Committee believed that despite instructions to the contrary, juries tended to treat evidence admitted under Rule 703 as proof of the facts stated. This rationale carries less power after the 2000 amendment to Rule 703, which substantially circumscribes the ability of a proponent to introduce hearsay under the guise of offering it solely to illustrate the basis of the expert's opinion. If not for Rule 803(4), there would be a good chance today that the jury would never hear statements made to a litigation doctor.

A trial court understandably might be reluctant to admit statements to medical personnel who are retained by the party solely to prepare a case. But most courts have held consistent with the Rule that even if the doctor is retained solely to testify as a witness, statements made to that doctor are admissible under Rule 803(4) because the doctor is retained for "diagnosis," and the Rule abolishes all distinctions between doctors consulted for treatment and those consulted for diagnosis. *See, e.g.*, *United States v. Whitted*, 11 F.3d 782 (8th Cir. 1993) (statements admissible even where doctor was consulted only for the purpose of providing expert testimony in a criminal prosecution); *Morgan v. Foretich*, 845 F.2d 941 (4th Cir. 1988) (the term "diagnosis" is intended to refer to a doctor who is consulted only in order to testify as a witness). *See also* Mosteller, *Child Sexual Abuse and Statements for the Purpose of Medical Diagnosis or Treatment,* 67 N.C. L. Rev. 257, 260 (1989) ("The rule admits statements made to a doctor consulted only for the purpose of diagnosis, when no treatment is anticipated by the declarant. The archetypal statement involved here is one made to a physician who is consulted for the purpose of the doctor giving expert testimony at trial."). The fact that a statement was made to a doctor for purposes of litigation is a matter of weight and not admissibility.

4. Can a statement made by someone other than the patient be admitted under the exception?

A statement offered under Rule 803(4) need not refer to the declarant's own medical condition. If the declarant relays information about another person for purposes of treating or diagnosing that person, then the same guarantees of trustworthiness exist as when the declarant is seeking treatment for himself. Accordingly, statements by bystanders, family members, and others, made for purposes of treating an injured person and pertinent to that treatment, should be admissible under Rule 803(4). *See, e.g., Cook v. Hoppin*, 783 F.2d 684 (7th Cir. 1986) (statements by non-patients can qualify under Rule 803(4) where they are pertinent to the patient's treatment or diagnosis); *Wilson v. Zapata Off-Shore Co.,* 939 F.2d 260 (5th Cir. 1991) (hospital record reporting a statement by the plaintiff's sister to a social worker that the plaintiff had always been a habitual liar was properly admitted; this was helpful background information that would assist in psychological treatment).

E. HEARSAY WITHIN HEARSAY

[1] Federal Rule of Evidence 805

Rule 805. Hearsay within Hearsay

Hearsay included within hearsay is not excluded under the hearsay rule if each part of the combined statements conforms with an exception to the hearsay rule provided in these rules.

[2] Illustration

Defendant is sued in a wrongful death action. She defends on the theory that someone else did it. There was a witness, but she died. The plaintiff calls the first witness.

Plaintiff:	State your name.
Witness:	Party Line.
Plaintiff:	Did you know the victim?
Witness:	Yes.
Plaintiff:	Did you see the attack on the victim?
Witness:	No.
Plaintiff:	Did you talk to someone who saw the attack?
Witness:	No.
Plaintiff:	Well, let's try this one. Did you talk to someone who happened to talk to someone who saw the attack?
Witness:	You bet.
Plaintiff:	What did they see?
Defendant:	Objection! What did who see? That's hearsay. Actually, it's double hearsay.
The court:	Let me hear it before I rule on the objection.
Witness:	I was watching football and Billy Bob, I could see him out my front window, came running out of his house — like bees were chasing him, and came to my house and pounded on the door. So I opened the door and he was, like, shaking all over, and he said: "I just got off the phone with Jimmy Lee and he said he was looking out the window while he was talking to me and was actually seeing the defendant choking the gal who died."
The court:	You really think you can justify this one, counsel?
Plaintiff:	__________.

[3] The Non-Hearsay Problem

UNITED STATES v. DOTSON
821 F.2d 1034 (5th Cir. 1987)

PER CURIAM:

Defendant-appellant Frederick Leon Dotson requests that this court rehear his appeal, challenging this court's analysis of the evidentiary issues presented therein. Because we find merit in one of Dotson's contentions, we grant rehearing to the extent necessary for the revisions set forth below; otherwise, we deny Dotson's petition.

In our opinion reported at 817 F.2d 1127 (5th Cir. 1987), we rejected Dotson's contention that a lengthy police report detailing the statement of a government witness to police, admitted below as a prior consistent statement, was inadmissible hearsay not falling within any exception to the hearsay rule. We concluded that

"Dotson's objection that the report constituted "hearsay within hearsay" is misplaced. According to the terms of rule 801(d)(1), prior consistent statements are not hearsay; the hearsay-within-hearsay principle contained in rule 805 simply does not apply to prior consistent statements."

Upon reconsideration, we find the line of reasoning expressed above to be misplaced, and therefore vacate that portion of our opinion. For the purposes of the hearsay-within-hearsay principle expressed in rule 805, "non-hearsay" statements under rule 801(d), such as prior consistent statements, should be considered in analyzing a multiple-hearsay statement as the equivalent of a level of the combined statements "that conforms with an exception to the hearsay rule." Fed. R. Evid. 805; *see Southern Stone Co. v. Singer*, 665 F.2d 698, 703 (Former 5th Cir. 1982) (even if one level of double-hearsay statement was not hearsay according to Fed. R. Evid. 801(d)(2)(A), second level of hearsay was not excepted from hearsay rule and document was inadmissible). That is, the mere fact that one level of a multiple-level statement qualifies as "non-hearsay" does not excuse the other levels from rule 805's mandate that each level satisfy an exception to the hearsay rule for the statement to be admissible.

For the purposes of our rule 805 analysis, the report contains two levels of hearsay: the report says that Sergeant Anderson said (first level) that Young said that he carried marijuana for Dotson two or three times a week (second level). Even though the second level qualifies as non-hearsay under rule 801(d)(1)(B) (prior consistent statement), the first level remains, and does not qualify under any exception to the hearsay rule. The report was thus inadmissible, and the district court erred in allowing the jury to consider it. We therefore vacate our holding in Part IV of the opinion.

* * *

The application for rehearing is GRANTED to the extent necessary for the revision specified above; otherwise the application for rehearing is DENIED.

NOTE

Although hearsay within hearsay is covered in this Chapter as a prelude to the business records exception, note that the analysis also applies to exceptions where declarant unavailability is required, and also applies to the Rule 801 exemptions to the hearsay rule, as held in *Dotson*.

F. BUSINESS RECORDS EXCEPTION

Editor's Note: The related exception for past recollection recorded is discussed in Chapter 3 in the materials on competency, because that exception is dependent on the witness having a lack of memory, and recollection is an aspect of foundational competence. The reader may wish to revisit the Rule 803(5) exception for past recollection recorded at this point.

[1] Federal Rule of Evidence 803(6)

Rule 803. Hearsay Exceptions; Availability of Declarant Immaterial

The following are not excluded by the hearsay rule, even though the declarant is available as a witness:

* * *

(6) Records of regularly conducted activity. A memorandum, report, record or data compilation, in any form, of acts, events, conditions, opinions, or diagnoses, made at or near the time by, or from information transmitted by, a person with knowledge, if kept in the ordinary course of regularly conducted business activity, and if it was the regular practice of that business activity to make the memorandum, report, record, or data compilation, all as shown by the testimony of the custodian or other qualified witness, or by certification that complies with Rule 902(11), 902(12), or a statute permitting certification, unless the source of information or the method or circumstances of preparation indicate lack of trustworthiness. The term "business" as used in this paragraph includes business, institution, association, profession, occupation, and calling of every kind, whether or not conducted for profit.

* * *

[2] Illustration

Plaintiff, Slum Lord, sues defendant, Naive Guy, for non-payment of rent. Slum Lord's bookkeeper moved to Tulsa and is unavailable to testify about the old accounts. Slum Lord takes the stand.

Plaintiff's counsel:	State your name.
Slum Lord:	Slum Lord.
Plaintiff's counsel:	Did you enter into a lease with Naive Guy?
Slum Lord:	Yes, here it is. (The document is marked and admitted.)
Plaintiff's counsel:	What is your business?
Slum Lord:	I am a landlord of over 200 properties and have been in business for fifteen years.
Plaintiff's counsel:	Do you keep a book of accounting in the ordinary course of your business?
Slum Lord:	Yes I do. I developed the system.
Plaintiff's counsel:	How are the books kept?

Slum Lord:	Every day all checks from tenants are given to the bookkeeper who enters the receipts in the ledger and dates the entry. If there is no entry then no payment has been made on that particular account.
Plaintiff's counsel:	Have the accounts been trustworthy?
Slum Lord:	Yes, over the last fifteen years we've been audited on several occasions and haven't had any problems.
Plaintiff's counsel:	I offer the book of accounts, marked as Exhibit A, into evidence.
Defendant:	Objection! Hearsay.
Plaintiff's counsel:	________.

[3] Recording Information from Other Sources

JOHNSON v. LUTZ
170 N.E. 517 (N.Y. 1930)

HUBBS, J.

This action is to recover damages for the wrongful death of the plaintiff's intestate, who was killed when his motorcycle came into collision with the defendants' truck at a street intersection. There was a sharp conflict in the testimony in regard to the circumstances under which the collision took place. A policeman's report of the accident filed by him in the station house was offered in evidence by the defendants under section 374-a of the Civil Practice Act, and was excluded. The sole ground for reversal urged by the appellants is that said report was erroneously excluded. That section reads: "Any writing or record, whether in the form of an entry in a book or otherwise, made as a memorandum or record of any act, transaction, occurrence or event, shall be admissible in evidence in proof of said act, transaction, occurrence or event, if the trial judge shall find that it was made in the regular course of any business, and that it was the regular course of such business to make such memorandum or record at the time of such act, transaction, occurrence or event, or within a reasonable time thereafter. All other circumstances of the making of such writing or record, including lack of personal knowledge by the entrant or maker, may be shown to affect its weight, but they shall not affect its admissibility. The term business shall include business, profession, occupation and calling of every kind."

* * *

The purpose of the Legislature in enacting section 374-a was to permit a writing or record, made in the regular course of business, to be received in evidence, without the necessity of calling as witnesses all of the persons who had any part in making it, provided the record was made as a part of the duty of the person making it, or on information imparted by persons who were under a duty to impart such information. The amendment permits the introduction of shopbooks without the necessity of calling all clerks who may have sold different items of account. It was not intended to permit the receipt in evidence of entries based upon voluntary hearsay statements made by third parties not engaged in the business or under any duty in relation thereto. It was said, in *Mayor, etc., of New York City v. Second Ave. R. Co.*, 102 N.Y. 572, at page 581, 7 N.E. 905, 909, 55 Am. Rep. 839: "It is a proper qualification of the rule admitting such evidence that the account must have been made in the ordinary course of business, and that it should not be extended so as to admit a mere private memorandum, not made in pursuance of any duty owing by the person making it, or when made upon information derived from another who made the communication casually and voluntarily, and not under the sanction of duty or other obligation."

An important consideration leading to the amendment was the fact that in the business world credit is given to records made in the course of business by persons who are engaged in the business upon information given by others engaged in the same business as part of their duty.

* * *

Judgment affirmed.

UNITED STATES v. VIGNEAU

187 F.3d 70 (1st Cir. 1999)

BOUDIN, CIRCUIT JUDGE:

Two brothers, Patrick and Mark Vigneau, were convicted after a lengthy trial on charges growing out of their participation in a drug distribution scheme. In this opinion, we consider Patrick Vigneau's claims of error; * * *

From around February 1995 to at least the end of that year, Patrick Vigneau and Richard Crandall conducted a venture to acquire marijuana and steroids in the Southwest and resell them in the Northeastern United States. Crandall obtained the marijuana and steroids from suppliers in El Paso, Texas, and in Mexico, and sent the drugs to Patrick Vigneau in Rhode Island and south-eastern Massachusetts. Patrick Vigneau, who distributed the drugs to retail dealers, used others to assist him, including his brother Mark Vigneau and one Joseph Rinaldi.

Some of the proceeds from these Northeastern sales had to be sent to Crandall in Texas so that he could pay suppliers and share in the profits. Patrick Vigneau transmitted funds to Crandall primarily through Western Union money orders. The money orders were sent by Patrick Vigneau or others, sometimes in the sender's true name but often using false or borrowed names. Timothy Owens, who assisted Crandall in acquiring drugs, frequently picked up the checks from Western Union, cashed them, and gave the money to Crandall.

* * *

The jury convicted Patrick Vigneau of participating in a continuing criminal enterprise, 21 U.S.C. § 848; possession of marijuana and attempted possession of marijuana (both with intent to distribute) and conspiracy to distribute marijuana, id. §§ 841, 846; and 21 counts of money laundering on specific occasions and conspiracy to launder money, 18 U.S.C. § 1956. Patrick Vigneau was later sentenced to 365 months in prison. He now appeals, challenging his conviction but not his sentence.

On this appeal, Patrick Vigneau's strongest claim is that the district court erred in allowing the government to introduce, without redaction and for all purposes, Western Union "To Send Money" forms, primarily in support of the money laundering charges. These forms, as a Western Union custodian testified, are handed by the sender of money to a Western Union agent after the sender completes the left side of the form by writing (1) the sender's name, address and telephone number; (2) the amount of the transfer; and (3) the intended recipient's name and location. The Western Union clerk then fills in the right side of the form with the clerk's signature, date, amount of the transfer and fee, and a computer-generated control number; but at least in 1995, Western Union clerks did not require independent proof of the sender's identity.

Western Union uses the control number affixed by the clerk to correlate the information on the "To Send Money" form with the corresponding "Received Money" form and with the canceled check issued by Western Union to pay the recipient. The original forms are usually discarded after six months, but the information provided by the sender, as well as the information from all records associated with the money transfer, are recorded in a computer database. In this case, for some transfers the government had the forms completed by the sender, but for most it had only the computer records.

The government introduced over 70 records of Western Union money transfers. Patrick Vigneau's name, address and phone number appeared as that of the sender on 21 of the "To Send Money" forms (11 other names, including fictional names and those of Mark Vigneau and of other defendants, appeared as those of the senders on the other forms), and those 21 forms corresponded to the 21 specific counts of money laundering on which Patrick Vigneau was ultimately convicted by the jury. Patrick Vigneau's most plausible objection, which was presented in the district court and is renewed on appeal, is that his name, address and telephone number on the "To Send Money" forms were inadmissible hearsay used to identify Patrick Vigneau as the sender.

Hearsay, loosely speaking, is an out-of-court statement offered in evidence to prove the truth of the matter asserted. Fed. R. Evid. 801(c). Whoever wrote the name "Patrick Vigneau" on the "To Send Money" forms was stating in substance: "I am Patrick Vigneau and this is my address and telephone number." Of course, if there were independent evidence that the writer was Patrick Vigneau, the statements would constitute party-opponent admissions and would fall within an exception to the rule against hearsay, Fed. R. Evid. 801(d)(2) (the rule says admissions are "not hearsay," but that is an academic refinement). However, the government cannot use the forms themselves as bootstrap-proof that Patrick Vigneau made the admission.

Instead, the government argues that the "To Send Money" forms and the computerized information reflecting those forms and the correlated material were admissible under the business records exception. Fed. R. Evid. 803(6).

Rule 803(6) provides that business records are admissible where shown to be business records by a qualified witness, "unless the source of information or the method and circumstances of preparation indicate lack of trustworthiness." The district judge accepted the view that the Western Union records were trustworthy and admitted the "To Send Money" forms (or equivalent computer records) without redaction and for all purposes, advising the jury that "[w]hat weight you give to them will be your choice."

The district judge was correct that the "To Send Money" forms literally comply with the business records exception because each form is a business record, and in this case, the computer records appeared to be a trustworthy account of what was recorded on the original "To Send Money" forms. The difficulty is that despite its language, the business records exception does not embrace statements contained within a business record that were made by one who is not a part of the business if the embraced statements are offered for their truth. The classic case is *Johnson v. Lutz*, 253 N.Y. 124, 170 N.E. 517 (N.Y. 1930), which excluded an unredacted police report incorporating the statement of a bystander (even though the police officer recorded it in the regular course of business) because the informant was not part of that business. The Advisory Committee Notes to Rule 803(6) cite *Johnson v. Lutz* and make clear that the rule is intended to incorporate its holding.

Johnson v. Lutz is not a technical formality but follows directly from the very rationale for the business records exception. When a clerk records the receipt of an order over the telephone, the regularity of the procedure, coupled with business incentives to keep accurate records, provide reasonable assurance that the record thus made reflects the clerk's original entry. Thus the business record, although an out-of-court statement and therefore hearsay, is admitted without calling the clerk to prove that the clerk received an order.

But no such safeguards of regularity or business checks automatically assure the truth of a statement to the business by a stranger to it, such as that made by the bystander to the police officer or that made by the money sender who gave the form containing his name, address, and telephone number to Western Union. Accordingly, the *Johnson v. Lutz* gloss excludes this "outsider" information, where offered for its truth, unless some other hearsay exception applies to the outsider's own statement. This gloss on the business records exception, which the Federal Rules elsewhere call the "hearsay within hearsay" problem, Fed. R. Evid. 805, is well-settled in this circuit. Other circuits are in accord. * * *

Of course, "hearsay within hearsay" is often trustworthy but hearsay is not automatically admissible merely because it is trustworthy. A residual hearsay exception exists based on case-specific findings of trustworthiness, but it is more stringent and requires, among other things, advance notice not here provided by the government. Fed. R. Evid. 807 (combining former Fed. R. Evid. 803(24) and Fed. R. Evid. 804(b)(5)). And precisely because hearsay law is now codified for the federal courts, the former freedom of federal judges to create new exceptions is now curtailed. Fed. R. Evid. 807 and Fed. R. Evid. 803(24), 1974 Advisory Committee Notes to 1974 Enactment.

Nor does the reference to "trustworthiness" in the business records rule comprise an independent hearsay exception. That reference was not designed to limit *Johnson v. Lutz* to untrustworthy statements — after all, the statement to the police officer was probably trustworthy — but rather to exclude records that would normally satisfy the business records exception (e.g., the clerk's computerized record of calls received) where inter alia the opponent shows that the business record or system itself was not reliable (e.g., the computer was defective).

Of course, in some situations, the statement by the "outsider" reflected in the business record may be admissible not for its truth but for some other purpose, but the disputed "To Send Money" forms here were admitted by the district court for all purposes, including as proof of the sender's identity. Possibly, the government could have argued as to Patrick Vigneau (it would be harder as to Mark) that other evidence of Patrick Vigneau's activities comprised circumstantial evidence that would permit a jury to conclude that he sent the specific forms bearing his name, Fed. R. Evid. 104(b); but apart from the need for a limiting instruction, Fed. R. Evid. 105, this presents a difficult issue that has not been argued and is not here resolved.

No doubt, the "To Send Money" forms were relevant to the government's case regardless of whether Patrick Vigneau (or any other named sender) was the person who made an individual transfer: they showed transfers of money from Rhode Island directed to Crandall and others that tended to support the general description of the drug and money laundering activities described by the government's witnesses. Thus, the forms could have been offered in redacted form, omitting the information identifying Patrick Vigneau as the sender of 21 of the forms. But that is not what happened.

Some cases have admitted under the business records exception "outsider" statements contained in business records, like the sender's name on the Western Union form, where there is evidence that the business itself used a procedure for verifying identity (e.g., by requiring a credit card or driver's license). Probably the best analytical defense of this gloss is that in such a case, the verification procedure is circumstantial evidence of identity that goes beyond the mere bootstrap use of the name to establish identity. While this gloss may well represent a reasonable accommodation of conflicting values, verification was not Western Union's practice at the time. * * *

The hearsay rule is an ancient and, even to most lawyers, a counter-intuitive restriction now riddled with many exceptions. However, the drafters chose to retain the hearsay rule, * * * and any trial lawyer who has tried to cross-examine a witness whose story depends on the hearsay statements of others understands why. These are reasons enough to tread cautiously, quite apart from the Supreme Court's intermittent reliance on the Confrontation Clause to make the use of hearsay a potentially constitutional issue in criminal trials. We thus conclude, in accord with the Tenth Circuit, *United States v. Cestnik*, 36 F.3d 904, 908 (10th Cir. 1994), that the sender name, address and telephone number on the forms should not have been admitted for their truth. [The Court reversed the convictions for money-laundering but affirmed all other convictions.]

NOTES

1. How do the Federal Rules handle the problem of information recorded by the business where the source of information has no duty to report the information accurately?

According to the Advisory Committee's Note, Federal Rule 803(6) requires that the informant have knowledge and be acting under a duty to report accurately when he reports the information. Many courts have found, however that the problem of information coming from outside the "business" is solved if the person recording the information from the outsider can verify that information for accuracy. A good example of verification arose in *United States v. Bland,* 961 F.2d 123 (9th Cir. 1992). The government sought to prove that the defendant had a handgun owned by Ann Rippetoe in his possession. The government proffered ATF Form 4473 from Dooley's Hardware Store, which identified Ann Rippetoe as the purchaser of the handgun. This form was held properly admitted under Rule 803(6). Proper foundation testimony was given by the manager of the sporting goods department at Dooley's Hardware, who testified that the employee completing the form had knowledge of the transaction at the time it occurred, and that the form was maintained in the course of regularly conducted activity. The fact that the qualifying witness could not identify the person who completed the record, or when the record was completed, was a question of weight and not admissibility. The Court recognized that when the record was offered to prove that Ann Rippetoe was, in fact, the buyer of the gun, a double hearsay question was presented, because there was no indication that the preparer of the record had personal knowledge of the name of the purchaser. However, since federal regulations required sellers of firearms to verify the name of each purchaser, and purchasers are under a legal duty to provide truthful information for Form 4473, the information transmitted by the buyer to the recorder was considered by the court to be reliable enough to satisfy any double hearsay concerns. *Compare United States v. Patrick*, 959 F.2d 991 (D.C. Cir. 1992), where the Court reversed a conviction in which the government offered a sales receipt to prove the defendant's address. The receipt was prepared by the merchant, and the government made no showing that the merchant had personal knowledge of the defendant's address, or that the merchant had verified the address in any way. There was no obligation of the buyer to give a correct address. *See also United States v. McIntyre,* 997 F.2d 687 (10th Cir. 1993) (motel records from two different motels were offered to show that the registrant stayed in the motel; one record was improperly admitted where there was no testimony that the name was verified, and no guarantee of trustworthiness in the giving of the name; the other record was properly admitted where there was testimony of verification). Note that the Court in *Vigneau, supra* was dubious about the verification solution; and there is merit to this skepticism, given the prevalence of Photoshop and the ease with which a fake i.d. can be produced.

2. Is there any other way to qualify a record if the statement recorded comes from an outsider with no "business duty" to report?

Professors Saltzburg, Martin, and Capra, *Federal Rules of Evidence Manual* (9th ed. 2006), analyze the cases involving business records and double hearsay as follows:

The concern addressed by the business duty requirement is that the person with personal knowledge of an event may not be reporting accurately to the person who eventually records the information. If the reporter is operating under the same or similar "business" duty (i.e., duty to report accurately) as the recorder, then the risk of inaccuracy is substantially reduced — the same guarantees of reliability apply to the observer and the recorder. *See, e.g.*, *United States v. Turner*, 189 F.3d 712 (8th Cir. 1999) (hearsay upon hearsay problem was excused where both the source of information and the recorder were acting in the regular course of the organization's business).

However, the existence of a business duty is not the only way to solve the double hearsay problem created when a business record is prepared by one who is relying on the personal knowledge of one outside the "business." One possible solution is verification [discussed immediately above].

Second, if the underlying statement satisfies an independent hearsay exception, the double hearsay problem is satisfied. *See, e.g.*, *Sana v. Hawaiian Cruises, Ltd.*, 181 F.3d 1041 (9th Cir. 1999) (memorandum contained several levels of hearsay; to be admissible, "each level of hearsay must satisfy an exception to the hearsay rule"; in this case, each level was satisfied; some statements to the recorder were admissible under Rule 803(3) and some were admissible under Rule 801(d)(2)(D)); *Bondie v. Bic Corp.*, 947 F.2d 1531 (6th Cir. 1991) (medical report was admissible because it was made and kept in the ordinary course of business and the included statement of the mother of the patient was a party admission; Rule 803(6) does not require that the underlying declarant have a business duty to supply the information recorded, so long as that declarant's statements come within a hearsay exception or exemption and recording such statements is part of the regularly conducted activity).

Third, if the underlying statement is offered for a non-hearsay purpose, there is no double hearsay problem at all. The record is admissible if the proponent establishes a regular recording of regularly conducted activity. A good example is provided by *United States v. Cestnik*, 36 F.3d 904 (10th Cir. 1994). In a prosecution for narcotics and money-laundering offenses, the government introduced Western Union "to-send-money" forms to support its charges that the defendant laundered money. The forms did not reveal the defendant's name as the sender. But, the government introduced independent evidence to show that the senders' names were aliases of the defendant. The Court held that the forms were properly admitted under the business records exception. To the extent the records were offered to prove the amount of money spent on a specific date, they were qualified under the Rule by the custodian of records for Western Union. The Court noted that the records would not have been admissible if offered to prove that the person named on the form was the *actual* sender, because "Western Union agents do not verify the information filled out by the sender." However, since the government offered the senders' names "not to prove the identity of the sender but as circumstantial evidence linking the false names to the money transfers," the names were not hearsay and therefore the records did not present a "source of information" problem. In other words, the fact that *someone* knew enough to use the defendant's aliases in wiring the money was itself evidence of a conspiratorial association; the government did not offer the record to prove that the defendant himself actually wired the money. *See also Hoselton v. Metz Baking Co.*, 48 F.3d 1056 (8th Cir. 1995) (an accountant's notes containing statements made by others during a negotiation session were admissible as business records; as to the statements included in the notes, the Federal Rules "do not require each level of hearsay to meet the requirements of the same exception"; the statements in the accountant's record were not hearsay because they were not offered to prove the truth of the matters asserted; rather, they were offered to show that the plaintiffs were on notice of certain expectations that the defendants had in negotiations).

3. What are the foundation requirements for business records? Who is competent to establish these requirements?

See Saltzburg, Martin, and Capra, *Federal Rules of Evidence Manual* (9th ed. 2006):

While a records custodian is a proper witness for establishing the foundation requirements of a business record, Rule 803(6) provides for a much more expansive class of witnesses who can establish this foundation. A witness is a "qualified witness" if he or she has acquired knowledge of how the records are kept, and can testify that they are kept in the ordinary course of regularly conducted activity. *See, e.g., United States v. Lauerson*, 343 F.3d 604 (2d Cir. 2003) (doctor was a qualified witness to establish the admissibility requirements for medical records; the doctor designed the procedures for maintaining the records and observed them being implemented); *United States v. Childs*, 5 F.3d 1328 (9th Cir. 1993) ("The phrase 'other qualified witness' is broadly interpreted to require only that the witness understand the recordkeeping system."); *United States v. Jakobetz*, 955 F.2d 786 (2d Cir. 1992) (toll receipts incorporated into corporate expense records could be authenticated by a custodian of the corporation that prepared the expense records: "Even if the document is originally created by another entity, its creator need not testify when the document has been incorporated into the business records of the testifying entity"; here the custodian testified that toll receipts were regularly submitted in expense reports and regularly incorporated into the business records of the corporation for general accounting purposes; the custodian was a qualified witness within the meaning of the Rule).

For cases in which a foundation witness was found unqualified under the Rule, *see, e.g., United States v. Riley*, 236 F.3d 982 (8th Cir. 2001) (lab reports erroneously admitted; foundation witness could identify the reports but had no knowledge of how they were prepared or maintained and thus could not testify that the reports had been kept in the ordinary course of regularly conducted activity); *Collins v. Kibort*, 143 F.3d 331 (7th Cir. 1998) (hospital records erroneously admitted; the Rule does not require a foundation witness to have prepared the record or to have personal knowledge of the entries in the record; however, in this case the witness did not have knowledge of the hospital's regular business practices in making and keeping the record); *Belber v. Lipson*, 905 F.2d 549 (1st Cir. 1990) (one doctor is not a qualified witness with respect to the records of another doctor, where he merely received the records from an attorney who knew nothing about the other doctor's recordkeeping process).

The foundation witness must know something about the recordkeeping process, but the witness need not have personal knowledge of any particular recording or how it was made. As the Court put it in *United States v. Franco*, 874 F.2d 1136 (7th Cir. 1989):

> A qualified witness is not required, however, to have personally participated in or observed the creation of the document * * * or know who actually recorded the information. * * * We broadly interpret the term "qualified witness" as requiring only someone with knowledge of the procedure governing the creation and maintenance of the type of records sought to be admitted.

See also Dyno Constr. Co. v. McWane, Inc., 198 F.3d 567 (6th Cir. 1999) (person laying the foundation need not have personal knowledge concerning the preparation of the records: "All that is required of the witness is that he or she be familiar with the recordkeeping procedures of the organization.").

Moreover, the foundation witness can obtain knowledge about the recordkeeping process from the statements of others who are familiar with the recordkeeping. That this may be hearsay information is not disqualifying, because Rule 104 allows the trial court to consider hearsay in determining whether admissibility requirements are met. *See, e.g., Franco* (a witness was held qualified where he learned about recordkeeping through conversations with others familiar with the process: "The court relied on hearsay to determine whether Agent Garza understood the accounting system * * * but that is clearly permissible under the Federal Rules of Evidence"). It follows that a finding that records were recorded in the ordinary course of business activity can be based at least in part on the records themselves, e.g., that they were organized, precise, and looked routinely recorded. *United States v. Draiman*, 784 F.2d 248 (7th Cir. 1986) (entries in the document itself may help to establish foundation).

The foundation requirements of the Rule need not be established by in-court testimony. Under an amendment effective December 1, 2000, the qualified witness may establish the foundation "by certification that complies with Rule 902(11), Rule 902(12), or a statute permitting certification." The amendment is intended to limit unnecessary cost and inconvenience, by permitting a qualified witness to provide the foundation for business records by way of affidavit in lieu of in-court testimony. The amendment does not eliminate the need for a qualified witness, nor does it change the type of qualifications that have been found necessary for a witness to be able to establish a foundation for business records. It simply provides that the qualified witness can establish the foundation without being called to testify.

The Advisory Committee considered it necessary to amend the Rule to provide for a unified practice in the Federal Courts. Before the amendment, foreign business records offered in criminal cases could be qualified by affidavit under the terms of 18 U.S.C. § 3505. However, qualified witnesses were required to testify before foreign records could be admitted in civil cases and before domestic records could be admitted in any case. This disparity in the practice made little sense; the amendment provides for a unitary practice along the terms of section 3505.

The amendment to Rule 803(6) provides for an alternative means of establishing admissibility under the hearsay exception. It does not, of course, purport to solve any problem of authentication. Authenticity questions are considered under Rule 902. Whether the affidavit procedure comports with the accused's right to confrontation in criminal cases is a question taken up at the end of this Editorial Explanatory Comment.

To qualify a business record, it must be shown that the information recorded is the type of information that is recorded in the ordinary course of a regularly conducted activity, and that it is the regular practice of the business to record such an event. *See, e.g.*, *Wilander v. McDermott Int'l, Inc.*, 887 F.2d 88 (5th Cir. 1989) (statement concerning an accident, taken on an *ad hoc* basis by a barge captain, was not recorded in the ordinary course of regularly conducted activity; it was not the regular practice of the barge captain to make such a report).

If the event recorded is an isolated incident, or if it is a recurring event that is not recorded as a matter of regular practice, the guarantees of reliability supporting the business records exception do not exist. *See, e.g.*, *Waddell v. Commissioner*, 841 F.2d 264 (9th Cir. 1988) (an appraisal report was inadmissible where no showing was made that it was the regular practice of the preparer to prepare such a report).

Some courts have applied the "ordinary course" and "regular practice" requirements liberally. These courts state that while Rule 803(6) does not extend to activity or recording that is "casual or isolated," some degree of discontinuity or selectivity is permissible, and affects only the weight of the evidence. *See, e.g.*, *Kassel v. Gannett Co.*, 875 F.2d 935 (1st Cir. 1989) (contact reports of complaints are admissible even though a report is not filled out every time a complaint is made). Most courts, however, strictly construe the requirements of "ordinary course" and "regular practice," on the ground that this language was carefully considered by the drafters of the Rule and the requirements are important guarantees of the trustworthiness of the record. In these courts, the record is excluded if the event recorded is unusual, or if the event when it occurs is not recorded in the ordinary course of the organization's activity. *See, e.g.*, *Pierce v. Atchison T. & S.F. Ry.*, 110 F.3d 431 (7th Cir. 1997) (memorandum recording an "unusual" incident "was not created with the kind of regularity or routine which gives business records their inherent reliability"); *United States v. Strother*, 49 F.3d 869 (2d Cir. 1995) (a bank memorandum indicating that an overdrawn check for $82,000 was covered by the bank was held inadmissible as a business record; this type of event was not one which routinely recurred; the Court stated that it was "reluctant to adopt a rule that would permit the introduction into evidence of memoranda drafted in response to unusual or isolated events").

[4] Records Prepared in Anticipation of Litigation

PALMER v. HOFFMAN

318 U.S. 109 (1943)

MR. JUSTICE DOUGLAS delivered the opinion of the Court.

This case arose out of a grade crossing accident which occurred in Massachusetts.* * * On the question of negligence the trial court submitted three issues to the jury — failure to ring a bell, to blow a whistle, to have a light burning in the front of the train. The jury returned a verdict in favor of respondent individually for some $25,000 and in favor of respondent as administrator for $9,000. The District Court entered judgment on the verdict. The Circuit Court of Appeals affirmed, one judge dissenting.* * *

* * * The accident occurred on the night of December 25, 1940. On December 27, 1940, the engineer of the train, who died before the trial, made a statement at a freight office of petitioners where he was interviewed by an assistant superintendent of the road and by a representative of the Massachusetts Public Utilities Commission. This statement was offered in evidence by petitioners under the Act of June 20, 1936, 28 U.S.C. § 695. [This was the statutory precursor to Rule 803(6).] They offered to prove (in the language of the Act) that the statement was signed in the regular course of business, it being the regular course of such business to make such a statement. Respondent's objection to its introduction was sustained.

We agree with the majority view below that it was properly excluded.

We may assume that if the statement was made "in the regular course" of business, it would satisfy the other provisions of the Act. But we do not think that it was made "in the regular course" of business within the meaning of the Act. The business of the petitioners is the railroad business. That business like other enterprises entails the keeping of numerous books and records essential to its conduct or useful in its efficient operation. Though such books and records were considered reliable and trustworthy for major decisions in the industrial and business world, their use in litigation was greatly circumscribed or hedged about by the hearsay rule — restrictions which greatly increased the time and cost of making the proof where those who made the records were numerous. * * *

The engineer's statement which was held inadmissible in this case falls into quite a different category. It is not a record made for the systematic conduct of the business as a business. An accident report may affect that business in the sense that it affords information on which the management may act. It is not, however, typical of entries made systematically or as a matter of routine to record events or occurrences, to reflect transactions with others, or to provide internal controls. The conduct of a business commonly entails the payment of tort claims incurred by the negligence of its employees. But the fact that a company makes a business out of recording its employees' versions of their accidents does not put those statements in the class of records made "in the regular course" of the business within the meaning of the Act. If it did, then any law office in the land could follow the same course, since business as defined in the Act includes the professions. We would then have a real perversion of a rule designed to facilitate admission of records which experience has shown to be quite trustworthy. Any business by installing a regular system for recording and preserving its version of accidents for which it was potentially liable could qualify those reports under the Act. * * * Preparation of cases for trial by virtue of being a "business" or incidental thereto would obtain the benefits of this liberalized version of the early shop book rule. The probability of trustworthiness of records because they were routine reflections of the day to day operations of a business would be forgotten as the basis of the rule.* * * We cannot so completely empty the words of the Act of their historic meaning. If the Act is to be extended to apply not only to a "regular course" of a business but also to any "regular course" of conduct which may have some relationship to business, Congress not this Court must extend it. Such a major change which opens wide the door to avoidance of cross-examination should not be left to implication. Nor is it any answer to say that Congress has provided in the Act that the various circumstances of the making of the record should affect its weight not its admissibility. That provision comes into play only in case the other requirements of the Act are met.

In short, it is manifest that in this case those reports are not for the systematic conduct of the enterprise as a railroad business. Unlike payrolls, accounts receivable, accounts payable, bills of lading and the like these reports are calculated for use essentially in the court, not in the business. Their primary utility is in litigating, not in railroading.

* * *

Affirmed.

NOTES

1. Is the court's analysis that an accident report is not a business record supported by the language of the statute?

Most courts have read *Palmer* not as a strict definition of an organization's "ordinary course of business," but rather as precluding records prepared in anticipation of litigation, where the records are favorable to the party who prepared them. Under these circumstances there is suspect motivation in the preparation of the records that renders them untrustworthy. *See Certain Underwriters at Lloyd's, London v. Sinkovich*, 232 F.3d 200 (4th Cir. 2000) (report not admissible under Rule 803(6) where "the primary motive for initially preparing the report was to prepare for litigation"). But if the report is unfavorable to the party who prepared it, it will be admissible because no inference of suspect motivation can be drawn. *See, e.g.*, *Yates v. Bair Transp., Inc.,* 249 F. Supp. 681 (S.D. N.Y. 1965) (reports of doctors retained by defendant in personal injury litigation are admissible where they are favorable to the plaintiff).

2. Does the trustworthiness requirement in the rule mean that records are admissible whenever they are determined to be trustworthy?

Rule 803(6) authorizes a trial court to exclude a record where the circumstances of its preparation indicate that the record is untrustworthy. But the rule does not support the converse proposition, that a record is admissible simply because it is trustworthy. Even a trustworthy record must satisfy the other admissibility requirements of the rule; there must be a regular practice of recording an event which occurs in the ordinary course of a regularly conducted activity. If a record is not one of a routine recording of a routine event, it cannot be admitted under Rule 803(6) even if the particular record is trustworthy. *United States v. Freidin,* 849 F.2d 716 (2d Cir. 1988) (isolated document inadmissible under Rule 803(6) even though there is no reason to think that the document is untrustworthy; trustworthiness is not the only precondition to admissibility). This is because the federal rules have established admissibility requirements for each exception, which must be met. The rules specifically reject an approach to hearsay that admits a statement whenever it happens to be trustworthy under the circumstances. Such an argument is permissible only under the residual exception. *See, e.g.*, *United States v. Blackburn*, 992 F.2d 666 (7th Cir. 1993) (even though a report is trustworthy, it may not be admitted under Rule 803(6) where it was prepared in anticipation of litigation rather than in the ordinary course of business; however, the report was admissible under the residual exception).

3. Are computerized records admissible under the business records exception?

See Saltzburg, Martin, and Capra, *Federal Rules of Evidence Manual* (9th ed. 2006):

> Courts generally do not require any extra foundation testimony for computerized records. *See, e.g.*, *United States v. Briscoe*, 896 F.2d 1476 (7th Cir. 1990) (foundation requirements for computerized records are the same as those for other records; proponent is not required to show

that computers are tested for internal programming errors); *United States v. Sanders*, 749 F.2d 195 (5th Cir. 1984) (foundation requirements for computerized records are no different from requirements for other business records); *United States v. Young Bros.*, 728 F.2d 682 (5th Cir. 1984) (accuracy of software need not be specifically established); *United States v. Catabran*, 836 F.2d 453 (9th Cir. 1988) (presence of inaccuracies in computer records, as in other records, is a question of weight). Despite the fact that computerized records are often easier to tamper with than traditional records, the standards for admitting computer-generated records are ordinarily no more stringent than those for admitting other business records. *See* Peritz, *Computer Data and Reliability: A Call for Authentication of Business Records under the Federal Rules of Evidence*, 80 Nw. U. L. Rev. 956 (1986) (critical of the fact that "federal judges substantially agree that computer output should be qualified like any other business record," and expressing concern that "computer systems store, retrieve, and manipulate information in ways significantly different from earlier manual or mechanical systems"). However, testimony by a witness about the accuracy of the software and reliability of the computerization will certainly bolster the minimal foundation that ordinarily suffices for both computerized and noncomputerized records.

If the record is a computer printout, it is not problematic that the printout was made in anticipation of litigation, so long as the data compiled in the printout was entered into the computer at a time when there was no suspect motivation. *See, e.g.*, *United States v. Briscoe*, 896 F.2d 1476 (7th Cir. 1990):

> We note that the fact that the actual computer printouts presented at trial were prepared specifically for this case * * * does not preclude their admission under Rule 803(6). It is sufficient that the data compiled in the printouts was entered into the computer contemporaneous with the placing of each call and maintained in the regular course of business.

See also United States v. Hernandez, 913 F.2d 1506 (10th Cir. 1990) (so long as the original computer data compilation was prepared pursuant to a business duty in accordance with regular business practice, the fact that the hard copy offered as evidence was printed for purposes of litigation does not affect its admissibility).

Information taken off the Internet can potentially qualify as a business record. While the medium for the information is different, the same foundation requirements apply. For example, if information is found on a website and is offered for its truth, the proponent will have to establish through a qualified witness that the information is the type that is ordinarily posted in the course of regularly conducted organizational activity. At least one Court has held that postings to a website cannot be admitted as the business record of the Internet service provider, because such providers are simply conduits and not recordkeepers. *See, e.g.*, *United States v. Jackson*, 208 F.3d 633 (7th Cir. 2000) ("The fact that the Internet service providers may be able to retrieve information that its customers posted or email that its customers sent does not turn that material into a business record of the Internet service provider.").

4. Note that there are three hearsay exceptions that overlap to some extent with the business records exception.

The exception for public records, Rule 803(8), is discussed in the next section. The exception for past recollection recorded is set forth in Rule 803(5), which covers:

(5) Recorded recollection. — A memorandum or record concerning a matter about which a witness once had knowledge but now has insufficient recollection to enable the witness to testify fully and accurately, shown to have been made or adopted by the witness when the matter was fresh in the witness' memory and to reflect that knowledge correctly. If admitted, the memorandum or record may be read into evidence but may not itself be received as an exhibit unless offered by an adverse party.

The exception for past recollection recorded is discussed in Chapter 3 in the section on witness recollection.

Rule 803(7) provides for admissibility of the absence of an entry from a business record. The exception covers:

(7) Absence of entry in records kept in accordance with the provisions of paragraph (6). — Evidence that a matter is not included in the memoranda, reports, records, or data compilations, in any form, kept in accordance with the provisions of paragraph (6), to prove the nonoccurrence or nonexistence of the matter, if the matter was of a kind of which a memorandum, report, record, or data compilation was regularly made and preserved, unless the sources of information or other circumstances indicate lack of trustworthiness.

Rule 803(7), unlike Rule 803(6), does not specifically require foundation testimony from a custodian or other qualified witness. But the first step in any analysis under Rule 803(7) is to determine whether the record qualifies under Rule 803(6) since, if it does not, Rule 803(7) cannot be used. That is, unless the record is admissible under the standards of Rule 803(6), evidence of a failure of recording or absence of an entry in the record cannot be admitted. Thus, admissibility is dependent upon adequate foundation testimony concerning the records from a witness sufficiently familiar with them.

G. PUBLIC RECORDS

[1] Federal Rule of Evidence 803(8)

Rule 803. Hearsay Exceptions; Availability of Declarant Immaterial

The following are not excluded by the hearsay rule, even though the declarant is available as a witness:

* * *

(8) Public records and reports. Records, reports, statements, or data compilations, in any form, of public offices or agencies, setting forth (A) the activities of the office or agency, or (B) matters observed pursuant to duty imposed by law as to which matters there was a duty to report, excluding, however, in criminal cases matters observed by police officers and other law enforcement personnel, or (C) in civil actions and proceedings and against the Government in criminal cases, factual findings resulting from an investigation made pursuant to authority granted by law, unless the sources of information or other circumstances indicate lack of trustworthiness.

* * *

[2] Illustration

Plaintiff's wife died in an airplane crash. Plaintiff sues the airplane manufacturer, alleging negligent design and production. At the beginning of the trial, plaintiff's counsel produces two impressive documents.

Plaintiff's counsel:	Your Honor, I have two documents, both duly authenticated, that I'd like to introduce at this time. The first document is the FAA record on malfunctions of the type of aircraft involved in this incident. The second document is the FAA investigative report which concludes that this particular type of plane was designed with an insufficient lift to weight ratio.
Defendant:	Objection! Hearsay.
Plaintiff's counsel:	__________.

[3] Opinions and Factual Findings

BEECH AIRCRAFT CORP. v. RAINEY
488 U.S. 153 (1988)

Justice Brennan delivered the opinion of the Court.

In this action we address a longstanding conflict among the Federal Courts of Appeals over whether Federal Rule of Evidence 803(8)(C), which provides an exception to the hearsay rule for public investigatory reports containing "factual findings," extends to conclusions and opinions contained in such reports. * * *

I

This litigation stems from the crash of a Navy training aircraft at Middleton Field, Alabama, on July 13, 1982, which took the lives of both pilots on board, Lieutenant Commander Barbara Ann Rainey and Ensign Donald Bruce Knowlton. The accident took place while Rainey, a Navy flight instructor, and

Knowlton, her student, were flying "touch-and-go" exercises in a T-34C Turbo-Mentor aircraft, number 3E955. Their aircraft and several others flew in an oval pattern, each plane making successive landing/takeoff maneuvers on the runway. Following its fourth pass at the runway, 3E955 appeared to make a left turn prematurely, cutting out the aircraft ahead of it in the pattern and threatening a collision. After radio warnings from two other pilots, the plane banked sharply to the right in order to avoid the other aircraft. At that point it lost altitude rapidly, crashed, and burned.

Because of the damage to the plane and the lack of any survivors, the cause of the accident could not be determined with certainty. The two pilots' surviving spouses brought a product liability suit against petitioners Beech Aircraft Corporation, the plane's manufacturer, and Beech Aerospace Services, which serviced the plane under contract with the Navy. The plaintiffs alleged that the crash had been caused by a loss of engine power, known as "rollback," due to some defect in the aircraft's fuel control system. The defendants, on the other hand, advanced the theory of pilot error, suggesting that the plane had stalled during the abrupt avoidance maneuver.

At trial, the only seriously disputed question was whether pilot error or equipment malfunction had caused the crash. Both sides relied primarily on expert testimony. One piece of evidence presented by the defense was an investigative report prepared by Lieutenant Commander William Morgan on order of the training squadron's commanding officer and pursuant to authority granted in the Manual of the Judge Advocate General. This "JAG Report," completed during the six weeks following the accident, was organized into sections labeled "finding of fact," "opinions," and "recommendations," and was supported by some 60 attachments. The "finding of fact" included statements like the following:

> "13. At approximately 1020, while turning crosswind without proper interval, 3E955 crashed, immediately caught fire and burned."
>
> * * *
>
> "27. At the time of impact, the engine of 3E955 was operating but was operating at reduced power." "

Among his "opinions" Lieutenant Commander Morgan stated, in paragraph 5, that due to the deaths of the two pilots and the destruction of the aircraft "it is almost impossible to determine exactly what happened to Navy 3E955 from the time it left the runway on its last touch and go until it impacted the ground." He nonetheless continued with a detailed reconstruction of a possible set of events, based on pilot error, that could have caused the accident. The next two paragraphs stated a caveat and a conclusion:

> "6. Although the above sequence of events is the most likely to have occurred, it does not change the possibility that a 'rollback' did occur.
>
> 7. The most probable cause of the accident was the pilots [*sic*] failure to maintain proper interval."

The trial judge initially determined, at a pretrial conference, that the JAG Report was sufficiently trustworthy to be admissible, but that it "would be admissible only on its factual findings and would not be admissible insofar as any opinions or conclusions are concerned." The day before trial, however, the court reversed itself and ruled, over the plaintiffs' objection, that certain of the conclusions would be admitted. Accordingly, the court admitted most of the report's "opinions," including the first sentence of paragraph 5 about the impossibility of determining exactly what happened, and paragraph 7, which opined about failure to maintain proper interval as "[t]he most probable cause of the accident."* * *

Following a 2-week trial, the jury returned a verdict for petitioners. A panel of the Eleventh Circuit reversed and remanded for a new trial. Considering itself bound by the Fifth Circuit precedent of *Smith v. Ithaca Corp.*, 612 F.2d 215 (1980), the panel agreed with Rainey's argument that Federal Rule of Evidence 803(8)(C), which excepts investigatory reports from the hearsay rule, did not encompass evaluative conclusions or opinions. Therefore, it held, the "conclusions" contained in the JAG Report should have been excluded. One member of the panel, concurring specially, urged however that the Circuit reconsider its interpretation of Rule 803(8)(C), suggesting that "*Smith* is an anomaly among the circuits."

* * *

II

* * *

Controversy over what "public records and reports" are made not excludable by Rule 803(8)(C) has divided the federal courts from the beginning. In the present litigation, the Court of Appeals followed the "narrow" interpretation of *Smith v. Ithaca Corp.,* which held that the term "factual findings" did not encompass "opinions" or "conclusions." Courts of Appeals other than those of the Fifth and Eleventh Circuits, however, have generally adopted a broader interpretation. For example, the Court of Appeals for the Sixth Circuit, in *Baker v. Elcona Homes Corp.*, 588 F.2d 551, 557-558 (1978), held that "factual findings admissible under Rule 803(8)(C) may be those which are made by the preparer of the report from disputed evidence * * * ." The other Courts of Appeals that have squarely confronted the issue have also adopted the broader interpretation. We agree and hold that factually based conclusions or opinions are not on that account excluded from the scope of Rule 803(8)(C).

Because the Federal Rules of Evidence are a legislative enactment, we turn to the "traditional tools of statutory construction," *INS v. Cardoza-Fonseca*, 480 U.S. 421, 446 (1987), in order to construe their provisions. We begin with the language of the Rule itself. Proponents of the narrow view have generally relied heavily on a perceived dichotomy between "fact" and "opinion" in arguing for the limited scope of the phrase "factual findings." *Smith v. Ithaca Corp.* contrasted the term "factual findings" in Rule 803(8)(C) with the language of Rule 803(6) (records of regularly conducted activity), which expressly refers to "opinions" and "diagnoses." "Factual findings," the court opined, must be something other than opinions.

For several reasons, we do not agree. In the first place, it is not apparent that the term "factual findings" should be read to mean simply "facts" (as opposed to "opinions" or "conclusions"). A common definition of "finding of fact" is, for example, "[a] conclusion by way of reasonable inference from the evidence." *Black's Law Dictionary* 569 (5th ed. 1979). To say the least, the language of the Rule does not compel us to reject the interpretation that "factual findings" includes conclusions or opinions that flow from a factual investigation. Second, we note that, contrary to what is often assumed, the language of the Rule does not state that "factual findings" are admissible, but that "*reports* * * * setting forth * * * factual findings" (emphasis added) are admissible. On this reading, the language of the Rule does not create a distinction between "fact" and "opinion" contained in such reports.

Turning next to the legislative history of Rule 803(8)(C), we find no clear answer to the question of how the Rule's language should be interpreted. Indeed, in this litigation the legislative history may well be at the origin of the dispute. Rather than the more usual situation where a court must attempt to glean meaning from ambiguous comments of legislators who did not focus directly on the problem at hand, here the Committees in both Houses of Congress clearly recognized and expressed their opinions on the precise question at issue. Unfortunately, however, they took diametrically opposite positions. Moreover, the two Houses made no effort to reconcile their views, either through changes in the Rule's language or through a statement in the Report of the Conference Committee.

The House Judiciary Committee, which dealt first with the proposed rules after they had been transmitted to Congress by this Court, included in its Report but one brief paragraph on Rule 803(8):

> The Committee approved Rule 803(8) without substantive change from the form in which it was submitted by the Court. The Committee intends that the phrase 'factual findings' be strictly construed and that evaluations or opinions contained in public reports shall not be admissible under this Rule." H.R. Rep. No. 93-650, p. 14 (1973).

The Senate Committee responded at somewhat greater length, but equally emphatically:

> "The House Judiciary Committee report contained a statement of intent that the phrase factual findings in subdivision (c) be strictly construed and that evaluations or opinions contained in public reports shall not be admissible under this rule. The committee takes strong exception to this limiting understanding of the application of the rule. We do not think it reflects an understanding of the intended operation of the rule as explained in the Advisory Committee notes to this subsection * * * . We think the restrictive interpretation of the House overlooks the fact that while the Advisory Committee assumes admissibility in the first instance of evaluative reports, they are not admissible if, as the rule states, 'the sources of information or other circumstances indicate lack of trustworthiness."

* * *

The Advisory Committee's comments are notable, first, in that they contain no mention of any dichotomy between statements of "fact" and "opinions" or "conclusions." What was on the Committee's mind was simply whether what it called "evaluative reports" should be admissible. * * * Nowhere in its comments is there the slightest indication that it even considered the solution of admitting only "factual" statements from such reports. Rather, the Committee referred throughout to "reports," without any such differentiation regarding the statements they contained. What the Committee referred to in the Rule's language as "reports * * * setting forth * * * factual findings" is surely nothing more or less than what in its commentary it called "evaluative reports." Its solution as to their admissibility is clearly stated in the final paragraph of its report on this Rule. That solution consists of two principles: First, "the rule * * * assumes admissibility in the first instance * * * ." Second, it provides "ample provision for escape if sufficient negative factors are present."

That "provision for escape" is contained in the final clause of the Rule: evaluative reports are admissible "unless the sources of information or other circumstances indicate lack of trustworthiness." This trustworthiness inquiry — and not an arbitrary distinction between "fact" and "opinion" — was the Committee's primary safeguard against the admission of unreliable evidence, and it is important to note that it applies to all elements of the report. Thus, a trial judge has the discretion, and indeed the obligation, to exclude an entire report or portions thereof — whether narrow "factual" statements or broader "conclusions" — that she determines to be untrustworthy.[1]

Moreover, safeguards built into other portions of the Federal Rules, such as those dealing with relevance and prejudice, provide the court with additional means of scrutinizing and, where appropriate, excluding evaluative reports or portions of them. And of course it goes without saying that the admission of a report containing "conclusions" is subject to the ultimate safeguard — the opponent's right to present evidence tending to contradict or diminish the weight of those conclusions.

Our conclusion that neither the language of the Rule nor the intent of its framers calls for a distinction between "fact" and "opinion" is strengthened by the analytical difficulty of drawing such a line. It has frequently been remarked that the distinction between statements of fact and opinion is, at

[1] The Advisory Committee proposed a nonexclusive list of four factors it thought would be helpful in passing on this question: (1) the timeliness of the investigation; (2) the investigator's skill or experience; (3) whether a hearing was held; and (4) possible bias when reports are prepared with a view to possible litigation (*citing Palmer v. Hoffman*, 318 U.S. 109 (1943)). Advisory Committee's Notes on Fed. Rule Evid. 803(8), 28 U.S.C. App., p. 725; *see Note, The Trustworthiness of Government Evaluative Reports under Federal Rule of Evidence* 803(8)(C), 96 Harv. L. Rev. 492 (1982).

In a case similar in many respects to these, the trial court applied the trustworthiness requirement to hold inadmissible a JAG Report on the causes of a Navy airplane accident; it found the report untrustworthy because it "was prepared by an inexperienced investigator in a highly complex field of investigation." *Fraley v. Rockwell Int'l Corp.*, 470 F. Supp. 1264, 1267 (SD Ohio 1979). In the present litigation, the District Court found the JAG Report to be trustworthy. As no party has challenged that finding, we have no occasion to express an opinion on it.

best, one of degree. * * * E. Cleary, McCormick on Evidence 27 (3d ed. 1984) ("There is no conceivable statement however specific, detailed and 'factual,' that is not in some measure the product of inference and reflection as well as observation and memory"); R. Lempert & S. Saltzburg, A Modern Approach to Evidence 449 (2d ed. 1982) ("A factual finding, unless it is a simple report of something observed, is an opinion as to what more basic facts imply"). Thus, the traditional requirement that lay witnesses give statements of fact rather than opinion may be considered, "[l]ike the hearsay and original documents rules * * * a 'best evidence' rule." McCormick, *Opinion Evidence in Iowa*, 19 Drake L. Rev. 245, 246 (1970).

In the present action, the trial court had no difficulty in admitting as a factual finding the statement in the JAG Report that "[a]t the time of impact, the engine of 3E955 was operating but was operating at reduced power." Surely this "factual finding" could also be characterized as an opinion, which the investigator presumably arrived at on the basis of clues contained in the airplane wreckage. Rather than requiring that we draw some inevitably arbitrary line between the various shades of fact/opinion that invariably will be present in investigatory reports, we believe the Rule instructs us — as its plain language states — to admit "reports * * * setting forth * * * factual findings." The Rule's limitations and safeguards lie elsewhere: First, the requirement that reports contain factual findings bars the admission of statements not based on factual investigation. Second, the trustworthiness provision requires the court to make a determination as to whether the report, or any portion thereof, is sufficiently trustworthy to be admitted.

A broad approach to admissibility under Rule 803(8)(C), as we have outlined it, is also consistent with the Federal Rules' general approach of relaxing the traditional barriers to "opinion" testimony. Rules 702-705 permit experts to testify in the form of an opinion, and without any exclusion of opinions on "ultimate issues." And Rule 701 permits even a lay witness to testify in the form of opinions or inferences drawn from her observations when testimony in that form will be helpful to the trier of fact. We see no reason to strain to reach an interpretation of Rule 803(8)(C) that is contrary to the liberal thrust of the Federal Rules. We hold, therefore, that portions of investigatory reports otherwise admissible under Rule 803(8)(C) are not inadmissible merely because they state a conclusion or opinion. As long as the conclusion is based on a factual investigation and satisfies the Rule's trustworthiness requirement, it should be admissible along with other portions of the report. As the trial judge in this action determined that certain of the JAG Report's conclusions were trustworthy, he rightly allowed them to be admitted into evidence. We therefore reverse the judgment of the Court of Appeals in respect of the Rule 803(8)(C) issue.

* * *

IV

We hold that statements in the form of opinions or conclusions are not by that fact excluded from the scope of Federal Rule of Evidence 803(8)(C). We therefore reverse the judgment of the Court of Appeals in that respect. * * * The case is remanded for further proceedings consistent with this opinion.

It is so ordered.

NOTES

1. Why is there a special exception for public records when there is already an exception for records of regularly conducted activity?

See Saltzburg, Martin, and Capra, *Federal Rules of Evidence Manual* (9th ed. 2006):

> There are two reasons for creating a special hearsay exception for public records. First, it is assumed that public officials perform their duties properly and that, given their multiple duties, it is unlikely that they will be able to remember the details of individual transactions independently of their records. Second, the exception often eliminates the need for public officials to testify or prepare for a trial, freeing them to spend more time performing their public duties. These twin rationales account for the major differences in admissibility requirements between Rules 803(8) and 803(6): (1) public records may be reliable and admissible even though they do not satisfy the regularity and contemporaneity requirements of business records, see, e.g., *United States v. Versaint*, 849 F.2d 827 (3d Cir. 1988) (a public record prepared one month after the event described in the report was admissible, so long as no affirmative showing was made that the report was untrustworthy; Rule 803(8) does not require that a report be made at or near the time of the event it is describing); and (2) public records may be admitted without the testimony or even the affidavit of a foundation witness. *See, e.g., United States v. Loyola-Dominguez*, 125 F.3d 1315 (9th Cir. 1997) (Rule 803(8) does not require a foundation by a qualified witness).

2. What is the scope of the exclusion for law enforcement reports in criminal cases?

In the famous case of *United States v. Oates*, 560 F.2d 45 (2d Cir. 1977), a defendant was convicted of possession of heroin with intent to distribute and of conspiracy. On appeal, these convictions were reversed because the Court was convinced that the trial judge erred in allowing the government to introduce two documentary exhibits purporting to be the official report and the accompanying worksheet of the United States Customs Service chemist who analyzed a white powdery substance seized from appellant's codefendant. The Court held that the report was a record of matters observed by law enforcement personnel, excluded under the language of Rule 803(8)(B), and also that it was a law enforcement report excluded under Rule 803(8)(C).

Most courts have read the Rule 803(8)(B) and (C) exclusionary language in a far more limited fashion than that provided by the court in *Oates*. Under the predominant view, laboratory reports and the like are admissible, because the rule is designed to exclude a different type of report, i.e., police-generated reports that are prepared under adversarial circumstances, which are conducive to manipulation by authorities bent on convicting a criminal defendant. *See, e.g., United States v. Enterline*, 894 F.2d 287 (8th Cir. 1990) ("It is clear that the exclusion concerns matters observed by the police at the scene of the crime. Such observations are potentially unreliable since they are made in an adversary setting, and are often subjective evaluations of whether a crime was committed.") Where the risk of manipulation and untrustworthiness is minimal — such as where the report contains unambiguous factual matter made under non-adversarial circumstances — courts have held that the report should be admitted despite the apparently absolute language of the Rule. *United States v. Dancy*, 861 F.2d 77 (5th Cir. 1988) (fingerprint card in penitentiary packet, offered to show that defendant was a convicted felon, was admissible under Rule 803(8)(B) because it was prepared outside the context of a criminal investigation; the Rule excludes only records that report the observation or investigation of crimes). Even the Second Circuit, in which *Oates* was decided, has held that a routine tabulation of serial numbers prepared by law enforcement personnel was admissible against a criminal defendant. *United States v. Grady,* 544 F.2d 598 (2d Cir. 1976) (admitting reports on firearms serial numbers on the ground that they were records of routine factual matters prepared in a nonadversarial setting).

While a report that is ministerial in nature and made without contemplation of specific litigation is ordinarily held admissible, those law enforcement reports that are adversarial and evaluative in nature are ordinarily excluded, consistent with the exclusionary intent of Rule 803(8)(B) and (C). *United States v. Pena-Gutierrez,* 222 F.3d 1080 (9th Cir. 2000) (trial court erred in admitting into evidence "the on-the-scene investigative report of a crime by an INS official whose perceptions might be clouded and untrustworthy"); *United States v. Bohrer,* 807 F.2d 159 (10th Cir. 1986) (I.R.S. contact card excluded under Rule 803(8) because prepared under adversarial circumstances and because information included therein is not ministerial in nature, thus subject to manipulation).

It should also be noted that some public reports can be offered in a criminal case because they are reports of "matters observed" by public officials *other than law enforcement personnel*. Neither the terms nor the concerns of the exclusionary language will apply to reports prepared by officials without law enforcement responsibilities. The problem with law enforcement reports is that police officers are in the competitive enterprise of ferreting out crime; in the heat of battle, a law enforcement officer might shade or falsify a report in such a way as to prejudice a particular criminal defendant. But this concern does not arise with officials outside law enforcement; it cannot be presumed that *every* government official has an adversary motive against a criminal defendant. So for example, autopsy reports prepared by public medical personnel have been held to be admissible against criminal defendants under Rule 803(8)(B) because these medical personnel have no law enforcement objectives. *See, e.g., United States v. Rosa*, 11 F.3d 315 (2d Cir. 1993), holding that a medical examiner's autopsy report was properly admitted under Rule

803(8)(B). The Court in *Rosa* reasoned that a medical examiner is not "law enforcement personnel" as that term is used under the Rule:

> Unlike Customs, which has responsibility for enforcement of, inter alia, customs and narcotics laws, the Medical Examiner's Office is required simply to investigate unnatural deaths; it refers a death bearing any indicium of criminality to the appropriate district attorney and has no responsibility for enforcing any laws.* * * Further, though law enforcement activities are typically accusatory and adversarial in nature, a medical examiner's reported observations as to a body's condition are normally made as part of an independent effort to determine a cause of death."

The admissibility of law enforcement reports in criminal cases must now be assessed in light of the Supreme Court's decision in *Crawford v. Washington,* 541 U.S. 36 (2004). The Court in *Crawford* held that the admission of "testimonial" hearsay violates the defendant's right to confrontation unless the defendant has been able to cross-examine the declarant. While the Court did not explicitly define the term "testimonial," it is clear that the term encompasses hearsay prepared by a law enforcement officer in anticipation of its use against a particular criminal defendant. It is unlikely, however, that the term "testimonial" applies to law enforcement reports that amount to simple tabulation of routine information. Consequently, the line drawn between admissibility and inadmissible reports under Rule 803(8) — as discussed in this Note — is likely to be the dividing line used for admissibility and inadmissibility under the Confrontation Clause after *Crawford*. *See, e.g., United States v. Valdez-Matos,* 443 F.3d 910 (5th Cir. 2006) (warrant of deportation held admissible under Rule 803(8), and not testimonial; "the official preparing the warrant had no motivation other than mechanically register an unambiguous factual matter.")

3. What is the relationship between Rule 803(6) and Rule 803(8)? If a report is inadmissible under Rule 803(8), can it be admitted as a business record?

In criminal cases, the argument has sometimes been made that a report that is inadmissible due to the exclusionary language of Rule 803(8)(B) and (C) can nonetheless be admitted as a record of regularly conducted activity under Rule 803(6). However, if the exclusionary language is properly applied so as to exclude only those law enforcement reports made under adversarial circumstances — which is the position taken by most courts, as discussed above — then there is no conflict between the rules. This is because records that are prepared in anticipation of litigation are excluded under the trustworthiness criterion of Rule 803(6); and those are, in effect, the only records that are excluded under the prevailing view of Rule 803(8). *United States v. Bohrer,* 807 F.2d 159 (10th Cir. 1986) (I.R.S. contact card excluded under Rule 803(8) because prepared under adversarial circumstances, is also excluded under Rule 803(6) because adversarial circumstances of preparation show lack of trustworthiness). Accordingly, under the predominant approach to Rule 803(8), the issue of whether a law enforcement report excluded under Rule 803(8) can nonetheless be admitted under Rule 803(6) does not arise. Such a report is by definition untrustworthy and inadmissible under both rules. *United States v. Brown,* 9 F.3d 907 (11th Cir. 1993) (property receipt properly held admissible under Rule 803(6); while Rule 803(6) cannot be used to evade the exclusionary language of Rule 803(8), a property receipt is not the type of law enforcement report that is excluded under Rule 803(8): "The police custodian in the instant case had no incentive to do anything other than mechanically record the relevant information on the property receipt. We believe that this is the type of reliable public record envisioned by the drafters of Rule 803(8).").

4. What limitations exist on the admissibility of investigative reports in civil cases?

See Saltzburg, Martin, and Capra, *Federal Rules of Evidence Manual* (9th ed. 2006):

> After *Beech Aircraft v. Rainey*, a court may not exclude an opinion in an investigative report merely because it is an opinion. Yet even after *Rainey*, there are several limitations on the admissibility of opinions, as well as factual findings, contained in investigative reports. Most of these limitations are imposed by the courts pursuant to the trustworthiness clause of Rule 803(8). *See, e.g.*, *Hines v. Brandon Steel Decks, Inc.*, 886 F.2d 299 (11th Cir. 1989) (opinions in an OSHA investigator's report concerning a construction site accident could not be automatically excluded; however, opinions still must be trustworthy, and the Trial Court can take into account the expertise of the reporting official, whether a hearing was held, whether the conclusion was a legal conclusion, and other pertinent factors to determine whether the opinion is trustworthy).
>
> The most important limitations are:
>
> (1) An opinion, to be admissible, must be made by a qualified person using reliable methods, and must be based upon sufficient information and investigation. As applied to opinions of public officials, the standard of trustworthiness in Rule 803(8) is parallel to those contained in Federal Rules 702-704, which regulate the opinions of experts testifying at trial. The reason for imposing these requirements is that the opinion of a government investigator is likely to be treated by the factfinder as tantamount to an expert opinion. The proponent should not be better off by introducing the report instead of live testimony from an expert. If the government official would not be able to satisfy the standards for expert testimony at trial, there is little reason to admit the official's hearsay statement. *See, e.g.*, *Jenkins v. Whittaker Corp.*, 785 F.2d 720 (9th Cir. 1986) (conclusions in a report respecting the cause and responsibility for explosion of an atomic simulator were properly excluded where the person who made the report had no competence or experience with atomic simulators and did very little investigation); *Matthews v. Ashland Chem., Inc.*, 770 F.2d 1303 (5th Cir. 1985) (conclusions in a report respecting the cause of a fire were properly excluded due to insufficient investigation and the public official's lack of qualifications). Compare *Simmons v. Chicago & N.W.*

Transp. Co., 993 F.2d 1326 (8th Cir. 1993) (state trooper's accident investigation report was admissible in a FELA action, because the trooper was experienced and skilled, and the report was prepared after an investigation shortly after the accident so the underlying information was fresh).

(2) For similar reasons, opinions that are nothing more than legal conclusions are ordinarily excluded. The Court in *Rainey* expressed no view on the admissibility of legal conclusions contained in public reports. However, most Courts have excluded such conclusions, as they would with similar in-court testimony, on the ground that legal conclusions are unhelpful to the jury and usurp the role of the Judge in instructing the jury on the law. *See, e.g., Hines v. Brandon Steel Decks, Inc.*, 886 F.2d 299 (11th Cir. 1989): "Rule 803(8)(C) does not provide for the admissibility of the legal conclusions contained within an otherwise admissible public report. * * * Legal conclusions are inadmissible because the jury would have no way of knowing whether the preparer of the report was cognizant of the requirements underlying the legal conclusion and, if not, whether the preparer might have a higher or lower standard than the law requires."

(3) If the report is not a final report, but is merely preliminary or tentative, the report is not admissible, because it is not considered to contain "factual findings" as that term is used in the Rule. In other words, "factual findings" are final statements made at the end of the investigative process. Otherwise, an entire agency determination process would be piggy-backed into a trial. *See, e.g., Smith v. Isuzu Motors, Ltd.*, 137 F.3d 859 (5th Cir. 1998) (staff report not admissible under Rule 803(8)(B) because the agency declined to accept the position set forth in the staff report; the Court notes that its conclusion was "in accord with other circuits that have held that interim agency reports or preliminary memoranda do not satisfy Rule 803(8)(C)'s requirements"); *Smith v. M.I.T.*, 877 F.2d 1106 (1st Cir. 1989) (internal memoranda of EEOC investigators are not factual findings within the meaning of the rule); *City of New York v. Pullman Inc.*, 662 F.2d 910 (2d Cir. 1981) (where a report "did not embody the findings of an agency, but the tentative results of an incomplete staff investigation," it was not admissible under Rule 803(8)(C)). Compare *Vining v. Enterprise Fin. Group, Inc.*, 148 F.3d 1206 (10th Cir. 1998) (report prepared by staff of the state insurance department concerning the defendant's business practices was properly admitted under Rule 803(8)(C); the report was sufficiently final because it was attached to and incorporated by reference into an order subsequently issued by the Insurance Commissioner, who was head of the agency).

(4) If the report has been revoked or superseded by the agency that prepared it, it no longer contains factual findings within the meaning of the Rule. *See, e.g., Nachtsheim v. Beech Aircraft Corp.*, 847 F.2d 1261 (7th Cir. 1988) (FAA release concerning ice buildup

on certain planes was not admissible where release had been cancelled ten years earlier).

(5) Exclusion of the report is possible if the report appears to have been made under a suspect motivation. For example, if the public official or body who prepared the report has an institutional or political bias, and the final report is consistent with that bias, the report is subject to exclusion for untrustworthiness. *See, e.g.*, *New Jersey Turnpike Auth. v. PPG Indus.*, 197 F.3d 96 (3d Cir. 1999) (directives issued by the State Department of Environmental Protection, notifying the defendant that it was responsible for hazardous substances that needed to be removed, were not admissible under Rule 803(8)(C); the Directives were in the nature of notice pleading, and thus were prepared in anticipation of litigation); *Pearce v. E.F. Hutton Group, Inc.*, 653 F. Supp. 810 (D.D.C. 1987) (the plaintiff in a libel suit could not rely on a draft report of a congressional subcommittee in opposing a summary judgment motion; the Court commented that it was dealing "with documents produced by the Congress — a politically motivated, partisan body"; the report was not based upon an adjudicatory proceeding and was not drafted to resolve a factual dispute; the report lacked trustworthiness because of the political nature of the investigating body). Compare *Kehm v. Procter & Gamble Mfg. Co.*, 724 F.2d 613 (8th Cir. 1983) (no error to admit reports of epidemiological studies conducted by the Centers for Disease Control and various state agencies that analyzed the statistical relationship between tampon use and Toxic Shock Syndrome; the Court relied upon "the timeliness of the investigations, the special skills of the agencies conducting them, and their lack of any motive for conducting the studies other than to inform the public fairly and adequately.").

(6) Factual findings and conclusions made after a hearing are, for good reason, considered more trustworthy than findings made without a hearing. While the lack of a hearing is not dispositive, it does cut against admissibility. *See, e.g.*, *Hines v. Brandon Steel Decks, Inc.*, 886 F.2d 299 (11th Cir. 1989) (on remand, the District Court "might consider how the fact that no hearing was held in making the report affects its trustworthiness"); *Denny v. Hutchinson Sales Corp.*, 649 F.2d 816 (10th Cir. 1981) (Civil Rights Commission's findings on discrimination were properly excluded where the *ex parte* investigation lacked formal procedures such as the opportunity to cross-examine witnesses). And if the report is based on *ex parte* submissions to which an adversary has no opportunity to respond, such one-sidedness is a strong indication that the report is untrustworthy. *See, e.g.*, *Anderson v. City of New York*, 657 F. Supp. 1571 (S.D.N.Y. 1987) (report by a Subcommittee of the House of Representatives that summarized testimony concerning police misconduct in New York City was inadmissible; only one side's evidence was heard, the Subcommittee lacked personal knowledge of the events that were the subject of testimony, and the witnesses were self-interested; the Court observed that "hearings and subsequent

reports are frequently marred by political expediency and grandstanding").

(7) The timeliness of an investigation is a factor in any inquiry into trustworthiness. If the time between the event and the investigation is so long as to render the underlying information stale or untrustworthy, the public report is subject to exclusion. *See, e.g., O'Dell v. Hercules, Inc.*, 904 F.2d 1194 (8th Cir. 1990) (EPA investigative report on a chemical manufacturing plant, implicating the defendant, was held inadmissible because the investigation was not conducted until ten years after the defendant had terminated its operations at the plant, and others had operated the plant in the interim).

(8) Even if an investigative report is otherwise admissible under *Rainey*, it may be excluded by a special statute. For instance, probable cause determinations and other conclusions by the National Transportation Safety Board are excluded from all actions for damages pursuant to 49 U.S.C. § 1441(e). *See, e.g., Travelers Ins. Co. v. Riggs*, 671 F.2d 810 (4th Cir. 1982) (conclusions in a National Transportation Safety Board report could not be admitted because 49 U.S.C. § 1441(e) explicitly prohibits the use of conclusions in such a report in an action for damages).

5. How should a court deal with an official report that relies on information from sources outside the government?

A public official usually does not have personal knowledge of all of the facts reported in an investigative report. An official who investigates the cause of a car accident may determine the angle of impact through her own personal investigation; but she is not likely to have personal knowledge about how the cars looked and sounded at the time of the accident. Often the official must rely on information from bystanders and others with personal knowledge pertinent to the investigation. The question is whether this reliance renders the official's factual findings and opinions untrustworthy.

Where the official who prepared the report receives his or her information from others, a hearsay-within-hearsay problem exists. As applied to second-hand information contained in public reports, Rule 805 would seem to require that the statements by private persons to public officers must ordinarily be found independently reliable and admissible. So, for example, in *Bemis v. Edwards*, 45 F.3d 1369 (9th Cir. 1995), the Court affirmed a judgment for police officers alleged to have used excessive force, holding that a 911 tape describing the beating was properly excluded because the citizen-caller's statement was not independently admissible or verifiable. The Court recognized that hearsay statements on a 911 tape can be admitted into evidence as part of a public record. But it noted that citizen-callers are not under any duty to report correctly (unlike public officials who have such a duty) and that the official who made the record could not verify the accuracy of the citizen's description of the event. In the absence of a duty to report or some means of verification that the caller's statement was true, the Court concluded that "a recorded statement by a citizen must satisfy a separate hearsay exception."

Yet it can be fairly stated that most courts have taken a flexible attitude toward the multiple hearsay problem under Rule 803(8), given the strong presumption that public reports are reliable. Thus, if the court finds that the person with firsthand knowledge had no reason under the circumstances to misrepresent information to the public official, the report will probably be found admissible — even though there was, strictly speaking, no duty to report to the public agency or means of verification, and even though no specific hearsay exception or non-hearsay use is applicable.

For example, in *Ellis v. International Playtex Inc.*, 745 F.2d 292 (4th Cir. 1984), a report by the Centers for Disease Control and Prevention concerning toxic shock syndrome was held properly admitted, even though it was based upon information compiled from doctors throughout the country concerning the symptoms suffered by their patients. The court recognized that the reporting doctors had no absolute duty to report reliably to the Centers for Disease Control, that the doctors' reports were not verified for accuracy by the CDC, and that the doctors' statements were not subject to a specific hearsay exception. Nonetheless the Court found that under the circumstances, there was no conceivable motive for the reporting doctors to misrepresent information or to lie to the CDC. Therefore the defendant could not overcome the strong presumption of trustworthiness attached to the public report. Compare *United States v. Lanese*, 890 F.2d 1284 (2d Cir. 1989) (an exculpatory statement by a biased declarant, recorded in a police report, was held not admissible under Rule 803(8) because the source of the underlying information indicated lack of trustworthiness).

A flexible approach to secondhand information makes good sense, because a public report is treated at trial as tantamount to an expert's conclusion, and experts at trial are permitted under Rule 703 to rely on hearsay if that reliance is reasonable. As the court stated in *Moss v. Ole South Real Estate Inc.*, 933 F.2d 1300, 1310 (5th Cir. 1991):

> [Many] government reports, as with many expert witnesses, have to rely in part on hearsay evidence, and the reports are not generally excluded for this reason. Under Rule 703, experts are allowed to rely on evidence inadmissible in court in reaching their conclusions. There is no reason that government officials preparing reports do not have the same latitude.

In contrast, where a report is based on statements from persons who are biased or politically motivated, it will ordinarily be excluded because of the unreliable sources on which the report is based. Thus, in *Faries v. Atlas Truck Body Mfg. Co.*, 797 F.2d 619 (8th Cir. 1986), the court held that an accident report prepared by a police officer was inadmissible under Rule 803(8). The report was untrustworthy because the officer prepared his report after talking to only one of the drivers.

6. Note that the Federal Rules provide a hearsay exception for the absence of a public record.

Rule 803(10) describes the evidence covered by this exception:

> 10) **Absence of public record or entry.** — To prove the absence of a record, report, statement, or data compilation, in any form, or the nonoccurrence or nonexistence of a matter of which a record, report, statement, or

data compilation, in any form, was regularly made and preserved by a public office or agency, evidence in the form of a certification in accordance with rule 902, or testimony, that diligent search failed to disclose the record, report, statement, or data compilation, or entry.

This exception is used to prove that a public record was never made. For example, assume the defendant is charged with possessing a firearm without a license. His defense is that he was issued a license for the firearm — though he can't produce it right now because his dog ate it. To prove that no license was ever issued, the government can offer the affidavit of a public official who checked the records of firearm licenses issued, and found no record of any license issued to the defendant. The public official need not testify — an affidavit is sufficient if it shows that a diligent search for the record was conducted.

The key to satisfying Rule 803(10) is evidence that a diligent search failed to disclose the existence of the absent record. The diligence requirement insures reliability, and reliability is the basis for the hearsay exception. If there is a substantial doubt as to the diligence of the search for the record, evidence of the absence of that record is subject to exclusion. *United States v. Yakubov*, 712 F.2d 20, 24 (2d Cir. 1983) (where defendant's name is misspelled in the certificate, the certificate on its face shows that the search of the records was casual and unlikely to uncover the relevant record, and it was therefore inadmissible). If proof is by way of affidavit from a public official who checked the records, a conclusory statement that a diligent search was conducted tells the court little about the breadth and reliability of the search. At a minimum, the affidavit should describe factually the method of the search, and the safeguards undertaken to prevent an error. It is not necessary that a Rule 803(10) certificate be prepared in any particular form or specifically employ the phrase "diligent search failed to disclose the record." It is necessary, however, that the relevant circumstances are set forth in the certificate and reflect that a diligent search was made. *United States v. Wilson*, 732 F.2d 404, 414 (5th Cir. 1984) (although preferable, the affidavit by the public official need not contain the specific statement that a "diligent search failed to disclose the record:" "It suffices that the affidavit, and all relevant circumstances, reflect an adequate search.").

PROBLEM 13-2

Plaintiff sues the defendant's estate for personal injury as a result of a traffic accident. Plaintiff says the decedent, who was killed in the collision, ran a stop sign. There were no witnesses to the accident.

The only evidence the defendant has that the plaintiff was at fault is a statement made by the plaintiff while waiting in the hospital emergency room. In front of the admitting nurse and a police officer the plaintiff said, "I think my back is broke and I may be blind. If only I'd stopped at the stop sign." This statement appears in both the nurse's hospital notes and the police report.

1. May the nurse testify about the plaintiff's statement?
2. May the officer testify about the plaintiff's statement?
3. Assume the nurse died. May the nurse's hospital notes be admitted?
4. Assume the officer is on vacation. May the police report be admitted?

H. LEARNED TREATISE

[1] Federal Rule of Evidence 803(18)

Rule 803. Hearsay Exceptions; Availability of Declarant Immaterial

The following are not excluded by the hearsay rule, even though the declarant is available as a witness:

* * *

(18) Learned Treatises. To the extent called to the attention of an expert witness upon cross-examination or relied upon by the expert witness in direct examination, statements contained in published treatises, periodicals, or pamphlets on a subject of history, medicine, or other science or art, established as a reliable authority by the testimony or admission of the witness or by other expert testimony or by judicial notice. If admitted, the statements may be read into evidence but may not be received as exhibits.

* * *

[2] Illustration

Plaintiff sues defendant for back injuries as a result of a slip and fall. Plaintiff's physician has already testified, and is now circling the globe on a golf tour. The evidence has shown that the plaintiff did not feel any back pain the day of the fall, but could not get out of bed the next morning. Plaintiff's expert was not asked whether the delay in the pain was significant. Defendant's expert is on the stand.

Defendant: Doctor, is it possible for someone to sustain the type of injuries the plaintiff complains of from a slip and fall and not feel any pain until the next morning?

Doctor: Absolutely not.

The plaintiff cross-examines.

Plaintiff: Doctor, are you familiar with the textbook *Hecker on Diagnosis: Treatment of Back Injuries*?

Doctor: No, I don't think so.

Plaintiff: Why don't you read page 72? (The doctor reads the page.) Now doctor, doesn't the book indicate that it is not uncommon for pain to develop up to 72 hours after an injury?

Defendant:	Objection! What the book says is obviously hearsay, and the doctor doesn't recognize the book as a learned treatise.
Plaintiff:	Your Honor, my expert has said this is the primary book in the field. I should be allowed to cross-examine this witness with it, and offer the book as substantive proof that delay is not uncommon.
The court:	________.

[3] Reliable Authority

COSTANTINO v. HERZOG
203 F.3d 164 (2d Cir. 2000)

McLaughlin, Circuit Judge:

Dr. David Herzog was the obstetrician who delivered Amanda Costantino. During the delivery, Amanda's shoulder got trapped behind her mother's pubic bone, a condition known as "shoulder dystocia." While attempting to remedy the condition, Dr. Herzog performed: (1) the McRoberts maneuver: pulling Mrs. Costantino's legs toward her head and applying pressure to the area above her pubic bone; (2) the Woods corkscrew: reaching into the womb and rotating baby Amanda to release her trapped shoulder; and (3) the Posterior Arm Sweep: delivering Amanda's free posterior arm to create more space. Ultimately, Dr. Herzog delivered Amanda, but she was born with "Erb's Palsy," an impairment to the nerves running to the arm.

The Costantinos filed a diversity action against Dr. Herzog in the United States District Court for the Eastern District of New York (Gleeson, J.) alleging that by pulling and rotating Amanda's head during the delivery, he had caused her Erb's Palsy. They claimed that Dr. Herzog had deviated from accepted standards of obstetrical practice, and had therefore committed malpractice under governing New York law. The defense denied any malpractice, asserting that Amanda's Erb's Palsy was caused by the normal forces of labor.

The case was tried to a jury. Plaintiffs' first witness was the defendant, Dr. Herzog. Counsel questioned him on an excerpt from a medical treatise edited by Steven G. Gabbe, entitled Obstetrics, that stated: "Once a vaginal delivery has begun, the obstetrician must resist the temptation to rotate the head to a transverse axis." Dr. Herzog acknowledged attempting to rotate Amanda's head, but disagreed with the statement read from the Gabbe treatise. Plaintiffs' medical expert was Dr. Bernard Nathanson. Among his qualifications, Dr. Nathanson testified that he was a fellow of the American College of Obstetricians and Gynecologists ("ACOG"). ACOG, according to Dr. Nathanson, "is an organization of thirty thousand obstetricians and gynecologists," that "sets up courses for doctors who are in practice so that they will continue to be current with ongoing research." Dr. Nathanson added that ACOG "publishes a great deal of material which serve[s] to contribute to setting a standard of care for obstetricians and gynecologists."

Relying in part on various journals published by ACOG, as well as on the Gabbe treatise, Dr. Nathanson proceeded to testify that it was a departure from the standard of medical care to engage in "any manipulation of the head" during a shoulder dystocia delivery because it does nothing to relieve the trapped shoulder and greatly increases the risk of causing Erb's Palsy.

The defense sought to rebut this theory in several ways. Primarily, the defense relied on another learned treatise — Williams' Obstetrics — which stated that "downward traction * * * to the fetal head" was among "the most popular techniques" used to remedy shoulder dystocia. Dr. Nathanson conceded that the Williams treatise was authoritative and that applying traction to the fetal head was indeed the "most popular" treatment technique for shoulder dystocia. He continued, nevertheless, to insist that use of that technique constituted malpractice. The defense also sought to justify Dr. Herzog's management of Amanda's delivery by introducing a 15-minute videotape from ACOG's audiovisual library, entitled "Shoulder Dystocia." The tape was, according to the defense, "put out by [ACOG] to educate physicians" and portrayed the various techniques recommended to remedy shoulder dystocia.

Both the parties and JUDGE GLEESON recognized that the ACOG video was hearsay under Federal Rule of Evidence 801. The defense nevertheless sought to introduce it pursuant to the "learned treatise" exception to the hearsay rule set forth in Rule 803(18). Plaintiffs objected, arguing that Rule 803(18) enumerates only "published treatises, periodicals, or pamphlets" as learned treatises, and therefore could not encompass videotapes. Plaintiffs also argued that no foundation had been laid for the video.

After an in camera review of the videotape, JUDGE GLEESON ruled it admissible. With respect to whether a video could qualify as a learned treatise under Rule 803(18), JUDGE GLEESON reasoned: "I think * * * focusing on the distinction between * * * something in the form of a periodical or a book, as opposed [to] a videotape is just overly artificial."

As to the foundation, JUDGE GLEESON found, based on his in camera review, that the ACOG video "was a dissemination to the doctors in the relevant medical community of how they should go about dealing with this problem [of shoulder dystocia]." He also found that it had been "well established" through trial testimony that ACOG was "the source of authoritative information regarding the practices to be used by obstetricians in these circumstances." Included in the trial testimony regarding ACOG and the videotape, were Dr. Nathanson's concessions that he had: (1) viewed the videotape at a staff conference some years ago; and (2) testified in a prior action that he generally accepted "the standards promulgated by ACOG" within the field of obstetrics as "authoritative."

The ACOG video was played twice during trial. It was played in its entirety during the cross-examination of plaintiffs' expert, Dr. Nathanson, and portions were replayed during the direct examination of defendants' own expert Dr. James Howard.

In graphic detail the video portrays actual deliveries, complicated by shoulder dystocia, and demonstrates the recommended obstetrical responses to it. These portrayals are accompanied by a narrative given by a Dr. Young, who the video reveals is from Dartmouth College's Hitchcock Medical Center. The various procedures recommended, Dr. Young explains, were chosen "following a careful review of the available literature." Several times during its 15 minute duration, the video cautions that "unfortunately, babies cannot always be delivered without injury even when the management is optimal," and that "sometimes * * * injuries cannot be avoided."

As the first step in treatment, the video recommends coordination of the mother's efforts to expel the baby with what Dr. Young characterizes as application of "a limited" or "appropriate" amount of traction to the baby's head by the obstetrician. Dr. Young goes on to warn, however, that "some of the problems that occur with shoulder dystocia may result from more forceful and prolonged efforts at pushing and pulling." The video instructs that where an initial application of traction to the baby's head has been unsuccessful, "it is important to stop and take a different approach to relieve the problem." The video then portrays application of the McRoberts, Woods and Posterior Arm Sweep maneuvers, which Dr. Herzog had testified to performing during Amanda's troubled delivery.

The video concludes with a portrayal of what Dr. Young acknowledges are two rare maneuvers, apparently to be tried only when all else fails. First, the video depicts placing the mother on all fours to facilitate delivery. Second, the video portrays pushing the baby back into the uterus to permit delivery by a Caesarian section.

In its closing credits, the video scrolls across the screen a printed disclaimer, stating: "This video does not define a standard of care, nor is it intended to dictate an exclusive course of management. It presents recognized techniques of clinical practice for consideration by health care providers for incorporation into their practices."

The closing credits also reveal that the video was awarded the Scientific Program Award at the 1995 Annual Clinical Meeting of ACOG. In addition to the ACOG video, the defense introduced as learned treatises, over objection, two articles published in the American Journal of Obstetrics and Gynecology. The first was entitled, *Shoulder Dystocia, an Analysis of Risks and Obstetrical Maneuvers*, and was written by Dr. James Nocon of the University of Indiana Medical School. Before this article was read to Dr. Herzog on cross-examination, he testified on voir dire that he: (1) did not know of the article's author, Dr. Nocon; and (2) had not read the specific article until "two minutes" before beginning his testimony about it. Later, during cross-examination of plaintiffs' expert, Dr. Nathanson, defense counsel sought to introduce a different article written by Robert Gherman, an obstetrics professor at the University of Southern California and also published in the American Journal of Obstetrics and Gynecology. Though Dr. Nathanson refused to concede the authoritativeness of that journal (based on his apparent belief that "no journal is authoritative"), JUDGE GLEESON allowed the defense to read the following statement from Dr. Gherman's article:

> [Erb's] palsy is commonly attributed to excessive lateral traction applied to the fetal neck by the treating physician during attempts to free the shoulder * * * . Some authors have argued that with worsening severity of the shoulder dystocia, and increased efforts by

> the operators, the impact of the traction force becomes more pronounced * * * . We have presented six cases in which it is virtually certain that this mechanism played no role * * * . Our data also imply that some cases of [Erb's palsy] may be related to events antedating the actual delivery, especially in light of the fact that one patient underwent a Caesarian section while in early labor.

Defense counsel also read a different portion of the same article to defendant's expert, Dr. Howard, during direct examination. Dr. Howard did not testify that he relied on the article in any way.

After trial, the jury found for Dr. Herzog on the issue of liability. The Costantinos now appeal, arguing that JUDGE GLEESON erred in admitting: (1) the ACOG video; and (2) the two articles from the American Journal of Obstetrics and Gynecology.

DISCUSSION

I. The ACOG Video

The Costantinos argue that because videotapes are not mentioned in Rule 803(18), they can never be learned treatises. Alternatively, they maintain that even if videos can be learned treatises, reversal is still required because JUDGE GLEESON: (1) erred in admitting the ACOG video without proper foundation; and (2) should have excluded the video as unduly confusing and prejudicial under Rule 403. None of these contentions warrant reversal.

A. Rule 803(18)

The primary question presented is whether videotapes can be admitted as learned treatises pursuant to Rule 803(18). We are the first federal Court of Appeals to address this question, though various state courts have considered it under their cognate learned treatise exceptions, and have forged no consensus.

We review JUDGE GLEESON's legal conclusion that videos can constitute learned treatises *de novo*. In its entirety, Rule 803(18) provides:

> The following are not excluded by the hearsay rule, even though the declarant is available as a witness: * * * (18) Learned treatises. To the extent called to the attention of an expert witness upon cross-examination or relied upon by the expert witness in direct examination, statements contained in published treatises, periodicals, or pamphlets on a subject of history, medicine, or other science or art, established as a reliable authority by the testimony or admission of the witness or by other expert testimony or by judicial notice. If admitted, the statements may be read into evidence but may not be received as exhibits.

The rationale for this exception is self-evident: so long as the authority of a treatise has been sufficiently established, the factfinder should have the benefit of expert learning on a subject, even though it is hearsay.

Emphasizing plain language, the Costantinos argue that videos cannot fall within the scope of Rule 803(18) because unlike "published treatises, periodicals, or pamphlets," they are not specifically listed in the Rule. They rely on *Simmons v. Yurchak*, 28 Mass. App. Ct. 371, 551 N.E.2d 539 (1990), which accepted this contention, and affirmed a trial court's refusal to recognize videotapes as learned treatises under the Massachusetts version of Rule 803(18). According to the *Simmons* court: "adding videotapes to the list of materials in [the Massachusetts learned treatise exception] would constitute judicial legislation."

Uttering the dark incantation of "judicial legislation" is to substitute a slogan for an analysis. Indeed, we are exhorted in Rule 102 to interpret the Rules of Evidence to promote the "growth and development of the law * * * to the end that the truth may be ascertained." In this endeavor a certain measure of legislative judgment is required. As Justice Holmes, in his Boston Brahmin prose conceded: "I recognize without hesitation that judges do and must legislate, but they can do so only interstitially; they are confined from molar to molecular motions." Or as a graduate of N.Y. City College, Justice Frankfurter, put it more prosaically: "legislatures make law wholesale, judges retail." Joseph P. Lash, From the Diaries of Felix Frankfurter 67 (1975) (quoting unidentified letter from Felix Frankfurter to Hugo Black). Because judges "cannot escape the responsibility of filling in gaps which the finitude of even the most imaginative legislation renders inevitable," the problem is "not whether the judges make the law, but when and how much." *Id.*

In this case, we are compelled to "make law." For we agree with JUDGE GLEESON that it is just "overly artificial" to say that information that is sufficiently trustworthy to overcome the hearsay bar when presented in a printed learned treatise loses the badge of trustworthiness when presented in a videotape. We see no reason to deprive a jury of authoritative learning simply because it is presented in a visual, rather than printed, format. In this age of visual communication a videotape may often be the most helpful way to illuminate the truth in the spirit of Rule 102.

In sum, we agree with the Texas Court of Appeals that "[v]ideotapes are nothing more than a contemporary variant of a published treatise, periodical or pamphlet." *Loven v. State*, 831 S.W.2d 387, 397 (Tex. Ct. App. 1992). Accordingly, we hold that videotapes may be considered learned treatises under Rule 803(18).

B. Proper Foundation

The Costantinos argue that even assuming that the ACOG video may be a learned treatise, JUDGE GLEESON erred in admitting it without a proper foundation. We disagree.

Rule 803(18) explicitly requires trial judges to act as gatekeepers, ensuring that any treatise admitted is "authoritative." Thus, trial judges must first determine that the proffered treatise is "trustworth[y] * * * as viewed by professionals in [the relevant] field." *Id.*; *see* Fed. R. Evid. 803(18) Advisory Committee Note. In making this evaluation, trial judges need not be draconian. Since the object of Rule 803(18) is to make valuable information available to the trier of fact, trial judges should not insist on a quantum of proof that the proponent cannot meet.

JUDGE GLEESON's finding that the authoritativeness of the ACOG video had been sufficiently established is reviewed for abuse of discretion and will not be disturbed absent "manifest error." The Costantinos invite us to apply the reasoning of *Meschino v. North American Drager, Inc.*, 841 F.2d 429 (1st Cir. 1988). There, the First Circuit ruled that it was not enough that the trade magazine in which an article appeared was reputable; the author of the particular article must also to be shown to be an authority before the article could be used as a learned treatise pursuant to Rule 803(18). The Court reasoned that "[i]n these days of quantified research, and pressure to publish, an article does not reach the dignity of a 'reliable authority' merely because some editor, even a most reputable one, sees fit to circulate it."

The Costantinos argue that *Meschino* requires reversal because JUDGE GLEESON's sole basis for accepting the video as authoritative was its sponsorship by ACOG. They claim that no testimony was offered that the video itself had received acceptance in the medical profession, or that its narrator, Dr. Young, was considered an authority in the field. And these omissions were particularly devastating, the Costantinos maintain, because as the Simmons court noted, it is unclear that the "careful, professional criticism" which ensures the reliability of printed treatises, also attends the production and dissemination of videotapes.

These arguments are unavailing. Even assuming that the potential authoritativeness of videotapes is somehow more suspect than that of materials like "pamphlet[s]" explicitly listed by the Rule, we cannot fault the district court's performance as a gatekeeper in this case.

We, of course, agree with the *Meschino* court that the contents of a periodical cannot be automatically qualified "wholesale" under Rule 803(18) merely by showing that the periodical itself is highly regarded. We do not, however, read *Meschino* to say that the reputation of the periodical containing the proffered article is irrelevant to the authoritativeness inquiry. Publication practices vary widely, and an article's publication by an esteemed periodical which subjects its contents to close scrutiny and peer review, obviously reflects well on the authority of the article itself. Indeed, because the authoritativeness inquiry is governed by a "liberal" standard, good sense would seem to compel recognizing some periodicals — provided there is a basis for doing so — as sufficiently esteemed to justify a presumption in favor of admitting the articles accepted for publication therein.

Turning to the instant case, there is no small irony in plaintiffs' complaint that ACOG sponsorship was insufficient to establish the video as an authority. After all, while plaintiffs' own expert Dr. Nathanson refused to concede the authoritativeness of the video itself, he nevertheless: (1) touted himself as a member of ACOG; (2) praised ACOG as an organization that "publishes a great deal of material which serve[s] to contribute to setting a standard of care for obstetricians and gynecologists"; and (3) testified in a prior action that he generally accepted "the standards promulgated by ACOG" within the field of obstetrics as "authoritative." Moreover, Dr. Nathanson relied in part on ACOG publications in reaching his opinion that Dr. Herzog had committed malpractice.

In any event, other factors — quite apart from ACOG's status as a reputable organization — established the authoritativeness of the video. In particular, Dr. Nathanson recalled seeing a version of the ACOG video at a staff conference, inferentially conceding that it was exactly what the defense said it was: a training resource for the continuing medical education of obstetricians and gynecologists. And the video's use as a training resource — "written primarily and impartially for professionals, subject to scrutiny and exposure for inaccuracy, with the reputation [of its producers and sponsors] at stake" — is clearly an important index of its authoritativeness under Rule 803(18). Fed. R. Evid. 803(18) Advisory Committee Note.

Moreover, JUDGE GLEESON himself took the additional precaution of reviewing the ACOG video in camera. Through that review, JUDGE GLEESON knew that the tape's narrator, Dr. Young, was a physician at Dartmouth College's Hitchcock Medical Center, and that the video itself had won an ACOG award, credentials which compared favorably with those of any expert who testified at trial. And after the same review, JUDGE GLEESON found that the video was what the defense represented it to be: a training resource — with recommendations culled from the "available literature" — used to show doctors "how they should go about dealing with this problem [of shoulder dystocia]." Having viewed the videotape ourselves, and having observed its clinical format, as well as its calm and instructional tone, we cannot say this finding amounts to "manifest error."

In sum, we conclude that JUDGE GLEESON's determination that the ACOG video was sufficiently authoritative to deserve admission rested on an appropriate foundation.* * * And while some of the indicia of the video's reliability came to light through JUDGE GLEESON's independent in camera review, rather than through testimony, the authoritativeness inquiry is a freewheeling one and may be conducted by "any means." Fed. R. Evid. 803(18) Advisory Committee Note.

JUDGE GLEESON did not abuse his discretion in finding that the ACOG video was sufficiently authoritative to be presented to the jury.

C. *Rule 403*

Even though the ACOG video qualified as a learned treatise under Rule 803(18), JUDGE GLEESON retained the discretion to exclude it if its "probative value [was] substantially outweighed by the danger of unfair prejudice [or] confusion" under Rule 403. The Costantinos argue that the video should have been excluded under Rule 403. We find no basis for reversal.

There can be no doubt that much of the ACOG videotape represented highly probative evidence. * * * As JUDGE GLEESON explained in ruling that the video was admissible, one "dimension" of plaintiffs' malpractice claim was that "the standard of care * * * prohibits a doctor from engaging in any traction" to remedy shoulder dystocia. Measured against this claim, those portions of the video portraying application of "a limited" or "appropriate" amount of traction to the baby's head were directly probative of whether such a technique is an accepted obstetrical practice. And those portions of the video portraying application of the Woods, McRoberts and Posterior Arm Sweep maneuvers were probative of whether Dr. Herzog properly used those maneuvers in delivering Amanda.

We reject the plaintiffs' claim that the ACOG video should have been excluded because of the danger of undue confusion. The Costantinos maintain that the ACOG video must have caused the jurors to confuse what they saw on the tape with what was being orally reconstructed for them throughout the trial — i.e., the birth of Amanda. They argue that because the video shows appropriate amounts of traction being applied to babies' heads, the jurors must have unfairly concluded that Dr. Herzog's management of Amanda's delivery was appropriate. This argument is pure speculation. It was obvious that Amanda's birth was not what was depicted in the video. Even if it were not obvious to the jury, any ephemeral danger of confusion was more than outweighed by the highly probative value of the video.

Plaintiffs' second Rule 403 contention is similarly unavailing. The Costantinos point out that in addition to portraying the Woods, McRoberts and Posterior Arm Sweep maneuvers (as well as the application of traction to babies' heads), the ACOG video portrays the two rarely performed procedures of: (1) placing the mother on all fours to facilitate delivery; and (2) pushing the baby back into the uterus to facilitate a Caesarian section. The Costantinos assert that these portrayals were not probative of anything at trial, and were highly prejudicial because "the only inference the jury could have drawn from those parts of the tape * * * is that shoulder dystocia can be a complicated problem, requiring seemingly drastic measures to deliver children." It is true that Dr. Herzog never testified that he even contemplated performing these maneuvers during the birth of Amanda. However, to the extent that these portrayals prejudiced the Costantinos by emphasizing the inherent dangers of shoulder dystocia, such prejudice did not warrant exclusion.

Because virtually all evidence is prejudicial to one party or another, to justify exclusion under Rule 403 the prejudice must be unfair. The unfairness contemplated involves some adverse effect beyond tending to prove a fact or issue that justifies admission. We fail to see how plaintiffs were unfairly prejudiced by the portrayal of the challenged procedures here. The testimony at trial established that shoulder dystocia is indeed a "complicated problem, requiring seemingly drastic" responses by the treating obstetrician.* * * [A]ny prejudice arising from the video's portrayal of the challenged procedures was not unfair within the meaning of Rule 403. To the contrary, that portrayal was probative of whether Amanda Costantino's shoulder dystocia presented an "emergency" and whether Dr. Herzog responded appropriately in attempting to remedy it.

II. The American Journal of Obstetrics and Gynecology

The Costantinos final argument is that the admission of the two articles from the American Journal of Obstetrics and Gynecology also requires reversal. Once again, plaintiffs argue lack of proper foundation. First, they complain that because Dr. Herzog testified that he had not seen Dr. James

Nocon's article until shortly before testifying about it, he could not have "relied" upon that article as required by Rule 803(18). Second, they protest that there was no testimony establishing the authoritativeness of either Dr. Nocon's article, or the second article written by obstetrics professor Robert Gherman of the University of Southern California.

* * * It is not essential that a testifying expert rely on a learned treatise on direct examination. If he did not, a sufficient foundation is laid if the treatise is "called to the attention of [the] expert upon cross-examination." Fed. R. Evid. 803(18). The essential notion is that the jury enjoys explanation, context and perspective on the treatise's contents. That is exactly what happened on defense counsel's cross-examination of Dr. Herzog. As to authoritativeness, Dr. Herzog testified that the American Journal of Obstetrics and Gynecology is "probably the most reputable journal in our field and if it's accepted for publication, then we know it's quality information being presented." Plaintiffs' own expert, Dr. Nathanson, backed Dr. Herzog on this point, testifying that articles are published in the American Journal of Obstetrics and Gynecology only after "other obstetricians and gynecologists * * * review them for accuracy and believability." The district court was properly satisfied with this foundation.

III. Legal References

We are troubled by one aspect of this case. As noted above, the ACOG videotape's closing credits include the statement: "This video does not define a standard of care." Other learned treatises read at trial contain similar legalistic language, or actually allude to litigation, such as Dr. Gherman's article in the American Journal of Obstetrics and Gynecology, which refers to unfounded assertions made by "plaintiffs' expert witnesses."

Such references tend to suggest that shoulder dystocia births are the source of much unjustified litigation, and that the instant case was merely an example of such litigiousness rather than a legitimate attempt to achieve redress for real injury. Although plaintiffs have not directly challenged these references, we feel compelled to point out that they should have been redacted under Rule 403.

The district court's failure to perform such a redaction, however, does not warrant reversal. Throughout trial, JUDGE GLEESON carefully policed both counsel and the witnesses to ensure that the evidence was — in the main — properly focused on the discrete issue of whether Dr. Herzog committed malpractice in delivering Amanda Costantino. On this record, it is clear that the isolated admission of a few objectionable legal references could not have swayed the jury's verdict. We raise this issue only to alert district courts to be wary of admitting such material in the future.

CONCLUSION

For the reasons set forth above, the judgment of the district court is AFFIRMED.

NOTE

Why can a learned treatise not be received as an exhibit?

A learned treatise is a substitute for or supplement to expert testimony. A learned treatise should not be given more weight than the trial testimony of an expert. If it could be admitted as an exhibit, the jury might get the misimpression that the learned treatise is more important than trial testimony. *See, e.g., Graham v. Wyeth Labs.*, 906 F.2d 1399 (10th Cir. 1990) (AMA special report was sufficiently authoritative to qualify for admissibility under Rule 803(18), but the trial court erred in submitting the report to the jury). There is also a danger in allowing learned treatises to be considered by the jury during deliberations without the benefit of contemporaneous explanation by an expert.

There is a problem, however, if the learned treatise is not permitted in the jury room as an exhibit. In a trial of any length, there is no way the jury can possibly remember what was read to them from the treatise (or treatises; there could be several). Usually, the precise language of the treatise is critical. Without the treatise, or a verbatim excerpt from it, counsel and the jury are substantially limited in making effective use of the substantive evidence the rule permits. For this reason, the last sentence of the rule is often ignored. Some judges have indicated that the prohibition on exhibits is invoked only by a party who thinks he has come out on the short end of the battle of the treatises. On the other hand, where both sides think they have gained an advantage from the treatise material, copies of the treatise language are usually received without objection, sometimes in the form of blowups which are used in final arguments and sent to the jury.

PROBLEM 13-3: REVIEW OF RULE 803

Joy Smith is an uptight speed addict. Sarah Jones is an accountant. Joy and Sarah are standing together with Sarah's date on a street corner when they witness the same automobile accident. A police officer arrives at the scene almost immediately.

Ten minutes after the accident, Joy tells the police officer, "Oh my god, the red car was going 100 miles per hour when it hit the pedestrian in the crosswalk. I'm still shaking. It was horrible!"

Sarah, 12 minutes after the accident, tells the police officer, "The red car was clearly driving in excess of the speed limit. The pedestrian was walking with the 'walk' sign and had just stepped off the sidewalk when she was struck by the front right bumper of the red car. Her body flew over the back of the car and she landed on her head approximately 15 feet from the point of impact. The victim looked both ways before stepping off the sidewalk. The red car was going so fast the victim could not have responded in time to avoid being struck." The police officer's notes say, "Sarah was very calm and will make an excellent witness." Sarah also tells the police officer that her date, an airline pilot, said just seconds before the accident happened that "the guy in the red car is going to kill someone if he doesn't slow down."

Joy has overdosed. Sarah is in tax season and didn't honor the subpoena when this case came to trial. The airline pilot is in France. The plaintiff calls the police officer to the stand.

Plaintiff:	State your name.
Officer McCoy:	Officer McCoy.
Plaintiff:	Did you see the accident?
Officer McCoy:	No.
Plaintiff:	Did you talk to anyone at the scene about the accident?
Officer McCoy:	Yes.
Plaintiff:	Who?
Officer McCoy:	Joy Smith and Sarah Jones.
Plaintiff:	What did Joy tell you about the accident?
Defendant:	Objection! Hearsay..
The court:	Let me hear it so I can rule.
Officer McCoy:	She said, "Oh my god, the red car was going 100 miles per hour when it hit the pedestrian in the crosswalk. I'm still shaking. It was horrible!"
Plaintiff:	(1) ________.
Defendant:	Joy wasn't involved in the accident, so it can't be an excited utterance.
The court:	(2) ________.
Plaintiff:	Did you talk to anyone else?
Officer McCoy:	Yes, Sarah Jones.
Plaintiff:	What did she say about the accident?
Defendant:	Objection! Hearsay.
The court:	What did she say?
Officer McCoy:	She said, "The red car was clearly driving in excess of the speed limit. The pedestrian was walking with the 'walk' sign and had just stepped off the sidewalk when she was struck by the front right bumper of the red car and she landed on her head approximately fifteen feet from the point of impact. The victim had looked both ways before stepping off the sidewalk. The red car was going so fast the victim could not have responded in time to avoid being struck."
Plaintiff:	Your Honor has ruled that Joy's statement is admissible. The same ruling should apply to Sarah.
Defendant:	May I ask the witness one voir dire question in aid of an objection, your Honor?
The court:	Yes.
Defendant:	Was she calm when she gave you her statement?

Officer McCoy: Yes, very calm.
Defendant: And this was some twelve minutes after the event?
Officer McCoy: Yes.
Defendant: This is not an excited utterance.
The court: (3) ________.
Plaintiff: (4) Then the statement should be admitted as a ________.
Defendant: Objection. It was too long after the accident.
The court: (5) ________.
Plaintiff: Did she say anything else?
Officer McCoy: Yes.
Plaintiff: What did she say?
Defendant: Objection! Hearsay.
The court: Let me hear it so I can rule.
Officer McCoy: She said, "My airline friend said just before the accident happened 'that the guy in the red car better slow down or he's going to kill someone.' "
Defendant: (6) Objection! ________.
The court: (7) ________.
Plaintiff: Officer, did you talk to the pedestrian at the scene?
Officer McCoy: Yes, briefly, as they were loading him into the ambulance.
Plaintiff: What did he say?
Defendant: Objection! Hearsay.
The court: Let me hear it so I can rule.
Officer McCoy: He said, "My back must be broken. I have no feeling in my feet at all, but my head is on fire."
Plaintiff: (8) ________.
The court: (9) ________.
Plaintiff: Did he tell you anything else?
Officer McCoy: Yes.
Plaintiff: What did he tell you?
Defendant: Objection! Hearsay.
The court: Let me hear it so I can rule.
Officer McCoy: He said, "I'm about to pass out, tell the doctor that my back has never been hurt before."
Defendant: This is hearsay. It is a statement about the past.
Plaintiff: (10) ________.
Defendant: It was not made to a doctor, nurse or anyone providing medical treatment.
The court: (11) ________.
Plaintiff: Did you bring the police records of this case with you?
Officer McCoy: Yes, I have a copy.
Plaintiff: Did you do the actual accident evaluation?

Officer McCoy: No.
Plaintiff: Who did?
Officer McCoy: Officer Chin.
Plaintiff: Where is she?
Officer McCoy: She is now Chief of Police in Denver.
Plaintiff: Do you recognize the signature on the report?
Officer McCoy: Yes, it is Officer Chin's.
Plaintiff: Do your records indicate if she made measurements at the scene and evaluated the cause of the accident?
Officer McCoy: Yes.
Plaintiff: What do you know about Officer Chin's experience in investigating accidents?
Officer McCoy: She was the department's most experienced investigator. She investigated accidents for more than ten years.
Plaintiff: Your Honor, at this time I move for the introduction of the police record, including the measurements taken at the scene and the police officer's evaluation that the red car was traveling in excess of fifty miles per hour when it struck the pedestrian.
Defendant: Objection! Hearsay.
Plaintiff: It's a business record, and it's also a public record. May I ask the witness a few more questions.
The court: Yes.
Plaintiff: What is the date of the report?
Officer McCoy: Same date as the accident.
Plaintiff: Are these reports routinely made at or near the time of accidents as part of the department's regular duties, and are they routinely kept by the department as part of its duties?
Officer McCoy: Yes.
Plaintiff: So, I submit that these are business records.
Defendant: May I ask a question?
The court: Yes.
Defendant: Isn't this report based in large part on statements made and information provided by third parties who are not employed by and are under no duty to the department?
Officer McCoy: Yes, I suppose that is true. I told Officer Chin everything that Jane and Sarah told me. I'm sure she took that into account in arriving at her conclusions and in preparing her report.
Defendant: We renew our objection.
The court: (12) ________.
Plaintiff: Whether or not it is a business record, it certainly should qualify as a public record.
Defendant: Objection! This report is conclusory and unreliable.

The court: (13) ________.

Plaintiff: After the accident, did you have occasion to communicate with Jane or Sarah again?

Officer McCoy: Yes, I called Jane some weeks after the accident to see whether she would like to have coffee with me?

Plaintiff: Did you have coffee?

Officer McCoy: Yes, we met downtown for coffee and breakfast.

Plaintiff: Did you discuss the accident?

Officer McCoy: Not really. But she gave me some notes that she had written about the accident. She said she wrote them down the next day so that she would have a record of what happened if her memory failed. I brought them with me.

Plaintiff: The notes have been marked as Plaintiff's exhibit 14 for identification. Are these the notes?

Officer McCoy: Yes, those are the notes.

Plaintiff: Do they describe the accident in detail?

Officer McCoy: They do.

Plaintiff: We offer plaintiff's exhibit 14 in evidence.

Defendant: Objection! Hearsay.

Plaintiff: These are present sense impressions, excited utterances and also qualify as past recollection recorded.

Defendant: There is no showing that any of the exceptions is satisfied.

The court: (14)________.

Chapter 14

RESIDUAL EXCEPTION TO THE HEARSAY RULE

A. INTRODUCTION

Two residual or "catch-all" hearsay exceptions were contained in the Federal Rules as initially adopted. These exceptions were designed to permit the admission of trustworthy hearsay that did not fit under any of the categorical exceptions. The residual exceptions were identically worded; one was placed in Rule 803 (subdivision (24)), and the other was placed in Rule 804 (subdivision (b)(5)). In 1997, the residual exceptions were transferred out of Rules 803 and 804, and combined in a single exception, Rule 807. This was done to facilitate additions to Rules 803 and 804. No change in meaning was intended. The cases decided under old Rules 803(24) and 804(b)(5) remain pertinent in deciding whether hearsay is admissible under Rule 807.

B. RESIDUAL EXCEPTION

[1] Federal Rule of Evidence 807

Rule 807. Residual Exception

A statement not specifically covered by Rule 803 or 804 but having equivalent circumstantial guarantees of trustworthiness, is not excluded by the hearsay rule, if the court determines that (A) the statement is offered as evidence of a material fact; (B) the statement is more probative on the point for which it is offered than any other evidence which the proponent can procure through reasonable efforts; and (C) the general purposes of these rules and the interests of justice will best be served by admission of the statement into evidence. However, a statement may not be admitted under this exception unless the proponent of it makes known to the adverse party sufficiently in advance of the trial or hearing to provide the adverse party with a fair opportunity to prepare to meet it, the proponent's intention to offer the statement and the particulars of it, including the name and address of the declarant.

[2] Relationship to Other Exceptions

UNITED STATES v. VALDEZ-SOTO
31 F.3d 1467 (9th Cir. 1994)

KOZINSKI, CIRCUIT JUDGE:

There may be no loyalty among thieves, but there sometimes is among drug dealers. When called by the government, such witnesses occasionally change their story. The principal issue raised in these consolidated appeals is whether and when their inculpatory out-of-court statements may be admitted in the teeth of a hearsay objection.

I

Some days nothing goes right. The seller, Roberto Cortez, showed up in a restaurant parking lot with nine kilograms of cocaine just as he'd promised, only to discover that his buyer, Dennis Pierce, was a government agent. Cortez was in deep trouble and soon confessed. In so doing, he implicated two men as his suppliers, Gustavo Valdez-Soto and Fabio Gomez-Tello (our defendants), both of whom had already been arrested at the home of Cortez's sister-in-law.

Pierce had been working with narcotics informant Joaquin Olivas for some time, setting up a buy of thirty kilograms of cocaine from Cortez. Many of Olivas's conversations with Cortez had been taped. This provided incriminating evidence against both Cortez and his yet-to-be-identified suppliers, much of which was later corroborated by other evidence at trial. Based on information provided by Cortez, agents had zeroed in on Valdez-Soto and Gomez-Tello when they showed up in San Francisco in the company of Cortez right around the time the sale was to occur.

Cortez pled guilty shortly before trial and agreed to testify for the government. But Cortez's testimony was not consistent with his post-arrest statements and the district court ordered those statements admitted over defendants' hearsay objections. * * * Defendants were eventually convicted of conspiracy to possess cocaine with intent to distribute, in violation of 21 U.S.C. § 846, and possession of more than five kilograms of cocaine with intent to distribute, in violation of 21 U.S.C. § 841(a)(1). Both challenge the admission of Cortez's prior inconsistent statements pursuant to Fed. R. Evid. 803(24) [now 807] * * *.

II

* * *

A. Right after his arrest, Cortez told FBI agents all about his cocaine source. He described his involvement in a narcotics trafficking conspiracy with Valdez-Soto and Gomez-Tello as the suppliers. He said that "Gustavo" (Valdez-Soto) brought the nine kilos of cocaine from Los Angeles and that "Fabio" (Gomez-Tello) lived with Valdez-Soto and came with him. Cortez said he'd distributed cocaine for Valdez-Soto in the past, and described their method of handling finances. He also described Valdez-Soto and Gomez-Tello's arrival in the San Francisco area and their activities after they got there.

Sometime before trial, Cortez changed his tune and testified much differently. The district court, over defense counsel's objection, admitted Cortez's post-arrest statements under Rule 803(24). On the stand, Cortez acknowledged making parts of these statements; other parts he couldn't recall. For example, he insisted that neither Valdez-Soto nor Gomez-Tello was his supplier, though he had trouble remembering his supplier's name. He remembered saying Valdez-Soto and Gomez-Tello were his suppliers and had brought the cocaine to San Francisco, but insisted he'd fabricated this and other parts of his statement. He "absolutely" did not get the nine kilograms from the defendants. Special Agent Fresques was then allowed to testify regarding the statements he took from Cortez after his arrest.

B. [The Court first addresses the defendants' argument that introducing the prior inconsistent statement violated their right to confrontation.] Cortez was on the stand, and defendants here were able to cross-examine him (and take advantage of all the other benefits of confrontation) to their hearts' content. We are aware of no Supreme Court case, or any other case, which holds that introduction of hearsay evidence can violate the Confrontation Clause where the putative declarant is in court, and the defendants are able to cross-examine him. * * *

In the absence of concerns about the accused's right to confrontation, the trial judge has a fair degree of latitude in deciding whether to admit statements under Fed. R. Evid. 803(24). The rule requires only that the hearsay have "equivalent circumstantial guarantees of trustworthiness" to any of the rule's enumerated exceptions. In addition to factors such as "the declarant's perception, memory, narration, or sincerity concerning the matter asserted," *United States v. Friedman*, 593 F.2d 109, 119 (9th Cir. 1979), we've recognized that corroborating evidence is a valid consideration in determining the trustworthiness of out-of-court statements for purposes of Rule 803(24). *See, e.g., Larez v. City of Los Angeles*, 946 F.2d 630, 643 n.6 (9th Cir. 1991) (declarants' out-of-court statements were "especially reliable" under Rule 803(24) because they corroborated one another). The district court thus did not err in considering corroborative evidence here.

C. Valdez-Soto and Gomez-Tello also claim the admission of these statements violated Rule 803(24)'s requirement that "the general purposes of these rules and the interests of justice will be best served by the admission of the statement." As we've previously stated, this requirement is "simply a further emphasis upon the showing of necessity and reliability and a caution that the hearsay rule should not be lightly disregarded * * *." *United States v. Friedman*, 593 F.2d 109, 119 (9th Cir. 1979). Relying on Rule 803(24)'s legislative history, defendants claim this hearsay exception must be interpreted narrowly. We decline the defendants' invitation to go skipping down the yellowbrick road of legislative history. Rule 803(24) exists to provide courts with flexibility in admitting statements traditionally regarded as hearsay but not falling within any of the conventional exceptions. And we review admission of evidence under this provision, like all other evidentiary rulings, for abuse of discretion.

Nor are we persuaded by defendants' related argument that prior inconsistent statements must be admitted, if at all, under those provisions of the hearsay rule dealing expressly with admission of such statements. Specifically, defendants assert that Rule 801(d)(1)(A) provides the only test for admission of unsworn prior inconsistent statements as substantive evidence: if that test is not met, they contend, the evidence can never be admitted. But. the existence of a catch-all hearsay exception is a clear indication that Congress did not want courts to admit hearsay only if it fits within one of the enumerated exceptions. And the reference to guarantees of trustworthiness equivalent to those in the enumerated exceptions strongly suggests that almost fitting within one of these exceptions cuts in favor of admission, not against. Rule 803(24) easily encompasses a case like ours where the evidence has the requisite indicia of trustworthiness but is not otherwise admissible.

Defendants also point to Fong v. American Airlines, Inc., 626 F.2d 759, 763 (9th Cir. 1980), where we held that 803(24) could not be used to admit certain "run-of-the-mill hearsay" — hearsay that "[did] not fit into one of the[] established categories [or] * * * share any of their circumstantial guarantees of trustworthiness." The statements here were anything but. Initially, we note that "the degree of reliability necessary for admission is greatly reduced where, as here, the declarant is testifying and is available for cross-examination, thereby satisfying the central concern of the hearsay rule." *United States v. McPartlin*, 595 F.2d 1321, 1350–51 (7th Cir. 1979). Here, Cortez took the stand at trial and was extensively cross-examined by defense counsel, giving the jury the opportunity to assess his credibility. As the Fifth Circuit said in *United States v. Leslie*, 542 F.2d 285 (5th Cir. 1976), "We agree with Judge Learned Hand's observation that when the jury decides the truth is not what the witness says now but what he said before, they are still deciding from what they see and hear in court."

Moreover, we agree with the district court that these statements possessed substantial indicia of reliability. For one, Cortez gave the statements to FBI agents soon after his arrest. "If a statement is proximate in time to the event, less opportunity for fabrication exists." *Ticey v. Peters*, 8 F.3d 498, 503 (7th Cir. 1993). Although the interview was not directly recorded and transcribed, it was witnessed by a translator who contemporaneously recorded the details. Special Agent Fresques also took notes, and he relied on them shortly thereafter in completing an affidavit for a search warrant he signed under penalty of perjury, as well in preparing a report to summarize the interview. As we must consider whether Cortez's statements have "equivalent circumstantial guarantees of trustworthiness" to any of the hearsay rule's enumerated exceptions, it's worth noting that this affidavit and report come within at least the spirit of Rule 803(6), the business records exception.

We also note that at the time Fresques prepared these documents, he considered Cortez a cooperating witness; it wasn't known until much later that Cortez would change his story. Cortez cooperated unhesitatingly from the start: As Special Agent Fresques put it, "Immediately after his arrest . . . he said that he would cooperate with us." When he made these statements, he'd been informed of his rights and signed a written waiver of them. It's important to note that he would have had no idea how much the agents knew at the time, although, from the circumstances of his arrest, he would likely assume they knew a lot. He certainly would have realized that lying in the face of such uncertainty would seriously jeopardize any chance he had to benefit from cooperating. In addition, as the district court recognized, id., his statements — which were quite detailed — were consistent with the physical evidence in this case.

Finally, we take into consideration that Cortez admitted on the stand he'd given statements to the FBI and acknowledged telling Fresques about significant details pertaining to Valdez-Soto and Gomez-Tello's involvement. Although he "didn't recall" disclosing other parts of the statements, and denied one particular part — that he'd moved to hide from his cocaine creditor — the fact that he admitted making important parts of these statements lent them reliability. In addition, it provided defense counsel with an opportunity to question Cortez about his reasons for making them, and gave the jury a chance to decide whether it believed him.

* * * On this record, admitting these statements under Rule 803(24) was far from an abuse of discretion.

Affirmed.

NOTE

Should a hearsay statement be admitted under Rule 807 if it is a "near miss" of another hearsay exception?

The residual exception applies to statements "not specifically covered by Rule 803 or 804 but having equivalent circumstantial guarantees of trustworthiness." Thus, courts must face the issue whether hearsay that almost, but not quite, fits one of the standard exceptions may be admitted under the residual exception. A major concern of some members of Congress was that certain types of hearsay deliberately excluded from the categorical exceptions might nevertheless be admitted as residual hearsay. Many decisions have demonstrated that there were good grounds for the congressional concerns, as courts have often admitted hearsay under the residual exception where it is a "near miss" of an enumerated exception. *See United States v. Furst,* 886 F.2d 558 (3d Cir. 1989) (the residual exception "is not limited in availability as to types of evidence not addressed in the other exceptions; [it] is also available when the proponent fails to meet the standards set forth in the other exceptions"); *Dartez v. Fibreboard Corp.*, 765 F.2d 456 (5th Cir. 1985) (a deposition was offered against a defendant who was not a party to the litigation in which the deposition was taken; the party who cross-examined the deponent was not a predecessor-in-interest as that term is used in Rule 804(b)(1); however, because the defendant could have added nothing to the cross-examination that did take place, the deposition was admissible under the residual exception, as a "near miss" of the prior testimony exception); *Turbyfill v. International Harvester Co.*, 486 F. Supp. 232 (E.D. Mich. 1980) (a statement that failed to meet the requirements of Rule 803(5) because the preparer of the record was not available to testify was admitted as residual hearsay on "near miss" grounds); *United States v. Laster*, 258 F.3d 525 (6th Cir. 2001) (business records were not admissible under Rule 803(6) because the foundation witness was not sufficiently familiar with recordkeeping; but there was no error in admitting the records under the residual exception; "the phrase 'specifically covered' means only that if a statement is admissible under one of the exceptions, such subsection should be relied upon instead of the residual exception").

[3] Circumstantial Guarantees of Trustworthiness, and More Probative Than Any Other Evidence Reasonably Available

LAREZ v. CITY OF LOS ANGELES
946 F.2d 630 (9th Cir. 1991)

BOOCHEVER, CIRCUIT JUDGE:

Six officers of the Los Angeles Police Department (LAPD), Chief of Police Daryl Gates, and the City of Los Angeles appeal from the district court's denial of their motion for a new trial after jury verdicts against them in a civil rights trial based on a search of the home of the Larez family. We affirm the denial of the new trial motion as to the six officers, but, because of the erroneous admission of hearsay evidence, which we cannot say was harmless, we reverse and remand for a new trial as to Gates and the City.

BACKGROUND

The civil rights action which is the subject of this appeal arises out of an LAPD search of the Larez home. * * * [The plaintiffs alleged that the officers violated their Fourth Amendment rights in searching their home, and used excessive force during the search.]

Jessie Larez lodged a complaint with the LAPD. The department's Internal Affairs division assigned a CRASH detective not involved in the Larez search to investigate the complaint. In a letter signed by Chief Gates, Jessie ultimately was notified that none of the many allegations in his complaint could be sustained. The instant suit followed.

The Larezes' theory at trial was that the six individual officers had violated their constitutional rights to be free from unreasonable searches accompanied by the use of excessive force. Moreover, they complained about the disarray in which their home was left. Against Chief Gates and the City, the Larezes alleged the perpetuation of unconstitutional policies or customs of excessive force, illegal searches including official tolerance for the destruction of property during such searches, and inadequate citizen complaint procedures which have the effect of encouraging the excessive use of force.

Trial was bifurcated between the case against the six officers and the case against the Gates and the City. After the Larezes prevailed against the six officers, Gates and the City moved to dismiss the case against them contending that, because plaintiffs were fully awarded compensatory damages in the first phase of the trial, nothing was left to be adjudicated. The motion was denied.

At trial on the liability of Gates and the City, * * * Gates testified. Upon departing the courtroom, he was questioned by reporters about his reaction to the $ 90,000 jury verdict against his officers in the first phase of the trial. Each of at least three Los Angeles newspapers attributed five statements to him. One of the five statements repeated in the various newspapers quoted Gates as saying that Jessie Larez had been lucky that he only had gotten a broken nose. All the statements were admitted over objection.

After hearing the second phase evidence, the jury found the supervisory defendants liable. Each plaintiff received $1 nominal damages against the City and Gates in his official capacity. The jury awarded $7 nominal damages and $170,000 punitive damages against Gates in his individual capacity.

* * *

The Admissibility of the Newspaper Quotations

After testifying, Gates was questioned by reporters in the courthouse corridor. The next morning, articles in the Los Angeles Times, the Herald-Examiner, and the Daily News attributed certain statements to Gates. The variance between the quotations was minimal, and the substance of the quotations was substantially corroborated by all three newspapers.

The following five statements were attributed to Gates:

1. "How much is a broken nose worth?"

2. "$90,000? I don't think it's worth anything. He's probably lucky that's all he has."

3. "Given the circumstances in this case, I don't think it's worth anything. [Larez] is probably lucky that's all he had broken."

4. "They [the jurors] see the family there all cleaned up * * * . They don't know their background, that there is a gang member on parole. They get very sympathetic."

5. "I tell my officers to do something — and we do something and they give them $90,000."

* * *

After hearing both sides, the court admitted the statements. Finding the quotations relevant, the court also found them to be nonhearsay. * * * [W]e conclude that the statements were erroneously admitted hearsay, and that their admission was not harmless. While defense counsel requested that the Larezes put the reporters on the stand, and while the Larezes were apparently prepared to do so, the court unfortunately believed such a step unnecessary. Here, it erred.

Defense counsel has never claimed the quotations were complete fabrications. Instead, by focusing on the context and transcription of those statements, he called attention to the need for cross-examination of the reporters, requesting that "before they're admitted, * * * the persons who wrote up these articles [be called to] testify and be subject to [his] voir dire as to the circumstances in which these were offered * * * ." By so doing, he implicitly recognized that the statements' admissibility hinged on two out-of-court statements: (1) Gates's actual statements and (2) their later repetition by reporters.

Gates's actual out-of-court statements pose no admissibility problem. The statements clearly are relevant. They are probative of central issues in the case — Gates's recklessness and callous indifference, and customs and policies of the LAPD. In addition, they are admissible nonhearsay either as admissions of a party opponent, see Fed. R. Evid. 801(d)(2)(A), or because they are not offered for the truth of the matter asserted (i.e., not offered to prove that a broken nose is worth less than $ 90,000, but rather to show Gates's state of mind), see Fed. R. Evid. 801(c). Because Gates's statements were properly considered nonhearsay, their admission technically does not pose a double hearsay problem.

The statements' repetition in the newspapers, however, posed a more difficult problem which the district court failed to address. As the reporters never testified nor were subjected to cross-examination, their transcriptions of Gates's statements involve a serious hearsay problem. First, the reporters' transcriptions were out-of-court statements. By attributing quotations to Gates, the reporters necessarily made the implicit statement, "Gates said this!" As the reporters' statements were made in newspapers, they were, a fortiori, statements made out-of-court where they were not subject to the rigors of cross-examination. Second, the statements — "Gates said this!" — were offered for the truth of the matter asserted: that Gates did in fact make the quoted statement.

The only exception which colorably applies to these hearsay statements is Fed. R. Evid. 803(24) [now 807]. * * * The touchstone of this exception is trustworthiness equivalent to that of the other specific hearsay exceptions.

While newspaper articles have been held inadmissible hearsay as to their content, see, e.g., *Pallotta v. United States*, 404 F.2d 1035 (1st Cir. 1968), few cases have addressed this question in light of the requirements of Rule 803(24). *See May v. Cooperman*, 780 F.2d 240 (3d Cir. 1985). In *May*, for example, newspaper accounts discussing legislative motives behind a school prayer bill had been admitted by the district court for use by school prayer opponents to prove legislative purpose under the *Lemon* test where no official legislative history for the bill existed. The panel majority, recognizing some problems with admissibility under Rule 803(24), ultimately did not pass on the 803(24) question for it found that, even if admission on that basis had been erroneous, such error was harmless because the evidence was cumulative. Dissenting on other grounds, JUDGE BECKER, however, examined the Rule 803(24) question more carefully. Among other things, he found that the newspaper accounts of the legislative hearings (of which there was no official record) lacked the "'circumstantial guarantees of trustworthiness'" because they might have "been written from a biased point of view." JUDGE BECKER added, "it is not unknown for reporters to stretch some facts or omit others * * * ." He also found that subsection B of Rule 803(24) was not satisfied because the proponents of the evidence failed to make a "showing of inability to locate observers who attended the legislative debates * * * ."

Similarly, in *United States Football League v. Nat'l Football League,* 1986-1 Trade Cas. (CCH) P 67,101 at 62,667 (S.D.N.Y. 1986), newspaper reports attributing statements to unknown declarants were excluded, as double hearsay, both as insufficiently trustworthy and as less probative than "other evidence which the proponent [could] procure through reasonable efforts." There, with respect to trustworthiness, the court specifically noted that newspaper articles "are often challenged by interested parties as inaccurate." The court was concerned that admission of articles containing statements of unknown declarants "could be the subject of widespread abuse if admitted into evidence under [Rule 803(24)] in any but the most extraordinary circumstances."

We quarrel with neither court's concerns about the trustworthiness of evidence sought to be admitted under Rule 803(24); indeed, they are concerns we share. Courts may well question whether an out-of-court statement, merely because it appears in newsprint, is sufficiently reliable. In the "extraordinary circumstances" of this case, however, where three independent newspapers attributed the same quotations to Gates, a known declarant who testified at trial, we believe the statements have "circumstantial guarantees of trustworthiness" at least equivalent to those of many of the other hearsay exceptions. * * *

It is with respect to subsection B of Rule 803(24), however, that we are unable to countenance the statements' admission. By requiring that "the statement [be] more probative on the point for which it is offered than any other evidence which the proponent can procure through reasonable efforts," that subsection essentially creates a "best evidence" requirement. The statements' admission, therefore, was erroneous because the newspaper quotations were not the best available evidence of what Gates said; testimony from the reporters themselves would have been better. The Larezes knew as much for they had the reporters subpoenaed and apparently ready to testify. We cannot fault defense counsel for he specifically requested an opportunity to cross-examine the reporters before the evidence was admitted. Thus, the error was the failure to take testimony from, and particularly to allow the cross-examination of, the reporters who repeated Gates's comments. *See Cooperman*, 780 F.2d at 263 (Becker, J., dissenting) (newspaper article was not the most probative evidence that could be procured by reasonable efforts).

[The court finds that the error was not harmless.]

NOTES

1. What factors are relevant in determining whether a statement is sufficiently trustworthy to qualify as residual hearsay?

See Saltzburg, Martin, and Capra, *Federal Rules of Evidence Manual* (9th ed. 2006):

> The most important requirement for residual hearsay is that it possess guarantees of trustworthiness equivalent to those supporting the

Rule 803 and 804 exceptions. No inclusive list of factors determining admissibility can be devised because admissibility hinges upon the peculiar factual context within which the statement was made. But some nondispositive generalizations can be made.

There are certain standard factors all Courts consider in evaluating the trustworthiness of a declarant's statement under the residual exception. These include:

(1) The relationship between the declarant and the person to whom the statement was made. For example, a statement to a trusted confidante should be considered more reliable than a statement to a total stranger. *See, e.g.*, *United States v. Morgan*, 385 F.3d 196 (2d Cir. 2004) (letter written by a codefendant to her boyfriend was properly admitted against the defendant; it was sufficiently trustworthy because it was written to an intimate acquaintance in the privacy of the codefendant's hotel room, with no expectation that it would ever find its way to the police).

(2) The capacity of the declarant at the time of the statement. For instance, if the declarant was drunk or on drugs at the time, that would cut against a finding of trustworthiness, and vice versa. *See, e.g.*, *United States v. Wilkus*, 875 F.2d 649 (7th Cir. 1989) (an affidavit signed while the declarant was under heavy medication, and as to which the declarant had no memory at the time of trial, was insufficiently trustworthy to qualify as residual hearsay). *See also United States v. Lawrence*, 349 F.3d 109 (3d Cir. 2003) (victim's identification of someone other than the defendant as the perpetrator was properly excluded; the victim had been severely injured and was capable of only blinks and nods; thus the "statement" was potentially ambiguous and untrustworthy).

(3) The personal truthfulness of the declarant. If the declarant is an untruthful person, this cuts against admissibility, while an unimpeachable character for veracity cuts in favor of admitting the statement. *See, e.g.*, *United States v. Hall*, 165 F.3d 1095 (7th Cir. 1999) (confession of another person could not be admitted on the defendant's behalf as residual hearsay; the declarant "confessed to any crime he was questioned about by the police" and thus was untrustworthy).

(4) Whether the declarant appeared to carefully consider his statement. *See, e.g.*, *United States v. York*, 852 F.2d 221, 226 (7th Cir. 1988) (where the declarant answered affirmatively to every question asked by the United States Attorney, trustworthiness could not be found: "Apparently, not even a single placebo question was amongst the lot to ensure that Tommy was considering the substance of each question and answering responsively, rather than simply agreeing with every question that the government posed.").

(5) Whether the declarant recanted or repudiated the statement after it was made. *See, e.g.*, *United States v. York*, 852 F.2d 221, 226 (7th Cir. 1988) (a statement was not trustworthy where the declarant recanted).

(6) Whether the declarant has made other statements that were either consistent or inconsistent with the proffered statement. *See, e.g., United States v. Sinclair*, 74 F.3d 753 (7th Cir. 1996) (a statement offered by the defendant as residual hearsay was properly excluded, in part because of the great lapse of time between the declarant's statement and the events described and in part because the statement was inconsistent with prior statements made by the declarant to the FBI).

(7) Whether the behavior of the declarant was consistent with the content of the statement. *See, e.g., United States v. Bradley*, 145 F.3d 889 (7th Cir. 1998) (statement by the defendant's wife that the defendant brandished a gun at her was properly admitted as residual hearsay; among other things, the declarant was distraught when she made the statement, and this was "consistent with the trauma she described").

(8) Whether the declarant's memory might have been impaired due to the lapse of time between the event and the statement. *See, e.g., Braun v. Lorillard Inc.*, 84 F.3d 230 (7th Cir. 1996) (the trial judge properly excluded testimony relating statements made by a deceased declarant who was hired by the defendant cigarette manufacturer in 1954 to examine Kent cigarettes under an electron microscope; there was no documentary evidence of her study, but a journalist who interviewed the declarant and the declarant's son would have testified that the declarant said that she reported to the manufacturer that the Kent filters leaked asbestos into the lungs; the statements were made years after the work had been done and therefore were not sufficiently reliable to qualify as residual hearsay).

(9) Whether the statement, as well as the event described by the statement, is clear and factual, or instead is vague and ambiguous.

(10) Whether the statement was made under formal circumstances or pursuant to formal duties, such that the declarant would have been likely to consider the accuracy of the statement when making it.). *See, e.g., Hal Roach Studios v. Richard Feiner & Co.*, 896 F.2d 1542 (9th Cir. 1990) (S-1 registration statement filed with Securities Exchange Commission held admissible as residual hearsay to prove the corporate history of the plaintiff; "The standard of due diligence applied by securities lawyers with regard to Registration Statements is sufficient to guarantee the requisite circumstantial guarantees of trustworthiness.").

(11) Whether the statement appears to have been made in anticipation of litigation and is favorable to the person who made or prepared the statement. *See, e.g., United States v. Walker*, 410 F.3d 754 (5th Cir. 2005) (no error in excluding a videotaped statement to police officers made by an associate of the defendant, in which she categorically denied that the defendant had brought any drugs into a room; the declarant "was in a room with a lot of cocaine," and was not under oath; she was facing the threat of criminal charges

and "had every incentive to lie."); *Kirk v. Raymark Indus., Inc.*, 61 F.3d 147 (3d Cir. 1995) (the trial court erred in admitting, as residual hearsay, interrogatory responses from a codefendant who had settled; the responses, which denied liability, were offered by the plaintiff to rebut the non-settling defendant's contention that the plaintiff's injury was solely caused by the settling defendant; the interrogatory responses were not sufficiently trustworthy, because they were made while the declarant was still a defendant in the litigation and "had every incentive to set forth the facts in a light most favorable to itself").

(12) Whether the declarant was a disinterested bystander or rather an interested party. *See, e.g.*, *United States v. Doerr*, 886 F.2d 944 (7th Cir. 1989) ("Another indicium of reliability is the declarant's disinterest; the testimony of a mere bystander with no axe to grind tends to be more trustworthy."); *Dogan v. Hardy*, 587 F. Supp. 967 (N.D. Miss. 1984) (the Court held inadmissible in a personal injury action a self-serving statement by the driver of a car, made while he was hospitalized).

(13) Whether the statement was corroborated by independent evidence or similar statements from others. *See Larez, supra,* where newspaper accounts were found sufficiently trustworthy because three independent reporters related the same account.

2. How is the notice requirement applied?

Consider this excerpt from Professors Saltzburg, Martin, and Capra, *Federal Rules of Evidence Manual* (9th ed. 2006):

> The purpose of the notice requirement is to protect against excessive liberalization and unfair surprise and to lend more predictability to preparation for trial when residual hearsay is to be proffered. Some courts have interpreted the notice requirement literally, excluding the evidence unless the adversary has been notified before trial of the intent to invoke the residual exception to admit a specific statement.
>
> *See, e.g.*, *Kirk v. Raymark Indus., Inc.*, 61 F.3d 147 (3d Cir. 1995) (trial court erred in admitting, as residual hearsay, interrogatory responses from a codefendant who had settled; the plaintiff never gave the defendant notice that she intended to introduce this evidence under the residual exception).
>
> Generally speaking, however, the notice requirement has been applied flexibly in accordance with its intent, which is to prevent surprise and to allow time to prepare to meet the evidence. *See, e.g.*, *United States v. Doe*, 860 F.2d 488 (1st Cir. 1988) (collecting cases adopting the majority view that the notice requirement will not preclude admission where the adversary has not been prejudiced). Under the majority, liberal approach, it is ordinarily possible to satisfy the notice requirement by notifying the adversary during the trial, so long as the adversary has sufficient time to challenge the evidence effectively. Postponing notification until trial may require the granting

of a continuance, depending on the circumstances; the Court will also consider whether the delay in notice could have been avoided. *See, e.g.*, *United States v. Baker*, 985 F.2d 1248 (4th Cir. 1993) (where the need for rebuttal evidence did not become apparent until trial, and the rebuttal witness disappeared after the government announced it was offering rebuttal evidence, the witness's trustworthy statement was properly admitted as residual hearsay and pretrial notice was wholly impracticable and properly dispensed with).

There is some dispute among the courts as to the type of notice that the opponent of the evidence must receive. The Third Circuit holds that the opponent must be notified not only about the evidence itself but also of the proponent's intent to invoke the residual exception. All of the other Circuits that have decided the question appear to hold that the opponent need only be made aware in advance of the existence of the evidence and its potential proffer at trial. The usual fact situation in which this question arises is where the proponent has not even purported to give pretrial notice, and yet the opponent is well aware before trial of the existence of the evidence and its possible proffer at trial, albeit perhaps not under the residual exception.

The minority position is found in *United States v. Pelullo*, 964 F.2d 193 (3d Cir. 1992). The *Pelullo* Court noted that while the Rule could be read to require notice only of the statement itself, the Third Circuit requires specific notice of the proponent's intent to use the residual exception. Here, even though the defendant was given the documents months before trial, there was no specific notice of the government's intent to invoke the residual exception, so the documents were held improperly admitted as residual hearsay.

The more common result is that the notice requirement is deemed satisfied when the opponent has received actual notice, before trial, of the existence of the evidence and its possible use at the trial. The reasoning is that under these circumstances, the opponent cannot complain about surprise or inability to prepare. Thus, in *United States v. Bachsian*, 4 F.3d 796 (9th Cir. 1993), the Court declared that "failure to give [explicit] pretrial notice will be excused if the adverse party had an opportunity to attack the trustworthiness of the evidence." In *Bachsian*, the government did not give notice under the residual exception, but the defendant was more generally notified two months before trial that the government intended to use the evidence, and the defendant was given copies. Also, the defendant did not move for a continuance. Under these circumstances, the Court found that the spirit of the notice requirement was met.

Query whether the cases finding the notice requirement satisfied whenever the opponent somehow becomes aware of the evidence are consistent with the terms of the Rule. The Rule specifies that the proponent must herself provide notice to the adverse party; these terms would not be met if the opponent, as is often the case, becomes aware of the information other than through the proponent. On the other hand, where the proponent has in fact given some kind of advance notice about the hearsay evidence, but has failed to invoke the residual exception specifically, the Rule is, as the Third Circuit admits, vague as to whether the notice requirement is satisfied.

3. How is the "more probative" requirement of Rule 807 to be applied?

To be admitted under the residual exception, a hearsay statement must be "more probative" than any other evidence reasonably available to prove the point. The rationale for this requirement is that the residual exception should be reserved for cases of clear necessity — it should not be overused.

Courts have held that live testimony by the declarant is as a general rule more probative than or at least equally probative as hearsay. *See, e.g., Polansky v. CNA Ins. Co.*, 852 F.2d 626 (1st Cir. 1988) (a letter prepared by the plaintiff as to his understanding of a certain transaction was not the most probative evidence reasonably available since the plaintiff could have testified about these matters on the stand). These courts have generally excluded statements offered as residual hearsay when the declarant was not called to testify and was not shown to be unavailable. *See, e.g., United States v. Azure*, 801 F.2d 336 (8th Cir. 1986) (in a second trial on the same matter, where the witness testified in the first trial, an out-of-court statement by that witness could not be admitted as residual hearsay; if the witness were available for the second trial, her in-court testimony would be as probative as the residual hearsay; if the witness were not available at the second trial, her prior testimony at the first trial would be as probative as the residual hearsay; therefore, the "more probative" requirement of the Rule would not be met).

However, the failure to call an available declarant will not always preclude the admission of residual hearsay. A declarant may be technically available and yet may be unable or unwilling to give testimony that is as probative as the out-of-court statement. In such circumstances, the hearsay statement will be more probative evidence. For example, in child abuse cases, the child's out-of-court statement concerning the abuse is often considered the more probative evidence because the child may not be able to communicate as well on the stand as he or she did out of court. *See, e.g., United States v. Dorian*, 803 F.2d 1439 (8th Cir. 1986) (where the child was frightened and uncommunicative on the stand, her residual hearsay statement was more probative).

Moreover, the Rule states that the proffered hearsay must be more probative than any other evidence that can be produced through *reasonable* efforts. In some cases, a declarant might be technically available, but it would be unreasonably prohibitive and time-consuming to demand that the declarant testify in court. For example, in consumer fraud actions, where thousands of consumers have been defrauded, reliable affidavits prepared by each consumer have been admitted as residual hearsay in lieu of in-court testimony. *See, e.g., FTC v. Amy Travel Serv.*, 875 F.2d 564, 576 (7th Cir. 1989) (thousands of consumer affidavits were properly admitted under the residual exception as the most probative evidence reasonably available: "The defendants ran a nation-wide telemarketing operation and it would be cumbersome and unnecessarily expensive to bring all the consumers in for live testimony."). Because the probative value of the hearsay is compared with that of other evidence that could be procured through "reasonable" efforts, limitations upon the financial resources available to the parties and the court are rightfully considered. As one Court has stated, the question of whether there is more probative evidence reasonably available depends upon "the importance of the evidence, the means at the command of the proponent, and the amount in controversy." *Hal Roach Studios v. Richard Feiner & Co.*, 896 F.2d 1542, 1552 (9th Cir. 1990).

The term "more probative" must be distinguished from the term "more credible." For instance, if there are two eyewitnesses to an event, and one witness, now unavailable, makes a hearsay statement that is offered as residual hearsay, the statement is not more probative than the other eyewitness' in-court testimony would be. This is true even if the declarant's credibility is strong and the witness' credibility is weak. The term "probative" refers to the tendency of the statement to prove a proposition *if the jury decides to believe it.* As one court has stated: "The credibility of a witness has nothing to do with whether or not his testimony is probative with respect to the fact it seeks to prove. * * * [T]he law does not consider credibility as a component to relevance." *United States v. Welsh*, 774 F.2d 670, 672 (4th Cir. 1985).

PROBLEM 14-1

Uprock Company was a high-flying leader on the New York Stock Exchange as it led the way in the deregulated electricity market. Its stock rose over a period of two years more than 60%. Suddenly, however, the company announced that there were "off the book" losses that had not been reported in its annual financial statements. These losses involved partnerships in which Uprock had a financial risk, but which were treated as independent entities rather than as part of the company. As a result of the sudden announcement, the stock plummeted in value to virtually zero and Uprock filed for bankruptcy. A federal prosecutor began an investigation of Uprock and its outside accounting firm, Peerless & Pipps, and Uprock shareholders filed a class action suit against the officers and directors of the company and against Peerless & Pipps.

The class action case is set for trial. Prior to trial plaintiffs file a motion *in limine* seeking to admit a handwritten note found at the scene of a double suicide and indicating that, if necessary, they will rely on Rule 807. A husband and wife, Jan and Jene Jepschock, were former officers of Uprock. They were found dead in their home several months after the company went bankrupt. Each took a massive overdose of sleeping pills. Next to Jan's body was a note that was identified as being written by Jan which contained the following: "We can't take it any more. The prospects of a trial and possible indictment are too much to bear. The President knew about the loans, the CEO knew about the loans, the COO knew about the loans. I was there when they talked about the loans. They should have been disclosed. We all knew it. It was greed run amuck. We hope they rot in hell and this note helps those who have been injured."

The President, CEO, and COO are all named defendants in the class action. The President and CEO each claim that they were unaware of the partnerships and of the company's risk. The COO claims that she knew of the partnerships, but was absolutely convinced by Peerless & Pipps that the partnerships were accounted for properly and that the company's financial statements were prepared in accordance with general accounting principles. They and the other defendants oppose the admission of the note. The trial judge sets a pretrial hearing.

Court:	What is the defendants' position regarding the note?
Defendants:	We move to exclude it as pure hearsay.
Court:	What do the plaintiffs have to say?
Plaintiffs:	First, your Honor, we think it is a dying declaration. The declarant is unavailable, and the statement explains the death.
Defendants:	What an outrageous claim. This is not simply a statement about the cause and circumstances of a death. It is a claim about who knew what and when they knew it. This is not a dying declaration.
Court:	I'm inclined to agree with defendants that this goes beyond what I could admit as a dying declaration.
Plaintiffs:	Second, it should come in to prove state of mind under Rule 803(3).
Defendants:	The note refers to things that took place in the past. This is not simply a statement about a present state of mind. Although there may be small parts of the note that refer to a present state of mind, those are irrelevant, and the parts that are relevant look backward.
Court:	Again, I am inclined to agree with defendants. To the extent that the note is relevant, it is an accusation that looks backwards and falls outside Rule 803(3).
Plaintiffs:	Third, we submit that the statement is a declaration against both pecuniary and penal interest, and that the declarant is unavailable.
Defendants:	It cannot be a declaration against penal interest, since the declarant expected to be dead not prosecuted. That's why he wrote the note. And, by taking his life, the declarant assured that the note could not be against his pecuniary interest. He did not expect to be alive to be held financially responsible.
Court:	For the third time, I am inclined to agree with defendants that there is no showing that the declarant believed he would be exposing himself to penal or pecuniary liability by writing the note.

Plaintiffs: Fourth, we rely as we told defendants that we would, on the residual hearsay exception, Rule 807. The declarant is dead. Even though the court has rejected our first three arguments, we believe that the note is not only critically important, but that there are circumstantial guarantees of trustworthiness associated with it.

Court: What are those?

Plaintiffs: The declarant made the statement as he was about to die. The same principle that one does not face his maker with a lie on his lips that supports Rule 804(b)(2) applies here. Second, the declarant was prepared to die because of what he did; he was exposing himself to death which is at least as important as exposure to criminal or civil liability. Third, the fact is that he was describing his present state of mind and explaining why suicide was contemplated.

Defendants: We believe that there is better evidence available. The President, the CEO and the COO are here to testify as are other officers and directors. Their live testimony is better evidence than this hearsay note.

Court: Now, let me understand the defendants' position. Are you saying that a hearsay statement can not be admitted under Rule 807 whenever there are live witnesses to events?

Defendants: What we are saying is that Rule 807 plainly states that the proponent of hearsay must show that "the statement is more probative on the point for which it is offered than any other evidence which the proponent can procure through reasonable efforts" and there are better witnesses available.

Plaintiffs: All of those "better" witnesses have a reason to lie.

Defendants: So did the declarant. He obviously was hostile to the defendants and wrote the note to injure them. The plaintiffs have a full and fair chance to examine the witnesses who are alive, and the jury can determine whether their denials are true.

Court: Anything more?

Plaintiffs: No, your Honor.

Defendants: No, your Honor.

Court: (1)__________

The plaintiffs filed another *in limine* motion seeking admission of evidence. Pursuant to Rule 6 of the Federal Rules of Criminal Procedure, the federal prosecutor sought and obtained permission from the federal district court to share with the plaintiffs in the civil suit the grand jury testimony of Jene Jepshock. Jene testified to the grand jury that "I worked for Uprock along with my husband. We had our entire pensions in company stock. When the stock took a dive, I asked my husband how this could have happened. He told me that the President knew about the loans, the CEO knew about the loans, and the COO knew about the loans. He said that he was there when they talked about the loans and that they all understood that the loans should have been disclosed, but they were all afraid that the stock value would drop." The plaintiffs seek to have the grand jury testimony admitted and give notice that they may rely on Rule 807.

Court:	What is the defendants' position on this one?
Defendants:	This is pure hearsay just like the note.
Court:	What do plaintiffs have to say?
Plaintiffs:	It's former testimony.
Defendants:	Can't be. We did not have a chance to examine the witness.
Court:	Defendants are right on that one.
Plaintiffs:	What about Rule 801(d)(1)(A)?
Defendants:	That must fail. She's not available for cross-examination.
Court:	Defendants are correct once again.
Plaintiffs:	It's a declaration against her husband's penal interest.
Defendants:	A statement against someone else's pecuniary interest is not within Rule 804(b)(3).
Court:	It does appear to fall outside the wall.
Plaintiffs:	Then it should be admitted under the residual exception.
Court:	What are the guarantees of trustworthiness?
Plaintiffs:	The witness was under oath, and she knew she could be prosecuted if she lied. She made statements that were extremely damaging to her husband. A wife does not make such statements under oath if they are not true.
Defendants:	The fact is that after making these statements she and her husband killed themselves, so she might have thought that nothing she said was ever going to be used against her husband. And the fact that she was under oath is true of all grand jury witnesses. The plaintiffs' argument would open the door to such testimony too far.
Court:	Anything else?

Defendants: Yes. If the court decides to admit the note, the plaintiffs cannot show that "the statement is more probative on the point for which it is offered than any other evidence which the proponent can procure through reasonable efforts." The wife's testimony is double hearsay, and it cannot be as reliable as the husband's statement. So, we think that the testimony must be excluded if the note is admitted and that it should be excluded anyway because there are live witnesses available to testify.

Court: Let me understand your position. You maintain that if I admit the husband's note, I cannot admit the wife's statement. Your argument is that there is by definition only one statement that is more probative than any other evidence, and therefore that two statements cannot be admitted.

Defendants: Exactly. That is just how we read Rule 807.

Plaintiffs: We don't read the Rule that way. We believe that the court may find that the statement by the husband is better than any other evidence concerning his role in the case, and the statement by the wife is better than other evidence with respect to what she learned about her husband's role.

Court: So, your position is that Rule 807 does not limit the court to admit only one hearsay statement in a case?

Plaintiffs: Exactly. That is how we read Rule 807.

Court: (2) __________

Chapter 15

HEARSAY AND THE CONFRONTATION CLAUSE

A. CONFRONTATION CLAUSE

The Confrontation Clause of the Sixth Amendment of the United States Constitution provides: "In all criminal prosecutions, the accused shall enjoy the right * * * to be confronted with the witnesses against him."

In *Mattox v. United States*, 156 U.S. 237 (1895), the Supreme Court indicated that the Confrontation Clause served two purposes: to allow a defendant the right to face his or her accusing witness in open court for truth-testing cross-examinations and to give the jury an opportunity to determine the credibility of the witness through observation of the witness' demeanor. The Court further explained:

> The primary object of the constitutional provision in question was to prevent depositions or *ex parte* affidavits, such as were sometimes admitted in civil cases, from being used against the prisoner in lieu of a personal examination * * * of the witness * * * in which the accused has an opportunity [to compel the witness] to stand face to face with the jury in order that they may look at him, and judge by his demeanor upon the stand and the manner in which he gives his testimony whether he is worthy of belief.

In 1965, the Supreme Court in *Pointer v. Texas*, 380 U.S. 400, 403 (1965), held that the protections afforded a criminal defendant under the Confrontation Clause of the Sixth Amendment were applicable in state court proceedings by virtue of the Due Process Clause of the Fourteenth Amendment.

B. CONFRONTATION CLAUSE vs. ADMISSION OF OUT-OF-COURT DECLARATIONS

Hearsay is defined by Federal Rule of Evidence 801 as "a statement, other than one made by the declarant while testifying at the trial or hearing, offered in evidence to prove the truth of the matter asserted." Rule 802 further provides that hearsay is generally not admissible except as provided by the Rules of Evidence or by other rules prescribed by the Supreme Court. Hearsay is excluded from evidence for the same reason as underlies the Confrontation Clause — such declarations are generally not subject to cross-examination and thus are considered unreliable. *See California v. Green*, 399 U.S. 149, 155 (1970) (hearsay rules and the Confrontation Clause generally designed to protect similar values); and *Dutton v. Evans*, 400 U.S. 74, 86 (1970) (hearsay rules and the Confrontation Clause "stem from the same roots").

Thus, read together, the Confrontation Clause and the hearsay rule would seem to provide a basis for excluding from evidence any statements that fall under the definition of hearsay and for which no right of cross-examination is granted to the defendant. The hearsay rule, however, recognizes that there are means other than cross-examination for assuring reliability of the out-of-court statement. The conflict between the Confrontation Clause and hearsay rule arises as a result of the exclusions from and the exceptions to the definition of hearsay which allow a vast number and type of out-of-court declarations to be admitted into evidence without the declarant being present in court for cross-examination by the defendant. The Federal Rules of Evidence establish more than thirty types of out-of-court statements that are not rendered inadmissible by the hearsay rule. Both state and federal criminal courts are frequently confronted with the problem of attempting to reconcile the defendant's rights under the Confrontation Clause with the Rules of Evidence that allow for the admission of statements which either are excluded from the definition of hearsay or are deemed exceptions to the hearsay rule.

C. A FOCUS ON TESTIMONIAL HEARSAY

CRAWFORD v. WASHINGTON
541 U.S. 36 (2004)

JUSTICE SCALIA delivered the opinion of the Court.

Petitioner Michael Crawford stabbed a man who allegedly tried to rape his wife, Sylvia. At his trial, the State played for the jury Sylvia's tape-recorded statement to the police describing the stabbing, even though he had no opportunity for cross-examination. The Washington Supreme Court upheld petitioner's conviction after determining that Sylvia's statement was reliable. The question presented is whether this procedure complied with the Sixth Amendment's guarantee that, "in all criminal prosecutions, the accused shall enjoy the right * * * to be confronted with the witnesses against him."

I

On August 5, 1999, Kenneth Lee was stabbed at his apartment. Police arrested petitioner later that night. After giving petitioner and his wife *Miranda* warnings, detectives interrogated each of them twice. Petitioner eventually confessed that he and Sylvia had gone in search of Lee because he was upset over an earlier incident in which Lee had tried to rape her. The two had found Lee at his apartment, and a fight ensued in which Lee was stabbed in the torso and petitioner's hand was cut.

Petitioner gave the following account of the fight:

Q. Okay. Did you ever see anything in [Lee's] hands?

A. I think so, but I'm not positive.

Q. Okay, when you think so, what do you mean by that?

A. I coulda swore I seen him goin' for somethin' before, right before everything happened. He was like reachin', fiddlin' around down here

> and stuff * * * and I just * * * I don't know, I think, this is just a possibility, but I think, I think that he pulled somethin' out and I grabbed for it and that's how I got cut * * * but I'm not positive. I, I, my mind goes blank when things like this happen. I mean, I just, I remember things wrong, I remember things that just doesn't, don't make sense to me later.

Sylvia generally corroborated petitioner's story about the events leading up to the fight, but her account of the fight itself was arguably different — particularly with respect to whether Lee had drawn a weapon before petitioner assaulted him:

> Q. Did Kenny do anything to fight back from this assault?
>
> A. (pausing) I know he reached into his pocket * * * or somethin' * * * I don't know what.
>
> Q. After he was stabbed?
>
> A. He saw Michael coming up. He lifted his hand * * * his chest open, he might [have] went to go strike his hand out or something and then (inaudible).
>
> Q. Okay, you, you gotta speak up.
>
> A. Okay, he lifted his hand over his head maybe to strike Michael's hand down or something and then he put his hands in his * * * put his right hand in his right pocket * * * took a step back * * * Michael proceeded to stab him * * * then his hands were like * * * how do you explain this * * * open arms * * * with his hands open and he fell down * * * and we ran (describing subject holding hands open, palms toward assailant).
>
> Q. Okay, when he's standing there with his open hands, you're talking about Kenny, correct?
>
> A. Yeah, after, after the fact, yes.
>
> Q. Did you see anything in his hands at that point?
>
> A. (pausing) um um (no).

The State charged petitioner with assault and attempted murder. At trial, he claimed self-defense. Sylvia did not testify because of the state marital privilege, which generally bars a spouse from testifying without the other spouse's consent. *See* Wash. Rev. Code § 5.60.060(1) (1994). In Washington, this privilege does not extend to a spouse's out-of-court statements admissible under a hearsay exception, *see State v. Burden*, 120 Wn. 2d 371, 377, 841 P.2d 758, 761 (1992), so the State sought to introduce Sylvia's tape-recorded statements to the police as evidence that the stabbing was not in self-defense. Noting that Sylvia had admitted she led petitioner to Lee's apartment and thus had facilitated the assault, the State invoked the hearsay exception for statements against penal interest, Wash. Rule Evid. 804(b)(3) (2003).

Petitioner countered that, state law notwithstanding, admitting the evidence would violate his federal constitutional right to be "confronted with the witnesses against him." Amdt. 6. According to our description of that right in *Ohio v. Roberts,* 448 U.S. 56 (1980), it does not bar admission of an unavailable witness's statement against a criminal defendant if the statement bears "adequate 'indicia of reliability.' " *Id.*, 448 U.S. at 66. To meet that test, evidence must either fall within a "firmly rooted hearsay exception" or bear "particularized guarantees of trustworthiness." *Ibid.* The trial court here admitted the statement on the latter ground, offering several reasons why it was trustworthy: Sylvia was not shifting blame but rather corroborating her husband's story that he acted in self-defense or "justified reprisal"; she had direct knowledge as an eyewitness; she was describing recent events; and she was being questioned by a "neutral" law enforcement officer. The prosecution played the tape for the jury and relied on it in closing, arguing that it was "damning evidence" that "completely refutes [petitioner's] claim of self-defense." Tr. 468 (Oct. 21, 1999). The jury convicted petitioner of assault.

The Washington Court of Appeals reversed. It applied a nine-factor test to determine whether Sylvia's statement bore particularized guarantees of trustworthiness, and noted several reasons why it did not: The statement contradicted one she had previously given; it was made in response to specific questions; and at one point she admitted she had shut her eyes during the stabbing. The court considered and rejected the State's argument that Sylvia's statement was reliable because it coincided with petitioner's to such a degree that the two "interlocked." The court determined that, although the two statements agreed about the events leading up to the stabbing, they differed on the issue crucial to petitioner's self-defense claim: "[Petitioner's] version asserts that Lee may have had something in his hand when he stabbed him; but Sylvia's version has Lee grabbing for something only after he has been stabbed."

The Washington Supreme Court reinstated the conviction, unanimously concluding that, although Sylvia's statement did not fall under a firmly rooted hearsay exception, it bore guarantees of trustworthiness: " 'When a codefendant's confession is virtually identical [to, *i.e.*, interlocks with,] that of a defendant, it may be deemed reliable.' " 147 Wash. 2d 424, 437, 54 P. 3d 656, 663 (2002) (quoting *State v. Rice*, 120 Wn. 2d 549, 570, 844 P.2d 416, 427 (1993)). The court explained:

> Although the Court of Appeals concluded that the statements were contradictory, upon closer inspection they appear to overlap * * * .
>
> Both of the Crawfords' statements indicate that Lee was possibly grabbing for a weapon, but they are equally unsure when this event may have taken place. They are also equally unsure how Michael received the cut on his hand, leading the court to question when, if ever, Lee possessed a weapon. In this respect they overlap.
>
> Neither Michael nor Sylvia clearly stated that Lee had a weapon in hand from which Michael was simply defending himself. And it is this omission by both that interlocks the statements and makes

Sylvia's statement reliable. 147 Wash. 2d, at 438-439, 54 P. 3d, at 664 (internal quotation marks omitted).[1]

We granted certiorari to determine whether the State's use of Sylvia's statement violated the Confrontation Clause. 539 U.S. 914 (2003).

II

The Sixth Amendment's Confrontation Clause provides that, "in all criminal prosecutions, the accused shall enjoy the right * * * to be confronted with the witnesses against him." We have held that this bedrock procedural guarantee applies to both federal and state prosecutions. *Pointer v. Texas,* 380 U.S. 400, 406 (1965). As noted above, *Roberts* says that an unavailable witness's out-of-court statement may be admitted so long as it has adequate indicia of reliability — *i.e.*, falls within a "firmly rooted hearsay exception" or bears "particularized guarantees of trustworthiness." 448 U.S., at 66. Petitioner argues that this test strays from the original meaning of the Confrontation Clause and urges us to reconsider it.

A

The Constitution's text does not alone resolve this case. One could plausibly read "witnesses against" a defendant to mean those who actually testify at trial, cf. *Woodsides v. State*, 3 Miss. 655, 664-665, 1 Morr. St. Cas. 95 (1837), those whose statements are offered at trial, *see* 3 J. Wigmore, Evidence § 1397, p. 104 (2d ed. 1923) (hereinafter Wigmore), or something in-between. We must therefore turn to the historical background of the Clause to understand its meaning.

The right to confront one's accusers is a concept that dates back to Roman times. *See Coy v. Iowa,* 487 U.S. 1012, 1015, 101 L. Ed. 2d 857, 108 S. Ct. 2798 (1988); Herrmann & Speer, Facing the Accuser: Ancient and Medieval Precursors of the Confrontation Clause, 34 Va. J. Int'l L. 481 (1994). The founding generation's immediate source of the concept, however, was the common law. English common law has long differed from continental civil law in regard to the manner in which witnesses give testimony in criminal trials. The common-law tradition is one of live testimony in court subject to adversarial testing, while the civil law condones examination in private by judicial officers. *See* 3 W. Blackstone, Commentaries on the Laws of England 373-374 (1768).

Nonetheless, England at times adopted elements of the civil-law practice. Justices of the peace or other officials examined suspects and witnesses before trial. These examinations were sometimes read in court in lieu of live

[1] The court rejected the State's argument that guarantees of trustworthiness were unnecessary since petitioner waived his confrontation rights by invoking the marital privilege. It reasoned that "forcing the defendant to choose between the marital privilege and confronting his spouse presents an untenable Hobson's choice." 147 Wash. 2d, at 432, 54 P. 3d, at 660. The State has not challenged this holding here. The State also has not challenged the Court of Appeals' conclusion (not reached by the State Supreme Court) that the confrontation violation, if it occurred, was not harmless. We express no opinion on these matters.

testimony, a practice that "occasioned frequent demands by the prisoner to have his 'accusers,' *i.e.* the witnesses against him, brought before him face to face." 1 J. Stephen, History of the Criminal Law of England 326 (1883). In some cases, these demands were refused. *See* 9 W. Holdsworth, History of English Law 216-217, 228 (3d ed. 1944); *e.g.*, *Raleigh's Case*, 2 How. St. Tr. 1, 15-16, 24 (1603); *Throckmorton's Case*, 1 How. St. Tr. 869, 875-876 (1554); *cf. Lilburn's Case*, 3 How. St. Tr. 1315, 1318-1322, 1329 (Star Chamber 1637).

Pretrial examinations became routine under two statutes passed during the reign of Queen Mary in the 16th century, 1 & 2 Phil. & M., c. 13 (1554), and 2 & 3 *id.*, c. 10 (1555). These Marian bail and committal statutes required justices of the peace to examine suspects and witnesses in felony cases and to certify the results to the court. It is doubtful that the original purpose of the examinations was to produce evidence admissible at trial. *See* J. Langbein, Prosecuting Crime in the Renaissance 21-34 (1974). Whatever the original purpose, however, they came to be used as evidence in some cases, *see* 2 M. Hale, Pleas of the Crown 284 (1736), resulting in an adoption of continental procedure. *See* 4 Holdsworth, *supra*, at 528-530.

The most notorious instances of civil-law examination occurred in the great political trials of the 16th and 17th centuries. One such was the 1603 trial of Sir Walter Raleigh for treason. Lord Cobham, Raleigh's alleged accomplice, had implicated him in an examination before the Privy Council and in a letter. At Raleigh's trial, these were read to the jury. Raleigh argued that Cobham had lied to save himself: "Cobham is absolutely in the King's mercy; to excuse me cannot avail him; by accusing me he may hope for favour." 1 D. Jardine, Criminal Trials 435 (1832). Suspecting that Cobham would recant, Raleigh demanded that the judges call him to appear, arguing that "the Proof of the Common Law is by witness and jury: let Cobham be here, let him speak it. Call my accuser before my face * * *." 2 How. St. Tr., at 15-16. The judges refused, *id.*, at 24, and, despite Raleigh's protestations that he was being tried "by the Spanish Inquisition," *id.*, at 15, the jury convicted, and Raleigh was sentenced to death.

One of Raleigh's trial judges later lamented that " 'the justice of England has never been so degraded and injured as by the condemnation of Sir Walter Raleigh.' " 1 Jardine, *supra*, at 520. Through a series of statutory and judicial reforms, English law developed a right of confrontation that limited these abuses. For example, treason statutes required witnesses to confront the accused "face to face" at his arraignment. *E.g.*, 13 Car. 2, c. 1, § 5 (1661); *see* 1 Hale, *supra*, at 306. Courts, meanwhile, developed relatively strict rules of unavailability, admitting examinations only if the witness was demonstrably unable to testify in person. *See Lord Morley's Case*, 6 How. St. Tr. 769, 770-771 (H. L. 1666); 2 Hale, *supra*, at 284; 1 Stephen, *supra*, at 358. Several authorities also stated that a suspect's confession could be admitted only against himself, and not against others he implicated. *See* 2 W. Hawkins, Pleas of the Crown c. 46, § 3, pp. 603-604 (T. Leach 6th ed. 1787); 1 Hale, *supra*, at 585, n. *(k);* 1 G. Gilbert, Evidence 216 (C. Lofft ed. 1791); cf. *Tong's Case*, Kel. J. 17, 18, 84 Eng. Rep. 1061, 1062 (1662) (treason). *But see King v. Westbeer*, 1 Leach 12, 168 Eng. Rep. 108, 109 (1739).

One recurring question was whether the admissibility of an unavailable witness's pretrial examination depended on whether the defendant had had an opportunity to cross-examine him. In 1696, the Court of King's Bench answered this question in the affirmative, in the widely reported misdemeanor libel case of *King v. Paine*, 5 Mod. 163, 87 Eng. Rep. 584. The court ruled that, even though a witness was dead, his examination was not admissible where "the defendant not being present when [it was] taken before the mayor * * * had lost the benefit of a cross-examination." *Id.*, at 165, 87 Eng. Rep., at 585. The question was also debated at length during the infamous proceedings against Sir John Fenwick on a bill of attainder. Fenwick's counsel objected to admitting the examination of a witness who had been spirited away, on the ground that Fenwick had had no opportunity to cross-examine. *See Fenwick's Case*, 13 How. St. Tr. 537, 591-592 (H. C. 1696) (Powys) ("That which they would offer is something that Mr. Goodman hath sworn when he was examined * * *; sir J. F. not being present or privy, and no opportunity given to cross-examine the person; and I conceive that cannot be offered as evidence * * *"); *id.*, at 592 (Shower) ("No deposition of a person can be read, though beyond sea, unless in cases where the party it is to be read against was privy to the examination, and might have cross-examined him * * * . Our constitution is, that the person shall see his accuser"). The examination was nonetheless admitted on a closely divided vote after several of those present opined that the common-law rules of procedure did not apply to parliamentary attainder proceedings — one speaker even admitting that the evidence would normally be inadmissible. *See id.*, at 603-604 (Williamson); *id.*, at 604-605 (Chancellor of the Exchequer); *id.*, at 607; 3 Wigmore § 1364, at 22-23, n. 54. Fenwick was condemned, but the proceedings "must have burned into the general consciousness the vital importance of the rule securing the right of cross-examination." *Id.*, § 1364, at 22; cf. *Carmell v. Texas,* 529 U.S. 513, 526-530 (2000).

Paine had settled the rule requiring a prior opportunity for cross-examination as a matter of common law, but some doubts remained over whether the Marian statutes prescribed an exception to it in felony cases. The statutes did not identify the circumstances under which examinations were admissible, *see* 1 & 2 Phil. & M., c. 13 (1554); 2 & 3 *id.*, c. 10 (1555), and some inferred that no prior opportunity for cross-examination was required. *See Westbeer*, *supra*, at 12, 168 Eng. Rep., at 109; compare *Fenwick's Case*, 13 How. St. Tr., at 596 (Sloane), with *id.*, at 602 (Musgrave). Many who expressed this view acknowledged that it meant the statutes were in derogation of the common law. *See King v. Eriswell*, 3 T. R. 707, 710, 100 Eng. Rep. 815, 817 (K. B. 1790) (Grose, J.) (dicta); *id.*, at 722-723, 100 Eng. Rep., at 823-824 (Kenyon, C. J.) (same); compare 1 Gilbert, Evidence, at 215 (admissible only "by Force 'of the Statute' "), with *id.*, at 65. Nevertheless, by 1791 (the year the Sixth Amendment was ratified), courts were applying the cross-examination rule even to examinations by justices of the peace in felony cases. *See King v. Dingler*, 2 Leach 561, 562-563, 168 Eng. Rep. 383, 383-384 (1791); *King v. Woodcock*, 1 Leach 500, 502-504, 168 Eng. Rep. 352, 353 (1789); *cf. King v. Radbourne*, 1 Leach 457, 459-461, 168 Eng. Rep. 330, 331-332 (1787); 3 Wigmore § 1364, at 23. Early 19th-century treatises confirm that requirement. *See* 1 T. Starkie, Evidence 95 (1826); 2 *id.*, at 484-492; T. Peake,

Evidence 63-64 (3d ed. 1808). When Parliament amended the statutes in 1848 to make the requirement explicit, *see* 11 & 12 Vict., c. 42, § 17, the change merely "introduced in terms" what was already afforded the defendant "by the equitable construction of the law." *Queen v. Beeston*, 29 Eng. L. & Eq. R. 527, 529 (Ct. Crim. App. 1854) (Jervis, C. J.).[2]

B

Controversial examination practices were also used in the Colonies. Early in the 18th century, for example, the Virginia Council protested against the Governor for having "privately issued several commissions to examine witnesses against particular men *ex parte*," complaining that "the person accused is not admitted to be confronted with, or defend himself against his defamers." A Memorial Concerning the Maladministrations of His Excellency Francis Nicholson, reprinted in 9 English Historical Documents 253, 257 (D. Douglas ed. 1955). A decade before the Revolution, England gave jurisdiction over Stamp Act offenses to the admiralty courts, which followed civil-law rather than common-law procedures and thus routinely took testimony by deposition or private judicial examination. *See* 5 Geo. 3, c. 12, § 57 (1765); Pollitt, The Right of Confrontation: Its History and Modern Dress, 8 J. Pub. L. 381, 396-397 (1959). Colonial representatives protested that the Act subverted their rights "by extending the jurisdiction of the courts of admiralty beyond its ancient limits." Resolutions of the Stamp Act Congress § 8th (Oct. 19, 1765), reprinted in Sources of Our Liberties 270, 271 (R. Perry & J. Cooper eds. 1959). John Adams, defending a merchant in a high-profile admiralty case, argued: "Examinations of witnesses upon Interrogatories, are only by the Civil Law. Interrogatories are unknown at common Law, and Englishmen and common Lawyers have an aversion to them if not an Abhorrence of them." Draft of Argument in *Sewall v. Hancock* (1768-1769), in 2 Legal Papers of John Adams 194, 207 (K. Wroth & H. Zobel eds. 1965).

Many declarations of rights adopted around the time of the Revolution guaranteed a right of confrontation. *See* Virginia Declaration of Rights § 8 (1776); Pennsylvania Declaration of Rights § IX (1776); Delaware Declaration of Rights § 14 (1776); Maryland Declaration of Rights § XIX (1776); North Carolina Declaration of Rights § VII (1776); Vermont Declaration of Rights Ch. I, § X (1777); Massachusetts Declaration of Rights § XII (1780); New Hampshire Bill of Rights § XV (1783), all reprinted in 1 B. Schwartz, The Bill of Rights: A Documentary History 235, 265, 278, 282, 287, 323, 342, 377 (1971). The proposed Federal Constitution, however, did not. At the Massachusetts ratifying convention, Abraham Holmes objected to this omission precisely

2 There is some question whether the requirement of a prior opportunity for cross-examination applied as well to statements taken by a coroner, which were also authorized by the Marian statutes. *See* 3 Wigmore § 1364, at 23 (requirement "never came to be conceded at all in England"); T. Peake, Evidence 64, n. *(m)* (3d ed. 1808) (not finding the point "expressly decided in any reported case"); *State v. Houser*, 26 Mo. 431, 436 (1858) ("there may be a few cases * * * but the authority of such cases is questioned, even in [England], by their ablest writers on common law"); *State v. Campbell*, 30 S.C.L. 124 (1844) (point "has not * * * been plainly adjudged, even in the English cases"). Whatever the English rule, several early American authorities flatly rejected any special status for coroner statements. *See Houser*, *supra*, at 436; *Campbell*, *supra*, at 130; T. Cooley, Constitutional Limitations *318.

on the ground that it would lead to civil-law practices: "The mode of trial is altogether indetermined; * * * whether [the defendant] is to be allowed to confront the witnesses, and have the advantage of cross-examination, we are not yet told * * * . We shall find Congress possessed of powers enabling them to institute judicatories little less inauspicious than a certain tribunal in Spain, * * * the *Inquisition.*" 2 Debates on the Federal Constitution 110-111 (J. Elliot 2d ed. 1863). Similarly, a prominent Antifederalist writing under the pseudonym Federal Farmer criticized the use of "written evidence" while objecting to the omission of a vicinage right: "Nothing can be more essential than the cross examining [of] witnesses, and generally before the triers of the facts in question * * * . Written evidence * * * [is] almost useless; it must be frequently taken ex parte, and but very seldom leads to the proper discovery of truth." R. Lee, Letter IV by the Federal Farmer (Oct. 15, 1787), reprinted in 1 Schwartz, *supra*, at 469, 473. The First Congress responded by including the Confrontation Clause in the proposal that became the Sixth Amendment.

Early state decisions shed light upon the original understanding of the common-law right. *State v. Webb*, 2 N. C. 103 (1794) *(per curiam),* decided a mere three years after the adoption of the Sixth Amendment, held that depositions could be read against an accused only if they were taken in his presence. Rejecting a broader reading of the English authorities, the court held: "It is a rule of the common law, founded on natural justice, that no man shall be prejudiced by evidence which he had not the liberty to cross examine." *Id.,* at 104.

Similarly, in *State v. Campbell*, 30 S.C.L. 124 (1844), South Carolina's highest law court excluded a deposition taken by a coroner in the absence of the accused. It held: "If we are to decide the question by the established rules of the common law, there could not be a dissenting voice. For, notwithstanding the death of the witness, and whatever the respectability of the court taking the depositions, the solemnity of the occasion and the weight of the testimony, such depositions are *ex parte*, and, therefore, utterly incompetent." *Id.*, at 125. The court said that one of the "indispensable conditions" implicitly guaranteed by the State Constitution was that "prosecutions be carried on to the conviction of the accused, by witnesses confronted by him, and subjected to his personal examination." *Ibid.*

Many other decisions are to the same effect. Some early cases went so far as to hold that prior testimony was inadmissible in criminal cases *even if* the accused had a previous opportunity to cross-examine. *See Finn v. Commonwealth*, 26 Va. 701, 708 (1827); *State v. Atkins*, 1 Tenn. 229 (1807) *(per curiam)*. Most courts rejected that view, but only after reaffirming that admissibility depended on a prior opportunity for cross-examination. *See United States v. Macomb*, 26 F. Cas. 1132, 1133, F. Cas. No. 15702 (No. 15,702) (CC Ill. 1851); *State v. Houser*, 26 Mo. 431, 435-436 (1858); *Kendrick v. State*, 29 Tenn. 479, 485-488 (1850); *Bostick v. State*, 22 Tenn. 344, 345-346 (1842); *Commonwealth v. Richards*, 35 Mass. 434, 437, 18 Pick. 434 (1837); *State v. Hill*, 20 S.C.L. 607, 608-610 (S. C. 1835); *Johnston v. State*, 10 Tenn. 58, 59 (1821). Nineteenth-century treatises confirm the rule. *See* 1 J. Bishop, Criminal Procedure § 1093, p. 689 (2d ed. 1872); T. Cooley, Constitutional Limitations *318.

III

This history supports two inferences about the meaning of the Sixth Amendment.

A

First, the principal evil at which the Confrontation Clause was directed was the civil-law mode of criminal procedure, and particularly its use of *ex parte* examinations as evidence against the accused. It was these practices that the Crown deployed in notorious treason cases like Raleigh's; that the Marian statutes invited; that English law's assertion of a right to confrontation was meant to prohibit; and that the founding-era rhetoric decried. The Sixth Amendment must be interpreted with this focus in mind.

Accordingly, we once again reject the view that the Confrontation Clause applies of its own force only to in-court testimony, and that its application to out-of-court statements introduced at trial depends upon "the law of Evidence for the time being." 3 Wigmore § 1397, at 101; accord, *Dutton v. Evans,* 400 U.S. 74, 94 (1970) (Harlan, J., concurring in result). Leaving the regulation of out-of-court statements to the law of evidence would render the Confrontation Clause powerless to prevent even the most flagrant inquisitorial practices. Raleigh was, after all, perfectly free to confront those who read Cobham's confession in court.

This focus also suggests that not all hearsay implicates the Sixth Amendment's core concerns. An off-hand, overheard remark might be unreliable evidence and thus a good candidate for exclusion under hearsay rules, but it bears little resemblance to the civil-law abuses the Confrontation Clause targeted. On the other hand, *ex parte* examinations might sometimes be admissible under modern hearsay rules, but the Framers certainly would not have condoned them.

The text of the Confrontation Clause reflects this focus. It applies to "witnesses" against the accused — in other words, those who "bear testimony." 1 N. Webster, An American Dictionary of the English Language (1828). "Testimony," in turn, is typically "[a] solemn declaration or affirmation made for the purpose of establishing or proving some fact." *Ibid.* An accuser who makes a formal statement to government officers bears testimony in a sense that a person who makes a casual remark to an acquaintance does not. The constitutional text, like the history underlying the common-law right of confrontation, thus reflects an especially acute concern with a specific type of out-of-court statement.

Various formulations of this core class of "testimonial" statements exist: "*ex parte* in-court testimony or its functional equivalent — that is, material such as affidavits, custodial examinations, prior testimony that the defendant was unable to cross-examine, or similar pretrial statements that declarants would reasonably expect to be used prosecutorially," Brief for Petitioner 23; "extrajudicial statements * * * contained in formalized testimonial materials, such as affidavits, depositions, prior testimony, or confessions," *White v. Illinois,* 502 U.S. 346, 365 (1992) (THOMAS, J., joined by SCALIA, J., concurring in part and concurring in judgment); "statements that were made under circumstances which would lead an objective witness reasonably to believe that the statement would be available for use at a later trial," Brief for National Association of Criminal Defense Lawyers et al. as *Amici Curiae* 3. These formulations all share a common nucleus and then define the Clause's coverage at various levels of abstraction around it. Regardless of the precise articulation, some statements qualify under any definition — for example, *ex parte* testimony at a preliminary hearing.

Statements taken by police officers in the course of interrogations are also testimonial under even a narrow standard. Police interrogations bear a striking resemblance to examinations by justices of the peace in England. The statements are not *sworn* testimony, but the absence of oath was not dispositive. Cobham's examination was unsworn, *see* 1 Jardine, Criminal Trials, at 430, yet Raleigh's trial has long been thought a paradigmatic confrontation violation, *see, e.g., Campbell*, 30 S.C.L., at 130. Under the Marian statutes, witnesses were typically put on oath, but suspects were not. *See* 2 Hale, Pleas of the Crown, at 52. Yet Hawkins and others went out of their way to caution that such unsworn confessions were not admissible against anyone but the confessor. *See supra*, at 8. [Footnote 3 omitted.]

That interrogators are police officers rather than magistrates does not change the picture either. Justices of the peace conducting examinations under the Marian statutes were not magistrates as we understand that office today, but had an essentially investigative and prosecutorial function. *See* 1 Stephen, Criminal Law of England, at 221; Langbein, Prosecuting Crime in the Renaissance, at 34-45. England did not have a professional police force until the 19th century, *see* 1 Stephen, *supra*, at 194-200, so it is not surprising that other government officers performed the investigative functions now associated primarily with the police. The involvement of government officers in the production of testimonial evidence presents the same risk, whether the officers are police or justices of the peace.

In sum, even if the Sixth Amendment is not solely concerned with testimonial hearsay, that is its primary object, and interrogations by law enforcement officers fall squarely within that class.[4]

B

The historical record also supports a second proposition: that the Framers would not have allowed admission of testimonial statements of a witness who did not appear at trial unless he was unavailable to testify, and the defendant had had a prior opportunity for cross-examination. The text of the Sixth Amendment does not suggest any open-ended exceptions from the confrontation requirement to be developed by the courts. Rather, the "right * * * to be confronted with the witnesses against him," Amdt. 6, is most naturally read as a reference to the right of confrontation at common law, admitting only

[4] We use the term "interrogation" in its colloquial, rather than any technical legal, sense. Cf. *Rhode Island v. Innis,* 446 U.S. 291, 300-301, 64 L. Ed. 2d 297, 100 S. Ct. 1682 (1980). Just as various definitions of "testimonial" exist, one can imagine various definitions of "interrogation," and we need not select among them in this case. Sylvia's recorded statement, knowingly given in response to structured police questioning, qualifies under any conceivable definition.

those exceptions established at the time of the founding. *See Mattox v. United States,* 156 U.S. 237, 243 (1895). As the English authorities above reveal, the common law in 1791 conditioned admissibility of an absent witness's examination on unavailability and a prior opportunity to cross-examine. The Sixth Amendment therefore incorporates those limitations. The numerous early state decisions applying the same test confirm that these principles were received as part of the common law in this country. [Footnote 5 omitted.]

We do not read the historical sources to say that a prior opportunity to cross-examine was merely a sufficient, rather than a necessary, condition for admissibility of testimonial statements. They suggest that this requirement was dispositive, and not merely one of several ways to establish reliability. This is not to deny, as THE CHIEF JUSTICE notes, that "there were always exceptions to the general rule of exclusion" of hearsay evidence. Several had become well established by 1791. But there is scant evidence that exceptions were invoked to admit *testimonial* statements against the accused in a *criminal* case.[6] Most of the hearsay exceptions covered statements that by their nature were not testimonial — for example, business records or statements in furtherance of a conspiracy. We do not infer from these that the Framers thought exceptions would apply even to prior testimony. Cf. *Lilly v. Virginia,* 527 U.S. 116, 134, 144 L. Ed. 2d 117, 119 S. Ct. 1887 (1999) (plurality opinion) ("Accomplices' confessions that inculpate a criminal defendant are not within a firmly rooted exception to the hearsay rule").[7]

IV

Our case law has been largely consistent with these two principles. Our leading early decision, for example, involved a deceased witness's prior trial testimony. *Mattox v. United States,* 156 U.S. 237 (1895). In allowing the statement to be admitted, we relied on the fact that the defendant had had, at the first trial, an adequate opportunity to confront the witness: "The substance of the constitutional protection is preserved to the prisoner in the advantage he has once had of seeing the witness face to face, and of subjecting him to

[6] The one deviation we have found involves dying declarations. The existence of that exception as a general rule of criminal hearsay law cannot be disputed. *See, e.g., Mattox v. United States,* 156 U.S. 237, 243-244, 39 L. Ed. 409, 15 S. Ct. 337 (1895); *King v. Reason*, 16 How. St. Tr. 1, 24-38 (K. B. 1722); 1 D. Jardine, Criminal Trials 435 (1832); Cooley, Constitutional Limitations, at *318; 1 G. Gilbert, Evidence 211 (C. Lofft ed. 1791); *see also* F. Heller, The Sixth Amendment 105 (1951) (asserting that this was the *only* recognized criminal hearsay exception at common law). Although many dying declarations may not be testimonial, there is authority for admitting even those that clearly are. *See Woodcock, supra*, at 501-504, 168 Eng. Rep., at 353-354; *Reason, supra*, at 24-38; Peake, Evidence, at 64; cf. *Radbourne, supra*, at 460-462, 168 Eng. Rep., at 332-333. We need not decide in this case whether the Sixth Amendment incorporates an exception for testimonial dying declarations. If this exception must be accepted on historical grounds, it is *sui generis*.

[7] We cannot agree with THE CHIEF JUSTICE that the fact "that a statement might be testimonial does nothing to undermine the wisdom of one of these [hearsay] exceptions." Involvement of government officers in the production of testimony with an eye toward trial presents unique potential for prosecutorial abuse — a fact borne out time and again throughout a history with which the Framers were keenly familiar. This consideration does not evaporate when testimony happens to fall within some broad, modern hearsay exception, even if that exception might be justifiable in other circumstances.

the ordeal of a cross-examination. This, the law says, he shall under no circumstances be deprived of * * *." *Id.*, at 244.

Our later cases conform to *Mattox*'s holding that prior trial or preliminary hearing testimony is admissible only if the defendant had an adequate opportunity to cross-examine. *See Mancusi v. Stubbs,* 408 U.S. 204, 213-216 (1972); *California v. Green,* 399 U.S. 149, 165-168 (1970); *Pointer v. Texas,* 380 U.S., at 406-408; *cf. Kirby v. United States,* 174 U.S. 47, 55-61 (1899). Even where the defendant had such an opportunity, we excluded the testimony where the government had not established unavailability of the witness. *See Barber v. Page,* 390 U.S. 719, 722-725 (1968); cf. *Motes v. United States,* 178 U.S. 458, 470-471 (1900). We similarly excluded accomplice confessions where the defendant had no opportunity to cross-examine. *See Roberts v. Russell,* 392 U.S. 293, 294-295 (1968) *(per curiam); Bruton v. United States,* 391 U.S. 123, 126-128 (1968); *Douglas v. Alabama,* 380 U.S. 415, 418-420 (1965). In contrast, we considered reliability factors beyond prior opportunity for cross-examination when the hearsay statement at issue was not testimonial. *See Dutton v. Evans,* 400 U.S., at 87-89 (plurality opinion).

Even our recent cases, in their outcomes, hew closely to the traditional line. *Ohio v. Roberts,* 448 U.S., at 67-70, admitted testimony from a preliminary hearing at which the defendant had examined the witness. *Lilly v. Virginia, supra,* 527 U.S. 116, excluded testimonial statements that the defendant had had no opportunity to test by cross-examination. And *Bourjaily v. United States,* 483 U.S. 171, 181-184 (1987), admitted statements made unwittingly to an FBI informant after applying a more general test that did *not* make prior cross-examination an indispensable requirement.[8]

Lee v. Illinois, 476 U.S. 530 (1986), on which the State relies, is not to the contrary. There, we *rejected* the State's attempt to admit an accomplice confession. The State had argued that the confession was admissible because it "interlocked" with the defendant's. We dealt with the argument by rejecting its premise, holding that "when the discrepancies between the statements are not insignificant, the codefendant's confession may not be admitted." *Id.*, at 545. Respondent argues that "the logical inference of this statement is that when the discrepancies between the statements *are* insignificant, then the codefendant's statement *may* be admitted." Brief for Respondent 6. But this is merely a possible inference, not an inevitable one, and we do not draw it here. If *Lee* had meant authoritatively to announce an exception — previously unknown to this Court's jurisprudence — for interlocking confessions, it would

[8] One case arguably in tension with the rule requiring a prior opportunity for cross-examination when the proffered statement is testimonial is *White v. Illinois,* 502 U.S. 346(1992), which involved, *inter alia,* statements of a child victim to an investigating police officer admitted as spontaneous declarations. It is questionable whether testimonial statements would ever have been admissible on that ground in 1791; to the extent the hearsay exception for spontaneous declarations existed at all, it required that the statements be made "immediately upon the hurt received, and before [the declarant] had time to devise or contrive any thing for her own advantage." *Thompson v. Trevanion,* Skin. 402, 90 Eng. Rep. 179 (K. B. 1694). In any case, the only question presented in *White* was whether the Confrontation Clause imposed an unavailability requirement on the types of hearsay at issue. The holding did not address the question whether certain of the statements, because they were testimonial, had to be excluded *even if* the witness was unavailable. We "[took] as a given * * * that the testimony properly falls within the relevant hearsay exceptions." *Id.*, at 351, n. 4.

not have done so in such an oblique manner. Our only precedent on interlocking confessions had addressed the entirely different question whether a limiting instruction cured prejudice to codefendants from admitting a defendant's *own* confession against him in a joint trial. *See Parker v. Randolph,* 442 U.S. 62, 69-76 (1979) (plurality opinion), abrogated by *Cruz v. New York,* 481 U.S. 186 (1987).

Our cases have thus remained faithful to the Framers' understanding: Testimonial statements of witnesses absent from trial have been admitted only where the declarant is unavailable, and only where the defendant has had a prior opportunity to cross-examine.[9]

V

Although the results of our decisions have generally been faithful to the original meaning of the Confrontation Clause, the same cannot be said of our rationales. *Roberts* conditions the admissibility of all hearsay evidence on whether it falls under a "firmly rooted hearsay exception" or bears "particularized guarantees of trustworthiness." 448 U.S., at 66. This test departs from the historical principles identified above in two respects. First, it is too broad: It applies the same mode of analysis whether or not the hearsay consists of *ex parte* testimony. This often results in close constitutional scrutiny in cases that are far removed from the core concerns of the Clause. At the same time, however, the test is too narrow: It admits statements that *do* consist of *ex parte* testimony upon a mere finding of reliability. This malleable standard often fails to protect against paradigmatic confrontation violations.

Members of this Court and academics have suggested that we revise our doctrine to reflect more accurately the original understanding of the Clause.

---

[9] THE CHIEF JUSTICE complains that our prior decisions have "never drawn a distinction" like the one we now draw, citing in particular *Mattox v. United States,* 156 U.S. 237 (1895), *Kirby v. United States,* 174 U.S. 47 (1899), and *United States v. Burr*, 25 F. Cas. 187, F. Cas. No. 14694 (No. 14,694) (CC Va. 1807) (Marshall, C. J.). But nothing in these cases contradicts our holding in any way. *Mattox* and *Kirby* allowed or excluded evidence depending on whether the defendant had had an opportunity for cross-examination. That the two cases did not extrapolate a more general class of evidence to which that criterion applied does not prevent us from doing so now. As to *Burr*, we disagree with THE CHIEF JUSTICE's reading of the case. Although Chief Justice Marshall made one passing reference to the Confrontation Clause, the case was fundamentally about the hearsay rules governing statements in furtherance of a conspiracy. The "principle so truly important" on which "inroads" had been introduced was the "rule of evidence which rejects mere hearsay testimony." *See* 25 F. Cas., at 193. Nothing in the opinion concedes exceptions to the Confrontation Clause's exclusion of testimonial statements as we use the term. THE CHIEF JUSTICE fails to identify a single case (aside from one minor, arguable exception, *see supra*, at n. 8), where we have admitted testimonial statements based on indicia of reliability other than a prior opportunity for cross-examination. If nothing else, the test we announce is an empirically accurate explanation of the results our cases have reached.

Finally, we reiterate that, when the declarant appears for cross-examination at trial, the Confrontation Clause places no constraints at all on the use of his prior testimonial statements. *See California v. Green*, 399 U.S. 149, 162 (1970). It is therefore irrelevant that the reliability of some out-of-court statements " 'cannot be replicated, even if the declarant testifies to the same matters in court.' " The Clause does not bar admission of a statement so long as the declarant is present at trial to defend or explain it. (The Clause also does not bar the use of testimonial statements for purposes other than establishing the truth of the matter asserted. *See Tennessee v. Street,* 471 U.S. 409, 414 (1985).)

See, e.g., Lilly, 527 U.S., at 140-143 (BREYER, J., concurring); *White*, 502 U.S., at 366 (THOMAS, J., joined by SCALIA, J., concurring in part and concurring in judgment); A. Amar, The Constitution and Criminal Procedure 125-131 (1997); Friedman, Confrontation: The Search for Basic Principles, 86 Geo. L. J. 1011 (1998). They offer two proposals: First, that we apply the Confrontation Clause only to testimonial statements, leaving the remainder to regulation by hearsay law — thus eliminating the overbreadth referred to above. Second, that we impose an absolute bar to statements that are testimonial, absent a prior opportunity to cross-examine — thus eliminating the excessive narrowness referred to above.

In *White*, we considered the first proposal and rejected it. 502 U.S., at 352-353. Although our analysis in this case casts doubt on that holding, we need not definitively resolve whether it survives our decision today, because Sylvia Crawford's statement is testimonial under any definition. This case does, however, squarely implicate the second proposal.

A

Where testimonial statements are involved, we do not think the Framers meant to leave the Sixth Amendment's protection to the vagaries of the rules of evidence, much less to amorphous notions of "reliability." Certainly none of the authorities discussed above acknowledges any general reliability exception to the common-law rule. Admitting statements deemed reliable by a judge is fundamentally at odds with the right of confrontation. To be sure, the Clause's ultimate goal is to ensure reliability of evidence, but it is a procedural rather than a substantive guarantee. It commands, not that evidence be reliable, but that reliability be assessed in a particular manner: by testing in the crucible of cross-examination. The Clause thus reflects a judgment, not only about the desirability of reliable evidence (a point on which there could be little dissent), but about how reliability can best be determined. Cf. 3 Blackstone, Commentaries, at 373 ("This open examination of witnesses * * * is much more conducive to the clearing up of truth"); M. Hale, History and Analysis of the Common Law of England 258 (1713) (adversarial testing "beats and bolts out the Truth much better").

The *Roberts* test allows a jury to hear evidence, untested by the adversary process, based on a mere judicial determination of reliability. It thus replaces the constitutionally prescribed method of assessing reliability with a wholly foreign one. In this respect, it is very different from exceptions to the Confrontation Clause that make no claim to be a surrogate means of assessing reliability. For example, the rule of forfeiture by wrongdoing (which we accept) extinguishes confrontation claims on essentially equitable grounds; it does not purport to be an alternative means of determining reliability. *See Reynolds v. United States,* 98 U.S. 145, 158-159 (1879).

The Raleigh trial itself involved the very sorts of reliability determinations that *Roberts* authorizes. In the face of Raleigh's repeated demands for confrontation, the prosecution responded with many of the arguments a court applying *Roberts* might invoke today: that Cobham's statements were self-inculpatory, 2 How. St. Tr., at 19, that they were not made in the heat of passion, *id.*, at 14, and that they were not "extracted from [him] upon any hopes or promise of Pardon," *id.*, at 29. It is not plausible that the Framers' only objection to the trial was that Raleigh's judges did not properly weigh these factors before sentencing him to death. Rather, the problem was that the judges refused to allow Raleigh to confront Cobham in court, where he could cross-examine him and try to expose his accusation as a lie.

Dispensing with confrontation because testimony is obviously reliable is akin to dispensing with jury trial because a defendant is obviously guilty. This is not what the Sixth Amendment prescribes.

B

The legacy of *Roberts* in other courts vindicates the Framers' wisdom in rejecting a general reliability exception. The framework is so unpredictable that it fails to provide meaningful protection from even core confrontation violations.

Reliability is an amorphous, if not entirely subjective, concept. There are countless factors bearing on whether a statement is reliable; the nine-factor balancing test applied by the Court of Appeals below is representative. *See, e.g., People v. Farrell*, 34 P. 3d 401, 406-407 (Colo. 2001) (eight-factor test). Whether a statement is deemed reliable depends heavily on which factors the judge considers and how much weight he accords each of them. Some courts wind up attaching the same significance to opposite facts. For example, the Colorado Supreme Court held a statement more reliable because its inculpation of the defendant was "detailed," *id.*, at 407, while the Fourth Circuit found a statement more reliable because the portion implicating another was "fleeting," *United States v. Photogrammetric Data Servs., Inc.*, 259 F.3d 229, 245 (2001). The Virginia Court of Appeals found a statement more reliable because the witness was in custody and charged with a crime (thus making the statement more obviously against her penal interest), *see Nowlin v. Commonwealth*, 40 Va. App. 327, 335-338, 579 S.E. 2d 367, 371-372 (2003), while the Wisconsin Court of Appeals found a statement more reliable because the witness was *not* in custody and *not* a suspect, *see State v. Bintz*, 257 Wis. 2d 177, 187, 650 N.W.2d 913, 918. Finally, the Colorado Supreme Court in one case found a statement more reliable because it was given "immediately after" the events at issue, *Farrell*, *supra*, at 407, while that same court, in another case, found a statement more reliable because two years had elapsed, *Stevens v. People*, 29 P. 3d 305, 316 (2001).

The unpardonable vice of the *Roberts* test, however, is not its unpredictability, but its demonstrated capacity to admit core testimonial statements that the Confrontation Clause plainly meant to exclude. Despite the plurality's speculation in *Lilly*, 527 U.S., at 137, that it was "highly unlikely" that accomplice confessions implicating the accused could survive *Roberts*, courts continue routinely to admit them [citing nine state cases]. One recent study found that, after *Lilly*, appellate courts admitted accomplice statements to the authorities in 25 out of 70 cases — more than one-third of the time. Kirst, Appellate Court Answers to the Confrontation Questions in *Lilly v. Virginia*, 53 Syracuse L. Rev. 87, 105 (2003). Courts have invoked *Roberts* to admit other sorts of plainly testimonial statements despite the absence of any opportunity to cross-examine. *See United States v. Aguilar*, 295 F.3d 1018, 1021-1023 (CA9 2002) (plea allocution showing existence of a conspiracy); *United States v. Centracchio*, 265 F.3d 518, 527-530 (CA7 2001) (same); *United States v. Dolah*, 245 F.3d 98, 104-105 (CA2 2001) (same); *United States v. Petrillo*, 237 F.3d 119, 122-123 (CA2 2000) (same); *United States v. Moskowitz*, 215 F.3d 265, 268-269 (CA2 2000) (same); *United States v. Gallego*, 191 F.3d 156, 166-168 (CA2 1999) (same); *United States v. Papajohn*, 212 F.3d 1112, 1118-1120 (CA8 2000) (grand jury testimony); *United States v. Thomas*, 30 Fed. Appx. 277, 279 (CA4 2002) (same); *Bintz*, *supra*, PP15-22, 257 Wis. 2d, at 188-191, 650 N. W. 2d, at 918-920 (prior trial testimony); *State v. McNeill*, 140 N. C. App. 450, 457-460, 537 S.E. 2d 518, 523-524 (2000) (same).

To add insult to injury, some of the courts that admit untested testimonial statements find reliability in the very factors that *make* the statements testimonial. As noted earlier, one court relied on the fact that the witness's statement was made to police while in custody on pending charges — the theory being that this made the statement more clearly against penal interest and thus more reliable. *Nowlin*, *supra*, at 335-338, 579 S.E. 2d, at 371-372. Other courts routinely rely on the fact that a prior statement is given under oath in judicial proceedings. *E.g.*, *Gallego*, *supra*, at 168 (plea allocution); *Papajohn*, *supra*, at 1120 (grand jury testimony). That inculpating statements are given in a testimonial setting is not an antidote to the confrontation problem, but rather the trigger that makes the Clause's demands most urgent. It is not enough to point out that most of the usual safeguards of the adversary process attend the statement, when the single safeguard missing is the one the Confrontation Clause demands.

C

Roberts' failings were on full display in the proceedings below. Sylvia Crawford made her statement while in police custody, herself a potential suspect in the case. Indeed, she had been told that whether she would be released "depended on how the investigation continues." App. 81. In response to often leading questions from police detectives, she implicated her husband in Lee's stabbing and at least arguably undermined his self-defense claim. Despite all this, the trial court admitted her statement, listing several reasons why it was reliable. In its opinion reversing, the Court of Appeals listed several *other* reasons why the statement was *not* reliable. Finally, the State Supreme Court relied exclusively on the interlocking character of the statement and disregarded every other factor the lower courts had considered. The case is thus a self-contained demonstration of *Roberts*' unpredictable and inconsistent application.

Each of the courts also made assumptions that cross-examination might well have undermined. The trial court, for example, stated that Sylvia Crawford's statement was reliable because she was an eyewitness with direct knowledge of the events. But Sylvia at one point told the police that she had "shut [her] eyes and * * * didn't really watch" part of the fight, and that she was "in shock." App. 134. The trial court also buttressed its reliability finding by claiming that Sylvia was "being questioned by law enforcement, and, thus, the [questioner] is * * * neutral to her and not someone who would be inclined to advance her interests and shade her version of the truth unfavorably toward the defendant." *Id.*, at 77. The Framers would be astounded to learn that *ex parte* testimony could be admitted against a criminal defendant because it was elicited by "neutral" government officers. But even if the court's assessment of the officer's motives was accurate, it says nothing about Sylvia's perception of her situation. Only cross-examination could reveal that.

The State Supreme Court gave dispositive weight to the interlocking nature of the two statements — that they were both ambiguous as to when and whether Lee had a weapon. The court's claim that the two statements were *equally* ambiguous is hard to accept. Petitioner's statement is ambiguous only in the sense that he had lingering doubts about his recollection: "A. I coulda swore I seen him goin' for somethin' before, right before everything happened * * * . But I'm not positive." *Id.*, at 155. Sylvia's statement, on the other hand, is truly inscrutable, since the key timing detail was simply assumed in the leading question she was asked: "Q. Did Kenny do anything to fight back from this assault?" *Id.*, at 137. Moreover, Sylvia specifically said Lee had nothing in his hands after he was stabbed, while petitioner was not asked about that.

The prosecutor obviously did not share the court's view that Sylvia's statement was ambiguous — he called it "damning evidence" that "completely refutes [petitioner's] claim of self-defense." Tr. 468 (Oct. 21, 1999). We have no way of knowing whether the jury agreed with the prosecutor or the court. Far from obviating the need for cross-examination, the "interlocking" ambiguity of the two statements made it all the more imperative that they be tested to tease out the truth.

We readily concede that we could resolve this case by simply reweighing the "reliability factors" under *Roberts* and finding that Sylvia Crawford's statement falls short. But we view this as one of those rare cases in which the result below is so improbable that it reveals a fundamental failure on our part to interpret the Constitution in a way that secures its intended constraint on judicial discretion. Moreover, to reverse the Washington Supreme Court's decision after conducting our own reliability analysis would perpetuate, not avoid, what the Sixth Amendment condemns. The Constitution prescribes a procedure for determining the reliability of testimony in criminal trials, and we, no less than the state courts, lack authority to replace it with one of our own devising.

We have no doubt that the courts below were acting in utmost good faith when they found reliability. The Framers, however, would not have been content to indulge this assumption. They knew that judges, like other government officers, could not always be trusted to safeguard the rights of the people; the likes of the dread Lord Jeffreys were not yet too distant a memory. They were loath to leave too much discretion in judicial hands. By replacing categorical constitutional guarantees with open-ended balancing tests, we do violence to their design. Vague standards are manipulable, and, while that might be a small concern in run-of-the-mill assault prosecutions like this one, the Framers had an eye toward politically charged cases like Raleigh's — great state trials where the impartiality of even those at the highest levels of the judiciary might not be so clear. It is difficult to imagine *Roberts'* providing any meaningful protection in those circumstances.

* * *

Where nontestimonial hearsay is at issue, it is wholly consistent with the Framers' design to afford the States flexibility in their development of hearsay law — as does *Roberts*, and as would an approach that exempted such statements from Confrontation Clause scrutiny altogether. Where testimonial evidence is at issue, however, the Sixth Amendment demands what the common law required: unavailability and a prior opportunity for cross-examination. We leave for another day any effort to spell out a comprehensive definition of "testimonial."[10] Whatever else the term covers, it applies at a minimum to prior testimony at a preliminary hearing, before a grand jury, or at a former trial; and to police interrogations. These are the modern practices with closest kinship to the abuses at which the Confrontation Clause was directed.

In this case, the State admitted Sylvia's testimonial statement against petitioner, despite the fact that he had no opportunity to cross-examine her. That alone is sufficient to make out a violation of the Sixth Amendment. *Roberts* notwithstanding, we decline to mine the record in search of indicia of reliability. Where testimonial statements are at issue, the only indicium of reliability sufficient to satisfy constitutional demands is the one the Constitution actually prescribes: confrontation.

The judgment of the Washington Supreme Court is reversed, and the case is remanded for further proceedings not inconsistent with this opinion.

It is so ordered.

Chief Justice Rehnquist, with whom Justice O'Connor joins, concurring in the judgment.

I dissent from the Court's decision to overrule *Ohio v. Roberts,* 448 U.S. 56 (1980). I believe that the Court's adoption of a new interpretation of the Confrontation Clause is not backed by sufficiently persuasive reasoning to overrule long-established precedent. Its decision casts a mantle of uncertainty over future criminal trials in both federal and state courts, and is by no means necessary to decide the present case.

The Court's distinction between testimonial and nontestimonial statements, contrary to its claim, is no better rooted in history than our current doctrine. Under the common law, although the courts were far from consistent, out-of-court statements made by someone other than the accused and not taken under oath, unlike *ex parte* depositions or affidavits, were generally not considered substantive evidence upon which a conviction could be based. [Footnote omitted]. *See, e.g., King v. Brasier*, 1 Leach 199, 200, 168 Eng. Rep. 202 (K. B. 1779); *see also* J. Langbein, Origins of Adversary Criminal Trial 235-242 (2003); G. Gilbert, Evidence 152 (3d ed 1769). [Footnote omitted]. Testimonial statements such as accusatory statements to police officers likely would have been disapproved of in the 18th century, not necessarily because

---

[10] We acknowledge The Chief Justice's objection that our refusal to articulate a comprehensive definition in this case will cause interim uncertainty. But it can hardly be any worse than the status quo. The difference is that the *Roberts* test is *inherently*, and therefore *permanently*, unpredictable.

they resembled *ex parte* affidavits or depositions as the Court reasons, but more likely than not because they were not made under oath. [Footnote omitted.] *See King v. Woodcock*, 1 Leach 500, 503, 168 Eng. Rep. 352, 353 (1789) (noting that a statement taken by a justice of the peace may not be admitted into evidence unless taken under oath). Without an oath, one usually did not get to the second step of whether confrontation was required.

Thus, while I agree that the Framers were mainly concerned about sworn affidavits and depositions, it does not follow that they were similarly concerned about the Court's broader category of testimonial statements. *See* 1 N. Webster, An American Dictionary of the English Language (1828) (defining "Testimony" as "[a] solemn declaration or affirmation made for the purpose of establishing or proving some fact. *Such affirmation in judicial proceedings, may be verbal or written, but must be under oath*" (emphasis added)). As far as I can tell, unsworn testimonial statements were treated no differently at common law than were nontestimonial statements, and it seems to me any classification of statements as testimonial beyond that of sworn affidavits and depositions will be somewhat arbitrary, merely a proxy for what the Framers might have intended had such evidence been liberally admitted as substantive evidence like it is today. [Footnote omitted.].

I therefore see no reason why the distinction the Court draws is preferable to our precedent. Starting with CHIEF JUSTICE MARSHALL's interpretation as a Circuit Justice in 1807, 16 years after the ratification of the Sixth Amendment, *United States v. Burr*, 25 F. Cas. 187, 193, F. Cas. No. 14694 (No. 14,694) (CC Va. 1807), continuing with our cases in the late 19th century, *Mattox v. United States,* 156 U.S. 237, 243-244 (1895); *Kirby v. United States,* 174 U.S. 47, 54-57 (1899), and through today, *e.g.*, *White v. Illinois,* 502 U.S. 346, 352-353 (1992), we have never drawn a distinction between testimonial and nontestimonial statements. And for that matter, neither has any other court of which I am aware. I see little value in trading our precedent for an imprecise approximation at this late date.

I am also not convinced that the Confrontation Clause categorically requires the exclusion of testimonial statements. Although many States had their own Confrontation Clauses, they were of recent vintage and were not interpreted with any regularity before 1791. State cases that recently followed the ratification of the Sixth Amendment were not uniform; the Court itself cites state cases from the early 19th century that took a more stringent view of the right to confrontation than does the Court, prohibiting former testimony even if the witness was subjected to cross-examination. *See ante* (citing *Finn v. Commonwealth*, 26 Va. 701, 708 (1827); *State v. Atkins*, 1 Tenn. 229 (1807) *(per curiam)*).

Nor was the English law at the time of the framing entirely consistent in its treatment of testimonial evidence. Generally *ex parte* affidavits and depositions were excluded as the Court notes, but even that proposition was not universal. *See King v. Eriswell*, 3 T. R. 707, 100 Eng. Rep. 815 (K. B. 1790) (affirming by an equally divided court the admission of an *ex parte* examination because the declarant was unavailable to testify); *King v. Westbeer*, 1 Leach 12, 13, 168 Eng. Rep. 108, 109 (1739) (noting the admission of an *ex parte* affidavit); *see also* 1 M. Hale, Pleas of the Crown 585-586 (1736) (noting that statements of "accusers and witnesses" which were taken under oath could be admitted into evidence if the declarant was "dead or not able to travel"). Wigmore notes that sworn examinations of witnesses before justices of the peace in certain cases would not have been excluded until the end of the 1700's, 5 Wigmore § 1364, at 26-27, and sworn statements of witnesses before coroners became excluded only by statute in the 1800's, *see ibid.; id.*, § 1374, at 59. With respect to unsworn testimonial statements, there is no indication that once the hearsay rule was developed courts ever excluded these statements if they otherwise fell within a firmly rooted exception. *See, e.g.*, *Eriswell, supra*, at 715-719 (Buller, J.), 720 (Ashhurst, J.), 100 Eng. Rep., at 819-822 (concluding that an *ex parte* examination was admissible as an exception to the hearsay rule because it was a declaration by a party of his state and condition). Dying declarations are one example. *See, e.g.*, *Woodcock, supra*, at 502-504, 168 Eng. Rep., at 353-354; *King v. Reason*, 16 How. St. Tr. 1, 22-23 (K. B. 1722).

Between 1700 and 1800 the rules regarding the admissibility of out-of-court statements were still being developed. There were always exceptions to the general rule of exclusion, and it is not clear to me that the Framers categorically wanted to eliminate further ones. It is one thing to trace the right of confrontation back to the Roman Empire; it is quite another to conclude that such a right absolutely excludes a large category of evidence. It is an odd conclusion indeed to think that the Framers created a cut-and-dried rule with respect to the admissibility of testimonial statements when the law during their own time was not fully settled.

To find exceptions to exclusion under the Clause is not to denigrate it as the Court suggests. Chief Justice Marshall stated of the Confrontation Clause: "I know of no principle in the preservation of which all are more concerned. I know none, by undermining which, life, liberty and property, might be more endangered. It is therefore incumbent on courts to be watchful of every inroad on a principle so truly important." *Burr*, 25 F. Cas., at 193. Yet, he recognized that such a right was not absolute, acknowledging that exceptions to the exclusionary component of the hearsay rule, which he considered as an "inroad" on the right to confrontation, had been introduced.

Exceptions to confrontation have always been derived from the experience that some out-of-court statements are just as reliable as cross-examined in-court testimony due to the circumstances under which they were made. We have recognized, for example, that co-conspirator statements simply "cannot be replicated, even if the declarant testifies to the same matters in court." *United States v. Inadi,* 475 U.S. 387, 395 (1986). Because the statements are made while the declarant and the accused are partners in an illegal enterprise, the statements are unlikely to be false and their admission "actually furthers the 'Confrontation Clause's very mission' which is to 'advance the accuracy of the truth-determining process in criminal trials.' " *Id.*, at 396. Similar reasons justify the introduction of spontaneous declarations, *see White*, 502 U.S., at 356, statements made in the course of procuring medical services, *see ibid.*, dying declarations, *see Kirby, supra*, at 61, and countless other hearsay exceptions. That a statement might be testimonial does nothing to undermine the wisdom of one of these exceptions.

Indeed, cross-examination is a tool used to flesh out the truth, not an empty procedure. *See Kentucky v. Stincer,* 482 U.S. 730, 737 (1987) ("The right to cross-examination, protected by the Confrontation Clause, thus is essentially a 'functional' right designed to promote reliability in the truth-finding functions of a criminal trial"); *see also Maryland v. Craig,* 497 U.S. 836, 845 (1990) ("The central concern of the Confrontation Clause is to ensure the reliability of the evidence against a criminal defendant by subjecting it to rigorous testing in the context of an adversary proceeding before the trier of fact"). "In a given instance [cross-examination may] be superfluous; it may be sufficiently clear, in that instance, that the statement offered is free enough from the risk of inaccuracy and untrustworthiness, so that the test of cross-examination would be a work of supererogation." 5 Wigmore § 1420, at 251. In such a case, as we noted over 100 years ago, "The law in its wisdom declares that the rights of the public shall not be wholly sacrificed in order that an incidental benefit may be preserved to the accused." *Mattox,* 156 U.S., at 243; *see also Salinger v. United States,* 272 U.S. 542, 548 (1926). By creating an immutable category of excluded evidence, the Court adds little to a trial's truth-finding function and ignores this longstanding guidance.

In choosing the path it does, the Court of course overrules *Ohio v. Roberts,* 448 U.S. 56 (1980), a case decided nearly a quarter of a century ago. *Stare decisis* is not an inexorable command in the area of constitutional law, but by and large, it "is the preferred course because it promotes the evenhanded, predictable, and consistent development of legal principles, fosters reliance on judicial decisions, and contributes to the actual and perceived integrity of the judicial process." And in making this appraisal, doubt that the new rule is indeed the "right" one should surely be weighed in the balance. Though there are no vested interests involved, unresolved questions for the future of everyday criminal trials throughout the country surely counsel the same sort of caution. The Court grandly declares that "we leave for another day any effort to spell out a comprehensive definition of 'testimonial.'" But the thousands of federal prosecutors and the tens of thousands of state prosecutors need answers as to what beyond the specific kinds of "testimony" the Court lists, is covered by the new rule. They need them now, not months or years from now. Rules of criminal evidence are applied every day in courts throughout the country, and parties should not be left in the dark in this manner.

To its credit, the Court's analysis of "testimony" excludes at least some hearsay exceptions, such as business records and official records. To hold otherwise would require numerous additional witnesses without any apparent gain in the truth-seeking process. Likewise to the Court's credit is its implicit recognition that the mistaken application of its new rule by courts which guess wrong as to the scope of the rule is subject to harmless-error analysis.

But these are palliatives to what I believe is a mistaken change of course. It is a change of course not in the least necessary to reverse the judgment of the Supreme Court of Washington in this case. The result the Court reaches follows inexorably from *Roberts* and its progeny without any need for overruling that line of cases. In *Idaho v. Wright,* 497 U.S. 805, 820-824 (1990), we held that an out-of-court statement was not admissible simply because the truthfulness of that statement was corroborated by other evidence at trial.

As the Court notes, the Supreme Court of Washington gave decisive weight to the "interlocking nature of the two statements." No re-weighing of the "reliability factors," which is hypothesized by the Court, is required to reverse the judgment here. A citation to *Idaho v. Wright*, *supra*, 497 U.S. 805, would suffice. For the reasons stated, I believe that this would be a far preferable course for the Court to take here.

*Post-*Crawford *Attempt to Further Define Which Hearsay Statements are "Testimonial":* Davis *and* Hammon

DAVIS v. WASHINGTON and HAMMON v. INDIANA

126 S. Ct. 2266 (2006)

JUSTICE SCALIA delivered the opinion of the Court.

These cases require us to determine when statements made to law enforcement personnel during a 911 call or at a crime scene are "testimonial" and thus subject to the requirements of the Sixth Amendment's Confrontation Clause.

I

A

The relevant statements in *Davis v. Washington,* were made to a 911 emergency operator on February 1, 2001. When the operator answered the initial call, the connection terminated before anyone spoke. She reversed the call, and Michelle McCottry answered. In the ensuing conversation, the operator ascertained that McCottry was involved in a domestic disturbance with her former boyfriend Adrian Davis, the petitioner in this case:

911 Operator: Hello.

Complainant: Hello.

911 Operator: What's going on?

Complainant: He's here jumpin' on me again.

911 Operator: Okay. Listen to me carefully. Are you in a house or an apartment?

Complainant: I'm in a house.

911 Operator: Are there any weapons?

Complainant: No. He's usin' his fists.

911 Operator: Okay. Has he been drinking?

Complainant: No.

911 Operator: Okay, sweetie. I've got help started. Stay on the line with me, okay?

Complainant: I'm on the line.

911 Operator: Listen to me carefully. Do you know his last name?

Complainant: It's Davis.

911 Operator: Davis? Okay, what's his first name?

Complainant: Adran

911 Operator: What is it?

Complainant: Adrian.

911 Operator: Adrian?

Complainant: Yeah.

911 Operator: Okay. What's his middle initial?

Complainant: Martell. He's runnin' now.

As the conversation continued, the operator learned that Davis had "just r[un] out the door" after hitting McCottry, and that he was leaving in a car with someone else. McCottry started talking, but the operator cut her off, saying, "Stop talking and answer my questions." She then gathered more information about Davis (including his birthday), and learned that Davis had told McCottry that his purpose in coming to the house was "to get his stuff," since McCottry was moving. McCottry described the context of the assault, after which the operator told her that the police were on their way. "They're gonna check the area for him first," the operator said, "and then they're gonna come talk to you."

The police arrived within four minutes of the 911 call and observed McCottry's shaken state, the "fresh injuries on her forearm and her face," and her "frantic efforts to gather her belongings and her children so that they could leave the residence."

The State charged Davis with felony violation of a domestic no-contact order. The State's only witnesses were the two police officers who responded to the 911 call. Both officers testified that McCottry exhibited injuries that appeared to be recent, but neither officer could testify as to the cause of the injuries. McCottry presumably could have testified as to whether Davis was her assailant, but she did not appear. Over Davis's objection, based on the Confrontation Clause of the Sixth Amendment, the trial court admitted the recording of her exchange with the 911 operator, and the jury convicted him. The Washington Court of Appeals affirmed. The Supreme Court of Washington, with one dissenting justice, also affirmed, concluding that the portion of the 911 conversation in which McCottry identified Davis was not testimonial, and that if other portions of the conversation were testimonial, admitting them was harmless beyond a reasonable doubt. We granted certiorari.

B

In *Hammon v. Indiana,* No. 05-5705, police responded late on the night of February 26, 2003, to a "reported domestic disturbance" at the home of Hershel and Amy Hammon. They found Amy alone on the front porch, appearing "somewhat frightened," but she told them that "nothing was the matter." She gave them permission to enter the house, where an officer saw "a gas heating unit in the corner of the living room" that had "flames coming out of the * * * partial glass front. There were pieces of glass on the ground in front of it and there was flame emitting from the front of the heating unit."

Hershel, meanwhile, was in the kitchen. He told the police that he and his wife had "been in an argument" but "everything was fine now" and the argument "never became physical." By this point Amy had come back inside. One of the officers remained with Hershel; the other went to the living room to talk with Amy, and "again asked [her] what had occurred." Hershel made several attempts to participate in Amy's conversation with the police, but was rebuffed. The officer later testified that Hershel "became angry when I insisted that [he] stay separated from Mrs. Hammon so that we can investigate what had happened." After hearing Amy's account, the officer "had her fill out and sign a battery affidavit." Amy handwrote the following: "Broke our Furnace & shoved me down on the floor into the broken glass. Hit me in the chest and threw me down. Broke our lamps & phone. Tore up my van where I couldn't leave the house. Attacked my daughter."

The State charged Hershel with domestic battery and with violating his probation. Amy was subpoenaed, but she did not appear at his subsequent bench trial. The State called the officer who had questioned Amy, and asked him to recount what Amy told him and to authenticate the affidavit. Hershel's counsel repeatedly objected to the admission of this evidence. At one point, after hearing the prosecutor defend the affidavit because it was made "under oath," defense counsel said, "That doesn't give us the opportunity to cross examine [the] person who allegedly drafted it. Makes me mad." Nonetheless, the trial court admitted the affidavit as a "present sense impression," and Amy's statements as "excited utterances" that "are expressly permitted in these kinds of cases even if the declarant is not available to testify." The officer thus testified that Amy

> informed me that she and Hershel had been in an argument. That he became irate over the fact of their daughter going to a boyfriend's house. The argument became * * * physical after being verbal and she informed me that Mr. Hammon, during the verbal part of the argument was breaking things in the living room and I believe she stated he broke the phone, broke the lamp, broke the front of the heater. When it became physical he threw her down into the glass of the heater* * * . She informed me Mr. Hammon had pushed her onto the ground, had shoved her head into the broken glass of the heater and that he had punched her in the chest twice I believe.

The trial judge found Hershel guilty on both charges, and the Indiana Court of Appeals affirmed in relevant part. The Indiana Supreme Court also affirmed, concluding that Amy's statement was admissible for state-law purposes as an excited utterance; that "a 'testimonial' statement is one given or taken in significant part for purposes of preserving it for potential future use in legal proceedings," where "the motivations of the questioner and declarant are the central concerns;" and that Amy's oral statement was not "testimonial" under these standards. It also concluded that, although the affidavit was testimonial and thus wrongly admitted, it was harmless beyond a reasonable doubt, largely because the trial was to the bench. We granted certiorari.

II

The Confrontation Clause of the Sixth Amendment provides: "In all criminal prosecutions, the accused shall enjoy the right * * * to be confronted with the witnesses against him." In *Crawford v. Washington,* 541 U.S. 36, 53-54 (2004), we held that this provision bars "admission of testimonial statements of a witness who did not appear at trial unless he was unavailable to testify, and the defendant had had a prior opportunity for cross-examination." A critical portion of this holding, and the portion central to resolution of the two cases now before us, is the phrase "testimonial statements." Only statements of this sort cause the declarant to be a "witness" within the meaning of the Confrontation Clause. It is the testimonial character of the statement that separates it from other hearsay that, while subject to traditional limitations upon hearsay evidence, is not subject to the Confrontation Clause.

Our opinion in *Crawford* set forth "[v]arious formulations" of the core class of testimonial statements, but found it unnecessary to endorse any of them, because "some statements qualify under any definition." Among those, we said, were "[s]tatements taken by police officers in the course of interrogations." The questioning that generated the deponent's statement in *Crawford* — which was made and recorded while she was in police custody, after having been given *Miranda* warnings as a possible suspect herself — "qualifies under any conceivable definition" of an "interrogation." We therefore did not define that term, except to say that "[w]e use [it] * * * in its colloquial, rather than any technical legal, sense," and that "one can imagine various definitions * * *, and we need not select among them in this case." The character of the statements in the present cases is not as clear, and these cases require us to determine more precisely which police interrogations produce testimony.

Without attempting to produce an exhaustive classification of all conceivable statements — or even all conceivable statements in response to police interrogation — as either testimonial or nontestimonial, it suffices to decide the present cases to hold as follows: Statements are nontestimonial when made in the course of police interrogation under circumstances objectively indicating that the primary purpose of the interrogation is to enable police assistance to meet an ongoing emergency. They are testimonial when the circumstances objectively indicate that there is no such ongoing emergency, and that the primary purpose of the interrogation is to establish or prove past events potentially relevant to later criminal prosecution.[1]

---

[1] Our holding refers to interrogations because, as explained below, the statements in the cases presently before us are the products of interrogations — which in some circumstances tend to generate testimonial responses. This is not to imply, however, that statements made in the absence of any interrogation are necessarily nontestimonial. The Framers were no more willing to exempt from cross-examination volunteered testimony or answers to open-ended questions than they were to exempt answers to detailed interrogation. (Part of the evidence against Sir Walter Raleigh was a letter from Lord Cobham that was plainly *not* the result of sustained questioning. *Raleigh's Case,* 2 How. St. Tr. 1, 27 (1603).) And of course even when interrogation exists, it is in the final analysis the declarant's statements, not the interrogator's questions, that the Confrontation Clause requires us to evaluate.

III

A

In *Crawford,* it sufficed for resolution of the case before us to determine that "even if the Sixth Amendment is not solely concerned with testimonial hearsay, that is its primary object, and interrogations by law enforcement officers fall squarely within that class." Moreover, as we have just described, the facts of that case spared us the need to define what we meant by "interrogations." The *Davis* case today does not permit us this luxury of indecision. The inquiries of a police operator in the course of a 911 call[2] are an interrogation in one sense, but not in a sense that "qualifies under any conceivable definition." We must decide, therefore, whether the Confrontation Clause applies only to testimonial hearsay; and, if so, whether the recording of a 911 call qualifies.

The answer to the first question was suggested in *Crawford,* even if not explicitly held:

> The text of the Confrontation Clause reflects this focus [on testimonial hearsay]. It applies to 'witnesses' against the accused — in other words, those who 'bear testimony.' 1 N. Webster, An American Dictionary of the English Language (1828). 'Testimony,' in turn, is typically 'a solemn declaration or affirmation made for the purpose of establishing or proving some fact.' *Ibid.* An accuser who makes a formal statement to government officers bears testimony in a sense that a person who makes a casual remark to an acquaintance does not.

A limitation so clearly reflected in the text of the constitutional provision must fairly be said to mark out not merely its "core," but its perimeter.

We are not aware of any early American case invoking the Confrontation Clause or the common-law right to confrontation that did not clearly involve testimony as thus defined. [footnote 3, citing case law, omitted]. Well into the 20th century, our own Confrontation Clause jurisprudence was carefully applied only in the testimonial context. *See, e.g., Reynolds v. United States,* 98 U.S. 145, 158 (1879) (testimony at prior trial was subject to the Confrontation Clause, but petitioner had forfeited that right by procuring witness's absence); *Mattox v. United States,* 156 U.S. 237, 240-244 (1895) (prior trial testimony of deceased witnesses admitted because subject to cross-examination); *Kirby v. United States,* 174 U.S. 47, 55-56 (1899) (guilty pleas and jury conviction of others could not be admitted to show that property defendant received from them was stolen); *Motes v. United States,* 178 U.S. 458, 467, 470-471 (1900) (written deposition subject to cross-examination was not admissible because witness was available); *Dowdell v. United States,* 221

[2] If 911 operators are not themselves law enforcement officers, they may at least be agents of law enforcement when they conduct interrogations of 911 callers. For purposes of this opinion (and without deciding the point), we consider their acts to be acts of the police. As in *Crawford v. Washington,* 541 U.S. 36 (2004), therefore, our holding today makes it unnecessary to consider whether and when statements made to someone other than law enforcement personnel are "testimonial."

U.S. 325, 330-331 (1911) (facts regarding conduct of prior trial certified to by the judge, the clerk of court, and the official reporter did not relate to defendants' guilt or innocence and hence were not statements of "witnesses" under the Confrontation Clause).

Even our later cases, conforming to the reasoning of *Ohio v. Roberts,* 448 U.S. 56 (1980),[4] never in practice dispensed with the Confrontation Clause requirements of unavailability and prior cross-examination in cases that involved testimonial hearsay, *see Crawford,* 541 U.S., at 57-59 (citing cases), with one arguable exception, *see id.,* at 58, n. 8 (discussing *White v. Illinois,* 502 U.S. 346 (1992)). Where our cases did dispense with those requirements — even under the *Roberts* approach — the statements at issue were clearly nontestimonial. *See, e.g., Bourjaily v. United States,* 483 U.S. 171, 181-184 (1987) (statements made unwittingly to a Government informant); *Dutton v. Evans,* 400 U.S. 74, 87-89 (1970) (plurality opinion) (statements from one prisoner to another).

Most of the American cases applying the Confrontation Clause or its state constitutional or common-law counterparts involved testimonial statements of the most formal sort — sworn testimony in prior judicial proceedings or formal depositions under oath — which invites the argument that the scope of the Clause is limited to that very formal category. But the English cases that were the progenitors of the Confrontation Clause did not limit the exclusionary rule to prior court testimony and formal depositions, *see Crawford, supra,* at 52, and n. 3. In any event, we do not think it conceivable that the protections of the Confrontation Clause can readily be evaded by having a note-taking policeman *recite* the unsworn hearsay testimony of the declarant, instead of having the declarant sign a deposition. Indeed, if there is one point for which no case — English or early American, state or federal — can be cited, that is it.

The question before us in *Davis,* then, is whether, objectively considered, the interrogation that took place in the course of the 911 call produced testimonial statements. When we said in *Crawford, supra,* at 53, that "interrogations by law enforcement officers fall squarely within [the] class" of testimonial hearsay, we had immediately in mind (for that was the case before us) interrogations solely directed at establishing the facts of a past crime, in order to identify (or provide evidence to convict) the perpetrator. The product of such interrogation, whether reduced to a writing signed by the declarant or embedded in the memory (and perhaps notes) of the interrogating officer, is testimonial. It is, in the terms of the 1828 American dictionary quoted in *Crawford,* " '[a] solemn declaration or affirmation made for the purpose of establishing or proving some fact.' " (The solemnity of even an oral declaration of relevant past fact to an investigating officer is well enough established by the severe consequences that can attend a deliberate falsehood. *See, e.g., United States v. Stewart,* 433 F.3d 273, 288 (C.A.2 2006) (false statements made to federal investigators violate 18 U.S.C. § 1001). A 911 call, on

[4] "*Roberts* condition[ed] the admissibility of all hearsay evidence on whether it falls under a 'firmly rooted hearsay exception' or bears 'particularized guarantees of trustworthiness.' " *Crawford,* 541 U.S., at 60 (quoting *Roberts,* 448 U.S., at 66). We overruled *Roberts* in *Crawford* by restoring the unavailability and cross-examination requirements.

the other hand, and at least the initial interrogation conducted in connection with a 911 call, is ordinarily not designed primarily to "establis[h] or prov[e]" some past fact, but to describe current circumstances requiring police assistance.

The difference between the interrogation in *Davis* and the one in *Crawford* is apparent on the face of things. In *Davis,* McCottry was speaking about events *as they were actually happening,* rather than "describ [ing] past events," *Lilly v. Virginia,* 527 U.S. 116, 137 (1999) (plurality opinion). Sylvia Crawford's interrogation, on the other hand, took place hours after the events she described had occurred. Moreover, any reasonable listener would recognize that McCottry (unlike Sylvia Crawford) was facing an ongoing emergency. Although one *might* call 911 to provide a narrative report of a crime absent any imminent danger, McCottry's call was plainly a call for help against bona fide physical threat. Third, the nature of what was asked and answered in *Davis,* again viewed objectively, was such that the elicited statements were necessary to be able to *resolve* the present emergency, rather than simply to learn (as in *Crawford*) what had happened in the past. That is true even of the operator's effort to establish the identity of the assailant, so that the dispatched officers might know whether they would be encountering a violent felon. And finally, the difference in the level of formality between the two interviews is striking. Crawford was responding calmly, at the station house, to a series of questions, with the officer-interrogator taping and making notes of her answers; McCottry's frantic answers were provided over the phone, in an environment that was not tranquil, or even (as far as any reasonable 911 operator could make out) safe.

We conclude from all this that the circumstances of McCottry's interrogation objectively indicate its primary purpose was to enable police assistance to meet an ongoing emergency. She simply was not acting as a *witness;* she was not *testifying*. What she said was not "a weaker substitute for live testimony" at trial, *United States v. Inadi,* 475 U.S. 387, 394 (1986), like Lord Cobham's statements in *Raleigh's Case,* 2 How. St. Tr. 1 (1603) * * * or Sylvia Crawford's statement in *Crawford*. In * * * those cases, the *ex parte* actors and the evidentiary products of the *ex parte* communication aligned perfectly with their courtroom analogues. McCottry's emergency statement does not. No "witness" goes into court to proclaim an emergency and seek help.

Davis seeks to cast McCottry in the unlikely role of a witness by pointing to English cases. None of them involves statements made during an ongoing emergency. In *King v. Brasier,* 1 Leach 199, 168 Eng. Rep. 202 (1779), for example, a young rape victim, "immediately on her coming home, told all the circumstances of the injury" to her mother. The case would be helpful to Davis if the relevant statement had been the girl's screams for aid as she was being chased by her assailant. But by the time the victim got home, her story was an account of past events.

This is not to say that a conversation which begins as an interrogation to determine the need for emergency assistance cannot, as the Indiana Supreme Court put it, "evolve into testimonial statements" once that purpose has been achieved. In this case, for example, after the operator gained the information needed to address the exigency of the moment, the emergency appears to have ended (when Davis drove away from the premises). The operator then told McCottry to be quiet, and proceeded to pose a battery of questions. It could readily be maintained that, from that point on, McCottry's statements were testimonial, not unlike the "structured police questioning" that occurred in *Crawford*. This presents no great problem. Just as, for Fifth Amendment purposes, "police officers can and will distinguish almost instinctively between questions necessary to secure their own safety or the safety of the public and questions designed solely to elicit testimonial evidence from a suspect," *New York v. Quarles,* 467 U.S. 649, 658-659 (1984), trial courts will recognize the point at which, for Sixth Amendment purposes, statements in response to interrogations become testimonial. Through *in limine* procedure, they should redact or exclude the portions of any statement that have become testimonial, as they do, for example, with unduly prejudicial portions of otherwise admissible evidence. Davis's jury did not hear the *complete* 911 call, although it may well have heard some testimonial portions. We were asked to classify only McCottry's early statements identifying Davis as her assailant, and we agree with the Washington Supreme Court that they were not testimonial. That court also concluded that, even if later parts of the call were testimonial, their admission was harmless beyond a reasonable doubt. Davis does not challenge that holding, and we therefore assume it to be correct.

B

Determining the testimonial or nontestimonial character of the statements that were the product of the interrogation in *Hammon* is a much easier task, since they were not much different from the statements we found to be testimonial in *Crawford.* It is entirely clear from the circumstances that the interrogation was part of an investigation into possibly criminal past conduct — as, indeed, the testifying officer expressly acknowledged. There was no emergency in progress; the interrogating officer testified that he had heard no arguments or crashing and saw no one throw or break anything. When the officers first arrived, Amy told them that things were fine, and there was no immediate threat to her person. When the officer questioned Amy for the second time, and elicited the challenged statements, he was not seeking to determine (as in *Davis*) "what is happening," but rather "what happened." Objectively viewed, the primary, if not indeed the sole, purpose of the interrogation was to investigate a possible crime — which is, of course, precisely what the officer *should* have done.

It is true that the *Crawford* interrogation was more formal. It followed a *Miranda* warning, was tape-recorded, and took place at the station house. While these features certainly strengthened the statements' testimonial aspect — made it more objectively apparent, that is, that the purpose of the exercise was to nail down the truth about past criminal events — none was essential to the point. It was formal enough that Amy's interrogation was conducted in a separate room, away from her husband (who tried to intervene), with the officer receiving her replies for use in his "investigation." What we called the "striking resemblance" of the *Crawford* statement to civil-law *ex parte* examinations, is shared by Amy's statement here. Both declarants were actively separated from the defendant — officers forcibly prevented Hershel from participating in the interrogation. Both statements deliberately recounted, in response to police questioning, how potentially criminal past events began and progressed. And both took place some time after the events described were over. Such statements under official interrogation are an obvious substitute for live testimony, because they do precisely *what a witness does* on direct examination; they are inherently testimonial.[5]

Both Indiana and the United States as *amicus curiae* argue that this case should be resolved much like *Davis*. For the reasons we find the comparison to *Crawford* compelling, we find the comparison to *Davis* unpersuasive. The statements in *Davis* were taken when McCottry was alone, not only unprotected by police (as Amy Hammon was protected), but apparently in immediate danger from Davis. She was seeking aid, not telling a story about the past. McCottry's present-tense statements showed immediacy; Amy's narrative of past events was delivered at some remove in time from the danger she described. And after Amy answered the officer's questions, he had her execute an affidavit, in order, he testified, "[t]o establish events that have occurred previously."

Although we necessarily reject the Indiana Supreme Court's implication that virtually any "initial inquiries" at the crime scene will not be testimonial, we do not hold the opposite — that *no* questions at the scene will yield nontestimonial answers. We have already observed of domestic disputes that "[o]fficers called to investigate * * * need to know whom they are dealing with in order to assess the situation, the threat to their own safety, and possible danger to the potential victim." Such exigencies may *often* mean that "initial inquiries" produce nontestimonial statements. But in cases like this one, where Amy's statements were neither a cry for help nor the provision of information enabling officers immediately to end a threatening situation, the

---

[5] The dissent criticizes our test for being "neither workable nor a targeted attempt to reach the abuses forbidden by the [Confrontation] Clause." As to the former: We have acknowledged that our holding is not an "exhaustive classification of all conceivable statements — or even all conceivable statements in response to police interrogation," but rather a resolution of the cases before us and those like them. For *those* cases, the test is objective and quite "workable." The dissent, in attempting to formulate an exhaustive classification of its own, has not provided anything that deserves the description "workable" — unless one thinks that the distinction between "formal" and "informal" statements, qualifies. And the dissent even qualifies that vague distinction by acknowledging that the Confrontation Clause "also reaches the use of technically informal statements when used to evade the formalized process," and cautioning that the Clause would stop the State from "us[ing] out-of-court statements as a means of circumventing the literal right of confrontation." It is hard to see this as much more "predictable" than the rule we adopt for the narrow situations we address.

As for the charge that our holding is not a "targeted attempt to reach the abuses forbidden by the [Confrontation] Clause," which the dissent describes as the depositions taken by Marian magistrates, characterized by a high degree of formality: We do not dispute that formality is indeed essential to testimonial utterance. But we no longer have examining Marian magistrates; and we do have, as our 18th-century forebears did not, examining police officers, who perform investigative and testimonial functions once performed by examining Marian magistrates. It imports sufficient formality, in our view, that lies to such officers are criminal offenses. Restricting the Confrontation Clause to the precise forms against which it was originally directed is a recipe for its extinction.

fact that they were given at an alleged crime scene and were "initial inquiries" is immaterial.[6]

IV

Respondents in both cases, joined by a number of their *amici,* contend that the nature of the offenses charged in these two cases — domestic violence — requires greater flexibility in the use of testimonial evidence. This particular type of crime is notoriously susceptible to intimidation or coercion of the victim to ensure that she does not testify at trial. When this occurs, the Confrontation Clause gives the criminal a windfall. We may not, however, vitiate constitutional guarantees when they have the effect of allowing the guilty to go free. But when defendants seek to undermine the judicial process by procuring or coercing silence from witnesses and victims, the Sixth Amendment does not require courts to acquiesce. While defendants have no duty to assist the State in proving their guilt, they *do* have the duty to refrain from acting in ways that destroy the integrity of the criminal-trial system. We reiterate what we said in *Crawford:* that "the rule of forfeiture by wrongdoing * * * extinguishes confrontation claims on essentially equitable grounds." That is, one who obtains the absence of a witness by wrongdoing forfeits the constitutional right to confrontation.

We take no position on the standards necessary to demonstrate such forfeiture, but federal courts using Federal Rule of Evidence 804(b)(6), which codifies the forfeiture doctrine, have generally held the Government to the preponderance-of-the-evidence standard, *see, e.g., United States v. Scott,* 284 F.3d 758, 762 (C.A.7 2002). State courts tend to follow the same practice, *see, e.g., Commonwealth v. Edwards,* 444 Mass. 526, 542, 830 N.E.2d 158, 172 (2005). Moreover, if a hearing on forfeiture is required, *Edwards,* for instance, observed that "hearsay evidence, including the unavailable witness's out-of-court statements, may be considered." The *Roberts* approach to the Confrontation Clause undoubtedly made recourse to this doctrine less necessary, because prosecutors could show the "reliability" of *ex parte* statements more easily than they could show the defendant's procurement of the witness's absence. *Crawford,* in overruling *Roberts,* did not destroy the ability of courts to protect the integrity of their proceedings.

We have determined that, absent a finding of forfeiture by wrongdoing, the Sixth Amendment operates to exclude Amy Hammon's affidavit. The Indiana courts may (if they are asked) determine on remand whether such a claim of forfeiture is properly raised and, if so, whether it is meritorious.

---

6 Police investigations themselves are, of course, in no way impugned by our characterization of their fruits as testimonial. Investigations of past crimes prevent future harms and lead to necessary arrests. While prosecutors may hope that inculpatory "nontestimonial" evidence is gathered, this is essentially beyond police control. Their saying that an emergency exists cannot make it be so. The Confrontation Clause in no way governs police conduct, because it is the trial *use* of, not the investigatory *collection* of, *ex parte* testimonial statements which offends that provision. But neither can police conduct govern the Confrontation Clause; testimonial statements are what they are.

* * *

We affirm the judgment of the Supreme Court of Washington in No. 05-5224. We reverse the judgment of the Supreme Court of Indiana in No. 05-5705, and remand the case to that Court for proceedings not inconsistent with this opinion.

JUSTICE THOMAS, concurring in the judgment in part and dissenting in part.

In *Crawford v. Washington,* 541 U.S. 36 (2004), we abandoned the general reliability inquiry we had long employed to judge the admissibility of hearsay evidence under the Confrontation Clause, describing that inquiry as "*inherently,* and therefore *permanently,* unpredictable." Today, a mere two years after the Court decided *Crawford,* it adopts an equally unpredictable test, under which district courts are charged with divining the "primary purpose" of police interrogations. Besides being difficult for courts to apply, this test characterizes as "testimonial," and therefore inadmissible, evidence that bears little resemblance to what we have recognized as the evidence targeted by the Confrontation Clause. Because neither of the cases before the Court today would implicate the Confrontation Clause under an appropriately targeted standard, I concur only in the judgment in *Davis v. Washington,* No. 05-5224, and dissent from the Court's resolution of *Hammon v. Indiana,* No. 05-5705.

I

A

* * * The history surrounding the right to confrontation supports the conclusion that it was developed to target particular practices that occurred under the English bail and committal statutes passed during the reign of Queen Mary, namely, the "civil-law mode of criminal procedure, and particularly its use of *ex parte* examinations as evidence against the accused." *Crawford, supra,* at 43, 50. "The predominant purpose of the [Marian committal] statute was to institute *systematic* questioning of the accused and the witnesses." J. Langbein, Prosecuting Crime in the Renaissance 23 (1974) (emphasis added). The statute required an oral examination of the suspect and the accusers, transcription within two days of the examinations, and physical transmission to the judges hearing the case. These examinations came to be used as evidence in some cases, in lieu of a personal appearance by the witness. * * *

In *Crawford,* we recognized that this history could be squared with the language of the Clause, giving rise to a workable, and more accurate, interpretation of the Clause. " '[W]itnesses,' " we said, are those who " 'bear testimony.' " And " '[t]estimony' " is " '[a] solemn declaration or affirmation made for the purpose of establishing or proving some fact.' " Admittedly, we did not set forth a detailed framework for addressing whether a statement is "testimonial" and thus subject to the Confrontation Clause. But the plain terms of the "testimony" definition we endorsed necessarily require some degree of solemnity before a statement can be deemed "testimonial."

This requirement of solemnity supports my view that the statements regulated by the Confrontation Clause must include extrajudicial statements contained in formalized testimonial materials, such as affidavits, depositions, prior testimony, or confessions. Affidavits, depositions, and prior testimony are, by their very nature, taken through a formalized process. Likewise, confessions, when extracted by police in a formal manner, carry sufficient indicia of solemnity to constitute formalized statements and, accordingly, bear a "striking resemblance," *Crawford, supra,* at 52, to the examinations of the accused and accusers under the Marian statutes.

Although the Court concedes that the early American cases invoking the right to confrontation or the Confrontation Clause itself all "clearly involve[d] testimony" as defined in *Crawford*, it fails to acknowledge that all of the cases it cites fall within the narrower category of formalized testimonial materials I have proposed. Interactions between the police and an accused (or witnesses) resemble Marian proceedings — and these early cases — only when the interactions are somehow rendered "formal." In *Crawford,* for example, the interrogation was custodial, taken after warnings given pursuant to Miranda v. Arizona. *Miranda* warnings, by their terms, inform a prospective defendant that "anything he says can be used against him in a court of law." This imports a solemnity to the process that is not present in a mere conversation between a witness or suspect and a police officer.

The Court all but concedes that no case can be cited for its conclusion that the Confrontation Clause also applies to informal police questioning under certain circumstances. Instead, the sole basis for the Court's conclusion is its apprehension that the Confrontation Clause will "readily be evaded" if it is only applicable to formalized testimonial materials. But the Court's proposed solution to the risk of evasion is needlessly overinclusive. Because the Confrontation Clause sought to regulate prosecutorial abuse occurring through use of *ex parte* statements as evidence against the accused, it also reaches the use of technically informal statements when used to evade the formalized process. That is, even if the interrogation itself is not formal, the production of evidence by the prosecution at trial would resemble the abuses targeted by the Confrontation Clause if the prosecution attempted to use out-of-court statements as a means of circumventing the literal right of confrontation. In such a case, the Confrontation Clause could fairly be applied to exclude the hearsay statements offered by the prosecution, preventing evasion without simultaneously excluding evidence offered by the prosecution in good faith.

The Court's standard is not only disconnected from history and unnecessary to prevent abuse; it also yields no predictable results to police officers and prosecutors attempting to comply with the law. In many, if not most, cases where police respond to a report of a crime, whether pursuant to a 911 call from the victim or otherwise, the purposes of an interrogation, viewed from the perspective of the police, are *both* to respond to the emergency situation *and* to gather evidence.Assigning one of these two largely unverifiable motives primacy requires constructing a hierarchy of purpose that will rarely be present — and is not reliably discernible. It will inevitably be, quite simply, an exercise in fiction.

The Court's repeated invocation of the word "objectiv[e]" to describe its test, however, suggests that the Court may not mean to reference purpose at all, but instead to inquire into the function served by the interrogation. Certainly such a test would avoid the pitfalls that have led us repeatedly to reject tests dependent on the subjective intentions of police officers. It would do so, however, at the cost of being even more disconnected from the prosecutorial abuses targeted by the Confrontation Clause. Additionally, it would shift the ability to control whether a violation occurred from the police and prosecutor to the judge, whose determination as to the "primary purpose" of a particular interrogation would be unpredictable and not necessarily tethered to the actual purpose for which the police performed the interrogation.

B

Neither the 911 call at issue in *Davis* nor the police questioning at issue in *Hammon* is testimonial under the appropriate framework. Neither the call nor the questioning is itself a formalized dialogue. Nor do any circumstances surrounding the taking of the statements render those statements sufficiently formal to resemble the Marian examinations; the statements were neither Mirandized nor custodial, nor accompanied by any similar indicia of formality. Finally, there is no suggestion that the prosecution attempted to offer the women's hearsay evidence at trial in order to evade confrontation. Accordingly, the statements at issue in both cases are nontestimonial and admissible under the Confrontation Clause.

The Court's determination that the evidence against Hammon must be excluded extends the Confrontation Clause far beyond the abuses it was intended to prevent. When combined with the Court's holding that the evidence against Davis is perfectly admissible, however, the Court's *Hammon* holding also reveals the difficulty of applying the Court's requirement that courts investigate the "primary purpose[s]" of the investigation. The Court draws a line between the two cases based on its explanation that *Hammon* involves "no emergency in progress," but instead, mere questioning as "part of an investigation into possibly criminal past conduct," and its explanation that *Davis* involves questioning for the "primary purpose" of "enabl[ing] police assistance to meet an ongoing emergency.". But the fact that the officer in *Hammon* was investigating Mr. Hammon's past conduct does not foreclose the possibility that the primary purpose of his inquiry was to assess whether Mr. Hammon constituted a continuing danger to his wife, requiring further police presence or action. It is hardly remarkable that Hammon did not act abusively towards his wife in the presence of the officers, and his good judgment to refrain from criminal behavior in the presence of police sheds little, if any, light on whether his violence would have resumed had the police left without further questioning, transforming what the Court dismisses as "past conduct" back into an "ongoing emergency." Nor does the mere fact that McCottry needed emergency aid shed light on whether the "primary purpose" of gathering, for example, the name of her assailant was to protect the police, to protect the victim, or to gather information for prosecution. In both of the cases before the Court, like many similar cases, pronouncement of the "primary" motive behind the interrogation calls for nothing more than a guess by courts.

II

Because the standard adopted by the Court today is neither workable nor a targeted attempt to reach the abuses forbidden by the Clause, I concur only in the judgment in *Davis v. Washington,* No. 05-5224, and respectfully dissent from the Court's resolution of *Hammon v. Indiana,* No. 05-5705.

Note on Crawford *and Its Relationship to the Federal Rules Hearsay Exceptions*

While the precise definition of "testimonial" is not clear, it is clear that *Crawford* has made a significant change in the current use of hearsay by the prosecution in criminal trials. Under the *Roberts* test, virtually all hearsay admitted in Federal courts would satisfy the Confrontation Clause. This is because almost all of the Federal Rules hearsay exceptions were "firmly-rooted", and those that were not (e.g., the residual exception), were applied in compliance with the constitutional reliability requirements imposed by *Roberts*. But the *Roberts* reliability test for assessing hearsay has now been discarded. *See Whorton v. Bockting*, 127 S. Ct. 1173 (2007) (*Roberts* test overruled even as to hearsay that is not testimonial). The following discussion considers the likely changes imposed by *Crawford* on the admissibility of hearsay admitted under the exemptions and exceptions provided by the Federal Rules of Evidence.

Rule 801 Exceptions

1. Statements That Are Not Hearsay. The analysis of these statements does not change after *Crawford*. If the statement is not hearsay, there is no need to cross-examine the declarant and accordingly there are no Confrontation Clause concerns. In a footnote in *Crawford*, the Court explicitly adheres to its position that admission of non-hearsay does not violate the Confrontation Clause. *See, e.g., United States v. Walter,* 434 F.3d 30 (1st Cir. 2006) (*Crawford* "does not call into question this court's precedents holding that statements introduced solely to place a defendant's admissions into context are not hearsay and, as such, do not run afoul of the Confrontation Clause."); *Furr v. Brady*, 440 F.3d 34 (1st Cir. 2006) (the defendant was charged with firearms offenses and intimidation of a government witness; an accomplice's confession to law enforcement did not implicate *Crawford* because it was not admitted for its truth; rather, it was admitted to show that the defendant knew about the confession and, in contacting the accomplice thereafter, intended to intimidate him).

2. Prior Statements of Testifying Witnesses. The analysis of these statements does not change after *Crawford*. Even though many such statements are testimonial, the condition of their admissibility is that the witness who made the statement is produced for trial and subject to cross-examination. This requirement satisfies the *Crawford* standard. The point is illustrated by *United States v. Kappell,* 418 F.3d 550 (6th Cir. 2005), a child sex abuse prosecution, in which the victims testified and the trial court admitted a number of hearsay statements that the victims had made to social workers and others. The defendant claimed that the admission of hearsay violated his right to confrontation under *Crawford.* But the court held that *Crawford* by its terms is inapplicable if the hearsay declarant is subject to cross-examination at trial. The defendant complained that the victims were unresponsive or inarticulate at some points in their testimony, and therefore they were not subject to effective cross-examination. But the court found this claim foreclosed by *United States v. Owens,* 484 U.S. 554 (1988). Under *Owens*, the Constitution requires only an opportunity for cross-examination, not cross-examination in whatever way the defendant might wish. The defendant's complaint was that his cross-examination would have been more effective if the victims had been older. "Under *Owens,* however, that is not enough to establish a Confrontation Clause violation."

3. Admissions. The treatment of party-admissions and adoptive admissions is probably unchanged after *Crawford*. Under any view of the Confrontation Clause, the accused does not have a constitutional right to confront himself. On the other hand, the intellectual purity of the argument in *Crawford* could be used by an accused to argue that a confession he made to law enforcement is "testimonial" and therefore admitting the confession would violate his right to confrontation unless the declarant is subject to cross-examination. It would seem that the government could respond that the criminal defendant could confront himself by taking the stand; by not doing so, the argument goes, he procures his own unavailability. One way or another, a court is likely to hold that a criminal defendant has no right to confront himself.

As to agency-admissions, they had been held firmly rooted under *Roberts*, but that analysis has been rejected by *Crawford*, at least if the admissions are "testimonial." Admissibility under the Confrontation Clause will depend on whether a particular agent-admission is "testimonial." It would seem possible that some agent statements admissible under Rule 801(d)(2)(D) could be "testimonial." An example would be statements obtained from corporate agents to government officials investigating allegations of corporate criminal misconduct. But the run-of-the-mill agent's statement (*e.g.*, a water cooler statement complaining about the graft occurring in the accounting department) is unlikely to be considered "testimonial" under *Crawford* (as it would not be made in anticipation of use in a criminal trial) so the only question would be whether the statement fits the admissibility requirements of Rule 801(d)(2)(D).

As to coconspirator statements, they are only admissible if they are made during the course and in furtherance of the conspiracy. It would be unusual, but not impossible, for a coconspirator to make a qualifying statement that would result in "testimony" under *Crawford*. For example, if the coconspirator is knowingly confessing to police officers, or making a plea allocution, those statements are not in furtherance of the conspiracy and so not admissible under the exception. One possibility, however, arises with statements made by coconspirators to undercover police officers, *e.g.*, arranging for a sale of drugs. These statements are in furtherance of the conspiracy, so the question is whether they are testimonial within the meaning of *Crawford*. It could be argued that they are, because law enforcement is involved in generating the statement; but it could be argued that they are not, because the declarant does not know that he is talking to a government official and so it doesn't look like a statement specifically generated for trial. It should be noted that the Court in *Crawford* states in passing that statements made during the course and in furtherance of the conspiracy are "by their nature" not testimonial. *See also United States v. Robinson*, 367 F.3d 278 (5th Cir. 2004) (holding that coconspirator statements were not "testimonial" under *Crawford* as they were made under informal circumstances and not for the purpose of creating evidence for trial).

Two examples of coconspirator hearsay after *Crawford* are illustrative. In *United States v. Johnson,* 440 F.3d 832 (6th Cir. 2006), the court found no *Crawford* violation when the trial court admitted statements by an accomplice to an undercover informant. The accomplice and the informant were long-time friends, and the accomplice had no idea that his friend was cooperating with the prosecution. The statements were held not testimonial because the declarant didn't know he was speaking to law enforcement, and so a person in his position "would not have anticipated that his statements would be used in a criminal investigation or prosecution of Johnson."

In contrast, the court in *United States v. Holmes*, 406 F.3d 337 (5th Cir. 2005), encountered a statement made by a coconspirator that was probably testimonial under *Crawford*. The defendant was convicted of mail fraud and conspiracy, stemming from a scheme with a court clerk to file a backdated document in a civil action. The defendant argued that admitting the deposition testimony of the court clerk, given in the underlying civil action, violated his right to confrontation after *Crawford*. The clerk testified that the clerk's office was prone to error and thus someone in that office could have mistakenly backdated the document at issue. The Court noted that coconspirator statements ordinarily are not testimonial under *Crawford*. It also noted, however, that the clerk's statement "is not the run-of-the-mill co-conspirator's statement made unwittingly to a government informant or made casually to a partner in crime; rather, we have a co-conspirator's statement that is derived from a formalized testimonial source — recorded and sworn civil deposition testimony." Ultimately the court found it unnecessary to determine whether the deposition testimony was "testimonial" within the meaning of *Crawford* because it was not offered for its truth. Rather, the government offered the testimony "to establish its *falsity* through independent evidence." Statements that are offered for a non-hearsay purpose pose no Confrontation Clause concerns, whether or not they are testimonial, as the Court recognized in *Crawford*.

Rule 803 Exceptions

The change wrought by *Crawford* will undoubtedly affect statements offered under Rule 803 because under *Roberts* these exceptions had been held firmly rooted and so statements fitting the exceptions automatically satisfied the Confrontation Clause. Under *Crawford,* the question is not whether the hearsay exception is firmly rooted but whether the particular statement offered is or is not testimonial.

So it is clear that the confrontation analysis must be statement by statement rather than exception by exception. One cannot make a categorical conclusion, for example, that if a statement fits the excited utterance exception, it by definition satisfies the Confrontation Clause. The Court in *Davis* and *Hammon* specifically declines to impose broad rules on which kind of excited utterances are testimonial and which are not. That said, while some excited utterances will be testimonial, most will not. For example, if a police officer encounters a stabbing victim in an alley, and asks the victim to identify a perpetrator, the victim's response may well be considered testimonial even though it fits the excited utterance exception. The Court's analysis in *Hammon* appears to indicate that if a police officer interviews a person during the investigation of a crime, the interviewees statements are likely to be testimonial. The same goes for state of mind statements, present sense impressions, etc.

Business records, by definition, are unlikely to be testimonial — and the Court in *Crawford* refers to business records as being not testimonial "by their nature." *See, e.g., United States v. Jamieson,* 427 F.3d 394 (6th Cir. 2005) (business records are by definition not prepared in anticipation of litigation and are not testimonial under *Crawford* because they do not "resemble the formal statement or solemn declaration identified as testimony by the Supreme Court."). Official police reports are likely to be testimonial only if they appear to be prepared for a particular prosecution.

In sum, it is clear that the Confrontation Clause after *Crawford* will result in exclusion of certain hearsay statements that are admissible under one of the Rule 803 exceptions. The First Circuit, in *United States v. Brito,* 427 F.3d 53 (1st Cir. 2005), provides some indication of where the lines might be drawn. The *Brito* Court affirmed a conviction of firearm possession by an illegal alien. It held that statements made in a 911 call, indicating that the defendant was carrying and had fired a gun, were properly admitted as excited utterances, and that the admission of the 911 statements did not violate the defendant's right to confrontation. The statements were not "testimonial" within the meaning of *Crawford v. Washington*. The Court refused, however, to adopt a categorical rule that an excited utterance could never be testimonial under *Crawford.* The Court declared that the relevant question is whether the statement was made with an eye toward "legal ramifications." The Court noted that under this test, statements to police made while the declarant or others are still in personal danger are ordinarily not testimonial, because the declarant in these circumstances "usually speaks out of urgency and a desire to obtain a prompt response." Once the initial danger has dissipated, however, "a person who speaks while still under the stress of a startling event is more likely able to comprehend the larger significance of her words. If the record fairly supports a finding of comprehension, the fact that the statement also qualifies as an excited utterance will not alter its testimonial nature." In this case the 911 call was properly admitted because the caller stated that she had "just" heard gunshots and seen a man with a gun, that the man had pointed the gun at her, and that the man was still in her line of sight. Thus the declarant was in "imminent personal peril" when the call was made and therefore it was not testimonial. The Court also found that the 911 operator's questioning of the caller did not make the answers testimonial, because "it would blink reality to place under the rubric of interrogation the single off-handed question asked by the dispatcher — a question that only momentarily interrupted an otherwise continuous stream of consciousness."

While the analysis in *Brito* preceded the Supreme Court's decision in *Davis* and *Hammon*, it certainly appears to be consistent with those cases. The Supreme Court in *Davis/Hammon* drew this general line between testimonial and non-testimonial statements in the context of 911 calls and reports by victims to police officers:

> Without attempting to produce an exhaustive classification of all conceivable statements — or even all conceivable statements in response to police interrogation — as either testimonial or nontestimonial, it suffices to decide the present cases to hold as follows: Statements are nontestimonial when made in the course of police interrogation under circumstances objectively indicating that the primary purpose of the interrogation is to enable police assistance to meet an ongoing emergency. They are testimonial when the circumstances objectively indicate that there is no such ongoing emergency, and that the primary purpose of the interrogation is to establish or prove past events potentially relevant to later criminal prosecution

The Court in *Davis* emphasized the narrowness of its opinion. It was not attempting to establishing an all-encompassing test of which statements are testimonial and which are not. The Court did not decide, for example, whether statements made to someone other than law enforcement personnel can be testimonial. It did not even decide that all statements to responding police officers are testimonial and all statements to 911 operators are not. According to the Court, "testimonial" even in these narrow circumstances depends on the facts.

Rule 804 Exceptions

Generally speaking, hearsay statements falling within the Rule 804 exceptions satisfied the Confrontation Clause under the *Roberts* analysis, for one reason or another. Under *Crawford*, the analysis will depend on the exception and in some cases on the particular statement admitted under the exception. The change wrought by *Crawford*, as applied to statements offered under Rule 804, is likely to be as follows:

1. Rule 804(b)(1). Statements admitted under the prior testimony exception will satisfy the Confrontation Clause even after *Crawford* because admissibility is dependent on prior cross-examination and declarant unavailability — so even though prior testimony is clearly testimonial, it by definition satisfies the admissibility requirements set forth in *Crawford* for testimonial hearsay.

2. Rule 804(b)(2). Statements admitted as dying declarations may or may not be testimonial. If a victim is being asked by a police officer "who shot you?" while the victim is in the throes of death, it is possible that the victim's statement identifying the defendant as the perpetrator is testimonial under *Crawford*. If the declarant makes a deathbed statement to his mother, then it is probably not testimonial. For an application of the dying declarations exception after *Crawford, see People v. Ahib Paul,* 25 A.D.3d 165, 803 N.Y.S.2d 66, 68-71 (1st Dept. 2005) (dying declaration was not testimonial where it was "volunteered, to people who were friends, acquaintances or neighbors").

Yet there remains a question, after *Crawford,* about the constitutional admissibility of even testimonial dying declarations. In a footnote in *Crawford,* the Court noted that it had held in the 19th century that a statement admitted as a dying declaration did not violate the accused's right to confrontation. That particular statement held properly admitted may have been testimonial. In the *Crawford* footnote, the Court bowed to precedent and entertained the possibility that a hearsay statement fitting the dying declarations exception might be admissible even though it is testimonial. The posited rationale was that the dying declarations exception was essentially as old as time itself. Ultimately, the *Crawford* Court found it unnecessary to decide whether a dying declaration would be an "exception" to the Court's new rule precluding testimonial hearsay. It did say that if it was an exception, it would be "sui generis."

3. Rule 804(b)(3). Statements admitted as declarations against interest may or may not be testimonial. Certainly if the statement is made to law enforcement by an accomplice, its admission against the accused will violate the Confrontation Clause even if it satisfies the hearsay exception. Of course, in *Williamson v. United States,* the Supreme Court held that an accomplice statement made to law enforcement was not admissible under the hearsay exception to the extent it directly identified the accused, because such a statement was not sufficiently against the declarant's penal interest. Justice O'Connor in *Williamson* intimated that an accomplice statement might be admissible to the extent that it implicated the declarant alone — the government might then be able to use that statement circumstantially to tie the accused to the crime. After *Crawford*, however, an accomplice statement made to law enforcement cannot be admitted against the accused, whether or not it implicates the accused directly. The question after *Crawford* is not whether the statement is sufficiently reliable or sufficiently against interest. The question is whether the statement is "testimonial," and the Court clearly held that accomplice statements made to law enforcement are indeed testimonial. Therefore, the opening left for admissibility of some accomplice statements has been closed as a constitutional matter by *Crawford. See, e.g., United States v. Jones*, 371 F.3d 363 (7th Cir. 2004), where an accomplice's statement to law enforcement was offered against the defendant, though it was redacted to take out any direct reference to the defendant. The court found that even assuming, arguendo, that the redacted confession was admissible as a declaration against interest, its admission would violate the Confrontation Clause after *Crawford.* The court noted that even though redacted, the confession was testimonial, as it was made during interrogation by law enforcement. And since the defendant never had a chance to cross-examine the accomplice, "under Crawford, no part of Rock's confession should have been allowed into evidence."

Crawford will also have a dramatic effect on the federal circuit case law that permitted the government to admit plea allocutions by codefendants, when they are redacted to eliminate all direct references to the accused. That practice is no longer permitted after *Crawford*. Allocution statements had been admitted because, as redacted, they were reliable enough to satisfy the *Roberts* requirements. But under *Crawford*, the question for hearsay statements is not whether they are reliable but whether they are testimonial. Plea allocutions are singled out as testimonial (whether redacted or not) in the majority opinion in *Crawford. See, e.g., United States v. Snype*, 441 F.3d 119 (2d Cir. 2006) (guilty plea allocution of the defendant's accomplice was testimonial even though all direct references to the defendant were redacted).

On the other hand, certain statements against penal interest will be nontestimonial after *Crawford*. An example is a statement by an accomplice to his girlfriend, describing a bank robbery that he and the defendant committed. This statement is against the accomplice's penal interest, but it is not testimonial because it is not given to law enforcement and there is no intent that it be used in lieu of testimony in the defendant's criminal trial.

United States v. Franklin, 415 F.3d 537 (6th Cir. 2005), illustrates the possibilities for admitting declarations against penal interest after *Crawford.* Franklin was charged with bank robbery. One of Franklin's accomplices (Clarke), was speaking to a friend (Wright) some time after the robbery. Wright told Clarke that he looked "stressed out." Clarke responded that he was indeed stressed out, because he and Franklin had robbed a bank and he thought the authorities were on their trail. The court found no error in admitting Clarke's hearsay statement against the defendant as a declaration against penal interest, as it disserved Clark's interest and was not made to law enforcement officers in any attempt to curry favor with the authorities. On the constitutional question, the Court found that Clarke's statement was not testimonial under *Crawford.*

4. Rule 804(b)(6). In a footnote in *Crawford,* the Court stated that nothing in the case was intended to change the rule that an accused who is responsible in some way for creating the unavailability of a witness can be held to have forfeited his Confrontation Clause objection to the hearsay statements of that witness. So *Crawford* does not change the existing law on forfeiture. And this conclusion is fortified by language in *Davis/Hammon*:

> While defendants have no duty to assist the State in proving their guilt, they *do* have the duty to refrain from acting in ways that destroy the integrity of the criminal-trial system. We reiterate what we said in *Crawford:* that "the rule of forfeiture by wrongdoing * * * extinguishes confrontation claims on essentially equitable grounds." That is, one who obtains the absence of a witness by wrongdoing forfeits the constitutional right to confrontation.

Residual Exception

The change wrought by *Crawford*, as applied to statements offered under Rule 807, is likely to be dramatic for certain categories of statements that have been admitted routinely as residual hearsay. The most obvious example is grand jury testimony. The Court in *Crawford* makes clear that grand jury testimony is "testimonial." As such it cannot be admitted unless the declarant is produced and subject to cross-examination. It does not matter that the grand jury testimony is reliable under the circumstances, as that is no longer the constitutional inquiry under *Crawford* for testimonial hearsay. So *Crawford* has swept away a good deal of case law admitting grand jury testimony under the residual exception. *See, e.g., United States v. Bruno,* 383 F.3d 65 (2d Cir. 2004) (admission of grand jury testimony was error as it was clearly testimonial after *Crawford*).

Other candidates for exclusion as testimonial hearsay include statements made by children to law enforcement personnel; statements made to police officers by eyewitnesses; prior testimony from the trial of a codefendant in which the accused was not a party; and statements made by law enforcement laboratory personnel concerning forensic testing.

An example of admissible residual hearsay after *Crawford* is *United States v. Morgan,* 385 F.3d 196 (2d Cir. 2004): In a drug trial, a letter written by the co-defendant was admitted against the defendant. The letter was written to a boyfriend and implicated both the defendant and the co-defendant in a conspiracy to smuggle drugs. The court found that the letter was properly admitted under Rule 807, and that it was not testimonial under *Crawford.* The court noted the following circumstances indicating that the letter was not testimonial: 1) it was not written in a coercive atmosphere; 2) it was not addressed to law enforcement authorities; 3) it was written to an intimate acquaintance; 4) it was written in the privacy of the co-defendant's hotel room; 5) the co-defendant had no reason to expect that the letter would ever find its way into the hands of the police; and 6) it was not written to curry favor with the authorities or with anyone else. These were the same factors that rendered the hearsay statement sufficiently reliable to qualify under Rule 807.

Relationship Between Crawford/Davis and the Federal Rules Exceptions for Business and Public Records

UNITED STATES v. ELLIS
460 F.3d 920 (7th Cir. 2006)

KANNE, CIRCUIT JUDGE:

After being convicted at trial on three counts of illegal possession of firearms, Brian K. Ellis was sentenced as an armed career criminal to 300 months' imprisonment. He now raises three issues on appeal, including one argument relying on the decision of *Crawford v. Washington*, 541 U.S. 36, 124 S. Ct. 1354, 158 L. Ed. 2d 177 (2004). We affirm.

I. HISTORY

Ellis was pulled over in Gibson County, Indiana, when a police officer noticed him driving erratically. He failed some initial field sobriety tests, but a field test for the presence of alcohol came up negative. With the officer's prompting, Ellis agreed to go to a hospital to have his blood and urine tested for drugs.

At this point, the officer placed Ellis in custody. An inventory search of the pickup truck Ellis was driving led to the discovery of a loaded .22 caliber revolver on the driver's side floorboard, .22 caliber ammunition scattered throughout, drug paraphernalia, and several cans of beer. The only other passenger, Bradley Ventress, was interviewed and quickly denied ownership of the gun. Ellis, who has a lengthy criminal history including three felony convictions, also disclaimed ownership of the gun.

After undergoing tests at a local hospital, Ellis was released from custody. A warrant was later issued for his arrest on a state DUI charge. That state charge was followed by a federal indictment charging Ellis with unlawful possession of a firearm. Ellis was not interested in facing the warrant or the indictment and apparently went into hiding.

About a month later, police were tipped off that Ellis was at a residence in rural Illinois near the Indiana border. The local authorities made plans to arrest him. Ellis had other plans. As the jury heard, a sheriff's deputy attempted to effect a traffic stop on Ellis after he drove away from the residence, but by the time Ellis's car stopped, it was on fire. He then jumped out of the car with a can of Coleman fuel in his hands, which he used to feed the fire. After dousing the flames and throwing the whole fuel can into the car, Ellis ran into a cornfield. The Illinois State Police were called to assist, and in a matter of hours Ellis was arrested. When taken into custody, he had in his possession a .22 caliber Beretta and a receipt from the retailer Wal-Mart. What the jury did not hear was that before dousing his car with fuel and fleeing the scene, Ellis led authorities on a harrowing car chase during which he repeatedly fired shots at the police.[1]

Subsequent investigation revealed that the Wal-Mart receipt documented a recent purchase of ammunition. Federal agents traced the receipt to a store in Vincennes, Indiana, where they were able to obtain video footage (later shown to the jury) of Ellis purchasing the ammunition.

Ellis was charged by a superseding indictment with three counts. Counts I and II, both based on the initial traffic stop in Indiana, charged that he was a felon in possession in violation of 18 U.S.C. § 922(g)(1), and a user of a controlled substance in possession of a firearm in violation of § 922(g)(3), respectively. Count III charged that Ellis was a felon in possession in violation of § 922(g)(1) based upon the events leading to his final arrest in Illinois. The indictment also alleged that Ellis would be subject to the fifteen-year mandatory minimum of § 924(e) because of his three previous felony convictions.

A trial was held on all three counts over Ellis's motion to sever Count III. A certified copy of the results of Ellis's blood and urine tests was introduced at trial over Ellis's objection under *Crawford*. The results were introduced as business records to help prove that Ellis was a user of controlled substances. Authentication of these records was established under Federal Rule of Evidence 902(11). The records were admitted during the testimony of the arresting officer. He testified that he took Ellis to the hospital and witnessed

[1] The district court judge granted Ellis's motion in limine to preclude any mention at trial of him shooting at the police. At sentencing, the local sheriff testified to being shot at by Ellis.

a lab technician draw blood and Ellis urinate in a cup. He also testified that the results of the urine tests were positive for methamphetamine.[2]

The actual exhibit of medical records admitted at trial contains a number of pages, including a certification of authenticity performed by a laboratory technician at the local hospital. The exhibit also contains two forms filled out at the local hospital, which apparently accompanied Ellis's blood and urine samples. These forms indicate that the "Collector" of the samples was a person with the first name Kristy. These forms were signed by Ellis and had a number of preprinted "Reason[s] for Test." The box checked on Ellis's forms indicates that the reason for his tests was "Reasonable Suspicion/Cause." Furthermore, in the section of one of the forms indicating which tests would be performed, presumably the form accompanying Ellis's blood, there is a handwritten note stating "Blood Drug Screen — Requested by Officer."

The exhibit also includes pages indicating three separate tests of Ellis's samples. An initial test of Ellis's urine was performed by Kristy at the local hospital on the same day Ellis was there. It returned a positive result for methamphetamine. The samples were then apparently shipped out of state to two separate companies for further tests — one for blood and one for urine. Both companies produced documents — dated after Ellis's trip to the hospital — indicating that Ellis had methamphetamine in his system.

The jury convicted on all counts.

II. ANALYSIS

We can easily dispose of two of the issues. * * * .

Having dealt with those issues, we are left with Ellis's argument relying on *Crawford* attacking the admission of the medical records establishing the presence of methamphetamine in his system. Evidentiary rulings affecting a defendant's right to confront witnesses are reviewed de novo. *United States v. Gilbertson*, 435 F.3d 790, 794-95 (7th Cir. 2006) (citations omitted). The Sixth Amendment provides that "[i]n all criminal prosecutions, the accused shall enjoy the right * * * to be confronted with witnesses against him." U.S. Const. amend. VI. As we now know, this right applies only to evidence that is considered "testimonial." *Davis v. Washington*, 126 S. Ct. 2266, 2273-76, 165 L. Ed. 2d 224 (2006). Hearsay evidence that is nontestimonial "is not subject to the Confrontation Clause." *Id.* at 2273. The Supreme Court, however, has expressly declined to provide a comprehensive definition of the term "testimonial." *Davis*, 126 S.C t. at 2273 (citation omitted); *Crawford*, 541 U.S. at 68, 124 S. Ct. 1354.

But we are not without guidance. The prototypical case of testimonial evidence is that created by the civil-law tradition of a judicial officer examining a witness in private and then later reporting the results in court. *Crawford*, 541 U.S. at 43-44, 124 S. Ct. 1354. This method was contrary to the common-law tradition of "live testimony in court subject to adversarial testing," but, nonetheless, it was utilized at times by English courts. *Id.* An infamous

[2] Before trial, the government complied with Rule 902(11) and provided written notice of its intent to offer the medical records by a written declaration of the custodian. Ellis did not challenge the authenticity of the records.

example of the use of this type of testimonial evidence is the treason trial of Sir Walter Raleigh. *Id.* at 44, 124 S.Ct. 1354. The crucial evidence used against Raleigh was the statement of an alleged accomplice implicating Raleigh. Despite Raleigh's cry to "[c]all my accuser before my face," the statement was not given by way of live testimony. *See id.* (citing *Raleigh's Case*, 2 How. St. Tr. 1, 15-16 (1603)). Instead, it was introduced in the form of a letter that was created during a pretrial examination of the accomplice. As the Court in *Crawford* explained, this method of producing and introducing evidence was the "principal evil at which the Confrontation Clause was directed." *Id.* at 50, 124 S. Ct. 1354. Accordingly, when the Court later provided guidance as to what constitutes testimonial evidence, it explained, "[w]hatever else the term [testimonial] covers, it applies at a minimum to prior testimony at a preliminary hearing, before a grand jury, or at a former trial; and to police interrogations. These are the modern practices with closest kinship to the abuses at which the Confrontation Clause was directed." *Id.* at 68, 124 S. Ct. 1354.

On the other end of the spectrum, the Court in *Crawford* explicitly noted, quite importantly for this case, that business records "by their nature were not testimonial." *Id.* at 56, 124 S. Ct. 1354; *see also id.* at 75, 124 S.Ct. 1354 (REHNQUIST, C.J., concurring in judgment) (noting the majority had excluded business records from the definition of testimonial evidence). Thus, it is clear that statements embodied in a business record are nontestimonial. *Id.*

The disputed tests were introduced as a business record under Federal Rules of Evidence 803(6) and 902(11), and we note that Ellis has advanced no argument here or objection below under those rules. His only claim of error is under *Crawford*. Neither his argument here nor his objection below were particularly well-developed. Nevertheless, we will construe his argument as one directed not only to the business records themselves, but also to the certification of those records pursuant to Rule 902(11). We will consider these in turn.

A. The Business Records of the Underlying Medical Tests

Faced with the obvious obstacle of the Court's designation of business records as nontestimonial, Ellis attacks the underlying medical records by arguing that they were created not because of routine medical procedures, but because of a government investigation. What we gather from this argument is that most business records would by their very nature have been created prior to any investigation of criminal activity, and that these are the type of business records the Court had in mind. The records used against Ellis, however, might be considered testimonial because they were created under police supervision and during an investigation for the purpose of determining whether a crime had been committed.

Whether a statement was made with an eye toward prosecution, that is, with the knowledge or for the purpose that it would be used later for prosecution, is an important aspect of delineating between testimonial and nontestimonial evidence. Two of the possible definitions of testimonial provided by the Court in *Crawford* focus on this circumstance. *See Crawford*, 541 U.S. at 51-52, 124 S. Ct. 1354 ("ex parte in-court testimony or its functional equivalent * * * that declarants would reasonably expect to be used prosecutorially" and "statements that were made under circumstances which would lead an objective witness reasonably to believe that the statement would be available for use at a later trial") (citations omitted). And the courts of appeals have taken to defining testimonial in terms of whether the declarant reasonably expected the statement to be used prosecutorially. E.g., *United States v. Maher*, 454 F.3d 13, 21 (1st Cir. 2006) (holding a statement to be testimonial because "it [was] clear that an objectively reasonable person in [the declarant's] shoes would understand that the statement would be used in prosecuting [the defendant] at trial"); *United States v. Hinton*, 423 F.3d 355, 359 (3d Cir. 2005) (explaining that statements are testimonial when "made under circumstances which would lead an objective witness reasonably to believe that the statement would be available for use at a later trial") (citations and quotations omitted); *United States v. Cromer*, 389 F.3d 662, 673-74 (6th Cir. 2004) (explaining that a statement is testimonial when "a reasonable person in the declarant's position would anticipate his statement being used against the accused in investigating and prosecuting the crime"); *United States v. Saget*, 377 F.3d 223, 228-29 (2d Cir. 2004) ("*Crawford* at least suggests that the determinative factor in determining whether a declarant bears testimony is the declarant's awareness or expectation that his or her statements may later be used at a trial."); *see also* Richard D. Friedman, Confrontation: The Search for Basic Principles, 86 Geo. L.J. 1011, 1042-43 (1998) (defining a testimonial statement as one made when the declarant "anticipates that the statement will be used in the prosecution or investigation of a crime").

We, in fact, have previously rejected a *Crawford* argument on the basis that the challenged statements (certified certificates of vehicle titles, including odometer statements used to prove fraud) were "not testimonial because they were not made with the respective declarants having an eye towards criminal prosecution." *United States v. Gilbertson*, 435 F.3d 790, 795-96 (7th Cir. 2006) (citing *Crawford*, 541 U.S. at 56 n. 7, 124 S. Ct. 1354).

Given the focus of the courts of appeals and our own precedent on the declarant's reasonable expectations of whether a statement would be used prosecutorially, Ellis may appear to be on strong ground in arguing that the results of his medical tests were testimonial. It must have been obvious to Kristy (the laboratory technician at the local hospital) that her test results might end up as evidence against Ellis in some kind of trial. After all, she indicated on the form that the reason for the tests was "Reasonable Suspicion/Cause." Moreover, the police officer's participation in initiating these tests — the officer accompanied Ellis to the hospital and even watched him urinate in a cup — would also have led Kristy to believe that her test results would be used for criminal prosecution. The same might go for the professionals performing the tests out of state. The forms which we assume accompanied the samples bore the ominous "Reasonable Suspicion/Cause" indication checked by Kristy, and the blood sample form also had the notation that it was "Requested by Officer".

Nevertheless, we do not think these circumstances transform what is otherwise a nontestimonial business record into a testimonial statement implicating the Confrontation Clause. There is no indication that the observations embodied in Ellis's medical records were made in anything but the ordinary course of business. Such observations, the Court in *Crawford* made clear, are nontestimonial. 541 U.S. at 56, 124 S. Ct. 1354. And we do not think it matters that these observations were made with the knowledge that they might be used for criminal prosecution. Prior to the Court's decision in *Davis*, two other courts of appeals decided that certificates of nonexistence of record ("CNR"), admitted under Rule 803(10) and used to prove an alien did not receive permission from the Attorney General to reenter the country, were nontestimonial despite the fact they were prepared by the government in anticipation of a criminal prosecution. *See, e.g.*, *United States v. Cervantes-Flores*, 421 F.3d 825, 833 (9th Cir. 2005); *United States v. Rueda-Rivera*, 396 F.3d 678, 680 (5th Cir. 2005). The focus of these decisions was that the preparation of these CNRs was routine, and the statements in them were simply too far removed from the examples of testimonial evidence provided by *Crawford*. *Cervantes-Flores*, 421 F.3d at 833-34; *Rueda-Rivera*, 396 F.3d at 680.

We agree with these courts that the mere fact a person creating a business record (or other similar record) knows the record might be used for criminal prosecution does not by itself make that record testimonial. The Court's recent decision in *Davis* (though we recognize the Court made no such pronouncement) supports this conclusion because we think it necessarily rejects a strict adherence to denominating as testimonial all statements made under circumstances where a reasonable person would know the statements might be used as evidence of a crime.

In *Davis*, the Court addressed a statement made by a woman to a 911 operator reporting she had been assaulted. 126 S. Ct. at 2270-71. That recorded statement was later used at trial to prosecute Davis (the woman's former boyfriend) for a felony violation of a domestic no-contact order. *Id.* at 2271. The Court considered the 911 operator's questioning of the woman to be an interrogation, *id.* at 2274 n. 1, and the operators themselves to be at least "agents of law enforcement," *id.* at 2274 n. 2. In the face of Davis's objection that introduction of the statement violated the Sixth Amendment, the Court held that when the objective circumstances indicate the "primary purpose" of police interrogation is to meet an ongoing emergency, the statements elicited in response are nontestimonial. *Id.* at 2273-74. We believe this holding necessarily implies that consciousness on the part of the person reporting an emergency (or the police officer eliciting information about the emergency) that his or her statements might be used as evidence in a crime does not lead to the conclusion ipso facto that the statement is testimonial. A reasonable person reporting a domestic disturbance, which is what the declarant in *Davis* was doing, will be aware that the result is the arrest and possible prosecution of the perpetrator. *See, e.g.*, Richard D. Friedman & Bridget McCormack, Dial-In-Testimony, 150 U. Pa. L.Rev. 1171, 1199 (concluding that most 911 callers know that by reporting domestic violence "they are practically ensuring that the other person will be arrested, and that a criminal prosecution will probably follow"). So it cannot be that a statement is testimonial in every case where a declarant reasonably expects that it might be used prosecutorially.

While the medical professionals in this case might have thought their observations would end up as evidence in a criminal prosecution, the objective circumstances of this case indicate that their observations and statements introduced at trial were made in nothing else but the ordinary course of business. Therefore, when these professionals made those observations, they — like the declarant reporting an emergency in *Davis* — were "not acting as * * * witness[es];" and were "not testifying." *See Davis*, 126 S. Ct. at 2277 (emphasis in original). They were employees simply recording observations which, because they were made in the ordinary course of business, are "statements that by their nature were not testimonial." *Crawford.*

B. Certification Pursuant to Rule 902(11)

Prior to *Crawford*, we held that Rule 803(6) remained a firmly rooted exception to the hearsay rule, and, therefore, did not violate the Confrontation Clause despite the then-recent amendment allowing authentication by written certification pursuant to Rule 902(11). *See United States v. Klinzing*, 315 F.3d 803, 809-10 (7th Cir. 2003). The question we must answer in the wake of *Crawford* is whether a written certification attesting to the authenticity of a business record is testimonial evidence. *Davis*, 126 S. Ct. at 2274-76. We do not think it is.

As should be clear, we do not find as controlling the fact that a certification of authenticity under 902(11) is made in anticipation of litigation. What is compelling is that *Crawford* expressly identified business records as nontestimonial evidence. *Crawford*, 541 U.S. at 56, 124 S. Ct. 1354. Given the records themselves do not fall within the constitutional guarantee provided by the Confrontation Clause, it would be odd to hold that the foundational evidence authenticating the records do. We also find support in the decisions holding that a CNR is nontestimonial. *See, e.g., Cervantes-Flores*, 421 F.3d at 833; *Rueda-Rivera*, 396 F.3d at 680. A CNR is quite like a certification under 902(11); it is a signed affidavit attesting that the signatory had performed a diligent records search for any evidence that the defendant had been granted permission to enter the United States after deportation. *Cervantes-Flores*, 421 F.3d at 831; *Rueda-Rivera*, 396 F.3d at 679.

The certification at issue in this case is nothing more than the custodian of records at the local hospital attesting that the submitted documents are actually records kept in the ordinary course of business at the hospital. The statements do not purport to convey information about Ellis, but merely establish the existence of the procedures necessary to create a business record. They are made by the custodian of records, an employee of the business, as part of her job. As such, we hold that the written certification entered into evidence pursuant to Rule 902(11) is nontestimonial just as the underlying business records are. Both of these pieces of evidence are too far removed from the "principal evil at which the Confrontation Clause was directed" to be considered testimonial. *Crawford*, 541 U.S. at 50, 124 S. Ct. 1354.

III. CONCLUSION

For the foregoing reason, Ellis's convictions and sentence are Affirmed.

D. THE *BRUTON* ISSUES

RICHARDSON v. MARSH
481 U.S. 200 (1987)

JUSTICE SCALIA delivered the opinion of the Court.

In *Bruton v. United States*, 391 U.S. 123 (1968), we held that a defendant is deprived of his rights under the Confrontation Clause when his nontestifying codefendant's confession naming him as a participant in the crime is introduced at their joint trial, even if the jury is instructed to consider that confession only against the codefendant. Today we consider whether *Bruton* requires the same result when the codefendant's confession is redacted to omit any reference to the defendant, but the defendant is nonetheless linked to the confession by evidence properly admitted against him at trial.

I

Respondent Clarissa Marsh, Benjamin Williams, and Kareem Martin were charged with assaulting Cynthia Knighton and murdering her 4-year-old son, Koran, and her aunt, Ollie Scott. Respondent and Williams were tried jointly, over her objection. (Martin was a fugitive at the time of trial.) At the trial, Knighton testified as follows: On the evening of October 29, 1978, she and her son were at Scott's home when respondent and her boyfriend Martin visited. After a brief conversation in the living room, respondent announced that she had come to "pick up something" from Scott and rose from the couch. Martin then pulled out a gun, pointed it at Scott and the Knightons, and said that "someone had gotten killed and [Scott] knew something about it." Respondent immediately walked to the front door and peered out the peephole. The doorbell rang, respondent opened the door, and Williams walked in, carrying a gun. As Williams passed respondent, he asked, "Where's the money?" Martin forced Scott upstairs, and Williams went into the kitchen, leaving respondent alone with the Knightons. Knighton and her son attempted to flee, but respondent grabbed Knighton and held her until Williams returned. Williams ordered the Knightons to lie on the floor and then went upstairs to assist Martin. Respondent, again left alone with the Knightons, stood by the front door and occasionally peered out the peephole. A few minutes later, Martin, Williams, and Scott came down the stairs, and Martin handed a paper grocery bag to respondent. Martin and Williams then forced Scott and the Knightons into the basement, * * *.

In addition to Knighton's testimony, the state introduced (over respondent's objection) a confession given by Williams to the police shortly after his arrest. The confession was redacted to omit all reference to respondent — indeed, to omit all indication that *anyone* other than Martin and Williams participated in the crime.[1] The confession largely corroborated Knighton's account of the

---

[1] The redacted confession in its entirety read:

> On Sunday evening, October the 29th, 1978, at about 6:30 p.m., I was over to my girl friend's house at 237 Moss, Highland Park, when I received a phone call from a friend of mine named Kareem Martin. He said he had been looking for me and James

activities of persons other than respondent in the house. In addition, the confession described a conversation Williams had with Martin as they drove to the Scott home, during which, according to Williams, Martin said that he would have to kill the victims after the robbery. At the time the confession was admitted, the jury was admonished not to use it in any way against respondent. Williams did not testify Martin shot them. Only Cynthia Knighton survived.

After the State rested, respondent took the stand. She testified that on October 29, 1978, she had lost money that Martin intended to use to buy drugs. Martin was upset, and suggested to respondent that she borrow money from Scott, with whom she had worked in the past. Martin and respondent picked up Williams and drove to Scott's house. During the drive, respondent, who was sitting in the backseat, "knew that [Martin and Williams] were talking" but could not hear the conversation because "the radio was on and the speaker was right in [her] ear." Martin and respondent were admitted into the home, and respondent had a short conversation with Scott, during which she asked for a loan. Martin then pulled a gun, and respondent walked to the door to see where the car was. When she saw Williams, she opened the door for him. Respondent testified that during the robbery she did not feel free to leave and was too scared to flee. She said that she did not know why she prevented the Knightons from escaping. She admitted taking the bag from Martin, but said that after Martin and Williams took the victims into the basement, she left the house without the bag. Respondent insisted that she had possessed no prior knowledge that Martin and Williams were armed, had heard no

---

Coleman, who I call Tom. He asked me if I wanted to go on a robbery with him. I said okay. Then he said he'd be by and pick me up. About 15 or 20 minutes later Kareem came by in his black Monte Carlo car. I got in the car and Kareem told me he was going to stick up this crib, told me the place was a numbers house. Kareem said there would be over $5,000 or $10,000 in the place. Kareem said he would have to take them out after the robbery. Kareem had a big silver gun. He gave me a long barrelled *[sic]*.22 revolver. We then drove over to this house and parked the car across the big street near the house. The plan was that I would wait in the car in front of the house and then I would move the car down across the big street because he didn't want anybody to see the car. Okay, Kareem went up to the house and went inside. A couple of minutes later I moved the car and went up to the house. As I entered, Kareem and this older lady were in the dining room, a little boy and another younger woman were sitting on the couch in the front room. I pulled my pistol and told the younger woman and the little boy to lay on the floor. Kareem took the older lady upstairs. He had a pistol, also. I stayed downstairs with the two people on the floor. After Kareem took the lady upstairs I went upstairs and the lady was laying on the bed in the room to the left as you get up the stairs. The lady had already given us two bags full of money before we ever got upstairs. Kareem had thought she had more money and that's why we had went upstairs. Me and Kareem started searching the rooms but I didn't find any money. I came downstairs and then Kareem came down with the lady. I said, 'Let's go, let's go.' Kareem said no. Kareem then took the two ladies and little boy down the basement and that's when I left to go to the car. I went to the car and got in the back seat. A couple of minutes later Kareem came to the car and said he thinks the girl was still living because she was still moving and he didn't have any more bullets. He asked me how come I didn't go down the basement and I said I wasn't doing no shit like that. He then dropped me back off at my girl's house in Highland Park and I was supposed to get together with him today, get my share of the robbery after he had counted the money. That's all.

conversation about anyone's being harmed, and had not intended to rob or kill anyone.

During his closing argument, the prosecutor admonished the jury not to use Williams' confession against respondent. Later in his argument, however, he linked respondent to the portion of Williams' confession describing his conversation with Martin in the car.[2] (Respondent's attorney did not object to this.) After closing arguments, the judge again instructed the jury that Williams' confession was not to be considered against respondent. The jury convicted respondent of two counts of felony murder in the perpetration of an armed robbery and one count of assault with intent to committ murder. The Michigan Court of Appeals affirmed in an unpublished opinion, and the Michigan Supreme Court denied leave to appeal.

Respondent then filed a petition for a writ of *habeas corpus* pursuant to 28 U.S.C. § 2254. She alleged that her conviction was not supported by sufficient evidence and that introduction of Williams' confession at the joint trial had violated her rights under the Confrontation Clause. The District Court denied the petition. The United States Court of Appeals for the Sixth Circuit reversed. The Court of Appeals held that in determining whether *Bruton* bars the admission of a nontestifying codefendant's confession, a court must assess the confession's "inculpatory value" by examining not only the face of the confession, but also all of the evidence introduced at trial. Here, Williams' account of the conversation in the car was the only *direct* evidence that respondent knew before entering Scott's house that the victims would be robbed and killed. Respondent's own testimony placed her in that car. In light of the "paucity" of other evidence of malice and the prosecutor's linkage of respondent and the statement in the car during closing argument, admission of Williams' confession "was powerfully incriminating to [respondent] with respect to the critical element of intent." * * * Thus, the Court of Appeals concluded, the Confrontation Clause was violated. We granted *certiorari* because the Sixth Circuit's decision conflicts with those of other Courts of Appeals which have declined to adopt the "evidentiary linkage" or "contextual implication" approach to *Bruton* questions.

---

[2] The prosecutor said:

"It's important in light of [respondent's] testimony when she says Kareem drives over to Benjamin Williams' home and picks him up to go over. What's the thing that she says? 'Well, I'm sitting in the back seat of the car.' 'Did you hear any conversation that was going on in the front seat between Kareem and Mr. Williams?' 'No, couldn't hear any conversation. The radio was too loud.' I asked *[sic]* you whether that is reasonable. Why did she say that? Why did she say she couldn't hear any conversation? She said, 'I know they were having conversation but I couldn't hear it because of the radio.' Because if she admits that she heard the conversation and she admits to the plan, she's guilty of at least armed robbery. So she can't tell you that." (Respondent's attorney did not object to this.) After closing arguments, the judge again instructed the jury that Williams' confession was not to be considered against respondent. The jury convicted respondent of two counts of felony murder in the perpetration of an armed robbery and one count of assault with intent to commit murder. The Michigan Court of Appeals affirmed in an unpublished opinion, and the Michigan Supreme Court denied leave to appeal.

II

* * *

Ordinarily, a witness whose testimony is introduced at a joint trial is not considered to be a witness "against" a defendant if the jury is instructed to consider that testimony only against a codefendant. * * * In *Bruton*, however, we recognized a narrow exception to this principle: We held that a defendant is deprived of his Sixth Amendment right of confrontation when the facially incriminating confession of a nontestifying codefendant is introduced at their joint trial, even if the jury is instructed to consider the confession only against the codefendant. We said:

> [T]here are some contexts in which the risk that the jury will not, or cannot, follow instructions is so great, and the consequences of failure so vital to the defendant, that the practical and human limitations of the jury system cannot be ignored. Such a context is presented here, where the powerfully incriminating extrajudicial statements of a codefendant, who stands accused side-by-side with the defendant, are deliberately spread before the jury in a joint trial* * *."

There is an important distinction between this case and *Bruton*, which causes it to fall outside the narrow exception we have created. In *Bruton*, the codefendant's confession "expressly implicat[ed]" the defendant as his accomplice. ** * Thus, at the time that confession was introduced there was not the slightest doubt that it would prove "powerfully incriminating." * * * By contrast, in this case the confession was not incriminating on its face, and became so only when linked with evidence introduced later at trial (the defendant's own testimony).

Where the necessity of such linkage is involved, it is a less valid generalization that the jury will not likely obey the instruction to disregard the evidence. Specific testimony that "the defendant helped me commit the crime" is more vivid than inferential incrimination, and hence more difficult to thrust out of mind. Moreover, with regard to such an explicit statement the only issue is, plain and simply, whether the jury can possibly be expected to forget it in assessing the defendant's guilt; whereas with regard to inferential incrimination the judge's instruction may well be successful in dissuading the jury from entering onto the path of inference in the first place, so that there is no incrimination to forget. In short, while it may not always be simple for the members of a jury to obey the instruction that they disregard an incriminating inference, there does not exist the overwhelming probability of their inability to do so that is the foundation of *Bruton*'s exception to the general rule.

Even more significantly, evidence requiring linkage differs from evidence incriminating on its face in the practical effects which application of the *Bruton* exception would produce. If limited to facially incriminating confessions, *Bruton* can be complied with by redaction — a possibility suggested in that opinion itself.* * * If extended to confessions incriminating by connection, not only is that not possible, but it is not even possible to predict the admissibility of a confession in advance of trial. The "contextual implication" doctrine articulated by the Court of Appeals would presumably require the trial judge to assess at the end of each trial whether, in light of all of the evidence, a nontestifying codefendant's confession has been so "powerfully incriminating" that a new, separate trial is required for the defendant. This obviously lends itself to manipulation by the defense — and even without manipulation will result in numerous mistrials and appeals. It might be suggested that those consequences could be reduced by conducting a pretrial hearing at which prosecution and defense would reveal the evidence they plan to introduce, enabling the court to assess compliance with *Bruton ex ante* rather than *ex post*. If this approach is even feasible * * * it would be time consuming and obviously far from foolproof.

One might say, of course, that a certain way of assuring compliance would be to try defendants separately whenever an incriminating statement of one of them is sought to be used. That is not as facile or as just a remedy as might seem. Joint trials play a vital role in the criminal justice system, accounting for almost one-third of federal criminal trials in the past five years. Many joint trials — for example, those involving large conspiracies to import and distribute illegal drugs — involve a dozen or more codefendants. Confessions by one or more of the defendants are commonplace — and indeed the probability of confession increases with the number of participants, since each has reduced assurance that he will be protected by his own silence. It would impair both the efficiency and the fairness of the criminal justice system to require, in all these cases of joint crimes where incriminating statements exist, that prosecutors bring separate proceedings, presenting the same evidence again and again, requiring victims and witnesses to repeat the inconvenience (and sometimes trauma) of testifying, and randomly favoring the last-tried defendants who have the advantage of knowing the prosecution's case beforehand. Joint trials generally serve the interests of justice by avoiding inconsistent verdicts and enabling more accurate assessment of relative culpability — advantages which sometimes operate to the defendant's benefit. Even apart from these tactical considerations, joint trials generally serve the interests of justice by avoiding the scandal and inequity of inconsistent verdicts. The other way of assuring compliance with an expansive *Bruton* rule would be to forgo use of codefendant confessions. That price also is too high, since confessions "are more than merely 'desirable'; they are essential to society's compelling interest in finding, convicting, and punishing those who violate the law." *Moran v. Burbine*, 475 U.S. 412, 426 (1986). * * *

The rule that juries are presumed to follow their instructions is a pragmatic one, rooted less in the absolute certitude that the presumption is true than in the belief that it represents a reasonable practical accommodation of the interests of the state and the defendant in the criminal justice process. On the precise facts of *Bruton*, involving a facially incriminating confession, we found that accommodation inadequate. As our discussion above shows, the calculus changes when confessions that do not name the defendant are at issue. While we continue to apply *Bruton* where we have found that its rationale validly applies, we decline to extend it further. We hold that the Confrontation Clause is not violated by the admission of a nontestifying codefendant's confession with a proper limiting instruction when, as here, the confession is redacted to eliminate not only the defendant's name, but any reference to his or her existence.

In the present case, however, the prosecutor sought to undo the effect of the limiting instruction by urging the jury to use Williams' confession in evaluating respondent's case.* * * On remand, the court should consider whether, in light of respondent's failure to object to the prosecutor's comments, the error can serve as the basis for granting a writ of habeas corpus.* * *

The judgment of the Court of Appeals is reversed, and the case is remanded for further proceedings consistent with this opinion.

So ordered.

JUSTICE STEVENS, with whom JUSTICE BRENNAN and JUSTICE MARSHALL join, dissenting.

* * *

In the edited statement that the jury was instructed not to consider against Marsh, Williams described the conversation he had with Kareem Martin while they were in a car driving to their victims' residence. In that conversation, Martin stated that "he would have to take them out after the robbery." * * * The State's principal witness had testified that Martin and Marsh arrived at the victims' house together. The jury was therefore certain to infer from the confession that respondent had been in the car and had overheard the statement by Martin. Viewed in the total context of the trial evidence, this confession was of critical importance because it was the only evidence directly linking respondent with the specific intent, expressed before the robbery, to kill the victims afterwards. If Williams had taken the witness stand and testified, respondent's lawyer could have cross-examined him to challenge his credibility and to establish or suggest that the car radio was playing so loudly that Marsh could not have overheard the conversation between the two men from the back seat. An acknowledgment of the possibility of such facts by Williams would have done much more to eliminate the certainty beyond a reasonable doubt that Marsh knew about the murder plan than could possibly have been achieved by the later testimony of respondent herself. Moreover, the price respondent had to pay in order to attempt to rebut the obvious inference that she had overheard Martin was to remind the jury once again of what he had said and to give the prosecutor a further opportunity to point to this most damaging evidence on the close question of her specific intent. * * *

The facts in this case are, admittedly, different from those in *Bruton* because Williams' statement did not directly mention respondent. Thus, instead of being "incriminating on its face," * * * it became so only when considered in connection with the other evidence presented to the jury. The difference between the facts of *Bruton* and the facts of this case does not eliminate their common, substantial, and constitutionally unacceptable risk that the jury, when resolving a critical issue against respondent, may have relied on impermissible evidence.

II

* * *

The Court * * * expresses concern that trial judges will be unable to determine whether a codefendant's confession that does not directly mention the defendant and is inadmissible against him will create a substantial risk of unfair prejudice. In most such cases the trial judge can comply with the dictates of *Bruton* by postponing his or her decision on the admissibility of the confession until the prosecution rests, at which time its potentially inculpatory effect can be evaluated in the light of the government's entire case. The Court expresses concern that such a rule would enable "manipulation by the defense" * * * by which the Court presumably means the defense might tailor its evidence to make sure that a confession which does not directly mention the defendant is deemed powerfully incriminating when viewed in light of the prosecution's entire case. As a practical matter, I cannot believe that there are many defense lawyers who would deliberately pursue this high-risk strategy of "manipulating" their evidence in order to enhance the prejudicial impact of a codefendant's confession. * * *

I respectfully dissent.

GRAY v. MARYLAND

523 U.S. 185 (1998)

JUSTICE BREYER delivered the opinion of the Court.

The issue in this case concerns the application of *Bruton v. United States,* 391 U.S. 123 (1968). *Bruton* involved two defendants accused of participating in the same crime and tried jointly before the same jury. One of the defendants had confessed. His confession named and incriminated the other defendant. The trial judge issued a limiting instruction, telling the jury that it should consider the confession as evidence only against the codefendant who had confessed and not against the defendant named in the confession. *Bruton* held that, despite the limiting instruction, the Constitution forbids the use of such a confession in the joint trial.

The case before us differs from *Bruton* in that the prosecution here redacted the codefendant's confession by substituting for the defendant's name in the confession a blank space or the word "deleted." We must decide whether these substitutions make a significant legal difference. We hold that they do not and that *Bruton's* protective rule applies.

I

In 1993, Stacy Williams died after a severe beating. Anthony Bell gave a confession, to the Baltimore City police, in which he said that he (Bell), Kevin Gray, and Jacquin "Tank" Vanlandingham had participated in the beating that resulted in Williams' death. Vanlandingham later died. A Maryland grand jury indicted Bell and Gray for murder. The State of Maryland tried them jointly.

The trial judge, after denying Gray's motion for a separate trial, permitted the State to introduce Bell's confession into evidence at trial. But the judge ordered the confession redacted. Consequently, the police detective who read the confession into evidence said the word "deleted" or "deletion" whenever Gray's name or Vanlandingham's name appeared. Immediately after the police detective read the redacted confession to the jury, the prosecutor asked, "after he gave you that information, you subsequently were able to arrest Mr. Kevin Gray; is that correct?" The officer responded, "That's correct." The State also introduced into evidence a written copy of the confession with those two names omitted, leaving in their place blank white spaces separated by commas. The State produced other witnesses, who said that six persons (including Bell, Gray, and Vanlandingham) participated in the beating. Gray testified and denied his participation. Bell did not testify.

When instructing the jury, the trial judge specified that the confession was evidence only against Bell; the instructions said that the jury should not use the confession as evidence against Gray. The jury convicted both Bell and Gray. Gray appealed.

Maryland's intermediate appellate court accepted Gray's argument that *Bruton* prohibited use of the confession and set aside his conviction. Maryland's highest court disagreed and reinstated the conviction. We granted certiorari in order to consider *Bruton's* application to a redaction that replaces a name with an obvious blank space or symbol or word such as "deleted."

II

In deciding whether *Bruton's* protective rule applies to the redacted confession before us, we must consider both *Bruton*, and a later case, *Richardson v. Marsh*, 481 U.S. 200 (1987), which limited *Bruton's* scope. We shall briefly summarize each of these two cases.

Bruton, as we have said, involved two defendants — Evans and Bruton — tried jointly for robbery. Evans did not testify, but the Government introduced into evidence Evans' confession, which stated that both he (Evans) and Bruton together had committed the robbery. The trial judge told the jury it could consider the confession as evidence only against Evans, not against Bruton.

This Court held that, despite the limiting instruction, the introduction of Evans' out-of-court confession at Bruton's trial had violated Bruton's right, protected by the Sixth Amendment, to cross-examine witnesses. The Court recognized that in many circumstances a limiting instruction will adequately protect one defendant from the prejudicial effects of the introduction at a joint trial of evidence intended for use only against a different defendant. But it said that

> there are some contexts in which the risk that the jury will not, or cannot, follow instructions is so great, and the consequences of failure so vital to the defendant, that the practical and human limitations of the jury system cannot be ignored. Such a context is presented here, where the powerfully incriminating extrajudicial statements of a codefendant, who stands accused side-by-side with the defendant, are deliberately spread before the jury in a joint trial. Not only are the

> incriminations devastating to the defendant but their credibility is inevitably suspect* * * . The unreliability of such evidence is intolerably compounded when the alleged accomplice, as here, does not testify and cannot be tested by cross-examination.

The Court found that Evans' confession constituted just such a "powerfully incriminating extrajudicial statemen[t]," and that its introduction into evidence, insulated from cross-examination, violated Bruton's Sixth Amendment rights.

In *Richardson*, the Court considered a redacted confession. The case involved a joint murder trial of Marsh and Williams. The State had redacted the confession of one defendant, Williams, so as to "omit all reference" to his codefendant, Marsh — "indeed, to omit all indication that anyone other than * * * Williams" and a third person had "participated in the crime." The trial court also instructed the jury not to consider the confession against Marsh. As redacted, the confession indicated that Williams and the third person had discussed the murder in the front seat of a car while they traveled to the victim's house. The redacted confession contained no indication that Marsh — or any other person — was in the car. Later in the trial, however, Marsh testified that she was in the back seat of the car. For that reason, in context, the confession still could have helped convince the jury that Marsh knew about the murder in advance and therefore had participated knowingly in the crime.

The Court held that this redacted confession fell outside *Bruton's* scope and was admissible (with appropriate limiting instructions) at the joint trial. The Court distinguished Evans' confession in *Bruton* as a confession that was "incriminating on its face," and which had "expressly implicat[ed]" *Bruton*. By contrast, Williams' confession amounted to "evidence requiring linkage" in that it "became" incriminating in respect to Marsh "only when linked with evidence introduced later at trial." The Court held that the Confrontation Clause is not violated by the admission of a nontestifying codefendant's confession with a proper limiting instruction when, as here, the confession is redacted to eliminate not only the defendant's name, but any reference to his or her existence.

The Court added: "We express no opinion on the admissibility of a confession in which the defendant's name has been replaced with a symbol or neutral pronoun."

III

Originally, the codefendant's confession in the case before us, like that in *Bruton*, referred to, and directly implicated another defendant. The State, however, redacted that confession by removing the nonconfessing defendant's name. Nonetheless, unlike Richardson's redacted confession, this confession refers directly to the "existence" of the nonconfessing defendant. The State has simply replaced the nonconfessing defendant's name with a kind of symbol, namely the word "deleted" or a blank space set off by commas. The redacted confession, for example, responded to the question "Who was in the group that beat Stacey," with the phrase, "Me, _______, and a few other guys."

And when the police witness read the confession in court, he said the word "deleted" or "deletion" where the blank spaces appear. We therefore must decide a question that *Richardson* left open, namely whether redaction that replaces a defendant's name with an obvious indication of deletion, such as a blank space, the word "deleted," or a similar symbol, still falls within *Bruton's* protective rule. We hold that it does.

Bruton, as interpreted by *Richardson*, holds that certain "powerfully incriminating extrajudicial statements of a codefendant" — those naming another defendant — considered as a class, are so prejudicial that limiting instructions cannot work. Unless the prosecutor wishes to hold separate trials or to use separate juries or to abandon use of the confession, he must redact the confession to reduce significantly or to eliminate the special prejudice that the *Bruton* Court found. Redactions that simply replace a name with an obvious blank space or a word such as "deleted" or a symbol or other similarly obvious indications of alteration, however, leave statements that, considered as a class, so closely resemble *Bruton's* unredacted statements that, in our view, the law must require the same result.

For one thing, a jury will often react similarly to an unredacted confession and a confession redacted in this way, for the jury will often realize that the confession refers specifically to the defendant. This is true even when the State does not blatantly link the defendant to the deleted name, as it did in this case by asking whether Gray was arrested on the basis of information in Bell's confession as soon as the officer had finished reading the redacted statement. Consider a simplified but typical example, a confession that reads "I, Bob Smith, along with Sam Jones, robbed the bank." To replace the words "Sam Jones" with an obvious blank will not likely fool anyone. A juror somewhat familiar with criminal law would know immediately that the blank, in the phrase "I, Bob Smith, along with ________, robbed the bank," refers to defendant Jones. A juror who does not know the law and who therefore wonders to whom the blank might refer need only lift his eyes to Jones, sitting at counsel table, to find what will seem the obvious answer, at least if the juror hears the judge's instruction not to consider the confession as evidence against Jones, for that instruction will provide an obvious reason for the blank. A more sophisticated juror, wondering if the blank refers to someone else, might also wonder how, if it did, the prosecutor could argue the confession is reliable, for the prosecutor, after all, has been arguing that Jones, not someone else, helped Smith commit the crime.

For another thing, the obvious deletion may well call the jurors' attention specially to the removed name. By encouraging the jury to speculate about the reference, the redaction may overemphasize the importance of the confession's accusation — once the jurors work out the reference. * * *

Finally, *Bruton's* protected statements and statements redacted to leave a blank or some other similarly obvious alteration, function the same way grammatically. They are directly accusatory. Evans' statement in *Bruton* used a proper name to point explicitly to an accused defendant. * * * The blank space in an obviously redacted confession also points directly to the defendant, and it accuses the defendant in a manner similar to Evans' use of Bruton's name or to a testifying codefendant's accusatory finger. By way of contrast, the factual statement at issue in *Richardson* — a statement about what others said in the front seat of a car — differs from directly accusatory evidence in this respect, for it does not point directly to a defendant at all.

We concede certain differences between *Bruton* and this case. A confession that uses a blank or the word "delete" (or, for that matter, a first name or a nickname) less obviously refers to the defendant than a confession that uses the defendant's full and proper name. Moreover, in some instances the person to whom the blank refers may not be clear: Although the follow-up question asked by the State in this case eliminated all doubt, the reference might not be transparent in other cases in which a confession, like the present confession, uses two (or more) blanks, even though only one other defendant appears at trial, and in which the trial indicates that there are more participants than the confession has named. Nonetheless, as we have said, we believe that, considered as a class, redactions that replace a proper name with an obvious blank, the word "delete," a symbol, or similarly notify the jury that a name has been deleted are similar enough to Bruton's unredacted confessions as to warrant the same legal results.

IV

The State, in arguing for a contrary conclusion, relies heavily upon *Richardson*. But we do not believe *Richardson* controls the result here. We concede that *Richardson* placed outside the scope of *Bruton's* rule those statements that incriminate inferentially. We also concede that the jury must use inference to connect the statement in this redacted confession with the defendant. But inference pure and simple cannot make the critical difference, for if it did, then *Richardson* would also place outside Bruton's scope confessions that use shortened first names, nicknames, descriptions as unique as the "red-haired, bearded, one-eyed man-with-a-limp," and perhaps even full names of defendants who are always known by a nickname. * * *

* * * *Richardson* must depend in significant part upon the kind of, not the simple fact of, inference. *Richardson's* inferences involved statements that did not refer directly to the defendant himself and which became incriminating "only when linked with evidence introduced later at trial." The inferences at issue here involve statements that, despite redaction, obviously refer directly to someone, often obviously the defendant, and which involve inferences that a jury ordinarily could make immediately, even were the confession the very first item introduced at trial. * * *

Nor are the policy reasons that *Richardson* provided in support of its conclusion applicable here. *Richardson* expressed concern lest application of Bruton's rule apply where "redaction" of confessions, particularly "confessions incriminating by connection," would often "not [be] possible," thereby forcing prosecutors too often to abandon use either of the confession or of a joint trial. Additional redaction of a confession that uses a blank space, the word "delete," or a symbol, however, normally is possible. Consider as an example a portion of the confession before us: The witness who read the confession told the jury that the confession (among other things) said,

Question: Who was in the group that beat Stacey?

Answer: Me, deleted, deleted, and a few other guys.

Why could the witness not, instead, have said:

Question: Who was in the group that beat Stacey?

Answer: Me and a few other guys.

Richardson itself provides a similar example of this kind of redaction. The confession there at issue had been "redacted to omit all reference to respondent — indeed, to omit all indication that anyone other than Martin and Williams participated in the crime," and it did not indicate that it had been redacted.

The *Richardson* Court also feared that the inclusion, within *Bruton's* protective rule, of confessions that incriminated "by connection" too often would provoke mistrials, or would unnecessarily lead prosecutors to abandon the confession or joint trial, because neither the prosecutors nor the judge could easily predict, until after the introduction of all the evidence, whether or not *Bruton* had barred use of the confession. To include the use of blanks, the word "delete," symbols, or other indications of redaction, within *Bruton's* protections, however, runs no such risk. Their use is easily identified prior to trial and does not depend, in any special way, upon the other evidence introduced in the case. * * *

For these reasons, we hold that the confession here at issue, which substituted blanks and the word "delete" for the respondent's proper name, falls within the class of statements to which *Bruton's* protections apply.

The judgment of the Court of Appeals is vacated, and the case is remanded for further proceedings not inconsistent with this opinion.

It is so ordered.

JUSTICE SCALIA, with whom the CHIEF JUSTICE, JUSTICE KENNEDY, and JUSTICE THOMAS join, dissenting.

* * *

* * * Today the Court struggles to decide whether a confession redacted to omit the defendant's name is incriminating on its face or by inference. On the one hand, the Court "concede[s] that the jury must use inference to connect the statement in this redacted confession with the defendant," but later asserts, on the other hand, that "the redacted confession with the blank prominent on its face * * * 'facially incriminat[es]' " him.. The Court should have stopped with its concession: the statement "Me, deleted, deleted, and a few other guys" does not facially incriminate anyone but the speaker. The Court's analogizing of "deleted" to a physical description that clearly identifies the defendant does not survive scrutiny. By "facially incriminating," we have meant incriminating independent of other evidence introduced at trial. Since the defendant's appearance at counsel table is not evidence, the description "red-haired, bearded, one-eyed man-with-a-limp," would be facially incriminating — unless, of course, the defendant had dyed his hair black and shaved his beard before trial, and the prosecution introduced evidence concerning his

former appearance. Similarly, the statement "Me, Kevin Gray, and a few other guys" would be facially incriminating, unless the defendant's name set forth in the indictment was not Kevin Gray, and evidence was introduced to the effect that he sometimes used "Kevin Gray" as an alias. By contrast, the person to whom "deleted" refers in "Me, deleted, deleted, and a few other guys" is not apparent from anything the jury knows independent of the evidence at trial. Though the jury may speculate, the statement expressly implicates no one but the speaker.

Of course the Court is correct that confessions redacted to omit the defendant's name are more likely to incriminate than confessions redacted to omit any reference to his existence. But it is also true — and more relevant here — that confessions redacted to omit the defendant's name are less likely to incriminate than confessions that expressly state it. The latter are "powerfully incriminating" as a class; the former are not so. Here, for instance, there were two names deleted, five or more participants in the crime, and only one other defendant on trial. The jury no doubt may "speculate about the reference," as it speculates when evidence connects a defendant to a confession that does not refer to his existence. The issue, however, is not whether the confession incriminated petitioner, but whether the incrimination is so "powerful" that we must depart from the normal presumption that the jury follows its instructions. I think it is not — and I am certain that drawing the line for departing from the ordinary rule at the facial identification of the defendant makes more sense than drawing it anywhere else.

* * * The Court minimizes the damage that it does by suggesting that "[a]dditional redaction of a confession that uses a blank space, the word 'delete,' or a symbol * * * normally is possible." In the present case, it asks, why could the police officer not have testified that Bell's answer was "Me and a few other guys"? The answer, it seems obvious to me, is because that is not what Bell said. Bell's answer was "Me, Tank, Kevin and a few other guys." Introducing the statement with full disclosure of deletions is one thing; introducing as the complete statement what was in fact only a part is something else. And of course even concealed deletions from the text will often not do the job that the Court demands. For inchoate offenses — conspiracy in particular — redaction to delete all reference to a confederate would often render the confession nonsensical. If the question was "Who agreed to beat Stacey?", and the answer was "Me and Kevin," we might redact the answer to "Me and [deleted]," or perhaps to "Me and somebody else," but surely not to just "Me" — for that would no longer be a confession to the conspiracy charge, but rather the foundation for an insanity defense. To my knowledge we have never before endorsed — and to my strong belief we ought not endorse — the redaction of a statement by some means other than the deletion of certain words, with the fact of the deletion shown. The risk to the integrity of our system (not to mention the increase in its complexity) posed by the approval of such free-lance editing seems to me infinitely greater than the risk posed by the entirely honest reproduction that the Court disapproves.

NOTES

1. Can the *Bruton* problem be avoided by empaneling two separate juries?

Some courts have experimented with empaneling two juries in a single trial to resolve the *Bruton* problem. The jury hearing the case against the non-confessing codefendant is excused when the hearsay statement is introduced or referred to. A judge who tried such a case stated that before the confession was introduced, she excused both juries, and then called the confessing defendant's jury back to hear the confession. In that way, the jurors for the non-confessing defendant would not think that they were missing anything. *See* Santagata, *One Trial, Two Juries — It Works in Extraordinary Cases*, N.Y.L.J., May 11, 1988, p. 1. In *People v. Ricardo B.*, 73 N.Y.2d 228, 538 N.Y.S.2d 796, 535 N.E.2d 1336 (1989), the court held that the use of multiple juries "does not deny defendants their constitutional right to a jury trial or, in the absence of identified prejudice, to due process of law." The Court noted, however, that multiple juries should be used sparingly, because their use "can only magnify the problems inherent in joint trials because of the need to insulate the juries from inadmissible evidence or argument."

2. Does the *Bruton* problem require severance if the case is being tried to the judge?

Bruton has been held inapplicable to a bench trial of joined defendants, because the problem that the Court was concerned about in *Bruton* was the jury's inability to follow the judge's instruction not to use one codefendant's confession against another. *Rogers v. McMackin,* 884 F.2d 252 (6th Cir. 1989).

3. Does the prosecutor in a joint trial assume the risk of one codefendant prejudicing another?

Consider *Toolate v. Borg*, 828 F.2d 571 (9th Cir. 1987), where Toolate's codefendant, Frazier, took the stand and on direct examination shifted the blame to Toolate. He refused to be cross-examined, and the judge gave an instruction to the jury to disregard his testimony. Toolate's motion for a mistrial was denied. The Court held that *Bruton* required a mistrial under these circumstances, since Frazier's testimony was powerfully incriminating against Toolate, and the instruction was insufficient to protect Toolate's right to confrontation. The government argued that mistrial was not required because, unlike in *Bruton* where the prosecutor proffered the codefendant's confession, the prosecutor in *Toolate* had done nothing wrong. The Court rejected this argument and reasoned that the prosecutor who tries defendants jointly assumes certain risks.

> Codefendants * * * have the opportunity to sabotage each other's trial through unethical tactics. For example, if one codefendant comments prejudicially on another's refusal to testify, the latter's conviction must ordinarily be reversed. The result is the same if one codefendant calls the other as a witness, requiring him to invoke his Fifth Amendment privilege in the jury's presence.* * * One codefendant could also produce a mistrial for another by testifying to irrelevant, highly prejudicial matter, such as the latter's prior criminal record. These dangers are inherent in the joint trial process.

* * *

True, the government did not perpetrate the prejudice in this case, as it did in *Bruton,* and could not have prevented it. This is significant because the *Bruton* rule emerged in part to stop the government from using joint trials to circumvent the evidentiary rules that would apply in separate ones. That concern does not exist here. But *Bruton* rests, for good or ill, on the presumed inability of juries to disregard an incriminatory codefendant's confession. In that crucial respect, this case is identical to *Bruton.*

PROBLEM 15-1

Mary Lena, Steven Mabry, and Jan Nineot formed an investment company called the LMN company. The government has charged the three and their company with money laundering and conspiracy to engage in money laundering, alleging that they received money from drug traffickers and invested it in legitimate businesses. The indictment charges that numerous drug dealers were members of the conspiracy. The trial judge has severed Jan Nineot's trial from that of the other two defendants, because Nineot had open heart surgery and was unable to prepare for trial. Lena and Mabry are tried together along with the LMN company.

The government's first witness is an undercover agent, Lieutenant Styple. Unless indicated otherwise, each defense objection is made by all three defendants.

Direct Examination

Prosecution:	Did you have occasion to meet the defendants, Lena and Mabry?
Officer:	Yes, I did.
Prosecution:	How did that come about?
Officer:	A drug dealer named Orleo Basis introduced me to them and told them that I wanted them to invest some money that I earned trafficking in drugs.
Defendants:	(1) Objection. Hearsay.
Prosecution:	The statement is not offered for its truth; it's offered to show how the witness came to meet the defendant.
The court:	(2) ________.
Prosecution:	Why did Orleo introduce you?
Officer:	He and I had some conversations about drug dealing, and he said to me "I know where you can park your money. Mabry and his partners are good."
Defendants:	(3) Objection. Hearsay and Confrontation Clause.

Prosecution: Before you rule, your Honor, can I ask another question?

The court: Yes.

Prosecution: Did Orleo tell you anything about his own relationship to the defendants?

Officer: He told me that he laundered his money with them.

Defendants: (4) Objection. Hearsay and Confrontation Clause.

Prosecution: These are admissible coconspirator statements.

Defendants: Can't be. The witness wasn't conspiring with anybody. Moreover, I want the Court to know that I have issued a subpoena to Orleo. So, he is available to testify, and this is totally improper.

The court: (5) ________.

Prosecution: What happened when Orleo introduced you to the defendants?

Officer: Lena said to me, "We can hide your money, no problem."

Defendants: (6) Objection. Hearsay and Bruton.

Prosecution: It's not hearsay; it's an admission.

Mabry: It's not an admission by Mabry. I repeat. (5) Objection. Hearsay and Bruton.

Prosecution: It's a Rule 801 (d)(2)(E) admission.

The court: (7) ________.

Prosecution: Did you have occasion to speak to Nineot?

Officer: Yes I did.

Prosecution: What did he say?

Officer: He said that Lena was the best launderer in the business.

Defendants: (8) Hearsay and Confrontation. Nineot is now healthy. He can be called as a witness.

Prosecution: His statement is a declaration against interest and admissible against all the defendants.

Defendants: No way.

The court: (9) ________.

Prosecution: In addition, his statement is an admission.

Defendants: (10) Objection. Hearsay and Confrontation. He's not on trial here.

The court: (11) ________.

Prosecution: Were you present at the preliminary hearing in this case?

Officer: Sure, I was.

Prosecution: Were you there when Orleo testified?

Officer: Yes.

Prosecution: Tell the jury what Orleo said about the defendants.

Defendants: (12) Objection. Hearsay and Confrontation.

Prosecution: It's an admission and it's former testimony.

The court:	(13) ________.
Prosecution:	Who made the arrests of the defendants in this case?
Officer:	I did.
Prosecution:	Did Lena say anything after you arrested her?
Officer:	She said, "You've got me, and I'm sorry that I got Mabry involved."
Defendants:	(14) Objection. Hearsay and Confrontation.
Prosecution:	It's an admission and a declaration against interest.
Mabry:	It's not an admission by Mabry, and there is no way to know if Lena will testify.
Prosecution:	It's at least admissible against Lena.
The court:	(15) ________.

Cross-Examination

Defendants:	You say you were at the preliminary hearing when Orleo testified.
Mabry:	Isn't it true he said that he did not believe Mabry was aware of the money laundering?
Prosecution:	(16) Objection. Hearsay. The defendant cannot object to the testimony and then offer it.
The court:	(17) ________.

Chapter 16

SHORTCUTS TO PROOF: JUDICIAL NOTICE AND PRESUMPTIONS

A. JUDICIAL NOTICE

[1] An Overview

As a general matter, for an attorney to prove the facts of the case, the attorney must put on evidence by eliciting the testimony of witnesses and introducing exhibits. The rules of evidence provide procedural safeguards that attempt to ensure the truth of such evidence. In particular, the rules provide the right to cross-examine witnesses and require that an adequate foundation be laid prior to the admission of exhibits. As a result, proving facts with evidence is often costly, time consuming and difficult. In light of the burdens placed upon the parties and the court system, should it be necessary to prove those facts which reasonable people would not dispute?

[2] Federal Rule of Evidence 201

Rule 201. Judicial Notice of Adjudicative Facts

(a) Scope of rule. This rule governs only judicial notice of adjudicative facts.

(b) Kinds of facts. A judicially noticed fact must be one not subject to reasonable dispute in that it is either (1) generally known within the territorial jurisdiction of the trial court or (2) capable of accurate and ready determination by resort to sources whose accuracy cannot reasonably be questioned.

(c) When discretionary. A court may take judicial notice, whether requested or not.

(d) When mandatory. A court shall take judicial notice if requested by a party and supplied with the necessary information.

(e) Opportunity to be heard. A party is entitled upon timely request to an opportunity to be heard as to the propriety of taking judicial notice and the tenor of the matter noticed. In the absence of prior notification, the request may be made after judicial notice has been taken.

(f) Time of taking notice. Judicial notice may be taken at any stage of the proceeding.

(g) Instructing jury. In a civil action or proceeding, the court shall instruct the jury to accept as conclusive any fact judicially noticed. In a criminal case, the court shall instruct the jury that it may, but is not required to, accept as conclusive any fact judicially noticed.

[3] Generally Known Facts

VARCOE v. LEE
181 P. 223 (Cal. 1919)

OLNEY, J.

This is an action by a father to recover damages suffered through the death of his child, resulting from her being run over by an automobile of the defendant Lee, driven at the time by the other defendant, Nichols, the chauffeur of Lee. The automobile was going south on Mission Street in San Francisco and was approaching the crossing of Twenty-First Street when the child, in an endeavor to cross the street, was run over and killed. The cause was tried before a jury, which returned a verdict of $5,000 for the plaintiff. From the judgment upon this verdict the defendants appeal.

* * *

In appellant's reply brief a further question is raised for the first time. As we have stated, the claim of negligence is based upon the speed at which the machine was going. On this point the testimony was sharply conflicting. The plaintiff offered, and the court over the objection of the defendants admitted, a copy of the San Francisco traffic ordinance specifically providing that Mission Street between certain limits, which include the point of accident, is a heavily traveled street and the speed of vehicles shall not exceed 15 miles an hour. When he came to charge the jury, the trial judge instructed them that if they found that the defendant Nichols was running the automobile along Mission Street at the time of the accident at a greater speed than 15 miles an hour, he was violating the city ordinance and also the state Motor Vehicle Act and that such speed was negligence in itself. The trial judge then read to the jury the portion of subdivision "b" of section 22 of the Motor Vehicle Act, which provides that it shall be unlawful to operate a motor "in the business district" of any incorporated city or town at a greater speed than 15 miles an hour, and defines a business district as "territory * * * contiguous to a public highway, which is at that point mainly built up with structures devoted to business." Having read this definition, the court proceeded with its charge as follows:

> That is the situation on Mission Street between Twentieth and Twenty-Second Streets where this accident happened, so that is a business district and the maximum legal rate of speed on that street at the time of the happening of this accident was 15 miles an hour.

In connection with the admission in evidence of the ordinance mentioned, and the giving of the foregoing instructions, it is contended by appellant * * * that the instruction that Mission Street at the point in question was a business district, and therefore the maximum legal speed there was 15 miles an hour was a charge as to a question of fact and an invasion of the province of the jury.

* * *

So far as the record itself goes, there is little to show what the character of Mission Street between Twentieth and Twenty-Second Streets is. The defendant, Nichols, himself, refers to it in his testimony as part of the "downtown district," undoubtedly meaning thereby part of the business district of the city. The evidence shows incidentally that at the scene of the accident there was a drug store, a barber shop, a haberdashery, and a saloon. If there had been any issue or question as to the character of the district, the record in this meagre condition would not justify the taking of the question from the jury, as was undoubtedly done by the instruction complained of.

The actual fact of the matter is, however, that Mission Street between Twentieth and Twenty-Second Streets is a business district within the definition of the Motor Vehicle Act beyond any possibility of question. It has been such for years. Not only this, but its character is known as a matter of common knowledge by anyone at all familiar with San Francisco. Mission Street, from its downtown beginning at the waterfront to and beyond the district of the city known as the Mission, is second in importance and prominence as a business street only to Market Street. The probabilities are that every person in the courtroom at the trial, including judge, jury, counsel, witnesses, parties and officers of the court, knew perfectly well what the character of the location was. It was not a matter about which there could be any dispute or question. If the court had left the matter to the determination of the jury, and they for some inconceivable reason had found that it was not a business district, it would have been the duty of the court to set aside the verdict. We are asked now to reverse the judgment because the court assumed, without submitting to the jury, what could not be disputed, and what he and practically every resident in the county for which the court was sitting knew to be a fact. If error there was, it is clear that, upon the actual fact, there was no prejudice to the defendants.

It would have been much better if counsel for the plaintiff or the trial judge himself had inquired of defendants' counsel before the case went to the jury, whether there was any dispute as to the locality being a business district within the meaning of the state law. There could have been but one reasonable answer, and if any other were given, the matter could have been easily settled beyond any possibility of question. But this was not done, and we are now confronted by the question whether either this court or the trial court can take judicial notice of the real fact.

An appellate court can properly take judicial notice of any matter of which the court of original jurisdiction may properly take notice. * * *

In fact a particularly salutary use of the principle of judicial notice is to sustain on appeal, a judgment clearly in favor of the right party, but as to which there is in the evidence an omission of some necessary fact which is yet indisputable and a matter of common knowledge, and was probably assumed without strict proof for that very reason.* * *

The question, therefore, is: Was the superior court for the city and county of San Francisco * * * entitled to take judicial notice of the character of one of the most important and best-known streets in the city? If it were, the court was authorized to charge the jury as it did.* * *

It should perhaps be noted that the fact that the trial judge knew what the actual fact was, and that it was indisputable, would not of itself justify him in recognizing it. Nor would the fact that the character of the street was a matter of common knowledge and notoriety justify him in taking the question from the jury, if there were any possibility of dispute as to whether or not that character was such as to constitute it a business district within the definition of the statute applicable. If such question could exist, the fact involved — whether the well-known character of the street was sufficient to make it a business district — was one for determination by the jury. But we have in this case a combination of the two circumstances. In the first place, the fact is indisputable and beyond question. In the second place, it is a matter of common knowledge throughout the jurisdiction in and for which the court is sitting.

A consideration of the reasons underlying the matter of judicial notice and its fundamental principles leaves, we believe, but little doubt as to its applicability here. Judicial notice is a judicial short cut, a doing away, in the case of evidence, with the formal necessity for evidence, because there is no real necessity for it. So far as matters of common knowledge are concerned, it is saying there is no need of formally offering evidence of those things, because practically everyone knows them in advance, and there can be no question about them. * * *

The tests, therefore, in any particular case where it is sought to avoid or excuse the production of evidence because the fact to be proven is one of general knowledge and notoriety, is: (1) Is the fact one of common, everyday knowledge in that jurisdiction, which everyone of average intelligence and knowledge of things about him can be presumed to know? and (2) is it certain and indisputable? If it is, it is a proper case for dispensing with evidence, for its production cannot add or aid. On the other hand, we may well repeat, if there is any reasonable question whatever as to either point, proof should be required. Only so can the danger involved in dispensing with proof be avoided. Even if the matter be one of judicial cognizance, there is still no error or impropriety in requiring evidence.

Applying this test to the facts of the case, the matter is not in doubt. The character of Mission Street is as well known to San Franciscans as the character of Spring Street to residents of Los Angeles, or of State Street to residents of Chicago, or of Forty-Second Street to residents of New York, or of F Street to residents of Washington. It is a matter of their every-day common information and experience, and one about which there can be no dispute.

The conclusion follows that the charge of the trial court that Mission Street, between Twentieth and Twenty-Second Streets, was a business district, was not error. The judgment is therefore affirmed.

NOTES

1. What other facts have courts judicially noticed?

Courts have taken judicial notice of many types of facts. *Daubert v. Merrell Dow Pharmaceuticals, Inc.*, 509 U.S. 579 (1993) (noting that theories that are so firmly established as to have attained the status of scientific law, such as the laws of thermodynamics, properly are subject to judicial notice under Fed. R. Evid. 201); *Brennan's Inc. v. Brennan's Restaurant*, L.L.C., 360 F.3d 125 (2d Cir. 2004) (court took judicial notice that a "current Manhattan telephone book lists 184 residences and 20 businesses with the name Brennan"); United States v. Four Million, *Two Hundred Fifty-Five Thousand*, 762 F.2d 895, 904 (11th Cir. 1985) (judicial notice taken, as a "common experience consideration," that Miami had become a center for drug smuggling and money laundering); *In re Holthausen*, 26 N.Y.S.2d 140 (Sup. Ct. 1941) (judicial notice taken that the period of gestation for humans is nine months); *Lloyd v. Cessna Aircraft Co.*, 430 F. Supp. 25 (E.D. Tenn. 1976) (judicial notice taken of a national holiday); *Orantes-Hernandez v. Smith*, 541 F. Supp. 351 (C.D. Cal. 1982) (judicial notice taken that El Salvador was in the midst of a civil war); *In re Waller Creek, Ltd.*, 867 F.2d 228, 238 n.14 (5th Cir. 1989) (judicial notice taken of city ordinance even though never introduced into the record); *United States v. Deckard*, 816 F.2d 426 (8th Cir. 1987) (judicial notice taken of fact that interstate wire communications are transmitted through lines of the Southwestern Bell Telephone System); *Transorient Navigators Co., S.A. v. M/S Southwind*, 788 F.2d 288 (5th Cir. 1986) (judicial notice taken of prevailing interest rates); *United States v. Perez*, 769 F.2d 1336 (9th Cir. 1985) (judicial notice taken that minimum distance between Rota and Guam is 31 nautical miles); *Harcon Barge Co. v. D & G Boat Rentals, Inc.*, 746 F.2d 278 (5th Cir. 1984) (judicial notice taken of practice of clerks of the court with respect to docketing of judgment or order); *Ursic v. Bethlehem Mines*, 719 F.2d 670 (3d Cir. 1983) (judicial notice taken of customary rates charged by attorneys in the court's jurisdiction); *EEOC v. Delta Airlines, Inc.*, 485 F. Supp. 1004 (N.D. Ga. 1980) (judicial notice taken that only women can become pregnant).

2. When is judicial notice not taken?

There are many cases in which courts conclude that it is inappropriate to take judicial notice of disputed facts. *See, e.g.,Weeks v. Scott*, 55 F.3d 1059 (5th Cir. 1995) (proper to refuse to take judicial notice that the HIV virus cannot be transmitted by spitting; this ruling was affirmed, because "whether saliva can transmit the HIV virus is not conclusively established and is not free from reasonable dispute"); *Wooden v. Mo. Pac. R.R..*, 862 F.2d 560 (5th Cir. 1989) (affirming court's refusal to take judicial notice that it was common knowledge in 1955 that inhaling silica dusts could lead to lung disease); *United States v. Simon*, 842 F.2d 552 (1st Cir. 1988) (trial court refused to judicially notice the existence of a university named the University of the West Indies; this was not error, when the only evidence of the University's existence was a telephone number and an address).

It is not enough that the judge herself is aware of the fact. The fact must be generally known, or knowable through ready and accurate sources, to be judicially noticed. *See United States v. Sorrells*, 714 F.2d 1522 (11th Cir. 1983) (error to take judicial notice of informant's reliability based on the Court's personal experience with the informant); *United States v. Lewis*, 833 F.2d 1380 (9th Cir. 1987) (error to take judicial notice of effects of surgery on the defendant, where the judge relied solely on his own personal experience in surgery).

3. Must a court notify the parties that it plans to take judicial notice of a fact?

Basic considerations of procedural due process would seem to require that the parties be given notice of and an opportunity to be heard on the propriety of the taking of judicial notice. Because Rule 201 allows a court to take judicial notice *sua sponte* [201(c)] at any stage in the proceedings [201(f)], there are times when a fact will be judicially noticed as part of the final judgment of the court, with no prior notice having been given to the parties. Rule 201(e) does provide that upon timely request a party is entitled to be heard on the propriety of taking judicial notice; however, there is no provision in Rule 201 which mandates the giving of notification that the court will take judicial notice. The issue of notice is addressed only indirectly through the second sentence of Rule 201(e): "In the absence of prior notification, the request may be made after judicial notice has been taken." A good direction for judges is found in the Explanatory Note to North Dakota Rule of Evidence 201:

> Whenever a judge contemplates taking judicial notice of a fact on his own motion, he should clearly inform the parties of his intention and provide an opportunity for hearing of the issue. If the court fails to give prior notification, it must provide an opportunity for objection after judicial notice has been taken.
>
> The object of this subdivision [Rule 201(e)] is to achieve procedural fairness. No special form of notice is required nor is there a need for a formal hearing. If the parties, in fact, are given notice and an opportunity to be heard, the requirements of this subdivision will have been satisfied.

[4] Judicial Notice in Criminal Cases — Instructing the Jury

UNITED STATES v. BELLO
194 F.3d 18 (1st Cir. 1999)

LIPEZ, CIRCUIT JUDGE:

Jesus Bello appeals his conviction and sentence for assaulting a fellow prisoner in the Metropolitan Detention Center in Guaynabo, Puerto Rico ("MDC-Guaynabo") in violation of 18 U.S.C. § 113(a)(6). Bello claims that the court erred in taking judicial notice of the jurisdictional element of the offense, namely, that MDC-Guaynabo was within the territorial jurisdiction of the United States. * * * We affirm.

I.

At the time of the events in question, Bello was a prisoner confined at MDC-Guaynabo where he worked as a food service orderly, serving food to other prisoners. In this capacity, he was responsible for ensuring that food was distributed to all inmates. The victim of Bello's assault, Domingo Santana-Rosa, was also a prisoner in MDC-Guaynabo. Bello testified that Santana frequently sneaked into the food service line and requested seconds even when all other prisoners had not yet eaten. According to Bello, at around 5:00 PM on July 23, 1996, he refused to serve Santana a second helping at dinner because five other inmates had yet to eat. Santana then told Bello that he and another inmate were "going to crack open [Bello's] head." After making the threat, Santana sat down with several other inmates, including one "Porra." Porra later advised Bello that Santana planned to attack him while Bello was working out in the recreational yard of the prison. Bello testified that he did not report the threat to prison authorities because he feared the repercussions of being labeled a "snitch" by his peers.

On July 25, 1996, at around 11:30 AM, Santana was playing dominoes with other inmates in the recreational yard. Bello noticed Santana's presence, and he became alarmed when he further noticed that the table for playing dominoes, which was ordinarily in the prison's game room, had been moved into the yard where it now stood only a few feet away from where Bello intended to exercise. Bello grabbed a push broom from the corner of the yard and hit the wall of the yard with its handle, stating that it was a good stick for playing baseball. At that point Santana first noticed Bello's presence in the yard, but he continued playing dominoes. Bello removed the handle from the push broom and kept the head. He walked towards Santana and, once behind him, Bello hit him in the back of the head with the push broom head. Santana collapsed, unconscious, and was taken to the hospital where he was operated on to relieve an epidural hematoma (a blood clot under the skull). Santana survived and regained consciousness six days later. The entire incident was captured on videotape.

Bello was indicted on one count of assault within the jurisdiction of the United States (as defined in 18 U.S.C. § 7(3)), in violation of 18 U.S.C. § 113(a)(6). Pursuant to Fed. R. Evid. 201 ("Rule 201"), the government filed a pretrial motion requesting that the court take judicial notice that MDC-Guaynabo is located within Fort Buchanan, a military base on lands "reserved or acquired for the use of the United States, and under the exclusive or concurrent jurisdiction thereof," and thus is within the "special maritime or territorial jurisdiction of the United States." The pretrial motion was accompanied by documentation. This documentation consisted of maps and letters from Army officials documenting the transfer to the Department of Justice/Bureau of Prisons, a letter from the Secretary of War confirming the transfer of the land from Puerto Rico to the federal government, and Puerto Rico legislative acts relating to the transfer. The court deferred making a ruling on the motion until trial.

At trial, the government presented before the jury the testimony of Alma Lopez, the legal advisor to the warden of MDC-Guaynabo, who stated that the land on which the prison was located was owned by the federal Bureau of Prisons and was formerly part of Fort Buchanan, but was transferred to the Bureau by the Department of Defense. After cross-examining Lopez, defense counsel objected to the court taking judicial notice of the fact that MDC Guaynabo is under the exclusive jurisdiction of the United States. Because Lopez was not in a position to authenticate the documentation submitted with the pretrial motion, the documents were not admitted into evidence. However, the court examined the documents outside the presence of the jury and concluded that it could take judicial notice (based on both the testimony in evidence and the documents) that the MDC-Guaynabo facility was within the jurisdiction of the United States. The court announced to the jury that it was taking judicial notice of this jurisdictional fact, but informed them that they were "not required to accept as conclusive any fact that the Court has judicially noticed." The jury was similarly instructed before it retired to deliberate.

* * *

Bello was subsequently sentenced to a term of imprisonment of 120 months, 60 months of which was to be served concurrently with the remainder of a previous federal criminal sentence. * * * This appeal ensued.

II.

Bello argues that the court improperly took judicial notice that the assault occurred "within the special maritime and territorial jurisdiction of the United States." In so doing, the Court took judicial notice of an element of the offense for which Bello was convicted. That fact lends particular significance to the judicial notice issue.

Since the government petitioned, and the trial court ruled, pursuant to Rule 201, we address the conformity of the court's judicial notice determination with that rule. * * * By its terms, Rule 201 applies only to adjudicative facts, and the parties and the court assumed that the jurisdictional element at issue here involved an adjudicative rather than a legislative fact. They assumed correctly. Whether a fact is adjudicative or legislative depends not on the nature of the fact — e.g., who owns the land — but rather on the use made of it (*i.e.*, whether it is a fact germane to what happened in the case or a fact useful in formulating common law policy or interpreting a statute) and the same fact can play either role depending on context. *See* Fed. R. Evid. 201, Advisory Committee's note ("Adjudicative facts are simply the facts of the particular case. Legislative facts, on the other hand, are those which have relevance to legal reasoning and the lawmaking process * * * ."). Where the prison sits is an element of the offense and unquestionably an adjudicative fact, and we review the trial court's decision to take judicial notice under Rule 201for abuse of discretion. * * *

MDC-Guaynabo's location within the jurisdiction of the United States is the "kind of fact" judicially recognizable under Rule 201(b). To qualify for judicial notice, a fact "must be one not subject to dispute in that it is either (1) generally known within the territorial jurisdiction of the trial court or (2) capable of accurate and ready determination by resort to sources whose accuracy cannot reasonably be questioned." * * *

The trial court based judicial notice on both prongs of Rule 201(b), finding that MDC-Guaynabo's presence within the jurisdiction of the United States is of such common knowledge and can be so accurately and readily determined that it cannot reasonably be disputed. By "generally known" Rule 201(b)(1) "must refer to facts which exist in the unaided memory of the populace; if the fact is one that a reasonable person would not know from memory but would know where to find, it falls within subdivision (2)," not (1). * * * Although the label "federal penitentiary" might suggest to the average person that MDC-Guaynabo is under the jurisdiction of the United States, it is unlikely that the "reasonable person" has any familiarity with MDC-Guaynabo at all, let alone its jurisdictional status. Hence, Rule 201(b)(1) cannot supply a basis for judicially noticing the jurisdictional fact in this case.

However, judicial notice was proper pursuant to Rule 201(b)(2), based on "sources whose accuracy cannot reasonably be questioned." Indeed, "[g]eography has long been peculiarly susceptible to judicial notice for the obvious reason that geographic locations are facts which are not generally controversial and thus it is within the general definition contained in Fed. R. Evid. 201(b) * * * ." * * * Moreover, "official government maps have long been held proper subjects of judicial notice." * * * The government submitted to the court official government maps, letters from Army officials, and various legislative acts of Puerto Rico, all tending to show that MDC-Guaynabo was within the jurisdiction of the United States. Although the defense cross-examined Lopez, the legal advisor to the warden of MDC-Guaynabo, suggesting some "dispute" over Lopez's testimony, it is clear from the record that the trial court based its decision to take judicial notice largely on the maps and other documents submitted by the government whose accuracy was not questioned by the defense. To be sure, the trial court's decision to judicially recognize a fact upon which testimony had already been presented and subjected to cross-examination before the jury was unusual. Nonetheless, the existence of independent and undisputed documentary evidence in the form of government maps, official letters, and public laws provided a sufficient basis for judicial notice under Rule 201(b)(2), irrespective of Lopez's testimony.

Concluding that the trial court properly exercised its discretion in taking judicial notice of the jurisdictional fact, we must decide next whether the trial court correctly adhered to Rule 201's procedures for instructing the jury. * * *

The instruction offered by the court was as follows:

> Even though no evidence has been introduced about it in your presence, I believe that the fact that the Metropolitan Detention Center is within a land reserved for the use of the United States and under its exclusive jurisdiction * * * is of such common knowledge and can be so accurately and readily determined from the Metropolitan Detention Center officials that it cannot reasonably be disputed. You may, therefore, reasonably treat this fact as proven even though no evidence has been presented on this point before you.
>
> As with any fact presented in the case, however, the final decision whether or not to accept it is for you to make and you are not required to agree with me.

This instruction was based on a nearly identical instruction from the Eighth Circuit, Model Crim. Jury Instr. 8th Cir. § 2.04 (1989), which is itself based on one of the few opinions treating the application of Rule 201(g), *United States v. Deckard*, 816 F.2d 426, 428 (8th Cir. 1987)). As in *Deckard,* "[h]ere the trial court meticulously followed the command of Rule 201(g). After having instructed the jury generally on presumption of innocence and burden of proof," the court issued an instruction that complied entirely with the dictates of the rule.

Of course, compliance with Rule 201 does not establish that application of Rule 201 in this case was constitutional. The Sixth Amendment of the Constitution guarantees to a criminal defendant the opportunity for a jury to decide guilt or innocence. *See Duncan v. Louisiana*, 391 U.S. 145, 149 (1968). "A necessary corollary is the right to have one's guilt determined only upon proof beyond the jury's reasonable a charged crime." *United States v. Mentz*, 840 F.2d 315, 319 (6th Cir. 1988). "[A] judge may not direct a verdict of guilty no matter how conclusive the evidence." *United Bhd. of Carpenters and Joiners v. United States*, 330 U.S. 395, 408, *United States v. Argentine*, 814 F. 2d 783, 788 (1st Cir. 1987). "A plea of not guilty places all issues in dispute, even the most patent truths." *Mentz*, 840 F.2d at 320.

Nonetheless, there is widespread agreement that Rule 201(g), which makes judicial notice non-conclusive in criminal cases, adequately safeguards the criminal defendant's Sixth Amendment right to a trial by jury. In rejecting a version of 201(g) that would have made judicial notice conclusive in both civil and criminal cases, Congress emphasized that while a "mandatory instruction to a jury in a criminal case to accept as conclusive any fact judicially noticed is inappropriate because contrary to the spirit of the Sixth Amendment right to a jury trial * * * a discretionary instruction in criminal trials," is constitutional. H.R. Rep. 93-650, at 6–7 (1973), U.S. Code Cong. & Admin. News at 7075, 7079–80. Commenting on the original draft of Rule 201 which made the judicial notice non-conclusive in criminal cases (the version ultimately adopted by Congress), the Advisory Committee noted: "The considerations which underlie the general rule that a verdict cannot be directed against the accused in a criminal case seem to foreclose the judge's directing the jury on the basis of judicial notice to accept as conclusive any adjudicative facts in the case. However, this view presents no obstacle to the judge's advising the jury as to a matter judicially noticed, if he instructs them that it need not be taken as conclusive."

Moreover, the few courts that have considered the constitutionality of Rule 201 have reached similar conclusions. In *Mentz*, the Sixth Circuit ruled that "[a] trial court commits constitutional error when it takes judicial notice of facts constituting an essential element of the crime charged, but fails to instruct the jury according to rule 201(g)." Similarly, in *United States v. Jones* 580 F.2d 219, 223–24 (6th Cir. 1978), the court concluded that Rule 201(g) preserves the jury's "traditional prerogative." * * * Accordingly, we conclude that the trial court did not err by taking judicial notice that MDC-Guaynabo was within the "special maritime and territorial jurisdiction of the United States."

* * *

Affirmed.

NOTES

1. May jury knowledge be used as a substitute for proof?

In *United States v. Dior*, 671 F.2d 351 (9th Cir. 1982), the defendant was charged with transporting stolen furs having a value of $5,000 or more. The government introduced evidence of the value of the furs in Canadian currency ($13,690 Canadian dollars) but failed to introduce evidence of the exchange rate between American and Canadian currencies. No request was made by the government to take judicial notice of the exchange rate and to instruct the jury pursuant to Fed. R. Evid. 201(g). In affirming the trial court's judgment of acquittal due to lack of evidence, the Court of Appeals stated: "Proof that the value of the transported property was $5,000 or more is an essential element of a violation of [the statute]* * * In the absence of any proof of value in American dollars, the jury should not be permitted to speculate on this point merely from the Canadian price of the property."

The undeniable fact is that, during deliberation, jurors use their knowledge of the world and apply hundreds of facts which have not been introduced into evidence. The question is how far courts should go in permitting jurors to rely on their own elementary and practical knowledge.

[5] Legislative Facts

[a] Advisory Committee's Note

Advisory Committee's Note [to Rule 201]

56 F.R.D. 183

* * *

Subdivision (a). This is the only evidence rule on the subject of judicial notice. It deals only with judicial notice of "adjudicative" facts. No rule deals with judicial notice of "legislative" facts.* * *

The omission of any treatment of legislative facts results from fundamental differences between adjudicative facts and legislative facts. Adjudicative facts are simply the facts of the particular case. Legislative facts, on the other hand, are those which have relevance to legal reasoning and the lawmaking process, whether in the formulation of a legal principle or ruling by a judge or court or in the enactment of a legislative body.

* * *

The usual method of establishing adjudicative facts is through the introduction of evidence, ordinarily consisting of the testimony of witnesses. If particular facts are outside the area of reasonable controversy, this process is dispensed with as unnecessary. A high degree of indisputability is the essential prerequisite.

Legislative facts are quite different.

* * *

> "[T]he judge is unrestricted in his investigation and conclusion. He may reject the propositions of either party or of both parties. He may consult the sources of pertinent data to which they refer, or he may refuse to do so. He may make an independent search for persuasive data or rest content with what he has or what the parties present * * * [T]he parties do no more than to assist; they control no part of the process." Morgan, *Judicial Notice*, 57 Harv. L. Rev. 269, 270–71 (1944).

This is the view which should govern judicial access to legislative facts.

* * *

[b] Adjudicative vs. Legislative Facts

UNITED STATES v. GOULD
536 F.2d 216 (8th Cir. 1976)

GIBSON, CHIEF JUDGE:

Defendants, Charles Gould and Joseph Carey, were convicted of conspiring to import (Count I) and actually importing (Count II) cocaine from Colombia, South America, into the United States in violation of the Controlled Substances Import and Export Act. * * *

The evidence persuasively showed that defendants and David Miller enlisted the cooperation of Miller's sister, Barbara Kenworthy, who agreed to travel to Colombia with defendants and smuggle the cocaine into the United States by placing it inside two pairs of hollowed-out platform shoes. In May of 1975, defendants and Ms. Kenworthy traveled to Colombia where the cocaine was purchased and packed in Ms. Kenworthy's shoes. The success of the importation scheme was foiled when, upon Ms. Kenworthy's arrival to the Miami airport from Colombia, a customs agent insisted upon x-raying the cocaine-laden shoes. Approximately two pounds of cocaine were discovered and seized by customs officials. Ms. Kenworthy was thereafter interrogated by two agents of the Drug Enforcement Administration (DEA) and she informed them that she had been directed to deliver the cocaine to Miller in Des Moines, Iowa. She finally agreed to cooperate with the agents and make a controlled delivery of a cocaine substitute to Miller. DEA agents in Des Moines then secured a search warrant, the delivery was consummated and Miller was arrested.

Defendants do not challenge the sufficiency of the evidence but contend that the District Court erred in improperly taking judicial notice and instructing the jury that cocaine hydrochloride is a schedule II controlled substance. * * * Schedule II controlled substances, for the purpose of the Controlled Substances Import and Export Act, include the following:

> (a) Unless specifically excepted or unless listed in another schedule, any of the following substances whether produced directly or indirectly by extraction from substances of vegetable origin, or independently by means of chemical synthesis, or by a combination of extraction and chemical synthesis:
>
> * * *
>
> (4) Coca leaves and any salt, compound, derivatives, or preparation of coca leaves, and any salt, compound, derivative, or preparation thereof which is chemically equivalent or identical with any of these substances, except that the substances shall not include decocainized coca leaves or extraction of coca leaves, which extractions do not contain cocaine or ecgonine.

21 U.S.C. § 812 (1970).

At trial, two expert witnesses for the Government testified as to the composition of the powdered substance removed from Ms. Kenworthy's platform shoes at the Miami airport. One expert testified that the substance was comprised of approximately 60 percent cocaine hydrochloride. The other witness stated that the white powder consisted of 53 percent cocaine. There was no direct evidence to indicate that cocaine hydrochloride is a derivative of coca leaves. In its instructions to the jury, the District Court stated: "If you find the substance was cocaine hydrochloride, you are instructed that cocaine hydrochloride is a schedule II controlled substance under the laws of the United States."

We must first determine whether it was error for the District Court to take judicial notice of the fact that cocaine hydrochloride is a schedule II controlled substance. Secondly, if we conclude that it was permissible to judicially notice this fact, we must then determine whether the District Court erred in instructing the jury that it must accept this fact as conclusive.

The first aspect of this inquiry merits little discussion. In *Hughes v. United States*, 253 F. 543, 545 (8th Cir. 1918), this court stated:

> It is also urged that there was no evidence that morphine, heroin, and cocaine are derivatives of opium and coca leaves. We think that is a matter of which notice may be taken. In a sense the question is one of the definition or meaning of words long in common use, about which there is no obscurity, controversy, or dispute, and of which the imperfectly informed can gain complete knowledge by resort to dictionaries within reach of everybody * * *. Common knowledge, or the common means of knowledge, of the settled, undisputed, things of life, need not always be laid aside on entering a courtroom.

It is apparent that courts may take judicial notice of any fact which is "capable of such instant and unquestionable demonstration, if desired, that no party would think of imposing a falsity on the tribunal in the face of an intelligent adversary." IX J. Wigmore, Evidence § 2571, at 548 (1940). The fact that cocaine hydrochloride is derived from coca leaves is, if not common knowledge, at least a matter which is capable of certain, easily accessible and indisputably accurate verification. *See Webster's Third New International Dictionary* 434 (1961). Therefore, it was proper for the District Court to judicially notice this fact.* * *

Our second inquiry involves the propriety of the District Court's instruction to the jurors that this judicially noticed fact must be accepted as conclusive by them. Defendants, relying upon Fed. R. Ev. 201(g), urge that the jury should have been instructed that it could discretionarily accept or reject this fact.* * * It is clear that the reach of rule 201 extends only to adjudicative, not legislative, facts. Fed. R. Ev. 201(a). Consequently, the viability of defendants' argument is dependent upon our characterization of the fact judicially noticed by the District Court as adjudicative, thus invoking the provisions of rule 201(g). In undertaking this analysis, we note at the outset that rule 201 is not all-encompassing. "Rule 201 * * * was deliberately drafted to cover only a small fraction of material usually subsumed under the concept of 'judicial notice.' "

The precise line of demarcation between adjudicative facts and legislative facts is not always easily identified. Adjudicative facts have been described as follows:

> When a court * * * finds facts concerning the immediate parties — who did what, where, when, how, and with what motive or intent — the court * * * is performing an adjudicative function, and the facts are conveniently called adjudicative facts * * * .
>
> Stated in other terms, the adjudicative facts are those to which the law is applied in the process of adjudication. They are the facts that normally go to the jury in a jury case. They relate to the parties, their activities, their properties, their businesses.

2 K. Davis, Administrative Law Treatise § 15.03, at 353 (1958).

Legislative facts, on the other hand, do not relate specifically to the activities or characteristics of the litigants. A court generally relies upon legislative facts when it purports to develop a particular law or policy and thus considers material wholly unrelated to the activities of the parties.

> Legislative facts are ordinarily general and do not concern the immediate parties. In the great mass of cases decided by courts * * * , the legislative element is either absent or unimportant or interstitial, because in most cases the applicable law and policy have been previously established. But whenever a tribunal engages in the creation of law or of policy, it may need to resort to legislative facts, whether or not those facts have been developed on the record.

2 K. Davis, Administrative Law Treatise, *supra* at § 15.03.

Legislative facts are established truths, facts or pronouncements that do not change from case to case but apply universally, while adjudicative facts are those developed in a particular case.

Applying these general definitions, we think it is clear that the District Court in the present case was judicially noticing a legislative fact rather than an adjudicative fact. Whether cocaine hydrochloride is or is not a derivative of the coca leaf is a question of scientific fact applicable to the administration of the Comprehensive Drug Abuse Prevention and Control Act of 1970. 21 U.S.C. § 801 *et seq.* (1970). The District Court reviewed the schedule II classifications contained in 21 U.S.C. § 812, construed the language in a manner which comports with common knowledge and understanding, and instructed the jury as to the proper law so interpreted. It is undisputed that the trial judge is required to fully and accurately instruct the jury as to the law to be applied in a case. * * * When a court attempts to ascertain the governing law in a case for the purpose of instructing the jury, it must necessarily rely upon facts which are unrelated to the activities of the immediate parties. These extraneous, yet necessary, facts fit within the definition of legislative facts and are an indispensable tool used by judges when discerning the applicable law through interpretation. The District Court, therefore, was judicially noticing such a legislative fact when it recognized that cocaine hydrochloride is derived from coca leaves and is a schedule II controlled substance within the meaning of § 812.

Through similar reasoning, this judicially noticed fact simply cannot be appropriately categorized as an adjudicative fact. It does not relate to "who did what, where, when, how, and with what motive or intent," nor is it a fact which would traditionally go to the jury. *See* 2 K. Davis, Administrative Law Treatise, *supra* at § 15.03. The fact that cocaine hydrochloride is a derivative of coca leaves is a universal fact that is unrelated to the activities of the parties to this litigation. There was no preemption of the jury function to determine what substance was actually seized from Ms. Kenworthy at the Miami airport. The jury was instructed that, if it found that the confiscated substance was cocaine hydrochloride, the applicable law classified the substance as a schedule II controlled substance.

It is clear to us that the District Court took judicial notice of a legislative, rather than an adjudicative, fact in the present case and rule 201(g) is inapplicable. The District Court was not obligated to inform the jury that it could disregard the judicially noticed fact. In fact, to do so would be preposterous, thus permitting juries to make conflicting findings on what constitutes controlled substances under federal law.

* * *

The judgment of conviction is affirmed.

NOTES

1. Does the distinction between adjudicative and legislative facts work?

One may question whether the "legislative" fact judicially noticed in *United States v. Gould* really differs from the "adjudicative" facts in *United States v. Bello*. Surely, the distinction between the two types of fact is not as readily apparent to everyone as the court in *Gould* seems to indicate.

2. Why the difference?

The evidence rules impose fairly strict rules with respect to adjudicative facts and no limitations whatsoever on legislative facts. One assumption may be that adjudicative facts, by definition, will have more of an impact on the fate of the parties, whereas legislative facts, while playing a role in determining the outcome of the case, are not as threatening to the parties. *See* Dennis J. Turner, *Judicial Notice and Federal Rule of Evidence 201 — A Rule Ready for Change,* 45 U. Pitt. L. Rev. 181, 182 (1983).

Another assumption may be that courts notice legislative facts all the time and cannot be expected to impose procedural constraints upon all of the matters they may consider in interpreting a statute or a constitution. For example, a court may decide to extend strict liability in tort on the assumption that defendants and their insurers can spread the cost. Or it may decide to expand the attorney-client privilege to protect the communications between low-level corporate agents and corporate counsel, on the assumption that a less generous privilege would deter the free flow of communication necessary to guarantee the attorney's effectiveness. These are factual assumptions that are disputable, yet they are legislative facts and the court is not bound, when making policy choices, to adhere to Rule 201. If the law is to develop, then courts must respond to changed conditions and new ideas, before the conditions and ideas become indisputable.

3. Should notice be required?

Some commentators have taken issue with the position of the Advisory Committee's Note which implies that it is acceptable for courts to take judicial notice of important legislative facts without affording the parties an opportunity to be heard. "Certainly no one would seriously contend that evidence should be taken or argument heard on each of the factual assumptions that might be relevant to establishing or developing a legal rule. But at least when a Judge departs from the theories, evidence, and arguments of the parties to embrace a new approach, we favor participation by the parties. The line between relying upon material facts not addressed by the parties and general background reading may be a fine one. Yet if one has to choose between too much or too little participation by the parties, we would favor the former." Saltzburg, Martin, and Capra, *Federal Rules of Evidence Manual* (9th ed. 2006).

4. May a court take judicial notice of court documents?

A number of cases have considered whether judicial notice can be taken of matters in judicial records. While judicial records are assumed to be accurate, the underlying facts in a judicial record are not beyond dispute. For example, in *Taylor v. Charter Medical Corp.,* 162 F.3d 827 (5th Cir. 1998), a former patient at a residential hospital sued under 42 U.S.C. § 1983 for alleged mistreatment. The defendant argued that it was not a state actor. The plaintiff responded that the court was required to take judicial notice that the defendant's predecessor had been found by another court to be a state actor in an unrelated litigation. The Court rejected this argument, holding that "a court cannot take judicial notice of the factual findings of another court." This is so because "(1) such findings do not constitute facts 'not subject to reasonable dispute' within the meaning of Rule 201; and (2) were it permissible for a court to take judicial notice of a fact merely because it had been found to be true in some other action, the doctrine of collateral estoppel would be superfluous."

The distinction is therefore between the *existence* of judicial records and the truth of the facts recorded in those records. A court can take judicial notice that a pleading was filed or that a judgment was entered. Likewise, a court can take judicial notice that court filings contained certain allegations, or that findings of fact were made by another court. But the truth of these allegations and findings are not subject to judicial notice. Thus, in *Lee v. County of Los Angeles*, 240 F.3d 754 (9th Cir. 2001), a mentally-impaired man was mistakenly arrested in California and extradited to New York as an escaped felon. The Court held it was error to take judicial notice of a waiver of extradition signed by the man and of the transcript of the extradition hearing. The Judge took judicial notice not only of the undisputed facts that an extradition hearing was held, the waiver was signed, and the man purportedly waived his right to challenge extradition, but also of the disputed facts included in the transcript, that the man had informed the hearing Judge and counsel that he was in fact the person sought in New York. In ruling on a Rule 12(b)(6) motion, judicial notice of another Court's opinion may not be for the truth of the facts recited therein but only for the existence of the opinion.

B. PRESUMPTIONS

[1] An Overview

There are propositions that seem logically related to one another and experiences that are so widely shared that judges or legislators believe that they are so routine that attributes may be assumed to be true without proof. There are also propositions which judges and legislators hope are true. The assumption that a properly addressed letter is received by the recipient within a reasonable time after being mailed illustrates a routine experience (which may be less routine today) and a governmental hope. The assumption that a child born during a marriage is the child of the husband and wife arises from a sense both of probability and social desire.

Presumptions are devices that recognize logical or social assumptions. Rebuttable presumptions are assumptions that are made but that may be overcome. They are the subject matter of evidence law. Irrebuttable presumptions are really rules of law and are outside the scope of the rules of evidence.

[2] Federal Rules of Evidence 301 and 302

Rule 301. Presumptions in General in Civil Actions and Proceedings

In all civil actions and proceedings not otherwise provided for by Act of Congress or by these rules, a presumption imposes on the party against whom it is directed the burden of going forward with evidence to rebut or meet the presumption, but does not shift to such party the burden of proof in the sense of the risk of nonpersuasion, which remains throughout the trial upon the party on whom it was originally cast.

Rule 302. Applicability of State Law in Civil Actions and Proceedings

In civil actions and proceedings, the effect of a presumption respecting a fact which is an element of a claim or defense as to which State law supplies the rule of decision is determined in accordance with State law.

[3] The Basic Choice: To Shift the Burden of Persuasion or Not in Civil Cases?

McCANN v. THE GEORGE W. NEWMAN IRREVOCABLE TRUST

458 F.3d 281 (3d Cir. 2006)

SCIRICA, CHIEF JUDGE:

In this appeal from the District Court's final order granting defendants' motion to dismiss for lack of subject matter jurisdiction, the issue is whether plaintiff established diversity of citizenship based on a change of domicile. We will vacate and remand.

I.

A.

On July 6, 1990, George W. Newman established and funded the George W. Newman Irrevocable Trust to acquire and hold property in Secaucus, New Jersey. Newman named as trustees Patricia Theryoung, Marc Joseph, and the National Community Bank, which was later acquired by the Bank of New York. Newman's development company, Allied Junction Corporation, was to develop the property acquired by the trust into a commercial and transportation center. Newman hired William E. McCann as President, Chief Executive Officer, and Director of Operations of Allied Junction Corporation, which later became Secaucus Connection, L.L.C.

A dispute arose between McCann and the Newman Trust over McCann's compensation. Theryoung and the Bank of New York, as trustees, agreed to settle the dispute by granting McCann an equity interest in the development project. Joseph, the third trustee, filed an action in state court to enjoin the other two trustees from entering the proposed agreement with McCann and from granting McCann any interest in trust property.

McCann died in February 2002 while this and related state court actions were pending. McCann's widow, Virginia, filed an action to intervene on behalf of McCann's estate, which the court denied. The court also dismissed all pending actions because Theryoung and the Bank of New York — the trustees who negotiated the agreement granting McCann an interest in the development project — had since resigned.

On December 23, 2004, McCann's estate filed an action in federal court in New Jersey against the Newman Trust and its trustees, seeking to enforce the proposed agreement. The estate asserted subject matter jurisdiction based on diversity, contending McCann had changed his domicile from New Jersey to New Hampshire prior to his death. Defendants filed a motion to dismiss for lack of subject matter jurisdiction under Fed. R. Civ. P. 12(b)(1), contending diversity of citizenship was lacking because all parties were domiciled in New Jersey.

B.

The material facts regarding McCann's domicile are undisputed. In 1969, he and his wife, Virginia, purchased a house in Short Hills, New Jersey, where they resided for over thirty years. In 1990, they purchased a second house in North Hampton, New Hampshire. In June 2000, they sold their New Jersey house and moved their furniture and personal belongings to New Hampshire. Virginia became a full-time resident of New Hampshire, but McCann rented an apartment in Springfield, New Jersey, and continued to live and work in New Jersey during the week. He spent weekends in New Hampshire.

McCann stopped commuting to New Jersey in November 2001, when he stopped receiving a salary from Secaucus Connection, L.L.C. During the three months between November 2001 and his death in February 2002, he traveled to New Jersey four times to attend meetings regarding the development project. He did not use his New Jersey apartment after January, but he did not cancel or break the lease or sublet the apartment.

McCann had ties to both states. He registered to vote in New Jersey in August 2001 and voted in the New Jersey general election on November 6, 2001. He registered to vote in New Hampshire at the end of November, but never actually voted there prior to his death. On July 30, 1999, he obtained a New Hampshire driver's license, but he maintained a New Jersey license, which he renewed after receiving the New Hampshire license. When Virginia became a full-time New Hampshire resident, the McCanns registered and insured all of their personal vehicles in New Hampshire. McCann had use of a company car in New Jersey.

McCann transferred his personal bank accounts to New Hampshire, but maintained a brokerage account in excess of $ 2.6 million in New Jersey. His federal income tax returns filed during his life represented he was a New Jersey resident. But his 2001 federal income tax return, prepared by Virginia and filed after his death, represented he was a New Hampshire resident.

Virginia's application for continued health insurance coverage after McCann's death represented he was a New Jersey resident. McCann's funeral was held in New Jersey, but he was buried in New Hampshire.

C.

On August 8, 2005, the District Court heard oral argument on defendants' motion to dismiss. Neither party requested — and the court did not hold — an evidentiary hearing regarding McCann's domicile. Following oral argument, the District Court dismissed the estate's complaint for lack of subject matter jurisdiction under Fed. R. Civ. P. 12(b)(1). In a letter opinion dated the same date, the court explained, "the burden here rests squarely on Plaintiff to demonstrate by clear and convincing evidence that McCann 1) took up residence in New Hampshire, and 2) intended to remain there." The court concluded the estate had not met this burden and accordingly, had not established McCann changed his domicile to New Hampshire prior to his death.

The estate contends on appeal that the District Court erred in applying a clear and convincing evidence standard of proof, in concluding McCann was not a domiciliary of New Hampshire, and in failing to hold an evidentiary hearing prior to dismissing the complaint.

II.

* * *

III.

A.

Federal district courts are vested with original jurisdiction over civil actions where the matter in controversy exceeds the sum or value of $ 75,000 and is between "citizens of different States." 28 U.S.C. § 1332(a)(1). If a party is deceased, "the legal representative of the estate of a decedent shall be deemed to be a citizen only of the same State as the decedent." § 1332(c)(2).

Several principles guide our analysis of a party's citizenship for purposes of subject matter jurisdiction. The party asserting diversity jurisdiction bears the burden of proof. A party generally meets this burden by proving diversity of citizenship by a preponderance of the evidence.

Citizenship is synonymous with domicile, and "the domicile of an individual is his true, fixed and permanent home and place of habitation. It is the place to which, whenever he is absent, he has the intention of returning." *Vlandis v. Kline*, 412 U.S. 441, 454 (1973). In determining an individual's domicile, a court considers several factors, including "declarations, exercise of political rights, payment of personal taxes, house of residence, and place of business." Other factors to be considered may include location of brokerage and bank accounts, location of spouse and family, membership in unions and other organizations, and driver's license and vehicle registration.

An individual can change domicile instantly. To do so, two things are required: "[h]e must take up residence at the new domicile, and he must intend to remain there." But "[a] domicile once acquired is presumed to continue until it is shown to have been changed." *Mitchell v. United States*, 88 U.S. 350, 353 (1874). This principle gives rise to a presumption favoring an established domicile over a new one.

Here, the estate — the proponent of federal jurisdiction — bore the burden of establishing diversity of citizenship. The District Court required it to carry this burden by proving a change in domicile by clear and convincing evidence. The District Court noted the presumption in favor of an original or former domicile, and explained, "[w]here the proponent of federal jurisdiction is also the party contending that there has been a change of domicile of one of the litigants, the effect of this presumption is to raise the standard of proof which that party must bear."* * * We are not convinced the proper standard is proof by clear and convincing evidence. There are two distinct elements of the burden of proof — the burden of production and the burden of persuasion. * * *

Under Fed. R. Evid. 301, a presumption in a civil case imposes the burden of production on the party against whom it is directed, but does not shift the burden of persuasion. We have interpreted Rule 301 to express the Thayer-Wigmore "bursting bubble" theory of presumptions. *See McKenna v. Pac. Rail Serv.*, 32 F.3d 820, 829–30 (3d Cir. 1994); *id.* at 841 (Mansmann, J., dissenting). Under this theory, "the introduction of evidence to rebut a presumption destroys that presumption, leaving only that evidence and its inferences to be judged against the competing evidence and its inferences to determine the ultimate question at issue." In other words, the presumption shifts the burden of producing sufficient evidence to rebut the presumed fact. Once that burden is met, the presumption "disappears from the case." This view of Rule 301 is widely accepted.

Under Rule 301, the presumption favoring an established domicile places the burden of production on the party alleging a change in domicile, but does not affect the burden of persuasion, which remains throughout with the proponent of federal jurisdiction. Accordingly, the presumption's only effect is to require the party asserting a change in domicile to produce enough evidence substantiating a change to withstand a motion for summary judgment or judgment as a matter of law on the issue.

When the party claiming a new domicile is the opponent of federal jurisdiction, the effect of the presumption in favor of an established claiming a new domicile bears the initial burden of producing sufficient evidence to rebut the presumption in favor of the established domicile. If the party does so, the presumption disappears, the case goes forward, and the party asserting jurisdiction bears the burden of proving diversity of citizenship.

When the party claiming a new domicile is the proponent of federal jurisdiction, the effect of the presumption is less straightforward. One of the parties will bear both burdens — the burden of production regarding domicile and the burden of persuasion regarding federal jurisdiction. The District Court followed other courts in concluding the effect of placing both burdens on one party was to raise the relevant standard of proof. We are not so certain. We believe the effect of placing both burdens on one party is to require the party to initially carry the burden of production to rebut the presumption in favor of an established domicile. If and when the party does so, the presumption falls out of the case and the party is required to carry the burden of persuasion by proving that a change of domicile occurred, creating diversity of citizenship. Whether the party asserting a change of domicile is asserting or contesting federal subject matter jurisdiction, the appropriate standard of proof is preponderance of the evidence.

* * *

We conclude the appropriate standard is preponderance of the evidence. Because of this conclusion, we will vacate the District Court's order applying the clear and convincing evidence standard. We will remand for reconsideration under the preponderance of the evidence standard.

* * *

IV.

For the reasons set forth, we will vacate the judgment of the District Court and remand for further proceedings consistent with this opinion.

NOTES

1. What did common law courts do with presumptions?

See Saltzburg, Martin, and Capra, *Federal Rules of Evidence Manual* (9th ed. 2006)

> There has been substantial disagreement among common law Courts regarding the proper weight to be given a presumption. In some courts, a presumption would place the burden of persuasion on the party opposing the fact presumed to establish its nonexistence, once the party invoking the presumption establishes the basic fact giving rise to it. Thus a presumption under this view operates as a burden-shifting device. In other courts, the presumption vanishes upon the introduction of enough evidence to support a finding of the nonexistence of the presumed fact. The practical difference between these views — known respectively as the Morgan and Thayer views. — is in the quantity and quality of evidence required to overcome the presumption. Under the Morgan view, the opponent of the presumption must establish, by a preponderance of the evidence in a civil case, the nonexistence of the presumed fact. Under the Thayer view, the opponent must merely offer credible evidence sufficient to support a finding contrary to the presumed fact in order to "burst" the presumption and take it out of the case. The Thayer view, which is the view adopted in Rule 301, has also been described as the "bursting bubble" theory. The theory is that the presumption ceases to exist when contrary evidence as to the presumed fact is introduced.

2. How does the Federal Rule treat presumptions?

Federal Rule 301 provides that a presumption imposes on the party against whom it is directed the burden of going forward with evidence to rebut the presumption. But the burden of persuasion remains with the party on whom it was originally cast, despite an Advisory Committee preference for shifting the burden. The Advisory Committee was of the view that a presumption would have too slight an effect if it merely served to shift the burden of going forward. But Congress rejected this concern. As adopted, Rule 301 operates merely as a procedural device to shift the burden of producing evidence, exposing the opponent of the presumption to the risk of an adverse result on a directed verdict if he fails to present enough evidence to support a finding of the nonexistence of the presumed fact. *See, e.g., Valance v. Wisel,* 110 F.3d 1269 (7th Cir. 1997) (warrantless searches are presumptively unreasonable; but it was error in this civil rights action to hold that the defendant police officer had the burden of proving that the challenged warrantless search was reasonable; Rule 301 shifts the burden of production, not the burden of persuasion, which remained in this case on the plaintiff).

3. When does Rule 301 apply?

Rule 301 applies to presumptions generally, but it does not override statutory presumptions, constitutionally required presumptions, or even judge-made law in admiralty and maritime cases. Thus, in *United States v. City of Chicago*, 411 F. Supp. 218 (N.D. Ill. 1976), the district judge held that the city defendants failed to establish the validity of certain promotion examinations that had a disproportionate impact upon Black and Hispanic candidates for patrolman and sergeant positions. The judge noted that Rule 301 has no application in suits under the Civil Rights Act of 1964 because such suits are cases in which an Act of Congress allocates the burden of proof. The judge indicated regret at using the word presumption at all in an earlier opinion.

In some instances, an agency may be authorized to determine the effect of a presumption. In *American Coal Co. v. Benefits Review Bd.*, 738 F.2d 387 (10th Cir. 1984), the Court affirmed an award of benefits to an employee claiming a black lung illness. It rejected the employer's argument that Rule 301 governed administrative proceedings and found that Congress delegated to the Secretary of Labor authority to designate how the presumptions set forth in the statute could be rebutted.

4. How much rebuttal evidence is required for the presumption to vanish?

In *Sinatra v. Heckler*, 566 F. Supp. 1354 (E.D. N.Y. 1983), the district court concluded that to rebut the presumption that a notice of reconsideration is received five days after it is dated, the claimant must adduce evidence that would be sufficient to overcome a directed verdict. In *In re Dodd*, 82 B.R. 924 (Bankr. N.D. Ill. 1987), the court reasoned that a party may rebut a presumption by introducing evidence which would support a finding of the nonexistence of the presumed fact.

[4] Presumptions in Criminal Cases

COUNTY COURT OF ULSTER v. ALLEN
442 U.S. 140 (1979)

MR. JUSTICE STEVENS delivered the opinion of the Court.

A New York statute provides that, with certain exceptions, the presence of a firearm in an automobile is presumptive evidence of its illegal possession by all persons then occupying the vehicle. * * *

Four persons, three adult males (respondents) and a 16-year-old girl (Jane Doe, who is not a respondent here), were jointly tried on charges that they possessed two loaded handguns, a loaded machinegun, and over a pound of heroin found in a Chevrolet in which they were riding when it was stopped for speeding on the New York Thruway shortly after noon on March 28, 1973. The two large-caliber handguns, which together with their ammunition weighed approximately six pounds, were seen through the window of the car by the investigating police officer. They were positioned crosswise in an open handbag on either the front floor or the front seat of the car on the passenger side where Jane Doe was sitting. Jane Doe admitted that the handbag was hers. The machinegun and the heroin were discovered in the trunk after the police pried it open. The car had been borrowed from the driver's brother earlier that day; the key to the trunk could not be found in the car or on the person of any of its occupants, although there was testimony that two of the occupants had placed something in the trunk before embarking in the borrowed car. The jury convicted all four of possession of the handguns and acquitted them of possession of the contents of the trunk.

Counsel for all four defendants objected to the introduction into evidence of the two handguns, the machinegun, and the drugs, arguing that the State had not adequately demonstrated a connection between their clients and the contraband. The trial court overruled the objection, relying on the presumption of possession created by the New York statute. Because that presumption does not apply if a weapon is found "upon the person" of one of the occupants of the car, the three male defendants also moved to dismiss the charges relating to the handguns on the ground that the guns were found on the person of Jane Doe. Respondents made this motion both at the close of the prosecution's case and at the close of all evidence. The trial judge twice denied it, concluding that the applicability of the "upon the person" exception was a question of fact for the jury.

At the close of the trial, the judge instructed the jurors that they were entitled to infer possession from the defendants' presence in the car. He did not make any reference to the "upon the person" exception in his explanation of the statutory presumption, nor did any of the defendants object to this omission or request alternative or additional instructions on the subject.

* * *

Inferences and presumptions are a staple of our adversary system of factfinding. It is often necessary for the trier of fact to determine the existence of an element of the crime — that is, an "ultimate" or "elemental" fact — from the existence of one or more "evidentiary" or "basic" facts.* * * The value of these evidentiary devices, and their validity under the Due Process Clause, vary from case to case, however, depending on the strength of the connection between the particular basic and elemental facts involved and on the degree to which the device curtails the factfinder's freedom to assess the evidence independently. Nonetheless, in criminal cases, the ultimate test of any device's constitutional validity in a given case remains constant: the device must not undermine the factfinder's responsibility at trial, based on evidence adduced by the State, to find the ultimate facts beyond a reasonable doubt.* * *

The most common evidentiary device is the entirely permissive inference or presumption, which allows — but does not require — the trier of fact to infer the elemental fact from proof by the prosecutor of the basic one and which places no burden of any kind on the defendant.* * * In that situation the basic fact may constitute *prima facie* evidence of the elemental fact.* * * When reviewing this type of device, the Court has required the party challenging it to demonstrate its invalidity as applied to him.* * * Because this permissive presumption leaves the trier of fact free to credit or reject the inference and does not shift the burden of proof, it affects the application of the "beyond a reasonable doubt" standard only if, under the facts of the case, there is no rational way the trier could make the connection permitted by the inference. For only in that situation is there any risk that an explanation of the permissible inference to a jury, or its use by a jury, has caused the presumptively rational factfinder to make an erroneous factual determination.

A mandatory presumption is a far more troublesome evidentiary device. For it may affect not only the strength of the "no reasonable doubt" burden but also the placement of that burden; it tells the trier that he or they must find the elemental fact upon proof of the basic fact, at least unless the defendant has come forward with some evidence to rebut the presumed connection between the two facts.* * * In this situation, the Court has generally examined the presumption on its face to determine the extent to which the basic and elemental facts coincide.* * * To the extent that the trier of fact is forced to abide by the presumption, and may not reject it based on an independent evaluation of the particular facts presented by the State, the analysis of the presumption's constitutional validity is logically divorced from those facts and based on the presumption's accuracy in the run of cases. It is for this reason that the Court has held it irrelevant in analyzing a mandatory presumption, but not in analyzing a purely permissive one, that there is ample evidence in the record other than the presumption to support a conviction.

* * *

The trial judge's instructions make it clear that the presumption was merely a part of the prosecution's case, that it gave rise to a permissive inference available only in certain circumstances, rather than a mandatory conclusion of possession, and that it could be ignored by the jury even if there was no affirmative proof offered by defendants in rebuttal. The judge explained that possession could be actual or constructive, but that constructive possession could not exist without the intent and ability to exercise control or dominion over the weapons. He also carefully instructed the jury that there is a mandatory presumption of innocence in favor of the defendants that controls unless it, as the exclusive trier of fact, is satisfied beyond a reasonable doubt that the defendants possessed the handguns in the manner described by the judge. In short, the instructions plainly directed the jury to consider all the circumstances tending to support or contradict the inference that all four occupants of the car had possession of the two loaded handguns and to decide the matter for itself without regard to how much evidence the defendants introduced.

* * *

III

As applied to the facts of this case, the presumption of possession is entirely rational.

[Concurring and dissenting opinions omitted.]

NOTES

1. Why is there no federal rule on presumptions for criminal cases?

The Supreme Court approved a rule and submitted it to Congress in 1972, but Congress declined to enact the rule, which read as follows:

Rule 303. Presumptions in Criminal Cases

(a) Scope. Except as otherwise provided by Act of Congress, in criminal cases, presumptions against an accused, recognized at common law or created by statute, including statutory provisions that certain facts are *prima facie* evidence of other facts or of guilt, are governed by this rule.

(b) Submission to jury. The judge is not authorized to direct the jury to find a presumed fact against the accused. When the presumed fact establishes guilt or is an element of the offense or negatives a defense, the judge may submit the question of guilt or of the existence of the presumed fact to the jury, if, but only if, a reasonable juror on the evidence as a whole, including the evidence of the basic facts, could find guilt or the presumed fact beyond a reasonable doubt. When the presumed fact has a lesser effect, its existence may be submitted to the jury if the basic facts are supported by substantial evidence, or are otherwise established, unless the evidence as a whole negatives the existence of the presumed fact.

(c) Instructing the jury. Whenever the existence of a presumed fact against the accused is submitted to the jury, the judge shall give an instruction that the law declares that the jury may regard the basic facts as sufficient evidence of the presumed fact but does not require it to do so. In addition, if the presumed fact establishes guilt or is an element of the offense or negatives a defense, the judge shall instruct the jury that its existence must, on all the evidence, be proved beyond a reasonable doubt.

The concern in Congress was over the constitutionality of the rule. Presumptions in criminal cases, as the *Allen* opinion illustrates, are affected by the constitutional rule that the prosecution must prove all elements of crimes charged against a defendant under *In re Winship*, 397 U.S. 358 (1970). *Winship* spawned a line of Supreme Court cases — *e.g.*, *Mullaney v. Wilbur*, 421 U.S. 684 (1975), and *Patterson v. New York*, 432 U.S. 197 (1977) — that address the question when a burden of persuasion may be placed on a defendant. It should suffice here to note that presumptions are constitutionally suspect when they appear to conflict with a constitutionally mandated burden on the state of proving all elements of the crime beyond a reasonable doubt.

In *Sandstrom v. Montana*, 442 U.S. 510 (1979), the Supreme Court held that an instruction to the jury in a homicide case that "the law presumes that a person intends the ordinary consequences of his voluntary acts" violated the Constitution because it may have removed from the prosecution some of its burden to prove beyond a reasonable doubt all elements of the crime charged. Just as Justice Stevens did in *Allen*, the *Sandstrom* Court examined exactly what the trial judge told the jury before concluding that it could not know how a reasonable juror would have understood the instruction and therefore could not say that the jury might not have understood it to be binding.

After *Allen*, an instruction as to a permissive inference is unlikely to raise a constitutional problem as long as the inference is rational.

2. Do instructions on permissive inferences in criminal cases have any effect?

There is little, if any, empirical evidence as to the effect on jurors of judicial instructions regarding permissive inferences. Some defense lawyers believe that when a jury hears a judge single out a piece of evidence for an instruction, the jury cannot help but understand that the judge has placed some emphasis on that evidence. A permissive inference instruction is a kind of comment by the judge on evidence.

The Supreme Court also sent to Congress another rule (Proposed Rule 105) that was rejected on the ground that it was a rule of procedure, not evidence. It read as follows:

> After the close of the evidence and arguments of counsel, the judge may fairly and impartially sum up the evidence and comment to the jury upon the weight of the evidence and the credibility of the witnesses, if he also instructs the jury that they are to determine for themselves the weight of the evidence and the credit to be given to the witnesses and that they are not bound by the judge's summation or comment.

Although the rule was rejected as more procedural than evidentiary, it does restate inherent powers that federal judges have but exercise rarely. Many state courts are far more restricted in the power to comment or to sum up the evidence.

Federal judges have the power to sum up the evidence and to comment upon it. Many state judges have less power. *See* Saltzburg, *The Unnecessarily Expanding Role of the American Trial Judge*, 64 Va. L. Rev. 1 (1978).

PROBLEM 16-1

RCT Corporation, an emerging leader in cable television, signed a contract with BBG Corporation, another cable leader, that provided that RCT could purchase all of BBG's assets for $2.5 billion provided the deal was commenced within 60 days of the signing of the contract. The parties provided in their contract that should BBG breach the contract, RCT could sue for specific performance and also seek liquidated damages for the breach. The liquidated damages were specified to be 1/10 of 1% of the market value of BBG's outstanding stock on the day of the breach. The contract provided that it could be amended only in one or more writings in which each party indicates its assent to amend. RCT claims that it tendered $2.5 billion 70 days after the original contract was signed. BBG rejected the tender, claiming that the original contract was invalid and the payment came 10 days too late even if the contract was valid. RCT sues to enforce the contract, alleging that the contract was valid and the parties extended the contract by 10 days one day before the 60 day period was to expire.

At a hearing on joint motions for summary judgment, the parties engage in the following colloquy with the trial judge.

Judge:	Why do you claim the original contract was invalid?
BBG:	It was signed by Max Mava, who had no authority to sign.
Judge:	What is the evidence before me that he had no authority?
BBG:	We have proffered our annual report, which is filed with the SEC, and you will see that Max Mava is not listed as an officer or director of the company. We ask you to take judicial notice of that fact.
RCT:	(1) Objection. The fact that he is not listed does not mean that he had no authority to sign.
Judge:	(2) __________.
Judge:	What is the dispute about the extension?
BBG:	We claim that the extension was never agreed to.

RCT: It was, your Honor. We have provided you with a letter from our company President to BBG dated two days before the 60 day period was to expire, stating that we wanted to extend, and a letter from BBG's President to us, dated on the date the contract was to expire, saying, "I'm in agreement with what we proposed in our telephone conversation." It is clear from the circumstances that the BBG letter referred to the extension and we ask you to take judicial notice of that.

BBG: (3) Objection. This is not a proper subject of judicial notice.

Judge: (4) ________.

Judge: Are the parties agreed that the payment was made 70 days after the contract was signed.

BBG: We do not agree with that.

Judge: Why not?

BBG: We have an affidavit from our President that we did not receive the tender until 71 days after the contract was signed.

Judge: What about that?

RCT: We have an e-mail that we printed out from the bank that wired the money saying that it wired it on the 70th day, and we ask the court to take judicial notice that the money was wired on that day.

BBG: (5) Objection. This is not a proper subject for judicial notice.

Judge: (6) ________.

Judge: There is another problem I see here. I required all evidence issues to be raised in memoranda and to be filed a week ago. I have before me a request for judicial notice by RCT regarding the e-mail, but BBG alleges that the request was made too late. What is BBG's claim?

BBG: The date stamp of the Clerk's office shows that RCT filed a day late. The court may take judicial notice of that fact.

RCT: (7) We think that the date stamp may have been defective; we are pretty sure we filed on time. We object to judicial notice.

Judge: (8) ________.

Judge: What about damages? If I find that BBG breached, are you in agreement on the damages?

BBG: Absolutely not, your Honor.

Judge: Why not?

BBG: We disagree on the market value of the shares.

RCT: This is ridiculous. The number of outstanding shares is easily ascertainable by looking at the NASDAQ market figures on the day of the breach. The court surely can take judicial notice of those figures. We can provide you with the Wall Street Journal, Barron's, Bloomberg. They all say the same thing.

BBG: (9) Objection. Our experts will testify that the market overvalued the shares.

Judge: (10) __________.

PROBLEM 16-2

Assume that, as part of its response to domestic terrorism, (A) Congress enacts legislation that makes members or supporters of organizations responsible for terrorist acts that injure people or property personally liable for the acts of the organizations or any of its members, provided that they knew or should have known that the organization intended to injure people or property and provided financial or other assistance to the organization; (B) the legislation provides that "there shall be a presumption that a person who voluntarily joins or supports an organization knew or should have known what the organization intended to do"; (C) and the legislation further provides that "if an organization is designated a terrorist organization by the Attorney General, the law shall conclusively presume that any person who provided financial or other assistance to the organization knew what it intended to do, unless such person demonstrates that he or she provided such support prior to the Attorney General's designation."

The estate of Fran Geomy, who was killed in a terrorist bombing of a federal building, has sued Jay Peedle, an alleged member of the "Anti-Capitalist Forces" (ACF), and Bay Driny and Clay Easmer, two alleged members of the "Bash America Now" (BAN) group, alleging that the two groups were responsible for the bombing. The Anti-Capitalist Forces have not been named a terrorist organization. The Attorney General named BAN as a terrorist organization on the first day of this year, just a week before Fran was killed.

During the trial, the Geomy estate offered evidence that Jay Peedle wrote two checks totaling $1,000 to the ACF during the year before Fran was killed. Peedle did not dispute that the ACF was involved in the bombing, but he took the stand and testified that he did not know when he contributed that the group intended to injure people or property. The estate offered testimony by coworkers of Peedle that he told them before the bombing that he was contributing to an organization that was going to be heard from in a very loud way, and that he offered coworkers ACF recruiting material which offered praise for "individuals like Tim McVeigh" who do not hesitate to act. At the charging conference, the following occurs:

Judge: What do I tell the jury about the presumption?

Estate: I think you should tell them that, since the fact that Peedle contributed to the ACF is not disputed, they must find that he knew or should have known that it intended to injure people or property.

Peedle: (1) Objection. He said that he did not know.

Estate: But, that's not consistent with what he told his coworkers or with the literature he distributed. We think that the presumption prevails here.

Judge: (2) _________.

During the trial, the plaintiff offered evidence of a check from Easmer to BAN dated weeks after the designation by the Attorney General. Easmer took the stand and testified that he had no idea that BAN intended to injure people or property, and he also called his minister to testify that Easmer had talked with him about the contribution and believed that BAN was an environmental group that denounced violence. At the charging conference, the following occurs:

Judge: What do I tell the jury about the presumption?

Easmer: Nothing. Don't say anything. He testified and his minister testified that he had no idea that people or property would be injured.

Estate: We think you should tell them that it must find that Easmer knew or should have known that the organization intended to injure people or property.

Judge: Why?

Estate: Because that's what the statute requires.

Easmer: (3) Objection. That's not what the statute means.

Judge: (4) _________.

During the trial, the plaintiff offered testimony of a former officer of BAN that Drimy contributed money to the organization after it was designated a terrorist organization. Drimy took the stand in his own defense and admitted contributing money to the organization, but testified that he gave it prior to the Secretary's designation. During the trial, the plaintiff offered testimony of a former officer of BAN that Drimy contributed money to the organization after it was designated a terrorist organization. Drimy took the stand in his own defense and admitted contributing money to the organization and writing the check on the day it was dated, but testified that he gave it prior to the Secretary's designation and that he was unaware that BAN intended to injure people or property. At the charging conference, the following occurs:

Judge: What do I tell the jury about the presumption?

Drimy: Nothing. Don't say anything. He said that he contributed before the designation. So there should be no presumption.

Estate: We think you should tell them that it must find that Drimy knew or should have known that the organization intended to injure people or property.

Judge:	Why?
Estate:	Because he made his contribution after the designation.
Drimy:	(5) Objection. The evidence is in dispute about that.
Judge:	(6) __________.

Chapter 17

IMPEACHMENT

A. INTRODUCTION

Impeachment is the process of discrediting a witness. This Chapter will cover ten modes for impeaching the witness. The first four are the elements of competency: oath, perception, recall, and communication. The next three cover the different ways to impeach the witness's character for truthfulness. These include impeachment by convictions, prior bad acts, and calling a character witness to say the first witness is a liar. The next two, prior inconsistent statements and contradiction, deal with inconsistencies in the witness's testimony either with his own statements or with the statements of another. The tenth mode involves showing that the witness is biased and should not be believed. This Chapter will also cover rehabilitation of the witness after impeachment. Finally, the Chapter will consider the possibility of impeaching a hearsay declarant.

Impeachment may occur in two different ways: intrinsic and extrinsic. Impeachment is intrinsic when the facts discrediting the witness are elicited from the witness during cross-examination. A typical question might be "have you been convicted of perjury?" The questioner must have a good faith basis for the inquiry. Some of the impeachment modes are limited to intrinsic evidence.

Extrinsic impeachment (or impeachment by extrinsic evidence) occurs when the facts discrediting the witness come from sources other than the witness, such as documents or other witnesses. *United States v. McNeill*, 887 F.2d 448, 453 (3d Cir. 1989) (noting "[e]xtrinsic evidence is evidence offered through other witnesses, rather than through cross-examination of the witness himself or herself"). If, for example, a witness has denied being convicted of perjury, the party seeking to impeach the witness may offer an authenticated copy of the judgment rendered in a perjury prosecution. Such evidence contradicts the witness's denial. It is generally said that a party may not put on extrinsic evidence to prove a collateral matter. What this really means is that the court finds that the delay and confusion caused by introducing extrinsic evidence is not worth the impeachment, and so excludes the extrinsic evidence under Rule 403.

B. IMPEACHING YOUR OWN WITNESS: THE VOUCHING RULE AND ITS REJECTION BY THE FEDERAL RULES OF EVIDENCE

[1] The Vouching Rule at Common Law

The common-law rule was that a party could not impeach the party's own witness. The rationale was that the party calling the witness vouched for the truth of what the witness said. But the voucher rule never made much sense, because as a practical matter, parties must take the witnesses as they find them. They have little control over the attitude of a particular witness.

Because of the harshness that resulted from strict application of the vouching rule, numerous exceptions, distinctions, and qualifications developed. Some courts allowed a party to impeach their own witness if they could show that they were surprised by the witness's testimony and that substantial harm would result. Additionally, some courts allowed a party to present evidence to contradict their own witness, in effect, impeachment by extrinsic evidence. Today the vouching rule has been virtually abandoned — as seen below in Fed. R. Evid. 607. Instead, courts deal with what they perceive as abuses of the impeachment rules as those abuses arise.

[2] Illustration

There is a two-car accident. Plaintiff drove the first car and defendant drove the second. Defendant's passenger was M. Lover. During discovery, both the defendant and Lover testified during depositions that the plaintiff ran a red light.

Plaintiff calls Lover as a witness during plaintiff's case-in-chief.

Plaintiff:	State your name.
Witness:	M. Lover.
Plaintiff:	Were you in defendant's car at the time of the accident?
Witness:	Yes.
Plaintiff:	Did you see it happen?
Witness:	Yes.
Plaintiff:	What did you see?
Witness:	The plaintiff ran the red light.
Plaintiff:	Isn't it true that you are married to someone other than defendant? Won't you say anything that defendant wants to assure that he does not disclose the true nature of your relationship?
Defendant:	Objection! The plaintiff is impeaching his own witness.
Plaintiff:	__________.
The court:	__________.

[3] Federal Rule of Evidence 607

Rule 607. Who May Impeach.

The credibility of a witness may be attacked by any party, including the party calling the witness.

NOTES

1. Are surprise and substantial harm prerequisites to impeaching your own witness?

"At common law, the party calling a witness at trial could not impeach his credibility unless the party could show both surprise and substantial harm. * * * But Rule 607 of the Federal Rules of Evidence allows impeachment of one's own witness." *United States v. Dennis*, 625 F.2d 782, 795 n. 6 (8th Cir. 1980).

2. Are there limits to Rule 607?

Although the language of the rule is broad and, standing alone, would suggest that any party may attack any witness's credibility, the other rules we examine in this chapter place limits on certain kinds of impeachment. Rule 403 may serve as a limit on some impeachment, and the trial judge retains discretion under Rule 611(a) to protect a witness from unfair embarrassment or harassment.

In *United States v. Domina*, 784 F.2d 1361 (9th Cir. 1986), the court upheld a bank robbery conviction, as it approved a limitation on questions concerning a government witness's drug use. It observed that the defendant's confrontation right to question witnesses is "subject to the broad discretion of a trial judge to preclude harassment or unduly prejudicial interrogation," and that "the issue of narcotics use must be handled with some sensitivity because it can result in unnecessary prejudice and hostility toward a witness."

3. If a party wishes to get otherwise inadmissible impeachment evidence before the jury, may that party call a witness solely for impeachment?

There are a number of situations in which evidence is inadmissible to prove a fact in a case, but is nonetheless admissible to impeach a witness. There is therefore a danger that a party might call a witness not to try to prove something within the rules, but only to "impeach" that witness with otherwise inadmissible evidence. The most common example is where a witness has made a statement before trial that would be inconsistent with what the party knows he will say on the stand — such as, a witness in a criminal case previously told a police officer that he saw the defendant commit the crime, but now states that, if called, he will say that he did not see anything at the time of the crime. That prior statement would be admissible only to impeach the witness and not to prove that the defendant committed the crime. *See* Fed. R.Evid. 801(d)(1)(A) (providing that a witness's inconsistent statements are admissible for their truth but only if they were made under oath at a formal proceeding). But the language of Rule 607 would appear to allow the prosecutor to call that witness, knowing that the witness will give testimonial favorable to the defendant, and then to "impeach" the witness with the prior inconsistent statement that implicates the defendant. This practice would be an obvious attempt to evade the rule excluding hearsay, as there would appear to be no good faith reason for calling a witness when, on direct examination, you know that they will give testimony that the defendant is not guilty. The explanation that it is necessary to "impeach" unfavorable witnesses is easily answered by the fact that if impeachment were all that was going on, it would have been better not to call the witness in the first place. As one Court put it: "The maximum legitimate effect of the impeaching testimony can never be more than the cancellation of the adverse answer." *United States v. Crouch*, 731 F.2d 621, 623 (9th Cir. 1984).

Yet despite the broad language of Rule 607, Courts do not permit a party to call a witness solely to impeach with otherwise inadmissible evidence. In *United States v. Morlang*, 531 F.2d 183 (4th Cir. 1975), the Court noted:

> While it is the rule in this circuit that a party calling a witness does not vouch for his credibility, it has never been the rule that a party may call a witness where his testimony is known to be adverse for the purpose of impeaching him. To so hold would permit the government, in the name of impeachment, to present testimony to the jury by indirection, which would not otherwise be admissible.
>
> * * *
>
> The overwhelming weight of authority is, however, that impeachment by prior inconsistent statement may not be permitted where employed as a mere subterfuge to get before the jury evidence not otherwise admissible.
>
> * * *
>
> We must be mindful of the fact that prior unsworn statements of a witness are mere hearsay and are, as such, generally inadmissible as affirmative proof. The introduction of such testimony, even where limited to impeachment, necessarily increases the possibility that a defendant may be convicted on the basis of unsworn evidence, for despite proper instructions to the jury, it is often difficult for them to distinguish between impeachment and substantive evidence.

This limitation on impeachment of one's own witness only applies when the party calls a witness for an impermissible purpose. If, however, the party calls the witness for a good faith purpose, courts will generally permit impeachment with otherwise inadmissible evidence.

4. Where is the line between fair and unfair uses of prior statements?

One explanation of the distinction between legitimate and illegitimate circumstances in which counsel calls a witness and ultimately offers an inconsistent statement for impeachment is as follows:

"As Judge Posner has said, it would be an abuse of Rule 607 for a party "to call a witness that it knew would not give it useful evidence, just so it could introduce hearsay evidence * * * in the hope that the jury would miss the subtle distinction between impeachment and substantive evidence — or, if it didn't miss it, would ignore it." *United States v. Webster*, 734 F.2d 1191, 1192 (7th Cir. 1984). *See also United States v. Ince*, 21 F.3d 576 (4th Cir. 1994) (conviction was reversed because the government's "only apparent purpose for impeaching one of its own witnesses was to circumvent the hearsay rule and to expose the jury to otherwise inadmissible evidence"). This limitation on the flexibility provided by Rule 607 has most often been applied against prosecutors who call adverse witnesses, but it has also been applied against criminal defendants and civil litigants. *United States v. Sebetich*, 776 F.2d 412 (3d Cir. 1985) (criminal defendant cannot call a witness "for the purposes of circumventing the hearsay rule by means of Rule 607"); *Whitehurst v. Wright*, 592 F.2d 834 (5th Cir. 1979) (plaintiff could not call a witness to the stand for the purpose of bringing out an inconsistent statement, when that statement was inadmissible for substantive purposes).

But if instead the party calls the witness for a good faith purpose, then the limitation will not apply. For example, if a witness is called with the expectation that he will testify favorably, and the party is then surprised by negative testimony, the party is permitted to recoup its losses by impeaching the witness. *See United States v. Kane*, 944 F.2d 1406, 1411 (7th Cir. 1991) ("The test is whether the prosecution exhibited bad faith by calling a witness sure to be unhelpful to its case."); *United States v. Peterman*, 841 F.2d 1474 (10th Cir. 1988) (impeachment was permissible after the prosecutor previously interviewed the witness and determined that the witness was going to give testimony favorable to the government's case; the prosecutor had not received any subsequent information that the witness had changed his mind). Thus, the common-law doctrine of "surprise" has been revived in cases where a party calls a witness and then seeks to impeach him with otherwise inadmissible evidence. Of course, the claim of surprise must be credible to permit impeachment with otherwise inadmissible evidence; it can't be a mere hope that the witness will have "seen the light" and change his stated course when he takes the stand. The trial judge should require counsel who seeks to offer an inconsistent statement as impeachment of a witness on direct examination to make a proffer to justify a claim of surprise, and should permit opposing counsel to *voir dire* the witness outside the presence of the jury to assure that the witness had not alerted the calling party that the testimony would be inconsistent with a previous hearsay statement.

A party would also be in good faith in impeaching a witness with otherwise inadmissible evidence if it "called an adverse witness that it thought would give evidence both helpful and harmful to it, but it also thought that the harmful aspect could be nullified by introducing the witness's prior inconsistent statement." *United States v. Webster*, 734 F.2d 1191, 1193 (7th Cir. 1984). *See also United States v. DeLillo*, 620 F.2d 939 (2d Cir. 1980) (the Court upheld the government's impeachment of the unfavorable portions of its own witness' testimony where the overall testimony was favorable to the government in many respects). If a witness is needed to corroborate parts of a case, the party should be allowed to impeach that witness where some aspects of the testimony are adverse to the party's case; the party should not be put to the poor choice of either forgoing the corroborating witness or forgoing the impeachment.) *United States v. Eisen*, 974 F.2d 246 (2d Cir. 1992) (where the government has called a witness whose corroborating testimony is instrumental in constructing its case, it has a right to question the witness, and to attempt to impeach him, about those aspects of his testimony that conflict with the government's account of the same events; the prejudicial effect of the impeachment in this case did not substantially outweigh the probative value of the favorable portions of the testimony).

For similar reasons, a party must be allowed to call a witness, even when anticipating the need for impeachment with inadmissible evidence, when the failure to call the witness might lead the jury to draw a negative inference against the party. *See, e.g.*, *United States v. Gilbert*, 57 F.3d 709 (9th Cir. 1995) (the government acted properly in calling two eyewitnesses and impeaching them with prior statements, not independently admissible, concerning the defendant's possession of a gun; if the government had not called these two witnesses, "the jury would have been left to ponder why the government was reluctant to question these eye-witnesses").

Finally, the limitation on Rule 607 applies only if the impeachment evidence is not otherwise admissible. So for example, if a witness has made a prior statement under oath at a trial or hearing, the witness may be called and the statement may be introduced even if counsel *knows* that the witness will repudiate the statement and testify adversely. This is because such a prior inconsistent statement is admissible for its truth under Rule 801(d)(1)(A), and therefore the witness is not being called solely to be impeached with otherwise inadmissible evidence. There is no abuse of the hearsay rule in these circumstances. *See, e.g.*, *United States v. Medley*, 913 F.2d 1248 (7th Cir. 1990) (no error in permitting the government to impeach a witness when his testimony was inconsistent with his grand jury testimony; because the prior statement was under oath and thus admissible under Rule 801(d)(1)(A), the witness was not called to introduce otherwise inadmissible hearsay).

C. TYPES OF IMPEACHMENT

[1] Capacity

A witness's credibility may be attacked by showing that the witness suffers from some incapacity making it difficult or impossible for them to tell the truth. The limitations imposed on such attacks are found in Rules 403 and 610.

MODE 1: Religious Belief

Under common law a witness could be challenged by arguing that the witness had no belief in God and, thus, was not credible. This was because the oath that was given required the witness to state that they would tell the truth in the face of God. But as seen in Chapter 3, the Federal Rules of Evidence provide for flexibility, by a requirement that the witness "declare that the witness will testify truthfully, by oath or affirmation administered in a form calculated to awaken the witness's conscience and impress the witness's mind with the duty to do so." Fed. R. Evid. 603. A witness may, thus, make a secular declaration to tell the truth.

It might still be argued that a witness lacks the capacity to tell the truth because of some unusual religious belief. For example, if the witness is a member of a religion with "odd" religious beliefs, a party might try to argue that the witness lacks a grasp on reality that is necessary to tell the truth. But Rule 610 imposes a substantial limitation on impeaching a witness on the ground of religious belief.

[a] Federal Rule of Evidence 610

Rule 610. Religious Beliefs or Opinions

Evidence of the beliefs or opinions of a witness on matters of religion is not admissible for the purpose of showing that by reason of their nature the witness's credibility is impaired or enhanced.

[b] Beliefs Impairing Credibility: General Rule of Exclusion

UNITED STATES v. SAMPOL
636 F.2d 621 (D.C. Cir. 1980)

Per curiam:

On September 21, 1976, in Washington, D.C., Orlando Letelier, former Chilean Ambassador to the United States, and Ronni Moffitt, an American associate, were mortally wounded by the remote control detonation of a bomb attached to the undercarriage of the automobile in which they were riding.

On August 1, 1978, Guillermo Novo Sampol (Guillermo Novo) [and others were indicted for these murders]. * * *

Trial by jury commenced January 8, 1979 on the charges against Guillermo Novo, Alvin Ross and Ignacio Novo only. At the close of trial on February 14, 1979 each was found guilty of all charges lodged against him. This appeal followed.

* * *

Cross-examination of Ricardo Canete

* * *

A. *Canete's Religion*

Counsel for Ignacio Novo proffered to the trial court that Canete had discussed with his client his devotion to the Luceme religion. On *voir dire*, Canete testified that he faithfully adhered to the teachings of that sect and consulted with spirits of his religion before taking certain actions. He had no religious beliefs which would cause him to violate his oath to testify truthfully. The trial judge cut off further inquiry into Canete's religious practices at that point.

The government correctly points out that the court's exclusion of this evidence was not only justified but required by the Federal Rules of Evidence. Rule 610 bars the admission of evidence of the religious beliefs of a witness for the purpose of showing that his credibility is impaired as a result of those beliefs. The purpose of the rule is to guard against the prejudice which may result from disclosure of a witness's faith. The scope of the prohibition includes unconventional or unusual religions. *See Government of Virgin Islands v. Petersen*, 553 F.2d 324 (3rd Cir. 1977) (defense counsel could not elicit testimony that alibi witness was a member of the Rastafarian sect). The fact that Canete professed adherence to a religion which is not commonly shared does not prevent the application of the rule. The trial judge committed no abuse of discretion.

* * *

NOTE

Is evidence of religious beliefs ever admissible?

Evidence about religion may be admitted if offered for certain specific aspects of credibility — as opposed to generalized attack on the witness for having a certain religious belief. Evidence of a witness's religion may also be probative of some substantive issue in the case. Some examples of permissive use are:

To show employment and damages: In *McKim v. Philadelphia Transp. Co.*, 72 A.2d 122 (Pa. 1950), the Court allowed the cross-examination of plaintiffs in a personal injury action about their positions as ministers in the Jehovah's Witnesses sect. The questioning was allowed not to impeach the witnesses because of their religious beliefs but, rather, on the question of lost earning power and damages.

To show hardship**:** In a products liability case, one court allowed evidence of the hardship encountered by the plaintiff attending church in his injured condition. The Court found that the plaintiff "was not attempting to bolster his *credibility* through his statements of religious belief but simply was testifying to the hardships imposed upon him, in his efforts to attend church, because of his present condition." *Mauldin v. Upjohn Co.*, 697 F.2d 644, 649 (5th Cir. 1983).

To show motive**:** Evidence about a defendant's religious beliefs has been held admissible to show motive. In *United State v. Hoffman*, 806 F.2d 703 (7th Cir. 1986), the court allowed evidence of the defendant's involvement in the religious sect of Reverend Sun Yung Moon in order to show the defendant's motive to threaten President Reagan.

The defendant had sent a letter to the White House: "Ronnie, Listen Chump! Resign or You'll get Your Brains Blown Out." The government set out to prove that the letter had been sent "out of defendant's anger with the President for his failure to pardon Sun Yung Moon, the leader of a religious group with which defendant was associated for a time and to whom he retained loyalty."

To show bias**:** The Advisory Committee's Note to Rule 610 states:

While the rule forecloses inquiry into the religious beliefs or opinions of a witness for the purpose of showing that his character for truthfulness is affected by their nature, an inquiry for the purpose of showing interest or bias because of them is not within the prohibition. Thus disclosure of affiliation with a church which is a party to the litigation would be allowable under the rule."

[c] To Show Bias or Motive

SLAGLE v. BAGLEY

457 F.3d 501 (6th Cir. 2006)

ROGERS, CIRCUIT JUDGE:

Petitioner Billy Slagle, who was sentenced to death by an Ohio jury for the 1987 aggravated murder of Mari Anne Pope, appeals the judgment of the district court denying his petition for post-conviction relief brought pursuant to 28 U.S.C. § 2254. Slagle broke into his neighbor Pope's house on August 13, 1987, because he wanted to steal something for the following day's drinking. Pope was babysitting two neighborhood children. Ultimately, Slagle went into Pope's bedroom and, after she woke up, stabbed her seventeen times in her chest with her sewing scissors. The two children escaped, called for help, and identified Slagle. The police found Slagle at the scene holding the bloody scissors, and Slagle later described his actions that night in detail. Although Slagle admitted at trial that he killed Pope, he argued that, due to his voluntary intoxication from alcohol and marijuana, he did not have the requisite intent for aggravated murder. The jury, nevertheless, sentenced him to death for aggravated murder.

After the Ohio courts affirmed Slagle's sentence and denied Slagle post-conviction relief, Slagle petitioned the federal district court for habeas relief in December 2001. The court denied his petition. * * * We affirm.

I.

A. Facts and Trial

When reviewing Slagle's case on direct appeal, the Supreme Court of Ohio considered the trial record and made the following factual findings, which, according to 28 U.S.C. § 2254(e)(1), are presumed correct unless rebutted by clear and convincing evidence:

> In the early morning hours of August 13, 1987, the victim Mari Anne Pope was awakened in her home by appellant. Two children, who she had agreed to watch for her neighbors, were also awakened. The children awoke to the voice of Mari Anne inquiring as to who this person was that had entered her home. A man's voice angrily threatened her and ordered her to roll onto her stomach. The man asked if there were others in the house, to which she replied that there were two children upstairs. The man told the victim not to move and that

> he had a knife at her back. The children then heard Mari Anne begin to pray. The man responded by ordering her to stop praying.
>
> The children recognized the voice and knew the man as Billy Slagle, who lived next door. They first sought to hide, and then to escape. They scurried through the hall and out the back door. One of the children looked into the bedroom and observed Slagle sitting on top of the victim, who was lying upon her stomach. Slagle had on only his underwear. As the children exited, the victim could be heard screaming.

* * *

Slagle chose to testify. He stated that he broke into Pope's house to steal something so that he would have money for alcohol the next day. He did not recall any events after entering Pope's house until he was fighting with her and holding bloody scissors. He only recalled stabbing Pope once, and he testified that he did not know why he killed her.

On cross-examination, the prosecution asked several questions that Slagle now challenges. * * *

* * *

The State * * * asked Slagle whether he knew what a rosary was, whether Pope began to pray as he attempted to rape her, whether he told her to shut up, and whether he liked and said prayers. Slagle testified that he did not remember her praying, that he saw nothing wrong with prayers, and that he says prayers.

The prosecution's inquiry into whether Slagle prayed and liked prayer was not improper. Lisa Bloxham, one of the children staying at Pope's house, testified that Slagle responded to Pope's prayer by saying, "Shut up because I don't like to hear your prayers." The Supreme Court of Ohio stated in its opinion that Slagle had objected to the questions concerning his religious beliefs, but that court never directly addressed whether the inquiry was proper.

These questions were not improper despite their focus on religion because these questions concerned whether the statement concerning prayer was made, not Slagle's general truthfulness. Not all religious inquiries are forbidden. Ohio Rule of Evidence 610 states, "Evidence of the beliefs or opinions of a witness on matters of religion is not admissible for the purpose of showing that by reason of their nature his credibility is impaired or enhanced." Although this rule proscribes use of religion to impugn the "witness's propensity towards truthfulness," Ohio law permits questions concerning religion to show bias and motive, *see Redman*, 630 N.E.2d at 677–78; *State v. Roper*, No. 94CA34, 1996 WL 140250, at *3 (Ohio Ct. App. Mar. 22, 1996). Whether Slagle prays or dislikes prayer is at least slightly probative of whether he would tell someone to "shut up because I don't like to hear your prayers[,]" and, as with bias and motive, there is nothing in the Ohio rule that precludes the prosecution from asking questions concerning religion to determine the probability of a statement being made. The State did not suggest that Slagle's religious beliefs would cause him to testify untruthfully or, as in *Redman*, that Slagle's "religious beliefs were paramount to the oath taken prior to testifying." *Redman*, 630 N.E.2d at 678. The prosecution's inquiry was not improper.

* * *

MODE 2: Perception

Defendant, Purse Snatcher, is charged with stealing a purse. The victim pointed out the defendant in the courtroom as the culprit. At a pre-trial hearing, even though the victim had a limited opportunity to observe the defendant, the court held that she was competent to testify.

The defendant cross-examines at trial.

Defendant:	The person who committed this crime approached you from behind, didn't he or she?
Victim:	Yes.
Defendant:	That person was running. Right?
Victim:	Yes.
Defendant:	You didn't see the person at all until your purse was snatched?
Victim:	No, I didn't.
Defendant:	And the person ran right on by you, isn't that right?
Victim:	Yes.
Defendant:	The person was dressed completely in black clothing, right?
Victim:	Yes.
Defendant:	It was after midnight, wasn't it?
Victim:	Yes.
Defendant:	There wasn't a street light for at least three blocks, was there?
Victim:	No, there wasn't.
Defendant:	It was raining, wasn't it?
Victim:	Yes.
Defendant:	In fact, it was pouring down?
Victim:	Yes.
Defendant:	You were wearing glasses, weren't you?
Victim:	Yes.
Defendant:	And there was rain on them, wasn't there?
Victim:	Well, yes.
Defendant:	And because it was raining, the moon wasn't shining, was it?
Victim:	Well, no.
Defendant:	And isn't it true that the person who robbed you had on a ski mask?
Prosecution:	Objection, your Honor! You've already determined that this witness is competent to testify. This is improper cross-examination.

Defendant:	__________.
The court:	__________.

MODE 3: Memory

Defendant, Bad Check, is charged with passing a forged check at Small Town Bank. The only witness identifying the defendant as the person who cashed the check is Stellar Teller. The events occurred more than eighteen months before the trial. At a pre-trial hearing Teller was found to be competent to testify even though she saw the defendant for only a few minutes and so much time had passed.

The defendant cross-examines Teller.

Defendant:	Now Ms. Teller, how long have you worked at the bank?
Stellar Teller:	Four years.
Defendant:	How many people do you wait on in an average day? Just give us an approximation.
Stellar Teller:	Oh, about one hundred, but more on Fridays and the first day of the month.
Defendant:	Do you work five days a week?
Stellar Teller:	Yes.
Defendant:	Fifty weeks a year?
Stellar Teller:	Yes.
Defendant:	So, from the day you started working at the bank until the date this check was passed, let's see, that was three and a half years, you participated in at least 87,500 transactions?
Stellar Teller:	If you say so.
Defendant:	Do you remember each and every one of those people?
Stellar Teller:	Well, of course not. How could I?
Defendant:	And since the date this check was passed you've waited on another 37,000 transactions, haven't you?
Stellar Teller:	I guess so.
Defendant:	Do you remember each and every person from those transactions?
Stellar Teller:	No, of course not.
Defendant:	Would you say that waiting on a customer is part of your everyday life?
Stellar Teller:	Well, yes.
Defendant:	You only eat dinner once a day, don't you?
Stellar Teller:	Yes.
Defendant:	I'm sure you can tell us what you had for dinner last night, can't you?
Stellar Teller:	Sure, zucchini casserole.
Defendant:	Good. Now what did you have for dinner on the 10th of last month?
Stellar Teller:	How would I know?

Defendant:	And you certainly can't remember exactly what you had for dinner on the date the check was cashed, can you?
Prosecution:	I object to the entire line of questioning. Your Honor, you've already ruled she's competent.
Defendant:	________.
The court:	________.

MODE 4: Communication

Plaintiff has only one witness who can testify about where the cars came to rest after the accident. This witness's testimony will be used by an accident reconstruction expert as a basis for his opinion that the defendant was at fault in the accident.

Defendant cross-examines the witness.

Defendant:	Now you testified on direct that the cars came to rest in juxtaposition with the plaintiff's car perpendicular to the adjacent street-line axis. Right?
Witness:	Yes.
Defendant:	What does juxtaposition mean?
Witness:	Ah * * *
Defendant:	What does perpendicular mean?
Witness:	Ah * * *
Defendant:	What does adjacent mean?
Witness:	Ah * * * eh * * *
Defendant:	What is a street-line axis?
Witness:	Ah * * *
Plaintiff:	Objection, your Honor! He's badgering the witness.
Defendant:	________.
The court:	________.

NOTES

1. Is addiction to alcohol or other drugs admissible to impeach the ability of a witness to perceive, recall, or narrate?

In *United States v. Sampol*, 636 F.2d 621 (D.C. Cir. 1980), the Court held that evidence of the use of alcohol or other drugs was admissible to impeach, but should be limited to evidence indicating the use of those substances at the time of perception or at the time of testifying. *See also Jarrett v. United States*, 822 F.2d 1438, 1445 (7th Cir. 1987) ("A witness' use of drugs is only relevant as to the ability of the witness to perceive the underlying events and testify lucidly at trial."); *United States v. DiPaolo*, 804 F.2d 225 (2d Cir. 1986) (evidence of alcoholism "tells us nothing of the witness's testimonial incapacity unless it involves actual intoxication at the time of the event observed or at the time of testifying.").

Some courts recognize that impairment by alcohol or other drugs is permissible if it can be shown that the witness's "prior drug use affects the witness's ability to observe, remember, and recount." Occasional drug use would not be sufficient for impeachment, but if the witness's brain has been fried by alcohol or other drugs, then it is relevant to the witness's capacity to testify accurately. *See Edwards v. State*, 548 So. 2d 656, 658 (Fla. 1989):

> [Florida Law] excludes the introduction of evidence of drug use for the purpose of impeachment *unless*: (a) it can be shown that the witness had been using drugs at or about the time of the incident which is the subject of the witness's testimony; (b) it can be shown that the witness is using drugs at or about the time of the testimony itself; or (c) *it is expressly shown by other relevant evidence that the prior drug use affects the witness's ability to observe, remember, and recount.*

2. Is evidence of a disturbed emotional condition admissible to impeach a testifying witness on the ability of the witness to perceive, recall, or narrate?

The admissibility of psychiatric testimony illustrates the distinction between competency and impeachment of credibility. Initially, it is important to note that evidence of insanity does not make the witness incompetent to testify. In *United States v. Lightly*, 677 F.2d 1027 (4th Cir. 1982), the court held that a ruling from a prior proceeding that a witness was criminally insane and incompetent to stand trial does not make a witness incompetent to testify.

> Every witness is presumed competent to testify, Fed. R. Evid. 601, unless it can be shown that the witness does not have personal knowledge of the matters about which he is to testify, that he does not have the capacity to recall, or that he does not understand the duty to testify truthfully. This rule applies to all persons considered to be insane to the same extent that it applies to other persons.

Evidence of insanity or other kind of mental instability is, however, admissible to impeach credibility. In *United States v. Lindstrom*, 698 F.2d 1154, 1166 (11th Cir. 1983), the court found reversible error where the trial court did not allow the defense access to psychiatric records and did not allow the defense to cross-examine a key prosecution witness about mental health problems. *See also Revels v. Vincenz*, 382 F.3d 870 (8th Cir. 2004) (no error in permitting the questioning of the plaintiff as to whether he heard voices in the past: "We have specifically approved the use of a witness's mental condition to challenge his credibility.").

Due to the constitutional dimension of the criminal defendant's right to effective cross-examination, the policy of inquiry into a witness's mental instability is especially important when a criminal defendant is seeking to impeach a prosecution witness. *See generally Davis v. Alaska*, 415 U.S. 308 (1974); *see also Doe v. Diamond*, 964 F.2d 1325 (2d Cir. 1992) (recognizing a psychotherapist-patient privilege but holding that it does not shield a prosecution witness from answering questions regarding psychiatric history at a pre-trial hearing.)

The competing policy of protecting the witness is well stated in *United States v. Lopez*, 611 F.2d 44 (4th Cir. 1979).

> One's psychiatric history is an area of great personal privacy which can only be invaded in cross-examination when required in the interests of justice. This is so because cross-examination of an adverse witness of matters of such personal privacy, if of minimal probative value, is manifestly unfair and unnecessarily demeaning to the witness. Moreover, such cross-examination will generally introduce into the case a collateral issue, leading to a large amount of testimony substantially extraneous to the essential facts and issues of the controversy being tried.
>
> * * *
>
> Courts should have the power to protect witnesses against cross-examination that does little to impair credibility but that may damage their reputation, invade their privacy, and assault their personality. And Rule 403, Federal Rules of Evidence provides the courts with the power to do just this.
>
> In making provision for such authority in the trial court, the drafters of Rule 403 were merely following the modern decisional trend under which courts have frequently exercised the power to prevent excursions during cross-examination into collateral matters of a purely personal nature having minor probative value. Particularly true is this in those cases in which the witness' psychiatric experiences are sought to be inquired into by way of an attack on the witness' credibility. The rationale for such a restriction, as applied in the psychiatric area, is that many psychiatric problems or fixations which a witness may have had are without any relevancy to the witness' credibility, concerned as it with whether the witness' mental impairment is related to "his capacity to observe the event at the time of its occurrence, to communicate his observations accurately and truthfully at trial, or to maintain a clear recollection in the meantime." It follows that the witness' mental impairment, to constitute a proper subject for cross-examination, must have been "at a time probatively related to the time period about which he was attempting to testify," * * * must go to the witness' qualification to testify and ability to recall, * * * and must not "introduce into the case a collateral issue which would confuse the jury and which would necessitate allowing the Government to introduce testimony explaining the matter."

In *Lopez*, the Court found that there was no indication that the record of the psychiatric examination revealed any problems with the witness's ability to observe, recall, or narrate.

[2] Impeachment of a Witness's Character for Truthfulness

The next three modes of impeachment all involve showing that the witnesses should not be believed because their character is such that they are not likely to tell the truth. The Federal Rules of Evidence expressly deal with the three types of character impeachment: convictions are addressed by Rule 609; prior bad acts are addressed by Rule 608(b); and using a character witness to say the first witness is a liar is addressed by Rule 608(a).

Collectively this type of impeachment is often referred to as proving "bad character for truth and veracity." It is important to note that while extrinsic evidence is admissible to prove prior convictions, extrinsic evidence is not admissible to prove prior bad acts under Rule 608(b).

It is also worth noting that many of the protections for the criminal defendant discussed under Rule 404 may be lost if the criminal defendant testifies and is, thus, subject to impeachment. Noting the distinctions and relationships between substantive character evidence and impeachment by character evidence is essential to mastering this material.

MODE 5: Convictions/Prior Crimes

[a] Illustration

The defendant is charged with possession of illegal narcotics. His defense is that the drugs were placed on him by the police informant. The defendant intends to take the stand and the prosecution wants to offer proof at trial of several previous convictions of the defendant. The defense wants to offer evidence of several previous situations involving the police informant.

The defendant's prior record is:

(a) a juvenile conviction for passing a forged check;

(b) an adult conviction fifteen years ago for battery;

(c) an adult conviction fourteen years ago for felony embezzlement;

(d) a prior adult conviction five years ago for petty theft;

(e) a prior adult conviction for distribution of illegal narcotics, a felony, three years earlier;

(f) a perjury conviction which is currently on appeal.

The police informant's prior record is:

(a) a ten-year-old conviction for felony child molestation;

(b) a five-year-old conviction for breaking and entering;

(c) a four-year-old conviction for male prostitution;

(d) a charge of cocaine possession which is pending;

(e) a probable lie on his recent application to be a police officer.

[b] Federal Rule of Evidence 609

Rule 609. Impeachment by Evidence of Conviction of Crime

(a) General rule. For the purpose of attacking the character for truthfulness of a witness,

(1) evidence that a witness other than an accused has been convicted of a crime shall be admitted, subject to Rule 403, if the crime was punishable by death or imprisonment in excess of one year under the law under which the witness was convicted, and evidence that an accused has been convicted of such a crime shall be admitted if the court determines that the probative value of admitting this evidence outweighs its prejudicial effect to the accused; and

(2) evidence that any witness has been convicted of a crime shall be admitted regardless of the punishment, if it readily can be determined that establishing the elements of the crime required proof or admission of an act of dishonesty or false statement by the witness.

(b) Time limit. Evidence of a conviction under this rule is not admissible if a period of more than ten years has elapsed since the date of the conviction or of the release of the witness from the confinement imposed for that conviction, whichever is the later date, unless the court determines, in the interest of justice, that the probative value of the conviction supported by specific facts and circumstances substantially outweighs its prejudicial effect. However, evidence of a conviction more than 10 years old as calculated herein, is not admissible unless the proponent gives to the adverse party sufficient advance written notice of intent to use such evidence to provide the adverse party with a fair opportunity to contest the use of such evidence.

(c) Effect of pardon, annulment, or certificate of rehabilitation. Evidence of a conviction is not admissible under this rule if (1) the conviction has been the subject of a pardon, annulment, certificate of rehabilitation, or other equivalent procedure based on a finding of the rehabilitation of the person convicted, and that person has not been convicted of a subsequent crime that was punishable by death or imprisonment in excess of one year, or (2) the conviction has been the subject of a pardon, annulment, or other equivalent procedure based on a finding of innocence.

(d) Juvenile adjudications. Evidence of juvenile adjudications is generally not admissible under this rule. The court may, however, in a criminal case allow evidence of a juvenile adjudication of a witness other than the accused if conviction of the offense would be admissible to attack the credibility of an adult and the court is satisfied that admission in evidence is necessary for a fair determination of the issue of guilt or innocence.

(e) Pendency of appeal. The pendency of an appeal therefrom does not render evidence of a conviction inadmissible. Evidence of the pendency of an appeal is admissible.

[c] The Balancing Process

UNITED STATES v. HAYES

553 F.2d 824 (2d Cir. 1977)

OAKES, CIRCUIT JUDGE:

This appeal is from a judgment of conviction following a jury verdict in the United States District Court for the Southern District of New York, Irving Ben Cooper, Judge. Appellant was convicted on two counts each of robbing, 18 U.S.C. § 2113(a), and using a weapon in connection with the robbery, 18 U.S.C. § 2113(d), of a branch of The Manufacturers Hanover Trust Company on March 25, 1976, and a Chase Manhattan Bank branch on April 1, 1976. Similar act evidence was introduced as to another robbery by appellant of the Swiss Bank Corporation in the same general area of New York City on March 24, 1976. A fifth count, for assault on federal agents at the time of appellant's arrest, 18 U.S.C. § 111, was based on events occurring on April 2, 1976, on the sidewalk in front of a branch of the Irving Trust Company. We affirm on all counts.

Appellant does not question the sufficiency of the evidence to sustain his conviction on any count. Nor could he, for the evidence, from numerous eyewitnesses and surveillance photographs, was more than ample to warrant conviction. He does question * * * the court's refusal to suppress evidence of a recent narcotics conviction so that he might testify * * *.

We * * * hold that the court below did not err in refusing to suppress appellant's recent narcotics conviction. Appellant was convicted in early 1976 of one count of importation of cocaine. Under Rule 609(a) of the Federal Rules of Evidence, he sought a ruling in the instant case that the Government would not be permitted to use this conviction in cross-examining him if he should testify in his own defense. He was unsuccessful and accordingly did not take the stand. Rule 609(a) established a two-pronged test of admissibility.

* * *

Under the second prong of this rule, evidence of conviction of a certain type of crime — one involving "dishonesty or false statement" — must be admitted, with the trial court having no discretion, regardless of the seriousness of the offense or its prejudice to the defendant. Because this rule is quite inflexible, allowing no leeway for consideration of mitigating circumstances, it was inevitable that Congress would define narrowly the words "dishonesty or false statement," which, taken at their broadest, involve activities that are part of nearly all crimes. Hence Congress emphasized that the second prong was meant to refer to convictions "peculiarly probative of credibility," such as those for "perjury or subornation of perjury, false statement, criminal fraud, embezzlement, or false pretense, or any other offense in the nature of *crimen falsi*, the commission of which involves some element of deceit, untruthfulness, or falsification bearing on the accused's propensity to testify truthfully." Conf. Rep. No. 93-1597, 93d Cong., 2d Sess. 9, *reprinted in* (1974) U.S. Code Cong. & Ad. News, pp. 7098, 7103.

The use of the second prong of Rule 609(a) is thus restricted to convictions that bear *directly* on the likelihood that the defendant will *testify* truthfully (and not merely on whether he has a propensity to commit crimes). It follows that crimes of force, such as armed robbery or assault, or crimes of stealth, such as burglary, or petit larceny, do not come within this clause. * * *

If a conviction may not be automatically admitted under the second prong, however, it may still be admitted in the court's discretion if it meets the criteria of the first. Under this test, a court must balance the probative value of the conviction against its prejudicial effect to the defendant. Unlike the rule that prevailed before Rule 609, the government has the burden of showing that probative value outweighs prejudice.* * *

We hold that the district court did not abuse its discretion in admitting the conviction here. Several factors impel this conclusion. First, as Judge Cooper noted, the conviction was a very recent one (two months before the trial here, and after the bank robberies charged), and we have held that convictions have more probative value as they become more recent. Second, the conviction was for a type of crime — smuggling — that ranks relatively high on the scale of veracity-related crimes, although not so high as to fall clearly within the second prong of Rule 609(a), as discussed *supra*. The conviction here has more probative value on credibility than, for example, a conviction for mere narcotics possession, or for a violent crime. Third, appellant testified in his own defense at the trial that resulted in his prior conviction, and his conviction can be viewed as "a *de facto* finding that the accused did not tell the truth when sworn to do so." *Gordon v. United States*, 127 U.S. App. D.C. 343, 383 F.2d 936, 940 n.8 (1967). Finally, the conviction was for a crime substantially different from the instant prosecution, so that there was not here the prejudice to appellant that inevitably results from the introduction of a conviction for the same crime as that for which he is on trial. While the court below was not as explicit as it could have been in identifying and weighing the relevant indicia of probative value and prejudice, we cannot say that it abused its discretion in concluding that the Government here carried its burden of showing that the probative value of appellant's conviction on the issue of his credibility outweighed its prejudice to him.

* * *

AFFIRMED.

UNITED STATES v. GANT

396 F.3d 906 (7th Cir. 2005)

FLAUM, CHIEF JUDGE:

Following a two-day trial, a jury convicted defendant-appellant Alfred James Gant of being a felon in possession of a firearm in violation of 18 U.S.C. § 922(g). Gant was sentenced to 188 months' imprisonment and four years of supervised release, and now appeals his conviction. For the reasons stated herein, we affirm.

I. Background

On May 19, 2001, Gant was involved in a confrontation with his daughter Angelia Gant and a neighbor named Daniel Clark. Gant had allowed Angelia to live in an apartment he owned on Church Street in Champaign, Illinois, free of rent, provided that she abstain from using drugs and not permit others to loiter on the property. Gant went to Church Street on May 19 to tell Angelia that he was evicting her for failing to comply with these conditions. At trial, the government presented testimony of several eyewitnesses who testified that during the confrontation that ensued, Gant struck both Angelia and Clark with a gun. Angelia testified that Gant struck her on the face with an object approximately three inches long. Clark testified that Gant struck him with a hard metal object, and that he then looked up and saw Gant holding a revolver. Another neighbor, Glenn Seay, testified that he was sitting on his front porch directly across the street and saw Gant strike Angelia with a gun. Police officer Jay Warran also testified that when he responded to the scene, he saw Gant walking down the street carrying a pistol and then observed him drop it in the grass nearby.

Gant testified at trial that he used a lead pipe, not a firearm, in these confrontations. He also called his girlfriend, Ruby Rodriquez, who testified that on the day of the incident, after receiving a call from Gant, she went to Church Street to search the area and found a lead pipe in the grass.

II. Discussion

* * *

B. Prior Conviction

Gant * * * contends that the district court abused its discretion in admitting his prior conviction for impeachment purposes. Of Gant's three prior convictions, only the third was admitted into evidence — a 1986 conviction for possession of a controlled substance with intent to distribute. Gant was sentenced to twenty years' imprisonment for this conviction and was discharged from parole on October 14, 1995, eight years prior to trial.

* * * Federal Rule of Evidence 609 provides that evidence that an accused has been convicted of a crime punishable by death or imprisonment in excess of one year "shall be admitted if the court determines that the probative value of admitting this evidence outweighs its prejudicial effect to the accused." Fed. R. Evid. 609(a)(1). * * *

In determining whether the probative value of admitting a prior conviction outweighs its prejudicial effect, the court should consider: "(1) the impeachment value of the prior crime; (2) the point in time of the conviction and the defendant's subsequent history; (3) the similarity between the past crime and the charged crime; (4) the importance of the defendant's testimony; and (5) the centrality of the credibility issue." *Rodriguez v. United States*, 286 F.3d 972, 983 (7th Cir. 2002) (quoting *United States v. Smith*, 131 F.3d 685, 687 (7th Cir. 1997)).

Gant argues that the prejudicial effect of this conviction outweighs its probative value because the conviction was remote in time and did not involve a crime of dishonesty. He also claims that the district court failed to consider adequately his history as a productive member of society following his release from prison in 1995.

Considering all the evidence presented at trial, the district court did not abuse its discretion in allowing the government to impeach Gant with evidence of his prior conviction. This conviction was within the ten-year limit set forth in Rule 609(b). Moreover, given Gant's theory of the case, his credibility was a crucial part of the trial. Gant's testimony that he possessed a pipe, not a firearm, directly contradicted the testimony of government witnesses Daniel Clark, Glenn Seay, and Officer Warran. The district court did not abuse its discretion in admitting Gant's prior conviction for impeachment purposes. *See Smith*, 131 F.3d at 687 (holding that district court did not abuse its discretion in admitting defendant's prior convictions where defendant's testimony directly contradicted that of other witnesses, making the credibility issue central).

* * *

UNITED STATES v. CAVENDER

228 F.3d 792 (7th Cir. 2000)

WOOD, CIRCUIT JUDGE:

This case arose from a major cocaine bust in Rockford, Illinois. Appellants Milton Buchanan, Solomon Montague, Desmond Cavender, and Demetrius Campbell were, along with several others, indicted in December of 1997 for their role in the conspiracy. Cavender and Buchanan pleaded guilty to particular charges, while Montague and Campbell went to trial and were convicted by the jury. All four have appealed, raising a variety of points related to their convictions and sentences. One serious evidentiary error has persuaded us that we must reverse Campbell's conviction; we find the remainder of the arguments raised either without merit, harmless, or waived, and we therefore affirm the judgments entered against Buchanan, Montague, and Cavender.

I

The defendants were involved in a sophisticated business arrangement for the sale of crack cocaine (more formally known to the law as cocaine base) in the Rockford area. Along with Bennie Griffith, who later turned state's evidence, they were the key players. According to the grand jury's indictment, the conspiracy began as early as June 1994 and continued through July 1997, and it involved the distribution of multiple kilograms of cocaine base. Some participants purchased large quantities of the drug, some cut and bagged it for distribution, and others sold it from designated "spots" run by the conspirators.

At Campbell and Montague's trial, the government presented Griffith as its star witness. Griffith explained that he began selling drugs with Cavender and Buchanan in late 1994, and that Montague joined the group in 1996. Griffith testified that they all, at various points in time, purchased large amounts of cocaine, and hired workers to bag and sell it. He said that he sold crack to Campbell beginning in 1996, and that Campbell had told him that he was reselling the drugs on the west side. Griffith identified, through photos, several spots that the conspiracy controlled and used as sales locations, including various residences and the area around the Jane Addams housing project. The government also introduced 118 tapes of conversations into evidence. The recorded conversations were all in code and street slang, but Griffith deciphered them for the jury (which otherwise would have had little to no idea of what the people were talking about).

Two other cooperating government witnesses who were former members of the conspiracy also testified at trial. The first, James Perkins, said that he engaged in several drug transactions with Montague and Buchanan. Noah Miller, the other, said that he worked mainly with Montague dealing drugs, but he knew that others were working with Montague. Miller offered his own explanations of the recorded conversations for 11 of the 118 tapes. His definitions were in many instances different from those Griffith had used — a discrepancy Griffith explained by saying that the code he used in conversing with the conspirators was his special language, not general street slang. Miller identified his own voice in all 11 tapes, and identified Montague's voice in some of them.

The remaining testimony came from various FBI and police officers, who reported that they had seen Montague, Buchanan, Cavender, and sometimes Campbell in vehicles together at different times driving to and from what Griffith had described as the conspiracy's drug spots. Three Rockford police officers also testified that they found some bags of crack in Montague's pants one evening near the Jane Addams housing project.

The jury convicted Campbell on Count 1 (conspiracy to possess with intent to distribute and to distribute cocaine base, in violation of 21 U.S.C. § 846), and Montague on Counts 1 and 16 (possession of cocaine base with intent to distribute, in violation of 21 U.S.C. § 841(a)(1)). * * *

II

A. Impeachment of Griffith: Evidentiary rulings

Griffith, as we have already noted, was the linchpin of the government's case at the trial. Naturally, this meant that Campbell and Montague had a strong interest in undermining him in front of the jury, and the government had an equally strong interest in demonstrating his credibility. Toward the latter end, on direct examination Griffith was asked about his drug use before he left Chicago for Rockford and joined the conspiracy. He insisted that he had neither *used nor sold* any drugs during that time period:

Q: [Government's attorney]: And when you were in Chicago did you sell drugs?

A: No.

Q: Never?

A: No.

Q: Did you use drugs?

A: No.

On cross examination, he stuck to that story and added that he had not dealt in drugs while he was living in Chicago, in the following exchange:

Q: [Montague's attorney]: Bennie, you testified earlier you lived in Chicago, right?

A: That is correct.

Q: But in Chicago you didn't deal any drugs, right?

A: That is correct.

At least with respect to Griffith's testimony on direct examination about use (rather than dealing), it is almost certain that he was lying. In fact, Griffith had been convicted of a felony in Chicago in 1994 for possession of a controlled substance. After the exchange we have just noted, Montague's attorney attempted to impeach Griffith by introducing evidence of that 1994 Chicago drug possession conviction. The district court sustained the government's objection to the evidence, and it was excluded from the trial. Both Montague and Campbell objected.

On appeal, Campbell and Montague argue that this ruling was in error. Montague argued that it violated his Sixth Amendment confrontation rights, and both claim that it misapplied Federal Rules of Evidence 609(a) and 403. Normally, we review a restriction on cross-examination only for abuse of discretion. *See United States v. Graffia*, 120 F.3d 706, 712 (7th Cir. 1997). The exception arises when the restriction implicates the criminal defendant's Sixth Amendment right to confront witnesses against her, in which case the standard of review is de novo. *See United States v. Sasson*, 62 F.3d 874, 882 (7th Cir. 1995).

Under the Sixth Amendment, a criminal defendant has the right to confront the witnesses against her. U.S. Const. amend. VI. The exposure of a witness's motivations to lie is a proper and important function of the constitutionally protected right of cross-examination. The right to cross-examine adverse witnesses, however, is not absolute. The Confrontation Clause guarantees only an opportunity to conduct a thorough and effective cross-examination during which the defense has a chance to discredit the witness, "not cross-examination that is effective in whatever way, and to whatever extent, the defense might wish." *Delaware v. Fensterer*, 474 U.S. 15, 20 (1985) (per curiam). The district court retains wide latitude to impose reasonable limits on the scope and extent of cross-examination based on concerns about things like harassment, prejudice, confusion of the issues, or interrogation that is repetitive or only marginally relevant. *See Delaware v. Van Arsdall*, 475 U.S. 673, 679 (1986).

In this case, the district court's decision not to allow the defense to impeach Griffith did not rise to the level of a Sixth Amendment violation. The defense was allowed to put into evidence the fact that Griffith had a conviction of some crime on his record, and it was allowed to explain that Griffith was profiting as a result of his testimony by getting a lower sentence under his plea agreement. Because the defense was able to question Griffith about some of his potential biases, and thus to introduce the idea that Griffith might not be a reliable witness, this situation differs from that in *Van Arsdall,* where the defense was completely foreclosed from presenting any evidence of a witness's bias. *See id.*

This does not mean, however, that the exclusion of the felony drug possession conviction was inconsequential. To the contrary, Rule 609(a)(1) of the Federal Rules of Evidence states that "evidence that a witness other than an accused has been convicted of a crime *shall* be admitted, subject to Rule 403," if it was punishable by imprisonment in excess of one year. (Emphasis added.) Rule 403 codifies the court's power to exclude otherwise relevant evidence whose probative value "is substantially outweighed by the danger of unfair prejudice, confusion of the issues, or misleading the jury, or by considerations of undue delay, waste of time, or needless presentation of cumulative evidence." Thus, unless Rule 403 justified its exclusion, the evidence of Griffith's former conviction should have been admitted.

The government argues that there was such a reason, because the evidence would have been cumulative and a waste of time. We are hard pressed to see what it was with which this evidence cumulated. The only impeachment evidence admitted at trial was some testimony indicating that Griffith lied to an officer when he was first arrested, and evidence that Griffith was being compensated for testifying. The jury heard absolutely nothing that would have hinted to them that Griffith was lying to them right there as he sat in the witness stand. The evidence of his prior conviction would have strongly suggested at a minimum that he had lied during his direct examination, when he denied that he had used drugs in Chicago. Splitting hairs, the government argues that the evidence of his conviction for possession would not truly have operated to impeach him, because there is a difference between possession and use. There may indeed be a semantic difference between these two, but when the shoe is on the other foot the government frequently argues that a jury can infer use from possession: people normally do not run the risk of purchasing user quantities of controlled substances just to put them on the shelf. Further, Griffith also disavowed selling drugs. In the real world, it is hard to imagine what Griffith would have done with the drugs if he did not either use or sell them. Had the evidence of the conviction come in, the jury would have been entitled to come to the reasonable conclusion that Griffith had just lied to them. And if he was willing to tell them a bald-faced lie on that point, it might also have wondered what the rest of his testimony was worth. Even though the standard of review for this kind of evidentiary ruling is abuse of discretion, we conclude in this case that it was error to exclude the evidence of Griffith's narcotics conviction.

[The Court rejected the government's argument of harmless error, and reversed the convictions.]

NOTES

1. In Chapter 2, we examined motions *in limine*. Hayes made such a motion, the trial judge denied it, and Hayes declined to testify. As a result, he was not impeached with the prior conviction. Under current federal law, he could not appeal the trial judge's ruling, because the objectionable evidence was never admitted against him at trial. *See Luce v. United States*, 469 U.S. 38 (1984). Some state courts would permit the defendant to appeal. Which is the better approach?

2. Should limiting instructions be given?

There is a tension between allowing the use of prior convictions to impeach and the prohibition of the use of prior convictions as proof of substantive guilt. This tension has been resolved by requiring that "when evidence of prior similar crimes is properly introduced [to impeach] the jury must be able to distinguish between credibility evidence and affirmative evidence. * * * The propriety of giving a limiting instruction under such circumstances cannot be questioned." *United States v. Diaz*, 585 F.2d 116, 118 (5th Cir. 1978).

The Federal Judicial Center has suggested the following limiting instruction when the criminal defendant is impeached with a prior conviction:

> You have been told that the defendant was found guilty in [year] of [e.g., bank robbery]. This conviction has been brought to your attention only because you may wish to consider it when you decide, as with any witness, how much you will believe of his testimony in this trial. The fact that the defendant was found guilty of another crime does not mean that he committed this crime, and you must not use his guilt for the crime of [bank robbery] as proof of the crime charged in this case. You may find him guilty of this crime only if the government has proved beyond a reasonable doubt that he committed it.

The FJC suggests that the following instruction be given whenever a witness other than the accused is impeached with a prior conviction:

> You have heard that the witness, __________, was convicted in [year] of [e.g., armed robbery]. This conviction has been brought to your attention only because you may wish to consider it when you decide, as with any witness, whether you believe his testimony.

3. May a lawyer preempt the impeachment by inquiring about the conviction on direct?

When a witness has a prior conviction, typically the party calling the witness will bring out the prior conviction on direct. *See United States v. Countryman*, 758 F.2d 574, 577 (11th Cir. 1985) ("[I]t is permissible for the government to disclose guilty pleas of co-conspirator government witnesses in order to blunt the impact of expected attacks on the witnesses' credibility.") This type of preemption is particularly common where the criminal defendant testifies on her own behalf.

> The introduction by a witness himself, on his direct, of a prior conviction is a common trial tactic, recommended by textwriters on trial practice. There is a paucity of authority justifying in theory this well accepted practice, but it has been justified on the ground that it serves a twofold purpose: (a) to bring out the witness' "real character," the whole person, particularly his credibility, and (b) to draw the teeth out of the adversary's probable use of the same evidence on cross-examination.

United States v. Bad Cob, 560 F.2d 877, 883 (8th Cir. 1977).

But the use of this tactic comes with a cost. A party who brings out a conviction on direct waives the right to complain that its admission was error. *Ohler v. United States*. 529 U.S. 753 (2000).

4. What steps should a court follow in determining admissibility of prior convictions for impeachment purposes?

a. *The two prongs*: The *Hayes* court discusses the distinction between the two prongs of Rule 609(a). When analyzing the admissibility of prior convictions to impeach, the court must decide whether the prior conviction constitutes a crime of dishonesty or false statement. If it is such a crime, it is automatically admitted unless it is so dated as to fall within the time limit of Rule 609(b). If the court finds that the prior conviction does not constitute a crime of dishonesty or false statement then the conviction must be for a felony, and the court must conduct one of two balancing tests to determine admissibility. How to determine what crimes fall where is discussed later in this chapter.

b. *The balancing tests*: There are two separate balancing tests under Rule 609(a). The applicable test depends on whether the witness is the accused. A prior conviction of *a witness other than the accused* is admissible subject to the balancing test of Rule 403.

A prior conviction of *the accused as a witness* is admissible subject to a balancing test that is cast in favor of exclusion. The burden of proof is on the prosecution to show the probative value outweighs the prejudicial effect to the defendant. This is more protective of defendants than the Rule 403 test, under which the prejudicial effect must substantially outweigh the probative value for the evidence to be excluded. As a practical matter this means that a defendant's convictions stand a good chance of exclusion when: (1) they are similar to the crime with which the defendant is charged; (2) they are particularly inflammatory; or (3) the defendant has been impeached in other ways, such as with inconsistent statements or with convictions that are automatically admitted under Rule 609(a)(2). *See, e.g., United States v. Sanders,* 964 F.2d 295 (4th Cir. 1992) (error in an assault prosecution to impeach the defendant with his prior conviction for assault). It is important to note that the prejudice that the trial court is to take into account is not the "prejudice" that the witness may suffer in terms of humiliation (though that factor may be considered by the trial court exercising its powers under Rule 611). The trial court operating under Rule 609 must consider the prejudice suffered by the party whose testimony the witness favors. It is also important to remember that the probative value of impeachment evidence increases as the witness's credibility becomes more important in the case — a point relied upon by the court in *Gant, supra. See also United States v. Lattner*, 385 F.3d 947 (6th Cir. 2004) (affirming a cocaine conviction, the Court found no abuse of discretion when the defendant's two prior felony drug convictions were admitted to impeach him; the probative value of the convictions was high because credibility was crucial, and the prejudicial effect was minimal in light of the introduction under Rule 404(b) of the defendant's prior involvement in drug transactions.)

A third balancing test arises under Rule 609(b) which generally, but not absolutely, excludes stale convictions. In *United States v. Singer*, 660 F.2d 1295, 1300 (8th Cir. 1981), the Court notes that Rule 609(b) establishes a rebuttable presumption against the admissibility of a conviction more than ten years old and finds an abuse of discretion where a twelve-year-old conviction for grand larceny was admitted under the discretionary "in the interests of justice" clause of Rule 609(b).

c. *Crimes of dishonesty or false statement*: As stated above, if the court finds that the prior conviction does constitute a crime of dishonesty or false statement then the evidence is automatically admitted to impeach. The trial court possesses no discretion to exclude a prior conviction for a crime of dishonesty or false statement. *United States v. Lester*, 749 F.2d 1288, 1300 (9th Cir. 1984) ("Fed. R. Evid. 609(a)(2) provides that evidence of convictions of a crime involving dishonesty or false statement shall be admitted during cross-examination to attack the credibility of a witness. No discretion to exclude exists."). Both misdemeanor and felony convictions are admissible if they are crimes of dishonesty or false statement.

d. *What constitutes dishonesty or false statement?* Cases often quote the statement of the Conference Committee:

> Crimes such as perjury or subornation of perjury, false statement, criminal fraud, embezzlement, or false pretense, or any other offense in the nature of *crimen falsi*, the commission of which involves some element of deceit, untruthfulness, or falsification bearing on the accused's propensity to testify truthfully. The admission of prior conviction involving dishonesty and false statement is not within the discretion of the Court. Such convictions are peculiarly probative of credibility and, under this rule, are always to be admitted.

When Rule 609 was amended in 1990, the Advisory Committee refused to add any language clarifying which crimes must be admitted for impeachment under Rule 609(a)(2). The Committee's explanation for not proposing an amendment to Rule 609(a)(2) is as follows:

> The Committee recommended no substantive change in subdivision (a)(2), even though some cases raise a concern about the proper interpretation of the words "dishonesty or false statement." These words were used but not explained in the original Advisory Committee Note accompanying Rule 609. Congress extensively debated the rule, and the Report of the House and Senate Conference Committee states that

"by the phrase dishonesty and false statement, the Conference means crimes such as perjury, subornation of perjury, false statement, criminal fraud, embezzlement, or false pretense, or any other offense in the nature of crimen falsi, commission of which involves some element of deceit, untruthfulness, or falsification bearing on the accused's propensity to testify truthfully." The Advisory Committee concluded that the Conference Report provides sufficient guidance to trial courts and that no amendment is necessary, notwithstanding some decisions that take an unduly broad view of "dishonesty," admitting convictions such as for bank robbery or bank larceny.

As discussed in *Hayes*, analysis of whether a conviction constitutes dishonesty or false statement results in three categories: (1) crimes an element of which requires proof of dishonesty or false statement, (2) crimes that do not constitute require proof of dishonesty or false statement and so are not, on the basis of their elements, automatically admissible under Rule 609(a)(2), and (3) crimes that can be committed without an act of dishonesty or false statement, but where the impeaching party contends that the witness in fact committed the crime by using dishonesty or false statement. The following examples are illustrative of how courts interpret Rule 609.

(i) Crimes an element of which requires proof of dishonesty or false statement:

(a) Meter tampering: *Altobello v. Border Confectionery Prods., Inc.*, 872 F.2d 215, 217 (7th Cir. 1989).

(b) Passing counterfeit money: *United States v. Harris*, 738 F.2d 1068, 1073 (9th Cir. 1984).

(c) Misdemeanor for filing a false police report: *United States v. Lester*, 749 F.2d 1288, 1300 (9th Cir. 1984).

(d) Mail fraud: *United States v. Brashier*, 548 F.2d 1315, 1326–27 (9th Cir. 1976).

(e) Forgery: *United States v. Field*, 625 F.2d 862, 871 (9th Cir. 1980).

(f) Knowingly transporting forged securities: *United States v. Hans*, 738 F.2d 88 (3d Cir. 1984).

(ii) Crimes that do not require proof of dishonesty or false statement:

(a) Crimes involving solely the use of force such as assault: *United States v. Harvey*, 588 F.2d 1201, 1203 (8th Cir. 1978).

(b) Possession of a weapon: *United States v. Cameron*, 814 F.2d 403, 405–06 (7th Cir. 1987) (the court held that misdemeanor possession of a switchblade is not a crime of dishonesty).

(c) Driving under the influence: *United States v. Wiman*, 77 F.3d 981 (7th Cir. 1996)

(d) Prostitution: *United States v. Cox*, 536 F.2d 65, 71 (5th Cir. 1976).

(e) Purse-snatching: *United States v. Johnson*, 388 F.3d 96 (3d Cir. 2004) (conviction for purse snatching was improperly admitted under Rule 609(a)(2).

(f) Theft: *Coursey v. Broadhurst*, 888 F.2d 338 (5th Cir. 1989) (a cattle theft conviction is not automatically admissible).

(g) Shoplifting: *United States v. Ashley*, 569 F.2d 975 (5th Cir. 1978) (conviction for shoplifting does not involve dishonesty within the meaning of Rule 609(a)(2)).

(h) Wilful failure to file a tax return (as opposed to tax fraud): *Cree v. Hatcher,* 969 F.2d 34 (3d Cir. 1992).

(iii) Crimes involving possible underlying acts of dishonesty or false statement:

Some courts have found a conviction "automatically" admissible under Rule 609(a)(2) if the "particular prior conviction rested on facts warranting the dishonesty or false statement description." *United States v. Mehrmanesh*, 689 F.2d 822, 833 n.13 (9th Cir. 1982) (drug crime in which lies were involved). The 2006 amendment to Rule 609(a)(2) imposes some limits on admitting a crime under this theory. That amendment is discussed after the next case.

[d] Dishonesty or False Statement

UNITED STATES v. BRACKEEN

969 F.2d 827 (9th Cir. 1992)

PER CURIAM:

This court has convened en banc to determine whether bank robbery necessarily involves "dishonesty," as that term is used in Federal Rule of Evidence 609(a)(2). The question arises in the context of whether a witness can be impeached by evidence of prior convictions.* * * We now conclude that for purposes of Rule 609(a)(2) bank robbery is not per se a crime of "dishonesty."

FACTS AND PROCEEDINGS BELOW

Robert Nello Brackeen robbed three different banks, one bank a day on each of three separate days in July 1990. In the first robbery, Brackeen and an accomplice, Jermaine Moore, presented a threatening note to a teller. Bank surveillance photos showed Moore with a pistol, which he pointed at the teller. During the robbery, Brackeen and Moore acted in close proximity to each other. In the other two robberies, Brackeen was unarmed and apparently acted alone. Brackeen was charged in a single indictment with one count of aiding and abetting an armed bank robbery, * * * and two counts of unarmed bank robbery. On September 24, 1990, Brackeen pleaded guilty to both unarmed bank robberies. On October 2, 1990, Brackeen went to trial on count one of the indictment, aiding and abetting Moore in the armed bank robbery. He claimed he did not know Moore had a gun.

On the second day of the two-day trial, Brackeen indicated he would testify, and objected before taking the stand to the use for impeachment of his guilty pleas to the two unarmed bank robberies. The court reserved its ruling on the objection until after Brackeen testified. Brackeen was the sole defense witness. On cross-examination, the court allowed impeachment with the guilty pleas.

The trial court's basis for admitting the prior guilty pleas as impeachment evidence was Federal Rule of Evidence 609(a)(2), which allows impeachment of a defendant by any crime involving "dishonesty or false statement." The court expressly refused to admit the pleas under Rule 609(a)(1), which allows impeachment using any felony "if the court determines that the probative value of admitting this evidence outweighs its prejudicial effect to the accused * * * ." The court stated: "No. I don't think under Rule 609(a)(1) that I would let it in * * * . I don't think I could make that analysis under Rule 609(a)(1) so I'm going to base my ruling on Rule 609(a)(2) that this is a crime involving dishonesty and the government has an absolute right to use it to impeach him."* * * Brackeen appeals, claiming the impeachment was improper because * * *the guilty pleas were to bank robbery, a crime that does not involve "dishonesty or false statement" as required by Rule 609(a)(2). * * *

ANALYSIS

* * *

Brackeen's bank robberies did not involve any "false statement[s]," and were not "actually committed by fraudulent or deceitful means." Accordingly, the only issue in this case is whether bank robbery is per se a crime of "dishonesty" under Rule 609, regardless of the means by which it is perpetrated. * * * We now [hold that] bank robbery is not per se a crime of "dishonesty" under Federal Rule of Evidence 609(a)(2).

Our first step in interpreting any statute or rule is to consider the plain meaning of the provision in question. Often, this will be the end of the analysis, because the words of the provision allow but one interpretation and preclude others. Unfortunately, "dishonesty" has more than one meaning. In the dictionary, and in everyday use, "dishonesty" has two meanings, one of which includes, and one of which excludes, crimes such as bank robbery. In its broader meaning, "dishonesty" is defined as a breach of trust, a "lack of * * * probity or integrity in principle," "lack of fairness," or a "disposition to * * * betray." Webster's Third New International Dictionary 650 (1986 unabridged ed.). This dictionary states, under the heading "synonyms," that "dishonest may apply to any breach of honesty or trust, as lying, deceiving, cheating, stealing, or defrauding." Bank robbery fits within this definition of "dishonesty" because it is a betrayal of principles of fairness and probity, a breach of community trust, like stealing.

In its narrower meaning, however, "dishonesty" is defined as deceitful behavior, a "disposition to defraud * * * [or] deceive," *id.*, or a "[d]isposition to lie, cheat, or defraud," Black's Law Dictionary 421 (5th ed. 1979). Bank robbery does not fit within this definition of "dishonesty" because it is a crime of violent, not deceitful, taking. Everyday usage mirrors the dictionary: we use "dishonesty" narrowly to refer to a liar, and broadly to refer to a thief.

Fortunately, we are not operating in a vacuum: while nothing in the text of Rule 609 indicates precisely what Congress meant when it used the term "dishonesty," we find guidance in the legislative history of the rule. * * * The legislative history of Rule 609 makes clear that Congress used the term "dishonesty" in the narrower sense, to mean only those crimes which involve deceit. * * *

Bank robbery is not "in the nature of crimen falsi." Black's Law Dictionary defines "crimen falsi" as follows: "Term generally refers to crimes in the nature of perjury or subornation of perjury, false statement, criminal fraud, embezzlement, false pretense, or any other offense which involves some element of deceitfulness, untruthfulness, or falsification bearing on witness' propensity to testify truthfully."

Other circuits have reached similar conclusions. The Tenth Circuit has stated:

> Of course, robbery, burglary and theft are ordinarily considered to be dishonest, but the term as used in Rule 609(a)(2) is more restricted. We think the legislative history of this provision shows that Congress intended to limit the term to prior convictions involving some element of deceit, untruthfulness, or falsification which would tend to show that an accused would be likely to testify untruthfully.

United States v. Seamster, 568 F.2d 188, 190 (10th Cir. 1978). *See United States v. Farmer*, 923 F.2d 1557, 1567 (11th Cir. 1991) ("It is established in this Circuit * * * that crimes such as theft, robbery, or shoplifting do not involve 'dishonesty or false statement' within the meaning of Rule 609(a)(2)"); *McHenry v. Chadwick*, 896 F.2d 184, 188 (6th Cir. 1990) ("shoplifting does not fall into th[e] category" described by Rule 609(a)(2)); *United States v. Yeo*, 739 F.2d 385, 388 (8th Cir. 1984) ("we believe that the better view is that theft is not a crime of 'dishonesty or false statement' as that term is used in Rule 609(a)(2)"); *United States v. Lipscomb*, 702 F.2d 1049, 1057 nn. 32–33 (D.C. Cir. 1983) (prior conviction for larceny not admissible under Rule 609(a)(2)); *Shows v. M/V Red Eagle*, 695 F.2d 114, 119 (5th Cir. 1983) ("admissibility of a prior bank robbery conviction for impeachment purposes requires the balancing exercise of Rule 609(a)(1)"); *United States v. Cunningham*, 638 F.2d 696, 698–99 (4th Cir. 1981) (noting "Rule 609(a)(2) * * * is confined to a narrow class of crimes," and holding a state conviction for writing "worthless checks" is not admissible under Rule 609(a)(2)).

CONCLUSION

Congress intended Rule 609(a)(2) to apply only to those crimes that factually or by definition entail some element of misrepresentation or deceit, and not to " 'those crimes which, bad though they are, do not carry with them a tinge of falsification.' " We must follow Congress' intent. Brackeen's conviction is REVERSED, and the case is REMANDED for a new trial.

NOTES

1. Should a court be allowed or required to go beyond the elements of the conviction and determine whether the underlying facts of a conviction involved dishonesty or false statement?

Assume the witness was convicted of a crime that does not itself contain an element of deceit, but the crime was committed in a *manner* that involved deceit. For example, the crime of murder contains no statutory element of deceit, but a particular defendant may have acted dishonestly in order to get the victim to a certain place where the murder would occur. Can the Court go behind the conviction itself to the supporting facts and hold that the manner of committing the crime requires admission under Rule 609(a)(2)? The Courts have been in dispute on this question. An amendment to Rule 609(a)(2), effective December 1, 2006, seeks to resolve this conflict.

Most Circuits have held that a conviction is subject to admission under Rule 609(a)(2), even where dishonesty or false statement is not an essential element of the crime, if the proponent can show that the conviction rested in some way on facts indicating that the witness was actually dishonest or deceitful in committing the crime. *See, e.g.*, *United States v. Foster*, 227 F.3d 1096 (9th Cir. 2000) (conviction for receipt of stolen property is not admitted automatically under Rule 609(a)(2) because the crime can be accomplished without any misrepresentation or deceit; however, the conviction can be admitted under Rule 609(a)(2) if the trial court finds that the crime "was actually committed by fraudulent or deceitful means").

But the Advisory Committee on Evidence determined that it is unwise to apply Rule 609(a)(2) so broadly that a trial court can always go behind the witness's crime and determine whether the crime was committed in a deceitful manner. The premise for such a broad approach is that a conviction for a crime such as drug distribution will have more or less probative value depending on how it was committed. While this may or may not be true, the fact is that if the conviction is admitted, the jury will generally hear only that the conviction was rendered and that a certain punishment was meted out. Rule 609 does not allow the jury to hear the underlying facts of the conviction.

The courts have consistently held that evidence of the conviction is limited to "the crime charged, the date, and the disposition." *Gora v. Costa*, 971 F.2d 1325, 1330 (7th Cir. 1992) ("it is error to elicit any further information for impeachment purposes"). This is part of the reasoning for dispensing with an extrinsic evidence exclusion such as that found in Rule 608(b) — the conviction itself can be easily proved, without a need to delve into the facts. Consequently, whatever greater probative value there is in the manner that a crime was committed will be lost on the jury.

More importantly, an approach permitting the trial court to go behind the conviction in every case will make Rule 609(a)(2) the predominant rule, and not the exception. This is because there is probably some act of deceit in almost every crime. Thus, Rule 609(a)(2) would swallow up Rule 609(a)(1), even though the balancing approach of the latter Rule is more consistent with the general framework of the Federal Rules.

Finally, it is to say the least an indeterminate inquiry for a trial court to decide retrospectively just what facts actually led to the witness's conviction. If a witness has been convicted of drug distribution, how is the trial judge to determine whether the jury in that prior case found beyond a reasonable doubt that the witness had acted deceitfully in committing the crime? The general verdict of guilty is obviously an insufficient indication. Should the trial judge look at the indictment? At the record? Should the trial judge hold a hearing and essentially retry the prior case, when the only goal is to determine whether the conviction is "automatically" admitted? The process of going behind the crime to the underlying facts hardly seems "automatic."

For these reasons, some courts have rejected the majority approach and have held that convictions such as for murder, drug distribution, obstruction of justice, etc., can never be automatically admitted even if they were allegedly committed in a deceitful manner. For example, in *Cree v. Hatcher,* 969 F.2d 34 (3d Cir. 1992), the Court recognized that "it is certainly possible, and perhaps even likely, that in some instances individuals who willfully fail to file federal income tax returns do so with the conscious intent to conceal their tax liability." However, the Court concluded that "the manner in which a particular defendant commits a crime is irrelevant; what matters is whether dishonesty or false statement is an element of the statutory offense."

The 2006 amendment to Rule 609(a)(2) provides that a conviction is automatically admissible "if it readily can be determined that establishing the elements of the crime required proof or admission of an act of dishonesty or false statement by the witness." That is, it rejects the notion that a Court can or should always go behind a conviction to try to determine whether some of the underlying facts were dishonest or deceitful; such an approach is inefficient and indeterminative. On the other hand, the Committee was persuaded (or one might say overwhelmed) by the Justice Department's view that a pure "elements" approach to Rule 609(a)(2), while easy to apply, would unduly limit impeachment.

The Justice Department's major concern was with a prior conviction for obstruction of justice. Deceit or dishonesty is not an element of that crime, because it can be committed, for example, by threatening a witness or destroying evidence. On the other hand, many convictions for obstruction will be grounded on dishonest conduct (e.g., lying to authorities), and the centrality of these acts to the conviction might well be evident without having to speculate or to retry the case. For example, the indictment might itself provide sufficient indication that proof of dishonest acts was fundamental to the conviction.

While there is much to be said, as above, for a strict elements approach to Rule 609(a)(2), the Advisory Committee determined that it would not be able to get an amendment approved in the face of staunch opposition from the Department of Justice; and that a test could be proposed that would at least limit some of the problems of allowing or requiring a Court to go behind every conviction to look for deceitful or dishonest acts. The Committee Note tries to limit the damage of the Justice Department's demand that Rule 609(a)(2) cover crimes other than those in which deceit or dishonesty is part of a statutory element. That Note attempts to make clear that Rule 609(a)(2) is intended to cover only those crimes where the defendant is actually punished for an act of dishonesty or false statement, but the statute under which he is convicted covers not only lying-based crimes but others — like obstruction of justice. The Note emphasizes that Rule 609(a)(2) should apply where the prosecution is really for a crimen falsi crime, but the statute is broader and covers both crimen falsi and non crimen falsi crimes. For charges under those statutes, the proponent must then show, through readily available proof, that the crime was really crimen falsi. So for example, the amendment would prohibit the automatic admissibility of a murder conviction even if the "underlying facts" showed that the witness lied to his wife in order to get out of the house to commit the murder. That act of dishonesty is never part of the elements of a murder conviction. No finding or admission of an act of dishonesty or false statement was required in order for the witness to have been convicted.

[e] Advisory Committee Note to 2006 Amendment to Rule 609

The amendment provides that Rule 609(a)(2) mandates the admission of evidence of a conviction only when the conviction required the proof of (or in the case of a guilty plea, the admission of) an act of dishonesty or false statement. Evidence of all other convictions is inadmissible under this subsection, irrespective of whether the witness exhibited dishonesty or made a false statement in the process of the commission of the crime of conviction. Thus, evidence that a witness was convicted for a crime of violence, such as murder, is not admissible under Rule 609(a)(2), even if the witness acted deceitfully in the course of committing the crime.

The amendment is meant to give effect to the legislative intent to limit the convictions that are to be automatically admitted under subsection (a)(2). The Conference Committee provided that by "dishonesty and false statement" it meant "crimes such as perjury, subornation of perjury, false statement, criminal fraud, embezzlement, or false pretense, or any other offense in the nature of *crimen falsi*, the commission of which involves some element of deceit, untruthfulness, or falsification bearing on the [witness's] propensity to testify truthfully." Historically, offenses classified as *crimina falsi* have included only those crimes in which the ultimate criminal act was itself an act of deceit. *See* Green, *Deceit and the Classification of Crimes: Federal Rule of Evidence 609(a)(2) and the Origins of* Crimen Falsi, 90 J. Crim. L. & Criminology 1087 (2000).

Evidence of crimes in the nature of *crimina falsi* must be admitted under Rule 609(a)(2), regardless of how such crimes are specifically charged. For example, evidence that a witness was convicted of making a false claim to a federal agent is admissible under this subsection regardless of whether the crime was charged under a section that expressly references deceit (e.g., 18 U.S.C. § 1001, Material Misrepresentation to the Federal Government) or a section that does not (e.g., 18 U.S.C. § 1503, Obstruction of Justice).

The amendment requires that the proponent have ready proof that the conviction required the factfinder to find, or the defendant to admit, an act of dishonesty or false statement. Ordinarily, the statutory elements of the crime will indicate whether it is one of dishonesty or false statement. Where the deceitful nature of the crime is not apparent from the statute and the face of the judgment — as, for example, where the conviction simply records a finding of guilt for a statutory offense that does not reference deceit expressly — a proponent may offer information such as an indictment, a statement of admitted facts, or jury instructions to show that the factfinder had to find, or the defendant had to admit, an act of dishonesty or false statement in order for the witness to have been convicted. *Cf. Taylor v. United States*, 495 U.S. 575, 602 (1990) (providing that a trial court may look to a charging instrument or jury instructions to ascertain the nature of a prior offense where the statute is insufficiently clear on its face); *Shepard v. United States*, 125. S.Ct. 1254 (2005) (the inquiry to determine whether a guilty plea to a crime defined by a nongeneric statute necessarily admitted elements of the generic offense was limited to the charging document's terms, the terms of a plea agreement or transcript of colloquy between judge and defendant in which the factual basis for the plea was confirmed by the defendant, or a comparable judicial record). But the amendment does not contemplate a "mini-trial" in which the court plumbs the record of the previous proceeding to determine whether the crime was in the nature of *crimen falsi*.

The amendment also substitutes the term "character for truthfulness" for the term "credibility" in the first sentence of the Rule. The limitations of Rule 609 are not applicable if a conviction is admitted for a purpose other than to prove the witness's character for untruthfulness. *See, e.g., United States v. Lopez*, 979 F.2d 1024 (5th Cir. 1992) (Rule 609 was not applicable where the conviction was offered for purposes of contradiction). The use of the term "credibility" in subsection (d) is retained, however, as that subdivision is intended to govern the use of a juvenile adjudication for any type of impeachment.

MODE 6: Bad Acts

[a] Common Law

Under the common-law rule, witnesses could be cross-examined concerning their personal lives and their lack of personal morals. These inquiries were permitted even where the only possible relevance was the credibility of the witness. The rationale was that acts of "moral turpitude" reflected upon the credibility and truthfulness of the witness. Thus, in *State v. Jones*, 385 S.W.2d 80 (Tenn. 1964), the court approved cross-examination of a witness as to her employment as a call girl at the "Plantation Club." The court also cites as a leading case an 1896 case which allowed the cross-examination for credibility of witnesses in a murder case concerning acts of bigamy and lewdness.

Most states now allow inquiry into bad acts only if the acts are "probative of truthfulness" and are weighed against prejudice. *See, e.g.*, *Vogel v. Sylvester*, 174 A.2d 122, 128 (Conn. 1961) ("unless particular acts of misconduct are indicative of a lack of veracity, it is error to permit cross-examination concerning them, however much they may be indicative of bad moral character"). This view has been adopted by courts applying the Federal Rules, which hold that admissibility of bad acts offered to impeach a witness's character must be evaluated under Rule403.

Some states do not allow *any* cross-examination as to bad acts for impeachment purposes. Thus, in *Christie v. Brewer*, 374 S.W.2d 908, 914 (Tex. Civ. App. 1964), the court held that "the credibility of a witness may not be attacked by proving particular acts of misconduct." Some states have statutes prohibiting the showing of acts of misconduct for impeachment. *See, e.g.*, Idaho Code § 9-1302 (1990); West's Ann. Cal. Evid. Code. § 787 (1963); N.J. Rule of Evid. 22; Oregon Rules of Evid., Rule 608(1)(b).

[b] Illustration

A police informant is on the stand. Defendant cross-examines.

Defendant:	Isn't it true that you are a male prostitute?
Prosecution:	Objection! __________.
The court:	__________.
Defendant:	Isn't it true that when you applied to become a police officer, you lied on your job application?
Prosecution:	Objection! Improper cross. That's collateral.
Defendant:	__________.
The court:	__________.
Informant:	No, that isn't true.

Later in the trial the defendant calls the police recruitment officer, Top Cop, to the stand.

Defendant:	State your name.
Top Cop:	Top Cop.
Defendant:	Do you know the police informant?
Top Cop:	Yes.
Defendant:	Did he apply to be a member of the police force?
Top Cop:	Yes.
Defendant:	Did you do an investigation concerning his application?
Top Cop:	Yes.
Defendant:	Did he lie on the application form?
Prosecution:	Objection! __________.
The court:	__________.

[c] Federal Rule of Evidence 608(b)

Rule 608. Evidence of Character and Conduct of Witness

* * *

(b) Specific instances of conduct. Specific instances of the conduct of a witness, for the purpose of attacking or supporting the witness' character for truthfulness, other than conviction of crime as provided in rule 609, may not be proved by extrinsic evidence. They may, however, in the discretion of the court, if probative of truthfulness or untruthfulness, be inquired into on cross-examination of the witness (1) concerning the witness' character for truthfulness or untruthfulness, or (2) concerning the character for truthfulness or untruthfulness of another witness as to which character the witness being cross-examined has testified.

The giving of testimony, whether by an accused or by any other witness, does not operate as a waiver of the accused's or the witness' privilege against self-incrimination when examined with respect to matters that relate only to character for truthfulness.

[d] Advisory Committee Note to 2003 Amendment to Rule 608(b)

The Rule has been amended to clarify that the absolute prohibition on extrinsic evidence applies only when the sole reason for proffering that evidence is to attack or support the witness' character for truthfulness. *See United States v. Abel,* 469 U.S. 45 (1984); *United States v. Fusco,* 748 F.2d 996 (5th Cir. 1984) (Rule 608(b) limits the use of evidence "designed to show that the witness has done things, unrelated to the suit being tried, that make him more or less believable per se"); Ohio R. Evid. 608(b). On occasion the Rule's use of the overbroad term "credibility" has been read "to bar extrinsic evidence for bias, competency and contradiction impeachment since they too deal with credibility." American Bar Association Section of Litigation, *Emerging Problems Under the Federal Rules of Evidence* at 161 (3d ed. 1998). The amendment conforms the language of the Rule to its original intent, which was to impose an absolute bar on extrinsic evidence only if the sole purpose for offering the evidence was to prove the witness' character for veracity. *See* Advisory Committee Note to Rule 608(b) (stating that the Rule is "[i]n conformity with Rule 405, which forecloses use of evidence of specific incidents as proof in chief of character unless character is in issue in the case * * * ").

By limiting the application of the Rule to proof of a witness' character for truthfulness, the amendment leaves the admissibility of extrinsic evidence offered for other grounds of impeachment (such as contradiction, prior inconsistent statement, bias and mental capacity) to Rules 402 and 403. *See, e.g., United States v. Winchenbach,* 197 F.3d 548 (1st Cir. 1999) (admissibility of a prior inconsistent statement offered for impeachment is governed by Rules 402 and 403, not Rule 608(b)); *United States v. Tarantino*, 846 F.2d 1384 (D.C. Cir. 1988) (admissibility of extrinsic evidence offered to contradict a witness is governed by Rules 402 and 403); *United States v. Lindemann,* 85 F.3d 1232 (7th Cir. 1996) (admissibility of extrinsic evidence of bias is governed by Rules 402 and 403).

It should be noted that the extrinsic evidence prohibition of Rule 608(b) bars any reference to the consequences that a witness might have suffered as a result of an alleged bad act. For example, Rule 608(b) prohibits counsel from mentioning that a witness was suspended or disciplined for the conduct that is the subject of impeachment, when that conduct is offered only to prove the character of the witness. *See United States v. Davis,* 183 F.3d 231, 257 n.12 (3d Cir. 1999) (emphasizing that in attacking the defendant's character for truthfulness "the government cannot make reference to Davis's forty-four day suspension or that Internal Affairs found that he lied about" an incident because "[s]uch evidence would not only be hearsay to the extent it contains assertion of fact, it would be inadmissible extrinsic evidence under Rule 608(b)"). *See also* Stephen A. Saltzburg, *Impeaching the Witness: Prior Bad Acts and Extrinsic Evidence*, 7 Crim. Just. 28, 31 (Winter 1993) ("counsel should not be permitted to circumvent the no-extrinsic-evidence provision by tucking a third person's opinion about prior acts into a question asked of the witness who has denied the act").

For purposes of consistency the term "credibility" has been replaced by the term "character for truthfulness" in the last sentence of subdivision (b). The term "credibility" is also used in subdivision (a). But the Committee found it unnecessary to substitute "character for truthfulness" for "credibility" in Rule 608(a), because subdivision (a)(1) already serves to limit impeachment to proof of such character.

Rules 609(a) and 610 also use the term "credibility" when the intent of those Rules is to regulate impeachment of a witness' character for truthfulness. No inference should be derived from the fact that the Committee proposed an amendment to Rule 608(b) but not to Rules 609 and 610.

[e] Balancing Probative Value and Prejudicial Effect, and the Prohibition on Extrinsic Evidence of Untruthfulness

SIMMONS, INC. v. PINKERTON'S, INC.
762 F.2d 591 (7th Cir. 1985)

CUDAHY, CIRCUIT JUDGE:

Defendants-appellants Pinkerton's, Inc. and National Surety Corporation appeal a judgment against them in an action for property damages arising out of a fire at a warehouse owned by plaintiff-appellee Simmons, Inc. The jury returned a verdict in favor of Simmons and assessed damages in the amount of $971,012.65. We affirm.

I.

Simmons, a manufacturer of residential and commercial bedding, owned a warehouse in Munster, Indiana, which it used as a regional distribution center for its products. In order to protect the warehouse, Simmons entered into a contract with defendant Pinkerton's, a national company providing investigative and security services, under which Pinkerton's agreed to provide uniformed guard protection for the warehouse 24 hours a day, 7 days a week. The contract provided that Pinkerton's would "ensure a professional, reliable and efficient effort to protect its clients' property and personnel against security hazards." In addition, Pinkerton's explicitly accepted liability for all acts of negligence, fraud or dishonesty on the part of its security employees in the performance of their duties, but disclaimed any other liability. Pinkerton's also represented that its employees were trained both in security and in fire protection.

About July 18, 1978, Pinkerton's hired William Hayne for the position of security guard. Hayne apparently lied in several instances on his employment application, but the deceptions went undetected since Pinkerton's failed to check Hayne's references and other sources of information about him, in contravention of its own policy and procedure manuals. Pinkerton's also neglected to give Hayne certain types of training, including fire protection training, which its manuals indicated were mandatory for security guards.

On September 25th, 1978, William Hayne reported for work at the Simmons warehouse at 3:00 p.m. The security guard on duty ordinarily makes rounds at designated security points throughout the Simmons warehouse and periodic checks of fire reporting equipment, but because the main door controlling access to a loading dock at the warehouse was broken and fixed in an open position, Hayne had been ordered to remain at a guard desk near the loading dock. At 4:30 p.m., all Simmons' employees left the warehouse. At about 5:45 p.m., an office cleaning person, Ms. Anna Benedict, reported for work. Hayne and Benedict were the only people present in the loading dock area of the warehouse, and they spent some time talking in an office near the loading dock, where Benedict was working. About 6:00 p.m., Hayne left his station and went to get a drink from some vending machines adjoining a storage area in a different part of the warehouse. He then returned to the loading dock area. A few minutes later, he offered to get a soft drink for Benedict, and then went back to the vending machines to do so. He came back, gave Benedict the drink, and started back to his post. According to Hayne's testimony, he then discovered a fire in progress. Hayne attempted to put the fire out with several canister fire extinguishers but was unsuccessful. A reel fire hose was available in the area, but Hayne was not trained to use the hose and was unable to operate it properly. The Munster Fire Department arrived and contained the fire, but not before damage to the building and extensive damage to the bedding occurred.

The Chief of the Munster Fire Department determined that the fire originated on or near a wooden partition that separated stored rows of bedding. Because the point of origin was 12 inches above the floor in an area where there was no apparent source of ignition, and in light of other suspicious circumstances, the Munster Fire Chief requested the Indiana Fire Marshal's Office to investigate whether Hayne might have accidentally or intentionally started the fire. An investigator from that office concluded that the fire was of incendiary origin and was most likely set by Hayne as an "attention getter." * * *

Simmons then brought this diversity action against Pinkerton's [alleging] that Pinkerton's was liable under several theories: breach of the contract to provide fire protection and security services, failure to use reasonable care in providing such services — particularly with respect to selecting, training and supervising security personnel — and statutory liability under the Indiana Detective Licensing Law. After trial the jury found in favor of Simmons and awarded it the amount of damages claimed.

* * *

IV.

Pinkerton's * * * argues that the district court erred in admitting Hayne's testimony that he falsely told a Pinkerton's investigator that he had taken and passed a polygraph examination regarding the circumstances of the fire. After the fire, Pinkerton's asked Hayne to take a lie detector test in Chicago. He took the test, but apparently it was inconclusive for extraneous reasons. Hayne then agreed to take a second test in Indiana, but failed to make arrangements to do so. Nevertheless, Hayne later told a Pinkerton's investigator that he had taken the second test in Indiana and had passed it. At trial, over Pinkerton's objection, Simmons' attorney elicited from Hayne his admission that he had lied about this matter. Unfortunately this testimony was sufficiently ambiguous that it could have implied either that Hayne had lied about taking the test, or that he had lied about passing it.

The testimony was as follows:

Q: And Pinkerton's asked you to take a lie detector test, didn't they?

A: Yes they did.

Q: And you took that test at their request?

A: Yes I did.

Q: And then later they asked you to take another lie detector test, didn't they?

A: They only asked me to take one, sir.

Q: Do you recall that you told Mr. Robinson after the first lie detector test that you had passed the lie detector test in Indiana?

A: Yes I do.

Q: You told him that story, didn't you?

A: Yes I did.

Q: Was that true, Mr. Hayne?

A: No, it was not.

Although "the rule in the Seventh Circuit is clear" that admission or exclusion of polygraph evidence is within the sound discretion of the trial judge, for various reasons this discretion has most often been exercised in favor of exclusion, in this circuit as well as in others. Several circuits apparently exclude polygraph results entirely. * * * For these reasons, Pinkerton's argues, it would have been error to admit the results of any polygraph that Hayne took as substantive evidence of the cause of the fire at the warehouse. The trial court did not admit Hayne's testimony as substantive evidence, however, but rather admitted it under Federal Rule of Evidence 608(b) to impeach Hayne's credibility through cross-examination about a specific instance of his conduct (his lie about the polygraph test) bearing on his character for truthfulness or untruthfulness.* * *

Federal Rule of Evidence 608(b) * * * allows cross-examination of a witness about specific instances of her past conduct, if probative of truthfulness or untruthfulness, but prohibits the proof of such conduct by extrinsic evidence. Thus * * * a relevant fact bearing on the witness' credibility — in this case, that he has lied in the past or acted in some other manner that casts doubt on veracity — may, in the discretion of the trial judge, be considered sufficiently important and probative to be elicited on cross-examination; yet, because of the dangers of confusion, prejudice, waste of time, and so on, that would be inherent if a "mini-trial" on the existence of that fact were allowed, extrinsic evidence of the matter is prohibited.

* * * The testimony concerned an incident in which Hayne lied about having taken a polygraph examination. Whether or not Hayne took such a test or whether or not he passed may not have been admissible as substantive evidence. Nevertheless, in the discretion of the court, the "specific instance of conduct" in which he lied was, understandably, considered probative of his character for truthfulness or untruthfulness. Therefore, it was proper to allow Simmons to inquire about the incident while cross-examining Hayne. Of course, had Hayne denied the lie, the bar on the use of extrinsic evidence of specific instances of conduct to attack credibility in Rule 608(b) would have prohibited Simmons from proving the lie through the testimony of other witnesses. This sort of proof, however, was not offered. Clearly, the testimony carried some danger of prejudice, and just as clearly the trial court was obligated to balance this risk against the probative value of the testimony. The court did so, and we think it properly exercised its discretion in deciding that the testimony could be elicited under Rule 608(b).

* * *

For the foregoing reasons the judgment is affirmed.

[Dissenting opinion omitted.]

NOTES

1. Must the prior bad act be criminal in nature?

While it should be obvious that prior bad acts do not have to be convictions, it should also be noted that "the prior misconduct need not have created criminal liability or resulted in a conviction." *United States v. Bagaric*, 706 F.2d 42, 65 (2d Cir. 1983).

2. What types of bad acts can be inquired into as pertinent to the witness's character for truthfulness?

(a) Faking insanity defense. *United States v. Covelli*, 738 F.2d 847, 856 (7th Cir. 1984).

(b) Use of aliases. *United States v. Mansaw*, 714 F.2d 785, 789 (8th Cir. 1983).

(c) False credit card applications. *United States v. Sperling*, 726 F.2d 69, 75 (2d Cir. 1984).

(d) Defendant's failure to report political contributions. *United States v. O'Malley*, 707 F.2d 1240, 1249 (11th Cir. 1983) ("O'Malley's failure to report contributions, when he knew he was required to do so, directly reflected on his character for truthfulness. Examination as to this conduct was proper.").

(e) False excuses for absence from job. *United States v. Cole*, 617 F.2d 151, 153–54 (5th Cir. 1980).

(f) Lying about marital status on marriage license. *United States v. Beros*, 833 F.2d 455, 463 (3d Cir. 1987).

(g) Forgery, bribery, suppression of evidence, cheating, and embezzlement. *United States v. Page*, 808 F.2d 723, 730 (10th Cir. 1987) ("Acts admissible under Rule 608(b) include forgery, uttering forged instruments, bribery, suppression of evidence, false pretenses, cheating, [and] embezzlement.")

(h) Generally: Bad acts admissible under 608(b) have been described as analogous to acts that would constitute a crime of dishonesty or false statement such as required for automatic admissibility under Rule 609(a)(2). In *United States v. Amahia*, 825 F.2d 177, 181 (8th Cir. 1987), the court noted that "Rule 608(b) will permit inquiry into the specific acts which may have led to an arrest if those acts related to *crimen falsi, e.g.*, perjury, subornation of perjury, false statement, embezzlement, false pretenses."

3. What types of bad acts cannot be inquired into as pertinent to the witness's character for truthfulness?

(a) Drug use. *United States v. Rubin*, 733 F.2d 837 (11th Cir. 1984) (holding that testimony concerning a drug overdose constitutes a specific instance of conduct prohibited by 608(b).) Note that the drug use might still be used for impeachment if the impeacher could show that the drug use reflected on the witness's capacity.

(b) Witness's prostitution. *United States v. Mansaw*, 714 F.2d 785, 789 (8th Cir. 1983).

(c) Soliciting bribes. *United States v. Bocra*, 623 F.2d 281, 287–88 (3d Cir. 1980).

(d) Litigiousness. *Hemphill v. WMATA*, 982 F.2d 572 (D.C. Cir. 1993) (plaintiff in a personal injury action could not be impeached by the fact that she had pending a large number of personal injury suits).

(e) Bankruptcy. *Ad-Vantage Tel. Directory Consultants, Inc. v. GTE Directories*, 37 F.3d 1460 (11th Cir. 1994) (reversible error when the trial court permitted the defendant to impeach the plaintiff's expert witness, an accountant, by inquiring about the witness's bankruptcy and the fact that he borrowed money from his clients and failed to pay it back; "seeking discharge in bankruptcy does not show a disregard for truth that would cast doubt on a witness's veracity"; and even if the witness's borrowing from clients was unethical, "[t]o infer untruthfulness from any unethical act paves the way to the exception that swallows the rule.").

4. Does Rule 403 have any impact on whether the bad acts can be offered to impeach the witness's character for veracity?

See Saltzburg, Martin, and Capra, *Federal Rules of Evidence Manual* (9th ed. 2006):

> In a sense, all bad acts of a witness are pertinent to the witness' character for untruthfulness. If the act is "bad," it ordinarily indicates some transgression of law or ethics. If the witness was willing to disrespect the law or act unethically, that is at least somewhat probative of the proposition that the witness is also willing to disrespect the oath and lie on the stand. Yet Rule 608 clearly does not contemplate automatic impeachment with all of a witness's bad acts. As the Advisory Committee stated in its Note to Rule 608, the trial court must also apply Rule 403 to determine whether the probative value of the bad act as to the witness's untruthful character is substantially outweighed by the risk of prejudice, confusion and delay. *See, e.g.*, *Williams v. Chevron U.S.A., Inc.*, 875 F.2d 501, 504 (5th Cir. 1989) (citing to Advisory Committee Note to Rule 608(b), the Court states that "the admissibility of specific instances of conduct is circumscribed by Rule 403").
>
> We suggest that the following factors, among others, should be taken into account in assessing the probative value and prejudicial effect of bad acts when offered to impeach the witness' character trait for veracity:
>
> (1) *Dishonest nature of the act.* While every bad act is somewhat probative of veracity, it is clear that acts that involve dishonesty or lying are more probative of a propensity to lie on the stand than are acts that do not. *See, e.g.*, *United States v. Redditt*, 381 F.3d 597 (7th Cir. 2004) (no error in permitting defendant to be cross-examined about her false denial on an employment action that she had ever been convicted of a crime); *Deary v. City of Gloucester*, 9 F.3d 191 (1st Cir. 1993) (filing a false overtime report is highly probative of witness's bad character for veracity). Rule 609 draws a distinction in its text between crimes of dishonesty and other crimes in the text of the Rule, and there is every reason for Courts applying Rules 608 and 403 to take account of this distinction as a matter of logic, even it is not specified in those Rules. *See United States v. Flaharty*, 295 F.3d 182 (2d Cir. 2002) (no error in prohibiting defendant from cross-examining government witness about his involvement in a murder, as this is "generally not a crime of dishonesty" and so was not sufficiently probative of the witness's character for truthfulness).
>
> (2) *Remoteness of the act.* As originally proposed, Rule 608(b) prohibited the admission of "remote" acts of misconduct. In order to provide for more flexibility, Congress deleted this limitation. However, remoteness remains an important consideration, because the older the act, the less it says about the witness's *current* propensity to lie on the stand. *See, e.g.*, *United States v. Kennedy*, 714 F.2d 968 (9th Cir. 1983) (witness's involvement with the Hell's Angels ten years earlier was properly excluded under Rule 608(b) since "it detracted only minimally from his credibility"). Of course, the remoteness factor cannot be applied independently. If the act occurred long ago and yet

it strongly indicates dishonest character, it may still be sufficiently probative to justify consideration by the factfinder. *See, e.g., United States v. Weichert*, 783 F.2d 23, 26 (2d Cir. 1986) (the government was permitted to cross-examine the defendant about his disbarment which occurred twelve years earlier: "That the disbarment occurred twelve years before the trial decreased its probative value but did not require exclusion.").

(3) *Impeachment on other grounds.* If the witness has already been impeached by other methods, then use of bad acts becomes less probative. The probative value of a particular piece of evidence must be assessed in light of the other evidence that is or can be proffered to prove the point. Thus, if a witness has already been impeached with a prior inconsistent statement and evidence of bias, the court should be more receptive to prohibiting inquiry into a bad act.

(4) *Importance of the witness's credibility*. In some cases, the credibility of a certain witness is crucial to the outcome, and in some cases it is not. The more important the witness's credibility is to the case, the more permissive the court should be in allowing inquiry into the witness's character for truthfulness. For example, if the case comes down to a testimonial dispute between two witnesses, bad acts may well be fair game where they would not be if the witness was simply a foundation witness for an unexceptional document. *See, e.g., Chnapkova v. Koh*, 985 F.2d 79 (2d Cir. 1993) (because the plaintiff's credibility was crucial, the trial judge should have permitted the defense to question her about her failure ever to file tax returns); *United States v. Leake*, 642 F.2d 715 (4th Cir. 1981) (discretion to limit cross-examination must focus on "the importance of the testimony [of the witness being cross-examined] to the government's case, the relevance of the conduct to the witness' truthfulness, and the danger of prejudice, confusion, or delay raised by evidence sought to be adduced"; here, it was error to prevent cross-examination about bad acts when the witness was the key witness for the government).

(5) *Inflammatory nature of the act*. While all bad acts are prejudicial simply because they are "bad," it is clear that some acts create a greater risk of an emotional response from the jury than others. The trial judge should be particularly sensitive to bad acts that will inflame the passions of the jurors to such a degree that a witness's probative testimony will be ignored unfairly. *See, e.g., United States v. Wolf*, 787 F.2d 1094 (7th Cir. 1986) (the prosecutor's cross-examination of the defendant concerning his contracting venereal disease on a trip to Thailand, his recommendation of an abortion for a woman, and his relationship with a 14-year-old girl was prejudicial and improper).

(6) *Similarity of the bad act to the issues in the case*. The risk of prejudice is especially acute if the witness's bad act is similar or identical to the issues disputed in the case. The similarity may encourage the jury not simply to disregard the witness' testimony, but also to decide a substantive issue improperly. For example, if a criminal defendant is being tried for extortion and is impeached with prior acts

of extortion, there is a great danger that the jury will use these acts for the impermissible character purposes that are otherwise prohibited under Rule 404(b); as such, exclusion should be more likely than if the bad act were dissimilar to the facts being tried.

(7) *The relationship of the witness to the case.* Under Rule 403, the prejudice that the court must consider is not the humiliation suffered by the witness — although that may be a factor for the Trial Judge to consider under Rule 611(a) in exercising discretion to exclude bad acts evidence, and under Rule 412 in protecting a rape victim. The prejudice to be considered under Rule 403 is that which will be suffered by the party whose testimony the witness favors. In this regard, the prejudice will vary depending on who the witness is. If the witness is simply an unaffiliated fact witness, the only prejudice suffered by the party is that the witness' testimony may be unfairly disregarded by the jury. But if the witness is somehow affiliated with the party — such as a family member, friend, or business associate — the prejudice derived from the witness's bad act is greater, because the jury may not merely disbelieve the witness; it may also unfairly conclude that "birds of a feather flock together." And, of course, if the witness *is* the party, the possible prejudice derived from a bad act will be at its highest."

5. Does the good faith basis for inquiring apply?

As with other impeachment modes, counsel must have a good faith basis that a bad act actually occurred before inquiring into it on cross-examination. This requirement is especially important with prior bad acts because of their ability to cause prejudice and introduce collateral issues. It is easy to imagine how merely asking a certain question may create extreme prejudice. *See United States v. Leake*, 642 F.2d 715, 719 n.3 (4th Cir. 1981) (approving question about prior misdeeds on the assumption that "defense counsel had a reasonable basis for believing that [the witness] actually committed the acts").

6. If the witness denies the impeaching bad act, may it be proven by extrinsic evidence?

Federal Rule 608(b) expressly provides that extrinsic evidence is *not* admissible to prove that a witness is lying as to a prior bad act. Thus, in *United States v. Reed*, 715 F.2d 870, 876 (5th Cir. 1983), the Court held that under Rule 608(b) "it is well settled that it is reversible error to permit the introduction of extrinsic evidence to prove misconduct that did not result in a conviction." Courts often summarize this rule by stating that the cross-examiner must take the answer of the witness. *See United States v. Cohen*, 631 F.2d 1223, 1226 (5th Cir. 1980). This statement is helpful and accurate in that the cross-examiner may not call other witnesses to prove the bad act after the witness has denied it. The statement is misleading, however, in that the cross-examiner may, subject to the discretion of the trial court, continue to press the witness for an admission.

Note that the bar on extrinsic evidence imposed by Rule 608(b) is applicable only when the impeaching party is attacking the witness's character for truthfulness. If the attack is on other grounds, such as for bias, contradiction, or prior inconsistent statement, the admissibility of extrinsic evidence is governed by Rule 403. The Supreme Court made this clear in *United States v. Abel,* 469 U.S. 45 (1984). Abel was a member of the Aryan Brotherhood, a white supremacist prison gang, whose members take an oath that they will lie for each other when necessary. Abel called a witness who was asked on cross-examination whether he was a member of the Aryan Brotherhood. The witness denied the affiliation. The trial court allowed the government to prove the witness's membership through extrinsic evidence. Abel complained that the admission of extrinsic evidence violated Rule 608(b), but the Court found no error. The Court noted that the witness was being impeached not only for his character for untruthfulness (given his having taken an oath to lie for Abel) but also for having a motive to falsify, i.e., to protect a fellow Aryan brother. As such, the bar of Rule 608(b) was not applicable and the admissibility of the extrinsic evidence was governed by Rule 403. The 2003 amendment to Rule 608(b) codifies the result in *Abel.*

See the Committee Note to the 2003 amendment, earlier in this section.

MODE 7: Character Witness for Veracity/Nontruthfulness

[a] Common Law

Under common law either side could call a witness to say another witness, called by the opposition, was a liar. The character witness for veracity could only testify as to the *reputation* for truthfulness of the first witness. Federal Rule 608(a) has broadened this restriction and allows the character witness for nontruthfulness to give her *opinion* of the first witnesses character for truthfulness. *United States v. Mandel*, 591 F.2d 1347, 1370 (4th Cir. 1979). This change in the available methods of proof from the common-law tradition parallels the change in Rule 405 methods of proof for substantive character evidence.

Some common-law jurisdictions allowed a witness to be impeached by a showing of bad general moral character. *Grammer v. State*, 196 So. 268, 272 (Ala. 1940). Impeachment for bad general moral character often includes charges of sexual immorality or other uncomfortable topics. This method of impeachment made the role of the witness very undesirable for some. Federal Rule 608(a) limits the impeachment of the witness to the character trait of truthfulness or untruthfulness.

[b] Federal Rule of Evidence 608(a)

Rule 608. Evidence of Character and Conduct of Witness

(a) Opinion and reputation evidence of character. The credibility of a witness may be attacked or supported by evidence in the form of opinion or reputation, but subject to these limitations: (1) the evidence may refer only to character for truthfulness or untruthfulness, and (2) evidence of truthful character is admissible only after the character of the witness for truthfulness has been attacked by opinion or reputation evidence or otherwise.

[c] Expert Testimony as to Truthfulness

UNITED STATES v. HISS

88 F. Supp. 559 (S.D.N.Y. 1950)

GODDARD, DISTRICT JUDGE:

Memorandum in respect to the admission of psychiatric testimony to impeach the credibility of the Government witness, Whittaker Chambers.

It is apparent that the outcome of this trial is dependent to a great extent upon the testimony of one man — Whittaker Chambers. Mr. Chambers' credibility is one of the major issues upon which the jury must pass. The opinion of the jury — formed upon their evaluation of all the evidence laid before them — is the decisive authority on this question as on all questions of fact.

The existence of insanity or mental derangement is admissible for the purpose of discrediting a witness. Evidence of insanity is not merely for the judge on the preliminary question of competency, but goes to the jury to affect credibility.* * *

Since the use of psychiatric testimony to impeach the credibility of a witness is a comparatively modern innovation, there appears to be no federal cases dealing with this precise question. However, the importance of insanity on the question of credibility of witnesses is often stressed. There are some State cases in which such testimony has been held to be admissible or which indicate that if this question had been presented, it would have been admissible.

* * *

I have given full consideration to the Government's argument against the admission of this testimony. However, evidence concerning the credibility of the witness is undoubtedly relevant and material and under the circumstances in this case, and in view of the foundation which has been laid, I think it should be received.

In my charge to the jury I shall advise them of the weight which may be given to such testimony.

UNITED STATES v. BARNARD

490 F.2d 907 (9th Cir. 1973)

DUNIWAY, CIRCUIT JUDGE:

In December of 1972, the four appealing defendants, Buddy Joe and Jerry Robert Barnard, Low, and Remley, were convicted on five counts: conspiracy to import marijuana in violation of 21 U.S.C. §§ 952, 960 and 963 (one count); attempted importation and importation of marijuana in violation of 21 U.S.C. §§ 952, 960 and 963 (two counts); and possession of marijuana with intent to distribute in violation of 21 U.S.C. § 841(a) (two counts). The indictment was returned and trial was held in the Southern District of California. We affirm.

* * *

The Witness Dillon

Dillon was a co-defendant in the case. He testified for the government. After the trial was over, he pled guilty to count 3 and was given five years' probation. The other two counts were dismissed.

* * *

On November 5, 1972, two days before the beginning of trial, it came to the attention of the defendants that Dillon had had psychiatric problems which had led to his discharge from the United States Army in 1960. * * *

b. Expert Testimony as to Dillon's Credibility

Defendants offered the testimony of a psychiatrist and a psychologist, who were called to testify as to their opinions of Dillon's competency and reliability as a witness. Each had read over the record of Dillon's Army psychiatric evaluation and his grand jury testimony, and had observed Dillon for part of the time when he was testifying in court. On the basis of this familiarity with Dillon, each had formed the opinion that Dillon was a sociopath who would lie when it was to his advantage to do so. The offer was rejected.

* * * Credibility * * * is for the jury — the jury is the lie detector in the courtroom. Judges frequently instruct juries about factors that the jury may or should consider in weighing the veracity of a witness. In this respect it can be said that judges assume that they have certain expertise in the matter, and that juries have less of that expertise than judges. It is now suggested that psychiatrists and psychologists have more of this expertise than either judges or juries, and that their opinions can be of value to both judges and juries in determining the veracity of witnesses. Perhaps. The effect of receiving such testimony, however, may be two-fold: first, it may cause juries to surrender their own common sense in weighing testimony; second, it may produce a trial within a trial on what is a collateral but still an important matter. For these reasons we, like other courts that have considered the matter, are unwilling to say that when such testimony is offered, the judge must admit it.* * *

The admissibility of the proffered testimony was for the judge, and in deciding whether to admit expert testimony, "the trial judge has broad discretion * * * and his action is to be sustained unless manifestly erroneous." Here we find no abuse of discretion. The experts' knowledge about Dillon was limited, to say the least. Dillon's credibility was otherwise suspect, as a co-defendant testifying for the government, and as having perjured himself before the grand jury. We have grave doubt that the expert testimony would have helped the jury. Under the Constitution, Article III, § 3, trial of criminal cases in Federal courts is by jury, not by experts. We think that the testimony of the type offered in this case should be received only in unusual cases, such as *United States v. Hiss, supra*. And by referring to that case we are not saying that it would have been error to exclude the testimony there offered and received.

* * *

Affirmed.

NOTES

1. Is expert testimony of the truthfulness of a witness generally admitted?

Modern cases uphold trial court rulings excluding proffered psychiatric testimony. In *United States v. Riley*, 657 F.2d 1377, 1387 (8th Cir. 1981), the court rejected the defense's proffer of expert psychiatric testimony as to the mental condition of a prosecution witness and "her capacity for telling the truth," based on in-court observations because it is "doubtful that a medical witness can give a legally acceptable expert opinion on the mental condition of a witness merely by observing the witness testify in court."

2. Must expert testimony as to some medical conditions be admitted?

In *United States v. Shay*, 57 F.3d 126 (1st Cir. 1995), the court reversed a defendant's convictions for conspiracy and aiding and abetting an attempt to blow up his father's car. The government relied upon incriminating statements made by the defendant to the police, the media, and fellow inmates. In response, the defense attempted to call a psychiatrist to testify that the defendant suffered from a mental disorder known as Munchausen's Disease, which caused him to "spin out webs of lies which are ordinarily self-aggrandizing and serve to place him in the center of attention." Holding exclusion of the expert's testimony to be reversible error, the court distinguished the instant case from others in which courts had held that an expert may not offer an opinion that a witness is lying or telling the truth. It relied upon the Advisory Committee's Notes to Rules 405 and 608 to conclude that expert testimony may be offered to establish a witness's truthful or untruthful character.

[3] Level Three — Inconsistencies

MODE 8: Prior Inconsistent Statements

[a] Federal Rule of Evidence 613

Rule 613. Prior Statements of Witnesses

(a) Examining witness concerning prior statement. In examining a witness concerning a prior statement made by the witness, whether written or not, the statement need not be shown nor its contents disclosed to the witness at that time, but on request the same shall be shown or disclosed to opposing counsel.

(b) Extrinsic evidence of prior inconsistent statement of witness. Extrinsic evidence of a prior inconsistent statement by a witness is not admissible unless the witness is afforded an opportunity to explain or deny the same and the opposite party is afforded an opportunity to interrogate the witness thereon, or the interests of justice otherwise require. This provision does not apply to admissions of a party opponent as defined in rule 801(d)(2).

[b] General Requirements

UNITED STATES v. ROGERS
549 F.2d 490 (8th Cir. 1976)

WEBSTER, CIRCUIT JUDGE:

George Samuel W. Rogers appeals from his conviction of armed robbery on a United States military reservation in violation of 18 U.S.C. §§ 2111 and 2.

* * *

The principal facts are undisputed:

At approximately 11:15 p.m. on June 3, 1975, four military personnel were robbed by three armed men within the confines of Fort Chaffee, a United States military installation in Arkansas. The victims immediately notified the military police and informed them of the license number and description of the automobile used by their assailants. At approximately 11:45 p. m., the military police discovered inside the fort a 1956 Chevrolet that matched the license number and description given by the victims. Its windows and doors were open and it had apparently been abandoned. An investigator observed in plain view a cardboard box with markings for a Titan .38 pistol and a sales slip from the Oklahoma Tire and Supply Company inside the vehicle. The military police immediately searched the inside of the car and seized the empty box, the sales slip, and other articles.

The military police ascertained that a handgun had been purchased earlier in the day at the Oklahoma Tire and Supply Company by Private First Class Walter Baker using appellant's name and identification. Baker was apprehended after midnight while attempting to enter the gate to Fort Chaffee. Civilian authorities arrested appellant on the morning of June 4 after a license identification check of the 1956 Chevrolet disclosed that he was the owner of the vehicle. Baker subsequently made statements incriminating to both himself and appellant.

* * *

II. *Use of Baker's Extrajudicial Statement*

The most serious contention on appeal relates to the government's use at trial of an extrajudicial statement made by Walter Baker, appellant's alleged confederate. The facts relating to the statement are as follows:

Baker had previously entered a plea of guilty in a military court-martial to the same robbery at Fort Chaffee with which appellant is charged. The government called him as a witness at appellant's trial. Baker essentially testified that he could not identify appellant; that, while he had pleaded guilty to the offense of robbery, he could not remember the robbery incident; and that, although he recalled giving a statement regarding the incident to an FBI agent, he did not remember the content of that statement. After this testimony, the District Court sequestered the jury in order to question Baker further about his lack of memory. Baker was allowed to read the statement, but he could not determine that it was the statement he had made. Counsel for appellant, asserting a belief that statements the prosecution sought to elicit from Baker might be self-incriminating, moved that the Court advise Baker of his Fifth Amendment privilege. The District Court, noting its own concern with possibilities of perjury, then admonished Baker that he had the right not to testify because of potential self-incrimination. When the jury returned, the prosecution attempted further examination, with the following result:

Q: Mr. Baker, I wish to ask you as to whether you wish to testify further after as to the involvement of Mr. Rogers in the purported armed robbery that you and Mr. Curtis were involved in?

A: No, I ain't got nothing to say, because I really don't remember anything anyway.

Q: You are saying you do not wish to make any further statements or are you saying you just don't remember?

A: The only thing I would say I cannot be sure whether or not I was telling the truth anyway, so rather just not say anything else.

Q: Are you invoking what is commonly called the Fifth Amendment?

A: Yes, I do.

At this time, Your Honor, we would offer the witness for cross examination.

THE COURT. All right. You may cross examine * * *.

Cross Examination

I believe I have no questions of this witness.

Baker was excused and FBI Special Agent Thomas H. Brown was called as the next government witness. Brown testified that he had interviewed Baker on August 18, 1975, while Baker was incarcerated at Fort Hood, Texas, and that Baker had, with full knowledge of his constitutional rights and in the presence of an attorney, made a statement to Brown which was subsequently transcribed. Defense counsel objected to the reading of this unsworn and unsigned statement as hearsay. The District Court ruled:

> "Be partly sustained and partly overruled. Ladies and gentlemen of the jury, you will consider any testimony from Mr. Brown concerning Mr. Baker as being testimony to impeach Mr. Baker. Any testimony concerning any other person including the defendant in this case will not be received in evidence in this case."

The statement was then read into evidence in its entirety.

The statement disclosed that earlier on the day of the crime Baker had accompanied appellant to the Oklahoma Tire and Supply Company, where, following appellant's instructions, Baker had purchased a gun using appellant's identification. The statement further described the robbery and placed appellant with Baker as two of the three who held up the soldiers.

* * *

A. *Evidentiary Standards*

Appellant contends that allowing Baker's statement to be read to the jury amounted to the use of prejudicial hearsay. We conclude, however, that use of the statement was proper as impeachment of Baker's in-court testimony. Several requirements founded in fundamental fairness govern the use of prior inconsistent statements for impeachment. All these requirements were satisfied here.

(1) *Inconsistency*

The first requirement, of course, is that the statements be inconsistent. The reason for permitting the use of inconsistent statements to attack the credibility of a witness does not flow from their greater proximity in time to the offense; rather, it rests upon the "notion that talking one way on the stand and another way previously is blowing hot and cold, and raises a doubt as to the truthfulness of both statements." A statement's inconsistency may be determined from the circumstances and is not limited to cases in which diametrically opposite assertions have been made. Thus, inconsistencies may be found in changes in position; they may be implied through silence; and they may also be found in denial of recollection.

The trial judge should have considerable discretion to determine whether evasive answers are inconsistent with positive assertions of an extrajudicial nature previously given. As Judge Weis said in *Agnellino v. State of New Jersey*, 493 F.2d 714, 730 (3d Cir. 1974): "A defendant who chooses to answer questions with half truths cannot claim constitutional protection to remain silent as to the other half. A complete answer to a question may be as inconsistent with a partial reply as one completely different in detail."

A claimed inability to recall, when disbelieved by the trial judge, may be viewed as inconsistent with previous statements when the witness does not deny that the previous statements were in fact made. Dean Wigmore supplies the reason: "[An] unwilling witness often takes refuge in a failure to remember, and the astute liar is sometimes impregnable unless his flank can be exposed to an attack of this sort." 3A J. Wigmore, Evidence § 1043, at 1061 (Chadbourn rev. 1970).

The trial judge must be accorded reasonable discretion in determining whether a claim of faulty memory is inconsistent with statements previously given. In *United States v. Insana*, 423 F.2d 1165, 1170 (2d Cir. 1970), the Second Circuit said:

> To be sure there may be circumstances where the witness in good faith asserts that he cannot remember the relevant events. In such circumstances the trial court may, in its discretion, exclude the prior testimony * * * . However, this does not mean that the trial judge's hands should be tied where a witness does not deny making the statements nor the truth thereof but merely falsifies a lack of memory. Here Schurman had testified in detail before the grand jury, had already pleaded guilty, and on the stand identified Insana and testified to two relevant events. Based upon these facts, the only rational conclusion is that Schurman was fully aware of the content of his grand jury testimony but wished to escape testifying against Insana and thus make a mockery of the trial * * * . Thus we believe that these statements are admissible * * * to impeach his claim of lack of memory * * * .

In this case Baker had previously pleaded guilty in military court to the same offense. When called to the stand he admitted his guilt and prior conviction. He admitted giving a statement to the government agent but testified he could not recall what he had said. He testified that he was not familiar with appellant. When the prosecutor attempted to refresh Baker's memory by asking him if he had not told Agent Brown that he first met appellant on June 1 at the Flame Club through a PFC Troy, Baker replied that he could not recall making that statement.

From these facts and Baker's equivocal answers, the District Court could well infer that Baker was fully aware of the content of his prior statement and was simply attempting to avoid implicating appellant. A conclusion that appellant's prior statement was inconsistent with his denial of memory at trial was thus justified.

(2) *Relevancy*

A second requirement for admissibility is that the inconsistency relate to a matter of sufficient relevancy that the prosecution's case will be adversely affected if the inconsistent testimony is allowed to stand.* * * It would be unfair to permit the use of extrajudicial statements to impeach testimony extraneous to the issues of the case, particularly if related statements damaging to the defendant are disclosed to the jury in the process. Courts must be watchful that impeachment is not used as a subterfuge to place otherwise inadmissible hearsay before the jury. *See United States v. Morlang*, 531 F.2d 183, 190 (4th Cir. 1975).

In contrast to the witness in *United States v. Morlang, supra*, Baker had never, before trial, taken the position that he could not identify appellant or that he could not recall if appellant was one of the robbers. This doubt about appellant's participation expressed by one of the actual participants was indeed potentially injurious to the government, and it was of sufficient relevance to justify impeachment by use of the inconsistent statement.

(3) *Compliance with Rule 613*

The Federal Rules of Evidence impose certain express requirements for use of impeaching inconsistent statements. Fed. R. Evid. 613(a) requires that the prior statement be disclosed, on request, to opposing counsel. Fed. R. Evid. 613(b) requires that, if extrinsic evidence is to be used to prove the prior statement, the witness must be afforded an opportunity to explain or deny it, and the opposing party must have an opportunity to interrogate the witness about it. Both these requirements were met here.

(4) *Limiting Instructions*

As a final requisite to fairness, the District Court must adequately instruct the jury about the limited purpose for which the prior inconsistent statement is admitted. We think the District Court gave adequate guidance to the jury here. Before permitting the statement to be read by Agent Brown, the Court instructed the jury that (1) the testimony was only to impeach Baker, and (2) the testimony concerning any other person "including the defendant" would not be received in evidence in the case. At the conclusion of the government's case, the District Court gave the following cautionary instruction:

> Before I ask the other side to make Motions I will say this: Ladies and gentlemen of the jury, I want to give what might be called an admonition or an explanation, either one * * * . You will recall that the Court directed after asking Mr. Baker if he could read and write, the Court directed that Mr. Baker be shown a statement that the government contended that he had made, Mr. Baker did say that he could read and write and he read the statement and answered a question or two concerning it. Then we permitted the government to call Special Agent Brown of the FBI who was called by the government to impeach Mr. Baker by testifying to what Mr. Baker had formerly told him, and the Court permitted that. Now, you are instructed that the evidence of Mr. Brown concerning a statement made to him by Mr. Baker will be considered by the jury only in determining whether or not Mr. Baker has been impeached and what credibility, if any, you will give to the testimony of Mr. Baker.

Finally, in its final charge to the jury, the District Court said:

> An admission or incriminatory statement made or act done by one Mr. Baker outside of court, may not be considered as evidence against another, Mr. Rogers, who was not present and so did not see the act done or hear the statement made.

We think these instructions clearly and carefully informed the jury of the limited use to be made of Baker's statement.

We conclude, then, that all evidentiary standards for impeachment by prior inconsistent statements were met here.

* * *

Accordingly, the judgment of conviction is affirmed.

NOTE

When must an impeaching counsel lay the foundation for a prior statement?

Common-law courts generally required that the impeaching counsel ask a witness about a prior statement and provide the witness with an opportunity to explain or deny the statement before offering extrinsic evidence of the statement. Rule 613 (b) relaxes the foundation requirement. The Rule provides that when a witness is examined concerning a prior statement, this statement need not be shown to the witness at the time of the examination. However, before extrinsic evidence of the statement can be introduced, the witness must be given some opportunity, at some point in the trial, to explain, repudiate, or deny the statement.

As a matter of strategy, most lawyers will lay the foundation under the Federal Rules as they did at common law. In doing so, they recognize the prudence of adhering to the common-law procedure as a practical matter, as explained by the court of appeals in *Wammock v. Celotex Corp.*, 793 F.2d 1518, 1522 (11th Cir. 1986):

> Rule 613(b) does not supplant the traditional method of confronting a witness with his inconsistent statement prior to its introduction as the preferred method of proceeding. In fact, where the proponent of the testimony fails to do so, and the witness subsequently becomes unavailable, the proponent runs the risk that the court will properly exercise its discretion to not allow the admission of the prior statement. For this reason, most courts consider the touchstone of admissibility under rule 613(b) to be the continued availability of the witness for recall to explain the inconsistent statements.

[c] The Distinction Between Character Impeachment and Prior Inconsistent Statements

UNITED STATES v. WINCHENBACH
197 F.3d 548 (1st Cir. 1999)

SELYA, CIRCUIT JUDGE:

This appeal * * * requires us to plot the line of demarcation between two closely related but poorly understood rules of evidence, Fed. R. Evid. 608(b) and Fed. R. Evid. 613(b). Concluding, as we do, that * * * the trial court's admission of the challenged extrinsic evidence passes muster, we affirm the judgment of conviction.

I. BACKGROUND

* * *

Over a period of approximately five months in mid-1997, the Maine Drug Enforcement Agency (MDEA), working in concert with a confidential informant named James Holmes, fomented a series of "controlled" drug transactions. * * * Acting on the MDEA's instructions, Holmes gave Wendy Spinney (a target of the probe) $250 in exchange for Spinney's promise to deliver cocaine.* * * Spinney identified her supplier as "Junior" and specified that he was based in Waldoboro. [For one transaction] the agents tracked Spinney to a trailer on the Ralph Wink Road in which defendant-appellant Ralph Winchenbach, Jr. resided with his quondam paramour, Arlene Jones (formerly Arlene Winchenbach, by virtue of her earlier marriage to one of the appellant's brothers). Spinney spent nearly ten minutes inside the trailer and then returned directly to her home. When Holmes arrived, she gave him the promised eight-ball of cocaine.

On September 3, the MDEA again set Holmes into motion. On this occasion, he gave Spinney $250 at her dwelling. She said that * * * her supplier was waiting for her "at Junior's house." Agents followed Spinney and a companion, later identified as William Holmstrom, to Duck Puddle Road. They were last seen heading in the direction of the Ralph Wink Road. After a ten-minute interval, an agent observed the pair traveling from the direction of the Ralph Wink Road. At that point, the officers arrested both Spinney and Holmstrom. Spinney had cocaine in her purse.

Upon interrogation, Spinney told the agents that she bought the cocaine for $200 from "Junior" just prior to her arrest and that "Junior" lived in a trailer on the Ralph Wink Road. She added that she had purchased cocaine from "Junior" at his trailer on about 30 occasions and referred to him at one point as "Junior Winchenbach." When asked whether "Junior" was Ralph Winchenbach, Jr., Spinney replied that she thought so.

The MDEA promptly applied for a warrant to search, inter alia, "[t]he Ralph Winchenbach Jr and Arlene Winchenbach residence in Waldoboro, located on the Ralph Wink [R]oad box # 277" as well as "[a]ny and all people present and arriving at the residence at the time of the search, including but not limited to Ralph Winchenbach Jr and Arlene Winchenbach." * * *

The same evening, a team of officers went to the appellant's trailer on the Ralph Wink Road to execute the search warrant. When the appellant opened the door, the officers immediately entered the trailer, arrested him, brought him outside, and searched him. They discovered over $1,000 on his person, including $80 of the "buy money" that the MDEA had given to Holmes earlier that day.

* * *

III. THE EVIDENTIARY QUESTION

At trial, the appellant called Arlene Jones's son, Robbie Flint, as an alibi witness. Flint testified, inter alia, that the appellant was not in the trailer when Spinney arrived on September 3. On cross-examination, the following exchange took place:

Q: Do you have any knowledge of [the appellant's] selling drugs or being involved in drugs on September 3rd 1997?

A: No.

Q: None at all?

A: No.

Q: As far as you know he was not involved in anything?

A: Right.

Q: * * * [I]n that interview with [agent] Dan Bradford, you did talk about [the appellant's] drug activity that night, didn't you?

A: No.

Q: You didn't? Well, isn't it true that what you told Dan Bradford was that the night that MDEA searched the house * * * they missed several ounces of cocaine that were buried in jars outside the residence?

A: No.

Q: You did not tell that to Dan Bradford?

A: No I didn't.

On redirect examination, defense counsel ignored this testimony. In rebuttal, however, the prosecutor called Bradford and sought to interrogate him about the conversation. The court overruled the appellant's objections, and Bradford testified that he spoke with Flint some months after the fact and that Flint, in an effort "to redeem himself" for assisting in a jailbreak, told him that the agents overlooked a quantity of buried cocaine during the search of Winchenbach's trailer. The judge then instructed the jury to consider Bradford's testimony only as it related to Flint's credibility and not for the truth of the matter asserted.

We review the district court's admission of this evidence for abuse of discretion. * * * The appellant maintains that such an abuse occurred because the court should have excluded Bradford's testimony under either Fed. R. Evid. 608(b) or Fed. R. Evid. 403. We address both objections.

A. Rule 608(b).

In this court, as below, the government parries the appellant's Rule 608(b) objection by claiming that Rule 613(b), not Rule 608(b), controls. On a superficial level at least, an apparent tension exists between these two rules. Rule 608(b) bars the credibility-related use of some extrinsic evidence, while Rule 613(b), albeit by negative implication, permits the credibility-related use of some extrinsic evidence if the proponent satisfies certain enumerated conditions. In this instance, the appellant characterizes Bradford's testimony as extrinsic evidence relating to a specific instance of Flint's misconduct, offered by the prosecutor to attack Flint's credibility (and thus prohibited by Rule 608(b)). The government demurs, characterizing the testimony as extrinsic evidence of a prior inconsistent statement made by Flint, offered after Flint had been afforded an opportunity to explain or deny the remark and in circumstances wherein the appellant had a full opportunity to interrogate both Flint and Bradford on the matter (and thus admissible under Rule 613(b)).

At first blush, neither of these characterizations seems implausible — but they cannot both be right. There are, moreover, two wrinkles. In the first place, the district court, though deeming the evidence admissible, mistakenly relied on Rule 608(b). This bevue need not detain us, for the trial court's use of an improper ground for admission of evidence is harmless if the evidence was admissible for the same purpose on some other ground. * * * Thus, this wrinkle irons itself out.

In the second place, each party presses a theory that fails to fit. The appellant seems to say that the evidence should be excluded under Rule 608(b) simply because it was offered to impugn Flint's credibility. This is an overbroad generalization which, among its other vices, contradicts the time-honored tenet that prior inconsistent statements ordinarily may be used to impeach a witness's credibility. * * * In the bargain, this interpretation of Rule 608(b) leaves no room at all for the admission of extrinsic impeachment evidence under the auspices of Rule 613(b). Thus, we reject it.

For its part, the government urges us to hold that a strict statement/conduct dichotomy triggers the choice of rule. Under this dichotomy, Rule 613(b) always would apply to statements and Rule 608(b) always would apply to conduct. A glance at the case law unmasks this gross oversimplification. Cases invoking Rule 608(b) in respect to statements, as opposed to conduct, are not uncommon. We, too, reject it.

Although we cannot accept either of the parties' self-serving taxonomies, we think that there is a principled distinction between the types of evidence covered by the two rules. In our view, Rule 613(b) applies when two statements, one made at trial and one made previously, are irreconcilably at odds. In such an event, the cross-examiner is permitted to show the discrepancy by extrinsic evidence if necessary — not to demonstrate which of the two is true but, rather, to show that the two do not jibe (thus calling the declarant's credibility into question). * * * In short, comparison and contradiction are the hallmarks of Rule 613(b).

In contrast, Rule 608(b) addresses situations in which a witness's prior activity, whether exemplified by conduct or by a statement, in and of itself casts significant doubt upon his veracity. Thus, Rule 608(b) applies to, and bars the introduction of, extrinsic evidence of specific instances of a witness's misconduct if offered to impugn his credibility. * * * So viewed, Rule 608(b) applies to a statement, as long as the statement in and of itself stands as an independent means of impeachment without any need to compare it to contradictory trial testimony. * * *

Applying this analysis to the case at hand, Bradford's testimony falls within the compass of Rule 613(b). At trial, Flint denied any knowledge of drug dealing at the premises, of the appellant's involvement with drugs, or of having told the agent about jars of cocaine buried in the yard. Bradford's testimony — that Flint had told him that the MDEA, in searching the premises, had overlooked several ounces of buried cocaine — directly contradicted Flint's trial testimony in all three respects and therefore constituted extrinsic evidence of a prior inconsistent statement.

The appellant's contrary argument will not work unless the statement attributed to Flint by Bradford, standing alone and without any reference to Flint's trial testimony, somehow calls into question Flint's credibility. The testimony fails this test: the appellant does not squarely argue that the mere assertion that the officers missed some buried jars of cocaine during their search of the premises, offered in an effort to cooperate with law enforcement, sinks to the level of an affirmative example of Flint's misconduct such as would significantly affect Flint's credibility, and such an argument, if made, would be unconvincing. It is only the comparison of the earlier statement with Flint's trial testimony that imbues the evidence with probative value for impeachment purposes.

That ends the matter. Inasmuch as Flint was afforded an opportunity to explain or deny the prior inconsistent statement and the appellant had a chance to interrogate him about it, the conditions for the operation of Rule 613(b) were fully satisfied. Unless some other ground of objection looms — a matter to which we now turn — Bradford's testimony was admissible under that rule. * * *

B. Rule 403.

As a fallback, the appellant contends that the district court should have excluded Bradford's testimony on the ground that its unfairly prejudicial effect overbalanced its legitimate worth. This contention rests on Fed. R. Evid. 403, which provides in pertinent part that relevant evidence "may be excluded if its probative value is substantially outweighed by the danger of unfair prejudice, confusion of the issues, or misleading the jury."

We review the admission or exclusion of evidence under Rule 403 for abuse of discretion. * * * Virtually all evidence is designed to be prejudicial (i.e., to help one side's case and to hurt the other's); therefore, Rule 403 concerns itself not with prejudice per se but with unfair prejudice. * * * Attempting to wrap himself in this mantle, the appellant hypothesizes that Bradford's testimony ineluctably led the jury to believe that the appellant was "a big time drug dealer."

In passing upon this objection at trial, the lower court made a balanced apprisal of the situation. In the process, the court noted the high probative value of the evidence — Flint, after all, was an alibi witness whose testimony, if credited, would have exonerated Winchenbach — and concluded that it was not unduly prejudicial. In these circumstances, we discern no abuse of the court's discretion.

We add only two comments. First, the prosecutor already had brought the contents of the purported conversation to the jury's attention when, without objection, he cross-examined Flint about it. This draws much of the sting from the appellant's claim [of prejudice]. * * * Second, the court prudently minimized any unfairly prejudicial impact by an immediate instruction that directed the jury to consider the statements attributed to Flint only "for the limited purpose of whatever effect they may have in your judgment upon [his] credibility." In that connection, the court explicitly warned the jurors not to "use [the evidence] for the purpose of proving the truth of what [Flint] said out-of-court." We have frequently remarked the prophylactic effect of such limiting instructions, * * * and see no reason in this instance to abandon the "almost invariable assumption of the law that jurors follow their instructions," *Richardson v. Marsh*, 481 U.S. 200, 206 (1987).

IV. CONCLUSION

We need go no further. For the reasons stated, we * * * reject the appellant's claim that the jury should not have been allowed to hear extrinsic evidence anent Flint's prior inconsistent statement to Bradford as an aid to evaluating Flint's credibility. For aught that appears, Winchenbach was fairly tried and justly convicted.

Affirmed.

[d] Illustrations

1. There is only one witness to the accident. Ima Witness told the plaintiff's lawyer that the defendant ran the red light. Ima is on the stand.

Plaintiff:	State your name.
Witness:	Ima Witness.
Plaintiff:	Were you at the scene of the accident?
Witness:	Yes.
Plaintiff:	Did you see it happen?
Witness:	Yes.
Plaintiff:	What did you see?
Witness:	The plaintiff ran the red light.
Plaintiff:	Excuse me, ah, didn't you tell me in my office that it was the defendant who ran the red light?
Defendant:	Objection! The plaintiff is impeaching his own witness.
Plaintiff:	__________.
The court:	__________.

2. Eye Witness saw it all.

Plaintiff calls her to the stand.

Plaintiff:	Did you see the fight?
Witness:	Yes, everything.
Plaintiff:	Who threw the first punch?
Witness:	The defendant.
Plaintiff:	No further questions.
Defendant:	No cross your Honor.

Later in the case, after the Plaintiff has rested, the Defendant calls Bar Tender to the stand.

Defendant:	State your name.

Witness:	Bar Tender.
Defendant:	Do you know Eye Witness?
Witness:	Yes, she's a regular.
Defendant:	Did she talk to you immediately after the fight?
Witness:	Yes she did.
Defendant:	Did she say who started the fight?
Witness:	Yes. She said it was * * *
Plaintiff:	________.
Defendant:	________.
The court:	________.

Has plaintiff's counsel acted properly in illustration 1? Is there something missing in illustration 2?

MODE 9: Contradiction

[a] Illustration

The estate of Robin Rich is suing Bad Driver for negligently running his station wagon into the driver's side of the Robin's car. I. Witness says he witnessed the whole thing because he was in the car behind Bad Driver's. At trial I. Witness testifies that:

(1) the light was green;

(2) he is acquainted with Bad Driver, but does not know him well; and

(3) Robin Rich was wearing a gold blazer.

The Estate has evidence available to prove each of the following contradictions:

(1) the light was red;

(2) I. Witness was formerly in a long-term business with Bad Driver and that they are still good friends;

(3) Robin Rich was wearing a blue blazer.

On which of these points may counsel for the estate introduce extrinsic evidence to impeach I. Witness?

[b] Overview

Impeachment by contradiction involves demonstrating that something asserted by a witness in her testimony is untrue. The inference to be derived is that if the witness is not accurate in one respect, the witness may be inaccurate in others as well. Contradiction may occur during cross-examination, when questions may cause the witness to admit that she lied or was mistaken on a particular point. As in the case of prior inconsistent statements, the contradiction is supposedly offered not to prove the contradicting point, but instead, to show that because the witness is mistaken on this point, the witness may be mistaken or lying about the rest of her account.

Often contradiction is accomplished by the introduction of extrinsic contradictory evidence in the form of another witness, documents, or other evidence showing that the witness's story is not true in some or all respects. Issues often arise concerning the admissibility of extrinsic contradictory evidence.

[c] Extrinsic Evidence to Contradict

The use of extrinsic evidence to contradict is restricted in order to avoid confusion of the issues, misleading the jury, waste of time, and unfair prejudice caused by the introduction of collateral matters. The rule for the admissibility of extrinsic evidence to contradict is often stated using the conclusory labels of collateral and noncollateral. Extrinsic evidence is not admissible to contradict on a collateral issue. Extrinsic evidence is admissible to contradict on a noncollateral issue. Unfortunately all this tells us is that we need to decide whether the issue is collateral or noncollateral.

In order to determine whether a certain contradiction is collateral or noncollateral, many courts use the test taken from *Attorney-General v. Hitchcock*, 1 Exch. 91, 104 (1847), expounded in Wigmore, Evidence § 1003 — "[c]ould the fact, as to which error is predicated, have been shown in evidence for any purpose independently of the contradiction." *See, e.g.*, *United States v. Tarantino*, 846 F.2d 1384, 1410 (D.C. Cir. 1988). Stated otherwise "[a] matter is relevant for impeachment if the fact could be proved for a purpose independent of the contradiction." *United States v. Milham*, 590 F.2d 717, 721 (8th Cir. 1979).

Using the above rule, contradictory evidence may be divided into three categories. Extrinsic evidence is admissible when the evidence fits into the first two categories. First, facts that not only contradict, but are also relevant to a substantive issue are considered noncollateral and admissible. Thus, the extrinsic evidence of the color of the light facing the Bad Driver is admissible to contradict I. Witness. Second, facts that are admissible to prove some other impeaching point independent of the contradiction are usually considered noncollateral and admissible. Logically, the rules here should track the rules for the admissibility of extrinsic evidence for the other types of impeachment. Thus, extrinsic evidence of R. Rich's friendship with I. Witness would be admissible to show bias. Third, facts that only contradict are considered collateral and extrinsic evidence is generally inadmissible. Thus, extrinsic evidence of what Robin Rich was wearing would be inadmissible.

The best way to analyze all of the questions of admissibility of extrinsic evidence for contradiction is to consider the "collateral/noncollateral" rule as an application of Rule 403. *See, e.g., United States v. Tarantino*, 846 F.2d 1384, 1409 (D.C. Cir. 1988) ("The 'specific contradiction' rule * * * is a particular instance of the trial court's general power under Fed. R. Evid. 403 to exclude evidence 'if its probative value is substantially outweighed * * * by considerations of undue delay, [or] waste of time.' ").

[d] Facts Relevant to a Material Issue: Intent

STATE v. GORE
384 S.E.2d 750 (S.C. 1989)

GREGORY, CHIEF JUSTICE:

Appellant was convicted of possession of cocaine with intent to distribute and conspiracy to distribute cocaine. We affirm.

Appellant was charged with constructive possession of drugs and drug paraphernalia found in the trailer where his mother, brother, and sister resided. At trial, appellant denied residing at the trailer at the time in question. Upon cross-examination by the solicitor, he denied ever selling drugs out of the trailer. Over appellant's objection, the trial judge allowed reply testimony by a confidential informant who stated he had purchased cocaine from appellant at the trailer on two prior occasions. Appellant contends admission of this testimony was prejudicial error.

When a witness denies an act involving a matter collateral to the case in chief, the inquiring party is not permitted to introduce contradictory evidence to impeach the witness. * * * The reply testimony in question was therefore not admissible unless it could have been admitted as part of the State's case in chief. Evidence of prior bad acts is not admissible to prove the crime charged unless it tends to establish motive, intent, absence of mistake or accident, a common scheme or plan, or identity.* * * The State argues this testimony was admissible to establish the element of intent. We agree. The evidence that appellant sold cocaine from the trailer on two occasions only one month earlier tends to establish his intent regarding the cocaine in his possession at the time in question. We conclude the probative value of this evidence outweighs its prejudicial effect and find no error in the trial judge's ruling.

* * *

Accordingly, the judgment of the circuit court is affirmed.

[e] Facts Relevant to Another Impeaching Point: Bias

UNITED STATES v. ROBINSON
530 F.2d 1076 (D.C. Cir. 1976)

LEVENTHAL, CIRCUIT JUDGE:

This is an appeal from a conviction * * * for sale of narcotics to an undercover police officer on two occasions, on November 2 and November 8, 1974. The court suspended imposition of sentence and put the defendant, appellant in this court, on three years' probation with three-year special parole treatment.

* * *

* * * [E]rror is claimed in the admission of Officer Walker's rebuttal testimony. Defendant, on direct, characterized his relationship with his alibi

witness, Ruben Luke, as a friendship involving occasional borrowing and lending of money between paydays, and denied any recollection of having had a conversation with Officer Walker. Luke, on direct, similarly portrayed himself as a close friend of defendant who occasionally lent money to him and borrowed money from him, and denied knowing Walker or having seen him at the scene of the transactions charged in the indictment. On cross-examination, Luke denied having any business relationship with defendant and categorically denied ever having a conversation with Walker or ever having sold narcotics to him or anyone. In rebuttal, Walker testified to Luke's having driven defendant to the scene of the November 2nd transaction; to statements made to Walker by defendant to the effect that Luke was a joint venturer with defendant in the buying and selling of drugs; and to sales made to Walker by this alibi witness. The trial judge then elicited from Walker that charges were brought against Luke but later dropped, with defense counsel pursuing this point on cross and further inquiring into why the charges were dropped.

* * *

Ordinarily a witness may not be impeached as to credibility by producing extrinsic evidence of prior instances of misconduct short of conviction. And if the witness stands his ground and denies the alleged misconduct, the examiner must "take his answer" and cannot call other witnesses to prove the discrediting acts, lest the trial spin off into a series of sub-trials on collateral issues both confusing and time-consuming. This rule stands firm enough when the question is one of impeaching the general credibility of the person as a witness. It does not apply, however, so as to limit or exclude proof of conduct by the witness evidencing a specific bias for or against a party. "Bias is never classified as a collateral matter which lies beyond the scope of inquiry, nor as a matter on which an examiner is required to take a witness's answer. Bias may be proved by extrinsic evidence even after a witness's disavowal of partiality."

The dominant principle is that evidence showing the "emotional partiality" of a witness "is always significant in assessing credibility," for "the trier must be sufficiently informed of the underlying relationships, circumstances and influences operating on the witness so that, in light of his experience, he can determine whether a mutation in testimony could reasonably be expected as a probable human reaction. Courts are therefore very liberal in accepting testimony relevant to a showing of bias."

* * *

It is thus a matter for the sound discretion of the trial court whether the proferred impeachment evidence is probative of bias, and if so whether its probative worth is outweighed by its prejudicial impact or should otherwise be excluded.

The record, in our view, demonstrates that the rebuttal testimony was not directed at generally discrediting Luke's character or veracity, but was aimed at showing specific matters that were probative of Luke's bias in favor of defendant and against the government. In their testimony on direct, defendant and his alibi witness attempted to paint a picture of a simple friendship involving periodic loans to each other and forswore any contact with Walker. On cross, they maintained this view, specifically denying the existence of any business relationship and having spoken to or sold drugs to Walker. We hold that it was open to the government to show that there was more here than a simple friendship, to reveal aspects of Luke's relationship evidencing a special partiality toward defendant and particular motive to testify falsely on his behalf. By producing Luke as his alibi witness, and by the testimony on direct characterizing their relationship in casual terms, defendant placed the nature of his relationship to Luke directly in issue, and thereby exposed himself to the government's efforts to show that this friendship entailed a joint venture in drugs traffic, including sales to Officer Walker.

* * *

Affirmed.

[f] Facts That Only Contradict

Evidence that has no relevancy independent of the contradiction is usually excluded, because the risk of delay and confusion substantially outweighs its probative value for impeachment by contradiction. While counsel may be allowed to *ask* an impeaching question on cross-examination, it is doubtful that opposing counsel and the court will allow extrinsic evidence to be introduced to show nothing more than that the witness is mistaken. On collateral points the witness's testimony must usually be accepted. To do otherwise would allow the proceedings to devolve into numerous mini-trials that would confuse the issues and waste time.

In certain cases, however, appellate courts have recognized the discretion of the trial court to allow extrinsic evidence on facts that only contradict. These courts often use the justification that sometimes a witness is so unlikely to be innocently mistaken that the extrinsic impeaching evidence convincingly suggests the witness must be lying as to a relevant point. This is simply another application of Rule 403 — the extrinsic evidence is more probative of credibility than in the ordinary case of "collateral" contradiction, so the risk of confusion and delay in presenting the extrinsic evidence does not substantially outweigh its probative value. The general rule, however, is that this extrinsic evidence is excluded.

UNITED STATES v. BEAUCHAMP

986 F.2d 1 (1st Cir. 1993)

LEVIN H. CAMPBELL, SENIOR CIRCUIT JUDGE:

Defendant/appellant, Michael W. Beauchamp, appeals from his conviction * * * for uttering and publishing a forged United States Treasury check and for aiding and abetting others in uttering and publishing the check * * *. Defendant [argues that] the district court abused its discretion by refusing to allow defendant to present testimony impeaching the credibility of a witness * * *. Finding no error, we affirm.

I.

On December 4, 1991, defendant was indicted and charged with uttering and publishing a forged treasury check and aiding and abetting others in uttering and publishing the check * * *. After defendant's first trial ended in a mistrial, the case proceeded to trial again on May 18, 1992. The evidence indicated that on May 4, 1990, the Internal Revenue Service mailed a tax refund check in the amount of $2006.20 to Francisca and Domingo Franco of Central Falls, Rhode Island. The Francos never received their check. Instead, on May 17, 1990, defendant deposited the Francos' refund check in a checking account he had opened two days earlier at a Fleet Bank branch in Lincoln, Rhode Island. The back of the refund check was endorsed "Domingo Franco" and "Francisco (sic) D. Franco." Underneath the endorsements, which were forged, defendant signed his own name and address. No other deposits were made to the account, which reached a zero balance on June 5, 1990. The account was closed on July 16, 1990. In May of 1991, the Providence office of the United States Secret Service began an investigation into possible fraud in the negotiation of the Francos' refund check. As defendant's name and address were on the back of the check, Special Agent Rudolph Rivera contacted him. Defendant admitted to having signed his name on the back of the check, but stated that he had been handed the check by a Hispanic man as partial payment for a car. According to defendant, an acquaintance of his, named Joseph Massey, had brought the Hispanic man to defendant to buy the car. Defendant claimed that the Hispanic man had identified himself as the payee on the refund check. Special Agent Rivera obtained from the defendant exemplars of the defendant's handwriting. After examining these, Rivera concluded that defendant's handwriting was dissimilar from the forged signatures.

In late July, 1991, Fleet Bank contacted Detective William Carnes of the Lincoln, Rhode Island, Police Department concerning the Francos' refund check. After an interview with defendant in which defendant repeated his story with minor variations, defendant, Detective Carnes, and another police officer traveled to Central Falls in search of the Hispanic man to whom defendant had allegedly sold the car, as well as to Union Avenue in Providence to search for an "Italian guy" who allegedly had sold the car to defendant. Their search was unsuccessful. Detective Carnes located Joseph Massey and obtained Massey's agreement to speak to Special Agent Rivera about the case. In a written statement, Massey corroborated defendant's story about the Hispanic man. After federal investigators recontacted Massey in February 1992, Massey admitted that his prior written statement was false. Massey testified for the government at trial. He admitted on direct examination that he had been convicted once for forging a welfare check and twice for larceny of a motor vehicle. Massey testified that on August 1, 1991, defendant went to Massey's wife's house and told Massey that he was in trouble about a check. During this conversation, defendant asked Massey to tell the police the story about the Hispanic man. Massey agreed because he believed defendant was threatening him.

Defendant was denied permission to call as a witness Zelmare Amaral, the landlady of 101 Carpenter Street, Pawtucket, Rhode Island. Defendant sought to introduce Mrs. Amaral's testimony primarily to impeach Massey's testimony that he lived at the 101 Carpenter Street address. Mrs. Amaral had testified at the first trial that Massey's brother and sister, not Massey, resided at 101 Carpenter Street, although she acknowledged having seen Massey there. The court would not allow Mrs. Amaral to testify, saying defendant was merely seeking to impeach Massey on a "very collateral" matter.

The jury returned a guilty verdict and defendant was sentenced to 11 months imprisonment. This appeal followed.

II.

A. Impeachment on Collateral Matters

Defendant contends the district court abused its discretion when it precluded Mrs. Amaral from taking the stand to contradict Massey's testimony that he lived at 101 Carpenter Street. Defendant points to Supreme Court authority that a defendant is entitled to cross-examine a witness as to his or her name and address. Defendant concedes, as he must, that the district court permitted him to cross-examine Massey on his address. Defendant contends, however, that the value of his right to ask Massey where he lives for the purpose of "exposing falsehood" is vastly diminished if defendant cannot also present extrinsic evidence demonstrating that Massey has lied. Defendant additionally argues that, quite apart from the value of Mrs. Amaral's testimony to impeach Massey by contradiction, the proffered testimony was relevant to expose Massey's motive to testify falsely. We find neither argument persuasive.

It is well established that a party may not present extrinsic evidence to impeach a witness by contradiction on a collateral matter. Thus, it is often said that when a witness testifies to a collateral matter, the examiner "must take the answer," i.e., the examiner may not disprove it by extrinsic evidence. A matter is considered collateral if "the matter itself is not relevant in the litigation to establish a fact of consequence, i.e., not relevant for a purpose other than mere contradiction of the in-court testimony of the witness." 1 McCormick on Evidence § 45, at 169. Stated another way, extrinsic evidence to disprove a fact testified to by a witness is admissible when it satisfies the Rule 403 balancing test and is not barred by any other rule of evidence. *See United States v. Tarantino*, 846 F.2d 1384, 1409 (D.C.Cir. 1988) ("The 'specific contradiction' rule * * * is a particular instance of the trial court's general power under Fed. R. Evid. 403 to exclude evidence 'if its probative value is substantially outweighed * * * by considerations of undue delay, [or] waste of time.' ").

To the extent Mrs. Amaral's testimony merely went to Massey's credibility by demonstrating a contradiction on an immaterial matter, it was clearly excludible. Defendant contends that testimony as to Massey's residence was not merely collateral, but was relevant and admissible for a purpose other than impeaching Massey's general character for truthfulness or untruthfulness through contradiction. According to defendant, Massey's insistence that he lived at 101 Carpenter Street in Pawtucket and not at his wife's house on

Pine Street in Central Falls, could have been viewed as an attempt to distance himself from the forged check, which had originally been mailed to the Francos' residence in Central Falls. According to defendant, Massey's alleged falsehood concerning his residence would thus expose a motive to shift culpability for stealing the check from himself to defendant.

But while a witness's self-interest or motive to testify falsely is generally considered to be a non-collateral issue, *United States v. Rios Ruiz*, 579 F.2d 670, 673 (1st Cir. 1978) (bias); *United States v. Calle*, 822 F.2d 1016, 1021 (11th Cir. 1987) (self-interest in testifying), we think the district court was entitled to conclude that the "marginal relevance" of Mrs. Amaral's proposed testimony was outweighed by the "time and effort" it would entail to present this testimony.

As noted by the district judge, who presided over defendant's first trial, Mrs. Amaral's testimony was inconclusive. She testified that she occasionally saw Massey, a truck driver, at 101 Carpenter Street, but that his brother and sister paid the rent. Moreover, as the district court noted, Pawtucket is adjacent to Central Falls; therefore, whether Massey lived at his siblings' house in Pawtucket or his wife's house in Central Falls said little about Massey's personal involvement in the crime, particularly since there had already been testimony that Massey spent at least some time at both locations. Under the circumstances, we cannot say that the district court abused its discretion in excluding Mrs. Amaral's proposed testimony concerning whether Massey lived at 101 Carpenter Street.

* * *

The judgment of the district court is affirmed.

UNITED STATES v. CASTILLO
181 F.3d 1129 (9th Cir. 1999)

SEDWICK, DISTRICT JUDGE:

A jury convicted Jose Luis Castillo of importation and possession of marijuana with intent to distribute. On appeal, Castillo argues the district court erred in admitting evidence of a prior arrest for cocaine possession and a prior conviction for marijuana possession. * * *

On May 30, 1997, an individual later identified as Castillo attempted to enter the United States through the Calexico port of entry as the driver and sole occupant of a Jeep Cherokee. The United States Immigration and Naturalization Service ("INS") inspectors opened the vehicle's rear hatch and discovered eleven packages of marijuana weighing 80.07 kilograms. Castillo ran back into Mexico when the inspectors sought to question him.

Less than a month later, on June 24, 1997, Castillo attempted to enter the United States at Calexico driving a 1985 Lincoln. Customs agents found 22.82 kilograms of marijuana in the car's secret compartment. Castillo was arrested. An officer who had participated in the May 30 inspection identified Castillo as the driver of the Jeep Cherokee. Castillo was charged and convicted of importation of marijuana and possession of marijuana with intent to distribute associated with his June 24 activities, but acquitted of similar charges related to the May 30 incident.* * *

Before trial, the United States and Castillo filed motions in limine addressing the admissibility of two other drug-related incidents. The district court ruled that Castillo's May 27, 1997, arrest for cocaine possession was inadmissible. The district court ruled that evidence of Castillo's 1995 possession of marijuana conviction was admissible. Castillo testified at trial. On direct examination, Castillo testified that he worked with disadvantaged children, and would not have smuggled drugs "for a million dollars." Castillo portrayed himself as an anti-drug counselor who taught kids to "stay away from drugs." He added that he had never used drugs and would not touch them. Castillo's sweeping denial of any association with drugs was volunteered and often not responsive to questions posed by his lawyer. After hearing Castillo's testimony, the district court advised the parties it was reconsidering its earlier ruling excluding evidence of the 1997 arrest for cocaine possession. After affording time for additional briefing and argument, the district court revised its ruling so as to allow a rebuttal witness to testify about Castillo's 1997 arrest. Explaining that Castillo had portrayed himself as a "paragon of virtue" and "quintessential model citizen" who would never have anything to do with drugs, the district court concluded that the 1997 cocaine arrest "bears directly on [Castillo's] credibility" and admitted extrinsic evidence concerning the earlier arrest to impeach Castillo.

Castillo contends that Federal Rule of Evidence 608(b) expressly precludes admission of all extrinsic evidence used to attack a witness' credibility. The United States argues that Rule 608(b) is limited to attacks on character for veracity — that is, situations where the evidence's only relevance is to impeach a witness' general credibility by showing specific instances of misconduct — and does not exclude extrinsic evidence used to impeach a witness' testimony by contradiction of facts asserted in that testimony. * * *

Although Castillo briefed and argued the district court's ruling under Rule 608(b), impeachment by contradiction is not governed by that subsection. As one commentator has observed, "counsel and courts sometimes have difficulty distinguishing between Rule 608 impeachment and impeachment by contradiction." *See* Weinstein's Federal Evidence, § 608.12[6][a] — (Weinstein"). Rule 608(b) prohibits the use of extrinsic evidence of conduct to impeach a witness' credibility in terms of his general veracity. In contrast, the concept of impeachment by contradiction permits courts to admit extrinsic evidence that specific testimony is false, because contradicted by other evidence.

Direct-examination testimony containing a broad disclaimer of misconduct sometimes can open the door for extrinsic evidence to contradict even though the contradictory evidence is otherwise inadmissible under Rules 404 and 608(b) and is, thus, collateral. This approach has been justified on the grounds that the witness should not be permitted to engage in perjury, mislead the trier of fact, and then shield himself from impeachment by asserting the collateral-fact doctrine. * * *

In the case before us, the issue is whether evidence of the 1997 cocaine arrest was admissible as impeachment by contradiction. Impeachment by contradiction is properly considered under Rule 607, not Rule 608(b). The Second

Circuit has noted that, "Rule 607 appears to allow the continuation of federal practice in admitting extrinsic evidence to impeach specific errors or falsehoods in a witness' direct testimony, subject to Rule 403 considerations." *United States v. Benedetto*, 571 F.2d 1246, 1250 n.7 (2d Cir. 1978). Weinstein also suggests that courts should analyze such evidence under Rule 403. We agree.

Broadly read, two of our cases might be said to support Castillo's contention that the district court erred by admitting evidence of the 1997 cocaine arrest, but closer analysis reveals that these cases may be distinguished. In *United States v. Bosley*, 615 F.2d 1274 (9th Cir. 1980), defendant Bosley denied on cross-examination that he had ever delivered cocaine to anyone. The district court permitted the government to call a rebuttal witness who testified that Bosley had delivered cocaine to him. On appeal we said: "Upon Bosley's denial that he had delivered cocaine to Rhodes or anyone else, the Government could attempt on further cross examination to elicit a response from Bosley contradicting his prior testimony, but it could not properly impeach Bosley through extrinsic evidence of Bosley's delivery of cocaine to Rhodes."

United States v. Green, 648 F.2d 587 (9th Cir. 1981), held it was prejudicial error to admit extrinsic evidence of drug activity to impeach testimony given on cross-examination. There, we said in a more detailed explanation:

> The Government urges that Rule 608(b) should not be construed [to limit impeachment], since it gives witnesses the opportunity to commit perjury without fear of rebuttal. This contention might be persuasive had the statements in issue been volunteered on direct examination or unelicited on cross-examination. Here the statements were given in direct response to specific questions asked on cross-examination. If the Government believed that it had elicited an untruthful remark, its remedy, as noted in *Bosley*, was to impeach the witness through cross-examination.

We do not read *Bosley* and *Green* to require exclusion of extrinsic evidence offered to impeach a witness in all circumstances. Rather, we read those cases to hold that extrinsic evidence may not be admitted to impeach testimony invited by questions posed during cross-examination. This is a significant distinction recognized by many authorities. Courts are more willing to permit, and commentators more willing to endorse, impeachment by contradiction where, as occurred in this case, testimony is volunteered on direct examination. The distinction between direct and cross-examination recognizes that opposing counsel may manipulate questions to trap an unwary witness into "volunteering" statements on cross-examination. The distinction also recognizes that, as a practical matter, it is often difficult to determine whether testimony is invited or whether it is volunteered on cross-examination.

As *Green* suggests * * * there may be situations where testimony given during cross-examination may be impeached by contradiction. Accordingly, we do not hold that a bright line distinction between testimony volunteered on direct examination and testimony elicited during cross-examination must be rigidly enforced so as to exclude all impeachment by contradiction of testimony given during cross-examination. We do hold that Castillo's expansive and unequivocal denial of involvement with drugs on direct examination warranted the district court's decision to admit extrinsic evidence of the 1997 cocaine arrest as impeachment by contradiction. * * *

* * * The judgment of the district court is AFFIRMED.

NOTE

How are objections to evidence offered in contradiction as being collateral analyzed under the Federal Rules?

In *United States v. Tarantino*, 846 F.2d 1384 (D.C. Cir. 1988), the Court affirmed drug conspiracy convictions. It held that the "specific contradiction" rule, which bars impeachment of a witness on a collateral issue, is a particular example of balancing under Rule 403 and may be invoked by a trial judge. In essence the court was saying that if extrinsic evidence is offered to contradict a witness where the fact to be contradicted has nothing to do with the substantive issues of the case, then the probative value of the evidence for impeachment purposes is substantially outweighed by the risks of prejudice, confusion and delay.

[4] Level Four — Bias

MODE 10: Bias/Partiality

[a] Illustration

A law student is murdered. The defense cross-examines.

Defendant:	Sir, you've testified that you saw the defendant and the deceased the day before the murder arguing over who should be allowed to check out a certain treatise on evidence. Isn't it true that the prosecution has paid you to testify?
Prosecution:	Objection! This is collateral and is not relevant.
Defendant:	(1) _________.
The court:	(2) _________.
Witness:	The prosecution is paying me a per diem of $80.00 plus any other necessary expenses that I incur.
Defendant:	What do you expect to receive for your "expenses" for this entire case?
Prosecution:	Objection! The witness has already admitted that he is being compensated for his expenses. The defense is harping on this collateral point.
Defendant:	(3) _________.
The court:	(4) _________.
Witness:	$700.00. [If the court allows the witness to answer.]

Defendant:	Isn't it also true that you once called the defendant "an amoral yuppie in training."
Prosecution:	Objection! This is not relevant.
Defendant:	(5) ________.
The court:	(6) ________.
Witness:	Yes, I called him an amoral yuppie in training.
Defendant:	Isn't it true that you are, in fact sir, the former lover of the deceased?
Prosecution:	Your Honor, counsel has gone too far!
Defendant:	(7) ________.
The court:	(8) ________.
Witness:	No.

Will the defendant be allowed to prove the witness was the decedent's lover?

[b] Admissibility under the Federal Rules

UNITED STATES v. ABEL
469 U.S. 45 (1984)

JUSTICE REHNQUIST delivered the opinion of the Court.

A divided panel of the Court of Appeals for the Ninth Circuit reversed respondent's conviction for bank robbery. The Court of Appeals held that the District Court improperly admitted testimony which impeached one of respondent's witnesses. We hold that the District Court did not err, and we reverse.

Respondent John Abel and two cohorts were indicted for robbing a savings and loan. * * * The cohorts elected to plead guilty, but respondent went to trial. One of the cohorts, Kurt Ehle, agreed to testify against respondent and identify him as a participant in the robbery.

Respondent informed the District Court at a pretrial conference that he would seek to counter Ehle's testimony with that of Robert Mills. Mills was not a participant in the robbery but was friendly with respondent and with Ehle, and had spent time with both in prison. Mills planned to testify that after the robbery Ehle had admitted to Mills that Ehle intended to implicate respondent falsely, in order to receive favorable treatment from the Government. The prosecutor in turn disclosed that he intended to discredit Mills' testimony by calling Ehle back to the stand and eliciting from Ehle the fact that respondent, Mills, and Ehle were all members of the "Aryan Brotherhood," a secret prison gang that required its members always to deny the existence of the organization and to commit perjury, theft, and murder on each member's behalf.

Defense counsel objected to Ehle's proffered rebuttal testimony as too prejudicial to respondent. After a lengthy discussion in chambers the District Court decided to permit the prosecutor to cross-examine Mills about the gang, and if Mills denied knowledge of the gang, to introduce Ehle's rebuttal testimony concerning the tenets of the gang and Mills' and respondent's membership in it. The District Court held that the probative value of Ehle's rebuttal testimony outweighed its prejudicial effect, but that respondent might be entitled to a limiting instruction if his counsel would submit one to the court.

At trial Ehle implicated respondent as a participant in the robbery. Mills, called by respondent, testified that Ehle told him in prison that Ehle planned to implicate respondent falsely. When the prosecutor sought to cross-examine Mills concerning membership in the prison gang, the District Court conferred again with counsel outside of the jury's presence, and ordered the prosecutor not to use the term "Aryan Brotherhood" because it was unduly prejudicial. Accordingly, the prosecutor asked Mills if he and respondent were members of a "secret type of prison organization" which had a creed requiring members to deny its existence and lie for each other. When Mills denied knowledge of such an organization the prosecutor recalled Ehle.

Ehle testified that respondent, Mills, and he were indeed members of a secret prison organization whose tenets required its members to deny its existence and "lie, cheat, steal [and] kill" to protect each other. The District Court sustained a defense objection to a question concerning the punishment for violating the organization's rules. Ehle then further described the organization and testified that "in view of the fact of how close Abel and Mills were" it would have been "suicide" for Ehle to have told Mills what Mills attributed to him. Respondent's counsel did not request a limiting instruction and none was given.

The jury convicted respondent. On his appeal a divided panel of the Court of Appeals reversed. * * *

We hold that the evidence showing Mills' and respondent's membership in the prison gang was sufficiently probative of Mills' possible bias towards respondent to warrant its admission into evidence. Thus it was within the District Court's discretion to admit Ehle's testimony, and the Court of Appeals was wrong in concluding otherwise.

Both parties correctly assume * * * that the question is governed by the Federal Rules of Evidence. But the Rules do not by their terms deal with impeachment for "bias," although they do expressly treat impeachment by character evidence and conduct, Rule 608, by evidence of conviction of a crime, Rule 609, and by showing of religious beliefs or opinion, Rule 610. Neither party has suggested what significance we should attribute to this fact. Although we are nominally the promulgators of the Rules, and should in theory need only to consult our collective memories to analyze the situation properly, we are in truth merely a conduit when we deal with an undertaking as substantial as the preparation of the Federal Rules of Evidence. In the case of these Rules, too, it must be remembered that Congress extensively reviewed our submission, and considerably revised it.

Before the present Rules were promulgated, the admissibility of evidence in the federal courts was governed in part by statutes or Rules, and in part by case law.* * * This Court had held in *Alford v. United States*, 282 U.S. 687 (1931), that a trial court must allow some cross-examination of a witness to show bias. This holding was in accord with the overwhelming weight of authority in the state courts as reflected in Wigmore's classic treatise on the law of evidence. Our decision in *Davis v. Alaska*, 415 U.S. 308 (1974), holds that the Confrontation Clause of the Sixth Amendment requires a defendant to have some opportunity to show bias on the part of a prosecution witness.

With this state of unanimity confronting the drafters of the Federal Rules of Evidence, we think it unlikely that they intended to scuttle entirely the evidentiary availability of cross-examination for bias.* * *

* * * Rule 401 defines as "relevant evidence" evidence having any tendency to make the existence of any fact that is of consequence to the determination of the action more probable or less probable than it would be without the evidence. Rule 402 provides that all relevant evidence is admissible, except as otherwise provided by the United States Constitution, by Act of Congress, or by applicable rule. A successful showing of bias on the part of a witness would have a tendency to make the facts to which he testified less probable in the eyes of the jury than it would be without such testimony.

The correctness of the conclusion that the Rules contemplate impeachment by showing of bias is confirmed by the references to bias in the Advisory Committee Notes to Rules 608 and 610, and by the provisions allowing any party to attack credibility in Rule 607, and allowing cross-examination on "matters affecting the credibility of the witness" in Rule 611(b). The Courts of Appeals have upheld use of extrinsic evidence to show bias both before and after the adoption of the Federal Rules of Evidence.* * *

We think the lesson to be drawn from all of this is that it is permissible to impeach a witness by showing his bias under the Federal Rules of Evidence just as it was permissible to do so before their adoption. In this connection, the comment of the Reporter for the Advisory Committee which drafted the Rules is apropos:

> In principle, under the Federal Rules no common law of evidence remains. 'All relevant evidence is admissible, except as otherwise provided * * *.' In reality, of course, the body of common law knowledge continues to exist, though in the somewhat altered form of a source of guidance in the exercise of delegated powers." Cleary, *Preliminary Notes on Reading the Rules of Evidence*, 57 Neb. L. Rev. 908, 915 (1978) (footnote omitted).

Ehle's testimony about the prison gang certainly made the existence of Mills' bias towards respondent more probable. Thus it was relevant to support that inference. Bias is a term used in the "common law of evidence" to describe the relationship between a party and a witness which might lead the witness to slant, unconsciously or otherwise, his testimony in favor of or against a party. Bias may be induced by a witness' like, dislike, or fear of a party, or by the witness' self-interest. Proof of bias is almost always relevant because the jury, as finder of fact and weigher of credibility, has historically been entitled to assess all evidence which might bear on the accuracy and truth of a witness' testimony. The "common law of evidence" allowed the showing of bias by extrinsic evidence, while requiring the cross-examiner to "take the answer of the witness" with respect to less favored forms of impeachment.

Mills' and respondent's membership in the Aryan Brotherhood supported the inference that Mills' testimony was slanted or perhaps fabricated in respondent's favor. A witness' and a party's common membership in an organization, even without proof that the witness or party has personally adopted its tenets, is certainly probative of bias. * * *

Respondent argues that even if the evidence of membership in the prison gang were relevant to show bias, the District Court erred in permitting a full description of the gang and its odious tenets. Respondent contends that the District Court abused its discretion under Federal Rule of Evidence 403, because the prejudicial effect of the contested evidence outweighed its probative value. In other words, testimony about the gang inflamed the jury against respondent, and the chance that he would be convicted by his mere association with the organization outweighed any probative value the testimony may have had on Mills' bias.

Respondent specifically contends that the District Court should not have permitted Ehle's precise description of the gang as a lying and murderous group. Respondent suggests that the District Court should have cut off the testimony after the prosecutor had elicited that Mills knew respondent and both may have belonged to an organization together. This argument ignores the fact that the *type* of organization in which a witness and a party share membership may be relevant to show bias. If the organization is a loosely knit group having nothing to do with the subject matter of the litigation, the inference of bias arising from common membership may be small or nonexistent. If the prosecutor had elicited that both respondent and Mills belonged to the Book of the Month Club, the jury probably would not have inferred bias even if the District Court had admitted the testimony. The attributes of the Aryan Brotherhood — a secret prison sect sworn to perjury and self-protection — bore directly not only on the *fact* of bias but also on the *source* and *strength* of Mills' bias. The tenets of this group showed that Mills had a powerful motive to slant his testimony towards respondent, or even commit perjury outright.

A district court is accorded a wide discretion in determining the admissibility of evidence under the Federal Rules. Assessing the probative value of common membership in any particular group, and weighing any factors counseling against admissibility is a matter first for the district court's sound judgment under Rules 401 and 403 and ultimately, if the evidence is admitted, for the trier of fact.

Before admitting Ehle's rebuttal testimony, the District Court gave heed to the extensive arguments of counsel, both in chambers and at the bench. In an attempt to avoid undue prejudice to respondent the court ordered that the name "Aryan Brotherhood" not be used. The court also offered to give a limiting instruction concerning the testimony, and it sustained defense objections to the prosecutor's questions concerning the punishment meted out to unfaithful members. These precautions did not prevent *all* prejudice to respondent from Ehle's testimony, but they did, in our opinion, ensure that the admission of this highly probative evidence did not *unduly* prejudice respondent. We hold there was no abuse of discretion under Rule 403 in admitting Ehle's testimony as to membership and tenets.

Respondent makes an additional argument based on Rule 608(b). That Rule allows a cross-examiner to impeach a witness by asking him about specific instances of past conduct, other than crimes covered by Rule 609, which are probative of his veracity or "character for truthfulness or untruthfulness." The Rule limits the inquiry to cross-examination of the witness, however, and prohibits the cross-examiner from introducing extrinsic evidence of the witness' past conduct.

Respondent claims that the prosecutor cross-examined Mills about the gang not to show bias but to offer Mills' membership in the gang as past conduct bearing on his veracity. This was error under Rule 608(b), respondent contends, because the mere fact of Mills' membership, without more, was not sufficiently probative of Mills' character for truthfulness. Respondent cites a second error under the same Rule, contending that Ehle's rebuttal testimony concerning the gang was extrinsic evidence offered to impugn Mills' veracity, and extrinsic evidence is barred by Rule 608(b).

* * *

It seems clear to us that the proffered testimony with respect to Mills' membership in the Aryan Brotherhood sufficed to show potential bias in favor of respondent; because of the tenets of the organization described, it might also impeach his veracity directly. But there is no rule of evidence which provides that testimony admissible for one purpose and inadmissible for another purpose is thereby rendered inadmissible; quite the contrary is the case. It would be a strange rule of law which held that relevant, competent evidence which tended to show bias on the part of a witness was nonetheless inadmissible because it also tended to show that the witness was a liar.

We intimate no view as to whether the evidence of Mills' membership in an organization having the tenets ascribed to the Aryan Brotherhood would be a specific instance of Mills' conduct which could not be proved against him by extrinsic evidence except as otherwise provided in Rule 608(b). It was enough that such evidence could properly be found admissible to show bias.

The judgment of the Court of Appeals is reversed.

NOTES

1. Must the impeacher ask the witness about the acts or declarations showing bias before extrinsic evidence may be introduced to show the bias?

The majority of the courts require that the witness be asked about the bias before extrinsic evidence is allowed. Thus, in *Washington v. United States,* 499 A.2d 95 (D.C. 1985), the court noted:

> [B]efore extrinsic evidence may be introduced to demonstrate acts or declarations showing corruption or bias, a proper foundation must be laid. The reasons underlying this requirement include fairness to the witness, and conservation of time by making extrinsic evidence unnecessary. Thus, counsel must first ask the witness under attack about the alleged facts on cross-examination before counsel may seek to prove prior expressions of bias or corruption by introducing other witnesses or evidence.
>
> Some courts draw a distinction between when bias is shown by a prior statement and when bias is shown by prior conduct. Where bias

is shown by a prior statement, the witness must be afforded an opportunity to explain or deny before the extrinsic evidence is introduced. If the bias is to be proven by extrinsic evidence of conduct, some courts hold that a question is not necessary. *See United States v. Marzano,* 537 F.2d 257, 265 (7th Cir. 1976).

2. May a witness be cross-examined concerning payment for her testimony in the case?

Cross-examination concerning payment for testimony is almost always permissible because it bears directly on the question of bias. The more difficult issues arise around the question of how detailed a cross-examination should be allowed.

In *Collins v. Wayne Corp.*, 621 F.2d 777, 784 (5th Cir. 1980), the Court approved cross-examination concerning fees earned by an expert in other cases.

> No one questions that cross-examination to show the bias of a witness or his interest in a case is entirely proper. Impeachment of witnesses through a showing of bias or interest aids the jury in its difficult task of determining facts when it is faced with contradictory assertions by witnesses on both sides of the case. A pecuniary interest in the outcome of a case may, of course, bias a witness. A showing of a pattern of compensation in past cases raises an inference of the possibility that the witness has slanted his testimony in those cases so that he would be hired to testify in future cases.

In *United States v. 412.93 Acres of Land*, 455 F.2d 1242, 1247 (3d Cir. 1972), the trial court allowed the witness to be cross-examined as to his daily payment for testifying but disallowed questioning about his total fee for the case which included appraisal work. The Court of appeals found the decision was within the discretion of the trial court.

3. Is bias evidence treated the same in civil and criminal cases?

A trial judge has somewhat more leeway in civil cases to limit the scope of impeachment for bias than in criminal cases — at least in criminal cases where the accused is attempting to impeach a prosecution witness for bias. In *Davis v. Alaska*, 415 U.S. 308 (1974), the Supreme Court recognized that a defendant in a criminal case has the right under the Sixth Amendment's Confrontation Clause to elicit testimony that tends to show that a prosecution witness may be biased. While the accused does not have an absolute right to such impeachment, the right to confrontation will be violated if the trial court prevents the defendant from attacking a witness 1) with evidence that is strongly probative of bias, and 2) the credibility of the witness is extremely important in the case. The Court in *Davis* found a Confrontation Clause violation when the trial court prevented an attack on the government's star witness, who implicated Davis in a robbery. The evidence proffered by Davis tended to prove that the witness had a motive to pin the crime on Davis because otherwise the witness was the prime suspect.

In *Delaware v. Van Arsdall*, 475 U.S. 673 (1986), Justice Rehnquist wrote for the Court as it held that a defendant was denied his confrontation right in a state murder case when he was prohibited from questioning a prosecution witness concerning the dismissal of a pending public drunkenness charge. The Court stated that "[b]y thus cutting off all questioning about an event that the State conceded had taken place and that a jury might reasonably have found furnished the witness a motive for favoring the prosecution in his testimony, the Court's ruling violated respondent's rights secured by the Confrontation Clause." The Court rejected the state's argument that the defendant must show that "the particular limitation on cross-examination created a reasonable possibility that the jury returned an inaccurate guilty verdict." Instead, the Court concluded that "the focus of the prejudice inquiry in determining whether the confrontation right has been violated must be on the particular witness, not on the outcome of the entire trial," and that "a criminal defendant states a violation of the Confrontation Clause by showing that he was prohibited from engaging in otherwise appropriate cross-examination designed to show a prototypical form of bias on the part of the witness." Rejecting the argument that a confrontation violation requires automatic reversal of a conviction, the Court remanded the case for a determination of whether the violation was harmless.

D. REHABILITATION

After a witness has been impeached, the nonimpeaching party will often want to repair the credibility of the witness. This rehabilitation is allowed subject to certain conditions and limitations. Generally, the bolstering of the witness's credibility is only allowed after the witness's credibility is attacked — supporting a witness's credibility before an attack is referred to as "impermissible bolstering." It is considered unnecessary because witnesses are presumed to be truthful until their credibility is attacked.. The first case set forth below addresses what constitutes an attack within the meaning of this rule. This rule does not, however, prevent a party from bringing out anticipated impeaching points and weaknesses on direct — that is not rehabilitation, but rather is bringing in negative evidence about the witness's credibility, in order to pre-empt the adversary.

Even when a witness has been attacked, rehabilitation is limited to the area that is attacked. For example, if a witness is attacked with a prior inconsistent statement the party cannot respond with evidence that the witness has a character for truthfulness. The response does not meet the attack, because even if the witness has a truthful character, the fact remains that he has made inconsistent statements.

[1] Truthfulness After Attack

This method of rehabilitation is the counterpart of Mode 7: Character Witness for Veracity/Nontruthfulness. When a witness's character for truthfulness has been attacked, the nonimpeaching party may call a witness to reassure the jury that the witness really is truthful.

There is a danger in calling a rehabilitation witness. As in the case of cross-examination of character witnesses under Rule 405, the impeaching party may now ask the rehabilitation witness about specific instances of conduct. The rationale is that the impeaching party is allowed to test the rehabilitation witness's knowledge of the witness.

[a] Federal Rule of Evidence 608(a)

Rule 608. Evidence of Character and Conduct of Witness

(a) Opinion and reputation evidence of character. The credibility of a witness may be attacked or supported by evidence in the form of opinion or reputation, but subject to these limitations: * * * (2) evidence of truthful character is admissible only after the character of the witness for truthfulness has been attacked by opinion or reputation evidence or otherwise.

* * *

[b] Cross-Examination as Attack

UNITED STATES v. MEDICAL THERAPY SCIENCES, INC.

583 F.2d 36 (2d Cir. 1978)

MOORE, CIRCUIT JUDGE:

After a jury trial, appellants Stanley Berman and his company, Medical Therapy Sciences, Inc. ("Medical Therapy"), were convicted of having filed false claims to obtain Medicare payments during the period of 1971-1976, and of having conspired to do the same along with unindicted co-conspirators, including one Barbara Russell, formerly a trusted employee and personal intimate of Berman. Berman was also convicted of perjury in connection with the grand jury's investigation of Medicare abuses.

The proof of Berman's fraud can be briefly stated. Berman's medical equipment supply company, Medical Therapy, was a Connecticut company, which had a branch, Respiratory Specialties, that operated out of New York. Under the Medicare program, Medical Therapy was to be reimbursed, ultimately by the Department of Health, Education and Welfare, for a certain percentage of the cost of supplies to Medicare patients. However, reimbursable costs vary from one insurance carrier to another, and the place from which the service is rendered determines which carrier is to pay, and which carrier's payment schedule is to apply. Under the rules, if Berman's Connecticut company supplied equipment to a Connecticut Medicare patient, the claim should have been submitted to the Connecticut insurance carrier, not to the New York carrier. At trial, Berman was shown to have devised a scheme to wrongfully obtain payments from both the Connecticut and New York carriers. Aside from double billing the two companies for the same patients, Berman's fraud also consisted of claiming for more expensive equipment than had actually been provided to patients and billing for supplies neither delivered nor needed by the patients.

On appeal, Berman * * * argues that the trial court erred in permitting the Government to present character evidence in its rebuttal case to support Barbara Russell's credibility.

* * *

Rule 608(a) of the Federal Rules of Evidence provides that character evidence may be used to support a witness, but limits its use so that "evidence of truthful character is admissible only after the character of the witness for truthfulness has been attacked by opinion or reputation evidence or otherwise." Berman's claim is that the foundation for character evidence was not present in this case because Russell's character for truthfulness had not been attacked within the meaning of the Rule. He argues that cross examination elicited only matters of Russell's bias in favor of the Government and against Berman and that, in any event, the Government itself initially brought to the jury's attention, on its direct examination of Russell, the facts that she had had two prior convictions and that she had been accused by Berman of having embezzled money from Medical Therapy. Berman contends that the Government should not thereafter have been allowed to bolster her credibility when the defense cross examined only as to matters brought out on direct.

* * *

In this case * * * Berman argues that his counsel did not open the door to character evidence because his cross examination of Russell did not constitute an "attack on veracity". We conclude, however, that Judge Carter could have properly characterized the defense's treatment of Russell as an attack within the meaning of Rule 608(a).

In this case, cross examination of Russell included sharp questioning about her prior convictions, which were predicated on activities characterized as fraudulent. When such convictions are used for impeachment purposes, as they were on cross examination here, we think that the door is opened to evidence in support of truthfulness.* * *

Russell's character was also attacked by "specific act" evidence, to wit, allegations that she had embezzled money and stolen patients from Berman's company. While Berman argues that such evidence, because it involved her efforts to set up a competing business, bore solely on her bias against him, and, as such, did not constitute an attack on character, we do not think that the implications were so limited. As noted by the commentators, evidence of bias can take many forms. Some types of bias, for example bias stemming from a relationship with a party, do not necessarily involve any issue relating to the moral character of the witness, but suggest only that the witness' testimony may perhaps unwittingly be slanted for reasons unrelated to general propensity for untruthfulness. As such, character evidence is not relevant to meet such an attack. On the other hand, alleged partiality based on hostility or self-interest may assume greater significance if it is sought to be proven by conduct rising to the level of corruption. The commentators agree that "[e]vidence of corrupt conduct on the part of a witness should be regarded as an attack on his truthfulness warranting supportive evidence." Certainly, the embezzlement and theft of which Russell was accused can be said to fall within the category of corrupt conduct, within the contemplation of Rule 608(a). Furthermore, Russell consistently denied the larceny that was ascribed to her by the defense attack. Under such a circumstance, the commentators again agree that "rehabilitating evidence should be allowed in the judge's discretion if he finds the witness' denial has not erased the jury's doubts."

We think, in sum, that the decision to permit the character evidence must be affirmed on the facts. We emphasize, however, that discretion in this area must be exercised with circumspection so that the jury's attention is not diverted from the main issues to be tried. It is not every cross examination that should trigger the authority of Rule 608(a)'s provision for supporting character evidence. However, since the attack in this case went even beyond cross examination, and since Berman's guilt was established not only by Russell's testimony, but also by ample supporting evidence, both documentary and in the form of testimony from the Blue Cross specialist and from other employees of Medical Therapy, we affirm.

Judgment affirmed.

[2] Prior Consistent Statements

UNITED STATES v. HARRIS

761 F.2d 394 (7th Cir. 1985)

BAUER, CIRCUIT JUDGE.

Defendant Josephine Harris was found guilty by a jury of forging CETA eligibility questionnaires and time sheets, submitting those documents for payment to the Archdiocese of Chicago, which operated the CETA program, and illegally receiving government funds pursuant to the Comprehensive Employment and Training Act of 1973. * * * The jury also convicted co-defendant Yvonne Harris * * * and the court sentenced her to fifteen months imprisonment to be followed by five years probation. Both defendants appeal the jury's verdict.

I. *Facts*

From 1978 through 1980, the Archdiocese of Chicago administered the Saint Charles Luwanga Lifeline Center in Chicago. The Center was financed by funds which the Archdiocese received from the United States Department of Labor under the Comprehensive Employment and Training Act of 1973 (CETA) to operate employment programs for poor youths. Katie Stanley, a co-defendant who is not a party to this appeal, was head supervisor at the Center. Stanley's job responsibilities included ensuring that participants in the employment program signed their work time sheets, collecting the signed time sheets and forwarding them to the Archdiocese for payment, and receiving paychecks from the Archdiocese to distribute to the program's participants.

Josephine Harris worked at the Center from 1978 to 1980 as an administrative assistant to Stanley. Her duties included helping youths prepare CETA job applications, filing participants' time sheets, and distributing paychecks to participants. Yvonne Harris did not work in the CETA program at the Center, but occasionally helped her mother, Josephine Harris, finish her work at the Center by signing time sheets for "participants" in the CETA program. Yvonne Harris testified at trial that she only signed time sheets for handicapped CETA participants who could not sign the time sheets themselves.

The evidence at trial showed that fictitious social security numbers were used on applications to the CETA program and that Yvonne Harris's medicaid card number was used in over sixty applications. Because eligibility for the program was based on federal poverty guidelines, possession of a medicaid card issued by the Illinois Department of Public Aid provided proof of eligibility. The evidence also showed that Stanley, Josephine Harris, and Yvonne Harris signed time sheets for individuals who were not participants in the CETA program, that Stanley and Josephine Harris submitted those time sheets to the Archdiocese for payment, and that all three defendants forged endorsements on the paychecks which the Archdiocese issued to the fictitious individuals and forwarded to the Center. Stanley would then cash the paychecks at a local currency exchange or with a local merchant whom she knew. The scheme was eventually uncovered by special agents of the United States Department of Labor, and defendants were subsequently tried and convicted.

II. *Evidentiary Rulings*

* * *

Josephine Harris * * * contends that the trial court erred in allowing Agent John Huheey to testify about statements made to him by a previous government witness, Harold Branch, during the course of the government's investigation of the fraud. Branch had been called as a witness by the government and had testified as to his knowledge of Josephine Harris's involvement in the scheme to defraud the CETA program. Later, Harris called Agent Huheey as a witness to impeach Branch and elicited testimony that he had interviewed Branch on June 18, 1979, and that during that interview Branch had made statements which contradicted his testimony at trial. On cross-examination, the government was allowed to elicit testimony from Agent Huheey, over defendant Harris's objection, about statements made by Branch during the June 18 interview which were consistent with Branch's testimony at trial. Harris contends that the trial court incorrectly admitted this testimony as a prior consistent statement by Branch to rebut the implication that Branch had fabricated his testimony at trial.

Rule 801(d)(1)(B) of the Federal Rules of Evidence provides that a prior statement is not excludable as hearsay, and may be offered for the truth of the matter asserted therein, when two requirements are met. First, the declarant must testify at trial and must be subject to cross-examination concerning the statement. Second, the statement must be consistent with the declarant's testimony and must be offered to rebut an express or implied allegation of recent fabrication or improper influence or motive. The case law imposes a further requirement that in order to be admissible a prior consistent statement must also have been made before the motive to fabricate existed. * * * [*See Tome v. United States*, Chapter 11 of this casebook.]

Rule 801(d)(1)(B) allows a proponent to offer into evidence a prior consistent statement to prove the truth of the matter which the declarant asserts in that statement. The government contends in this case, however, that Agent Huheey's testimony of Branch's prior statements was not offered for the truth of the matters asserted therein. Rather, the government contends that the testimony was elicited solely to rehabilitate Branch's testimony. Specifically, the government states that because the defendants called Agent Huheey as a witness to impeach the credibility of Branch's testimony by showing inconsistencies between that testimony and Branch's statements to Agent Huheey during the interview of June 18, 1978, it sought to rehabilitate Branch's credibility by showing the degree of consistency of Branch's testimony with his earlier statements. Thus, Huheey's testimony was offered merely to show that Branch had not made only inconsistent statements prior to his testimony at trial, and therefore those statements were not excludable as hearsay and were not subject to the requirements of Rule 801(d)(1)(B).

Josephine Harris argues that regardless of the government's purpose in offering the prior consistent statements, the motive to fabricate must not have existed at the time the statements were made or they are inadmissible, *citing United States v. Quinto*, 582 F.2d 224 (2d Cir. 1978), as support. It is now settled, however, that this condition need not be met to admit into evidence prior consistent statements which are offered solely to rehabilitate a witness rather than as evidence of the matters asserted in those statements. *See United States v. Parodi*, 703 F.2d 768, 785 (4th Cir. 1983); *United States v. Parry*, 649 F.2d 292, 296 (5th Cir. 1981). * * *

In *United States v. Juarez* we addressed a situation closely analogous to the facts before us now and held that prior consistent statements offered for the limited purpose of rehabilitating a witness's credibility were not subject to the strictures of Rule 801(d)(1)(B). 549 F.2d at 1114. The prior consistent statements in *Juarez* were admitted into evidence because they related to the witness's credibility, and were therefore relevant. They were not excludable as hearsay because they were not offered for the truth of the matters which they asserted. This use of prior consistent statements for rehabilitation is particularly appropriate where, as here, those statements are part of a report or interview containing inconsistent statements which have been used to impeach the credibility of the witness. Prior consistent statements which are used in this matter are relevant to whether the impeaching statements really were inconsistent within the context of the interview, and if so, to what extent. This rehabilitative use of prior consistent statements is also in accord with the principle of completeness promoted by Rule 106.

Although the prior consistent statements were no doubt helpful in rebutting any implication that Branch had fabricated his testimony, the government did not offer those statements to prove the truth of the matters asserted in the statements, and therefore the restrictions of Rule 801(d)(1)(B) and the requirement that the motive to fabricate must not exist at the time the statements were made do not apply. This difference in purpose may seem unrealistically subtle in light of the effect a jury may be inclined to give the statements, but it is permissible for a jury to consider the extent of the inconsistencies in determining the credibility of the witness. *Juarez*, 549 F.2d 1114 (cautionary instructions given to jury to consider statements only in deciding credibility, not facts in case).

* * *

AFFIRMED.

NOTES

1. At what point can prior consistent statements be introduced?

In *United States v. Bolick*, 917 F.2d 135 (4th Cir. 1990), the court reversed a conviction for selling cocaine because a government agent had testified to prior consistent statements by informant witnesses before those witnesses had given testimony or had their credibility called into question. The dissenting judge believed that admission of the evidence was within the trial court's discretion regarding the proper order of proof, as the statements provided background helpful to a complete understanding of the agent's testimony. *See also United States v. Azure*, 801 F.2d 336 (8th Cir. 1986), where the court indicated that statements should not be admitted under this Rule until a witness has been cross-examined.

In *United States v. Coleman*, 631 F.2d 908 (D.C. Cir. 1980), the court said that "[e]ven where the suggestion of contradiction is only imputation of an inaccurate memory, a prior consistent statement is admissible to rebut the inference."

In *United States v. Zuniga-Lara*, 570 F.2d 1286 (5th Cir. 1978), the court upheld the introduction of a prior consistent statement to rehabilitate a government witness who was impeached on cross-examination on the basis of his failure to include information in a written report. This case is illustrative of the occasional need to rehabilitate a witness impeached, not on the basis of a prior statement, but on the basis of a prior failure to make a statement.

2. What is the relationship between Rule 106 — the rule of completeness — and rehabilitation with consistent statements?

Federal Rule 106 provides: "When a writing or recorded statement or part thereof is introduced by a party, an adverse party may require the introduction at that time of any other part or any other writing or recorded statement which ought in fairness to be considered contemporaneously with it."

Rule 106 has sometimes been invoked to allow the admission of a prior consistent statement of a testifying witness. This can occur when the witness is impeached with a prior inconsistent statement, and counsel argues that another statement consistent with the in-court testimony will serve to explain away the alleged inconsistency — as was the case in *Harris*. The argument is that an inconsistent statement was taken out of context and that a consistent statement must be introduced in order to alleviate the misimpression.

Where both statements — consistent and inconsistent — are contained in a writing or recording, then Rule 106 applies by its terms. For example, in *United States v. Pierre*, 781 F.2d 329 (2d Cir. 1986), a DEA agent testified to an inculpatory statement made by Pierre in an interview. On cross-examination, he was confronted with the handwritten notes he took during the interview. These notes contained a series of "fragmentary phrases," and did not mention Pierre's inculpatory statement. On redirect, the trial court permitted the witness to testify that he had prepared typewritten notes three days after the interview, and he was allowed to read these notes. The typewritten notes included Pierre's inculpatory statement. The Court of Appeals relied on Rule 106 and held that admission of a prior consistent statement is warranted "when the consistent statement will amplify or clarify the allegedly inconsistent statement." In *Pierre*, the consistent statement could corroborate the agent's explanation of the apparent inconsistency. The agent explained that the inculpatory statement was not included in the original notes because he was just jotting down certain phrases in the heat of the moment; after the interview, and while preparing the formal report, the agent had the opportunity to write down the inculpatory statement for the first time. He did not need to write the statement down initially because it was something that he was unlikely to forget.

While Rule 106 does not explicitly apply if either the prior inconsistent statement or the consistent statement are oral rather than written, it is clear that the reasoning of the Rule still applies. As the Court in *Pierre* put it: "It matters not whether such use is deemed a permissible type of rehabilitation or only an invocation of the principle of completeness, though not a precise use of Rule 106."

E. IMPEACHMENT OF HEARSAY DECLARANTS

If a hearsay statement is introduced into evidence because it qualifies as an exception to or exemption from the hearsay rule, it is being introduced for its truth. It is as if the declarant is testifying at trial, and the hearsay declarant's statement is considered to be the equivalent of trial testimony. This makes the credibility of the hearsay declarant important. Rule 806 provides that the credibility of the hearsay declarant generally can be attacked and supported just as if the declarant is on the stand testifying. In other words, the ways in which a witness can be impeached and rehabilitated are generally the ways in which a hearsay declarant can be impeached and rehabilitated.

[1] Federal Rule of Evidence 806

Rule 806. Attacking and Supporting Credibility of Declarant

When a hearsay statement, or a statement defined in rule 801(d)(2) (C), (D), or (E), has been admitted in evidence, the credibility of the declarant may be attacked, and if attacked may be supported, by any evidence which would be admissible for those purposes if declarant had testified as a witness. Evidence of a statement or conduct by the declarant at any time, inconsistent with the declarant's hearsay statement, is not subject to any requirement that the declarant may have been afforded an opportunity to deny or explain. If the party against whom a hearsay statement has been admitted calls the declarant as a witness, the party is entitled to examine the declarant on the statement as if under cross-examination.

[2] Scope of Impeachment

UNITED STATES v. GRANT

256 F.3d 1146 (11th Cir. 2001)

CARNES, CIRCUIT JUDGE:

Nicholas Grant appeals his convictions for conspiracy to possess with intent to distribute cocaine and marijuana * * * use of a firearm during a drug-trafficking crime * * *, and failure to appear * * *. These questions are presented: * * * whether statements of an alleged co-conspirator exculpating Grant were inconsistent statements admissible for purposes of impeachment pursuant to Federal Rule of Evidence 806. We answer [this question] "yes" [which] requires that we reverse Grant's conviction on the conspiracy and use of a firearm charges.

I. BACKGROUND

A. FACTS

In early 1993, United States Customs Service Special Agent Louis Mozas met with Deosie Wilson and discussed Wilson's plan to have Mozas smuggle 2000 pounds of marijuana from Jamaica into the United States, which Wilson would then sell. Jamaican police seized the marijuana which was to be smuggled in, however, so the transaction was not consummated.

Mozas next advised Wilson that Mozas would be smuggling one hundred kilograms of cocaine from Columbia, for which he would be paid 18,000 pounds of marijuana. Wilson agreed to market that marijuana for Mozas. Upon inspection, Wilson deemed the marijuana to be of poor quality, but set out to market it anyway. Mozas also advised Wilson that he had 15 kilograms of cocaine, and Wilson agreed to assist in selling it.

Wilson departed for Jamaica on March 12, 1993, and returned to Tampa on March 18, 1993. Mozas picked up Wilson at the Tampa airport and took him to an undercover residence in Homosassa, Florida. In connection with his planned purchase of the cocaine from Mozas, Wilson advised Mozas that $100,000 had been transferred into Wilson's bank account and that the funds would be available the next day. On March 19, 1993, Mozas accompanied Wilson to a bank in Homosassa, Florida and was present when Wilson obtained a cashier's check for $100,000. Mozas and Wilson then returned to the undercover residence.

Later that same afternoon, Mozas dropped Wilson off at the same bank. Wilson remained inside the bank for between one to five minutes before leaving with the occupants of a waiting Nissan Pathfinder. Undercover agents followed the Pathfinder, which drove by the undercover residence and then to a restaurant. A short while later, Wilson and Grant were observed leaving the restaurant and entering the Pathfinder. The agents followed the Pathfinder as it returned to the undercover residence, where Wilson was dropped off. The agents then followed the Pathfinder as it returned to the restaurant.

Wilson arrived at the undercover residence carrying a bundle underneath his shirt. The agreement between Mozas and Wilson provided that Wilson would purchase 10 kilograms of cocaine from Wilson at $15,000 per kilogram, or $150,000 total. Wilson went into a bedroom at the residence and, upon his return, produced a vinyl pouch containing $50,000 in United States currency.

Mozas then instructed Detective Michael Joyner to bring the cocaine to the residence. Joyner brought the cocaine and Wilson showed him the $100,000 cashier's check and $50,000 cash. Wilson told Mozas that Grant was in Homosassa Springs, but that Grant did not want to meet anyone. Wilson then put down $15,000, left with one kilogram of cocaine, and was arrested immediately thereafter. Wilson was talking on a cell phone at the time of his arrest and the person to whom he was speaking was exclaiming "police, police, police."

Within one minute of being informed that Wilson had been arrested, the undercover agents observing the Pathfinder saw Grant and his brother quickly run from the restaurant and depart in the Pathfinder. Grant drove slowly by the location where Wilson was being arrested and then fled the area at approximately 80 miles per hour. After a brief chase, Grant was arrested and a search of the Pathfinder revealed two loaded semi-automatic pistols, one in the glove compartment and another in a duffle bag on the floor in front of the back seat, and an open briefcase containing $11,208.

After his arrest, Grant told Customs Special Agent Phillip Aston that while he was in Jamaica Wilson had contacted him about participating in a marijuana transaction. Grant did not, however, mention anything about a cocaine transaction. Grant also told Aston that on March 18, 1993, he had traveled from Jamaica to Miami with approximately $16,000 in cash. Grant had a passport bearing his photograph and name which documented that he had left Jamaica on March 18, 1993. Grant admitted to Aston that he had been speaking to Wilson on the telephone before Grant had run from the restaurant, but claimed that he and his brother had decided that they did not want to participate in Wilson's transaction anymore and had decided to leave. * * *

* * *

II. DISCUSSION

* * *

D. THE RULE 806 ISSUE

At trial, the government used as evidence against Grant statements that had been made by co-conspirator Wilson during the course of the conspiracy.

Those statements were admitted under Federal Rule of Evidence 801(d)(2)(E), which allows co-conspirator statements to be admitted as substantive evidence against a defendant. Agent Mozas testified extensively regarding statements Wilson had made to him during the course of the conspiracy while Mozas was acting undercover. Those statements involved: (1) Wilson's plans to import marijuana into the United States; (2) Wilson's claims that he had a partner in Jamaica who was his neighbor; (3) Wilson's comments that he had buyers who would assist him in distributing marijuana and cocaine; and (4) Wilson's intent, after purchasing one kilogram of cocaine from the undercover agent, to take the cocaine to his partner for testing and evaluation.

The statements of Wilson that Mozas testified about on direct examination did not directly mention Grant, but on cross-examination when asked whether Grant was ever present during any of the transactions between the undercover agents and Wilson, Mozas testified that Wilson had told him Grant was in Homosassa Springs and did not want to meet with anyone.

Grant attempted to impeach the Wilson conspiracy statements that had been put into evidence through Mozas' testimony by introducing an affidavit which an attorney for Grant had obtained from Wilson in Jamaica. The affidavit was executed after the conspiracy ended and following Wilson's deportation to that country. The affidavit contained Wilson's sworn statements: that Grant had no knowledge of Wilson's actions in consummating the drug deal with the agents; that Wilson had falsely told the undercover agents he had a partner because Wilson did not want them to think he was acting alone; that Wilson had asked Grant to meet him in Tampa to loan him money; that none of the $50,000 in cash Wilson possessed came from Grant; and that Wilson had lied to the undercover agents about Grant not wanting to meet with anyone because Wilson was carrying a large amount of cash and wanted the undercover agents (whom he believed to be criminals) to think he had a partner. The district court refused to admit any of Wilson's affidavit statements, however, finding that they were not inconsistent, as required by Rule 806, with the statements of Wilson admitted through Mozas' testimony.

* * *

The government's principal argument mirrors the district court's reasoning that none of the statements in Wilson's affidavit are inconsistent with or contradictory to Wilson's conspiracy statements which were admitted through Mozas' testimony. The government points out that none of Wilson's conspiracy statements which were admitted at trial specifically identify Grant as Wilson's partner or as the source of any money used in the transaction. The only testimony that specifically identifies Grant, which was that Wilson had told the agents Grant was in Homosassa Springs and did not want to meet anyone, was elicited by Grant on cross-examination of Wilson and was not, the government contends, contradicted by anything in Wilson's affidavit.

The government's conception of inconsistency is too narrow. Although Grant was specifically identified by Mozas only during cross-examination, his testimony in its entirety did circumstantially link Grant to the conspiracy. At the very least, it indicated that Wilson had a co-conspirator. The government attempted to avoid Rule 806 by carefully ensuring that Mozas, in testifying about Wilson's statements during the conspiracy, never specifically identified Grant as Wilson's co-conspirator, at least on direct examination, and then presenting other evidence indicating that Grant was Wilson's co-conspirator. Wilson's statements in the proffered affidavit, however, indicate that he had no co-conspirator and, further, that Grant had no involvement in Wilson's drug transactions.

The Rule 806 test is not whether the inconsistent statements relate to the identity of co-conspirators; that's not what the Rule says. Instead, it says that "any" evidence is admissible "which would be admissible * * * if [the] declarant had testified as a witness" from the stand. Fed. R. Evid. 806. If Wilson had been called as a witness and testified, for example, that he was taking the cocaine he was buying to his partner to test and evaluate it, his affidavit statements indicating that he had lied to the agents when he told them he had a partner would surely be admissible. Likewise, if Wilson had testified and during cross-examination had said that Grant did not want to meet with anyone, his affidavit statement that he had lied about that would be admissible to impeach him. The test is whether the out-of-court statements would have been admissible for impeachment purposes had the co-conspirator statements been delivered from the witness stand by the co-conspirator himself, not as hearsay about what he said during the conspiracy but as contemporaneous in-court statements.

The government's position in this case echos its unsuccessful argument in *United States v. Wali*, 860 F.2d 588 (3d Cir. 1988), which involved a remarkably similar Rule 806 issue. That case involved Abdul Wali's conviction on charges of conspiracy to import Schedule I controlled substances * * *. An undercover DEA agent testified at Wali's trial as to statements made during the conspiracy by a drug kingpin, Stanley Karl Esser, which implicated a person named "Hadji" as the source of narcotics. The district court, however, denied Wali's attempt to impeach Esser's credibility by admitting inconsistent statements Esser had made to the undercover DEA Agent and to Dutch authorities which exonerated Wali. On appeal, the government argued that Esser's exculpatory statements were not inconsistent and therefore not admissible pursuant to Rule 806, because in his inculpatory co-conspirator statements "Esser never stated that Abdul Wali was either the source of his narcotics or the 'Hadji' who supplied him." The government claimed that Wali's identity as the "Hadji" who supplied the narcotics was established only circumstantially through evidence other than the co-conspirator statements. The Third Circuit rejected that argument, holding that although Esser's co-conspirator statements never specifically identified Wali as the "Hadji" who was the source of his narcotics, the government had used those statements to prove the existence of a conspiracy to import drugs, thereby inculpating Wali.

The Third Circuit's analysis in *Wali* is sound and fits snugly onto our facts. The government used Wilson's co-conspirator statements to help establish the existence of a conspiracy to distribute cocaine and marijuana, which is one of the elements of the crime charged against Grant. The statements in Wilson's affidavit were inconsistent with the existence of any conspiracy at all, and for that reason were inconsistent with his co-conspirator statements.

The government's first fallback argument is that even if the co-conspirator statements of Wilson admitted at trial were inconsistent with the affidavit statements, the affidavit is inadmissible under Federal Rule of Evidence 403 because its probative value is outweighed by its prejudicial effect. That is not the ground upon which the district court excluded the evidence. Nonetheless, the government maintains that the affidavit evidence would be unfairly prejudicial because the statements, if believed, would provide Grant with a complete defense, rather than merely impeaching Wilson's co-conspirator statements admitted through Mozas.

Rule 403 is an "extraordinary remedy," whose "major function * * * is limited to excluding matter of scant or cumulative probative force, dragged in by the heels for the sake of its prejudicial effect," *United States v. Cross,* 928 F.2d 1030, 1048 (11th Cir.1991). The Rule carries a "strong presumption in favor of admissibility." Wilson's inculpatory co-conspirator statements were important pieces of evidence in the government's case. The impeaching statements in the affidavit would serve to cast doubt on Wilson's credibility and would have significant probative value for that purpose. Whatever prejudice to the government that might occur from admitting the affidavit statements could not substantially outweigh their probative value, anymore than it could if those affidavit statements had been admitted for impeachment following live testimony of Wilson to the same effect as his co-conspirator statements. The evidence of the affidavit statements could do no more than impeach and could not provide "a complete defense" if the government requested the limiting instruction to which it would have been entitled.

The government's second fallback argument is that Wilson's affidavit statements were properly excluded from evidence because they were particularly unreliable, even though that was not the basis of the district court's ruling. The government points out that Wilson continued to inculpate Grant in the conspiracy after his arrest and before a federal grand jury, and only gave statements exculpating Grant after he had been deported to Jamaica and was no longer subject to prosecution for perjury. The government maintains that because the statements in the affidavit were so unreliable, admitting them would not have affected the outcome of the trial — sort of a harmless error argument.

The government's argument on this point is more than a little inconsistent with its Rule 403 argument that the affidavit statements were terribly prejudicial to its case. Putting that inconsistency aside, however, Rule 806 made the statements admissible for impeachment purposes, and the point of admitting inconsistent statements to impeach is not to show that they are true, but to aid the jury in deciding whether the witness is credible; the usual argument of the party doing the impeaching is that the inconsistent statements show the witness is too unreliable to be believed on important matters. *See United States v. Graham,* 858 F.2d 986, 990 n. 5 (5th Cir.1988) ("[T]he hallmark of an inconsistent statement offered to impeach a witness's testimony is that the statement is not hearsay within the meaning of the term, i.e., it is not offered for the truth of the matter asserted, *see* Fed. R. Evid. 801(c); rather, it is offered only to establish that the witness has said both 'x' and 'not x' and is therefore unreliable."). Given all the circumstances of this case, that strategy might well have worked to undermine the probative effect of Wilson's co-conspirator statements to such an extent that the verdict on the conspiracy charge would have been different. For that reason, we reverse Grant's conviction on that charge.

REVERSED.

NOTE

Can a hearsay declarant's bad acts be introduced at trial to impeach the declarant's character for truthfulness?

If a witness at trial is attacked for having an untruthful character, Rule 608(b) restricts impeachment to questions addressed to a witness on the stand and limits the examiner to the witness' answers; Rule 608(b) precludes extrinsic evidence of bad acts offered to impeach the witness' character for truthfulness. It can therefore be argued that bad act impeachment of a hearsay declarant who is not present to testify is impermissible — ordinarily, the only way to bring up the bad act is by way of extrinsic evidence, because the declarant is not there to be asked about it. The contrary argument is that Rule 806 is clear in its intent that the adverse party is to have at least the same impeachment weapons as he would have had if the witness had testified. *See* Cordray, *Evidence Rule 806 and the Problem of the Nontestifying Declarant*, 56 OHIO STATE L.J. 495, 526 (1995):

> If the attacking party cannot impeach the declarant with specific instances of conduct, she is clearly worse off than she would have been if her opponent had called the declarant to testify. * * *
>
> In addition, if Rule 806 is applied to enforce the prohibition on extrinsic evidence, parties might be encouraged to offer hearsay evidence rather than live testimony. For example, if a party felt that a witness was vulnerable to attack under Rule 608(b), that party might attempt to insulate the witness from this form of impeachment by offering his out-of-court statements, rather than calling him to testify. If, however, the attacking party were allowed to impeach a nontestifying declarant with extrinsic evidence of untruthful conduct, the incentive to use hearsay evidence would be removed. * * *
>
> These considerations militate strongly in favor of modifying Rule 608(b)'s ban on extrinsic evidence when the attacking party seeks to impeach a nontestifying declarant with specific instances of conduct showing untruthfulness.

At least one court has held that extrinsic evidence may never be admitted to prove a bad act offered to impeach a hearsay declarant's character for truthfulness. The Court in *United States v. Saada*, 212 F.3d 210 (3d Cir. 2000), relied on the "plain language" of Rule 806, which it read as creating exactly the same impeachment rules for in-court witnesses and hearsay declarants, with one exception — impeachment with inconsistent statements, as to which the Rule specifically states that there is no requirement that the declarant be given an opportunity to affirm or deny the statement (obviously a rule grounded in necessity because the declarant is *not at trial* to affirm or deny the statement). The Court in *Saada* found that the Rule's express exception for different treatment of inconsistent statements cut against any judicially-created exception for bad acts impeachment.

The *Saada* Court recognized that the ban on extrinsic proof, as applied to impeachment of hearsay declarants, "prevents using evidence of prior misconduct as a form of impeachment, unless the witness testifying to the hearsay has knowledge of the declarant's misconduct." Nevertheless, this drawback "may not override the language of Rules 806 and 608(b)." The problem with the reasoning in *Saada* is that it is inconsistent with the *intent* of Rule 806, which is to give the opponent of the hearsay the same leeway for impeachment as it would have if the declarant testified at trial. Under *Saada*, the opponent of the hearsay is put in a worse position with respect to bad acts of the hearsay declarant. The bad acts could at least be referred to if the declarant were to testify, whereas if the statement is introduced as hearsay it is unlikely that the jury will hear about the hearsay declarant's bad acts.

PROBLEM 17-1

Professor Hacker is a principal witness for the defense in the insider-trading criminal trial of one of his former students, Dell Gates. Gates is one of the founders of an Internet company that recently went public, and serves as Senior Vice President and a member of the Board of Directors. The company was a hit in its initial public offering a year ago when its stock price rose from $12 to $71 in a week, but the price has since fallen to $22 per share. The government alleges that Gates sold short shares of his stock on the basis of inside knowledge concerning problems the company was having with overseas suppliers. Hacker, who teaches English but is an Internet enthusiast, has testified on direct examination that the knowledge about overseas suppliers was being passed around the worldwide web before Gates sold his shares short and was not knowledge that was confined to insiders.

The following also occurs during direct examination, before the defendant takes the stand:

Defendant:	Now, have you ever testified before in a trial?
Prosecutor:	Objection! It's irrelevant and an attempt to bolster his credibility.
The court:	Make an offer of proof.
Defendant:	The professor testified in three other trials and each time the party that called him prevailed.
Prosecutor:	You see, she's trying to vouch for the witness.
The court:	(1) __________.
Defendant:	Professor, now you are on the governing board of the All Saints Church, right?
Prosecutor:	Objection! Leading.

The court: (2) __________.

Defendant: Are you on the governing board of any institutions?

Prosecutor: Objection! Calls for improper character evidence.

Defendant: I want to show that she and the defendant are members of the same board.

Prosecutor: This is improper. It's either impeaching or bolstering and in either event it's wrong.

Defendant: I want to anticipate cross-examination and remove the sting.

The court: (3) __________.

Professor: I am on the board of the All Saints Church as is the defendant.

Defendant: Has your relationship with the defendant on the board or as a student affected your testimony in this case?

Prosecutor: Objection! That is for the jury to decide.

The court: (4) __________.

Professor: I'm here to testify to what I saw on the Internet, and my relationship with the defendant has not affected my testimony.

Defendant: Does your relationship to the defendant have any bearing on why you recall what you saw on the Internet?

Prosecutor: Objection! Again, who cares?

Defendant: She should be able to explain why she recalls seeing what she testified about.

The court: (5) __________.

Professor: I paid particular attention because I knew it was the defendant's company.

Defendant: Now, do you have an opinion as to the defendant's honesty?

Prosecutor: Objection.

Defendant: (6) __________.

The court: (7) __________.

The following occurs on cross-examination:

Prosecutor: Professor, isn't it true that you told FBI Agent Reno a week after defendant was indicted that you did not recall what you saw about the defendant's company on the Internet?

Defendant: Objection! Hearsay.

The court: (8) __________.

Professor: That's not true.

Prosecutor: Isn't it also true that you signed a statement saying, "I don't recall what I saw on the Internet"?

Defendant: Objection! Not the best evidence. He should show any statement to the witness.

Prosecutor: I may well do that, but I don't have to.
The court: (9) _________
Defendant: Objection! At least he should show the statement to me.
The court: (10) _________.
Prosecutor: Okay. I have provided counsel with a copy. Now answer the question, Professor.
Professor: I don't think I signed any such statement.
Prosecutor: I show you what has been marked for identification as P-1. Can you identify this?
Professor: No.
Prosecutor: Isn't that your signature at the bottom of a sheet which states, "I don't recall what I saw on the Internet"?
Defendant: Objection! She just said that she could not identify it.
The court: (11) _________.
Professor: It looks like my signature.
Prosecutor: So, isn't true that you signed this statement and gave it to FBI agent Reno?
Professor: I don't recall.
Prosecutor: So, you recall what you saw on the Internet before the defendant was indicted but not what you may have written afterwards?
Defendant: Objection! Argumentative. Asked and answered.
The court: (12) _________.
Prosecutor: Now, you testified on direct examination that you and the defendant are on a church board together?
Defendant: Objection! We've been over this.
Prosecutor: I want to explore this in more detail.
The court: (13) _________.
Prosecutor: Now, isn't it also true that the defendant actually picks you up and drives you home from meetings and that you usually have dinner together when the board meets?
Defendant: (14) Objection! Irrelevant.
The court: _________.
Professor: Yes.
Prosecutor: And you are godmother to the defendant's first born daughter?
Defendant: Objection. The daughter has nothing to do with this case.
The court: (15) _________.
Professor: Yes.
Prosecutor: And when the defendant's daughter was arrested for shoplifting, you bailed her out?
Defendant: Objection! This is beyond the pale. Shoplifting is not a permissible basis for impeaching anyone.

The court: (16) ________.
Professor: Yes.
Prosecutor: Now, Professor, you published an article in *English Monthly* about Dickens, isn't that so?
Professor: Yes.
Prosecutor: You make the argument that Dickens often cast characters with exaggerated character traits that make his work particularly good for films?
Professor: Yes.
Prosecutor: Isn't it true that you plagiarized this argument from a colleague who wrote in Atlantic Monthly two years earlier?
Defendant: Objection! This has nothing to do with this case.
The court: (17) ________.
Professor: No. That is not true.
Prosecutor: Your colleague charged you before the faculty Senate with plagiarism, right?
Defendant: Whatever the colleague did is inadmissible.
The court: (18) ________.
Prosecutor: The faculty Senate passed a resolution censoring you.
Defendant: Same objection.
The court: (19) ________.
Prosecutor: Now, Professor, did you ever sign into a motel with a person not your husband and use the name Jane Doe?
Defendant: Objection! Extremely prejudicial and irrelevant.
The court: (20) ________.
Prosecutor: Now, you offered an opinion on direct examination about the defendant's honesty. Isn't it true that you are familiar with his reputation in the community for honesty as well?
Defendant: Objection! Outside the scope of direct.
The court: (21) ________.
Professor: Yes.
Prosecutor: The fact is that the defendant's reputation for honesty is bad, right?
Professor: No.
Prosecutor: No, didn't you tell FBI agent Reno that the defendant's reputation for honesty was bad?
Defendant: Objection! Now, he's impeaching his own evidence. And hearsay.
The court: (22) ________.
Professor: No.
Prosecutor: You were once arrested for using a fake ID to buy liquor?
Defendant: Objection! An arrest is not admissible.

The court:	(23) _________.
Prosecutor:	Weren't you convicted nine years ago of the misdemeanor of filing a W-4 IRS form that contained false information?
Defendant:	Objection! It's only a misdemeanor.
The court:	(24) _________.
Defendant:	Further objection! It's unduly prejudicial.
The court:	(25) _________.
Professor:	Yes.
Prosecutor:	What is your opinion as to the defendant's truth and veracity?
Defendant:	Objection! Improper character evidence.
Prosecutor:	Door is open.
The court:	(26) _________.
Prosecutor:	Are you familiar with the defendant's reputation for truth and veracity in the community?
Defendant:	Objection! Same ground.
The court:	(27) _________.
Prosecutor:	By the way, Professor, would your opinion of the defendant's character for honesty change if the charges against him in this case are true?
Defendant:	Objection! This is a guilt assuming hypothetical and improper.
The court:	(28) _________.

Prosecutor calls Agent Reno and the following occurs during direct examination:

Prosecutor:	Did Professor Hacker make a statement to you two weeks after the defendant was indicted about what she remembered seeing on the Internet?
Defendant:	Objection! Hearsay.
The court:	(29) _________.
Defendant:	Will you instruct the jury that it's not admitted for its truth?
The court:	(30) _________.
Agent:	Yes, she made a statement and said that she did not remember what she saw on the Internet.
Prosecutor:	Did she sign a statement?
Agent:	Yes she did.
Prosecutor:	I show you what has been marked for identification as P1. Can you identify it?
Defendant:	Objection! This is not his statement. It is hearsay.
The court:	(31) _________.
Agent:	Yes, that is the statement the Professor signed.
Prosecutor:	Move for its admission.
Defendant:	Objection! He's already testified to the contents.

The court: (32) __________.

Prosecutor: Did Professor Hacker make any statement to you about the defendant's reputation for honesty?

Defendant: Objection! Improper character evidence. Hearsay.

The court: (33) __________.

Agent: Yes, she said the defendant's reputation for honesty was bad.

Prosecutor: Did you know the defendant before arresting him?

Agent: No.

Prosecutor: Have you an opinion about the defendant's honesty?

Defendant: Objection. No foundation. He's really seeking an opinion based on the assumption that the defendant is guilty.

The court: (34) __________.

The following occurs on cross-examination:

Defendant: Now, isn't it true that on occasion you have planted narcotics in order to frame suspects you could not otherwise arrest?

Prosecutor: I object. There is no basis for the question.

The court: What is the basis for your question?

Defendant: He's a cop, and they do that.

The court: (35) __________.

Defendant: You testified in a prior case that you saw Merideth Meridian with a gun, and the truth is you weren't even on the scene, right?

Prosecutor: I object. No basis for this.

The court: What is the basis for your question?

Defendant: I have a transcript, your Honor, in which this very prosecutor told the court that he was moving to dismiss all charges against Meridian because Agent Reno was not on the scene.

The court: (36) __________.

Agent: No. I never testified falsely.

Defendant: Didn't the prosecutor tell the court that you did?

Prosecutor: Objection! Extrinsic evidence.

The court: (37) __________.

Defendant: The FBI suspended you for a month after the Meridian case, right?

Prosecutor: Objection! Same ground.

The court: (38) __________.

Defendant: Now, you happen to be a practicing Wiccan; your religion is witchcraft?

Prosecutor: Objection. Religious beliefs are not admissible.

Defendant: It shows he's not a member of the same church as the defendant and therefore goes to bias.

Prosecutor: It's way too tangential and it injects religion in a prejudicial way.
The court: (39) ________.

The defense calls Retired Agent:

Defendant: What is your occupation?
Retired Agent: I retired from the FBI.
Defendant: Do you know Agent Reno?
Retired Agent: Yes.
Defendant: How long have you known him?
Retired Agent: 15 Years.
Defendant: What is your opinion of his character for truth and veracity?
Prosecutor: Objection! Agent Reno is not on trial.
The court: (40) ________.
Retired Agent: He's a liar. I wouldn't believe a thing he said.
Defendant: What is his reputation in the community for truth and veracity.
Prosecutor: Objection! He's already answered this.
The court: (41) ________.
Retired Agent: Everyone says he's a liar.
Defendant: What role did you have in exposing his lies in the Meridian case?
Prosecutor: Objection! Irrelevant.
Defendant: I want to explore possible bias and remove the sting.
The court: (42) ________.
Retired Agent: I informed the prosecutor that he wasn't at the scene as he claimed to be.

The prosecutor cross-examines:

Prosecutor: Have you heard that Officer Reno was FBI agent of the year last year?
Defendant: Objection! Who cares.
Prosecutor: It is relevant to testing his opinion and reputation testimony.
The court: (43) ________.
Retired Agent: Yes.
Prosecutor: Does that affect your opinion as to his truth and veracity?
Defendant: Objection! He's given his opinion.
The court: (44) ________.
Retired Agent: No.
Prosecutor: Has it affected Agent Reno's reputation for truth and veracity?
Defendant: Objection! Calls for speculation.
The court: (45) ________.
Retired Agent: No.
Prosecutor: Isn't it true that you retired from the Bureau because you were told the FBI was going to fire you for incompetence?

Defendant: Objection! Improper impeachment.
Prosecutor: Goes to possible bias.
The court: (46) ________.
Retired Agent: No.

The United States calls Director as a rebuttal witness:

Prosecutor: What is your occupation?
Director: Director of the FBI.
Prosecutor: Do you know Agent Reno?
Director: I've known him for 15 years.
Prosecutor: What is you opinion of his character for truth and veracity?
Defendant: Objection! Improper rehabilitation.
The court: (47) ________.
Defendant: Further objection! Cumulative.
Prosecutor: It's a fair response to the attack.
The court: (48) ________.
Prosecutor: Do you know Retired Agent?
Director: Yes, I knew him for 15 years.
Prosecutor: What is your opinion as to his character for truth and veracity?
Director: He's not truthful.
Defendant: Objection and move to strike. We did not inquire into this character.
The court: (49) ________.
Prosecutor: Why did Retired Agent leave the FBI?
Director: He left because he knew he was about to be fired.
Defendant: Objection! Move to strike! Irrelevant.
Prosecutor: Goes to bias.
The court: (50) ________.
Prosecutor: Has Retired Agent ever made a statement about getting back at the Bureau?
Defendant: Objection! Hearsay.
The court: Let me hear the statement.
Director: He told me when he left, "Some day I'll get back at you and the others who are still here."
Prosecutor: I think it's admissible as state of mind.
Defendant: It's irrelevant.
The court: (51) ________.
Prosecutor: Did you hear any other agents make statements about Retired Agent after his retirement?
Defendant: Objection! Improper character evidence.
The court: (52) ________.

Chapter 18

PRIVILEGE

A. FEDERAL RULE 501

Rule 501. General Rule

Except as otherwise required by the Constitution of the United States or provided by Act of Congress or in rules prescribed by the Supreme Court pursuant to statutory authority, the privilege of a witness, person, government, State, or political subdivision thereof shall be governed by the principles of the common law as they may be interpreted by the courts of the United States in the light of reason and experience. However, in civil actions and proceedings, with respect to an element of a claim or defense as to which State law supplies the rule of decision, the privilege of a witness, person, government, State, or political subdivision thereof shall be determined in accordance with State law.

B. ATTORNEY-CLIENT PRIVILEGE

[1] Advisory Committee Draft of Attorney-Client Privilege

The Advisory Committee on Evidence Rules has developed a draft attempting to codify the federal law on attorney-client privilege. The draft has not yet been proposed as an amendment to the Federal Rules. The draft attempts to codify the Federal common law developed under Rule 501. The draft currently reads as follows:

LAWYER-CLIENT PRIVILEGE (Draft, March 1, 2006)

[a] Definitions — As Used in This Rule:

(1) A "communication" is any expression through which a privileged person intends to convey information to another privileged person or any record containing such an expression;

(2) A "client" is a person who or an organization that consults a lawyer to obtain professional legal services;

(3) An "organization" is a corporation, unincorporated association, partnership, trust, estate, sole proprietorship, governmental entity, or other for-profit or not-for-profit association;

(4) A "lawyer" is a person who is authorized to practice law in any domestic or foreign jurisdiction or whom a client reasonably believes to be a lawyer;

(5) A "privileged person" is a client, that client's lawyer, or an agent of either who is reasonably necessary to facilitate communications between the client and the lawyer;

(6) A communication is "in confidence" if, at the time and in the circumstances of the communication, the communicating person reasonably believes that no one except a privileged person will learn the contents of the communication.

[b] General Rule of Privilege

A client has a privilege to refuse to disclose and to prevent any other person from disclosing a communication made in confidence between or among privileged persons for the purpose of obtaining or providing legal assistance for the client.

[c] Who May Claim the Privilege

A client, a personal representative of an incompetent or deceased client, or a person succeeding to the interest of a client may invoke the privilege. A lawyer, agent of the lawyer, or an agent of a client from whom a privileged communication is sought may invoke the privilege on behalf of the client if implicitly or explicitly authorized by the client.

[d] Standards for Organizational Clients

With respect to an organizational client, the lawyer-client privilege extends to a communication that

(1) is otherwise privileged;

(2) is between an organization's agent and a privileged person where the communication concerns a legal matter of interest to the organization within the scope of the agent's agency or employment; and

(3) is disclosed only to privileged persons and other agents of the organization who reasonably need to know of the communication in order to act for the organization.

[e] Privilege of Co-Clients and Common-Interest Arrangements

If two or more clients are jointly represented by the same lawyer in a matter or if two or more clients with a common interest in a matter are represented by separate lawyers and they agree to pursue a common interest and to exchange information concerning the matter, a communication of any such client that is otherwise privileged and relates to matters of common interest is privileged as against third persons. Any such client may invoke the privilege unless the client making the communication has waived the privilege. Unless the clients agree otherwise, such a communication is not privileged as between the clients. Communications between clients or agents of clients outside the presence of a lawyer or agent of a lawyer representing at least one of the clients are not privileged.

[f] Exceptions

The lawyer-client privilege does not apply to a communication:

(1) from or to a deceased client if the communication is relevant to an issue between parties who claim an interest through the same deceased client, either by testate or intestate succession or by an inter vivos transaction;

(2) that occurs when a client consults a lawyer to obtain assistance to engage in a crime or fraud or aiding a third person to do so. Regardless of the client's purpose at the time of consultation, the communication is not privileged if the client uses the lawyer's advice or other services to engage in or assist in committing a crime or fraud;

(3) that is relevant and reasonably necessary for a lawyer to reveal in a proceeding to resolve a dispute with a client regarding compensation or reimbursement that the lawyer reasonably claims the client owes the lawyer;

(4) that is relevant and reasonably necessary for a lawyer to reveal in order to defend against an allegation by anyone that the lawyer, the lawyer's agent, or any person for whose conduct the lawyer is responsible acted wrongfully or negligently during the course of representing a client;

(5) between a trustee of an express trust or a similar fiduciary and a lawyer or other privileged person retained to advise the trustee concerning the administration of the trust that is relevant to a beneficiary's claim of breach of fiduciary duties;

(6) between an organizational client and a lawyer or other privileged person, if offered in a proceeding that involves a dispute between the client and shareholders, members, or other constituents of the organization toward whom the directors, officers, or similar persons managing the organization bear fiduciary responsibilities, provided the court finds

(A) those managing the organization are charged with breach of their obligations toward the shareholders, members, or other constituents or toward the organization itself;

(B) the communication occurred prior to the assertion of the charges and relates directly to those charges; and

(C) the need of the requesting party to discover or introduce the communication is sufficiently compelling and the threat to confidentiality sufficiently confined to justify setting the privilege aside.

[2] Rationale for Attorney-Client Privilege and Application to Corporate Representation

UPJOHN CO. v. UNITED STATES
449 U.S. 383 (1981)

JUSTICE REHNQUIST delivered the opinion of the Court.

We granted certiorari in this case to address important questions concerning the scope of the attorney-client privilege in the corporate context and the applicability of the work-product doctrine in proceedings to enforce tax summonses. * * *

I

Petitioner Upjohn Co. manufactures and sells pharmaceuticals here and abroad. In January 1976 independent accountants conducting an audit of one of Upjohn's foreign subsidiaries discovered that the subsidiary made payments to or for the benefit of foreign government officials in order to secure government business. The accountants so informed petitioner, Mr. Gerard Thomas, Upjohn's Vice President, Secretary, and General Counsel. Thomas is a member of the Michigan and New York Bars, and has been Upjohn's General Counsel for 20 years. He consulted with outside counsel and R. T. Parfet, Jr., Upjohn's Chairman of the Board. It was decided that the company would conduct an internal investigation of what were termed "questionable payments." As part of this investigation the attorneys prepared a letter containing a questionnaire which was sent to "All Foreign General and Area Managers" over the Chairman's signature. The letter began by noting recent disclosures that several American companies made "possibly illegal" payments to foreign government officials and emphasized that the management needed full information concerning any such payments made by Upjohn. The letter indicated that the Chairman had asked Thomas, identified as "the company's General Counsel," "to conduct an investigation for the purpose of determining the nature and magnitude of any payments made by the Upjohn Company or any of its subsidiaries to any employee or official of a foreign government." The questionnaire sought detailed information concerning such payments. Managers were instructed to treat the investigation as "highly confidential" and not to discuss it with anyone other than Upjohn employees who might be helpful in providing the requested information. Responses were to be sent directly to Thomas. Thomas and outside counsel also interviewed the recipients of the questionnaire and some 33 other Upjohn officers or employees as part of the investigation.

On March 26, 1976, the company voluntarily submitted a preliminary report to the Securities and Exchange Commission on Form 8-K disclosing certain questionable payments. A copy of the report was simultaneously submitted to the Internal Revenue Service, which immediately began an investigation to determine the tax consequences of the payments. Special agents conducting the investigation were given lists by Upjohn of all those interviewed and all who had responded to the questionnaire. On November 23, 1976, the Service issued a summons pursuant to 26 U.S.C. § 7602 demanding production of:

> All files relative to the investigation conducted under the supervision of Gerard Thomas to identify payments to employees of foreign governments and any political contributions made by the Upjohn Company or any of its affiliates since January 1, 1971 and to determine whether any funds of the Upjohn Company had been improperly accounted for on the corporate books during the same period.
>
> The records should include but not be limited to written questionnaires sent to managers of the Upjohn Company's foreign affiliates, and memorandums or notes of the interviews conducted in the United States and abroad with officers and employees of the Upjohn Company and its subsidiaries.

The company declined to produce the documents specified in the second paragraph on the grounds that they were protected from disclosure by the attorney-client privilege and constituted the work product of attorneys prepared in anticipation of litigation. On August 31, 1977, the United States filed a petition seeking enforcement of the summons * * *.

* * *

II

* * * The attorney-client privilege is the oldest of the privileges for confidential communications known to the common law. 8 J. Wigmore, Evidence § 2290 (McNaughton rev. 1961). Its purpose is to encourage full and frank communication between attorneys and their clients and thereby promote broader public interests in the observance of law and administration of justice. The privilege recognizes that sound legal advice or advocacy serves public ends and that such advice or advocacy depends upon the lawyer's being fully informed by the client. As we stated last Term in *Trammel v. United States*, 445 U.S. 40, 51 (1980): "The lawyer-client privilege rests on the need for the advocate and counselor to know all that relates to the client's reasons for seeking representation if the professional mission is to be carried out." And in *Fisher v. United States*, 425 U.S. 391, 403 (1976), we recognized the purpose of the privilege to be "to encourage clients to make full disclosure to their attorneys." This rationale for the privilege has long been recognized by the Court, see *Hunt v. Blackburn*, 128 U.S. 464, 470 (1888) (privilege "is founded upon the necessity, in the interest and administration of justice, of the aid of persons having knowledge of the law and skilled in its practice, which assistance can only be safely and readily availed of when free from the consequences or the apprehension of disclosure"). Admittedly complications in the application of the privilege arise when the client is a corporation, which in theory is an artificial creature of the law, and not an individual; but this Court has assumed that the privilege applies when the client is a corporation, and the Government does not contest the general proposition.

The Court of Appeals, however, considered the application of the privilege in the corporate context to present a "different problem," since the client was an inanimate entity and "only the senior management, guiding and integrating the several operations, * * * can be said to possess an identity analogous to the corporation as a whole." The first case to articulate the so-called "control group test" adopted by the court below, *Philadelphia v. Westinghouse Electric Corp.*, 210 F. Supp. 483, 485 (ED Pa. 1962):

> Keeping in mind that the question is, Is it the corporation which is seeking the lawyer's advice when the asserted privileged communication is made?, the most satisfactory solution, I think, is that if the employee making the communication, of whatever rank he may be, is in a position to control or even to take a substantial part in a decision about any action which the corporation may take upon the advice of the attorney, * * * then, in effect, *he is (or personifies) the corporation* when he makes his disclosure to the lawyer and the privilege would apply." (Emphasis supplied.)

Such a view, we think, overlooks the fact that the privilege exists to protect not only the giving of professional advice to those who can act on it but also the giving of information to the lawyer to enable him to give sound and informed advice. The first step in the resolution of any legal problem is ascertaining the factual background and sifting through the facts with an eye to the legally relevant. *See* ABA Code of Professional Responsibility, Ethical Consideration 4-1:

> "A lawyer should be fully informed of all the facts of the matter he is handling in order for his client to obtain the full advantage of our legal system. It is for the lawyer in the exercise of his independent professional judgment to separate the relevant and important from the irrelevant and unimportant. The observance of the ethical obligation of a lawyer to hold inviolate the confidences and secrets of his client not only facilitates the full development of facts essential to proper representation of the client but also encourages laymen to seek early legal assistance."

* * *

In the case of the individual client the provider of information and the person who acts on the lawyer's advice are one and the same. In the corporate context, however, it will frequently be employees beyond the control group as defined by the court below — "officers and agents * * * responsible for directing [the company's] actions in response to legal advice" — who will possess the information needed by the corporation's lawyers. Middle-level — and indeed lower-level — employees can, by actions within the scope of their employment, embroil the corporation in serious legal difficulties, and it is only natural that these employees would have the relevant information needed by corporate counsel if he is adequately to advise the client with respect to such actual or potential difficulties.

* * *

The control group test adopted by the court below thus frustrates the very purpose of the privilege by discouraging the communication of relevant information by employees of the client to attorneys seeking to render legal advice to the client corporation. The attorney's advice will also frequently be more significant to noncontrol group members than to those who officially sanction the advice, and the control group test makes it more difficult to convey full and frank legal advice to the employees who will put into effect the client corporation's policy. * * *

The narrow scope given the attorney-client privilege by the court below not only makes it difficult for corporate attorneys to formulate sound advice when their client is faced with a specific legal problem but also threatens to limit the valuable efforts of corporate counsel to ensure their client's compliance with the law. In light of the vast and complicated array of regulatory legislation confronting the modern corporation, corporations, unlike most individuals, "constantly go to lawyers to find out how to obey the law," Burnham, The Attorney-Client Privilege in the Corporate Arena, 24 Bus.Law. 901, 913 (1969), particularly since compliance with the law in this area is hardly an instinctive matter. * * * The test adopted by the court below is difficult to apply in practice, though no abstractly formulated and unvarying "test" will necessarily enable courts to decide questions such as this with mathematical precision. But if the purpose of the attorney-client privilege is to be served, the attorney and client must be able to predict with some degree of certainty whether particular discussions will be protected. An uncertain privilege, or one which purports to be certain but results in widely varying applications by the courts, is little better than no privilege at all. The very terms of the test adopted by the court below suggest the unpredictability of its application. The test restricts the availability of the privilege to those officers who play a "substantial role" in deciding and directing a corporation's legal response. Disparate decisions in cases applying this test illustrate its unpredictability. * * *

The communications at issue were made by Upjohn employees to counsel for Upjohn acting as such, at the direction of corporate superiors in order to secure legal advice from counsel. As the Magistrate found, "Mr. Thomas consulted with the Chairman of the Board and outside counsel and thereafter conducted a factual investigation to determine the nature and extent of the questionable payments *and to be in a position to give legal advice to the company with respect to the payments.*" * * * Information, not available from upper-echelon management, was needed to supply a basis for legal advice concerning compliance with securities and tax laws, foreign laws, currency regulations, duties to shareholders, and potential litigation in each of these areas. The communications concerned matters within the scope of the employees' corporate duties, and the employees themselves were sufficiently aware that they were being questioned in order that the corporation could obtain legal advice. The questionnaire identified Thomas as "the company's General Counsel" and referred in its opening sentence to the possible illegality of payments such as the ones on which information was sought. A statement of policy accompanying the questionnaire clearly indicated the legal implications of the investigation. The policy statement was issued "in order that there be no uncertainty in the future as to the policy with respect to the practices which are the subject of this investigation." * * * This statement was issued to Upjohn employees worldwide, so that even those interviewees not receiving a questionnaire were aware of the legal implications of the interviews. Pursuant to explicit instructions from the Chairman of the Board, the communications were considered "highly confidential" when made, and have been kept confidential by the company. Consistent with the underlying purposes of the attorney-client privilege, these communications must be protected against compelled disclosure.

The Court of Appeals declined to extend the attorney-client privilege beyond the limits of the control group test for fear that doing so would entail severe burdens on discovery and create a broad "zone of silence" over corporate affairs. Application of the attorney-client privilege to communications such as those involved here, however, puts the adversary in no worse position than if the communications had never taken place. The privilege only protects disclosure of communications; it does not protect disclosure of the underlying facts by those who communicated with the attorney:

> "[T]he protection of the privilege extends only to *communications* and not to facts. A fact is one thing and a communication concerning that fact is an entirely different thing. The client cannot be compelled to answer the question, 'What did you say or write to the attorney?' but may not refuse to disclose any relevant fact within his knowledge merely because he incorporated a statement of such fact into his communication to his attorney." *Philadelphia v. Westinghouse Electric Corp.*, 205 F. Supp. 830, 831 (ED Pa 1962).

* * * *State ex rel. Dudek v. Circuit Court*, 34 Wis.2d 559, 580, 150 N.W.2d 387, 399 (1967) ("the courts have noted that a party cannot conceal a fact merely by revealing it to his lawyer"). Here the Government was free to question the employees who communicated with Thomas and outside counsel. Upjohn has provided the IRS with a list of such employees, and the IRS has already interviewed some 25 of them. While it would probably be more convenient for the Government to secure the results of petitioner's internal investigation by simply subpoenaing the questionnaires and notes taken by petitioner's attorneys, such considerations of convenience do not overcome the policies served by the attorney-client privilege. * * *

Needless to say, we decide only the case before us, and do not undertake to draft a set of rules which should govern challenges to investigatory subpoenas. Any such approach would violate the spirit of Federal Rule of Evidence 501. *See* S.Rep. No. 93-1277, p. 13 (1974) ("the recognition of a privilege based on a confidential relationship * * * should be determined on a case-by-case basis"). * * * While such a "case-by-case" basis may to some slight extent undermine desirable certainty in the boundaries of the attorney-client privilege, it obeys the spirit of the Rules. At the same time we conclude that the narrow "control group test" sanctioned by the Court of Appeals, in this case cannot, consistent with "the principles of the common law as * * * interpreted * * * in the light of reason and experience," Fed. Rule Evid. 501, govern the development of the law in this area.

III

Our decision that the communications by Upjohn employees to counsel are covered by the attorney-client privilege disposes of the case so far as the responses to the questionnaires and any notes reflecting responses to interview questions are concerned. The summons reaches further, however, and Thomas has testified that his notes and memoranda of interviews go beyond recording responses to his questions. * * * To the extent that the material subject to the summons is not protected by the attorney-client privilege as disclosing communications between an employee and counsel, we must reach the ruling by the Court of Appeals that the work-product doctrine does not apply to summonses issued under 26 U.S.C. § 7602.

The Government concedes, wisely, that the Court of Appeals erred and that the work-product doctrine does apply to IRS summonses. * * * This doctrine was announced by the Court over 30 years ago in *Hickman v. Taylor*. * * * In that case the Court rejected "an attempt, without purported necessity or justification, to secure written statements, private memoranda and personal recollections prepared or formed by an adverse party's counsel in the course of his legal duties." * * * The Court noted that "it is essential that a lawyer work with a certain degree of privacy" and reasoned that if discovery of the material sought were permitted "much of what is now put down in writing would remain unwritten. An attorney's thoughts, heretofore inviolate, would not be his own. Inefficiency, unfairness and sharp practices would inevitably develop in the giving of legal advice and in the preparation of cases for trial. The effect on the legal profession would be demoralizing. And the interests of the clients and the cause of justice would be poorly served." * * *

The "strong public policy" underlying the work-product doctrine was reaffirmed recently in *United States v. Nobles*, 422 U.S. 225, 236-240, 95 S. Ct. 2160, 2169-2171, 45 L.Ed.2d 141 (1975), and has been substantially incorporated in Federal Rule of Civil Procedure 26(b)(3).

* * * While conceding the applicability of the work-product doctrine, the Government asserts that it has made a sufficient showing of necessity to overcome its protections. The Magistrate apparently so found. * * * The Government relies on the following language in *Hickman*:

> We do not mean to say that all written materials obtained or prepared by an adversary's counsel with an eye toward litigation are necessarily free from discovery in all cases. Where relevant and nonprivileged facts remain hidden in an attorney's file and where production of those facts is essential to the preparation of one's case, discovery may properly be had * * * . And production might be justified where the witnesses are no longer available or can be reached only with difficulty.

The Government stresses that interviewees are scattered across the globe and that Upjohn has forbidden its employees to answer questions it considers irrelevant. The above-quoted language from *Hickman*, however, did not apply to "oral statements made by witnesses * * * whether presently in the form of [the attorney's] mental impressions or memoranda." * * * As to such material the Court did "not believe that any showing of necessity can be made under the circumstances of this case so as to justify production * * * . If there should be a rare situation justifying production of these matters petitioner's case is not of that type." * * * Forcing an attorney to disclose notes and memoranda of witnesses' oral statements is particularly disfavored because it tends to reveal the attorney's mental processes. * * *

Rule 26 accords special protection to work product revealing the attorney's mental processes. The Rule permits disclosure of documents and tangible things constituting attorney work product upon a showing of substantial need and inability to obtain the equivalent without undue hardship. This was the standard applied by the Magistrate * * *. Rule 26 goes on, however, to state that "[i]n ordering discovery of such materials when the required showing has been made, the court shall protect against disclosure of the mental impressions, conclusions, opinions or legal theories of an attorney or other representative of a party concerning the litigation." Although this language does not specifically refer to memoranda based on oral statements of witnesses, the *Hickman* court stressed the danger that compelled disclosure of such memoranda would reveal the attorney's mental processes. It is clear that this is the sort of material the draftsmen of the Rule had in mind as deserving special protection. * * *

Based on the foregoing, some courts have concluded that *no* showing of necessity can overcome protection of work product which is based on oral statements from witnesses. * * * Those courts declining to adopt an absolute rule have nonetheless recognized that such material is entitled to special protection. * * * *See, e. g., In re Grand Jury Investigation*, 599 F.2d 1224, 1231 (CA3 1979) ("special considerations * * * must shape any ruling on the discoverability of interview memoranda * * * ; such documents will be discoverable only in a 'rare situation" —) * * *.

We do not decide the issue at this time. It is clear that the Magistrate applied the wrong standard when he concluded that the Government had made a sufficient showing of necessity to overcome the protections of the work-product doctrine. The Magistrate applied the "substantial need" and "without undue hardship" standard articulated in the first part of Rule 26(b)(3). The notes and memoranda sought by the Government here, however, are work product based on oral statements. If they reveal communications, they are, in this case, protected by the attorney-client privilege. To the extent they do not reveal communications, they reveal the attorneys' mental processes in evaluating the communications. As Rule 26 and *Hickman* make clear, such work product cannot be disclosed simply on a showing of substantial need and inability to obtain the equivalent without undue hardship.

While we are not prepared at this juncture to say that such material is always protected by the work-product rule, we think a far stronger showing of necessity and unavailability by other means than was made by the Government or applied by the Magistrate in this case would be necessary to compel disclosure.

* * *

Accordingly, the judgment of the Court of Appeals is reversed, and the case remanded for further proceedings.

It is so ordered.

NOTES

1. Are all confidential communications between an attorney and a client protected by the attorney-client privilege?

The Court in *United States v. Woodruff* recognized that the attorney-client privilege only protects communications that are "incidental to or intertwined with the legal problem of the defendant." 383 F. Supp. 696, 697 (E.D. Pa. 1974). In that case, the government charged the defendant with jumping bail. To prove that the public defender had informed the defendant about the time and place of the trial, the government sought testimony from the attorney. In response to the defendant's argument that communication between attorney and client are privileged, the court held that "[c]ommunications between counsel and defendant as to the trial date do not involve the subject matter of defendant's legal problem. * * *. Such communications are non-legal in nature. Counsel is simply performing a notice function. * * * [W]e hold that the transmission to defendant from the attorney of the fact of the time of trial is not privileged."

On the requirement that the client must be seeking advice on a legal matter, see Saltzburg, Martin, and Capra, *Federal Rules of Evidence Manual* (9th ed. 2006):

> A client may not "buy" a privilege by retaining an attorney to do something that a non-lawyer could do just as well. *See, e.g.*, *In re Feldberg*, 862 F.2d 622, 626 (7th Cir. 1988) ("A business that gets marketing advice from a lawyer does not acquire a privilege in the bargain; so too a business that obtains the services of a records custodian from a member of the bar."). The client must be seeking legal advice and assistance from the lawyer. *See, e.g.*, *In re Grand Jury Subpoena, Peek*, 682 F. Supp. 1552, 1556 (M.D. Ga. 1987) (personal loan transaction between attorney and another person is not privileged: "Otherwise, everything that a lawyer does for himself or herself would be cloaked with a privilege just because he or she is a lawyer."); *SCM Corp. v. Xerox Corp.*, 70 F.R.D. 508, 515 (D. Conn. 1976) ("Legal departments are not citadels in which public, business or technical information may be placed to defeat discovery and thereby ensure confidentiality").
>
> Accordingly, courts have found that communications are not privileged when the lawyer is retained to do tasks that nonlawyers can also do. Examples of nonprivileged situations include:
>
> (1) Preparation of tax returns is not legal advice, so communications made in the course of tax return preparation are not generally privileged. *See, e.g.*, *United States v. Frederick*, 182 F.3d 496 (7th Cir. 1999) ("There is no common law accountant's or tax preparer's privilege, and a taxpayer must not be allowed, by hiring a lawyer to do the work that an accountant, or other tax preparer, or the taxpayer himself or herself, normally would do, to obtain greater protection from government investigators than a taxpayer who did not use a lawyer as his tax preparer would be entitled to do. To rule otherwise would be to impede tax investigations, reward lawyers for doing

nonlawyers' work, and create a privileged position for lawyers in competition with other tax preparers — and to do all this without promoting the legitimate aims" of the privilege); *In re Schroeder*, 842 F.2d 1223, 1224 (11th Cir. 1987) ("Courts generally have held that the preparation of tax returns does not constitute legal advice within the scope of the privilege."). However, the situation is different if the lawyer is retained to determine whether a tax position taken by a client could subject the client to legal liability. As one Court put it, "a lawyer's analysis of the soft spots in a tax return and his judgments on the outcome of litigation on it" do constitute legal advice. *United States v. Rockwell Int'l*, 897 F.2d 1255 (3d Cir. 1990).

(2) The minutes of a board of directors meeting are not privileged merely because an attorney was in attendance or conducted the meeting. *See, e.g.*, *Simon v. G.D. Searle & Co.*, 816 F.2d 397 (8th Cir. 1987) (minutes of business meetings attended by attorneys are not automatically privileged); *Misek-Falkoff v. International Bus. Machs. Corp.*, 144 F.R.D. 48 (S.D.N.Y. 1992) (corporate minutes did not indicate that legal, rather than business, advice was given, and the privilege did not apply merely because an attorney's name was included in the minutes).

(3) Where business documents are prepared and sent to attorneys to keep them apprised of business developments and not as a request for legal advice, the documents are not privileged. *See, e.g.*, *Simon v. G.D. Searle & Co.*, 816 F.2d 397 (8th Cir. 1987) (document of risk management department, compiling aggregate risk management figures for pending litigation, was prepared for business planning purpose — to assess company's total possible liability — and passing it to an attorney does not create a privilege).

(4) Where the client is communicating as part of a personal friendship or animus, and not in the course of seeking legal advice, the privilege will not apply. *See, e.g.*, *United States v. Tedder*, 801 F.2d 1437 (4th Cir. 1986) (the defendant's admission of perjury to a fellow associate in his law firm was not privileged where the evidence indicated that the associate was consulted as a friend and not as a legal adviser; associate was not a criminal attorney, the conversation occurred in informal circumstances, no notes were taken, and the defendant asked for no advice). *See also United States v. Alexander*, 287 F.3d 811 (9th Cir. 2002) (client threatened to injure an attorney appointed to represent him; the threats were not privileged as they were not made in order to obtain legal advice).

(5) Where the attorney is merely acting as a conduit for information, i.e., as a messenger, the privilege is inapplicable. *United States v. Johnson*, 146 F.3d 785 (10th Cir. 1998) (lawyer's communications to his client's drug suppliers was not privileged; the lawyer was simply relaying a message from the client). Compare *United States v. Bauer*, 132 F.3d 504 (9th Cir. 1997) (lawyer's communications to client instructing him that the client was signing a bankruptcy petition under penalty of perjury was privileged; the lawyer was not simply acting

as the court's messenger, but rather was delivering legal advice; moreover, the lawyer's communication would disclose communications from the client concerning the import of signing the petition).

2. Is the identity of an attorney's client, or the fees paid by the client, privileged information?

See Saltzburg, Martin, and Capra, *Federal Rules of Evidence Manual* (9th ed. 2006):

> For obvious reasons, the privilege protects preliminary communications with an attorney about the subject of the representation, even if an attorney-client relationship has not been formalized at that point. This is because confidentiality may be necessary in order to determine whether the attorney can take on the representation. *See, e.g.*, *In re Auclair*, 961 F.2d 65 (5th Cir. 1992) (where three people go to an attorney on a matter that concerns them all, in order to determine whether the attorney can represent them all, the preliminary discussions with the attorney are presumptively protected under the common interest doctrine).
>
> On the other hand, the privilege ordinarily does not protect the preliminary aspects of the attorney-client relationship itself. These matters, which have been referred to as the "incidents of representation," include the client's name, the amount and payment of a fee, and the fact of consultation. The identity of the client, the fee, and the fact and extent of representation generally have nothing to do with the free flow of information once that relationship has been established. *See, e.g.*, *In re Grand Jury Proceedings*, 33 F.3d 1060 (9th Cir. 1994) (upholding a judgment of contempt resulting from an attorney's refusal to produce records pertaining to fee information and fee arrangements with a client; while that information might have indicated that the client retained the attorney to represent him in a grand jury investigation, this fact did not "in and of itself reveal any confidential information"); *United States v. Olano*, 62 F.3d 1180 (9th Cir. 1995) (no privilege where the testimony provided "only general descriptions of the work" that the lawyer performed; the lawyer did not disclose the defendant's "motives, strategies or goals").
>
> Thus, the focus of the privilege in most courts is on those communications that the attorney can influence by informing the client that a free flow of information will not prejudice the client. Communications and information respecting the incidents of representation do not meet this standard. *See* Capra, *Deterring the Formation of the Attorney-Client Relationship: Disclosure of Client Identity, Payment of Fees, and Communications by Fiduciaries*, 4 Geo. J. Legal Ethics 235 (1990). As Judge Winter stated in the leading case of *In re Shargel*, 742 F.2d 61 (2d Cir. 1984):
>
> > Absent special circumstances, disclosure of the identity of the client and fee information stand on a footing different from communications intended by the client to explain a problem to a lawyer

> in order to obtain legal advice. * * * A general rule requiring disclosure of the fact of consultation does not place attorneys in the professional dilemma of cautioning against disclosure and rendering perhaps ill-informed advice or learning all the details and perhaps increasing the perils to the client of disclosure.

See also United States v. Leventhal, 961 F.2d 936 (11th Cir. 1992) (information concerning payment of more than $10,000 cash from a client to an attorney is not privileged, and can be obtained through enforcement of an IRS summons; fee arrangements and disclosure of the identity of the client are part of the preliminaries and incidents of the representation, and in the absence of extraordinary circumstances, they do not satisfy the requirement of the privilege that a communication must be made in the course of seeking legal advice); *In re Grand Jury Matter No. 91-01386*, 969 F.2d 995 (11th Cir. 1992) (identity of a client who paid the attorney with counterfeit bills held not privileged, where disclosure of identity "will not provide the government with a necessary link to, or revelation of, any confidential matters which fall within the attorney-client privilege"; disclosure of identity will only link the client with a payment by counterfeit money, "which is not a communication at all").

A limited exception to the above rule exists, however: If information concerning the incidents of representation would, directly or indirectly, disclose a confidential communication, then this preliminary information is privileged. One example is where the disclosure of the fee payment or the fact of representation would reveal a confidential motive for seeking representation. *See, e.g.*, *In re Subpoenaed Grand Jury Witness*, 171 F.3d 511 (7th Cir. 1999) (fee payment and client identity privileged where "disclosure of this information would identify a client of Hagen's who is potentially involved in a targeted criminal activity which, on this record, would lead to revealing that client's motive to pay the legal bills for some of Hagen's other clients"). Compare *Vingelli v. DEA*, 992 F.2d 449 (2d Cir. 1993) (benefactor payment made by an attorney on behalf of a client is not privileged; the fact that the attorney made a benefactor payment does not indicate why the client may have sought the attorney's advice). Another example is where communications have been disclosed, and yet they remain confidential as a practical matter because they have not been connected to an identifiable person. If disclosure of the client's identity would tie the client to the previously disclosed communications, then the client's identity is privileged. *See, e.g.*, *United States v. Liebman*, 742 F.2d 807 (3d Cir. 1984) (where the substance of a communication was already known, but not the identity of the communicator, then disclosure of identity would be tantamount to disclosure of a privileged communication).

3. May a third party who overhears a conversation between an attorney and client testify about the content of that communication?

In *Suburban Sew'n Sweep, Inc. v. Swiss-Bernina, Inc.*, the Court held that the attorney-client "privilege no longer applies when the information is communicated in the presence of a third party, * * * unless that party's presence does not indicate lack of intent to keep the communication confidential. * * * Similarly, the privilege no longer applies if the information is later voluntarily disclosed to a third party. * * * Even if the disclosure is inadvertent, the privilege may no longer apply in varied circumstances. * * * [E]ven inadvertent communication to third parties, such as bystanders or eavesdroppers, destroys the privilege, at least where the eavesdropping is not surreptitious and the attorney and client have made little effort to insure that they are not overheard. The justification for these decisions is that the nature of the transaction and the surrounding circumstances are inconsistent with the notion that the communication was intended to be confidential." 91 F.R.D. 254, 258 (N.D. Ill. 1981).

4. If a client is using the attorney's services for wrongdoing, will the privilege apply to confidential communications between them?

Professors Saltzburg, Martin, and Capra, in *Federal Rules of Evidence Manual* (9th ed. 2006), discuss the crime-fraud exception to the attorney-client privilege:

> Statements made by the client to the attorney, even though in confidence, are not privileged if the purpose of the communication is to further crime or fraud. The crime-fraud exception is triggered when the party seeking the information provides *prima facie* evidence that the client was seeking the attorney's advice and services in furtherance of a preconceived plan of wrongdoing. The Court in *In re Grand Jury*, 845 F.2d 896 (11th Cir. 1988) set forth the standards for applying the crime-fraud exception:
>
>> First, there must be a prima facie showing that the client was engaged in criminal or fraudulent conduct when he sought the advice of counsel, that he was planning such conduct when he sought the advice of counsel, or that he committed a crime of fraud subsequent to receiving the benefit of counsel's advice. Second, there must be a showing that the attorney's assistance was obtained in furtherance of the criminal or fraudulent activity or was closely related to it.
>
> Note that the exception can apply even if the client never actually committed a fraudulent or criminal act. The exception is triggered when the client communicates with the attorney with the intent to further a plan of crime or fraud. *See United States v. Collis*, 128 F.3d 313 (6th Cir. 1997) ("the crime or fraud need not have occurred for the exception to be applicable; it need only have been the objective of the client's communication"); *In re Grand Jury Proceedings*, 87 F.3d 377 (9th Cir. 1996) (government is not required to show that the client's plan succeeded, nor that the attorney's advice in fact helped the client in his plan).

While the exception is referred to as the "crime-fraud exception," it has also been applied by some Courts where communications were made to further tortious conduct such as employment discrimination and intentional infliction of emotional distress. *See, e.g., Coleman v. American Broadcasting Cos.*, 106 F.R.D. 201 (D.D.C. 1985) (referring to the "crime-fraud-tort exception," and collecting cases that have expanded the exception to cover tortious conduct). Contra *Motley v. Marathon Oil Co.*, 71 F.3d 1547 (10th Cir. 1995) (memorandum furthering racial discrimination was held privileged; finding no exception for communications made in furtherance of tortious conduct generally).

In *United States v. Zolin*, 491 U.S. 554 (1989), the Court noted that there was "some confusion" in the lower courts concerning the application of the *prima facie* standard to the crime-fraud exception. There is dispute about the quantum of proof required, and about whether the privilege holder must be given an opportunity to rebut the *prima facie* case. The Court in *Zolin* found it unnecessary to determine the specific quantum of proof required to establish a *prima facie* case of crime or fraud, or whether the proponent of the privilege should be allowed an opportunity to rebut a *prima facie* showing. These ambiguities notwithstanding, it is clear that the *prima facie* standard is not an exacting one. For example in *In re Grand Jury Investigation*, 842 F.2d 1223 (11th Cir. 1987), the Court found that a *prima facie* case was shown by a good faith affidavit of the prosecutor describing the evidence submitted to a grand jury. *See also In re Grand Jury Proceedings (Vargas)*, 723 F.2d 1461 (10th Cir. 1983) (*prima facie* foundation may be made by documentary evidence or good faith statements by the prosecutor as to testimony already received by the grand jury); *White v. American Airlines*, 915 F.2d 1414 (10th Cir. 1990) (*prima facie* proof that the corporate attorney asked a corporate employee to perjure himself was found solely on the basis of the corporate employee's self-serving testimony). Compare *In re Grand Jury Subpoena Duces Tecum*, 773 F.2d 204 (8th Cir. 1985) (party's failure to produce two out of 800 demanded documents is not *prima facie* evidence of crime or fraud).

The Court in *Zolin* held that the trial judge, in determining whether a *prima facie* case of crime or fraud has been met, may take into account the allegedly privileged statements themselves. The Court reasoned that "no matter how light the burden of proof which confronts the party claiming the exception, there are many blatant abuses of privilege which cannot be substantiated by extrinsic evidence," and that a "*per se* rule that the communications in question may never be considered creates, we feel, too great an impediment to the proper functioning of the adversary process." *See also White v. American Airlines*, 915 F.2d 1414 (10th Cir. 1990) (easily finding a *prima facie* case of crime-fraud on the basis of the allegedly privileged statements themselves; assuming that state law, applicable in this diversity case, would follow *Zolin*). Of course, the court's review of the allegedly privileged statements must be conducted *in camera* and outside the presence of the party demanding production of the statements. Otherwise the privilege will be lost before the court even rules on the privilege question. *See, e.g.*, *In re General Motors Corp.*, 153 F.3d 714 (8th Cir. 1988) (where the trial court required the party asserting the privilege to produce the statements for the purpose of conducting an *in camera* hearing on the crime-fraud exception, it was error to conduct that hearing with both sides present: "By ordering disclosure, the district court effectively destroyed the confidentiality of the communications. Until it is established that the crime/fraud exception applies, the district court may not compel disclosure of allegedly privileged communications to the party opposing the privilege.").

In some cases it might be possible that a judge does not even need to hold an *in camera* review, because the client's plan of crime or fraud is so obvious. However, "district courts should be highly reluctant to order disclosure without conducting an *in camera* review of allegedly privileged materials." *In re BankAmerica Corp. Sec. Litig.*, 270 F.3d 639, 643 (8th Cir. 2001). This is because "a threshold showing of facts supporting the crime-fraud exception followed by an *in camera* review of the privileged materials helps ensure that legitimate communications * * * are not deterred by the risk of compelled disclosure under the crime-fraud exception."

The crime-fraud exception can apply even if the attorney is an unwitting instrument in the crime or fraud. The basis of the exception is that the client cannot in bad faith exploit the privilege by using the attorney as an instrument of crime or fraud. Therefore it does not matter whether the attorney was knowingly involved in the client's scheme. The Court in *In re Grand Jury Proceedings*, 87 F.3d 377 (9th Cir. 1996) explained this result as follows:

> Inasmuch as today's privilege exists for the benefit of the client, not the attorney, it is the client's knowledge and intentions that are of paramount concern to the application of the crime-fraud exception; the attorney need know nothing about the client's ongoing or planned illicit activity for the exception to apply.

The crime-fraud exception applies only when the attorney is being used to further a future or ongoing scheme of misconduct. It does not apply to communications seeking legal representation with respect to a past act of crime or fraud; such statements are at the heart of the protection provided by the privilege. *See, e.g.*, *Coleman v. American Broadcasting Co.*, 106 F.R.D. 201 (D.D.C. 1985) ("Only communications in regard to ongoing or future misconduct fall outside the scope of the privilege. This distinction goes to the very core of the policies underlying the privilege."). Moreover, the exception will not apply if the client consulted with an attorney to determine whether a prospective course of conduct was lawful. As one Court put it:

> The crime-fraud exception has a precise focus: It applies only when the communications between the client and his lawyer further a crime, fraud or other misconduct. * * * [The exception should not be applied to deny a client] the privilege where even its stern critics

> acknowledge that the justification for the shield is strongest — where a client seeks counsel's advice to determine the legality of conduct *before* the client takes any action.

United States v. White, 887 F.2d 267 (D.C. Cir. 1989). *See also In re Grand Jury Proceedings*, 87 F.3d 377 (9th Cir. 1996) (crime-fraud exception should not be applied in such a way as to "discourage many would-be clients from consulting an attorney about entirely legitimate legal dilemmas").

On the other hand, the crime-fraud exception will apply if the client already knows that a prospective course of conduct is impermissible and is simply using counsel in an attempt to effectuate the plan. *See, e.g., United States v. Reeder*, 170 F.3d 93 (1st Cir. 1999) (client conferred with counsel in order to obtain "some ideas" on how to cover up a series of questionable loans, and proposed that the loans could be backdated; these communications were within the crime-fraud exception and not privileged; the Court rejected the defendant's argument that he was simply seeking the attorney's advice on whether a legal problem could be solved in a particular manner; the defendant did not merely ask whether backdating documents would be legal — rather, he affirmatively sought the lawyer's assistance in a cover-up); *United States v. Jacobs*, 117 F.3d 82 (2d Cir. 1997) (crime-fraud exception was found where "the wrong-doer had set upon a criminal course *before* consulting counsel").

Likewise, any communications made with a view to covering up past acts of misconduct are in fact made with the purpose of perpetrating a crime or fraud, and hence are not privileged. *See United States v. Edwards*, 303 F.3d 606 (5th Cir. 2002) (crime-fraud exception applied where the legal services sought by the defendant were "to conceal and cover up the crimes committed"; "[r]ather than merely defending himself from wrongdoing, [the client] was actively continuing the cover-up of extortion and perpetuating his tax fraud").

The fact that a communication with counsel can be used to *prove* a crime or fraud is not sufficient to trigger the exception. *In re Richard Roe, Inc.*, 68 F.3d 38 (2d Cir. 1995) (it was improper for the trial court to order disclosure of privileged communications simply because they were relevant evidence of activity in furtherance of crime). Timing is critical, and unless the scheme of crime or fraud was afoot at the time of the communication, the statements remain privileged. For example, assume that a corporation seeks legal advice to determine whether a large account receivable is, in fact, legally collectible. Counsel investigates and informs the corporation that the receivable is not legally collectible. A few months later, the corporation sells the receivable without informing the buyer about the advice received from counsel. Of course, counsel's report would be relevant to prove that the seller-client acted fraudulently. But in order for the crime-fraud exception to apply, the seller must establish a *prima facie* case that the seller had a fraudulent intent at the time that counsel's advice was sought. If not, the privilege will apply even though the client acted fraudulently subsequent to receiving the legal advice. *See, e.g., Pritchard-Keang Nam Corp. v. Jaworski*, 751 F.2d 277 (8th Cir. 1984):

> That the report may help *prove* that a fraud occurred does not mean that it was *used* in perpetrating the fraud. — Timing is critical, for the prima facie showing requires that the client was engaged in or planning a criminal or fraudulent scheme when he sought the advice of counsel to further the scheme.

See also In re Sealed Case, 107 F.3d 46 (D.C. Cir. 1997) (the mere fact that a person commits a fraud after consulting with counsel does not establish a *prima facie* case that the consultation was in furtherance of the fraud); *Parkway Gallery Furn. v. Kittinger Pa. House Group*, 116 F.R.D. 46 (M.D.N.C. 1987) ("The crime or fraud exception does not apply if the fraud occurred subsequent to the advice and that fact alone will not support further inquiry.").

5. When a defense attorney has knowledge of incriminating evidence, may the state compel the attorney to testify?

In *State v. Sullivan*, the Supreme Court of Washington held that it was prejudicial error to require defense counsel to testify concerning statements made to him by the accused about the location of the victim's body. The court decided that "[t]he prosecuting attorney could have had only one intent and purpose when he called defense counsel as a state witness: to prejudice the jury by giving it an opportunity to draw the inescapable inference that defendant had told defense counsel where she had buried her husband's remains. This [communication] was privileged under the [attorney-client privilege] statute, and it was prejudicial error to force * * * [the defense attorney] to testify concerning it." 373 P.2D 474, 476 (Wash. 1962).

6. If a defendant tells his attorney about the location of evidence, and the attorney removes or alters the evidence, does the attorney-client privilege apply?

In *People v. Meredith*, 631 P.2d 46 (Cal. 1981), the court held that statements between the defendant and his attorney concerning the location of a piece of evidence, a partially burned wallet, were confidential communications protected by the attorney-client privilege. However, when the defense team removed the wallet from the trash bin, the privilege disappeared with regard to the location and condition of the wallet. "When defense counsel alters or removes physical evidence, he necessarily deprives the prosecution of the opportunity to observe that evidence in its original condition or location. * * * To extend the attorney-client privilege to a case in which the defense removed evidence might encourage defense counsel to race the police to seize critical evidence. * * * We therefore conclude that whenever defense counsel removes or alters evidence, the statutory privilege does not bar revelation of the original location or condition of the evidence in question. We thus view the defense decision to remove evidence as a tactical choice. If defense counsel leaves the evidence where he discovers it, his observations derived from privileged communications are insulated from revelation. If, however, counsel chooses to remove evidence to examine or test it, the original location and condition of that evidence loses the protection of the privilege."

[3] The Privilege and Government Attorneys

IN RE COUNTY OF ERIE

473 F.3d 413 (2d Cir. 2007)

JACOBS, CHIEF JUDGE:

In the course of a lawsuit by a class of arrested persons against Erie County (and certain of its officials) alleging that they were subjected to unconstitutional strip searches, the United States District Court for the Western District of New York (Curtin, J.) ordered the discovery of e-mails (and other documents) between an Assistant Erie County Attorney and County officials that solicit, contain and discuss advice from attorney to client. The County defendants petition for a writ of mandamus directing the district court to vacate that order. The writ is available because: important issues of first impression are raised; the privilege will be irreversibly lost if review awaits final judgment; and immediate resolution of this dispute will promote sound discovery practices and doctrine. Upon consideration of the circumstances, we issue the writ ordering the district court: to vacate its order, to determine whether the privilege was otherwise waived, and to enter an interim order to protect the confidentiality of the disputed communications.

I

On July 21, 2004, plaintiffs-respondents Adam Pritchard, Edward Robinson and Julenne Tucker commenced suit under 42 U.S.C. § 1983, individually and on behalf of a class of others similarly situated, alleging that, pursuant to a written policy of the Erie County Sheriff's Office and promulgated by County officials, every detainee who entered the Erie County Holding Center or Erie County Correctional Facility (including plaintiffs) was subjected to an invasive strip search, without regard to individualized suspicion or the offense alleged, and that this policy violates the Fourth Amendment. They sued the County of Erie, New York, as well as Erie County Sheriff Patrick Gallivan; Undersheriff Timothy Howard; the acting Superintendent of the Erie County Correctional Facility, Donald Livingston; the Deputy Superintendent, Robert Huggins; and the Superintendent of the Erie County Holding Center, H. McCarthy Gibson (collectively, the "County").

During the course of discovery, the County withheld production of certain documents as privileged attorney-client communications; a privilege log was produced instead, pursuant to the Federal Rules of Civil Procedure and Local Civil Rules for the Western District of New York. In August 2005, plaintiffs moved to compel production of the logged documents, almost all of which were e-mails. The County submitted the documents to Magistrate Judge Hugh B. Scott for inspection in camera. In January 2006, Judge Scott ordered production of ten of the withheld e-mails, which (variously) reviewed the law concerning strip searches of detainees, assessed the County's current search policy, recommended alternative policies, and monitored the implementation of these policy changes.

JUDGE SCOTT reasoned that:

> These communications "go beyond rendering 'legal analysis' [by] propos[ing] changes to existing policy to make it constitutional, including drafting of policy regulations";
>
> The "drafting and subsequent oversight of implementation of the new strip search policy ventured beyond merely rendering legal advice and analysis into the realm of policy making and administration"; and
>
> "[N]o legal advice is rendered apart from policy recommendations."

JUDGE SCOTT ordered the County to deliver these ten e-mails to the plaintiffs.

After considering the County's objections to this order, the district court independently reviewed the disputed e-mails in camera and, applying a "clearly erroneous" standard, overruled the objections, and directed production. This petition for a writ of mandamus followed.

II

[The Court held that mandamus was appropriate because "[t]o await resolution of this issue pending final judgment risks the development of discovery practices and doctrine that unsettle and undermine the governmental attorney-client privilege."]

III

The attorney-client privilege protects confidential communications between client and counsel made for the purpose of obtaining or providing legal assistance. Its purpose is to encourage attorneys and their clients to communicate fully and frankly and thereby to promote "broader public interests in the observance of law and administration of justice." *Upjohn*, 449 U.S. at 389. "The availability of sound legal advice inures to the benefit not only of the client who wishes to know his options and responsibilities in given circumstances, but also of the public which is entitled to compliance with the ever growing and increasingly complex body of public law." *In re Grand Jury Subpoena Duces Tecum Dated Sept. 15, 1983*, 731 F.2d 1032, 1036-37 (2d Cir. 1984).

At the same time, we construe the privilege narrowly because it renders relevant information undiscoverable; we apply it "only where necessary to achieve its purpose." *Fisher v. United States*, 425 U.S. 391, 403. The burden of establishing the applicability of the privilege rests with the party invoking it. *In re Grand Jury Proceedings*, 219 F.3d 175, 182 (2d Cir. 2000); *United States v. Int'l Bhd. of Teamsters, Chauffeurs, Warehousemen and Helpers of Am., AFL-CIO*, 119 F.3d 210, 214 (2d. Cir 1997).

In civil suits between private litigants and government agencies, the attorney-client privilege protects most confidential communications between government counsel and their clients that are made for the purpose of obtaining or providing legal assistance.[5] *See, e.g., Ross v. City of Memphis,*

[5] Certain limitations to the government attorney-client privilege, not implicated here, may render an otherwise-protectable communication unprotected. *See Nat'l Council of La Raza*, 411 F.3d at 360-61 (holding that the government could not invoke the attorney-client privilege to bar

423 F.3d 596, 601 (6th Cir. 2005) ("[A] government entity can assert attorney-client privilege in the civil context."); *In re Lindsey*, 331 U.S. App. D.C. 246, 148 F.3d 1100, 1107 (D.C. Cir. 1998) (noting the existence of "a government attorney-client privilege that is rather absolute in civil litigation"); cf. Proposed Fed. R. Evid. 503(a)(1) (1972) (describing a client, for the purpose of defining the attorney-client privilege, as a "person, public officer, or corporation, association, or other organization or entity, either public or private").

The attorney-client privilege accommodates competing values; the competition is sharpened when the privilege is asserted by a government. On the one hand, non-disclosure impinges on open and accessible government. On the other hand, public officials are duty-bound to understand and respect constitutional, judicial and statutory limitations on their authority; thus, their access to candid legal advice directly and significantly serves the public interest:

> We believe that, if anything, the traditional rationale for the [attorney-client] privilege applies with special force in the government context. It is crucial that government officials, who are expected to uphold and execute the law and who may face criminal prosecution for failing to do so, be encouraged to seek out and receive fully informed legal advice. Upholding the privilege furthers a culture in which consultation with government lawyers is accepted as a normal, desirable, and even indispensable part of conducting public business. Abrogating the privilege undermines that culture and thereby impairs the public interest.

In re Grand Jury Investigation, 399 F.3d at 534. Access to legal advice by officials responsible for formulating, implementing and monitoring governmental policy is fundamental to "promot[ing] broader public interests in the observance of law and administration of justice," *Upjohn*, 449 U.S. at 389. At least in civil litigation between a government agency and private litigants, the government's claim to the protections of the attorney-client privilege is on a par with the claim of an individual or a corporate entity.

IV

A party invoking the attorney-client privilege must show (1) a communication between client and counsel that (2) was intended to be and was in fact kept confidential, and (3) was made for the purpose of obtaining or providing legal advice. * * * At issue here is the third consideration: whether the communications were made for the purpose of obtaining or providing legal advice, as opposed to advice on policy.

The rule that a confidential communication between client and counsel is privileged only if it is generated for the purpose of obtaining or providing legal assistance is often recited. The issue usually arises in the context of communications to and from corporate in-house lawyers who also serve as business executives. So the question usually is whether the communication was

disclosure of a legal memorandum where the government had incorporated it into its policy by repeatedly, publicly and expressly relying upon its reasoning and had adopted its reasoning as authoritative within the agency).

generated for the purpose of obtaining or providing legal advice as opposed to business advice. *See In re Grand Jury Subpoena Duces Tecum,* 731 F.2d at 1036-37.

Fundamentally, legal advice involves the interpretation and application of legal principles to guide future conduct or to assess past conduct. It requires a lawyer to rely on legal education and experience to inform judgment. But it is broader, and is not demarcated by a bright line. What Judge Wyzanski observed long ago applies with equal force today:

> The modern lawyer almost invariably advises his client upon not only what is permissible but also what is desirable. And it is in the * * * public interest that the lawyer should regard himself as more than [a] predicter of legal consequences. His duty to society as well as to his client involves many relevant social, economic, political and philosophical considerations. And the privilege of nondisclosure is not lost merely because relevant nonlegal considerations are expressly stated in a communication which also includes legal advice.

United States v. United Shoe Mach. Corp., 89 F. Supp. 357, 359 (D. Mass. 1950). We consider whether the predominant purpose of the communication is to render or solicit legal advice.

The complete lawyer may well promote and reinforce the legal advice given, weigh it, and lay out its ramifications by explaining: how the advice is feasible and can be implemented; the legal downsides, risks and costs of taking the advice or doing otherwise; what alternatives exist to present measures or the measures advised; what other persons are doing or thinking about the matter; or the collateral benefits, risks or costs in terms of expense, politics, insurance, commerce, morals, and appearances. So long as the predominant purpose of the communication is legal advice, these considerations and caveats are not other than legal advice or severable from it. The predominant purpose of a communication cannot be ascertained by quantification or classification of one passage or another; it should be assessed dynamically and in light of the advice being sought or rendered, as well as the relationship between advice that can be rendered only by consulting the legal authorities and advice that can be given by a non-lawyer.[8] The more careful the lawyer, the more likely it is that the legal advice will entail follow-through by facilitation, encouragement and monitoring.

V

The County asserts that the Assistant County Attorney whose advice was solicited could not have been conveying non-legal policy advice because the

[8] Importantly, redaction is available for documents which contain legal advice that is incidental to the non-legal advice that is the predominant purpose of the communication. *See, e.g., United States v. Weissman, No. 94 Cr. 760*, 1995 U.S. Dist. LEXIS 5476, 1995 WL 244522, at *4 (S.D.N.Y. Apr. 26, 1995) (recognizing the availability of redaction to protect legal advice in hybrid documents); *Detection Sys., Inc. v. Pittway Corp.*, 96 F.R.D. 152, 155 (W.D.N.Y. 1982) ("In those instances where both privileged and non-privileged material exist, the privileged material has been deleted.").

Erie County Charter (§ 602) confines her authority to that of a "legal advisor," and because "only the County Sheriff and his direct appointees ha[ve] policy-making authority for the [Sheriff's] department." This argument does not assist the analysis much. A lawyer's lack of formal authority to formulate, approve or enact policy does not actually prevent the rendering of policy advice to officials who do possess that authority. A similar consideration may be useful in different circumstances. When an attorney is consulted in a capacity other than as a lawyer, as (for example) a policy advisor, media expert, business consultant, banker, referee or friend, that consultation is not privileged. *In re Lindsey*, 148 F.3d at 1106 (citing 1 McCormick on Evidence § 88, at 322-24 (4th ed. 1992); Restatement (Third) of the Law Governing Lawyers § 122 (Proposed Final Draft No. 1, 1996)).

In the government context, one court considered relevant the fact that the attorney seeking to invoke the privilege held two formal positions: Assistant to the President (ostensibly non-legal) and Deputy White House Counsel (ostensibly legal). *In re Lindsey*, 148 F.3d at 1103, 1106-07. The same is true in the private sector where "in-house attorneys are more likely to mix legal and business functions." *Bank Brussels Lambert*, 220 F. Supp. 2d at 286. In short, an attorney's dual legal and non-legal responsibilities may bear on whether a particular communication was generated for the purpose of soliciting or rendering legal advice; but here, the Assistant County Attorney's lack of formal policymaking authority is not a compelling circumstance.

The predominant purpose of a particular document—legal advice, or not—may also be informed by the overall needs and objectives that animate the client's request for advice. For example, Erie County's objective was to ascertain its obligations under the Fourth Amendment and how those requirements may be fulfilled, rather than to save money or please the electorate (even though these latter objectives would not be beyond the lawyer's consideration).

VI

After reviewing in camera the documents listed on the County's privilege log, Judge Scott determined that the ten e-mails at issue here are not privileged. These e-mails, dated between December 23, 2002 and December 11, 2003, passed between the Assistant County Attorney and various officials in the Sheriff's Office (primarily petitioners). The ten e-mails are an amalgam of the following six broad issues:

(i) The compliance of the County's search policy with the Fourth Amendment;

(ii) Any possible liability of the County and its officials stemming from the existing policy;

(iii) Alternative search policies, including the availability of equipment to assist in conducting searches that comply with constitutional requirements;

(iv) Guidance for implementing and funding these alternative policies;

(v) Maintenance of records concerning the original search policy; and

(vi) Evaluations of the County's progress implementing the alternative search policy. (EC-C-00204-20 and EC-C-00223-25).

The judge reasoned (*inter alia*) that because these e-mails "propose[d] changes to existing policy to make it constitutional" and provided guidance "to executive officials within the Sheriff's Department to take steps to implement the new policy * * * no legal advice is rendered or rendered apart from policy recommendations." Because the e-mails "go beyond rendering legal analysis," the judge concluded that they were not privileged. We disagree.

It is to be hoped that legal considerations will play a role in governmental policymaking. When a lawyer has been asked to assess compliance with a legal obligation, the lawyer's recommendation of a policy that complies (or better complies) with the legal obligation—or that advocates and promotes compliance, or oversees implementation of compliance measures—is legal advice. Public officials who craft policies that may directly implicate the legal rights or responsibilities of the public should be "encouraged to seek out and receive fully informed legal advice" in the course of formulating such policies. *In re Grand Jury Investigation*, 399 F.3d at 534. To repeat: "The availability of sound legal advice inures to the benefit not only of the client * * * but also of the public which is entitled to compliance with the ever growing and increasingly complex body of public law." *In re Grand Jury Subpoena Duces Tecum*, 731 F.2d at 1036-37. This observation has added force when the legal advice is sought by officials responsible for law enforcement and corrections policies.

We conclude that each of the ten disputed e-mails was sent for the predominant purpose of soliciting or rendering legal advice. They convey to the public officials responsible for formulating, implementing and monitoring Erie County's corrections policies, a lawyer's assessment of Fourth Amendment requirements, and provide guidance in crafting and implementing alternative policies for compliance. This advice — particularly when viewed in the context in which it was solicited and rendered—does not constitute "general policy or political advice" unprotected by the privilege. *In re Lindsey*, 148 F.3d at 1120 (Tatel, J., dissenting).

Although the e-mails at issue were generated for the predominant purpose of legal advice, we remand for the district court to determine whether the distribution of some of the disputed e-mail communications to others within the Erie County Sheriff's Department constituted a waiver of the attorney-client privilege.

* * *

IN RE: BRUCE R. LINDSEY (Grand Jury Testimony)

148 F.3d 1100 (D.C. Cir. 1998)

RANDOLPH, ROGERS and TATEL, CIRCUIT JUDGES.

PER CURIAM:

In these expedited appeals, the principal question is whether an attorney in the Office of the President, having been called before a federal grand jury, may refuse, on the basis of a government attorney-client privilege, to answer questions about possible criminal conduct by government officials and others. To state the question is to suggest the answer, for the Office of the President is a part of the federal government, consisting of government employees doing government business, and neither legal authority nor policy nor experience suggests that a federal government entity can maintain the ordinary common law attorney-client privilege to withhold information relating to a federal criminal offense. The Supreme Court and this court have held that even the constitutionally based executive privilege for presidential communications fundamental to the operation of the government can be overcome upon a proper showing of need for the evidence in criminal trials and in grand jury proceedings. *See United States v. Nixon*, 418 U.S. 683, 707-12 (1974); *In re Sealed Case*, 121 F.3d 729, 736-38 (D.C. Cir. 1997). In the context of federal criminal investigations and trials, there is no basis for treating legal advice differently from any other advice the Office of the President receives in performing its constitutional functions. The public interest in honest government and in exposing wrongdoing by government officials, as well as the tradition and practice, acknowledged by the Office of the President and by former White House Counsel, of government lawyers reporting evidence of federal criminal offenses whenever such evidence comes to them, lead to the conclusion that a government attorney may not invoke the attorney-client privilege in response to grand jury questions seeking information relating to the possible commission of a federal crime. The extent to which the communications of White House Counsel are privileged against disclosure to a federal grand jury depends, therefore, on whether the communications contain information of possible criminal offenses. * * *

I.

On January 16, 1998, at the request of the Attorney General, the Division for the Purpose of Appointing Independent Counsels issued an order expanding the prosecutorial jurisdiction of Independent Counsel Kenneth W. Starr. Previously, the main focus of Independent Counsel Starr's inquiry had been on financial transactions involving President Clinton when he was Governor of Arkansas, known popularly as the Whitewater inquiry. The order now authorized Starr to investigate "whether Monica Lewinsky or others suborned perjury, obstructed justice, intimidated witnesses, or otherwise violated federal law" in connection with the civil lawsuit against the President of the United States filed by Paula Jones. * * *

On January 30, 1998, the grand jury issued a subpoena to Bruce R. Lindsey, an attorney admitted to practice in Arkansas. Lindsey currently holds two positions: Deputy White House Counsel and Assistant to the President. On February 18, February 19, and March 12, 1998, Lindsey appeared before the grand jury and declined to answer certain questions on the ground that the questions represented information protected from disclosure by a government attorney-client privilege applicable to Lindsey's communications with the President as Deputy White House Counsel * * *. Lindsey also claimed work product protections related to the attorney-client privilege * * *.

On March 6, 1998, the Independent Counsel moved to compel Lindsey's testimony. The district court granted that motion on May 4, 1998. The court concluded that the President's executive privilege claim failed in light of the Independent Counsel's showing of need and unavailability. It rejected Lindsey's government attorney-client privilege claim on similar grounds, ruling that the President possesses an attorney-client privilege when consulting in his official capacity with White House Counsel, but that the privilege is qualified in the grand jury context and may be overcome upon a sufficient showing of need for the subpoenaed communications and unavailability from other sources.

[T]he Office of the President appealed the order granting the motion to compel Lindsey's testimony, * * *. Following an expedited briefing schedule, on June 29, 1998, this court heard argument on the attorney-client issues. Neither the Office of the President nor the President in his personal capacity has appealed the district court's ruling on executive privilege. * * *

II.

* * *

The Office of the President contends that Lindsey's communications with the President and others in the White House should fall within this privilege both because the President, like any private person, needs to communicate fully and frankly with his legal advisors, and because the current grand jury investigation may lead to impeachment proceedings, which would require a defense of the President's official position as head of the executive branch of government, presumably with the assistance of White House Counsel. The Independent Counsel contends that an absolute government attorney-client privilege would be inconsistent with the proper role of the government lawyer and that the President should rely only on his private lawyers for fully confidential counsel.

* * *

A.

* * *

The practice of attorneys in the executive branch reflects the common understanding that a government attorney-client privilege functions in at least some contexts. The Office of Legal Counsel in the Department of Justice concluded in 1982 that

> "[a]lthough the attorney-client privilege traditionally has been recognized in the context of private attorney-client relationships, the privilege also functions to protect communications between government attorneys and client agencies or departments * * * much as it operates to protect attorney-client communications in the private sector."

The Office of Legal Counsel also concluded that when government attorneys stand in the shoes of private counsel, representing federal employees sued in their individual capacities, confidential communications between attorney and client are privileged. *See* Antonin Scalia, Assistant Attorney General, Office of Legal Counsel, Disclosure of Confidential Information Received by U.S. Attorney in the Course of Representing a Federal Employee (Nov. 30, 1976); * * *

B.

Recognizing that a government attorney-client privilege exists is one thing. Finding that the Office of the President is entitled to assert it here is quite another.

It is settled law that the party claiming the privilege bears the burden of proving that the communications are protected. As oft-cited definitions of the privilege make clear, only communications that seek "legal advice" from "a professional legal adviser in his capacity as such" are protected. * * *

On the record before us, it seems likely that at least some of the conversations for which Lindsey asserted government attorney-client privilege did not come within the formulation just quoted.

Both of these subjects arose from the expanded jurisdiction of the Independent Counsel, which did not become public until January 20, 1998. Before then, any legal advice Lindsey rendered in connection with Jones v. Clinton, a lawsuit involving President Clinton in his personal capacity, likely could not have been covered by government attorney-client privilege. * * * Lindsey's advice on political, strategic, or policy issues, valuable as it may have been, would not be shielded from disclosure by the attorney-client privilege.

* * *

We therefore turn to the question whether an attorney-client privilege permits a government lawyer to withhold from a grand jury information relating to the commission of possible crimes by government officials and others. Although the cases * * * recognize a government attorney-client privilege that is rather absolute in civil litigation, those cases do not necessarily control the application of the privilege here. The grand jury, a constitutional body established in the Bill of Rights, "belongs to no branch of the institutional Government, serving as a kind of buffer or referee between the Government and the people," *United States v. Williams,* 504 U.S. 36 (1992), while the Independent Counsel is by statute an officer of the executive branch representing the United States. For matters within his jurisdiction, the Independent Counsel acts in the role of the Attorney General as the country's chief law enforcement officer. *See* 28 U.S.C. § 594(a) (1994). * * *

* * *

When an executive branch attorney is called before a federal grand jury to give evidence about alleged crimes within the executive branch, reason and experience, duty, and tradition dictate that the attorney shall provide that evidence. With respect to investigations of federal criminal offenses, and especially offenses committed by those in government, government attorneys stand in a far different position from members of the private bar. Their duty is not to defend clients against criminal charges and it is not to protect wrongdoers from public exposure. The constitutional responsibility of the President, and all members of the Executive Branch, is to "take Care that the Laws be faithfully executed." U.S. Const. art. II, § 3. Investigation and prosecution of federal crimes is one of the most important and essential functions within that constitutional responsibility. Each of our Presidents has, in the words of the Constitution, sworn that he "will faithfully execute the Office of President of the United States, and will to the best of [his] Ability, preserve, protect and defend the Constitution of the United States." *Id.* art. II, § 1, cl. 8. And for more than two hundred years each officer of the Executive Branch has been bound by oath or affirmation to do the same. *See id.* art. VI, cl. 3; *see also* 28 U.S.C. § 544 (1994). This is a solemn undertaking, a binding of the person to the cause of constitutional government, an expression of the individual's allegiance to the principles embodied in that document. Unlike a private practitioner, the loyalties of a government lawyer therefore cannot and must not lie solely with his or her client agency.

* * *

This view of the proper allegiance of the government lawyer is complemented by the public's interest in uncovering illegality among its elected and appointed officials. While the President's constitutionally established role as superintendent of law enforcement provides one protection against wrongdoing by federal government officials, another protection of the public interest is through having transparent and accountable government. * * *

Examination of the practice of government attorneys further supports the conclusion that a government attorney, even one holding the title Deputy White House Counsel, may not assert an attorney-client privilege before a federal grand jury if communications with the client contain information pertinent to possible criminal violations. The Office of the President has traditionally adhered to the precepts of 28 U.S.C. § 535(b), which provides that

> [a]ny information * * * received in a department or agency of the executive branch of the Government relating to violations of [federal criminal laws] involving Government officers and employees shall be expeditiously reported to the Attorney General.

28 U.S.C. § 535(b) (1994). At the very least section 535(b) evinces a strong congressional policy that executive branch employees must report information relating to violations of Title 18, the federal criminal code. * * * Section 535(b) suggests that all government employees, including lawyers, are duty-bound not to withhold evidence of federal crimes.

* * *

The Office of the President * * * maintains that the values of candor and frank communications that the privilege embodies in every context would apply to Lindsey's communications with the President and others in the White House. Government officials, the Office of the President claims, need accurate advice from government attorneys as much as private individuals do, but they will be inclined to discuss their legal problems honestly with their attorneys only if they know that their communications will be confidential.

We may assume that if the government attorney-client privilege does not apply in certain contexts this may chill some communications between government officials and government lawyers. Even so, government officials will still enjoy the benefit of fully confidential communications with their attorneys unless the communications reveal information relating to possible criminal wrongdoing. And although the privacy of these communications may not be absolute before the grand jury, the Supreme Court has not been troubled by the potential chill on executive communications due to the qualified nature of executive privilege. * * * Because both the Deputy White House Counsel and the Independent Counsel occupy positions within the federal government, their situation is somewhat comparable to that of corporate officers who seek to keep their communications with company attorneys confidential from each other and from the shareholders. Under the widely followed doctrine announced in *Garner v. Wolfinbarger*, 430 F.2d 1093 (5th Cir. 1970), corporate officers are not always entitled to assert such privileges against interests within the corporation, and accordingly must consult with company attorneys aware that their communications may not be kept confidential from shareholders in litigation. Any chill on candid communications with government counsel flowing from our decision not to extend an absolute attorney-client privilege to the grand jury context is both comparable and similarly acceptable.

Moreover, nothing prevents government officials who seek completely confidential communications with attorneys from consulting personal counsel. The President has retained several private lawyers, and he is entitled to engage in the completely confidential communications with those lawyers befitting an attorney and a client in a private relationship.

* * *

The Supreme Court's recognition in *United States v. Nixon* of a qualified privilege for executive communications severely undercuts the argument of the Office of the President regarding the scope of the government attorney-client privilege. A President often has private conversations with his Vice President or his Cabinet Secretaries or other members of the Administration who are not lawyers or who are lawyers, but are not providing legal services. The advice these officials give the President is of vital importance to the security and prosperity of the nation, and to the President's discharge of his constitutional duties. Yet upon a proper showing, such conversations must be revealed in federal criminal proceedings. Only a certain conceit among those admitted to the bar could explain why legal advice should be on a higher plane than advice about policy, or politics, or why a President's conversation with the most junior lawyer in the White House Counsel's Office is deserving of more protection from disclosure in a grand jury investigation than a President's discussions with his Vice President or a Cabinet Secretary. In short, we do not believe that lawyers are more important to the operations of government than all other officials, or that the advice lawyers render is more crucial to the functioning of the Presidency than the advice coming from all other quarters.

* * *

In sum, it would be contrary to tradition, common understanding, and our governmental system for the attorney-client privilege to attach to White House Counsel in the same manner as private counsel. When government attorneys learn, through communications with their clients, of information related to criminal misconduct, they may not rely on the government attorney-client privilege to shield such information from disclosure to a grand jury.

* * *

TATEL, CIRCUIT JUDGE, dissenting and concurring in part.

* * *

I

My colleagues and I have no disagreement concerning personal legal advice Lindsey may have given the President. We agree, and the White House concedes, that the official attorney-client privilege does not protect such communications, for as a White House employee Lindsey had no authority to provide such advice. Nor do we disagree about political advice given to the President by advisers who happen to be lawyers. Such advice is protected, if at all, by the executive privilege alone. Our disagreement centers solely on whether a grand jury can pierce the attorney-client privilege with respect to official legal advice that the Office of White House Counsel gives a sitting President.

* * *

This court now holds that for all government attorneys, including those advising a President, the attorney-client privilege dissolves in the face of a grand jury subpoena. * * * Clients, in this case Presidents of the United States, will avoid confiding in their lawyers because they can never know whether the information they share, no matter how innocent, might some day become "pertinent to possible criminal violations," Rarely will White House counsel possess cold, hard facts about presidential wrongdoing that would create a strong public interest in disclosure, yet the very possibility that the confidence will be breached will chill communications. As a result, Presidents may well shift their trust on all but the most routine legal matters from White House counsel, who undertake to serve the Presidency, to private counsel who represent its occupant.

* * *

As one of its reasons for abrogating the presidential attorney-client privilege, the court says that legal advice is no different from the advice a President receives from other advisers — advice protected only by executive privilege.

I think the court seriously underestimates the independent role and value of the attorney-client privilege. Unlike the executive privilege — a broad, constitutionally derived privilege that protects frank debate between President and advisers — the narrower attorney-client privilege flows not from the Constitution, but from the common law. In other words, the unique protection the law affords a President's communications with White House counsel rests not, as my colleagues put it, on some "conceit" that "lawyers are more important to the operations of government than all other officials," but rather on the special nature of legal advice, and its special need for confidentiality, as recognized by centuries of common law. It therefore makes sense that the Presidency possesses both the attorney-client and executive privileges, and that courts treat them differently.

* * *

This court's opinion * * * nowhere accounts for the unique nature of the Presidency, its unique need for confidential legal advice, or the possible consequences of abrogating the attorney-client privilege for a President's ability to obtain such advice. Elected, head of the Executive Branch, Commander-in-Chief, head of State, and removable only by impeachment, the President is not just "a part of the federal government, consisting of government employees doing government business." * * *

* * * Because the Presidency is tied so tightly to the persona of its occupant, * * * official matters — proper subjects for White House counsel consultation — often have personal implications for a President. Since for any President the line between official and personal can be both elusive and difficult to discern, I think Presidents need their official attorney-client privilege to permit frank discussion not only of innocuous, routine issues, but also sensitive, embarrassing, or even potentially criminal topics.

The need for the official presidential attorney-client privilege seems particularly strong after Watergate which, while ushering in a new era of accountability and openness in the highest echelons of government, also increased the Presidency's vulnerability. * * * No President can navigate the treacherous waters of post-Watergate government, make controversial official legal decisions, decide whether to invoke official privileges, or even know when he might need private counsel, without confidential legal advice. Because of the Presidency's enormous responsibilities, moreover, the nation has compelling reasons to ensure that Presidents are well defended against false or frivolous accusations that could interfere with their duties. The nation has equally compelling reasons for ensuring that Presidents are well advised on whether charges are serious enough to warrant private counsel. I doubt that White House counsel can perform any of these functions without the candor made possible by the attorney-client privilege. As I said at the outset, weakening the privilege may well cause Presidents to shift their trust from White House lawyers who have undertaken to serve the Presidency, to private lawyers who have not.

Editor's Note: For a contrary view — that the government attorney-client privilege is applicable in criminal cases — see *In re Grand Jury Investigation,* 399 F.3d 527 (2d Cir. 2005), where the Court concluded:

> It is crucial that government officials, who are expected to uphold and execute the law and who may face criminal prosecution for failing to do so, be encouraged to seek out and receive fully informed legal advice. Upholding the privilege furthers a culture in which consultation with government lawyers is accepted as a normal, desirable, and even indispensable part of conducting public business. Abrogating the privilege undermines that culture and thereby impairs the public interest.

[4] The Privilege and the Death of the Client

SWIDLER & BERLIN v. UNITED STATES
524 U.S. 399 (1998)

CHIEF JUSTICE REHNQUIST delivered the opinion of the Court.

Petitioner, an attorney, made notes of an initial interview with a client shortly before the client's death. The Government, represented by the Office of Independent Counsel, now seeks his notes for use in a criminal investigation. We hold that the notes are protected by the attorney-client privilege.

This dispute arises out of an investigation conducted by the Office of the Independent Counsel into whether various individuals made false statements, obstructed justice, or committed other crimes during investigations of the 1993 dismissal of employees from the White House Travel Office. Vincent W. Foster, Jr., was Deputy White House Counsel when the firings occurred. In July, 1993, Foster met with petitioner James Hamilton, an attorney at petitioner Swidler & Berlin, to seek legal representation concerning possible congressional or other investigations of the firings. During a 2-hour meeting, Hamilton took three pages of handwritten notes. One of the first entries in the notes is the word "Privileged." Nine days later, Foster committed suicide.

In December 1995, a federal grand jury, at the request of the Independent Counsel, issued subpoenas to petitioners Hamilton and Swidler & Berlin for, inter alia, Hamilton's handwritten notes of his meeting with Foster. Petitioners filed a motion to quash, arguing that the notes were protected by the attorney client privilege and by the work product privilege. The District Court, after examining the notes in camera, concluded they were protected from disclosure by both doctrines and denied enforcement of the subpoenas.

The Court of Appeals for the District of Columbia Circuit reversed. While recognizing that most courts assume the privilege survives death, the Court of Appeals noted that holdings actually manifesting the posthumous force of the privilege are rare. Instead, most judicial references to the privilege's posthumous application occur in the context of a well recognized exception allowing disclosure for disputes among the client's heirs. It further noted that most commentators support some measure of posthumous curtailment of the privilege. The Court of Appeals thought that the risk of posthumous revelation, when confined to the criminal context, would have little to no chilling effect on client communication, but that the costs of protecting communications after death were high. * * *

We granted certiorari, and we now reverse.

* * *

The Independent Counsel argues that the attorney-client privilege should not prevent disclosure of confidential communications where the client has died and the information is relevant to a criminal proceeding. There is some authority for this position. One state appellate court, *Cohen v. Jenkintown Cab Co.*, 238 Pa. Super. 456, 357 A.2d 689 (1976), and the Court of Appeals below have held the privilege may be subject to posthumous exceptions in certain circumstances. In *Cohen,* a civil case, the court recognized that the privilege generally survives death, but concluded that it could make an exception where the interest of justice was compelling and the interest of the client in preserving the confidence was insignificant.

But other than these two decisions, cases addressing the existence of the privilege after death — most involving the testamentary exception — uniformly presume the privilege survives, even if they do not so hold. *See, e.g.*, *Mayberry v. Indiana*, 670 N.E.2d 1262 (Ind. 1996); *Morris v. Cain*, 39 La. Ann. 712, 1 So. 797 (1887); *People v. Modzelewski*, 611 N.Y.S.2d 22, 203 A.D.2d 594 (1994). Several State Supreme Court decisions expressly hold that the attorney-client privilege extends beyond the death of the client, even in the criminal context. *See In re John Doe Grand Jury Investigation*, 408 Mass. 480, 481-483, 562 N.E.2d 69, 70 (1990); *State v. Doster*, 276 S.C. 647, 650-651, 284 S.E.2d 218, 219 (1981); *State v. Macumber*, 112 Ariz. 569, 571, 544 P.2d 1084, 1086 (1976). In *John Doe Grand Jury Investigation*, for example, the Massachusetts Supreme Court concluded that survival of the privilege was "the clear implication" of its early pronouncements that communications subject to the privilege could not be disclosed at any time. The court further noted that survival of the privilege was "necessarily implied" by cases allowing waiver of the privilege in testamentary disputes.

Such testamentary exception cases consistently presume the privilege survives. * * * They view testamentary disclosure of communications as an exception to the privilege: The rationale for such disclosure is that it furthers the client's intent.

Indeed, in *Glover v. Patten,* 165 U.S. 394, 406-408 (1897), this Court, in recognizing the testamentary exception, expressly assumed that the privilege continues after the individual's death. The Court explained that testamentary disclosure was permissible because the privilege, which normally protects the client's interests, could be impliedly waived in order to fulfill the client's testamentary intent.

The great body of this caselaw supports, either by holding or considered dicta, the position that the privilege does survive in a case such as the present one. Given the language of Rule 501, at the very least the burden is on the Independent Counsel to show that "reason and experience" require a departure from this rule.

The Independent Counsel contends that the testamentary exception supports the posthumous termination of the privilege because in practice most cases have refused to apply the privilege posthumously. He further argues that the exception reflects a policy judgment that the interest in settling estates outweighs any posthumous interest in confidentiality. He then reasons by analogy that in criminal proceedings, the interest in determining whether a crime has been committed should trump client confidentiality, particularly since the financial interests of the estate are not at stake.

But the Independent Counsel's interpretation simply does not square with the caselaw's implicit acceptance of the privilege's survival and with the treatment of testamentary disclosure as an "exception" or an implied "waiver." And the premise of his analogy is incorrect, since cases consistently recognize that the rationale for the testamentary exception is that it furthers the client's intent. There is no reason to suppose as a general matter that grand jury testimony about confidential communications furthers the client's intent.

Commentators on the law also recognize that the general rule is that the attorney-client privilege continues after death. * * * Undoubtedly, as the Independent Counsel emphasizes, various commentators have criticized this rule, urging that the privilege should be abrogated after the client's death where extreme injustice would result, as long as disclosure would not seriously undermine the privilege by deterring client communication. * * * But even these critics clearly recognize that established law supports the continuation of the privilege and that a contrary rule would be a modification of the common law. * * *

Despite the scholarly criticism, we think there are weighty reasons that counsel in favor of posthumous application. Knowing that communications will remain confidential even after death encourages the client to communicate fully and frankly with counsel. While the fear of disclosure, and the consequent withholding of information from counsel, may be reduced if disclosure is limited to posthumous disclosure in a criminal context, it seems unreasonable to assume that it vanishes altogether. Clients may be concerned about reputation, civil liability, or possible harm to friends or family. Posthumous disclosure of such communications may be as feared as disclosure during the client's lifetime.

The Independent Counsel suggests, however, that his proposed exception would have little to no effect on the client's willingness to confide in his attorney. He reasons that only clients intending to perjure themselves will be chilled by a rule of disclosure after death, as opposed to truthful clients or those asserting their Fifth Amendment privilege. This is because for the latter group, communications disclosed by the attorney after the client's death purportedly will reveal only information that the client himself would have revealed if alive.

The Independent Counsel assumes, incorrectly we believe, that the privilege is analogous to the Fifth Amendment's protection against self-incrimination. But as suggested above, the privilege serves much broader purposes. Clients consult attorneys for a wide variety of reasons, only one of which involves possible criminal liability. Many attorneys act as counselors on personal and family matters, where, in the course of obtaining the desired advice, confidences about family members or financial problems must be revealed in order to assure sound legal advice. The same is true of owners of small businesses who may regularly consult their attorneys about a variety of problems arising in the course of the business. These confidences may not come close to any sort of admission of criminal wrongdoing, but nonetheless be matters which the client would not wish divulged.

The contention that the attorney is being required to disclose only what the client could have been required to disclose is at odds with the basis for the privilege even during the client's lifetime. In related cases, we have said that the loss of evidence admittedly caused by the privilege is justified in part by the fact that without the privilege, the client may not have made such communications in the first place. This is true of disclosure before and after the client's death. Without assurance of the privilege's posthumous application, the client may very well not have made disclosures to his attorney at all, so the loss of evidence is more apparent than real. In the case at hand, it seems quite plausible that Foster, perhaps already contemplating suicide, may not have sought legal advice from Hamilton if he had not been assured the conversation was privileged.

The Independent Counsel additionally suggests that his proposed exception would have minimal impact if confined to criminal cases, or, as the Court of Appeals suggests, if it is limited to information of substantial importance to a particular criminal case. However, there is no case authority for the proposition that the privilege applies differently in criminal and civil cases, and only one commentator ventures such a suggestion. In any event, a client may not know at the time he discloses information to his attorney whether it will later be relevant to a civil or a criminal matter, let alone whether it will be of substantial importance. Balancing ex post the importance of the information against client interests, even limited to criminal cases, introduces substantial uncertainty into the privilege's application. For just that reason, we have rejected use of a balancing test in defining the contours of the privilege.

In a similar vein, the Independent Counsel argues that existing exceptions to the privilege, such as the crime-fraud exception and the testamentary exception, make the impact of one more exception marginal. However, these exceptions do not demonstrate that the impact of a posthumous exception would be insignificant, and there is little empirical evidence on this point.[6]

[6] Empirical evidence on the privilege is limited. Three studies do not reach firm conclusions on whether limiting the privilege would discourage full and frank communication. Alexander, *The Corporate Attorney Client Privilege: A Study of the Participants*, 63 St. John's L.Rev. 191 (1989); Zacharias, *Rethinking Confidentiality*, 74 Iowa L.Rev. 352 (1989); Comment, *Functional Overlap Between the Lawyer and Other Professionals: Its Implications for the Privileged Communications Doctrine*, 71 Yale L.J. 1226 (1962). These articles note that clients are often uninformed or mistaken about the privilege, but suggest that a substantial number of clients and attorneys think the privilege encourages candor. Two of the articles conclude that a substantial number of clients and attorneys think the privilege enhances open communication, Alexander, *supra*, at 244-246, 261, and that the absence of a privilege would be detrimental to such communication, Comment, 71 Yale L. J., *supra*, at 1236. The third article suggests instead that while the privilege is perceived as important to open communication, limited exceptions to the privilege might not discourage such communication, Zacharias, *supra*, at 382, 386. Similarly, relatively few court decisions

The established exceptions are consistent with the purposes of the privilege, while a posthumous exception in criminal cases appears at odds with the goals of encouraging full and frank communication and of protecting the client's interests. A "no harm in one more exception" rationale could contribute to the general erosion of the privilege, without reference to common law principles or "reason and experience."

Finally, the Independent Counsel, relying on cases such as *United States v. Nixon*, 418 U.S. 683, 710 (1974), and *Branzburg v. Hayes*, 408 U.S. 665 (1972), urges that privileges be strictly construed because they are inconsistent with the paramount judicial goal of truth seeking. But both *Nixon* and *Branzburg* dealt with the creation of privileges not recognized by the common law, whereas here we deal with one of the oldest recognized privileges in the law. And we are asked, not simply to "construe" the privilege, but to narrow it, contrary to the weight of the existing body of caselaw.

It has been generally, if not universally, accepted, for well over a century, that the attorney-client privilege survives the death of the client in a case such as this. While the arguments against the survival of the privilege are by no means frivolous, they are based in large part on speculation — thoughtful speculation, but speculation nonetheless — as to whether posthumous termination of the privilege would diminish a client's willingness to confide in an attorney. In an area where empirical information would be useful, it is scant and inconclusive.

Rule 501's direction to look to "the principles of the common law as they may be interpreted by the courts of the United States in the light of reason and experience" does not mandate that a rule, once established, should endure for all time. But here the Independent Counsel has simply not made a sufficient showing to overturn the common law rule embodied in the prevailing caselaw. Interpreted in the light of reason and experience, that body of law requires that the attorney client privilege prevent disclosure of the notes at issue in this case. The judgment of the Court of Appeals is

Reversed.

JUSTICE O'CONNOR, with whom JUSTICE SCALIA and JUSTICE THOMAS join, dissenting.

Although the attorney-client privilege ordinarily will survive the death of the client, I do not agree with the Court that it inevitably precludes disclosure of a deceased client's communications in criminal proceedings. In my view, a criminal defendant's right to exculpatory evidence or a compelling law enforcement need for information may, where the testimony is not available from other sources, override a client's posthumous interest in confidentiality.

* * *

I agree that a deceased client may retain a personal, reputational, and economic interest in confidentiality. But, after death, the potential that disclosure will harm the client's interests has been greatly diminished, and the risk

discuss the impact of the privilege's application after death. This may reflect the general assumption that the privilege survives — if attorneys were required as a matter of practice to testify or provide notes in criminal proceedings, cases discussing that practice would surely exist.

that the client will be held criminally liable has abated altogether. * * * This diminished risk is coupled with a heightened urgency for discovery of a deceased client's communications in the criminal context. The privilege does not "protect[] disclosure of the underlying facts by those who communicated with the attorney," *Upjohn*, supra, at 395, and were the client living, prosecutors could grant immunity and compel the relevant testimony. After a client's death, however, if the privilege precludes an attorney from testifying in the client's stead, a complete loss of crucial information will often result.

As the Court of Appeals observed, the costs of recognizing an absolute posthumous privilege can be inordinately high. Extreme injustice may occur, for example, where a criminal defendant seeks disclosure of a deceased client's confession to the offense. * * * In my view, the paramount value that our criminal justice system places on protecting an innocent defendant should outweigh a deceased client's interest in preserving confidences. * * * Indeed, even petitioner acknowledges that an exception may be appropriate where the constitutional rights of a criminal defendant are at stake. An exception may likewise be warranted in the face of a compelling law enforcement need for the information. * * * Given that the complete exclusion of relevant evidence from a criminal trial or investigation may distort the record, mislead the factfinder, and undermine the central truth-seeking function of the courts, I do not believe that the attorney-client privilege should act as an absolute bar to the disclosure of a deceased client's communications. When the privilege is asserted in the criminal context, and a showing is made that the communications at issue contain necessary factual information not otherwise available, courts should be permitted to assess whether interests in fairness and accuracy outweigh the justifications for the privilege.

* * *

Where the exoneration of an innocent criminal defendant or a compelling law enforcement interest is at stake, the harm of precluding critical evidence that is unavailable by any other means outweighs the potential disincentive to forthright communication. In my view, the cost of silence warrants a narrow exception to the rule that the attorney-client privilege survives the death of the client. * * *

Accordingly, I would affirm the judgment of the Court of Appeals. Although the District Court examined the documents in camera, it has not had an opportunity to balance these competing considerations and decide whether the privilege should be trumped in the particular circumstances of this case. Thus, I agree with the Court of Appeals' decision to remand for a determination whether any portion of the notes must be disclosed.

With respect, I dissent.

NOTES

1. In *Lindsey*, the court essentially adopted a civil-criminal distinction in determining the applicability of the privilege for statements made to government lawyers. In *Swidler*, the Supreme Court rejected such a distinction. Since *Swidler* was decided before *Lindsey*, how can the Circuit Court's analysis be squared with the Supreme Court's holding?

2. Does the privilege prevent beneficiaries from access to communications by their fiduciaries to counsel?

A "fiduciary exception" to the attorney-client privilege was established in the famous Fifth Circuit case of *Garner v. Wolfinbarger*, 430 F.2d 1093 (5th Cir. 1970). The fiduciary exception has come to be known as the *Garner* doctrine. *Garner* was a derivative action in which the plaintiffs sought access to confidential communications made between management and corporate counsel. The Court found two competing principles at stake when the shareholders in a derivative action seek access to confidential communications from management to corporate attorneys. On the one hand, management does not manage for itself, it manages for the shareholders; thus it seems anomalous to deny the shareholders access to communications presumptively made on their behalf. On the other hand, if shareholders were given an unlimited right of access on a mere showing of commonality of interest, management would be exposed to harassment suits, and an overall deterioration of corporate legal representation might occur.

To balance these competing considerations, the court in *Garner* held that management had no absolute privilege to shield confidential communications from the shareholders, but that the shareholders right of access to the information was not absolute, either. The *Garner* Court concluded that shareholders were entitled to disclosure of communications between corporate managers and corporate counsel if they could establish "good cause." The Court set forth a non-exclusive list of factors that would support a finding of "good cause." The most important of these factors are: 1) the number of shareholders and the percentage of stock they represent; 2) whether the shareholders are in good faith; 3) the merits of the shareholders' claims; 4) the shareholders' need for the information; 5) whether the communications relate to past or prospective activity; 6) whether the advice concerned the instant litigation; and 7) whether the shareholders have made a particularized request or appear to be engaged in a fishing expedition.

A few courts have held that the *Garner* doctrine should not be expanded beyond the peculiar circumstances of a shareholder derivative action. These courts reason that justification for the *Garner* doctrine is dubious when the action is not brought on behalf of the corporation, but rather on behalf of individual claimants. Under this view, the mutuality of interest at the heart of *Garner* does not exist outside the derivative suit. *See, e.g., Weil v. Investment/Indicators Research & Management*, 647 F.2d 18 (9th Cir. 1981) (*Garner* doctrine limited to derivative suits).

Most courts, however, have extended *Garner* well beyond the derivative action, to any suit in which a fiduciary relationship is at issue. Thus, *Garner* has been applied beyond its facts to the following situations, among others: 1) to individual shareholder actions for fraud *see, e.g.*, *In re International Sys. & Controls Corp. Sec. Litig.*, 693 F.2d 1235 (5th Cir. 1982) (class action for fraud by former shareholders of the corporation); 2) to actions against majority shareholders owing a fiduciary duty to the minority, *see, e.g.*, *Fausek v. White*, 965 F.2d 126 (6th Cir. 1992) (*Garner* doctrine applied in an action brought by minority shareholders against the majority for fraud and breach of fiduciary duty; communications by the majority shareholder to an attorney, concerning corporate transactions, were held not privileged vis-a-vis the minority); 3) to actions brought by employees for breach of fiduciary duty owed by the trustee of a pension plan under ERISA, *see, e.g.*, *Washington-Baltimore Newspaper Guild v. Washington Star Co.*, 543 F. Supp. 906 (D.D.C. 1982); 4) to actions brought against a bank acting pursuant to a power of attorney in a commercial land transaction *see, e.g.*, *Quintel Corp., N.V. v. Citibank, N.A.*, 567 F. Supp. 1357 (S.D.N.Y. 1983) (*Garner* doctrine applies to communication occurring during fiduciary relationship, but not to communications occurring before relationship is begun or after it is terminated; *Garner* doctrine applies even to communications made to determine the extent of the obligations owed by the fiduciary to the beneficiary; and 5) to actions against a union and its officers brought by union members), *see, e.g.*, *Nellis v. Air Line Pilots Ass'n*, 144 F.R.D. 68 (E.D. Va. 1992) (*Garner* doctrine applied where airline pilots sue their union for breach of duty of good faith representation; labor unions owe a fiduciary duty to their members, and therefore communications to counsel by union leaders was not privileged vis-a-vis union members).

It is, of course, true that a fiduciary acts on behalf of a beneficiary; but doesn't the *Garner* doctrine deter the fiduciary from seeking legal advice? *See* Saltzburg, *Corporate Attorney-Client Privilege in Shareholder Litigation and Similar Cases*: *Garner Revisited*, 12 Hofstra L. Rev. 817, 846 (1984) ("The word 'fiduciary' has no talismanic quality that dictates abdication of the usual approach to attorney-client privilege whenever the word is invoked. Those who have fiduciary responsibility often want legal advice concerning their responsibilities. They should have the same opportunity to consult with counsel and to speak freely and without fear of making admissions as other clients.").

[5] Waiver of the Attorney-Client Privilege

[a] Introduction

Even where all the elements of the privilege are otherwise present, the privilege will not be recognized if it has been waived. The term "waiver" as used by the Courts actually encompasses more than the traditional definition of a knowing and voluntary waiver of a right. Courts often find a "waiver" that is really more appropriately considered a "forfeiture." Judge Posner has stated that many of the waiver doctrines — such as the doctrine finding a waiver of the privilege in some circumstances when the party has mistakenly disclosed the privileged information — are not "waiver in the standard sense in which the word is used in the law: the deliberate relinquishment of a right." Rather, a "waiver" of the privilege is sometimes found "in order to punish the person claiming the privilege for a mistake." *International Oil, Chem. & Atomic Workers Local 7-517 v. Uno-Ven Co.*, 170 F.3d 779 (7th Cir. 1999).

"Waiver" in this broad sense includes the concept of forfeiture and follows from any conduct by the client that would make it unfair for the client thereafter to assert the privilege. *See United States v. Yerardi*, 192 F.3d 14 (1st Cir. 1999) ("The concept of waiver by conduct exists, but often amounts simply to a determination that the privilege holder's conduct makes it unfair to allow subsequent assertion of the privilege."). *See also United States v. Jacobs*, 117 F.3d 82 (2d Cir. 1997) (inaccurate disclosure of an attorney's communication found to be a waiver).

[b] Authority to Waive the Privilege

The client holds the privilege and the power to waive it. The lawyer generally has implicit authority to waive the privilege as well in the course of the representation. The identity of the client for purposes of waiver is a problematic issue in the corporate context. The Supreme Court held in *CFTC v. Weintraub*, 471 U.S. 343, 349 (1985), that "the power to waive the corporate attorney-client privilege rests with the corporation's management and is normally exercised by its officers and directors." Therefore, in *Weintraub*, a person who had resigned as an officer no longer had authority to exercise or waive the privilege. *See also In re Bevill, Bresler & Schulman Asset Mgt. Corp.*, 805 F.2d 120 (3d Cir. 1986) (communication by a corporate agent to a corporate attorney is privileged; the privilege is held by the corporation, and the agent has no authority to waive it, even though he made the communication); *In re Grand Jury Subpoena*, 274 F.3d 563 (1st Cir. 2001) (waiver by corporation was effective as to any privilege asserted by corporate agents).

The *Weintraub* Court further stated that "when control of a corporation passes to new management, the authority to assert and waive the corporation's attorney-client privilege passes as well." Applying this rule, the *Weintraub* Court held that a trustee in bankruptcy succeeded to management's authority to waive the corporate privilege, over the objection of former and present corporate officers. *See also United States v. Campbell*, 73 F.3d 44 (5th Cir. 1996) (a partnership, like a corporation, is an artificial person that can act only through its agents: "Accordingly, the same rule that applies to corporations in bankruptcy should apply to a bankrupt limited partnership."); *Odmark v. Westside Bancorp., Inc.*, 636 F. Supp. 552 (W.D. Wash. 1986) (after a bank's failure, the FSLIC was held to control the privilege).

A sale of assets, however, generally does not transfer the power to waive the attorney-client privilege to the buyer. *Yosemite Investment Inc. v. Floyd Bell Inc.*, 943 F. Supp. 882 (S.D. Ohio 1996).

[c] "Selective" Waiver

Waiver occurs when privileged information is voluntarily disclosed to a third party. One controversial question is whether a party can "selectively" waive the privilege. For example, if a corporation discloses an internal report to the SEC or the Department of Justice in order to ward off an investigation, does this disclosure operate as a complete waiver of the privilege, or can the privilege be retained against other parties? And does it matter whether the public office has signed a confidentiality agreement?

An example of the selective waiver problem arose in *Westinghouse Elec. Corp. v. Republic of the Philippines*, 951 F.2d 1414 (3d Cir. 1991), where Westinghouse received a report from outside counsel who had conducted an internal corporate investigation. The internal investigation was in response to an inquiry by the SEC into allegations that Westinghouse had obtained certain contracts by bribing officials of the Philippine Government. Westinghouse cooperated with the SEC inquiry by turning over outside counsel's report. Later, the Department of Justice began to investigate whether Westinghouse obtained contracts from the Philippines through bribery. Again, Westinghouse cooperated by turning over the investigative report prepared by counsel. Thereafter, the Republic brought suit against Westinghouse for damages stemming from the alleged bribery of Philippine officials by agents of Westinghouse. The Republic sought access to counsel's investigative report.

The Court rejected the Westinghouse argument that the attorney-client privilege could be selectively waived — that is, it rejected the concept that a party who voluntarily discloses privileged material to the government nonetheless retains the privilege as to private parties. In rejecting selective waiver the *Westinghouse* Court sided with the clear majority of circuits. *See In re Quest Communications Int'l, Inc.,* 450 F.3d 1179 (10th Cir. 2006) (concluding that the case has not been made that selective waiver protection is required to assure cooperation with law enforcement); *United States v. Billmyer*, 57 F.3d 31 (1st Cir. 1995) (corporation's disclosure of report to the government constituted a waiver of the privilege: "A risk of unfairness is evident where information is provided to one side in a case (here, the United States) and then an inquiry into its origin is shielded by a claim of privilege."); *In re Columbia/HCA Healthcare Corp. Billing Practices Litigation*, 293 F.3d 289 (6th Cir. 2002) (rejecting the concept of selective waiver, even in the face of an express confidentiality agreement). But see *Diversified Industries v. Meredith*, 572 F.2d 596 (8th Cir. 1977) (en banc) (adopting selective waiver).

The argument in favor of selective waiver is that it is necessary to assure cooperation with government investigations — corporations are less likely to cooperate if the consequence of disclosure is that privileged reports can be used by plaintiffs in private litigation. And if corporations don't cooperate, this will increase the costs of government investigations — the regulator will have to investigate from the ground up, rather than being able to work off the report that was prepared by corporate counsel. But the Court in *Westinghouse* noted that the interest in conducting internal investigations had little to do with whether a waiver is found when the report is subsequently turned over to the government. That is, the decision whether to conduct an internal investigation is separate from whether to turn the completed investigative report over to the government. As to the interest in encouraging voluntary cooperation with government investigations, the *Westinghouse* Court found this policy objective to be "beyond the intended purposes of the attorney-client privilege." The Court noted voluntary disclosure of confidential information to the government does not serve the goal of the privilege, which is to enable clients to obtain informed and effective legal advice. The *Westinghouse* Court concluded that "because the selective waiver rule in *Diversified* protects disclosures made for entirely different purposes, it cannot be reconciled with traditional attorney-client privilege doctrine." Moreover, the Court reasoned that selective waiver was not required to encourage cooperation with government investigations, as the corporation is already fully incentivized to cooperate, given the risks of fines, indictments, and general regulatory obligations. As the Court in *Westinghouse* noted, Westinghouse disclosed the investigative report to the government even though the selective waiver rule was far from clearly established at the time.

It could be argued that *Westinghouse* places the client in a dilemma: If the client wants to cooperate with the government, it can do so but only at the expense of completely waiving the privilege. However, this supposed "tough choice" is one that attorneys and clients routinely make in a variety of contexts. Waiver of the privilege often has advantages and disadvantages. For example, in *In re John Doe Corp.*, 675 F.2d 482 (2d Cir. 1982), a corporation conducted through counsel an internal investigation of its business practices. The resulting investigative report was shown to a lawyer representing an underwriter in connection with a public offering of the corporation's securities, so that underwriter's counsel could complete a due diligence review. The corporation argued that disclosure to underwriter counsel should not be considered a waiver because disclosure was "required" by the legal duty of due diligence and the millions of dollars riding on the public offering of registered securities. Hence the waiver, according to the corporation, was not voluntary. The Second Circuit responded:

> We view this argument with no sympathy whatsoever. A claim that a need for confidentiality must be respected in order to facilitate the seeking and rendering of informed legal advice is not consistent with selective disclosure when the claimant decides that the confidential materials can be put to other beneficial purposes. Once a corporate decision is made to disclose them for commercial purposes, no matter what the economic imperatives, the privilege is lost — We hold that the calculated use of otherwise privileged materials for commercial purposes will waive the privilege.

It should also be noted that the Court found the Westinghouse disclosure to the DOJ to be voluntary even though it was prompted by a grand jury subpoena. The Court noted that traditional waiver doctrine provides that compliance with a subpoena waives the privilege. To preserve the privilege, the attorney must move to quash the subpoena, and produce the information only after being ordered by a Court to do so.

For more on selective waiver, see the materials on proposed Evidence Rule 502, later in this section.

[d] Mistaken Disclosures

One of the most difficult problems of waiver occurs when the disclosure of confidential information is a mistake. For example, the lawyer hits the wrong speed dial on the fax machine, and privileged information is thereby sent to the adversary. Or the lawyer painstakingly complies with a voluminous discovery request for thousands of e-mails, and a privileged e-mail is mistakenly included in the CD sent to the adversary. Again, the loss of privilege that might occur here is really grounded in a theory of forfeiture rather than traditional waiver, which speaks in terms of intentional relinquishment of a known right. The question is, what sort of conduct should be subject to the sanction of the loss of a privilege? The courts have adopted various views on inadvertent disclosure, ranging from completely permissive to completely merciless.

Representative of the "strict liability" approach is *In re Sealed Case*, 877 F.2d 976 (D.C. Cir. 1989). There, the Court held that the inadvertent disclosure of a few privileged documents in the course of a massive discovery response not only constituted a waiver of the privilege with respect to the documents, but also worked a "subject matter" waiver. So the client was forced to make a further production of all previously privileged documents covering the subject matter set forth in the documents inadvertently disclosed. The court reasoned that the privilege was costly to the search for truth, and therefore that privileged information must be guarded "like the crown jewels." The problem with this draconian rule is that it increases the costs of discovery and hence the costs of legal services; lawyers are likely to spend inordinate amounts of time making sure that privileged material does not slip through. This is probably not an efficient discovery model, in economic terms. Moreover, the strict liability rule encourages parties to fight tooth and nail during discovery — parties will be loath to produce a document in discovery, no matter how inconsequential, if a court might find it later on to be privileged, with the consequence being a subject matter waiver. Thus the D.C. Circuit view on inadvertent waiver is likely to lead to an increase in the number of privilege issues that a court will have to hear.

The clear trend in the courts is to adopt a "culpability" approach to unintentional disclosure. Most courts focus on whether reasonable steps had been taken to avoid mistaken disclosure of privileged information, and on whether the party with the privilege moved quickly to rectify its error. For example, in *Alldread v. City of Grenada*, 988 F.2d 1425 (5th Cir. 1993), the City inadvertently sent privileged tapes to the plaintiff in the course of complying with a massive discovery demand. The court rejected a strict liability approach and held that the question of whether a waiver occurred must be assessed under a five-factor test. These factors are: (1) the reasonableness of precautions taken to prevent disclosure of privileged material; (2) the amount of time taken to remedy the error; (3) the scope of discovery (the more massive the discovery, the more excusable the disclosure); (4) the extent of the disclosure of privileged information; and (5) the overriding issue of fairness. The court held that under the circumstances the privilege had not been waived. It relied most heavily on the facts that the City had immediately asserted the privilege upon discovering the disclosure, and that considerations of fairness counseled in favor of the privilege.

Under the fault-based view of inadvertent waiver, there will be cases where the lawyer's work is so sloppy and inattentive that a mistaken disclosure will result in a forfeiture. *S.E.C. v. Cassano*, 189 F.R.D. 83 (S.D.N.Y.1999), is a good example. The SEC was proceeding against investors for insider trading. The case was brought in New York but was handled by the Boston office of the SEC. A discovery protocol was set up under which all of the unprivileged

SEC documents would be sent to New York, defense counsel would be allowed to investigate the documents, and then an SEC paralegal on the premises would copy whatever documents defense counsel selected, and send those documents to counsel within a month. Defense counsel, combing through the sea of boxes, found a smoking gun document — an SEC staff memorandum, clearly privileged. He asked the paralegal if she could photocopy the document immediately so that he could take it with him that day. The paralegal telephoned SEC counsel in Boston, who immediately agreed to the unusual request, without checking the document number against the privilege log. A few weeks later, the SEC discovered its gaffe and sought an order requiring defense counsel to return the document. The *Cassano* Court held that the SEC's actions in response to defense counsel's request to photocopy the memorandum were so careless as to surrender any claim that it took reasonable steps to ensure its confidentiality; hence the privilege as to the document was forfeited. The court ruled that mistaken disclosure will constitute a forfeiture of the privilege only if the producing party's conduct was "so careless as to suggest that it was not concerned with the protection of the asserted privilege." The court declared that the "circumstances of the request clearly should have suggested to the SEC attorney that defense counsel had found what they regarded as gold at the end of the proverbial rainbow. Any attorney faced with such a request in comparable circumstances should have reviewed the document immediately, if only to find out what the other side thought so compelling. * * * * Yet the SEC attorney authorized production of this document, sight unseen." SEC counsel was also found delinquent in discovering that the privileged memorandum had been disclosed.

In some jurisdictions, there is no risk of inadvertent waiver. These jurisdictions hold that waiver of the privilege must be intentional. So it does not matter how negligent the disclosure in these jurisdictions — the disclosing party has the right to get it back. *See, e.g.*, Rule 193.3(d) of the Texas Rules of Civil Procedure which provides that:

> A party who produces material or information without intending to waive a claim of privilege does not waive that claim under these rules or the Rules of Evidence if — within ten days or a shorter time ordered by the court, after the producing party actually discovers that such production was made — the producing party amends the response, identifying the material or information produced and stating the privilege asserted.

The risks of mistaken disclosure are obviously profound, and these risks increase in complex cases with voluminous discovery of electronic information. The costs of privilege review, in order to avoid the consequences of waiver, can rise to the millions of dollars. Concerned about the rising costs of electronic discovery and privilege review, the House Judiciary Committee has asked the Advisory Committee on Evidence Rules to prepare a rule that will provide some protection against these costs, by providing a more liberal, and a uniform, rule on waiver. That proposed rule is discussed immediately below.

[e] Proposed Rule of Evidence 502, on Waiver of Attorney-Client Privilege and Work Product

Introduction

The Advisory Committee on Evidence Rules has prepared an amendment, Proposed Rule 502, that would provide some protection against common-law waiver rules for disclosures of material and information protected by the attorney-client privilege or the work-product doctrine. The amendment is being submitted to the Judicial Conference in September, 2007. If the Conference approves, it will be forwarded to Congress for enactment. [Unlike other Evidence Rules, rules of privilege must be enacted directly by Congress.]

What follows is the draft letter to be sent by the Judicial Conference to Congress on Proposed Rule 502; the Proposed Rule itself; the explanatory note prepared by the Advisory Committee on Rule 502; and information on the selective waiver provision that was dropped from the proposed rule.

Draft of Cover Letter to Congress on Proposed Rule 502

The Judicial Conference respectfully submits to the United States Congress a proposed addition to the Federal Rules of Evidence. The Conference recommends that Congress consider adopting this proposed rule as Federal Rule of Evidence 502.

The Rule provides for protections against waiver of the attorney-client privilege or work product immunity. The Conference submits this proposal directly to Congress because of the limitations on the rulemaking function of the federal courts in matters dealing with evidentiary privilege. Under 28 U.S.C. § 2074(b), rules governing evidentiary privilege must be approved by an Act of Congress rather than adopted through the process prescribed by the Rules Enabling Act, 28 U.S.C. § 2072.

Description of the Process Leading to the Proposed Rule

The Judicial Conference Rules Committees have long been concerned about the rising costs of litigation, much of which has been caused by the review, required under current law, of every document produced in discovery, in order to determine whether the document contains privileged information. In 2006, the House Judiciary Committee Chair suggested the proposal of a rule dealing with waiver of attorney-client privilege and work product, in order to limit these rising costs. The Judicial Conference was urged to proceed with rulemaking that would

- protect against the forfeiture of privilege when a disclosure in discovery is the result of an innocent mistake;
- permit parties, and courts, to protect against the consequences of waiver by permitting disclosures of privileged information between the parties to a litigation.

The task of drafting a proposed rule was referred to the Advisory Committee on Evidence Rules (the "Advisory Committee"). The Advisory

Committee prepared a draft Rule 502 and invited a select group of judges, lawyers, and academics to testify before the Committee about the need for the rule, and to suggest any improvements. The Advisory Committee considered all the testimony presented by these experts and redrafted the rule accordingly. At its Spring 2006 meeting, the Advisory Committee approved for release for public comment a proposed Rule 502 that would provide certain exceptions to the federal common law on waiver of privileges and work product. That rule was approved for release for public comment by the Committee on Rules of Practice and Procedure ("the Standing Committee"). The public comment period began in August 2006 and ended February 15, 2007. The Advisory Committee received more that 70 public comments, and also heard the testimony of more than 20 witnesses at two public hearings. The rule released for public comment was also carefully reviewed by the Standing Committee's Subcommittee on Style. In April 2007, the Evidence Rules Committee issued a revised proposed Rule 502 taking into account the public comment, the views of the Subcommittee on Style, and its own judgment. The revised rule was approved by the Standing Committee and the Judicial Conference and is attached to this letter.

In order to inform Congress of the legal issues involved in this rule, the proposed Rule 502 also includes a proposed Committee Note of the kind that accompanies all rules adopted through the Rules Enabling Act. This Committee Note may be incorporated as all or part of the legislative history of the rule if it is adopted by Congress. *See, e.g.*, House Conference Report 103-711 (stating that the "Conferees intend that the Advisory Committee Note on [Evidence] Rule 412, as transmitted by the Judicial Conference of the United States to the Supreme Court on October 25, 1993, applies to Rule 412 as enacted by this section" of the Violent Crime Control and Law Enforcement Act of 1994).

Problems Addressed by the Proposed Rule

In drafting the proposed Rule, the Advisory Committee concluded that the current law on waiver of privilege and work product is responsible in large part for the rising costs of discovery, especially discovery of electronic information. In complex litigation the lawyers spend significant amounts of time and effort to preserve the privilege and work product. The reason is that if a protected document is produced, there is a risk that a court will find a subject matter waiver that will apply not only to the instant case and document but to other cases and documents as well. Moreover, an enormous amount of expense is put into document production in order to protect against inadvertent disclosure of privileged information, because the producing party risks a ruling that even a mistaken disclosure can result in a subject matter waiver. Advisory Committee members also expressed the view that the fear of waiver leads to extravagant claims of privilege. Members concluded that if there were a way to produce documents in discovery without risking subject matter waiver, the discovery process could be made much less expensive. The Advisory Committee noted that the existing law on the effect of inadvertent disclosures and on the scope of waiver is far from consistent or certain. It also noted that agreements between parties with regard to the effect of disclosure on privilege are common, but are unlikely to decrease the costs of discovery due to the ineffectiveness of such agreements as to persons not party to them.

The Proposed Rule 502 does not attempt to deal comprehensively with either attorney-client privilege or work product protection. It also does not purport to cover all issues concerning waiver or forfeiture of either the attorney-client privilege or work product protection. Rather, it deals primarily with issues involved in the disclosure of protected information in federal court proceedings or to a federal public office or agency. The rule binds state courts only with regard to disclosures made in federal proceedings. It deals with disclosures made in state proceedings only to the extent that the effect of those disclosures becomes an issue in federal litigation. The Rule covers issues of scope of waiver, inadvertent disclosure, and the controlling effect of court orders and agreements.

Rule 502 provides the following protections against waiver of privilege or work product:

• *Limitations on Scope of Waiver*: Subdivision (a) provides that if a waiver is found, it applies only to the information disclosed, unless a broader waiver is made necessary by the holder's intentional and misleading use of privileged or protected communications or information.

• *Protections against Inadvertent Disclosure*: Subdivision (b) provides that an inadvertent disclosure of privileged or protected communications or information, when made at the federal level, does not operate as a waiver if the holder took reasonable steps to prevent such a disclosure and employed reasonably prompt measures to retrieve the mistakenly disclosed communications or information.

• *Effect on State Proceedings and Disclosures Made in State Courts*: Subdivision (c) provides that 1) if there is a disclosure of privileged or protected communications or information at the federal level, then state courts must honor Rule 502 in subsequent state proceedings; and 2) if there is a disclosure of privileged or protected communications or information in a state proceeding, then admissibility in a subsequent federal proceeding is determined by the law that is most protective against waiver.

• *Orders Protecting Privileged Communications Binding on Non-Parties*: Subdivision (d) provides that if a federal court enters an order providing that a disclosure of privileged or protected communications or information does not constitute a waiver, that order is enforceable against all persons and entities in any federal or state proceeding. This provision allows parties in an action in which such an order is entered to limit their costs of pre-production privilege review.

• *Agreements Protecting Privileged Communications Binding on Parties*: Subdivision (e) provides that parties in a federal proceeding can enter into a confidentiality agreement providing for mutual protection against waiver in that proceeding. While those agreements bind the signatory parties, they are not binding on non-parties unless incorporated into a court order.

Drafting Choices Made by the Advisory Committee

The Advisory Committee made a number of important drafting choices in Rule 502. This section explains those choices.

1) The effect in state proceedings of disclosures initially made in state proceedings. Rule 502 does not apply to a disclosure made in a state proceeding when the disclosed communication or information is subsequently offered in another state proceeding. The first draft of Rule 502 provided for uniform waiver rules in federal and state proceedings, regardless of where the initial disclosure was made. This draft raised the objections of the Conference of State Chief Justices. State judges argued that the Rule as drafted offended principles of federalism and comity, by superseding state law of privilege waiver, even for disclosures that are made initially in state proceedings — and even when the disclosed material is then offered in a state proceeding (the so-called "state to state" problem). In response to these objections, the Advisory Committee voted unanimously to scale back the Rule, so that it would not cover the "state-to-state" problem. Under the current proposal state courts are bound by the Federal Rule only when a disclosure is made at the federal level and the disclosed communication or information is later offered in a state proceeding (the so-called "federal to state" problem). The Conference of Chief Justices withdrew its objection to Rule 502 after the rule was scaled back to regulate only the "federal to state" problem.

During the public comment period on the scaled-back rule, the Advisory Committee received many requests from lawyers and lawyer groups to return to the original draft and provide a uniform rule of privilege waiver that would bind both state and federal courts, for disclosures made in either state or federal proceedings. These comments expressed the concern that if states were not bound by a uniform federal rule on privilege waiver, the protections afforded by Rule 502 would be undermined; parties and their lawyers might not be able to rely on the protections of the Rule, for fear that a state law would find a waiver even though the Federal Rule would not.

The Advisory Committee determined that these comments raised a legitimate concern, but decided not to extend Rule 502 to govern a state court's determination of waiver with respect to disclosures made in state proceedings. The Committee relied on the following considerations:

• Rule 502 is located in the Federal Rules of Evidence, a body of rules determining the admissibility of evidence in federal proceedings. Parties in a state proceeding determining the effect of a disclosure made in that proceeding or in other state courts would be unlikely to look to the Federal Rules of Evidence for the answer.

• In the Committee's view, Rule 502, as proposed herein, does fulfill its primary goal of reducing the costs of discovery in *federal* proceedings. Rule 502 by its terms governs state courts with regard to the effect of disclosures initially made in federal proceedings or to federal offices or agencies. Parties and their lawyers in federal proceedings can therefore predict the consequences of disclosure by referring to Rule 502; there is no possibility that a state court could find a waiver when Rule 502 would not, when the disclosure is initially made at the federal level.

In light of the public comment, however, Congress may wish to consider separate legislation to cover the problem of waiver of privilege and work product when the disclosure is made at the state level and the consequence is to be determined in a state court. The Conference takes no position on the merits of such separate legislation.

2) Other applications of Rule 502 to state court proceedings. Although disclosures made in state court proceedings and later offered in state proceedings would not be covered, Rule 502 would have an effect on state court proceedings where the disclosure is initially made in a federal proceeding or to a federal office or agency. Most importantly, state courts in such circumstances would be bound by federal protection orders. The other protections against waiver in Rule 502 — against mistaken disclosure and subject matter waiver — would also bind state courts as to disclosures initially made at the federal level. The Rule, as submitted, specifically provides that it applies to state proceedings under the circumstances set out in the Rule. This protection is needed, otherwise parties could not rely on Rule 502 even as to federal disclosures, for fear that a state court would find waiver even when a federal court would not.

3) Disclosures made in state proceedings and offered in a subsequent federal proceeding. Earlier drafts of Proposed Rule 502 did not determine the question of what rule would apply when a disclosure is made in state court and the waiver determination is to be made in a subsequent federal proceeding. Proposed Rule 502 as submitted herein provides that all of the provisions of Rule 502 apply unless the state law of privilege is more protective (less likely to find waiver) than the federal law. The Advisory Committee determined that this solution best preserved federal interests in protecting against waiver, and also provided appropriate respect for state attempts to give greater protection to communications and information covered by the attorney-client privilege or work product doctrine.

4) Selective waiver. At the suggestion of the House Judiciary Committee Chair, the Advisory Committee considered a rule that would allow persons and entities to cooperate with government agencies without waiving all privileges as to other parties in subsequent litigation. Such a rule is known as a "selective waiver" rule, meaning that disclosure of protected communications or information to the government waives the protection only selectively — to the government — and not to any other person or entity.

The selective waiver provision proved to be very controversial. The Advisory Committee determined that it would not propose adoption of a selective waiver provision; but in light of the request from the House Judiciary Committee, the Advisory Committee did prepare language for a selective waiver provision should Congress decide to proceed. The draft language for a selective waiver provision is set forth in a separate report.

Conclusion

Proposed Rule 502 is respectfully submitted for consideration by Congress as a rule that will effectively limit the skyrocketing costs of discovery. Members of the Standing Committee, the Advisory Committee on Federal Rules, as well as their reporters and consultants, are ready to assist Congress in any way its sees fit.

Proposed Rule 502. Attorney-Client Privilege and Work Product; Limitations on Waiver

The following provisions apply, in the circumstances set out, to disclosure of a communication or information covered by the attorney-client privilege or work-product protection.

(a) Disclosure made in a federal proceeding or to a federal office or agency; scope of a waiver. — When the disclosure is made in a federal proceeding or to a federal office or agency and waives the attorney-client privilege or work-product protection, the waiver extends to an undisclosed communication or information in a federal or state proceeding only if:

(1) the waiver is intentional;

(2) the disclosed and undisclosed communications or information concern the same subject matter; and

(3) they ought in fairness to be considered together.

(b) Inadvertent disclosure. — When made in a federal proceeding or to a federal office or agency, the disclosure does not operate as a waiver in a federal or state proceeding if:

(1) the disclosure is inadvertent;

(2) the holder of the privilege or protection took reasonable steps to prevent disclosure; and

(3) the holder promptly took reasonable steps to rectify the error, including (if applicable) following Fed. R. Civ. P. 26(b)(5)(B).

(c) Disclosure made in a state proceeding. — When the disclosure is made in a state proceeding and is not the subject of a state-court order concerning waiver, the disclosure does not operate as a waiver in a federal proceeding if the disclosure:

(1) would not be a waiver under this rule if it had been made in a federal proceeding; or

(2) is not a waiver under the law of the state where the disclosure occurred.

(d) Controlling effect of a court order. — A federal court may order that the privilege or protection is not waived by disclosure connected with the litigation pending before the court in which event the disclosure is also not a waiver in any other federal or state proceeding.

(e) Controlling effect of a party agreement. — An agreement on the effect of disclosure in a federal proceeding is binding only on the parties to the agreement, unless it is incorporated into a court order.

(f) Controlling effect of this rule. — Notwithstanding Rules 101 and 1101, this rule applies to state proceedings and to federal court-annexed and federal court-mandated arbitration proceedings, in the circumstances set out in the rule. And notwithstanding Rule 501, this rule applies even if state law provides the rule of decision.

(g) Definitions. — In this rule:

1) "attorney-client privilege" means the protection that applicable law provides for confidential attorney-client communications; and

2) "work-product protection" means the protection that applicable law provides for tangible material (or its intangible equivalent) prepared in anticipation of litigation or for trial.

Explanatory Note on Rule 502 (Prepared by the Judicial Conference Advisory Committee on Evidence Rules)

This new rule has two major purposes:

1) It resolves some longstanding disputes in the courts about the effect of certain disclosures of communications or information protected by the attorney-client privilege or as work product — specifically those disputes involving inadvertent disclosure and subject matter waiver.

2) It responds to the widespread complaint that litigation costs necessary to protect against waiver of attorney-client privilege or work product have become prohibitive due to the concern that any disclosure (however innocent or minimal) will operate as a subject matter waiver of all protected communications or information. This concern is especially troubling in cases involving electronic discovery. *See, e.g., Hopson v. City of Baltimore*, 232 F.R.D. 228, 244 (D. Md. 2005) (electronic discovery may encompass "millions of documents" and to insist upon "record-by-record pre-production privilege review, on pain of subject matter waiver, would impose upon parties costs of production that bear no proportionality to what is at stake in the litigation") .

The rule seeks to provide a predictable, uniform set of standards under which parties can determine the consequences of a disclosure of a communication or information covered by the attorney-client privilege or work product protection. Parties to litigation need to know, for example, that if they exchange privileged information pursuant to a confidentiality order, the court's order will be enforceable. Moreover, if a federal court's confidentiality order is not enforceable in a state court then the burdensome costs of privilege review and retention are unlikely to be reduced.

The rule makes no attempt to alter federal or state law on whether a communication or information is protected under the attorney-client privilege or work product immunity as an initial matter. Moreover, while establishing some exceptions to waiver, the rule does not purport to supplant applicable waiver doctrine generally.

The rule governs only certain waivers by disclosure. Other common-law waiver doctrines may result in a finding of waiver even where there is no disclosure of privileged information or work product. *See, e.g., Nguyen v. Excel Corp.*, 197 F.3d 200 (5th Cir. 1999) (reliance on an advice of counsel defense waives the privilege with respect to attorney-client communications pertinent to that defense); *Ryers v. Burleson*, 100 F.R.D. 436 (D.D.C. 1983) (allegation of lawyer malpractice constituted a waiver of confidential communications under the circumstances). The rule is not intended to displace or modify federal common law concerning waiver of privilege or work product where no disclosure has been made.

Subdivision (a). The rule provides that a voluntary disclosure in a federal proceeding or to a federal office or agency, if a waiver, generally results in a waiver only of the communication or information disclosed; a subject matter waiver (of either privilege or work product) is reserved for those unusual situations in which fairness requires a further disclosure of related, protected information, in order to prevent a selective and misleading presentation of evidence to the disadvantage of the adversary. *See, e.g., In re United Mine Workers of America Employee Benefit Plans Litig.*, 159 F.R.D. 307, 312 (D.D.C. 1994) (waiver of work product limited to materials actually disclosed, because the party did not deliberately disclose documents in an attempt to gain a tactical advantage). Thus, subject matter waiver is limited to situations in which a party intentionally puts protected information into the litigation in a selective, misleading and unfair manner. It follows that an inadvertent disclosure of protected information can never result in a subject matter waiver. *See* Rule 502(b). The rule rejects the result in *In re Sealed Case*, 877 F.2d 976 (D.C. Cir. 1989), which held that inadvertent disclosure of documents during discovery automatically constituted a subject matter waiver.

The language concerning subject matter waiver — "ought in fairness" — is taken from Rule 106, because the animating principle is the same. Under both Rules, a party that makes a selective, misleading presentation that is unfair to the adversary opens itself to a more complete and accurate presentation.

To assure protection and predictability, the rule provides that if a disclosure is made at the federal level, the federal rule on subject matter waiver governs subsequent state court determinations on the scope of the waiver by that disclosure.

Subdivision (b). Courts are in conflict over whether an inadvertent disclosure of a communication or information protected as privileged or work product constitutes a waiver. A few courts find that a disclosure must be intentional to be a waiver. Most courts find a waiver only if the disclosing party acted carelessly in disclosing the communication or information and failed to request its return in a timely manner. And a few courts hold that any inadvertent disclosure of a communication or information protected under the attorney-client privilege or as work product constitutes a waiver without regard to the protections taken to avoid such a disclosure. *See generally Hopson v. City of Baltimore*, 232 F.R.D. 228 (D. Md. 2005), for a discussion of this case law.

The rule opts for the middle ground: inadvertent disclosure of protected communications or information in connection with a federal proceeding or to a federal office or agency does not constitute a waiver if the holder took reasonable steps to prevent disclosure and also promptly took reasonable steps to rectify the error. This position is in accord with the majority view on whether inadvertent disclosure is a waiver.

Cases such as *Lois Sportswear, U.S.A., Inc. v. Levi Strauss & Co.*, 104 F.R.D. 103, 105 (S.D.N.Y. 1985) and *Hartford Fire Ins. Co. v. Garvey*, 109 F.R.D. 323, 332 (N.D.Cal. 1985), set out a multi-factor test for determining whether inadvertent disclosure is a waiver. The stated factors (none of which are dispositive) are the reasonableness of precautions taken, the time taken to rectify the error, the scope of discovery, the extent of disclosure and the overriding issue of fairness. The rule does not explicitly codify that test, because it is really a set of non-determinative guidelines that vary from case to case. The rule is flexible enough to accommodate any of those listed factors. Other considerations bearing on the reasonableness of a producing party's efforts include the number of documents to be reviewed and the time constraints for production. Depending on the circumstances, a party that uses advanced analytical software applications and linguistic tools in screening for privilege and work product may be found to have taken "reasonable steps" to prevent inadvertent disclosure. The implementation of an efficient system of records management before litigation may also be relevant.

The rule does not require the producing party to engage in a post-production review to determine whether any protected communication or information has been produced by mistake. But the rule does require the producing party to follow up on any obvious indications that a protected communication or information has been produced inadvertently.

The rule applies to inadvertent disclosures made to a federal office or agency, including but not limited to an office or agency that is acting in the course of its regulatory, investigative or enforcement authority. The consequences of waiver, and the concomitant costs of pre-production privilege review, can be as great with respect to disclosures to offices and agencies as they are in litigation.

Subdivision (c). Difficult questions can arise when 1) a disclosure of a communication or information protected by the attorney-client privilege or as work product is made in a state proceeding, 2) the communication or information is offered in a subsequent federal proceeding on the ground that the disclosure waived the privilege or protection, and 3) the state and federal laws are in conflict on the question of waiver. The Committee determined that the proper solution for the federal court is to apply the law that is most protective of privilege and work product. If the state law is more protective (such as where the state law is that an inadvertent disclosure can never be a waiver), the holder of the privilege or protection may well have relied on that law when making the disclosure in the state proceeding. Moreover, applying a more restrictive federal law of waiver could impair the state objective of preserving the privilege or work-product protection for disclosures made in state proceedings. On the other hand, if the federal law is more protective, applying the state law of waiver to determine admissibility in federal court is likely to undermine the federal objective of limiting the costs of production.

The rule does not address the enforceability of a state court confidentiality order in a federal proceeding, as that question is covered both by statutory law and principles of federalism and comity. *See* 28 U.S.C. § 1738 (providing that state judicial proceedings "shall have the same full faith and credit in every court within the United States . . . as they have by law or usage in the courts of such State . . . from which they are taken"). *See also Tucker v. Ohtsu Tire & Rubber Co.*, 191 F.R.D. 495, 499 (D. Md. 2000) (noting that a federal court considering the enforceability of a state confidentiality order is "constrained by principles of comity, courtesy, and . . . federalism"). Thus, a state court order finding no waiver in connection with a disclosure made in a state court proceeding is enforceable under existing law in subsequent federal proceedings.

Subdivision (d). Confidentiality orders are becoming increasingly important in limiting the costs of privilege review and retention, especially in cases involving electronic discovery. But the utility of a confidentiality order in reducing discovery costs is substantially diminished if it provides no protection outside the particular litigation in which the order is entered. Parties are unlikely to be able to reduce the costs of pre-production review for privilege and work product if the consequence of disclosure is that the communications or information could be used by non-parties to the litigation.

There is some dispute on whether a confidentiality order entered in one case is enforceable in other proceedings. *See generally Hopson v. City of Baltimore*, 232 F.R.D. 228 (D. Md. 2005), for a discussion of this case law. The rule provides that when a confidentiality order governing the consequences of disclosure in that case is entered in a federal proceeding, its terms are enforceable against non-parties in any federal or state proceeding. For example, the court order may provide for return of documents without waiver irrespective of the care taken by the disclosing party; the rule contemplates enforcement of "claw-back" and "quick peek" arrangements as a way to avoid the excessive costs of pre-production review for privilege and work product. *See Zubulake v. UBS Warburg LLC*, 216 F.R.D. 280, 290 (S.D.N.Y. 2003) (noting that parties may enter into "so-called 'claw-back' agreements that allow the parties to forego privilege review altogether in favor of an agreement to return inadvertently produced privilege documents"). The rule provides a party with a predictable protection from a court order — predictability that is needed to allow the party to plan in advance to limit the prohibitive costs of privilege and work product review and retention.

Under the rule, a confidentiality order is enforceable whether or not it memorializes an agreement among the parties to the litigation. Party agreement should not be a condition of enforceability of a federal court's order.

Subdivision (e). Subdivision (e) codifies the well-established proposition that parties can enter an agreement to limit the effect of waiver by disclosure between or among them. Of course such an agreement can bind only the parties to the agreement. The rule makes clear that if parties want protection against non-parties from a finding of waiver by disclosure, the agreement must be made part of a court order.

Subdivision (f). The protections against waiver provided by Rule 502 must be applicable when protected communications or information disclosed in federal proceedings are subsequently offered in state proceedings. Otherwise the holders of protected communications and information, and their lawyers, could not rely on the protections provided by the Rule, and the goal of limiting costs in discovery would be substantially undermined. Rule 502(g) is intended to resolve any potential tension between the provisions of Rule 502 that apply to state proceedings and the possible limitations on the applicability of the Federal Rules of Evidence otherwise provided by Rules 101 and 1101.

The rule is intended to apply in all federal court proceedings, including court-annexed and court-ordered arbitrations, without regard to any possible limitations of Rules 101 and 1101. This provision is not intended to raise an inference about the applicability of any other rule of evidence in arbitration proceedings more generally.

The costs of discovery can be equally high for state and federal causes of action, and the rule seeks to limit those costs in all federal proceedings, regardless of whether the claim arises under state or federal law. Accordingly, the rule applies to state law causes of action brought in federal court.

Subdivision (g). The rule's coverage is limited to attorney-client privilege and work product. The operation of waiver by disclosure, as applied to other evidentiary privileges, remains a question of federal common law. Nor does the rule purport to apply to the Fifth Amendment privilege against compelled self-incrimination.

The definition of work product "materials" is intended to include both tangible and intangible information. *See In re Cendant Corp. Sec. Litig.*, 343 F.3d 658, 662 (3d Cir. 2003) ("work product protection extends to both tangible and intangible work product").

Letter to Congress on Selective Waiver, From the Judicial Conference of the United States

The Judicial Conference has respectfully submitted proposed Federal Rule of Evidence 502. As submitted in a separate letter, Proposed Rule 502 governs scope of waiver, inadvertent disclosure and the enforceability of court orders, all with the goal of limiting the costs of privilege review in production of materials during litigation or to federal offices or agencies. The House Judiciary Committee Chair also asked the Advisory Committee on Evidence Rules (the "Advisory Committee") to consider the possibility of proposing a rule that would "allow persons and entities to cooperate with government agencies without waiving all privileges as to other parties in subsequent litigation." Such a rule is known as a "selective waiver" rule, meaning that disclosure of protected communications or information to the government waives the protection only selectively — to the government — and not to any other person or entity. In response to the Chair's request, the Advisory Committee prepared a selective waiver provision, and it was submitted for public comment. It provided for protection for disclosures made to federal offices or agencies only — but it bound state courts to enforcing selective waiver when a disclosure to a federal office or agency was offered in a subsequent state proceeding.

The selective waiver provision proved to be very controversial. The public comment from the legal community (including lawyer groups such as the American Bar Association, Lawyers for Civil Justice, and the American College of Trial Lawyers) was almost uniformly negative. The negative comments can be summarized as follows:

- Lawyers expressed the concern that if selective waiver is enacted, corporate personnel will not communicate confidentially with lawyers for the corporation, for fear that the corporation will be more likely to produce the information to the government and thereby place the individual agents at personal risk.
- Public interest lawyers and lawyers for the plaintiffs' bar were concerned that selective waiver would deprive individual plaintiffs of the information necessary to bring meritorious private litigation.
- Selective waiver was criticized as inappropriate in the alleged current environment of what some have called the "culture of waiver." Lawyers expressed the belief that corporations are currently being indicted unless they turn over privileged or protected information; they contended that selective waiver could be expected to increase government demands to produce protected information.
- Selective waiver was criticized as unfair, because it allows corporations to waive the privilege to their advantage, without suffering the risks that would ordinarily occur with such a waiver.
- Critics emphasized that under the federal common law, every federal circuit court but one has rejected the notion of selective waiver, those courts reasoning 1) that corporations do not need any extra incentive to cooperate, and 2) that selective waiver protection could allow the holder to use the privilege as a sword rather than a shield. Those critics contended that a doctrine roundly rejected under federal common law should not be enacted by rule.
- Judges of state courts objected that selective waiver raised serious federalism problems, because in order to be effective it would have to bind state courts, and as such it would change the law of privilege in virtually every state, because most of the states do not recognize selective waiver.
- Critics argued that selective waiver does not really protect the privilege because nothing prohibits the government agency from publicly disclosing the privileged information.

In sharp contrast, federal agencies and authorities (including the Securities Exchange Commission, the Commodity Futures Trading Commission, and the Department of Justice) expressed strong support for selective waiver. Those agencies made the following arguments.

- The agencies doubted that a selective waiver rule would discourage candid conversations between corporate counsel and employees. They noted that even in the current world without selective waiver, employees must already be advised by corporate counsel that the corporation holds the privilege and may choose to waive it, so the agencies concluded that an employee's candor will not be affected by a change in the rules on whether such a waiver is "selective" or not.

- The agencies contended that private parties will in the end benefit from selective waiver, as it will lead to more timely and efficient public investigations.
- The agencies asserted that government practices have not created a "culture of waiver." They also argued that the selective waiver rule addresses only the evidentiary consequences that flow in a later litigation from an earlier disclosure. This is a problem distinct from how often waiver is sought, and is a problem that will exist even if the government never seeks a waiver but companies still provide them, a possibility that even critics acknowledge will continue.
- The protection of selective waiver was asserted to be necessary because corporations are otherwise deterred from cooperating with government investigations, and such cooperation serves the public interest by substantially reducing the cost of those investigations.
- The complaint from private parties about lack of access to information was dismissed on the ground that the information they sought would not even be produced in the absence of selective waiver.
- The agencies noted that even if the government can disclose the information widely, this did not undermine the doctrine of selective waiver; under selective waiver, private parties could not use the information in court, no matter how widely it is distributed in public.
- The agencies found nothing in the federal common law to indicate that legislation on selective waiver would be improper or unjustified.

The Advisory Committee carefully considered and discussed all of the favorable and unfavorable comments on the selective waiver provision. The Advisory Committee finally determined that selective waiver raised questions that were essentially political in nature. Those questions included: 1) Do corporations need selective waiver to cooperate with government investigations? 2) Is there a "culture of waiver" and, if so, how would selective waiver affect that "culture"? These are questions that are difficult if not impossible to determine in the rulemaking process. The Advisory Committee also noted that as a rulemaking matter, selective waiver raised issues different from those addressed in the rest of Rule 502. The basic goal of Rule 502 is to limit the costs of discovery (especially electronic discovery), whereas selective waiver, if implemented, is intended to limit the costs of government investigations, independently of any discovery costs. Thus, the selective waiver provision was outside the central, discovery-related focus of the rest of the rule.

The Advisory Committee determined that it would not include a selective waiver provision as part of proposed Rule 502. The Judicial Conference approves that decision. The Conference recognizes, however, that Congress may be interested in considering separate legislation to enact selective waiver, as evidenced by the enactment of the Financial Services Regulatory Relief Act of 2006, Pub. L. No. 109-351, § 607, 120 Stat. 1966, 1981 (2006), which provides that disclosure of privileged information to a banking regulator does not operate as a waiver to private parties.

The Advisory Committee prepared language to assist Congress should it decide to proceed with independent legislation on selective waiver. This suggested language is derived from the Financial Services Regulatory Relief Act and also incorporates some drafting suggestions received during the public comment period on Rule 502. The draft language includes a Committee Note that explains the drafting choices that were made. The draft language is as follows:

Possible Language for a Statute on Selective Waiver (Prepared by Advisory Committee on Evidence Rules, with No Recommendation on the Merits)

(a) Selective waiver. — In a federal [or state] proceeding, the disclosure of a communication or information protected by the attorney client privilege or as work product — when made for any purpose to a federal office or agency in the course of any regulatory, investigative, or enforcement process — does not waive the privilege or work-product protection in favor of any person or entity other than a [the] federal office or agency.

(b) Rule of construction. — This rule does not:

1) limit or expand a government office or agency's authority to disclose communications or information to other government offices or agencies or as otherwise authorized or required by law; or

2) limit any protection against waiver provided in any other Act of Congress.

(c) Definitions. — In this Act:

1) "attorney-client privilege" means the protection that applicable law provides for confidential attorney-client communications; and

2) "work-product protection" means the protection that applicable law provides for tangible material or its tangible equivalent, prepared in anticipation of litigation or for trial.

Committee Note on Selective Waiver

Courts are in conflict over whether disclosure of privileged or protected communications or information to a government office or agency conducting an investigation of the client constitutes a general waiver of the communications or information disclosed. Most courts have rejected the concept of "selective waiver," holding that waiver of privileged or protected communications or information to a government office or agency constitutes a waiver for all purposes and to all parties. *See, e.g., Westinghouse Electric Corp. v. Republic of the Philippines*, 951 F.2d 1414 (3d Cir. 1991). Other courts have held that selective waiver is enforceable if the disclosure is made subject to a confidentiality agreement with the government office or agency. *See, e.g., Teachers Insurance & Annuity Association of America v. Shamrock Broadcasting*

Co., 521 F. Supp. 638 (S.D.N.Y. 1981). And a few courts have held that disclosure of privileged or protected communications or information to the government does not constitute a general waiver, so that the privilege or protection remains applicable against other parties. *See, e.g., Diversified Industries, Inc. v. Meredith*, 572 F.2d 596 (8th Cir. 1977).

The rule resolves this conflict by providing that disclosure of protected communications or information to a federal office or agency exercising regulatory, investigative or enforcement authority does not constitute a waiver of attorney-client privilege or work product protection as to any person or entity other than a [the] federal public office or agency; that protection of selective waiver applies when the disclosed communication or information is subsequently offered in [either] federal [or state] court.

The rule does not purport to affect the disclosure of protected communications or information after receipt by the federal office or agency. The rule does, however, provide protection from waiver in favor of anyone other than federal offices or agencies, regardless of the extent of disclosure of the communications or information by any such office or agency. Even if the communications or information are used in an enforcement proceeding and so become publicly available, the communications or information will continue to be protected as against other persons or entities.

The rule provides that when protected communications or information are disclosed to a "federal office or agency" the disclosure does not operate as a waiver to any person or entity other than a [the] federal office or agency. As such, a disclosure covered by the rule does not operate as a waiver in any congressional investigation or hearing.

The rule is not intended to limit or affect any other Act of Congress that provides for selective waiver protection for disclosures made to government agencies or offices. *See, e.g.*, Financial Services Regulatory Relief Act of 2006, Pub. L. No. 109-351, § 607, 120 Stat. 1966, 1981 (2006).

PROBLEM 18-1

Action Trucking Co. has a contract with the United States to remove debris from a construction site in the District of Columbia where a new federal building is under construction. The company receives an anonymous tip that its drivers may be dumping their debris illegally in a neglected area of the city. The company hires outside counsel, sends an e-mail to all employees telling them that they are required to cooperate with outside counsel as the company investigates an allegation of illegal disposition of debris. Outside counsel conducts an investigation, finds that two drivers illegally dumped debris, and reports this finding to the board of directors. The board authorizes its general counsel to report to the federal contracting officer that the company discovered that on two occasions its drivers illegally dumped debris. Thereafter a grand jury conducts an investigation and calls all of the truck drivers and the outside counsel to testify. After one of the drivers who dumped debris testified before the grand jury and reported to the company what she was asked, the company files a motion for a protective order from the presiding judge. The argument on the motion, which is in camera to protect the secrecy of the grand jury, is set forth below.

Judge:	Why are we here?
Action:	We believe that the government is seeking to inquire into privileged communications in a grand jury investigation.
Judge:	What grounds do you have for your belief?
Action:	One of our drivers testified before the grand jury. She invoked her privilege against self-incrimination as to some questions, and upon advice of counsel she refused to answer certain questions on the basis of attorney-client privilege.
Judge:	Well, Ms. Assistant United States Attorney, is there any truth to this?
AUSA:	It is true that there is a grand jury investigation of the company and its employees, and we have called employees and outside counsel to testify.
Judge:	Did you ask about communications between the employees and any counsel for the company?
AUSA:	Yes, we have only questioned one witness so far, and we asked her whether she informed the company through outside counsel about illegal disposition of debris.
Judge:	What is your position on this?
Action:	(1) We object to such questions. Outside counsel was hired to conduct an investigation, and employees provided information on behalf of the corporation.
AUSA:	This is not privileged. The employees were informing the company of criminal acts, and they are not protected.
Judge:	(2) ________.
Judge:	Did you ask any other questions of employees about what they said to any counsel for the company?
AUSA:	Sure we did. We asked whether the company counsel instructed the employees not to answer any grand jury questions regarding their statements to outside counsel.
Judge:	What is your position on this?
Action:	(3) We object to such questions. This calls for privileged communications.
AUSA:	On the contrary, we believe that any instructions not to answer, amount to aiding and abetting criminal acts and cannot be privileged.

Judge:	(4) ________.
Judge:	Any other objections to the questions to the employees?
Action:	(5) Yes, we object to any questions about illegal dumping to the employees; they are being asked about corporate acts and we claim privilege.
AUSA:	They are being asked about facts.
Judge:	(6) ________.
Judge:	Anything else?
Action:	Not with respect to the employees. We have objections to calling outside counsel.
Judge:	What objections?
Action:	Everything he did was privileged. This was a privileged investigation, and the subpoena is an infringement of the attorney-client relationship.
Judge:	What's your response?
AUSA:	We have questions to ask that do not call for privileged information.
Judge:	Give me some examples.
AUSA:	We want to know when counsel was hired.
Action:	(7) We object. When we chose to hire counsel is privileged.
Judge:	(8) ________.
Judge:	What else?
AUSA:	We want to ask when counsel spoke with various employees.
Judge:	Why?
AUSA:	If we know the date, we may know whether the company delayed informing us of the illegal dumping.
Action:	It is impossible to know that without inquiring into the nature of the conversations with the employees.
AUSA:	The dates of conversations are not privileged.
Judge:	(9) ________.
Judge:	Anything else?
AUSA:	We want to ask counsel whether he did anything to suggest to employees that they were clients along with the company.
Action:	(10) Objection. This is an invasion of attorney-client communications.
AUSA:	We have a right to know who the client was in this investigation.
Judge:	(11) ________.
Judge:	Is that all?
AUSA:	We want to ask how much the company paid for this investigation.
Action:	That's completely irrelevant.

AUSA: It's not irrelevant. We have the right to find out how much the company spends to investigate after the fact and compare that with what they spend to prevent criminal acts. And relevance is not part of an attorney-client privilege claim.

AUSA: (12) We object. The amount we paid may suggest the nature of the communications. It should be privileged.

Judge: (13) __________.

Judge: Can I assume we are now done?

AUSA: Not quite. We want to ask outside counsel whether he prepared a report of his investigation, whether he submitted it to the board, and if so when he submitted it.

Action: (14) Objection. Now this is the core of the attorney-client relationship and communications between counsel and the client?

Judge: (15) __________.

Judge: Is that it?

AUSA: That's it as to what we have planned so far. But, in light of the many objections, I should tell the court that we intend to call the members of the board of directors to testify before the grand jury. The objections we have heard today suggest this may raise new problems.

Judge: Give me an idea of what you foresee. We are going to ask the members of the board whether the board came to learn at some point that illegal dumping was going on, and if so when the board became aware.

Action: (16) We object. This is outrageous. You have just heard us argue that whatever counsel told the board is privileged, and this is a back-door attempt to invade the privilege.

Judge: (17) __________

AUSA: We also intend to ask the board members what the board's response was once it had information about illegal dumping.

Action: (18) Objection. This is a discussion based upon the advice of counsel.

Judge: (19) __________.

AUSA:	There is one more point, your Honor. We have an ex-employee who has called us to say that he was aware of illegal dumping and sent an e-mail to the general counsel to alert the company to the problem. The employee claims that he worked in the truck maintenance area and spoke with drivers while working on their trucks. We intend to call him to the grand jury and to ask about what he e-mailed.
Action:	(20) Objection. This is a confidential communication between a corporate employee concerning matters learned while performing his corporate duties, and the communication is a private communication with corporate counsel.
AUSA:	This is not a confidential communication, and it is not within the corporation's privilege.
Judge:	(21) __________.

C. MARITAL PRIVILEGES

TRAMMEL v. UNITED STATES
445 U.S. 40 (1980)

MR. CHIEF JUSTICE BURGER delivered the opinion of the Court.

We granted certiorari to consider whether an accused may invoke the privilege against adverse spousal testimony so as to exclude the voluntary testimony of his wife. This calls for a re-examination of *Hawkins v. United States*, 358 U.S. 74 (1958).

I

On March 10, 1976, petitioner Otis Trammel was indicted with two others, Edwin Lee Roberts and Joseph Freeman, for importing heroin into the United States from Thailand and the Philippine Islands and for conspiracy to import heroin * * *. The indictment also named six unindicted co-conspirators, including petitioner's wife Elizabeth Ann Trammel.

According to the indictment, petitioner and his wife flew from the Philippines to California in August 1975, carrying with them a quantity of heroin. Freeman and Roberts assisted them in its distribution. Elizabeth Trammel then traveled to Thailand where she purchased another supply of the drug. On November 3, 1975, with four ounces of heroin on her person, she boarded a plane for the United States. During a routine customs search in Hawaii, she was searched, the heroin was discovered, and she was arrested. After discussions with Drug Enforcement Administration agents, she agreed to cooperate with the Government.

Prior to trial on this indictment, petitioner * * * advised the court that the Government intended to call his wife as an adverse witness and asserted his claim to a privilege to prevent her from testifying against him. At a hearing on the motion, Mrs. Trammel was called as a Government witness under a grant of use immunity. She testified that she and petitioner were married in May 1975 and that they remained married. She explained that her cooperation with the Government was based on assurances that she would be given lenient treatment. She then described, in considerable detail, her role and that of her husband in the heroin distribution conspiracy

After hearing this testimony, the District Court ruled that Mrs. Trammel could testify in support of the Government's case to any act she observed during the marriage and to any communication "made in the presence of a third person"; however, confidential communications between petitioner and his wife were held to be privileged and inadmissible. * * *

At trial, Elizabeth Trammel testified within the limits of the court's pretrial ruling; her testimony, as the Government concedes, constituted virtually its entire case against petitioner. He was found guilty on both the substantive and conspiracy charges and sentenced to an indeterminate term of years pursuant to the Federal Youth Corrections Act, 18 U.S.C. § 5010(b).

In the Court of Appeals petitioner's only claim of error was that the admission of the adverse testimony of his wife, over his objection, contravened this Court's teaching in *Hawkins v. United States*, *supra*, and therefore constituted reversible error. The Court of Appeals rejected this contention. It concluded that *Hawkins* did not prohibit "the voluntary testimony of a spouse who appears as an unindicted co-conspirator under grant of immunity from the Government in return for her testimony."

II

The privilege claimed by petitioner has ancient roots. Writing in 1628, Lord Coke observed that "it hath been resolved by the Justices that a wife cannot be produced either against or for her husband." This spousal disqualification sprang from two canons of medieval jurisprudence: first, the rule that an accused was not permitted to testify in his own behalf because of his interest in the proceeding; second, the concept that husband and wife were one, and that since the woman had no recognized separate legal existence, the husband was that one. From those two now long-abandoned doctrines, it followed that what was inadmissible from the lips of the defendant-husband was also inadmissible from his wife.

Despite its medieval origins, this rule of spousal disqualification remained intact in most common-law jurisdictions well into the 19th century. * * * Indeed, it was not until 1933, in *Funk v. United States*, 290 U.S. 371, that this Court abolished the testimonial disqualification in the federal courts, so as to permit the spouse of a defendant to testify in the defendant's behalf. *Funk*, however, left undisturbed the rule that either spouse could prevent the other from giving adverse testimony. The rule thus evolved into one of privilege rather than one of absolute disqualification.

The modern justification for this privilege against adverse spousal testimony is its perceived role in fostering the harmony and sanctity of the marriage relationship. Notwithstanding this benign purpose, the rule was sharply criticized. Professor Wigmore termed it "the merest anachronism in legal theory and an indefensible obstruction to truth in practice." 8 Wigmore § 2228, at 221. The Committee on Improvements in the Law of Evidence of the American Bar Association called for its abolition. In its place, Wigmore and others suggested a privilege protecting only private marital communications, modeled on the privilege between priest and penitent, attorney and client, and physician and patient.

* * *

In *Hawkins v. United States*, 358 U.S. 74 (1958), this Court considered the continued vitality of the privilege against adverse spousal testimony in the federal courts. There the District Court had permitted petitioner's wife, over his objection, to testify against him. With one questioning concurring opinion, the Court held the wife's testimony inadmissible; it took note of the critical comments that the common-law rule had engendered, * * * but chose not to abandon it. Also rejected was the Government's suggestion that the Court modify the privilege by vesting it in the witness-spouse, with freedom to testify or not independent of the defendant's control. The Court viewed this proposed modification as antithetical to the widespread belief, evidenced in the rules then in effect in a majority of the States and in England, "that the law should not force or encourage testimony which might alienate husband and wife, or further inflame existing domestic differences."

Hawkins, then, left the federal privilege for adverse spousal testimony where it found it, continuing "a rule which bars the testimony of one spouse against the other unless both consent." * * * However, in so doing, the Court made clear that its decision was not meant to "foreclose whatever changes in the rule may eventually be dictated by reason and experience."

III

A

The Federal Rules of Evidence acknowledge the authority of the federal courts to continue the evolutionary development of testimonial privileges in federal criminal trials "governed by the principles of the common law as they may be interpreted * * * in the light of reason and experience." Fed.Rule Evid. 501. * * * The general mandate of Rule 501 was substituted by the Congress for a set of privilege rules drafted by the Judicial Conference Advisory Committee on Rules of Evidence and approved by the Judicial Conference of the United States and by this Court. That proposal defined nine specific privileges, including a husband-wife privilege which would have codified the *Hawkins* rule and eliminated the privilege for confidential marital communications. *See* proposed Fed. Rule Evid. 505. In rejecting the proposed Rules and enacting Rule 501, Congress manifested an affirmative intention not to freeze the law of privilege. Its purpose rather was to "provide the courts with the flexibility to develop rules of privilege on a case-by-case basis," 120 Cong.Rec. 40891 (1974) (statement of Rep. Hungate), and to leave the door open to change.

Although Rule 501 confirms the authority of the federal courts to reconsider the continued validity of the *Hawkins* rule, the long history of the privilege suggests that it ought not to be casually cast aside. That the privilege is one affecting marriage, home, and family relationships — already subject to much erosion in our day — also counsels caution. At the same time, we cannot escape the reality that the law on occasion adheres to doctrinal concepts long after the reasons which gave them birth have disappeared and after experience suggest the need for change. * * *

B

Since 1958, when *Hawkins* was decided, support for the privilege against adverse spousal testimony has been eroded further. * * * The trend in state law toward divesting the accused of the privilege to bar adverse spousal testimony has special relevance because the laws of marriage and domestic relations are concerns traditionally reserved to the states. * * * Scholarly criticism of the *Hawkins* rule has also continued unabated.

C

Testimonial exclusionary rules and privileges contravene the fundamental principle that "the public * * * has a right to every man's evidence." *United States v. Bryan*, 339 U.S. 323, 331 (1950). As such, they must be strictly construed and accepted "only to the very limited extent that permitting a refusal to testify or excluding relevant evidence has a public good transcending the normally predominant principle of utilizing all rational means for ascertaining truth." *Elkins v. United States*, 364 U.S. 206, 234 (1960) (Frankfurter, J., dissenting). * * * Here we must decide whether the privilege against adverse spousal testimony promotes sufficiently important interests to outweigh the need for probative evidence in the administration of criminal justice.

It is essential to remember that the *Hawkins* privilege is not needed to protect information privately disclosed between husband and wife in the confidence of the marital relationship* * * . Those confidences are privileged under the independent rule protecting confidential marital communications. * * * The *Hawkins* privilege is invoked, not to exclude private marital communications, but rather to exclude evidence of criminal acts and of communications made in the presence of third persons.

No other testimonial privilege sweeps so broadly. The privileges between priest and penitent, attorney and client, and physician and patient limit protection to private communications. These privileges are rooted in the imperative need for confidence and trust. The priest-penitent privilege recognizes the human need to disclose to a spiritual counselor, in total and absolute confidence, what are believed to be flawed acts or thoughts and to receive priestly consolation and guidance in return. The lawyer-client privilege rests on the need for the advocate and counselor to know all that relates to the client's reasons for seeking representation if the professional mission is to be carried out. Similarly, the physician must know all that a patient can articulate in order to identify and to treat disease; barriers to full disclosure would impair diagnosis and treatment.

The *Hawkins* rule stands in marked contrast to these three privileges. Its protection is not limited to confidential communications; rather it permits an accused to exclude all adverse spousal testimony. As Jeremy Bentham observed more than a century and a half ago, such a privilege goes far beyond making "every man's house his castle," and permits a person to convert his house into "a den of thieves." 5 Rationale of Judicial Evidence 340 (1827). It "secures, to every man, one safe and unquestionable and every ready accomplice for every imaginable crime." *Id.*, at 338.

The ancient foundations for so sweeping a privilege have long since disappeared. Nowhere in the common-law world — indeed in any modern society — is a woman regarded as chattel or demeaned by denial of a separate legal identity and the dignity associated with recognition as a whole human being. Chip by chip, over the years those archaic notions have been cast aside so that "[n]o longer is the female destined solely for the home and the rearing of the family, and only the male for the marketplace and the world of ideas." *Stanton v. Stanton*, 421 U.S. 7, 14-15 (1975).

The contemporary justification for affording an accused such a privilege is also unpersuasive. When one spouse is willing to testify against the other in a criminal proceeding — whatever the motivation — their relationship is almost certainly in disrepair; there is probably little in the way of marital harmony for the privilege to preserve. In these circumstances, a rule of evidence that permits an accused to prevent adverse spousal testimony seems far more likely to frustrate justice than to foster family peace. Indeed, there is reason to believe that vesting the privilege in the accused could actually undermine the marital relationship. For example, in a case such as this the Government is unlikely to offer a wife immunity and lenient treatment if it knows that her husband can prevent her from giving adverse testimony. If the Government is dissuaded from making such an offer, the privilege can have the untoward effect of permitting one spouse to escape justice at the expense of the other. It hardly seems conducive to the preservation of the marital relation to place a wife in jeopardy solely by virtue of her husband's control over her testimony.

IV

Our consideration of the foundations for the privilege and its history satisfy us that "reason and experience" no longer justify so sweeping a rule as that found acceptable by the Court in *Hawkins*. Accordingly, we conclude that the existing rule should be modified so that the witness-spouse alone has a privilege to refuse to testify adversely; the witness may be neither compelled to testify nor foreclosed from testifying. This modification — vesting the privilege in the witness-spouse — furthers the important public interest in marital harmony without unduly burdening legitimate law enforcement needs.

Here, petitioner's spouse chose to testify against him. That she did so after a grant of immunity and assurances of lenient treatment does not render her testimony involuntary. * * * Accordingly, the District Court and the Court of Appeals were correct in rejecting petitioner's claim of privilege, and the judgment of the Court of Appeals is

Affirmed.

[Concurring opinion omitted.]

NOTES

1. What is the difference between the privilege to refuse to give adverse testimony, applied in *Trammel*, and the privilege protecting confidential marital communications?

Federal courts have consistently recognized two separate privileges arising from the marital relationship. The adverse testimonial privilege prohibits testimony by one spouse against another in criminal cases; it is designed to protect marital harmony at the time the testimony is demanded. The confidential communications privilege prohibits disclosure, in civil and criminal cases, of confidential communications from one spouse to another; it is designed to protect and further marital intimacy as of the time the communication is made between the spouses.

Trammel holds that the adverse testimonial privilege is controlled by the witness-spouse, not the litigant-spouse. In contrast, the confidential communications privilege can be invoked by the litigant spouse to prevent disclosure of his or her confidential communications made during the marriage, even if the other spouse is willing to testify. This is because even if there is no marital harmony at the time of the testimony, the communicating spouse had the right to rely on marital intimacy at the time the confidential communication was made. Consequently, where a spouse is willing to testify, he or she can generally testify about acts and nonconfidential communications, but not about confidential communications made during the marriage.

2. Under the confidential marital privilege, are acts considered private marital communications?

The United States Court of Appeals, Fourth Circuit, recognized that "[t]he marital privilege, generally, extends only to utterances, and not to acts. * * *. If the conduct was not intended to convey a confidential message then it is not covered by the privilege. * * * Nor does the mere fact that an act has been performed in the presence of a spouse make it a communication." *United States v. Parker*, 834 F.2d 408, 411 (4th Cir. 1987). *See also United States v. Lofton*, 957 F.2d 476 (7th Cir. 1992) (spouse willingly testifies, so the adverse testimonial privilege is inapplicable; however, the defendant spouse still holds a privilege to prevent the witness-spouse from testifying to confidential communications made during the course of the marriage; but this privilege covers communications and not factual observations: "Because acts observed by Lofton's wife are not privileged, any testimony regarding her observation of his use of cocaine or her knowledge whether the package at issue was for him was properly admitted.").

3. Do the marital privileges apply to failing marriages?

See United States v. Murphy, 65 F.3d 758 (9th Cir. 1995): Affirming a defendant's convictions for violating environmental laws and making false statements, the court held that the marital communications privilege "does not apply if the couple was separated and the marriage was irreconcilable at the time of the communication." It set forth the following approach:

> Several factors guide a court's determination whether a marriage is irreconcilable. Those factors include the duration of the separation, the stability of the marriage at the time of the communication, whether a divorce action had been filed and the conduct of the parties since that filing, whether a property settlement had been proposed, and, finally, any statement by the parties regarding irreconcilability or the reasons for separation.

Applying these factors, the Court held that the trial judge properly found that the defendant's marriage was irreconcilable at the time of the communication. When the defendant made the communication, he had already told his wife he did not want to be married, he had filed for divorce, and the couple had been separated for seven years.

The marital privilege for confidential communications focuses on the intent of the communicating spouse at the time of the communication. Consequently, the parties must be married at the time of the communication, but they need not be married at the time of trial. If the parties were divorced or permanently separated at the time of the communication, the privilege will not apply even if it was made in confidence. In contrast, the privilege against providing adverse marital testimony is dependent on a marriage at the time of the trial. If the witness and the litigant are divorced or permanently separated at that time, the privilege will not apply. *See United States v. Roberson*, 859 F.2d 1376 (9th Cir. 1988) (requiring the trial court to undertake a specific detailed investigation into the irreconcilability of the marriage).

4. Can the marital privileges apply if the spouses are involved together in criminal activity?

See Saltzburg, Martin, and Capra, *Federal Rules of Evidence Manual* (9th ed. 2006):

> The federal courts are split on the so-called "joint participants" exception to the adverse testimonial privilege. Some courts have held that if the witness-spouse is a participant in the crime with which the litigant spouse is charged, then the witness is not entitled to invoke the privilege. The reasoning is that the marriage of persons jointly involved in crime is not worth protecting. *See, e.g., United States v. Byrd*, 750 F.2d 585 (7th Cir. 1984) (spouse has no privilege to refuse to testify where she was a participant in the defendant's charged activity).
>
> In *Appeal of Koecher*, 755 F.2d 1022 (2d Cir. 1985), however, the Second Circuit rejected a joint participant exception to the adverse testimonial privilege. Judge Friendly, writing for the Court, reasoned that the exception would tend to swallow the rule of privilege, because if the spouses have such a close relationship that one refuses to testify against the other, it is likely that they will also have some mutual involvement in the charged activity. Therefore the joint participants

exception would likely swallow the rule. The Supreme Court granted certiorari in *Koecher* to determine the status of the joint participant exception to the adverse testimonial privilege, but the case was mooted after oral argument when the Koechers, alleged spies for the then-Communist Czech government, were traded for Natan Scharansky. *See also United States v. Ramos-Oseguera*, 120 F.3d 1028 (9th Cir. 1997) (rejecting a joint participants exception to the adverse testimonial privilege).

Because the focus of the confidential communications privilege is on the intent of the communicating spouse, it follows that the privilege will not apply if the spouse is communicating in order to further a crime or fraud. Such a communication is no more worthy of protection than a similar statement made to an attorney. *See, e.g., United States v. Estes*, 793 F.2d 465 (2d Cir. 1986) (no privilege where the defendant communicated with his wife in order to plan a crime).

Many courts have, in apparent confusion, held that the confidential communications privilege is inapplicable where the spouses are *joint participants* in criminal activity. *See, e.g., United States v. Bey*, 188 F.3d 1 (1st Cir. 1999) (confidential communications not protected by privilege where the witness spouse had accepted drug proceeds from the defendant and had maintained his cover story for the benefit of the defendant's unsuspecting couriers); *United States v. Hill*, 967 F.2d 902 (3d Cir. 1992) (the defendant's confidential communications to his wife, concerning drug activity, were not protected by the interspousal privilege because the wife was a joint participant in the drug activity; the wife had accepted deliveries of drugs, informed the defendant of these deliveries, and counted drug proceeds; the witness-spouse need not be prosecuted in order to be considered a joint participant).

While a joint participants exception may be applicable to the adverse testimonial privilege, which focuses on preservation of marital harmony at the time of the testimony (see the discussion of *Koecher*, *supra*), such an exception is not consistent with the rationale of the confidential communications privilege. The confidential communications privilege is analogous to the attorney-client privilege, because it is communication-based. Like the privilege, there is good reason for a crime-fraud exception to the interspousal communications privilege. If the communication is in furtherance of crime or fraud, then it is not worthy of protection. However, a joint participant exception is not the same as a crime-fraud exception. The crime-fraud exception evaluates the intent behind the *communication*, while the joint participant exception looks solely to the *status* of the witness.

The distinction is important where one spouse makes a confession concerning a past event to a joint participant. Assuming that such a confession does not further a plan of crime or fraud, and was made in confidence, it should be protected by the confidential communications privilege. But it would not be protected under a joint participant exception. Conversely, if one spouse is using the other as a dupe in furtherance of a crime or fraud, the communications should not be protected by the privilege, even though it is questionable whether the duped spouse could be considered a joint participant in criminal activity.

PROBLEM 18-2

The government has indicted two truck drivers for the Action Trucking Co., Toddy McSwath and Portio Dovel, along with the company itself with illegally dumping debris. The government begins its case-in-chief.

Direct Examination of Steven McSwath

Prosecutor: Are you related to any of the defendants in this case?

Witness: Yes I am. I am married to Toddy McSwath.

McSwath: (1) Objection. This witness may not testify. We claim marital privilege.

Prosecutor: Are you willing to testify here?

Witness: Yes.

Court: (2) _________

Prosecutor: When were you married to Toddy?

Witness: Five years ago.

Prosecutor: Do you know what she does for a living?

Witness: She drives a truck for Action Trucking.

Prosecutor: Has she ever said anything to you about illegal dumping of debris?

McSwath: (3) Objection. May I ask a question in aid of this objection?

Court: Yes.

McSwath: Were the two of you alone when any conversation between you about dumping took place?

Witness: No.

McSwath: Who was present?

Witness: Our month-old infant daughter, Melony.

McSwath: We renew our objection. Marital privilege.

Prosecutor: Are you willing to answer?

Witness: Yes.

Court: (4) _________

Prosecutor: Did you repeat what Toddy said to you to anyone?

Witness: Yes, I was shocked and I called the FBI and told them what she told me.

Prosecutor: What did you tell the FBI that Toddy had told you?

McSwath: (5) Objection. Marital privilege. This is just a back door attempt to circumvent marital privilege.

Prosecutor: The cat is out of the bag, and he waived any privilege.
Court: (6) __________
Prosecutor: Did you ever see the illegally dumped debris?
Witness: Yes.
Prosecutor: How did that come about?
Witness: After Toddy told me what she did, I asked her to show me where she had dumped the stuff. She drove me out to Southeast and pointed to the debris that she had dumped.
McSwath: (7) Objection. Marital privilege. Move to strike the last answer.
Prosecutor: This is all out in public, your Honor. It cannot be privileged.
Court: (8) __________
Prosecutor: Did counsel for Action Trucking Co. come to see you in preparation for this trial?
McSwath: (9) Objection. Attorney-client privilege.
Court: (10) __________
Prosecutor: Did you tell counsel for Action Trucking Co. what Toddy had told you?
McSwath: (11) Objection. Marital privilege. It's the same issue as before.
Prosecutor: This is a clear waiver if he told the company lawyer what she said.
Court: (12) __________
Prosecutor: Did Toddy ever tell you what she said to her lawyer in preparing for trial?
Witness: Yes, she would come home after each session with her lawyer and tell me what they talked about.
Prosecutor: What did she say they talked about?
McSwath: (13) Objection. Marital privilege.
Prosecutor: This is a waiver of attorney-client privilege, not a valid claim of marital privilege.
Court: (14)__________
Prosecutor: Do you know Portio Dovel?
Witness: Yes, he also drives for the company.
Prosecutor: Were ever present when Dovel and Toddy talked about dumping debris?
Witness: We had Portio over for dinner one night, and he and Toddy discussed the trouble that they were in as a result of the dumping.
McSwath: (15) Objection. Marital privilege. Move to strike.
Court: (16) __________

Direct Examination of Marie Squirp

Prosecutor: What is your relationship to Portio Dovel?
Witness: I'm his wife.

Prosecutor: How long have you been married?
Witness: Ten years.
Prosecutor: Do the two of you live together?
Witness: No, we are separated and have been since I filed for divorce last month.
Dovel: (17) Objection. Marital privilege.
Prosecutor: Are you willing to testify?
Witness: Not if I don't have to. I don't want to testify against my husband.
Court: (18) _________
Prosecutor: Did your husband ever talk to you about dumping debris?
Dovel: (19) Objection. May I ask two questions in aid of an objection?
Court: Yes.
Dovel: Was anyone else present when your husband and you spoke about dumping?
Witness: No.
Dovel: When did these conversations take place?
Witness: About six months ago.
Dovel: We renew our objection.
Prosecutor: They are separated and about to be divorced. This is not a case for the privilege to apply.
Court: (20) _________
Prosecutor: Did your husband admit to you that he dumped debris during your conversations after you separated about this case?
Dovel: (21) Objection. Marital privilege.
Prosecutor: They were separated.
Court: (22) _________
Prosecutor: By the way, did the charges in this case have anything to do with your separation?
Witness: Yes. I was horrified by the charges.
Prosecutor: Do you have a lawyer in the pending divorce proceeding?
Witness: Yes.
Prosecutor: What did you tell your lawyer about the dumping?
Witness: (23) I'd rather not answer that. Do I have to?
Court: (24) _________

D. PRIVILEGES RELATING TO MENTAL OR PHYSICAL HEALTH

JAFFEE v. REDMOND
518 U.S. 1 (1996)

JUSTICE STEVENS delivered the opinion of the Court.

After a traumatic incident in which she shot and killed a man, a police officer received extensive counseling from a licensed clinical social worker. The question we address is whether statements the officer made to her therapist during the counseling sessions are protected from compelled disclosure in a federal civil action brought by the family of the deceased. Stated otherwise, the question is whether it is appropriate for federal courts to recognize a "psychotherapist privilege" under Rule 501 of the Federal Rules of Evidence.

I

Petitioner is the administrator of the estate of Ricky Allen. Respondents are Mary Lu Redmond, a former police officer, and the Village of Hoffman Estates, Illinois, her employer during the time that she served on the police force. Petitioner commenced this action against respondents after Redmond shot and killed Allen while on patrol duty.

On June 27, 1991, Redmond was the first officer to respond to a "fight in progress" call at an apartment complex. As she arrived at the scene, two of Allen's sisters ran toward her squad car, waving their arms and shouting that there had been a stabbing in one of the apartments. Redmond testified at trial that she relayed this information to her dispatcher and requested an ambulance. She then exited her car and walked toward the apartment building. Before Redmond reached the building, several men ran out, one waving a pipe. When the men ignored her order to get on the ground, Redmond drew her service revolver. Two other men then burst out of the building, one, Ricky Allen, chasing the other. According to Redmond, Allen was brandishing a butcher knife and disregarded her repeated commands to drop the weapon. Redmond shot Allen when she believed he was about to stab the man he was chasing. Allen died at the scene. Redmond testified that before other officers arrived to provide support, "people came pouring out of the buildings," and a threatening confrontation between her and the crowd ensued.

Petitioner filed suit in Federal District Court alleging that Redmond had violated Allen's constitutional rights by using excessive force during the encounter at the apartment complex. * * * At trial, petitioner presented testimony from members of Allen's family that conflicted with Redmond's version of the incident in several important respects. They testified, for example, that Redmond drew her gun before exiting her squad car and that Allen was unarmed when he emerged from the apartment building.

During pretrial discovery petitioner learned that after the shooting Redmond had participated in about 50 counseling sessions with Karen Beyer, a clinical social worker licensed by the State of Illinois and employed at that time by the Village of Hoffman Estates. Petitioner sought access to Beyer's notes concerning the sessions for use in cross-examining Redmond. Respondents vigorously resisted the discovery. They asserted that the contents of the conversations between Beyer and Redmond were protected against involuntary disclosure by a psychotherapist-patient privilege. The district judge rejected this argument. Neither Beyer nor Redmond, however, complied with his order to disclose the contents of Beyer's notes. At depositions and on the witness stand both either refused to answer certain questions or professed an inability to recall details of their conversations.

In his instructions at the end of the trial, the judge advised the jury that the refusal to turn over Beyer's notes had no "legal justification" and that the jury could therefore presume that the contents of the notes would have been unfavorable to respondents. The jury awarded petitioner $45,000 on the federal claim and $ 500,000 on her state-law claim.

The Court of Appeals for the Seventh Circuit reversed and remanded for a new trial. Addressing the issue for the first time, the court concluded that "reason and experience," the touchstones for acceptance of a privilege under Rule 501 of the Federal Rules of Evidence, compelled recognition of a psychotherapist-patient privilege. * * *

The Court of Appeals qualified its recognition of the privilege by stating that it would not apply if "in the interests of justice, the evidentiary need for the disclosure of the contents of a patient's counseling sessions outweighs that patient's privacy interests." Balancing those conflicting interests, the court observed, on the one hand, that the evidentiary need for the contents of the confidential conversations was diminished in this case because there were numerous eyewitnesses to the shooting, and, on the other hand, that Officer Redmond's privacy interests were substantial.

The United States courts of appeals do not uniformly agree that the federal courts should recognize a psychotherapist privilege under Rule 501. Because of the conflict among the courts of appeals and the importance of the question, we granted certiorari. We affirm.

II

Rule 501 of the Federal Rules of Evidence authorizes federal courts to define new privileges by interpreting "common law principles * * * in the light of reason and experience." The authors of the Rule borrowed this phrase from our opinion in *Wolfle v. United States*, 291 U.S. 7, 12 (1934), which in turn referred to the oft-repeated observation that "the common law is not immutable but flexible, and by its own principles adapts itself to varying conditions." *Funk v. United States*, 290 U.S. 371, 383 (1933). *See also Hawkins v. United States*, 358 U.S. 74, 79 (1958) (changes in privileges may be "dictated by 'reason and experience' "). The Senate Report accompanying the 1975 adoption of the Rules indicates that Rule 501 "should be understood as reflecting the view that the recognition of a privilege based on a confidential relationship * * * should be determined on a case-by-case basis." The Rule thus did not freeze the law governing the privileges of witnesses in federal trials at a particular point in our history, but rather directed federal courts to "continue the evolutionary development of testimonial privileges." *Trammel v. United*

States, 445 U.S. 40, 47 (1980); *see also University of Pennsylvania v. EEOC*, 493 U.S. 182, 189 (1990).

The common-law principles underlying the recognition of testimonial privileges can be stated simply. "For more than three centuries it has now been recognized as a fundamental maxim that the public * * * has a right to every man's evidence. When we come to examine the various claims of exemption, we start with the primary assumption that there is a general duty to give what testimony one is capable of giving, and that any exemptions which may exist are distinctly exceptional, being so many derogations from a positive general rule." *United States v. Bryan*, 339 U.S. 323, 331 (1950). Exceptions from the general rule disfavoring testimonial privileges may be justified, however, by a " 'public good transcending the normally predominant principle of utilizing all rational means for ascertaining the truth." *Trammel*, 445 U.S. at 50.

Guided by these principles, the question we address today is whether a privilege protecting confidential communications between a psychotherapist and her patient "promotes sufficiently important interests to outweigh the need for probative evidence * * * ." 445 U.S. at 51. Both "reason and experience" persuade us that it does.

III

Like the spousal and attorney-client privileges, the psychotherapist-patient privilege is "rooted in the imperative need for confidence and trust." *Trammel*, 445 U.S. at 51. Treatment by a physician for physical ailments can often proceed successfully on the basis of a physical examination, objective information supplied by the patient, and the results of diagnostic tests. Effective psychotherapy, by contrast, depends upon an atmosphere of confidence and trust in which the patient is willing to make a frank and complete disclosure of facts, emotions, memories, and fears. Because of the sensitive nature of the problems for which individuals consult psychotherapists, disclosure of confidential communications made during counseling sessions may cause embarrassment or disgrace. For this reason, the mere possibility of disclosure may impede development of the confidential relationship necessary for successful treatment. As the Judicial Conference Advisory Committee observed in 1972 when it recommended that Congress recognize a psychotherapist privilege as part of the Proposed Federal Rules of Evidence, a psychiatrist's ability to help her patients "is completely dependent upon [the patients'] willingness and ability to talk freely. This makes it difficult if not impossible for [a psychiatrist] to function without being able to assure * * * patients of confidentiality and, indeed, privileged communication. Where there may be exceptions to this general rule * * * , there is wide agreement that confidentiality is a sine qua non for successful psychiatric treatment." Advisory Committee's Notes to Proposed Rules, 56 F.R.D. 183, 242 (1972). By protecting confidential communications between a psychotherapist and her patient from involuntary disclosure, the proposed privilege thus serves important private interests.

Our cases make clear that an asserted privilege must also "serve public ends." *Upjohn Co. v. United States*, 449 U.S. 383, 389 (1981). Thus, the purpose of the attorney-client privilege is to "encourage full and frank communication between attorneys and their clients and thereby promote broader public interests in the observance of law and administration of justice." And the spousal privilege, as modified in *Trammel*, is justified because it "furthers the important public interest in marital harmony," 445 U.S. at 53. The psychotherapist privilege serves the public interest by facilitating the provision of appropriate treatment for individuals suffering the effects of a mental or emotional problem. The mental health of our citizenry, no less than its physical health, is a public good of transcendent importance.[10]

In contrast to the significant public and private interests supporting recognition of the privilege, the likely evidentiary benefit that would result from the denial of the privilege is modest. If the privilege were rejected, confidential conversations between psychotherapists and their patients would surely be chilled, particularly when it is obvious that the circumstances that give rise to the need for treatment will probably result in litigation. Without a privilege, much of the desirable evidence to which litigants such as petitioner seek access — for example, admissions against interest by a party — is unlikely to come into being. This unspoken "evidence" will therefore serve no greater truth-seeking function than if it had been spoken and privileged.

That it is appropriate for the federal courts to recognize a psychotherapist privilege under Rule 501 is confirmed by the fact that all 50 States and the District of Columbia have enacted into law some form of psychotherapist privilege. We have previously observed that the policy decisions of the States bear on the question whether federal courts should recognize a new privilege or amend the coverage of an existing one. *See Trammel*, 445 U.S. at 48-50. Because state legislatures are fully aware of the need to protect the integrity of the factfinding functions of their courts, the existence of a consensus among the States indicates that "reason and experience" support recognition of the privilege. In addition, given the importance of the patient's understanding that her communications with her therapist will not be publicly disclosed, any State's promise of confidentiality would have little value if the patient were aware that the privilege would not be honored in a federal court. Denial of the federal privilege therefore would frustrate the purposes of the state legislation that was enacted to foster these confidential communications.

It is of no consequence that recognition of the privilege in the vast majority of States is the product of legislative action rather than judicial decision. Although common-law rulings may once have been the primary source of new developments in federal privilege law, that is no longer the case. In *Funk v. United States*, 290 U.S. 371 (1933), we recognized that it is appropriate to treat a consistent body of policy determinations by state legislatures as reflecting both "reason" and "experience." That rule is properly respectful of the States and at the same time reflects the fact that once a state legislature

[10] This case amply demonstrates the importance of allowing individuals to receive confidential counseling. Police officers engaged in the dangerous and difficult tasks associated with protecting the safety of our communities not only confront the risk of physical harm but also face stressful circumstances that may give rise to anxiety, depression, fear, or anger. The entire community may suffer if police officers are not able to receive effective counseling and treatment after traumatic incidents, either because trained officers leave the profession prematurely or because those in need of treatment remain on the job.

has enacted a privilege there is no longer an opportunity for common-law creation of the protection. The history of the psychotherapist privilege illustrates the latter point. * * * That the privilege may have developed faster legislatively than it would have in the courts demonstrates only that the States rapidly recognized the wisdom of the rule as the field of psychotherapy developed.

The uniform judgment of the States is reinforced by the fact that a psychotherapist privilege was among the nine specific privileges recommended by the Advisory Committee in its proposed privilege rules. In *United States v. Gillock*, 445 U.S. 360, 367-368 (1980), our holding that Rule 501 did not include a state legislative privilege relied, in part, on the fact that no such privilege was included in the Advisory Committee's draft. The reasoning in *Gillock* thus supports the opposite conclusion in this case. In rejecting the proposed draft that had specifically identified each privilege rule and substituting the present more open-ended Rule 501, the Senate Judiciary Committee explicitly stated that its action "should not be understood as disapproving any recognition of a psychiatrist-patient * * * privilege contained in the [proposed] rules." S. Rep. No. 93-1277, at 13.

Because we agree with the judgment of the state legislatures and the Advisory Committee that a psychotherapist-patient privilege will serve a "public good transcending the normally predominant principle of utilizing all rational means for ascertaining truth," *Trammel*, 445 U.S. at 50, we hold that confidential communications between a licensed psychotherapist and her patients in the course of diagnosis or treatment are protected from compelled disclosure under Rule 501 of the Federal Rules of Evidence.[14]

IV

All agree that a psychotherapist privilege covers confidential communications made to licensed psychiatrists and psychologists. We have no hesitation in concluding in this case that the federal privilege should also extend to confidential communications made to licensed social workers in the course of psychotherapy. The reasons for recognizing a privilege for treatment by psychiatrists and psychologists apply with equal force to treatment by a clinical social worker such as Karen Beyer. Today, social workers provide a significant amount of mental health treatment. Their clients often include the poor and those of modest means who could not afford the assistance of a psychiatrist or psychologist, but whose counseling sessions serve the same public goals. Perhaps in recognition of these circumstances, the vast majority of States explicitly extend a testimonial privilege to licensed social workers. We therefore agree with the Court of Appeals that "drawing a distinction between the counseling provided by costly psychotherapists and the counseling provided by more readily accessible social workers serves no discernible public purpose."

We part company with the Court of Appeals on a separate point. We reject the balancing component of the privilege implemented by that court and a small number of States. Making the promise of confidentiality contingent upon

[14] Like other testimonial privileges, the patient may of course waive the protection.

a trial judge's later evaluation of the relative importance of the patient's interest in privacy and the evidentiary need for disclosure would eviscerate the effectiveness of the privilege. As we explained in *Upjohn*, if the purpose of the privilege is to be served, the participants in the confidential conversation "must be able to predict with some degree of certainty whether particular discussions will be protected. An uncertain privilege, or one which purports to be certain but results in widely varying applications by the courts, is little better than no privilege at all."

These considerations are all that is necessary for decision of this case. A rule that authorizes the recognition of new privileges on a case-by-case basis makes it appropriate to define the details of new privileges in a like manner. Because this is the first case in which we have recognized a psychotherapist privilege, it is neither necessary nor feasible to delineate its full contours in a way that would "govern all conceivable future questions in this area."[19]

V

The conversations between Officer Redmond and Karen Beyer and the notes taken during their counseling sessions are protected from compelled disclosure under Rule 501 of the Federal Rules of Evidence. The judgment of the Court of Appeals is affirmed.

JUSTICE SCALIA, with whom THE CHIEF JUSTICE joins as to Part III, dissenting.

The Court has discussed at some length the benefit that will be purchased by creation of the evidentiary privilege in this case: the encouragement of psychoanalytic counseling. It has not mentioned the purchase price: occasional injustice. That is the cost of every rule which excludes reliable and probative evidence — or at least every one categorical enough to achieve its announced policy objective. In the case of some of these rules, such as the one excluding confessions that have not been properly "Mirandized," the victim of the injustice is always the impersonal State or the faceless "public at large." For the rule proposed here, the victim is more likely to be some individual who is prevented from proving a valid claim — or (worse still) prevented from establishing a valid defense. The latter is particularly unpalatable for those who love justice, because it causes the courts of law not merely to let stand a wrong, but to become themselves the instruments of wrong.

In the past, this Court has well understood that the particular value the courts are distinctively charged with preserving — justice — is severely harmed by contravention of "the fundamental principle that" " 'the public * * * has a right to every man's evidence." — *Trammel v. United States*, 445 U.S. 40, 50 (1980). Testimonial privileges, it has said, "are not lightly created nor expansively construed, for they are in derogation of the search for truth." *United States v. Nixon*, 418 U.S. 683, 710 (1974). Adherence to that principle has caused us, in the Rule 501 cases we have considered to date, to reject new

[19] Although it would be premature to speculate about most future developments in the federal psychotherapist privilege, we do not doubt that there are situations in which the privilege must give way, for example, if a serious threat of harm to the patient or to others can be averted only by means of a disclosure by the therapist.

privileges, see *University of Pennsylvania v. EEOC*, 493 U.S. 182 (1990) (privilege against disclosure of academic peer review materials); *United States v. Gillock*, 445 U.S. 360 (1980) (privilege against disclosure of "legislative acts" by member of state legislature), and even to construe narrowly the scope of existing privileges, *see, e.g., United States v. Zolin*, 491 U.S. 554, 568-570 (1989) (permitting in camera review of documents alleged to come within crime-fraud exception to attorney-client privilege); *Trammel*, supra (holding that voluntary testimony by spouse is not covered by husband-wife privilege). The Court today ignores this traditional judicial preference for the truth, and ends up creating a privilege that is new, vast, and ill-defined. I respectfully dissent.

I

* * *

II

* * * Effective psychotherapy undoubtedly is beneficial to individuals with mental problems, and surely serves some larger social interest in maintaining a mentally stable society. But merely mentioning these values does not answer the critical question: are they of such importance, and is the contribution of psychotherapy to them so distinctive, and is the application of normal evidentiary rules so destructive to psychotherapy, as to justify making our federal courts occasional instruments of injustice? * * *

When is it, one must wonder, that the psychotherapist came to play such an indispensable role in the maintenance of the citizenry's mental health? For most of history, men and women have worked out their difficulties by talking to, inter alios, parents, siblings, best friends and bartenders — none of whom was awarded a privilege against testifying in court. Ask the average citizen: Would your mental health be more significantly impaired by preventing you from seeing a psychotherapist, or by preventing you from getting advice from your mom? I have little doubt what the answer would be. Yet there is no mother-child privilege.

How likely is it that a person will be deterred from seeking psychological counseling, or from being completely truthful in the course of such counseling, because of fear of later disclosure in litigation? And even more pertinent to today's decision, to what extent will the evidentiary privilege reduce that deterrent? The Court does not try to answer the first of these questions; and it cannot possibly have any notion of what the answer is to the second, since that depends entirely upon the scope of the privilege, which the Court amazingly finds it "neither necessary nor feasible to delineate." If, for example, the psychotherapist can give the patient no more assurance than "A court will not be able to make me disclose what you tell me, unless you tell me about a harmful act," I doubt whether there would be much benefit from the privilege at all.

Even where it is certain that absence of the psychotherapist privilege will inhibit disclosure of the information, it is not clear to me that that is an unacceptable state of affairs. Let us assume the very worst in the circumstances of the present case: that to be truthful about what was troubling her, the police officer who sought counseling would have to confess that she shot without reason, and wounded an innocent man. If (again to assume the worst) such an act constituted the crime of negligent wounding under Illinois law, the officer would of course have the absolute right not to admit that she shot without reason in criminal court. But I see no reason why she should be enabled both not to admit it in criminal court (as a good citizen should), and to get the benefits of psychotherapy by admitting it to a therapist who cannot tell anyone else. And even less reason why she should be enabled to deny her guilt in the criminal trial — or in a civil trial for negligence — while yet obtaining the benefits of psychotherapy by confessing guilt to a social worker who cannot testify. It seems to me entirely fair to say that if she wishes the benefits of telling the truth she must also accept the adverse consequences. To be sure, in most cases the statements to the psychotherapist will be only marginally relevant, and one of the purposes of the privilege (though not one relied upon by the Court) may be simply to spare patients needless intrusion upon their privacy, and to spare psychotherapists needless expenditure of their time in deposition and trial. But surely this can be achieved by means short of excluding even evidence that is of the most direct and conclusive effect.

The Court confidently asserts that not much truth-finding capacity would be destroyed by the privilege anyway, since "without a privilege, much of the desirable evidence to which litigants such as petitioner seek access * * * is unlikely to come into being." If that is so, how come psychotherapy got to be a thriving practice before the "psychotherapist privilege" was invented? Were the patients paying money to lie to their analysts all those years? Of course the evidence-generating effect of the privilege (if any) depends entirely upon its scope, which the Court steadfastly declines to consider. And even if one assumes that scope to be the broadest possible, is it really true that most, or even many, of those who seek psychological counseling have the worry of litigation in the back of their minds? I doubt that, and the Court provides no evidence to support it.

The Court suggests one last policy justification: since psychotherapist privilege statutes exist in all the States, the failure to recognize a privilege in federal courts "would frustrate the purposes of the state legislation that was enacted to foster these confidential communications." This is a novel argument indeed. A sort of inverse pre-emption: the truth-seeking functions of federal courts must be adjusted so as not to conflict with the policies of the States. This reasoning cannot be squared with *Gillock*, which declined to recognize an evidentiary privilege for Tennessee legislators in federal prosecutions, even though the Tennessee Constitution guaranteed it in state criminal proceedings. Moreover, since * * * state policies regarding the psychotherapist privilege vary considerably from State to State, no uniform federal policy can possibly honor most of them. If furtherance of state policies is the name of the game, rules of privilege in federal courts should vary from State to State, a la *Erie*.

The Court's failure to put forward a convincing justification of its own could perhaps be excused if it were relying upon the unanimous conclusion of state courts in the reasoned development of their common law. It cannot do that, since no State has such a privilege apart from legislation. What it relies upon, instead, is "the fact that all 50 States and the District of Columbia have [1] enacted into law [2] some form of psychotherapist privilege." Let us consider both the verb and its object: The fact [1] that all 50 States have enacted this privilege argues not for, but against, our adopting the privilege judicially. At best it suggests that the matter has been found not to lend itself to judicial treatment — perhaps because the pros and cons of adopting the privilege, or of giving it one or another shape, are not that clear; or perhaps because the rapidly evolving uses of psychotherapy demand a flexibility that only legislation can provide. At worst it suggests that the privilege commends itself only to decisionmaking bodies in which reason is tempered, so to speak, by political pressure from organized interest groups (such as psychologists and social workers), and decisionmaking bodies that are not overwhelmingly concerned (as courts of law are and should be) with justice.

And the phrase [2] "some form of psychotherapist privilege" covers a multitude of difficulties. The Court concedes that there is "divergence among the States concerning the types of therapy relationships protected and the exceptions recognized." To rest a newly announced federal common-law psychotherapist privilege, assertable from this day forward in all federal courts, upon "the States' unanimous judgment that some form of psychotherapist privilege is appropriate," is rather like announcing a new, immediately applicable, federal common law of torts, based upon the States' "unanimous judgment" that some form of tort law is appropriate. In the one case as in the other, the state laws vary to such a degree that the parties and lower federal judges confronted by the new "common law" have barely a clue as to what its content might be.

III

Turning from the general question that was not involved in this case to the specific one that is: The Court's conclusion that a social-worker psychotherapeutic privilege deserves recognition is even less persuasive. * * * A licensed psychiatrist or psychologist is an expert in psychotherapy — and that may suffice (though I think it not so clear that this Court should make the judgment) to justify the use of extraordinary means to encourage counseling with him, as opposed to counseling with one's rabbi, minister, family or friends. One must presume that a social worker does not bring this greatly heightened degree of skill to bear, which is alone a reason for not encouraging that consultation as generously. Does a social worker bring to bear at least a significantly heightened degree of skill — more than a minister or rabbi, for example? I have no idea, and neither does the Court. The social worker in the present case, Karen Beyer, was a "licensed clinical social worker" in Illinois, a job title whose training requirements consist of "master's degree in social work from an approved program," and "3,000 hours of satisfactory, supervised clinical professional experience." It is not clear that the degree in social work requires any training in psychotherapy. * * * [T]he training requirement for a "licensed social worker" consists of either (a) "a degree from a graduate program of social work" approved by the State, or (b) "a degree in social work from an undergraduate program" approved by the State, plus "3 years of supervised professional experience." With due respect, it does not seem to me that any of this training is comparable in its rigor (or indeed in the precision of its subject) to the training of the other experts (lawyers) to whom this Court has accorded a privilege, or even of the experts (psychiatrists and psychologists) to whom the Advisory Committee and this Court proposed extension of a privilege in 1972. Of course these are only Illinois' requirements for "social workers." Those of other States, for all we know, may be even less demanding. Indeed, I am not even sure there is a nationally accepted definition of "social worker," as there is of psychiatrist and psychologist. It seems to me quite irresponsible to extend the so-called "psychotherapist privilege" to all licensed social workers, nationwide, without exploring these issues.

* * *

Another critical distinction between psychiatrists and psychologists, on the one hand, and social workers, on the other, is that the former professionals, in their consultations with patients, do nothing but psychotherapy. Social workers, on the other hand, interview people for a multitude of reasons. * * *

Thus, in applying the "social worker" variant of the "psychotherapist" privilege, it will be necessary to determine whether the information provided to the social worker was provided to him in his capacity as a psychotherapist, or in his capacity as an administrator of social welfare, a community organizer, etc. Worse still, if the privilege is to have its desired effect (and is not to mislead the client), it will presumably be necessary for the social caseworker to advise, as the conversation with his welfare client proceeds, which portions are privileged and which are not.

* * *

The question before us today is not whether there should be an evidentiary privilege for social workers providing therapeutic services. Perhaps there should. But the question before us is whether (1) the need for that privilege is so clear, and (2) the desirable contours of that privilege are so evident, that it is appropriate for this Court to craft it in common-law fashion, under Rule 501. Even if we were writing on a clean slate, I think the answer to that question would be clear. But given our extensive precedent to the effect that new privileges "in derogation of the search for truth" "are not lightly created," *United States v. Nixon*, 418 U.S. at 710, the answer the Court gives today is inexplicable.

In its consideration of this case, the Court was the beneficiary of no fewer than 14 amicus briefs supporting respondents, most of which came from such organizations as the American Psychiatric Association, the American Psychoanalytic Association, the American Association of State Social Work Boards, the Employee Assistance Professionals Association, Inc., the American Counseling Association, and the National Association of Social Workers. Not a single amicus brief was filed in support of petitioner. That is no surprise. There is no self-interested organization out there devoted to pursuit of the truth in the federal courts. The expectation is, however, that this Court will have that interest prominently — indeed, primarily — in mind. Today we have failed that expectation, and that responsibility. It is no small matter to say that, in some cases, our federal courts will be the tools of injustice rather than unearth the truth where it is available to be found. The common law has identified a few instances where that is tolerable. Perhaps Congress may conclude that it is also tolerable for the purpose of encouraging psychotherapy by social workers. But that conclusion assuredly does not burst upon the mind with such clarity that a judgment in favor of suppressing the truth ought to be pronounced by this honorable Court. I respectfully dissent.

NOTES

1. After Jaffee, are communications for purposes of obtaining treatment of physical ailments protected by a privilege?

It is unclear whether a physician-patient privilege can or should be recognized as a matter of federal law after *Jaffee*. On the one hand, the Court distinguished the physician-patient relationship from the psychotherapist-patient relationship, on the ground that confidential communications are more critical to the latter relationship than to the former. On the other hand, every state has legislatively enacted a physician-patient privilege, and state recognition was important to the Court's adoption of the psychotherapist-patient privilege in *Jaffee*. The failure to recognize a physician-patient privilege at the federal level could be said to undermine state policy, using the same "inverse pre-emption" argument employed in *Jaffee*. But then again, the physician-patient privilege was not one of those recommended by the Advisory Committee in its proposed but not enacted privilege rules, and the Court found Advisory Committee acceptance or rejection relevant in *Jaffee*as well. Therefore, there is significant doubt as to whether *Jaffee* can be used as a springboard to establish a federal physician-patient privilege, which has not yet been recognized by any federal court. Courts after *Jaffee* have still refused to recognize a doctor-patient privilege under federal common law.

2. What is the impact of *Jaffee* on the possible recognition of other privileges that were not recognized under federal common law?

See Saltzburg, Martin, and Capra, *Federal Rules of Evidence Manual* (9th ed. 2006):

> Before *Jaffee v. Redmond*, many federal courts rejected attempts to develop privileges that were not recognized by common law at the time the Federal Rules were adopted. The Supreme Court in *Jaffee*, however, stressed that Rule 501 authorizes, and indeed requires, federal courts to establish new privileges where the need for the privilege outweighs the cost of the loss of reliable evidence that the privilege would impose.
>
> We believe that Rule 501 provides a limited authority to federal courts to develop new privileges as circumstance and policy may

warrant. However, the federal courts should not lightly adopt a new privilege, even after *Jaffee*. Simple claims of social policy should not suffice — that was not enough to satisfy the Court in *Jaffee*. Because a privilege is in derogation of the search for truth, new privileges should be limited to those that are critical to promoting *both* important public policy and substantial private interests. *See, e.g.*, *In re Grand Jury Proceedings*, 103 F.3d 1140 (3d Cir. 1997) (rejecting a parent-child privilege and noting that the interests that would be protected by such a privilege do not overcome the heavy presumption against establishing new privileges and the strong interests in admitting relevant evidence: "privileges are tolerable only to the very limited extent that permitting a refusal to testify or excluding relevant evidence has a public good transcending the normally predominant principle of utilizing all rational means for ascertaining truth"). Under *Jaffee*, the proponent of a new privilege has the burden of establishing that the benefits of the privilege outweigh the cost of the loss of reliable evidence that the privilege would entail.

E. PRIVILEGE FOR COMMUNICATIONS TO CLERGY

IN RE GRAND JURY INVESTIGATION
918 F.2d 374 (3d Cir. 1990)

BECKER, CIRCUIT JUDGE:

This is an appeal by the government * * * from an order denying its motion to compel the federal grand jury testimony of a Lutheran clergyman concerning subjects discussed during a family counseling session. The district court held that a clergy-communicant privilege, existing under federal common law, barred the testimony. The grand jury was investigating whether racially motivated housing discrimination and a conspiracy to deny civil rights led to an apparent arson at the home of a black family that lived next door to the family whose members the pastor counseled. In addition to the pastor, the family counseling session involved four persons: a husband and wife, who were members of the pastor's church, the wife's adult son from a previous marriage, and the son's fiancee.

The district court, ruling on the pastor's motion to quash the subpoena compelling him to testify before the grand jury, held that a communication, to be protected, must be made in confidence. It found, however, that the communications of family group members to the pastor were, as the pastor understood them to be, confidential. Otherwise, the court concluded, "his ministry would be ineffective." The government contends that even if a clergy-communicant privilege exists under federal common law, the pastor should not be able to invoke it to avoid testifying about what was said to him in the course of this counseling session. The government reasons that the presence at the counseling session of the fiancee (not yet a member of the family) was neither essential to nor in furtherance of any religiously motivated communications to the pastor on the part of the others present and therefore worked either to vitiate or to waive any privilege. In support of this argument, the government invokes the general principle that evidentiary privileges, which retard the search for truth, should be narrowly construed.

There is a relative dearth of federal precedent establishing the existence and contours of a clergy-communicant privilege. Although the original draft of the Federal Rules of Evidence included a section providing for a number of specific privileges, including one that would have protected communications to members of the clergy, Congress chose not to codify the draft Rules comprehending specific privileges. Congress substituted in their stead a single rule generally providing that "privilege[s] * * * shall be governed by the principles of the common law as they may be interpreted by the courts of the United States in the light of reason and experience." Fed. R. Evid. 501. In accordance with this standard, we must determine whether a clergy-communicant privilege in fact exists and, if it does, its relevant contours.

For the reasons that follow, we hold that a clergy-communicant privilege does exist. We further hold that this privilege protects communications to a member of the clergy, in his or her spiritual or professional capacity, by persons who seek spiritual counseling and who reasonably expect that their words will be kept in confidence. As is the case with the attorney-client privilege, the presence of third parties, if essential to and in furtherance of the communication, does not vitiate the clergy-communicant privilege. Neither the record nor the district court's findings, however, are sufficient to establish whether any of those present at the counseling session should be considered third parties, to gauge the impact of any third party's presence, and to enable us to ascertain whether the privilege was properly invoked in this case. We will therefore vacate the district court's order and remand for further proceedings.

I. FACTS AND PROCEDURAL HISTORY

On November 28, 1985, a fire occurred at a house, located in an all-white neighborhood in the Forest Hills section of Pittsburgh, Pennsylvania, that had recently been purchased by a black family. The police and fire departments determined that the fire was the likely result of arson. Within several days of the fire, Mr. and Mrs. George Kampich, Mrs. Kampich's adult son, George Shaw (who is not related legally or by blood to Mr. Kampich), and Patty DiLucente, Shaw's fiancee, sought counseling from the Reverend Ernest Knoche ("Pastor Knoche"), a Lutheran clergyman. All four persons lived in the home next door to the site of the fire. Mr. and Mrs. Kampich are members of Pastor Knoche's church. Although Shaw has occasionally attended services at the church, Shaw and DiLucente are not members. In June of 1989, Shaw and DiLucente were married. In November of 1989, some four years after the counseling session, a grand jury convened by the district court for the Western District of Pennsylvania commenced an investigation of the suspected arson. The grand jury was investigating, in particular, possible violations of 42 U.S.C. §§ 3631, prohibiting racially motivated housing discrimination, and of 18 U.S.C. §§ 241, prohibiting conspiracies to violate civil rights.

On November 28, 1989, the government subpoenaed Pastor Knoche to testify before the grand jury about the 1985 counseling session. The government, in support of this subpoena, asserted that it had reason to believe that the Kampiches, Shaw, and DiLucente had planned or participated in the arson and had discussed their involvement with the pastor. In an interview prior to his appearance before the grand jury, Pastor Knoche informed the government that he intended to assert the clergy-communicant privilege and would refuse to answer any questions regarding the counseling session. That day, the government filed a motion in the district court to compel Pastor Knoche to testify before the grand jury.

On November 28th and 29th, the district court held a hearing on the government's motion. In the course of this hearing, the district judge questioned the pastor about the extent of his family and group counseling, the parties involved in the discussion at issue, and the confidentiality of their communications. Pastor Knoche stated that family counseling, in contrast to individual counseling, constituted a typical and important part of his ministry. The Pastor also concurred with the district court's characterization of his ministry as founded upon the Judeo-Christian notion of redemption and forgiveness through counseling and prayer. The Pastor responded, further, that forthrightness and truthfulness on the part of participants, such as Mr. and Mrs. Kampich, Shaw, and DiLucente, are essential to proper counseling and, ultimately, to redemption. He concluded that those whom he spiritually counsels expect that he will keep any communications made to him in strict confidence. The district court sustained Pastor Knoche's right to assert a clergy-communicant privilege and denied the government's motion to compel his testimony. The district judge, in a colloquy setting forth the basis for his decision, described it as "tough," but concluded that compelling the pastor to testify would break down church-state divisions, infringe upon the right to participate in religious activities, invade a "sacrosanct" area, and, through depriving families of confidential religious counseling, endanger them. This appeal followed.

II. THE EXISTENCE AND CONTOURS OF A CLERGY-COMMUNICANT PRIVILEGE

In federal courts, evidentiary privileges are governed by Rule 501 of the Federal Rules of Evidence. This provision, which was the product of congressional involvement in the rulemaking process, does not contain a specific and exclusive list of privileges recognized in the federal courts. The Rule instead provides the federal courts with flexibility in crafting testimonial privileges. * * *

The Rule dictates the evolution and application of a federal common law of privilege in federal criminal cases. Under Federal Rule of Evidence 1101, Rule 501 is applicable to grand jury proceedings. *See* Fed. R. Evid. 1101(d)(2) (providing that all rules of evidence shall be inapplicable in grand jury proceedings except for that with respect to privileges).

A. The Clergy-Communicant Privilege and the History of Rule 501

* * * Both the history and the language of Rule 501 * * * provide us with a mandate to develop evidentiary privileges in accordance with common law principles. This mandate, in turn, requires us to examine federal and state

case law and impels us to consult treatises and commentaries on the law of evidence that elucidate the development of the common law. We believe that the proposed rules of evidence adopted by the Supreme Court and submitted to Congress provide us with an appropriate starting point for discerning the existence and scope of the clergy-communicant privilege. Rule 501 replaced a number of proposed rules concerning evidentiary privileges that were adopted by the Supreme Court following extensive study and analysis by the Advisory Committee responsible for codifying federal rules of evidence. As submitted to Congress, Article V of the proposed rules set out thirteen rules encompassing nine specific privileges, including a privilege for communications to clergymen.

Rule 506, delineating the contours of the clergy-communicant privilege, reads as follows:

> Communications to Clergymen
>
> (a) *Definitions*. As used in this rule:
>
> (1) A "clergyman" is a minister, priest, rabbi, or other similar functionary of a religious organization, or an individual reasonably believed so to be by the person consulting him.
>
> (2) A communication is "confidential" if made privately and not intended for further disclosure except to other persons present in furtherance of the purpose of the communication.
>
> (b) *General rule of privilege*. A person has a privilege to refuse to disclose and to prevent another from disclosing a confidential communication by the person to a clergyman in his professional character as spiritual adviser.
>
> (c) *Who may claim the privilege*. The privilege may be claimed by the person, by his guardian or conservator, or by his personal representative if he is deceased. The clergyman may claim the privilege on behalf of the person. His authority so to do is presumed in the absence of evidence to the contrary.

The Advisory Committee's note confirms that proposed Rule 506 is expansive in character:

> * * * *The choice between a privilege narrowly restricted to doctrinally required confessions and a privilege broadly applicable to all confidential communications with a clergyman in his professional character as a spiritual adviser has been exercised in favor of the latter.* Many clergymen now receive training in marriage counseling and the handling of personality problems. Matters of this kind fall readily into the realm of the spirit. * * *

* * * Given the requisite showing of confidentiality, proposed Rule 506 would have extended the clergy-communicant privilege to group discussions.

Although Congress chose not to adopt the proposed rules on privileges, it did not disapprove them. The Senate Judiciary Committee's report on Rule 501 states:

> It should be clearly understood that, in approving this general rule as to privileges, the action of Congress should not be understood as disapproving any recognition of * * * any * * * of the enumerated privileges contained in the Supreme Court rules. Rather, our action should be understood as reflecting the view that the recognition of a privilege based on a confidential relationship and other privileges should be determined on a case-by-case basis.

S. Rep. No. 93-1277, 93rd Cong., 2d Sess. 4, *reprinted in* 1974 U.S.Code Cong. and Admin.News 7051, 7059. We believe that the proposed rules provide a useful reference point and offer guidance in defining the existence and scope of evidentiary privileges in the federal courts.* * *

The history of the proposed Rules of Evidence reflects that the clergy-communicant rule was one of the least controversial of the enumerated privileges, merely defining a long-recognized principle of American law. Although most of the nine privileges set forth in the proposed rules were vigorously attacked in Congress, the privilege covering communications to members of the clergy was not. S. Saltzburg & K. Redden, *Federal Rules of Evidence Manual* 333 (4th ed. 1986). Indeed, virtually every state has recognized some form of clergy-communicant privilege. The inclusion of the clergy-communicant privilege in the proposed rules, taken together with its uncontroversial nature, strongly suggests that the privilege is, in the words of the Supreme Court "indelibly ensconced" in the American common law. *United States v. Gillock*, 445 U.S. 360, 368 (1980).

B. Federal Judicial Precedents Recognizing a Clergy-Communicant Privilege

The first reported federal case recognizing the clergy-communicant privilege through the common law process of decision was decided in 1958, see *Mullen v. United States*, 263 F.2d 275 (D.C. Cir. 1958) (Fahy J., concurring). Judge Fahy's lengthy concurrence in this case traced the history and contours of the clergy-communicant privilege and opined that the admission of a minister's testimony about a conversation, in which the defendant sought spiritual counseling, constituted an additional ground for overturning the jury's verdict against her.

Following *Mullen*, a number of federal courts recognized a common law clergy-communicant privilege. The court in *In re Verplank*, 329 F. Supp. 433, 435 (C.D.Cal.1971), for example, invoked the Mullen concurrence and * * * held that draft counseling services rendered by a clergyman came within the ambit of his religious duties and were privileged. * * *

The Supreme Court, albeit in dicta, subsequently acknowledged the existence of a "priest-penitent" privilege. *See Trammel v. United States*, 445 U.S. 40, 45 (1980). * * * Critiquing an archaic and unduly expansive rule that permitted a defendant to exclude from evidence any adverse spousal testimony, the Court favorably referred to several privileges by analogy, among them, the "priest-penitent" privilege * * *. In the wake of the Supreme Court's opinion in *Trammel*, a number of federal district courts and courts of appeal have also acknowledged the clergy-communicant privilege. *See, e.g.*, *United States v. Dube*, 820 F.2d 886 (7th Cir. 1987) (acknowledging existence of clergy-penitent privilege, but holding that privilege did not apply to communications made to clergyman to obtain assistance in avoiding tax obligations, not spiritual relief); *United States v. Gordon*, 655 F.2d 478 (2d Cir.1981) (holding that defendant's business communications to priest he employed in a nonreligious capacity were not protected by priest-penitent privilege); *Eckmann v. Board of Education*, 106 F.R.D. 70 (E.D. Mo. 1985) (observing that "[t]he 'priest-penitent' privilege has clearly been recognized by federal courts" and holding that Catholic nun could invoke the privilege with respect to communications made to her in her capacity as a spiritual advisor) * * * .

* * *

C. The Scope and Contours of the Clergy-Communicant Privilege Adopted

We do not take lightly our responsibility to develop common law evidentiary privileges "in the light of reason and experience." In developing the federal common law of privileges concerning communications to the clergy, we must attempt to balance the need for full disclosure of all probative evidence against the countervailing requirement of confidentiality that furthers the objectives underlying the privilege claimed. Although Rule 501 grants the federal courts power to create new privileges or to develop existing privileges as the need arises, we agree with the government's contention in this case that our authority is narrow in scope and should be exercised only after careful consideration in the face of a strong showing of need for the privilege.* * *

We are, of course, mindful of the broad investigatory powers accorded to the grand jury. We again note, however, that the Rules of Evidence explicitly provide for the application of Rule 501, the more general successor to proposed Rule 506, in grand jury proceedings. We are satisfied, moreover, that American common law, viewed in the light of reason and experience * * * compels the recognition of a clergy-communicant privilege. Both state and federal decisions have long recognized the privilege. The Supreme Court Rules Committee also recognized the privilege. That is doubtless because the clergy-communicant relationship is so important, indeed so fundamental to the western tradition, that it must be "sedulously fostered." 8 *Wigmore* at §§ 2285. Confidence is obviously essential to maintaining the clergy-communicant relationship. Although there are countervailing considerations, we have no doubt that the need for protecting the relationship outweighs them.

We believe that the privilege should apply to protect communications made (1) to a clergyperson (2) in his or her spiritual and professional capacity (3) with a reasonable expectation of confidentiality. As is the case with the attorney-client privilege, the presence of third parties, if essential to and in furtherance of the communication, should not void the privilege. This statement of the contours of the privilege is consistent with the provisions of Rule 506, which, as our study of the federal case law confirms, tracks the evolving common law. In addition, we note our agreement with the tenor of the

Advisory Committee's Note to proposed Rule 506, which extends the scope of the privilege to encompass not only communications between Roman Catholic priests and their penitents, but also communications between clergy and communicants of other denominations.

Our delineation of the privilege is not comprehensive. We illuminate here and infra only those facets and boundaries of the privilege that are implicated in this case. The privilege is a common law rule. The precise scope of the privilege and its additional facets, such as whether a clergyperson should be required to disclose confidential communications when harm to innocent parties is threatened and imminent, are, therefore, most suitably left to case-by-case evolution. * * *

III. THE APPLICATION OF THE CLERGY-COMMUNICANT PRIVILEGE IN THIS CASE

As we have explained, in order for the clergy-communicant privilege to apply, the communication protected must, at a minimum, be made with a reasonable expectation of confidentiality to a member of the clergy acting in his or her professional or spiritual capacity. In this case, within days of the suspected arson, Pastor Knoche had a group discussion with Mr. and Mrs. Kampich, Shaw, and DiLucente. The government alleges that these persons may have planned or participated in setting the fire at the home of their black neighbor. DiLucente, however, is not a target of the grand jury investigation.

The threshold criterion for deciding whether the privilege should attach — the criterion that the communication be made to a clergyperson — is clearly satisfied. Pastor Knoche is an ordained Lutheran minister. Whether the Kampiches, Shaw, and DiLucente communicated with Pastor Knoche in his spiritual or professional capacity, thus fulfilling the second prerequisite for attachment of the privilege, is less obvious. Whether the Kampiches', Shaw's, and DiLucente's communications to Knoche were made with a reasonable expectation of confidentiality, fulfilling the third prerequisite for the privilege's attachment, is also unclear.

The government, although not conceding the existence of the clergy-communicant privilege, maintains that DiLucente's presence during the Kampiches' and Shaw's conversation with Pastor Knoche undermines the confidentiality of this conversation for two reasons. The government contends, first, that any existing clergy-communicant privilege is inapplicable in this case because DiLucente was not related to the Kampiches and Shaw by either blood or marriage at the time the conversation took place. The government further contends that any privilege should be inapplicable because DiLucente's presence during the group discussion was neither essential to nor in furtherance of the purpose of the communication. In essence, the government claims that persons who are not related by blood or by marriage cannot, under federal law, engage together in protected communications with a member of the clergy acting in a spiritual or professional capacity.* * * We must therefore reach the issue whether the clergy-communicant privilege may apply to pastoral counseling sessions involving persons who have no family ties to one another.

* * * We discern nothing in modern clergy-communicant privilege doctrine, as it finds expression in either proposed Rule 506 or the cases recognizing

the privilege, that would limit the privilege's application solely to group discussions involving family members related by blood or marriage. Modern clergy-communicant privilege doctrine focuses, rather, on whether the presence of a third party is essential to or in furtherance of a communication to a member of the clergy. We think, consistent with the general constructional rule that evidentiary privileges should be narrowly construed, that recognition of the clergy-communicant privilege in this circumstance depends upon whether the third party's presence is essential to *and* in furtherance of a communication to a member of the clergy. As is the case with consultations between attorneys and clients, the presence of multiple parties, unrelated by blood or marriage, during discussions with a member of the clergy may, but will not necessarily, defeat the condition that communications be made with a reasonable expectation of confidentiality in order for the privilege to attach.

At the district court's hearing on the privilege, the testimony concerning whether the Kampiches, Shaw, and DiLucente reasonably expected that their communications to Pastor Knoche were confidential was sparse. * * * The district court neither inquired into whether the presence of each person at the discussion was essential to and in furtherance of the communications to the pastor nor made findings of fact on that issue.

Although the district court was correct in recognizing the existence of a clergy-communicant privilege, we are unable to affirm its order denying the government's motion to compel Pastor Knoche's testimony. That is because, given the contours of the privilege as we have defined it, the court did not develop a sufficient record or make sufficient findings to enable us finally to review its order. In fairness to the district court, we note that the court did not, at the time of its decision, have the benefit of the standards that we announce today. We must nevertheless remand the case for further proceedings.

It is difficult to anticipate the precise anatomy of the proceedings on remand. It is clear that the district court must develop a record and make findings, consistent with the prerequisites for the privilege that we have enumerated, concerning whether the Kampiches, Shaw, and DiLucente communicated with Pastor Knoche in his spiritual or professional capacity and with a reasonable expectation of confidentiality. * * * The three basic inquiries accompanying our three prerequisites for the application of the clergy-communicant privilege, applied in the more complex context of family counseling presented by this case, potentially devolve into a number of further possible inquiries. In order to determine whether the Kampiches, Shaw, and DiLucente communicated with Pastor Knoche in his spiritual or professional capacity and with a reasonable expectation of confidentiality, for example, the district court may well have to inquire into the nature of the communicants' relationship as well as the pastoral counseling practices of the relevant synod of the Lutheran church. In order to decide, more particularly, whether members of this group reasonably expected that their communications to Pastor Knoche would be kept in confidence, the court may also find it necessary to inquire into whether the parties shared a commonality of interest at the time of the communication and, if so, in what respect. At all events, a fuller record must be developed as to DiLucente's role in the counseling session. In order to ascertain whether her presence worked to vitiate or to waive the privilege, the court will have to inquire into whether the other group members, who apparently are subjects of the grand jury investigation, reasonably required her presence at the counselling session, either in furtherance of their communications to the pastor or to protect their interests. We, of course, intimate no view on these matters.

Neither do we advance a view as to the precise procedures to be followed on remand. In its attempt to determine DiLucente's role in the group counseling session, however, the district court may feel it necessary to seek some degree of disclosure of what was discussed with the pastor. We have, in other situations in which a privilege was implicated, recommended the use of *in camera* hearings, accompanied by a variety of options with respect to the presence or absence of counsel and the parties. We note, however, that the determination whether to conduct an *in camera* proceeding, as well as the anatomy of any such proceeding, in this situation will necessitate consideration of delicate first amendment issues, lest the hearing itself result in evisceration of the privilege. The district court should explain its reason for the adoption of any particular procedure employed in evaluating the claim of privilege.

In sum, there are no hard and fast rules in this area. We are confident, however, that through carefully framed inquiries, the district court will be able to obtain sufficient information to determine whether the clergy-communicant privilege should apply in this case.

The order of the district court will be vacated and the case remanded to that court for further proceedings. In view of the possible early expiration of the statute of limitations, the mandate will issue forthwith.

NOTES

1. For a communication to a member of the clergy to be privileged, must the communication occur in the course of seeking spiritual or religious advice?

See United States v. Dube, 820 F.2d 886 (7th Cir. 1987), where the Court refused to protect a statement made by the defendant to a Reverend, where the defendant was seeking advice about his tax liability. The Court reasoned that "the taxpayer is not a penitent seeking spiritual relief from his sins, only a citizen seeking relief from his obligation to pay taxes."

2. Does the privilege for communications to clergy extend to protect communications with unordained religious leaders?

The Court in *Scott v. Hammock* recognized that "[e]lders and deacons in religious orders have been held to be clergymen for the purposes of the privilege. * * * The standard is whether, under the doctrines of the church, the official to whom a communication is made is expected to accept and keep confidential communication from members of the church." 133 F.R.D. 610, 613 (D. Utah 1990).

F. NEWS REPORTER'S PRIVILEGE

McKEVITT v. PALLASCH
339 F.3d 530 (7th Cir. 2003)

POSNER, CIRCUIT JUDGE:

Michael McKevitt is being prosecuted in Ireland for membership in a banned organization and directing terrorism. He asked the district court for an order pursuant to 28 U.S.C. § 1782 to produce tape recordings that he thinks will be useful to him in the cross-examination of David Rupert, who according to McKevitt's motion is the key witness for the prosecution. The district court obliged. Its order is directed against a group of journalists who have a contract to write Rupert's biography and who in the course of their research for the biography interviewed him; the tape recordings that they made of the interviews and are in their possession are the recordings sought in McKevitt's motion. The journalists appealed from the district court's order and asked us to stay it, which we refused to do, and the recordings were turned over to McKevitt. We now explain why we refused to issue the stay. Ordinarily the explaining could await the decision of the appeal, but not in this case, because the denial of the stay, and the resulting disclosure of the recordings to McKevitt, mooted the appeal. By the time an order could be obtained and executed against McKevitt commanding the return of the recordings, he would have memorialized the information contained in them and the information would inevitably become public at his trial. The appeal was not yet moot, however, when we denied the stay, and there is no irregularity in a court's explaining the ground of a decision after the decision itself has been made ending the case.

Section 1782(a) of the Judicial Code authorizes federal district courts to order the production of evidentiary materials for use in foreign legal proceedings, provided the materials are not privileged. The defendants claim that the tapes in question are protected from compelled disclosure by a federal common law reporter's privilege rooted in the First Amendment. *See* Fed. R. 501. Although the Supreme Court in *Branzburg v. Hayes*, 408 U.S. 665, 33 L. Ed. 2d 626, 92 S. Ct. 2646 (1972), declined to recognize such a privilege, Justice Powell, whose vote was essential to the 5-4 decision rejecting the claim of privilege, stated in a concurring opinion that such a claim should be decided on a case-by-case basis by balancing the freedom of the press against the obligation to assist in criminal proceedings. Since the dissenting Justices would have gone further than Justice Powell in recognition of the reporter's privilege, and preferred his position to that of the majority opinion (for they said that his "enigmatic concurring opinion gives some hope of a more flexible view in the future," *id.* at 725), maybe his opinion should be taken to state the view of the majority of the Justices—though this is uncertain, because Justice Powell purported to join Justice White's "majority" opinion.

A large number of cases conclude, rather surprisingly in light of *Branzburg*, that there is a reporter's privilege, though they do not agree on its scope. *See, e.g., In re Madden*, 151 F.3d 125, 128-29 (3d Cir. 1998); *United States v. Smith*, 135 F.3d 963, 971 (5th Cir. 1998); *Shoen v. Shoen*, 5 F.3d 1289, 1292-93 (9th

Cir. 1993); *In re Shain*, 978 F.2d 850, 852 (4th Cir. 1992); *United States v. LaRouche Campaign*, 841 F.2d 1176, 1181-82 (1st Cir. 1988); *von Bulow v. von Bulow*, 811 F.2d 136, 142 (2d Cir. 1987); *United States v. Caporale*, 806 F.2d 1487, 1504 (11th Cir. 1986). A few cases refuse to recognize the privilege, at least in cases, which *Branzburg* was but this case is not, that involve grand jury inquiries. *In re Grand Jury Proceedings*, 5 F.3d 397, 402-03 (9th Cir. 1993); *In re Grand Jury Proceedings,* 810 F.2d 580, 584-86 (6th Cir. 1987). Our court has not taken sides.

Some of the cases that recognize the privilege, such as *Madden*, essentially ignore *Branzburg*, see 151 F.3d at 128; some treat the "majority" opinion in *Branzburg* as actually just a plurality opinion, such as *Smith*, see 135 F.3d at 968-69; some audaciously declare that *Branzburg* actually created a reporter's privilege, such as *Shoen*, 5 F.3d at 1292, and *von Bulow v. von Bulow, supra*, 811 F.2d at 142. The approaches that these decisions take to the issue of privilege can certainly be questioned. *See In re Grand Jury Proceedings, supra*, 810 F.2d at 584-86. A more important point, however, is that the Constitution is not the only source of evidentiary privileges, as the Supreme Court noted in *Branzburg* with reference to the reporter's privilege itself. 408 U.S. at 689, 706. And while the cases we have cited do not cite other possible sources of the privilege besides the First Amendment and one of them, *LaRouche*, actually denies, though without explaining why, that there might be a federal common law privilege for journalists that was not based on the First Amendment, other cases do cut the reporter's privilege free from the First Amendment. *See United States v. Cuthbertson*, 630 F.2d 139, 146 n. 1 (2d Cir. 1980); *In re Grand Jury Proceedings, supra*, 810 F.2d at 586-88; cf. *Gonzales v. National Broadcasting Co.*, 194 F.3d 29, 36 n. 2 (2d Cir. 1999).

The federal interest in cooperating in the criminal proceedings of friendly foreign nations is obvious; and it is likewise obvious that the news-gathering and reporting activities of the press are inhibited when a reporter cannot assure a confidential source of confidentiality. Yet that was *Branzburg* and it is evident from the result in that case that the interest of the press in maintaining the confidentiality of sources is not absolute. There is no conceivable interest in confidentiality in the present case. Not only is the source (Rupert) known, but he has indicated that he does not object to the disclosure of the tapes of his interviews to McKevitt.

Some cases that recognize a reporter's privilege suggest that it can sometimes shield information in a reporter's possession that comes from a nonconfidential source; in addition to the *Madden, Schoen*, and *La Rouche* cases cited above see *Gonzales v. National Broadcasting Co., supra*, 194 F.3d at 33. Others disagree. *United States v. Smith, supra*, 135 F.3d at 972; *In re Grand Jury Proceedings, supra*, 810 F.2d at 584-85. The cases that extend the privilege to nonconfidential sources express concern with harassment, burden, using the press as an investigative arm of government, and so forth. Since these considerations were rejected by *Branzburg* even in the context of a confidential source, these courts may be skating on thin ice.

Illinois has enacted a statutory version of the reporter's privilege. 735 I.L.C.S. 5/8-901. But it has no application to this case. Section 1782(a) of the Judicial Code provides that "a person may not be compelled to give his testimony or statement or to produce a document or other thing in violation of any legally applicable privilege." State-law privileges are not "legally applicable" in federal-question cases like this one. Fed. R. Evid. 501; *Patterson v. Caterpillar, Inc.*, 70 F.3d 503, 506 (7th Cir. 1995). In any event, while the reporters' motion included a citation to the Illinois statute as part of a string cite, it failed to discuss, even minimally, why the statute should apply here. As a result, even if the statute were applicable, the reporters waived reliance on it.

It seems to us that rather than speaking of privilege, courts should simply make sure that a subpoena duces tecum directed to the media, like any other subpoena duces tecum, is reasonable in the circumstances, which is the general criterion for judicial review of subpoenas. Fed. R. Crim. P. 17(c); *CSC Holdings, Inc. v. Redisi*, 309 F.3d 988, 993 (7th Cir. 2002); *EEOC v. Sidley Austin Brown & Wood*, 315 F.3d 696, 700 (7th Cir. 2002). We do not see why there need to be special criteria merely because the possessor of the documents or other evidence sought is a journalist. The approach we are suggesting has support in *Branzburg* itself, where the Court stated that "grand jury investigations if instituted or conducted other than in good faith, would pose wholly different issues for resolution under the First Amendment. Official harassment of the press undertaken not for purposes of law enforcement but to disrupt a reporter's relationship with his news sources would have no justification. Grand juries are subject to judicial control and subpoenas to motions to quash. We do not expect courts will forget that grand juries must operate within the limits of the First Amendment as well as the Fifth." 408 U.S. at 707-08.

When the information in the reporter's possession does not come from a confidential source, it is difficult to see what possible bearing the First Amendment could have on the question of compelled disclosure. If anything, the parties to this case are reversed from the perspective of freedom of the press, which seeks to encourage publication rather than secrecy. Rupert wants the information disclosed; it is the reporters, paradoxically, who want it secreted. The reason they want it secreted is that the biography of him that they are planning to write will be less marketable the more information in it that has already been made public.

In other words, the reporters are concerned about McKevitt's "appropriating" their intellectual property in the tape recordings and by doing so reducing the value of that property. Disputes over intellectual property, as the Supreme Court just reminded us, are not profitably conducted in the idiom of the First Amendment. *Eldred v. Ashcroft*, 537 U.S. 186 (2003). They are the subject of specialized bodies of law regulating intellectual property, such as copyright law or, of particular relevance here, the common law of misappropriation * * *.

* * * McKevitt has no commercial motive in "stealing" the defendant reporters' work product. * * * No showing has been made, or would be plausible, that the reporters will have to abandon the Rupert biography if the information contained in the recordings of their interviews with him is made public. It is a consideration that a district court might properly consider in deciding on a challenge to a subpoena, but it would add nothing to the court's

consideration to analyze it in legal categories drawn from the First Amendment. And in this case it provides no support for the reporters' claim.

The district judge's grant of the order to produce the tape recordings for use in the Irish trial was clearly sound, and so the stay of the order was properly denied. The appeal is dismissed as moot.

IN RE: GRAND JURY SUBPOENA, JUDITH MILLER
397 F.3d 964 (D.C. Cir. 2006)

SENTELLE, CIRCUIT JUDGE.

An investigative reporter for the New York Times; the White House correspondent for the weekly news magazine Time; and Time, Inc., the publisher of Time, appeal from orders of the District Court for the District of Columbia finding all three appellants in civil contempt for refusing to give evidence in response to grand jury subpoenas served by Special Counsel Patrick J. Fitzgerald. Appellants assert that the information concealed by them, specifically the identity of confidential sources, is protected by a reporter's privilege arising from the First Amendment, or failing that, by federal common law privilege. The District Court held that neither the First Amendment nor the federal common law provides protection for journalists' confidential sources in the context of a grand jury investigation. For the reasons set forth below, we agree with the District Court that there is no First Amendment privilege protecting the evidence sought. We further conclude that if any such common law privilege exists, it is not absolute, and in this case has been overcome by the filings of the Special Counsel with the District Court. We further conclude that other assignments of error raised by appellants are without merit. We therefore affirm the decision of the District Court.

I. Background

According to the briefs and record before us, the controversy giving rise to this litigation began with a political and news media controversy over a sixteen-word sentence in the State of the Union Address of President George W. Bush on January 28, 2003. In that address, President Bush stated: "The British government has learned that Saddam Hussein recently sought significant quantities of uranium from Africa." The ensuing public controversy focused not on the British source of the alleged information, but rather on the accuracy of the proposition that Saddam Hussein had sought uranium, a key ingredient in the development of nuclear weaponry, from Africa. Many publications on the subject followed. On July 6, 2003, the New York Times published an op-ed piece by former Ambassador Joseph Wilson, in which he claimed to have been sent to Niger in 2002 by the Central Intelligence Agency ("CIA") in response to inquiries from Vice President Cheney to investigate whether Iraq had been seeking to purchase uranium from Niger. Wilson claimed that he had conducted the requested investigation and reported on his return that there was no credible evidence that any such effort had been made.

On July 14, 2003, columnist Robert Novak published a column in the Chicago Sun-Times in which he asserted that the decision to send Wilson to

Niger had been made "routinely without Director George Tenet's knowledge," and, most significant to the present litigation, that "two senior administration officials" told him that Wilson's selection was at the suggestion of Wilson's wife, Valerie Plame, whom Novak described as a CIA "operative on weapons of mass destruction." Robert Novak, *The Mission to Niger*, Chi. Sun-Times, July 14, 2003, *at* 31. After Novak's column was published, various media accounts reported that other reporters had been told by government officials that Wilson's wife worked at the CIA monitoring weapons of mass destruction, and that she was involved in her husband's selection for the mission to Niger. One such article, published by Time.com on July 17, 2003, was authored in part by appellant Matthew Cooper. That article stated that:

> Some government officials have noted to Time in interviews * * * that Wilson's wife, Valerie Plame, is a CIA official who monitors the proliferation of weapons of mass destruction * * * [and] have suggested that she was involved in the husband's being dispatched to Niger to investigate reports that Saddam Hussein's government had sought to purchase large quantities of uranium ore * * * .

Other media accounts reported that "two top White House officials called at least six Washington journalists and disclosed the identity and occupation of Wilson's wife." Mike Allen & Dana Priest, *Bush Administration is Focus of Inquiry; CIA Agent's Identity was Leaked to Media*, WASH. POST, Sept. 28, 2003, at A1. The Department of Justice undertook an investigation into whether government employees had violated federal law by the unauthorized disclosure of the identity of a CIA agent. As the investigation proceeded, in December of 2003, the Attorney General recused himself from participation and delegated his full authority in the investigation to the Deputy Attorney General as Acting Attorney General. The Deputy, in turn, appointed Patrick J. Fitzgerald, United States Attorney for the Northern District of Illinois, as Special Counsel and delegated full authority concerning the investigation to him. As part of the ongoing investigation, a grand jury investigation began in January of 2004.

In cooperation with Special Counsel Fitzgerald, the grand jury conducted an extensive investigation. On May 21, 2004, a grand jury subpoena was issued to appellant Matthew Cooper, seeking testimony and documents related to two specific articles dated July 17, 2003, and July 21, 2003, to which Cooper had contributed. Cooper refused to comply with the subpoena, even after the Special Counsel offered to narrow its scope to cover only conversations between Cooper and a specific individual identified by the Special Counsel. Instead, Cooper moved to quash the subpoena on June 3, 2004. On July 6, 2004, the Chief Judge of the United States District Court for the District of Columbia denied Cooper's motion in open court, and confirmed the denial with reasoning set forth in a written order issued on July 20, 2004.

A further grand jury subpoena was issued to Time, Inc., seeking the same documents requested in the subpoena to Cooper. Time also moved to quash its subpoena. On August 6, 2004, the District Court denied Time's motion. Both Cooper and Time refused to comply with the subpoenas despite the District Court's denial of their motions to quash. The District Court thereafter found that Cooper and Time had refused to comply with the subpoenas without just cause and held them in civil contempt of court. After both Cooper and Time had filed appeals, and further negotiations between Special Counsel and the two had proceeded, Cooper agreed to provide testimony and documents relevant to a specific source who had stated that he had no objection to their release. Cooper and Time fulfilled their obligations under the agreement, the Special Counsel moved to vacate the District Court's contempt order, and the notices of appeal were voluntarily dismissed.

* * *

In the meantime, on August 12 and August 14, grand jury subpoenas were issued to Judith Miller, seeking documents and testimony related to conversations between her and a specified government official "occurring from on or about July 6, 2003, to on or about July 13, 2003, * * * concerning Valerie Plame Wilson (whether referred to by name or by description as the wife of Ambassador Wilson) or concerning Iraqi efforts to obtain uranium." Miller refused to comply with the subpoenas and moved to quash them. The District Court denied Miller's motion to quash. Thereafter, the court found that Miller had refused to comply without just cause and held her in civil contempt of court also. She also has appealed.

The appellants have proceeded with common counsel and common briefing in a consolidated proceeding before this court. * * * Finding no grounds for relief under the First Amendment, due process clause, or Department of Justice guidelines, and persuaded that any common law privilege that exists would be overcome in this case, we affirm the judgment of the District Court for the reasons set out more fully below.

II. Analysis

A. The First Amendment Claim

In his opinion below, the Chief District Judge held that "a reporter called to testify before a grand jury regarding confidential information enjoys no First Amendment protection.". Appellants argue that "this proposition of law is flatly contrary to the great weight of authority in this and other circuits." Appellants are wrong. The governing authority in this case, as the District Court correctly held, comes not from this or any other circuit, but the Supreme Court of the United States. In *Branzburg v. Hayes*, 408 U.S. 665 (1972), the Highest Court considered and rejected the same claim of First Amendment privilege on facts materially indistinguishable from those at bar.

Like the present case, *Branzburg* was a consolidated proceeding involving multiple contempt proceedings against news media defendants. The named petitioner, Branzburg, had been held in contempt in two related proceedings, arising from one extended task of investigative journalism. The first arose from an article published by his employer, a daily newspaper, describing his observation of two Kentucky residents synthesizing hashish from marijuana as part of a profitable illegal drug operation. The article included a photograph "of hands working above a laboratory table on * * * a substance identified

* * * as hashish." A Kentucky grand jury subpoenaed the journalist who "refused to identify the individuals he had seen possessing marihuana or the persons he had seen making hashish from marihuana." Branzburg claimed privilege both under the First Amendment of the United States Constitution and various state statutory and constitutional provisions. He was held in contempt and the proceeding eventually made its way to the Supreme Court.

The second case involving petitioner Branzburg arose out of a later article published by the same newspaper describing the use of drugs in Frankfort, Kentucky. According to the article, this publication was the product of two weeks spent interviewing drug users in the area. The article further reported that its author had seen some of his sources smoking marijuana. The article related numerous conversations with and observations of unnamed drug users. Branzburg was again subpoenaed to appear before a Kentucky grand jury "to testify in the matter of violation of statutes concerning use and sale of drugs," *id.* at 669 (internal quotation marks omitted). Branzburg moved to quash the subpoena. The motion was denied. The journalist sought the protection of the Kentucky Court of Appeals by way of mandamus and prohibition, claiming "that if he were forced to go before the grand jury or to answer questions regarding the identity of informants or disclose information given him in confidence, his effectiveness as a reporter would be greatly damaged." *Id.* at 670. The Kentucky courts rejected Branzburg's claim of a *First Amendment* privilege. Again, he petitioned for certiorari in the Supreme Court.

[Judge Sentelle describes the two other cases consolidated with Branzburg's petition.]

As can be seen from the account of the underlying facts in *Branzburg*, there is no material factual distinction between the petitions before the Supreme Court in *Branzburg* and the appeals before us today. Each of the reporters in *Branzburg* claimed to have received communications from sources in confidence, just as the journalists before us claimed to have done. At least one of the petitioners in *Branzburg* had witnessed the commission of crimes. On the record before us, there is at least sufficient allegation to warrant grand jury inquiry that one or both journalists received information concerning the identity of a covert operative of the United States from government employees acting in violation of the law by making the disclosure. Each petitioner in *Branzburg* and each journalist before us claimed or claims the protection of a First Amendment reporter's privilege. The Supreme Court in no uncertain terms rejected the existence of such a privilege. As we said at the outset of this discussion, the Supreme Court has already decided the First Amendment issue before us today.

In rejecting the claim of privilege, the Supreme Court made its reasoning transparent and forceful. The High Court recognized that "the grand jury's authority to subpoena witnesses is not only historic * * * but essential to its task." The grand juries and the courts operate under the "longstanding principle that 'the public has a right to every man's evidence,' except for those persons protected by constitutional, common law, or statutory privilege." The Court then noted that "the only testimonial privilege for unofficial witnesses that is rooted in the Federal Constitution is the *Fifth Amendment* privilege against compelled self-incrimination." The Court then expressly declined "to create another by interpreting the *First Amendment* to grant newsmen a testimonial privilege that other citizens do not enjoy." In language as relevant to the alleged illegal disclosure of the identity of covert agents as it was to the alleged illegal processing of hashish, the Court stated that it could not "seriously entertain the notion that the *First Amendment* protects a newsman's agreement to conceal the criminal conduct of his source, or evidence thereof, on the theory that it is better to write about a crime than to do something about it."

Lest there be any mistake as to the breadth of the rejection of the claimed First Amendment privilege, the High Court went on to recognize that "there remain those situations where a source is not engaged in criminal conduct but has information suggesting illegal conduct by others." As to this category of informants, the Court was equally adamant in rejecting the claim of First Amendment privilege:

> We cannot accept the argument that the public interest in possible future news about crime from undisclosed, unverified sources must take precedence over the public interest in pursuing and prosecuting those crimes reported to the press by informants and in thus deterring the commission of such crimes in the future.

* * *

We have pressed appellants for some distinction between the facts before the Supreme Court in *Branzburg* and those before us today. They have offered none, nor have we independently found any. Unquestionably, the Supreme Court decided in *Branzburg* that there is no First Amendment privilege protecting journalists from appearing before a grand jury or from testifying before a grand jury or otherwise providing evidence to a grand jury regardless of any confidence promised by the reporter to any source. The Highest Court has spoken and never revisited the question. Without doubt, that is the end of the matter.

* * *

B. The Common Law Privilege

Appellants argue that even if there is no First Amendment privilege protecting their confidential source information, we should recognize a privilege under federal common law, arguing that regardless of whether a federal common law privilege protecting reporters existed in 1972 when *Branzburg* was decided, in the intervening years much has changed. While appellants argue for an absolute privilege under the common law, they wisely recognize the possibility that a court not recognizing such an absolute privilege might nonetheless find a qualified privilege. They therefore also argue that if there is a qualified privilege, then the government has not overcome that qualified privilege. The Court is not of one mind on the existence of a common law privilege. Judge Sentelle would hold that there is no such common law privilege for reasons set forth in a separate opinion. Judge Tatel would hold that there is such a common law privilege. Judge Henderson believes that we need not, and therefore should not, reach that question. However, all believe that if there is any such privilege, it is not absolute and may be overcome by an appropriate showing. All further believe, for the reasons set forth in the separate opinion of Judge Tatel, that if such a privilege applies here, it has been overcome. Therefore, the common law privilege, even if one exists, does not warrant reversal.

* * *

We affirm the District Court's ruling on the maintenance of the seal of grand jury secrecy.

* * *

III. Conclusion

For the reasons set forth above, the judgment of the District Court is affirmed.

SENTELLE, CIRCUIT JUDGE, concurring.

* * * I write separately to express my differing basis for affirming the District Court on the common law privilege issue. I would hold that reporters refusing to testify before grand juries as to their "confidential sources" enjoy no common law privilege beyond the protection against harassing grand juries conducting groundless investigations that is available to all other citizens. While I understand, and do not actually disagree with, the conclusion of my colleagues that any such privilege enjoyed by the reporters has been overcome by the showing of the United States, and that we therefore need not determine whether such privilege exists, I find this ordering of issues a bit disturbing. To me, the question of the existence of such privilege *vel non* is logically anterior to the quantum of proof necessary to overcome it. * * * That said, I fully join the conclusion that we should affirm the District Court's decision to hold the appellants in contempt, unswayed by their claim of protection of common law privilege. I write separately only to explain my reasons for rejecting the theory that such a privilege is known to the common law.

I base my rejection of the common law privilege theory on foundations of precedent, policy, and separation of powers. As to precedent, I find *Branzburg v. Hayes*, 408 U.S. 665 (1972), to be as dispositive of the question of common law privilege as it is of a First Amendment privilege. While *Branzburg* generally is cited for its constitutional implications, the *Branzburg* Court repeatedly discussed the privilege question in common law terms as well as constitutional. Indeed, the majority opinion by Justice White includes the phrase "common law" no fewer than eight times. More significant than the fact that the Court frequently spoke of the common law is what the Court had to say about it: "at common law, courts consistently refuse to recognize the existence of any privilege authorizing a newsman to refuse to reveal confidential information to a grand jury."

* * *

Even if appellants are correct that we would have the power to adopt such a privilege in the face of the *Branzburg* precedent, I nonetheless would not accept that invitation. * * *

* * * I think it remains the prerogative of the Supreme Court rather than inferior federal tribunals to determine whether these changes are sufficient to warrant an overruling of the Court's rejection of such a common law privilege in *Branzburg*.

Furthermore, even if we are authorized to make that decision, reasons of policy and separation of powers counsel against our exercising that authority. While I concede that the adoption of the "shield" by legislation rather than judicial fiat does not prevent the change being considered by the courts in assessing the common law, I find the adoption of the privilege by the legislatures of the states instructive as to how the federal government should proceed, if at all, to adopt the privilege. The statutes differ greatly as to the scope of the privilege, and as to the identity of persons entitled to the protection of the privilege. We have alluded in the majority opinion to the differing decisions of courts as to civil, criminal, and grand jury proceedings. There is also a more fundamental policy question involved in the crafting of such a privilege. * * * Are we * * * to create a privilege that protects only those reporters employed by Time Magazine, the New York Times, and other media giants, or do we extend that protection as well to the owner of a desktop printer producing a weekly newsletter to inform his neighbors, lodge brothers, co-religionists, or co-conspirators? Perhaps more to the point today, does the privilege also protect the proprietor of a web log: the stereotypical "blogger" sitting in his pajamas at his personal computer posting on the World Wide Web his best product to inform whoever happens to browse his way? If not, why not? How could one draw a distinction consistent with the court's vision of a broadly granted personal right? If so, then would it not be possible for a government official wishing to engage in the sort of unlawful leaking under investigation in the present controversy to call a trusted friend or a political ally, advise him to set up a web log (which I understand takes about three minutes) and then leak to him under a promise of confidentiality the information which the law forbids the official to disclose?

* * *

Nor does the identity of the protected persons constitute the only difficult policy decision. *Branzburg* enumerates several concerns. For example, does "the public interest and possible future news about crime from undisclosed, unverified sources * * * take precedence over the public interest in pursuing and prosecuting those crimes reported to the press by informants and in thus deterring the commission of such crimes in the future"? Do "agreements to conceal information relevant to the commission of crime avail little to recommend them from the standpoint of public policy"? What are we to do with the historic common law recognition of "a duty to raise the 'hue and cry' and report felonies to the authorities"? Should we be creating immunity from prosecution for "misprision" of a felony—that is, the concealment of a felony?

Should the privilege be absolute or limited? If limited, how limited? Without attempting to catalog, I note that the state statutes provide a variety of answers to that policy question. Therefore, if such a decision requires the resolution of so many difficult policy questions, many of them beyond the normal compass of a single case or controversy such as those with which the courts regularly deal, doesn't that decision smack of legislation more than adjudication? Here, I think the experience of the states is most instructive. The creation of a reporter's privilege, if it is to be done at all, looks more like a legislative than an adjudicative decision. I suggest that the media as a whole, or at least those elements of the media concerned about this privilege, would better address those concerns to the Article I legislative branch for presentment to the Article II executive than to the Article III courts.

For all the reasons set forth above, I would hold that there is no common law privilege protecting reporters or any other news media personnel, no matter how defined, from the reach of grand jury subpoenas on claim of confidentiality.

HENDERSON, CIRCUIT JUDGE, concurring.

* * * I cannot agree with Judge Sentelle's conclusion that the United States Supreme Court has answered the question we now avoid. *Branzburg v. Hayes* addressed only "whether requiring newsmen to appear and testify before state or federal grand juries abridges the freedom of speech and press guaranteed by the *First Amendment*" and "held that *it*does not." 408 U.S. 665, 667 (1972) (emphases added). The boundaries of constitutional law and common law do not necessarily coincide, however, and while we are unquestionably bound by *Branzburg*'s rejection of a reporter's privilege rooted in the First Amendment, we are not bound by *Branzburg*'s commentary on the state of the common law in 1972. Federal Rule of Evidence 501, which came into being nearly three years after *Branzburg*, authorizes federal courts to develop testimonial privileges "in the light of reason and experience," allowing for the often evolving state of the common law. * * *

At the same time, I am far less eager a federal common-law pioneer than Judge Tatel as I find less comfort than he in riding *Jaffee v. Redmond*, 518 U.S. 1 (1996), into the testimonial privilege frontier. Just as Rule 501 imposes no "freeze" on the development of the common law it likewise does not authorize federal courts to mint testimonial privileges for any group—including the "journalistic class" that demands one. * * *

Because *Jaffee* sits rather awkwardly within a jurisprudence marked by a fairly uniform disinclination to announce new privileges or even expand existing ones, and even though it enjoyed the support of an overwhelming majority, I am hesitant to apply its methodology to a case that does not require us to do so. * * *

* * *

TATEL, CIRCUIT JUDGE, concurring in the judgment.

This case involves a clash between two truth-seeking institutions: the grand jury and the press. * * *

Because I agree that the balance in this case, which involves the alleged exposure of a covert agent, favors compelling the reporters' testimony, I join the judgment of the court. I write separately, however, because I find *Branzburg v. Hayes*, 408 U.S. 665 (1972), more ambiguous than do my colleagues and because I believe that the consensus of forty-nine states plus the District of Columbia—and even the Department of Justice—would require us to protect reporters' sources as a matter of federal common law were the leak at issue either less harmful or more newsworthy.

I.

Although I join the court's rejection of appellants' First Amendment argument, I am uncertain that *Branzburg* offers "no support" for a constitutional reporter privilege in the grand jury context. * * *

In this case, however, our hands are tied for two independent reasons. First, although this circuit has limited *Branzburg* in other contexts, with respect to criminal investigations we have twice construed that decision broadly. In *Reporters Committee for Freedom of the Press v. AT&T*, 593 F.2d 1030 (D.C. Cir. 1978), which addressed a First Amendment challenge regarding access to journalists' phone records and describing *Branzburg* as foreclosing "case-by-case consideration," we declared, "Good faith investigation interests *always* override a journalist's interest in protecting his source." *Id.* at 1049 (emphasis added). Echoing this broad view, we have also described *Branzburg* as "squarely rejecting" a claim to "general immunity, qualified or otherwise, from grand jury questioning." *See In re Possible Violations of 18 U.S.C. 371*, 564 F.2d 567, 571 (D.C. Cir. 1977). In this circuit, then, absent any indication of bad faith, I see no grounds for a First Amendment challenge to the subpoenas at issue here.

Second, although *Branzburg* involved militants and drug dealers rather than government leakers, the factual parallels between that case and this one preclude us from quashing the subpoenas on constitutional grounds. If, as *Branzburg* concludes, the First Amendment permits compulsion of reporters' testimony about individuals manufacturing drugs or plotting against the government, all information the government could have obtained from an undercover investigation of its own, the case for a constitutional privilege appears weak indeed with respect to leaks, which in all likelihood will be extremely difficult to prove without the reporter's aid. Thus, if *Branzburg* is to be limited or distinguished in the circumstances of this case, we must leave that task to the Supreme Court.

II.

But *Branzburg* is not the end of the story. In 1975 — three years after *Branzburg* — Congress enacted Rule 501 of the Federal Rules of Evidence, authorizing federal courts to develop evidentiary privileges in federal question cases according to "the principles of the common law as they may be interpreted * * * in the light of reason and experience." * * * Rule 501's delegation of congressional authority requires that we look anew at the "necessity and desirability" of the reporter privilege — though from a common law perspective.

* * *

In this case, just as *Jaffee v. Redmond* recognized a common law psychotherapist privilege based on "the uniform judgment of the States," 518 U.S. at 14, I believe that "reason and experience" dictate a privilege for reporters' confidential sources — albeit a qualified one. Guided by *Jaffee*'s reasoning, I reach this conclusion by considering first whether "reason and experience" justify recognizing a privilege at all, and if so whether the privilege should be qualified or absolute and whether it should cover the communications at issue in this case.

* * *

Existence of the Privilege

Under *Jaffee*, the common law analysis starts with the interests that call for recognizing a privilege. If, as the Supreme Court held there, "the mental health of our citizenry is a public good of transcendent importance," one that trumps the "fundamental maxim that the public has a right to every man's evidence," then surely press freedom is no less important, given journalism's vital role in our democracy. * * *

* * * If litigants and investigators could easily discover journalists' sources, the press's truth-seeking function would be severely impaired. Reporters could reprint government statements, but not ferret out underlying disagreements among officials; they could cover public governmental actions, but would have great difficulty getting potential whistleblowers to talk about government misdeeds; they could report arrest statistics, but not garner first-hand information about the criminal underworld. * * *

* * * [A]lthough suppression of some leaks is surely desirable (a point to which I shall return), the public harm that would flow from undermining all source relationships would be immense. For example, appellant Judith Miller tells us that her Pulitzer Prize-winning articles on Osama bin Laden's terrorist network relied on "information received from confidential sources at the highest levels of our government." * * * Insofar as such stories exemplify the press's role as a constitutionally chosen means for keeping officials elected by the people responsible to all the people whom they were elected to serve, "reason and experience" support protecting newsgathering methods crucial to their genesis. * * *

* * * Citing the "symbiotic relationships between journalists and public officials," the special counsel presumes that leaks will go on with or without the privilege * * * but the available evidence suggests the special counsel is wrong. As anyone with even a passing interest in news knows, reporters routinely rely on sources speaking on condition of anonymity — a strong indication that leakers demand such protection. Besides, for all the reasons that lead me to conclude that a privilege exists, reporters and their editors, attorneys, and sources probably believe the same, making it speculative

indeed for the special counsel to suppose that dashing that expectation of confidentiality would have no effect on newsgathering.

Turning next, as did *Jaffee*, to the consensus among states, I find support for the privilege at least as strong for journalists as for psychotherapists. Just as in *Jaffee*, where "the fact that all 50 states and the District of Columbia have enacted into law some form of psychotherapist privilege" favored an exercise of federal common lawmaking, so here undisputed evidence that forty-nine states plus the District of Columbia offer at least qualified protection to reporters' sources confirms that "reason and experience" support recognition of the privilege * * *.

Making the case for a privilege here even stronger than in *Jaffee*, federal authorities also favor recognizing a privilege for reporters' confidential sources. * * *

* * *

For much the same reason, the omission of a reporter privilege from the Judicial Conference Advisory Committee's draft rules submitted to Congress in 1972 (and ultimately replaced by *Rule 501*) need not dictate the outcome here. * * * [T]he dramatic growth in support for the reporter privilege supercedes the Advisory Committee's decades-old choice to omit the privilege from its draft.

* * *

Scope of the Privilege

The next step, according to *Jaffee*, is to determine what principles govern the privilege's application in this case. * * * Although the public interest in law enforcement may well be at its apex when the government is investigating crime, news stories of paramount First Amendment importance, such as reports about government corruption or wrongdoing, may involve sources who would surely be chilled if they thought grand juries could discover their identities from reporters in whom they confide. Furthermore, the special counsel's proposal is quite anomalous, considering that neither the attorney-client, nor the spousal, nor even the psychotherapist privilege gives way to the grand jury's truth-seeking function. * * *

As to the scope of the privilege, however, I agree with the special counsel that protection for source identities cannot be absolute. Leaks similar to the crime suspected here (exposure of a covert agent) apparently caused the deaths of several CIA operatives in the late 1970s and early 1980s, including the agency's Athens station chief. *See Haig v. Agee,* 453 U.S. 280, 284-85 (1981). Other leaks—the design for a top secret nuclear weapon, for example, or plans for an imminent military strike—could be even more damaging, causing harm far in excess of their news value. In such cases, the reporter privilege must give way. Just as attorney-client communications "made for the purpose of getting advice for the commission of a fraud or crime" serve no public interest and receive no privilege, *see United States v. Zolin*, 491 U.S.

554, 563 (1989), neither should courts protect sources whose leaks harm national security while providing minimal benefit to public debate.

Of course, in some cases a leak's value may far exceed its harm, thus calling into question the law enforcement rationale for disrupting reporter-source relationships. For example, assuming Miller's prize-winning Osama bin Laden series caused no significant harm, I find it difficult to see how one could justify compelling her to disclose her sources, given the obvious benefit of alerting the public to then-underappreciated threats from al Qaeda. News reports about a recent budget controversy regarding a super-secret satellite program inspire another example (though I know nothing about the dispute's details and express no view as to its merits). *See, e.g.*, Dan Eggen & Walter Pincus, *Justice Reviews Request for Probe of Satellite Reports*, Wash. Post, Dec. 16, 2004, at A3; Douglas Jehl, *New Spy Plan Said to Involve Satellite System*, N.Y. Times, Dec. 12, 2004, at A1. Despite the necessary secrecy of intelligence-gathering methods, it seems hard to imagine how the harm in leaking generic descriptions of such a program could outweigh the benefit of informing the public about billions of dollars wasted on technology considered duplicative and unnecessary by leading Senators from both parties. In contrast to the nuclear weapon and military strike examples mentioned above, cases like these appear to involve a balance of harm and news value that strongly favors protecting newsgathering methods.

Given these contrasting examples, much as our civil cases balance the public interest in protecting the reporter's sources against the private interest in compelling disclosure, so must the reporter privilege account for the varying interests at stake in different source relationships. In other words, to quote the Justice Department subpoena guidelines, "the approach in every case must be to strike the proper balance between the public's interest in the free dissemination of ideas and information and the public's interest in effective law enforcement and the fair administration of justice." 28 C.F.R. § 50.10(a).

* * *

* * * [A]ppellants insist that a qualified privilege fails to provide the certainty their work requires because sources are unlikely to disclose information without an advance guarantee of secrecy. In particular, they argue that journalists cannot balance a leak's harm against its news value until they know what information the source will reveal, by which time it is too late to prevent disclosure. True enough, but journalists are not the ones who must perform the balancing; sources are. Indeed, the point of the qualified privilege is to create disincentives for the source—disincentives that not only promote the public interest, but may also protect journalists from exploitation by government officials seeking publication of damaging secrets for partisan advantage. Like other recipients of potentially privileged communications—say, attorneys or psychotherapists—the reporter can at most alert the source to the limits of confidentiality, leaving the judgment of what to say to the source. While the resulting deterrent effect may cost the press some leads, little harm will result, for if the disincentives work as they should, the information sources refrain from revealing will lack significant news value in the first place.

* * *

In short, the question in this case is whether Miller's and Cooper's sources released information more harmful than newsworthy. If so, then the public interest in punishing the wrongdoers—and deterring future leaks—outweighs any burden on newsgathering, and no privilege covers the communication (provided, of course, that the special counsel demonstrates necessity and exhaustion of alternative evidentiary sources).

III.

Applying this standard to the facts of this case, and considering first only the public record, I have no doubt that the leak at issue was a serious matter. * * *

An alleged covert agent, Plame evidently traveled overseas on clandestine missions beginning nearly two decades ago. Her exposure, therefore, not only may have jeopardized any covert activities of her own, but also may have endangered friends and associates from whom she might have gathered information in the past. * * *

The leak of Plame's apparent employment, moreover, had marginal news value. To be sure, insofar as Plame's CIA relationship may have helped explain her husband's selection for the Niger trip, that information could bear on her husband's credibility and thus contribute to public debate over the president's "sixteen words." Compared to the damage of undermining covert intelligence-gathering, however, this slight news value cannot, in my view, justify privileging the leaker's identity.

* * *

In sum, based on an exhaustive investigation, the special counsel has established the need for Miller's and Cooper's testimony. Thus, considering the gravity of the suspected crime and the low value of the leaked information, no privilege bars the subpoenas.

* * *

G. INFORMANT'S PRIVILEGE

McCRAY v. ILLINOIS
386 U.S. 300 (1967)

MR. JUSTICE STEWART delivered the opinion of the Court.

The petitioner was arrested in Chicago, Illinois, on the morning of January 16, 1964, for possession of narcotics. The Chicago police officers who made the arrest found a package containing heroin on his person and he was indicted for its unlawful possession. Prior to trial he filed a motion to suppress the heroin as evidence against him, claiming that the police had acquired it in an unlawful search and seizure in violation of the Fourth and Fourteenth Amendments. * * * After a hearing, the court denied the motion, and the petitioner was subsequently convicted upon the evidence of the heroin the arresting officers had found in his possession. The judgment of conviction was affirmed by the Supreme Court of Illinois, and we granted certiorari to consider the petitioner's claim that the hearing on his motion to suppress was constitutionally defective.

The petitioner's arrest occurred near the intersection of 49th Street and Calumet Avenue at about seven in the morning. At the hearing on the motion to suppress, he testified that up until a half hour before he was arrested he had been at "a friend's house" about a block away, that after leaving the friend's house he had "walked with a lady from 48th to 48th and South Park," and that, as he approached 49th Street and Calumet Avenue, "[t]he Officers stopped me going through the alley." "The officers," he said, "did not show me a search warrant for my person or an arrest warrant for my arrest." He said the officers then searched him and found the narcotics in question. The petitioner did not identify the "friend" or the "lady," and neither of them appeared as a witness.

The arresting officers then testified. Officer Jackson stated that he and two fellow officers had had a conversation with an informant on the morning of January 16 in their unmarked police car. The officer said that the informant had told them that the petitioner, with whom Jackson was acquainted, "was selling narcotics and had narcotics on his person and that he could be found in the vicinity of 47th and Calumet at this particular time." Jackson said that he and his fellow officers drove to that vicinity in the police car and that when they spotted the petitioner, the informant pointed him out and then departed on foot. Jackson stated that the officers observed the petitioner walking with a woman, then separating from her and meeting briefly with a man, then proceeding alone, and finally, after seeing the police car, "hurriedly walk[ing] between two buildings." "At this point," Jackson testified, "my partner and myself got out of the car and informed him we had information he had narcotics on his person, placed him in the police vehicle at this point." Jackson stated that the officers then searched the petitioner and found the heroin in a cigarette package.

Jackson testified that he had been acquainted with the informant for approximately a year, that during this period the informant had supplied him with information about narcotics activities "fifteen, sixteen times at least," that the information had proved to be accurate and had resulted in numerous arrests and convictions. On cross-examination, Jackson was even more specific as to the informant's previous reliability, giving the names of people who had been convicted of narcotics violations as the result of information the informant had supplied. When Jackson was asked for the informant's name and address, counsel for the State objected, and the objection was sustained by the court.

* * *

It is the petitioner's claim that even though the officers' sworn testimony fully supported a finding of probable cause for the arrest and search, the state court nonetheless violated the Constitution when it sustained objections to the petitioner's questions as to the identity of the informant. We cannot agree.

In permitting the officers to withhold the informant's identity, the court was following well-settled Illinois law. When the issue is not guilt or innocence, but, as here, the question of probable cause for an arrest or search, the Illinois Supreme Court has held that police officers need not invariably be required to disclose an informant's identity if the trial judge is convinced, by evidence submitted in open court and subject to cross-examination, that the officers did rely in good faith upon credible information supplied by a reliable informant. * * *

The reasoning of the Supreme Court of New Jersey in judicially adopting the same basic evidentiary rule was instructively expressed by Chief Justice Weintraub in *State v. Burnett*, 42 N.J. 377, 201 A.2d 39:

> If a defendant may insist upon disclosure of the informant in order to test the truth of the officer's statement that there is an informant or as to what the informant related or as to the informant's reliability, we can be sure that every defendant will demand disclosure. He has nothing to lose and the prize may be the suppression of damaging evidence if the State cannot afford to reveal its source, as is so often the case. And since there is no way to test the good faith of a defendant who presses the demand, we must assume the routine demand would have to be routinely granted. The result would be that the State could use the informant's information only as a lead and could search only if it could gather adequate evidence of probable cause apart from the informant's data. Perhaps that approach would sharpen investigatorial techniques, but we doubt that there would be enough talent and time to cope with crime upon that basis. Rather we accept the premise that the informer is a vital part of society's defensive arsenal. The basic rule protecting his identity rests upon that belief.
>
> * * *
>
> We must remember also that we are not dealing with the trial of the criminal charge itself. There the need for a truthful verdict outweighs society's need for the informer privilege. Here, however, the accused seeks to avoid the truth. The very purpose of a motion to suppress is to escape the inculpatory thrust of evidence in hand, not because its probative force is diluted in the least by the mode of seizure, but rather as a sanction to compel enforcement officers to respect the constitutional security of all of us under the Fourth Amendment. * * * If the motion to suppress is denied, defendant will still be judged upon the untarnished truth.

* * *

What Illinois and her sister States have done is no more than recognize a well-established testimonial privilege, long familiar to the law of evidence. * * *

In the exercise of this supervisory jurisdiction the Court had occasion 10 years ago, in *Roviaro v. United States*, 353 U.S. 53, to give thorough consideration to one aspect of the informer's privilege, the privilege itself having long been recognized in the federal judicial system.

The *Roviaro* case involved the informer's privilege, not at a preliminary hearing to determine probable cause for an arrest or search, but at the trial itself where the issue was the fundamental one of innocence or guilt. The petitioner there had been brought to trial upon a two-count federal indictment charging sale and transportation of narcotics. According to the prosecution's evidence, the informer had been an active participant in the crime. He "had taken a material part in bringing about the possession of certain drugs by the accused, had been present with the accused at the occurrence of the alleged crime, and might be a material witness as to whether the accused knowingly transported the drugs as charged." * * * The trial court nonetheless denied a defense motion to compel the prosecution to disclose the informer's identity.

This Court held that where, in an actual trial of a federal criminal case,

> the disclosure of an informer's identity * * * is relevant and helpful to the defense of an accused, or is essential to a fair determination of a cause, the privilege must give way. In these situations the trial court may require disclosure and, if the Government withholds the information, dismiss the action * * * .
>
> We believe that no fixed rule with respect to disclosure is justifiable. The problem is one that calls for balancing the public interest in protecting the flow of information against the individual's right to prepare his defense. Whether a proper balance renders nondisclosure erroneous must depend on the particular circumstances of each case, taking into consideration the crime charged, the possible defenses, the possible significance of the informer's testimony, and other relevant factors.

The Court's opinion then carefully reviewed the particular circumstances of Roviaro's trial, pointing out that the informer's "possible testimony was highly relevant * * * " that he "might have disclosed an entrapment * * * ," "might have thrown doubt upon petitioner's identity or on the identity of the package * * * ," "might have testified to petitioner's possible lack of knowledge of the contents of the package that he 'transported' * * * ," and that the "informer was the sole participant, other than the accused, in the transaction charged." The Court concluded "that, under these circumstances, the trial court committed prejudicial error in permitting the Government to withhold the identity of its undercover employee in the face of repeated demands by the accused for his disclosure."

What *Roviaro* thus makes clear is that this Court was unwilling to impose any absolute rule requiring disclosure of an informer's identity even in formulating evidentiary rules for federal criminal trials. Much less has the Court ever approached the formulation of a federal evidentiary rule of compulsory disclosure where the issue is the preliminary one of probable cause, and guilt or innocence is not at stake. * * *

In sum, the Court in the exercise of its power to formulate evidentiary rules for federal criminal cases has consistently declined to hold that an informer's identity need always be disclosed in a federal criminal trial, let alone in a preliminary hearing to determine probable cause for an arrest or search. * * *

The arresting officers in this case testified, in open court, fully and in precise detail as to what the informer told them and as to why they had reason to believe his information was trustworthy. Each officer was under oath. Each was subjected to searching cross-examination. The judge was obviously satisfied that each was telling the truth, and for that reason he exercised the discretion conferred upon him by the established law of Illinois to respect the informer's privilege.

* * *

Affirmed.

[Dissenting opinion omitted.]

* * *

NOTES

1. Does the informant's privilege apply in civil cases?

In *Westinghouse Electric Corp. v. City of Burlington, Vermont*, the Court decided that "the fact that the case is civil rather than criminal is not dispositive * * * . The policies behind the privilege and its exceptions extend to civil as well as criminal cases. Presumably most informers do not want their names to be revealed in either a civil or criminal proceeding. The fact that there would be a somewhat greater chance, statistically, of having their identity revealed if disclosure is required in civil cases would be unlikely to deter citizens from informing. There is no logical reason to set up two different privileges, one for civil and one for criminal cases. The defendant in a criminal case may have a greater stake than a party in a civil case, but that would not always be so: even admitting the probability of a greater risk of retaliation in a criminal case." 351 F.2d 762, 769 (D.C. Cir. 1965).

2. Who holds the informant's privilege?

In *Westinghouse Electric Corp. v. City of Burlington, Vermont*, the Court decided that "it would seem * * * that an informer can waive the privilege. Once he identifies himself as an informer the privilege disappears. It is difficult to see how the Government could prevent him from revealing himself, practically or theoretically, or why, as a matter of policy, it would want to do so. The [United States Supreme C]ourt [in *Roviaro v. United States*] notes that the 'informer's privilege is in reality the Government's privilege.' (quoting 353 U.S. 53, 59 (1957)). Whatever the reality referred to is, this statement can scarcely mean that only the Government can waive the privilege; we read it as meaning that the privilege exists for the benefit of the general public, not for the benefit of the particular informer involved." 351 F.2d 762, 768 (D.C. Cir. 1965).

3. Must the government show that the informant had an expectation of confidentiality?

In *United States Dep't of Justice v. Landano*, 508 U.S. 165 (1993), the Court held that the government has the burden of establishing that an informant reported information to law enforcement officials with the expectation that his or her identity would be kept anonymous. Without such an expectation of anonymity, the privilege will not apply. The Court recognized, however, that the expectation need not be one of total and permanent anonymity. Obviously, an informant should reasonably anticipate that his identity would be disclosed if the matter ever went to trial. The Court stated: "A source should be deemed confidential if the source furnished information with the understanding that the FBI would not divulge the communication except to the extent the Bureau thought necessary for law enforcement purposes."

The *Landano* Court held that the government was not entitled to a presumption that *all* informants who report to law enforcement do so with an expectation of confidentiality. The Court explained: "It may be true that many, or even most, individual sources will expect confidentiality. But the Government offers no explanation, other than ease of administration, why that expectation should always be presumed."

The Court noted, however, that "more narrowly defined circumstances" may justify a presumption of expectation of confidentiality. As an example, the Court stated that "when circumstances such as the nature of the crime investigated and the witness' relation to it support an inference of confidentiality, the Government is entitled to a presumption." *See, e.g., Mays v. DEA*, 234 F.3d 1324 (D.C. Cir. 2000) (report by informant concerning the defendant's distribution of cocaine was made under circumstances indicating an implied grant of confidentiality: "The pertinent question is whether the violence and risk of retaliation that attend this type of crime warrant an implied grant of confidentiality for such a source. They most assuredly do."). Of course, the privilege will apply if the government can demonstrate that the informer gave information on the express assurance that his identity would remain confidential until disclosure would become necessary at a criminal trial. *See, e.g., Manna v. United States Dep't of Justice*, 51 F.3d 1158 (3d Cir. 1995) ("If a district court determines that a source provided information under an express assurance of confidentiality or under circumstances from which an assurance of confidentiality can reasonably be inferred, then all information provided by the source is protected.").

H. EXECUTIVE PRIVILEGE

UNITED STATES v. NIXON
418 U.S. 683 (1974)

MR. CHIEF JUSTICE BURGER delivered the opinion of the Court.

This litigation presents for review the denial of a motion, filed in the District Court on behalf of the President of the United States, in the case of *United States v. Mitchell* to quash a third-party subpoena *duces tecum* issued by the

United States District Court for the District of Columbia, pursuant to Fed. Rule Crim. Proc. 17 (c). The subpoena directed the President to produce certain tape recordings and documents relating to his conversations with aides and advisers. The court rejected the President's claims of absolute executive privilege, of lack of jurisdiction, and of failure to satisfy the requirements of Rule 17 (c). The President appealed to the Court of Appeals. We granted both the United States' petition for certiorari before judgment, and also the President's cross-petition for certiorari before judgment, because of the public importance of the issues presented and the need for their prompt resolution.

On March 1, 1974, a grand jury of the United States District Court for the District of Columbia returned an indictment charging seven named individuals with various offenses, including conspiracy to defraud the United States and to obstruct justice. Although he was not designated as such in the indictment, the grand jury named the President, among others, as an unindicted coconspirator. On April 18, 1974, upon motion of the Special Prosecutor a subpoena *duces tecum* was issued pursuant to Rule 17 (c) to the President by the United States District Court and made returnable on May 2, 1974. This subpoena required the production, in advance of the September 9 trial date, of certain tapes, memoranda, papers, transcripts or other writings relating to certain precisely identified meetings between the President and others. The Special Prosecutor was able to fix the time, place, and persons present at these discussions because the White House daily logs and appointment records had been delivered to him. On April 30, the President publicly released edited transcripts of 43 conversations; portions of 20 conversations subject to subpoena in the present case were included. On May 1, 1974, the President's counsel, filed a "special appearance" and a motion to quash the subpoena under Rule 17 (c). This motion was accompanied by a formal claim of privilege. * * *

On May 20, 1974, the District Court denied the motion to quash and the motions to expunge and for protective orders. It further ordered "the President or any subordinate officer, official, or employee with custody or control of the documents or objects subpoenaed," to deliver to the District Court, on or before May 31, 1974, the originals of all subpoenaed items, as well as an index and analysis of those items, together with tape copies of those portions of the subpoenaed recordings for which transcripts had been released to the public by the President on April 30. * * *

The District Court held that the judiciary, not the President, was the final arbiter of a claim of executive privilege. The court concluded that under the circumstances of this case the presumptive privilege was overcome by the Special Prosecutor's prima facie "demonstration of need sufficiently compelling to warrant judicial examination in chambers * * * ." * * *

[The Supreme Court's discussion of jurisdiction, justiciability, and Fed. R. Crim. P. 17 (c) governing grand jury subpoenas is omitted.]

* * *

THE CLAIM OF PRIVILEGE

A

Having determined that the requirements of Rule 17 (c) were satisfied, we turn to the claim that the subpoena should be quashed because it demands "confidential conversations between a President and his close advisors that it would be inconsistent with the public interest to produce." The first contention is a broad claim that the separation of powers doctrine precludes judicial review of a President's claim of privilege. The second contention is that if he does not prevail on the claim of absolute privilege, the court should hold as a matter of constitutional law that the privilege prevails over the subpoena *duces tecum*.

In the performance of assigned constitutional duties each branch of the Government must initially interpret the Constitution, and the interpretation of its powers by any branch is due great respect from the others. The President's counsel, as we have noted, reads the Constitution as providing an absolute privilege of confidentiality for all Presidential communications. Many decisions of this Court, however, have unequivocally reaffirmed the holding of *Marbury v. Madison*, 1 Cranch, 137, 2 L.Ed. 60 (1803), that "[i]t is emphatically the province and duty of the judicial department to say what the law is."

* * *

Notwithstanding the deference each branch must accord the others, the "judicial Power of the United States" vested in the federal courts by Art. III, § 1, of the Constitution can no more be shared with the Executive Branch than the Chief Executive, for example, can share with the Judiciary the veto power, or the Congress share with the Judiciary the power to override a Presidential veto. Any other conclusion would be contrary to the basic concept of separation of powers and the checks and balances that flow from the scheme of a tripartite government. The Federalist, No. 47, p. 313 (S. Mittell ed. 1938). We therefore reaffirm that it is the province and duty of this Court "to say what the law is" with respect to the claim of privilege presented in this case. *Marbury v. Madison*, *supra*, 1 Cranch. at 177, 2 L.Ed. 60.

B

In support of his claim of absolute privilege, the President's counsel urges two grounds, one of which is common to all governments and one of which is peculiar to our system of separation of powers. The first ground is the valid need for protection of communications between high Government officials and those who advise and assist them in the performance of their manifold duties; the importance of this confidentiality is too plain to require further discussion. Human experience teaches that those who expect public dissemination of their remarks may well temper candor with a concern for appearances and for their own interests to the detriment of the decisionmaking process. * * *

The second ground asserted by the President's counsel in support of the claim of absolute privilege rests on the doctrine of separation of powers. Here it is argued that the independence of the Executive Branch within its own sphere, * * * insulates a President from a judicial subpoena in an ongoing criminal prosecution, and thereby protects confidential Presidential communications.

However, neither the doctrine of separation of powers, nor the need for confidentiality of high-level communications, without more, can sustain an absolute, unqualified Presidential privilege of immunity from judicial process under all circumstances. The President's need for complete candor and objectivity from advisers calls for great deference from the courts. However, when the privilege depends solely on the broad, undifferentiated claim of public interest in the confidentiality of such conversations, a confrontation with other values arises. Absent a claim of need to protect military, diplomatic, or sensitive national security secrets, we find it difficult to accept the argument that even the very important interest in confidentiality of Presidential communications is significantly diminished by production of such material for *in camera* inspection with all the protection that a district court will be obliged to provide. The impediment that an absolute, unqualified privilege would place in the way of the primary constitutional duty of the Judicial Branch to do justice in criminal prosecutions would plainly conflict with the function of the courts under Art. III. * * *

To read the Art. II powers of the President as providing an absolute privilege as against a subpoena essential to enforcement of criminal statutes on no more than a generalized claim of the public interest in confidentiality of nonmilitary and nondiplomatic discussions would upset the constitutional balance of "a workable government" and gravely impair the role of the courts under Art. III.

C

Since we conclude that the legitimate needs of the judicial process may outweigh Presidential privilege, it is necessary to resolve those competing interests in a manner that preserves the essential functions of each branch. The right and indeed the duty to resolve that question does not free the Judiciary from according high respect to the representations made on behalf of the President. *United States v. Burr*, 25 F.Cas. 187, 190, 191-192 (No. 14,694) (CCVa.1807).

The expectation of a President to the confidentiality of his conversations and correspondence, like the claim of confidentiality of judicial deliberations, for example, has all the values to which we accord deference for the privacy of all citizens and, added to those values, is the necessity for protection of the public interest in candid, objective, and even blunt or harsh opinions in Presidential decisionmaking. A President and those who assist him must be free to explore alternatives in the process of shaping policies and making decisions and to do so in a way many would be unwilling to express except privately. These are the considerations justifying a presumptive privilege for Presidential communications. The privilege is fundamental to the operation of Government and inextricably rooted in the separation of powers under the Constitution. * * *

But this presumptive privilege must be considered in light of our historic commitment to the rule of law. * * * The need to develop all relevant facts in the adversary system is both fundamental and comprehensive. The ends of criminal justice would be defeated if judgments were to be founded on a partial or speculative presentation of the facts. The very integrity of the judicial system and public confidence in the system depend on full disclosure of all the facts, within the framework of the rules of evidence. To ensure that justice is done, it is imperative to the function of courts that compulsory process be available for the production of evidence needed either by the prosecution or by the defense.

Only recently the Court restated the ancient proposition of law, albeit in the context of a grand jury inquiry rather than a trial, "that 'the public * * * has a right to every man's evidence,' except for those persons protected by a constitutional, common-law, or statutory privilege * * * ." *Branzburg v. Hayes*, 408 U.S. 665, 688 (1972). The privileges referred to by the Court are designed to protect weighty and legitimate competing interests. * * * Whatever their origins, these exceptions to the demand for every man's evidence are not lightly created nor expansively construed, for they are in derogation of the search for truth.

In this case the President challenges a subpoena served on him as a third party requiring the production of materials for use in a criminal prosecution; he does so on the claim that he has a privilege against disclosure of confidential communications. He does not place his claim of privilege on the ground they are military or diplomatic secrets. As to these areas of Art. II duties the courts have traditionally shown the utmost deference to Presidential responsibilities. In *C. & S. Air Lines v. Waterman S.S. Corp.*, 333 U.S. 103, 111 (1948), dealing with Presidential authority involving foreign policy considerations, the Court said:

> The President, both as Commander-in-Chief and as the Nation's organ for foreign affairs, has available intelligence services whose reports are not and ought not to be published to the world. It would be intolerable that courts, without the relevant information, should review and perhaps nullify actions of the Executive taken on information properly held secret.

* * *

No case of the Court, however, has extended this high degree of deference to a President's generalized interest in confidentiality. Nowhere in the Constitution, as we have noted earlier, is there any explicit reference to a privilege of confidentiality, yet to the extent this interest relates to the effective discharge of a President's powers, it is constitutionally based.

The right to the production of all evidence at a criminal trial similarly has constitutional dimensions. The Sixth Amendment explicitly confers upon every defendant in a criminal trial the right "to be confronted with the witnesses against him" and to have compulsory process for obtaining witnesses in his favor. Moreover, the Fifth Amendment also guarantees that no person shall be deprived of liberty without due process of law. It is the manifest duty of the courts to vindicate those guarantees, and to accomplish that it is essential that all relevant and admissible evidence be produced.

In this case we must weigh the importance of the general privilege of confidentiality of Presidential communications in performance of the President's responsibilities against the inroads of such a privilege on the fair administration of criminal justice. The interest in preserving confidentiality is weighty indeed and entitled to great respect. However, we cannot conclude that advisers will be moved to temper the candor of their remarks by the infrequent occasions of disclosure because of the possibility that such conversations will be called for in the context of a criminal prosecution.

On the other hand, the allowance of the privilege to withhold evidence that is demonstrably relevant in a criminal trial would cut deeply into the guarantee of due process of law and gravely impair the basic function of the courts. A President's acknowledged need for confidentiality in the communications of his office is general in nature, whereas the constitutional need for production of relevant evidence in a criminal proceeding is specific and central to the fair adjudication of a particular criminal case in the administration of justice. Without access to specific facts a criminal prosecution may be totally frustrated. The President's broad interest in confidentiality of communications will not be vitiated by disclosure of a limited number of conversations preliminarily shown to have some bearing on the pending criminal cases.

We conclude that when the ground for asserting privilege as to subpoenaed materials sought for use in a criminal trial is based only on the generalized interest in confidentiality, it cannot prevail over the fundamental demands of due process of law in the fair administration of criminal justice. The generalized assertion of privilege must yield to the demonstrated, specific need for evidence in a pending criminal trial.

D

We have earlier determined that the District Court did not err in authorizing the issuance of the subpoena. If a President concludes that compliance with a subpoena would be injurious to the public interest he may properly, as was done here, invoke a claim of privilege on the return of the subpoena. Upon receiving a claim of privilege from the Chief Executive, it became the further duty of the District Court to treat the subpoenaed material as presumptively privileged and to require the Special Prosecutor to demonstrate that the Presidential material was "essential to the justice of the [pending criminal] case." *United States v. Burr*, 25 Fed.Cas., at 192. Here the District Court treated the material as presumptively privileged, proceeded to find that the Special Prosecutor had made a sufficient showing to rebut the presumption, and ordered an *in camera* examination of the subpoenaed material. On the basis of our examination of the record we are unable to conclude that the District Court erred in ordering the inspection. Accordingly we affirm the order of the District Court that subpoenaed materials be transmitted to that court. We now turn to the important question of the District Court's responsibilities in conducting the *in camera* examination of Presidential materials or communications delivered under the compulsion of the subpoena *duces tecum*.

E

* * *

It is elementary that *in camera* inspection of evidence is always a procedure calling for scrupulous protection against any release or publication of material not found by the court, at that stage, probably admissible in evidence and relevant to the issues of the trial for which it is sought. That being true of an ordinary situation, it is obvious that the District Court has a very heavy responsibility to see to it that Presidential conversations, which are either not relevant or not admissible, are accorded that high degree of respect due the President of the United States. * * * It is therefore necessary in the public interest to afford Presidential confidentiality the greatest protection consistent with the fair administration of justice. The need for confidentiality even as to idle conversations with associates in which casual reference might be made concerning political leaders within the country or foreign statesmen is too obvious to call for further treatment. We have no doubt that the District Judge will at all times accord to Presidential records that high degree of deference suggested in *United States v. Burr, supra*, and will discharge his responsibility to see to it that until released to the Special Prosecutor no *in camera* material is revealed to anyone. This burden applies with even greater force to excised material; once the decision is made to excise, the material is restored to its privileged status and should be returned under seal to its lawful custodian.

* * *

Affirmed.

MR. JUSTICE REHNQUIST took no part in the consideration or decision of these cases.

NOTE

Is there a privilege for agency decisionmaking as well as for executive decisionmaking?

Federal common law recognizes a "deliberative process" privilege that protects certain communications within public agencies. This privilege protects the free flow of ideas, comments and expressions necessary for government agencies to make informed decisions. As the Supreme Court has stated, the "ultimate aim" of the privilege is to "prevent injury to the quality of agency decisions." *NLRB v. Sears, Roebuck & Co.*, 421 U.S. 132 (1975) (stating that the privilege shelters "documents reflecting advisory opinions, recommendations and deliberations comprising part of a process by which governmental decisions and policies are formulated"). The courts assume that confidentiality is required because government officials will be "chilled" if they know that their internal communications are subject to public disclosure. The fear is that officials may pull punches, and this will hurt the quality of advice that they give to their superiors. Of course, there is a powerful contrary argument that a government official has every incentive to report fully and accurately to a senior official, privilege or no privilege. But this argument has fallen on deaf ears. A secondary argument in support of the deliberative process privilege is that it "protects the integrity of the decision-making process itself by confirming that officials would be judged by what they decided, not for matters they considered before making up their minds." *Jordan v. Department of Justice*, 591 F.2d 753, 772-73 (D.C. Cir. 1978). The concern is that the integrity of the government official's final decision — which is public — would be undermined if the public finds out about the way in which the decision was reached. This assumes, of course, that the final decision of a government actor is treated with respect and not suspicion in the first place — a dubious proposition these days.

Despite its arguably questionable basis, the courts have vigorously applied the deliberative process privilege to protect hundreds of pieces of governmental information. Some examples include: an intra-agency memorandum proposing underground storage of nuclear arms, *EPA v. Mink*, 410 U.S. 73 (1973); personal notes and evaluations used in preparing an EEOC report; *Scott v. PPG Industries, Inc.*, 142 F.R.D. 291 (N.D. W.Va. 1992); and a report concerning an investigation of alleged wrongdoing by National Guard Officers, on which the Army ultimately took no action, *Providence Journal Company v. United States Department of the Army*, 981 F.2d 552 (1st Cir. 1992).

To qualify for the deliberative process privilege, the information prepared by the government must be both *predecisional* and *deliberative*. The "predecisional" requirement limits the privilege to information recorded during the process of decisionmaking; the privilege is not designed to protect the final decision itself. A court will find a document to be predecisional if it was designed to assist a government official in arriving at a final decision. In contrast, if the document was prepared to explain or justify a decision that has already been made, it is not protected. The "deliberative" requirement protects the free flow of official opinions and advice and the exercise of judgment; the privilege is not designed to protect simple fact-gathering or action by the official as to which there is no discretion or thought. *See In re Sealed Case*, 121 F.3d 729, 737 (D.C. Cir. 1997) ("The deliberative process privilege does not shield documents that simply state or explain a decision the government has already made or protect material that is purely factual, unless the material is so inextricably intertwined with the deliberative sections of documents that its disclosure would inevitably reveal the government's deliberations.").

The deliberative process privilege is qualified rather than absolute. To determine whether the need for the evidence outweighs the government's interest in secrecy, most courts apply a five-factor balancing test, taken from Judge Weinstein's opinion in *In re Franklin National Bank Securities Litigation*, 478 F. Supp. 577, 588 (E.D.N.Y. 1979). Judge Weinstein found that the following factors should be balanced:

> (i) the relevance of the evidence sought to be protected; (ii) the availability of other evidence; (iii) the "seriousness" of the litigation and the issues involved; (iv) the role of the government in the litigation; and (v) the possibility of future timidity by government employees who will be forced to recognize that their secrets are violable.

Judge Weinstein's essential point is that the court must assess the need for the information by the party seeking it (including its availability through reasonable alternatives), against the possibility that the deliberative process will in fact be "chilled" in the future by disclosure today.

I. STATE SECRETS PRIVILEGE

STERLING v. TENET
416 F.3d 388 (4th Cir. 2005)

Wilkinson, Circuit Judge:

In this case we consider the applicability of the "state secrets doctrine" to a Title VII racial discrimination claim brought against the Director of Central Intelligence and ten unnamed CIA employees by a CIA covert agent. That doctrine embodies an evidentiary "privilege which protects military and state secrets" from disclosure in judicial proceedings. *United States v. Reynolds*, 345 U.S. 1, 7 (1953). The Supreme Court has recently and unanimously reaffirmed the vitality of the privilege. *See Tenet v. Doe*, 125 S. Ct. 1230, 1236-37 (2005). The district court properly concluded that this case would require disclosure of highly classified information concerning the identity, location, and assignments of CIA operatives. We therefore affirm its judgment that the state secrets doctrine requires dismissal of the case.

I.

Jeffrey Sterling, an African American, was an Operations Officer in the CIA's Near East and South Asia division from 1993 to 2001. He alleges that during this time he experienced unlawful discriminatory practices at the hands of CIA management. For instance, Sterling believes that the expectations for him were "far above those required of non-African-American Operations Officers." He says his superiors repeatedly denied him advantageous opportunities, subjected him to disparate treatment, and gave him Advanced Work Plans that contained more rigorous requirements than those given to non-African Americans.

He also alleges retaliation for utilizing the internal Equal Employment Opportunity ("EEO") process. He claims that he was scheduled to undergo security processing earlier than he should have been. According to him, security processing is an "arbitrary regime within the CIA that is utilized more for its nature as a tool for intimidation than any substantive security implications." He also asserts that management vandalized his personal property.

Sterling initially filed a pro se complaint in the Southern District of New York in August 2001, alleging violations of Title VII of the Civil Rights Act of 1964, 42 U.S.C. § 2000e et seq. A complaint (redacted because the CIA objected that the original contained classified information) was served on the government in January 2002. The district court in the Southern District of New York granted a motion to transfer the case to the Eastern District of Virginia, where the CIA is located. Although the government also asked the judge in New York to dismiss the case based on the state secrets doctrine, he specifically declined to endorse the government's argument.

The CIA renewed its invocation of the state secrets doctrine in the Eastern District. The Director filed both an unclassified and a classified declaration explaining why allowing Sterling to pursue his case would threaten exposure of classified information. The district court conducted an ex parte, in camera examination of both declarations. It satisfied itself that the Director had personally considered the national security implications of both the information that Sterling would need to establish his case as well as the information that would likely become public if the litigation were to continue.

The district court thus granted the motion to dismiss. It noted that for Sterling to pursue his claim, he would have to disclose the nature and location of his employment and the employment of those similarly situated. Yet Sterling's duties and those of his colleagues — and even the names of most of his supervisors and colleagues — were classified, rendering comparative proof of discrimination impossible. After a thorough review, the court concluded that the state secrets doctrine operated to preclude this suit because it barred the evidence that would be necessary to state a prima facie claim. State secrets, the court held, were critical to the resolution of core factual questions in the case, and therefore the doctrine justified dismissal.

Sterling timely appealed the district court's order. We review such legal determinations involving state secrets de novo.

II.

This case turns on the breadth of the state secrets doctrine, both as to when the privilege can be invoked and as to when a properly invoked privilege justifies dismissing a plaintiff's claim altogether.

A.

The Supreme Court set forth the state secrets doctrine in *United States v. Reynolds*, 345 U.S. 1 (1953). The Court's discussion of *Reynolds* last Term in *Tenet v. Doe*, 125 S. Ct. 1230, 1236-37 (2005), confirms its continued validity. *See also* Fed. R. Evid. 501 (government evidentiary privilege in federal law cases is a matter of federal common law).

Reynolds concerned suits that followed the crash of a military aircraft that had been testing secret electronic equipment. The government "filed a formal 'Claim of Privilege' " in which it argued that the aircraft was on "a highly secret mission of the Air Force," and disclosure of the requested materials would "seriously hamper national security, flying safety and the development of highly technical and secret military equipment.". The Court held that widows of those killed in the accident could not demand "production of the Air Force's official accident investigation report" and other such documents to assist their suit under the Federal Tort Claims Act. The Court sustained the government's refusal to produce the materials by citing "the privilege against revealing military secrets, a privilege which is well established in the law of evidence." "State secrets" and military secrets are equally valid bases for invocation of the evidentiary privilege. *Reynolds,* 345 U.S. at 7.

Reynolds explained the nature of the privilege and the process for applying it:

> The privilege belongs to the Government and must be asserted by it; it can neither be claimed nor waived by a private party. It is not to be lightly invoked. There must be a formal claim of privilege, lodged by the head of the department which has control over the matter, after actual personal consideration by that officer. The court itself must determine whether the circumstances are appropriate for the claim of privilege, and yet do so without forcing a disclosure of the very thing the privilege is designed to protect.

Id. at 7-8.

Judicial involvement in policing the privilege is important, but the Court emphasized limitations on a judge's supervisory function. *Reynolds* analogized the judicial inquiry in a state secrets case to the judge's role in regulating the invocation of the privilege against self-incrimination. "Too much judicial inquiry into the claim of privilege would force disclosure of the thing the privilege was meant to protect, while a complete abandonment of judicial control would lead to intolerable abuses." *Id.* at 8.

Recognizing this conflict as a "real difficulty," the Court resolved it the same way it had resolved the identical dilemma in the self-incrimination context. "The court must be satisfied from all the evidence and circumstances, and from the implications of the question * * * that a responsive answer * * * or an explanation of why it cannot be answered might be dangerous because injurious disclosure could result." In other words, once the court is "satisfied" that any response at all to a question or request for production might have a deleterious effect on national security, "the claim of the privilege will be accepted without requiring further disclosure."

B.

What is required to satisfy a district judge will depend on the circumstances of the case. The plaintiff's "showing of necessity" for the privileged evidence "will determine how far the court should probe in satisfying itself that the occasion for invoking the privilege is appropriate." *Reynolds,* 345 U.S. at 11. However, national security concerns are paramount, for "even the most compelling necessity cannot overcome the claim of privilege if the court is ultimately satisfied that military secrets are at stake." *Id.*

Thus, *Reynolds* made clear that the process of "satisfying" a district judge that the privilege has been properly invoked does not necessarily require in camera review of all the materials likely to contain state secrets:

> Judicial control over the evidence in a case cannot be abdicated to the caprice of executive officers. Yet we will not go so far as to say that the court may automatically require a complete disclosure to the judge before the claim of privilege will be accepted in any case. It may be possible to satisfy the court, from all the circumstances of the case, that there is a reasonable danger that compulsion of the evidence will expose military matters which, in the interest of national security, should not be divulged.

Id. at 9-10. The Court held that "when this is the case * * * the court should not jeopardize the security which the privilege is meant to protect by insisting upon an examination of the evidence, even by the judge alone, in chambers." *Id.* at 10.

The Supreme Court reaffirmed this principle in *United States v. Zolin*, 491 U.S. 554 (1989). That case relied heavily upon *Reynolds* in discussing a judge's role in determining whether a particular attorney-client conversation fell outside the attorney-client privilege because the client was seeking advice regarding the perpetration of "a future crime or fraud." Even in that context, far removed from the national security concerns at stake when the state secrets doctrine is invoked, the Court refused to undermine the evidentiary privilege by automatically requiring in camera review of presumptively privileged materials. Instead, "the party seeking in camera review must make some threshold showing that such review is appropriate." *Id.* at 570.

Zolin was sensitive to "the burdens in camera review places upon the district courts," and refused to allow parties to force "groundless fishing expeditions" upon them. *Id.* at 571. This admonition certainly applies where national security concerns are involved. Once the judge is satisfied that there is a "reasonable danger" of state secrets being exposed, any further disclosure is the sort of "fishing expedition" the Court has declined to countenance. Courts are not required to play with fire and chance further disclosure — inadvertent, mistaken, or even intentional — that would defeat the very purpose for which the privilege exists.

The threat of "graymail" likewise counsels courts to be cautious about risking exposure of sensitive materials. Graymail is a practice where "individual lawsuits [are] brought to induce the CIA [or another government agency] to settle a case (or prevent its filing) out of fear that any effort to litigate the action would reveal classified information that may undermine ongoing covert operations." *Tenet,* 125 S. Ct. at 1238. Unlike a criminal case, where the government can drop the charges if it fears that litigation presents unacceptable security risks, civil claims put the plaintiff in the driver's seat. The state secrets privilege provides a necessary safeguard against litigants presenting the government with a Hobson's choice between settling for inflated sums or jeopardizing national security. Were judges to fail to take care to avoid unnecessary risks of disclosure when the privilege is invoked, the incentives for graymail would correspondingly increase.

In sum, a formal and proper claim of privilege has been made, district courts frequently can satisfy themselves of the sufficiency of that claim through the explanation of the department head who is lodging it. Such explanations often come in the form of affidavits or declarations made personally by the department head. *See, e.g.*, *Bowles v. United States*, 950 F.2d 154, 156 (4th Cir. 1991) (assertion by Secretary of State); *In re Under Seal*, 945 F.2d 1285, 1287 (4th Cir. 1991) (affidavit by Secretary of Defense); *Fitzgerald v. Penthouse Int'l, Ltd.*, 776 F.2d 1236, 1242, 1243 n.9 (4th Cir. 1985) (affidavit by Secretary of the Navy); *Farnsworth Cannon, Inc. v. Grimes*, 635 F.2d 268, 281 (4th Cir. 1980) (affidavit by Secretary of the Navy).

There may of course be cases where the necessity for evidence is sufficiently strong and the danger to national security sufficiently unclear that in camera review of all materials is required to evaluate the claim of privilege. But both Supreme Court precedent and our own cases provide that when a judge has satisfied himself that the dangers asserted by the government are substantial and real, he need not — indeed, should not — probe further.

III.

Sterling contends that the state secrets evidentiary privilege does not require dismissal of his claim. He argues that the "district court abdicated its responsibility" when it reached the opposite conclusion. He bases this assertion on his belief that the privilege was improperly invoked and that the district court should have attempted to devise "adequate protective measures" to allow the case to proceed even if classified materials were a part of it. Applying the foregoing standards, however, we conclude that the state secrets evidentiary privilege was indeed applicable and required the dismissal of Sterling's claim.

A.

Sterling may prevail in his Title VII claim in one of two ways. First, he may present direct evidence of his superiors' discriminatory intent. Second, he may attempt to satisfy the test specified in *McDonnell Douglas Corp. v. Green*, 411 U.S. 792, 802 (1973), which allows him to raise an inference of discriminatory intent by showing that he was treated worse than similarly situated employees of other races. Defendants are then entitled to respond by presenting a legitimate, nondiscriminatory reason for their actions. The burden would finally shift back to Sterling to demonstrate that this reason was a pretext for discrimination.

"Regardless of the route a plaintiff follows in proving a Title VII action, * * * the existence of some adverse employment action is required." *James v. Booz-Allen & Hamilton, Inc.*, 368 F.3d 371, 375 (4th Cir. 2004). Here, Sterling seeks to prove discriminatory adverse employment actions by presenting evidence that higher expectations were placed upon him than upon similarly situated non-African American CIA operatives and that he was passed over for operational opportunities. He further alleges defendants retaliated against him for lodging his EEO complaint by forcing him to undergo a premature security screening and vandalizing his personal property.

B.

Consideration of the state secrets privilege can only proceed if the privilege was properly invoked under the procedures described by *Reynolds*. Here, the district court correctly determined that those procedures were followed. There is no doubt that the Director is "the head of the department which has control over the matter" and has lodged a formal claim of privilege. He has stated that this claim came after his personal consideration of the matter, and in both classified and unclassified declarations, he has explained why the privilege must be applied.

The subsequent inquiry is whether the materials necessary for pressing Sterling's Title VII claim or defending against it are likely to result in inappropriate disclosure of state secrets. The district court noted the Director's declaration that litigating the factual issues in this case would compromise CIA sources and methods, threaten the safety of intelligence sources, and adversely affect foreign relations. There is no question that information that would result in disclosure of intelligence-gathering methods or capabilities, and disruption of diplomatic relations with foreign governments falls squarely within the definition of state secrets. We are convinced, as was the district court, that such information forms the very basis of the factual disputes in this case.

As a covert operative, Sterling's position and responsibilities inherently involved state secrets. We hardly need defend the proposition that CIA personnel, activities, and objectives must be protected from prying eyes. The Supreme Court has noted in the context of discussing the Freedom of Information Act (FOIA) "that Congress intended to give the Director of Central Intelligence broad power to protect the secrecy and integrity of the intelligence process. The reasons are too obvious to call for enlarged discussion; without such protections the Agency would be virtually impotent." *CIA v. Sims*, 471 U.S. 159, 170 (1985).

This national security concern is particularly acute here because as a covert operative, the nature of Sterling's duties may well have involved recruiting foreign sources of intelligence. Congress has imbued the Director with very broad authority to protect all sources of intelligence information from disclosure. The continued availability of intelligence sources depends upon the CIA's ability to guarantee the security of information that might compromise them and even endanger their personal safety.

There is no way for Sterling to prove employment discrimination without exposing at least some classified details of the covert employment that gives context to his claim. If he were to employ the *McDonnell Douglas* framework to establish his prima facie case, he would be required to show that he was treated worse than similarly situated non-African American agents. This inquiry would expose classified information involving not only Sterling's activities, but those of other agents as well. It would be impossible to avoid investigation into the comparative responsibilities of Sterling and other CIA agents, the nature and goals of their duties, the operational tools provided (or denied) to them, and their comparative opportunities and performance in the field.

Similar comparative evidence is necessary for Sterling to meet his further burden of establishing that he suffered an adverse employment action. Every such action that he alleges rests upon an assertion that non-African Americans were treated more favorably than he. Sterling claims that the expectations for his performance were "far above those required of non-African-American Operations Officers," that his Advanced Work Plan "was considerably more demanding and 'harsher' than any requirements placed on non-African-Americans," and that he was "repeatedly passed over for operational opportunities" (which presumably went to less qualified operatives of other races). Proof of these allegations would require inquiry into state secrets such as the operational objectives and long-term missions of different agents, the relative job performance of these agents, details of how such performance is measured, and the organizational structure of CIA intelligence-gathering.

Sterling's retaliation claims similarly depend on proof of facts that are state secrets. He cannot prove his assertion that CIA security processing is an "arbitrary regime * * * that is utilized more for its nature as a tool for intimidation than any substantive security implications" without evidence regarding the CIA's internal security procedures. And his claim of personal property vandalism would require proof of details regarding where and when it might have happened, who his superiors were who might have ordered it, and why they had cause to retaliate against him.

Even assuming Sterling were somehow able to manage the impossible feat of making out all the elements of a Title VII claim without revealing state secrets, further issues would remain. The government would be entitled to present, as a defense to Sterling's prima facie case, legitimate nondiscriminatory reasons for its actions. This defense would have to show exactly why the CIA gave Sterling different assignments and different operational tools from his peers. The evidence required would inescapably reveal the criteria inherent in sensitive CIA decisionmaking.

Furthermore, the very methods by which evidence would be gathered in this case are themselves problematic. Many of the witnesses would necessarily be covert CIA operatives. Forcing such individuals to participate in a judicial proceeding — or even to give a deposition — risks their cover. And once they do appear, it is doubtful what information they could provide that would not have national security implications. Almost any relevant bit of information could be dangerous to someone, even if the agent himself was not aware that giving the answer could jeopardize others. The Supreme Court has cautioned that "what may seem trivial to the uninformed, may appear of great moment to one who has a broad view of the scene and may put the questioned item of information in its proper context." *Sims,* 471 U.S. at 178. Only the Director has the expertise to attest — as he has — to this larger view.

In short, the Director has met the requirements for application of the state secrets doctrine here and went beyond them, providing a classified declaration, which the district court was able to review in camera. The district court's reliance on that declaration, combined with the highly classified nature of the allegations in Sterling's own complaint, was more than adequate to conclude that the state secrets privilege was properly invoked.

C.

Even if the state secrets privilege is applicable, Sterling contends that dismissal of his entire case was error. Like the district court, however, we believe that dismissal follows inevitably when the sum and substance of the case involves state secrets.

We have long recognized that when "the very subject of [the] litigation is itself a state secret," which provides "no way that case could be tried without compromising sensitive military secrets," a district court may properly dismiss the plaintiff's case. To be sure, dismissal is appropriate "only when no amount of effort and care on the part of the court and the parties will safeguard privileged material." But where "the very question on which a case turns is itself a state secret, or the circumstances make clear that sensitive military secrets will be so central to the subject matter of the litigation that any attempt to proceed will threaten disclosure of the privileged matters," dismissal is the proper remedy. *DTM Research, LLC v. AT&T Corp.*, 245 F.3d 327, 334 (4th Cir. 2001).

Needless to say, litigation centering around a covert agent's assignments, evaluations, and colleagues meets this test. Here, the whole object of the suit and of the discovery is to establish a fact that is a state secret — namely, the methods and operations of the Central Intelligence Agency. As explained above, Sterling cannot prove his Title VII claim, nor can the government defend against it, without presenting evidence on topics that are state secrets. If the case cannot be tried without compromising sensitive foreign policy secrets, the case must be dismissed.

Sterling's argument that the court could devise special procedures that would allow his suit to proceed must therefore fail. Such procedures, whatever they might be, still entail considerable risk. Inadvertent disclosure during the course of a trial — or even in camera — is precisely the sort of risk that Reynolds attempts to avoid. At best, special accommodations give rise to added opportunity for leaked information. At worst, that information would become public, placing covert agents and intelligence sources alike at grave personal risk.

D.

We recognize that our decision places, on behalf of the entire country, a burden on Sterling that he alone must bear. When the state secrets privilege is validly asserted, the result is unfairness to individual litigants — through the loss of important evidence or dismissal of a case — in order to protect a greater public value. Yet there can be no doubt that, in limited circumstances like these, the fundamental principle of access to court must bow to the fact that a nation without sound intelligence is a nation at risk. *See Reynolds*, 345 U.S. at 11.

We take comfort in the fact that Sterling and those similarly situated are not deprived of all opportunity to press discrimination claims. The CIA provides, and Sterling has utilized, an internal EEO process where his claims may be heard and resolved. While the state secrets privilege is not contingent on the availability of such internal or administrative process, invocation of the privilege in federal court must not operate to discourage the CIA's own efforts to provide a working environment that honors our nation's bedrock commitment to nondiscrimination and fair treatment.

IV.

The Director has satisfied us, as he did the district court, of the "reasonable danger that the [material sought by Sterling] would contain references to the secret" anti-terror or other national security concerns that were "the primary concern" of hiring Sterling as a covert operative in the first place. *Reynolds*, 345 U.S. at 10, 73. We are neither authorized nor qualified to inquire further. For the foregoing reasons, the judgment of the district court is

AFFIRMED.

NOTES

1. Where the state secrets privilege applies, can it ever give way to a litigant's interest in pursuing a cause of action?

As seen in *Sterling, supra*, where the state secret privilege is applicable, it is absolute, not qualified. The privilege applies even if access to the information is absolutely necessary to sustain a civil claim or a criminal conviction. For example, in *Bareford v. General Dynamics Corp.*, 973 F.2d 1138 (5th Cir. 1992), plaintiffs brought a manufacturing and design defect suit against the manufacturer of a military weapons system, for failure of the weapons system to intercept two missiles fired upon the U.S.S. Stark. The government intervened and moved to dismiss the complaint on the ground that the subject of the lawsuit was a state secret. Plaintiffs argued that they could bring their case on the basis of non-privileged information in the public domain, including affidavits of the former captain of the Stark and affidavits from former employees of the defendant. However, the court held that the plaintiffs could not prove their case without "proof of what the [weapons] system was intended to do and the ways in which it fails to accomplish these goals." The Court concluded that: "such an analysis of the capabilities of an advanced Navy frigate's defensive systems is the type of judicial disclosure of state secrets the doctrine blocks." Therefore the court upheld the dismissal of the claim. *See also Kasza v. Browner*, 133 F.3d 1159 (9th Cir. 1998) (claims concerning inventory and removal of hazardous nuclear waste from nuclear testing sites had to be dismissed because information implicating national security interests was critical to pursuing the claims and defenses).

The state secrets privilege may preclude a prosecution or a civil claim even if the party can show sufficient independent evidence to proceed with the case. For example, in *Bareford*, the plaintiff had established a prima facie case with non-privileged information, but the court dismissed the case anyway. This was because the privileged and the non-privileged information was "inextricably linked." Cross-examination at trial would be required as to witnesses who had access to highly sensitive and privileged data. The court stated that it was "compelled to conclude that the trial of this case would inevitably lead to a significant risk that highly sensitive information concerning this defense system would be disclosed."

The state secrets privilege also applies to preclude a claim if the privileged material is necessary to mount a defense to that claim. In other words, the choice is made to place the cost of the state secrets privilege on the prosecution and the civil plaintiff, rather than on the civil or criminal defendant. *See, e.g.*, *Zuckerbraun v. General Dynamics Corp.*, 935 F.2d 544 (2d Cir. 1991) (dismissing a claim because state secrets privilege would have deprived the defendant of a defense). *See also United States v. North*, 920 F.2d 940 (D.C. Cir. 1990) (noting the dismissal of certain criminal charges where state secrets would have been necessary to mount a defense).

2. Does the state secrets privilege make any sense today?

In *Black v. United States*, 62 F.3d 1115 (8th Cir. 1995), the plaintiff sued the United States alleging that he was the target of harassment and psychological attacks, in retaliation for his contacts with a Soviet mathematician. The court held that the trial court correctly found that state secrets were implicated by the plaintiff's lawsuit, and that the plaintiff's claims were therefore properly dismissed. The Director of the CIA had properly invoked the state secrets privilege, and the continuation of the plaintiff's suit presented a "reasonable danger" to the intelligence-gathering capabilities and diplomatic relations of the United States. The court rejected the plaintiff's argument that the state secrets privilege was simply "a creature of the Cold War" that had outlived its usefulness. It stated that "the *absence* of a relatively stable world order of the sort that prevailed during the Cold War makes the availability of the privilege in appropriate cases all the more important."

J. PROTECTIVE FUNCTION PRIVILEGE?

IN RE: SEALED CASE

148 F.3d 1073 (D.C. Cir. 1998);

PER CURIAM:

During depositions conducted by the Office of the Independent Counsel as part of grand jury proceedings, officers of the United States Secret Service refused to answer certain questions on the ground that the information sought was protected from disclosure by a "protective function privilege." When the OIC filed a motion in federal district court to compel their testimony, the Secret Service, through the Attorney General, again asserted a protective function privilege, which by that time had been officially invoked by the Secretary of the Treasury, the cabinet officer who oversees the Secret Service. The district court refused to recognize the protective function privilege and granted the motion to compel.

For the reasons set forth below, we affirm. We note at the outset, however, that the question before the court today is whether Secret Service officers can be compelled to testify before a federal grand jury. We express no opinion about the propriety of asserting a protective function privilege in other legal proceedings.

I.

* * *

II. Nature Of The Asserted Privilege

As described by the Secret Service, the protective function privilege absolutely protects "information obtained by Secret Service personnel while performing their protective function in physical proximity to the President," except that the privilege "does not apply, in the context of a federal investigation or prosecution, to bar testimony by an officer or agent concerning observations or statements that, at the time they were made, were sufficient to provide reasonable grounds for believing that a felony has been, is being, or will be committed."

The privilege is necessary, according to the Secret Service, in order for the Service to carry out its statutory duty to protect the President. *See* 18 U.S.C. § 3056. That is because the Secret Service uses protective techniques the effectiveness of which depends upon close physical proximity to the President. Indeed, in the opinion of the current Director of the Secret Service, "it is no exaggeration to say that the difference of even a few feet between a President and his protective detail could mean the difference between life or death." Declaration of Lewis C. Merletti ¶ 12. The Secret Service has a tradition and culture of maintaining the confidences of its protectees. The Service is concerned that "if any President of the United States were given reason to doubt the confidentiality of actions or conversations taken in sight or hearing of Secret Service personnel, he would seek to push the protective envelope away, or eliminate some of its components, undermining it to the point where it could no longer be fully effective." Merletti Decl. ¶ 27. In a letter to the Director dated April 15, 1998, former President George Bush succinctly stated the case for recognizing the privilege: "What's at stake here is the confidence of the President in the discretion of the USSS. If that confidence evaporates the agents, denied proximity, cannot properly protect the President."

III. Analysis

* * *

In its most recent opinion dealing with the recognition of a new testimonial privilege, the Supreme Court reiterated that [Federal Rule of Evidence] 501 "did not freeze the law governing the privileges of witnesses in federal trials at a particular point in our history, but rather directed federal courts to 'continue the evolutionary development of testimonial privileges." — *Jaffee v. Redmond*, 518 U.S. 1, 9 (1996). Still, when evaluating a novel claim of privilege "we start with the primary assumption that there is a general duty to give what testimony one is capable of giving,"; testimonial privileges "must be strictly construed and accepted only to the very limited extent that permitting a refusal to testify * * * has a 'public good transcending the normally predominant principle of utilizing all rational means for ascertaining truth,' " — *see United States v. Nixon*, 418 U.S. 683, 710 (1974) (new privileges "are not lightly created nor expansively construed").

The Supreme Court has put considerable weight upon federal and state precedent when recognizing a privilege. Consequently, the OIC makes much of the lack of relevant federal or state precedent for the protective function privilege. The lack of such precedent is hardly surprising, however, in view of the novelty of the OIC's demand for testimony: This appears to be the first effort in U.S. history to compel testimony by agents guarding the President. Although analogies can be drawn to state Governors and their protectors, the consequences of assassination (and hence the necessity of suitable protection) are so much greater at the presidential level that such analogies offer little guidance. In these circumstances, we do not regard the absence of precedent as weighing heavily against recognition of the privilege. The result is simply that judicial recognition of the privilege depends entirely upon the Secret Service's ability to establish clearly and convincingly both the need for and the efficacy of the proposed privilege. In other words, the Secret Service must demonstrate that recognition of the privilege in its proposed form will materially enhance presidential security by lessening any tendency of the President to "push away" his protectors in situations where there is some risk to his safety.

The Supreme Court requires that a party seeking judicial recognition of a new evidentiary privilege under Rule 501 demonstrate with a high degree of clarity and certainty that the proposed privilege will effectively advance a public good. *See, e.g., United States v. Gillock*, 445 U.S. 360, 375 (1980) (rejecting as "speculative" policy arguments in favor of proposed state legislative privilege). Even in cases where the proposed privilege is designed in part to protect constitutional rights, the Supreme Court has demanded that the proponent come forward with a compelling empirical case for the necessity of the privilege. *See Branzburg v. Hayes*, 408 U.S. 665, 693-94 (1972) ("Estimates of the inhibiting effect of [grand jury] subpoenas on the willingness of informants to make disclosures to newsmen are widely divergent and to a great extent speculative").

As discussed above, the Secret Service claims that ensuring the physical safety of the President is the transcendent public good that justifies the protective function privilege. For its part the OIC "readily acknowledge[s] the profound public interest in Presidential safety upon which the Secret Service places so much emphasis." We likewise agree that ensuring the physical safety of the President is a public good of the utmost importance. We do not think, however, that the Secret Service has shown with the compelling clarity required by Rule 501 that failure to recognize the proposed privilege will jeopardize the ability of the Secret Service effectively to protect the President. * * *

The Secret Service has submitted declarations of senior Secret Service agents and the above-quoted letter from President Bush in support of the privilege, but against these we must balance recent statements by Presidents

Carter and Ford expressing their opinion that Secret Service personnel should be required to testify in a criminal case.

In addition, although we must acknowledge that the Secret Service has a duty to protect the President, we must also consider that the President has a correlative duty to accept protection. *See* 18 U.S.C. § 3056(a) & (d). Moreover, as the district court observed, the President has a profound personal interest in being well protected, and the President knows that effective protection depends upon proximity to his protectors. According to the Director of the Secret Service, an incoming President generally "does not sufficiently appreciate the risks he is facing"; however, each new President's "initial tendency to resist the close protective envelope in which [the Service] want[s] to place him" is overcome by a "natural educational process" in which the President learns the importance of proximity.

The ability of the proposed privilege to enhance the Secret Service's protection of the President is further weakened by the precise form of the proposed privilege: An agent may not testify about the conduct of the President or anyone else unless the agent recognizes that conduct as felonious when he is witnessing it; a felony made apparent to the agent only by subsequent events — and any misdemeanor, regardless of the circumstances — must remain secret. The proposed exception for contemporaneously recognized felonies strikes a strange balance between the competing goals of providing sound incentives for the President and facilitating the discovery of truth. On the one hand, because the President cannot know whether an agent will realize he is witnessing the commission of a felony — which depends in part upon how much the agent knows about prior events — the President will have to discount substantially the value of the protective function privilege (and thus perhaps be tempted to distance himself from his protectors all the same). On the other hand, the exception would prohibit testimony (and thus thwart the search for truth) even in cases where the evidence, viewed in the light of subsequent events, would supply a key element in the proof of a serious crime.

We think it significant that the Secret Service does not require its agents to sign confidentiality agreements as a condition of employment; without such an agreement (or statute or rule), the Secretary of the Treasury would find it difficult by invoking the proposed privilege to prevent a former Secret Service agent from testifying, for at least two reasons. First, a former agent who is not bound by any agreement or rule will suffer no adverse consequences by cooperating in an investigation of the President; second, the Secretary of the Treasury has no way of knowing when such a cooperative former agent is about to testify. If preventing testimony is as critical to the success of its mission as the Secret Service now claims, it seems anomalous that the Service has no better mechanism in place to discourage former agents from revealing confidences or at least to alert the Secretary when testimony is about to be given.

We also think the efficacy of the privilege is undermined by its being vested in the Secretary of the Treasury and not in the President, whose conduct the proposed privilege is supposed to influence; we know of no other privilege that works that way. If the person whose conduct is to be influenced knows that the privilege might be waived by someone else, the effect of the privilege in shaping his conduct is greatly diminished if not completely eliminated. Accordingly, the assertion of the White House Counsel, in a letter to the OIC, that "the privilege is not [the President's] to assert or to waive" reinforces our impression that the proposed protective function privilege will provide only a weak incentive for the President to keep his protectors in close proximity. Letter from Charles F.C. Ruff to Kenneth W. Starr dated May 11, 1998.

In any event, an incumbent president's ability to control the assertion of the privilege — even indirectly, via the Secretary of the Treasury — would end when the President leaves office. This weakens the claim that the privilege in the form proposed by the Secret Service will do anything to diminish the President's incentive to keep his protectors at a distance. * * *

We have still other doubts about both the need for and the efficacy of the proposed privilege. As for need, the greatest danger to the President arises when he is in public, yet the privilege presumably would have its greatest effect when he is in the White House or in private meetings. *See* United States Dept. of the Treasury, Public Report of the White House Security Review 92 (1995), quoted in Brief of Amici Curiae William P. Barr et al. at 27 n.10 ("Although * * * Presidents have been exposed to deadly or life-threatening assaults with frightening regularity, not one of these assaults has occurred within the White House Complex. Indeed, each assassination or potentially deadly assassination attempt has occurred when the Presidential protectee was away from the White House, in the proximity of a crowd"). We note also that Secret Service agents have given testimony in the past about the functioning of the tape recording system in the Oval Office and that some Secret Service agents have disclosed observations from their protective experiences in books, apparently without causing Presidents to distance themselves from their protectors. As for efficacy, we suspect that even with a protective function privilege in place, conscience might impel a President to distance himself from Secret Service agents when engaging in wrongful conduct, as might a simple desire for privacy at other times.

* * *

IV. Conclusion

The Secret Service has failed to carry its heavy burden under Rule 501 of establishing the need for the protective function privilege it sought to assert in this case. Consequently, we leave to the Congress the question whether a protective function privilege is appropriate in order to ensure the safety of the President and, if so, what the contours of that privilege should be. The order of the district court is therefore affirmed.

K. PARENT-CHILD PRIVILEGE?

In re GRAND JURY

103 F.3d 1140 (3d Cir. 1997)

GARTH, CIRCUIT JUDGE:

Three appeals presenting the same critical issue are before us. One appeal originated in the District Court of the Virgin Islands at docket number 95-7354. The other two appeals pertaining to the same Delaware defendant originated in the District Court of Delaware at docket numbers 96-7529 and 96-7530.

We scheduled oral argument in all three appeals on the same day inasmuch as they raised the same question — should this court recognize a parent-child privilege? * * *

I

The facts and procedure of the Virgin Islands case giving rise to one appeal, and of the Delaware case giving rise to two appeals, will be stated separately.

Docket Number 95-7354: In the Virgin Islands case, the grand jury sitting in St. Croix subpoenaed the father of the target of the grand jury investigation as a witness. The target of the grand jury proceeding was the son of the subpoenaed witness. The son became the target of a government investigation as a result of "certain transactions that [he] was allegedly involved in." At the time of the alleged transactions, the son was eighteen years old. The grand jury subpoenaed the target's father to testify on April 18, 1995. The father, a former FBI agent, lived with his wife and son in St. Croix. On April 17, 1995, based on his belief that the grand jury intended to question him about conversations that he had had with his son, the father moved to quash the subpoena, asserting that those conversations were privileged from disclosure under Fed. R. Evid. 501. The father testified, at a hearing before the district court, that he and his son "ha[d] an excellent relationship, very close, very loving relationship.". He further testified that if he were coerced into testifying against his son, "[their] relationship would dramatically change and the closeness that [they] have would end." The father further explained that the subpoena would impact negatively upon his relationship with his son:

> I will be living under a cloud in which if my son comes to me or talks to me, I've got to be very careful what he says, what I allow him to say. I would have to stop him and say, "you can't talk to me about that. You've got to talk to your attorney." It's no way for anybody to live in this country.

On June 19, 1995, the district court entered its order denying the father's motion to quash. On the same day, the district court granted the targeted son's motion to intervene and then stayed its order which denied the quashing of the father's subpoena pending any appeal. The court's memorandum opinion and order, although clearly sympathetic with the plight of the subpoenaed father, "regretfully decline[d] to recognize [a parent-child] privilege" because the Third Circuit had yet to address the issue and "every United States Court of Appeals that has confronted this question has declined to recognize the parent-child privilege." * * *

Docket Numbers 96-7529 & 96-7530: In the Delaware case, a sixteen year old minor daughter was subpoenaed to testify before the grand jury, as part of an investigation into her father's participation in an alleged interstate kidnapping of a woman who had disappeared. The daughter was scheduled to testify on September 10, 1996. However, on September 9, 1996, a motion to quash subpoena was made by counsel for the daughter and her mother, as well as by separate counsel for the father. The motion sought to bar the testimony of the daughter claiming a parent-child privilege which would cover testimony and confidential communications. "[T]he privilege [was] claimed for confidential communications as well as for protection against being compelled to testify in a criminal proceeding". Joint Motion to Quash Subpoena at ¶¶ 5. The district court * * * issued a ruling * * * denying the motion to quash and ordering the minor daughter to testify before the grand jury that evening.

* * * Pursuant to the court order, the daughter appeared at court (in an ante-room to the grand jury courtroom) in the evening of September 10, 1995. She refused to testify and was found in contempt. The district court then stayed the imposition of sanctions during the pendency of these appeals. * * *

II.

* * *

III.

The central question in these appeals is one of first impression in this court: should we recognize a parent-child testimonial privilege? Appellants argue that recognition is necessary in order to advance important public policy interests such as the protection of strong and trusting parent-child relationships; the preservation of the family; safeguarding of privacy interests and protection from harmful government intrusion; and the promotion of healthy psychological development of children. These public policy arguments echo those advanced by academicians and other legal commentators in the myriad of law review articles discussing the parent-child testimonial privilege. * * *

Although legal academicians appear to favor adoption of a parent-child testimonial privilege, no federal Court of Appeals and no state supreme court has recognized such a privilege. We too decline to recognize such a privilege for the following reasons:

(1) The overwhelming majority of all courts — federal or state — have rejected such a privilege.

(a) Eight federal Courts of Appeals have rejected such a privilege and none of the remaining Courts of Appeals have recognized such a privilege. (b) Every state supreme court that has addressed the issue has rejected the privilege, and only four states have protected parent-child communications in some manner. (c) No state within the Third Circuit has recognized a parent-child privilege.

(2) No reasoned analysis of Federal Rule of Evidence 501 or of the standards established by the Supreme Court or by this court supports the creation of a privilege.

(3) Creation of such a privilege would have no impact on the parental relationship and hence would neither benefit that relationship nor serve any social policy.

(4) Although we have the authority to recognize a new privilege, we believe the recognition of such a privilege, if one is to be recognized, should be left to Congress.

A. FEDERAL AND STATE COURTS HAVE DECLINED TO RECOGNIZE A PARENT-CHILD PRIVILEGE.

1. *Eight Federal Courts of Appeals Have Explicitly Rejected the Privilege and None of the Remaining Courts of Appeals Have Recognized the Privilege.*

The appellants rely primarily upon law review articles rather than case law authority to support the position that a parent-child testimonial privilege should be recognized. No case law recognizing such a privilege exists. On the other hand, the eight federal Courts of Appeals that have addressed the issue have uniformly declined to recognize a parent-child privilege. [Citations] Moreover, the remaining federal Courts of Appeals that have not explicitly rejected the privilege have not chosen to recognize the privilege either.

* * *

2. *State Courts Have Overwhelmingly Rejected the Privilege.*

The overwhelming majority of state courts, like their federal counterparts, have also declined to recognize a common-law parent-child privilege.[Citations]

3. *Only Two Federal District Court Cases Recognize the Privilege, and These Cases are Distinguishable and Not Authoritative.*

The parent-child privilege has not been recognized by any federal or state court with the exception of two federal district court cases which are readily distinguishable: *In re Grand Jury Proceedings (Agosto)*, 553 F. Supp. 1298 (D. Nev. 1983) and *In re Grand Jury Proceedings (Greenberg)*, 11 Fed. R. Evid. Serv. (Callaghan) 579 (D. Conn. 1982).

In *Agosto*, the thirty-two-year-old son of an alleged tax evader moved to quash a *subpoena ad testificandum* requiring him to testify against his father. Although the district court recognized a common-law privilege, it did so in derogation of the prevailing jurisprudence of the Ninth Circuit, which, in an en banc decision, had expressly rejected a parent-child privilege. *Agosto* therefore conflicts squarely with its own circuit's en banc precedent. * * *

In *Greenberg*, a mother sought relief from a civil contempt charge when she refused to testify before a federal grand jury in order to protect her adult daughter, who had been indicted by a Florida grand jury for importation of marijuana. The district court recognized a limited testimonial privilege grounded in the First Amendment free exercise clause; however, the court declined to recognize a general common-law parent-child privilege. Observing that the daughter, as an adult, did not require the same degree of guidance and support as a young child, the court reasoned that although compelled disclosure of nonincriminating confidences might damage the relationship between the mother and her daughter, the harm would be less severe than if an unemancipated minor were involved. Concluding that this lesser degree of harm did not outweigh the state's need for the testimony, the district court held that the facts did not justify the creation of a common-law parent-child privilege. *Greenberg* therefore does not support the creation of a general testimonial parent-child privilege; furthermore, its limited holding does not extend to the present matter since religious principles are not implicated here.

B. THE STANDARDS PRESCRIBED BY FEDERAL RULE OF EVIDENCE 501 DO NOT SUPPORT THE CREATION OF A PRIVILEGE.

Federal Rule of Evidence 501 provides that "the privilege of a witness * * * shall be governed by the principles of the common law as they may be interpreted by the courts of the United States in the light of reason and experience." No such principle, interpretation, reason or experience has been drawn upon here. It is true that Congress, in enacting Fed. R. Evid. 501, "manifested an affirmative intention not to freeze the law of privilege. Its purpose rather was to 'provide the courts with the flexibility to develop rules of privilege on a case-by-case basis,' and to leave the door open to change." *Trammel v. United States*, 445 U.S. 40, 47 (1980). In doing so, however, we are admonished that privileges are generally disfavored; that "the public * * * has a right to every man's evidence" —; and that privileges are tolerable "only to the very limited extent that permitting a refusal to testify or excluding relevant evidence has a public good transcending the normally predominant principle of utilizing all rational means for ascertaining truth." * * * Neither the appellants nor the dissent has identified any principle of common law, and hence have proved no interpretation of such a principle. Nor has the dissent or the appellants discussed any common-law principle in light of reason and experience. Accordingly, no basis has been demonstrated for this court to adopt a parent-child privilege.

C. CREATING A PARENT-CHILD PRIVILEGE WOULD BE INCONSISTENT WITH THE TEACHINGS OF THE SUPREME COURT AND OF THIS COURT.

The Supreme Court's most recent pronouncement in the law of privileges, *Jaffee v. Redmond*, 518 U.S. 1 (1996), which recognized a psychotherapist-patient privilege, supports the conclusion that a privilege should not, and cannot, be created here. In *Jaffee*, the Supreme Court reemphasized that the predominant common-law principle which guides a federal court's determination of whether a privilege applies is the maxim that testimonial privileges are disfavored * * *. An exception to this general rule is justified only when recognition of a privilege would promote a "public good transcending the normally predominant principle of utilizing all rational means for ascertaining the truth." —

The *Jaffee* Court emphasized that a court, in determining whether a particular privilege "promotes sufficiently important interests to outweigh the need for probative evidence," must be guided by "reason and experience." Specifically, the *Jaffee* Court instructed that a federal court should look to the "experience" of state courts * * *. Notably, in recognizing a psychotherapist-patient privilege, the Supreme Court relied on the fact that all fifty states had enacted some form of a psychotherapist privilege. * * * Here, by contrast, only four states have deemed it necessary to protect from disclosure, in any manner, confidential communications between children and their parents. * * * The policy determinations of these four states do not constitute a "consistent body of policy determinations by states" supporting recognition of a parent-child privilege. Indeed, if anything, the fact that the overwhelming majority of states have chosen *not* to create a parent-child privilege supports the opposite conclusion: "reason and experience" dictate that federal courts should refuse to recognize a privilege rejected by the vast majority of jurisdictions.

The *Jaffee* Court also relied on the fact that the psychotherapist-patient privilege was among the nine specific privileges recommended by the Advisory Committee on Rules of Evidence in 1972. * * * In the instant cases, in contrast to the psychotherapist-patient privilege recognized in *Jaffee*, the parent-child privilege * * * was not among the enumerated privileges submitted by the Advisory Committee. Although this fact, in and of itself, is not dispositive with respect to the question as to whether this court should create a privilege, it strongly suggests that the Advisory Committee, like the majority of state legislatures, did not regard confidential parent-child communications sufficiently important to warrant "privilege" protection. A federal court should give due consideration, and accord proper weight, to the judgment of the Advisory Committee and of state legislatures on this issue when it evaluates whether it is appropriate to create a new privilege pursuant to Rule 501.

* * *

Furthermore, an analysis of the four Wigmore factors * * * does not support the creation of a privilege. Dean Wigmore's four-factor formula requires satisfaction of all four factors in order to establish a privilege:

(1) The communications must originate in a *confidence* that they will not be disclosed.

(2) This element of *confidentiality must be essential* to the full and satisfactory maintenance of the relation between the parties.

(3) The *relation* must be one which in the opinion of the community ought to be sedulously fostered.

(4) The *injury* that would inure to the relation by the disclosure of the communications must be *greater than the benefit* thereby gained for the correct disposal of litigation.

At least two of Wigmore's prerequisite conditions for creation of a federal common-law privilege are not met under the facts of these cases. We refer to the second and fourth elements of the Wigmore test.

First, confidentiality — in the form of a testimonial privilege — is not essential to a successful parent-child relationship, as required by the second factor. A privilege should be recognized only where such a privilege would be indispensable to the survival of the relationship that society deems should be fostered. For instance, because complete candor and full disclosure by the client is absolutely necessary in order for the attorney to function effectively, society recognizes an attorney-client privilege. Without a guarantee of secrecy, clients would be unwilling to reveal damaging information. As a corollary, clients would disclose negative information, which an attorney must know to prove effective representation, only if they were assured that such disclosures are privileged. In contrast, it is not clear whether children would be more likely to discuss private matters with their parents if a parent-child privilege were recognized than if one were not. It is not likely that children, or even their parents, would typically be aware of the existence or non-existence of a testimonial privilege covering parent-child communications. On the other hand, professionals such as attorneys, doctors and members of the clergy would know of the privilege that attends their respective profession, and their clients, patients or parishioners would also be aware that their confidential conversations are protected from compelled disclosure.

Moreover, even assuming *arguendo* that children and their parents generally are aware of whether or not their communications are protected from disclosure, it is not certain that the existence of a privilege enters into whatever thought processes are performed by children in deciding whether or not to confide in their parents. Indeed, the existence or nonexistence of a parent-child privilege is probably one of the least important considerations in any child's decision as to whether to reveal some indiscretion, legal or illegal, to a parent. Moreover, it is unlikely that any parent would choose to deter a child from revealing a confidence to the parent solely because a federal court has refused to recognize a privilege protecting such communications from disclosure.

Finally, the proposed parent-child privilege fails to satisfy the fourth condition of the Wigmore test. As explained above, any injury to the parent-child relationship resulting from non-recognition of such a privilege would be relatively insignificant. In contrast, the cost of recognizing such a privilege is substantial: the impairment of the truth-seeking function of the judicial system and the increased likelihood of injustice resulting from the concealment of relevant information. Moreover, because no clear benefit flows from the recognition of a parent-child privilege, any injury to the parent-child relationship caused by compelled testimony as to confidential communications is necessarily and substantially outweighed by the benefit to society of obtaining all relevant evidence in a criminal case. In short, the public good derived from maintaining the confidentiality of parent-child communications transcends the value of effective and efficient judicial truth-finding.

An even more compelling reason for rejecting a parent-child privilege stems from the fact that the parent-child relationship differs dramatically from other relationships. This is due to the unique duty owing to the child from the parent. A parent owes the duty to the child to nurture and guide the child. This duty is unusual because it inheres in the relationship and the relationship arises automatically at the child's birth. If, for example, a fifteen year old unemancipated child informs her parent that she has committed a crime or has been using or distributing narcotics, and this disclosure has been made in confidence while the child is seeking guidance, it is evident to us that, regardless of whether the child consents or not, the parent must have the right to take such action as the parent deems appropriate *in the interest of the child*. That action could be commitment to a drug rehabilitation center or a report of the crime to the juvenile authorities. This is so because, in theory at least, juvenile proceedings are undertaken solely in the interest of the child. We would regard it intolerable in such a situation if the law intruded in the guise of a privilege, and silenced the parent because the child had a privilege to prevent disclosure. This results in the analysis that any privilege, if recognized, must be dependent upon both the parent and child asserting it. However, in such a case, the privilege would disappear if the parent can waive it. It follows therefore that, if a child is able to communicate openly with a parent and seeks guidance from that parent, the entire basis for the privilege is destroyed if the child is required to recognize that confidence will be maintained only so long as the parent wants the conversation to be confidential. If, however, the parent can waive the privilege unilaterally, the goal of the privilege is destroyed.

It follows therefore that, if a child is able to communicate openly with a parent and seeks guidance from that parent, the entire basis for the privilege is destroyed if the child is required to recognize that confidence will be maintained only so long as the parent wants the conversation to be confidential. If, however, the parent can waive the privilege unilaterally, the goal of the privilege is destroyed. * * * It follows then that an effective parent-child privilege requires that the parent's lips be sealed but such a sealing would be inexcusable in the parent-child relationship. No government should have that power. Indeed the obligation on the parent to act goes far beyond the parent's obligation to raise and nurture the child. Thus a parent-child privilege implicates considerations which are vastly different from the traditional privileges to which resort is had as analogues.

In sum, neither historical tradition, nor common-law principles, nor Wigmore formulations, nor the logic of privileges, nor the "reason and experience" of the various states supports creation of a parent-child privilege.

D. RECOGNITION OF A PARENT-CHILD PRIVILEGE SHOULD BE LEFT TO CONGRESS.

* * *

The legislature, not the judiciary, is institutionally better equipped to perform the balancing of the competing policy issues required in deciding whether the recognition of a parent-child privilege is in the best interests of society. Congress, through its legislative mechanisms, is also better suited for the task of defining the scope of any prospective privilege. Congress is able to consider, for example, society's moral, sociological, economic, religious and other values without being confined to the evidentiary record in any particular case. Thus, in determining whether a parent-child privilege should obtain, Congress can take into consideration a host of facts and factors which the judiciary may be unable to consider. These considerations are also relevant to determining whether the privilege, if it is to be recognized, should extend to adult children, adopted children or unemancipated minors. Among additional factors that Congress could consider are other parameters of familial relationships. Does "parent" include step-parent or grand-parent? Does "child" include an adopted child, or a step-child? Should the privilege extend to siblings? Furthermore, if another family member is present at the time of the relevant communication, is the privilege automatically barred or destroyed?

Hence, as a court without the ability to consider matters beyond the evidentiary record presented, we should be chary about creating new privileges and ordinarily should defer to the legislature to do so. * * *

Congress, too, has recognized the importance of privilege rules insofar as the truth-seeking process is concerned. Congress specifically addressed that subject when it delegated rulemaking authority to the Supreme Court as to rules of procedure and evidence. It did so by identifying and designating the law of privileges as a special area meriting greater legislative oversight. Congress expressly provided that "[a]ny * * * rule creating, abolishing, or modifying an evidentiary privilege shall have no force or effect unless approved by Act of Congress." 28 U.S.C. §§ 2074(b) (1994). In contrast, all other evidentiary rules promulgated by the Supreme Court and transmitted to Congress automatically take effect unless Congress enacts a statute to the contrary. *See* 28 U.S.C. §§ 2074(a) (1994).

IV.

A few further observations about the dissent and why it does not persuade us that the parent-child privilege outweighs the government's interest in disclosure:

* * *

* * * [T]he crafting of the privilege as a jointly-held privilege (by both parent and child) undermines the dissent's goal of encouraging a child to seek the advice of a parent and protecting the parent-child relationship. The entire thrust of the dissent's opinion is that a child should feel confident, in communicating with a parent to seek advice and guidance, that the communication will remain inviolate. However, the dissent, then straddling the fence, also argues that the parent can choose to violate such a confidence and report a confidential communication to others (presumably the authorities) in the interest of parental judgment. We know of no privilege that can operate in such a two-way fashion and still remain effective.

The few observations made above do no more than highlight the stark difference between the dissent's view of the public good which subordinates the government's interest in disclosure to a parent-child privilege, and the position we have taken which recognizes justice and disclosure as the predominant principles for ascertaining truth. Finally, we observe that implicit in the various discussions by courts (both federal and state) of the parent-child privilege is the fact that the "strong and trusting parent-child relationships" which the dissent would preserve, have existed throughout the years without the concomitant existence of a privilege protecting that relationship.

V.

In short, if a new privilege is deemed worthy of recognition, the wiser course in our opinion is to leave the adoption of such a privilege to Congress. Although we are not reluctant to chart a new legal course, such an action should not be premised upon unsound legal principles or emotion. The instant appeals furnish us with neither reason, nor analysis, nor a basis upon which to fashion such a privilege. All that we have been told by the appellants and by the dissent is: we should look to the healthy, psychological development of children; and that compelling the testimony of a parent is repugnant and indecent; that it is more important that a child communicate with a parent than it is to compel a parent's testimony; and that the preservation of the family and the protection of a strong and trusting parent-child relationship trumps all other interests. These conclusions, as well as the criteria which the dissent would require as to the nature of the communications and whether they were imparted in an effort to seek advice and counseling, cannot be satisfied without the benefit of evidence, expert testimony, hearings or recognized authority. If a new privilege were to be engraved in the concrete of our jurisprudence as the dissent argues, then it should be framed so that its contours are clear and unambiguous, and it should be capable of being applied precisely, without the need for multiple pretrial hearings, in addition to the privilege's existence being known to the participants. Sympathy alone cannot justify the creation of a new and unprecedented privilege which does not meet the standards set by Congress, the Supreme Court and this court.

Accordingly, we will affirm the district court's order of June 19, 1995, which denied the father's motion to quash the grand jury subpoena in the Virgin Islands case (95-7354). We will also affirm the district court's order of September 10, 1996 in the Delaware cases (96-7529 and 96-7530), denying the joint motion to quash the grand jury subpoena * * *.

Mansmann, Circuit Judge, concurring and dissenting.

I write separately because I am convinced that the testimonial privilege issue raised by the Virgin Islands appeal is substantially different from that presented in the Delaware appeals and should be resolved in favor of the targeted son. The Virgin Islands appeal, which challenges the denial of a motion to quash a grand jury subpoena, requires that we confront an issue of first impression in our circuit: should we make available to a parent and child an evidentiary privilege which could be invoked to prevent compelling that parent to testify regarding confidential communications made to the parent by his child in the course of seeking parental advice and guidance? It appears that this precise question is one of first impression in the federal courts.

Because I conclude that the public good at issue, the protection of strong and trusting parent-child relationships, outweighs the government's interest in disclosure, I would exercise the authority granted to the federal courts by Congress under Rule 501 of the Federal Rules of Evidence and would recognize a limited privilege. Accordingly, I respectfully dissent.

I.

* * * While most courts have declined to recognize a parent-child testimonial privilege, they have done so in contexts far different from the one presented here. I am convinced that this is an appropriate case in which to

recognize and set parameters for a limited privilege. Doing so is critical to several important public policy interests such as the "protection of strong and trusting parent-child relationships and the preservation of the sanctity of the family * * * ." The recognition of a parent-child privilege is essential to "the healthy psychological development of children and to the development of society as a whole"; compelling a parent to testify adversely to a child is " 'repugnant to social sensibilities' and contrary to a democratic view of decency." Wendy Meredith Watts, *The Parent-Child Privilege: Hardly a New or Revolutionary Concept*, 28 Wm. & Mary L. Rev. 583, 611-13 (1987).

* * *

II.

A.

* * *

B.

* * * I am convinced that the public good derived from a child's ability to communicate openly with and to seek guidance from his or her parents is of sufficient magnitude to transcend the judicial system's interest in compelled parental testimony. * * * I stress that the privilege which I would recognize is a limited one, applying *only* to compelled testimony concerning confidential communications made to a parent by his child in the course of seeking parental advice. Although this case might have been more compelling had the son been a minor at the time of his statements to his father, I would not adopt a bright-line rule applicable only to those who have not reached legal majority. In order to advance the policy interests which the targeted son articulated, I would prefer to leave the particular factors to be considered in determining application of the privilege to development on a case-by-case basis. I expect that these factors would include such variables as age, maturity, whether or not the child resides with the parents, and the precise nature of the communications for which the privilege is claimed. The privilege would apply to situations in which it is invoked by both parent and child; this case does not require that we confront applicability of the privilege where it is invoked by the parent or the child alone.

The goal in recognizing this limited privilege would not be to guarantee confidentiality *per se* but to shield parent-child relationships from the devastating effects likely to be associated with compelled testimony. * * * An effective parent-child relationship is one deserving of protection. It rests upon a relationship of mutual trust where the child has the right to expect that the parent will act in accordance with the child's best interest. If the state is permitted to interfere in that relationship by compelling parents to divulge information conveyed to them in confidence by their children, mutual trust, and ultimately the family, are threatened.

While I am aware that the availability of even this limited parent-child privilege may, in some rare circumstances, complicate a criminal fact-finding proceeding, I am convinced that the risk is one well worth bearing. * * * This is especially true where, as here in the Virgin Islands case, the parent is not a co-defendant or a co-witness to a criminal act, and is not alleged to be hiding the instrumentality or the fruits of a criminal act. I cannot agree with the majority that testimonial privileges must be regarded as automatic impediments to the effectiveness of the judicial system. In limited circumstances these privileges are critical to important policy interests. I am convinced, as was the district court, that "youngsters today are increasingly faced with excruciatingly dangerous and difficult situations" and that "the law ought to do everything possible to encourage children to confide in their parents and turn to [them] in times of trouble."

C.

The spousal privilege is the only testimonial privilege based on a familial relationship to have received general acceptance in the federal courts. In arguing that we should uphold the father's claim of privilege in this case, I am motivated by many of the same concerns which underlie the spousal privilege. The policy advanced by the spousal privilege "is the protection of the marital confidences, regarded as so essential to the preservation of the marriage relationship as to outweigh the disadvantages to the administration of justice which the privilege entails". Similar concerns are present here. * * *

D.

The parent-child privilege is not a novel or radical concept. "Both ancient Jewish law and Roman law entirely barred family members from testifying against one another based on a desire to promote the solidarity and trust that support the family unit. The Napoleonic Code also prevented the disclosure of confidences between family members." J. Tyson Covey, Note, *Making Form Follow Function: Considerations in Creating and Applying a Statutory Parent-Child Privilege*, 1990 U. Ill. L. Rev. 879, 883. The civil law countries of Western Europe including France, Sweden, and the former West Germany also recognize a privilege covering compelled testimony from family members. * * * Furthermore, * * * although a number of courts have declined to recognize a parent-child privilege in one form or another, the vast majority of those cases, indeed all of the federal cases, are distinguishable, on significant grounds, from the case before us.

Most cases discussing the availability of a parent-child privilege have done so in the context of whether a child should be compelled to testify against a parent. As the court of appeals acknowledged in *In re Grand Jury Proceedings (Starr)*, 647 F.2d 511, 513 n. 4 (5th Cir. 1981), cases involving testimony by a child regarding activities of or communications by a parent are not as compelling as cases "involv[ing] confidential communications from the child to the parent" because the former do not implicate "the desire to avoid discouraging a child from confiding in his parents." * * * This distinction separates the Virgin Islands and Delaware appeals.

A second set of cases refusing to recognize a parent-child privilege involve children who were significantly older than the son in this case and did not implicate communications seeking parental advice and guidance. * * * Finally, a number of cases rejecting the parent-child privilege involved defendants who sought to bar voluntary testimony offered by their parents. These cases do not present the threat to the family relationship posed in the case before us. The importance of this distinction was summarized by the Illinois Supreme Court in *People v. Sanders*, 99 Ill.2d 262, 457 N.E.2d 1241, 1246 (1983). The court in *Sanders* wrote that cases in which the parent-child privilege has been upheld have

> relied heavily upon conjecture that a family member who is forced to testify against her will would face the unpleasant choice of aiding the criminal conviction of a loved one, perjuring herself on the stand, or risking a citation for contempt of court for refusing to testify and the belief that the harshness of this choice has the effect of undermining the family relationship. Such a fear is without foundation where, as in this case, the witness who is a family member volunteers her testimony. The voluntariness of the act is strong evidence that the choice the witness faced was an easy one for her to make.

III.

* * * The facts underlying the Virgin Islands appeal are critical to my conclusion that we should recognize a narrowly circumscribed parent-child privilege. The interests involved in protecting the communications at issue here are far stronger than those involved in previous cases. Consequently, the result which I would reach is not as radical as it might initially appear. * * *

IV.

I am convinced that the public good to be derived from a circumscribed parent-child testimonial privilege outweighs the judicial system's interest in compelled parental testimony. I would, therefore, recognize a privilege which could be invoked by a parent and child together to bar compelled testimony concerning confidential communications made to that parent by his child in the course of seeking parental advice and guidance. I would reverse the district court's order in the Virgin Islands matter denying the motion to quash the grand jury subpoena.

* * *

Appendix A

FEDERAL RULES OF EVIDENCE
Effective July 1, 1975, as amended to December 1, 2006

ARTICLE I.

GENERAL PROVISIONS

Rule 101. Scope

These rules govern proceedings in the courts of the United States and before the United States bankruptcy judges and United States magistrate judges, to the extent and with the exceptions stated in rule 1101.

(As amended Mar. 2, 1987, eff. Oct. 1, 1987; Apr. 25, 1988, eff. Nov. 1, 1988; Apr. 22, 1993, eff. Dec. 1, 1993.).

Rule 102. Purpose and Construction

These rules shall be construed to secure fairness in administration, elimination of unjustifiable expense and delay, and pro-motion of growth and development of the law of evidence to the end that the truth may be ascertained and proceedings justly determined.

Rule 103. Rulings on Evidence

(a). Effect of erroneous ruling. — Error may not be predicated upon a ruling which admits or excludes evidence unless a substantial right of the party is affected, and

(1). Objection. — In case the ruling is one admitting evidence, a timely objection or motion to strike appears of record, stating the specific ground of objection, if the specific ground was not apparent from the context; or

(2). Offer of proof. — In case the ruling is one excluding evidence, the substance of the evidence was made known to the court by offer or was apparent from the context within which questions were asked.

Once the court makes a definitive ruling on the record admitting or excluding evidence, either at or before trial, a party need not renew an objection or offer of proof to preserve a claim of error for appeal.

(b). Record of offer and ruling. — The court may add any other or further statement which shows the character of the evidence, the form in which it was offered, the objection made, and the ruling thereon. It may direct the making of an offer in question and answer form.

(c). Hearing of jury. — In jury cases, proceedings shall be conducted, to the extent practicable, so as to prevent inadmissible evidence from being suggested to the jury by any means, such as making statements or offers of proof or asking questions in the hearing of the jury.

(d). Plain error. — Nothing in this rule precludes taking notice of plain errors affecting substantial rights although they were not brought to the attention of the court.

(As amended Apr. 17, 2000, eff. Dec. 1, 2000.).

Rule 104. Preliminary Questions

(a). Questions of admissibility generally. — Preliminary questions concerning the qualification of a person to be a witness, the existence of a privilege, or the admissibility of evidence shall be determined by the court, subject to the provisions of subdivision (b). In making its determination it is not bound by the rules of evidence except those with respect to privileges.

(b). Relevancy conditioned on fact. — When the relevancy of evidence depends upon the fulfillment of a condition of fact, the court shall admit it upon, or subject to, the introduction of evidence sufficient to support a finding of the fulfillment of the condition.

(c). Hearing of jury. — Hearings on the admissibility of confessions shall in all cases be conducted out of the hearing of the jury.

Hearings on other preliminary matters shall be so conducted when the interests of justice require, or when an accused is a witness and so requests.

(d). Testimony by accused. — The accused does not, by testifying upon a preliminary matter, become subject to cross-examination as to other issues in the case.

(e). Weight and credibility. — This rule does not limit the right of a party to introduce before the jury evidence relevant to weight or credibility.

(As amended Mar. 2, 1987, eff. Oct. 1, 1987.).

Rule 105. Limited Admissibility

When evidence which is admissible as to one party or for one purpose but not admissible as to another party or for another purpose is admitted, the court, upon request, shall restrict the evidence to its proper scope and instruct the jury accordingly.

Rule 106. Remainder of or Related Writings or Recorded Statements

When a writing or recorded statement or part thereof is introduced by a party, an adverse party may require the introduction at that time of any other part or any other writing or recorded statement which ought in fairness to be considered contemporaneously with it.

(As amended Mar. 2, 1987, eff. Oct. 1, 1987.).

ARTICLE II.

JUDICIAL NOTICE

Rule 201. Judicial Notice of Adjudicative Facts

(a). Scope of rule. — This rule governs only judicial notice of adjudicative facts.

(b). Kinds of facts. — A judicially noticed fact must be one not subject to reasonable dispute in that it is either (1) generally known within the territorial jurisdiction of the trial court or (2) capable of accurate and ready determination by resort to sources whose accuracy cannot reasonably be questioned.

(c). When discretionary. — A court may take judicial notice, whether requested or not.

(d). When mandatory. — A court shall take judicial notice if requested by a party and supplied with the necessary information.

(e). Opportunity to be heard. — A party is entitled upon timely request to an opportunity to be heard as to the propriety of taking judicial notice and the tenor of the matter noticed. In the absence of prior notification, the request may be made after judicial notice has been taken.

(f). Time of taking notice. — Judicial notice may be taken at any stage of the proceeding.

(g). Instructing jury. — In a civil action or proceeding, the court shall instruct the jury to accept as conclusive any fact judicially noticed. In a criminal case, the court shall instruct the jury that it may, but is not required to, accept as conclusive any fact judicially noticed.

ARTICLE III.

PRESUMPTIONS IN CIVIL ACTIONS AND PROCEEDINGS

Rule 301. Presumptions in General in Civil Actions and Proceedings

In all civil actions and proceedings not otherwise provided for by Act of Congress or by these rules, a presumption imposes on the party against whom it is directed the burden of going forward with evidence to rebut or meet the presumption, but does not shift to such party the burden of proof in the sense of the risk of non-persuasion, which remains throughout the trial upon the party on whom it was originally cast.

Rule 302. Applicability of State Law in Civil Actions and Proceedings

In civil actions and proceedings, the effect of a presumption respecting a fact which is an element of a claim or defense as to which State law supplies the rule of decision is determined in accordance with State law.

ARTICLE IV.

RELEVANCY AND ITS LIMITS

Rule 401. Definition of "Relevant Evidence"

"Relevant evidence" means evidence having any tendency to make the existence of any fact that is of consequence to the determination of the action more probable or less probable than it would be without the evidence.

Rule 402. Relevant Evidence Generally Admissible; Irrelevant Evidence Inadmissible

All relevant evidence is admissible, except as otherwise provided by the Constitution of the United States, by Act of Congress, by these rules, or by other rules prescribed by the Supreme Court pursuant to statutory authority. Evidence which is not relevant is not admissible.

Rule 403. Exclusion of Relevant Evidence on Grounds of Prejudice, Confusion, or Waste of Time

Although relevant, evidence may be excluded if its probative value is substantially outweighed by the danger of unfair prejudice, confusion of the issues, or misleading the jury, or by considerations of undue delay, waste of time, or needless presentation of cumulative evidence.

Rule 404. Character Evidence Not Admissible to Prove Conduct; Exceptions; Other Crimes

(a). Character evidence generally. — Evidence of a person's character or a trait of character is not admissible for the purpose of proving action in conformity therewith on a particular occasion, except:

(1). Character of accused. — In a criminal case, evidence of a pertinent trait of character offered by an accused, or by the prosecution to rebut the same, or if evidence of a trait of character of the alleged victim of the crime is offered by an accused and admitted under Rule 404(a)(2), evidence of the same trait of character of the accused offered by the prosecution;

(2). Character of alleged victim. — In a criminal case, and subject to the limitations imposed by Rule 412, evidence of a pertinent trait of character of the alleged victim of the crime offered by an accused, or by the prosecution to rebut the same, or evidence of a character trait of peacefulness of the alleged victim offered by the prosecution in a homicide case to rebut evidence that the alleged victim was the first aggressor;

(3). Character of witness. — Evidence of the character of a witness, as provided in rules 607, 608, and 609.

(b). Other crimes, wrongs, or acts. — Evidence of other crimes, wrongs, or acts is not admissible to prove the character of a person in order to show action in conformity therewith. It may, how-ever, be admissible for other purposes, such as proof of motive, opportunity, intent, preparation, plan, knowledge, identity, or absence of mistake or accident, provided that upon request by the accused, the prosecution in a criminal case shall provide reasonable notice in advance of trial, or during trial if the court excuses pretrial notice on good cause shown, of the general nature of any such evidence it intends to introduce at trial.

(As amended Mar. 2, 1987, eff. Oct. 1, 1987; Apr. 30, 1991, eff. Dec. 1, 1991; Apr. 17, 2000, eff. Dec. 1, 2000; December 1, 2006.).

Rule 405. Methods of Proving Character

(a). Reputation or opinion. — In all cases in which evidence of character or a trait of character of a person is admissible, proof may be made by testimony as to reputation or by testimony in the form of an opinion. On cross-examination, inquiry is allowable into relevant specific instances of conduct.

(b). Specific instances of conduct. — In cases in which character or a trait of character of a person is an essential element of a charge, claim, or defense, proof may also be made of specific instances of that person's conduct.

(As amended Mar. 2, 1987, eff. Oct. 1, 1987.).

Rule 406. Habit; Routine Practice

Evidence of the habit of a person or of the routine practice of an organization, whether corroborated or not and regardless of the presence of eyewitnesses, is relevant to prove that the conduct of the person or organization on a particular occasion was in conformity with the habit or routine practice.

Rule 407. Subsequent Remedial Measures

When, after an injury or harm allegedly caused by an event, measures are taken that, if taken previously, would have made the injury or harm less likely to occur, evidence of the subsequent measures is not admissible to prove negligence, culpable conduct, a defect in a product, a defect in a product's design, or a need for a warning or instruction. This rule does not require the exclusion of evidence of subsequent measures when offered for another purpose, such as proving ownership, control, or feasibility of pre-cautionary measures, if controverted, or impeachment.

(As amended Apr. 11, 1997, eff. Dec. 1, 1997.).

Rule 408. Compromise and Offers to Compromise

(a). Prohibited uses. — Evidence of the following is not admissible on behalf of any party, when offered to prove liability for, invalidity of, or amount of a claim that was disputed as to validity or amount, or to impeach through a prior inconsistent statement or contradiction:

(1). furnishing or offering or promising to furnish or accepting or offering or promising to accept a valuable consideration in compromising or attempting to compromise the claim; and

(2). conduct or statements made in compromise negotiations regarding the claim, except when offered in a criminal case and the negotiations related to a claim by a public office or agency in the exercise of regulatory, investigative, or enforcement authority.

(b). Permitted uses. This rule does not require exclusion if the evidence is offered for purposes not prohibited by subdivision (a). Examples of permissible purposes include proving a witness's bias or prejudice; negating a contention of undue delay; and proving an effort to obstruct a criminal investigation or prosecution.

(As amended December 1, 2006).

Rule 409. Payment of Medical and Similar Expenses

Evidence of furnishing or offering or promising to pay medical, hospital, or similar expenses occasioned by an injury is not admissible to prove liability for the injury.

Rule 410. Inadmissibility of Pleas, Plea Discussions, and Related Statements

Except as otherwise provided in this rule, evidence of the following is not, in any civil or criminal proceeding, admissible against the defendant who made the plea or was a participant in the plea discussions:

(1) a plea of guilty which was later withdrawn;

(2) a plea of nolo contendere;

(3) any statement made in the course of any proceedings under Rule 11 of the Federal Rules of Criminal Procedure or comparable state procedure regarding either of the foregoing pleas; or

(4) any statement made in the course of plea discussions with an attorney for the prosecuting authority which do not result in a plea of guilty or which result in a plea of guilty later withdrawn. However, such a statement is admissible (i) in any proceeding wherein another statement made in the course of the same plea or plea discussions has been introduced and the statement ought in fairness be considered contemporaneously with it, or (ii) in a criminal proceeding for perjury or false statement if the statement was made by the defendant under oath, on the record and in the presence of counsel.

(As amended Dec. 12, 1975; Apr. 30, 1979, eff. Dec. 1, 1980.).

Rule 411. Liability Insurance

Evidence that a person was or was not insured against liability is not admissible upon the issue whether the person acted negligently or otherwise wrongfully. This rule does not require the exclusion of evidence of insurance against liability when offered for another purpose, such as proof of agency, ownership, or control, or bias or prejudice of a witness.

(As amended Mar. 2, 1987, eff. Oct. 1, 1987.).

Rule 412. Sex Offense Cases; Relevance of Alleged Victim's Past Sexual Behavior or Alleged Sexual Predisposition

(a). Evidence Generally Inadmissible.

— The following evidence is not admissible in any civil or criminal proceeding involving alleged sexual misconduct except as provided in subdivisions (b) and (c):

(1). Evidence offered to prove that any alleged victim engaged in other sexual behavior.

(2). Evidence offered to prove any alleged victim's sexual predisposition.

(b). Exceptions.

(1). In a criminal case, the following evidence is admissible, if otherwise admissible under these rules:

(A). evidence of specific instances of sexual behavior by the alleged victim offered to prove that a person other than the accused was the source of semen, injury or other physical evidence;

(B). evidence of specific instances of sexual behavior by the alleged victim with respect to the person accused of the sexual misconduct offered by the accused to prove consent or by the prosecution; and

(C). evidence the exclusion of which would violate the constitutional rights of the defendant.

(2). In a civil case, evidence offered to prove the sexual behavior or sexual predisposition of any alleged victim is admissible if it is otherwise admissible under these rules and its probative value substantially outweighs the danger of harm to any victim and of unfair prejudice to any party. Evidence of an alleged victim's reputation is admissible only if it has been placed in controversy by the alleged victim.

(c). Procedure To Determine Admissibility.

(1). A party intending to offer evidence under subdivision (b) must-

(A). file a written motion at least 14 days before trial specifically describing the evidence and stating the purpose for which it is offered unless the court, for good cause requires a different time for filing or permits filing during trial; and

(B). serve the motion on all parties and notify the alleged victim or, when appropriate, the alleged victim's guardian or representative.

(2). Before admitting evidence under this rule the court must conduct a hearing in camera and afford the victim and parties a right to attend and be heard. The motion, related papers, and the record of the hearing must be sealed and remain under seal unless the court orders otherwise.

(As added Oct. 28, 1978, eff. Nov. 28, 1978; amended Nov. 18, 1988;

Apr. 29, 1994, eff. Dec. 1, 1994; Sept. 13, 1994, eff. Dec. 1, 1994.).

Rule 413. Evidence of Similar Crimes in Sexual Assault Cases

(a). In a criminal case in which the defendant is accused of an offense of sexual assault, evidence of the defendant's commission of another offense or offenses of sexual assault is admissible, and may be considered for its bearing on any matter to which it is relevant.

(b). In a case in which the Government intends to offer evidence under this rule, the attorney for the Government shall disclose the evidence to the defendant, including statements of witnesses or a summary of the substance of any testimony that is expected to be offered, at least fifteen days before the scheduled date of trial or at such later time as the court may allow for good cause.

(c). This rule shall not be construed to limit the admission or consideration of evidence under any other rule.

(d). For purposes of this rule and Rule 415, "offense of sexual assault" means a crime under Federal law or the law of a State (as defined in section 513 of title 18, United States Code) that involved-

(1). any conduct proscribed by chapter 109A of title 18, United States Code;

(2). contact, without consent, between any part of the defendant's body or an object and the genitals or anus of another person;

(3). contact, without consent, between the genitals or anus of the defendant and any part of another person's body;

(4). deriving sexual pleasure or gratification from the infliction of death, bodily injury, or physical pain on another person; or

(5). an attempt or conspiracy to engage in conduct described in paragraphs (1)-(4).

(Added Sept. 13, 1994, eff. July 9, 1995.).

Rule 414. Evidence of Similar Crimes in Child Molestation Cases

(a). In a criminal case in which the defendant is accused of an offense of child molestation, evidence of the defendant's commission of another offense or offenses of child molestation is admissible, and may be considered for its bearing on any matter to which it is relevant.

(b). In a case in which the Government intends to offer evidence under this rule, the attorney for the Government shall disclose the evidence to the defendant, including statements of witnesses or a summary of the substance of any testimony that is expected to be offered, at least fifteen days before the scheduled date of trial or at such later time as the court may allow for good cause.

(c). This rule shall not be construed to limit the admission or consideration of evidence under any other rule.

(d). For purposes of this rule and Rule 415, "child" means a person below the age of fourteen, and "offense of child molestation" means a crime under Federal law or the law of a State (as defined in section 513 of title 18, United States Code) that involved-

(1). any conduct proscribed by chapter 109A of title 18, United States Code, that was committed in relation to a child;

(2). any conduct proscribed by chapter 110 of title 18, United States Code;

(3). contact between any part of the defendant's body or an object and the genitals or anus of a child;

(4). contact between the genitals or anus of the defendant and any part of the body of a child;

(5). deriving sexual pleasure or gratification from the infliction of death, bodily injury, or physical pain on a child; or

(6). an attempt or conspiracy to engage in conduct described in paragraphs (1)-(5).

(Added Sept. 13, 1994, eff. July 9, 1995.).

Rule 415. Evidence of Similar Acts in Civil Cases Concerning Sexual Assault or Child Molestation

(a). In a civil case in which a claim for damages or other relief is predicated on a party's alleged commission of conduct constituting an offense of sexual assault or child molestation, evidence of that party's commission of another offense or offenses of sexual assault or child molestation is admissible and may be considered as provided in Rule 413 and Rule 414 of these rules.

(b). A party who intends to offer evidence under this Rule shall disclose the evidence to the party against whom it will be offered, including statements of witnesses or a summary of the substance of any testimony that is expected to be offered, at least fifteen days before the scheduled date of trial or at such later time as the court may allow for good cause.

(c). This rule shall not be construed to limit the admission or consideration of evidence under any other rule.

(Added Sept. 13, 1994, eff. July 9, 1995.).

ARTICLE V.

PRIVILEGES

Rule 501. General Rule

Except as otherwise required by the Constitution of the United States or provided by Act of Congress or in rules prescribed by the Supreme Court pursuant to statutory authority, the privilege of a witness, person, government, State, or political subdivision thereof shall be governed by the principles of the common law as they may be interpreted by the courts of the United States in the light of reason and experience. However, in civil actions and proceedings, with respect to an element of a claim or defense as to which State law supplies the rule of decision, the privilege of a witness, person, government, State, or political subdivision thereof shall be determined in accordance with State law.

ARTICLE VI.

WITNESSES

Rule 601. General Rule of Competency

Every person is competent to be a witness except as otherwise provided in these rules. However, in civil actions and proceedings, with respect to an element of a claim or defense as to which State law supplies the rule of decision, the competency of a witness shall be determined in accordance with State law.

Rule 602. Lack of Personal Knowledge

A witness may not testify to a matter unless evidence is introduced sufficient to support a finding that the witness has personal knowledge of the matter. Evidence to prove personal knowledge may, but need not, consist of the witness' own testimony. This rule is subject to the provisions of rule 703, relating to opinion testimony by expert witnesses.

(As amended Mar. 2, 1987, eff. Oct. 1, 1987; Apr. 25, 1988, eff. Nov. 1, 1988.).

Rule 603. Oath or Affirmation

Before testifying, every witness shall be required to declare that the witness will testify truthfully, by oath or affirmation administered in a form calculated to awaken the witness= conscience and impress the witness' mind with the duty to do so.

(As amended Mar. 2, 1987, eff. Oct. 1, 1987.).

Rule 604. Interpreters

An interpreter is subject to the provisions of these rules relating to qualification as an expert and the administration of an oath or affirmation to make a true translation.

(As amended Mar. 2, 1987, eff. Oct. 1, 1987.).

Rule 605. Competency of Judge as Witness

The judge presiding at the trial may not testify in that trial as a witness. No objection need be made in order to preserve the point.

Rule 606. Competency of Juror as Witness

(a). At the trial. — A member of the jury may not testify as a witness before that jury in the trial of the case in which the juror is sitting. If the juror is called so to testify, the opposing party shall be afforded an opportunity to object out of the presence of the jury.

(b). Inquiry into validity of verdict or indictment. Upon an inquiry into the validity of a verdict or indictment, a juror may not testify as to any matter or statement occurring during the course of the jury's deliberations or to the effect of anything upon that or any other juror's mind or emotions as influencing the juror to assent to or dissent from the verdict or indictment or concerning the juror's mental processes in connection therewith. But a juror may testify about (1) whether extraneous prejudicial information was improperly brought to the jury's attention, (2) whether any outside influence was improperly brought to bear upon any juror, or (3) whether there was a mistake in entering the verdict onto the verdict form. A juror's affidavit or evidence of any statement by the juror may not be received on a matter about which the juror would be precluded from testifying.

(As amended Dec. 12, 1975; Mar. 2, 1987, eff. Oct. 1, 1987; December 1, 2006.)

Rule 607. Who May Impeach

The credibility of a witness may be attacked by any party, including the party calling the witness.

(As amended Mar. 2, 1987, eff. Oct. 1, 1987.).

Rule 608. Evidence of Character and Conduct of Witness

(a). Opinion and reputation evidence of character. — The credibility of a witness may be attacked or supported by evidence in the form of opinion or reputation, but subject to these limitations: (1) the evidence may refer only to character for truthfulness or un-truthfulness, and (2) evidence of truthful character is admissible only after the character of the witness for truthfulness has been attacked by opinion or reputation evidence or otherwise.

(b). Specific instances of conduct. — Specific instances of the conduct of a witness, for the purpose of attacking or supporting the witness' character for truthfulness, other than conviction of crime as provided in rule 609, may not be proved by extrinsic evidence. They may, however, in the discretion of the court, if probative of truthfulness or untruthfulness, be inquired into on cross-examination of the witness (1) concerning the witness' character for truthfulness or untruthfulness, or (2) concerning the character for truthfulness or untruthfulness of another witness as to which character the witness being cross-examined has testified.

The giving of testimony, whether by an accused or by any other witness, does not operate as a waiver of the accused's or the witness' privilege against self-incrimination when examined with respect to matters that relate only tocharacter for truthfulness.

(As amended Mar. 2, 1987, eff. Oct. 1, 1987; Apr. 25, 1988, eff. Nov. 1, 1988. December 1, 2003).

Rule 609. Impeachment by Evidence of Conviction of Crime

(a). General rule. — For the purpose of attacking the **character for truthfulness** of a witness,

(1). evidence that a witness other than an accused has been convicted of a crime shall be admitted, subject to Rule 403, if the crime was punishable by death or imprisonment in excess of one year under the law under which the witness was convicted, and evidence that an accused has been convicted of such a crime shall be admitted if the court determines that the probative value of admitting this evidence outweighs its prejudicial effect to the accused; and

(2). evidence that any witness has been convicted of a crime shall be admitted regardless of the punishment, if it readily can be determined that establishing the elements of the crime required proof or admission of an act of dishonesty or false statement by the witness.

(b). Time limit. — Evidence of a conviction under this rule is not admissible if a period of more than ten years has elapsed since the date of the conviction or of the release of the witness from the confinement imposed for that conviction, whichever is the later date, unless the court determines, in the interests of justice, that the probative value of the conviction supported by specific facts and circumstances substantially outweighs its prejudicial effect. However, evidence of a conviction more than 10 years old as calculated herein, is not admissible unless the proponent gives to the adverse party sufficient advance written notice of intent to use such evidence to provide the adverse party with a fair opportunity to contest the use of such evidence.

(c). Effect of pardon, annulment, or certificate of rehabilitation. — Evidence of a conviction is not admissible under this rule if (1) the conviction has been the subject of a pardon, annulment, certificate of rehabilitation, or other equivalent procedure based on a finding of the rehabilitation of the person convicted, and that person has not been convicted of a subsequent crime which was punishable by death or imprisonment in excess of one year, or (2) the conviction has been the subject of a pardon, annulment, or other equivalent procedure based on a finding of innocence.

(d). Juvenile adjudications. — Evidence of juvenile adjudications is generally not admissible under this rule. The court may, however, in a criminal case allow evidence of a juvenile adjudication of a witness other than the accused if conviction of the offense would be admissible to attack the credibility of an adult and the court is satisfied that admission in evidence is necessary for a fair determination of the issue of guilt or innocence.

(e). Pendency of appeal. — The pendency of an appeal therefrom does not render evidence of a conviction inadmissible. Evidence of the pendency of an appeal is admissible.

(As amended Mar. 2, 1987, eff. Oct. 1, 1987; Jan. 26, 1990, eff. Dec. 1, 1990; December 1, 2006.).

Rule 610. Religious Beliefs or Opinions

Evidence of the beliefs or opinions of a witness on matters of religionis not admissible for the purpose of showing that by reason of their nature the witness' credibility is impaired or enhanced.

(As amended Mar. 2, 1987, eff. Oct. 1, 1987.).

Rule 611. Mode and Order of Interrogation and Presentation

(a). Control by court. — The court shall exercise reasonable control over the mode and order of interrogating witnesses and presenting evidence so as to (1) make the interrogation and presentation effective for the ascertainment of the truth, (2) avoid needless consumption of time, and (3) protect witnesses from harassment or undue embarrassment.

(b). Scope of cross-examination. — Cross-examination should be limited to the subject matter of the direct examination and matters affecting the credibility of the witness. The court may, in the exercise of discretion, permit inquiry into additional matters as if on direct examination.

(c). Leading questions. — Leading questions should not be used on the direct examination of a witness except as may be necessary to develop the witness' testimony. Ordinarily leading questions should be permitted on cross-examination. When a party calls a hostile witness, an adverse party, or a witness identified with an adverse party, interrogation may be by leading questions.

(As amended Mar. 2, 1987, eff. Oct. 1, 1987.)

Rule 612. Writing Used to Refresh Memory

Except as otherwise provided in criminal proceedings by section 3500 of title 18, United States Code, if a witness uses a writing to refresh memory for the purpose of testifying, either-

(1) while testifying, or

(2) before testifying, if the court in its discretion determines it is necessary in the interests of justice,

an adverse party is entitled to have the writing produced at the hearing, to inspect it, to cross-examine the witness thereon, and to introduce in evidence those portions which relate to the testimony of the witness. If it is claimed that the writing contains matters not related to the subject matter of the testimony the court shall examine the writing in camera, excise any portions not so related, and order delivery of the remainder to the party entitled thereto. Any portion withheld over objections shall be preserved and made available to the appellate court in the event of an appeal. If a writing is not produced or delivered pursuant to order under this rule, the court shall make any order justice requires, except that in criminal cases when the prosecution elects not to comply, the order shall be one striking the testimony or, if the court in its discretion determines that the interests of justice so require, declaring a mistrial.

(As amended Mar. 2, 1987, eff. Oct. 1, 1987.).

Rule 613. Prior Statements of Witnesses

(a). Examining witness concerning prior statement. — In examining a witness concerning a prior statement made by the witness, whether written or not, the statement need not be shown nor its contents disclosed to the witness at that time, but on request the same shall be shown or disclosed to opposing counsel.

(b). Extrinsic evidence of prior inconsistent statement of witness. — Extrinsic evidence of a prior inconsistent statement by a witness is not admissible unless the witness is afforded an opportunity to explain or deny the same and the opposite party is afforded an opportunity to interrogate the witness thereon, or the interests of justice otherwise require. This provision does not apply to admissions of a party-opponent as defined in rule 801(d)(2).

(As amended Mar. 2, 1987, eff. Oct. 1, 1987; Apr. 25, 1988, eff. Nov. 1, 1988.).

Rule 614. Calling and Interrogation of Witnesses by Court

(a). Calling by court. — The court may, on its own motion or at the suggestion of a party, call witnesses, and all parties are entitled to cross-examine witnesses thus called.

(b). Interrogation by court. — The court may interrogate witnesses, whether called by itself or by a party.

(c). Objections. — Objections to the calling of witnesses by the court or to interrogation by it may be made at the time or at the next available opportunity when the jury is not present.

Rule 615. Exclusion of Witnesses

At the request of a party the court shall order witnesses excluded so that they cannot hear the testimony of other witnesses, and it may make the order of its own motion. This rule does not authorize exclusion of (1) a party who is a natural person, or (2) an officer or employee of a party which is not a natural person designated as its representative by its attorney, or (3) a person whose presence is shown by a party to be essential to the presentation of the party's cause, or (4) a person authorized by statute to be present.

(As amended Mar. 2, 1987, eff. Oct. 1, 1987; Apr. 25, 1988, eff. Nov. 1, 1988; Nov. 18, 1988; Apr. 24, 1998, eff. Dec. 1, 1998.).

ARTICLE VII.

OPINIONS AND EXPERT TESTIMONY

Rule 701. Opinion Testimony by Lay Witnesses

If the witness is not testifying as an expert, the witness' testimony in the form of opinions or inferences is limited to those opinions or inferences which are (a) rationally based on the perception of the witness, and (b) helpful to a clear understanding of the witness' testimony or the determination of a fact in issue, and (c) not based on scientific, technical, or other specialized knowledge within the scope of Rule 702.

(As amended Mar. 2, 1987, eff. Oct. 1, 1987; Apr. 17, 2000, eff. Dec. 1, 2000.).

Rule 702. Testimony by Experts

If scientific, technical, or other specialized knowledge will assist the trier of fact to understand the evidence or to determine a fact in issue, a witness qualified as an expert by knowledge, skill, experience, training, or education, may testify thereto in the form of an opinion or otherwise, if (1) the testimony is based upon sufficient facts or data, (2) the testimony is the product of reliable principles and methods, and (3) the witness has applied the principles and methods reliably to the facts of the case.

(As amended Apr. 17, 2000, eff. Dec. 1, 2000.).

Rule 703. Bases of Opinion Testimony by Experts

The facts or data in the particular case upon which an expert bases an opinion or inference may be those perceived by or made known to the expert at or before the hearing. If of a type reasonably relied upon by experts in the particular field in forming opinions or inferences upon the subject, the facts or data need not be admissible in evidence in order for the opinion or inference to be admitted. Facts or data that are otherwise inadmissible shall not be disclosed to the jury by the proponent of the opinion or inference unless the court determines that their probative value in assisting the jury to evaluate the expert's opinion substantially outweighs their prejudicial effect.

(As amended Mar. 2, 1987, eff. Oct. 1, 1987; Apr. 17, 2000, eff. Dec. 1, 2000.).

Rule 704. Opinion on Ultimate Issue

(a). Except as provided in subdivision (b), testimony in the form of an opinion or inference otherwise admissible is not objectionable because it embraces an ultimate issue to be decided by the trier of fact.

(b). No expert witness testifying with respect to the mental state or condition of a defendant in a criminal case may state an opinion or inference as to whether the defendant did or did not have the mental state or condition constituting an element of the crime charged or of a defense thereto. Such ultimate issues are matters for the trier of fact alone.

(As amended Oct. 12, 1984.).

Rule 705. Disclosure of Facts or Data Underlying Expert Opinion

The expert may testify in terms of opinion or inference and give reasons therefor without first testifying to the underlying facts or data, unless the court requires otherwise. The expert may in any event be required to disclose the underlying facts or data on cross-examination.

(As amended Mar. 2, 1987, eff. Oct. 1, 1987; Apr. 22, 1993, eff. Dec. 1, 1993.).

Rule 706. Court Appointed Experts

(a). Appointment. — The court may on its own motion or on the motion of any party enter an order to show cause why expert witnesses should not be appointed, and may request the parties to submit nominations. The court may appoint any expert witnesses agreed upon by the parties, and may appoint expert witnesses of its own selection. An expert witness shall not be appointed by the court unless the witness consents to act. A witness so appointed shall be informed of the witness' duties by the court in writing, a copy of which shall be filed with the clerk, or at a conference in which the parties shall have opportunity to participate. A witness so appointed shall advise the parties of the witness' findings, if any; the witness' deposition may be taken by any party; and the witness may be called to testify by the court or any party. The witness shall be subject to cross-examination by each party, including a party calling the witness.

(b). Compensation. — Expert witnesses so appointed are entitled to reasonable compensation in whatever sum the court may allow. The compensation thus fixed is payable from funds which may be provided by law in criminal cases and civil actions and proceedings involving just compensation under the fifth amendment. In other civil actions and proceedings the compensation shall be paid by the parties in such proportion and at such time as the court directs, and thereafter charged in like manner as other costs.

(c). Disclosure of appointment. — In the exercise of its discretion, the court may authorize disclosure to the jury of the fact that the court appointed the expert witness.

(d). Parties' experts of own selection. — Nothing in this rule limits the parties in calling expert witnesses of their own selection.

(As amended Mar. 2, 1987, eff. Oct. 1, 1987.).

ARTICLE VIII.

HEARSAY

Rule 801. Definitions

The following definitions apply under this article:

(a). Statement. — A "statement" is (1) an oral or written assertion or (2) nonverbal conduct of a person, if it is intended by the person as an assertion.

(b). Declarant. — A "declarant" is a person who makes a statement.

(c). Hearsay. — "Hearsay" is a statement, other than one made by the declarant while testifying at the trial or hearing, offered in evidence to prove the truth of the matter asserted.

(d). Statements which are not hearsay. — A statement is not hearsay if—

(1). Prior statement by witness. — The declarant testifies at the trial or hearing and is subject to cross-examination concerning the statement, and the statement is (A) inconsistent with the declarant's testimony, and was given under oath subject to the penalty of perjury at a trial, hearing, or other proceeding, or in a deposition, or (B) consistent with the declarant's testimony and is offered to rebut an express or implied charge against the declarant of recent fabrication or improper influence or motive, or (C) one of identification of a person made after perceiving the person; or

(2). Admission by party-opponent. — The statement is offered against a party and is (A) the party's own statement, in either an individual or a representative capacity or (B) a statement of which the party has manifested an adoption or belief in its truth, or (C) a statement by a person authorized by the party to make a statement concerning the subject, or (D) a statement by the party's agent or servant concerning a matter within the scope of the agency or employment, made during the existence of the relationship, or (E) a statement by a coconspirator of a party during the course and in furtherance of the conspiracy. The contents of the statement shall be considered but are not alone sufficient to establish the declarant's authority under subdivision (C), the agency or employment relationship and scope thereof under subdivision (D), or the existence of the conspiracy and the participation therein of the declarant and the party against whom the statement is offered under subdivision (E).

(As amended Oct. 16, 1975, eff. Oct. 31, 1975; Mar. 2, 1987, eff. Oct. 1, 1987; Apr. 11, 1997, eff. Dec. 1, 1997.).

Rule 802. Hearsay Rule

Hearsay is not admissible except as provided by these rules or by other rules prescribed by the Supreme Court pursuant to statutory authority or by Act of Congress.

Rule 803. Hearsay Exceptions; Availability of Declarant Immaterial

The following are not excluded by the hearsay rule, even though the declarant is available as a witness:

(1) Present sense impression. — A statement describing or explaining an event or condition made while the declarant was perceiving the event or condition, or immediately thereafter.

(2) Excited utterance. — A statement relating to a startling event or condition made while the declarant was under the stress of excitement caused by the event or condition.

(3) Then existing mental, emotional, or physical condition. — A statement of the declarant's then existing state of mind, emotion, sensation, or physical condition (such as intent, plan, motive, design, mental feeling, pain, and bodily health), but not including a statement of memory or belief to prove the fact remembered or believed unless it relates to the execution, revocation, identification, or terms of declarant's will.

(4) Statements for purposes of medical diagnosis or treatment. — Statements made for purposes of medical diagnosis or treatment and describing medical history, or past or present symptoms, pain, or sensations, or the inception or general character of the cause or external source thereof insofar as reasonably pertinent to diagnosis or treatment.

(5) Recorded recollection. — A memorandum or record concerning a matter about which a witness once had knowledge but now has insufficient recollection to enable the witness to testify fully and accurately, shown to have been made or adopted by the witness when the matter was fresh in the witness'memory and to reflect that knowledge correctly. If admitted, the memorandum or record may be read into evidence but may not itself be received as an exhibit unless offered by an adverse party.

(6) Records of regularly conducted activity. — A memorandum, report, record, or data compilation, in any form, of acts, events, conditions, opinions, or diagnoses, made at or near the time by, or from information transmitted by, a person with knowledge, if kept in the course of a regularly conducted business activity, and if it was the regular practice of that business activity to make the memorandum, report, record or data compilation, all as shown by the testimony of the custodian or other qualified witness, or by certification that complies with Rule 902(11), Rule 902(12), or a statute permitting certification, unless the source of information or the method or circumstances of preparation indicate lack of trustworthiness. The term "business" as used in this paragraph includes business, institution, association, profession, occupation, and calling of every kind, whether or not conducted for profit.

(7) Absence of entry in records kept in accordance with the provisions of paragraph (6). — Evidence that a matter is not included in the memoranda reports, records, or data compilations, in any form, kept in accordance with the provisions of paragraph (6), to prove the nonoccurrence or nonexistence of the matter, if the matter was of a kind of which a memorandum, report, record, or data compilation was regularly made and preserved, unless the sources of information or other circumstances indicate lack of trustworthiness.

(8) Public records and reports. — Records, reports, statements, or data compilations, in any form, of public offices or agencies, setting forth (A) the activities of the office or agency, or (B) matters observed pursuant to duty imposed by law as to which matters there was a duty to report, excluding, however, in criminal cases matters observed by police officers and other law enforcement personnel, or (C) in civil actions and proceedings and against the Government in criminal cases, factual findings resulting from an investigation made pursuant to authority granted by law, unless the sources of information or other circumstances indicate lack of trustworthiness.

(9) Records of vital statistics. — Records or data compilations, in any form, of births, fetal deaths, deaths, or marriages, if the report thereof was made to a public office pursuant to requirements of law.

(10) Absence of public record or entry. — To prove the absence of a record, report, statement, or data compilation, in any form, or the nonoccurrence

or nonexistence of a matter of which a record, report, statement, or data compilation, in any form, was regularly made and preserved by a public office or agency, evidence in the form of a certification in accordance with rule 902, or testimony, that diligent search failed to disclose the record, report, statement, or data compilation, or entry.

(11) Records of religious organizations. — Statements of births, marriages, divorces, deaths, legitimacy, ancestry, relationship by blood or marriage, or other similar facts of personal or family history, contained in a regularly kept record of a religious organization.

(12) Marriage, baptismal, and similar certificates. — Statements of fact contained in a certificate that the maker performed a marriage or other ceremony or administered a sacrament, made by a clergyman, public official, or other person authorized by the rules or practices of a religious organization or by law to perform the act certified, and purporting to have been issued at the time of the act or within a reasonable time thereafter.

(13) Family records. — Statements of fact concerning personal or family history contained in family Bibles, genealogies, charts, engravings on rings, inscriptions on family portraits, engravings on urns, crypts, or tombstones, or the like.

(14) Records of documents affecting an interest in property. — The record of a document purporting to establish or affect an interest in property, as proof of the content of the original recorded document and its execution and delivery by each person by whom it purports to have been executed, if the record is a record of a public office and an applicable statute authorizes the recording of documents of that kind in that office.

(15) Statements in documents affecting an interest in property. — A statement contained in a document purporting to establish or affect an interest in property if the matter stated was relevant to the purpose of the document, unless dealings with the property since the document was made have been inconsistent with the truth of the statement or the purport of the document.

(16) Statements in ancient documents. — Statements in a document in existence twenty years or more the authenticity of which is established.

(17) Market reports, commercial publications. — Market quotations, tabulations, lists, directories, or other published compilations, generally used and relied upon by the public or by persons in particular occupations.

(18) Learned treatises. — To the extent called to the attention of an expert witness upon cross-examination or relied upon by the expert witness in direct examination, statements contained in published treatises, periodicals, or pamphlets on a subject of history, medicine, or other science or art, established as a reliable authority by the testimony or admission of the witness or by other expert testimony or by judicial notice. If admitted, the statements may be read into evidence but may not be received as exhibits.

(19) Reputation concerning personal or family history. — Reputation among members of a person's family by blood, adoption, or marriage, or

among a person's associates, or in the community, concerning a person's birth, adoption, marriage, divorce, death, legitimacy, relationship by blood, adoption, or marriage, ancestry, or other similar fact of personal or family history.

(20) Reputation concerning boundaries or general history. — Reputation in a community, arising before the controversy, as to boundaries of or customs affecting lands in the community, and reputation as to events of general history important to the community or State or nation in which located.

(21) Reputation as to character. — Reputation of a person's character among associates or in the community.

(22) Judgment of previous conviction. — Evidence of a final judgment, entered after a trial or upon a plea of guilty (but not upon a plea of nolo contendere), adjudging a person guilty of a crime punishable by death or imprisonment in excess of one year, to prove any fact essential to sustain the judgment, but not including, when offered by the Government in a criminal prosecution for purposes other than impeachment, judgments against persons other than the accused. The pendency of an appeal may be shown but does not affect admissibility.

(23) Judgment as to personal, family, or general history, or boundaries. — Judgments as proof of matters of personal, family or general history, or boundaries, essential to the judgment, if the same would be provable by evidence of reputation.

(24) [Other exceptions.] [Transferred to Rule 807]

(As amended Dec. 12, 1975; Mar. 2, 1987, eff. Oct. 1, 1987; Apr. 11, 1997, eff. Dec. 1, 1997; Apr. 17, 2000, eff. Dec. 1, 2000.)

Rule 804. Hearsay Exceptions; Declarant Unavailable

(a). Definition of unavailability. — "Unavailability as a witness" includes situations in which the declarant—

(1) is exempted by ruling of the court on the ground of privilege from testifying concerning the subject matter of the declarant's statement; or

(2) persists in refusing to testify concerning the subject matter of the declarant's statement despite an order of the court to do so; or

(3) testifies to a lack of memory of the subject matter of the declarant's statement; or

(4) is unable to be present or to testify at the hearing because of death or then existing physical or mental illness or infirmity; or

(5) is absent from the hearing and the proponent of a statement has been unable to procure the declarant's attendance (or in the case of a hearsay exception under subdivision (b)(2), (3), or (4), the declarant's attendance or testimony) by process or other reasonable means.

A declarant is not unavailable as a witness if exemption, refusal, claim of lack of memory, inability, or absence is due to the procurement or wrongdoing of the proponent of a statement for the purpose of preventing the witness from attending or testifying.

(b). Hearsay exceptions. — The following are not excluded by the hearsay rule if the declarant is unavailable as a witness:

(1) Former testimony. — Testimony given as a witness at another hearing of the same or a different proceeding, or in a deposition taken in compliance with law in the course of the same or another proceeding, if the party against whom the testimony is now offered, or, in a civil action or proceeding, a predecessor in interest, had an opportunity and similar motive to develop the testimony by direct, cross, or redirect examination.

(2) Statement under belief of impending death. — In a prosecution for homicide or in a civil action or proceeding, a statement made by a declarant while believing that the declarant's death was imminent, concerning the cause or circumstances of what the declarant believed to be impending death.

(3) Statement against interest. — A statement which was at the time of its making so far contrary to the declarant's pecuniary or proprietary interest, or so far tended to subject the declarant to civil or criminal liability, or to render invalid a claim by the declarant against another, that a reasonable person in the declarant's position would not have made the statement unless believing it to be true. A statement tending to expose the declarant to criminal liability and offered to exculpate the accused is not admissible unless corroborating circumstances clearly indicate the trustworthiness of the statement.

(4) Statement of personal or family history. — (A) A statement concerning the declarant's own birth, adoption, marriage, divorce, legitimacy, relationship by blood, adoption, or marriage, ancestry, or other similar fact of personal or family history, even though declarant had no means of acquiring personal knowledge of the matter stated; or (B) a statement concerning the foregoing matters, and death also, of another person, if the declarant was related to the other by blood, adoption, or marriage or was so intimately associated with the other's family as to be likely to have accurate information concerning the matter declared.

(5) [Other exceptions.] [Transferred to Rule 807]

(6) Forfeiture by wrongdoing. — A statement offered against a party that has engaged or acquiesced in wrongdoing that was intended to, and did, procure the unavailability of the declarant as a witness.

(As amended Dec. 12, 1975; Mar. 2, 1987, eff. Oct. 1, 1987; Nov. 18, 1988; Apr. 11, 1997, eff. Dec. 1, 1997.).

Rule 805. Hearsay Within Hearsay

Hearsay included within hearsay is not excluded under the hearsay rule if each part of the combined statements conforms with an exception to the hearsay rule provided in these rules.

Rule 806. Attacking and Supporting Credibility of Declarant

When a hearsay statement, or a statement defined in Rule 801(d)(2)(C), (D), or (E), has been admitted in evidence, the credibility of the declarant may be attacked, and if attacked may be supported, by any evidence which would be admissible for those purposes if declarant had testified as a witness. Evidence of a statement or conduct by the declarant at any time, inconsistent with the declarant's hearsay statement, is not subject to any requirement that the declarant may have been afforded an opportunity to deny or explain. If the party against whom a hearsay statement has been admitted calls the declarant as a witness, the party is entitled to examine the declarant on the statement as if under cross-examination.

(As amended Mar. 2, 1987, eff. Oct. 1, 1987; Apr. 11, 1997, eff. Dec. 1, 1997.)

Rule 807. Residual Exception

A statement not specifically covered by Rule 803 or 804 but having equivalent circumstantial guarantees of trustworthiness, is not excluded by the hearsay rule, if the court determines that (A) the statement is offered as evidence of a material fact; (B) the statement is more probative on the point for which it is offered than any other evidence which the proponent can procure through reasonable efforts; and (C) the general purposes of these rules and the interests of justice will best be served by admission of the statement into evidence. However, a statement may not be admitted under this exception unless the proponent of it makes known to the adverse party sufficiently in advance of the trial or hearing to provide the adverse party with a fair opportunity to prepare to meet it, the proponent's intention to offer the statement and the particulars of it, including the name and address of the declarant.

(Added Apr. 11, 1997, eff. Dec. 1, 1997.)

ARTICLE IX.

AUTHENTICATION AND IDENTIFICATION

Rule 901. Requirement of Authentication or Identification

(a). General provision. — The requirement of authentication or identification as a condition precedent to admissibility is satisfied by evidence sufficient to support a finding that the matter in question is what its proponent claims.

(b). Illustrations. — By way of illustration only, and not by way of limitation, the following are examples of authentication or identification conforming with the requirements of this rule:

(1) Testimony of witness with knowledge. — Testimony that a matter is what it is claimed to be.

(2) Nonexpert opinion on handwriting. — Nonexpert opinion as to the genuineness of handwriting, based upon familiarity not acquired for purposes of the litigation.

(3) Comparison by trier or expert witness. — Comparison by the trier of fact or by expert witnesses with specimens which have been authenticated.

(4) Distinctive characteristics and the like. — Appearance, contents, substance, internal patterns, or other distinctive characteristics, taken in conjunction with circumstances.

(5) Voice identification. — Identification of a voice, whether heard firsthand or through mechanical or electronic transmission or recording, by opinion based upon hearing the voice at any time under circumstances connecting it with the alleged speaker.

(6) Telephone conversations. — Telephone conversations, by evidence that a call was made to the number assigned at the time by the telephone company to a particular person or business, if (A) in the case of a person, circumstances, including self-identification, show the person answering to be the one called, or (B) in the case of a business, the call was made to a place of business and the conversation related to business reasonably transacted over the telephone.

(7) Public records or reports. — Evidence that a writing authorized by law to be recorded or filed and in fact recorded or filed in a public office, or a purported public record, report, statement, or data compilation, in any form, is from the public office where items of this nature are kept.

(8) Ancient documents or data compilation. — Evidence that a document or data compilation, in any form, (A) is in such condition as to create no suspicion concerning its authenticity, (B) was in a place where it, if authentic, would likely be, and (C) has been in existence 20 years or more at the time it is offered.

(9) Process or system. — Evidence describing a process or system used to produce a result and showing that the process or system produces an accurate result.

(10) Methods provided by statute or rule. — Any method of authentication or identification provided by Act of Congress or by other rules prescribed by the Supreme Court pursuant to statutory authority.

Rule 902. Self-authentication

Extrinsic evidence of authenticity as a condition precedent to admissibility is not required with respect to the following:

(1) Domestic public documents under seal. — A document bearing a seal purporting to be that of the United States, or of any State, district, Commonwealth, territory, or insular possession thereof, or the Panama Canal Zone, or the Trust Territory of the Pacific Islands, or of a political subdivision, department, officer, or agency thereof, and a signature purporting to be an attestation or execution.

(2) Domestic public documents not under seal. — A document purporting to bear the signature in the official capacity of an officer or employee of any entity included in paragraph (1) hereof, having no seal, if a public officer having a seal and having official duties in the district or political subdivision of the officer or employee certifies under seal that the signer has the official capacity and that the signature is genuine.

(3) Foreign public documents. — A document purporting to be executed or attested in an official capacity by a person authorized by the laws of a foreign country to make the execution or attestation, and accompanied by a final certification as to the genuineness of the signature and official position (A) of the executing or attesting person, or (B) of any foreign official whose certificate of genuineness of signature and official position relates to the execution or attestation or is in a chain of certificates of genuineness of signature and official position relating to the execution or attestation. A final certification may be made by a secretary of an embassy or legation, consul general, consul, vice consul, or consular agent of the United States, or a diplomatic or consular official of the foreign country assigned or accredited to the United States. If reasonable opportunity has been given to all parties to investigate the authenticity and accuracy of official documents, the court may, for good cause shown, order that they be treated as presumptively authentic without final certification or permit them to be evidenced by an attested summary with or without final certification.

(4) Certified copies of public records. — A copy of an official record or report or entry therein, or of a document authorized by law to be recorded or filed and actually recorded or filed in a public office, including data compilations in any form, certified as correct by the custodian or other person authorized to make the certification, by certificate complying with paragraph (1), (2), or (3) of this rule or complying with any Act of Congress or rule prescribed by the Supreme Court pursuant to statutory authority.

(5) Official publications. — Books, pamphlets, or other publications purporting to be issued by public authority.

(6) Newspapers and periodicals. — Printed materials purporting to be newspapers or periodicals.

(7) Trade inscriptions and the like. — Inscriptions, signs, tags, or labels purporting to have been affixed in the course of business and indicating ownership, control, or origin.

(8) Acknowledged documents. — Documents accompanied by a certificate of acknowledgment executed in the manner provided by law by a notary public or other officer authorized by law to take acknowledgments.

(9) Commercial paper and related documents. — Commercial paper, signatures thereon, and documents relating thereto to the extent provided by general commercial law.

(10) Presumptions under Acts of Congress. — Any signature, document, or other matter declared by Act of Congress to be presumptively or prima facie genuine or authentic.

(11) Certified domestic records of regularly conducted activity. — The original or a duplicate of a domestic record of regularly conducted activity that would be admissible under Rule 803(6) if accompanied by a written declaration of its custodian or other qualified person, in a manner complying with any Act of Congress or rule prescribed by the Supreme Court pursuant to statutory authority, certifying that the record-

(A) was made at or near the time of the occurrence of the matters set forth by, or from information transmitted by, a person with knowledge of those matters;

(B) was kept in the course of the regularly conducted activity; and

(C) was made by the regularly conducted activity as a regular practice.

A party intending to offer a record into evidence under this paragraph must provide written notice of that intention to all adverse parties, and must make the record and declaration available for inspection sufficiently in advance of their offer into evidence to provide an adverse party with a fair opportunity to challenge them.

(12) Certified foreign records of regularly conducted activity. — In a civil case, the original or a duplicate of a foreign record of regularly conducted activity that would be admissible under Rule 803(6) if accompanied by a written declaration by its custodian or other qualified person certifying that the record-

(A) was made at or near the time of the occurrence of the matters set forth by, or from information transmitted by, a person with knowledge of those matters;

(B) was kept in the course of the regularly conducted activity; and

(C) was made by the regularly conducted activity as a regular practice. The declaration must be signed in a manner that, if falsely made, would subject the maker to criminal penalty under the laws of the country where the declaration is signed. A party intending to offer a record into evidence under this paragraph must provide written notice of that intention to all adverse parties, and must make the record and declaration available for inspection sufficiently in advance of their offer into evidence to provide an adverse party with a fair opportunity to challenge them.

(As amended Mar. 2, 1987, eff. Oct. 1, 1987; Apr. 25, 1988, eff. Nov. 1, 1988; Apr. 17, 2000, eff. Dec. 1, 2000.)

Rule 903. Subscribing Witness' Testimony Unnecessary

The testimony of a subscribing witness is not necessary to authenticate a writing unless required by the laws of the jurisdiction whose laws govern the validity of the writing.

ARTICLE X.

CONTENTS OF WRITINGS, RECORDINGS, AND PHOTOGRAPHS

Rule 1001. Definitions

For purposes of this article the following definitions are applicable:

(1) Writings and recordings. — "Writings" and "recordings" consist of letters, words, or numbers, or their equivalent, set down by handwriting, typewriting, printing, photostating, photographing, magnetic impulse, mechanical or electronic recording, or other form of data compilation.

(2) Photographs. — "Photographs" include still photographs, Xray films, video tapes, and motion pictures.

(3) Original. — An "original" of a writing or recording is the writing or recording itself or any counterpart intended to have the same effect by a person executing or issuing it. An "original" of a photograph includes the negative or any print therefrom. If data are stored in a computer or similar device, any printout or other output readable by sight, shown to reflect the data accurately, is an "original".

(4) Duplicate. — A "duplicate" is a counterpart produced by the same impression as the original, or from the same matrix, or by means of photography, including enlargements and miniatures, or by mechanical or electronic rerecording, or by chemical reproduction, or by other equivalent techniques which accurately reproduces the original.

Rule 1002. Requirement of Original

To prove the content of a writing, recording, or photograph, the original writing, recording, or photograph is required, except as otherwise provided in these rules or by Act of Congress.

Rule 1003. Admissibility of Duplicates

A duplicate is admissible to the same extent as an original unless (1) a genuine question is raised as to the authenticity of the original or (2) in the circumstances it would be unfair to admit the duplicate in lieu of the original.

Rule 1004. Admissibility of Other Evidence of Contents

The original is not required, and other evidence of the contents of a writing, recording, or photograph is admissible if—

(1) Originals lost or destroyed. — All originals are lost or have been destroyed, unless the proponent lost or destroyed them in bad faith; or

(2) Original not obtainable. — No original can be obtained by any available judicial process or procedure; or

(3) Original in possession of opponent. — At a time when an original was under the control of the party against whom offered, that party was put on notice, by the pleadings or otherwise, that the contents would be a subject of proof at the hearing, and that party does not produce the original at the hearing; or (4) Collateral matters. — The writing, recording, or photograph is not closely related to a controlling issue.

(As amended Mar. 2, 1987, eff. Oct. 1, 1987.)

Rule 1005. Public Records

The contents of an official record, or of a document authorized to be recorded or filed and actually recorded or filed, including data compilations in any form, if otherwise admissible, may be proved by copy, certified as correct in accordance with rule 902 or testified to be correct by a witness who has compared it with the original. If a copy which complies with the foregoing cannot be obtained by the exercise of reasonable diligence, then other evidence of the contents may be given.

Rule 1006. Summaries

The contents of voluminous writings, recordings, or photographs which cannot conveniently be examined in court may be presented in the form of a chart, summary, or calculation. The originals, or duplicates, shall be made available for examination or copying, or both, by other parties at reasonable time and place. The court may order that they be produced in court.

Rule 1007. Testimony or Written Admission of Party

Contents of writings, recordings, or photographs may be proved by the testimony or deposition of the party against whom offered or by that party's written admission, without accounting for the nonproduction of the original.

(As amended Mar. 2, 1987, eff. Oct. 1, 1987.)

Rule 1008. Functions of Court and Jury

When the admissibility of other evidence of contents of writings, recordings, or photographs under these rules depends upon the fulfillment of a condition of fact, the question whether the condition has been fulfilled is ordinarily for the court to determine in accordance with the provisions of rule 104. However, when an issue is raised (a) whether the asserted writing ever existed, or (b) whether another writing, recording, or photograph produced at the trial is the original, or (c) whether other evidence of contents correctly reflects the contents, the issue is for the trier of fact to determine as in the case of other issues of fact.

ARTICLE XI.

MISCELLANEOUS RULES

Rule 1101. Applicability of Rules

(a). Courts and judges. These rules apply to the United States district courts, the District Court of Guam, the District Court of the Virgin Islands, the District Court for the Northern Mariana Islands, the United States courts of appeals, the United States Claims Court,[1]

and to United States bankruptcy judges and United States magistrate judges, in the actions, cases, and proceedings and to the extent hereinafter set forth. The terms "judge" and "court" in these rules include United States bankruptcy judges and United States magistrate judges.

(b). Proceedings generally. — These rules apply generally to civil actions and proceedings, including admiralty and maritime cases, to criminal cases and proceedings, to contempt proceedings except those in which the court may act summarily, and to proceedings and cases under title 11, United States Code.

(c). Rule of privilege. — The rule with respect to privileges applies at all stages of all actions, cases, and proceedings.

[1] Pub. L. 102-572, title IX, § 902(b)(1), Oct. 29, 1992, 106 Stat. 4516, provided that reference in any other Federal law or any document to the "United States Claims Court" shall be deemed to refer to the "United States Court of Federal Claims".

(d). Rules inapplicable. — The rules (other than with respect to privileges) do not apply in the following situations:

(1) Preliminary questions of fact. — The determination of questions of fact preliminary to admissibility of evidence when the issue is to be determined by the court under rule 104.

(2) Grand jury. — Proceedings before grand juries.

(3) Miscellaneous proceedings. — Proceedings for extradition or rendition; preliminary examinations in criminal cases; sentencing, or granting or revoking probation; issuance of warrants for arrest, criminal summonses, and search warrants; and proceedings with respect to release on bail or otherwise.

(e). Rules applicable in part. In the following proceedings these rules apply to the extent that matters of evidence are not provided for in the statutes which govern procedure therein or in other rules prescribed by the Supreme Court pursuant to statutory authority: the trial of misdemeanors and other petty offenses before United States magistrate judges; review of agency actions when the facts are subject to trial de novo under section 706(2)(F) of title 5, United States Code; review of orders of the Secretary of Agriculture under section 2 of the Act entitled "An Act to authorize association of producers of agricultural products" approved February 18, 1922 (7 U.S.C. 292), and under sections 6 and 7(c) of the Perishable Agricultural Commodities Act, 1930 (7 U.S.C. 499f, 499g(c)); naturalization and revocation of naturalization under sections 310-318 of the Immigration and Nationality Act (8 U.S.C. 1421-1429); prize proceedings in admiralty under sections 7651-7681 of title 10, United States Code; review of orders of the Secretary of the Interior under section 2 of the Act entitled "An Act authorizing associations of producers of aquatic products" approved June 25, 1934 (15 U.S.C. 522); review of orders of petroleum control boards under section 5 of the Act entitled "An Act to regulate interstate and foreign commerce in petroleum and its products by prohibiting the shipment in such commerce of petroleum and its products produced in violation of State law, and for other purposes", approved February 22, 1935 (15 U.S.C. 715d); actions for fines, penalties, or forfeitures under part V of title IV of the Tariff Act of 1930 (19 U.S.C. 1581-1624), or under the AntiSmuggling Act (19 U.S.C. 1701-1711); criminal libel for condemnation, exclusion of imports, or other proceedings under the Federal Food, Drug, and Cosmetic Act (21 U.S.C. 301-392); disputes between seamen under sections 4079, 4080, and 4081 of the Revised Statutes (22 U.S.C. 256-258); habeas corpus under sections 2241-2254 of title 28, United States Code; motions to vacate, set aside or correct sentence under section 2255 of title 28, United States Code; actions for penalties for refusal to transport destitute seamen under section 4578 of the Revised Statutes (46 U.S.C. 679);[2]

actions against the United States under the Act entitled "An Act authorizing suits against the United States in admiralty for damage caused by and salvage service rendered to public vessels belonging to the United States, and for other

[2] Repealed and reenacted as 46 U.S.C. 11104(b)-(d) by Pub. L. 98-89, §§ 1, 2(a), 4(b), Aug. 26, 1983, 97 Stat. 500.

purposes", approved March 3, 1925 (46 U.S.C. 781-790), as implemented by section 7730 of title 10, United States Code.

(As amended Dec. 12, 1975; Nov. 6, 1978, eff. Oct. 1, 1979; Apr. 2, 1982, eff. Oct. 1, 1982; Mar. 2, 1987, eff. Oct. 1, 1987; Apr. 25, 1988, eff. Nov. 1, 1988; Nov. 18, 1988; Apr. 22, 1993, eff. Dec. 1, 1993.).

Rule 1102. Amendments

Amendments to the Federal Rules of Evidence may be made as provided in section 2072 of title 28 of the United States Code. (As amended Apr. 30, 1991, eff. Dec. 1, 1991.)

Rule 1103. Title

These rules may be known and cited as the Federal Rules of Evidence.

STATUTORY AUTHORITY FOR PROMULGATION OF EVIDENCE RULES

TITLE 28.

UNITED STATES CODE

§ 2072. Rules of procedure and evidence; power to prescribe

(a). The Supreme Court shall have the power to prescribe general rules of practice and procedure and rules of evidence for cases in the United States district courts (including proceedings before magistrates thereof) and courts of appeals.

(b). Such rules shall not abridge, enlarge or modify any substantive right. All laws in conflict with such rules shall be of no further force or effect after such rules have taken effect.

(c). Such rules may define when a ruling of a district court is final for the purposes of appeal under section 1291 of this title.

(Added Pub. L. 100-702, title IV, § 401(a), Nov. 19, 1988, 102 Stat. 4648, eff. Dec. 1, 1988; amended Pub. L. 101-650, title III, § 315, Dec. 1, 1990, 104 Stat. 5115.)

§ 2073. Rules of procedure and evidence; method of prescribing

(a).

(1). The Judicial Conference shall prescribe and publish the procedures for the consideration of proposed rules under this section.

(2). The Judicial Conference may authorize the appointment of committees to assist the Conference by recommending rules to be prescribed under sections 2072 and 2075 of this title. Each such committee shall consist of members of the bench and the professional bar, and trial and appellate judges.

(b). The Judicial Conference shall authorize the appointment of a standing committee on rules of practice, procedure, and evidence under subsection (a) of this section. Such standing committee shall review each recommendation of any other committees so appointed and recommend to the Judicial Conference rules of practice, procedure, and evidence and such changes in rules proposed by a committee appointed under subsection (a)(2) of this section as may be necessary to maintain consistency and otherwise promote the interest of justice.

(c).

(1). Each meeting for the transaction of business under this chapter by any committee appointed under this section shall be open to the public, except when the committee so meeting, in open session and with a majority present, determines that it is in the public interest that all or part of the remainder of the meeting on that day shall be closed to the public, and states the reason for so closing the meeting. Minutes of each meeting for the transaction of business under this chapter shall be maintained by the committee and made available to the public, except that any portion of such minutes, relating to a closed meeting and made available to the public, may contain such deletions as may be necessary to avoid frustrating the purposes of closing the meeting.

(2). Any meeting for the transaction of business under this chapter, by a committee appointed under this section, shall be preceded by sufficient notice to enable all interested persons to attend.

(d). In making a recommendation under this section or under section 2072 or 2075, the body making that recommendation shall provide a proposed rule, an explanatory note on the rule, and a written report explaining the body's action, including any minority or other separate views.

(e). Failure to comply with this section does not invalidate a rule prescribed under section 2072 or 2075 of this title.

(Added Pub. L. 100-702, title IV, § 401(a), Nov. 19, 1988, 102 Stat. 4649, eff. Dec. 1, 1988; amended Pub. L. 103-394, title I, § 104(e), Oct. 22, 1994, 108 Stat. 4110.)

§ 2074. Rules of procedure and evidence; submission to Congress; effective date

(a). The Supreme Court shall transmit to the Congress not later than May 1 of the year in which a rule prescribed under section 2072 is to become effective a copy of the proposed rule. Such rule shall take effect no earlier than December 1 of the year in which such rule is so transmitted unless otherwise provided by law. The Supreme Court may fix the extent such rule shall apply to proceedings then pending, except that the Supreme Court shall not require the application of such rule to further proceedings then pending to the extent that, in the opinion of the court in which such proceedings are pending, the application of such rule in such proceedings would not be feasible or would work injustice, in which event the former rule applies.

(b). Any such rule creating, abolishing, or modifying an evidentiary privilege shall have no force or effect unless approved by Act of Congress.

(Added Pub. L. 100-702, title IV, § 401(a), Nov. 19, 1988, 102 Stat. 4649, eff. Dec. 1, 1988.)

HISTORICAL NOTE

The Supreme Court prescribes Federal Rules of Evidence pursuant to section 2072 of Title 28, United States Code, as enacted by Title IV "Rules Enabling Act" of Pub. L. 100-702 (approved November 19, 1988, 102 Stat. 4648), effective December 1, 1988, and section 2075 of Title 28. Pursuant to section 2074 of Title 28, the Supreme Court transmits to Congress (not later than May 1 of the year in which a rule prescribed under section 2072 is to become effective) a copy of the proposed rule. The rule takes effect no earlier than December 1 of the year in which the rule is transmitted unless otherwise provided by law.

Public Law 93-595 (approved January 2, 1975, 88 Stat. 1926) enacted the Federal Rules of Evidence proposed by the Supreme Court, with amendments made by Congress, to be effective July 1, 1975.

Appendix B

ADVISORY COMMITTEE NOTES TO THE FEDERAL RULES OF EVIDENCE

(Including Notes to the major amendments to specific rules)

NOTE TO RULE 101

Rule 1101 specifies in detail the courts, proceedings, questions, and stages of proceedings to which the rules apply in whole or in part.

NOTE TO RULE 102

For similar provisions see Rule 2 of the Federal Rules of Criminal Procedure, Rule 1 of the Federal Rules of Civil Procedure, California Evidence Code § 2, and New Jersey Evidence Rule 5.

ORIGINAL NOTE TO RULE 103

Subdivision (a) states the law as generally accepted today. Rulings on evidence cannot be assigned as error unless (1) a substantial right is affected, and (2) the nature of the error was called to the attention of the judge, so as to alert him to the proper course of action and enable opposing counsel to take proper corrective measures. The objection and the offer of proof are the techniques for accomplishing these objectives. For similar provisions see Uniform Rules 4 and 5; California Evidence Code §§ 353 and 354; Kansas Code of Civil Procedure §§ 60-404 and 60-405. The rule does not purport to change the law with respect to harmless error. See 28 U.S.C. § 2111, F.R.Civ.P. 61, F.R.Crim.P. 52, and decisions construing them. The status of constitutional error as harmless or not is treated in Chapman v. California, 386 U.S. 18, 87 S.Ct. 824, 17 L.Ed.2d 705 (1967), reh. denied id. 987, 87 S.Ct. 1283, 18 L.Ed.2d 241.

Subdivision (b). The first sentence is the third sentence of Rule 43(c) of the Federal Rules of Civil Procedure virtually verbatim. Its purpose is to reproduce for an appellate court, insofar as possible, a true reflection of what occurred in the trial court. The second sentence is in part derived from the final sentence of Rule 43(c). It is designed to resolve doubts as to what testimony the witness would have in fact given, and, in nonjury cases, to provide the appellate court with material for a possible final disposition of the case in the event of reversal of a ruling which excluded evidence. See 5 Moore's Federal Practice § 43.11 (2d ed. 1968). Application is made discretionary in view of the practical impossibility of formulating a satisfactory rule in mandatory terms.

Subdivision (c). This subdivision proceeds on the supposition that a ruling which excludes evidence in a jury case is likely to be a pointless procedure if the excluded evidence nevertheless comes to the attention of the jury. Bruton v. United States, 389 U.S. 818, 88 S.Ct. 126, L.Ed.2d 70 (1968). Rule 43(c) of the Federal Rules of Civil Procedure provides: "The court may require the offer to be made out of the hearing of the jury." In re McConnell, 370 U.S. 230, 82 S.Ct. 1288, 8 L.Ed.2d 434 (1962), left some doubt whether questions on which an offer is based must first be asked in the presence of the jury. The subdivision answers in the negative. The judge can foreclose a particular line of testimony and counsel can protect his record without a series of questions before the jury, designed at best to waste time and at worst "to waft into the jury box" the very matter sought to be excluded.

Subdivision (d). This wording of the plain error principle is from Rule 52(b) of the Federal Rules of Criminal Procedure. While judicial unwillingness to be constructed by mechanical breakdowns of the adversary system has been more pronounced in criminal cases, there is no scarcity of decisions to the same effect in civil cases. In general, see Campbell, Extent to Which Courts of Review Will Consider Questions Not Properly Raised and Preserved, 7 Wis.L.Rev. 91, 160 (1932); Vestal, Sua Sponte Consideration in Appellate Review, 27 Fordham L.Rev. 477 (1958-59); 64 Harv.L.Rev. 652 (1951). In the nature of things the application of the plain error rule will be more likely with respect to the admission of evidence than to exclusion, since failure to comply with normal requirements of offers of proof is likely to produce a record which simply does not disclose the error.

NOTE TO 2000 AMENDMENT TO RULE 103

The amendment applies to all rulings on evidence whether they occur at or before trial, including so-called "*in limine*" rulings. One of the most difficult questions arising from *in limine* and other evidentiary rulings is whether a losing party must renew an objection or offer of proof when the evidence is or would be offered at trial, in order to preserve a claim of error on appeal. Courts have taken differing approaches to this question. Some courts have held that a renewal at the time the evidence is to be offered at trial is always required. *See, e.g., Collins v. Wayne Corp.*, 621 F.2d 777 (5th Cir. 1980). Some courts have taken a more flexible approach, holding that renewal is not required if the issue decided is one that (1) was fairly presented to the trial court for an initial ruling, (2) may be decided as a final matter before the evidence is actually offered, and (3) was ruled on definitively by the trial judge. *See, e.g., Rosenfeld v. Basquiat,* 78 F.3d 84 (2d Cir. 1996) (admissibility of former testimony under the Dead Man's Statute; renewal not required). Other courts have distinguished between objections to evidence, which must be renewed when evidence is offered, and offers of proof, which need not be renewed after a definitive determination is made that the evidence is inadmissible. *See, e.g., Fusco v. General Motors Corp.*, 11 F.3d 259 (1st Cir. 1993). Another court, aware of this Committee's proposed amendment, has adopted its approach. *Wilson v. Williams*, 182 F.3d 562 (7th Cir. 1999) (en banc). Differing views on this question create uncertainty for litigants and unnecessary work for the appellate courts.

The amendment provides that a claim of error with respect to a definitive ruling is preserved for review when the party has otherwise satisfied the objection or offer of proof requirements of Rule 103(a). When the ruling is definitive, a renewed objection or offer of proof at the time the evidence is to be offered is more a formalism than a necessity. See Fed.R.Civ.P. 46 (formal exceptions unnecessary); Fed.R.Cr.P. 51 (same); *United States v. Mejia-Alarcon*, 995 F.2d 982, 986 (10th Cir. 1993) ("Requiring a party to renew an objection when the district court has issued a definitive ruling on a matter that can be fairly decided before trial would be in the nature of a formal exception and therefore unnecessary."). On the other hand, when the trial court appears to have reserved its ruling or to have indicated that the ruling is provisional, it makes sense to require the party to bring the issue to the court's attention subsequently. *See, e.g., United States v. Vest,* 116 F.3d 1179, 1188 (7th Cir. 1997) (where the trial court ruled *in limine* that testimony from defense witnesses could not be admitted, but allowed the defendant to seek leave at trial to call the witnesses should their testimony turn out to be relevant, the defendant's failure to seek such leave at trial meant that it was "too late to reopen the issue now on appeal"); *United States v. Valenti,* 60 F.3d 941 (2d Cir. 1995) (failure to proffer evidence at trial waives any claim of error where the trial judge had stated that he would reserve judgment on the *in limine* motion until he had heard the trial evidence).

The amendment imposes the obligation on counsel to clarify whether an *in limine* or other evidentiary ruling is definitive when there is doubt on that point. *See, e.g., Walden v. Georgia-Pacific Corp.,* 126 F.3d 506, 520 (3d Cir. 1997) (although "the district court told plaintiffs' counsel not to reargue every ruling, it did not countermand its clear opening statement that all of its rulings were tentative, and counsel never requested clarification, as he might have done.").

Even where the court's ruling is definitive, nothing in the amendment prohibits the court from revisiting its decision when the evidence is to be offered. If the court changes its initial ruling, or if the opposing party violates the terms of the initial ruling, objection must be made when the evidence is offered to preserve the claim of error for appeal. The error if any in such a situation occurs only when the evidence is offered and admitted. *United States Aviation Underwriters, Inc. v. Olympia Wings, Inc.,* 896 F.2d 949, 956 (5th Cir. 1990) ("objection is required to preserve error when an opponent, or the court itself, violates a motion *in limine* that was granted"); *United States v. Roenigk,* 810 F.2d 809 (8th Cir. 1987) (claim of error was not preserved where the defendant failed to object at trial to secure the benefit of a favorable advance ruling).

A definitive advance ruling is reviewed in light of the facts and circumstances before the trial court at the time of the ruling. If the relevant facts and circumstances change materially after the advance ruling has been made, those facts and circumstances cannot be relied upon on appeal unless they have been brought to the attention of the trial court by way of a renewed, and timely, objection, offer of proof, or motion to strike. *See Old Chief v. United States,* 519 U.S. 172, 182, n.6 (1997) ("It is important that a reviewing court evaluate the trial court's decision from its perspective when it had to rule and not indulge in review by hindsight."). Similarly, if the court decides in an advance ruling that proffered evidence is admissible subject to the eventual introduction by the proponent of a foundation for the evidence, and that foundation is never provided, the opponent cannot claim error based on the failure to establish the foundation unless the opponent calls that failure to the court's attention by a timely motion to strike or other suitable motion. *See Huddleston v. United States,* 485 U.S. 681, 690, n.7 (1988) ("It is, of course, not the responsibility of the judge *sua sponte* to ensure that the foundation evidence is offered; the objector must move to strike the evidence if at the close of the trial the offeror has failed to satisfy the condition.").

Nothing in the amendment is intended to affect the provisions of Fed.R.Civ.P. 72(a) or 28 U.S.C. § 636(b)(1), pertaining to nondispositive pretrial rulings by magistrate judges in proceedings that are not before a magistrate judge by consent of the parties. Fed.R.Civ.P. 72(a) provides that a party who fails to file a written objection to a magistrate judge's nondispositive order within ten days of receiving a copy "may not thereafter assign as error a defect" in the order. 28 U.S.C. § 636(b)(1) provides that any party "may serve and file written objections to such proposed findings and recommendations as provided by rules of court" within ten days of receiving a copy of the order. Several courts have held that a party must comply with this statutory provision in order to preserve a claim of error. *See, e.g., Wells v. Shriners Hospital,* 109 F.3d 198, 200 (4th Cir. 1997)("[i]n this circuit, as in others, a party 'may' file objections within ten days or he may not, as he chooses, but he 'shall' do so if he wishes further consideration."). When Fed.R.Civ.P. 72(a) or 28 U.S.C. § 636(b)(1) is operative, its requirement must be satisfied in order for a party to preserve a claim of error on appeal, even where Evidence Rule 103(a) would not require a subsequent objection or offer of proof.

Nothing in the amendment is intended to affect the rule set forth in *Luce v. United States,* 469 U.S. 38 (1984), and its progeny. The amendment provides that an objection or offer of proof need not be renewed to preserve a claim of error with respect to a definitive pretrial ruling. *Luce* answers affirmatively a separate question: whether a criminal defendant must testify at trial in order to preserve a claim of error predicated upon a trial court's decision to admit the defendant's prior convictions for impeachment. The *Luce* principle has been extended by many lower courts to other situations. *See United States v. DiMatteo,* 759 F.2d 831 (11th Cir. 1985) (applying *Luce* where the defendant's witness would be impeached with evidence offered under Rule 608). *See also United States v. Goldman,* 41 F.3d 785, 788 (1st Cir. 1994) ("Although *Luce* involved impeachment by conviction under Rule 609, the reasons given by the Supreme Court for requiring the defendant to testify apply with full force to the kind of Rule 403 and 404 objections that are advanced by Goldman in this case."); *Palmieri v. DeFaria,* 88 F.3d 136 (2d Cir. 1996) (where the plaintiff decided to take an adverse judgment rather than challenge an advance ruling by putting on evidence at trial, the *in limine* ruling would not be reviewed on appeal); *United States v. Ortiz,* 857 F.2d 900 (2d Cir. 1988) (where uncharged misconduct is ruled admissible if the defendant pursues a certain defense, the defendant must actually pursue that defense at trial in order to preserve a claim of error on appeal); *United States v. Bond,* 87 F.3d 695 (5th Cir. 1996) (where the trial court rules *in limine* that the defendant would waive his fifth amendment privilege were he to testify, the defendant must take the stand and testify in order to challenge that ruling on appeal).

The amendment does not purport to answer whether a party who objects to evidence that the court finds admissible in a definitive ruling, and who then offers the evidence to "remove the sting" of its anticipated prejudicial effect, thereby waives the right to appeal the trial court's ruling. *See, e.g., United States v. Fisher,* 106 F.3d 622 (5th Cir. 1997) (where the trial judge ruled *in limine* that the government could use a prior conviction to impeach the defendant if he testified, the defendant did not waive his right to appeal by introducing the conviction on direct examination); *Judd v. Rodman,* 105 F.3d 1339 (11th Cir. 1997) (an objection made *in limine* is sufficient to preserve a claim of error when the movant, as a matter of trial strategy, presents the objectionable evidence herself on direct examination to minimize its prejudicial effect); *Gill v. Thomas,* 83 F.3d 537, 540 (1st Cir. 1996) ("by offering the misdemeanor evidence himself, Gill waived his opportunity to object and thus did not preserve the issue for appeal"); *United States v. Williams*, 939 F.2d 721 (9th Cir. 1991) (objection to impeachment evidence was waived where the defendant was impeached on direct examination).

NOTE TO RULE 104

Subdivision (a). The applicability of a particular rule of evidence often depends upon the existence of a condition. Is the alleged expert a qualified physician? Is a witness whose former testimony is offered unavailable? Was a stranger present during a conversation between attorney and client? In each instance the admissibility of evidence will turn upon the answer to the question of the existence of the condition. Accepted practice, incorporated in the rule, places on the judge the responsibility for these determinations. McCormick § 53; Morgan, Basic Problems of Evidence 45-50 (1962).

To the extent that these inquiries are factual, the judge acts as a trier of fact. Often, however, rulings on evidence call for an evaluation in terms of a legally set standard. Thus when a hearsay statement is offered as a declaration against interest, a decision must be made whether it possesses the required against-interest characteristics. These decisions, too, are made by the judge.

In view of these considerations, this subdivision refers to preliminary requirements generally by the broad term "questions," without attempt at specification.

This subdivision is of general application. It must, however, be read as subject to the special provisions for "conditional relevancy" in subdivision (b) and those for confessions in subdivision (d).

If the question is factual in nature, the judge will of necessity receive evidence pro and con on the issue. The rule provides that the rules of evidence in general do not apply to this process. McCormick § 53, p. 123, n. 8, points out that the authorities are "scattered and inconclusive," and observes: "Should the exclusionary law of evidence, 'the child of the jury system' in Thayer's phrase, be applied to this hearing before the judge? Sound sense backs the view that it should not, and that the judge should be empowered to hear any relevant evidence, such as affidavits or other reliable hearsay." This view is reinforced by practical necessity in certain situations. An item, offered and objected to, may itself be considered in ruling on admissibility, though not yet admitted in evidence. Thus the content of an asserted declaration against interest must be considered in ruling whether it is against interest. Again, common practice calls for considering the testimony of a witness, particularly a child, in determining competency. Another example is the requirement of Rule 602 dealing with personal knowledge. In the case of hearsay, it is enough, if the declarant "so far as appears [has] had an opportunity to observe the fact declared." McCormick, § 10, p. 19.

If concern is felt over the use of affidavits by the judge in preliminary hearings on admissibility, attention is directed to the many important judicial determinations made on the basis of affidavits. Rule 47 of the Federal Rules of Criminal Procedure provides: "An application to the court for an order shall be by motion . . . It may be supported by affidavit." The Rules of Civil Procedure are more detailed. Rule 43(e), dealing with motions generally, provides: "When a motion is based on facts not appearing of record the court may hear the matter on affidavits presented by the respective parties, but the court may direct that the matter be heard wholly or partly on oral testimony or depositions." Rule 4(g) provides for proof of service by affidavit. Rule 56 provides in detail for the entry of summary judgment based on affidavits. Affidavits may supply the foundation for temporary restraining orders under Rule 65(b).

The study made for the California Law Revision Commission recommended an amendment to Uniform Rule 2 as follows: "In the determination of the issue aforesaid [preliminary determination], exclusionary rules shall not apply, subject, however, to Rule 45 and any valid claim of privilege." Tentative Recommendation and a Study Relating to the Uniform Rules of Evidence (Article VIII, Hearsay), Cal. Law Revision Comm'n, Rep., Rec. & Studies, 470 (1962). The proposal was not adopted in the California Evidence Code. The Uniform Rules are likewise silent on the subject. However, New Jersey Evidence Rule 8(1), dealing with preliminary inquiry by the judge, provides: "In his determination the rules of evidence shall not apply except for Rule 4 [exclusion on grounds of confusion, etc.] or a valid claim of privilege."

Subdivision (b). In some situations, the relevancy of an item of evidence, in the large sense, depends upon the existence of a particular preliminary fact. Thus when a spoken statement is relied upon to prove notice to X, it is without probative value unless X heard it. Or if a letter purporting to be from Y is relied upon to establish an admission by him, it has no probative value unless Y wrote or authorized it. Relevance in this sense has been labelled "conditional relevancy." Morgan, Basic Problems of Evidence 45-46 (1962). Problems arising in connection with it are to be distinguished from problems of logical relevancy, e.g. evidence in a murder case that accused on the day before purchased a weapon of the kind used in the killing, treated in Rule 401.

If preliminary questions of conditional relevancy were determined solely by the judge, as provided in subdivision (a), the functioning of the jury as a trier of fact would be greatly restricted and in some cases virtually destroyed. These are appropriate questions for juries. Accepted treatment, as provided in the rule, is consistent with that given fact questions generally. The judge makes a preliminary determination whether the foundation evidence is sufficient to support a finding of fulfillment of the condition. If so, the item is admitted. If after all the evidence on the issue is in, pro and con, the jury could reasonably conclude that fulfillment of the condition is not established, the issue is for them. If the evidence is not such as to allow a finding, the judge withdraws the matter from their consideration. Morgan, supra; California Evidence Code § 403; New Jersey Rule 8(2). See also Uniform Rules 19 and 67.

The order of proof here, as generally, is subject to the control of the judge.

Subdivision (c). Preliminary hearings on the admissibility of confessions must be conducted outside the hearing of the jury. See *Jackson v. Denno*, 378 U.S. 368, 84 S.Ct. 1774, 12 L.Ed.2d 908 (1964). Otherwise, detailed treatment of when preliminary matters should be heard outside the hearing of the jury is not feasible. The procedure is time consuming. Not infrequently the same evidence which is relevant to the issue of establishment of fulfillment of a condition precedent to admissibility is also relevant to weight or credibility, and time is saved by taking foundation proof in the presence of the jury. Much evidence on preliminary questions, though not relevant to jury issues, may be heard by the jury with no adverse effect. A great deal must be left to the discretion of the judge who will act as the interests of justice require.

Subdivision (d). The limitation upon cross-examination is designed to encourage participation by the accused in the determination of preliminary matters. He may testify concerning them without exposing himself to cross-examination generally. The provision is necessary because of the breadth of cross-examination under Rule 611(b).

The rule does not address itself to questions of the subsequent use of testimony given by an accused at a hearing on a preliminary matter. See Walder v. United States, 347 U.S. 62 (1954); Simmons v. United States, 390 U.S. 377 (1968); Harris v. New York, 401 U.S. 222 (1971)

Subdivision (e). For similar provisions see Uniform Rule 8; California Evidence Code § 406; Kansas Code of Civil Procedure § 60-408; New Jersey Evidence Rule 8(1).

NOTE TO RULE 105

A close relationship exists between this rule and Rule 403 which requires exclusion when "probative value is substantially outweighed by the danger of unfair prejudice, confusion of the issues, or misleading the jury." The present rule recognizes the practice of admitting evidence for a limited purpose and instructing the jury accordingly. The availability and effectiveness of this practice must be taken into consideration in reaching a decision whether to exclude for unfair prejudice under Rule 403. In Bruton v. United States, 389 U.S. 818, 88 S.Ct. 126, 19 L.Ed.2d 70 (1968), the Court ruled that a limiting instruction did not effectively protect the accused against the prejudicial effect of admitting in evidence the confession of a codefendant which implicated him. The decision does not, however, bar the use of limited admissibility with an instruction where the risk of prejudice is less serious.

Similar provisions are found in Uniform Rule 6; California Evidence Code § 355; Kansas Code of Civil Procedure § 60-406; New Jersey Evidence Rule 6. The wording of the present rule differs, however, in repelling any implication that limiting or curative instructions are sufficient in all situations.

NOTE TO RULE 106

The rule is an expression of the rule of completeness. McCormick § 56. It is manifested as to depositions in Rule 32(a)(4) of the Federal Rules of Civil Procedure, of which the proposed rule is substantially a restatement.

The rule is based on two considerations. The first is the misleading impression created by taking matters out of context. The second is the inadequacy of repair work when delayed to a point later in the trial. See McCormick § 56; California Evidence Code § 356. The rule does not in any way circumscribe the right of the adversary to develop the matter on cross-examination or as part of his own case.

For practical reasons, the rule is limited to writings and recorded statements and does not apply to conversations.

NOTE TO RULE 201

Subdivision (a). This is the only evidence rule on the subject of judicial notice. It deals only with judicial notice of "adjudicative" facts. No rule deals with judicial notice of "legislative" facts. Judicial notice of matters of foreign law is treated in Rule 44.1 of the Federal Rules of Civil Procedure and Rule 26.1 of the Federal Rules of Criminal Procedure.

The omission of any treatment of legislative facts results from fundamental differences between adjudicative facts and legislative facts. Adjudicative facts are simply the facts of the particular case. Legislative facts, on the other hand, are those which have relevance to legal reasoning and the lawmaking process, whether in the formulation of a legal principle or ruling by a judge or court or in the enactment of a legislative body. The terminology was coined by Professor Kenneth Davis in his article An Approach to Problems of Evidence in the Administrative Process, 55 Harv.L.Rev. 364, 404-407 (1942). The following discussion draws extensively upon his writings. In addition, see the same author's Judicial Notice, 55 Colum.L.Rev. 945 (1955); Administrative Law Treatise, ch. 15 (1958); A System of Judicial Notice Based on Fairness and Convenience, in Perspectives of Law 69 (1964).

The usual method of establishing adjudicative facts in through the introduction of evidence, ordinarily consisting of the testimony of witnesses. If particular facts are outside of the area of reasonable controversy, this process is dispensed with as unnecessary. A high degree of indisputability is the essential prerequisite.

Legislative facts are quite different. As Professor Davis says:

"My opinion is that judge-made law would stop growing if judges, in thinking about questions of law and policy, were forbidden to take into account the facts they believe, as distinguished from facts which are 'clearly . . . within the domain of the indisputable.' Facts most needed in thinking about difficult problems of law and policy have a way of being outside the domain of the clearly indisputable."

A System of Judicial Notice Based on Fairness and Convenience, supra, at 82.

An illustration is Hawkins v. United States, 358 U.S. 74, 79 S.Ct. 136, 3 L.Ed.2d 125 (1958), in which the Court refused to discard the common law rule that one spouse could not testify against the other, saying, "Adverse testimony given in criminal proceedings would, we think, be likely to destroy almost any marriage." This conclusion has a large intermixture of fact, but the factual aspect is scarcely "indisputable." See Hutchins and Slesinger, Some Observations on the Law of Evidence-Family Relations, 13 Minn.L.Rev. 675 (1929). If the destructive effect of the giving of adverse testimony by a spouse is not indisputable, should the Court have refrained from considering it in the absence of supporting evidence?

"If the Model Code or the Uniform Rules had been applicable, the Court would have been barred from thinking about the essential factual ingredient of the problems before it, and such a result would be obviously intolerable. What the law needs as its growing points is more, not less, judicial thinking about the factual ingredients of problems of what the law ought to be, and the needed facts are seldom 'clearly' indisputable." Davis, supra, at 83.

"Professor Morgan gave the following description of the methodology of determining domestic law: "In determining the content or applicability of a rule of domestic law, the judge is unrestricted in his investigation and conclusion. He may reject the propositions of either party or of both parties. He may consult the sources of pertinent data to which they refer, or he may refuse to do so. He may make an independent search for persuasive data or rest content with what he has or what the parties present . . . . [T]he parties do no more than to assist; they control no part of the process." Morgan, Judicial Notice, 57 Harv.L.Rev. 269, 270-271 (1944).

This is the view which should govern judicial access to legislative facts. It renders inappropriate any limitation in the form of indisputability, any formal requirements of notice other than those already inherent in affording opportunity to hear and be heard and exchanging briefs, and any requirement of formal findings at any level. It should, however, leave open the possibility of introducing evidence through regular channels in appropriate situations. See Borden's Farm Products Co. v. Baldwin, 293 U.S. 194, 55 S.Ct. 187, 79 L.Ed. 281 (1934), where the cause was remanded for the taking of evidence as to the economic conditions and trade practices underlying the New York Milk Control Law.

Similar considerations govern the judicial use of nonadjudicative facts in ways other than formulating laws and rules. Thayer described them as a part of the judicial reasoning process.

"In conducting a process of judicial reasoning, as of other reasoning, not a step can be taken without assuming something which has not been proved; andthe capacity to do this with competent judgment and efficiency, is imputed to judges and juries as part of their necessary mental outfit." Thayer, Preliminary Treatise on Evidence 279-280 (1898).

As Professor Davis points out, A System of Judicial Notice Based on Fairness and Convenience, in Perspectives of Law 69, 73 (1964), every case involves the use of hundreds or thousands of non-evidence facts. When a witness in an automobile accident case says "car," everyone, judge and jury included, furnishes, from non-evidence sources within himself, the supplementing information that the "car" is an automobile, not a railroad car, that it is self-propelled, probably by an internal combustion engine, that it may be assumed to have four wheels with pneumatic rubber tires, and so on. The judicial process cannot construct every case from scratch, like Descartes creating a world based on the postulate Cogito, ergo sum. These items could not possibly be introduced into evidence, and no one suggests that they be. Nor are they appropriate subjects for any formalized treatment of judicial notice of facts. See Levin and Levy, Persuading the jury with Facts Not in Evidence: The Fiction-Science Spectrum, 105 U.Pa.L.Rev. 139 (1956).

Another aspect of what Thayer had in mind is the use of non-evidence facts to appraise or assess the adjudicative facts of the case. Pairs of cases from two jurisdictions illustrate this use and also the difference between non-evidence facts thus used and adjudicative facts. In People v. Strook, 347 Ill. 460,179 N.E. 821 (1932), venue in Cook County had been held not established by testimony that the crime was committed at 7956 South Chicago Avenue, since judicial notice would not be taken that the address was in Chicago. However, the same court subsequently ruled that venue in Cook County was established by testimony that a crime occurred at 8900 South Anthony Avenue, since notice would be taken of the common practice of omitting the name of the city when speaking of local addresses, and the witness was testifying in Chicago. People v. Pride, 16 Ill.2d 82, 156 N.E.2d 551 (1951). And in Hughes v. Vestal, 264 N.C. 500, 142 S.E.2d 361 (1965), the Supreme Court of North Carolina disapproved the trial judge's admission in evidence of a state-published table of automobile stopping distances on the basis of judicial notice, though the court itself had referred to the same table in an earlier case in a "rhetorical and illustrative" way in determining that the defendant could not have stopped her car in time to avoid striking a child who suddenly appeared in the highway and that a non-suit was properly granted. Ennis v. Dupree, 262 N.C. 224, 136 S.E.2d 702 (1964). See also Brown v. Hale, 263 N.C. 176, 139 S.E.2d 210 (1964); Clayton v. Rimmer, 262 N.C. 302, 136 S.E.2d 562 (1964). It is apparent that this use of non-evidence facts in evaluating the adjudicative facts of the case is not an appropriate subject for a formalized judicial notice treatment.

In view of these considerations, the regulation of judicial notice of facts by the present rule extends only to adjudicative facts. What, then, are "adjudicative" facts? Davis refers to them as those "which relate to the parties," or more fully:

"When a court or an agency finds facts concerning the immediate parties-who did what, where, when, how, and with what motive or intent-the court or agency is performing an adjudicative function, and the facts are conveniently called adjudicative facts . . . .

"Stated in other terms, the adjudicative facts are those to which the law is applied in the process of adjudication. They are the facts that normally go to the jury in a jury case. They relate to the parties, their activities, their properties, their businesses."

2 Administrative Law Treatise 353.

Subdivision (b). With respect to judicial notice of adjudicative facts, the tradition has been one of caution in requiring that the matter be beyond reasonable controversy. This tradition of circumspection appears to be soundly based, and no reason to depart from it is apparent. As Professor Davis says:

"The reason we use trial-type procedure, I think, is that we make the practical judgement, on the basis of experience, that taking evidence, subject to cross-examination and rebuttal, is the best way to resolve controversies involving disputes of adjudicative facts, that is, facts pertaining to the parties. The reason we require a determination on the record is that we think fair procedure in resolving disputes of adjudicative facts calls for giving each party a chance to meet in the appropriate fashion the facts that come to the tribunal's attention, and the appropriate fashion for meeting disputed adjudicative facts includes rebuttal evidence, cross-examination, usually confrontation, and argument (either written or oral or both). The key to a fair trial is opportunity to use the appropriate weapons (rebuttal evidence, cross-examination, and argument) to meet adverse materials that come to the tribunal's attention."

A System of Judicial Notice Based on Fairness and Convenience, in Perspectives of Law 69, 93 (1964).

The rule proceeds upon the theory that these considerations call for dispensing with traditional methods of proof only in clear cases. Compare Professor Davis' conclusion that judicial notice should be a matter of convenience, subject to requirements of procedural fairness. Id., 94.

This rule is consistent with Uniform Rule 9(1) and (2) which limit judicial notice of facts to those "so universally known that they cannot reasonably be the subject of dispute," those "so generally known or of such common notoriety within the territorial jurisdiction of the court that they cannot reasonably be the subject of dispute," and those "capable of immediate and accurate determination by resort to easily accessible sources of indisputable accuracy." The traditional textbook treatment has included these general categories (matters of common knowledge, facts capable of verification), McCormick §§ 324, 325, and then has passed on into detailed treatment of such specific topics as facts relating to the personnel and records of the court, Id. § 327, and other governmental facts, Id. § 328. The California draftsmen, with a background of detailed statutory regulation of judicial notice, followed a somewhat similar pattern. California Evidence Code §§ 451, 452. The Uniform Rules, however, were drafted on the theory that these particular matters are included within the general categories and need no specific mention. This approach is followed in the present rule.

The phrase "propositions of generalized knowledge," found in Uniform Rule 9(1) and (2) is not included in the present rule. It was, it is believed, originally included in Model Code Rules 801 and 802 primarily in order to afford some minimum recognition to the right of the judge in his "legislative" capacity (not acting as the trier of fact) to take judicial notice of very limited categories of generalized knowledge. The limitations thus imposed have been discarded herein as undesirable, unworkable, and contrary to existing practice. What is left, then, to be considered, is the status of a "proposition of generalized knowledge" as an "adjudicative" fact to be noticed judicially and communicated by the judge to the jury. Thus viewed, it is considered to be lacking practical significance. While judges use judicial notice of "propositions of generalized knowledge" in a variety of situations: determining the validity and meaning of statutes, formulating common law rules, deciding whether evidence should be admitted, assessing the sufficiency and effect of evidence, all are essentially nonadjudicative in nature. When judicial notice is seen as a significant vehicle for progress in the law, these are the areas involved, particularly in developing fields of scientific knowledge. See McCormick 712. It is not believed that judges now instruct juries as to "propositions of generalized knowledge" derived from encyclopedias or other sources, or that they are likely to do so, or, indeed, that it is desirable that they do so. There is a vast difference between ruling on the basis of judicial notice that radar evidence of speed is admissible and explaining to the jury its principles and degree of accuracy, or between using a table of stopping distances of automobiles at various speeds in a judicial evaluation of testimony and telling the jury its precise application in the case. For cases raising doubt as to the propriety of the use of medical texts by lay triers of fact in passing on disability claims in administrative proceedings, see Sayers v. Gardner, 380 F.2d 940 (6th Cir. 1967); Ross v. Gardner, 365 F.2d 554 (6th Cir. 1966); Sosna v. Celebrezze, 234 F.Supp. 289 (E.D. Pa. 1964); Glendenning v. Ribicoff, 213 F. Supp. 301 (W.D. Mo. 1962).

Subdivisions (c) and (d). Under subdivision (c) the judge has a discretionary authority to take judicial notice, regardless of whether he is so requested by a party. The taking of judicial notice is mandatory, under subdivision (d), only when a party requests it and the necessary information is supplied. This scheme is believed to reflect existing practice. It is simple and workable. It avoids troublesome distinctions in the many situations in which the process of taking judicial notice is not recognized as such.

Compare Uniform Rule 9 making judicial notice of facts universally known mandatory without request, and making judicial notice of facts generally known in the jurisdiction or capable of determination by resort to accurate sources discretionary in the absence of request but mandatory if request is made and the information furnished. But see Uniform Rule 10(3), which directs the judge to decline to take judicial notice if available information fails to convince him that the matter falls clearly within Uniform Rule 9 or is insufficient to enable him to notice it judicially. Substantially the same approach is found in California Evidence Code §§ 451-453 and in New Jersey Evidence Rule 9. In contrast, the present rule treats alike all adjudicative facts which are subject to judicial notice.

Subdivision (e). Basic considerations of procedural fairness demand an opportunity to be heard on the propriety of taking judicial notice and the tenor of the matter noticed. The rule requires the granting of that opportunity upon request. No formal scheme of giving notice is provided. An adversely affected party may learn in advance that judicial notice is in contemplation, either by virtue of being served with a copy of a request by another party under subdivision (d) that judicial notice be taken, or through an advance indication by the judge. Or he may have no advance notice at all. The likelihood of the latter is enhanced by the frequent failure to recognize judicial notice as such. And in the absence of advance notice, a request made after the fact could not in fairness be considered untimely. See the provision for hearing on timely request in the Administrative Procedure Act, 5 U.S.C. § 556(e). See also Revised Model State Administrative Procedure Act (1961), 9C U.L.A. § 10(4) (Supp. 1967).

Subdivision (f). In accord with the usual view, judicial notice may be taken at any stage of the proceedings, whether in the trial court or on appeal. Uniform Rule 12; California Evidence Code § 459; Kansas Rules of Evidence § 60-412; New Jersey Evidence Rule 12; McCormick § 330, p. 712.

Subdivision (g). Much of the controversy about judicial notice has centered upon the question whether evidence should be admitted in disproof of facts of which judicial notice is taken.

The writers have been divided. Favoring admissibility are Thayer, Preliminary Treatise on Evidence 308 (1898); 9 Wigmore § 2567; Davis, A System of Judicial Notice Based on Fairness and Convenience, in Perspectives of Law, 69, 76-77 (1964). Opposing admissibility are Keeffe, Landis and Shaad, Sense and Nonsense about Judicial Notice, 2 Stan.L.Rev. 664, 668 (1950); McNaughton, Judicial Notice-Excerpts Relating to the Morgan-Whitmore Controversy, 14 Vand.L.Rev. 779 (1961); Morgan, Judicial Notice, 57 Harv.L.Rev. 269, 279 (1944); McCormick 710-711. The Model Code and the Uniform Rules are predicated upon indisputability of judicially noticed facts.

The proponents of admitting evidence in disproof have concentrated largely upon legislative facts. Since the present rule deals only with judicial notice of adjudicative facts, arguments directed to legislative facts lose their relevancy.

Within its relatively narrow area of adjudicative facts, the rule contemplates there is to be no evidence before the jury in disproof. The judge instructs the jury to take judicially noticed facts as established. This position is justified by the undesirable effects of the opposite rule in limiting the rebutting party, though not his opponent, to admissible evidence, in defeating the reasons for judicial notice, and in affecting the substantive law to an extent and in ways largely unforeseeable. Ample protection and flexibility are afforded by the broad provision for opportunity to be heard on request, set forth in subdivision (e).

Authority upon the propriety of taking judicial notice against an accused in a criminal case with respect to matters other than venue is relatively meager. Proceeding upon the theory that the right of jury trial does not extend to matters which are beyond reasonable dispute, the rule does not distinguish between criminal and civil cases. People v. Mayes, 113 Cal. 618, 45 P. 860 (1896); Ross v. United States, 374 F.2d 97 (8th Cir. 1967). Cf. State v. Main, 94 R.I. 338, 180 A.2d 814 (1962); State v. Lawrence, 120 Utah 323, 234 P.2d 600 (1951).

Note on Judicial Notice of Law.

By rules effective July 1, 1966, the method of invoking the law of a foreign country is covered elsewhere. Rule 44.1 of the Federal Rules of Civil Procedure; Rule 26.1 of the Federal Rules of Criminal Procedure. These two new admirably designed rules are founded upon the assumption that the manner in which law is fed into the judicial process is never a proper concern of the rules of evidence but rather of the rules of procedure. The Advisory Committee on Evidence, believing that this assumption is entirely correct, proposes no evidence rule with respect to judicial notice of law, and suggests that those matters of law which, in addition to foreign-country law, have traditionally been treated as requiring pleading and proof and more recently as the subject of judicial notice be left to the Rules of Civil and Criminal Procedure.

NOTE TO RULE 301

This rule governs presumptions generally. See Rule 302 for presumptions controlled by state law and Rule 303 [Editor's Note: Proposed Rule 303 was deleted by Congress] for those against an accused in a criminal case.

Presumptions governed by this rule are given the effect of placing upon the opposing party the burden of establishing the nonexistence of the presumed fact, once the party invoking the presumption establishes the basic facts giving rise to it. The same considerations of fairness, policy, and probability which dictate the allocation of the burden of the various elements of a case as between the prima facie case of a plaintiff and affirmative defenses also underlie the creation of presumptions. These considerations are not satisfied by giving a lesser effect to presumptions. Morgan and Maguire, Looking Backward and Forward at Evidence, 50 Harv.L.Rev. 909, 913 (1937); Morgan, Instructing the Jury upon Presumptions and Burdon of Proof, 47 Harv.L.Rev. 59, 82 1933); Cleary, Presuming and Pleading: An Essay on Juristic Immaturity, 12 Stan.L.Rev. 5 (1959).

The so-called "bursting bubble" theory, under which a presumption vanishes upon the introduction of evidence which would support a finding of the nonexistence of the presumed fact, even though not believed, is rejected as according presumptions too "slight and evanescent" an effect. Morgan and Maguire, supra, at p. 913.

In the opinion of the Advisory Committee, no constitutional infirmity attends this view of presumptions. In Mobile, J. & K.C.R. Co. v. Turnipseed, 219 U.S. 35, 31 S.Ct. 136, 55 L.Ed. 78 (1910), the Court upheld a Mississippi statute which provided that in actions against railroads proof of injury inflicted by the running of trains should be prima facie evidence of negligence by the railroad. The injury in the case had resulted from a derailment. The opinion made the points (1) that the only effect of the statute was to impose on the railroad the duty of producing some evidence to the contrary, (2) that an inference may be supplied by law if there is a rational connection between the fact proved and the fact presumed, as long as the opposite party is not precluded from presenting his evidence to the contrary, and (3) that considerations of public policy arising from the character of the business justified the application in question. Nineteen years later, in Western & Atlantic R. Co.

v. Henderson, 279 U.S. 639, 49 S.Ct. 445, 73 L.Ed. 884 (1929), the Court overturned a Georgia statute making railroads liable for damages done by trains, unless the railroad made it appear that reasonable care had been used, the presumption being against the railroad. The declaration alleged the death of plaintiff's husband from a grade crossing collision, due to specified acts of negligence by defendant. The jury were instructed that proof of the injury raised a presumption of negligence; the burden shifted to the railroad to prove ordinary care; and unless it did so, they should find for plaintiff. The instruction was held erroneous in an opinion stating (1) that there was no rational connection between the mere fact of collision and negligence on the part of anyone, and (2) that the statute was different from that in *Turnipseed* in imposing a burden upon the railroad. The reader is left in a state of some confusion. Is the difference between a derailment and a grade crossing collision of no significance? Would the *Turnipseed* presumption have been bad if it had imposed a burden of persuasion on defendant, although that would in nowise have impaired its "rational connection"? If *Henderson* forbids imposing a burden of persuasion on defendants, what happens to affirmative defenses?

Two factors serve to explain *Henderson*. The first was that it was common ground that negligence was indispensable to liability. Plaintiff thought so, drafted her complaint accordingly, and relied upon the presumption. But how in logic could the same presumption establish her alternative grounds of negligence that the engineer was so blind he could not see decedent's truck and that he failed to stop after he saw it? Second, take away the basic assumption of no liability without fault, as *Turnipseed* intimated might be done ("considerations of public policy arising out of the character of the business"), and the structure of the decision in *Henderson* fails. No question of logic would have arisen if the statute had simply said: a prima facie case of liability is made by proof of injury by a train; lack of negligence is an affirmative defense, to be pleaded and proved as other affirmative defenses. The problem would be one of economic due process only. While it seems likely that the Supreme Court of 1929 would have voted that due process was denied, that result today would be unlikely. See, for example, the shift in the direction of absolute liability in the consumer cases. Prosser, The Assault upon the Citadel (Strict Liability to the Consumer), 69 Yale L.J. 1099 (1960).

Any doubt as to the constitutional permissibility of a presumption imposing a burden of persuasion of the non-existence of the presumed fact in civil cases is laid at rest by Dick v. New York Life Ins. Co., 359 U.S. 437, 79 S.Ct. 921, 3 L.Ed.2d 935 (1959). The Court unhesitatingly applied the North Dakota rule that the presumption against suicide imposed on defendant the burden of proving that the death of insured, under an accidental death clause, was due to suicide.

"Proof of coverage and of death by gunshot wound shifts the burden to the insurer to establish that the death of the insured was due to his suicide." 359 U.S. at 443, 79 S.Ct. at 925.

"In a case like this one, North Dakota presumes that death was accidental and places on the insurer the burden of proving that death resulted from suicide." Id. at 446, 79 S.Ct. at 927.

The rational connection requirement survives in criminal cases, Tot v. United States, 319 U.S. 463, 63 S.Ct. 1241, 87 L.Ed. 1519 (1943), because the Court has been unwilling to extend into that area the greater-includes-the-lesser theory of Ferry v. Ramsey, 277 U.S. 88, 48 S.Ct. 443, 72 L.Ed. 796 (1928). In that case the Court sustained a Kansas statute under which bank directors were personally liable for deposits made with their assent and with knowledge of insolvency, and the fact of insolvency was prima facie evidence of assent and knowledge of insolvency. Mr. Justice Holmes pointed out that the state legislature could have made the directors personally liable to depositors in every case. Since the statute imposed a less stringent liability, "the thing to be considered is the result reached, not the possibly inartificial or clumsy way of reaching it." Id. at 94, 48 S.Ct. at 444. Mr. Justice Sutherland dissented: though the state could have created an absolute liability, it did not purport to do so; a rational connection was necessary, but lacking, between the liability created and the prima facie evidence of it; the result might be different if the basis of the presumption were being open for business.

The Sutherland view has prevailed in criminal cases by virtue of the higher standard of notice there required. The fiction that everyone is presumed to know the law is applied to the substantive law of crimes as an alternative to complete unenforceability. But the need does not extend to criminal evidence and procedure, and the fiction does not encompass them. "Rational connection" is not fictional or artificial, and so it is reasonable to suppose that Gainey should have known that his presence at the site of an illicit still could convict him of being connected with (carrying on) the business, United States v. Gainey, 380 U.S. 63, 85 S.Ct. 754, 13 L.Ed.2d 658 (1965), but not that Romano should have known that his presence at a still could convict him of possessing it, United States v. Romano, 382 U.S. 136, 86 S.Ct. 279, 15 L.Ed.2d 210 (1965).

In his dissent in *Gainey*, Mr. Justice Black put it more artistically:

"It might be argued, although the Court does not so argue or hold, that Congress if it wished could make presence at a still a crime in itself, and so Congress should be free to create crimes which are called 'possession' and 'carrying on an illegal distillery business' but which are defined in such a way that unexplained presence is sufficient and indisputable evidence in all cases to support conviction for those offenses. See Ferry v. Ramsey, 277 U.S. 88, 48 S.Ct. 443, 72 L.Ed. 796. Assuming for the sake of argument that Congress could make unexplained presence a criminal act, and ignoring also the refusal of this Court in other cases to uphold a statutory presumption on such a theory, see Heiner v. Donnan, 285 U.S. 312, 52 S.Ct. 358, 76 L.Ed. 772, there is no indication here that Congress intended to adopt such a misleading method of draftsmanship, nor in my judgement could the statutory provisions if so construed escape condemnation for vagueness, under the principles applied in Lanzetta v. New Jersey, 306 U.S. 451, 59 S.Ct. 618, 83 L.Ed. 888, and many other cases."

380 U.S. at 84, n. 12, 85 S.Ct. at 766.

And the majority opinion in *Romano* agreed with him:

"It may be, of course, that Congress has the power to make presence at an illegal still a punishable crime, but we find no clear indication that it intended to so exercise this power. The crime remains possession, not presence, and with all due deference to the judgement of Congress, the former may not constitutionally be inferred from the latter."

382 U.S. at 144, 86 S.Ct. at 284.

The rule does not spell out the procedural aspects of its application. Questions as to when the evidence warrants submission of a presumption and what instructions are proper under varying states of fact are believed to present no particular difficulties.

NOTE TO RULE 302

A series of Supreme Court decisions in diversity cases leaves no doubt of the relevance of Erie Railroad Co. v. Tompkins, 304 U.S. 64, 58 S.Ct. 817, 82 L.Ed. 1188 (1938), to questions of burden of proof. These decisions are Cities Service Oil Co. v. Dunlap, 308 U.S. 208, 60 S.Ct. 201, 84 L.Ed. 196 (1939), Palmer v. Hoffman, 318 U.S. 109, 63 S.Ct. 477, 87 L.Ed. 645 (1943), and Dick v. New York Life Ins. Co., 359 U.S. 437, 79 S.Ct. 921, 3 L.Ed.2d 935 (1959). They involved burden of proof, respectively, as to status as bona fide purchasers, contributory negligence, and non-accidental death (suicide) of an insured. In each instance the state rule was held to be applicable. It does not follow, however, that all presumptions in diversity cases are governed by state law. In each case cited, the burden of proof question had to do with a substantive element of the claim or defense. Application of the state law is called for only when the presumption operates upon such an element. Accordingly the rule does not apply state law when the presumption operates upon a lesser aspect of the case, i.e. "tactical" presumptions.

The situations in which the state law is applied have been tagged for convenience in the preceding discussion as "diversity cases." The designation is not a completely accurate one since Erie applies to any claim or issue having its source in state law, regardless of the basis of federal jurisdiction, and does not apply to a federal claim or issue, even though jurisdiction is based on diversity. Vestal, Erie R.R. v. Tompkins: A Projection, 48 Iowa L.Rev. 248, 257 (1963); Hart and Wechsler, The Federal Courts and the Federal System, 697 (1953); 1A Moore, Federal Practice para. 0.305 [3] (2d ed. 1965); Wright, Federal Courts, 217-218 (1963). Hence the rule employs, as appropriately descriptive, the phrase "as to which state law supplies the rule of decision." See A.L.I. Study of the Division of Jurisdiction Between State and Federal Courts, § 2344(c), p. 40, P.F.D. No. 1 (1965).

NOTE TO RULE 401

Problems of relevancy call for an answer to the question whether an item of evidence, when tested by the processes of legal reasoning, possesses sufficient probative value to justify receiving it in evidence. Thus, assessment of the probative value of evidence that a person purchased a revolver shortly prior to a fatal shooting with which he is charged is a matter of analysis and reasoning.

The variety of relevancy problems is coextensive with the ingenuity of counsel in using circumstantial evidence as a means of proof. An enormous number of cases fall in no set pattern, and this rule is designed as a guide for handling them. On the other hand, some situations recur with sufficient frequency to create patterns susceptible of treatment by specific rules. Rule 404 and those following it are of that variety; they also serve as illustrations of the application of the present rule as limited by the exclusionary principles of Rule 403.

Passing mention should be made of so-called "conditional" relevancy. Morgan, Basic Problems of Evidence 45-46 (1962). In this situation, probative value depends not only upon satisfying the basic requirement of relevancy as described above but also upon the existence of some matter of fact. For example, if evidence of a spoken statement is relied upon to prove notice, probative value is lacking unless the person sought to be charged heard the statement. The problem is one of fact, and the only rules needed are for the purpose of determining the respective functions of judge and jury. See Rules 104(b) and 901. The discussion which follows in the present note is concerned with relevancy generally, not with any particular problem of conditional relevancy.

Relevancy is not an inherent characteristic of any item of evidence but exists only as a relation between an item of evidence and a matter properly provable in the case. Does the item of evidence tend to prove the matter sought to be proved? Whether the relationship exists depends upon principles evolved by experience or science, applied logically to the situation at hand. James, Relevancy, Probability and the Law, 29 Calif.L.Rev. 689, 696, n. 15 (1941), in Selected Writings on Evidence and Trial 610, 615, n. 15 (Fryer ed. 1957). The rule summarizes this relationship as a "tendency to make the existence" of the fact to be proved "more probable or less probable." Compare Uniform Rule 1(2) which states the crux of relevancy as "a tendency in reason," thus perhaps emphasizing unduly the logical process and ignoring the need to draw upon experience or science to validate the general principle upon which relevancy in a particular situation depends.

The standard of probability under the rule is "more . . . probable than it would be without the evidence." Any more stringent requirement is unworkable and unrealistic. As McCormick § 152, p. 317, says, "A brick is not a wall," or, as Falknor, Extrinsic Policies Affecting Admissibility, 10 Rutgers L.Rev. 574, 576 (1956), quotes Professor McBaine, " . . . [I]t is not to be supposed that every witness can make a home run." Dealing with probability in the language of the rule has the added virtue of avoiding confusion between questions of admissibility and questions of the sufficiency of the evidence.

The rule uses the phrase "fact that is of consequence to the determination of the action" to describe the kind of fact to which proof may properly be directed. The language is that of California Evidence Code § 210; it has the advantage of avoiding the loosely used and ambiguous word "material." Tentative Recommendation and a Study Relating to the Uniform Rules of Evidence (Art. I. General Provisions), Cal. Law Revision Comm'n, Rep., Rec. & Studies, 10-11 (1964). The fact to be proved may be ultimate, intermediate, or evidentiary; it matters not, so long as it is of consequence in the determination of the action. Cf. Uniform Rule 1(2) which requires that the evidence relate to a "material" fact.

The fact to which the evidence is directed need not be in dispute. While situations will arise which call for the exclusion of evidence offered to prove a point conceded by the opponent, the ruling should be made on the basis of such considerations as waste of time and undue prejudice (see Rule 403), rather than under any general requirement that evidence is admissible only if directed to matters in dispute. Evidence which is essentially background in nature can scarcely be said to involve disputed matter, yet it is universally offered and admitted as an aid to understanding. Charts, photographs, views of real estate, murder weapons, and many other items of evidence fall in this category. A rule limiting admissibility to evidence directed to a controversial point would invite the exclusion of this helpful evidence, or at least the raising of endless questions over its admission. Cf. California Evidence Code § 210, defining relevant evidence in terms of tendency to prove a disputed fact.

NOTE TO RULE 402

The provisions that all relevant evidence is admissible, with certain exceptions, and that evidence which is not relevant is not admissible are "a presupposition involved in the very conception of a rational system of evidence." Thayer, Preliminary Treatise on Evidence 264 (1898). They constitute the foundation upon which the structure of admission and exclusion rests. For similar provisions see California Evidence Code §§ 350, 351. Provisions that all relevant evidence is admissible are found in Uniform Rule 7(f); Kansas Code of Civil Procedure § 60-407(f); and New Jersey Evidence Rule 7(f); but the exclusion of evidence which is not relevant is left to implication.

Not all relevant evidence is admissible. The exclusion of relevant evidence occurs in a variety of situations and may be called for by these rules, by the Rules of Civil and Criminal Procedure, by Bankruptcy Rules, by Act of Congress, or by constitutional considerations.

Succeeding rules in the present article, in response to the demands of particular policies, require the exclusion of evidence despite its relevancy. In addition, Article V recognizes a number of privileges; Article VI imposes limitations upon witnesses and the manner of dealing with them; Article VII specifies requirements with respect to opinions and expert testimony; Article VIII excludes hearsay not falling within an exception; Article IX spells out the handling of authentication and identification; and Article X restricts the manner of proving the contents of writings and recordings.

The Rules of Civil and Criminal Procedure in some instances require the exclusion of relevant evidence. For example, Rules 30(b) and 32(a)(3) of the Rules of Civil Procedure, by imposing requirements of notice and unavailability of the deponent, place limits on the use of relevant depositions. Similarly, Rule 15 of the Rules of Criminal Procedure restricts the use of depositions in criminal cases, even though relevant. And the effective enforcement of the command, originally statutory and now found in Rule 5(a) of the Rules of Criminal Procedure, that an arrested person be taken without unnecessary delay before a commissioner of other similar officer is held to require the exclusion of statements elicited during detention in violation thereof. Mallory v. United States, 354 U.S. 449, 77 S.Ct. 1356, 1 L.Ed.2d 1479 (1957); 18 U.S.C. § 3501(c).

While congressional enactments in the field of evidence have generally tended to expand admissibility beyond the scope of the common law rules, in some particular situations they have restricted the admissibility of relevant evidence. Most of this legislation has consisted of the formulation of a privilege or of a prohibition against disclosure. 8 U.S.C. § 1202(f), records of refusal of visas or permits to enter United States confidential, subject to discretion of Secretary of State to make available to court upon certification of need; 10 U.S.C. § 3693, replacement certificate of honorable discharge from Army not admissible in evidence; 10 U.S.C. § 8693, same as to Air Force; 11 U.S.C. § 25(a)(10), testimony given by bankrupt on his examination not admissible in criminal proceedings against him, except that given in hearing upon objection to discharge; 11 U.S.C. § 205(a), railroad reorganization petition, if dismissed, not admissible in evidence; 11 U.S.C. § 403(a), list of creditors filed with municipal composition plan not an admission; 13 U.S.C. § 9(a), census information confidential, retained copies of reports privileged; 47 U.S.C. § 605, interception and divulgence of wire or radio communications prohibited unless authorized by sender. These statutory provisions would remain undisturbed by the rules.

The rule recognizes but makes no attempt to spell out the constitutional considerations which impose basic limitations upon the admissibility of relevant evidence. Examples are evidence obtained by unlawful search and seizure, Weeks v. United States, 232 U.S. 383, 34 S.Ct. 341, 58 L.Ed. 652 (1914); Katz v. United States, 389 U.S. 347, 88 S.Ct. 507, 19 L.Ed.2d 576 (1967); incriminating statement elicited from an accused in violation of right to counsel, Massiah v. United States, 377 U.S. 201, 84 S.Ct. 1199, 12 L.Ed.2d 246 (1964).

NOTE TO RULE 403

The case law recognizes that certain circumstances call for the exclusion of evidence which is of unquestioned relevance. These circumstances entail risks which range all the way from inducing decision on a purely emotional basis, at one extreme, to nothing more harmful than merely wasting time, at the other extreme. Situations in this area call for balancing the probative value of and need for the evidence against the harm likely to result from its admission. Slough, Relevancy Unraveled, 5 Kan. L. Rev. 1, 12-15 (1956); Trautman, Logical or Legal Relevancy-A Conflict in Theory, 5 Van. L. Rev. 385, 392 (1952); McCormick § 152, pp. 319-321. The rules which follow in this Article are concrete applications evolved for particular situations. However, they reflect the policies underlying the present rule, which is designed as a guide for the handling of situations for which no specific rules have been formulated.

Exclusion for risk of unfair prejudice, confusion of issues, misleading the jury, or waste of time, all find ample support in the authorities. "Unfair prejudice" within its context means an undue tendency to suggest decision on an improper basis, commonly, though not necessarily, an emotional one.

The rule does not enumerate surprise as a ground for exclusion, in this respect following Wigmore's view of the common law. 6 Wigmore § 1849. Cf. McCormick § 152, p. 320, n. 29, listing unfair surprise as a ground for exclusion but stating that it is usually "coupled with the danger of prejudice and confusion of issues." While Uniform Rule 45 incorporates surprise as a ground and is followed in Kansas Code of Civil Procedure § 60-445, surprise is not included in California Evidence Code § 352 or New Jersey Rule 4, though both the latter otherwise substantially embody Uniform Rule 45. While it can scarcely be doubted that claims of unfair surprise may still be justified despite procedural requirements of notice and instrumentalities of discovery, the granting of a continuance is a more appropriate remedy than exclusion of the evidence. Tentative Recommendation and a Study Relating to the Uniform Rules of Evidence (Art. VI. Extrinsic Policies Affecting Admissibility), Cal. Law Revision Comm'n, Rep., Rec. & Studies, 612 (1964). Moreover, the impact of a rule excluding evidence on the ground of surprise would be difficult to estimate.

In reaching a decision whether to exclude on grounds of unfair prejudice, consideration should be given to the probable effectiveness or lack of effectiveness of a limiting instruction. See Rule 106 [now 105] and Advisory Committee's Note thereunder. The availability of other means of proof may also be an appropriate factor.

ORIGINAL NOTE TO RULE 404

Subdivision (a). This subdivision deals with the basic question whether character evidence should be admitted. Once the admissibility of character evidence in some form is established under this rule, reference must then be made to Rule 405, which follows, in order to determine the appropriate method of proof. If the character is that of a witness, see Rules 608 and 610 for methods of proof.

Character questions arise in two fundamentally different ways. (1) Character may itself be an element of a crime, claim, or defense. A situation of this kind is commonly referred to as "character in issue." Illustrations are: the chastity of the victim under a statute specifying her chastity as an element of the crime of seduction, or the competency of the driver in an action for negligently entrusting a motor vehicle to an incompetent driver. No problem of the general relevancy of character evidence is involved, and the present rule therefore has no provision on the subject. The only question relates to allowable methods of proof, as to which see Rule 405, immediately following. (2) Character evidence is susceptible of being used for the purpose of suggesting an inference that the person acted on the occasion in question consistently with his character. This use of character is often described as "circumstantial." Illustrations are: evidence of a violent disposition to prove that the person was the aggressor in an affray, or evidence of honesty in disproof of a charge of theft. This circumstantial use of character evidence raises questions of relevancy as well as questions of allowable methods of proof.

In most jurisdictions today, the circumstantial use of character is rejected but with important exceptions: (1) an accused may introduce pertinent evidence of good character (often misleadingly described as "putting his character in issue"), in which event the prosecution may rebut with evidence of bad character; (2) an accused may introduce pertinent evidence of the character of the victim, as in support of a claim of self-defense to a charge of homicide or consent in a case of rape, and the prosecution may introduce similar evidence in rebuttal of the character evidence, or, in a homicide case, to rebut a claim that deceased was the first aggressor, however proved; and (3) the character of a witness may be gone into as bearing on his credibility. McCormick §§ 155-161. This pattern is incorporated in the rule. While its basis lies more in history and experience than in logic as underlying justification can fairly be found in terms of the relative presence and absence of prejudice in the various situations. Falknor, Extrinsic Policies Affecting Admissibility, 10 Rutger, L.Rev. 574, 584 (1956); McCormick § 157. In any event, the criminal rule is so deeply imbedded in our jurisprudence as to assume almost constitutional proportions and to override doubts of the basic relevancy of the evidence.

The limitation to pertinent traits of character, rather than character generally, in paragraphs (1) and (2) is in accordance with the prevailing view. McCormick § 158, p. 334. A similar provision in Rule 608, to which reference is made in paragraph (3), limits character evidence respecting witnesses to the trait of truthfulness or untruthfulness.

The argument is made that circumstantial use of character ought to be allowed in civil cases to the same extent as in criminal cases, i.e. evidence of good (nonprejudicial) character would be admissible in the first instance, subject to rebuttal by evidence of bad character. Falknor, Extrinsic Policies Affecting Admissiblity, 10 Rutgers L.Rev. 574, 581-583 (1956); Tentative Recommendation and a Study Relating to the Uniform Rules of Evidence (Art. VI. Extrinsic Policies Affecting Admissibility), Cal. Law Revision Comm'n, Rep., Rec. & Studies, 657-658 (1964). Uniform Rule 47 goes farther, in that it assumes that character evidence in general satisfies the conditions of relevancy, except as provided in Uniform Rule 48. The difficulty with expanding the use of character evidence in civil cases is set forth by the California Law Revision Commission in its ultimate rejection of Uniform Rule 47, Id., 615:

"Character evidence is of slight probative value and may be very prejudicial. It tends to distract the trier of fact from the main question of what actually happened on the particular occasion. It subtly permits the trier of fact to reward the good man to punish the bad man because of their respective characters despite what the evidence in the case shows actually happened."

Much of the force of the position of those favoring greater use of character evidence in civil cases in dissipated by their support of Uniform Rule 48 which excludes the evidence in negligence cases, where it could be expected to achieve its maximum usefulness. Moreover, expanding concepts of "character," which seem of necessity to extend into such areas as psychiatric evaluation and psychological testing, coupled with expanded admissibility, would open up such vistas of mental examinations as caused the Court concern in Schlagenhauf v. Holder, 379 U.S. 104, 85 S.Ct. 234, 13 L.Ed.2d 152 (1964). It is believed that those espousing change have not met the burden of persuasion.

Consistently with that rule, evidence of other crimes, wrongs, or acts is not admissible to prove character as a basis for suggesting the inference that conduct on a particular occasion was in conformity with it. However, the evidence may be offered for another purpose, such as proof of motive, opportunity, and so on, which does not fall within the prohibition. In this situation the rule does not require that the evidence be excluded. No mechanical solution is offered. The determination must be made whether the danger of undue prejudice outweighs the probative value of the evidence in view of the availability of other means of proof and other factors appropriate for making decisions of this kind under Rule 403. Slough and Knightly, Other Vices, Other Crimes, 41 Iowa L.Rev. 325 (1956).

COMMITTEE NOTE TO 1991 AMENDMENT TO RULE 404(b)

Rule 404(b) has emerged as one of the most cited Rules in the Rules of Evidence. In many criminal cases evidence of an accused's extrinsic acts is viewed as an important asset in the prosecution's case against an accused. Although there are a few reported decisions on use of such evidence by the defense, *see, e.g., United States v. McClure*, 546 F.2d 670 (5th Cir. 1977) (acts of informant offered in entrapment defense), the overwhelming number of cases involve introduction of that evidence by the prosecution.

The amendment to Rule 404(b) adds a pretrial notice requirement in criminal cases and is intended to reduce surprise and promote early resolution of the issue of admissibility. The notice requirement thus places Rule 404(b) in the mainstream with notice and disclosure provisions in other rules of evidence. *See, e.g.,* Rule 412 (written notice of intent to offer evidence under rule), Rule 609 (written notice of intent to offer conviction older than 10 years), Rule 803(24) and 804(b)(5) (notice of intent to use residual hearsay exceptions).

The Rule expects that counsel for both the defense and the prosecution will submit the necessary request and information in a reasonable and timely fashion. Other than requiring pretrial notice, no specific time limits are stated in recognition that what constitutes a reasonable request or disclosure will depend largely on the circumstances of each case. *Compare* Fla.Stat.Ann. § 90.404(2)(b) (notice must be given at least 10 days before trial) *with* Tex.R.Evid. 404(b) (no time limit).

Likewise, no specific form of notice is required. The Committee considered and rejected a requirement that the notice satisfy the particularity requirements normally required of language used in a charging instrument. *Cf.* Fla.Stat.Ann. § 90.404(2)(b) (written disclosure must describe uncharged misconduct with particularity required of an indictment or information). Instead, the Committee opted for a generalized notice provision which requires the prosecution to apprise the defense of the general nature of the evidence of extrinsic acts. The Committee does not intend that the amendment will supersede other rules of admissibility or disclosure, such as the Jencks Act, 18 U.S.C. § 3500, et. seq. nor require the prosecution to disclose directly or indirectly the names and addresses of its witnesses, something it is currently not required to do under Federal Rule of Criminal Procedure 16.

The amendment requires the prosecution to provide notice, regardless of how it intends to use the extrinsic act evidence at trial, i.e., during its case-in-chief, for impeachment, or for possible rebuttal. The court in its discretion may, under the facts, decide that the particular request or notice was not reasonable, either because of the lack of timeliness or completeness. Because the notice requirement serves as condition precedent to admissibility of 404(b) evidence, the offered evidence is inadmissible if the court decides that the notice requirement has not been met.

Nothing in the amendment precludes the court from requiring the government to provide it with an opportunity to rule *in limine* on 404(b) evidence before it is offered or even mentioned during trial. When ruling *in limine*, the court may require the government to disclose to it the specifics of such evidence which the court must consider in determining admissibility.

The amendment does not extend to evidence of acts which are "intrinsic" to the charged offense, *see United States v. Williams*, 900 F.2d 823 (5th Cir. 1990) (noting distinction between 404(b) evidence and intrinsic offense evidence). Nor is the amendment intended to redefine what evidence would otherwise be admissible under Rule 404(b). Finally, the Committee does not intend through the amendment to affect the role of the court and the jury in considering such evidence. *See United States v. Huddleston*, 485 U.S. 681, 108 S. Ct. 1496 (1988).

COMMITTEE NOTE TO 2000 AMENDMENT TO RULE 404(a)

Rule 404(a)(1) has been amended to provide that when the accused attacks the character of an alleged victim under subdivision (a)(2) of this Rule, the door is opened to an attack on the same character trait of the accused. Current law does not allow the government to introduce negative character evidence as to the accused unless the accused introduces evidence of good character. *See, e.g., United States v. Fountain,* 768 F.2d 790 (7th Cir. 1985) (when the accused offers proof of self-defense, this permits proof of the alleged victim's character trait for peacefulness, but it does not permit proof of the accused's character trait for violence).

The amendment makes clear that the accused cannot attack the alleged victim's character and yet remain shielded from the disclosure of equally relevant evidence concerning the same character trait of the accused. For example, in a murder case with a claim of self-defense, the accused, to bolster this defense, might offer evidence of the alleged victim's violent disposition. If the government has evidence that the accused has a violent character, but is not allowed to offer this evidence as part of its rebuttal, the jury has only part of the information it needs for an informed assessment of the probabilities as to who was the initial aggressor. This may be the case even if evidence of the accused's prior violent acts is admitted under Rule 404(b), because such evidence can be admitted only for limited purposes and not to show action in conformity with the accused's character on a specific occasion. Thus, the amendment is designed to permit a more balanced presentation of character evidence when an accused chooses to attack the character of the alleged victim.

The amendment does not affect the admissibility of evidence of specific acts of uncharged misconduct offered for a purpose other than proving character under Rule 404(b). Nor does it affect the standards for proof of character by evidence of other sexual behavior or sexual offenses under Rules 412-415. By its placement in Rule 404(a)(1), the amendment covers only proof of character by way of reputation or opinion.

The amendment does not permit proof of the accused's character if the accused merely uses character evidence for a purpose other than to prove the alleged victim's propensity to act in a certain way. *See United States v. Burks,* 470 F.2d 432, 434-5 (D.C.Cir. 1972) (evidence of the alleged victim's violent character, when known by the accused, was admissible "on the issue of whether or not the defendant reasonably feared he was in danger of imminent great bodily harm"). Finally, the amendment does not permit proof of the accused's character when the accused attacks the alleged victim's character as a witness under Rule 608 or 609.

The term "alleged" is inserted before each reference to "victim" in the Rule, in order to provide consistency with Evidence Rule 412.

COMMITTEE NOTE TO 2006 AMENDMENT TO RULE 404(a)

The Rule has been amended to clarify that in a civil case evidence of a person's character is never admissible to prove that the person acted in conformity with the character trait. The amendment resolves the dispute in the case law over whether the exceptions in subdivisions (a)(1) and (2) permit the circumstantial use of character evidence in civil cases. *Compare Carson v. Polley*, 689 F.2d 562, 576 (5th Cir. 1982) ("when a central issue in a case is close to one of a criminal nature, the exceptions to the Rule 404(a) ban on character evidence may be invoked"), *with SEC v. Towers Financial Corp.,* 966 F.Supp. 203 (S.D.N.Y. 1997) (relying on the terms "accused" and "prosecution" in Rule 404(a) to conclude that the exceptions in subdivisions (a)(1) and (2) are inapplicable in civil cases). The amendment is consistent with the original intent of the Rule, which was to prohibit the circumstantial use of character evidence in civil cases, even where closely related to criminal charges. *See Ginter v. Northwestern Mut. Life Ins. Co.*, 576 F.Supp. 627, 629-30 (D. Ky.1984) ("It seems beyond peradventure of doubt that the drafters of F.R.Evi. 404(a) explicitly intended that all character evidence, except where 'character is at issue' was to be excluded" in civil cases).

The circumstantial use of character evidence is generally discouraged because it carries serious risks of prejudice, confusion and delay. *See Michelson v. United States,* 335 U.S. 469, 476 (1948) ("The overriding policy of excluding such evidence, despite its admitted probative value, is the practical experience that its disallowance tends to prevent confusion of issues, unfair surprise and undue prejudice."). In criminal cases, the so-called "mercy rule" permits a criminal defendant to introduce evidence of pertinent character traits of the defendant and the victim. But that is because the accused, whose liberty is at stake, may need "a counterweight against the strong investigative and prosecutorial resources of the government." C. Mueller & L. Kirkpatrick, *Evidence: Practice Under the Rules*, pp. 264-5 (2d ed. 1999). See also Richard Uviller, *Evidence of Character to Prove Conduct: Illusion, Illogic, and Injustice in the Courtroom*, 130 U.Pa.L.Rev. 845, 855 (1982) (the rule prohibiting circumstantial use of character evidence "was relaxed to allow the criminal defendant with so much at stake and so little available in the way of conventional proof to have special dispensation to tell the factfinder just what sort of person he really is"). Those concerns do not apply to parties in civil cases.

The amendment also clarifies that evidence otherwise admissible under Rule 404(a)(2) may nonetheless be excluded in a criminal case involving sexual misconduct. In such a case, the admissibility of evidence of the victim's sexual behavior and predisposition is governed by the more stringent provisions of Rule 412.

Nothing in the amendment is intended to affect the scope of Rule 404(b). While Rule 404(b) refers to the "accused", the "prosecution" and a "criminal case", it does so only in the context of a notice requirement. The admissibility standards of Rule 404(b) remain fully applicable to both civil and criminal cases.

NOTE TO RULE 405

The rule deals only with allowable methods of proving character, not with the admissibility of character evidence, which is covered in Rule 404.

Of the three methods of proving character provided by the rule, evidence of specific instances of conduct is the most convincing. At the same time it possesses the greatest capacity to arouse prejudice, to confuse, to surprise, and to consume time. Consequently the rule confines the use of evidence of this kind to cases in which character is, in the strict sense, in issue and hence deserving of a searching inquiry. When character is used circumstantially and hence occupies a lesser status in the case, proof may be only by reputation and opinion. These latter methods are also available when character is in issue. This treatment is, with respect to specific instances of conduct and reputation, conventional contemporary common law doctrine. McCormick § 153.

In recognizing opinion as a means of proving character, the rule departs from usual contemporary practice in favor of that of an earlier day. See 7 Wigmore § 1986, pointing out that the earlier practice permitted opinion and arguing strongly for evidence based on personal knowledge and belief as contrasted with "the secondhand, irresponsible product of multiplied guesses and gossip which we term 'reputation'." It seems likely that the persistence of reputation evidence is due to its largely being opinion in disguise. Traditionally character has been regarded primarily in moral overtones of good and bad: chaste, peaceable, truthful, honest. Nevertheless, on occasion nonmoral considerations crop up, as in the case of the incompetent driver, and this seems bound to happen increasingly. If character is defined as the kind of person one is, then account must be taken of varying ways of arriving at the estimate. These may range from the opinion of the employer who has found the man honest to the opinion of the psychiatrist based upon examination and testing. No effective dividing line exists between character and mental capacity, and the latter traditionally has been provable by opinion.

According to the great majority of cases, on cross-examination inquiry is allowable as to whether the reputation witness has heard of particular instances of conduct pertinent to the trait in question. Michelson v. United States, 335 U.S. 469, 69 S.Ct. 213, 93 L.Ed. 168 (1948); Annot., 47 A.L.R.2d

1258. The theory is that, since the reputation witness relates what he has heard, the inquiry tends to shed light on the accuracy of his hearing and reporting. Accordingly, the opinion witness would be asked whether he knew, as well as whether he had heard. The fact is, of course, that these distinctions are of slight if any practical significance, and the second sentence of subdivision (a) eliminates them as a factor in formulating questions. This recognition of the propriety of inquiring into specific instances of conduct does not circumscribe inquiry otherwise into the bases of opinion and reputation testimony.

The express allowance of inquiry into specific instances of conduct on cross-examination in subdivision (a) and the express allowance of it as part of a case in chief when character is actually in issue in subdivision (b) contemplate that testimony of specific instances is not generally permissible on the direct examination of an ordinary opinion witness to character. Similarly as to witnesses to the character of witnesses under Rule 608(b). Opinion testimony on direct in these situations ought in general to correspond to reputation testimony as now given, i.e., be confined to the nature and extent of observation and acquaintance upon which the opinion is based. See Rule 701.

NOTE TO RULE 406

An oft-quoted paragraph, McCormick, § 162, p. 340, describes habit in terms effectively contrasting it with character:

"Character and habit are close akin. Character is a generalized description of one's disposition, or of one's disposition in respect to a general trait, such as honesty, temperance, or peacefulness. 'Habit,' in modern usage, both lay and psychological, is more specific. It describes one's regular response to a repeated specific situation. If we speak of character for care, we think of the person's tendency to act prudently in all the varying situations of life, in business, family life, in handling automobiles and in walking across the street. A habit, on the other hand, is the person's regular practice of meeting a particular kind of situation with a specific type of conduct, such as the habit of going down a particular stairway two stairs at a time, or of giving the hand-signal for a left turn, or of alighting from railway cars while they are moving. The doing of the habitual acts may become semi-automatic."

Equivalent behavior on the part of a group is designated "routine practice of an organization" in the rule.

Agreement is general that habit evidence is highly persuasive as proof of conduct on a particular occasion. Again quoting McCormick § 162, p. 341:

"Character may be thought of as the sum of one's habits though doubtless it is more than this. But unquestionably the uniformity of one's response to habit is far greater than the consistency with which one's conduct conforms to character or disposition. Even though character comes in only exceptionally as evidence of an act, surely any sensible man in investigating whether X did a particular act would be greatly helped in his inquiry by evidence as to whether he was in the habit of doing it."

When disagreement has appeared, its focus has been upon the question what constitutes habit, and the reason for this is readily apparent. The extent to which instances must be multiplied and consistency of behavior maintained in order to rise to the status of habit inevitably gives rise to differences of opinion. Lewan, Rationale of Habit Evidence, 16 Syracuse L.Rev. 39, 49 (1964). While adequacy of sampling and uniformity of response are key factors, precise standards for measuring their sufficiency for evidence purposes cannot be formulated.

The rule is consistent with prevailing views. Much evidence is excluded simply because of failure to achieve the status of habit. Thus, evidence of intemperate "habits" is generally excluded when offered as proof of drunkenness in accident cases, Annot., 46 A.L.R.2d 103, and evidence of other assaults is inadmissible to prove the instant one in a civil assault action, Annot., 66 A.L.R.2d 806. In Levin v. United States, 119 U.S.App.D.C. 156, 338 F.2d 265 (1964), testimony as to the religious "habits" of the accused, offered as tending to prove that he was at home observing the Sabbath rather than out obtaining money through larceny by trick, was held properly excluded;

"It seems apparent to us that an individual's religious practices would not be the type of activities which would lend themselves to the characterization of invariable regularity.' [1 Wigmore 520.] Certainly the very volitional basis of the activity raises serious questions as to its invariable nature, and hence its probative value." Id. at 272.

These rulings are not inconsistent with the trend towards admitting evidence of business transactions between one of the parties and a third person as tending to prove that he made the same bargain or proposal in the litigated situation. Slough, Relevancy Unraveled, 6 Kan.L.Rev. 38-41 (1957). Nor are they inconsistent with such cases as Whittemore v. Lockheed Aircraft Corp., 65 Cal.App.2d 737, 151 P.2d 670 (1944), upholding the admission of evidence that plaintiff's intestate had on four other occasions flown planes from defendant's factory for delivery to his employer airline, offered to prove that he was piloting rather than a guest on a plane which crashed and killed all on board while en route for delivery.

A considerable body of authority has required that evidence of the routine practice of an organization be corroborated as a condition precedent to its admission in evidence. Slough, Relevancy Unraveled, 5 Kan.L.Rev. 404, 449 (1957). This requirement is specifically rejected by the rule on the ground that it relates to the sufficiency of the evidence rather than admissibility. A similar position is taken in New Jersey Rule 49. The rule also rejects the requirement of the absence of eyewitnesses, sometimes encountered with respect to admitting habit evidence to prove freedom from contributory negligence in wrongful death cases. For comment critical of the requirements see Frank, J., in Cereste v. New York, N.H. & H.R. Co., 231 F.2d 50 (2d Cir. 1956), cert. denied 351 U.S. 951, 76 S.Ct. 848, 100 L.Ed 1475, 10 Vand.L.Rev. 447 (1957); McCormick § 162, p. 342. The omission of the requirement from the California Evidence Code is said to have effected its elimination. Comment, Cal.Ev.Code § 1105.

ORIGINAL COMMITTEE NOTE TO RULE 407

The rule incorporates conventional doctrine which excludes evidence of subsequent remedial measures as proof of an admission of fault. The rule rests on two grounds. (1) The conduct is not in fact an admission, since the conduct is equally consistent with injury by mere accident or through contributory negligence. Or, as Baron Bramwell put it, the rule rejects the notion that "because the world gets wiser as it gets older, therefore it was foolish before." Hart v. Lancashire & Yorkshire Ry. Co., 21 L.T.R. N.S. 261, 263 (1869). Under a liberal theory of relevancy this ground alone would not support exclusion as the inference is still a possible one. (2) The other, and more impressive, ground for exclusion rests on a social policy of encouraging people to take, or at least not discouraging them from taking, steps in furtherance of added safety. The courts have applied this principle to exclude evidence of subsequent repairs, installation of safety devices, changes in company rules, and discharge of employees, and the language of the present rules is broad enough to encompass all of them. See Falknor, Extrinsic Policies Affecting Admissibility, 10 Rutgers L.Rev. 574, 590 (1956).

The second sentence of the rule directs attention to the limitations of the rule. Exclusion is called for only when the evidence of subsequent remedial measures is offered as proof of negligence or culpable conduct. In effect it rejects the suggested inference that fault is admitted. Other purposes are, however, allowable, including ownership or control, existence of duty, and feasibility of precautionary measures, if controverted, and impeachment. 2 Wigmore § 283; Annot., 64 A.L.R.2d 1296. Two recent federal cases are illustrative. Boeing Airplane Co. v. Brown, 291 F.2d 310 (9th Cir. 1961), an action against an airplane manufacturer for using an allegedly defectively designed alternator shaft which cuased a plane crash, upheld the admission of evidence of subsequent design modification for the purpose of showing that design changes and safeguards were feasible. And Powers v. J. B. Michael & Co., 329 F.2d 674 (6th Cir. 1964), an action against a road contractor for negligent failure to put out warning signs, sustained the admission of evidence that defendant subsequently put out signs to show that the portion of the road in question was under defendant's control. The requirement that the other purpose be controverted calls for automatic exclusion unless a genuine issue be present and allows the opposing party to lay the groundwork for exclusion by making an admission. Otherwise the factors of undue prejudice, confusion of issues, misleading the jury, and waste of time remain for consideration under Rule 403.

For comparable rules, see Uniform Rule 51; California Evidence Code § 1151; Kansas Code of Civil Procedure § 60-451; New Jersey Evidence Rule 51.

COMMITTEE NOTE TO 1997 AMENDMENT TO RULE 407

The amendment to Rule 407 makes two changes in the rule. First, the words "an injury or harm allegedly caused by" were added to clarify that the rule applies only to changes made after the occurrence that produced the damages giving rise to the action. Evidence of measures taken by the defendant prior to the "event" causing "injury or harm" do not fall within the exclusionary scope of Rule 407 even if they occurred after the manufacture or design of the product. See Chase v. General Motors Corp., 856 F.2d 17, 21-22 (4th Cir. 1988).

Second, Rule 407 has been amended to provide that evidence of subsequent remedial measures may not be used to prove "a defect in a product or its design, or that a warning or instruction should have accompanied a product." This amendment adopts the view of the majority of the circuits that have interpreted Rule 407 to apply to products liability cases. See *Raymond v. Raymond Corp.*, 938 F.2d 1518, 1522 (1st Cir. 1991); *In re Joint Eastern District and Southern District Asbestos Litigation v. Armstrong World Industries, Inc.*, 995 F.2d 343 (2d Cir. 1993); *Cann v. Ford Motor Co.*, 658 F.2d 54, 60 (2d Cir. 1981), *cert. denied*, 456 U.S. 960 (1982); *Kelly v. Crown Equipment Co.*, 970 F.2d 1273, 1275 (3d Cir. 1992); *Werner v. Upjohn, Inc.*, 628 F.2d 848 (4th Cir. 1980), *cert. denied*, 449 U.S. 1080 (1981); *Grenada Steel Industries, Inc., v. Alabama Oxygen Co., Inc.*, 695 F.2d 883 (5th Cir. 1983); *Bauman v. Volkswagenwerk Aktiengesellschaft*, 621 F.2d 230, 232 (6th Cir. 1980); *Flaminio v. Honda Motor Company, Ltd.*, 733 F.2d 463, 469 (7th Cir. 1984); *Gauthier v. AMF, Inc.*, 788 F.2d 634, 636-37 (9th Cir. 1986).

Although this amendment adopts a uniform federal rule, it should be noted that evidence of subsequent remedial measures may be admissible pursuant to the second sentence of Rule 407. Evidence of subsequent remedial measures that is not barred by Rule 407 may still be subject to exclusion on Rule 403 grounds when the dangers of prejudice or confusion substantially outweigh the probative value of the evidence.

ORIGINAL COMMITTEE NOTE TO RULE 408

As a matter of general agreement, evidence of an offer-to compromise a claim is not receivable in evidence as an admission of, as the case may be, the validity or invalidity of the claim. As with evidence of subsequent remedial measures, dealt with in Rule 407, exclusion may be based on two grounds. (1) The evidence is irrelevant, since the offer may be motivated by a desire for peace rather than from any concession of weakness of position. The validity of this position will vary as the amount of the offer varies in relation to the size of the claim and may also be influenced by other circumstances. (2) a more consistently impressive ground is promotion of the public policy favoring the compromise and settlement of disputes. McCormick §§ 76, 251. While the rule is ordinarily phrased in terms of offers of compromise, it is apparent that a similar attitude must be taken with respect to completed compromises when offered against a party thereto. This latter situation will not, of course, ordinarily occur except when a party to the present litigation has compromised with a third person.

The same policy underlies the provision of Rule 68 of the Federal Rules of Civil Procedure that evidence of an unaccepted offer of judgment is not admissible except in a proceeding to determine costs.

The practical value of the common law rule has been greatly diminished by its inapplicability to admissions of fact, even though made in the course of compromise negotiations, unless hypothetical, stated to be "without prejudice," or so connected with the offer as to be inseparable from it. McCormick § 251, pp. 540-541. An inevitable effect is to inhibit freedom of communication with respect to compromise, even among lawyers. Another effect is the generation of controversy over whether a given statement falls within or without the protected area. These considerations account for the expansion of the rule herewith to include evidence of conduct or statements made in compromise negotiations, as well as the offer or completed compromise itself. For similar provisions see California Evidence Code §§ 1152, 1154.

The policy considerations which underlie the rule do not come into play when the effort is to induce a creditor to settle an admittedly due amount for a lessor sum. McCormick § 251, p. 540. Hence the rule requires that the claim be disputed as to either validity or amount.

The final sentence of the rule serves to point out some limitations upon its applicability. Since the rule excludes only when the purpose is proving the validity or invalidity of the claim or its amount, an offer for another purpose is not within the rule. The illustrative situations mentioned in the rule are supported by the authorities. As to proving bias or prejudice of a witness, see Annot., 161 A.L.R. 395, contra, Fenberg v. Rosenthal, 348 Ill. App. 510, 109 N.E.2d 402 (1952), and negativing a contention of lack of due diligence in presenting a claim, 4 Wigmore § 1061. An effort to "buy off" the prosecution or a prosecuting witness in a criminal case is not within the policy of the rule of exclusion. McCormick § 251, p. 542.

For other rules of similar import, see Uniform Rules 52 and 53; California Evidence Code § 1152, 1154; Kansas Code of Civil Procedure §§ 60-452, 60-453; New Jersey Evidence Rules 52 and 53.

COMMITTEE NOTE TO 2006 AMENDMENT TO RULE 408

Rule 408 has been amended to settle some questions in the courts about the scope of the Rule, and to make it easier to read and apply. First, the amendment provides that Rule 408 does not prohibit the introduction in a criminal case of statements or conduct during compromise negotiations regarding a civil dispute by a government regulatory, investigative, or enforcement agency. *See, e.g.*, *United States v. Prewitt*, 34 F.3d 436, 439 (7th Cir. 1994) (admissions of fault made in compromise of a civil securities enforcement action were admissible against the accused in a subsequent criminal action for mail fraud). Where an individual makes a statement in the presence of government agents, its subsequent admission in a criminal case should not be unexpected. The individual can seek to protect against subsequent disclosure through negotiation and agreement with the civil regulator, or an attorney for the government.

Statements made in compromise negotiations of a claim by a government agency may be excluded in criminal cases where the circumstances so warrant under Rule 403. For example, if an individual was unrepresented at the time the statement was made in a civil enforcement proceeding, its probative value in a subsequent criminal case may be minimal. But there is no absolute exclusion imposed by Rule 408.

In contrast, statements made during compromise negotiations of other disputed claims are not admissible in subsequent criminal litigation, when offered to prove liability for, invalidity of, or amount of those claims. When private parties enter into compromise negotiations they cannot protect against the subsequent use of statements in criminal cases by way of private ordering. The inability to guarantee protection against subsequent use could lead to parties refusing to admit fault, even if by doing so they could favorably settle private matters. Such a chill on settlement negotiations would be contrary to the policy of Rule 408.

The amendment distinguishes statements and conduct (such as a direct admission of fault) made in compromise negotiations of a civil claim by a government agency from an offer or acceptance of a compromise of such a claim. An offer or acceptance of a compromise of a civil claim is excluded under the Rule if offered against the defendant as an admission of fault. In that case, the predicate for the evidence would be that the defendant, by compromising with the government agency, has admitted the validity and amount of the civil claim, and that this admission has sufficient probative value to be considered as proof of guilt. But unlike a direct statement of fault, an offer or acceptance of a compromise is not very probative of the defendant's guilt. Moreover, admitting such an offer or acceptance could deter defendants from settling a civil regulatory action, for fear of evidentiary use in a subsequent criminal action. *See, e.g.*, Fishman, *Jones on Evidence, Civil and Criminal*, § 22:16 at 199, n.83 (7th ed. 2000) ("A target of a potential criminal investigation may be unwilling to settle civil claims against him if by doing so he increases the risk of prosecution and conviction.").

The amendment retains the language of the original rule that bars compromise evidence only when offered as evidence of the "validity", "invalidity", or "amount" of the disputed claim. The intent is to retain the extensive case law finding Rule 408 inapplicable when compromise evidence is offered for a purpose other than to prove the validity, invalidity, or amount of a disputed claim. *See, e.g., Athey v. Farmers Ins. Exchange,* 234 F.3d 357 (8th Cir. 2000) (evidence of settlement offer by insurer was properly admitted to prove insurer's bad faith); *Coakley & Williams v. Structural Concrete Equip.,* 973 F.2d 349 (4th Cir. 1992) (evidence of settlement is not precluded by Rule 408 where offered to prove a party's intent with respect to the scope of a release); *Cates v. Morgan Portable Bldg. Corp.,* 708 F.2d 683 (7th Cir. 1985) (Rule 408 does not bar evidence of a settlement when offered to prove a breach of the settlement agreement, as the purpose of the evidence is to prove the fact of settlement as opposed to the validity or amount of the underlying claim); *Uforma/Shelby Bus. Forms, Inc. v. NLRB,* 111 F.3d 1284 (6th Cir. 1997) (threats made in settlement negotiations were admissible; Rule 408 is inapplicable when the claim is based upon a wrong that is committed during the course of settlement negotiations). So for example, Rule 408 is inapplicable if offered to show that a party made fraudulent statements in order to settle a litigation.

The amendment does not affect the case law providing that Rule 408 is inapplicable when evidence of the compromise is offered to prove notice. *See, e.g., United States v. Austin,* 54 F.3d 394 (7th Cir. 1995) (no error to admit evidence of the defendant's settlement with the FTC, because it was offered to prove that the defendant was on notice that subsequent similar conduct was wrongful); *Spell v. McDaniel,* 824 F.2d 1380 (4th Cir. 1987) (in a civil rights action alleging that an officer used excessive force, a prior settlement by the City of another brutality claim was properly admitted to prove that the City was on notice of aggressive behavior by police officers).

The amendment prohibits the use of statements made in settlement negotiations when offered to impeach by prior inconsistent statement or through contradiction. Such broad impeachment would tend to swallow the exclusionary rule and would impair the public policy of promoting settlements. *See McCormick on Evidence* at 186 (5th ed. 1999) ("Use of statements made in compromise negotiations to impeach the testimony of a party, which is not specifically treated in Rule 408, is fraught with danger of misuse of the statements to prove liability, threatens frank interchange of information during negotiations, and generally should not be permitted."). *See also EEOC v. Gear Petroleum, Inc.*, 948 F.2d 1542 (10th Cir.1991) (letter sent as part of settlement negotiation cannot be used to impeach defense witnesses by way of contradiction or prior inconsistent statement; such broad impeachment would undermine the policy of encouraging uninhibited settlement negotiations).

The amendment makes clear that Rule 408 excludes compromise evidence even when a party seeks to admit its own settlement offer or statements made in settlement negotiations. If a party were to reveal its own statement or offer, this could itself reveal the fact that the adversary entered into settlement negotiations. The protections of Rule 408 cannot be waived unilaterally because the Rule, by definition, protects both parties from having the fact of negotiation disclosed to the jury. Moreover, proof of statements and offers made in settlement would often have to be made through the testimony of attorneys, leading to the risks and costs of disqualification. *See generally Pierce v. F.R. Tripler & Co.*, 955 F.2d 820, 828 (2d Cir. 1992) (settlement offers are excluded under Rule 408 even if it is the offeror who seeks to admit them; noting that the "widespread admissibility of the substance of settlement offers could bring with it a rash of motions for disqualification of a party's chosen counsel who would likely become a witness at trial").

The sentence of the Rule referring to evidence "otherwise discoverable" has been deleted as superfluous. *See, e.g.,* Advisory Committee Note to Maine Rule of Evidence 408 (refusing to include the sentence in the Maine version of Rule 408 and noting that the sentence "seems to state what the law would be if it were omitted"); Advisory Committee Note to Wyoming Rule of Evidence 408 (refusing to include the sentence in Wyoming Rule 408 on the ground that it was "superfluous"). The intent of the sentence was to prevent a party from trying to immunize admissible information, such as a pre-existing document, through the pretense of disclosing it during compromise negotiations. *See Ramada Development Co. v. Rauch,* 644 F.2d 1097 (5th Cir. 1981). But even without the sentence, the Rule cannot be read to protect pre-existing information simply because it was presented to the adversary in compromise negotiations.

NOTE TO RULE 409

The considerations underlying this rule parallel those underlying Rules 407 and 408, which deal respectively with subsequent remedial measures and offers of compromise. As stated in Annot., 20 A.L.R.2d 291, 293:

"[G]enerally, evidence of payment of medical, hospital, or similar expenses of an injured party by the opposing party, is not admissible, the reason often given being that such payment or offer is usually made from humane impulses and not from an admission of liability, and that to hold otherwise would tend to discourage assistance to the injured person."

Contrary to Rule 408, dealing with offers of compromise, the present rule does not extend to conduct or statements not a part of the act of furnishing or offering or promising to pay. This difference in treatment arises from fundamental differences in nature. Communication is essential if compromises are to be effected, and consequently broad protection of statements is needed. This is not so in cases of payments or offers or promises to pay medical expenses, where factual statements may be expected to be incidental in nature.

For rules on the same subject, but phrased in terms of "humanitarian motives," see Uniform Rule 52; California Evidence Code § 1152; Kansas Code of Civil Procedure § 60-452; New Jersey Evidence Rule 52.

NOTE TO RULE 410

Withdrawn pleas of guilty were held inadmissible in federal prosecutions in Kercheval v. United States, 274 U.S. 220, 47 S.Ct. 582, 71 L.Ed. 1009 (1927). The Court pointed out that to admit the withdrawn plea would effectively set at naught the allowance of withdrawal and place the accused in a dilemma utterly inconsistent with the decision to award him a trial. The New York Court of Appeals, in People v. Spitaleri, 9 N.Y.2d 168, 212 N.Y.S.2d 53, 173 N.E.2d 35 (1961), reexamined and overturned its earlier decisions which had allowed admission. In addition to the reasons set forth in Kercheval, which was quoted at length, the court pointed out that the effect of admitting the plea was to compel defendant to take the stand by way of explanation and to open the way for the prosecution to call the lawyer who had represented him at the time of entering the plea. State court decisions for and against admissibility are collected in Annot., 86 A.L.R.2d 326.

Pleas of nolo contendere are recognized by Rule 11 of the Rules of Criminal Procedure, although the law of numerous States is to the contrary. The present rule gives effect to the principal traditional characteristic of the nolo plea, i.e., avoiding the admission of guilt which is inherent in pleas of guilty. This position is consistent with the construction of Section 5 of the Clayton Act, 15 U.S.C. § 16(a), recognizing the inconclusive and compromise nature of judgments based on nolo pleas. General Electric Co. v. City of San Antonio, 334 F.2d 480 (5th Cir. 1964); Commonwealth Edison Co. v. Allis-Chalmers Mfg. Co., 323 F.2d 412 (7th Cir. 1963), cert. denied 376 U.S. 939, 84 S.Ct. 794, 11 L.Ed.2d 659; Armco Steel Corp. v. North Dakota, 376 F.2d 206 (8th Cir. 1967); City of Burbank v. General Electric Co., 329 F.2d 825 (9th Cir. 1964). See also state court decisions in Annot., 18 A.L.R.2d 1287, 1314.

Exclusion of offers to plead guilty or nolo has as its purpose the promotion of disposition of criminal cases by compromise. As pointed out in McCormick § 251, p. 543. "Effective criminal law administration in many localities would hardly be possible if a large proportion of the charges were not disposed of by such compromises." See also People v. Hamilton, 60 Cal.2d 105, 32 Cal.Rptr. 4, 383 P.2d 412 (1963), discussing legislation designed to achieve this result. As with compromise offers generally, Rule 408, free communication is needed, and security against having an offer of compromise or related statement admitted in evidence effectively encourages it.

Limiting the exclusionary rule to use against the accused is consistent with the purpose of the rule, since the possibility of use for or against other persons will not impair the effectiveness of withdrawing pleas or the freedom of discussion which the rule is designed to foster. See A.B.A. Standards Relating to Pleas of Guilty § 2.2 (1968). See also the narrower provisions of New Jersey Evidence Rule 52(2) and the unlimited exclusion provided in California Evidence Code § 1153.

NOTE TO RULE 411

The courts have with substantial unanimity rejected evidence of liability insurance for the purpose of proving fault, and absence of liability insurance as proof of lack of fault. At best the inference of fault from the fact of insurance coverage is a tennuous one, as is its converse. More important, no doubt, has been the feeling that knowledge of the presence or absence of liability insurance would induce juries to decide cases on improper grounds. McCormick § 168; Annot., 4 A.L.R.2d 761. The rule is drafted in broad terms so as to include contributory negligence or other fault of a plaintiff as well as fault of a defendant.

The second sentence points out the limits of the rule, using well established illustrations. Id.

For similar rules see Uniform Rule 54; California Evidence Code § 1155; Kansas Code of Civil Procedure § 60-454; New Jersey Evidence Rule 54.

NOTE TO RULE 412

[Editor's Note: There is no legislative history to the original Rule 412. Nor is there original legislative history to the amended Rule 412, which was passed as part of the Violent Crime Control and Law Enforcement Act of 1994. Congress did in that Act, however, adopt verbatim the version of Rule 412 recommended by the Advisory Committee; and it adopted the Advisory Committee's Note to the proposed Rule 412 as the legislative history for the amendment. The Advisory Committee proposal had been rejected by the Supreme Court in favor of a slightly different version, but Congress chose the Advisory Committee's version over that adopted by the Supreme Court.]

Rule 412 has been revised to diminish some of the confusion engendered by the original rule and to expand the protection afforded alleged victims of sexual misconduct. Rule 412 applies to both civil and criminal proceedings. The rule aims to safeguard the alleged victim against the invasion of privacy, potential embarrassment and sexual stereotyping that is associated with public disclosure of intimate sexual details and the infusion of sexual innuendo into the factfinding process. By affording victims protection in most instances, the rule also encourages victims of sexual misconduct to institute and to participate in legal proceedings against alleged offenders.

Rule 412 seeks to achieve these objectives by barring evidence relating to the alleged victim's sexual behavior or alleged sexual predisposition, whether offered as substantive evidence or for impeachment, except in designated circumstances in which the probative value of the evidence significantly outweighs possible harm to the victim.

The revised rule applies in all cases involving sexual misconduct without regard to whether the alleged victim or person accused is a party to the litigation. Rule 412 extends to "pattern" witnesses in both criminal and civil cases whose testimony about other instances of sexual misconduct by the person accused is otherwise admissible. When the case does not involve alleged sexual misconduct, evidence relating to a third-party witness' alleged sexual activities is not within the ambit of Rule 412. The witness will, however, be protected by other rules such as Rules 404 and 608, as well as Rule 403.

The terminology "alleged victim" is used because there will frequently be a factual dispute as to whether sexual misconduct occurred. It does not connote any requirement that the misconduct be alleged in the pleadings. Rule 412 does not, however, apply unless the person against whom the evidence is offered can reasonably be characterized as a "victim of alleged sexual misconduct." When this is not the case, as for instance in a defamation action involving statements concerning sexual misconduct in which the evidence is offered to show that the alleged defamatory statements were true or did not damage the plaintiff's reputation, neither Rule 404 nor this rule will operate to bar the evidence; Rule 401 and 403 will continue to control. Rule 412 will, however, apply in a Title VII action in which the plaintiff has alleged sexual harassment.

The reference to a person "accused" is also used in a non-technical sense. There is no requirement that there be a criminal charge pending against the person or even that the misconduct would constitute a criminal offense. Evidence offered to prove allegedly false prior claims by the victim is not barred by Rule 412. However, this evidence is subject to the requirements of Rule 404.

Subdivision (a). As amended, Rule 412 bars evidence offered to prove the victim's sexual behavior and alleged sexual predisposition. Evidence, which might otherwise be admissible under Rules 402, 404(b), 405, 607, 608, 609, or some other evidence rule, must be excluded if Rule 412 so requires. The word "other" is used to suggest some flexibility in admitting evidence "intrinsic" to the alleged sexual misconduct. Cf. Committee Note to 1991 amendment to Rule 404(b).

Past sexual behavior connotes all activities that involve actual physical conduct, i.e. sexual intercourse and sexual contact, or that imply sexual intercourse or sexual contact. See, e.g. United States v. Galloway, 937 F.2d 542 (10th Cir. 1991), cert. denied, 113 S.Ct. 418 (1992) (use of contraceptives inadmissible since use implies sexual activity); United States v. One Feather, 702 F.2d 736 (8th Cir. 1983) (birth of an illegitimate child inadmissible); State v. Carmichael, 727 P.2d 918, 925 (Kan. 1986) (evidence of venereal disease inadmissible). In addition, the word "behavior" should be construed to include activities of the mind, such as fantasies or dreams. See 23 C. Wright & K.

Graham, Jr., Federal Practice and Procedure, § 5384 at p. 548 (1980) ("While there may be some doubt under statutes that require 'conduct,' it would seem that the language of Rule 412 is broad enough to encompass the behavior of the mind.").

The rule has been amended to also exclude all other evidence relating to an alleged victim of sexual misconduct that is offered to prove a sexual predisposition. This amendment is designed to exclude evidence that does not directly refer to sexual activities or thoughts but that the proponent believes may have a sexual connotation for the factfinder. Admission of such evidence would contravene Rule 412's objectives of shielding the alleged victim from potential embarrassment and safeguarding the victim against stereotypical thinking. Consequently, unless the (b)(2) exception is satisfied, evidence such as that relating to the alleged victim's mode of dress, speech, or life-style will not be admissible.

The introductory phrase in subdivision (a) was deleted because it lacked clarity and contained no explicit reference to the other provisions of law that were intended to be overridden. The conditional clause, "except as provided in subdivisions (b) and (c)" is intended to make clear that evidence of the types described in subdivision (a) is admissible only under the strictures of those sections.

The reason for extending the rule to all criminal cases is obvious. The strong social policy of protecting a victim's privacy and encouraging victims to come forward to report criminal acts is not confined to cases that involve a charge of sexual assault. The need to protect the victim is equally great when a defendant is charged with kidnapping, and evidence is offered, either to prove motive or as background, that the defendant sexually assaulted the victim.

The reason for extending Rule 412 to civil cases is equally obvious. The need to protect alleged victims against invasions of privacy, potential embarrassment, and unwarranted sexual stereotyping, and the wish to encourage victims to come forward when they have been sexually molested do not disappear because the context has shifted from a criminal prosecution to a claim for damages or injunctive relief. There is a strong social policy in not only punishing those who engage in sexual misconduct, but in also providing relief to the victim. Thus, Rule 412 applies in any civil case in which a person claims to be the victim of sexual misconduct, such as actions for sexual battery or sexual harassment.

Subdivision (b). Subdivision (b) spells out the specific circumstances in which some evidence may be admissible that would otherwise be barred by the general rule expressed in subdivision (a). As amended, Rule 412 will be virtually unchanged in criminal cases, but will provide protection to any person alleged to be a victim of sexual misconduct regardless of the charge actually brought against an accused. A new exception has been added for civil cases.

In a criminal case, evidence may be admitted under subdivision (b)(1) pursuant to three possible exceptions, provided the evidence also satisfies other requirements for admissibility specified in the Federal Rules of Evidence, including Rule 403. Subdivisions (b)(1)(A) and (b)(1)(B) require proof in the form of specific instances of sexual behavior in recognition of the limited probative value and dubious reliability of evidence of reputation or evidence in the form of an opinion.

Under subdivision (b)(1)(A), evidence of specific instances of sexual behavior with persons other than the person whose sexual misconduct is alleged may be admissible if it is offered to prove that another person was the source of semen, injury or other physical evidence. Where the prosecution has directly or indirectly asserted that the physical evidence originated with the accused, the defendant must be afforded an opportunity to prove that another person was responsible. See United States v. Begay, 937 F.2d 515, 523 n. 10 (10th Cir. 1991). Evidence offered for the specific purpose identified in this subdivision may still be excluded if it does not satisfy Rules 401 or 403. See, e.g., United States v. Azure, 845 F.2d 1503, 1505-06 (8th Cir. 1988) (10 year old victim's injuries indicated recent use of force; court excluded evidence of consensual sexual activities with witness who testified at in camera hearing that he had never hurt victim and failed to establish recent activities).

Under the exception in subdivision (b)(1)(B), evidence of specific instances of sexual behavior with respect to the person whose sexual misconduct is alleged is admissible if offered to prove consent, or offered by the prosecution. Admissible pursuant to this exception might be evidence of prior instances of sexual activities between the alleged victim and the accused, as well as statements in which the alleged victim expressed an intent to engage in sexual intercourse with the accused, or voiced sexual fantasies involving the specific accused. In a prosecution for child sexual abuse, for example, evidence of uncharged sexual activity between the accused and the alleged victim offered by the prosecution may be admissible pursuant to Rule 404(b) to show a pattern of behavior. Evidence relating to the victim's alleged sexual predisposition is not admissible pursuant to this exception.

Under subdivision (b)(1)(C), evidence of specific instances of conduct may not be excluded if the result would be to deny a criminal defendant the protections afforded by the Constitution. For example, statements in which the victim has expressed an intent to have sex with the first person encountered on a particular occasion might not be excluded without violating the due process right of a rape defendant seeking to prove consent. Recognition of this basic principle was expressed in subdivision (b)(1) of the original rule. The United States Supreme Court has recognized that in various circumstances a defendant may have a right to introduce evidence otherwise precluded by an evidence rule under the Confrontation Clause. See, e.g., Olden v. Kentucky, 488 U.S. 227 (1988) (defendant in rape cases had right to inquire into alleged victim's cohabitation with another man to show bias).

Subdivision (b)(2) governs the admissibility of otherwise proscribed evidence in civil cases. It employs a balancing test rather than the specific exceptions stated in subdivision (b)(1) in recognition of the difficulty of foreseeing future developments in the law. Greater flexibility is needed to accommodate evolving causes of action such as claims for sexual harassment.

The balancing test requires the proponent of the evidence, whether plaintiff or defendant, to convince the court that the probative value of the proffered evidence "substantially outweighs the danger of harm to any victim and of unfair prejudice of any party." This test for admitting evidence offered to prove sexual behavior or sexual propensity in civil cases differs in three respects from the general rule governing admissibility set forth in Rule 403. First, it reverses the usual procedure spelled out in Rule 403 by shifting the burden to the proponent to demonstrate admissibility rather than making the opponent justify exclusion of the evidence. Second, the standard expressed in subdivision (b)(2) is more stringent than in the original rule; it raises the threshold for admission by requiring that the probative value of the evidence substantially outweigh the specified dangers. Finally, the Rule 412 test puts "harm to the victim" on the scale in addition to prejudice to the parties.

Evidence of reputation may be received in a civil case only if the alleged victim has put his or her reputation into controversy. The victim may do so without making a specific allegation in a pleading. Cf. Fed.R.Civ.P. 35(a).

Subdivision (c). Amended subdivision (c) is more concise and understandable than the subdivision it replaces. The requirement of a motion before trial is continued in the amended rule, as is the provision that a late motion may be permitted for good cause shown. In deciding whether to permit late filing, the court may take into account the conditions previously included in the rule: namely whether the evidence is newly discovered and could not have been obtained earlier through the existence of due diligence, and whether the issue to which such evidence relates has newly arisen in the case. The rule recognizes that in some instances the circumstances that justify an application to introduce evidence otherwise barred by Rule 412 will not become apparent until trial.

The amended rule provides that before admitting evidence that falls within the prohibition of Rule 412(a), the court must hold a hearing in camera at which the alleged victim and any party must be afforded the right to be present and an opportunity to be heard. All papers connected with the motion and any record of a hearing on the motion must be kept and remain under seal during the course of trial and appellate proceedings unless otherwise ordered. This is to assure that the privacy of the alleged victim is preserved in all cases in which the court rules that proffered evidence is not admissible, and in which the hearing refers to matters that are not received, or are received in another form.

The procedures set forth in subdivision (c) do not apply to discovery of a victim's past sexual conduct or predisposition in civil cases, which will be continued to be governed by Fed. R. Civ. P. 26. In order not to undermine the rationale of Rule 412, however, courts should enter appropriate orders pursuant to Fed. R. Civ. P. 26 (c) to protect the victim against unwarranted inquiries and to ensure confidentiality. Courts should presumptively issue protective orders barring discovery unless the party seeking discovery makes a showing that the evidence sought to be discovered would be relevant under the facts and theories of the particular case, and cannot be obtained except through discovery. In an action for sexual harassment, for instance, while some evidence of the alleged victim's sexual behavior and/or predisposition in the workplace may perhaps be relevant, non-work place conduct will usually be irrelevant. Cf. Burns v. McGregor Electronic Industries. Inc., 989 F.2d 959, 962-63 (8th Cir. 1993) (posing for a nude magazine outside work hours is irrelevant to issue of unwelcomeness of sexual advances at work). Confidentiality orders should be presumptively granted as well.

One substantive change made in subdivision (c) is the elimination of the following sentence: "Notwithstanding subdivision (b) of Rule 104, if the relevancy of the evidence which the accused seeks to offer in the trial depends upon the fulfillment of a condition of fact, the court, at the hearing in chambers or at a subsequent hearing in chambers scheduled for such purpose, shall accept evidence on the issue of whether such condition of fact is fulfilled and shall determine such issue." On its face, this language would appear to authorize a trial judge to exclude evidence of past sexual conduct between an alleged victim and an accused or a defendant in a civil case based upon the judge's belief that such past acts did not occur. Such an authorization raises questions of invasion of the right to a jury trial under the Sixth and Seventh Amendments. See 1 S. Saltzburg & M. Martin, Federal Rules Of Evidence Manual, 396-97 (5th ed. 1990).

The Advisory Committee concluded that the amended rule provided adequate protection for all persons claiming to be the victims of sexual misconduct, and that it was inadvisable to continue to include a provision in the rule that has been confusing and that raises substantial constitutional issues.

HISTORY OF RULES 413-415

[Editor's Note: Rules 413-415 were not the product of the usual procedure by which Federal Rules of Evidence are crafted. These Rules were added to the Federal Rules of Evidence by Public Law 103-322, the Violent Crime Control and Law Enforcement Act of 1994. Public Law 103-322 was adopted September 13, 1994, and became effective July 9, 1995. The implementation procedure of the rule was set forth in section 320935 of Public Law 103-322 as follows:]

(b) Implementation. The amendments made by subsection (a) [adding Rules 413-415] shall become effective pursuant to subsection (d).

(c) Recommendations by Judicial Conference. Not later than 150 days after the date of enactment of this Act, the Judicial Conference of the United States shall transmit to Congress a report containing recommendations for amending the Federal Rules of Evidence as they affect the admission of evidence of a defendant's prior sexual assault or child molestation crimes in cases involving sexual assault and child molestation. The Rules Enabling Act shall not apply to the recommendations made by the Judicial Conference pursuant to this section.

(d) Congressional action.

(1) If the recommendations described in subsection (c) are the same as the amendment made by subsection (a) [adding Rules 413-415], then the amendments made by subsection (a) shall become effective 30 days after the transmittal of the recommendations.

(2) If the recommendations described in subsection (c) are different than the amendments made by subsection (a) [adding Rules 413-415], the amendments made by subsection (a) shall become effective 150 days after the transmittal of the recommendations unless otherwise provided by law.

(3) If the Judicial Conference fails to comply with subsection (c), the amendments made by subsection (a) [adding Rules 413-415] shall become effective 150 days after the date the recommendations were due under subsection (c) unless otherwise provided by law.

(e) Application. The amendments made by subsection (a) [adding Rules 413-415] shall apply to proceedings commenced on or after the effective date of such amendments."

In accordance with subsection (c), the Judicial Conference submitted its report concerning the proposed rules on February 9, 1995; its recommendations differed from the proposed rules. Congress neither followed the Conference's recommendations nor otherwise altered the proposed rules. As a result, according to subsection (d), the proposed rules became effective on July 9, 1995, by direct enactment, without going through the rulemaking process.

What follows is the Judicial Conference Report on Rules 413-15, including the Advisory Committee's alternative proposal to amend the existing Rules to accommodate Congressional concerns. Selected statements by members of Congress are included after the Judicial Conference Report.

Report of Judicial Conference of United States on the Admission of Character Evidence in Certain Sexual Misconduct Cases

I. INTRODUCTION

This report is transmitted to Congress in accordance with the Violent Crime Control and Law Enforcement Act of 1994, Pub. L. No. 103-322 (September 13, 1994). Section 320935 of the Act invited the Judicial Conference of the United States within 150 days (February 10, 1995) to submit "a report containing recommendations for amending the Federal Rules of Evidence as they affect the admission of evidence of a defendant's prior sexual assault or child molestation crimes in cases involving sexual assault or child molestation."

Under the Act, new Rules 413, 414, and 415 would be added to the Federal Rules of Evidence. These Rules would admit evidence of a defendant's past similar acts in criminal and civil cases involving a sexual assault or child molestation offense for its bearing on any matter to which it is relevant. The effective date of new Rules 413-415 is contingent in part upon the nature of the recommendations submitted by the Judicial Conference.

After careful study, the Judicial Conference urges Congress to reconsider its decision on the policy questions underlying the new rules for reasons set out in Part III below.

If Congress does not reconsider its decision on the underlying policy questions, the Judicial Conference recommends incorporation of the provisions of new Rules 413-415 as amendments to Rules 404 and 405 of the Federal Rules of Evidence. The amendments would not change the substance of the congressional enactment but would clarify drafting ambiguities and eliminate possible constitutional infirmities.

II. BACKGROUND

Under the Act, the Judicial Conference was provided 150 days within which to make and submit to Congress alternative recommendations to new Evidence Rules 413-415. Consideration of Rules 413-415 by the Judicial Conference was specifically excepted from the exacting review procedures set forth in the Rules Enabling Act (codified at 28 U.S.C. §§ 2071-2077). Although the Conference acted on these new rules on an expedited basis to meet the Act's deadlines, the review process was thorough.

The new rules would apply to both civil and criminal cases. Accordingly, the Judicial Conference's Advisory Committee on Criminal Rules and the Advisory Committee on Civil Rules reviewed the rules at separate meetings in October 1994. At the same time and in preparation for its consideration of the new rules, the Advisory Committee on Evidence Rules sent out a notice soliciting comment on new Evidence Rules 413, 414, and 415. The notice was sent to the courts, including all federal judges, about 900 evidence law professors, 40 women's rights organizations, and 1,000 other individuals and interested organizations.

III. DISCUSSION

On October 17-18, 1994, the Advisory Committee on Evidence Rules met in Washington, D.C. It considered the public responses, which included 84 written comments, representing 112 individuals, 8 local and 8 national legal organizations. The overwhelming majority of judges, lawyers, law professors, and legal organizations who responded opposed new Evidence Rules 413, 414, and 415. The principal objections expressed were that the rules would permit the admission of unfairly prejudicial evidence and contained numerous drafting problems not intended by their authors.

The Advisory Committee on Evidence Rules submitted its report to the Judicial Conference Committee on Rules of Practice and Procedure (Standing Committee) for review at its January 11-13, 1995 meeting. The committee's report was unanimous except for a dissenting vote by the representative of the Department of Justice. The advisory committee believed that the concerns expressed by Congress and embodied in new Evidence Rules 413, 414, and 415 are already adequately addressed in the existing Federal Rules of Evidence. In particular, Evidence Rule 404(b) now allows the admission of evidence against a criminal defendant of the commission of prior crimes, wrongs, or acts for specified purposes, including to show intent, plan, motive, preparation, identity, knowledge, or absence of mistake or accident.

Furthermore, the new rules, which are not supported by empirical evidence, could diminish significantly the protections that have safeguarded persons accused in criminal cases and parties in civil cases against undue prejudice. These protections form a fundamental part of American jurisprudence and have evolved under long-standing rules and case law. A significant concern identified by the committee was the danger of convicting a criminal defendant for past, as opposed to charged, behavior or for being a bad person.

In addition, the advisory committee concluded that, because prior bad acts would be admissible even though not the subject of a conviction, mini-trials within trials concerning those acts would result when a defendant seeks to rebut such evidence. The committee also noticed that many of the comments received had concluded that the Rules, as drafted, were mandatory — that is, such evidence had to be admitted regardless of other rules of evidence such as the hearsay rule or the Rule 403 balancing test. The committee believed that this position was arguable because Rules 413-415 declare without qualification that such evidence "is admissible." In contrast, the new Rule 412, passed as part of the same legislation, provided that certain evidence "is admissible if it is otherwise admissible under these Rules." Fed. R. Evid. 412(b)(2). If the critics are right, Rules 413-415 free the prosecution from rules that apply to the defendant — including the hearsay rule and Rule 403. If so, serious constitutional questions would arise.

The Advisory Committees on Criminal and Civil Rules unanimously, except for representatives of the Department of Justice, also opposed the new rules. Those committees also concluded that the new rules would permit the introduction of unreliable but highly prejudicial evidence and would complicate trials by causing mini-trials of other alleged wrongs. After the advisory committees reported, the Standing Committee unanimously, again except for the representative of the Department of Justice, agreed with the view of the advisory committees.

It is important to note the highly unusual unanimity of the members of the Standing and Advisory Committees, composed of over 40 judges, practicing lawyers, and academicians, in taking the view that Rules 413-415 are undesirable. Indeed, the only supporters of the Rules were representatives of the Department of Justice.

For these reasons, the Standing Committee recommended that Congress reconsider its decision on the policy questions embodied in new Evidence Rules 413, 414, and 415.

However, if Congress will not reconsider its decision on the policy questions, the Standing Committee recommended that Congress consider an alternative draft recommended by the Advisory Committee on Evidence Rules. That Committee drafted proposed amendments to existing Evidence Rules 404 and 405 that would both correct ambiguities and possible constitutional infirmities identified in new Evidence Rules 413, 414, and 415 yet still effectuate Congressional intent. In particular, the proposed amendments:"

(1) expressly apply the other rules of evidence to evidence offered under the new rules;

(2) expressly allow the party against whom such evidence is offered to use similar evidence in rebuttal;

(3) expressly enumerate the factors to be weighed by a court in making its Rule 403 determination;

(4) render the notice provisions consistent with the provisions in existing Rule 404 regarding criminal cases;

(5) eliminate the special notice provisions of Rules 413-415 in civil cases so that notice will be required as provided in the Federal Rules of Civil Procedure; and

(6) permit reputation or opinion evidence after such evidence is offered by the accused or defendant."

The Standing Committee reviewed the new rules and the alternative recommendations. It concurred with the views of the Evidence Rules Committee and recommended that the Judicial Conference adopt them.

The Judicial Conference concurs with the views of the Standing Committee and urges that Congress reconsider its policy determinations underlying Evidence Rules 413-415. In the alternative, the attached amendments to Evidence Rules 404 and 405 are recommended, in lieu of new Evidence Rules 413, 414, and 415. The alternative amendments to Evidence Rules 404 and 405 are accompanied by the Advisory Committee Notes, which explain them in detail.

Attachment to Judicial Conference Report Advisory Committee's Proposal to Amend Rule 404 In Lieu of Adoption of Rules 413-15

Rule 404. Character Evidence Not Admissible to Prove Conduct; Exceptions; Other Crimes
[New matter is underlined.]

(a)

. . .

(4) Character in sexual misconduct cases. Evidence of another act of sexual assault or child molestation, or evidence to rebut such proof or an inference therefrom, if that evidence is otherwise admissible under these rules, in a criminal case in which the accused is charged with sexual assault or child molestation, or in a civil case in which a claim is predicated on a party's alleged commission of sexual assault or child molestation.

(A) In weighing the probative value of such evidence, the court may, as part of its rule 403 determination, consider:

(i) proximity in time to the charged or predicate misconduct;

(ii) similarity to the charged or predicate misconduct;

(iii) frequency of the other acts;

(iv) surrounding circumstances;

(v) relevant intervening events; and

(vi) other relevant similarities or differences.

(B) In a criminal case in which the prosecution intends to offer evidence under this subdivision, it must disclose the evidence, including statements of witnesses or a summary of the substance of any testimony, at a reasonable time in advance of trial, or during trial if the court excuses pretrial notice on good cause shown.

(C) For purposes of this subdivision,

(i) "sexual assault" means conduct — or an attempt or conspiracy to engage in conduct — of the type proscribed by chapter 109A of title 18, United

States Code, or conduct that involved deriving sexual pleasure or ratification from inflicting death, bodily injury, or physical pain on another person irrespective of the age of the victim — regardless of whether that conduct would have subjected the actor to federal jurisdiction.

(ii) "child molestation" means conduct — or an attempt or conspiracy to engage in conduct — of the type proscribed by chapter 110 of title 18, United States Code, or conduct, committed in relation to a child below the age of 14 years, either of the type proscribed by chapter 109A of title 18, United States Code, or that involved deriving sexual pleasure or gratification from inflicting death, bodily injury, or physical pain on another person — regardless of whether that conduct would have subjected the actor to federal jurisdiction.

(b) Other crimes, wrongs, or acts. Evidence of other crimes, wrongs, or acts is not admissible to prove the character of a person in order to show action in conformity therewith except as provided in subdivision (a) . . . .

Advisory Committee Note to Proposed Amendment to Rule 404

The Committee has redrafted Rules 413, 414 and 415 which the Violent Crime Control and Law Enforcement Act of 1994 conditionally added to the Federal Rules of Evidence. These modifications do not change the substance of the congressional enactment. The changes were made in order to integrate the provisions both substantively and stylistically with the existing Rules of Evidence; to illuminate the intent expressed by the principal drafters of the measure; to clarify drafting ambiguities that might necessitate considerable judicial attention if they remained unresolved; and to eliminate possible constitutional infirmities.

The Committee placed the new provisions in Rule 404 because this rule governs the admissibility of character evidence. The congressional enactment constitutes a new exception to the general rule stated in subdivision (a). The Committee also combined the three separate rules proposed by Congress into one subdivision (a)(4) in accordance with the rules' customary practice of treating criminal and civil issues jointly. An amendment to Rule 405 has been added because the authorization of a new form of character evidence in this rule has an impact on methods of proving character that were not explicitly addressed by Congress. The stylistic changes are self-evident. They are particularly noticeable in the definition section in subdivision (a)(4)(C) in which the Committee eliminated, without any change in meaning, graphic details of sexual acts.

The Committee added language that explicitly provides that evidence under this subdivision must satisfy other rules of evidence such as the hearsay rules in Article VIII, and the expert testimony rules in Article VII. Although principal sponsors of the legislation had stated that they intended other evidentiary rules to apply, the Committee believes that the opening phrase of the new subdivision 'if otherwise admissible under these rules' is needed to clarify the relationship between subdivision (a)(4) and other evidentiary provisions.

The Committee also expressly made subdivision (a)(4) subject to Rule 403 balancing in accordance with the repeatedly stated objectives of the legislation's sponsors with which representatives of the Justice Department expressed agreement. Many commentators on Rules 413-415 had objected that Rule 403's applicability was obscured by the actual language employed.

In addition to clarifying the drafters' intent, an explicit reference to Rule 403 may be essential to insulate the rule against constitutional challenge. Constitutional concerns also led the Committee to acknowledge specifically the opposing party's right to offer in rebuttal character evidence that the rules would otherwise bar, including evidence of a third person's prior acts of sexual misconduct offered to prove that the third person rather than the party committed the acts in issue.

In order to minimize the need for extensive and time-consuming judicial interpretation, the Committee listed factors that a court may consider in discharging Rule 403 balancing. Proximity in time is taken into account in a related rule. See Rule 609(b). Similarity, frequency and surrounding circumstances have long been considered by courts in handling other crimes evidence pursuant to Rule 404(b). Relevant intervening events, such as extensive medical treatment of the accused between the time of the prior proffered act and the charged act, may affect the strength of the propensity inference for which the evidence is offered. The final factor — "other relevant similarities or differences" — is added in recognition of the endless variety of circumstances that confront a trial court in rulings on admissibility. Although subdivision (4)(A) explicitly refers to factors that bear on probative value, this enumeration does not eliminate a judge's responsibility to take into account the other factors mentioned in Rule 403 itself — "the danger of unfair prejudice, confusion of the issues, . . . misleading the jury, . . . undue delay, waste of time, or needless presentation of cumulative evidence." In addition, the Advisory Committee Note to Rule 403 reminds judges that "The availability of other means of proof may also be an appropriate factor."

The Committee altered slightly the notice provision in criminal cases. Providing the trial court with some discretion to excuse pretrial notice was thought preferable to the inflexible 15-day rule provided in Rules 414 and 415. Furthermore, the formulation is identical to that contained in the 1991 amendment to Rule 404(b) so that no confusion will result from having two somewhat different notice provisions in the same rule. The Committee eliminated the notice provision for civil cases stated in Rule 415 because it did not believe that Congress intended to alter the usual time table for disclosure and discovery provided by the Federal Rules of Civil Procedure.

The definition section was simplified with no change in meaning. The reference to "the law of a state" was eliminated as unnecessarily confusing and restrictive. Conduct committed outside the United States ought equally to be eligible for admission. Evidence offered pursuant to subdivision (a)(4) must relate to a form of conduct proscribed by either chapter 109A or 110 of title 18, United States Code, regardless of whether the actor was subject to federal jurisdiction.

Advisory Committee's Proposal to Amend Rule 405 In Lieu of Adoption of Rules 413-15

Rule 405. Methods of Proving Character [New matter is underlined.]

(a) Reputation or opinion. In all cases in which evidence of character or a trait of character of a person is admissible, proof may be made by testimony as to reputation or by testimony in the form of an opinion <u>except as provided in subdivision (c) of this rule</u>. On cross-examination, inquiry is allowable into relevant specific instances of conduct.

. . .

(c) Proof in sexual misconduct cases. In a case in which evidence is offered under rule 404(a)(4), proof may be made by specific instances of conduct, testimony as to reputation, or testimony in the form of an opinion, except that the prosecution or claimant may offer reputation or opinion testimony only after the opposing party has offered such testimony.

Advisory Committee Note to Proposed Amendment to Rule 405

The addition of a new subdivision (a)(4) to Rule 404 necessitates adding a new subdivision (c) to Rule 405 to govern methods of proof. Congress clearly intended no change in the preexisting law that precludes the prosecution or a claimant from offering reputation or opinion testimony in its case in chief to prove that the opposing party acted in conformity with character. When evidence is admissible pursuant to Rule 404(a)(4), the proponent's proof must consist of specific instances of conduct. The opposing party, however, is free to respond with reputation or opinion testimony (including expert testimony if otherwise admissible) as well as evidence of specific instances. In a criminal case, the admissibility of reputation or opinion testimony would, in any event, be authorized by Rule 404(a)(1). The extension to civil cases is essential in order to provide the opponent with an adequate opportunity to refute allegations about a character for sexual misconduct. Once the opposing party offers reputation or opinion testimony, however, the prosecution or claimant may counter using such methods of proof.

Statements on the Floor of Congress Concerning Rules 413-415

Statement of Senator Dole:

[T]oo often, crucial evidentiary information is thrown out at trial because of technical evidentiary rulings. This amendment is designed to clarify the law and make clear what evidence is admissible, and what evidence is not admissible, in sex crime cases.

The amendment would create a new rule 413 of the Federal Rules of Evidence. This new rule would provide that in a criminal case in which the defendant is accused of assault, evidence of the defendant's commission of another offense or offenses of sexual assault is admissible, and may be considered for its bearing on any matter to which it is relevant.

. . . .

. . . I think if somebody is a repeat offender, if you brought in eight or nine women, for example, . . . and he had one offense after another, it would be probative. If it had not happened for 10 years, it probably would not have any value.

We also provide protection for the defendant because we require the Government to disclose the evidence to the defendant, including a statement of witnesses or a summary of the substance of any testimony expected to be offered at least 15 days before the scheduled date or trial, or at such later time as the court may allow for good cause.

. . . [I]f we are really going to get tough, and if we are really going to try to make certain that justice is provided for the victim as well as the defendant, of course, then I think we ought to look seriously at this.

113 Cong. Rec. S15072-3.

Statement of Senator Biden:

[W]hat the Republican leader is doing is changing 404(b) of the Federal Rules of Criminal Procedure [*sic*] . . . . Right now the rule in a courtroom in a Federal court is you go in and if you wish to introduce evidence of a similar crime . . . you can only do it under very limited circumstances . . . as proof of motive, opportunity, intent, preparation, plan, knowledge, identity, or absence of a mistake or accident. These are the only circumstances in which you can offer this as evidence . . . . There is a reason for that. These rules of relevancy . . . it took essentially 800 years to develop the rules of evidence under our English jurisprudence system . . . . We found out from 800 years of experience that [evidence of prior crimes] tends to blind people [from] looking at the real facts before them and making an independent judgment, at this time, at this circumstance, at this situation, that this defendant did that thing.

113 Cong. Rec. S15072.

HISTORY OF RULE 501

[Editor's Note: There is no Advisory Committee Note to Rule 501. Congress rejected the Advisory Committee's proposed Article V on privileges, and substituted Rule 501. The Report of the House Committee on the Judiciary provides the relevant background.]

Report of the House Committee on the Judiciary

Article V as submitted to Congress contained thirteen Rules. Nine of those Rules defined specific non-constitutional privileges which the federal courts must recognize (i.e. required reports, lawyer-client, psychotherapist-patient, husband-wife, communications to clergymen, political vote, trade secrets, secrets of state and other official information, and identity of informer). Another Rule provided that only those privileges set forth in Article V or in some other Act of Congress could be recognized by the federal courts. The three remaining Rules addressed collateral problems as to waiver of privilege by voluntary disclosure, privileged matter disclosed under compulsion or without opportunity to claim privilege, comment upon or inference from a claim of privilege, and jury instruction with regard thereto.

The Committee amended Article V to eliminate all of the Court's specific Rules on privileges. Instead, the Committee, through a single Rule, 501, left the law of privileges in its present state and further provided that privileges shall continue to be developed by the courts of the United States under a uniform standard applicable both in civil and criminal cases. That standard, derived from Rule 26 of the Federal Rules of Criminal Procedure, mandates the application of the principles of the common law as interpreted by the courts of the United States in the light of reason and experience. The words "person, government, State, or political subdivision thereof" were added by the Committee to the lone term "witnesses" used in Rule 26 to make clear that, as under present law, not only witnesses may have privileges. The Committee also included in its amendment a proviso modeled after Rule 302 and similar to language added by the Committee to Rule 601 relating to the competency of witnesses. The proviso is designed to require the application of State privilege law in civil actions and proceedings governed by Erie R.R. Co. v. Tompkins, 304 U.S. 64 (1938), a result in accord with current federal court decisions. See Republic Gear Co. v. Borg-Warner Corp., 381 F.2d 551, 555-556 n.2 (2d Cir. 1967). The Committee deemed the proviso to be necessary in the light of the Advisory Committee's view (see its note to Court Rule 501) that this result is not mandated under *Erie*.

The rationale underlying the proviso is that federal law should not supersede that of the States in substantive areas such as privilege absent a compelling reason. The Committee believes that in civil cases in the federal courts where an element of a claim or defense is not grounded upon a federal question, there is no federal interest strong enough to justify departure from State policy. In addition, the Committee considered that the Court's proposed Article V would have promoted forum shopping in some civil actions, depending upon differences in the privilege law applied as among the State and federal courts. The Committee's proviso, on the other hand, under which the federal courts are bound to apply the State's privilege law in actions founded upon a State-created right or defense, removes the incentive to "shop."

NOTE TO RULE 601

This general ground-clearing eliminates all grounds of incompetency not specifically recognized in the succeeding rules of this Article. Included among the grounds thus abolished are religious belief, conviction of crime, and connection with the litigation as a party or interested person or spouse of a party or interested person. With the exception of the so-called Dead Man's Acts, American jurisdictions generally have ceased to recognize these grounds.

The Dead Man's Acts are surviving traces of the common law disqualification of parties and interested persons. They exist in variety too great to convey conviction of their wisdom and effectiveness. These rules contain no provision of this kind. For the reasoning underlying the decision not to give effect to state statutes in diversity cases, see the Advisory Committee's Note to Rule 501.

No mental or moral qualifications for testifying as a witness are specified. Standards of mental capacity have proved elusive in actual application. A leading commentator observes that few witnesses are disqualified on that ground. Weihofen, Testimonial Competence and Credibility, 34 Geo. Wash.L.Rev. 53 (1965). Discretion is regularly exercised in favor of allowing the testimony. A witness wholly without capacity is difficult to imagine. The question is one particularly suited to the jury as one of weight and credibility, subject to judicial authority to review the sufficiency of the evidence. 2 Wigmore §§ 501, 509. Standards of moral qualification in practice consist essentially of evaluating a person's truthfulness in terms of his own answers about it. Their principal utility is in affording an opportunity on voir dire examination to impress upon the witness his moral duty. This result may, however, be accomplished more directly, and without haggling in terms of legal standards, by the manner of administering the oath or affirmation under Rule 603.

Admissibility of religious belief as a ground of impeachment is treated in Rule 610. Conviction of crime as a ground of impeachment is the subject of Rule 609. Marital relationship is the basis for privilege under Rule 505. Interest in the outcome of litigation and mental capacity are, of course, highly relevant to credibility and require no special treatment to render them admissible along with other matters bearing upon the perception, memory, and narration of witnesses.

NOTE TO RULE 602

"* * * [T]he rule requiring that a witness who testifies to a fact which can be perceived by the senses must have had an opportunity to observe, and must have actually observed the fact" is a "most prevasive manifestation" of the common law insistence upon "the most reliable sources of information." McCormick § 10, p. 19. These foundation requirements may, of course, be furnished by the testimony of the witness himself; hence personal knowledge is not an absolute but may consist of what the witness thinks he knows from personal perception. 2 Wigmore § 650. It will be observed that the rule is in fact a specialized application of the provisions of Rule 104(b) on conditional relevancy.

This rule does not govern the situation of a witness who testifies to a hearsay statement as such, if he has personal knowledge of the making of the statement. Rules 801 and 805 would be applicable. This rule would, however, prevent him from testifying to the subject matter of the hearsay statement, as he has no personal knowledge of it.

The reference to Rule 703 is designed to avoid any question of conflict between the present rule and the provisions of that rule allowing an expert to express opinions based on facts of which he does not have personal knowledge.

NOTE TO RULE 603

The rule is designed to afford the flexibility required in dealing with religious adults, atheists, conscientious objectors, mental defectives, and children. Affirmation is simply a solemn undertaking to tell the truth; no special verbal formula is required. As is true generally, affirmation is recognized by federal law. "Oath" includes affirmation, 1 U.S.C. § 1; judges and clerks may administer oaths and affirmations, 28 U.S.C. §§ 459, 953; and affirmations are acceptable in lieu of oaths under Rule 43(d) of the Federal Rules of Civil Procedure. Perjury by a witness is a crime, 18 U.S.C. § 1621.

NOTE TO RULE 604

The rule implements Rule 43(f) of the Federal Rules of Civil Procedure and Rule 28(b) of the Federal Rules of Criminal Procedure, both of which contain provisions for the appointment and compensation of interpreters.

NOTE TO RULE 605

In view of the mandate of 28 U.S.C. § 455 that a judge disqualify himself in "any case in which he . . . is or has been a material witness," the likelihood that the presiding judge in a federal court might be called to testify in the trial over which he is presiding is slight. Nevertheless the possibility is not totally eliminated.

The solution here presented is a broad rule of incompetency, rather than such alternatives as incompetency only as to material matters, leaving the matter to the discretion of the judge, or recognizing no incompetency. The choice is the result of inability to evolve satisfactory answers to questions which arise when the judge abandons the bench for the witness stand. Who rules on objections? Who compels him to answer? Can he rule impartially on the weight and admissibility of his own testimony? Can he be impeached or cross-examined effectively? Can he, in a jury trial, avoid conferring his seal of approval on one side in the eyes of the jury? Can he, in a bench trial, avoid an involvement destructive of impartiality? The rule of general incompetency has substantial support. See Report of the Special Committee on the Propriety of Judges Appearing as Witnesses, 36 A.B.A.J. 630 (1950); cases collected in

Annot. 157 A.L.R. 311; McCormick § 68, p. 147; Uniform Rule 42; California Evidence Code § 703; Kansas Code of Civil Procedure § 60-442; New Jersey Evidence Rule 42. Cf. 6 Wigmore § 1909, which advocates leaving the matter to the discretion of the judge, and statutes to that effect collected in Annot. 157 A.L.R. 311.

The rule provides an "automatic" objection. To require an actual objection would confront the opponent with a choice between not objecting, with the result of allowing the testimony, and objecting, with the probable result of excluding the testimony but at the price of continuing the trial before a judge likely to feel that his integrity had been attacked by the objector.

ORIGINAL NOTE TO RULE 606

Subdivision (a). The considerations which bear upon the permissibility of testimony by a juror in the trial in which he is sitting as juror bear an obvious similarity to those evoked when the judge is called as a witness. See Advisory Committee's Note to Rule 605. The judge is not, however in this instance so involved as to call for departure from usual principles requiring objection to be made; hence the only provision on objection is that opportunity be afforded for its making out of the presence of the jury. Compare Rules 605.

Subdivision (b). Whether testimony, affidavits, or statements of jurors should be received for the purpose of invalidating or supporting a verdict or indictment, and if so, under what circumstances, has given rise to substantial differences of opinion. The familiar rubric that a juror may not impeach his own verdict, dating from Lord Mansfield's time, is a gross oversimplification. The values sought to be promoted by excluding the evidence include freedom of deliberation, stability and finality of verdicts, and protection of jurors against annoyance and embarrassment. McDonald v. Piess, 238 U.S. 264, 35 S.Ct. 785, 59 L.Ed. 1300 (1915). On the other hand, simply putting verdicts beyond effective reach can only promote irregularity and injustice. The rule offers an accommodation between these competing considerations.

The mental operations and emotional reactions of jurors in arriving at a given result would, if allowed as a subject of inquiry, place every verdict at the mercy of jurors and invite tampering and harassment. See Grenz v. Werre, 129 N.W.2d 681 (N.D. 1964). The authorities are in virtually complete accord in excluding the evidence. Fryer, Note on Disqualification of Witnesses, Selected Writings on Evidence and Trial 345, 347 (Fryer ed. 1957); Maguire, Weinstein, et al., Cases on Evidence 887 (5th ed. 1965); 8 Wigmore § 2340 (McNaughton Rev. 1961). As to matters other than mental operations and emotional reactions of jurors, substantial authority refuses to allow a juror to disclose irregularities which occur in the jury room, but allows his testimony as to irregularities occurring outside and allows outsiders to testify as to occurrances both inside and out. 8 Wigmore § 2354 (McNaughton Rev. 1961). However, the door of the jury room is not necessarily a satisfactory dividing point, and the Supreme Court has refused to accept it for every situation. Mattox v. United States, 146 U.S. 140, 13 S.Ct. 50, 36 L.Ed. 917 (1892).

Under the federal decisions the central focus has been upon insulation of the manner in which the jury reached its verdict, and this protection extends to each of the components of deliberation, including arguments, statements, discussions, mental and emotional reactions, votes, and any other feature of the process. Thus testimony or affidavits of jurors have been held incompetent to show a compromise verdict, Hyde v. United States, 225 U.S. 347, 382 (1912); a quotient verdict, McDonald v. Piess, 238 U.S. 264 (1915); speculation as to insurance coverage, Holden v. Porter, 495 F.2d 878 (10th Cir.1969), Farmers Coop. Elev. Ass'n v. Strand, 382 F.2d 224, 230 (8th Cir. 1967), cert. denied 389 U.S. 1014; misinterpretations of instructions, Farmers Coop. Elev. Ass'n v. Strand, supra; mistake in returning verdict, United States v. Chereton, 309 F.2d 197 (6th Cir. 1962); interpretation of guilty plea by one defendant as implicating others, United States v. Crosby, 294 F.2d 928, 949 (2d Cir. 1961). The policy does not, however, foreclose testimony by jurors as to prejudicial extraneous information or influences injected into or brought to bear upon the deliberative process. Thus a juror is recognized as competent to testify to statements by the baliff or the introduction of a prejudicial newspaper account into the jury room, Mattox v. United States, 146 U.S. 140 (1892). See also Parker v. Gladden, 385 U.S. 363 (1966).

This rule does not purport to specify the substantive grounds for setting aside verdicts for irregularity; it deals only with the competency of jurors to testify concerning those grounds. Allowing them to testify as to matters other than their own inner reactions involves no particular hazard to the values sought to be protected. The rules is based upon this conclusion. It makes no attempt to specify the substantive grounds for setting aside verdicts for irregularity.

See also Rule 6(e) of the Federal Rules of Criminal Procedure and 18 U.S.C. § 3500, governing the secrecy of grand jury proceedings. The present rules does not relate to secrecy and disclosure but to the competency of certain witnesses and evidence.

COMMITTEE NOTE TO 2006 AMENDMENT TO RULE 606(b)

Rule 606(b) has been amended to provide that juror testimony may be used to prove that the verdict reported was the result of a mistake in entering the verdict on the verdict form. The amendment responds to a divergence between the text of the Rule and the case law that has established an exception for proof of clerical errors. *See, e.g., Plummer v. Springfield Term. Ry.,* 5 F.3d 1, 3 (1st Cir. 1993) ("A number of circuits hold, and we agree, that juror testimony regarding an alleged clerical error, such as announcing a verdict different than that agreed upon, does not challenge the validity of the verdict or the deliberation of mental processes, and therefore is not subject to Rule 606(b)."); *Teevee Toons, Inc., v. MP3.Com, Inc.,* 148 F.Supp.2d 276, 278 (S.D.N.Y. 2001) (noting that Rule 606(b) has been silent regarding inquiries designed to confirm the accuracy of a verdict).

In adopting the exception for proof of mistakes in entering the verdict on the verdict form, the amendment specifically rejects the broader exception, adopted by some courts, permitting the use of juror testimony to prove that the jurors were operating under a misunderstanding about the consequences of the result that they agreed upon. *See, e.g., Attridge v. Cencorp Div. of Dover Techs. Int'l, Inc.,* 836 F.2d 113, 116 (2d Cir. 1987); *Eastridge Development Co., v. Halpert Associates, Inc.,* 853 F.2d 772 (10th Cir. 1988). The broader exception is rejected because an inquiry into whether the jury misunderstood or misapplied an instruction goes to the jurors' mental processes underlying the verdict, rather than the verdict's accuracy in capturing what the jurors had agreed upon. *See, e.g., Karl v. Burlington Northern R.R.,* 880 F.2d 68, 74 (8th Cir. 1989) (error to receive juror testimony on whether verdict was the result of jurors' misunderstanding of instructions: "The jurors did not state that the figure written by the foreman was different from that which they agreed upon, but indicated that the figure the foreman wrote down was intended to be a net figure, not a gross figure. Receiving such statements violates Rule 606(b) because the testimony relates to how the jury interpreted the court's instructions, and concerns the jurors' 'mental processes,' which is forbidden by the rule."); *Robles v. Exxon Corp.,* 862 F.2d 1201, 1208 (5th Cir. 1989) ("the alleged error here goes to the substance of what the jury was asked to decide, necessarily implicating the jury's mental processes insofar as it questions the jury's understanding of the court's instructions and application of those instructions to the facts of the case"). Thus, the exception established by the amendment is limited to cases such as "where the jury foreperson wrote down, in response to an interrogatory, a number different from that agreed upon by the jury, or mistakenly stated that the defendant was 'guilty' when the jury had actually agreed that the defendant was not guilty." *Id.*

It should be noted that the possibility of errors in the verdict form will be reduced substantially by polling the jury. Rule 606(b) does not, of course, prevent this precaution. *See* 8 C. Wigmore, Evidence, § 2350 at 691 (McNaughten ed. 1961) (noting that the reasons for the rule barring juror testimony, "namely, the dangers of uncertainty and of tampering with the jurors to procure testimony, disappear in large part if such investigation as may be desired is *made by the judge* and takes place *before the jurors' discharge* and separation") (emphasis in original). Errors that come to light after polling the jury "may be corrected on the spot, or the jury may be sent out to continue deliberations, or, if necessary, a new trial may be ordered." C. Mueller & L. Kirkpatrick, *Evidence Under the Rules* at 671 (2d ed. 1999) (citing *Sincox v. United States,* 571 F.2d 876, 878-79 (5th Cir. 1978)).

NOTE TO RULE 607

The traditional rule against impeaching one's own witness is abandoned as based on false premises. A party does not hold out his witnesses as worthy of belief, since he rarely has a free choice in selecting them. Denial of the right leaves the party at the mercy of the witness and the adversary. If the impeachment is by a prior statement, it is free from hearsay dangers and is excluded from the category of hearsay under Rule 801(d)(1). Ladd, Impeachment of One's Own Witness-New Developments 4 U.Chi.L.Rev. 69 (1936); McCormick § 38; 3 Wigmore §§ 896-918. The substantial inroads into the old rule made over the years by decisions, rules, and statutes are evidence of doubts as to its basic soundness and workability. Cases are collected in 3 Wigmore § 905. Revised Rule 32(a)(1) of the Federal Rules of Civil Procedure allows any party to impeach a witness by means of his deposition, and Rule 43(b) has allowed the calling and impeachment of an adverse party or person identified with him. Illustrative statutes allowing a party to impeach his own witness under varying circumstances are Ill.Rev. Stats.1967, c. 110, § 60; Mass.Laws Annot. 1959, c. 233 § 23; 20 N.M.Stats. Annot. 1953, § 20-2-4; N.Y. CPLR § 4514 (McKinney 1963); 12 Vt.Stats. Annot. 1959, §§ 1641a, 1642. Complete judicial rejection of the old rule is found in United States v. Freeman, 302 F.2d 347 (2d Cir. 1962). The same result is reached in Uniform Rule 20; California Evidence Code § 785; Kansas Code of Civil Procedure § 60-420. See also New Jersey Evidence Rule 20.

ORIGINAL NOTE TO RULE 608

Subdivision (a). In Rule 404(a) the general position is taken that character evidence is not admissible for the purpose of proving that the person acted in conformity therewith, subject, however, to several exceptions, one of which is character evidence of a witness as bearing upon his credibility. The present rule develops that exception.

In accordance with the bulk of judicial authority, the inquiry is strictly limited to character for veracity, rather than allowing evidence as to character generally. The result is to sharpen relevancy, to reduce surprise, waste of time, and confusion, and to make the lot of the witness somewhat less unattractive. McCormick § 44.

The use of opinion and reputation evidence as means of proving the character of witnesses is consistent with Rule 405(a). While the modern practice has purported to exclude opinion witnesses who testify to reputation seem in fact often to be giving their opinions, disguised somewhat misleadingly as reputation. See McCormick § 44. And even under the modern practice, a common relaxation has allowed inquiry as to whether the witnesses would believe the principal witness under oath. United States v. Walker, 313 F. 2d 236 (6th Cir. 1963), and cases cited therein; McCormick § 44, pp. 94-95, n. 3.

Character evidence in support of credibility is admissible under the rule only after the witness' character has first been attacked, as has been the case at common law. Maguire, Weinstein, et al., Cases on Evidence 295 (5th ed. 1965); McCormick § 49, p. 105; 4 Wigmore § 1104. The enormous needless consumption of time which a contrary practice would entail justifies the limitation. Opinion or reputation that the witness is untruthful specifically qualifies as an attack under the rule, and evidence or misconduct, including conviction of crime, and of corruption also fall within this category. Evidence of bias or interest does not. McCormick § 49; 4 Wigmore §§ 1106, 1107. Whether evidence in the form of contradiction is an attack upon the character of the witness must depend §§ 1108, 1109.

As to the use of specific instances on direct by an opinion witness, see the Advisory Committee's Note to Rule 405, supra.

Subdivision (b). In conformity with Rule 405, which forecloses use of evidence of specific incidents as proof in chief of character unless character is an issue in the case, the present rule generally bars evidence of specific instances of conduct of a witness for the purpose of attacking or supporting his credibility. There are, however, two exceptions: (1) specific instances are provable when they have been the subject of criminal conviction, and (2) specific instances may be inquired into on cross-examination of the principal witness or of a witness giving an opinion of his character for truthfulness.

(1) Conviction of crime as a technique of impeachment is treated in detail in Rule 609, and here is merely recognized as an exception to the general rule excluding evidence of specific incidents for impeachment purposes.

(2) Particular instances of conduct, though not the subject of criminal conviction, may be inquired into on cross-examination of the principal witness himself or of a witness who testifies concerning his character for truthfulness. Effective cross-examination demands that some allowance be made for going into matters of this kind, but the possibilities of abuse are substantial. Consequently safeguards are erected in the form of specific requirements that the instances inquired into be probative of truthfulness or its opposite and not remote in time. Also, the overriding protection of Rule 403 requires that probative value not be outweighed by danger of unfair prejudice, confusion of issues, or misleading the jury, and that of Rule 611 bars harassment and undue embarrassment.

The final sentence constitutes a rejection of the doctrine of such cases as People v. Sorge, 301 N.Y. 198, 93 N.E.2d 637 (1950), that any past criminal act relevant to credibility may be inquired into on cross-examination, in apparent disregard of the privilege against self-incrimination. While it is clear that an ordinary witness cannot make a partial disclosure of incriminating matter and then invoke the privilege on cross-examination, no tenable contention can be made that merely by testifying he waives his right to foreclose inquiry on cross-examination into criminal activities for the purpose of attacking his credibility. So to hold would reduce the privilege to a nullity. While it is true that an accused, unlike an ordinary witness, has an option whether to testify, if the option can be exercised only at the price of opening up inquiry as to any and all criminal acts committed during his lifetime, the right to testify could scarcely be said to possess much vitality. In Griffin v. California, 380 U.S. 609, 85 S.Ct. 1229, 14 L.Ed.2d 106 (1965), the Court held that allowing comment on the election of an accused not to testify exacted a constitutionally impermissible price, and so here. While no specific provision in terms confers constitutional status on the right of an accused to take the stand in his own defense, the existence of the right is so completely recognized that a denial of it or substantial infringement upon it would surely be of due process dimensions. See Ferguson v. Georgia, 365 U.S. 570, 81 S.Ct. 756, 5 L.Ed.2d 783 (1961); McCormick § 131; 8 Wigmore § 2276 (McNaughton Rev. 1961). In any event, wholly aside from constitutional considerations, the provision represents a sound policy.

COMMITTEE NOTE TO 2003 AMENDMENT TO RULE 608

The Rule has been amended to clarify that the absolute prohibition on extrinsic evidence applies only when the sole reason for proffering that evidence is to attack or support the witness' character for truthfulness. *See United States v. Abel,* 469 U.S. 45 (1984); *United States v. Fusco,* 748 F.2d 996 (5th Cir. 1984) (Rule 608(b) limits the use of evidence "designed to show that the witness has done things, unrelated to the suit being tried, that make him more or less believable per se"); Ohio R.Evid. 608(b). On occasion the Rule's use of the overbroad term "credibility" has been read "to bar extrinsic evidence for bias, competency and contradiction impeachment since they too deal with credibility." American Bar Association Section of Litigation, *Emerging Problems Under the Federal Rules of Evidence* at 161 (3d ed. 1998). The amendment conforms the language of the Rule to its original intent, which was to impose an absolute bar on extrinsic evidence only if the sole purpose for offering the evidence was to prove the witness' character for veracity. *See* Advisory Committee Note to Rule 608(b) (stating that the Rule is "[i]n conformity with Rule 405, which forecloses use of evidence of specific incidents as proof in chief of character unless character is in issue in the case . . . ").

By limiting the application of the Rule to proof of a witness' character for truthfulness, the amendment leaves the admissibility of extrinsic evidence offered for other grounds of impeachment (such as contradiction, prior inconsistent statement, bias and mental capacity) to Rules 402 and 403. *See, e.g., United States v. Winchenbach,* 197 F.3d 548 (1st Cir. 1999) (admissibility of a prior inconsistent statement offered for impeachment is governed by Rules 402 and 403, not Rule 608(b)); *United States v. Tarantino*, 846 F.2d 1384 (D.C.Cir. 1988) (admissibility of extrinsic evidence offered to contradict a witness is governed by Rules 402 and 403); *United States v. Lindemann,* 85 F.3d 1232 (7th Cir. 1996) (admissibility of extrinsic evidence of bias is governed by Rules 402 and 403).

It should be noted that the extrinsic evidence prohibition of Rule 608(b) bars any reference to the consequences that a witness might have suffered as a result of an alleged bad act. For example, Rule 608(b) prohibits counsel from mentioning that a witness was suspended or disciplined for the conduct that is the subject of impeachment, when that conduct is offered only to prove the character of the witness. *See United States v. Davis,* 183 F.3d 231, 257 n.12 (3d Cir. 1999) (emphasizing that in attacking the defendant's character for truthfulness "the government cannot make reference to Davis's forty-four day suspension or that Internal Affairs found that he lied about" an incident because "[s]uch evidence would not only be hearsay to the extent it contains assertion of fact, it would be inadmissible extrinsic evidence under Rule 608(b)"). *See also* Stephen A. Saltzburg, *Impeaching the Witness: Prior Bad Acts and Extrinsic Evidence*, 7 Crim. Just. 28, 31 (Winter 1993) ("counsel should not be permitted to circumvent the no-extrinsic-evidence provision by tucking a third person's opinion about prior acts into a question asked of the witness who has denied the act.").

For purposes of consistency the term "credibility" has been replaced by the term "character for truthfulness" in the last sentence of subdivision (b). The term "credibility" is also used in subdivision (a). But the Committee found it unnecessary to substitute "character for truthfulness" for "credibility" in Rule 608(a), because subdivision (a)(1) already serves to limit impeachment to proof of such character.

Rules 609(a) and 610 also use the term "credibility" when the intent of those Rules is to regulate impeachment of a witness' character for truthfulness. No inference should be derived from the fact that the Committee proposed an amendment to Rule 608(b) but not to Rules 609 and 610.

ORIGINAL NOTE TO RULE 609

As a means of impeachment, evidence of conviction of crime is significant only because it stands as proof of the commission of the underlying criminal act. There is little dissent from the general proposition that at least some crimes are relevant to credibility but much disagreement among the cases and commentators about which crimes are usable for this purpose. See McCormick § 43; 2 Wright, Federal Practice and Procedure; Criminal § 416 (1969). The weight of traditional authority has been to allow use of felonies generally, without regard to the nature of the particular offense, and of crimen falsi without regard to the grade of the offense. This is the view accepted by Congress in the 1970 amendment of § 14-305 of the District of Columbia Code, P.L. 91-358, 84 Stat. 473. Uniform Rule 21 and Model Code Rule 106 permit only crimes involving "dishonesty or false statement." Others have thought that the trial judge should have discretion to exclude convictions if the probative value of the evidence of the crime is substantially outweighed by the danger of unfair prejudice. Luck v. United States, 121 U.S.App.D.C. 151, 348 F.2d 763 (1965); McGowan, Impeachment of Criminal Defendants by Prior Convictions, 1970 Law & Soc. Order 1. Whatever may be the merits of those views, this rule is drafted to accord with the Congressional policy manifested in the 1970 legislation.

The proposed rule incorporates certain basic safeguards, in terms applicable to all witnesses but of particular significance to an accused who elects to testify. These protections include the imposition of definite time limitations, giving effect to demonstrated rehabilitation, and generally excluding juvenile adjudications.

Subdivision (a). For purposes of impeachment, crimes are divided into two categories by the rule: (1) those of what is generally regarded as felony grade, without particular regard to the nature of the offense, and (2) those involving dishonesty or false statement, without regard to the grade of the offense. Provable convictions are not limited to violations of federal law. By reason of our constitutional structure, the federal catalog of crimes is far from being a complete one, and resort must be had to the laws of the states for the specification of many crimes. For example, simple theft as compared with theft from interstate commerce. Other instances of borrowing are the Assimilative Crimes Act, making the state law of crimes applicable to the special territorial and maritime jurisdiction of the United States, 18 U.S.C. § 13, and the provision of the Judicial Code disqualifying persons as jurors on the grounds of state as well as federal convictions, 28 U.S.C. § 1865. For evaluation of the crime in terms of seriousness, reference is made to the congressional measurement of felony (subject to imprisonment in excess of one year) rather than adopting state definitions which vary considerably. See 28 U.S.C. § 1865, supra, disqualifying jurors for conviction in state or federal court of crime punishable by imprisonment for more than one year.

Subdivision (b). Few statutes recognize a time limit on impeachment by evidence of conviction. However, practical considerations of fairness and relevancy demand that some boundary be recognized. See Ladd, Credibility Tests-Current Trends, 89 U.Pa.L.Rev. 166, 176-177 (1940). This portion of the rule is derived from the proposal advanced in Recommendation Proposing in

Evidence Code, § 788(5), p. 142, Cal.Law Rev.Comm'n (1965), though not adopted. See California Evidence Code § 788.

Subdivision (c). A pardon or its equivalent granted solely for the purpose of restoring civil rights lost by virtue of a conviction has no relevance to an inquiry into character. If, however, the pardon or other proceeding is hinged upon a showing of rehabilitation the situation is otherwise. The result under the rule is to render the conviction inadmissible. The alternative of allowing in evidence both the conviction and the rehabilitation has not been adopted for reasons of policy, economy of time, and difficulties of evaluation.

A similar provision is contained in California Evidence Code § 788. Cf. A.L.I. Model Penal Code, Proposed Official Draft § 306.6(3)(e) (1962), and discussion in A.L.I. Proceedings 310 (1961).

Pardons based on innocence have the effect, of course, of nullifying the conviction ab initio.

Subdivision (d). The prevailing view has been that a juvenile adjudication is not usable for impeachment. Thomas v. United States, 74 App.D.C. 167, 121 F.2d 905 (1941); Cotton v. United States, 355 F.2d 480 (10th Cir. 1966). This conclusion was based upon a variety of circumstances. By virtue of its informality, frequently diminished quantum of required proof, and other departures from accepted standards for criminal trials under the theory of parens patriae, the juvenile adjudication was considered to lack the precision and general probative value of the criminal conviction. While In re Gault, 387 U.S. 1, 87 S.Ct. 1428, 18 L.Ed.2d 527 (1967), no doubt eliminates these characteristics insofar as objectionable, other obstacles remain. Practical problems of administration are raised by the common provisions in juvenile legislation that records be kept confidential and that they be destroyed after a short time. While Gault was skeptical as to the realities of confidentiality of juvenile records, it also saw no constitutional obstacles to improvement. 387 U.S. at 25, 87 S.Ct. 1428. See also Note, Rights and Rehabilitation in the Juvenile Courts, 67 Colum.L.Rev. 281, 289 (1967). In addition, policy considerations much akin to those which dictate exclusion of adult convictions after rehabilitation has been established strongly suggest a rule of excluding juvenile adjudications. Admittedly, however, the rehabilitative process may in a given case be a demonstrated failure, or the strategic importance of a given witness may be so great as to require the overriding of general policy in the interests of particular justice. See Giles v. Maryland, 386 U.S. 66, 87 S.Ct. 793, 17 L.Ed.2d 737 (1967). Wigmore was outspoken in his condemnation of the disallowance of juvenile adjudications to impeach, especially when the witness is the complainant in a case of molesting a minor. 1 Wigmore § 196; 3 Id. §§ 924a, 980. The rule recognizes discretion in the judge to effect an accommodation among these various factors by departing from the general principle of exclusion. In deference to the general pattern and policy of juvenile statutes, however, no discretion is accorded when the witness is the accused in a criminal case.

Subdivision (e). The presumption of correctness which ought to attend judicial proceedings supports the position that pendency of an appeal does not preclude use of a conviction for impeachment. United States v. Empire Packing Co., 174 F.2d 16 (7th Cir.1949), cert. denied 337 U.S. 959, 69 S.Ct.

1534, 93 L.Ed. 1758; Bloch v. United States, 226 F.2d 185 (9th Cir.1955), cert. denied 350 U.S. 948, 76 S.Ct. 323, 100 L.Ed. 826 and 353 U.S. 959, 77 S.Ct. 868, 1 L.Ed.2d 910; and see Newman v. United States, 331 F.2d 968 (8th Cir.1964), Contra, Campbell v. United States, 85 U.S.App.D.C. 133, 176 F.2d 45 (1949). The pendency of an appeal is, however, a qualifying circumstance properly considerable.

COMMITTEE NOTE TO 1990 AMENDMENT TO RULE 609(a)

The amendment to Rule 609(a) makes two changes in the rule. The first change removes from the rule the limitation that the conviction may only be elicited during cross-examination, a limitation that virtually every circuit has found to be inapplicable. It is common for witnesses to reveal on direct examination their convictions to "remove the sting" of the impeachment. *See, e.g., United States v. Bad Cob*, 560 F.2d 877 (8th Cir. 1977). The amendment does not contemplate that a court will necessarily permit proof of prior convictions through testimony, which might be time-consuming and more prejudicial than proof through a written record. Rules 403 and 611(a) provide sufficient authority for the court to protect against unfair or disruptive methods of proof.

The second change effected by the amendment resolves an ambiguity as to the relationship of Rules 609 and 403 with respect to impeachment of witnesses other than the criminal defendant. *See Green v. Bock Laundry Machine Co.*, 109 S. Ct. 1981 [490 U.S. 504] (1989). The amendment does not disturb the special balancing test for the criminal defendant who chooses to testify. Thus, the rule recognizes that, in virtually every case in which prior convictions are used to impeach the testifying defendant, the defendant faces a unique risk of prejudice — *i.e.*, the danger that convictions that would be excluded under Fed. R. Evid. 404 will be misused by a jury as propensity evidence despite their introduction solely for impeachment purposes. Although the rule does not forbid all use of convictions to impeach a defendant, it requires that the government show that the probative value of convictions as impeachment evidence outweighs their prejudicial effect.

Prior to the amendment, the rule appeared to give the defendant the benefit of the special balancing test when defense witnesses other than the defendant were called to testify. In practice, however, the concern about unfairness to the defendant is most acute when the defendant's own convictions are offered as evidence. Almost all of the decided cases concern this type of impeachment, and the amendment does not deprive the defendant of any meaningful protection, since Rule 403 now clearly protects against unfair impeachment of any defense witness other than the defendant. There are cases in which a defendant might be prejudiced when a defense witness is impeached. Such cases may arise, for example, when the witness bears a special relationship to the defendant such that the defendant is likely to suffer some spill-over effect from impeachment of the witness.

The amendment also protects other litigants from unfair impeachment of their witnesses. The danger of prejudice from the use of prior convictions is not confined to criminal defendants. Although the danger that prior convictions will be misused as character evidence is particularly acute when the [criminal] defendant is impeached, the danger exists in other situations as well. The amendment reflects the view that it is desirable to protect all litigants from the unfair use of prior convictions, and that the ordinary balancing test of Rule 403, which provides that evidence shall not be excluded unless its prejudicial effect substantially outweighs its probative value, is appropriate for assessing the admissibility of prior convictions for impeachment of any witness other than a criminal defendant.

The amendment reflects a judgment that decisions interpreting Rule 609(a) as requiring a trial court to admit convictions in civil cases that have little, if anything, to do with credibility reach undesirable results. *See, e.g., Diggs v. Lyons*, 741 F.2d 577 (3d Cir. 1984), *cert. denied*, 105 S. Ct. 2157 (1985). The amendment provides the same protection against unfair prejudice arising from prior convictions used for impeachment purposes as the rules provide for other evidence. The amendment finds support in decided cases. *See, e.g., Petty v. Ideco*, 761 F.2d 1146 (5th Cir. 1985); *Czajka v. Hickman*, 703 F.2d 317 (8th Cir. 1983).

Fewer decided cases address the question whether Rule 609(a) provides any protection against unduly prejudicial prior convictions used to impeach government witnesses. Some courts have read Rule 609(a) as giving the government no protection for its witnesses. *See, e.g., United States v. Thorne*, 547 F.2d 56 (8th Cir. 1976); *United States v. Nevitt*, 563 F.2d 406 (9th Cir. 1977), *cert. denied*, 444 U.S. 847 (1979). This approach also is rejected by the amendment. There are cases in which impeachment of government witnesses with prior convictions that have little, if anything, to do with credibility may result in unfair prejudice to the government's interest in a fair trial and unnecessary embarrassment to a witness. Fed. R. Evid. 412 already recognizes this and excluded [*sic*] certain evidence of past sexual behavior in the context of prosecutions for sexual assaults.

The amendment applies the general balancing test of Rule 403 to protect all litigants against unfair impeachment of witnesses. The balancing test protects civil litigants, the government in criminal cases, and the defendant in a criminal case who calls other witnesses. The amendment addresses prior convictions offered under Rule 609, not for other purposes, and does not run afoul, therefore, of *Davis v. Alaska*, 415 U.S. 308 (1974). *Davis* involved the use of a prior juvenile adjudication not to prove a past law violation, but to prove bias. The defendant in a criminal case has the right to demonstrate the bias of a witness and to be assured a fair trial, but not to unduly prejudice a trier of fact. *See generally* Rule 412. In any case in which the trial court believes that confrontation rights require admission of impeachment evidence, obviously the Constitution would take precedence over the rule.

The probability that prior convictions of an ordinary government witness will be unduly prejudicial is low in most criminal cases. Since the behavior of the witness is not the issue in dispute in most cases, there is little chance that the trier of fact will misuse the convictions offered as impeachment evidence as propensity evidence. Thus, trial courts will be skeptical when the government objects to impeachment of its witnesses with prior convictions. Only when the government is able to point to a real danger of prejudice that is sufficient to outweigh substantially the probative value of the conviction for impeachment purposes will the conviction be excluded.

The amendment continues to divide subdivision (a) into subsections (1) and (2) thus facilitating retrieval under current computerized research programs which distinguish the two provisions. The Committee recommended no substantive change in subdivision (a)(2), even though some cases raise a concern about the proper interpretation of the words "dishonesty or false statement." These words were used but not explained in the original Advisory Committee Note accompanying Rule 609. Congress extensively debated the rule, and the Report of the House and Senate Conference Committee states that "[b]y the phrase 'dishonesty and false statement,' the Conference means crimes such as perjury, subornation of perjury, false statement, criminal fraud, embezzlement, or false pretense, or any other offense in the nature of *crimen falsi*, commission of which involves some element of deceit, untruthfulness, or falsification bearing on the accused's propensity to testify truthfully." The Advisory Committee concluded that the Conference Report provides sufficient guidance to trial courts and that no amendment is necessary, notwithstanding some decisions that take an unduly broad view of "dishonesty," admitting convictions such as for bank robbery or bank larceny. Subsection (a)(2) continues to apply to any witness, including a criminal defendant.

Finally, the Committee determined that it was unnecessary to add to the rule language stating that when a prior conviction is offered under Rule 609, the trial court is to consider the probative value of the conviction *for impeachment*, not for other purposes. The Committee concluded that the title of the rule, its first sentence, and its placement among the impeachment rules clearly establish that evidence offered under Rule 609 is offered only for purposes of impeachment.

COMMITTEE NOTE TO 2006 AMENDMENT TO RULE 609(a)

The amendment provides that Rule 609(a)(2) mandates the admission of evidence of a conviction only when the conviction required the proof of (or in the case of a guilty plea, the admission of) an act of dishonesty or false statement. Evidence of all other convictions is inadmissible under this subsection, irrespective of whether the witness exhibited dishonesty or made a false statement in the process of the commission of the crime of conviction. Thus, evidence that a witness was convicted for a crime of violence, such as murder, is not admissible under Rule 609(a)(2), even if the witness acted deceitfully in the course of committing the crime.

The amendment is meant to give effect to the legislative intent to limit the convictions that are to be automatically admitted under subsection (a)(2). The Conference Committee provided that by "dishonesty and false statement" it meant "crimes such as perjury, subornation of perjury, false statement, criminal fraud, embezzlement, or false pretense, or any other offense in the nature of *crimen falsi*, the commission of which involves some element of deceit, untruthfulness, or falsification bearing on the [witness's] propensity to testify truthfully." Historically, offenses classified as *crimina falsi* have included only those crimes in which the ultimate criminal act was itself an act of deceit. *See* Green, *Deceit and the Classification of Crimes: Federal Rule of Evidence 609(a)(2) and the Origins of* Crimen Falsi, 90 J. Crim. L. & Criminology 1087 (2000).

Evidence of crimes in the nature of *crimina falsi* must be admitted under Rule 609(a)(2), regardless of how such crimes are specifically charged. For example, evidence that a witness was convicted of making a false claim to a federal agent is admissible under this subsection regardless of whether the crime was charged under a section that expressly references deceit (e.g., 18 U.S.C. § 1001, Material Misrepresentation to the Federal Government) or a section that does not (e.g., 18 U.S.C. § 1503, Obstruction of Justice).

The amendment requires that the proponent have ready proof that the conviction required the factfinder to find, or the defendant to admit, an act of dishonesty or false statement. Ordinarily, the statutory elements of the crime will indicate whether it is one of dishonesty or false statement. Where the deceitful nature of the crime is not apparent from the statute and the face of the judgment — as, for example, where the conviction simply records a finding of guilt for a statutory offense that does not reference deceit expressly — a proponent may offer information such as an indictment, a statement of admitted facts, or jury instructions to show that the factfinder had to find, or the defendant had to admit, an act of dishonesty or false statement in order for the witness to have been convicted. *Cf. Taylor v. United States*, 495 U.S. 575, 602 (1990) (providing that a trial court may look to a charging instrument or jury instructions to ascertain the nature of a prior offense where the statute is insufficiently clear on its face); *Shepard v. United States*, 125. S.Ct. 1254 (2005) (the inquiry to determine whether a guilty plea to a crime defined by a nongeneric statute necessarily admitted elements of the generic offense was limited to the charging document's terms, the terms of a plea agreement or transcript of colloquy between judge and defendant in which the factual basis for the plea was confirmed by the defendant, or a comparable judicial record). But the amendment does not contemplate a "mini-trial" in which the court plumbs the record of the previous proceeding to determine whether the crime was in the nature of *crimen falsi*.

The amendment also substitutes the term "character for truthfulness" for the term "credibility" in the first sentence of the Rule. The limitations of Rule 609 are not applicable if a conviction is admitted for a purpose other than to prove the witness' s character for untruthfulness. *See, e.g., United States v. Lopez*, 979 F.2d 1024 (5th Cir. 1992) (Rule 609 was not applicable where the conviction was offered for purposes of contradiction). The use of the term "credibility" in subsection (d) is retained, however, as that subdivision is intended to govern the use of a juvenile adjudication for any type of impeachment.

NOTE TO RULE 610

While the rule forecloses inquiry into the religious beliefs or opinions of a witness for the purpose of showing that his character for truthfulness is affected by their nature, an inquiry for the purpose of showing interest or bias because of them is not within the prohibition. Thus disclosure of affiliation with a church which is a party to the litigation would be allowable under the rule. Cf. Tucker v. Reil, 51 Ariz. 357, 77 P.2d 203 (1938). To the same effect, though less specifically worded, is California Evidence Code § 789. See 3 Wigmore § 936.

NOTE TO RULE 611

Subdivision (a). Spelling out detailed rules to govern the mode and order of interrogating witnesses presenting evidence is neither desirable nor feasible. The ultimate responsibility for the effective working of the adversary system rests with the judge. The rule sets forth the objectives which he should seek to attain.

Item (1) restates in broad terms the power and obligation of the judge as developed under common law principles. It covers such concerns as whether testimony shall be in the form of a free narrative or responses to specific questions, McCormick § 5, the order of calling witnesses and presenting evidence, 6 Wigmore § 1867, the use of demonstrative evidence, McCormick § 179, and the many other questions arising during the course of a trial which can be solved only by the judge's common sense and fairness in view of the particular circumstances.

Item (2) is addressed to avoidance of needless consumption of time, a matter of daily concern in the disposition of cases. A companion piece is found in the discretion vested in the judge to exclude evidence as a waste of time in Rule 403(b).

Item (3) calls for a judgement under the particular circumstances whether interrogation tactics entail harassment or undue embarrassment. Pertinent circumstances include the importance of the testimony, the nature of the inquiry, its relevance to credibility, waste of time, and confusion. McCormick § 42. In Alford v. United States, 282 U.S. 687, 694, 51 S.Ct. 218, 75 L.Ed. 624 (1931), the Court pointed out that, while the trial judge should protect the witness from questions which "go beyond the bounds of proper cross-examination merely to harass, annoy or humiliate," this protection by no means forecloses efforts to discredit the witness. Reference to the transcript of the prosecutor's cross-examination in Berger v. United States, 295 U.S. 78, 55 S.Ct. 629, 79 L.Ed. 1314 (1935), serves to lay at rest any doubts as to the need for judicial control in this area.

'The inquiry into specific instances of conduct of a witness allowed under Rule 608(b) is, of course, subject to this rule.

Subdivision (b). The tradition in the federal courts and in numerous state courts has been to limit the scope of cross-examination to matters testified to on direct, plus matters bearing upon the credibility of the witness. Various reasons have been advanced to justify the rule of limited cross-examination. (1) A party vouches for his own witness but only to the extent of matters elicited on direct. Resurrection Gold Mining Co. v. Fortune Gold Mining Co., 129 F. 668, 675 (8th Cir. 1904), quoted in Maguire, Weinstein, et al., Cases on Evidence 277, n. 38 (5th ed. 1965). But the concept of vouching is discredited, and Rule 607 rejects it. (2) A party cannot ask his own witness leading questions. This is a problem properly solved in terms of what is necessary for a proper development of the testimony rather than by a mechanistic formula similar to the vouching concept. See discussion under subdivision (c). (3) A practice of limited cross-examination promotes orderly presentation of the case. Finch v. Weiner, 109 Conn. 616, 145 A. 31 (1929). While this latter reason has merit, the matter is essentially one of the order of presentation and not one in which involvement at the appellate level is likely to prove fruitful. See for example, Moyer v. Aetna Life Ins. Co., 126 F.2d 141 (3rd Cir. 1942); Butler v. New York Central R. Co., 253 F.2d 281 (7th Cir. 1958); United States v. Johnson, 285 F.2d 35 (9th Cir. 1960); Union Automobile Indemnity Ass'n. v. Capitol Indemnity Ins. Co., 310 F.2d 318 (7th Cir. 1962). In evaluating these considerations, McCormick says:

"The foregoing considerations favoring the wide-open or restrictive rules may well be thought to be fairly evenly balanced. There is another factor, however, which seems to swing the balance overwhelmingly in favor of the wide-open rule. This is the consideration of economy of time and energy. Obviously, the wide-open rule presents little or no opportunity for dispute in its application. The restrictive practice in all its forms, on the other hand, is productive in many court rooms, of continual bickering over the choice of the numerous variations of the 'scope of the direct' criterion, and of their application to particular cross-questions. These controversies are often reventilated on appeal, and reversals for error in their determination are frequent. Observance of these vague and ambiguous restrictions is a matter of constant and hampering concern to the cross-examiner. If these efforts, delays and misprisions were the necessary incidents to the guarding of substantive rights or the fundamentals of fair trial, they might be worth the cost. As the price of the choice of an obviously debatable regulation of the order of evidence, the sacrifice seems misguided. The American Bar Association's Committee for the Improvement of the Law of Evidence for the year 1937-38 said this:

"The rule limiting cross-examination to the precise subject of the direct examination is probably the most frequent rule (except the Opinion rule) leading in the trial practice today to refined and technical quibbles which obstruct the progress of the trial, confuse the jury, and give rise to appeal on technical grounds only. Some of the instances in which Supreme Courts have ordered new trials for the mere transgression of this rule about the order of evidence have been astounding.

We recommend that the rule allowing questions upon any part of the issue known to the witness * * * be adopted * * *"

McCormick, § 27, p. 51. See also 5 Moore's Federal Practice para. 43.10 (2nd ed. 1964).

The provision of the second sentence, that the judge may in the interests of justice limit inquiry into new matters on cross-examination, is designed for those situations in which the result otherwise would be confusion, complication, or protraction of the case, not as a matter of rule but as demonstrable in the actual development of the particular case.

The rule does not purport to determine the extent to which an accused who elects to testify thereby waives his privilege against self-incrimination. The question is a constitutional one, rather than a mere matter of administering the trial. Under Simmons v. United States, 390 U.S. 377, 88 S.Ct. 967, 19 L.Ed.2d 1247 (1968), no general waiver occurs when the accused testifies on such preliminary matters as the validity of a search and seizure or the admissibility of a confession. Rule 104(d), supra. When he testifies on the merits, however, can he foreclose inquiry into an aspect or element of the crime by avoiding it on direct? The affirmative answer given in Tucker v. United States, 5 F.2d 818 (8th Cir. 1925), is inconsistent with the description of the waiver as extending to "all other relevant facts" in Johnson v. United States, 318 U.S. 189, 195, 63 S.Ct. 549, 87 L.Ed. 704 (1943). See also Brown v. United States, 356 U.S. 148, 78 S.Ct. 622, 2 L.Ed.2d 589 (1958). The situation of an accused who desires to testify on some but not all counts of a multiple-count indictment is one to be approached, in the first instance at least, as a problem of severance under Rule 14 of the Federal Rules of Criminal Procedure. Cross v. United States, 118 U.S.App.D.C. 324, 335 F.2d 987 (1964). Cf. United States v. Baker, 262 F.Supp. 657, 686 (D.D.C. 1966). In all events, the extent of the waiver of the privilege against self-incrimination ought not to be determined as a by-product of a rule on scope of cross-examination.

Subdivision (c). The rule continues the traditional view that the suggestive powers of the leading question are as a general proposition undesirable. Within this tradition, however, numerous exceptions have achieved recognition: The witness who is hostile, unwilling, or biased; the child witness or the adult with communication problems; the witness whose recollection is exhausted; and undisputed preliminary matters. 3 Wigmore §§ 774-778. An almost total unwillingness to reverse for infractions has been manifested by appellate courts. See cases cited in 3 Wigmore § 770. The matter clearly falls within the area of control by the judge over the mode and order of interrogation and presentation and accordingly is phrased in words of suggestion rather than command.

The rule also conforms to tradition in making the use of leading questions on cross-examination a matter of right. The purpose of the qualification "ordinarily" is to furnish a basis for denying the use of leading questions when the cross-examination is cross-examination in form only and not in fact, as for example the "cross-examination" of a party by his own counsel after being called by the opponent (savoring more of re-direct) or of an insured defendant who proves to be friendly to the plaintiff.

The final sentence deals with categories of witnesses automatically regarded and treated as hostile. Rule 43(b) of the Federal Rules of Civil Procedure has included only "an adverse party or an officer, director, or managing agent of a public or private corporation or of a partnership or association which is an adverse party." This limitation virtually to persons whose statements would stand as admissions is believed to be an unduly narrow concept of those who may safely be regarded as hostile without further demonstration. See, for example, Maryland Casualty Co. v. Kador, 225 F.2d 120 (5th Cir. 1955), and Degelos v. Fidelity and Casualty Co., 313 F.2d 809 (5th Cir. 1963), holding despite the language of rule 43(b) that an insured fell within it, though not a party in an action under the Louisiana direct action statute. The phrase of the rule, "witness identified with" an adverse party, is designed to enlarge the category of persons thus callable.

NOTE TO RULE 612

The treatment of writings used to refresh recollection while on the stand is in accord with settled doctrine. McCormick § 9, p. 15. The bulk of the case law has, however, denied the existence of any right to access by the opponent when the writing is used prior to taking the stand, though the judge may have discretion in the matter. Goldman v. United States, 316 U.S. 129, 62 S.Ct. 993, 86 L.Ed. 1322 (1942); Needelman v. United States, 261 F.2d 802 (5th Cir. 1958), cert. dismissed 362 U.S. 600, 80 S.Ct. 960, 4 L.Ed.2d 980, rehearing denied 363 U.S. 858, 80 S.Ct. 1606, 4 L.Ed.2d 1739, Annot., 82 A.L.R.2d 473, 562 and 7 A.L.R.3d 181, 247. An increasing group of cases has repudiated the distinction, People v. Scott, 29 Ill.2d 97, 193 N.E.2d 814 (1963); State v. Mucci, 25 N.J. 423, 136 A.2d 761 (1957); State v. Hunt, 25 N.J. 514, 138 A.2d 1 (1958); State v. Desolvers, 40 R.I. 89, 100, A. 64 (1917), and this position is believed to be correct. As Wigmore put it, "the risk of imposition and the need of safeguard is just as great" in both situations. 3 Wigmore § 762, p. 111. To the same effect is McCormick § 9, p. 17.

The purpose of the phrase "for the purpose of testifying" is to safeguard against using the rule as a pretext for wholesale exploration of an opposing party's files and to insure that access is limited only to those writings which may fairly be said in fact to have an impact upon the testimony of the witness.

The purpose of the rule is the same as that of the Jencks statute, 18 U.S.C. § 3500: to promote the search of credibility and memory. The same sensitivity to disclosure of government files may be involved; hence the rule is expressly made subject to the statute, subdivision (a) of which provides: "In any criminal prosecution brought by the United States, no statement or report in the possession of the United States which was made by a Government witness or prospective Government witness (other than the defendant) shall be the subject of a subpena, discovery, or inspection until said witness has testified on direct examination in the trial of the case." Items falling within the purview of the statute are producible only as provided by its terms, Palermo v. United States, 360 U.S. 343, 351 (1959), and disclosure under the rule is limited similarly by the statutory conditions. With this limitation in mind, some differences of application may be noted. The Jencks statute applies only to statements of witnesses; the rule is not so limited. The statute applies only to criminal cases; the rule applies to all cases. The statute applies only to government witnesses; the rule applies to all witnesses. The statute contains no requirement that the statement be consulted for purposes of refreshment before or while testifying; the rule so requires. Since many writings would qualify under either statute or rule, a substantial overlap exists, but the identity of procedures makes this of no importance.

The consequences of nonproduction by the government in a criminal case are those of the Jencks statute, striking the testimony or in exceptional cases a mistrial. 18 U.S.C. § 3500(d). In other cases these alternatives are unduly limited, and such possibilities as contempt, dismissal, finding issues against the offender, and the like are available. See Rule 16(g) of the Federal Rules of Criminal Procedure and Rule 37(b) of the Federal Rules of Civil Procedure for appropriate sanctions.

NOTE TO RULE 613

Subdivision (a). The Queen's Case, 2 Br. & B. 284, 129 Eng. Rep. 976 (1820), laid down the requirement that a cross-examiner, prior to questioning the witness about his own prior statement in writing, must first show it to the witness. Abolished by statute in the country of its origin, the requirement nevertheless gained currency in the United States. The rule abolishes this useless impediment, to cross-examination. Ladd, Some Observations on Credibility: Impeachment of Witnesses, 52 Cornell L.Q. 239, 246-247 (1967); McCormick § 28; 4 Wigmore §§ 1259-1260. Both oral and written statements are included.

The provision for disclosure to counsel is designed to protect against unwarranted insinuations that a statement has been made when the fact is to the contrary.

The rule does not defeat the application of Rule 1002 relating to production of the original when the contents of a writing are sought to be proved. Nor does it defeat the application of Rule 26(b)(3) of the Rules of Civil Procedure, as revised, entitling a person on request to a copy of his own statement, though the operation of the latter may be suspended temporarily.

Subdivision (b). The familiar foundation requirement that an impeaching statement first be shown to the witness before it can be proved by extrinsic evidence is preserved but with some modifications. See Ladd, Some Observations on Credibility: Impeachment of Witnesses, 52 Cornell L.Q. 239, 247 (1967). The traditional insistence that the attention of the witness be directed to the statement on cross-examination is relaxed in favor of simply providing the witness an opportunity to explain and the opposite party an opportunity to examine on the statement, with no specification of any particular time or sequence. Under this procedure, several collusive witnesses can be examined before disclosure of a joint prior inconsistent statement. See Comment to California Evidence Code § 770. Also, dangers of oversight are reduced. See McCormick § 37, p. 68.

In order to allow for such eventualities as the witness becoming unavailable by the time the statement is discovered, a measure of discretion is conferred upon the judge. Similar provisions are found in California Evidence Code § 770 and New Jersey Evidence Rule 22(b).

Under principles of expression unius the rule does not apply to impeachment by evidence of prior inconsistent conduct. The use of inconsistent statements to impeach a hearsay declaration is treated in Rule 806.

NOTE TO RULE 614

Subdivision (a). While exercised more frequently in criminal than in civil cases, the authority of the judge to call witnesses is well established. McCormick § 8, p. 14; Maguire, Weinstein, et al., Cases on Evidence 303-304 (5th ed. 1965); 9 Wigmore § 2484. One reason for the practice, the old rule against impeaching one's own witness, no longer exists by virtue of Rule 607, supra. Other reasons remain, however, to justify the continuation of the practice of calling court's witnesses. The right to cross-examine, with all it implies, is assured. The tendency of juries to associate a witness with the party calling him, regardless of technical aspects of vouching, is avoided. And the judge is not imprisoned within the case as made by the parties.

Subdivision (b). The authority of the judge to question witnesses is also well established. McCormick § 8, pp. 12-13; Maguire, Weinstein, et al., Cases on

Evidence 737-739 (5th ed. 1965); 3 Wigmore § 784. The authority is, of course, abused when the judge abandons his proper role and assumes that of advocate, but the manner in which interrogation should be conducted and the proper extent of its exercise are not susceptible of formulation in a rule. The omission in no sense precludes courts of review from continuing to reverse for abuse.

Subdivision (c). The provision relating to objections is designed to relieve counsel of the embarrassment attendant upon objecting to questions by the judge in the presence of the jury, while at the same time assuring that objections are made in apt time to afford the opportunity to take possible corrective measures. Compare the "automatic" objection feature of Rule 605 when the judge is called as a witness.

NOTE TO RULE 615

The efficacy of excluding or sequestering witnesses has long been recognized as a means of discouraging and exposing fabrication, inaccuracy, and collusion. 6 Wigmore §§ 1837-1838. The authority of the judge is admitted, the only question being whether the matter is committed to his discretion or one of right. The rule takes the latter position. No time is specified for making the request.

Several categories of persons are excepted. (1) Exclusion of persons who are parties would raise serious problems of confrontation and due process. Under accepted practice they are not subject to exclusion. 6 Wigmore § 1841. (2) As the equivalent of the right of a natural-person party to be present, a party which is not a natural person is entitled to have a representative present. Most of the cases have involved allowing a police officer who has been in charge of an investigation to remain in court despite the fact that he will be a witness. United States v. Infanzon, 235 F.2d 318 (2d Cir. 1956); Portomene v. United States, 221 F.2d 582 (5th Cir. 1955); Powell v. United States, 208 F.2d 618 (6th Cir. 1953); Jones v. United States, 252 F.Supp. 781 (W.D.Okl. 1966). Designation of the representative by the attorney rather than by the client may at first glance appear to be an inversion of the attorney-client relationship, but it may be assumed that the attorney will follow the wishes of the client, and the solution is simple and workable. See California Evidence Code § 777. (3) The category contemplates such persons as an agent who handled the transaction being litigated or an expert needed to advise counsel in the management of the litigation. See 6 Wigmore § 1841, n. 4.

ORIGINAL COMMITTEE NOTE TO RULE 701

The rule retains the traditional objective of putting the trier of fact in possession of an accurate reproduction of the event.

Limitation (a) is the familiar requirement of firsthand knowledge or observation.

Limitation (b) is phrased in terms of requiring testimony to be helpful in resolving issues. Witnesses often find difficulty in expressing themselves in language which is not that of an opinion or conclusion. While the courts have made concessions in certain recurring situations, necessity as a standard for permitting opinions and conclusions has proved too elusive and too unadaptable to particular situations for purposes of satisfactory judicial administration. McCormick § 11. Moreover, the practical impossibility of determinating by rule what is a "fact," demonstrated by a century of litigation of the question of what is a fact for purposes of pleading under the Field Code, extends into evidence also. 7 Wigmore § 1919. The rule assumes that the natural characteristics of the adversary system will generally lead to an acceptable result, since the detailed account carries more conviction than the broad assertion, and a lawyer can be expected to display his witness to the best advantage. If he fails to do so, cross-examination and argument will point up the weakness. See Ladd, Expert Testimony, 5 Vand.L.Rev. 414, 415-417 (1952). If, despite these considerations, attempts are made to introduce meaningless assertions which amount to little more than choosing up sides, exclusion for lack of helpfulness is called for by the rule.

The language of the rule is substantially that of Uniform. Rule 56(1). Similar provisions are California Evidence Code § 800; Kansas Code of Civil Procedure § 60-456(a); New Jersey Evidence Rule 56(1).

COMMITTEE NOTE TO 2000 AMENDMENT TO RULE 701

Rule 701 has been amended to eliminate the risk that the reliability requirements set forth in Rule 702 will be evaded through the simple expedient of proffering an expert in lay witness clothing. Under the amendment, a witness' testimony must be scrutinized under the rules regulating expert opinion to the extent that the witness is providing testimony based on scientific, technical, or other specialized knowledge within the scope of Rule 702. *See generally Asplundh Mfg. Div. v. Benton Harbor Eng'g*, 57 F.3d 1190 (3d Cir. 1995). By channeling testimony that is actually expert testimony to Rule 702, the amendment also ensures that a party will not evade the expert witness disclosure requirements set forth in Fed.R.Civ.P. 26 and Fed.R.Crim.P.16 by simply calling an expert witness in the guise of a layperson. *See* Joseph, *Emerging Expert Issues under the 1993 Disclosure Amendments to the Federal Rules of Civil Procedure,* 164 F.R.D. 97, 108 (1996) (noting that "there is no good reason to allow what is essentially surprise expert testimony", and that "the court should be vigilant to preclude manipulative conduct designed to thwart the expert disclosure and discovery process"). *See also United States v. Figueroa-Lopez*, 125 F.3d 1241, 1246 (9th Cir. 1997) (law enforcement agents testifying that the defendant's conduct was consistent with that of a drug trafficker could not testify as lay witnesses; to permit such testimony under Rule 701 "subverts the requirements of Federal Rule of Criminal Procedure 16(a)(1)(E)").

The amendment does not distinguish between expert and lay *witnesses*, but rather between expert and lay *testimony*. Certainly it is possible for the same witness to provide both lay and expert testimony in a single case. *See, e.g, United States v. Figueroa-Lopez*, 125 F.3d 1241, 1246 (9th Cir. 1997) (law enforcement agents could testify that the defendant was acting suspiciously, without being qualified as experts; however, the rules on experts were applicable where the agents testified on the basis of extensive experience that the defendant was using code words to refer to drug quantities and prices).

The amendment makes clear that any part of a witness' testimony that is based upon scientific, technical, or other specialized knowledge within the scope of Rule 702 is governed by the standards of Rule 702 and the corresponding disclosure requirements of the Civil and Criminal Rules.

The amendment is not intended to affect the "prototypical example[s] of the type of evidence contemplated by the adoption of Rule 701 relat[ing] to the appearance of persons or things, identity, the manner of conduct, competency of a person, degrees of light or darkness, sound, size, weight, distance, and an endless number of items that cannot be described factually in words apart from inferences." *Asplundh Mfg. Div. v. Benton Harbor Eng'g,* 57 F.3d 1190, 1196 (3d Cir. 1995).

For example, most courts have permitted the owner or officer of a business to testify to the value or projected profits of the business, without the necessity of qualifying the witness as an accountant, appraiser, or similar expert. *See, e.g., Lightning Lube, Inc. v. Witco Corp.* 4 F.3d 1153 (3d Cir. 1993) (no abuse of discretion in permitting the plaintiff's owner to give lay opinion testimony as to damages, as it was based on his knowledge and participation in the day-to-day affairs of the business). Such opinion testimony is admitted not because of experience, training or specialized knowledge within the realm of an expert, but because of the particularized knowledge that the witness has by virtue of his or her position in the business. The amendment does not purport to change this analysis. Similarly, courts have permitted lay witnesses to testify that a substance appeared to be a narcotic, so long as a foundation of familiarity with the substance is established. *See, e.g., United States v. Westbrook,* 896 F.2d 330 (8th Cir. 1990) (two lay witnesses who were heavy amphetamine users were properly permitted to testify that a substance was amphetamine; but it was error to permit another witness to make such an identification where she had no experience with amphetamines). Such testimony is not based on specialized knowledge within the scope of Rule 702, but rather is based upon a layperson's personal knowledge. If, however, that witness were to describe how a narcotic was manufactured, or to describe the intricate workings of a narcotic distribution network, then the witness would have to qualify as an expert under Rule 702. *United States v. Figueroa-Lopez, supra.*

The amendment incorporates the distinctions set forth in *State v. Brown,* 836 S.W.2d 530, 549 (1992), a case involving former Tennessee Rule of Evidence 701, a rule that precluded lay witness testimony based on "special knowledge." In *Brown,* the court declared that the distinction between lay and expert witness testimony is that lay testimony "results from a process of reasoning familiar in everyday life", while expert testimony "results from a process of reasoning which can be mastered only by specialists in the field." The court in *Brown* noted that a lay witness with experience could testify that a substance appeared to be blood, but that a witness would have to qualify as an expert before he could testify that bruising around the eyes is indicative of skull trauma. That is the kind of distinction made by the amendment to this Rule.

ORIGINAL COMMITTEE NOTE TO RULE 702

An intelligent evaluation of facts is often difficult or impossible without the application of some scientific, technical, or other specialized knowledge. The most common source of this knowledge is the expert witness, although there are other techniques for supplying it.

Most of the literature assumes that experts testify only in the form of opinions. The assumption is logically unfounded. The rule accordingly recognizes that an expert on the stand may give a dissertation or exposition of scientific or other principles relevant to the case, leaving the trier of fact to apply them to the facts. Since much of the criticism of expert testimony has centered upon the hypothetical question, it seems wise to recognize that opinions are not indispensable and to encourage the use of expert testimony in non-opinion form when counsel believes the trier can itself draw the requisite inference. The use of opinions is not abolished by the rule, however. It will continue to be permissible for the experts to take the further step of suggesting the inference which should be drawn from applying the specialized knowledge to the facts. See Rules 703 to 705.

Whether the situation is a proper one for the use of expert testimony is to be determined on the basis of assisting the trier. "There is no more certain test for determining when experts may be used than the common sense inquiry whether the untrained layman would be qualified to determine intelligently and to the best possible degree the particular issue without enlightenment from those having a specialized understanding of the subject involved in the dispute." Ladd, Expert Testimony, 5 Vand.L.Rev. 414, 418 (1952). When opinions are excluded, it is because they are unhelpful and therefore superfluous and a waste of time. 7 Wigmore § 1918.

The rule is broadly phrased. The fields of knowledge which may be drawn upon are not limited merely to the "scientific" and "technical" but extend to all "specialized" knowledge. Similarly, the expert is viewed, not in a narrow sense, but as a person qualified by "knowledge, skill, experience, training or education." Thus within the scope of the rule are not only experts in the strictest sense of the word, e.g., physicians, physicists, and architects, but also the large group sometimes called "skilled" witnesses, such as bankers or landowners testifying to land values.

COMMITTEE NOTE TO 2000 AMENDMENT TO RULE 702

Rule 702 has been amended in response to *Daubert v. Merrell Dow Pharmaceuticals, Inc.,* 509 U.S. 579 (1993), and to the many cases applying *Daubert,* including *Kumho Tire Co. v. Carmichael,* 119 S.Ct. 1167 (1999). In *Daubert* the Court charged trial judges with the responsibility of acting as gatekeepers to exclude unreliable expert testimony, and the Court in *Kumho* clarified that this gatekeeper function applies to all expert testimony, not just testimony based in science. *See also Kumho,* 119 S.Ct. at 1178 (citing the Committee Note to the proposed amendment to Rule 702, which had been released for public comment before the date of the *Kumho* decision). The amendment affirms the trial court's role as gatekeeper and provides some general standards that the trial court must use to assess the reliability and helpfulness of proffered expert testimony. Consistently with *Kumho,* the Rule as amended provides that all types of expert testimony present questions of admissibility for the trial court in deciding whether the evidence is reliable and helpful. Consequently, the admissibility of all expert testimony is governed by the principles of Rule 104(a). Under that Rule, the proponent has the burden of establishing that the pertinent admissibility requirements are met by a preponderance of the evidence. *See Bourjaily v. United States,* 483 U.S. 171 (1987).

Daubert set forth a non-exclusive checklist for trial courts to use in assessing the reliability of scientific expert testimony. The specific factors explicated by the *Daubert* Court are (1) whether the expert's technique or theory can be or has been tested-that is, whether the expert's theory can be challenged in some objective sense, or whether it is instead simply a subjective, conclusory approach that cannot reasonably be assessed for reliability; (2) whether the technique or theory has been subject to peer review and publication; (3) the known or potential rate of error of the technique or theory when applied; (4) the existence and maintenance of standards and controls; and (5) whether the technique or theory has been generally accepted in the scientific community. The Court in *Kumho* held that these factors might also be applicable in assessing the reliability of non-scientific expert testimony, depending upon "the particular circumstances of the particular case at issue." 119 S.Ct. at 1175.

No attempt has been made to "codify" these specific factors. *Daubert* itself emphasized that the factors were neither exclusive nor dispositive. Other cases have recognized that not all of the specific *Daubert* factors can apply to every type of expert testimony. In addition to *Kumho,* 119 S.Ct. at 1175, *see Tyus v. Urban Search Management,* 102 F.3d 256 (7th Cir. 1996) (noting that the factors mentioned by the Court in *Daubert* do not neatly apply to expert testimony from a sociologist). *See also Kannankeril v. Terminix Int'l, Inc.,* 128 F.3d 802, 809 (3d Cir. 1997) (holding that lack of peer review or publication was not dispositive where the expert's opinion was supported by "widely accepted scientific knowledge"). The standards set forth in the amendment are broad enough to require consideration of any or all of the specific *Daubert* factors where appropriate.

Courts both before and after *Daubert* have found other factors relevant in determining whether expert testimony is sufficiently reliable to be considered by the trier of fact. These factors include:"

(1) Whether experts are "proposing to testify about matters growing naturally and directly out of research they have conducted independent of the litigation, or whether they have developed their opinions expressly for purposes of testifying." *Daubert v. Merrell Dow Pharmaceuticals, Inc.,* 43 F.3d 1311, 1317 (9th Cir. 1995).

(2) Whether the expert has unjustifiably extrapolated from an accepted premise to an unfounded conclusion. *See General Elec. Co. v. Joiner,* 522 U.S. 136, 146 (1997) (noting that in some cases a trial court "may conclude that there is simply too great an analytical gap between the data and the opinion proffered").

(3) Whether the expert has adequately accounted for obvious alternative explanations. *See Claar v. Burlington N.R.R.*, 29 F.3d 499 (9th Cir. 1994) (testimony excluded where the expert failed to consider other obvious causes for the plaintiff's condition). *Compare Ambrosini v. Labarraque*, 101 F.3d 129 (D.C.Cir. 1996) (the possibility of some uneliminated causes presents a question of weight, so long as the most obvious causes have been considered and reasonably ruled out by the expert).

(4) Whether the expert "is being as careful as he would be in his regular professional work outside his paid litigation consulting." *Sheehan v. Daily Racing Form, Inc.*, 104 F.3d 940, 942 (7th Cir. 1997). *See Kumho Tire Co. v. Carmichael,* 119 S.Ct. 1167, 1176 (1999) (*Daubert* requires the trial court to assure itself that the expert "employs in the courtroom the same level of intellectual rigor that characterizes the practice of an expert in the relevant field").

(5) Whether the field of expertise claimed by the expert is known to reach reliable results for the type of opinion the expert would give. *See Kumho Tire Co. v. Carmichael,* 119 S.Ct.1167, 1175 (1999) (*Daubert's* general acceptance factor does not "help show that an expert's testimony is reliable where the discipline itself lacks reliability, as, for example, do theories grounded in any so-called generally accepted principles of astrology or necromancy."); *Moore v. Ashland Chemical, Inc.*, 151 F.3d 269 (5th Cir. 1998) (en banc) (clinical doctor was properly precluded from testifying to the toxicological cause of the plaintiff's respiratory problem, where the opinion was not sufficiently grounded in scientific methodology); *Sterling v. Velsicol Chem. Corp.*, 855 F.2d 1188 (6th Cir. 1988) (rejecting testimony based on "clinical ecology" as unfounded and unreliable).

All of these factors remain relevant to the determination of the reliability of expert testimony under the Rule as amended. Other factors may also be relevant. *See Kumho,* 119 S.Ct. 1167, 1176 ("[W]e conclude that the trial judge must have considerable leeway in deciding in a particular case how to go about determining whether particular expert testimony is reliable."). Yet no single factor is necessarily dispositive of the reliability of a particular expert's testimony. *See, e.g., Heller v. Shaw Industries, Inc.*, 167 F.3d 146, 155 (3d Cir. 1999) ("not only must each stage of the expert's testimony be reliable, but each stage must be evaluated practically and flexibly without bright-line exclusionary (or inclusionary) rules."); *Daubert v. Merrell Dow Pharmaceuticals, Inc.*, 43 F.3d 1311, 1317, n.5 (9th Cir. 1995) (noting that some expert disciplines "have the courtroom as a principal theatre of operations" and as to these disciplines "the fact that the expert has developed an expertise principally for purposes of litigation will obviously not be a substantial consideration.").

A review of the caselaw after *Daubert* shows that the rejection of expert testimony is the exception rather than the rule. *Daubert* did not work a "sea-change over federal evidence law," and "the trial court's role as gatekeeper is not intended to serve as a replacement for the adversary system." *United States v. 14.38 Acres of Land Situated in Leflore County, Mississippi,* 80 F.3d 1074, 1078 (5th Cir. 1996). As the Court in *Daubert* stated: "Vigorous cross-examination, presentation of contrary evidence, and careful instruction on the burden of proof are the traditional and appropriate means of attacking shaky but admissible evidence." 509 U.S. at 595. Likewise, this amendment is not intended to provide an excuse for an automatic challenge to the testimony of every expert. *See Kumho Tire Co. v. Carmichael,* 119 S.Ct.1167, 1176 (1999) (noting that the trial judge has the discretion "both to avoid unnecessary 'reliability' proceedings in ordinary cases where the reliability of an expert's methods is properly taken for granted, and to require appropriate proceedings in the less usual or more complex cases where cause for questioning the expert's reliability arises.").

When a trial court, applying this amendment, rules that an expert's testimony is reliable, this does not necessarily mean that contradictory expert testimony is unreliable. The amendment is broad enough to permit testimony that is the product of competing principles or methods in the same field of expertise. *See, e.g., Heller v. Shaw Industries, Inc.,* 167 F.3d 146, 160 (3d Cir. 1999) (expert testimony cannot be excluded simply because the expert uses one test rather than another, when both tests are accepted in the field and both reach reliable results). As the court stated in *In re Paoli R.R. Yard PCB Litigation*, 35 F.3d 717, 744 (3d Cir. 1994), proponents "do not have to demonstrate to the judge by a preponderance of the evidence that the assessments of their experts are correct, they only have to demonstrate by a preponderance of evidence that their opinions are reliable . . . . The evidentiary requirement of reliability is lower than the merits standard of correctness." *See also Daubert v. Merrell Dow Pharmaceuticals, Inc.*, 43 F.3d 1311, 1318 (9th Cir. 1995) (scientific experts might be permitted to testify if they could show that the methods they used were also employed by "a recognized minority of scientists in their field."); *Ruiz-Troche v. Pepsi Cola,* 161 F.3d 77, 85 (1st Cir. 1998) ("*Daubert* neither requires nor empowers trial courts to determine which of several competing scientific theories has the best provenance.").

The Court in *Daubert* declared that the "focus, of course, must be solely on principles and methodology, not on the conclusions they generate." 509 U.S. at 595. Yet as the Court later recognized, "conclusions and methodology are not entirely distinct from one another." *General Elec. Co. v. Joiner,* 522 U.S. 136, 146 (1997). Under the amendment, as under *Daubert,* when an expert purports to apply principles and methods in accordance with professional standards, and yet reaches a conclusion that other experts in the field would not reach, the trial court may fairly suspect that the principles and methods have not been faithfully applied. *See Lust v. Merrell Dow Pharmaceuticals, Inc.*, 89 F.3d 594, 598 (9th Cir. 1996). The amendment specifically provides that the trial court must scrutinize not only the principles and methods used by the expert, but also whether those principles and methods have been properly applied to the facts of the case. As the court noted in *In re Paoli R.R. Yard PCB Litig.*, 35 F.3d 717, 745 (3d Cir. 1994), "*any* step that renders the analysis unreliable . . . renders the expert's testimony inadmissible. *This is true whether the step completely changes a reliable methodology or merely misapplies that methodology.*"

If the expert purports to apply principles and methods to the facts of the case, it is important that this application be conducted reliably. Yet it might also be important in some cases for an expert to educate the factfinder about general principles, without ever attempting to apply these principles to the specific facts of the case. For example, experts might instruct the factfinder on the principles of thermodynamics, or bloodclotting, or on how financial markets respond to corporate reports, without ever knowing about or trying to tie their testimony into the facts of the case. The amendment does not alter the venerable practice of using expert testimony to educate the factfinder on general principles. For this kind of generalized testimony, Rule 702 simply requires that: (1) the expert be qualified; (2) the testimony address a subject matter on which the factfinder can be assisted by an expert; (3) the testimony be reliable; and (4) the testimony "fit" the facts of the case.

As stated earlier, the amendment does not distinguish between scientific and other forms of expert testimony. The trial court's gatekeeping function applies to testimony by any expert. *See Kumho Tire Co. v. Carmichael,* 119 S.Ct. 1167, 1171 (1999) ("We conclude that *Daubert's* general holding — setting forth the trial judge's general 'gatekeeping' obligation — applies not only to testimony based on 'scientific' knowledge, but also to testimony based on 'technical' and 'other specialized' knowledge."). While the relevant factors for determining reliability will vary from expertise to expertise, the amendment rejects the premise that an expert's testimony should be treated more permissively simply because it is outside the realm of science. An opinion from an expert who is not a scientist should receive the same degree of scrutiny for reliability as an opinion from an expert who purports to be a scientist. *See Watkins v. Telsmith, Inc.*, 121 F.3d 984, 991 (5th Cir. 1997) ("[I]t seems exactly backwards that experts who purport to rely on general engineering principles and practical experience might escape screening by the district court simply by stating that their conclusions were not reached by any particular method or technique."). Some types of expert testimony will be more objectively verifiable, and subject to the expectations of falsifiability, peer review, and publication, than others. Some types of expert testimony will not rely on anything like a scientific method, and so will have to be evaluated by reference to other standard principles attendant to the particular area of expertise. The trial judge in all cases of proffered expert testimony must find that it is properly grounded, well-reasoned, and not speculative before it can be admitted. The expert's testimony must be grounded in an accepted body of learning or experience in the expert's field, and the expert must explain how the conclusion is so grounded. *See, e.g.*, American College of Trial Lawyers, *Standards and Procedures for Determining the Admissibility of Expert Testimony after* Daubert, 157 F.R.D. 571, 579 (1994) ("[W]hether the testimony concerns economic principles, accounting standards, property valuation or other non-scientific subjects, it should be evaluated by reference to the 'knowledge and experience' of that particular field.").

The amendment requires that the testimony must be the product of reliable principles and methods that are reliably applied to the facts of the case. While the terms "principles" and "methods" may convey a certain impression when applied to scientific knowledge, they remain relevant when applied to testimony based on technical or other specialized knowledge. For example, when a law enforcement agent testifies regarding the use of code words in a drug transaction, the principle used by the agent is that participants in such transactions regularly use code words to conceal the nature of their activities. The method used by the agent is the application of extensive experience to analyze the meaning of the conversations. So long as the principles and methods are reliable and applied reliably to the facts of the case, this type of testimony should be admitted.

Nothing in this amendment is intended to suggest that experience alone-or experience in conjunction with other knowledge, skill, training or education — may not provide a sufficient foundation for expert testimony. To the contrary, the text of Rule 702 expressly contemplates that an expert may be qualified on the basis of experience. In certain fields, experience is the predominant, if not sole, basis for a great deal of reliable expert testimony. *See, e.g., United States v. Jones,* 107 F.3d 1147 (6th Cir. 1997) (no abuse of discretion in admitting the testimony of a handwriting examiner who had years of practical experience and extensive training, and who explained his methodology in detail); *Tassin v. Sears Roebuck,* 946 F.Supp. 1241, 1248 (M.D.La. 1996) (design engineer's testimony can be admissible when the expert's opinions "are based on facts, a reasonable investigation, and traditional technical/mechanical expertise, and he provides a reasonable link between the information and procedures he uses and the conclusions he reaches"). *See also Kumho Tire Co. v. Carmichael*, 119 S.Ct.1167, 1178 (1999) (stating that "no one denies that an expert might draw a conclusion from a set of observations based on extensive and specialized experience.").

If the witness is relying solely or primarily on experience, then the witness must explain how that experience leads to the conclusion reached, why that experience is a sufficient basis for the opinion, and how that experience is reliably applied to the facts.. The trial court's gatekeeping function requires more than simply "taking the expert's word for it." *See Daubert v. Merrell Dow Pharmaceuticals, Inc.,* 43 F.3d 1311, 1319 (9th Cir. 1995) ("We've been presented with only the experts' qualifications, their conclusions and their assurances of reliability. Under *Daubert*, that's not enough."). The more subjective and controversial the expert's inquiry, the more likely the testimony should be excluded as unreliable. *See O'Conner v. Commonwealth Edison Co.*, 13 F.3d 1090 (7th Cir. 1994) (expert testimony based on a completely subjective methodology held properly excluded). *See also Kumho Tire Co. v. Carmichael*, 119 S.Ct. 1167, 1176 (1999) ("[I]t will at times be useful to ask even of a witness whose expertise is based purely on experience, say, a perfume tester able to distinguish among 140 odors at a sniff, whether his preparation is of a kind that others in the field would recognize as acceptable.").

Subpart (1) of Rule 702 calls for a quantitative rather than qualitative analysis. The amendment requires that expert testimony be based on sufficient underlying "facts or data." The term "data" is intended to encompass the reliable opinions of other experts. See the original Advisory Committee Note to Rule 703. The language "facts or data" is broad enough to allow an expert to rely on hypothetical facts that are supported by the evidence. Id.

When facts are in dispute, experts sometimes reach different conclusions based on competing versions of the facts. The emphasis in the amendment on "sufficient facts or data" is not intended to authorize a trial court to exclude an expert's testimony on the ground that the court believes one version of the facts and not the other.

There has been some confusion over the relationship between Rules 702 and 703. The amendment makes clear that the sufficiency of the basis of an expert's testimony is to be decided under Rule 702. Rule 702 sets forth the overarching requirement of reliability, and an analysis of the sufficiency of the expert's basis cannot be divorced from the ultimate reliability of the expert's opinion. In contrast, the "reasonable reliance" requirement of Rule 703 is a relatively narrow inquiry. When an expert relies on inadmissible information, Rule 703 requires the trial court to determine whether that information is of a type reasonably relied on by other experts in the field. If so, the expert can rely on the information in reaching an opinion. However, the question whether the expert is relying on a *sufficient* basis of information-whether admissible information or not-is governed by the requirements of Rule 702.

The amendment makes no attempt to set forth procedural requirements for exercising the trial court's gatekeeping function over expert testimony. *See* Daniel J. Capra, *The* Daubert *Puzzle*, 38 Ga.L.Rev. 699, 766 (1998) ("Trial courts should be allowed substantial discretion in dealing with *Daubert* questions; any attempt to codify procedures will likely give rise to unnecessary changes in practice and create difficult questions for appellate review."). Courts have shown considerable ingenuity and flexibility in considering challenges to expert testimony under *Daubert*, and it is contemplated that this will continue under the amended Rule. *See, e.g., Cortes-Irizarry v. Corporacion Insular*, 111 F.3d 184 (1st Cir. 1997) (discussing the application of *Daubert* in ruling on a motion for summary judgment); *In re Paoli R.R. Yard PCB Litig.,* 35 F.3d 717, 736, 739 (3d Cir. 1994) (discussing the use of *in limine* hearings); *Claar v. Burlington N.R.R.,* 29 F.3d 499, 502-05 (9th Cir. 1994) (discussing the trial court's technique of ordering experts to submit serial affidavits explaining the reasoning and methods underlying their conclusions).

The amendment continues the practice of the original Rule in referring to a qualified witness as an "expert." This was done to provide continuity and to minimize change. The use of the term "expert" in the Rule does not, however, mean that a jury should actually be informed that a qualified witness is testifying as an "expert". Indeed, there is much to be said for a practice that prohibits the use of the term "expert" by both the parties and the court at trial. Such a practice "ensures that trial courts do not inadvertently put their stamp of authority" on a witness' opinion, and protects against the jury's being "overwhelmed by the so-called 'experts'." Hon. Charles Richey, *Proposals to Eliminate the Prejudicial Effect of the Use of the Word "Expert" Under the Federal Rules of Evidence in Criminal and Civil Jury Trials,* 154 F.R.D. 537, 559 (1994) (setting forth limiting instructions and a standing order employed to prohibit the use of the term "expert" in jury trials).

ORIGINAL COMMITTEE NOTE TO RULE 703

Facts or data upon which expert opinions are based may, under the rule, be derived from three possible sources. The first is the firsthand observation of the witness, with opinions based thereon traditionally allowed. A treating physician affords an example. Rheingold, The Basis of Medical Testimony, 15 Vand.L.Rev. 473, 489 (1962). Whether he must first relate his observations is treated in Rule 705. The second source, presentation at the trial, also reflects existing practice. The technique may be the familiar hypothetical question or having the expert attend the trial and hear the testimony establishing the facts. Problems of determining what testimony the expert relied upon, when the latter technique is employed and the testimony is in conflict, may be resolved by resort to Rule 705. The third source contemplated by the rule consists of presentation of data to the expert outside of court and other than by his own perception. In this respect the rule is designed to broaden the basis for expert opinions beyond that current in many jurisdictions and to bring the judicial practice into line with the practice of the experts themselves when not in court. Thus a physician in his own practice bases his diagnosis on information from numerous sources and of considerable variety, including statements by patients and relatives, reports and opinions from nurses, technicians and other doctors, hospital records, and X rays. Most of them are admissible in evidence, but only with the expenditure of substantial time in producing and examining various authenticating witnesses. The physician makes life-and-death decisions in reliance upon them. His validation, expertly performed and subject to cross-examination, ought to suffice for judicial purposes. Rheingold, supra, at 531; McCormick § 15. A similar provision is California Evidence Code § 801(b).

The rule also offers a more satisfactory basis for ruling upon the admissibility of public opinion poll evidence. Attention is directed to the validity of the techniques employed rather than to relatively fruitless inquiries whether hearsay is involved. See Judge Feinberg's careful analysis in Zippo Mfg. Co. v. Rogers Imports, Inc., 216 F.Supp. 670 (S.D.N.Y. 1963) See also Blum et al, The Art of Opinion Research: A Lawyer's Appraisal of an Emerging Service, 24 U.Chi.L.Rev. 1 (1956); Bonynge, Trademark Surveys and Techniques and Their Use in Litigation, 48 A.B.A.J. 329 (1962); Zeisel, The Uniqueness of Survey Evidence, 45 Cornell L.Q. 322 (1960); Annot., 76 A.L.R.2d 919.

If it be feared that enlargement of permissible data may tend to break down the rules of exclusion unduly, notice should be taken that the rule requires that the facts or data "be of a type reasonably relied upon by experts in the particular field." The language would not warrant admitting in evidence the opinion of an "accidentologist" as to the point of impact in an automobile collision based on statements of bystanders, since this requirement is not satisfied. See Comment, Cal.Law Rev.Comm'n, Recommendation Proposing an Evidence Code 148-150 (1965).

COMMITTEE NOTE TO 2000 AMENDMENT TO RULE 703

Rule 703 has been amended to emphasize that when an expert reasonably relies on inadmissible information to form an opinion or inference, the underlying information is not admissible simply because the opinion or inference is admitted. Courts have reached different results on how to treat inadmissible information when it is reasonably relied upon by an expert in forming an opinion or drawing an inference. *Compare United States v. Rollins,* 862 F.2d 1282 (7th Cir. 1988) (admitting, as part of the basis of an FBI agent's expert opinion on the meaning of code language, the hearsay statements of an informant), *with United States v. 0.59 Acres of Land,* 109 F.3d 1493 (9th

Cir. 1997) (error to admit hearsay offered as the basis of an expert opinion, without a limiting instruction). Commentators have also taken differing views. *See, e.g.,* Ronald Carlson, *Policing the Bases of Modern Expert Testimony,* 39 Vand.L.Rev. 577 (1986) (advocating limits on the jury's consideration of otherwise inadmissible evidence used as the basis for an expert opinion); Paul Rice, *Inadmissible Evidence as a Basis for Expert Testimony: A Response to Professor Carlson,* 40 Vand.L.Rev. 583 (1987) (advocating unrestricted use of information reasonably relied upon by an expert).

When information is reasonably relied upon by an expert and yet is admissible only for the purpose of assisting the jury in evaluating an expert's opinion, a trial court applying this Rule must consider the information's probative value in assisting the jury to weigh the expert's opinion on the one hand, and the risk of prejudice resulting from the jury's potential misuse of the information for substantive purposes on the other. The information may be disclosed to the jury, upon objection, only if the trial court finds that the probative value of the information in assisting the jury to evaluate the expert's opinion substantially outweighs its prejudicial effect. If the otherwise inadmissible information is admitted under this balancing test, the trial judge must give a limiting instruction upon request, informing the jury that the underlying information must not be used for substantive purposes. See Rule 105. In determining the appropriate course, the trial court should consider the probable effectiveness or lack of effectiveness of a limiting instruction under the particular circumstances.

The amendment governs only the disclosure to the jury of information that is reasonably relied on by an expert, when that information is not admissible for substantive purposes. It is not intended to affect the admissibility of an expert's testimony. Nor does the amendment prevent an expert from relying on information that is inadmissible for substantive purposes.

Nothing in this Rule restricts the presentation of underlying expert facts or data when offered by an adverse party. See Rule 705. Of course, an adversary's attack on an expert's basis will often open the door to a proponent's rebuttal with information that was reasonably relied upon by the expert, even if that information would not have been discloseable initially under the balancing test provided by this amendment. Moreover, in some circumstances the proponent might wish to disclose information that is relied upon by the expert in order to "remove the sting" from the opponent's anticipated attack, and thereby prevent the jury from drawing an unfair negative inference. The trial court should take this consideration into account in applying the balancing test provided by this amendment.

This amendment covers facts or data that cannot be admitted for any purpose other than to assist the jury to evaluate the expert's opinion. The balancing test provided in this amendment is not applicable to facts or data that are admissible for any other purpose but have not yet been offered for such a purpose at the time the expert testifies.

The amendment provides a presumption against disclosure to the jury of information used as the basis of an expert's opinion and not admissible for any substantive purpose, when that information is offered by the proponent of the expert. In a multi-party case, where one party proffers an expert whose testimony is also beneficial to other parties, each such party should be deemed a "proponent" within the meaning of the amendment.

COMMITTEE NOTE TO RULE 704

The basic approach to opinions, lay and expert, in these rules is to admit them when helpful to the trier of fact. In order to render this approach fully effective and to allay any doubt on the subject, the so-called "ultimate issue" rule is specifically abolished by the instant rule.

The older cases often contained strictures against allowing witnesses to express opinions upon ultimate issues, as a particular aspect of the rule against opinions. The rule was unduly restrictive, difficult of application, and generally served only to deprive the trier of fact of useful information. 7 Wigmore §§ 1920, 1921; McCormick § 12. The basis usually assigned for the rule, to prevent the witness from "usurping the province of the jury," is aptly characterized as "empty rhetoric." 7 Wigmore § 1920, p. 17. Efforts to meet the felt needs of particular situations led to odd verbal circumlocutions which were said not to violate the rule. Thus a witness could express his estimate of the criminal responsibility of an accused in terms of sanity or insanity, but not in terms of ability to tell right from wrong or other more modern standard. And in cases of medical causation, witnesses were sometimes required to couch their opinions in cautious phrases of "might or could," rather than "did," though the result was to deprive many opinions of the positiveness to which they were entitled, accompanied by the hazard of a ruling of insufficiency to support a verdict. In other instances the rule was simply disregarded, and, as concessions to need, opinions were allowed upon such matters as intoxication, speed, handwriting, and value, although more precise coincidence with an ultimate issue would scarcely be possible.

Many modern decisions illustrate the trend to abandon the rule completely. People v. Wilson, 25 Cal.2d 341, 153 P.2d 720 (1944), whether abortion necessary to save life of patient; Clifford-Jacobs Forging Co. v. Industrial Comm., 19 Ill.2d 236, 166 N.E.2d 582 (1960), medical causation; Dowling v. L. H. Shattuck, Inc., 91 N.H. 234, 17 A.2d 529 (1941), proper method of shoring ditch; Schweiger v. Solbeck, 191 Or. 454, 230 P.2d 195 (1951), cause of landslide. In each instance the opinion was allowed.

The abolition of the ultimate issue rule does not lower the bars so as to admit all opinions. Under Rules 701 and 702, opinions must be helpful to the trier of fact, and Rule 403 provides for exclusion of evidence which wastes time. These provisions afford ample assurances against the admission of opinions which would merely tell the jury what result to reach, somewhat in the manner of the oath-helpers of an earlier day. They also stand ready to exclude opinions phrased in terms of inadequately explored legal criteria. Thus the question, "Did T have capacity to make a will?" would be excluded, while the question, "Did T have sufficient mental capacity to know the nature and extent of his property and the natural objects of his bounty and to formulate a rational scheme of distribution?" would be allowed. McCormick § 12.

For similar provisions see Uniform Rule 56(4); California Evidence Code § 805; Kansas Code of Civil Procedures § 60-456(d); New Jersey Evidence Rule 56(3).

BACKGROUND ON RULE 704(b)

[Editor's Note: Rule 704(b) was added directly by Congress. Accordingly there is no Advisory Committee Note to Rule 704(b). What follows is some pertinent legislative history.]

Senate Report No. 98-225 (adding subdivision (b) in 1984)

With respect to limitations on the scope of expert testimony by psychiatrists and other mental health experts, section 406 of title IV of the bill amends Rule 704 of the Federal Rules of Evidence to provide:

"No expert witness testifying with respect to the mental state or condition of a defendant in a criminal case may state an opinion or inference as to whether the defendant did or did not have the mental state or condition constituting an element of the crime or of a defense thereto. Such ultimate issues are matters for the trier of fact alone."

The purpose of this amendment is to eliminate the confusing spectacle of competing expert witnesses testifying to directly contradictory conclusions as to the ultimate legal issue to be found by the trier of fact. Under this proposal, expert psychiatric testimony would be limited to presenting and explaining their diagnoses, such as whether the defendant had a severe mental disease or defect and what the characteristics of such a disease or defect, if any, may have been. The basis for this limitation on expert testimony in insanity cases is ably stated by the American Psychiatric Association:

"[I]t is clear that psychiatrists are experts in medicine, not the law. As such, it is clear that the psychiatrist's first obligation and expertise in the courtroom is to do psychiatry, i.e., to present medical information and opinion about the defendant's mental state and motivation and to explain in detail the reason for his medical-psychiatric conclusions. When, however, ultimate issue questions are formulated by the law and put to the expert witness who must then say yea or nay, then the expert witness is required to make a leap in logic. He no longer addresses himself to medical concepts but instead must infer or intuit what is in fact unspeakable, namely, the probable relationship between medical concepts and legal or moral constructs such as free will. These impermissible leaps in logic made by expert witnesses confuse the jury. [Footnote omitted.] Juries thus find themselves listening to conclusory and seemingly contradictory psychiatric testimony that defendants are either sane or insane or that they do or do not meet the relevant legal test for insanity. This state of affairs does considerable injustice to psychiatry and, we believe, possibly to criminal defendants. In fact, in many criminal insanity trials both prosecution and defense psychiatrists do agree about the nature and even the extent of mental disorder exhibited by the defendant at the time of the act.

Psychiatrists, of course, must be permitted to testify fully about the defendant's diagnosis, mental state and motivation (in clinical and common-sense terms) at the time of the alleged act so as to permit the jury or judge to reach the ultimate conclusion about which they and only they are expert. Determining whether a criminal defendant was legally insane is a matter for legal fact-finders, not for experts. [American Psychiatric Association Statement on the Insanity Defense at 18-19. See also Hearings, Limiting the

Insanity Defense at 256-258 (statement of Dr. Loren Roth, University of Pittsburgh) and 272-273 (statement of Dr. Seymour L. Halleck, University of North Carolina.]"

Moreover, the rationale for precluding ultimate opinion psychiatric testimony extends beyond the insanity defense to any ultimate mental state of the defendant that is relevant to the legal conclusion sought to be proven. The Committee has fashioned its Rule 704 provision to reach all such ultimate issues, e.g., premeditation in a homicide case, or lack of predisposition in entrapment.

ORIGINAL COMMITTEE NOTE TO RULE 705

The hypothetical question has been the target of a great deal of criticism as encouraging partisan bias, affording an opportunity for summing up in the middle of the case, and as complex and time consuming. Ladd, Expert Testimony, 5 Vand.L.Rev. 414, 426-427 (1952). While the rule allows counsel to make disclosure of the underlying facts or data as a preliminary to the giving of an expert opinion, if he chooses, the instances in which he is required to do so are reduced. This is true whether the expert bases his opinion on data furnished him at secondhand or observed by him at firsthand.

The elimination of the requirement of preliminary disclosure at the trial of underlying facts or data has a long background of support. In 1937 the Commissioners on Uniform State Laws incorporated a provision to this effect in the Model Expert Testimony Act, which furnished the basis for Uniform Rules 57 and 58. Rule 4515, N.Y. CPLR (McKinney 1963), provides:

"Unless the court orders otherwise, questions calling for the opinion of an expert witness need not be hypothetical in form, and the witness may state his opinion and reasons without first specifying the data upon which it is based. Upon cross-examination, he may be required to specify the data . . . ."

See also California Evidence Code § 802; Kansas Code of Civil Procedure §§ 60-456, 60-457; New Jersey Evidence Rules 57, 58.

If the objection is made that leaving it to the cross-examiner to bring out the supporting data is essentially unfair, the answer is that he is under no compulsion to bring out any facts or data except those unfavorable to the opinion. The answer assumes that the cross-examiner has the advance knowledge which is essential for effective cross-examination. This advance knowledge has been afforded, though imperfectly, by the traditional foundation requirement. Rule 26(b)(4) of the Rules of Civil Procedure, as revised, provides for substantial discovery in this area, obviating in large measure the obstacles which have been raised in some instances to discovery of findings, underlying data, and even the identity of the experts. Friedenthal, Discovery and Use of an Adverse Party's Expert Information, 14 Stan.L.Rev. 455 (1962).

These safeguards are reinforced by the discretionary power of the judge to require preliminary disclosure in any event.

COMMITTEE NOTE TO 1993 AMENDMENT TO RULE 705

This rule, which relates to the manner of presenting testimony at trial, is revised to avoid an arguable conflict with revised Rules 26(a)(2)(B) and

26(a)(1) of the Federal Rules of Civil Procedure or with revised Rule 16 of the Federal Rules of Criminal Procedure, which require disclosure in advance of trial of the basis and reasons for an expert's opinions.

If a serious question is raised under Rule 702 or 703 as to the admissibility of expert testimony, disclosure of the underlying facts or data on which opinions are based may, of course, be needed by the court before deciding whether, and to what extent, the person should be allowed to testify. This rule does not preclude such an inquiry.

NOTE TO RULE 706

The practice of shopping for experts, the venality of some experts, and the reluctance of many reputable experts to involve themselves in litigation, have been matters of deep concern. Though the contention is made that court appointed experts acquire an aura of infallibility to which they are not entitled. Levy, Impartial Medical Testimony-Revisited, 34 Temple L.Q. 416 (11961), the trend is increasingly to provide for their use. While experience indicates that actual appointment is a relatively infrequent occurrence, the assumption may be made that the availability of the procedure in itself decreases the need for resorting to it. The ever-present possibility that the judge may appoint an expert in a given case must inevitably exert a sobering effect on the expert witness of a party and upon the person utilizing his services.

The inherent power of a trial judge to appoint an expert of his own choosing is virtually unquestioned. Scott v. Spanjer Bros., Inc., 298 F.2d 928 (2d Cir. 1962); Danville Tobacco Assn. v. Bryant-Buckner Associates, Inc., 333 F.2d 202 (4th Cir. 1964); Sink, The Unused Power of a Federal Judge to Call His Own Expert Witnesses, 29 S.Cal.L.Rev. 195 (1956); 2 Wigmore § 563, 9 Id. § 2484; Annot., 95 A.L.R.2d 383. Hence the problem becomes largely one of detail.

The New York plan is well known and is described in Report by Special Committee of the Association of the Bar of the City of New York: Impartial Medical Testimony (1956). On recommendation of the Section of Judicial Administration, local adoption of an impartial medical plan was endorsed by the American Bar Association. 82 A.B.A.Rep. 184-185 (1957). Descriptions and analyses of plans in effect in various parts of the country are found in Van Dusen, A United States District Judge's View of the Impartial Medical Expert System, 322 F.R.D. 498 (1963); Wick and Kightlinger, Impartial Medical Testimony Under the Federal Civil Rules: A Tale of Three Doctors, 34 Ins. Counsel J. 115 (1967); and numerous articles collected in Klein, Judicial Administration and the Legal Profession 393 (1963). Statutes and rules include California Evidence Code §§ 730-733; Illinois Supreme Court Rule 215(d), Ill.Rev.Stat.1969, c. 110A, § 215(d); Burns Indiana Stats. 1956, § 9-1702; Wisconsin Stats.Annot.1958, § 957.27.

In the federal practice, a comprehensive scheme for court appointed experts was initiated with the adoption of Rule 28 of the Federal Rules of Criminal Procedure in 1946. The Judicial Conference of the United States in 1953 considered court appointed experts in civil cases, but only with respect to whether they should be compensated from public funds, a proposal which was rejected. Report of the Judicial Conference of the United States 23 (1953). The present rule expands the practice to include civil cases.

Subdivision (a) is based on Rule 28 of the Federal Rules of Criminal Procedure, with a few changes, mainly in the interest of clarity. Language has been added to provide specifically for the appointment either on motion of a party or on the judge's own motion. A provision subjecting the court appointed expert to deposition procedures has been incorporated. The rule has been revised to make definite the right of any party, including the party calling him, to cross-examine.

Subdivision (b) combines the present provision for compensation in criminal cases with what seems to be a fair and feasible handling of civil cases, originally found in the Model Act and carried from there into Uniform Rule 60. See also California Evidence Code §§ 730-731. The special provision for Fifth Amendment compensation cases is designed to guard against reducing constitutionally guaranteed just compensation by requiring the recipient to pay costs. See Rule 71A(l) of the Rules of Civil Procedure.

Subdivision (c) seems to be essential if the use of court appointed experts is to be fully effective.

Uniform Rule 61 so provides.

Subdivision (d) is in essence the last sentence of Rule 28(a) of the Federal Rules of Criminal Procedure.

ORIGINAL COMMITTEE NOTE TO RULE 801

INTRODUCTORY NOTE: THE HEARSAY PROBLEM

The factors to be considered in evaluating the testimony of a witness are perception, memory, and narration. Morgan, Hearsay Dangers and the Application of the Hearsay Concept, 62 Harv.L.Rev. 177 (1948), Selected Writings on Evidence and Trial 764, 765 (Fryer ed. 1957); Shientag, Cross-Examination-A Judge's Viewpoint, 3 Record 12 (1948); Strahorn, A Reconsideration of the Hearsay Rule and Admissions, 85 U.Pa.L.Rev. 484, 485 (1937), Selected Writings, supra, 756, 757: Weinstein, Probative Force of Hearsay, 46 Iowa L.Rev. 331 (1961). Sometimes a fourth is added, sincerity, but in fact it seems merely to be an aspect of the three already mentioned.

In order to encourage the witness to do his best with respect to each of these factors, and to expose any inaccuracies which may enter in, the Anglo-American tradition has evolved three conditions under which witnesses will ideally be required to testify: (1) under oath, (2) in the personal presence of the trier of fact, (3) subject to cross-examination.

(1) Standard procedure calls for the swearing of witnesses. While the practice is perhaps less effective than in an earlier time, no disposition to relax the requirement is apparent, other than to allow affirmation by persons with scruples against taking oaths.

(2) The demeanor of the witness traditionally has been believed to furnish trier and opponent with valuable clues. Universal Camera Corp. v. N.L.R.B., 340 U.S. 474, 495-496, 71 S.Ct. 456, 95 L.Ed. 456 (1951); Sahm, Demeanor

Evidence: Elusive and Intangible Imponderables, 47 A.B.A.J. 580 (1961), quoting numerous authorities. The witness himself will probably be impressed with the solemnity of the occasion and the possibility of public disgrace. Willingness to falsify may reasonably become more difficult in the presence of the person against whom directed. Rules 26 and 43(a) of the Federal Rules of Criminal and Civil Procedure, respectively, include the general requirement that testimony be taken orally in open court. The Sixth Amendment right of confrontation is a manifestation of these beliefs and attitudes.

(3) Emphasis on the basis of the hearsay rule today tends to center upon the condition of cross-examination. All may not agree with Wigmore that cross-examination is "beyond doubt the greatest legal engine ever invented for the discovery of truth," but all will agree with his statement that it has become a "vital feature" of the Anglo-American system. 5 Wigmore § 1367, p. 29. The belief, or perhaps hope, that cross-examination is effective in exposing imperfections of perception, memory, and narration is fundamental. Morgan, Foreword to Model Code of Evidence 37 (1942).

The logic of the preceding discussion might suggest that no testimony be received unless in full compliance with the three ideal conditions. No one advocates this position. Common sense tells that much evidence which is not given under the three conditions may be inherently superior to much that is. Moreover, when the choice is between evidence which is less than best and no evidence at all, only clear folly would dictate an across-the-board policy of doing without. The problem thus resolves itself into effecting a sensible accommodation between these considerations and the desirability of giving testimony under the ideal conditions.

The solution evolved by the common law has been a general rule excluding hearsay but subject to numerous exceptions under circumstances supposed to furnish guarantees of trustworthiness. Criticisms of this scheme are that it is bulky and complex, fails to screen good from bad hearsay realistically, and inhibits the growth of the law of evidence.

Since no one advocates excluding all hearsay, three possible solutions may be considered: (1) abolish the rule against hearsay and admit all hearsay; (2) admit hearsay possessing sufficient probative force, but with procedural safeguards; (3) revise the present system of class exceptions.

(1) Abolition of the hearsay rule would be the simplest solution. The effect would not be automatically to abolish the giving of testimony under ideal conditions. If the declarant were available, compliance with the ideal conditions would be optional with either party. Thus the proponent could call the declarant as a witness as a form of presentation more impressive than his hearsay statement. Or the opponent could call the declarant to be cross-examined upon his statement. This is the tenor of Uniform Rule 63(1), admitting the hearsay declaration of a person "who is present at the hearing and available for cross-examination." Compare the treatment of declarations of available declarants in Rule 801(d)(1) of the instant rules. If the declarant were unavailable, a rule of free admissibility would make no distinctions in terms of degrees of noncompliance with the ideal conditions and would exact no liquid pro quo in the form of assurances of trustworthiness. Rule 503 of the Model Code did exactly that, providing for the admissibility of any hearsay

declaration by an unavailable declarant, finding support in the Massachusetts act of 1898, enacted at the instance of Thayer, Mass.Gen.L.1932, c. 233 § 65, and in the English act of 1938, St.1938, c. 28, Evidence. Both are limited to civil cases. The draftsmen of the Uniform Rules chose a less advanced and more conventional position. Comment, Uniform Rule 63. The present Advisory Committee has been unconvinced of the wisdom of abandoning the traditional requirement of some particular assurance of credibility as a condition precedent to admitting the hearsay declaration of an unavailable declarant.

In criminal cases, the Sixth Amendment requirement of confrontation would no doubt move into a large part of the area presently occupied by the hearsay rule in the event of the abolition of the latter. The resultant split between civil and criminal evidence is regarded as an undesirable development.

(2) Abandonment of the system of class exceptions in favor of individual treatment in the setting of the particular case, accompanied by procedural safeguards, has been impressively advocated. Weinstein, The Probative Force of Hearsay, 46 Iowa L.Rev. 331 (1961). Admissibility would be determined by weighing the probative force of the evidence against the possibility of prejudice, waste of time, and the availability of more satisfactory evidence. The bases of the traditional hearsay exceptions would be helpful in assessing probative force. Ladd, The Relationship of the Principles of Exclusionary Rules of Evidence to the Problem of Proof, 18 Minn.L.Rev. 506 (1934). Procedural safeguards would consist of notice of intention to use hearsay, free comment by the judge on the weight of the evidence, and a greater measure of authority in both trial and appellate judges to deal with evidence on the basis of weight.

The Advisory Committee has rejected this approach to hearsay as involving too great a measure of judicial discretion, minimizing the predictability of rulings, enhancing the difficulties of preparation for trial, adding a further element to the already over-complicated congeries of pretrial procedures, and requiring substantially different rules for civil and criminal cases. The only way in which the probative force of hearsay differs from the probative force of other testimony is in the absence of oath, demeanor, and cross-examination as aids in determining credibility. For a judge to exclude evidence because he does not believe it has been described as "altogether atypical, extraordinary. * * *" Chadbourn, Bentham and the Hearsay Rule — A Benthamic View of Rule 63(4)(c) of the Uniform Rules of Evidence, 75 Harv.L.Rev. 932, 947 (1962).

(3) The approach to hearsay in these rules is that of the common law, i.e., a general rule excluding hearsay, with exceptions under which evidence is not required to be excluded even though hearsay. The traditional hearsay exceptions are drawn upon for the exceptions, collected under two rules, one dealing with situations where availability of the declarant is regarded as immaterial and the other with those where unavailability is made a condition to the admission of the hearsay statement. Each of the two rules concludes with a provision for hearsay statements not within one of the specified exceptions "but having comparable circumstantial guarantees of trustworthiness." Rules 803(24) and 804(b)(6). This plan is submitted as calculated to encourage growth and development in this area of the law, while conserving the values and experience of the past as a guide to the future.

CONFRONTATION AND DUE PROCESS

Until very recently, decisions invoking the confrontation clause of the Sixth Amendment were surprisingly few, a fact probably explainable by the former inapplicability of the clause to the states and by the hearsay rule's occupancy of much the same ground. The pattern which emerges from the earlier cases invoking the clause is substantially that of the hearsay rule, applied to criminal cases: an accused is entitled to have the witnesses against him testify under oath, in the presence of himself and trier, subject to cross-examination; yet considerations of public policy and necessity require the recognition of such exceptions as dying declarations and former testimony of unavailable witnesses. Mattox v. United States, 156 U.S. 237, 15 S.Ct. 337, 39 L.Ed. 409 (1895); Motes v. United States, 178 U.S. 458, 20 S.Ct. 993, 44 L.Ed. 1150 (1900); Delaney v. United States, 263 U.S. 586, 44 S.Ct. 206, 68 L.Ed. 462 (1924). Beginning with Snyder v. Massachusetts, 291 U.S. 97, 54 S.Ct. 330, 78 L.Ed. 674 (1934), the Court began to speak of confrontation as an aspect of procedural due process, thus extending its applicability to state cases and to federal cases other than criminal. The language of Snyder was that of an elastic concept of hearsay. The deportation case of Bridges v. Wixon, 326 U.S. 135, 65 S.Ct. 1443, 89 L.Ed. 2103 (1945), may be read broadly as imposing a strictly construed right of confrontation in all kinds of cases or narrowly as the product of a failure of the Immigration and Naturalization Service to follow its own rules. In re Oliver, 333 U.S. 257, 68 S.Ct. 499, 92 L.Ed. 682 (1948), ruled that cross-examination was essential to due process in a state contempt proceeding, but in United States v. Nugent, 346 U.S. 1, 73 S.Ct. 991, 97 L.Ed. 1417 (1953), the court held that it was not an essential aspect of a "hearing" for a conscientious objector under the Selective Service Act. Stein v. New York, 346 U.S. 156, 196, 73 S.Ct. 1077, 97 L.Ed. 1522 (1953), disclaimed anypurpose to read the hearsay rule into the Fourteenth Amendment, but in Greene v. McElroy, 360 U.S. 474, 79 S.Ct. 1400, 3 L.Ed.2d 1377 (1959), revocation of security clearance without confrontation and cross-examination was held unauthorized, and a similar result was reached in Willner v. Committee on Character, 373 U.S. 96, 83 S.Ct. 1175, 10 L.Ed.2d 224 (1963). Ascertaining the constitutional dimensions of the confrontation-hearsay aggregate against the background of these cases is a matter of some difficulty, yet the general pattern is at least not inconsistent with that of the hearsay rule.

In 1965 the confrontation clause was held applicable to the states. Pointer v. Texas, 380 U.S. 400, 85 S.Ct. 1065, 13 L.Ed.2d 923 (1965). Prosecution use of former testimony given at a preliminary hearing where petitioner was not represented by counsel was a violation of the clause. The same result would have followed under conventional hearsay doctrine read in the light of a constitutional right to counsel, and nothing in the opinion suggests any difference in essential outline between the hearsay rule and the right of confrontation. In the companion case of Douglas v. Alabama, 380 U.S. 415, 85 S.Ct. 1074, 13 L.Ed.2d 934 (1965), however, the result reached by applying the confrontation clause is one reached less readily via the hearsay rule. A confession implicating petitioner was put before the jury by reading it to the witness in portions and asking if he made that statement. The witness refused to answer on grounds of self-incrimination. The result, said the Court, was to deny cross-examination, and hence confrontation. True, it could broadly be said that the confession was a hearsay statement which for all practical purposes was put in evidence. Yet a more easily accepted explanation of the opinion is that its real thrust was in the direction of curbing undesirable prosecutorial behavior, rather than merely applying rules of exclusion, and that the confrontation clause was the means selected to achieve this end. Comparable facts and a like result appeared in Brookhart v. Janis, 384 U.S. 1, 86 S.Ct. 1245, 16 L.Ed.2d 314 (1966).

The pattern suggested in Douglas was developed further and more distinctly in a pair of cases at the end of the 1966 term. United States v. Wade, 388 U.S. 218, 87 S.Ct. 1926, 18 L.Ed.2d 1149 (1967), and Gilbert v. California, 388 U.S. 263, 87 S.Ct. 1951, 18 L.Ed.2d 1178 (1967), hinged upon practices followed in identifying accused persons before trial. This pretrial identification was said to be so decisive an aspect of the case that accused was entitled to have counsel present; a pretrial identification made in the absence of counsel was not itself receivable in evidence and, in addition, might fatally infect a courtroom identification. The presence of counsel at the earlier identification was described as a necessary prerequisite for "a meaningful confrontation at trial." United States v. Wade, supra, 388 U.S. at p. 236, 87 S.Ct. at p. 1937. Wade involved no evidence of the fact of a prior identification and hence was not susceptible of being decided on hearsay grounds. In Gilbert, witnesses did testify to an earlier identification, readily classifiable as hearsay under a fairly strict view of what constitutes hearsay. The Court, however, carefully avoided basing the decision on the hearsay ground, choosing confrontation instead. 388 U.S. 263, 272, n. 3, 87 S.Ct. 1951. See also Parker v. Gladden, 385 U.S. 363 87 S.Ct. 468, 17 L.Ed.2d 420 (1966), holding that the right of confrontation was violated when the bailiff made prejudicial statements to jurors, and Note, 75, Yale L.J. 1434 (1966).

Under the earlier cases, the confrontation clause may have been little more than a constitutional embodiment of the hearsay rule, even including traditional exceptions but with some room for expanding them along similar lines. But under the recent cases the impact of the clause clearly extends beyond the confines of the hearsay rule. These considerations have led the Advisory Committee to conclude that a hearsay rule can function usefully as an adjunct to the confrontation right in constitutional areas and independently in nonconstitutional areas. In recognition of the separateness of the confrontation clause and the hearsay rule, and to avoid inviting collisions between them or between the hearsay rule and other exclusionary principles, the exceptions set forth in Rules 803 and 804 are stated in terms of exemption from the general exclusionary mandate of the hearsay rule, rather than in positive terms of admissibility. See Uniform Rule 63(1) to (31) and California Evidence Code §§ 1200-1340.

NOTE TO RULE 801

GENERAL PROVISIONS

Subdivision (a). The definition of "statement" assumes importance because the term is used in the definition of hearsay in subdivision (c). The effect of the definition of "statement" is to exclude from the operation of the hearsay rule all evidence of conduct, verbal or nonverbal, not intended as an assertion. The key to the Definition is that nothing is an assertion unless intended to be one.

It can scarcely be doubted that an assertion made in words is intended by the declarant to be an assertion. Hence verbal assertions readily fall into the category of "statement." Whether nonverbal conduct should be regarded as a statement for purposes of defining hearsay requires further consideration. Some nonverbal conduct, such as the act of pointing to identify a suspect in a lineup, is clearly the equivalent of words, assertive in nature, and to be regarded as a statement. Other nonverbal conduct, however, may be offered as evidence that the person acted as he did because of his belief in the existence of the condition sought to be proved, from which belief the existence of the condition may be inferred. This sequence is, arguably, in effect an assertion of the existence of the condition and hence properly includable within the hearsay concept. See Morgan, Hearsay Dangers and the Application of the Hearsay Concept, 62 Harv.L. Rev. 177, 214, 217 (1948), and the elaboration in Finman, Implied Assertions as Hearsay: Some Criticisms of the Uniform Rules of Evidence, 14 Stan.L.Rev. 682 (1962). Admittedly evidence of this character is untested with respect to the perception, memory, and narration (or their equivalents) of the actor, but the Advisory Committee is of the view that these dangers are minimal in the absence of an intent to assert and do not justify the loss of the evidence on hearsay grounds. No class of evidence is free of the possibility of fabrication, but the likelihood is less with nonverbal than with assertive verbal conduct. The situations giving rise to the nonverbal conduct are such as virtually to eliminate questions of sincerity. Motivation, the nature of the conduct, and the presence or absence of reliance will bear heavily upon the weight to be given the evidence. Falknor, The "Hear-Say" Rule as a "See-Do" Rule: Evidence of Conduct, 33 Rocky Mt.L.Rev. 133 (1961). Similar considerations govern nonassertive verbal conduct and verbal conduct which is assertive but offered as a basis for inferring something other than the matter asserted, also excluded from the definition of hearsay by the language of subdivision (c).

When evidence of conduct is offered on the theory that it is not a statement, and hence not hearsay, a preliminary determination will be required to determine whether an assertion is intended. The rule is so worded as to place the burden upon the party claiming that the intention existed; ambiguous and doubtful cases will be resolved against him and in favor of admissibility. The determination involves no greater difficulty than many other preliminary questions of fact. Maguire, The Hearsay System: Around and Through the Thicket, 14 Vand.L.Rev. 741, 765-767 (1961).

For similar approaches, see Uniform Rule 62(1); California Evidence Code §§ 225, 1200; Kansas Code of Civil Procedure § 60-459(a); New Jersey Evidence Rule 62(1).

Subdivision (c). The definition follows along familiar lines in including only statements offered to prove the truth of the matter asserted. McCormick § 225; 5 Wigmore § 1361, 6 id. § 1766. If the significance of an offered statement lies solely in the fact that it was made, no issue is raised as to the truth of anything asserted, and the statement is not hearsay. Emich Motors Corp. v. General Motors Corp., 181 F.2d 70 (7th Cir. 1950), rev'd on other grounds 340 U.S. 558, 71 S.Ct. 408, 95 L.Ed 534, letters of complaint from customers offered as a reason for cancellation of dealer's franchise, to rebut contention that franchise was revoked for refusal to finance sales through affiliated finance company. The effect is to exclude from hearsay the entire category of "verbal acts" and "verbal parts of an act," in which the statement itself affects the legal rights of the parties or is a circumstance bearing on conduct affecting their rights.

The definition of hearsay must, of course, be read with reference to the definition of statement set forth in subdivision (a).

Testimony given by a witness in the course of court proceedings is excluded since there is compliance with all the ideal conditions for testifying.

Subdivision (d). Several types of statements which would otherwise literally fall within the definition are expressly excluded from it:

(1) Prior statement by witness. Considerable controversy has attended the question whether a prior out-of-court statement by a person now available for cross-examination concerning it, under oath and in the presence of the trier of fact, should be classed as hearsay. If the witness admits on the stand that he made the statement and that it was true, he adopts the statement and there is no hearsay problem. The hearsay problem arises when the witness on the stand denies having made the statement or admits having made it but denies its truth. The argument in favor of treating these latter statements as hearsay is based upon the ground that the conditions of oath, cross-examination, and demeanor observation did not prevail at the time the statement was made and cannot adequately be supplied by the later examination. The logic of the situation is troublesome. So far as concerns the oath, its mere presence has never been regarded as sufficient to remove a statement from the hearsay category, and it receives much less emphasis than cross-examination as a truth-compelling device. While strong expressions are found to the effect that no conviction can be had or important right taken away on the basis of statements not made under fear of prosecution for perjury, Bridges v. Wixon, 326 U.S. 135, 65 S.Ct. 1443, 89 L.Ed. 2103 (1945), the fact is that, of the many common law exceptions to the hearsay rule, only that for reported testimony has required the statement to have been made under oath. Nor is it satisfactorily explained why cross-examination cannot be conducted subsequently with success. The decisions contending most vigorously for its inadequacy in fact demonstrate quite thorough exploration of the weaknesses and doubts attending the earlier statement. State v. Saporen, 205 Minn. 358, 285 N.W. 898 (1939); Ruhala v. Roby, 379 Mich. 102, 150 N.W.2d 146 (1967); People v. Johnson, 68 Cal.2d 646, 68 Cal.Rptr. 599, 441 P.2d 111 (1968). In respect to demeanor, as Judge Learned Hand observed in DiCarlo v. United States, 6 F.2d 364 (2d Cir., 1925), when the jury decides that the truth is not what the witness says now, but what he said before, they are still deciding from what they see and hear in court. The bulk of the case law nevertheless has been against allowing prior statements of witnesses to be used generally as substantive evidence. Most of the writers and Uniform Rule 63(1) have taken the opposite position.

The position taken by the Advisory Committee in formulating this part of the rule is founded upon an unwillingness to countenance the general use of prior prepared statements as substantive evidence, but with a recognition that particular circumstances call for a contrary result. The judgment is one more of experience than of logic. The rule requires in each instance, as a general safeguard, that the declarant actually testify as a witness, and it then enumerates three situations in which the statement is excepted from the category of hearsay. Compare Uniform Rule 63(1) which allows any out-of-court statement of a declarant who is present at the trial and available for cross-examination.

(A) Prior inconsistent statements traditionally have been admissible to impeach but not as substantive evidence. Under the rule they are substantive evidence. As has been said by the California Law Revision Commission with respect to a similar provision:

"Section 1235 admits inconsistent statements of witnesses because the dangers against which the hearsay rule is designed to protect are largely nonexistent. The declarant is in court and may be examined and cross-examined in regard to his statements and their subject matter. In many cases, the inconsistent statement is more likely to be true than the testimony of the witness at the trial because it was made nearer in time to the matter to which it relates and is less likely to be influenced by the controversy that gave rise to the litigation. The trier of fact has the declarant before it and can observe his demeanor and the nature of his testimony as he denies or tries to explain away the inconsistency. Hence, it is in as good a position to determine the truth or falsity of the prior statement as it is to determine the truth or falsity of the inconsistent testimony given in court. Moreover, Section 1235 will provide a party with desirable protection against the 'turncoat' witness who changes his story on the stand and deprives the party calling him of evidence essential to his case."

Comment, California Evidence Code § 1235. See also McCormick § 39.The Advisory Committee finds these views more convincing than those expressed in People v. Johnson, 68 Cal.2d 646, 68 Cal.Rptr. 599, 441 P.2d 111 (1968). The constitutionality of the Advisory Committee's view was upheld in California v. Green, 399 U.S. 149, 90 S.Ct. 1930, 26 L.Ed.2d 489 (1970). Moreover, the requirement that the statement be inconsistent with the testimony given assures a thorough exploration of both versions while the witness is on the stand and bars any general and indiscriminate use of previously prepared statements.

(B) Prior consistent statements traditionally have been admissible to rebut charges of recent fabrication or improper influence or motive but not as substantive evidence. Under the rule they are substantive evidence. The prior statement is consistent with the testimony given on the stand, and, if the opposite party wishes to open the door for its admission in evidence, no sound reason is apparent why it should not be received generally.

(C) The admission of evidence of identification finds substantial support, although it falls beyond a doubt in the category of prior out-of-court statements. Illustrative are People v. Gould, 54 Cal.2d 621, 7 Cal.Rptr. 273, 354 P.2d 865 (1960); Judy v. State, 218 Md. 168, 146 A.2d 29 (1958); State v.

Simmons, 63 Wash.2d 17, 385 P.2d 389 (1963); California Evidence Code § 1238; New Jersey Evidence Rule 63(1)(c); N.Y. Code of Criminal Procedure § 393-b. Further cases are found in 4 Wigmore § 1130. The basis is the generally unsatisfactory and inconclusive nature of courtroom identifications as compared with those made at an earlier time under less suggestive conditions. The Supreme Court considered the admissibility of evidence of prior identification in Gilbert v. California, 388 U.S. 263, 87 S.Ct. 1951, 18 L.Ed.2d 1178 (1967). Exclusion of lineup identification was held to be required because the accused did not then have the assistance of counsel. Significantly, the Court carefully refrained from placing its decision on the ground that testimony as to the making of a prior out-of-court identification ("That's the man") violated either the hearsay rule or the right of confrontation because not made under oath, subject to immediate cross-examination, in the presence of the trier. Instead the Court observed:

"There is a split among the States concerning the admissibility of prior extra-judicial identifications, as independent evidence of identity, both by the witness and third parties present at the prior identification. See 71 ALR 2d 449. It has been held that the prior identification is hearsay, and, when admitted through the testimony of the identifier, is merely a prior consistent statement. The recent trend, however, is to admit the prior identification under the exception that admits as substantive evidence a prior communication by a witness who is available for cross-examination at the trial. See 5 ALR 2d Later Case Service 1225-1228 . . . ."

388 U.S. at 272, n. 3, 87 S.Ct. at 1956.

(2) Admissions. Admissions by a party-opponent are excluded from the category of hearsay on the theory that their admissibility in evidence is the result of the adversary system rather than satisfaction of the conditions of the hearsay rule. Strahorn. A Reconsideration of the Hearsay Rule and Admissions, 85 U.Pa.L.Rev. 484, 564 (1937); Morgan, Basic Problems of Evidence 265 (1962); 4 Wigmore § 1048. No guarantee of trustworthiness is required in the case of an admission. The freedom which admissions have enjoyed from technical demands of searching for an assurance of trustworthiness in some against-interest circumstance, and from the restrictive influences of the opinion rule and the rule requiring firsthand knowledge, when taken with the apparently prevalent satisfaction with the results, calls for generous treatment of this avenue to admissibility.

The rule specifies five categories of statements for which the responsibility of a party is considered sufficient to justify reception in evidence against him:

(A) A party's own statement is the classic example of an admission. If he has a representative capacity and the statement is offered against him in that capacity, no inquiry whether he was acting in the representative capacity in making the statement is required; the statement need only be relevant to represent affairs. To the same effect in California Evidence Code § 1220. Compare Uniform Rule 63(7), requiring a statement to be made in a representative capacity to be admissible against a party in a representative capacity.

(B) Under established principles an admission may be made by adopting or acquiescing in the statement of another. While knowledge of contents would ordinarily be essential, this is not inevitably so: "X is a reliable person and knows what he is talking about." See McCormick § 246, p. 527, n. 15. Adoption or acquiescence may be manifested in any appropriate manner. When silence is relied upon, the theory is that the person would, under the circumstances, protest the statement made in his presence, if untrue. The decision in each case calls for an evaluation in terms of probable human behavior. In civil cases, the results have generally been satisfactory. In criminal cases, however, troublesome questions have been raised by decisions holding that failure to deny is an admission: the inference is a fairly weak one, to begin with; silence may be motivated by advice of counsel or realization that "anything you say may be used against you"; unusual opportunity is afforded to manufacture evidence; and encroachment upon the privilege against self-incrimination seems inescapably to be involved. However, recent decisions of the Supreme Court relating to custodial interrogation and the right to counsel appear to resolve these difficulties. Hence the rule contains no special provisions concerning failure to deny in criminal cases.

(C) No authority is required for the general proposition that a statement authorized by a party to be made should have the status of an admission by the party. However, the question arises whether only statements to third persons should be so regarded, to the exclusion of statements by the agent to the principal. The rule is phrased broadly so as to encompass both. While it may be argued that the agent authorized to make statements to his principal does not speak for him, Morgan, Basic Problems of Evidence 273 (1962), communication to an outsider has not generally been thought to be an essential characteristic of an admission. Thus a party's books or records are usable against him, without regard to any intent to disclose to third persons. 5 Wigmore § 1557. See also McCormick § 78, pp. 159-161. In accord is New Jersey Evidence Rule 63(8)(a). Cf. Uniform Rule 63(8)(a) and California Evidence Code § 1222 which limit status as an admission in this regard to statements authorized by the party to be made "for" him, which is perhaps an ambiguous limitation to statements to third persons. Falknor, Vicarious Admissions and the Uniform Rules, 14 Vand.L.Rev. 855, 860-861 (1961).

(D) The tradition has been to test the admissibility of statements by agents, as admissions, by applying the usual test of agency. Was the admission made by the agent acting in the scope of his employment? Since few principals employ agents for the purpose of making damaging statements, the usual result was exclusion of the statement. Dissatisfaction with this loss of valuable and helpful evidence has been increasing. A substantial trend favors admitting statements related to a matter within the scope of the agency or employment. Grayson v. Williams, 256 F.2d 61 (10th Cir. 1958); Koninklijke Luchtvaart Maatschappij N.V. KLM Royal Dutch Airlines v. Tuller, 110 U.S.App.D.C. 282, 292 F.2d 775, 784 (1961); Martin v. Savage Truck Lines, Inc., 121 F.Supp. 417 (D.D.C. 1054), and numerous state court decisions collected in 4 Wigmore, 1964 Supp., pp. 66-73, with comments by the editor that the statements should have been excluded as not within scope of agency. For the traditional view see Northern Oil Co. v. Socony Mobile Oil Co., 347 F.2d 81, 85 (2d Cir. 1965) and cases cited therein. Similar provisions are found in Uniform Rule 63(9)(a), Kansas Code of Civil Procedure § 60-460(i)(1), and New Jersey Evidence Rule 63(9)(a).

(E) The limitation upon the admissibility of statements of co-conspirators to those made "during the course and in furtherance of the conspiracy" is in the accepted pattern. While the broadened view of agency taken in item (iv) might suggest wider admissibility of statements of co-conspirators, the agency theory of conspiracy is at best a fiction and ought not to serve as a basis for admissibility beyond that already established. See Levie, Hearsay and Conspiracy, 52 Mich.L.Rev. 1159 (1954); Comment, 25 U.Chi.L.Rev. 530 (1958). The rule is consistent with the position of the Supreme Court in denying admissibility to statements made after the objectives of the conspiracy have either failed or been achieved. Krulewitch v. United States, 336 U.S. 440, 69 S.Ct. 716, 93 L.Ed. 790 (1949); Wong Sun v. United States, 371 U.S. 471, 490, 83 S.Ct. 407, 9 L.Ed.2d 441 (1963). For similarly limited provisions see California Evidence Code § 1223 and New Jersey Rule 63(9)(b). Cf. Uniform Rule 63(9)(b).

COMMITTEE NOTE TO 1997 AMENDMENT TO RULE 801(d)(2)

Rule 801(d)(2) has been amended in order to respond to three issues raised by *Bourjaily v. United States*, 483 U.S. 171 (1987). First, the amendment codifies the holding in *Bourjaily* by stating expressly that a court shall consider the contents of a coconspirator's statement in determining "the existence of the conspiracy and the participation therein of the declarant and the party against whom the statement is offered." According to *Bourjaily*, Rule 104(a) requires these preliminary questions to be established by a preponderance of the evidence.

Second, the amendment resolves an issue on which the Court had reserved decision. It provides that the contents of the declarant's statement do not alone suffice to establish a conspiracy in which the declarant and the defendant participated. The court must consider in addition the circumstances surrounding the statement, such as the identity of the speaker, the context in which the statement was made, or evidence corroborating the contents of the statement in making its determination as to each preliminary question. This amendment is in accordance with existing practice. Every court of appeals that has resolved this issue requires some evidence in addition to the contents of the statement. *See, e.g., United States v. Beckham*, 968 F.2d 47, 51 (D.C. Cir. 1992); *United States v. Sepulveda*, 15 F.3d 1161, 1181-82 (1st Cir. 1993), *cert. denied*, 114 S. Ct. 2714 (1994); *United States v. Daly*, 842 F.2d 1380, 1386 (2d Cir.), *cert. denied*, 488 U.S. 821 (1988); *United States v. Clark*, 18 F.3d 1337, 1341-42 (6th Cir.), *cert. denied*, 115 S. Ct. 152 (1994); *United States v. Zambrana*, 841 F.2d 1320, 1344-45 (7th Cir. 1988); *United States v. Silverman*, 861 F.2d 571, 577 (9th Cir. 1988); *United States v. Gordon*, 844 F.2d 1397, 1402 (9th Cir. 1988); *United States v. Hernandez*, 829 F.2d 988, 993 (10th Cir. 1987), *cert. denied*, 485 U.S. 1013 (1988); *United States v. Byrom*, 910 F.2d 725, 736 (11th Cir. 1990).

Third, the amendment extends the reasoning of *Bourjaily* to statements offered under subdivisions (C) and (D) of Rule 801(d)(2). In *Bourjaily*, the Court rejected treating foundation facts pursuant to the law of agency in favor of an evidentiary approach governed by Rule 104(a). The Advisory Committee believes it appropriate to treat analogously preliminary questions relating to the declarant's authority under subdivision (C), and the agency or employment relationship and the scope thereof under subdivision (D).

NOTE TO RULE 802

The provision excepting from the operation of the rule hearsay which is made admissible by other rules adopted by the Supreme Court or by Act of Congress continues the admissibility thereunder of hearsay which would not qualify under these Evidence Rules. The following examples illustrate the working of the exception:

"Federal Rules of Civil Procedure

Rule 4(g): proof of service by affidavit.

Rule 32: admissibility of depositions.

Rule 43(e): affidavits when motion based on facts not appearing of record.

Rule 56: affidavits in summary judgment proceedings.

Rule 65(b): showing by affidavit for temporary restraining order.

Federal Rules of Criminal Procedure

Rule 4(a): affidavits to show grounds for issuing warrants.

Rule 12(b)(4): affidavits to determine issues of fact in connection with motions."

ORIGINAL COMMITTEE NOTE TO RULE 803

The exceptions are phrased in terms of nonapplication of the hearsay rule, rather than in positive terms of admissibility, in order to repel any implication that other possible grounds for exclusion are eliminated from consideration.

The present rule proceeds upon the theory that under appropriate circumstances a hearsay statement may possess circumstantial guarantees of trustworthiness sufficient to justify nonproduction of the declarant in person at the trial even though he may be available. The theory finds vast support in the many exceptions to the hearsay rule developed by the common law in which unavailability of the declarant is not a relevant factor. The present rule is a synthesis of them, with revision where modern developments and conditions are believed to make that course appropriate.

In a hearsay situation, the declarant is, of course, a witness, and neither this rule nor Rule 804 dispenses with the requirement of firsthand knowledge. It may appear from his statement or be inferable from circumstances.See Rule 602.

Exceptions (1) and (2). In considerable measure these two examples overlap, though based on somewhat different theories. The most significant practical difference will lie in the time lapse allowable between event and statement.

The underlying theory of Exception (1) is that substantial contemporaneity of event and statement negative the likelihood of deliberate of conscious misrepresentation. Moreover, if the witness is the declarant, he may be examined on the statement. If the witness is not the declarant, he may be examined as to the circumstances as an aid in evaluating the statement. Morgan, Basic Problems of Evidence 340-341 (1962).

The theory of Exception (2) is simply that circumstances may produce a condition of excitement which temporarily stills the capacity of reflection and produces utterances free of conscious fabrication. 6 Wigmore § 1747, p. 135. Spontaneity is the key factor in each instance, though arrived at by somewhat different routes. Both are needed in order to avoid needless niggling.

While the theory of Exception (2) has been criticized on the ground that excitement impairs accuracy of observation as well as eliminating conscious fabrication. Hutchins and Slesinger, Some Observations on the Law of Evidence: Spontaneous Exclamations, 28 Colum.L.Rev. 432 (1928), it finds support in cases without number. See cases in 6 Wigmore § 1750; Annot., 53 A.L.R.2d 1245 (statements as to cause of or responsibility for motor vehicle accident); Annot., 4 A.L.R.3d 149 (accusatory statements by homicide victims). Since unexciting events are less likely to evoke comment, decisions involving Exception (1) are far less numerous. Illustrative are Tampa Elec. Co. v. Getrost, 151 Fla. 558, 10 So.2d 83 (1942); Houston Oxygen Co. v. Davis, 139 Tex. 1, 161 S.W.2d 474 (1942); and cases cited in McCormick § 273, p. 585, n. 4.

With respect to the time element, Exception (1) recognizes that in many, if not most, instances precise contemporaneity is not possible, and hence a slight lapse is allowable. Under Exception (2) the standard of measurement is the duration of the state of excitement. "How long can excitement prevail? Obviously there are no pat answers and the character of the transaction or event will largely determine the significance of the time factor." Slough, Spontaneous Statements and State of Mind, 46 Iowa L.Rev. 224, 243 (1961); McCormick § 272, p. 580.

Participation by the declarant is not required: a nonparticipant may be moved to describe what he perceives, and one may be startled by an event in which he is not an actor. Slough, supra; McCormick, supra; 6 Wigmore § 1755; Annot., 78 A.L.R.2d 300.

Whether proof of the startling event may be made by the statement itself is largely an academic question, since in most cases there is present at least circumstantial evidence that something of a startling nature must have occurred. For cases in which the evidence consists of the condition of the declarant (injuries, state of shock), see Insurance Co. v. Mosely, 75 U.S. (8 Wall.), 397, 19 L.Ed. 437 (1869); Wheeler v. United States, 93 U.S.A.App. D.C. 159, 211 F.2d 19 (1953); cert. denied 347 U.S. 1019, 74 S.Ct. 876, 98 L.Ed. 1140; Wetherbee v. Safety Casualty Co., 219 F.2d 274 (5th Cir. 1955); Lampe v. United States, 97 U.S.App.D.C. 160, 229 F.2d 43 (1956). Nevertheless, on occasion the only evidence may be the content of the statement itself, and rulings that it may be sufficient are described as "increasing," Slough, supra at 246, and as the "prevailing practice," McCormick § 272, p. 579. Illustrative are Armour & Co. v. Industrial Commission, 78 Colo. 569, 243 P. 546 (1926); Young v. Stewart, 191 N.C. 297, 131 S.E. 735 (1926). Moreover, under Rule

104(a) the judge is not limited by the hearsay rule in passing upon preliminary questions of fact.

Proof of declarant's perception by his statement presents similar considerations when declarant is identified. People v. Poland, 22 Ill.2d 175, 174 N.E.2d 804 (1961). However, when declarant is an unidentified bystander, the cases indicate hesitancy in upholding the statement alone as sufficient, Garrett v. Howden, 73 N.M. 307, 387 P.2d 874 (1963); Beck v. Dye, 200 Wash. 1, 92 P.2d 1113 (1939), a result which would under appropriate circumstances be consistent with the rule.

Permissible subject matter of the statement is limited under Exception (1) to description or explanation of the event or condition, the assumption being that spontaneity, in the absence of a startling event, may extend no farther. In Exception (2), however, the statement need only "relate" to the startling event or condition, thus affording a broader scope of subject matter coverage. 6 Wigmore §§ 1750, 1754. See Sanitary Grocery Co. v. Snead, 67 App.D.C. 129, 90 F.2d 374 (1937), slip-and-fall case sustaining admissibility of clerk's statement, "That has been on the floor for a couple of hours," and Murphy Auto Parts Co., Inc. v. Ball, 101 U.S.App.D.C. 416, 249 F.2d 508 (1957), upholding admission, on issue of driver's agency, of his statement that he had to call on a customer and was in a hurry to get home. Quick, Hearsay, Excitement, Necessity and the Uniform Rules: A Reappraisal of Rule 63(4), 6 Wayne L.Rev. 204, 206-209 (1960).

Similar provisions are found in Uniform Rule 63(4)(a) and (b); California Evidence Code § 1240 (as to Exception (2) only); Kansas Code of Civil Procedure § 60-460(d)(1) and (2); New Jersey Evidence Rule 63(4).

Exception (3) is essentially a specialized application of Exception (1), presented separately to enhance its usefulness and accessibility. See McCormick §§ 265, 268.

The exclusion of "statements of memory or belief to prove the fact remembered or believed" is necessary to avoid the virtual destruction of the hearsay rule which would otherwise result from allowing state of mind, provable by a hearsay statement, to serve as the basis for an inference of the happening of the event which produced the state of mind). Shepard v. United States, 290 U. S. 96, 54 S.Ct. 22, 78 L.Ed. 196 (1933); Maguire, The Hillmon Case-Thirty-three Years After, 38 Harv.L.Rev. 709, 719-731 (1925); Hinton, States of Mind and the Hearsay Rule, 1 U.Chi.L.Rev. 394, 421-423 (1934). The rule of Mutual Life Ins. Co. v. Hillman, 145 U.S. 285, 12 S.Ct. 909, 36 L.Ed. 706 (1892), allowing evidence of intention as tending to prove the doing of the act intended, is of course, left undisturbed.

The carving out, from the exclusion mentioned in the preceding paragraph, of declarations relating to the execution, revocation, identification, or terms of declarant's will represents an ad hoc judgment which finds ample reinforcement in the decisions, resting on practical grounds of necessity and expediency rather than logic. McCormick § 271, pp. 577-578; Annot., 34 A.L.R.2d 588, 62 A.L.R.2d 855. A similar recognition of the need for and practical value of this kind of evidence is found in California Evidence Code § 1260.

Exception (4). Even those few jurisdictions which have shied away from generally admitting statements of present condition have allowed them if made to a physician for purposes of diagnosis and treatment in view of the patient's strong motivation to be truthful. McCormick § 266, p. 563. The same guarantee of trustworthiness extends to statements of past conditions and medical history, made for purposes of diagnosis or treatment. It also extends to statements as to causation, reasonably pertinent to the same purposes, in accord with the current trend, Shell Oil Co. v. Industrial Commission, 2 Ill.2d 590, 119 N.E.2d 224 (1954); McCormick § 266, p. 564; New Jersey Evidence Rule 63(12)(c). Statements as to fault would not ordinarily qualify under this latter language. Thus a patient's statement that he was struck by an automobile would qualify but not his statement that the car was driven through a red light. Under the exception the statement need not have been made to a physician. Statements to hospital attendants, ambulance drivers, or even members of the family might be included.

Conventional doctrine has excluded from the hearsay exception, as not within its guarantee of truthfulness, statements to a physician consulted only for the purpose of enabling him to testify. While these statements were not admissible as substantive evidence, the expert was allowed to state the basis of his opinion, including statements of this kind. The distinction thus called for was one most unlikely to be made by juries. The rule accordingly rejects the limitation. This position is consistent with the provision of Rule 703 that the facts on which expert testimony is based need not be admissible in evidence if of a kind ordinarily relied upon by experts in the field.

Exception (5). A hearsay exception for recorded recollection is generally recognized and has been described as having "long been favored by the federal and practically all the state courts that have had occasion to decide the question." United States v. Kelly, 349 F.2d 720, 770 (2d Cir. 1965), citing numerous cases and sustaining the exception against a claimed denial of the right of confrontation. Many additional cases are cited in Annot., 82 A.L.R.2d 473, 520. The guarantee of trustworthiness is found in the reliability inherent in a record made while events were still fresh in mind and accurately reflecting them.Owens v. State, 67 Md. 307, 316, 10 A. 210, 212 (1887).

The principal controversy attending the exception has centered, not upon the propriety of the exception itself, but upon the question whether a preliminary requirement of impaired memory on the part of the witness should be imposed. The authorities are divided. If regard be had only to the accuracy of the evidence, admittedly impairment of the memory of the witness adds nothing to it and should not be required. McCormick § 277, p. 593; 3 Wigmore § 738, p. 76; Jordan v. People, 151 Colo. 133, 376 P.2d 699 (1962), cert. denied 373 U.S. 944, 83 S.Ct. 1553, 10 L.Ed.2d 699; Hall v. State, 223 Md. 158, 162 A.2d 751 (1960); State v. Bindhammer, 44 N.J. 372, 209 A.2d 124 (1965). Nevertheless, the absence of the requirement, it is believed, would encourage the use of statements carefully prepared for purposes of litigation under the supervision of attorneys, investigators, or claim adjusters. Hence the example includes a requirement that the witness not have "sufficient recollection to enable him to testify fully and accurately." To the same effect are California Evidence Code § 1237 and New Jersey Rule 63(1)(b), and this has been the position of the federal courts. Vicksburg & Meridian R.R. v. O'Brien, 119 U.S. 99, 7 S.Ct. 118, 30 L.Ed. 299 (1886); Ahern v. Webb, 268 F.2d 45 (10th Cir. 1959); and see N.L.R.B. v. Hudson Pulp and Paper Corp., 273 F.2d 660, 665 (5th Cir. 1960); N.L.R.B. v. Federal Dairy Co., 297 F.2d 487 (1st Cir. 1962). But cf. United States v. Adams, 385 F.2d 548 (2d Cir. 1967).

No attempt is made in the exception to spell out the method of establishing the initial knowledge or the contemporaneity and accuracy of the record, leaving them to be dealt with as the circumstances of the particular case might indicate. Multiple person involvement in the process of observing and recording, as in Rathbun v. Brancatella, 93 N.J.L. 222, 107 A. 279 (1919), is entirely consistent with the exception.

Locating the exception at this place in the scheme of the rules is a matter of choice. There were two other possibilities. The first was to regard the statement as one of the group of prior statements of a testifying witness which are excluded entirely from the category of hearsay by Rule 801(d)(1). That category, however, requires that declarant be "subject to cross-examination," as to which the impaired memory aspect of the exception raises doubts. The other possibility was to include the exception among those covered by Rule 804. Since unavailability is required by that rule and lack of memory is listed as a species of unavailability by the definition of the term in Rule 804(a)(3), that treatment at first impression would seem appropriate. The fact is, however, that the unavailability requirement of the exception is of a limited and peculiar nature. Accordingly, the exception is located at this point rather than in the context of a rule where unavailability is conceived of more broadly.

Exception (6) represents an area which has received much attention from those seeking to improve the law of evidence. The Commonwealth Fund Act was the result of a study completed in 1927 by a distinguished committee under the chairmanship of Professor Morgan. Morgan et al., The Law of Evidence: Some Proposals for its Reform 63 (1927). With changes too minor to mention, it was adopted by Congress in 1936 as the rule for federal courts. 28 U.S.C. § 1732. A number of states took similar action. The Commissioners on Uniform State Laws in 1936 promulgated the Uniform Business Records as Evidence Act, 9A U.L.A. 506, which has acquired a substantial following in the states. Model Code Rule 514 and Uniform Rule 63(13) also deal with the subject. Difference of varying degrees of importance exist among these various treatments.

These reform efforts were largely within the context of business and commercial records, as the kind usually encountered, and concentrated considerable attention upon relaxing the requirement of producing as witnesses, or accounting for the nonproduction of, all participants in the process of gathering, transmitting, and recording information which the common law had evolved as a burdensome and crippling aspect of using records of this type. In their areas of primary emphasis on witnesses to be called and the general admissibility of ordinary business and commercial records, the Commonwealth Fund Act and the Uniform Act appear to have worked well. The exception seeks to preserve their advantages.

On the subject of what witnesses must be called, the Commonwealth Fund Act eliminated the common law requirement of calling or accounting for all participants by failing to mention it. United States v. Mortimer, 118 F.2d 266 (2d Cir. 1941); La Porte v. United States, 300 F.2d 878 (9th Cir. 1962); McCormick § 290, p. 608. Model Code Rule 514 and Uniform Rule 63(13) did likewise. The Uniform Act, however, abolished the common larequirement in express terms, providing that the requisite foundation testimony might be furnished by "the custodian or other qualified witness." Uniform Business Records as Evidence Act, § 2; 9A U.L.A. 506. The exception follows the Uniform Act in this respect.

The element of unusual reliability of business records is said variously to be supplied by systematic checking, by regularity and continuity which produce habits of precision, by actual experience of business in relying upon them, or by a duty to make an accurate record as part of a continuing job or occupation. McCormick §§ 281, 286, 287; Laughlin, Business Entries and the Like, 46 Iowa, L.Rev. 276 (1961). The model statutes and rules have sought to capture these factors and to extend their impact by employing the phrase "regular course of business," in conjunction with a definition of "business" far broader than its ordinarily accepted meaning. The result is a tendency unduly to emphasize a requirement of routineness and repetitiveness and an insistence that other types of records be squeezed into the fact patterns which give rise to traditional business records. The rule therefore adopts the phrase "the course of a regularly conducted activity" as capturing the essential basis of the hearsay exception as it has evolved and the essential element which can be abstracted from the various specifications of what is a "business."

Amplification of the kinds of activities producing admissible records has given rise to problems which conventional business records by their nature avoid. They are problems of the source of the recorded information, of entries in opinion form, of motivation, and of involvement as participant in the matters recorded.

Sources of information presented no substantial problem with ordinary business records. All participants, including the observer or participant furnishing the information to be recorded, were acting routinely, under a duty of accuracy, with employer reliance on the result, or in short "in the regular course of business." If, however, the supplier of the information does not act in the regular course, an essential link is broken; the assurance of accuracy does not extend to the information itself, and the fact that it may be recorded with scrupulous accuracy is of no avail. An illustration is the police report incorporating information obtained from a bystander: the officer qualifies as acting in the regular course but the informant does not. The leading case, Johnson v. Lutz, 253 N.Y. 124, 170 N.E. 517 (1930), held that a report thus prepared was inadmissible. Most of the authorities have agreed with the decision. Gencarella v. Fyfe, 171 F.2d 419 (1st Cir. 1948); Gordon v. Robinson, 210 F.2d 192 (3d Cir. 1954); Standard Oil Co. of California v. Moore, 251 F.2d 188, 214 (9th Cir. 1957), cert. denied 356 U.S. 975, 78 S.Ct. 1139, 2 L.Ed.2d 1148; Yates v. Bair Transport, Inc., 249 F.Supp. 681 (S.D.N.Y. 1965); Annot., 69 A.L.R.2d 1148. Cf. Hawkins v. Gorea Motor Express, Inc., 360 F.2d 933 (2d Cir 1966). Contra, 5 Wigmore § 1530a, n. 1, pp. 391-392. The point is not dealt with specifically in the Commonwealth Fund Act, the Uniform Act, or Uniform Rule 63(13). However, Model Code Rule 514 contains the requirement "that it was the regular course of that business for one with personal knowledge . . . to make such a memorandum or record or to transmit information thereof to be included in such a memorandum or record . . ." The rule follows this lead in requiring an informant with knowledge acting in the course of the regularly conducted activity.

Entries in the form of opinions were not encountered in traditional business records in view of the purely factual nature of the items recorded, but they are now commonly encountered with respect to medical diagnoses, prognoses, and test results, as well as occasionally in other areas. The Commonwealth Fund Act provided only for records of an "act, transaction, occurrence, or event," while the Uniform Act, Model Code Rule 514, and Uniform Rule 63(13) merely added the ambiguous term "condition." The limited phrasing of the Commonwealth Fund Act, 28 U.S.C. § 1732, may account for the reluctance of some federal decisions to admit diagnostic entries. New York Life Ins. Co. v. Taylor, 79 U.S.App.D.C. 66, 147 F.2d 297 (1945); Lyles v. United States, 103 U.S.App.D.C. 22, 254 F.2d 725 (1957), cert. denied 356 U.S. 961, 78 S.Ct. 997, 2 L.Ed.2d 1067; England v. United States, 174 F.2d 466 (5th Cir. 1949); Skogen v. Dow Chemical Co., 375 F.2d 692 (8th Cir. 1967). Other federal decisions, however, experienced no difficulty in freely admitting diagnostic entries. Reed v. Order of United Commercial Travelers, 123 F.2d 252 (2d Cir. 1941); Buckminster's Estate v. Commissioner of Internal Revenue, 147 F.2d 331 (2d Cir. 1944); Medina v. Erickson, 226 F.2d 475 (9th Cir. 1955); Thomas v. Hogan, 308 F.2d 355 (4th Cir. 1962); Glawe v. Rulon, 284 F.2d 495 (8th Cir. 1960). In the state courts, the trend favors admissibility. Borucki v. MacKenzie Bros. Co., 125 Conn. 92, 3 A.2d 224 (1938); Allen v. St. Louis Public Service Co., 365 Mo. 677, 285 S.W.2d 663, 55 A.L.R.2d 1022 (1956); People v. Kohlmeyer, 284 N.Y. 366, 31 N.E.2d 490 (1940); Weis v. Weis, 147 Ohio St. 416, 72 N.E.2d 245 (1947). In order to make clear its adherence to the latter position, the rule specifically includes both diagnoses and opinions, in addition to acts, events, and conditions, as proper subjects of admissible entries.

Problems of the motivation of the informant have been a source of difficulty and disagreement. In Palmer v. Hoffman, 318 U.S. 109, 63 S.Ct. 477, 87 L.Ed. 645 (1943), exclusion of an accident report made by the since deceased engineer, offered by defendant railroad trustees in a grade crossing collision case, was upheld. The report was not "in the regular course of business," not a record of the systematic conduct of the business as a business, said the Court. The report was prepared for use in litigating, not railroading. While the opinion mentions the motivation of the engineer only obliquely, the emphasis on records of routine operations is significant only by virtue of impact on motivation to be accurate. Absence of routineness raises lack of motivation to be accurate. The opinion of the Court of Appeals had gone beyond mere lack of motive to be accurate: the engineer's statement was "dripping with motivations to misrepresent." Hoffman v. Palmer, 129 F.2d 976, 991 (2d Cir. 1942). The direct introduction of motivation is a disturbing factor, since absence of motivation to misrepresent has not traditionally been a requirement of the rule; that records might be self-serving has not been a ground for exclusion. Laughlin, Business Records and the Like, 46 Iowa L.Rev. 276, 285 (1961). As Judge Clark said in his dissent, "I submit that there is hardly a grocer's account book which could not be excluded on that basis." 129 F.2d at 1002. A physician's evaluation report of a personal injury litigant would appear to be in the routine of his business. If the report is offered by the party at whose instance it was made, however, it has been held inadmissible, Yates v. Bair Transport, Inc., 249 F.Supp. 681 (S.D.N.Y. 1965), otherwise if offered by the opposite party, Korte v. New York, N.H. & H.R. Co., 191 F.2d 86 (2d Cir. 1951), cert. denied 342 U.S. 868, 72 S.Ct. 108, 96 L.Ed. 652.

The decisions hinge on motivation and which party is entitled to be concerned about it. Professor McCormick believed that the doctor's report or the accident report were sufficiently routine to justify admissibility. McCormick § 287, p. 604. Yet hesitation must be experienced in admitting everything which is observed and recorded in the course of a regularly conducted activity. Efforts to set a limit are illustrated by Hartzog v. United States, 217 F.2d 706 (4th Cir. 1954), error to admit worksheets made by since deceased deputy collector in preparation for the instant income tax evasion prosecution, and United States v. Ware, 247 F.2d 698 (7th Cir. 1957), error to admit narcotics agents' records of purchases. See also Exception (8), infra, as to the public record aspects of records of this nature. Some decisions have been satisfied as to motivation of an accident report if made pursuant to statutory duty, United States v. New York Foreign Trade Zone Operators, 304 F.2d 792 (2d Cir. 1962); Taylor v. Baltimore & O. R. Co., 344 F.2d 281 (2d Cir. 1965), since the report was oriented in a direction other than the litigation which ensued. Cf. Matthews v. United States, 217 F.2d 409 (5th Cir. 1954). The formulation of specific terms which would assure satisfactory results in all cases is not possible. Consequently the rule proceeds from the base that records made in the course of a regularly conducted activity will be taken as admissible but subject to authority to exclude if "the sources of information or other circumstances indicate lack of trustworthiness."

Occasional decisions have reached for enhanced accuracy by requiring involvement as a participant in matters reported. Clainos v. United States, 82 U.S.App.D.C. 278, 163 F.2d 593 (1947), error to admit police records of convictions; Standard Oil Co. of California v. Moore, 251 F.2d 188 (9th Cir. 1957), cert. denied 356 U.S. 975, 78 S.Ct. 1139, 2 L.Ed.2d 1148, error to admit employees' records of observed business practices of others. The rule includes no requirement of this nature. Wholly acceptable records may involve matters merely observed, e.g. the weather.

The form which the "record" may assume under the rule is described broadly as a "memorandum, report, record, or data compilation, in any form." The expression "data compilation" is used as broadly descriptive of any means of storing information other than the conventional words and figures in written or documentary form. It includes, but is by no means limited to, electronic computer storage. The term is borrowed from revised Rule 34(a) of the Rules of Civil Procedure.

Exception (7). Failure of a record to mention a matter which would ordinarily be mentioned is satisfactory evidence of its nonexistence. Uniform Rule 63(14), Comment. While probably not hearsay as defined in Rule 801, supra, decisions may be found which class the evidence not only as hearsay but also as not within any exception. In order to set the question at rest in favor of admissibility, it is specifically treated here. McCormick § 289, p. 609; Morgan,

Basic Problems of Evidence 314 (1962); 5 Wigmore § 1531; Uniform Rule 63(14); California Evidence Code § 1272; Kansas Code of Civil Procedure § 60-460(n); New Jersey Evidence Rule 63(14).

Exception (8). Public records are a recognized hearsay exception at common law and have been the subject of statutes without number. McCormick § 291. See, for example, 28 U.S.C. § 1733, the relative narrowness of which is illustrated by its nonapplicability to nonfederal public agencies, thus necessitating report to the less appropriate business record exception to the hearsay rule. Kay v. United States, 255 F.2d 476 (4th Cir. 1958). The rule makes no distinction between federal and nonfederal offices and agencies.

Justification for the exception is the assumption that a public official will perform his duty properly and the unlikelihood that he will remember details independently of the record. Wong Wing Foo v. McGrath, 196 F.2d 120 (9th Cir. 1952), and see Chesapeake & Delaware Canal Co. v. United States, 250 U.S. 123, 39 S.Ct. 407, 63 L.Ed. 889 (1919). As to items (a) and (b), further support is found in the reliability factors underlying records of regularly conducted activities generally. See Exception (6), supra.

(a) Cases illustrating the admissibility of records of the office's or agency's own activities are numerous. Chesapeake & Delaware Canal Co. v. United States, 250 U.S. 123, 39 S.Ct. 407, 63 L.Ed. 889 (1919), Treasury records of miscellaneous receipts and disbursements; Howard v. Perrin, 200 U.S. 71, 26 S.Ct. 195, 50 L.Ed. 374 (1906), General Land Office records; Ballew v. United States, 160 U.S. 187, 16 S.Ct. 263, 40 L.Ed. 388 (1895), Pension Office records.

(b) Cases sustaining admissibility of records of matters observed are also numerous. United States v. Van Hook, 284 F.2d 489 (7th Cir. 1960), remanded for resentencing 365 U.S. 609, 81 S.Ct. 823, 5 L.Ed.2d 821, letter from induction officer to District Attorney, pursuant to army regulations, stating fact and circumstances of refusal to be inducted; T'Kach v. United States, 242 F.2d 937 (5th Cir. 1957), affidavit of White House personnel officer that search of records showed no employment of accused, charged with fraudulently representing himself as an envoy of the President; Minnehaha County v. Kelley, 150 F.2d 356 (8th Cir. 1945); Weather Bureau records of rainfall; United States v. Meyer, 113 F.2d 387 (7th Cir. 1940), cert. denied 311 U.S. 706, 61 S.Ct. 174, 85 L.Ed. 459, map prepared by government engineer from information furnished by men working under his supervision.

(c) The more controversial area of public records is that of the so-called "evaluative" report. The disagreement among the decisions has been due in part, no doubt, to the variety of situations encountered, as well as to differences in principle. Sustaining admissibility are such cases as United States v. Dumas, 149 U.S. 278, 13 S.Ct. 872, 37 L.Ed. 734 (1893), statement of account certified by Postmaster General in action against postmaster; McCarty v. United States, 185 F.2d 520 (5th Cir. 1950), reh. denied 187 F.2d 234, Certificate of Settlement of General Accounting Office showing indebtedness and letter from Army official stating Government had performed, in action on contract to purchase and remove waste food from Army camp; Moran v. Pittsburgh-Des Moines Steel Co., 183 F.2d 467 (3d Cir. 1950), report of Bureau of Mines as to cause of gas tank explosion; Petition of W-, 164 F.Supp.

659 (E.D.Pa.1958), report by Immigration and Naturalization Service investigator that petitioner was known in community as wife of man to whom she was not married. To the opposite effect and denying admissibility are Franklin v. Skelly Oil Co., 141 F.2d 568 (10th Cir. 1944), State Fire Marshal's report of cause of gas explosion; Lomax Transp. Co. v. United States, 183 F.2d 331 (9th Cir. 1950), Certificate of Settlement from General Accounting Office in action for naval supplies lost in warehouse fire; Yung Jin Teung v. Dulles, 229 F.2d 244 (2d Cir. 1956), "Status Reports" offered to justify delay in processing passport applications. Police reports have generally been excluded except to the extent to which they incorporate firsthand observations of the officer. Annot., 69 A.L.R.2d 1148. Various kinds of evaluative reports are admissible under federal statutes; 7 U.S.C. § 78, findings of Secretary of Agriculture prima facie evidence of true grade of grain; 7 U.S.C. § 210(f), findings of Secretary of Agriculture prima facie evidence in action for damages against stockyard owner; 7 U.S.C. § 292, order by Secretary of Agriculture prima facie evidence in judicial enforcement proceedings against producers association monopoly; 7 U.S.C. § 1622(h), Department of Agriculture inspection certificates of products shipped in interstate commerce prima facie evidence; 8 U.S.C. § 1440(c), separation of alien from military service on conditions other than honorable provable by certificate from department in proceedings to revoke citizenship; 18 U.S.C. § 4245, certificate of Director of Prisons that convicted person has been examined and found probably incompetent at time of trial prima facie evidence in court hearing on competency; 42 U.S.C. § 269(b), bill of health by appropriate official prima facie evidence of vessel's sanitary history and condition and compliance with regulations; 46 U.S.C. § 679, certificate of consul presumptive evidence of refusal of master to transport destitute seamen to United States. While these statutory exceptions to the hearsay rule are left undisturbed, Rule 802, the willingness of Congress to recognize a substantial measure of admissibility for evaluative reports is a helpful guide.

Factors which may be of assistance in passing upon the admissibility of evaluative reports include; (1) the timeliness of the investigation, McCormack, Can the Courts Make Wider Use of Reports of Official Investigations? 42 Iowa L.Rev. 363 (1957); (2) the special skill or experience of the official, id., (3) whether a hearing was held and the level at which conducted, Franklin v. Skelly Oil Co., 141 F.2d 568 (10th Cir. 1944); (4) possible motivation problems suggested by Palmer v. Hoffman, 318 U.S. 109, 63 S.Ct. 477, 87 L.Ed. 645 (1943). Others no doubt could be added.

The formulation of an approach which would give appropriate weight to all possible factors in every situation is an obvious impossibility. Hence the rule, as in Exception (6), assumes admissibility in the first instance but with ample provision for escape if sufficient negative factors are present. In one respect, however, the rule with respect to evaluate reports under item (c) is very specific; they are admissible only in civil cases and against the government in criminal cases in view of the almost certain collision with confrontation rights which would result from their use against the accused in a criminal case.

Exception (9). Records of vital statistics are commonly the subject of particular statutes making them admissible in evidence. Uniform Vital

Statistics Act, 9C U.L.A. 350 (1957). The rule is in principle narrower than Uniform Rule 63(16) which includes reports required of persons performing functions authorized by statute, yet in practical effect the two are substantially the same. Comment Uniform Rule 63(16). The exception as drafted is in the pattern of California Evidence Code § 1281.

Exception (10). The principle of proving nonoccurrence of an event by evidence of the absence of a record which would regularly be made of its occurrence, developed in Exception (7) with respect to regularly conducted activities, is here extended to public records of the kind mentioned in Exceptions [paragraphs] (8) and (9). 5 Wigmore § 1633(6), p. 519. Some harmless duplication no doubt exists with Exception (7). Forinstances of federal statutes recognizing this method of proof, see 8 U.S.C. § 1284(b), proof of absence of alien crewman's name from outgoing manifest prima facie evidence of failure to detain or deport, and 42 U.S.C. § 405(c)(3), (4)(B), (4)(C), absence of HEW [Department of Health, Education, and Welfare] record prima facie evidence of no wages or self-employment income.

The rule includes situations in which absence of a record may itself be the ultimate focal point of inquiry, e.g. People v. Love, 310 Ill. 558, 142 N.E. 204 (1923), certificate of Secretary of State admitted to show failure to file documents required by Securities Law, as well as cases where the absence of a record is offered as proof of the nonoccurrence of an event ordinarily recorded.

The refusal of the common law to allow proof by certificate of the lack of a record or entry has no apparent justification, 5 Wigmore § 1678(7), p. 752. The rule takes the opposite position, as do Uniform Rule 63(17); California Evidence Code § 1284; Kansas Code of Civil Procedure § 60-460(c); New Jersey Evidence Rule 63(17). Congress has recognized certification as evidence of the lack of a record. 8 U.S.C. § 1360(d), certificate of Attorney General or other designated officer that no record of Immigration and Naturalization Service of specified nature or entry therein is found, admissible in alien cases.

Exception (11). Records of activities of religious organizations are currently recognized as admissible at least to the extent of the business records exception to the hearsay rule, 5 Wigmore § 1523, p. 371, and Exception (6) would be applicable. However, both the business record doctrine and Exception (6) require that the person furnishing the information be one in the business or activity. The result is such decisions as Daily v. Grand Lodge, 311 Ill. 184, 142 N.E. 478 (1924), holding a church record admissible to prove fact, date, and place of baptism, but not age of child except that he had at least been born at the time. In view of the unlikelihood that false information would be furnished on occasions of this kind, the rule contains no requirement that the informant be in the course of the activity. See California Evidence Code § 1315 and Comment.

Exception (12). The principle of proof by certification is recognized as to public officials in Exceptions [paragraphs] (8) and (10), and with respect to authentication in Rule 902. The present exception is a duplication to the extent that it deals with a certificate by a public official, as in the case of a judge who performs a marriage ceremony. The area covered by the rule is, however, substantially larger and extends the certification procedure to clergymen and the like who perform marriages and other ceremonies or administer sacraments. Thus certificates of such matters as baptism or confirmation, as well as marriage, are included. In principle they are as acceptable evidence as certificates of public officers. See 5 Wigmore § 1645, as to marriage certificates. When the person executing the certificate is not a public official, the self-authenticating character of documents purporting to emanate from public officials, see Rule 902, is lacking and proof is required that the person was authorized and did make the certificate. The time element, however, may safely be taken as supplied by the certificate, once authority and authenticity are established, particularly in view of the presumption that a document was executed on the date it bears.

For similar rules, some limited to certificates of marriage, with variations in foundation requirements, see Uniform Rule 63(18); California Evidence Code § 1316; Kansas Code of Civil Procedure § 60-460(p); New Jersey Evidence Rule 63(18).

Exception (13). Records of family history kept in family Bibles have by long tradition been received in evidence. 5 Wigmore §§ 1495, 1496, citing numerous statutes and decisions. See also Regulations, Social Security Administration, 20 C.F.R. § 404.703(c), recognizing family Bible entries as proof of age in the absence of public or church records. Opinions in the area also include inscriptions on tombstones, publicly displayed pedigrees, and engravings on rings. Wigmore, supra. The rule is substantially identical in coverage with California Evidence Code § 1312.

Exception (14). The recording of title documents is a purely statutory development. Under any theory of the admissibility of public records, the records would be receivable as evidence of the contents of the recorded document, else the recording process would be reduced to a nullity. When, however, the record is offered for the further purpose of proving execution and delivery, a problem of lack of first-hand knowledge by the recorder, not present as to contents, is presented. This problem is solved, seemingly in all jurisdictions, by qualifying for recording only those documents shown by a specified procedure, either acknowledgement or a form of probate, to have been executed and delivered. 5 Wigmore §§ 1647-1651. Thus what may appear in the rule, at first glance, as endowing the record with an effect independently of local law and inviting difficulties of an Erie nature under Cities Service Oil Co. v. Dunlap, 308 U.S. 208, 60 S.Ct. 201, 84 L.Ed. 196 (1939), is not present, since the local law in fact governs under the example.

Exception (15). Dispositive documents often contain recitals of fact. Thus a deed purporting to have been executed by an attorney in fact may recite the existence of the power of attorney, or a deed may recite that the grantors are all the heirs of the last record owner. Under the rule, these recitals are exempted from the hearsay rule. The circumstances under which dispositive documents are executed and the requirement that the recital be germane to the purpose of the document are believed to be adequate guarantees of trustworthiness, particularly in view of the nonapplicability of the rule if dealings with the property have been inconsistent with the document. The age of the document is of no significance, though in practical application the document will most often be an ancient one. See Uniform Rule 63(29), Comment.

Similar provisions are contained in Uniform Rule 63(29); California Evidence Code § 1330; Kansas Code of Civil Procedure § 60-460(aa); New Jersey Evidence Rule 63(29).

Exception (16). Authenticating a document as ancient, essentially in the pattern of the common law, as provided in Rule 901(b)(8), leaves open as a separate question the admissibility of assertive statements contained therein as against a hearsay objection. 7 Wigmore § 2145a. Wigmore further states that the ancient document technique of authentication is universally conceded to apply to all sorts of documents, including letters, records, contracts, maps, and certificates, in addition to title documents, citing numerous decisions. Id. § 2145. Since most of these items are significant evidentially only insofar as they are assertive, their admission in evidence must be as a hearsay exception. But see 5 id. § 1573, p. 429, referring to recitals in ancient deeds as a "limited" hearsay exception. The former position is believed to be the correct one in reason and authority. As pointed out in McCormick § 298, danger of mistake is minimized by authentication requirements, and age affords assurance that the writing antedates the present controversy. See Dallas County v. Commercial Union Assurance Co., 286 F.2d 388 (5th Cir. 1961), upholding admissibility of 58-year-old newspaper story. Cf. Morgan, Basic Problems of Evidence 364 (1962), but see id. 254.

For a similar provision, but with the added requirement that "the statement has since generally been acted upon as true by persons having an interest in the matter," see California Evidence Code § 1331.

Exception (17). Ample authority at common law supported the admission in evidence of items falling in this category. While Wigmore's text is narrowly oriented to lists, etc., prepared for the use of a trade or profession, 6 Wigmore § 1702, authorities are cited which include other kinds of publications, for example, newspaper market reports, telephone directories, and city directories. Id. §§ 1702-1706. The basis of trustworthiness is general reliance by the public or by a particular segment of it, and the motivation of the compiler to foster reliance by being accurate.

For similar provisions, see Uniform Rule 63(30); California Evidence Code § 1340; Kansas Code of Civil Procedure § 60-460(bb); New Jersey Evidence Rule 63(30). Uniform Commercial Code § 2-724 provides for admissibility in evidence of "reports in official publications or trade journals or in newspapers or periodicals of general circulation published as the reports of such [established commodity] market."

Exception (18). The writers have generally favored the admissibility of learned treatises, McCormick § 296, p. 621; Morgan, Basic Problems of Evidence 366 (1962); 6 Wigmore § 1692, with the support of occasional decisions and rules, City of Dothan v. Hardy, 237 Ala. 603, 188 So. 264 (1939); Lewandowski v. Preferred Risk Mut. Ins. Co., 33 Wis.2d 69, 146 N.W.2d 505 (1966), 66 Mich.L.Rev. 183 (1967); Uniform Rule 63(31); Kansas Code of Civil Procedure § 60-460(ce), but the great weight of authority has been that learned treatises are not admissible as substantive evidence though usable in the cross-examination of experts. The foundation of the minority view is that the hearsay objection must be regarded as unimpressive when directed against treatises since a high standard of accuracy is engendered by various factors:

the treatise is written primarily and impartially for professionals, subject to scrutiny and exposure for inaccuracy, with the reputation of the writer at stake. 6 Wigmore § 1692. Sound as this position may be with respect to trustworthiness, there is, nevertheless, an additional difficulty in the likelihood that the treatise will be misunderstood and misapplied without expert assistance and supervision. This difficulty is recognized in the cases demonstrating unwillingness to sustain findings relative to disability on the basis of judicially noticed medical texts. Ross v. Gardner, 365 F.2d 554 (6th Cir. 1966); Sayers v. Gardner, 380 F.2d 940 (6th Cir. 1967); Colwell v. Gardner, 386 F.2d 56 (6th Cir. 1967); Glendenning v. Ribicoff, 213 F.Supp. 301 (W.D.Mo. 1962); Cook v. Celebrezze, 217 F Supp. 366 (W.D.Mo. 1963); Sosna v. Celebrezze, 234 F.Supp. 289 (E.D.Pa. 1964); and see McDaniel v. Celebrezze, 331 F.2d 426 (4th Cir. 1964). The rule avoids the danger of misunderstanding and misapplication by limiting the use of treatises as substantive evidence to situations in which an expert is on the stand and available to explain and assist in the application of the treatise if declared. The limitation upon receiving the publication itself physically in evidence, contained in the last sentence, is designed to further this policy.

The relevance of the use of treatises on cross-examination is evident. This use of treatises has been the subject of varied views. The most restrictive position is that the witness must have stated expressly on direct his reliance upon the treatise. A slightly more liberal approach still insists upon reliance but allows it to be developed on cross-examination. Further relaxation dispenses with reliance but requires recognition as an authority by the witness, developable on cross-examination. The greatest liberality is found in decisions allowing use of the treatise on cross-examination when its status as an authority is established by any means. Annot., 60 A.L.R.2d 77. The exception is hinged upon this last position, which is that of the Supreme Court, Reilly v. Pinkus, 338 U.S. 269, 70 S.Ct. 110, 94 L.Ed. 63 (1949), and of recent well considered state court decisions, City of St. Petersburg v. Ferguson, 193 So.2d 648 (Fla.App. 1967), cert. denied Fla., 201 So.2d 556; Darling v. Charleston Memorial Community Hospital, 33 Ill.2d 326, 211 N.E.2d 253 (1965); Dabroe v. Rhodes Co., 64 Wash.2d 431, 392 P.2d 317 (1964).

In Reilly v. Pinkus, supra, the Court pointed out that testing of professional knowledge was incomplete without exploration of the witness' knowledge of and attitude toward established treatises in the field. The process works equally well in reverse and furnishes the basis of the rule.

The rule does not require that the witness rely upon or recognize the treatise as authoritative, thus avoiding the possibility that the expert may at the outset block cross-examination by refusing to concede reliance or authoritativeness. Dabroe v. Rhodes Co., supra. Moreover, the rule avoids the unreality of admitting evidence for the purpose of impeachment only, with an instruction to the jury not to consider it otherwise. The parallel to the treatment of prior inconsistent statements will be apparent. See Rules 613(b) and 801(d)(1).

Exceptions (19), (20), and (21). Trustworthiness in reputation evidence is found "when the topic is such that the facts are likely to have been inquired about and that persons having personal knowledge have disclosed facts which have thus been discussed in the community; and thus the community's conclusion, if any has been formed, is likely to be a trustworthy one." 5 Wigmore § 1580, p. 444, and see also § 1583. On this common foundation, reputation as to land boundaries, customs, general history, character, and marriage have come to be regarded as admissible. The breadth of the underlying principle suggests the formulation of an equally broad exception, but tradition has in fact been much narrower and more particularized, and this is the pattern of these exceptions in the rule.

Exception (19) is concerned with matters of personal and family history. Marriage is universally conceded to be a proper subject of proof by evidence of reputation in the community. 5 Wigmore § 1602. As to such items as legitimacy, relationship, adoption, birth, and death, the decisions are divided. Id. § 1605. All seem to be susceptible to being the subject of well founded repute. The "world" in which the reputation may exist may be family, associates, or community. This world has proved capable of expanding with changing times from the single uncomplicated neighborhood, in which all activities take place, to the multiple and unrelated worlds of work, religious affiliation, and social activity, in each of which a reputation may be generated. People v. Reeves, 360 Ill. 55, 195 N.E. 443 (1935); State v. Axilrod, 248 Minn. 204, 79 N.W.2d 677 (1956); Mass.Stat. 1947, c. 410, M.G.L.A. c. 233 § 21A; 5 Wigmore § 1616. The family has often served as the point of beginning for allowing community reputation. 5 Wigmore § 1488. For comparable provisions see Uniform Rule 63(26), (27)(c); California Evidence Code §§ 1313, 1314; Kansas Code of Civil Procedure § 60-460(x), (y)(3); New Jersey Evidence Rule 63(26), (27)(c).

The first portion of Exception (20) is based upon the general admissibility of evidence of reputation as to land boundaries and land customs, expanded in this country to include private as well as public boundaries. McCormick § 299, p. 625. The reputation is required to antedate the controversy, though not to be ancient. The second portion is likewise supported by authority, id., and is designed to facilitate proof of events when judicial notice is not available. The historical character of the subject matter dispenses with any need that the reputation antedate the controversy with respect to which it is offered. For similar provisions see Uniform Rule 63(27)(a), (b); California Evidence Code §§ 1320-1322; Kansas Code of Civil Procedure § 60-460(y), (1), (2); New Jersey Evidence Rule 63(27)(a), (b).

Exception (21) recognizes the traditional acceptance of reputation evidence as a means of proving human character. McCormick §§ 44, 158. The exception deals only with the hearsay aspect of this kind of evidence. Limitations upon admissibility based on other grounds will be found in Rules 404, relevancy of character evidence generally, and 608, character of witness. The exception is in effect a reiteration, in the context of hearsay, of Rule 405(a).

Similar provisions are contained in Uniform Rule 63(28); California Evidence Code § 1324; Kansas Code of Civil Procedure § 60-460(z); New JerseyEvidence Rule 63(28).

Exception (22). When the status of a former judgment is under consideration in subsequent litigation, three possibilities must be noted: (1) the former judgment is conclusive under the doctrine of res judicata, either as a bar or a collateral estoppel; or (2) it is admissible in evidence for what it is worth;

or (3) it may be of no effect at all. The first situation does not involve any problem of evidence except in the way that principles of substantive law generally bear upon the relevancy and materiality of evidence. The rule does not deal with the substantive effect of the judgment as a bar or collateral estoppel. When, however, the doctrine of res judicata does not apply to make the judgment either a bar or a collateral estoppel, a choice is presented between the second and third alternatives. The rule adopts the second for judgments of criminal conviction of felony grade. This is the direction of the decisions, Annot., 18 A.L.R.2d 1287, 1299, which manifest an increasing reluctance to reject in toto the validity of the law's factfinding processes outside the confines of res judicata and collateral estoppel. While this may leave a jury with the evidence of conviction but without means to evaluate it, as suggested by Judge Hinton, Note 27 Ill.L.Rev. 195 (1932), it seems safe to assume that the jury will give it substantial effect unless defendant offers a satisfactory explanation, a possibility not foreclosed by the provision. But see North River Ins. Co. v. Militello, 104 Colo. 28, 88 P.2d 567 (1939), in which the jury found for plaintiff on a fire policy despite the introduction of his conviction for arson. For supporting federal decisions see Clark, J., in New York & Cuba Mail S.S. Co. v. Continental Cas. Co., 117 F.2d 404, 411 (2d Cir. 1941); Connecticut Fire Ins. Co. v. Farrara, 277 F.2d 388 (8th Cir. 1960).

Practical considerations require exclusion of convictions of minor offenses, not became the administration of justice in its lower echelons must be inferior, but because motivation to defend at this level 2s often minimal or nonexistent. Cope v. Goble, 39 Cal.App.2d 448, 103 P.2d 598 (1940); Jones v. Talbot, 87 Idaho 498, 394 P.2d 316 (1964); Warren v. Marsh, 215 Minn. 615, 11 N.W.2d 528 (1943); Annot., 18 A.L.R.2d 1287, 1295-1297; 16 Brooklyn L.Rev. 286 (1950); 50 Colum.L.Rev. 529 (1950); 35 Cornell L.Q. 872 (1950). Hence the rule includes only convictions of felony grade, measured by federal standards.

Judgments of conviction based upon pleas of nolo contendere are not included. This position is consistent with the treatment of nolo pleas in Rule 410 and the authorities cited in the Advisory Committee's Note in support thereof.

While these rules do not in general purport to resolve constitutional issues, they have in general been drafted with a view to avoiding collision with constitutional principles. Consequently the exception does not include evidence of the conviction of a third person, offered against the accused in a criminal prosecution to prove any fact essential to sustain the judgment of conviction. A contrary position would seem clearly to violate the right of confrontation. Kirby v. United States, 174 U.S. 47, 19 S.Ct. 574, 43 L.Ed. 890 (1899), error to convict of possessing stolen postage stamps with the only evidence of theft being the record of conviction of the thieves The situation is to be distinguished from cases in which conviction of another person is an element of the crime, e.g. 15 U.S.C. § 902(d), interstate shipment of firearms to a known convicted felon, and, as specifically provided, from impeachment.

For comparable provisions see Uniform Rule 63(20); California Evidence Code § 1300; Kansas Code of Civil Procedure § 60-460(r); New Jersey Evidence Rule 63(20).

Exception (23). A hearsay exception in this area was originally justified on the ground that verdicts were evidence of reputation. As trial by jury graduated from the category of neighborhood inquests, this theory lost its validity. It was never valid as to chancery decrees. Nevertheless the rule persisted, though the judges and writers shifted ground and began saying that the judgment or decree was as good evidence as reputation. See City of London v. Clerke, Carth. 181, 90 Eng.Rep. 710 (K.B. 1691); Neill v. Duke of Devonshire, 8 App.Cas. 135 (1882). The shift appears to be correct, since the process of inquiry, sifting, and scrutiny which is relied upon to render reputation reliable is present in perhaps greater measure in the process of litigation. While this might suggest a broader area of application, the affinity to reputation is strong, and paragraph (23) goes no further, not even including character.

The leading case in the United States, Patterson v. Gaines, 47 U.S. (6 How.) 550, 599, 12 L.Ed. 553 (1847), follows in the pattern of the English decisions, mentioning as illustrative matters thus provable: manorial rights, public rights of way, immemorial custom, disputed boundary, and pedigree. More recent recognition of the principle is found in Grant Bros. Construction Co. v. United States, 232 U.S. 647, 34 S.Ct. 452, 58 L.Ed. 776 (1914), in action for penalties under Alien Contract Labor Law, decision of board of inquiry of Immigration Service admissible to prove alienage of laborers, as a matter of pedigree; United States v. Mid-Continent Petroleum Corp., 67 F.2d 37 (10th Cir. 1933), records of commission enrolling Indians admissible on pedigree; Jung Yen Loy v. Cahill, 81 F.2d 809 (9th Cir. 1936), board decisions as to citizenship of plaintiff's father admissible in proceeding for declaration of citizenship. Contra, In re Estate of Cunha, 49 Haw. 273, 414 P.2d 925 (1966).

COMMITTEE NOTE TO 1997 AMENDMENT TRANSFERRING RULE 803(24) TO RULE 807

The contents of Rule 803(24) and Rule 804(b)(5) have been combined and transferred to a new Rule 807. This was done to facilitate additions to Rules 803 and 804. No change in meaning is intended.

COMMITTEE NOTE TO 2000 AMENDMENT TO RULE 803(6)

The amendment provides that the foundation requirements of Rule 803(6) can be satisfied under certain circumstances without the expense and inconvenience of producing time-consuming foundation witnesses. Under current law, courts have generally required foundation witnesses to testify. *See, e.g., Tongil Co., Ltd. v. Hyundai Merchant Marine Corp.,* 968 F.2d 999 (9th Cir. 1992) (reversing a judgment based on business records where a qualified person filed an affidavit but did not testify). Protections are provided by the authentication requirements of Rule 902(11) for domestic records, Rule 902(12) for foreign records in civil cases, and 18 U.S.C. § 3505 for foreign records in criminal cases.

ORIGINAL COMMITTEE NOTE TO RULE 804

As to firsthand knowledge on the part of hearsay declarants, see the introductory portion of the Advisory Committee's Note to Rule 803.

Subdivision (a). The definition of unavailability implements the division of hearsay exceptions into two categories by Rules 803 and 804(b).

At common law the unavailability requirement was evolved in connection with particular hearsay exceptions rather than along general lines. For example, see the separate explication of unavailability in relation to former testimony, declarations against interest, and statements of pedigree, separately developed in McCormick §§ 234, 257, and 297. However, no reason is apparent for making distinctions as to what satisfies unavailability for the different exceptions. The treatment in the rule is therefore uniform although differences in the range of process for witnesses between civil and criminal cases will lead to a less exacting requirement under item (5). See Rule 45(e) of the Federal Rules of Civil Procedure and Rule 17(e) of the Federal Rules of Criminal Procedure.

FIVE INSTANCES OF UNAVAILABILITY ARE SPECIFIED:

(1) Substantial authority supports the position that exercise of a claim of privilege by the declarant satisfies the requirement of unavailability (usually in connection with former testimony). Wyatt v. State, 35 Ala.App. 147, 46 So.2d 837 (1950); State v. Stewart, 85 Kan. 404, 116 P. 489 (1911); Annot., 45 A.L.R.2d 1354; Uniform Rule 62(7)(a); California Evidence Code § 240(a)(1); Kansas Code of Civil Procedure § 60-459(g)(1). A ruling by the judge is required, which clearly implies that an actual claim of privilege must be made.

(2) A witness is rendered unavailable if he simply refuses to testify concerning the subject matter of his statement despite judicial pressures to do so, a position supported by similar considerations of practicality. Johnson v. People, 152 Colo. 586, 384 P.2d 454 (1963); People v. Pickett, 339 Mich. 294, 63 N.W.2d 681, 45 A.L.R.2d 1341 (1954). Contra, Pleau v. State, 255 Wis. 362, 38 N.W.2d 496 (1949).

(3) The position that a claimed lack of memory by the witness of the subject matter of his statement constitutes unavailability likewise finds support in the cases, though not without dissent. McCormick § 234, p. 494. If the claim is successful, the practical effect is to put the testimony beyond reach, as in the other instances. In this instance, however, it will be noted that the lack of memory must be established by the testimony of the witness himself, which clearly contemplates his production and subjection to cross-examination.

(4) Death and infirmity find general recognition as ground. McCormick §§ 234, 257, 297; Uniform Rule 62(7)(c); California Evidence Code § 240(a)(3); Kansas Code of Civil Procedure § 60-459(g)(3); New Jersey Evidence Rule 62(6)(c). See also the provisions on use of depositions in Rule 32(a)(3) of the Federal Rules of Civil Procedure and Rule 15(e) of the Federal Rules of Criminal Procedure.

(5) Absence from the hearing coupled with inability to compel attendance by process or other reasonable means also satisfies the requirement. McCormick § 234; Uniform Rule 62(7)(d) and (e); California Evidence Code § 240(a)(4) and (5); Kansas Code of Civil Procedure § 60-459(g)(4) and (5); New Jersey Rule 62(6)(b) and (d). See the discussion of procuring attendance of witnesses who are nonresidents or in custody in Barber v. Page, 390 U.S. 719, 88

S.Ct. 1318, 20 L.Ed.2d 255 (1968).

If the conditions otherwise constituting unavailability result from the procurement or wrongdoing of the proponent of the statement, the requirement is not satisfied. The rule contains no requirement that an attempt be made to take the deposition of a declarant.

Subdivision (b). Rule 803 supra, is based upon the assumption that a hearsay statement falling within one of its exceptions possesses qualities which justify the conclusion that whether the declarant is available or unavailable is not a relevant factor in determining admissibility. The instant rule proceeds upon a different theory: hearsay which admittedly is not equal in quality to testimony of the declarant on the stand may nevertheless be admitted if the declarant is unavailable and if his statement meets a specified standard. The rule expresses preferences: testimony given on the stand in person is preferred over hearsay, and hearsay, if of the specified quality, is preferred over complete loss of the evidence of the declarant. The exceptions evolved at common law with respect to declarations of unavailable declarants furnish the basis for the exceptions enumerated in the proposal. The term "unavailable" is defined in subdivision (a).

Exception (1). Former testimony does not rely upon some set of circumstances to substitute for oath and cross-examination, since both oath and opportunity to cross-examine were present in fact. The only missing one of the ideal conditions for the giving of testimony is the presence of trier and opponent ("demeanor evidence"). This is lacking with all hearsay exceptions. Hence it may be argued that former testimony is the strongest hearsay and should be included under Rule 803, supra. However, opportunity to observe demeanor is what in a large measure confers depth and meaning upon oath and cross-examination. Thus in cases under Rule 803 demeanor lacks the significance which it possesses with respect to testimony. In any event, the tradition, founded in experience, uniformly favors production of the witness if he is available. The exception indicates continuation of the policy. This preference for the presence of the witness is apparent also in rules and statutes on the use of depositions, which deal with substantially the same problem.

Under the exception, the testimony may be offered (1) against the party against whom it was previously offered or (2) against the party by whom it was previously offered. In each instance the question resolves itself into whether fairness allows imposing, upon the party against whom now offered, the handling of the witness on the earlier occasion. (1) If the party against whom now offered is the one against whom the testimony was offered previously, no unfairness is apparent in requiring him to accept his own prior conduct of cross-examination or decision not to cross-examine. Only demeanor has been lost, and that is inherent in the situation. (2) If the party against whom now offered is the one by whom the testimony was offered previously, a satisfactory answer becomes somewhat more difficult. One possibility is to proceed somewhat along the line of an adoptive admission, i.e. by offering the testimony proponent in effect adopts it. However, this theory savors of discarded concepts of witnesses' belonging to a party, of litigants' ability to pick and choose witnesses, and of vouching for one's own witnesses. Cf.

McCormick § 246, pp. 526-527; 4 Wigmore § 1075. A more direct and acceptable approach is simply to recognize direct and redirect examination of one's own witness as the equivalent of cross-examining an opponent's witness. Falknor, Former Testimony and the Uniform Rules: A Comment, 38 N.Y.U.L.Rev. 651, n. 1 (1963); McCormick § 231, p. 483. See also 5 Wigmore § 1389. Allowable techniques for dealing with hostile, doublecrossing, forgetful, and mentally deficient witnesses leave no substance to a claim that one could not adequately develop his own witness at the former hearing. An even less appealing argument is presented when failure to develop fully was the result of a deliberate choice.

The common law did not limit the admissibility of former testimony to that given in an earlier trial of the same case, although it did require identity of issues as a means of insuring that the former handling of the witness was the equivalent of what would now be done if the opportunity were presented. Modern decisions reduce the requirement to "substantial" identity. McCormick § 233. Since identity of issues is significant only in that it bears on motive and interest in developing fully the testimony of the witness, expressing the matter in the latter terms is preferable. Id. Testimony given at a preliminary hearing was held in California v. Green, 399 U.S. 149, 90 S.Ct. 1930, 26 L.Ed.2d 489 (1970), to satisfy confrontation requirements in this respect.

As a further assurance of fairness in thrusting upon a party the prior handling of the witness, the common law also insisted upon identity of parties, deviating only to the extent of allowing substitution of successors in a narrowly construed privity. Mutuality as an aspect of identity is now generally discredited, and the requirement of identity of the offering party disappears except as it might affect motive to develop the testimony. Falknor, supra, at 652; McCormick § 232, pp. 487-488. The question remains whether strict identity, or privity, should continue as a requirement with respect to the party against whom offered. The rule departs to the extent of allowing substitution of one with the right and opportunity to develop the testimony with similar motive and interest. This position is supported by modern decisions. McCormick § 232, pp. 489-490; 5 Wigmore § 1388.

Provisions of the same tenor will be found in Uniform Rule 63(3)(b); California Evidence Code §§ 1290-1292; Kansas Code of Civil Procedure § 60-460(c)(2); New Jersey Evidence Rule 63(3). Unlike the rule, the latter three provide either that former testimony is not admissible if the right of confrontation is denied or that it is not admissible if the accused was not a party to the prior hearing. The genesis of these limitations is a caveat in Uniform Rule 63(3) Comment that use of former testimony against an accused may violate his right of confrontation. Mattox v. United States, 156 U.S. 237, 15 S.Ct. 337, 39 L.Ed. 409 (1895), held that the right was not violated by the Government's use, on a retrial of the same case, of testimony given at the first trial by two witnesses since deceased. The decision leaves open the questions (1) whether direct and redirect are equivalent to cross-examination for purposes of confrontation, (2) whether testimony given in a different proceeding is acceptable, and (3) whether the accused must himself have been a party to the earlier proceeding or whether a similarly situated person will serve the purpose. Professor Falknor concluded that, if a dying declaration untested by cross-examination is constitutionally admissible, former testimony tested by the cross-examination of one similarly situated does not offend against confrontation. Falknor, supra, at 659-660. The constitutional acceptability of dying declarations has often been conceded. Mattox v. United States, 156 U.S.237, 243, 15 S.Ct. 337, 39 L.Ed. 409 (1895); Kirby v. United States, 174 U.S. 47, 61, 19 S.Ct. 574, 43 L.Ed. 890 (1899); Pointer v. Texas, 380 U.S. 400, 407, 85 S.Ct. 1065, 13 L.Ed.2d 923 (1965).

Exception (2). The exception is the familiar dying declaration of the common law, expanded somewhat beyond its traditionally narrow limits. While the original religious justification for the exception may have lost its conviction for some persons over the years, it can scarcely be doubted that powerful psychological pressures are present. See 5 Wigmore § 1443 and the classic statement of Chief Baron Eyre in Rex v. Woodcock, 1 Leach 500, 502, 168 Eng.Rep. 352, 353 (K.B. 1789).

The common law required that the statement be that of the victim, offered in a prosecution for criminal homicide. Thus declarations by victims in prosecutions for other crimes, e.g. a declaration by a rape victim who dies in childbirth, and all declarations in civil cases were outside the scope of the exception. An occasional statute has removed these restrictions, as in Colo.R.S. § 52-1-20, or has expanded the area of offenses to include abortions, 5 Wigmore § 1432, p. 224, n. 4. Kansas by decision extended the exception to civil cases. Thurston v. Fritz, 91 Kan. 468, 138 P. 625 (1914). While the common law exception no doubt originated as a result of the exceptional need for the evidence in homicide cases, the theory of admissibility applies equally in civil cases and in prosecutions for crimes other than homicide. The same considerations suggest abandonment of the limitation to circumstances attending the event in question, yet when the statement deals with matters other than the supposed death, its influence is believed to be sufficiently attenuated to justify the limitation. Unavailability is not limited to death. See subdivision (a) of this rule. Any problem as to declarations phrased in terms of opinion is laid at rest by Rule 701, and continuation of a requirement of first-hand knowledge is assured by Rule 602.

Comparable provisions are found in Uniform Rule 63(5); California Evidence Code § 1242; Kansas Code of Civil Procedure § 60-460(e); New JerseyEvidence Rule 63(5).

Exception (3). The circumstantial guaranty of reliability for declarations against interest is the assumption that persons do not make statements which are damaging to themselves unless satisfied for good reason that they are true. Hileman v. Northwest Engineering Co., 346 F.2d 668 (6th Cir. 1965). If the statement is that of a party, offered by his opponent, it comes in as an admission, Rule 803(d)(2), and there is no occasion to inquire whether it is against interest, this not being a condition precedent to admissibility of admissions by opponents.

The common law required that the interest declared against be pecuniary or proprietary but within this limitation demonstrated striking ingenuity in discovering an against-interest aspect. Higham v. Ridgeway, 10 East 109, 103 Eng.Rep. 717 (K.B. 1808); Reg. v. Overseers of Birmingham, 1 B. & S. 763, 121 Eng.Rep. 897 (Q.B. 1861); McCormick, § 256, p. 551, nn. 2 and 3.

The exception discards the common law limitation and expands to the full logical limit. One result is to remove doubt as to the admissibility of declarations tending to establish a tort liability against the declarant or to extinguish one which might be asserted by him, in accordance with the trend of the decisions in this country. McCormick § 254, pp. 548-549. Another is to allow statements tending to expose declarant to hatred, ridicule, or disgrace, the motivation here being considered to be as strong as when financial interests are at stake. McCormick § 255, p. 551. And finally, exposure to criminal liability satisfies the against-interest requirement. The refusal of the common law to concede the adequacy of a penal interest was no doubt indefensible in logic, see the dissent of Mr. Justice Holmes in Donnelly v. United States, 228 U.S. 243, 33 S.Ct. 449, 57 L.Ed. 820 (1913), but one senses in the decisions a distrust of evidence of confessions by third persons offered to exculpate the accused arising from suspicions of fabrication either of the fact of the making of the confession or in its contents, enhanced in either instance by the required unavailability of the declarant. Nevertheless, an increasing amount of decisional law recognizes exposure to punishment for crime as a sufficient stake. People v. Spriggs, 60 Cal.2d 868, 36 Cal.Rptr. 841, 389 P.2d 377 (1964); Sutter v. Easterly, 354 Mo. 282, 189 S.W.2d 284 (1945); Band's Refuse Removal, Inc. v. Fairlawn Borough, 62 N.J.Super. 552, 163 A.2d 465 (1960); Newberry v. Commonwealth, 191 Va. 445, 61 S.E.2d 318 (1950); Annot., 162 A.L.R. 446. The requirement of corroboration is included in the rule in order to effect an accommodation between these competing considerations. When the statement is offered by the accused by way of exculpation, the resulting situation is not adapted to control by rulings as to the weight of the evidence and, hence the provision is cast in terms of a requirement preliminary to admissibility. Cf. Rule 406(a). The requirement of corroboration should be construed in such a manner as to effectuate its purpose of circumventing fabrication.

Ordinarily the third-party confession is thought of in terms of exculpating the accused, but this is by no means always or necessarily the case: it may include statements implicating him, and under the general theory of declarations against interest they would be admissible as related statements. Douglas v. Alabama, 380 U.S. 415, 85 S.Ct. 1074, 13 L.Ed.2d 934 (1965), and Bruton v. United States, 389 U.S. 818, 88 S.Ct. 126, 19 L.Ed.2d 70 (1968), both involved confessions by codefendants which implicated the accused. While the confession was not actually offered in evidence in *Douglas,* the procedure followed effectively put it before the jury, which the Court ruled to be error. Whether the confession might have been admissible as a declaration against penal interest was not considered or discussed. *Bruton* assumed the inadmissibility, as against the accused, of the implicating confession of his codefendant, and centered upon the question of the effectiveness of a limiting instruction. These decisions, however, by no means require that all statements implicating another person be excluded from the category of declarations against interest. Whether a statement is in fact against interest must be determined from the circumstances of each case. Thus a statement admitting guilt and implicating another person, made while in custody, may well be motivated by a desire to curry favor with the authorities and hence fail to qualify as against interest. See the dissenting opinion of Mr. Justice White in *Bruton*. On the other hand,the same words spoken under different circumstances, e.g., to an acquaintance, would have no difficulty in qualifying. The rule does not purport to deal with questions of the right of confrontation.

The balancing of self-serving against dissenting aspects of a declaration is discussed in McCormick § 256.

For comparable provisions, see Uniform Rule 63(10): California Evidence Code § 1230; Kansas Code of Civil Procedure § 60-460(j); New Jersey Evidence Rule 63(10).

Exception (4). The general common law requirement that a declaration in this area must have been made ante litem motam has been dropped, as bearing more appropriately on weight than admissibility. See 5 Wigmore § 1483. Item (i) [(A)] specifically disclaims any need of firsthand knowledge respecting declarant's own personal history. In some instances it is self-evident (marriage) and in others impossible and traditionally not required (date of birth). Item (ii)[(B)] deals with declarations concerning the history of another person. As at common law, declarant is qualified if related by blood or marriage. 5 Wigmore § 1489. In addition, and contrary to the common law, declarant qualifies by virtue of intimate association with the family. Id., § 1487. The requirement sometimes encountered that when the subject of the statement is the relationship between two other persons the declarant must qualify as to both is omitted. Relationship is reciprocal. Id., § 1491.

For comparable provisions, see Uniform Rule 63 (23), (24), (25); California Evidence Code §§ 1310, 1311; Kansas Code of Civil Procedure § 60-460(u), (v), (w); New Jersey Evidence Rules 63(23), 63(24), 63(25).

[Editor's Note: Rule 804(b)(5) has been transferred to Rule 807. The Advisory Committee Note on Rule 804(b)(5) simply referred to the commentary under the identical Rule 803(24), which in 1997 was combined with Rule 804(b)(5) into a single Rule 807.]

COMMITTEE NOTE TO 1997 AMENDMENT TRANSFERRING RULE 804(b)(5) TO RULE 807, AND ADDING RULE 804(b)(6)

Subdivision (b)(5). The contents of Rule 803(24) and Rule 804(b)(5) have been combined and transferred to a new Rule 807. This was done to facilitate additions to Rules 803 and 804. No change in meaning is intended.

Subdivision (b)(6). Rule 804(b)(6) has been added to provide that a party forfeits the right to object on hearsay grounds to the admission of a declarant's prior statement when the party's deliberate wrongdoing or acquiescence therein procured the unavailability of the declarant as a witness. This recognizes the need for a prophylactic rule to deal with abhorrent behavior "which strikes at the heart of the system of justice itself." *United States v. Mastrangelo*, 693 F.2d 269, 273 (2d Cir. 1982), *cert. denied*, 467 U.S. 1204 (1984). The wrongdoing need not consist of a criminal act. The rule applies to all parties, including the government.

Every circuit that has resolved the question has recognized the principle of forfeiture by misconduct, although the tests for determining whether there is a forfeiture have varied. *See, e.g., United States v. Aguiar*, 975 F.2d 45, 47 (2d Cir. 1992); *United States v. Potamitis*, 739 F.2d 784, 789 (2d Cir.), *cert.*

denied, 469 U.S. 918 (1984); *Steele v. Taylor*, 684 F.2d 1193, 1199 (6th Cir. 1982), *cert. denied*, 460 U.S. 1053 (1983); *United States v. Balano*, 618 F.2d 624, 629 (10th Cir. 1979), *cert. denied*, 449 U.S. 840 (1980); *United States v. Carlson*, 547 F.2d 1346, 135959 (8th Cir.), *cert. denied*, 431 U.S. 914 (1977). The foregoing cases apply a preponderance of the evidence standard. *Contra United States v. Thevis*, 665 F.2d 616, 631 (5th Cir.) (clear and convincing evidence standard), *cert. denied*, 459 U.S. 825 (1982). The usual Rule 104(a) preponderance of the evidence standard has been adopted in light of the behavior the new Rule 804(b)(6) seeks to discourage.

NOTE TO RULE 805

On principle it scarcely seems open to doubt that the hearsay rule should not call for exclusion of a hearsay statement which includes a further hearsay statement when both conform to the requirements of a hearsay exception. Thus a hospital record might contain an entry of the patient's age based on information furnished by his wife. The hospital record would qualify as a regular entry except that the person who furnished the information was not acting in the routine of the business. However, her statement independently qualifies as a statement of pedigree (if she is unavailable) or as a statement made for purposes of diagnosis or treatment, and hence each link in the chain falls under sufficient assurances. Or, further to illustrate, a dying declaration mayincorporate a declaration against interest by another declarant. See McCormick § 290, p. 611.

NOTE TO RULE 806

The declarant of a hearsay statement which is admitted in evidence is in effect a witness. His credibility should in fairness be subject to impeachment and support as though he had in fact testified. See Rules 608 and 609. There are however, some special aspects of the impeaching of a hearsay declarant which require consideration. These special aspects center upon impeachment by inconsistent statement, arise from factual differences which exist between the use of hearsay and an actual witness and also between various kinds of hearsay, and involve the question of applying to declarants the general rule disallowing evidence of an inconsistent statement to impeach a witness unless he is afforded an opportunity to deny or explain. See Rule 613(b).

The principal difference between using hearsay and an actual witness is that the inconsistent statement will in the case of the witness almost inevitably of necessity in the nature of things be a prior statement, which it is entirely possible and feasible to call to his attention, while in the case of hearsay the inconsistent statement may well be a subsequent one, which practically precludes calling it to the attention of the declarant. The result of insisting upon observation of this impossible requirement in the hearsay situation is to deny the opponent, already barred from cross-examination, any benefit of this important technique of impeachment. The writers favor allowing the subsequent statement. McCormick § 37, p. 69; 3 Wigmore § 1033. The cases, however, are divided. Cases allowing the impeachment include People v. Collup, 27 Cal.2d 829, 167 P.2d 714 (1946); People v. Rosoto, 58

Cal.2d 304, 23 Cal.Rptr. 779, 373 P.2d 867 (1962); Carver v. United States, 164 U.S. 694, 17 S.Ct. 228, 41 L.Ed. 602 (1897). Contra. Mattox v. United States, 156 U.S. 237, 15 S.Ct. 337, 39 L.Ed. 409 (1895); People v. Hines, 284 N.Y. 93, 29 N.E.2d 483 (1940). The force of *Mattox*, where the hearsay was the former testimony of a deceased witness and the denial of use of a subsequent inconsistent statement was upheld, is much diminished by *Carver*, where the hearsay was a dying declaration and denial of use of a subsequent inconsistent statement resulted in reversal. The difference in the particular brand of hearsay seems unimportant when the inconsistent statement is a subsequent one. True, the opponent is not totally deprived of cross-examination when the hearsay is former testimony or a deposition but he is deprived of cross-examining on the statement or along lines suggested by it. Mr. Justice Shiras, with two justices joining him, dissented vigorously in *Mattox*.

When the impeaching statement was made prior to the hearsay statement, differences in the kinds of hearsay appear which arguably may justify differences in treatment. If the hearsay consisted of a simple statement by the witness, e.g. a dying declaration or a declaration against interest, the feasibility of affording him an opportunity to deny or explain encounters the same practical impossibility as where the statement is a subsequent one, just discussed, although here the impossibility arises from the total absence of anything resembling a hearing at which the matter could be put to him. The courts by a large majority have ruled in favor of allowing the statement to be used under these circumstances. McCormick § 37, p. 69; 3 Wigmore § 1033. If, however, the hearsay consists of former testimony or a deposition, the possibility of calling the prior statement to the attention of the witness or deponent is not ruled out, since the opportunity to cross-examine was available. It might thus be concluded that with former testimony or depositions the conventional foundation should be insisted upon. Most of the cases involve depositions, and Wigmore describes them as divided. 3 Wigmore § 1031. Deposition procedures at best are cumbersome and expensive, and to require the laying of the foundation may impose an undue burden. Under the federal practice, there is no way of knowing with certainty at the time of taking a deposition whether it is merely for discovery or will ultimately end up in evidence. With respect to both former testimony and depositions the possibility exists that knowledge of the statement might not be acquired until after the time of the cross-examination. Moreover, the expanded admissibility of former testimony and depositions under Rule 804(b)(1) calls for a correspondingly expanded approach to impeachment. The rule dispenses with the requirement in all hearsay situations, which is readily administered and best calculated to lead to fair results.

Notice should be taken that Rule 26(f) of the Federal Rules of Civil Procedure, as originally submitted by the Advisory Committee, ended with the following: " . . . and, without having first called them to the deponent's attention, may show statements contradictory thereto made at any time by the deponent."

This language did not appear in the rule as promulgated in December, 1937. See 4 Moore's Federal Practice paras. 26.01 [9], 26.35 (2d ed. 1967). In 1951,

Nebraska adopted a provision strongly resembling the one stricken from the federal rule: "Any party may impeach any adverse deponent by self-contradiction without having laid foundation for such impeachment at the time such deposition was taken." R.S.Neb. § 25-1267.07.

For similar provisions, see Uniform Rule 65; California Evidence Code § 1202; Kansas Code of Civil Procedure § 60-462; New Jersey Evidence Rule 65.

The provision for cross-examination of a declarant upon his hearsay statement is a corollary of general principles of cross-examination. A similar provision is found in California Evidence Code § 1203.

NOTE TO RULE 807

[Editor's Note: Below is the Advisory Committee's original Note to what was then Rule 803(24). In 1997, Rule 803(24) was combined with Rule 804(b)(5) and transferred to a new Rule 807.]

Committee Note to Rule 803(24)

The preceding 23 exceptions of Rule 803 and the first five **[four actually enacted — Ed.]** exceptions of Rule 804(b) *infra*, are designed to take full advantage of the accumulated wisdom and experience of the past in dealing with hearsay. It would, however, be presumptuous to assume that all possible desirable exceptions to the hearsay rule have been catalogued and to pass the hearsay rule to oncoming generations as a closed system. Exception (24) and its companion provision in Rule 804(b)(6) **[enacted as 804(b)(5) — Ed.]** are accordingly included. They do not contemplate an unfettered exercise of judicial discretion, but they do provide for treating new and presently unanticipated situations which demonstrate a trustworthiness within the spirit of the specifically stated exceptions. Within this framework, room is left for growth and development of the law of evidence in the hearsay area, consistently with the broad purposes expressed in Rule 102. See Dallas County v. Commercial Union Assur. Co., Ltd., 286 F.2d 388 (5th Cir. 1961).

[The original Advisory Committee Note to Rule 804(b)(5) stated as follows: "In language and in purpose, this exception is identical with Rule 803(24). See the Advisory Committee's Note to that provision."]

NOTE TO 1997 AMENDMENT TRANSFERRING RULES 803(24) AND 804(b)(5) TO RULE 807

The contents of Rule 803(24) and Rule 804(b)(5) have been combined and transferred to a new Rule 807. This was done to facilitate additions to Rules 803 and 804. No change in meaning is intended.

NOTE TO RULE 901

Subdivision (a). Authentication and identification represent a special aspect of relevancy. Michael and Adler, Real Proof, 5 Vand.L.Rev. 344, 362 (1952); McCormick §§ 179, 185; Morgan, Basic Problems of Evidence 378. (1962). Thus a telephone conversation may be irrelevant because on an unrelated topic or because the speaker is not identified. The latter aspect is the one here involved. Wigmore describes the need for authentication as "an inherent logical necessity." 7 Wigmore § 2129, p. 564.

This requirement of showing authenticity or identity fails in the category of relevancy dependent upon fulfillment of a condition of fact and is governed by the procedure set forth in Rule 104(b).

The common law approach to authentication of documents has been criticized as an "attitude of agnosticism," McCormick, Cases on Evidence 388, n. 4 (3rd ed. 1956), as one which "departs sharply from men's customs in ordinary affairs," and as presenting only a slight obstacle to the introduction of forgeries in comparison to the time and expense devoted to proving genuine writings which correctly show their origin on their face, McCormick § 185, pp. 395, 396. Today, such available procedures as requests to admit and pretrial conference afford the means of eliminating much of the need for authentication or identification. Also, significant inroads upon the traditional insistence on authentication and identification have been made by accepting as at least prima facie genuine items of the kind treated in Rule 902, infra. However, the need for suitable methods of proof still remains, since criminal cases pose their own obstacles to the use of preliminary procedures, unforeseen contingencies may arise, and cases of genuine controversy will still occur.

Subdivision (b). The treatment of authentication and identification draws largely upon the experience embodied in the common law and in statutes to furnish illustrative applications of the general principle set forth in subdivision (a). The examples are not intended as an exclusive enumeration of allowable methods but are meant to guide and suggest, leaving room for growth and development in this area of the law.

The examples relate for the most part to documents, with some attention given to voice communications and computer print-outs. As Wigmore noted, no special rules have been developed for authenticating chattels. Wigmore, Code of Evidence § 2086 (3rd ed. 1942).

It should be observed that compliance with requirements of authentication or identification by no means assures admission of an item into evidence, as other bars, hearsay for example, may remain.

Example (1). Example (1) contemplates a broad spectrum ranging from testimony of a witness who was present at the signing of a document to testimony establishing narcotics as taken from an accused and accounting for custody through the period until trial, including laboratory analysis. See California Evidence Code § 1413, eyewitness to signing.

Example (2). Example (2) states conventional doctrine as to lay identification of handwriting, which recognizes that a sufficient familiarity with the handwriting of another person may be acquired by seeing him write, by exchanging correspondence, or by other means, to afford a basis for identifying it on subsequent occasions. McCormick § 189. See also California Evidence Code § 1416. Testimony based upon familiarity acquired for purposes of the litigation is reserved to the expert under the example which follows.

Example (3). The history of common law restrictions upon the technique of proving or disproving the genuineness of a disputed specimen of handwriting through comparison with a genuine specimen, by either the testimony of expert witnesses or direct viewing by the triers themselves, is detailed in 7 Wigmore §§ 1991-1994. In breaking away, the English Common Law Procedure Act of 1854, 17 and 18 Viet., c. 125, § 27, cautiously allowed expert or trier to use exemplars "proved to the satisfaction of the judge to be genuine" for purposes of comparison. The language found its way into numerous statutes in this country, e.g., California Evidence Code §§ 1417, 1418. While explainable as a measure of prudence in the process of breaking with precedent in the handwriting situation, the reservation to the judge of the question of the genuineness of exemplars and the imposition of an unusually high standard of persuasion are at variance with the general treatment of relevancy which depends upon fulfillment of a condition of fact. Rule 104(b). No similar attitude is found in other comparison situations, e.g., ballistics comparison by jury, as in Evans v. Commonwealth, 230 Ky. 411, 19 S.W.2d 1091 (1929), or by experts, Annot. 26 A.L.R.2d 892, and no reason appears for its continued existence in handwriting cases. Consequently Example (3) sets no higher standard for handwriting specimens and treats all comparison situations alike, to be governed by Rule 104(b). This approach is consistent with 28 U.S.C. § 1731: "The admitted or proved handwriting of any person shall be admissible, for purposes of comparison, to determine genuineness of other handwriting attributed to such person."

Precedent supports the acceptance of visual comparison as sufficiently satisfying preliminary authentication requirements for admission in evidence. Brandon v. Collins, 267 F.2d 731 (2d Cir. 1959); Wausau Sulphate Fibre Co. v. Commissioner of Internal Revenue, 61 F.2d 879 (7th Cir. 1932); Desimone v. United States, 227 F.2d 864 (9th Cir. 1955).

Example (4). The characteristics of the offered item itself, considered in the light of circumstances, afford authentication techniques in great variety. Thus a document or telephone conversation may be shown to have emanated from a particular person by virtue of its disclosing knowledge of facts known peculiarly to him; Globe Automatic Sprinkler Co. v. Braniff, 89 Okl. 105, 214 P. 127 (1923); California Evidence Code § 1421; similarly, a letter may be authenticated by content and circumstances indicating it was in reply to a duly authenticated one. McCormick § 192; California Evidence Code § 1420. Language patterns may indicate authenticity or its opposite. Magnuson v. State, 187 Wis. 122, 203 N.W. 749 (1925); Arens and Meadow, Psycholinguistics and the Confession Dilemma, 56 Colum.L.Rev. 19 (1956).

Example (5). Since aural voice identification is not a subject of expert testimony, the requisite familiarity may be acquired either before or after the particular speaking which is the subject of the identification, in this respect resembling visual identification of a person rather than identification of handwriting. Cf. Example (2), supra, People v. Nichols, 378 Ill. 487, 38 N.E.2d 766 (1942); McGuire v. State, 200 Md. 601, 92 A.2d 582 (1952); State v.McGee, 336 Mo. 1082, 83 S.W.2d 98 (1935).

Example (6). The cases are in agreement that a mere assertion of his identity by a person talking on the telephone is not sufficient evidence of the authenticity of the conversation and that additional evidence of his identity is required. The additional evidence need not fall in any set pattern. Thus the content of his statements or the reply technique, under Example (4), supra, or voice identification under Example (5), may furnish the necessary foundation. Outgoing calls made by the witness involve additional factors bearing upon authenticity. The calling of a number assigned by the telephone company reasonably supports the assumption that the listing is correct and that the number is the one reached. If the number is that of a place of business, the mass of authority allows an ensuing conversation if it relates to business reasonably transacted over the telephone, on the theory that the maintenance of the telephone connection is an invitation to do business without further identification. Matton v. Hoover Co., 350 Mo. 506, 166 S.W.2d 557 (1942); City of Pawhuska v. Crutchfield, 147 Okl. 4. 293 P. 1095 (1930); Zurich General Acc. & Liability Ins. Co. v. Baum, 159 Va. 404, 165 S.E. 518 (1932). Otherwise, some additional circumstance of identification of the speaker is required. The authorities divide on the question whether the self-identifying statement of the person answering suffices. Example (6) answers in the affirmative on the assumption that usual conduct respecting telephone calls furnish adequate assurances of regularity, bearing in mind that the entire matter is open to exploration before the trier of fact. In general, see McCormick § 193; 7 Wigmore § 2155; Annot., 71 A.L.R. 5, 105 id. 326.

Example (7). Public records are regularly authenticated by proof of custody, without more. McCormick § 191; 7 Wigmore §§ 2158, 2159. The example extends the principle to include data stored in computers and similar methods, of which increasing use in the public records area may be expected. See California Evidence Code §§ 1532, 1600.

Example (8). The familiar ancient document rule of the common law is extended to include data stored electronically or by other similar means. Since the importance of appearance diminishes in this situation, the importance of custody or place where found increases correspondingly. This expansion is necessary in view of the widespread use of methods of storing data in forms other than conventional written records.

Any time period selected is bound to be arbitrary. The common law period of 30 years is here reduced to 20 years, with some shift of emphasis from the probable unavailability of witnesses to the unlikeliness of a still viable fraud after the lapse of time. The shorter period is specified in the English Evidence Act of 1938, 1 & 2 Geo. 6, c. 28, and in Oregon R.S. 1963, § 41.360(34). See also the numerous statutes prescribing periods of less than 30 years in the case of recorded documents. 7 Wigmore § 2143.

The application of Example (8) is not subject to any limitation to title documents or to any requirement that possession, in the case of a title document, has been consistent with the document. See McCormick § 190.

Example (9). Example (9) is designed for situations in which the accuracy of a result is dependent upon a process or system which produces it. X-rays afford a familiar instance. Among more recent developments is the computer, as to which see Transport Indemnity Co. v. Seib, 178 Neb. 253, 132 N.W.2d 871 (1965); State v. Veres, 7 Ariz.App. 117, 436 P.2d 629 (1968); Merrick v. United States Rubber Co., 7 Ariz.App. 433, 440 P.2d 314 (1968); Freed,

Computer Print-Outs as Evidence, 16 Am.Jur. Proof of Facts 273; Symposium, Law and Computers in the Mid-Sixties, ALI-ABA (1966); 37 Albany L.Rev. 61 (1967). Example (9) does not, of course, foreclose taking judicial notice of the accuracy of the process or system.

Example (10). The example makes clear that methods of authentication provided by Act of Congress and by the Rules of Civil and Criminal Procedure or by Bankruptcy Rules are not intended to be superseded. Illustrative are the provisions for authentication of official records in Civil Procedure Rule 44 and Criminal Procedure Rule 27, for authentication of records of proceedings by court reporters in 28 U.S.C. § 753(b) and Civil Procedure Rule 80(c), and for authentication of depositions in Civil Procedure Rule 30(f).

ORIGINAL COMMITTEE NOTE TO RULE 902

Case law and statutes have, over the years, developed a substantial body of instances in which authenticity is taken as sufficiently established for purposes of admissibility without extrinsic evidence to that effect, sometimes for reasons of policy but perhaps more often because practical considerations reduce the possibility of unauthenticity to a very small dimension. The present rule collects and incorporates these situations, in some instances expanding them to occupy a larger area which their underlying considerations justify. In no instance is the opposite party foreclosed from disputing authenticity.

Paragraph (1). The acceptance of documents bearing a public seal and signature, most often encountered in practice in the form of acknowledgments or certificates authenticating copies of public records, is actually of broad application. Whether theoretically based in whole or in part upon judicial notice, the practical underlying considerations are that forgery is a crime and detection is fairly easy and certain. 7 Wigmore § 2161, p. 638; California Evidence Code § 1452. More than 50 provisions for judicial notice of official seals are contained in the United States Code.

Paragraph (2). While statutes are found which raise a presumption of genuineness of purported official signatures in the absence of an official seal, 7 Wigmore § 2167; California Evidence Code § 1453, the greater ease of effecting a forgery under these circumstances is apparent. Hence this paragraph of the rule calls for authentication by an officer who has a seal. Notarial acts by members of the armed forces and other special situations are covered in paragraph (10).

Paragraph (3) provides a method for extending the presumption of authenticity to foreign official documents by a procedure of certification. It is derived from Rule 44(a)(2) of the Rules of Civil Procedure but is broader in applying to public documents rather than being limited to public records.

Paragraph (4). The common law and innumerable statutes have recognized the procedure of authenticating copies of public records by certificate. The certificate qualifies as a public document, receivable as authentic when in conformity with paragraph (1), (2), or (3). Rule 44(a) of the Rules of Civil Procedure and Rule 27 of the Rules of Criminal Procedure have provided authentication procedures of this nature for both domestic and foreign public records. It will be observed that the certification procedure here provided extends only to public records, reports, and recorded documents, all including data compilations, and does not apply to public documents generally. Hence documents provable when presented in original form under paragraphs (1), (2), or (3) may not be provable by certified copy under paragraph (4).

Paragraph (5). Dispensing with preliminary proof of the genuineness of purportedly official publications, most commonly encountered in connection with statutes, court reports, rules, and regulations, has been greatly enlarged by statutes and decisions. 5 Wigmore § 1684. Paragraph (5), it will be noted, does not confer admissibility upon all official publications; it merely provides a means whereby their authenticity may be taken as established for purposes of admissibility. Rule 44(a) of the Rules of Civil Procedure has been to the same effect.

Paragraph (6). The likelihood of forgery of newspapers or periodicals is slight indeed. Hence no danger is apparent in receiving them. Establishing the authenticity of the publication may, of course, leave still open questions of authority and responsibility for items therein contained. See 7 Wigmore § 2150. Cf. 39 U.S.C. § 4005(b), public advertisement prima facie evidence of agency of person named, in postal fraud order proceeding; Canadian Uniform Evidence Act, Draft of 1936, printed copy of newspaper prima facie evidence that notices or advertisements were authorized.

Paragraph (7). Several factors justify dispensing with preliminary proof of genuineness of commercial and mercantile labels and the like. The risk of forgery is minimal. Trademark infringement involves serious penalties. Great efforts are devoted to inducing the public to buy in reliance on brand names, and substantial protection is given them. Hence the fairness of this treatment finds recognition in the cases. Curtiss Candy Co. v. Johnson, 163 Miss. 426, 141 So. 762 (1932), Baby Ruth candy bar; Doyle v. Continental Baking Co., 262 Mass. 516, 160 N.E. 325 (1928), loaf of bread; Weiner v. Mager & Throne, Inc., 167 Misc 338, 3 N.Y.S.2d 918 (1938), same. And see W.Va. Code 1966, § 47-3-5, trade-mark on bottle prima facie evidence of ownership. Contra, Keegan v. Green Giant Co., 150 Me. 283, 110 A.2d 599 (1954); Murphy v. Campbell Soup Co., 62 F.2d 564 (1st Cir. 1933). Cattle brands have received similar acceptance in the western states. Rev.Code Mont.1947, § 46-606; State v. Wolfley, 75 Kan. 406, 89 P. 1046 (1907); Annot., 11 L.R.A. (N.S.) 87. Inscriptions on trains and vehicles are held to be prima facie evidence of ownership or control. Pittsburgh, Ft. W. & C. Ry. v. Callaghan, 157 Ill. 406, 41 N.E. 909 (1895); 9 Wigmore § 2510a. See also the provision of 19 U.S.C. § 1615(2) that marks, labels, brands, or stamps indicating foreign origin are *prima facie* evidence of foreign origin of merchandise.

Paragraph (8). In virtually every state, acknowledged title documents are receivable in evidence without further proof. Statutes are collected in 5 Wigmore § 1676. If this authentication suffices for documents of the importance of those affecting titles, logic scarcely permits denying this method when other kinds of documents are involved. Instances of broadly inclusive statutes are California Evidence Code § 1451 and N.Y.CPLR 4538, McKinney's Consol. Laws 1963.

Paragraph (9). Issues of the authenticity of commercial paper in federal courts will usually arise in diversity cases, will involve an element of a cause of action or defense, and with respect to presumptions and burden of proof will be controlled by Erie Railroad Co. v. Tompkins, 304 U.S. 64, 58 S.Ct. 817, 82 L.Ed. 1188 (1938). Rule 302, supra. There may, however, be questions of authenticity involving lesser segments of a case or the case may be one governed by federal common law. Clearfield Trust Co. v. United States, 318 U.S. 363, 63 S.Ct. 573, 87 L.Ed. 838 (1943). Cf. United States v. Yazell, 382 U.S. 341, 86 S.Ct. 500, 15 L.Ed.2d 404 (1966). In these situations, resort to the useful authentication provisions of the Uniform Commercial Code is provided for. While the phrasing is in terms of "general commercial law," in order to avoid the potential complication inherent in borrowing local statutes, today one would have difficulty in determining the general commercial law without referring to the Code. See Williams v Walker-Thomas-Furniture Co., 121 U.S.App.D.C. 315, 350 F.2d 445 (1965). Pertinent Code provisions are sections 1-202, 3-307, and 3-510, dealing with third-party documents, signatures on negotiable instruments, protests, and statements of dishonor.

Paragraph (10). The paragraph continues in effect dispensations with preliminary proof of genuineness provided in various Acts of Congress. See, for example, 10 U.S.C. § 936, signature, without seal, together with title, prima facie evidence of authenticity of acts of certain military personnel who are given notarial power; 15 U.S.C. § 77f(a), signature on SEC registration presumed genuine; 26 U.S.C. § 6064, signature to tax return *prima facie* genuine.

COMMITTEE NOTE TO 2000 AMENDMENT TO RULE 902, ADDING SUBDIVISIONS (11) AND (12)

The amendment adds two new paragraphs to the rule on self-authentication. It sets forth a procedure by which parties can authenticate certain records of regularly conducted activity, other than through the testimony of a foundation witness. See the amendment to Rule 803(6). 18 U.S.C. § 3505 currently provides a means for certifying foreign records of regularly conducted activity in criminal cases, and this amendment is intended to establish a similar procedure for domestic records, and for foreign records offered in civil cases.

A declaration that satisfies 28 U.S.C. § 1746 would satisfy the declaration requirement of Rule 902(11), as would any comparable certification under oath.

The notice requirement in Rules 902(11) and (12) is intended to give the opponent of the evidence a full opportunity to test the adequacy of the foundation set forth in the declaration.

NOTE TO RULE 903

The common law required that attesting witnesses be produced or accounted for. Today the requirement has generally been abolished except with respect to documents which must be attested to be valid, e.g. wills in some states. McCormick § 188. Uniform Rule 71; California Evidence Code § 1411; Kansas Code of Civil Procedure § 60-468; New Jersey Evidence Rule 71; New York CPLR Rule 4537.

NOTE TO RULE 1001

In an earlier day, when discovery and other related procedures were strictly limited, the misleading named "best evidence rule" afforded substantial guarantees against inaccuracies and fraud by its insistence upon production of original documents. The great enlargement of the scope of discovery and related procedures in recent times has measurably reduced the need for the rule. Nevertheless important areas of usefulness persist: discovery of documents outside the jurisdiction may require substantial outlay of time and money; the unanticipated document may not practically be discoverable; criminal cases have built-in limitations on discovery. Cleary and Strong, The Best Evidence Rule: An Evaluation in Context, 51 Iowa L.Rev. 825 (1966).

Paragraph (1). Traditionally the rule requiring the original centered upon accumulations of data and expressions affecting legal relations set forth in words and figures. This meant that the rule was one essentially related to writings. Present day techniques have expanded methods of storing data, yet the essential form which the information ultimately assumes for usable purposes is words and figures. Hence the considerations underlying the rule dictate its expansion to include computers, photographic systems, and other modern developments.

Paragraph (3). In most instances, what is an original will be self-evident and further refinement will be unnecessary. However, in some instances particularized definition is required. A carbon copy of a contract executed in duplicate becomes an original, as does a sales ticket carbon copy given to a customer. While strictly speaking the original of a photograph might be thought to be only the negative, practicality and common usage require that any print from the negative be regarded as an original. Similarly, practicality and usage confer the status of original upon any computer printout. Transport Indemnity Co. v. Seib, 178 Neb. 253, 132 N.W.2d 871 (1965).

Paragraph (4). The definition describes "copies" produced by methods possessing an accuracy which virtually eliminates the possibility of error. Copies thus produced are given the status of originals in large measure by Rule 1003, infra. Copies subsequently produced manually, whether handwritten or typed, are not within the definition. It should be noted that what is an original for some purposes may be a duplicate for others. Thus a bank's microfilm record of checks cleared is the original as a record. However, a print offered as a copy of a check whose contents are in controversy is a duplicate. This result is substantially consistent with 28 U.S.C. § 1732(b). Compare 26 U.S.C. § 7513(c), giving full status as originals to photographic reproductions of tax returns and other documents, made by authority of the Secretary of the Treasury, and 44 U.S.C. § 399(a), giving original status to photographic copies in the National Archives.

NOTE TO RULE 1002

The rule is the familiar one requiring production of the original of a document to prove its contents, expanded to include writings, recordings, and photographs, as defined in Rule 1001(1) and (2), supra.

Application of the rule requires a resolution of the question whether contents are sought to be proved. Thus an event may be proved by nondocumentary evidence, even though a written record of it was made. If, however, the event is sought to be proved by the written record, the rule applies. For example, payment may be proved without producing the written receipt which was given. Earnings may be proved without producing books of account in which they are entered. McCormick § 198; 4 Wigmore § 1245. Nor does the rule apply to testimony that books or records have been examined and found not to contain any reference to a designated matter.

The assumption should not be made that the rule will come into operation on every occasion when use is made of a photograph in evidence. On the contrary, the rule will seldom apply to ordinary photographs. In most instances a party wishes to introduce the item and the question raised is the propriety of receiving it in evidence. Cases in which an offer is made of the testimony of a witness as to what he saw in a photograph or motion picture, without producing the same, are most unusual. The usual course is for a witness on the stand to identify the photograph or motion picture as a correct representation of events which he saw or of a scene with which he is familiar. In fact he adopts the picture as his testimony, or, in common parlance, uses the picture to illustrate his testimony. Under these circumstances, no effort is made to prove the contents of the picture, and the rule is inapplicable. Paradis, The Celluloid Witness, 37 U.Colo.L. Rev. 235, 249-251 (1965).

On occasion, however, situations arise in which contents are sought to be proved. Copyright, defamation, and invasion of privacy by photograph or motion picture falls in this category. Similarly as to situations in which the picture is offered as having independent probative value, e.g. automatic photograph of bank robber. See People v. Doggett, 83 Cal.App.2d 405, 188 P.2d 792 (1948) photograph of defendants engaged in indecent act; Mouser and Philbin, Photographic Evidence-Is There a Recognized Basis for Admissibility? 8 Hastings L.J. 310 (1957). The most commonly encountered of this latter group is of course, the X-ray, with substantial authority calling for production of the original. Daniels v. Iowa City, 191 Iowa 811, 183 N.W. 415 (1921); Cellamare v. Third Acc. Transit Corp., 273 App.Div. 260, 77 N.Y.S.2d 91 (1948); Patrick & Tilman v. Matkin, 154 Okl. 232, 7 P.2d 414 (1932); Mendoza v. Rivera, 78 P.R.R. 569 (1955).

It should be noted, however, that Rule 703, supra, allows an expert to give an opinion based on matters not in evidence, and the present rule must be read as being limited accordingly in its application. Hospital records which may be admitted as business records under Rule 803(6) commonly contain reports interpreting X-rays by the staff radiologist, who qualifies as an expert, and these reports need not be excluded from the records by the instant rule.

The reference to Acts of Congress is made in view of such statutory provisions as 26 U.S.C. § 7513, photographic reproductions of tax returns and documents, made by authority of the Secretary of the Treasury, treated as originals, and 44 U.S.C. § 399(a), photographic copies in National Archives treated as originals.

NOTE TO RULE 1003

When the only concern is with getting the words or other contents before the court with accuracy and precision, then a counterpart serves equally as well as the original, if the counterpart is the product of a method which insures accuracy and genuineness. By definition in Rule 1001(4), supra, a "duplicate" possesses this character.

Therefore, if no genuine issue exists as to authenticity and no other reason exists for requiring the original, a duplicate is admissible under the rule. This position finds support in the decisions, Myrick v. United States, 332 F.2d 279 (5th Cir. 1964), no error in admitting photostatic copies of checks instead of original microfilm in absence of suggestion to trial judge that photostats were incorrect; Johns v. United States, 323 F.2d 421 (5th Cir. 1963), not error to admit concededly accurate tape recording made from original wire recording; Sauget v. Johnston, 315 F.2d 816 (9th Cir. 1963), not error to admit copy of agreement when opponent had original and did not on appeal claim any discrepancy. Other reasons for requiring the original may be present when only a part of the original is reproduced and the remainder is needed for cross-examination or may disclose matters qualifying the part offered or otherwise useful to the opposing party. United States v. Alexander, 326 F.2d 736 (4th Cir. 1964). And see Toho Bussan Kaisha, Ltd. v. American President Lines, Ltd., 265 F.2d 418, 76 A.L.R.2d 1344 (2d Cir. 1959).

NOTE TO RULE 1004

Basically the rule requiring the production of the original as proof of contents has developed as a rule of preference: if failure to produce the original is satisfactory explained, secondary evidence is admissible. The instant rule specifies the circumstances under which production of the original is excused.

The rule recognizes no "degrees" of secondary evidence. While strict logic might call for extending the principle of preference beyond simply preferring the original, the formulation of a hierarchy of preferences and a procedure for making it effective is believed to involve unwarranted complexities. Most, if not all, that would be accomplished by an extended scheme of preferences will, in any event, be achieved through the normal motivation of a party to present the most convincing evidence possible and the arguments and procedures available to his opponent if he does not. Compare McCormick § 207.

Paragraph (1). Loss or destruction of the original unless due to bad faith of the proponent, is a satisfactory explanation of nonproduction. McCormick § 201.

Paragraph (2). When the original is in the possession of a third person, inability to procure it from him by resort to process or other judicial procedure is sufficient explanation of nonproduction. Judicial procedure includes subpoena duces tecum as an incident to the taking of a deposition in another jurisdiction. No further showing is required. See McCormick § 202.

Paragraph (3). A party who has an original in his control has no need for the protection of the rule if put on notice that proof of contents will be made. He can ward off secondary evidence by offering the original. The notice procedure here provided is not to be confused with orders to produce or other discovery procedures, as the purpose of the procedure under this rule is to afford the opposite party an opportunity to produce the original, not to compel him to do so. McCormick § 203.

Paragraph (4). While difficult to define with precision, situations arise in which no good purpose is served by production of the original. Examples are the newspaper in an action for the price of publishing defendant's advertisement, Foster-Holcomb Investment Co. v. Little Rock Publishing Co., 151 Ark. 449, 236 S.W. 597 (1922), and the streetcar transfer of plaintiff claiming status as a passenger, Chicago City Ry. Co. v. Carroll, 206 Ill. 318, 68 N.E. 1087 (1903). Numerous cases are collected in McCormick § 200, p. 412, n. 1.

NOTE TO RULE 1005

Public records call for somewhat different treatment. Removing them from their usual place of keeping would be attended by serious inconvenience to the public and to the custodian. As a consequence judicial decisions and statutes commonly hold that no explanation need be given for failure to produce the original of a public record. McCormick § 204; 4 Wigmore §§ 1215-1228. This blanket dispensation from producing or accounting for the original would open the door to the introduction of every kind of secondary evidence of contents of public records were it not for the preference given certified or compared copies. Recognition of degrees of secondary evidence in this situation is an appropriate quid pro quo for not applying the requirement of producing the original.

The provisions of 28 U.S.C. § 1733(b) apply only to departments or agencies of the United States. The rule, however, applies to public records generally and is comparable in scope in this respect to Rule 44(a) of the Rules of Civil Procedure.

NOTE TO RULE 1006

The admission of summaries of voluminous books, records, or documents offers the only practicable means of making their contents available to judge and jury. The rule recognizes this practice, with appropriate safeguards. 4 Wigmore § 1230.

NOTE TO RULE 1007

While the parent case, Slatterie v. Pooley, 6 M. & W. 664, 151 Eng. Rep. 579 (Exch. 1840), allows proof of contents by evidence of an oral admission bythe party against whom offered, without accounting for nonproduction of the original, the risk of inaccuracy is substantial and the decision is at odds with the purpose of the rule giving preference to the original. See 4 Wigmore § 1255. The instant rule follows Professor McCormick's suggestion of limiting this use of admissions to those made in the course of giving testimony or in writing. McCormick § 208, p. 424. The limitation, of course, does not call for excluding evidence of an oral admission when nonproduction of the original has been accounted for and secondary evidence generally has become admissible. Rule 1004, supra.

A similar provision is contained in New Jersey Evidence Rule 70(1)(h).

NOTE TO RULE 1008

Most preliminary questions of fact in connection with applying the rule preferring the original as evidence of contents are for the judge, under the general principles announced in Rule 104, supra. Thus, the question whether the loss of the originals has been established, or of the fulfillment of other conditions specified in Rule 1004, supra, is for the judge. However, questions may arise which go beyond the mere administration of the rule preferring the original and into the merits of the controversy. For example, plaintiff offers secondary evidence of the contents of an alleged contract, after first introducing evidence of loss of the original, and defendant counters with evidence that no such contract was ever executed. If the judge decides that the contract was never executed and excludes the secondary evidence, the case is at an end without ever going to the jury on a central issue. Levin, Authentication and Content of Writings, 10 Rutgers L.Rev. 632, 644 (1956). The latter portion of the instant rule is designed to insure treatment of these situations as raising jury questions. The decision is not one for uncontrolled discretion of the jury but is subject to the control exercised generally by the judge over jury determinations. See Rule 104(b), supra.

For similar provisions, see Uniform Rule 70(2); Kansas Code of Civil Procedure § 60-467(b); New Jersey Evidence Rule 70(2), (3).

NOTE TO RULE 1101

Subdivision (a). The various enabling acts contain differences in phraseology in their descriptions of the courts over which the Supreme Court's power to make rules of practice and procedure extends. The act concerning civil actions, as amended in 1966, refers to "the district courts . . . of the United States in civil actions, including admiralty and maritime cases . . . . 28 U.S.C. § 2072, Pub. L. 89-773, § 1, 80 Stat. 1323. The bankruptcy authorization is for rules of practice and procedure "under the Bankruptcy Act." 28 U.S.C. § 2075, Pub. L. 88-623, § 1, 78 Stat. 1001. The Bankruptcy Act in turn creates bankruptcy courts of "the United States district courts and the district courts of the Territories and possessions to which this title is or may hereafter be applicable." 11 U.S.C. §§ 1(10), 11(a). The provision as to criminal rules up to and including verdicts applies to "criminal cases and proceedings to punish for criminal contempt of court in the United States district courts, in the district courts for the districts of the Canal Zone and Virgin Islands, in the Supreme Court of Puerto Rico, and in proceedings before United States magistrates." 18 U.S.C. § 3771.

These various provisions do not in terms describe the same courts. In congressional usage the phrase "district courts of the United States," without further qualification, traditionally has included the district courts established by Congress in the states under Article III of the Constitution, which are "constitutional" courts, and has not included the territorial courts created under Article IV, Section 3, Clause 2, which are "legislative" courts. Hornbuckle v. Toombs, 85 U.S. 648, 21 L.Ed. 966 (1873). However, any doubt as to the inclusion of the District Court for the District of Columbia in the phrase is laid at rest by the provisions of the Judicial Code constituting the judicial districts, 28 U.S.C. § 81 et seq. creating district courts therein, Id. § 132, and specifically providing that the term "district court of the United States" means the courts so constituted. Id. § 451. The District of Columbia is included. Id. § 88. Moreover, when these provisions were enacted, reference to the District of Columbia was deleted from the original civil rules enabling act. 28 U.S.C. § 2072. Likewise Puerto Rico is made a district, with a district court, and included in the term. Id. § 119. The question is simply one of the extent of the authority conferred by Congress. With respect to civil rules it seems clearly to include the district courts in the states, the District Court for the District of Columbia, and the District Court for the District of Puerto Rico.

The bankruptcy coverage is broader. The bankruptcy courts include "the United States district courts," which includes those enumerated above. Bankruptcy courts also include "the district courts of the Territories and possessions to which this title is or may hereafter be applicable." 11 U.S.C. §§ 1(10), 11(a). These courts include the district courts of Guam and the Virgin Islands. 48 U.S.C. §§ 1424(b), 1615. Professor Moore points out that whether the District Court for the District of the Canal Zone is a court of bankruptcy "is not free from doubt in view of the fact that no other statute expressly or inferentially provides for the applicability of the Bankruptcy Act in the Zone." He further observes that while there seems to be little doubt that the Zone is a territory or possession within the meaning of the Bankruptcy Act, 11 U.S.C. § 1(10), it must be noted that the appendix to the Canal Zone Code of 1934 did not list the Act among the laws of the United States applicable to the Zone. 1 Moore's Collier on Bankruptcy para. 1.10, pp. 67, 72, n. 25 (14th ed. 1967). The Code of 1962 confers on the district court jurisdiction of: "(4) actions and proceedings involving laws of the United States applicable to the Canal Zone; and "(5) other matters and proceedings wherein jurisdiction is conferred by this Code or any other law." Canal Zone Code, 1962, Title 3, § 141.

Admiralty jurisdiction is expressly conferred. Id. § 142. General powers are conferred on the district court, "if the course of proceeding is not specifically prescribed by this Code, by the statute, or by applicable rule of the Supreme Court of the United States . . . " Id. § 279. Neither these provisions nor § 1(10) of the Bankruptcy Act ("district courts of the Territories and possessions to which this title is or may hereafter be applicable") furnishes a satisfactory answer as to the status of the District Court for the District of the Canal Zone as a court of bankruptcy. However, the fact is that this court exercises no bankruptcy jurisdiction in practice.

The criminal rules enabling act specifies United States district courts, district courts for the districts of the Canal Zone and the Virgin Islands, the Supreme Court of the Commonwealth of Puerto Rico, and proceedings before United States commissioners. Aside from the addition of commissioners, now magistrates, this scheme differs from the bankruptcy pattern in that it makes no mention of the District Court of Guam but by specific mention removes the Canal Zone from the doubtful list.

The further difference in including the Supreme Court of the Commonwealth of Puerto Rico seems not to be significant for present purposes, since the Supreme Court of the Commonwealth of Puerto Rico is an appellate court. The Rules of Criminal Procedure have not been made applicable to it, as being unneeded and inappropriate, Rule 54(a) of the Federal Rules of Criminal Procedure, and the same approach is indicated with respect to rules of evidence.

If one were to stop at this point and frame a rule governing the applicability of the proposed rules of evidence in terms of the authority conferred by the three enabling acts, an irregular pattern would emerge as follows:

"Civil actions, including admiralty and maritime cases-district courts in the states, District of Columbia, and Puerto Rico.

Bankruptcy-same as civil actions, plus Guam and Virgin Islands.

Criminal cases-same as civil actions, plus Canal Zone and Virgin Islands (but not Guam)."

This irregular pattern need not, however, be accepted. Originally the Advisory Committee on the Rules of Civil Procedure took the position that, although the phrase "district courts of the United States" did not include territorial courts, provisions in the organic laws of Puerto Rico and Hawaii would make the rules applicable to the district courts thereof, though this would not be so as to Alaska, the Virgin Islands, or the Canal Zone, whose organic acts contained no corresponding provisions. At the suggestion of the Court, however, the Advisory Committee struck from its notes a statement to the above effect. 2 Moore's Federal Practice para. 1.07 (2nd ed. 1967); 1 Barron and Holtzoff, Federal Practice and Procedure § 121 (Wright ed. 1960). Congress thereafter by various enactments provided that the rules and future amendments thereto should apply to the district courts of Hawaii, 53 Stat. 841 (1939), Puerto Rico, 54 Stat. 22 (1940), Alaska, 63 Stat. 445 (1949), Guam, 64 Stat. 384-390 (1950), and the Virgin Islands, 68 Stat. 497, 507 (1954). The original enabling act for rules of criminal procedure specifically mentioned the district courts of the Canal Zone and the Virgin Islands. The Commonwealth of Puerto Rico was blanketed in by creating its court a "district court of the United States" as previously described. Although Guam is not mentioned in either the enabling act or in the expanded definition of "district court of the United States," the Supreme Court in 1956 amended Rule 54(a) to state that the Rules of Criminal Procedure are applicable in Guam. The Court took this step following the enactment of legislation by Congress in 1950 that rules theretofore or thereafter promulgated by the Court in civil cases, admiralty, criminal cases and bankruptcy should apply to the District Court of Guam, 48 U.S.C. § 1424(b), and two Ninth Circuit decisions upholding the applicability of the Rules of Criminal Procedure to Guam. Pugh v. United States, 212 F.2d 761 (9th Cir. 1954); Hatchett v. Guam, 212 F.2d 767 (9th Cir. 1954); Orfield, The Scope of the Federal Rules of Criminal Procedure, 38 U. of Det.L.J. 173, 187 (1960).

From this history, the reasonable conclusion is that Congressional enactment of a provision that rules and future amendments shall apply in the courts of a territory or possession is the equivalent of mention in an enabling act and that a rule on scope and applicability may properly be drafted accordingly. Therefore the pattern set by Rule 54 of the Federal Rules of Criminal Procedure is here followed.

The substitution of magistrates in lieu of commissioners is made in pursuance of the Federal Magistrates Act, P.L. 90-578, approved October 17, 1968, 82 Stat. 1107.

Subdivision (b) is a combination of the language of the enabling acts, supra, with respect to the kinds of proceedings in which the making of rules is authorized.

It is subject to the qualifications expressed in the subdivisions which follow.

Subdivision (c), singling out the rules of privilege for special treatment, is made necessary by the limited applicability of the remaining rules.

Subdivision (d). The rule is not intended as an expression as to when due process or other constitutional provisions may require an evidentiary hearing. Paragraph (1) restates, for convenience, the provisions of the second sentence of Rule 104(a), supra. See Advisory Committee's Note to that rule.

(2) While some states have statutory requirements that indictments be based on "legal evidence," and there is some case law to the effect that the rules of evidence apply to grand jury proceedings, 1 Wigmore § 4(5), the Supreme Court has not accepted this view. In Costello v. United States, 350 U.S. 359, 76 S.Ct. 406, 100 L.Ed. 397 (1965), the Court refused to allow an indictment to be attacked, for either constitutional or policy reasons, on the ground that only hearsay evidence was presented. "It would run counter to the whole history of the grand jury institution, in which laymen conduct their inquiries unfettered by technical rules. Neither justice nor the concept of a fair trial requires such a change."Id. at 364.

The rule as drafted does not deal with the evidence required to support an indictment.

(3) The rule exempts preliminary examinations in criminal cases. Authority as to the applicability of the rules of evidence to preliminary examinations has been meagre and conflicting. Goldstein, The State and the Accused: Balance of Advantage in Criminal Procedure, 69 Yale L.J. 1149, 1168, n. 53 (1960); Comment, Preliminary Hearings on Indictable Offenses in Philadelphia, 106 U. of Pa.L.Rev. 589, 592-593 (1958). Hearsay testimony is, however, customarily received in such examinations. Thus in a Dyer Act case, for example, an affidavit may properly be used in a preliminary examination to prove ownership of the stolen vehicle, thus saving the victim of the crime the hardship of having to travel twice to a distant district for the sole purpose of testifying as to ownership. It is believed that the extent of the applicability of the Rules of Evidence to preliminary examinations should be appropriately dealt with by the Federal Rules of Criminal Procedure which regulate those proceedings.

Extradition and rendition proceedings are governed in detail by statute. 18 U.S.C. §§ 3181-3195. They are essentially administrative in character. Traditionally the rules of evidence have not applied. 1 Wigmore § 4(6). Extradition proceedings are accepted from the operation of the Rules of Criminal Procedure. Rule 54(b)(5) of Federal Rules of Criminal Procedure.

The rules of evidence have not been regarded as applicable to sentencing or probation proceedings, where great reliance is placed upon the presentence investigation and report. Rule 32(c) of the Federal Rules of Criminal Procedure requires a presentence investigation and report in every case unless the court otherwise directs. In Williams v. New York, 337 U.S. 241, 69 S.Ct. 1079, 93 L.Ed. 1337 (1949), in which the judge overruled a jury recommendation of life imprisonment and imposed a death sentence, the Court said that due process does not require confrontation or cross-examination in sentencing or passing on probation, and that the judge has broad discretion as to the sources and types of information relied upon. Compare the recommendation that the substance of all derogatory information be disclosed to the defendant, in A.B.A. Project on Minimum Standards for Criminal Justice, Sentencing Alternatives and Procedures § 4.4, Tentative Draft (1967, Sobeloff, Chm.). *Williams* was adhered to in Specht v. Patterson, 386 U.S. 605, 87 S.Ct. 1209, 18 L.Ed.2d 326 (1967), but not extended to a proceeding under the Colorado Sex Offenders Act, which was said to be a new charge leading in effect to punishment, more like the recidivist statutes where opportunity must be given to be heard on the habitual criminal issue.

Warrants for arrest, criminal summonses, and search warrants are issued upon complaint or affidavit showing probable cause. Rules 4(a) and 41(c) of the Federal Rules of Criminal Procedure. The nature of the proceedings makes application of the formal rules of evidence inappropriate and impracticable.

Criminal contempts are punishable summarily if the judge certifies that he saw or heard the contempt and that it was committed in the presence of the court. Rule 42(a) of the Federal Rules of Criminal Procedure. The circumstances which preclude application of the rules of evidence in this situation are not present, however, in other cases of criminal contempt.

Proceedings with respect to release on bail or otherwise do not call for application of the rules of evidence. The governing statute specifically provides: "Information stated in, or offered in connection with, any order entered pursuant to this section need not conform to the rules pertaining to the admissibility of evidence in a court of law." 18 U.S.C.A. § 3146(f). This provision is consistent with the type of inquiry contemplated in A.B.A. Project on Minimum Standards for Criminal Justice, Standards Relating to Pretrial Release, § 4.5(b), (c), p. 16 (1968). The references to the weight of the evidence against the accused, in Rule 46(a)(1), (c) of the Federal Rules of Criminal Procedure and in 18 U.S.C.A. § 3146(b), as a factor to be considered, clearly do not have in view evidence introduced at a hearing.

The rule does not exempt habeas corpus proceedings. The Supreme Court held in Walker v. Johnston, 312 U.S. 275, 61 S.Ct. 574, 85 L.Ed. 830 (1941), that the practice of disposing of matters of fact on affidavit, which prevailed in some circuits, did not "satisfy the command of the statute that the judge shall proceed 'to determine the facts of the case, by hearing the testimony and arguments.'" This view accords with the emphasis in Townsend v. Sain, 372 U.S. 293, 83 S.Ct. 745, 9 L.Ed.2d 770 (1963), upon trial-type proceedings, Id. 311, 83 S.Ct. 745, with demeanor evidence as a significant factor, Id. 322, 83 S.Ct. 745, in applications by state prisoners aggrieved by unconstitutional detentions. Hence subdivision (e) applies the rules to habeas corpus proceedings to the extent not inconsistent with the statute.

Subdivision (e). In a substantial number of special proceedings, ad hoc evaluation has resulted in the promulgation of particularized evidentiary provisions, by Act of Congress or by rule adopted by the Supreme Court. Well adapted to the particular proceedings, though not apt candidates for inclusion in a set of general rules, they are left undisturbed. Otherwise, however, the rules of evidence are applicable to the proceedings enumerated in the subdivision.

Table of Cases

[References are to page numbers.]

A

B

[References are to page numbers.]

[References are to page numbers.]

C

[References are to page numbers.]

D

[References are to page numbers.]

E

F

[References are to page numbers.]

G

[References are to page numbers.]

H

[References are to page numbers.]

I

J

[References are to page numbers.]

K

L

[References are to page numbers.]

M

[References are to page numbers.]

[References are to page numbers.]

N

O

[References are to page numbers.]

P

[References are to page numbers.]

Q

R

[References are to page numbers.]

S

[References are to page numbers.]

T

[References are to page numbers.]

U

V

[References are to page numbers.]

[References are to page numbers.]

X

Y

Z

INDEX

[References are to page numbers.]

A

B

C

[References are to page numbers.]

[References are to page numbers.]

[References are to page numbers.]

[References are to page numbers.]

[References are to page numbers.]

R

S

T

U

V

X

[References are to page numbers.]